Y0-CAX-794

Patterns of
World History

Patterns of World History

Second Edition

Volume 2: Since 1400

Peter von Sivers
University of Utah

Charles A. Desnoyers
La Salle University

George B. Stow
La Salle University

New York   Oxford
OXFORD UNIVERSITY PRESS

Oxford University Press is a department of the University of Oxford.
It furthers the University's objective of excellence in research,
scholarship, and education by publishing worldwide.

Oxford   New York
Auckland   Cape Town   Dar es Salaam   Hong Kong   Karachi
Kuala Lumpur   Madrid   Melbourne   Mexico City   Nairobi
New Delhi   Shanghai   Taipei   Toronto

With offices in
Argentina   Austria   Brazil   Chile   Czech Republic   France   Greece
Guatemala   Hungary   Italy   Japan   Poland   Portugal   Singapore
South Korea   Switzerland   Thailand   Turkey   Ukraine   Vietnam

Copyright © 2015, 2012 by Oxford University Press.

For titles covered by Section 112 of the US Higher Education Opportunity Act,
please visit www.oup.com/us/he for the latest information about pricing and
alternate formats.

Published in the United States of America by
Oxford University Press
198 Madison Avenue, New York, NY 10016
http://www.oup.com

Oxford is a registered trade mark of Oxford University Press.

All rights reserved. No part of this publication may be reproduced,
stored in a retrieval system, or transmitted, in any form or by any means,
electronic, mechanical, photocopying, recording, or otherwise,
without the prior permission of Oxford University Press.

Library of Congress Cataloging-in-Publication Data
Von Sivers, Peter.
  Patterns of world history / Peter von Sivers, University of Utah, Charles A. Desnoyers, La Salle
University, George B. Stow, La Salle University. -- Second edition.
      pages cm.
  Includes bibliographical references and index.
   ISBN 978-0-19-939961-1 (pbk., combined volume : acid-free paper) -- ISBN 978-0-19-
939962-8 (pbk., v. 1 : acid-free paper) -- ISBN 978-0-19-939963-5 (pbk., v. 2 : acid-
paper) -- ISBN 978-0-19-939964-2 (pbk., v. 3 : acid-free paper) 1. World history--Textbooks.
I. Desnoyers, Charles, 1952- II. Stow, George B. III. Title.
   D21.V66 2014
   909--dc23

                                                                                    2014013433

About the Cover: This women's tunic, created sometime in the 19th or early 20th century, is
from Khotan, a town in today's Xinjiang region of China. The original wearer was likely from
the Uighur ethnic group. The neck and shoulder decoration is composed of bands of patterned
red and gold silk imported from India. Each strip was carefully teased into an arc shape as it
was sewn onto the tunic. The section forming the collar is evenly gathered. This effect was
achieved by inserting stiffeners secured by rows of stitching. The configuration of this applied
decoration denotes that the wearer was a married woman.

9 8 7 6 5 4 3 2 1

Printed in the United States of America
on acid-free paper

Coniugi Judithae dilectissimae

—Peter von Sivers

To all my students over the years, who have taught me at least as much as I've taught them; and most of all to my wife, Jacki, beloved in all things, but especially in her infinite patience and fortitude in seeing me through the writing of this book.

—Charles A. Desnoyers

For Susan and our children, Meredith and Jonathan.

—George B. Stow

—I hear and I forget; I see and I remember; I do and I understand
(Chinese proverb) 我听见我忘记;我看见我记住;我做我了解

Brief Contents

MAPS   xv

STUDYING WITH MAPS   xvi

PREFACE   xvii

NOTE ON DATES AND SPELLINGS   xxvi

ABOUT THE AUTHORS   xxvii

Part 3: The Formation of Religious Civilizations
600–1450 CE   272

15. The Rise of Empires in the Americas, 600–1550 CE   432

Part 4: Interactions across the Globe
1450–1750   460

16. The Western European Overseas Expansion and Ottoman–Habsburg Struggle, 1450–1650   462

17. The Renaissance, New Sciences, and Religious Wars in Europe, 1450–1750   494

18. New Patterns in New Worlds: Colonialism and Indigenous Responses in the Americas, 1500–1800   530

19. African Kingdoms, the Atlantic Slave Trade, and the Origins of Black America, 1450–1800   564

20. The Mughal Empire: Muslim Rulers and Hindu Subjects, 1400–1750   598

21. Regulating the "Inner" and "Outer" Domains: China and Japan, 1500–1800   626

Part 5: The Origins of Modernity
1750–1900   658

22. Patterns of Nation-States and Culture in the Atlantic World, 1750–1880   660

23. Creoles and Caudillos: Latin America in the Nineteenth Century, 1790–1917   694

24. The Challenge of Modernity: East Asia, 1750–1910   728

25. Adaptation and Resistance: The Ottoman and Russian Empires, 1683–1908   760

26. Industrialization and Its Discontents, 1750–1914   790

27. The New Imperialism in the Nineteenth Century, 1750–1914   822

Part 6: From Three Modernities to One
1914–Present   854

28. World Wars and Competing Visions of Modernity, 1900–1945   856

29. Reconstruction, Cold War, and Decolonization, 1945–1962   894

30. The End of the Cold War, Western Social Transformation, and the Developing World, 1963–1991   930

31. A Fragile Capitalist-Democratic World Order, 1991–2014   964

FURTHER RESOURCES   R-1

CREDITS   C-1

SUBJECT INDEX   I-1

Contents

MAPS   xv

STUDYING WITH MAPS   xvi

PREFACE   xvii

NOTE ON DATES AND SPELLINGS   xxvi

ABOUT THE AUTHORS   xxvii

PART THREE

The Formation of Religious Civilizations
600–1450 CE

272

Chapter 15

600–1550 CE

The Rise of Empires in the Americas

432

▶ The Legacy of Teotihuacán and the Toltecs in Mesoamerica   433

    Militarism in the Mexican Basin   434

    Late Maya States in Yucatán   436

▶ The Legacy of Tiwanaku and Wari in the Andes   438

    The Expanding State of Tiwanaku   438

    The Expanding City-State of Wari   440

▶ American Empires: Aztec and Inca Origins and Dominance   442

    The Aztec Empire of Mesoamerica   442

    The Inca Empire of the Andes   445

▶ Imperial Society and Culture   450

    Imperial Capitals: Tenochtitlán and Cuzco   450

    Power and Its Cultural Expressions   453

▶ Putting It All Together   456

Features:

Patterns Up Close:
Human Sacrifice
and Propaganda   454

Against the Grain:
Amazon Rain Forest
Civilizations   458

PART FOUR

Interactions across the Globe
1450–1750

460

Chapter 16

1450–1650

The Western European Overseas Expansion and Ottoman–Habsburg Struggle

462

▶ The Muslim–Christian Competition in the East and West,
1450–1600   463

    Iberian Christian Expansion, 1415–1498   464

    Rise of the Ottomans and Struggle with the Habsburgs for Dominance,
1300–1609   469

Features:

Patterns Up Close:
Shipbuilding   470

Against the Grain:
Tilting at Windmills   492

▶ **The Centralizing State: Origins and Interactions**   479
State Transformation, Money, and Firearms   479

▶ **Imperial Courts, Urban Festivities, and the Arts**   484
The Ottoman Empire: Palaces, Festivities, and the Arts   484
The Spanish Habsburg Empire: Popular Festivities and the Arts   487

Putting It All Together   490

Chapter 17
1450–1750

The Renaissance, New Sciences, and Religious Wars in Europe
494

Features:

Patterns Up Close:
Mapping the World   508

Against the Grain:
The Digger Movement   528

▶ **Cultural Transformations: Renaissance, Baroque, and New Sciences**   496
The Renaissance and Baroque Arts   496
The New Sciences   499
The New Sciences and Their Social Impact   502
The New Sciences: Philosophical Interpretations   506

▶ **Centralizing States and Religious Upheavals**   508
The Rise of Centralized Kingdoms   508
The Protestant Reformation, State Churches, and Independent Congregations   512
Religious Wars and Political Restoration   516

Putting It All Together   526

Chapter 18
1500–1800

New Patterns in New Worlds: Colonialism and Indigenous Responses in the Americas
530

Features:

Patterns Up Close:
The Columbian
Exchange   548

Against the Grain:
Juana Inés de la Cruz   562

▶ **The Colonial Americas: Europe's Warm-Weather Extension**   531
The Conquest of Mexico and Peru   532
The Establishment of Colonial Institutions   537

▶ **The Making of American Societies: Origins and Transformations**   547
Exploitation of Mineral and Tropical Resources   547
Social Strata, Castes, and Ethnic Groups   551
The Adaptation of the Americas to European Culture   557

Putting It All Together   560

Chapter 19
1450–1800

African Kingdoms, the Atlantic Slave Trade, and the Origins of Black America
564

Features:

Patterns Up Close:
Voodoo and Other New
World Slave Religions   590

Against the Grain:
Oglethorpe's Free
Colony   596

▶ **African States and the Slave Trade**   566
The End of Empires in the North and the Rise of States in the Center   567
Portugal's Explorations along the African Coast and Contacts with Ethiopia   570
Coastal Africa and the Atlantic Slave Trade   572

▶ **American Plantation Slavery and Atlantic Mercantilism**   577
The Special Case of Plantation Slavery in the Americas   578
Slavery in British North America   582
The Fatal Triangle: The Economic Patterns of the Atlantic Slave Trade   586

▶ **Culture and Identity in the African Diaspora**   589
A New Society: Creolization of the Early Atlantic World   589

Putting It All Together   594

Chapter 20
1400–1750

The Mughal Empire: Muslim Rulers and Hindu Subjects

598

▶ **History and Political Life of the Mughals**   599
From Samarkand to Hindustan   600
The Summer and Autumn of Empire   605

▶ **Administration, Society, and Economics**   611
Mansabdars and Bureaucracy   612
The Mughals and Early Modern Economics   613
Society, Family, and Gender   615

▶ **Science, Religion, and the Arts**   617
Science and Technology   617
Religion: In Search of Balance   618
Literature and Art   620

Putting It All Together   622

> Features:
> **Patterns Up Close:**
> Akbar's Attempt at
> Religious Synthesis   608
> **Against the Grain:**
> Sikhism in Transition   624

Chapter 21
1500–1800

Regulating the "Inner" and "Outer" Domains: China and Japan

626

▶ **Late Ming and Qing China to 1750**   627
From Expansion to Exclusion   628
The Spring and Summer of Power: The Qing to 1750   631
Village and Family Life   639
Science, Culture, and Intellectual Life   641

▶ **The Long War and Longer Peace: Japan, 1450–1750**   644
The Struggle for Unification   644
The Tokugawa *Bakufu* to 1750   646
Growth and Stagnation: Economy and Society   650
Hothousing "Japaneseness": Culture, Science, and Intellectual Life   653

Putting It All Together   654

> Features:
> **Patterns Up Close:**
> The "China" Trade   632
> **Against the Grain:**
> Seclusion's Exceptions   656

PART FIVE

The Origins of Modernity
1750–1900

658

Chapter 22
1750–1871

Patterns of Nation-States and Culture in the Atlantic World

660

▶ **Origins of the Nation-State, 1750–1815**   661
The American, French, and Haitian Revolutions   662

▶ Enlightenment Culture: Radicalism and Moderation   673
   The Enlightenment and Its Many Expressions   673
   The Other Enlightenment: The Ideology of Ethnolinguistic Nationalism   676

▶ The Growth of the Nation-State, 1815–1871   677
   Restoration Monarchies, 1815–1848   677
   Nation-State Building in Anglo-America, 1783–1900   682

▶ Romanticism and Realism: Philosophical
   and Artistic Expression to 1850   687
   Romanticism   687
   Realism   688

Putting It All Together   690

Chapter 23
1790–1917

Creoles and Caudillos: Latin America in the Nineteenth Century

                                                                                      694

▶ Independence, Constitutionalism, and Landed Elites   695
   Independence and Southern and Western South American Politics   696
   Independence and Development in Northern South America   699
   Independence and Political Development in the North: Mexico   702
   Brazil: From Kingdom to Republic   710

▶ Latin American Society and Economy in the Nineteenth Century   714
   Rebuilding Societies and Economies   715
   Export-Led Growth   718
   Culture, Family, and the Status of Women   723

Putting It All Together   724

Chapter 24
1750–1910

The Challenge of Modernity: East Asia

                                                                                      728

▶ China and Japan in the Age of Imperialism   730
   China and Maritime Trade, 1750–1839   730
   The Opium Wars and the Treaty Port Era   733
   Toward Revolution: Reform and Reaction to 1900   740
   In Search of Security through Empire: Japan in the Meiji Era   743

▶ Economics and Society in Late Qing China   747
   The Seeds of Modernity and the New Economic Order   747
   Culture, Arts, and Science   749

▶ Zaibatsu and Political Parties: Economics and Society
   in Meiji Japan   751
   Commerce and Cartels   752
   "Enlightenment and Progress": Science, Culture, and the Arts   755

Putting It All Together   756

Features:

Patterns Up Close:
The Guillotine   668

Against the Grain:
Defying the Third
Republic   692

Features:

Patterns Up Close:
Slave Rebellions
in Cuba and Brazil   712

Against the Grain:
Early Industrialization
in Chile?   726

Features:

Patterns Up Close:
Interaction and Adaptation:
"Self-Strengthening" and
"Western Science and
Eastern Ethics"   738

Against the Grain:
Reacting to Modernity   758

Chapter 25
1683–1908

Adaptation and Resistance:
The Ottoman and Russian Empires   760

▶ **Decentralization and Reforms in the Ottoman Empire**   762
Ottoman Imperialism in the 1600s and 1700s   762
The Western Challenge and Ottoman Responses   765
Iran's Effort to Cope with the Western Challenge   771

▶ **Westernization, Reforms, and Industrialization in Russia**   775
Russia and Westernization   776
Russia in the Early Nineteenth Century   777
The Great Reforms   780
Russian Industrialization   782
The Abortive Russian Revolution of 1905   785

Putting It All Together   786

Features:

Patterns Up Close:
Sunni and Shiite Islam   772

Against the Grain:
Precursor to Lenin   788

Chapter 26
1750–1914

Industrialization and Its Discontents   790

▶ **Origins and Growth of Industrialism, 1750–1914**   791
Early Industrialism, 1750–1870   791
The Spread of Early Industrialism   795
Later Industrialism, 1871–1914   796

▶ **The Social and Economic Impact of Industrialism, 1750–1914**   803
Demographic Changes   803
Industrial Society   804
Critics of Industrialism   808
Improved Standards of Living   810
Improved Urban Living   811
Big Business   812

▶ **Intellectual and Cultural Responses to Industrialism**   814
Scientific and Intellectual Developments   814
Toward Modernity in Philosophy and Religion   816
Toward Modernity in Literature and the Arts   817

Putting It All Together   818

Features:

Patterns Up Close:
"The Age of Steam"   798

Against the Grain:
The Luddites   820

Chapter 27
1750–1914

The New Imperialism in the Nineteenth Century   822

▶ **The British Colonies of India, Australia, and New Zealand**   823
The British East India Company   824
Direct British Rule   828
British Settler Colonies: Australia   831

▶ **European Imperialism in the Middle East and Africa**   833
The Rising Appeal of Imperialism in the West   834
The Scramble for Africa   838

Features:

Patterns Up Close:
Military Transformations and
the New Imperialism   832

Against the Grain:
An Anti-Imperial
Perspective   852

▶ **Western Imperialism and Colonialism in Southeast Asia**   844

The Dutch in Indonesia   844

Spain in the Philippines   846

The French in Vietnam   849

Putting It All Together   850

PART
SIX

From Three Modernities to One

1914–PRESENT   854

Chapter 28

1900–1945

World Wars and Competing Visions of Modernity   856

▶ **The Great War and Its Aftermath**   857

A Savage War and a Flawed Peace   858

America First: The Beginnings of a Consumer Culture and the Great Depression   862

Great Britain and France: Slow Recovery and Troubled Empires   868

Latin America: Independent Democracies and Authoritarian Regimes   874

▶ **New Variations on Modernity: The Soviet Union and Communism**   875

The Communist Party and Regime in the Soviet Union   875

The Collectivization of Agriculture and Industrialization   876

▶ **New Variations on Modernity: Supremacist Nationalism in Italy, Germany, and Japan**   877

From Fascism in Italy to Nazism in the Third Reich   878

Japan's "Greater East Asia Co-Prosperity Sphere" and China's Struggle for Unity   885

Putting It All Together   890

> **Features:**
>
> **Patterns Up Close:**
> The Harlem Renaissance and the African Diaspora   866
>
> **Against the Grain:**
> Righteous among the Nations   892

Chapter 29

1945–1962

Reconstruction, Cold War, and Decolonization   894

▶ **Superpower Confrontation: Capitalist Democracy and Communism**   895

The Cold War Era, 1945–1962   895

Society and Culture in Postwar North America, Europe, and Japan   905

▶ **Populism and Industrialization in Latin America**   907

Slow Social Change   908

Populist Guided Democracy   909

▶ **The End of Colonialism and the Rise of New Nations**   911

"China Has Stood Up"   911

Decolonization, Israel, and Arab Nationalism in the Middle East   913

Decolonization and the Cold War in Asia   917

Decolonization and Cold War in Africa   923

Putting It All Together   926

> **Features:**
>
> **Patterns Up Close:**
> Bandung and the Origins of the Non-Aligned Movement   920
>
> **Against the Grain:**
> Postwar Counterculture   928

Chapter 30
1963–1991

The End of the Cold War, Western Social Transformation, and the Developing World   930

▶ **The Climax of the Cold War**   931
The Soviet Superpower in Slow Decline   932

▶ **Transforming the West**   939
Civil Rights Movements   939

▶ **From "Underdeveloped" to "Developing" World, 1963–1991**   944
China: Cultural Revolution to Four Modernizations   946
Vietnam: War and Unification   951
The Middle East   952
Africa: From Independence to Development   955
Latin America: Proxy Wars   958

Putting It All Together   960

> Features:

Patterns Up Close:
From Women's Liberation
to Feminism   944

Against the Grain:
The African National
Congress   962

Chapter 31
1991–2014

A Fragile Capitalist-Democratic World Order   964

▶ **Capitalist Democracy: The Dominant Pattern of Modernity**   965
A Decade of Global Expansion: The United States and the World in the 1990s   966
Two Communist Holdouts: China and Vietnam   976
A Decade of Global Shifts: Twenty-First-Century Currents and Cross-Currents   977

▶ **The Environmental Limits of Modernity**   991

Putting It All Together   994

FURTHER RESOURCES   R-1
CREDITS   C-1
SUBJECT INDEX   I-1

> Features:

Patterns Up Close:
Social Networking   988

Against the Grain:
North Korea, Lone Holdout
against the World   996

Maps

Map 15.1   North America and Mesoamerica, ca. 1100   435
Map 15.2   Tiwanaku and Wari, ca. 1000   441
Map 15.3   The Aztec Empire, ca. 1520   444
Map 15.4   The Inca Empire, ca. 1525   446
Map 15.5   Tenochtitlán and the Mexican Basin   451
Map 15.6   Cuzco   453
Map 16.1   Africa, the Mediterranean, and the Indian Ocean, 1415–1498   465
Map 16.2   The Ottoman Empire, 1307–1683   473
Map 16.3   Europe and the Mediterranean, ca. 1560   475
Map 16.4   Ottoman–Portuguese Competition in the Indian Ocean, 1536–1580   477
Map 17.1   Centers of Learning in Europe, 1500–1770   504
Map 17.2   European Warfare, 1450–1750   511
Map 17.3   The Protestant Reformation, ca. 1580   515
Map 17.4   Europe in 1648   521
Map 17.5   The Expansion of Russia, 1462–1795   525
Map 18.1   The European Exploration of the Americas, 1519–1542   535
Map 18.2   The Colonization of Central and South America to 1750   539
Map 18.3   The Colonization of North America to 1763   544
Map 18.4   The Columbian Exchange   549
Map 19.1   Peoples and Kingdoms in Sub-Saharan Africa, 1450–1750   568
Map 19.2   Regions from which Captured Africans Were Brought to the Americas, 1501–1867   579
Map 19.3   Regions in which Enslaved Africans Landed, 1501–1867   583
Map 19.4   The North Atlantic System, ca. 1750   586
Map 19.5   Slave Revolts in the Americas, 1500–1850   594
Map 20.1   Area Subjugated by Timur-i Lang, 1360–1405   601
Map 20.2   The Conquests of Babur   602
Map 20.3   Mughal India under Akbar   604
Map 20.4   European Trading Ports in India and Southeast Asia, ca. 1690   614
Map 21.1   China in 1600   629
Map 21.2   World Trade Networks, ca. 1770   630
Map 21.3   Silver Flows and Centers of Porcelain Production   632
Map 21.4   China during the Reign of Qianlong   636
Map 21.5   The Campaigns of Hideyoshi   646
Map 21.6   Urban Population and Major Transport Routes in Japan, ca. 1800   651
Map 22.1   British North America in 1763   663
Map 22.2   The Haitian Revolution   671
Map 22.3   Napoleonic Europe, 1796–1815   672
Map 22.4   Europe after the Congress of Vienna   678
Map 22.5   Europe in 1871   682
Map 22.6   The Expanding United States in 1900   684
Map 23.1   The New Nation-States of Latin America and the Caribbean, 1831   704
Map 23.2   Mexico's Loss of Territory to the United States, 1824–1854   705
Map 23.3   The Economy of Latin America and the Caribbean, ca. 1900   715

Map 23.4   Non-Western Migrations in the Nineteenth Century   721
Map 24.1   The Opium Trade: Origins, Interactions, Adaptations   732
Map 24.2   Treaty Ports and Foreign Spheres of Influence in China, 1842–1907   735
Map 24.3   The Taiping Rebellion, 1851–1864   737
Map 24.4   Japanese Territorial Expansion, 1870–1905   746
Map 24.5   The Modernization of Japan to 1910   753
Map 25.1   The Decline of the Ottoman Empire, 1683–1923   764
Map 25.2   The Territorial Expansion of the Russian Empire, 1795–1914   778
Map 26.1   Industrializing Britain in 1850   794
Map 26.2   The Industrialization of Europe by 1914   797
Map 26.3   World Population Growth, 1700–1900   804
Map 26.4   European Population Movements, 1750–1914   806
Map 27.1   The Expansion of British Power in India, 1756–1805   826
Map 27.2   The British Empire in India, 1858–1914   829
Map 27.3   Competitive Imperialism: The World in 1914   834
Map 27.4   The Scramble for Africa   839
Map 27.5   The Spread of Islam and Christianity in Africa, 1860–1900   840
Map 27.6   Western Imperialism in Southeast Asia, 1870–1914   846
Map 28.1   Europe, the Middle East, and North Africa in 1914 and 1923   863
Map 28.2   European Empires, 1936   871
Map 28.3   World War II in Europe, 1939–1945   884
Map 28.4   World War II in the Pacific, 1937–1945   890
Map 29.1   The Cold War, 1947–1991   898
Map 29.2   Global Regime Changes Engineered by the CIA   900
Map 29.3   The Cuban Missile Crisis   905
Map 29.4   Urbanization and Population Growth in Latin America and the Caribbean, ca. 1950   909
Map 29.5   Decolonization in Africa, the Middle East, and Asia since 1945   914
Map 29.6   The Palestine Conflict, 1947–1949   915
Map 30.1   Communist Eastern Europe, 1945–1989   934
Map 30.2   The Fall of Communism in Eastern Europe and the Soviet Union   938
Map 30.3   Governmental Participation by Women   944
Map 30.4   Open Cities and Special Economic Zones in China, 1980–2000   949
Map 30.5   The Vietnam War   951
Map 30.6   The Arab–Israeli Wars, 1967 and 1973   953
Map 31.1   The Global Distribution of Wealth, 2012   967
Map 31.2   The Global Balance of Trade, 2008   969
Map 31.3   US Security Commitments since 1945   972
Map 31.4   World Map of Climate Change Performance   993

Studying with Maps

MAPS

World history cannot be fully understood without a clear comprehension of the chronologies and parameters within which different empires, states, and peoples have changed over time. Maps facilitate this understanding by illuminating the significance of time, space, and geography in shaping the patterns of world history.

Projection

A map *projection* portrays all or part of the earth, which is spherical, on a flat surface. All maps, therefore, include some distortion. The projections in *Patterns of World History* show the earth at global, continental, regional, and local scales.

Topography

Many maps in *Patterns of World History* show *relief*—the contours of the land. Topography is an important element in studying maps because the physical terrain has played a critical role in shaping human history.

Scale Bar

Every map in *Patterns of World History* includes a *scale* that shows distances in both miles and kilometers, and in some instances in feet as well.

Map Key

Maps use symbols to show the location of features and to convey information. Each symbol is explained in the map's *key*.

Global Locator

Many of the maps in *Patterns of World History* include *global locators* that show the area being depicted in a larger context.

The Inca Empire ca. 1525 CE

Inca expansion
To 1438
Under Pachacuti, 1438–1463
Under Pachacuti and Tupac Yupanqui, 1463–1471
Under Tupac Yupanqui, 1471–1493
Under Huayna Capac, 1493–1525
Imperial boundary
Boundary between the four quarters of the empire
Inca road
Imperial capital
Major Inca administrative center
PERU   Modern-day country

Preface

The response to the first edition of *Patterns of World History* has been extraordinarily gratifying to those of us involved in its development. The diversity of schools that have adopted the book—community colleges as well as state universities; small liberal arts schools as well as large private universities—suggests to us that its central premise of exploring *patterns* in world history is both adaptable to a variety of pedagogical environments and congenial to a wide body of instructors. Indeed, from the responses to the book we have received thus far, we expect that the level of writing, timeliness and completeness of the material, and analytical approach will serve it well as the discipline of world history continues to mature. These key strengths are enhanced in the second edition of *Patterns* by constructive, dynamic suggestions from the broad range of students and instructors who are using the book.

It is widely agreed that world history is more than simply the sum of all national histories. Likewise, *Patterns of World History*, Second Edition, is more than an unbroken sequence of dates, battles, rulers, and their activities, and it is more than the study of isolated stories of change over time. Rather, in this textbook we endeavor to present in a clear and engaging way how world history "works." Instead of merely offering a narrative history of the appearance of this or that innovation, we present an analysis of the process by which an innovation in one part of the world is diffused and carried to the rest of the globe. Instead of focusing on the memorization of people, places, and events, we strive to present important facts in context and draw meaningful connections, analyzing whatever patterns we find and drawing conclusions where we can. In short, we seek to examine the interlocking mechanisms and animating forces of world history, without neglecting the human agency behind them.

The *Patterns* Approach

Our approach in this book is, as the title suggests, to look for patterns in world history. We should say at the outset that we do not mean to select certain categories into which we attempt to stuff the historical events we choose to emphasize, nor do we claim that all world history is reducible to such patterns, nor do we mean to suggest that the nature of the patterns determines the outcome of historical events. We see them instead as broad, flexible organizational frameworks around which to build the structure of a world history in such a way that the enormous sweep and content of the past can be viewed in a comprehensible narrative, with sound analysis and ample scope for debate and discussion. In this sense, we view them much like the armatures in clay sculptures, giving support and structure to the final figure but not necessarily preordaining its ultimate shape.

From its origins, human culture grew through interactions and adaptations on all the continents except Antarctica. A voluminous scholarship on all regions of the world has thus been accumulated, which those working in the field have to attempt to master if their explanations and arguments are to sound even remotely persuasive. The sheer volume and complexity of the sources, however, mean that even the knowledge and expertise of the best scholars are going to be incomplete. Moreover, the humility with which all historians must approach their material contains within it the realization that no historical explanation is ever fully satisfactory or final: As a driving force in the historical process, creative human agency moves events in directions that are never fully predictable, even if they follow broad patterns. Learning to discern patterns in this process not only helps novice historians to appreciate the complex challenges (and rewards) of historical inquiry; it also develops critical thinking abilities in all students.

As we move through the second decade of the twenty-first century, world historians have long since left behind the "West plus the rest" approach that marked the field's early years, together with economic and geographical reductionism, in the search for a new balance between comprehensive cultural and institutional examinations on the one hand and those highlighting human agency on the other. All too often, however, this is reflected in texts that seek broad coverage at the expense of analysis, thus resulting in a kind of "world history lite." Our aim is therefore to simplify the study of the world—to make it accessible to the student—without making world history itself simplistic.

Patterns of World History, Second Edition, proposes the teaching of world history from the perspective of the relationship between continuity and change. What we advocate in this book is a distinct intellectual framework for this relationship and the role of innovation and historical change through patterns of origins, interactions, and adaptations. Each small or large technical or cultural innovation originated in one geographical center or independently in several different centers. As people in the centers interacted with their neighbors, the neighbors adapted to, and in many cases were transformed by, the innovations. By "adaptation" we include the entire spectrum of human responses, ranging from outright rejection to creative borrowing and, at times, forced acceptance.

Small technical innovations often went through the pattern of origin, interaction, and adaptation across the world without arousing much attention, even though they had major consequences. For example, the horse collar, which originated in ninth-century China and allowed for the replacement of oxen with stronger horses, gradually improved the productivity of agriculture in eleventh-century western Europe. More sweeping intellectual–cultural innovations, by contrast, such as the spread of universal religions like Buddhism, Christianity, and Islam and the rise of science, have often had profound consequences—in some cases leading to conflicts lasting centuries—and affect us even today.

Sometimes change was effected by commodities that to us seem rather ordinary. Take sugar, for example: It originated in southeast Asia and was traded and grown in the Mediterranean, where its cultivation on plantations created the model for expansion into the vast slave system of the Atlantic basin from the fifteenth through the nineteenth centuries, forever altering the histories of four continents. What would our diets look like today without sugar? Its history continues to unfold as we debate its merits and health risks and it supports huge multinational agribusinesses.

Or take a more obscure commodity: opium. Opium had been used medicinally for centuries in regions all over the world. But the advent of tobacco traded from the Americas to the Philippines to China, and the encouragement of Dutch traders in the region, created an environment in which the drug was smoked for the first time. Enterprising rogue British merchants, eager to find a way to crack closed Chinese markets

for other goods, began to smuggle it in from India. The market grew, the price went down, addiction spread, and Britain and China ultimately went to war over China's attempts to eliminate the traffic. Here, we have an example of an item generating interactions on a worldwide scale, with impacts on everything from politics to economics, culture, and even the environment. The legacies of the trade still weigh heavily on two of the rising powers of the twenty-first century: China and India. And opium and its derivatives, like morphine and heroin, continue to bring relief as well as suffering on a colossal scale to hundreds of millions of people.

What, then, do we gain by studying world history through the use of such patterns? First, if we consider innovation to be a driving force of history, it helps to satisfy an intrinsic human curiosity about origins—our own and others. Perhaps more importantly, seeing patterns of various kinds in historical development brings to light connections and linkages among peoples, cultures, and regions—as in the aforementioned examples—that might not otherwise present themselves.

Second, such patterns can also reveal differences among cultures that other approaches to world history tend to neglect. For example, the differences between the civilizations of the Eastern and Western Hemispheres are generally highlighted in world history texts, but the broad commonalities of human groups creating agriculturally based cities and states in widely separated areas also show deep parallels in their patterns of origins, interactions, and adaptations. Such comparisons are at the center of our approach.

Third, this kind of analysis offers insights into how an individual innovation was subsequently developed and diffused across space and time—that is, the patterns by which the new eventually becomes a necessity in our daily lives. Through all of this we gain a deeper appreciation of the unfolding of global history from its origins in small, isolated areas to the vast networks of global interconnectedness in our present world.

Finally, our use of a broad-based understanding of continuity, change, and innovation allows us to restore culture in all its individual and institutionalized aspects—spiritual, artistic, intellectual, scientific—to its rightful place alongside technology, environment, politics, and socioeconomic conditions. That is, understanding innovation in this way allows this text to help illuminate the full range of human ingenuity over time and space in a comprehensive, evenhanded, and open-ended fashion.

Options for Teaching with *Patterns of World History,* Second Edition

In response to requests from teachers who adopted the first edition, we now offer a version of *Patterns of World History* that includes a selection of primary-text and visual sources after every chapter. This section, called "Patterns of Evidence," enhances student engagement with key chapter patterns through contemporaneous voices and perspectives. Each source is accompanied by a concise introduction to provide chronological and geographical context; "Working with Sources" questions after each selection prompt students to make critical connections between the source and the main chapter narrative.

For the convenience of instructors teaching a course over two 15-week semesters, both versions of *Patterns* are limited to 31 chapters. For the sake of continuity and to accommodate the many different ways schools divide the midpoint of their world history sequence, Chapters 15–18 overlap in both volumes; in Volume 2, Chapter 15 is given as a "prelude" to Part Four. Those using a trimester system will also find divisions made in convenient places, with Chapter 10 coming at the beginning of Part Two and Chapter 22 at the beginning of Part Five. Finally, for those schools that offer a modern world history course that begins at approximately 1750, a volume is available that includes only the final two parts of the book.

Patterns of Change and Six Periods of World History

Similarly, *Patterns* is adaptable to both chronological and thematic styles of instruction. We divide the history of the world into six major time periods and recognize for each period one or two main patterns of innovation, their spread through interaction, and their adoption by others. Obviously, lesser patterns are identified as well, many of which are of more limited regional interactive and adaptive impact. We wish to stress again that these are broad categories of analysis and that there is nothing reductive or deterministic in our aims or choices. Nevertheless, we believe the patterns we have chosen help to make the historical process more intelligible, providing a series of lenses that can help to focus the otherwise confusing facts and disparate details that comprise world history.

Part One (Prehistory–600 BCE): Origins of human civilization—tool making and symbol creating—in Africa as well as the origins of agriculture, urbanism, and state formation in the three agrarian centers of the Middle East, India, and China.

Part Two (600 BCE–600 CE): Emergence of the axial-age thinkers and their visions of a transcendent god or first principle in Eurasia; elevation of these visions to the status of state religions in empires and kingdoms, in the process forming multiethnic and multilinguistic polities.

Part Three (600–1450): Disintegration of classical empires and formation of religious civilizations in Eurasia, with the emergence of religiously unified regions divided by commonwealths of multiple states.

Part Four (1450–1750): Rise of new empires; interaction, both hostile and peaceful, among the religious civilizations and new empires across all continents of the world. Origins of the New Science in Europe, based on the use of mathematics for the investigation of nature.

Part Five (1750–1900): Origins of scientific–industrial "modernity," simultaneous with the emergence of constitutional and ethnic nation-states, in the West (Europe and North America); interaction of the West with Asia and Africa, resulting in complex adaptations, both coerced as well as voluntary, on the part of the latter.

Part Six (1900–Present): Division of early Western modernity into the three competing visions: communism, supremacist nationalism, and capitalism. After two horrific world wars and the triumph of nation-state formation across the world, capitalism remains as the last surviving version of modernity. Capitalism is then reinvigorated by the increasing use of social networking tools, which popularizes both "traditional" religious and cultural ideas and constitutional nationalism in authoritarian states.

Chapter Organization and Structure

Each part of the book addresses the role of change and innovation on a broad scale in a particular time and/or region, and each chapter contains different levels of exploration to examine the principal features of particular cultural or national areas and how each affects, and is affected by, the patterns of origins, interactions, and adaptations:

- *Geography and the Environment*: The relationship between human beings and the geography and environment of the places they inhabit is among the most basic factors in understanding human societies. In this chapter segment, therefore, the topics under investigation involve the natural environment of a particular region and the general conditions affecting change and innovation. Climatic conditions, earthquakes, tsunamis, volcanic eruptions, outbreaks of disease, and so forth all have obvious effects on how humans react to the challenge of survival. The initial portions of chapters introducing new regions for study therefore include environmental and geographical overviews, which are revisited and expanded in later chapters as necessary. The larger issues of how decisive the impact of geography on the development of human societies is—as in the commonly asked question "Is geography destiny?"—are also examined here.
- *Political Developments*: In this segment, we ponder such questions as how rulers and their supporters wield political and military power. How do different political traditions develop in different areas? How do states expand, and why? How do different political arrangements attempt to strike a balance between the rulers and the ruled? How and why are political innovations transmitted to other societies? Why do societies accept or reject such innovations from the outside?

Are there discernible patterns in the development of kingdoms or empires or nation-states?
- *Economic and Social Developments*: The relationship between economics and the structures and workings of societies has long been regarded as crucial by historians and social scientists. But what patterns, if any, emerge in how these relationships develop and function among different cultures? This segment explores such questions as the following: What role does economics play in the dynamics of change and continuity? What, for example, happens in agrarian societies when merchant classes develop? How does the accumulation of wealth lead to social hierarchy? What forms do these hierarchies take? How do societies formally and informally try to regulate wealth and poverty? How are economic conditions reflected in family life and gender relations? Are there patterns that reflect the varying social positions of men and women that are characteristic of certain economic and social institutions? How are these in turn affected by different cultural practices?
- *Intellectual, Religious, and Cultural Aspects*: Finally, we consider it vital to include an examination dealing in some depth with the way people understood their existence and life during each period. Clearly, intellectual innovation—the generation of new ideas—lies at the heart of the changes we have singled out as pivotal in the patterns of origins, interactions, and adaptations that form the heart of this text. Beyond this, those areas concerned with the search for and construction of meaning—particularly religion, the arts, philosophy, and science—not only reflect shifting perspectives but also, in many cases, play a leading role in determining the course of events within each form of society. All of these facets of intellectual life are in turn manifested in new perspectives and representations in the cultural life of a society.

Features

- **Seeing Patterns/Thinking Through Patterns:** Successful history teachers often employ recursive, even reiterative, techniques in the classroom to help students more clearly perceive patterns. In a similar fashion, "Seeing Patterns" and "Thinking Through Patterns" use a question–discussion format in each chapter to pose several broad questions ("Seeing Patterns") as advance organizers for key themes, which are then matched up with short essays at the end ("Thinking Through Patterns") that examine these same questions in a sophisticated yet student-friendly fashion. Instructors who have class-tested *Patterns of World History* report that the "Thinking Through Patterns" essays, designed to foster discussion, also serve as excellent models for student writing.

- **Patterns Up Close:** Since students frequently better apprehend macro-level patterns when they see their contours brought into sharper relief, "Patterns Up Close" essays in each chapter highlight a particular innovation that demonstrates origins, interactions, and adaptations in action. Spanning technological, social, political, intellectual, economic, and environmental developments, the "Patterns Up Close" essays combine text, visuals, and graphics to consider everything from the pepper trade to the guillotine.

- **Marginal Glossary:** To avoid the necessity of having to flip pages back and forth, definitions of words that the reader may not know, as well as of key terms, are set directly in the margin at the point where they are introduced.

Today, more than ever, students and instructors are confronted by a vast welter of information on every conceivable subject. Beyond the ever-expanding print media, the Internet and the Web have opened hitherto unimaginable amounts of data to us. Despite such unprecedented access, however, all of us are too frequently overwhelmed by this undifferentiated—and all too often indigestible—mass. Nowhere is this more true than in world history, by definition the field within the historical profession with the broadest scope. Therefore, we think that an effort at synthesis—of narrative and analysis structured around a clear, accessible, widely applicable theme—is needed, an effort that seeks to explain critical patterns of the world's past behind the billions of bits of information accessible at the stroke of a key on a computer keyboard. We hope this text, in tracing the lines of transformative ideas and things that left their patterns deeply imprinted into the canvas of world history, will provide such a synthesis.

Changes to the Second Edition

Streamlined narrative To facilitate accessibility, we have shortened the overall length of the book by 20 percent. This reduction has not come at the expense of discarding essential topics. Instead, we have tightened the narrative, focusing even more on key concepts and (with the guidance of reviewers) discarding extraneous examples.

Revised and enhanced coverage of the Atlantic World In response to feedback from both users and nonusers of the text, we have substantially improved Part Five's coverage of the Atlantic World. The former Chapter 27, "Creoles and Caudillos," is now Chapter 23, allowing for a seamless continuation with the discussion of Atlantic revolutions in Chapter 22. "Industrialization and its Discontents," which formerly was Chapter 23, is now Chapter 26, while the former Chapter 26, "The New Imperialism," is now Chapter 27. The overall result of these organizational changes is to substantially enhance the book's coverage of Latin America in the eighteenth and nineteenth centuries. We are indebted to the guidance, scholarship, and close reading of the revised chapters in Part Five provided by Evan Ward of Brigham Young University.

NEW FEATURE "Against the Grain" At the end of each chapter, these brief narratives illustrate how the discernment of patterns allows for an appreciation of alternatives, even contradictions, brought about by creative human agency. Topics range from visionaries who challenged dominant religious patterns, including Akhenaten in ancient Egypt and the Cathars in medieval Europe; women who found agency, voice, and even power within patriarchal societies, such as Empress Wu in seventh-century China or Juana Inés de la Cruz in seventeenth-century Mexico; and agitators who fought for social and economic justice, including the outspoken critic of nineteenth-century British imperialism E. D. Morel and the fearless anti-apartheid movement led by the African National Congress.

- **NEW FEATURE Pull quotes** The pages of the second edition are enlivened by pithy quotes from a diverse array of contemporaneous voices, lending both context and commentary to the main narrative.
- New **"Patterns Up Close" essays** New topics for this popular feature include recent discoveries about early human/Neanderthal interaction; Islamic influence on European Gothic architecture; comparisons of Byzantine and Islamic art; global innovations in cartography that fueled the age of exploration; the Harlem Renaissance and the African diaspora; and the Non-Aligned Movement.

In addition to the substantive reworking of Part Five, all chapters of *Patterns* have benefited from the thoughtful suggestions of reviewers as well as feedback from instructors who are teaching with the book. Recent discoveries about our past as well as the rapid pace at which our contemporary world is changing are also reflected in the second edition. Here are some of the key changes we made to other parts of the book:

Part One Chapter 1 has been revised to incorporate recent scientific discoveries about hominid origins, Asian hominid finds, and the human presence in Beringia. A new "Patterns Up Close" essay considers new evidence about the Neanderthals. In Chapter 2, we expanded discussions of gender roles in early agrarian societies. Chapter 3 takes an enhanced look at the controversy surrounding putative Indo-European migration.

Part Two Chapter 6 examines new discoveries by tropical archaeologists that have enhanced our understanding of early plant domestication. Chapter 7 includes a broader discussion of the origins of early Greek literature. Chapter 8 offers a more nuanced discussion of the role of women in Hinduism.

Part Three In Chapter 10, discussion of the origins of the Islamic religious civilization has been significantly revised and streamlined, affording both greater clarity and sharper detail; discussion of Eastern Christian civilization and the rise of Byzantium has been enhanced; and a new "Patterns Up Close" essay thoughtfully compares Byzantine icons and Islamic miniatures. In Chapter 11, the "Patterns Up Close" essay has been revised to emphasize the pattern of origins and interactions shaping Gothic cathedrals, especially with Islamic architecture. Chapter 12 includes a refined examination of our interpretation of Indian syncretism. And Chapter 14 considers interactions between Chinese traders and Swahili merchants.

Part Four Chapter 16 includes a new "Patterns Up Close" essay exploring the differences between Sunni and Shiite Islam. Chapter 17 has been restructured; it now begins with a discussion of Renaissance culture. In addition, the discussion of Copernicus's connection between the discovery of America and the heliocentric theory of the planetary system has been enhanced, and a new "Patterns Up Close" essay describes the tremendous advances in cartography made by many cultures. Chapter 18 now considers the resistance of Native American peoples to Spanish colonization. Chapter 20 streamlines the discussion of the founding of the Timurids.

Part Five In addition to the structural changes described above, Chapter 22 now includes a section on the Haitian Revolution, to emphasize its proper place within the modern constitutional revolutions; new discussions of Native Americans appear throughout. Chapter 23 begins with a new vignette; the entire chapter has been largely rewritten to emphasize the contributions of the indigenous and subaltern populations of Latin America to the process of independence. In Chapter 26, the segment on innovations in communication technology was relocated in order to emphasize their importance.

Part Six Chapter 29 now includes a segment on the Central Intelligence Agency, along with a map showing its global involvement in regime change. A new "Patterns Up Close" essay describes the importance of the Bandung Conference. To Chapter 30 we added material in the segment on the American civil rights movement to include civil rights for Native Americans and the gay rights movement. We have also revised the "Patterns Up Close" essay on the women's liberation movement to emphasize global dimensions of the feminist movement. Chapter 31 has been enlarged, to bring world history up to 2014, through sections on Egypt, Syria, Iraq, Nigeria, and the Central African Republic.

Additional Learning Resources for *Patterns of World History*

Dashboard: Dashboard delivers quality content, tools, and assessments to track student progress in an intuitive, Web-based learning environment. Assessments are designed to accompany *Patterns of World History* and are automatically graded so instructors can easily check students' progress as they complete their assignments. The color-coded gradebook illustrates at a glance where students are succeeding and where they can improve so instructors can adapt lectures on the fly to student needs. Dashboard features a streamlined interface that connects instructors and students with the functions they perform most, and simplifies the learning experience by putting student progress first. All Dashboard content is engineered to work on mobile devices, including the iOS operating system. Our goal is to create a platform that is simple, informative, and mobile. Please contact your local Oxford University Press representative for a demonstration of Dashboard.

Oxford First Source (www.oup.com/us/first-source): Oxford First Source is an online database, with custom print capability, of primary source documents in world history. The continuously updated collection consists of approximately 300 documents, both textual and visual, selected and organized to complement any world history survey text. These documents cover a broad range of political, social, and cultural topics. The documents are indexed by date, title, subject, and region and are fully searchable. Each is accompanied by a headnote and study questions. Six-month access to Oxford First Source is free when bundled with *Patterns of World History*, or can be purchased standalone for $19.95. Please contact your local Oxford University Press representative for details.

Asset Resource Center (ARC): This online resource center, available to adopters of *Patterns of World History*, includes:

Instructor's Resource Manual: Includes, for each chapter, a detailed chapter outline, suggested lecture topics, learning objectives, map quizzes, geography exercises, classroom activities, "Patterns Up Close" activities, "Seeing Patterns and Making Connections" activities, "Against the Grain" exercises, biographical sketches, and suggested Web resources and digital media files. Also includes for each chapter approximately 40 multiple-choice, short-answer, true-or-false, and fill-in-the-blank as well as approximately 10 essay questions.

PowerPoints and Computerized Testbank: Includes PowerPoint slides and JPEG and PDF files for all the maps and photos in the text, an additional 400 map files from *The Oxford Atlas of World History*, and approximately 250 additional PowerPoint-based slides organized by theme and topic. Also includes approximately 1,500 questions that can be customized by the instructor.

Additional Resources

- *Sources in Patterns of World History*: **Volume 1: To 1600:** Completely revised, it includes approximately 75 text and visual sources in world history, organized by the chapter organization of *Patterns of World History*. Each source is accompanied by a headnote and reading questions.
- *Sources in Patterns of World History*: **Volume 2: Since 1400:** Completely revised, it includes approximately 90 text and visual sources in world history, organized by the chapter organization of *Patterns of World History*. Each source is accompanied by a headnote and reading questions.
- *Mapping Patterns of World History*, **Volume 1: To 1600:** Includes approximately 50 full-color maps, each accompanied by a brief headnote, as well as Concept Map exercises.
- *Mapping Patterns of World History*, **Volume 2: Since 1400:** Includes approximately 50 full-color maps, each accompanied by a brief headnote, as well as Concept Map exercises.
- **Companion Website (www.oup.com/us/vonsivers):** Includes quizzes, flashcards, map exercises, and links to YouTube videos.
- **E-book for Patterns of World History:** E-books of all the volumes are available for purchase at www.coursesmart.com.

Bundling Options

Patterns of World History can be bundled at a significant discount with any of the titles in the popular Very Short Introductions or Oxford World's Classics series, as well as other titles from the Higher Education division world history catalog (www.oup.com/us/catalog/he). Please contact your OUP representative for details.

Acknowledgments

Throughout the course of writing, revising, and preparing *Patterns of World History* for publication we have benefited from the guidance and professionalism accorded us by all levels of the staff at Oxford University Press. John Challice, vice president and publisher, had faith in the inherent worth of our project from the outset and provided the initial impetus to move forward. Meg Botteon guided us through the revisions and added a final polish, often helping us with substantive suggestions. Lynn Luecken carried out the thankless task of assembling the manuscript and did so with generosity and good cheer, helping us with many details in the final manuscript. Picture researcher Francelle Carapetyan diligently tracked down every photo request despite the sometimes sketchy sources we provided, Ben Sadock copyedited the manuscript with meticulous attention to detail, and Theresa Stockton steered us through the intricacies of production with the stoicism of a saint.

Most of all, we owe a special debt of gratitude to Charles Cavaliere, our editor. Charles took on the daunting task of directing the literary enterprise at a critical point in the book's career. He pushed this project to its successful completion, accelerated its schedule, and used a combination of flattery and hard-nosed tactics to make sure we stayed the course. His greatest contribution, however, is in the way he refined our original vision for the book with several important adjustments that clarified its latent possibilities. From the maps to the photos to the special features, Charles's high standards and concern for detail are evident on every page.

Developing a book like *Patterns of World History* is an ambitious project, a collaborative venture in which authors and editors benefit from the feedback provided by a team of outside readers and consultants.

We gratefully acknowledge the advice that the many reviewers, focus group participants, and class testers (including their students) shared with us along the way. We tried to implement all of the excellent suggestions. We owe a special debt of thanks to Evan R. Ward, who provided invaluable guidance for the revision of the coverage of Latin America and the Caribbean in Part 5, and to Jonathan S. Perry, who deftly assembled the documents for the "with Sources" version of *Patterns*. Of course, any errors of fact or interpretation that remain are solely our own.

Reviewers of the Second Edition

Michael Broyles, Macomb Community College Center Campus

Richard Garlitz, University of Tennessee at Martin

Marjorie L. Hilton, Murray State University

Ellen J. Jenkins, Arkansas Tech University

Michael Johnson, Northwest Arkansas Community College

Anthony Makowski, Delaware County Community College

Mary Jane Maxwell, Green Mountain College

Jason McCollom, University of Arkansas

Eva M. Mehl, University of North Carolina, Wilmington

George S. Pabis, Georgia Perimeter College

David Pizzo, Murray State University

Brian M. Puaca, Christopher Newport University

Jason Ripper, Everett Community College

Kira Robison, University of Alabama, Huntsville

Chad Ross, East Carolina University

Casey Schmitt, College of William and Mary

Jonathan Seitz, Drexel University

Teshale Tibebu, Temple University

Annamarie Vallis, California State University, Fresno

Gilmar Visoni, Queensborough Community College

Evan R. Ward, Brigham Young University

James Weiss, Salem State University

Reviewers of the First Edition

Stephanie Ballenger, Central Washington University

Alan Baumler, Indiana University of Pennsylvania

Robert Blackey, California State University

Robert Bond, San Diego Mesa College

Mauricio Borrero, St. John's University

Linda Bregstein-Scherr, Mercer County Community College

Scott Breuninger, University of South Dakota

Paul Brians, Washington State University

Gayle K. Brunelle, California State University, Fullerton

James De Lorenzi, City University of New York, John Jay College

Jennifer Kolpacoff Deane, University of Minnesota, Morris

Andrew D. Devenney, Grand Valley State University

Francis A. Dutra, University of California, Santa Barbara

Jeffrey Dym, Sacramento State University

Jennifer C. Edwards, Manhattan College

Lisa M. Edwards, University of Massachusetts Lowell

Charles T. Evans, Northern Virginia Community College

Christopher Ferguson, Auburn University

Scott Fritz, Western New Mexico State University

Arturo Giraldez, University of the Pacific

Candace Gregory-Abbott, California State University, Sacramento

Derek Heng, Ohio State University

Eric Hetherington, New Jersey Institute of Technology

Laura J. Hilton, Muskingum University

Elizabeth J. Houseman, State University of New York at Brockport

Hung-yok Ip, Oregon State University

Geoffrey Jensen, University of Arkansas

Roger E. Kanet, University of Miami

Kelly Kennington, Auburn University

Amelia M. Kiddle, University of Arizona

Frederic Krome, University of Cincinnati Clermont College

Mark W. Lentz, University of Louisiana, Lafayette

Heather Lucas, Georgia Perimeter College

Susan Mattern, University of Georgia

Susan A. Maurer, Nassau Community College

Jason McCollom, University of Arkansas

Douglas T. McGetchin, Florida Atlantic University

Stephen Morillo, Wabash College

Carolyn Neel, Arkansas Tech University

Kenneth J. Orosz, Buffalo State College

Alice K. Pate, Columbus State University

Patrick M. Patterson, Honolulu Community College

Daniel Pope, University of Oregon

G. David Price, Santa Fe College

Michael Redman, University of Louisville

Leah Renold, Texas State University

Jeremy Rich, Middle Tennessee State University

Jason Ripper, Everett Community College

Chad Ross, East Carolina University

Nana Yaw B. Sapong, Southern Illinois University

Daniel Sarefield, Fitchburg State College

Claire Schen, State University of New York, Buffalo

Robert C. Schwaller, University of North Carolina at Charlotte

George Sochan, Bowie State University

Ramya Sreenivasan, State University of New York, Buffalo

John Stanley, Kutztown University

Vladimir Steffel, Ohio State University

Anthony J. Steinhoff, University of Tennessee at Chattanooga

Micheal Tarver, Arkansas Tech University

Shane Tomashot, Georgia State University

Kate Transchel, California State University, Chico

Melanie Tubbs, Arkansas Tech University

Andrew Wackerfuss, Georgetown University

Evan R. Ward, Brigham Young University

Joseph K. S. Yick, Texas State University

Please let us know your experiences with *Patterns of World History* so that we may improve it in future editions. We welcome your comments and suggestions.

Peter von Sivers
pv4910@xmission.com

Charles A. Desnoyers
desnoyer@lasalle.edu

George B. Stow
gbsgeorge@aol.com

Note on Dates and Spellings

In keeping with widespread practice among world historians, we use "BCE" and "CE" to date events and the phrase "years ago" to describe developments from the remote past.

The transliteration of Middle Eastern words has been adjusted as much as possible to the English alphabet. Therefore, long vowels are not emphasized. The consonants specific to Arabic (alif, dhal, ha, sad, dad, ta, za, `ayn, ghayn, and qaf) are either not indicated or rendered with common English letters. A similar procedure is followed for Farsi. Turkish words follow the alphabet reform of 1929, which adds the following letters to the Western alphabet or modifies their pronunciation: c (pronounced "j"), ç (pronounced "tsh"), ğ (not pronounced but lengthening of preceding vowel), ı ("i" without dot, pronunciation close to short e), i/İ ("i" with dot, including in caps), ö (no English equivalent), ş ("sh"), and ü (no English equivalent). The spelling of common contemporary Middle Eastern and Islamic terms follows daily press usage (which, however, is not completely uniform). Examples are "al-Qaeda," "Quran," and "Sharia."

The system used in rendering the sounds of Mandarin Chinese—the northern Chinese dialect that has become in effect the national spoken language in China and Taiwan—into English in this book is *hanyu pinyin*, usually given as simply *pinyin*. This is the official romanization system of the People's Republic of China and has also become the standard outside of Taiwan, Republic of China. Most syllables are pronounced as they would be in English, with the exception of the letter *q*, which has an aspirated "ch" sound; *ch* itself has a less aspirated "ch" sound. *Zh* carries a hard "j" and *j* a soft, English-style "j." Some syllables also are pronounced— particularly in the regions around Beijing—with a retroflex *r* so that the syllable *shi*, for example, carries a pronunciation closer to "shir." Finally, the letter *r* in the *pinyin* system has no direct English equivalent, but an approximation may be had by combining the sounds of "r" and "j."

Japanese terms have been romanized according to a modification of the Hepburn system. The letter *g* is always hard; vowels are handled as they are in Italian— *e*, for example, carries a sound like "ay." We have not, however, included diacritical markings to indicate long vowel sounds for *u* or *o*. Where necessary, these have been indicated in the pronunciation guides.

For Korean terms, we have used a variation of the McCune-Reischauer system, which remains the standard romanization scheme for Korean words used in English academic writing, but eliminated any diacritical markings. Here again, the vowel sounds are pronounced more or less like those of Italian and the consonants, like those of English.

For Vietnamese words, we have used standard renditions based on the modern Quoc Ngu ("national language") system in use in Vietnam today. The system was developed by Jesuit missionaries and is based on the Portuguese alphabet. Once more, we have avoided diacritical marks, and the reader should follow the pronunciation guides for approximations of Vietnamese terms.

Latin American terms (Spanish, Nahua, or Quechua) generally follow local usage, including accents, except where they are Anglicized, per the *Oxford English Dictionary*. Thus, the Spanish-Quechua word "Tiahuanacu" becomes the Anglicized word "Tiwanaku."

We use the terms "Native American" and "Indian" interchangeably to refer to the peoples of the Americas in the pre-Columbian period and "Amerindian" in our coverage of Latin America since independence.

In keeping with widely recognized practice among paleontologists and other scholars of the deep past, we use the term "hominins" in Chapter 1 to emphasize their greater remoteness from apes and proximity to modern humans.

Phonetic spellings often follow the first appearance of a non-English word whose pronunciation may be unclear to the reader. We have followed the rules for capitalization per *The Chicago Manual of Style*.

About the Authors

Peter von Sivers is associate professor of Middle Eastern history at the University of Utah. He has previously taught at UCLA, Northwestern University, the University of Paris VII (Vincennes), and the University of Munich. He has also served as chair of the Joint Committee of the Near and Middle East, Social Science Research Council, New York, 1982–1985; editor of the *International Journal of Middle East Studies*, 1985–1989; member of the board of directors of the Middle East Studies Association of North America, 1987–1990; and chair of the SAT II World History Test Development Community of the Educational Testing Service, Princeton, NJ, 1991–1994. His publications include *Caliphate, Kingdom, and Decline: The Political Theory of Ibn Khaldun* (1968, in German), several edited books, and three dozen peer-reviewed chapters and articles on Middle Eastern and North African history, as well as world history. He received his Dr. phil. from the University of Munich.

Charles A. Desnoyers is professor of history and director of Asian Studies at La Salle University in Philadelphia. He has previously taught at Temple University, Villanova University, and Pennsylvania State University. In addition to serving as History Department chair from 1999–2007, he was a founder and long-time director of the Greater Philadelphia Asian Studies Consortium, and president (2011–2012) of the Mid-Atlantic Region Association for Asian Studies. He has served as a reader, table leader, and question writer for the AP European and World History exams. He is a lifetime member of the World History Association and served as editor of the organization's *Bulletin* from 1995–2001. In addition to numerous articles in peer-reviewed and general publications, his work includes *A Journey to the East: Li Gui's "A New Account of a Trip Around the Globe"* (2004, University of Michigan Press). He received his PhD from Temple University.

George B. Stow is professor of ancient and medieval history and director of the graduate program in history at La Salle University, Philadelphia. His teaching experience embraces a variety of undergraduate and graduate courses in ancient Greece and Rome, medieval England, and world history, and he has been awarded the Lindback Distinguished Teaching Award. Professor Stow is a member of the Medieval Academy of America and a Fellow of the Royal Historical Society. He is the recipient of a National Defense Education Act Title IV Fellowship, a Woodrow Wilson Foundation Fellowship, and research grants from the American Philosophical Society and La Salle University. His publications include a critical edition of a fourteenth-century monastic chronicle, *Historia Vitae et Regni Ricardi Secundi* (University of Pennsylvania Press, 1977), as well as numerous articles and reviews in scholarly journals including *Speculum, The English Historical Review, the Journal of Medieval History, the American Historical Review*, and several others. He received his PhD from the University of Illinois.

Patterns of
World History

Chapter 15 600–1550 CE

The Rise of Empires in the Americas

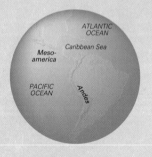

Just outside Lima, in a sandy and dry ravine 3 miles to the east of the city, is the shantytown of Túpac Amaru, named after the last Inca ruler, who died in 1572. People fleeing the Maoist Shining Path guerillas in the highlands southeast of Lima settled here during the 1980s. Archaeologists had known for years that the site was an ancient burial place called Puruchuco (Quechua "Feathered Helmet") but could not prevent the influx of settlers. By the late 1990s, the temporary shantytown had become an established settlement with masonry houses, streets, and a school. Dwellers were anxious to acquire title to their properties, introduce urban services and utilities, and clean up ground contaminated in many places by raw sewage. However, residents realized that archaeologists had to be called in before the shantytown could be officially recognized. Túpac Amaru was facing an increasingly familiar dilemma in the developing world, pitting modern needs against the wish to know the past through discovering and (if possible) preserving its last traces.

During emergency excavations from 1999 to 2001, the archaeologist Guillermo Cock, together with Túpac Amaru residents hired as field assistants, unearthed one of the most astounding treasures in the history of American archaeology. The team discovered some 2,200 mummies, most of them bundled up in blankets and perfectly preserved with their hair, skin,

ABOVE: **One of 2,200 mummies from the Inca period (1438–1533) excavated in Túpac Amaru, Peru.**

eyes, and genitals intact. Many bundles also contained rich burial gifts, including jewelry, corn, potatoes, peanuts, peppers, and coca leaves. Forty bundles had false heads made of cotton cloth, some topped with wigs, making the bundles look like oversized persons.

Scholars hope that in a few years, when all of the mummies have been unwrapped, answers can be given as to the social characteristics of the buried people. Were they members of an Inca colony planted into one of the empire's provinces? Or were they locals under their own lord, recognizing Inca overlordship? Were they specialized laborers, such as weavers, who produced cloth tributes for the Incas? Were children and women sacrificed to accompany the cotton king in his journey to the afterlife? Had assimilation between the conquerors and conquered begun? These questions are difficult to answer as so much about the Inca Empire that ruled the Andes from 1438 to 1533 remains unknown. Yet the questions are exciting precisely because they could not have been posed prior to the discovery of these mummies.

The Inca Empire and its contemporary the Aztec Empire (1427–1521) grew out of political, economic, and cultural patterns that began to form around 600 CE in Mesoamerica and the Andes (see Chapter 5). At that time, kingdoms had emerged out of chiefdoms in two small areas of Mesoamerica, the southern Yucatán Peninsula and the Mexican Basin. After 600, kingdom formation became more general across Mesoamerica and arose for the first time in the Andes. These kingdoms were states with military ruling classes that used new types of weapons and could conquer larger territories than was possible prior to the 600s. Military competition prepared the way for the origin of empires—multireligious, multilinguistic, and multiethnic states encompassing many thousands of square miles. Even though empires arrived later in the Americas than in Eurasia, they demonstrate that humans, once they had adopted agriculture, followed remarkably similar patterns of social and political formation across the world.

The Legacy of Teotihuacán and the Toltecs in Mesoamerica

As discussed in Chapter 5, the city-state of Teotihuacán had dominated northern Mesoamerica from 200 BCE to the late 500s CE. It fell into ruin probably as the result of an internal uprising against an overbearing ruling class. After its collapse, the surrounding towns and villages, as well as half a dozen other cities in and around the Mexican Basin, perpetuated the cultural legacy of Teotihuacán for centuries. Employing this legacy, the conquering state of the Toltecs unified a major part of the region for a short period from 900 to 1180. At the same time, after an internal crisis, the southern Maya kingdoms on the Yucatán Peninsula reached their late flowering, together with the northern state of Chichén Itzá.

▶ Within the patterns of state formation basic to the Americas, which types of states emerged in Mesoamerica and the Andes during the period 600–1550? What characterized these states?

▶ Why did the Tiwanaku and Wari states have ruling classes but no dynasties and central bureaucracies? How were these patterns expressed in the territorial organization of these states?

▶ What patterns of urban life characterized the cities of Tenochtitlán and Cuzco, the capitals of the Aztec and Inca Empires? In which ways were these cities similar to those of Eurasia and Africa?

Chapter Outline

- The Legacy of Teotihuacán and the Toltecs in Mesoamerica

- The Legacy of Tiwanaku and Wari in the Andes

- American Empires: Aztec and Inca Origins and Dominance

- Imperial Society and Culture

- Putting It All Together

Militarism in the Mexican Basin

After the ruling class of Teotihuacán disintegrated at the end of the sixth century, the newly independent local lords and their supporters in the small successor states of Mesoamerica continued Teotihuacán's cultural heritage. This heritage was defined by Teotihuacán's temple style, ceramics, textiles, and religious customs, especially the cult of the feathered serpent god Quetzalcoatl [ket-sal-COA]. The Toltecs, migrants from the north, militarized the Teotihuacán legacy and transformed it into a program of conquest.

Ceremonial Centers and Chiefdoms   In the three centuries after the end of the city-state of Teotihuacán, the local population declined from some 200,000 to about 30,000. Although largely ruined, the ceremonial center continued to attract pilgrims, but other places around the Mexican Basin and beyond rose in importance. The semiarid region to the northwest of the valley had an extensive mining industry, with many mine shafts extending a mile or more into the mountains. The region produced gemstones such as greenstone, turquoise, hematite, and cinnabar. Independent after 600, inhabitants built ceremonial centers and small states of their own, trading their gemstones to their neighbors in all directions.

To the north were the Pueblo cultures in today's southwestern United States. These cultures were based on sophisticated irrigated farming systems and are known for their distinctive painted pottery styles. They flourished between 700 and 1500 in the canyons of what are today the states of New Mexico, Arizona, southwestern Colorado, and southeastern Utah. In turn, these cultures might have been in contact with the Mississippi cultures, among which the ceremonial center and city of Cahokia (650–1400) near modern St. Louis is the best-known site. An obsidian scraper from the Pachuca region north of the Mexican Basin found in Spiro Mounds, Oklahoma, attests to at least occasional contacts between Mesoamerica and the Mississippi culture (see Map 15.1).

In western Mesoamerica, ceremonial centers and chiefdoms flourished on the basis of metallurgy, which arrived through Ecuadoran seaborne merchants ca. 600–800. The Ecuadorans received their copper from Peru, in return for seashells found in the warm waters off their coast as well as farther north. Copper, too soft for agricultural implements or military weapons, served mostly in households and as jewelry for the rich.

In the south, a number of small, fortified hilltop states flourished in the post-Teotihuacán period. Their inhabitants built moats and ramparts to protect these states. More than in other Mesoamerican states, the southern ruling classes were embroiled in fierce wars during 600–900, images of which are depicted in stone reliefs of gruesome battle scenes.

The Toltec Conquering State   Early after the collapse of Teotihuacán, craftspeople and farmers migrated some 60 miles north to Tula, a place on a ridge in the highlands watered by two tributaries of a river flowing into the Gulf of Mexico. They founded a small ceremonial center and town with workshops known for the high quality of the scrapers, knives, and spear points fabricated from the local Pachuca obsidian. Around 900, new migrants arrived from northwest Mexico as well as the Gulf Coast. The northerners spoke Nahuatl [NA-hua], the language of the later Aztecs, who considered Tula their ancestral city.

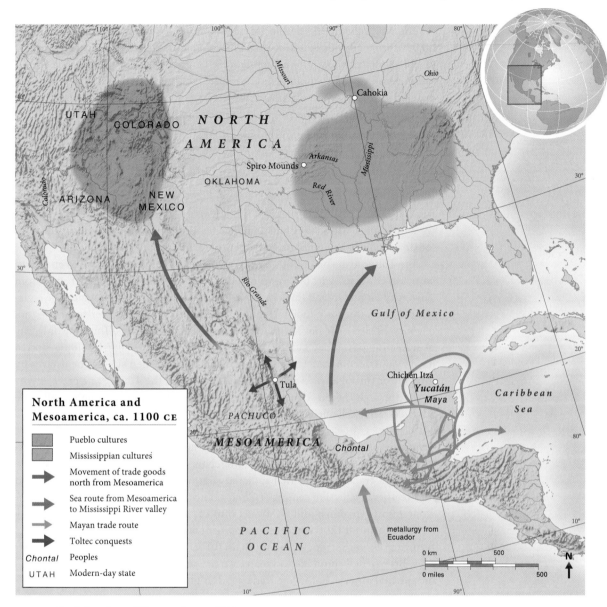

MAP **15.1 North America and Mesoamerica, ca. 1100.**

The integration of the new arrivals was apparently not peaceful, since it resulted in the abandonment of the temple and the departure of a defeated party of Tulans. This abandonment may well have been enshrined in the myth of Tolpiltzin, a priest-king of the feathered serpent god Quetzalcoatl, who after his departure to the east would one day return to restore the cult to its rightful center. Later, Spaniards used the myth to justify their rule in the Americas (see Chapter 18).

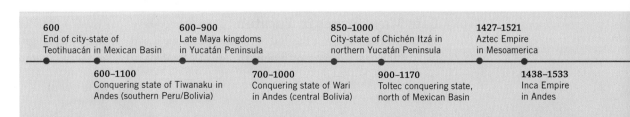

600	600–900	850–1000	1427–1521
End of city-state of Teotihuacán in Mexican Basin	Late Maya kingdoms in Yucatán Peninsula	City-state of Chichén Itzá in northern Yucatán Peninsula	Aztec Empire in Mesoamerica

600–1100	700–1000	900–1170	1438–1533
Conquering state of Tiwanaku in Andes (southern Peru/Bolivia)	Conquering state of Wari in Andes (central Bolivia)	Toltec conquering state, north of Mexican Basin	Inca Empire in Andes

The new Tula of 900 developed quickly into a large city with a new temple, 60,000 urban dwellers, and perhaps another 60,000 farmers on surrounding lands. It was the first city-centered state to give pictorial prominence to the sacrifice of captured warriors. As it evolved, Tula became the capital of the conquering state of the Toltecs, which imprinted its warrior culture on large parts of Mesoamerica from around 900 to 1180 (see Map 15.1).

The Toltecs introduced two innovations in weaponry that improved the effectiveness of hand-to-hand combat. First, there was the new weapon of a short (1.5-foot) sword made of hardwood with inlaid obsidian edges, which could slash as well as crush, in contrast to the obsidian-spiked clubs that had been the primary weapons in earlier times. Second, warriors wore obsidian daggers with wooden handles inside a band on the left arm, replacing simpler obsidian blades, which were difficult to use as they had no handles. Traditional dart throwers and slings for stone projectiles completed the offensive armament of the warriors.

The Toltec army of 13,000–26,000 soldiers was sufficiently large to engage in battles of conquest within an area of 4 days' march (roughly 40 miles) away from Tula. Any target beyond this range was beyond their capabilities, given the logistics of armor, weapons, food rations, narrow dirt roads, and uneven terrain—and, of course, Toltecs did not have the benefit of wheeled vehicles. Thus, the only way of projecting power beyond the range of 40 miles was to establish colonies and to have troops accompany traders, each of which could then supply themselves by foraging or through trade along the way. As a result, the Toltec state projected its power through the prestige of its large military, rather than through a full-scale administrative scheme with the imposition of governors, tributes, and taxes.

Trade   Apart from demonstrating military might, the Toltecs pursued the establishment of a large trade network. Merchants parlayed Tula's obsidian production into a trade network that radiated southward into the cacao, vanilla, and bird-feather production centers of Chiapas and Guatemala; to the north into gemstone mining regions; and westward into centers of metal mining. Metallurgy advanced around 1200 with the development of the technology of bronze casting. Bronze axes were stronger and more useful for working with wood than copper axes. Bronze bells produced a greater variety of sounds than those of copper. As ornamental objects, both were trade goods highly prized by the elites in Tula.

The Late Toltec Era   Toltec military power declined in the course of the twelfth century when the taxable grain yield around the city diminished, because of either prolonged droughts or a depletion of the topsoil on the terraces, or a combination of the two. Sometime around 1180, a new wave of foraging peoples from the northwest invaded, attacking with bows and arrows and using hit-and-run tactics against Toltec communication lines. The disruptions caused an internal revolt, which brought down the ceremonial center and its palaces. By 1200, Tula was a city with a burned-out center, like Teotihuacán six centuries earlier, and Mesoamerica relapsed into a period of small-state coexistence like that of the pre-600 period.

Late Maya States in Yucatán

Teotihuacán's demise at the end of the sixth century was paralleled by a realignment of the balance of power among the Maya kingdoms in the southern Yucatán lowlands of Mesoamerica. This realignment, accompanied by extensive warfare, was resolved by around 650. A period of late flowering spanned the next two centuries, followed by a shift of power from the southern to the northern part of the peninsula.

The Southern Kingdoms　At its height during the fourth and fifth centuries, Teotihuacán in the Mexican Basin had interjected itself into the delicate balance of power existing among the Maya kingdoms of southern Yucatán. Alliances among the states shifted, and prolonged wars of conquest racked the lowlands, destroying several older states. A dozen new kingdoms emerged and established a new balance of power among themselves. After a lengthy hiatus, Maya culture entered its final period (650–900).

The most striking phenomenon of the final period in the southern, rain forest–covered lowlands and adjacent highlands were massive new programs of agricultural expansion and ceremonial monument construction. Agriculture was expanded again through cutting down the rain forest on hillsides and terracing the hills for soil retention. The largest kingdoms grew to 50,000–60,000 inhabitants and reached astounding rural population densities of about 1,000 persons per square mile. (In comparison, England's most densely populated counties just prior to its agricultural expansion after 1700 were Middlesex and Surrey, with 221 and 207 persons per square mile, respectively.) Although the late Maya states were geographically small, they were administratively the most centralized polities ever created in indigenous American history.

The late Maya states did not last long. In spite of all efforts, the usually torrential downpours of the rainy season gradually washed the topsoil from the newly built hillside terraces. The topsoil, accumulating as alluvium in the flatlands, was initially quite fertile, but from around 800 onward it became more and more depleted of nutrients. In addition, in many wetlands, farmers found it difficult to prevent clay from forming over the alluvium and hardening in the process. Malnutrition resulting from the shrinking agricultural surface began to reduce the labor force. Ruling classes had to make do with fewer workers and smaller agricultural surpluses. In the end, even the ruling classes suffered, with members killing each other for what remained of these surpluses. By about 900, the Maya kingdoms in southern Yucatán had shriveled to the size of chiefdoms with small towns and villages.

Chichén Itzá in the North　A few small Maya states on the periphery survived. The most prominent among them was Chichén Itzá [chee-CHEN eat-SA] in the northern lowlands, which flourished from about 850 to 1000. At first glance the region would appear to be less than hospitable to a successful state. The climate in the north was much drier than that in the south. The surface was rocky or covered with thin topsoil, supporting mostly grass, scrub vegetation, and isolated forests. In many places, where the soil was too saline, agriculture was impossible, and the production of salt was the only source of income. There were no rivers, but many sinkholes in the porous limestone underneath the soil held water. Countless cisterns to hold additional amounts of water for year-round use were cut into the limestone and plastered to prevent seepage. This water, carried in jars to the surface, supported an intensive garden agriculture, productive enough to sustain entire towns and city-states.

Chacmool (Offering Table) at the Entrance to the Temple of Warriors, Chichén Itzá. Chacmools originated here and spread to numerous places in Mesoamerica, as far north as Tenochtitlán and Tula. Offerings to the gods included food, tobacco, feathers, and incense. Offerings might have included also human sacrifices. The table in the form of a prostrate human figure is in itself symbolic of sacrifice.

Chichén Itzá was founded during the phase of renewed urbanization in 650. It was built near two major sinkholes and several salt flats. The population was composed of local Maya as well as the Maya-speaking Chontal from the Gulf Coast farther west. Groups among these people engaged in long-distance trade, both overland and in boats along the coast. Since trade in the most lucrative goods (such as cacao, vanilla, jade, copper, bronze, turquoise, and obsidian) required contact with people well outside even the farthest political reach of either Teotihuacán or Tula, merchants (*pochtecas* [potsh-TAY-cas]) traveled in armed caravans. These merchant groups enjoyed considerable freedom and even sponsorship by the ruling classes of the states of Mesoamerica.

Chontal traders adopted Toltec culture, and when they based themselves in Chichén Itzá around 850 they superimposed their adopted culture over that of the original Maya. How the city was ruled is only vaguely understood, but there is some evidence that there were two partially integrated ruling factions, possibly descended from the Chontal and local Maya, sharing in the governance of the city. At the very end of the period of Teotihuacán, Maya, and Toltec cultural expansion, the three cultural traditions finally merged on the Yucatán Peninsula in only one geographically marginal place. This merger, however, did not last long; already around 1000 the ruling-class factions left the city-state for unknown reasons. As a result, the city-state diminished in size and power to town level.

The Legacy of Tiwanaku and Wari in the Andes

Mesoamerica and the Andes, from the time of chiefdom formation in 2500 BCE in Caral-Supé onward, shared the tradition of regional temple pilgrimages. In the Andes, the chiefdoms remained mostly coastal, with some inland extensions along valleys of the Andes. Around 600 CE, the two conquering states of Tiwanaku in the highlands of what are today southern Peru and Bolivia and Wari in central Peru emerged. Both states encompassed tens of thousands of inhabitants and represented a major step in the formation of larger, militarily organized polities.

The Expanding State of Tiwanaku

Tiwanaku was a political and cultural power center in the south-central Andes during the period 600–1100. It began as a ceremonial center with surrounding villages and gradually developed into a state dominating the region around Lake Titicaca. At its apogee it was an expanding state, planting colonies in regions far from the lake and conveying its culture through trade to peoples even beyond the colonies.

Agriculture on the High Plain   The Andes consist of two parallel mountain chains stretching along the west coast of South America. For the most part, these chains are close together, divided by small plains, valleys, and lower mountains. In southeastern Peru and western Bolivia an intermountain plain, 12,500 feet above sea level, extends as wide as 125 miles. At its northern end lies Lake Titicaca, subdivided into a larger and deeper northern basin and a smaller, shallower, swampy, and reed-covered southern basin. Five major and 20 smaller rivers coming from the eastern Andes chain feed Lake Titicaca, which has one outlet at its southern end, a river flowing into Lake Poopó [po-POH], a salt lake 150 miles south. The Lake Titicaca region, located above the tree line, receives winter rains sufficient for agriculture and grazing, whereas the southern plain around Lake Poopó is too dry to sustain more than steppes.

Tiwanaku, Kalassaya Gate. Within the Temple of the Sun, this gate is aligned with the sun's equinoxes and was used for festive rituals. Note the precise stone work, which the Incas later developed further.

In spite of its elevation, the region around Lake Titicaca offered nearly everything necessary for an advanced urbanization process. The lake's freshwater supported fish and resources such as reeds from the swamps, which served for the construction of boats and roofs. Corn flourished only in the lower elevations of the Andes and had to be imported, together with the corn-derived *chicha*, a beer-like drink. Instead of corn, the food staples were potatoes and quinoa. The grasslands of the upper hills served as pastures for llama and alpaca herds. Llamas were used as transportation animals, and alpacas provided wool. The meat of both animals—preserved for winter through drying—was a major protein source. Although frost was an ever-present danger in Tiwanaku, nutrition was quite diversified.

Farmers grew their crops on hillside terraces, where runoff water could be channeled, or on raised fields close to the lake. The raised-field system, which farmers had adopted through interaction with the peoples of the Maya lowlands, consisted of a grid of narrow strips of earth, separated from each other by channels. Mud from the channels, heaped onto the strips, replenished their fertility. A wooden foot plow, perhaps with a bronze blade, seems to have been the main farming implement, although hard archaeological proof is still elusive. By 500, the combined sustenance from fishing, hunting, farming, and herding supported dozens of villages and, by 700, the city of Tiwanaku and its 20,000 inhabitants.

Coordinated with the calendar as well as life-cycle events (such as initiation rituals), ceremonial feasts brought together elite lineages and clients, or ordinary craftspeople and villagers. Elites and clients cohered through **reciprocity**—that is, communal labor for the construction of the ceremonial centers and elaborate feasting, in which elite wealth was expended for the ceremonial leveling of status differences. Until shortly before the end of the state, it does not appear that this reciprocity gave way to more forcible ways of allocating labor through conscription or taxation.

Reciprocity: In its basic form, an informal agreement among people according to which a gift or an invitation has to be returned after a reasonable amount of time; in the pre-Columbian Americas, an arrangement of feasts instead of taxes shared by ruling classes and subjects in a state.

Expansion and Colonization   Like Tiwanaku, the core region around the southern basin of Lake Titicaca housed a set of related but competing elite–client hierarchies. Ruling clans with intermediate leaders and ordinary farmers in the villages comprised a state capable of imposing military power beyond the center. But counterbalancing clans at the head of similar hierarchies prevented the rise of dynasties that would command permanent, unified central administrations and military forces.

The projection of power over the northern lake, therefore, was not primarily of a military nature: The prevalent form of Tiwanaku authority was the outstanding prestige of its ceremonial center. This center attracted pilgrims not merely from the northern lake but also from more distant regions. Pilgrims partaking in Tiwanaku feasting ceremonies can be considered extensions of the reciprocity and clientage system of the ruling classes and, hence, of Tiwanaku power.

But there were also armed trading caravans and the foundation of colonies in the western valleys of the Andes, where military force played a role. Merchants accompanied by warriors and llama drivers crossed multiple polities in order to exchange textiles and ceramics for basalt cores in the south, metal ingots and obsidian cores in the north, and coca leaves and other psychotropic substances in the east, often hundreds of miles away. Settler colonies were additional forms of power projection, especially those established in the Moquegua [mow-KAY-gah] valley 200 miles, or 10–12 days of walking, to the west. Here, at some 2,800 feet above sea level, Tiwanaku emigrants established villages, which sent their corn or beer to the capital in return for salt, as well as stone and obsidian tools. Although overall less militarily inclined than the Mesoamerican states of the same time period, Tiwanaku wielded a visible influence over southern Peru (see Map 15.2).

The Expanding City-State of Wari

Little is known about early settlements in central Peru, some 450 miles, or 3–4 weeks of foot travel, north from Tiwanaku. The state of Wari emerged around 600 from a number of small polities organized around ceremonial centers. Expansion to the south put Wari into direct contact with Tiwanaku. The two states came to some form of mutual accommodation, and it appears that neither embarked on an outright conquest of the other. Their military postures remained limited to their regional spheres of influence.

Origins and Expansion   Wari was centered on the Ayacucho valley, a narrow plain in the highlands of northern Peru. Here, the land between the two chains of the Andes is mountainous, interspersed with valleys and rivers flowing to the Pacific or the Amazon. The elevation of 8,000 feet in the Ayacucho valley allowed for the cultivation of potatoes as well as corn and cotton. In the course of the seventh century, Wari grew into a city of 30,000 inhabitants and brought a number of neighboring cities under its control. It also pushed for an enlargement of the agricultural base through the expansion of terrace farming. Like Tiwanaku, Wari eventually became the center of a developed urbanism and a diversified agriculture.

In addition to maintaining control over the cities in its vicinity, Wari employed architects who constructed new towns. These planned centers included plazas, housing for laborers, and halls for feasting. Outside the core area, Wari elites established colonies between 100 and 450 miles away. It appears that Wari exercised much stronger political control over the elites of its core region than Tiwanaku and was more active in founding colonies.

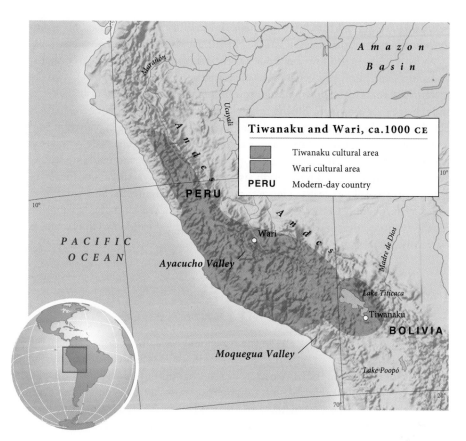

MAP 15.2 **Tiwanaku and Wari, ca. 1000.**

The Wari–Tiwanaku Frontier   Early on, Wari established a colony upstream in the Moquegua valley near southern Peru's west coast, some 100 miles southeast. The settlers built extensive terraces and canals together with protective walls and settlements on mountain peaks. This building activity coincided with the establishment by Tiwanaku of downstream farming colonies. It is possible that there was considerable tension with Tiwanaku during the initial period (650–800) over the division of water between the two colonies. But during 800–1000 the two agricultural communities developed closer ties, with indications that the two local elites engaged in a peaceful sharing of the water resources and common feasting activities. Very likely, the Moquegua valley was politically so far on the periphery of both states that neither had the means to impose itself on the other.

In its evolution, Wari was an expanding state very similar to Tiwanaku. Both were governed by elite clans under leaders who derived their strength from reciprocal patron–client organizations binding leaders to farmers and craftspeople. Extensive feasts strengthened the bond. Something must have happened to erode this bond, however, since there is evidence of increased internal tension after 950 in the two states. Groups arose which defaced sculptures, destroyed portals, and burned down edifices. Somehow, crowds previously happy to uphold elite control in return for participation in the lavish feasts provided by the elites must have become angry at these elites, their ceremonies, and the temple sculptures.

Scholars have argued that it was perhaps the fragility of power based on an increasingly unequal sharing that caused the rift between elites and subjects.

Why would elites allow reciprocity to be weakened to such a degree that it became a sham? Previous generations of scholars argued that climatic change deprived the elites of the wherewithal to throw large feasts. In the case of Tiwanaku there is evidence that a drought hit the high plain beginning in 1040, but this date is clearly a century too late for an explanation. A more convincing explanation suggests environmental degradation as the result of agricultural expansion. Land that was only marginally suitable for agriculture was exhausted and could no longer sustain a vastly increased population, as with the late Maya kingdoms. Unfortunately, there is still too little evidence to extend the environmental argument from the Maya kingdoms to the Andes highland and sierra. An ultimate explanation for the disintegration of the expanding states of Tiwanaku and Wari thus remains currently elusive.

American Empires: Aztec and Inca Origins and Dominance

Expanding and conquering states in the Andes and Mesoamerica gave way in the early fifteenth century to empires. At this time, demographic growth and the evolution of militarism in the Americas reached a point of transition to the pattern of imperial political formation. Conquering states had been cities with ceremonial centers, which dominated agricultural hinterlands and projected their prestige or power across regions. By contrast, the Aztec (1427–1521) and Inca (1438–1533) Empires in Mesoamerica and the Andes were states with capitals and ceremonial centers, vastly larger tributary hinterlands, and armies capable of engaging in campaigns at distances twice (or more) as far as previous states could. As in Eurasia, they were centralized multireligious, multiethnic, and multilinguistic polities: empires in every sense of the word.

The Aztec Empire of Mesoamerica

Forming part of the Uto-Aztecan–speaking group of Native Americans originating in the Great Basin of the American Southwest, the ancestors of the Aztecs entered Mexico at an unknown time as migrants in search of a better life. They found this life eventually as conquerors of the Mexican Basin, the site of today's Mexico City (after the drainage of most of the valley). In the course of the fifteenth century they conquered an empire that eventually encompassed Mesoamerica from the Pacific to the Gulf of Mexico and from the middle of modern northern Mexico to the Isthmus of Panama.

Settlement in the Mexican Valley   Once arrived in northern Mexico, the Aztecs traced their beginnings to a founding myth. According to this myth, the first Aztec was one of seven brothers born on an island in a lake or in a mountain cave 150 leagues (450 miles) northwest of the Mexican Basin. The distance, recorded by Spaniards in the sixteenth century, can be interpreted as corresponding to a mountain in the modern state of Guanajuato [goo-wa-na-hoo-WA-to]. This Aztec ancestor and his descendants migrated south as foragers dressed in skins and lacking agriculture and urban civilization. Their hunter–warrior patron god Huitzilpochtli [hoo-it-zil-POSHT-lee] guided them to a promised land of plenty.

After settling for a while in Tula (claimed later as a place of heritage), their god urged the foragers to move on to the Mexican Basin. Here, an eagle perched on a cactus commanded the Aztecs to settle and build a temple to their god. In this temple, they were to nourish him with the sacrificial blood of humans captured in war. Like many peoples in Eurasia as well as the contemporary Incas, the Aztecs contrasted their later empire and its glory with a myth of humble beginnings and long periods of wandering toward an eventual promised land.

The historical record in the Mexican Basin becomes clearer in the fourteenth century. In the course of this period, the Aztecs appeared as clients of two Toltec-descended overlords in states on the southwestern shore. Here, they created the two islands of Tenochtitlán [te-notsh-tit-LAN] and Tlatelolco [tla-te-LOL-co], founded a city with a ceremonial center on Tenochtitlán, engaged in farming and rendered military service to their overlords. Thanks to successes on the battlefield, Aztec leaders were able to marry into the elites of the neighboring city-states and gained the right to have their own ruler ("speaker," *tlatloani* [tla-tlo-AH-nee]) presiding over a council of leading members of the elite and priests. Toward the end of the fourteenth century, an emerging Aztec elite was firmly integrated with the ruling classes of many of the two dozen or so city-states in and around the valley.

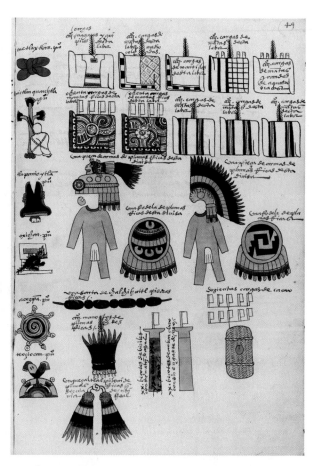

List of Tributes Owed to the Aztecs. The list includes quantities of cotton and wool textiles, clothes, headgear with feathers, and basketry. The Aztecs did not continue the complex syllabic script of the Maya but used instead images, including persons with speech bubbles, for communication. Spanish administrators and monks who copied the Aztec manuscripts added their own explanations to keep track of Native American tributes.

The Rise of the Empire   After a successful rebellion in 1428 of a triple alliance among the Aztec city-state of Tenochtitlán and two other vassal states against the reigning city-state in the Mexican Basin the Aztec leader Itzcóatl [its-CO-aw] (r. 1428–1440) emerged as the dominant figure. Itzcóatl and his three successors, together with the rulers of the two allied states, expanded their city-states on the two islands and the shore through conquests into a full-fledged empire. Tenochtitlán, on one of the islands, became the capital of what became an empire that consisted of a set of six "inner provinces" in the Mexican Basin. Local elites were left in place, but they were required to attend ceremonies in Tenochtitlán, bring and receive gifts, leave their sons as hostages, and intermarry with the elites of the triple alliance. Commoner farmers outside the cities had to provide tributes in the form of foodstuffs and labor services, making the imperial core self-sufficient.

After the middle of the fifteenth century, the triple alliance conquered a set of 55 city-states outside the valley as "outer provinces." It created an imperial polity from the Pacific to the Gulf, from Tarasco, 200 miles to the northwest, to Oaxaca, over 500 miles to the south (see Map 15.3). This state was now far more centralized than the preceding Teotihuacán and Toltec city-states. In this empire, local ruling families with their ceremonial centers and gods were generally left in place,

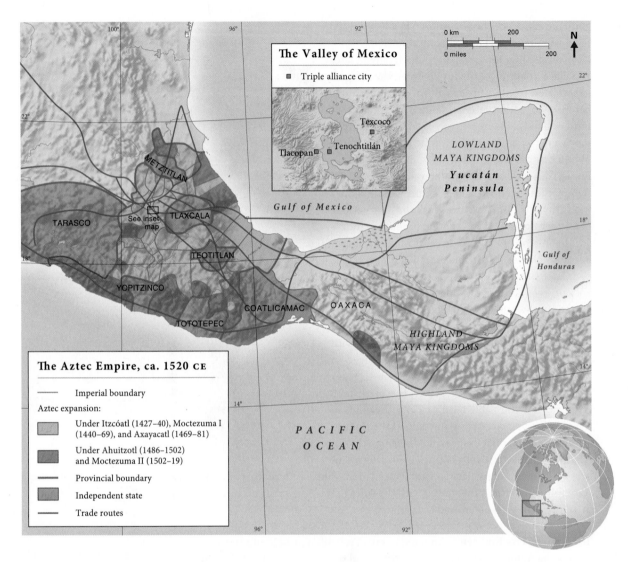

MAP 15.3 **The Aztec Empire, ca. 1520.**

but commoners had to produce tributes in the form of raw materials or lightweight processed and manufactured goods.

In some provinces, Aztec governors replaced the rulers; in most others, Aztec tribute collectors (supported by troops) held local rulers in check and supervised the transportation of the tributes by porters to the valley. Reciprocity, once of central importance in Mesoamerica, continued on a grand scale but was now clearly subordinate to military considerations.

The resulting multiethnic, multireligious, and multilinguistic empire of eventually some 19 million inhabitants was still a work in progress in the early sixteenth century when the Spanish arrived. Right in the middle of the empire, just 50 miles east of the Mexican Basin, the large state of Tlaxcala [tlash-KAH-lah], Nahuatl-speaking like the Aztecs, held out in opposition, together with multiple enemy states on the periphery. Although the ruling elites of the triple alliance did everything to expand, even inviting enemy rulers to their festivities in order to secure their loyalty through gestures of reciprocity, pockets of anti-Aztec states survived and eventually became crucial allies of the Spanish, providing the latter's tiny military forces with a critical mass of fighters.

Some outer provinces possessed strategic importance, with Aztec colonies implanted to prepare for eventual conquest of remaining enemies outside the empire. The most relentlessly pursued policy of continued expansion of Aztec central control was the threat of warfare, for the purpose of capturing rebels or enemies as prisoners of war to be sacrificed to the gods in the ceremonial centers. This fear-inducing tactic—or "power propaganda"—was an integral innovation in the imperialism of the Aztecs.

The Military Forces   The triple alliance ruled a Nahuatl-speaking population of some 1.5 million inhabitants in the core provinces of the Mexican Basin. This number yielded a maximum of a quarter of a million potential soldiers, taking into consideration that most soldiers were farmers with agricultural obligations. From this large number of adult males, the Aztecs assembled units of 8,000 troops each, which they increased as the need arose. Initially, the army was recruited from among the elite of the Aztecs and their allies. But toward the middle of the fifteenth century, Aztec rulers set up a military school system for the sons of the elite plus those commoners who were to become priests. A parallel school system for the sons of commoners, aged 15–20 years, also included military training. After graduation, recruits began as porters, carrying supplies for the combat troops—an Aztec innovation which considerably enlarged the marching range of armies on campaign. Soldiers rose in the army hierarchy on the basis of merit, particularly as demonstrated by their success in the capture of enemies for future sacrifice.

The Aztecs inherited the weaponry and armor of the Toltecs but also made some important innovations. The bow and arrow, which arrived from northwest Mexico at the end of Toltec rule, became a standard weapon in Aztec armies. In addition, perhaps as late as the fifteenth century, the Aztecs developed the three-foot obsidian-spiked broadsword, derived from the Toltec short sword, in order to enhance the latter's slashing force. As a result, clubs, maces, and axes declined in importance in the Aztec arsenal. Thrusting spears, dart throwers, and slings continued to be used as standard weapons. Body armor, consisting of quilted, sleeveless cotton shirts, thick cotton helmets, and round wooden or cane shields, was adopted from the Toltecs. With the arrival of the Aztecs, the Americas had acquired the heaviest infantry weaponry in their history, reflective of the intensity of militarism in their society—a militarism which was also typical of the earlier empires of the beginning Iron Age in the Middle East.

Aztec Weapons. Aztec weapons were well-crafted hardwood implements with serrated obsidian edges, capable of cutting through metal, including iron. As slashing weapons they were highly effective in close combat.

"When a child was born, his parents would put him into the Calmécac [elite school] or in the Telpochcalli [commoner school], that is, they would promise the child as a gift [to the patron divinity], . . . that he would become a priest . . . or . . . become a warrior."

—Florentine Codex

The Inca Empire of the Andes

After the disintegration of Tiwanaku and Wari around 1100, the central Andes returned to the traditional politics of local chiefdoms in small city-states with ceremonial centers and agricultural hinterlands. The best-known city-state was Chimú on the Peruvian coast, with its capital of Chan Chan numbering

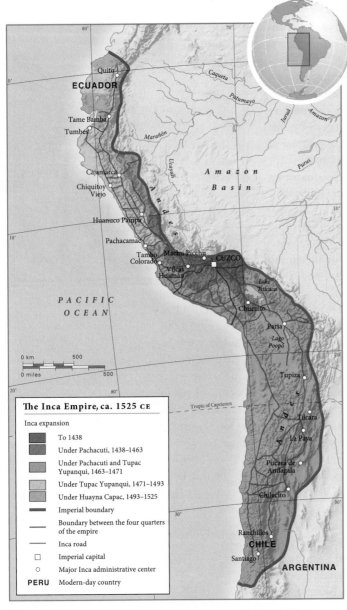

30,000 inhabitants. Tiwanaku cultural traditions, however, remained dominant and were expressed in religious ceremonies, textile motifs, and ceramic styles.

Given the fierce competition among the pilgrimage centers, insecurity was rampant during the period 1100–1400, with particular influence granted to charismatic military leaders who could project military force and pacify the land. After a gestation period during the fourteenth century, the southern Peruvian city-state of Cuzco with its Inca elite emerged in the early fifteenth century at the head of a highly militaristic conquering polity. Within another century, the Incas had established an empire, called Tawantinsuyu [ta-wan-tin-SOO-yuh] (Quechua "Four Regions"), symbolizing its geographical expanse. It stretched from Ecuador in the north to central Chile in the south, with extensions into the tropical upper Amazon region and western Argentinean steppes (see Map 15.4).

As in the case of the Aztecs, the founding myth of the Incas involves a cave, an island, and a promised land of rich agriculture. In one version, the creator god Viracocha [vee-rah-KO-chah] summoned four brothers and four sisters from caves seven leagues (21 miles) from Cuzco to the south, pairing them as couples and promising them a land of plenty. They would find this land when a golden rod, to be used on their wanderings, would get stuck in the soil. Alternatively, the sun god Inti [IN-tee] did the pairing of the couples on an island in Lake Titicaca and thereby bestowed the glory of Tiwanaku on them, before sending them with the golden rod to their promised land. Cuzco, where the rod plunged into the fertile soil, was settled land, however, and a war ensued in which the Incas drove out the existing farmers.

In the fourteenth century, Cuzco became a serious contender in the city-state competition. Like Wari, Cuzco was located at a highland elevation of 11,300 feet between the two Andes chains of southern Peru, roughly one-third of the way from Lake Titicaca north to Wari. Eight rulers (*curacas* [koo-RA-kas]) are said to have succeeded each other in the consolidation of Cuzco as a regional power. Although their names are recorded, events are hazy and dates are missing altogether. Firm historical terrain is reached with the ninth ruler, Pachacuti (r. 1438–1471). The history of the Incas from 1438 onwards is known much better, primarily because of the memories of the grandchildren of the fifteenth-century Inca conquerors, recorded by the Spanish who defeated them in their conquest.

Imperial Expansion   The system of reciprocity that characterized earlier Mesoamerican and Andean history continued under the Incas but was also, as in the case of Aztecs, decisively cast in the mold of power-enforced unilateralism. *Ayllu* [AY-yoo], the Quechua term for a household with an ancestral lineage, implied mutual obligations among groups of households, neighborhoods, villages, and city-states. To negotiate these obligations, Inca society—from households to provinces—was divided into two halves with roughly equal reciprocities. At the elite level, there were two sets of reciprocities, the first within two main branches of the elite and the second between the two branches of the elite and the subjects. The most important social expression of reciprocity remained the feast. In the Incan Empire, the state collected considerably more from the subject *ayllus* than Tiwanaku and Wari had done, but whether it returned comparable amounts through feasts and celebrations was a matter of contention, often leading to armed rebellion.

The earliest conquests under Pachacuti were toward the near south around Lake Titicaca, as well as the agriculturally rich lands north of the former Wari state. Thereafter, in the later fifteenth century, the Incas expanded 1,300 miles northward to southern Ecuador and 1,500 miles southward to Chile. The final provinces, added in the early sixteenth century, were in northern Ecuador as well as on the eastern slopes of the Andes, from the upper Amazon to western Argentina. The capital, Cuzco, which counted some 100,000 inhabitants in the early sixteenth century, was laid out in a cross-shaped grid of four streets leading out into the suburbs. Symbolically, as indicated by the empire's Quechua name, the capital reached out to the four regions of the empire—coast, north, south, and Amazon rain forest.

Administration   Ethnic Inca governors administered the four regions, which were subdivided into a total of some 80 provinces, each again with an Inca subgovernor. Most provinces were composites of former city-states, which remained under their local elites but had to accept a unique decimal system of population organization imposed by the Inca rulers. According to this system, members of the local elites commanded 10,000, 1,000, 100, and 10 household, or *ayllu*, heads for the purpose of recruiting the manpower for the *mit'a* [MIT-ah] ("to take a turn," in reference to service obligations rotating among the subjects). The services, which subjects owed the empire as a form of taxes, were in farming, herding, manufacturing, military service, and portage. In its structure it was not unlike the Ming and Qing Chinese systems of local organization called *baojia* (see Chapter 12).

The *mit'a* was perhaps the single most important innovation the Incas contributed to the history of the Americas. In contrast to the Aztecs, who shipped taxes in kind to their capital by boat, the Incas had no efficient means of transportation for long distances. The only way to make use of the taxes in kind was to store them locally. The Incas built tens of thousands of storehouses everywhere in their empire, requiring subjects to deliver a portion of their harvests, animal products, and domestically produced goods under *mit'a* obligations to the nearest storehouse in their vicinity. These supplies were available to officials and troops and enabled the Incas to conduct military campaigns far from Cuzco without the need for foraging among local farmers. In addition, it was through the *mit'a* that quotas of laborers were raised for the construction of inns, roads, ceremonial centers, palaces, terraces, and irrigation canals, often far away from the urban center. Finally, *mit'a* provided laborers for mines, quarries, state and temple farms, and colonies. No form of labor or service went untaxed.

To keep track of *mit'a* obligations, officials passed bundles of knotted cord (*quipú*, or *khipu* [KEE-poo], "knot") upward from level to level in the imperial administration. The numbers of knots on each cord in the bundles contained information on population figures and service obligations. As discussed in Chapter 5, the use of quipús was widespread in the Andes long before the Inca and can be considered as the Andean equivalent of a communication system. The only innovation contributed by the Incas seems to have been the massive scale on which these cord bundles were generated and employed. Some 700 have been preserved. Unfortunately, all modern attempts to decipher them have so far failed, and thus it is impossible to accurately outline the full picture of Inca service allocations.

Inca Roads. Inca roads were paths reserved for runners and the military. They were built on beds of rocks and rubble and connected strategic points in the most direct line possible.

Military Organization Perhaps the most important *mit'a* obligation which subject households owed to the Inca in the conquest phase of the empire was the service of young, able-bodied men in the military. Married men 25–30 years old were foot soldiers, often accompanied by wives and children; unmarried men 18–25 years of age served as porters or messengers. As in the Aztec Empire, administrators made sure that enough laborers remained in the villages to take care of their other obligations of farming, herding, transporting, and manufacturing. Sources report armies in the range of 35,000–140,000. Intermediate commanders came from the local and regional elites, and the top commanders were members of the two upper and lower Inca ruling elites.

Inca weaponry was comparable to that of the Aztecs, consisting of bows and arrows, dart throwers, slings, clubs with spiked bronze heads, wooden broadswords, bronze axes, and bronze-tipped javelins. Using Bolivian tin, Inca smiths were able to make a much harder and more useful bronze than was possible with earlier techniques. The Incas lacked the Aztec obsidian-serrated swords but used a snare (which the Aztecs did not possess) with attached stone or bronze weights to entangle the enemy's legs. Protective armor consisted of quilted cotton shirts, copper breastplates, cane helmets, and shields. These types of weapons and armor were widely found among the Incas and their enemies. The advantage enjoyed by the Incas resulted from the sheer massiveness of their weapons and supplies, procured from craftspeople through the *mit'a* and stored in strategically located armories.

During the second half of the fifteenth century the Incas turned from conquest to consolidation. Faced at that time with a number of rebellions, they deemphasized the decimal draft and recruited longer-serving troops from among a smaller number of select, trusted peoples. These troops garrisoned the forts distributed throughout the empire. They also were part of the settler colonies implanted in rebellious provinces and in border regions. The fiercest resistance came from the people of the former Tiwanaku state and from the northeast Peruvian provinces, areas with long state traditions of their own. Since elite infighting also became more pronounced toward the end of the fifteenth century, personal guards recruited from non-Inca populations and numbering up to 7,000 soldiers accompanied many leading ruling-class members. The professionalization of the Inca army, however, lagged behind that of the Aztecs, since the Incas did not have military academies open to their subjects.

Communications Although they lacked the military professionalization of the Aztecs, the Incas created an imperial communication and logistics structure that was unparalleled in the Americas. Early on, the Incas systematically improved on the road network that they inherited from Tiwanaku, Wari, and other states. Two parallel trunk roads extended from Cuzco nearly the entire length of the empire in both southerly and northerly directions. One followed the coast and western slopes of the western Andes chain; the other led through the mountain lands, valleys, and high plains between the western and eastern Andes chains. In numerous places, additional highways connected the two trunk roads. Suspension bridges made of thick ropes crossed gorges, while rafts were used for crossing rivers. The roads, 3–12 feet wide, crossed the terrain as directly as possible, often requiring extensive grounding, paving, staircasing, and tunneling. In many places, the 25,000-mile road network still exists today, attesting to the engineering prowess of the Incas.

The roads were reserved for troops, officials, and runners carrying messages. For their convenience, every 15 miles, or at the end of a slow 1-day journey, an inn provided accommodation. Larger armies stopped at barracks-like constructions or pitched tents on select campgrounds. Like the Romans, and despite the fact that they did not have wheeled transport, the Incas were well aware of how crucial paved and well-supplied roads were for infantry soldiers.

Imperial Society and Culture

As Mesoamerica and the Andes entered their imperial age, cosmopolitan capitals with monumental ceremonial centers and palaces emerged. The sizes of both capitals and monuments were visual expressions of the exalted power that the rulers claimed. Almost daily ceremonies and rituals, accompanied by feasts, further underscored the authority of rulers. These ceremonies and rituals expressed the American spiritual and polytheistic heritage but were modified to impress on enemies and subjects alike the irresistible might of the empires.

Imperial Capitals: Tenochtitlán and Cuzco

In the fifteenth century, the Aztec and Inca capitals were among the largest cities of the world, encompassing between 100,000 and 200,000 inhabitants. Both cities maintained their high degree of urbanism through a complex command system of labor, services, and goods. Although their monumental architecture followed different artistic traditions, both emphasized platforms and sanctuaries atop large pyramid-like structures as symbols of elevated power as well as closeness to the astral gods, especially those associated with the sun and Venus.

Tenochtitlán as an Urban Metropolis   More than half of the approximately 1.5 million people living during the fifteenth century in the Mexican Basin were urban dwellers, including elites, priests, administrators, military officers, merchants, traders, craftspeople, messengers, servants, and laborers. Such an extraordinary concentration of urban citizens was unique in the agrarian world prior to the industrialization of Europe (beginning around 1800), when cities usually held no more than 10 percent of the total population (see Map 15.5).

The center of Tenochtitlán, on the southern island, was a large platform where the Aztec settlers had driven pilings into marshy ground and heaped rocks and rubble. In an enclosure on this platform were the main pyramid, with temples to the Aztec gods on top, and a series of smaller ceremonial centers. Adjacent to this on the platform were a food market and a series of palaces of the ruling elite, which included guest quarters, administrative offices, storage facilities for tributes, kitchens, the high court for the elite and the court of appeals for commoners, the low court for civil cases, workshops for craftspeople, the prison, and councils for teachers and the military. Large numbers of Aztecs

Aqueduct from the Western Hills to Tenochtitlán. This aqueduct, still standing today, provided fresh water to the palace and mansions of the center of the island, to be used as drinking water and for washing.

and visitors assembled each day to pay respect to the ruler and to trade in the market in preparation for assemblies and feasts.

In 1473, the southern island was merged with the northern island to form a single unit. At the center of the northern island was a platform that contained the principal market of the combined islands. This daily market attracted as many as 40,000 farmers, craftspeople, traders, porters, and laborers on the main market day. The sophistication of the market was comparable to that of any market in Eurasia during the fifteenth century.

A number of causeways crossed the capital and linked it with the lakeshore. People also traveled inside the city on a number of main and branch canals. Dikes with sluices on the east side regulated both the water level and the salinity of the lake around the islands. The runoff during the summer rainy season from the southwestern mountains provided freshwater to dilute the lake's salinity, and the eastern dikes kept out salt water from the rest of the lake. Potable water arrived from the shore via an aqueduct on one of the western causeways. This aqueduct served mostly the ceremonial center and palace precinct, but branches brought potable water to a number of elite residences nearby as well. Professional water carriers took fresh water to commoners in the various quarters of the city; professional waste removers collected human waste from urban residences and took it to farmers for fertilizer. In short, Tenochtitlán possessed a fully developed urban infrastructure.

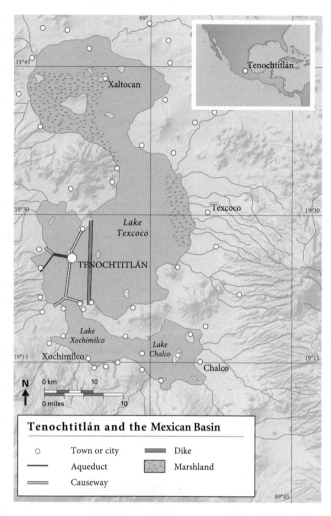

MAP **15.5** **Tenochtitlán and the Mexican Basin.**

The two city centers—the pyramid and palaces in the south and the market in the north—were surrounded by dozens of residential city quarters. Built on a layer of firm ground, many of these quarters were inhabited by craftspeople of a shared profession, who practiced their crafts in their residences. As discussed earlier in this chapter, merchants occupied a privileged position between the elite and the commoners. As militarily trained organizers of large caravans of porters, the merchants also provided the Aztec capital with luxury goods. Depending on their social rank, craftspeople occupied residences of larger or smaller size, usually grouped into compounds of related families. The rooms of the houses surrounded a central patio on which most of the household activities took place—an architectural preference common to Mesoamerica and the Andes, as well as the Middle East and Mediterranean.

Residents of quarters farther away from the center were farmers. In these quarters, making up nearly two-thirds of Tenochtitlán's surface, families engaged in intensive farming. Here, a grid of canals encased small, rectangular islands devoted to housing compounds and/or farming. People moved within these barrios by boat. Since the Mexican Basin received year-round rains that were often

Chinampas:
Mesoamerican
agricultural practice
by which farmers grew
crops upon small,
human-made islands
in Lake Texcoco.

insufficient for dry farming, a raised-field system prevailed, whereby farmers dredged the canals, heaped the fertile mud on top of the rectangular islands, called *chinampas,* and added water from the canals and waste from their households or brought by boat from the urban neighborhoods. In contrast to the luxurious palaces of the elite, housing for farmers consisted of plastered huts made of cane, wood, and reeds. As in all agrarian societies, farmers—subject to high taxes or rents—were among the poorest folk.

On the surface of the *chinampas,* farmers grew corn, beans, squash, amaranth, and peppers. These seed plants were supplemented by *maguey* [mag-AY], a large succulent agave. This evergreen plant grew in poor soils; had a large root system, which helped in stabilizing the ground; and produced fiber useful for weaving and pulp useful for making *pulque* [POOL-kay], a fermented drink. To plant these crops in the soft soil, a digging stick, slightly broadened at one end, was sufficient. Regular watering made multicropping of seed plants possible. Trees, planted at the edges, protected the *chinampas* against water erosion.

Ownership of the *chinampas* was vested in clans, which, under neighborhood leaders, were responsible for the allocation of land and adjudication of disputes as well as the payment of taxes in kind to the elite. But there were also members of the elite who, as absentee owners, possessed estates and employed managers to collect rents from the farmers. Whether there was a trend from taxes to rents (that is, from a central tax authority to a decentralized landowner class) is unknown. Given the high productivity of raised-field farming, which was similar to that of the Eurasian agrarian–urban centers, such a trend would not have been surprising.

Cuzco as a Ceremonial-Administrative City   The site of the Inca city of Cuzco was an elongated triangle formed by the confluence of two rivers. At one

Cuzco Stone Masonry. Inspired by the masonry of the people of Tiwanaku, the Inca built imposing structures with much larger blocks of limestone or granite. To cut the blocks, masons used copper and bronze chisels, making use of natural fissures in the stone.

end, opposite the confluence, was a hill with a number of structures, including the imperial armory and a temple dedicated to the sun god. Enormous, zigzagging walls followed the contours of the hill. The walls were built with stone blocks weighing up to 100 tons and cut so precisely that no mortar was needed, a technique which the Incas adopted from Tiwanaku.

Below, on the plain leading to the confluence, the city was laid out in a grid pattern. The residents of the city, all belonging to the upper and lower Inca ruling class, lived in adobe houses arranged in a block-and-courtyard pattern similar to that of Wari. Several squares and temples within the city served as ceremonial centers. One plaza contained a platform, with the imperial throne and a pillar placed symbolically atop what the Incas considered the earth's center or navel. The Coricancha [co-ri-CAN-tsha], the city's main temple, stood near the confluence of the rivers. This temple was a walled compound comprising six buildings set around a courtyard. Chambers in these buildings contained the Inca gods and goddesses as well as the divine statues or sacred objects confiscated from the provinces. Each year priests of the empire's ceremonial centers sent one such sacred object to the Coricancha, to demonstrate their obedience to the central Inca temple (see Map 15.6).

Across the rivers, in separate suburbs, were settlements for commoners with markets and storehouses. They were surrounded by fields, terraces, and irrigation canals. In the fields, interspersed stone pillars and shrines were aligned on sight lines radiating from the Coricancha, tying the countryside closely to the urban center. These alignments were reminiscent of the Nazca lines drawn half a millennium earlier in southern Peru (Chapter 9). Farther away were imperial estates with unfree laborers from outside the *mit'a* system and its reciprocal feasting. In contrast to the Aztec elite, which allowed meritorious generals to rise in the hierarchy, the Inca elite remained exclusionary, allowing no commoners to reside in Cuzco.

Power and Its Cultural Expressions

Ruling elites, as repeatedly emphasized in this chapter, put a strong emphasis on displaying their power during the period 600–1500. This was particularly true with the Aztecs and Incas during the fifteenth century. Among these displays were human sacrifices, mausoleums, and mummy burials. Although all three involved changes in social relations, these changes were accommodated in the existing overall religious culture.

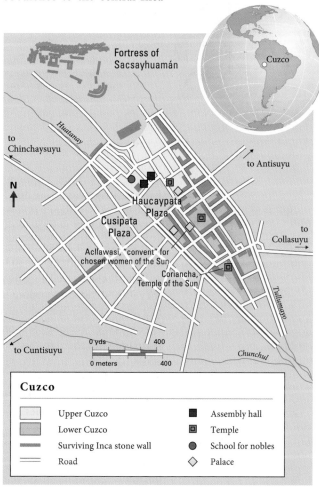

MAP **15.6 Cuzco.**

Human Sacrifice and Propaganda

In the first millennium CE, Mesoamerica and the Andes evolved from their early religious spirituality to polytheism. The spiritual heritage, however, remained a strong undercurrent. Both American regions engaged in human as well as animal and agricultural sacrifices. Rulers appeased the gods also through self-sacrifice—that is, the piercing of tongue and penis, as was the case among the Olmecs (1400–400 BCE) and Mayas (600 BCE–900 CE). The feathered serpent god Quetzalcoatl was the Mesoamerican deity of self-sacrifice, revered in the city-states of Teotihuacán (200 BCE–570 CE) and Tula (ca. 900 CE). Under the Toltecs and the Aztecs, this god receded into the background, in favor of warrior gods such as Tezcatlipoca and Huitzilpochtli. The survival of traditional blood rituals within polytheism was a pattern that distinguished the early American empires from their Eurasian counterparts.

Whether human sacrifices were prolific under Aztec and Inca imperialism is questionable. About the same number of human victims were excavated at the Feathered Serpent Temple of Teotihuacán and at the Templo Mayor of Tenochtitlán: 137 versus 126 skeletons. These numbers are minuscule in comparison to the impression created

Human Sacrifice. Human sacrifice among the pre-Columbian Mesoamericans and Andeans was based on the concept of a shared life spirit or mind, symbolized by the life substance of blood. In the American spiritual-polytheistic conceptualization, the gods sacrificed their blood, or themselves altogether, during creation; rulers pierced their earlobes, tongues, or penises for blood sacrifices; and war captives lost their lives when their hearts were sacrificed.

Inca Ruling Class Gender Relations   The ruling classes in the Inca Empire displayed their power in several ways. Among the examples were the "Houses of Chosen Women" in Cuzco and provincial colonies. The greatest honor for Inca girls was to enter at age 10–12 into the service of these houses. An inspector from Cuzco made regular visits to the villages of the empire to select attractive young girls for the service. The girls were marched to the capital or the colonies, where they were divided according to beauty, skills, and social standing. These houses had female instructors who provided the girls with a 4-year education in cooking, beer making, weaving, and officiating in the rituals and ceremonies of the Inca religion. After their graduation, the young women became virgin temple priestesses, were given in marriage to non-Incas honored for service to the ruler, or became palace servants, musicians, or concubines of the Inca elite. The collection of this girl tribute was separate from the reciprocity system. As such, it was an act of assigning gender roles in an emerging social hierarchy defined by power inequalities.

Traditionally, gender roles were less strictly divided than in Eurasia. The horticultural form of agriculture in Mesoamerica and the Andes gave males fewer opportunities to accumulate wealth and power than plow agriculture did in Eurasia. Hoes and foot plows distinguished men and women from each other less than plows and teams of oxen or horses did. Nevertheless, it comes as no surprise that

by the Spanish conquerors and encourage doubts about the magnitude of human sacrifices in temple ceremonies. It appears that even though the Aztec and Inca ruling classes were focused on war, the ritual of human sacrifice was not as pervasive as has been widely assumed.

Could it be that there was no significant increase in human sacrifice under the Aztecs and Incas, as the self-serving Spanish conquerors alleged? Were there perhaps, instead, imperial propaganda machines in the Aztec and Inca Empires, employed in the service of conquest and consolidation—similar to those of the Assyrians and Mongols in Eurasia—who sought to intimidate their enemies? In this case, the Aztec and Inca Empires would not be exceptional barbaric aberrations in world history. Instead, they would be but two typical examples of the general world-historical pattern of competitive militaristic states during the early agrarian era using propaganda to further their imperial power.

Questions

- In examining the question of whether empires such as the Inca and the Aztec employed human sacrifice for propaganda purposes, can this practice be considered an adaptation that evolved out of earlier rituals, such as royal bloodletting?
- If the Aztec and the Inca did indeed employ human sacrifice for propaganda purposes, what does this say about the ability of these two empires to use cultural and religious practices to consolidate their power?

the gradual agrarian–urban diversification of society, even if it was slower in the Americas than in Eurasia, proceeded along similar paths of increasing male power concentration in villages, ceremonial centers, temple cities, conquering states, and empires. Emphasizing gender differences, therefore, should be viewed as a characteristic phenomenon arising in imperial contexts.

Inca Mummy Veneration   Other houses in Cuzco were ghostly residences in which scores of attendants and servants catered to what were believed to be the earthly needs of deceased, mummified Inca emperors and their principal wives. During the mummification process attendants removed the cadaver's internal organs, placed them in special containers, and desiccated the bodies until they were completely mummified. Servants dressed the mummies (*mallquis* [MAY-kees]) in their finest clothing and placed them back into their residences amid their possessions, as if they had never died. The mummies received daily meals and were carried around by their retinues for visits to their mummified relatives. On special occasions, mummies were lined up according to rank on Cuzco's main plaza to participate in ceremonies and processions. In this way, they remained fully integrated into the daily life of the elite.

"We order that everyone bury their deceased in a chamber [*pucullo*, stone tomb], that the dead not be buried in their houses and that the deceased's spindle, dining service, food, drink, and garments be buried with them."

—Ordinances of the Inca, recorded by Felipe Guaman Poma de Ayala

"Ghost residences" with mummies can be considered an outgrowth of the old Andean custom of mummification. This custom was widely practiced among the elites of the ceremonial centers, who, however, generally placed their ancestors in temple tombs, shrines, or caves. Mummies were also buried in cemeteries, sometimes collectively in bundles with false heads made of cotton. Preserving the living spaces of the deceased obviously required considerable wealth—wealth provided only by imperial regimes for their elites.

As a general phenomenon in Andean society, of course, mummies were a crucial ingredient in the religious heritage, in which strong spiritual elements survived underneath the polytheistic overlay of astral gods. In the spiritual tradition, body and spirit cohabit more or less loosely. In a trance, a diviner's mind can travel, enter the minds of other people and animals, or make room for other people's minds. Similarly, in death a person's spirit, while no longer in the body, remains nearby and therefore still needs daily nourishment in order not to be driven away. Hence, even though non-Incan Andean societies removed the dead from their daily living spaces, descendants had to visit tombs regularly with food and beer or provide buried mummies with ample victuals.

The expenses for the upkeep of the mummy households were the responsibility of the deceased emperor's bloodline, headed by a surviving brother. As heirs of the emperor's estate, the members of the bloodline formed a powerful clan within the ruling class. The new emperor was excluded from this estate and had to acquire his own new one in the course of his rule, a mechanism evidently designed to intensify his imperial ambitions for conquest. In the early sixteenth century, however, when it became logistically difficult to expand much beyond the enormous territory already accumulated in the Andes, this ingenious mechanism of keeping the upper and lower rungs of the ruling class united became counterproductive. Emperors lacking resources had to contend with brothers richly endowed with inherited wealth and ready to engage in dynastic warfare—as actually occurred shortly before the arrival of the Spanish (1529–1532).

Putting It All Together

During the short time of their existence, the Aztec and Inca Empires unleashed extraordinary creative energies. Sculptors, painters, and (after the arrival of the Spanish) writers recorded the traditions as well as the innovations of the fifteenth century. Aztec painters produced codices, or illustrated manuscripts, that present the divine pantheons, myths, calendars, ceremonial activities, chants, poetry, and administrative activities of their societies in exquisite and colorful detail. They fashioned these codices using bark paper, smoothing it with plaster, and connecting the pages accordion-style. Today, a handful of these codices survive, preserved in Mexican and European libraries.

The Aztec and Inca Empires were polities that illustrate how humans not in contact with the rest of the world and living within an environment that was different from Eurasia and Africa in many respects developed patterns of innovation that were remarkably similar. On the basis of an agriculture that eventually produced ample surpluses, humans made the same choices as their cousins in Eurasia and Africa. Specifically, in the period 600–1500, they created temple-centered city-states, just like their Sumerian and Hindu counterparts. Their military states were not unlike the Chinese warring states. And, finally, their empires—although just beginning to flourish in the Bronze Age—were comparable to those of the New Kingdom Egyptians or Assyrians. The Americas had their own unique variations of these larger historical patterns, to be sure; but they nevertheless displayed the same humanity as found elsewhere.

For additional resources, including maps, primary sources, visuals, and quizzes, please go to www.oup.com/us/vonsivers. Please see the Further Resources section at the back of the book for additional readings and suggested websites.

Against the Grain

Amazon Rain Forest Civilizations

For many years, prevailing scholarly opinion held that the vast Amazonian river basin, covered by dense rain forest, was too inhospitable to allow for more than small numbers of widely dispersed foragers to subsist. Even farmers, living in more densely populated villages, could not possibly have founded complex, stratified societies. Slash-and-burn agriculture, the common form of farming on poor tropical soils even today, by definition prevented the advance of urban life: After exhausting the soil in a given area, whole villages had to pack up and move.

Beginning in the 1990s, however, a few scholars realized that this belief was erroneous. Modern farmers, increasingly encroaching on the rain forest, made these scholars aware of two hitherto neglected features. First, these farmers often advanced into stretches of forest and savanna on top of what is called in Portuguese *terra preta*—black soil so fertile that it did not require fertilizers for years. Second, as they slashed and burned the rain forest and savanna with their modern tools, they exposed monumental earthworks that had previously escaped attention under the cover of vegetation. The two features were actually connected. *Terra preta* was the result of centuries of patient soil enrichment by indigenous people who were also the builders of the earthworks. Instead of slashing and burning, these people had engaged in "slashing and charring"—that is, turning the trees into longer-lasting nutrient-rich charcoal rather than less fertile and quickly depleted ash.

Since the early 2000s, scholars have documented large-scale settlements in areas along the southern tributaries to the Amazon, describing large village clusters with central plazas, fortification walls, bridges, causeways, and waterworks. One such cluster is located on the upper Xingu, a tributary of the lower Amazon. A set of two clusters is situated near the upper reaches of the Purus, a tributary of the upper Amazon. One occupies a fertile flood plain, the other the less fertile highlands further away from the river. In the Purus region, researchers employing aerial photography revealed a huge area home to perhaps 60,000 inhabitants during a period around the late thirteenth century. This area is adjacent to the farthest northeastern extension of the Inca Empire into the Amazon, with fortresses being excavated by Finnish teams. Thus, when the Incas expanded into the rain forest, they clearly did so to incorporate flourishing, advanced societies into their empire. Thanks to scholars who challenged the orthodoxy of the "empty rain forest," we are rediscovering the Amazonian past.

- **Which is more important: to save the rain forest or uncover its archaeological past? Can the two objectives be combined?**

- **Compare the Amazonian earthworks to those of Benin in Africa during the same period (Chapter 14). Which similarities and differences can you discover?**

Thinking Through Patterns

▶ **Within the patterns of state formation basic to the Americas, which types of states emerged in Meso-america and the Andes during the period 600–1550? What characterized these states?**

The basic pattern of state formation in the Americas was similar to that of Eurasia and Africa. Historically, it began with the transition from foraging to agriculture and settled village life. As the population increased, villages under elders became chiefdoms, which in turn became city-states with temples. As in Eurasia and Africa, American city-states often became conquering states, beginning with the Maya kingdoms and Teotihuacán. Both, however, remained small. Military states, in which ruling classes sought to expand territories, such as Tula and, to a lesser degree, Tiwanaku and Wari, were characteristic for the early part of the period 600–1550. The successors of these—the Aztec and Inca Empires—were multiethnic, multilinguistic, and multireligious polities that dominated Mesoamerica and the Andes for about a century, before the Spanish conquest brought them to a premature end.

The states of Tiwanaku and Wari had more or less cohesive ruling classes but no dynasties of rulers and centralized bureaucracies. These ruling classes and their subjects—corn and potato farmers—were integrated with each other through systems of reciprocity—that is, military protection in return for foodstuffs. They customarily renewed the bonds of reciprocity in common feasts. After one or two centuries, however, tensions arose, either between stronger and weaker branches of the ruling classes or between rulers and subjects over questions of obligations and justice. When these tensions erupted into internal warfare, the states disintegrated, often in conjunction with environmental degradation and climate change.

▶ **Why did the Tiwanaku and Wari states have ruling classes but no dynasties and central bureaucracies? How were these patterns expressed in the territorial organization of these states?**

▶ **What patterns of urban life characterized the cities of Tenochtitlán and Cuzco, the capitals of the Aztec and Inca Empires? In which ways were these cities similar to those of Eurasia and Africa?**

Tenochtitlán and Cuzco, the capitals of the Aztec and Inca Empires, were two urban centers organized around temples and associated residences of the ruling dynasties and their priestly classes. They also contained large city quarters inhabited by craftspeople specializing in the production of woven textiles, pottery, leather goods, and weapons. Large central markets provided for the exchange of foodstuffs, crafts, and imported luxury goods. Armed caravans of merchants and porters transported the luxury goods, such as cacao, feathers, obsidian, and turquoise, across hundreds of miles. Tenochtitlán had an aqueduct for the supply of drinking water, and Cuzco was traversed by a river. Both capitals had agricultural suburbs in which farmers used irrigation for the production of the basic food staples.

PART FOUR

Interactions across the Globe

1450–1750

S tarting around 1450, important changes can be detected in the patterns of world history. The religious civilizations that had emerged in the period after 600 CE continued to evolve, but the competing states that constituted these civilizations began to give way to new empires, such as those of the Mughals, the Ottomans, the Safavids, and the Habsburgs. China, historically an empire, had already reconstituted itself under the Ming after the collapse of the Mongol superempire that had straddled Eurasia. Finally, on the Atlantic coast, smaller European countries, such as Portugal, Spain, the Netherlands, England, and France, were creating the first global seaborne empires. Large or small, land-based or maritime, however, all of these empires employed the vitally important innovation of firearms. In addition, many reorganized themselves as centralized polities based on money economies, large bureaucracies, and professional armies. Locked into far-flung competition for resources, markets, and ideological influence, they interacted with each other with increasing intensity.

While this renewal of the drive for empire among these civilizations was a significant turning point in world history, two new phenomena appeared during the three centuries in question that would have far-reaching implications. Indeed, they would ultimately provide the basis on which our modern society was to be built: the New Sciences (or Scientific Revolution) and the Enlightenment. Attempts to found an understanding of the universe on mathematics and experimentation would lead to the primacy of science as the chief mode of interpreting the physical realm. Attempts to apply the principles of science to understanding and improving human societies would lead to the concepts of individual rights, natural law, and popular sovereignty that would become the modern legacy of the Enlightenment. The combination of these two trends created the foundations of the *scientific–industrial society* that now dominates our modern global culture.

The process by which this took place was, of course, extremely complex, and it is impossible for us to do more than suggest some of the larger patterns of it here. Moreover, because of the long-standing argument in Western historiography for European "exceptionalism"—that there was something unique in the European historical experience that preordained it to rise to dominance—we must be careful to explore the various aspects of this process without sliding into easy assumptions

1440–1897
Benin kingdom, West Africa

1492
Spanish conquest of Granada, expulsion of Jews, and discovery of the Americas

ca. 1500
Beginning of Columbian Exchange

1514
Nicolaus Copernicus formulates the heliocentric model

1453
Ottoman capture of Constantinople

1498
Vasco da Gama's circumnavigation of Africa and journey to India

1511
First African slaves taken to Hispaniola

1517
Martin Luther posts his 95 theses; beginning of Protestant Reformation

about their inevitability. For example, one question that suggests itself is "To what extent did the societies of western Europe (what we have termed the 'religious civilization' of western Christianity) part ways with the other religious civilizations of the world?" Here, aspects of the question are tantalizingly complex and, thus, have recently been the subject of considerable debate:

- On the one hand, there appears to have been no movement comparable to that of the European Renaissance or Reformation arising during this time in the other parts of the world to create a new culture similar to that of Europe. The Middle East, India, and China for the most part continued ongoing cultural patterns, although often on considerably higher levels of refinement and sophistication. Recent scholarship on neglected cultural developments in these areas from 1450 to 1750 has provided ample proof for the continuing vitality of Islamic, Hindu, Buddhist, Confucian, and Daoist cultural traditions. Thus, former assumptions of stagnation or decline no longer seem supportable.

- On the other hand, Europe, like much of the rest of the world, remained rooted in agrarian–urban patterns until the effects of the Industrial Revolution began to be felt sometime after 1800. The centuries-old patterns in which the majority of the population was employed in agriculture, not cities, continued unchanged. Furthermore, through nearly this entire period, China and India were more populous and at least as wealthy and diversified in their economies and social structures as their European counterpart. The "great divergence," as scholars currently call it, happened only *after* the Western constitutional and industrial revolutions. Nonetheless, the overall wealth of European countries involved in the conquest and exploitation of the resources of the Americas and the development of global trading systems advanced immensely—as did knowledge of the globe as a whole. Thus, while India and China had possessed these resources partially or completely already for a long time, European countries were now utilizing them at an accelerating rate. This wealth and the patterns of its acquisition and distribution would soon have far-reaching consequences.

It is important to emphasize that those developments we deem crucial today were not immediately apparent to the people living at the time. Indeed, for the great majority of people, even in 1750, much seemed to go on as before. Everywhere in the world empires continued to grow and decline, religious tensions continued to erupt into warfare, and rulers continued to ground their authority not in their peoples but in the divine. Thus, for a full understanding of world history during 1450–1750, one has to carefully balance cultural, political, social, and economic factors and constantly keep in mind that although change was certainly occurring, it was often too imperceptible for contemporaries to detect.

Thinking Like a World Historian

▶ What new and different patterns characterized the development of states and empires in the period 1450–1750?

▶ How did the emergence of centralizing states lead to more intensive and frequent interactions among empires in the period 1450–1750?

▶ How did the New Sciences and the Enlightenment lay the foundation for the scientific–industrial society that dominates our global culture today?

▶ To what extent did the societies of western Europe diverge from other civilizations in the period 1450–1750? Why is the notion of "exceptionalism" problematic in examining this question?

1521, 1533
Spanish conquest of the Aztec and Inca Empires

1577
Matteo Ricci, first Jesuit missionary to arrive in China

1607
Founding of Jamestown, Virginia

1720
Edo, capital of Japan, world's largest city

1542–1605
Akbar, the most innovative of the Mughal rulers (India)

1604
Galileo Galilei formulates the mathematical law of falling bodies

1687
Isaac Newton unifies physics and astronomy

1736–1795
Reign of Qianlong emperor, China

Chapter 16 1450–1650

The Western European Overseas Expansion and Ottoman–Habsburg Struggle

Al-Hasan Ibn Muhammad al-Wazzan (ca. 1494–1550) was born into a family of bureaucrats in Muslim Granada soon after the Christian conquest of this kingdom in southern Iberia in 1492. Unwilling to convert to Christianity, Hasan's family emigrated to Muslim Morocco around 1499–1500 and settled in the city of Fez. Here, Hasan received a good education in religion, law, logic, and the sciences. After completing his studies, he entered the administration of the Moroccan sultan, traveling to sub-Saharan Africa and the Middle East on diplomatic missions.

In 1517, as he was returning home from a mission to Istanbul, Christian **corsairs** kidnapped him from his ship. Like their Muslim counterparts, these corsairs roamed the Mediterranean to capture unsuspecting travelers, whom they then held for ransom or sold into slavery. For a handsome sum of money, they turned the cultivated Hasan over to Pope Leo X (1513–1521), who ordered Hasan to convert to Christianity and baptized him with his own family name, Giovanni Leone di Medici. Hasan became known in Rome as Leo Africanus ("Leo the African"), in

ABOVE: An Officer in the Army of Charles V Buys the Freedom of two Christian Women from their Muslim Captor. Painting by Jan Cornelisz Vermeyen (ca. 1500–1559); he accompanied Emperor Charles V on his victorious campaign against Muslim Tunis in 1535.

reference to his travels in sub-Saharan Africa. He stayed for 10 years in Italy, initially at the papal court and later as an independent scholar in Rome. During this time, he taught Arabic to Roman clergymen, compiled an Arabic–Hebrew–Latin dictionary, and wrote an essay on famous Arabs. His most memorable and enduring work was a travelogue, first composed in Arabic and later translated into Italian, *Description of Africa*, which was for many years the sole source of information about sub-Saharan Africa in the western Christian world.

After 1527, however, life became difficult in Rome. In this year, Charles V (r. 1516–1558), king of Spain and emperor of the Holy Roman Empire of Germany, invaded Italy and sacked the city. Hasan survived the sack of Rome but departed for Tunis sometime after 1531, seeking a better life in Muslim North Africa. Unfortunately, all traces of Hasan after his departure from Rome are lost. It is possible that he perished in 1535 when Charles V attacked and occupied Tunis (1535–1574), although it is generally assumed that he lived there until around 1550.

The world in which Hasan lived and traveled was a Muslim–Christian world composed of the Middle East, North Africa, and Europe. Muslims on the Iberian Peninsula and in the Balkans bracketed this world, with the western Christians in the center. Although Muslims and Christians traveled in much of this world more or less freely—as merchants, mapmakers, adventurers, mercenaries, or corsairs—the two religious civilizations were locked in a pattern of fierce competition. During 800–1050, the Muslims justified their conquests as holy wars (*jihads*), and during 1050–1300 the Christians retaliated with their Crusades and the reconquest of Iberia.

By the fifteenth century, the Christians saw their liberation of Iberia and North Africa from Muslim rule and circumnavigation of the Muslims in the Mediterranean as stepping stones toward rebuilding the crusader kingdom of Jerusalem, which had been lost to the Muslims in 1291. Searching for a route that would take them around Africa, they hoped to defeat the Muslims in Jerusalem with an attack from the east. Driven at least in part by this search, the Christians discovered the continents of the Americas. For their part, the Muslims sought to conquer eastern and central Europe while simultaneously shoring up their defense of North Africa and driving the Portuguese out of the Indian Ocean. After a hiatus of several centuries—when commonwealths of states had characterized western Christian and Islamic civilizations—imperial polities reemerged, in the form of the Ottoman and Habsburg Empires vying for world rule.

The Muslim–Christian Competition in the East and West, 1450–1600

After a long period during which the Christian kings in Iberia found tributes by the Muslim emirs more profitable than war, in the second half of the fifteenth

Seeing Patterns

▶ What patterns characterized Christian and Muslim competition in the period 1300–1600? Which elements distinguished them from each other, and which elements were similar? How did the pattern change over time?

▶ How did centralizing states in the Middle East and Europe function in the period 1450–1600? How did economics, military power, and imperial objectives interact to create the centralizing state?

▶ Which patterns did cultural expressions follow in the Habsburg and Ottoman Empires? Why did the ruling classes of these empires sponsor these expressions?

Corsairs: In the context of this chapter, Muslim or Christian pirates who boarded ships, confiscated the cargoes, and held the crews and travelers for ransom; they were nominally under the authority of the Ottoman sultan or the pope in Rome but operated independently.

Chapter Outline

- The Muslim–Christian Competition in the East and West, 1450–1600

- The Centralizing State: Origins and Interactions

- Imperial Courts, Urban Festivities, and the Arts

- Putting It All Together

century the kings resumed the *Reconquista*. During the same time period, the small principality of the Ottomans took advantage of Mongol and Byzantine weakness to conquer lands in both Anatolia and the Balkans. After the Muslim conquest of Constantinople in 1453 and the western Christian conquest of Granada in 1492, the path was open for the emergence of the Ottoman and Habsburg Empires.

Iberian Christian Expansion, 1415–1498

During a revival of anti-Muslim Crusade passions in the fourteenth century, Portugal resumed its *Reconquista* policies by expanding to North Africa in 1415. Looking for a way to circumnavigate the Muslims, collect West African gold, and reach the Indian spice coast, Portuguese sailors and traders established fortified harbors along the African coastline. Castile and Aragon, not to be left behind, conquered Granada in 1492, occupied ports in North Africa, and sent Columbus to discover an alternate route to what the Portuguese were seeking. Although Columbus's discovery of America did not yield Indian spices, he delivered a new continent to the rulers of Castile and Aragon (see Map 16.1).

Maritime Explorations   Portugal's resumption of the *Reconquista* had its roots in its mastery of Atlantic seafaring. In 1277–1281, mariners of the Italian city-state of Genoa pioneered commerce by sea between the Mediterranean and northwestern Europe. One port on the route was Lisbon, where Portuguese shipwrights and their Genoese teachers teamed up to develop new ships suited for the stormy Atlantic seas. In the early fifteenth century they developed the *caravel*, a small ship with high, upward-extending fore and aft sides, a stern rudder, and square as well as triangular lateen sails. With their new ships, the Portuguese became important traders between England and the Mediterranean countries.

The sea trade stimulated an exploration of the eastern Atlantic. By the early fifteenth century, the Portuguese had discovered the uninhabited islands of the Azores and Madeira, while the Castilians, building their own caravels, began a century-long conquest of the Canary Islands. Here, the indigenous, still Neolithic Berber inhabitants, the Guanches, put up a fierce resistance. But settlers, with the backing of Venetian investors, carved out colonies on conquered parcels of land, on which they enslaved the Guanches to work in sugarcane plantations. They thus adopted the sugarcane plantation system from the eastern Mediterranean, where it had Byzantine and Crusader roots on the island of Cyprus, as discussed in greater detail in Chapter 18, and made it an Atlantic one.

Apocalyptic Expectations   Parallel with the Atlantic explorations, Iberian Christians began to rethink their relationship with the Muslims on the peninsula. The loss of the crusader kingdom in Palestine to the Muslim Mamluks in 1291 was an event that stirred deep feelings of guilt among the western Christians. Efforts to dispatch military expeditions to reconquer Jerusalem failed, however, mostly because rulers in Europe—busy centralizing their realms—were now more interested in warring against each other for territorial gain. The failure did not dampen spiritual revivals, however, especially among the monks of the Franciscan and **military orders** of Iberia. These monks, often well connected with the Iberian

Military orders: Ever since the early 1100s, the papacy encouraged the formation of monastic fighting orders, such as the Hospitalers and Templars, to combat the Muslims in the crusader kingdom of Jerusalem; similar *Reconquista* orders, such as the Order of Santiago and the Order of Christ, emerged in Iberia to eliminate Muslim rule.

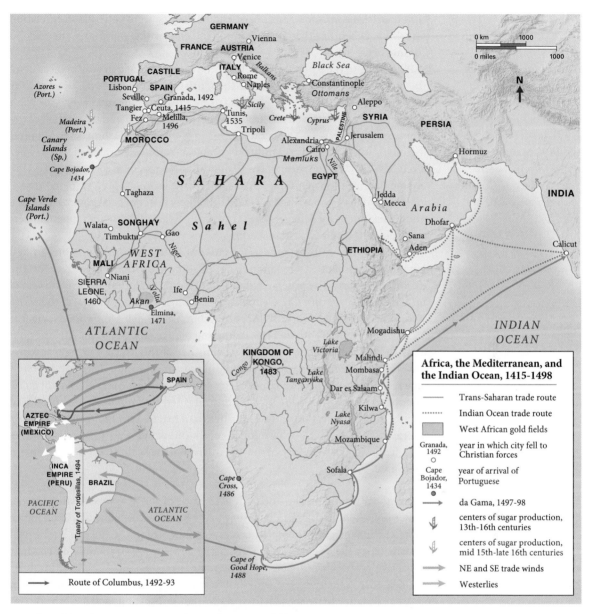

MAP **16.1 Africa, the Mediterranean, and the Indian Ocean, 1415–1498.**

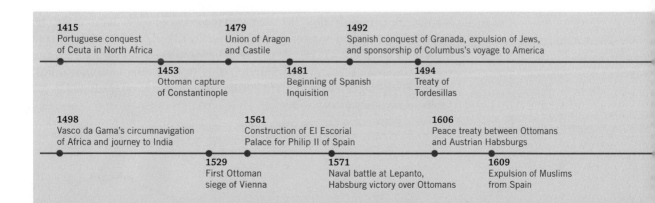

1415
Portuguese conquest
of Ceuta in North Africa

1453
Ottoman capture
of Constantinople

1479
Union of Aragon
and Castile

1481
Beginning of Spanish
Inquisition

1492
Spanish conquest of Granada, expulsion of Jews,
and sponsorship of Columbus's voyage to America

1494
Treaty of
Tordesillas

1498
Vasco da Gama's circumnavigation
of Africa and journey to India

1529
First Ottoman
siege of Vienna

1561
Construction of El Escorial
Palace for Philip II of Spain

1571
Naval battle at Lepanto,
Habsburg victory over Ottomans

1606
Peace treaty between Ottomans
and Austrian Habsburgs

1609
Expulsion of Muslims
from Spain

royal courts as confessors, preachers, and educators, were believers in revelation (Greek *apokalypsis*)—that is, the imminent end of the world and the Second Coming of Christ.

Apocalypse: In Greek, "revelation"—that is, unveiling the events at the end of history, before God's judgment; during the 1400s, expectation of the imminence of Christ's Second Coming, with precursors paving the way.

According to the **Apocalypse**, Christ's return could happen only in Jerusalem, which, therefore, made it urgent for the Christians to reconquer the city. They widely believed that they would be aided by Prester John, an alleged Christian ruler at the head of an immense army from Ethiopia or India. In the context of the intense religious fervor of the period, Christians as well as Muslims saw no contradiction between religion and military conquest. A providential God, so they believed, justified the conquest of lands and the enslavement of the conquered. The religious justification of military action, therefore, was not a pretext for more base material interests (though these would be a likely effect of such conquests) but a proud declaration by believers that God was on their side to help them convert and conquer the non-Christian world.

In Portugal, political claims in the guise of apocalyptic expectations guided the military orders in "reconquering" Ceuta, a northern port city of the Moroccan sultans. The orders argued that prior to the Berber–Arab conquest of the early eighth century CE, Ceuta had been Christian and that it was therefore lawful to undertake its capture. Accordingly, a fleet under Henry the Navigator (1394–1460) took Ceuta in 1415, capturing a huge stock of West African gold ready to be minted as money. Henry, a brother of the ruling Portuguese king, saw himself as a precursor in the unfolding of apocalyptic events and invested huge resources into the search for the *Rio de Oro*, the West African "river of gold" thought to be the place where Muslims obtained their gold. By the middle of the fifteenth century, Portuguese mariners had reached the "gold coast" of West Africa (today's Ghana), where local rulers imported gold from the interior Akan fields, near a tributary of the Niger River—the "gold river" of the Muslim merchants.

Reforms in Castile   The Portuguese renewal of the *Reconquista* stimulated a similar revival in Castile. For a century and a half, Castile had collected tributes from Granada instead of completing the reconquest of the peninsula. The revival occurred after the dynastic union of Castile and Aragon–Catalonia under their respective monarchs, Queen Isabella (r. 1474–1504) and King Ferdinand II (r. 1479–1516). The two monarchs embarked on a political and religious reform program designed to strengthen their central administrations and used the reconquest ideology to help speed up the reforms.

Among the political reforms was the recruitment of urban militias and judges, both under royal supervision, to check the military and judicial powers of the aristocracy. Religious reform focused on improved education for the clergy and stricter enforcement of Christian doctrine among the population at large. The new institution entrusted with the enforcement of doctrine was the Spanish Inquisition, a body of clergy first appointed by Isabella and Ferdinand in 1481 to ferret out any people whose beliefs and practices were deemed to violate Christian theology and church law. With their religious innovations, the monarchs regained the initiative from the popes and laid the foundations for increased state power.

The Conquest of Granada   The *Reconquista* culminated in a 10-year campaign (1482–1492), now fought with cannons on both sides. In the end, Granada fell into Christian hands because the Ottomans, still consolidating their power in the Balkans, sent only a naval commander who stationed himself in North Africa and harassed Iberian ships. The Mamluks of Egypt, less powerful than the Ottomans, sent an embassy to Granada that made a feeble threat of retribution against Christians in Egypt and Syria. Abandoned by the Muslim powers, the last emir of Granada negotiated terms for an honorable surrender. According to these terms, Muslims who chose to stay as subjects of the Castilian crown were permitted to do so, practicing their faith in their own mosques.

The treaty did not apply to the Jews of Granada, however, who were forced either to convert to Christianity or emigrate. In the 1300s, anti-Jewish preaching by the Catholic clergy and riots by Christians against Jews in Seville had substantially reduced the Jewish population of some 300,000 at its peak (ca. 1050) to a mere 80,000 in 1492. Of this remainder, a majority emigrated in 1492 to Portugal and the Ottoman Empire, strengthening the urban population of the latter with their commercial and crafts skills. Portugal adopted its own expulsion decree in 1497. Thus, the nearly millennium-and-a-half-long Jewish presence in Sefarad, as Spain was called in Hebrew, ended, with an expulsion designed to strengthen the Christian unity of Iberia.

After the expulsion of the Jews, it did not take long for the Christians to violate the Muslim treaty of surrender. The church engaged in forced conversions, the burning of Arabic books, and transformations of mosques into churches, triggering an uprising of Muslims in Granada (1499–1500). Christian troops crushed the uprising, and Isabella and Ferdinand used it as an excuse to abrogate the treaty of surrender. In one province after another during the early sixteenth century, Muslims were forced to convert, disperse to other provinces, or emigrate.

Columbus's Journey to the Caribbean   At the peak of their royal power in early 1492, Isabella and Ferdinand seized a golden opportunity to catch up quickly with the Portuguese in the Atlantic. They authorized the seasoned mariner Christopher Columbus (1451–1506) to build two caravels and a larger carrack and sail westward across the Atlantic. Columbus promised to reach India ahead of the Portuguese, who were attempting to find a route to India by sailing around Africa. The two monarchs pledged money for the construction of ships from Castilian and Aragonese Crusade levies collected from the Muslims.

In September, Columbus and his mariners departed from the Castilian Canary Islands, catching the favorable South Atlantic easterlies. After a voyage of a little over a month, Columbus landed on one of the Bahaman islands. From there he explored a number of Caribbean islands, mistakenly assuming that he was close to the Indian subcontinent. After a stay of 3 months, he left a small colony of settlers behind and returned to Iberia with seven captured Caribbean islanders and a small quantity of gold.

Columbus was a self-educated explorer. Through voracious but indiscriminate reading, he had accumulated substantial knowledge of such diverse subjects as geography, cartography, the Crusades, and the Apocalypse. On the basis of this reading (and his own faulty calculations), he insisted that the ocean stretching between western Europe and eastern Asia was relatively narrow. Furthermore, he fervently believed that God had made him the forerunner of an Iberian apocalyptic world ruler who would recapture Jerusalem from the Muslims just prior to the Second Coming of Christ.

For many years, Columbus had peddled his idea about reaching India (and subsequently Jerusalem) from the east at the Portuguese court. The Portuguese, however, while sharing Columbus's apocalyptic fervor, dismissed his Atlantic Ocean calculations as fantasies. Even in Castile, where Columbus went after his rejection in Portugal, it took several years and the victory over Granada before Queen Isabella finally listened to him. Significantly, it was at the height of their success at Granada in 1492 that Isabella and Ferdinand seized their chance to beat the Portuguese to Asia. Although disappointed by the meager returns of Columbus's first and subsequent voyages, Isabella and Ferdinand were delighted to have acquired new islands in the Caribbean, in addition to the Canaries. In one blow they had drawn even with Portugal.

Vasco da Gama's Journey to India   Portugal redoubled its efforts after 1492 to discover the way to India around Africa. In 1498, the king appointed an important court official and member of the crusading Order of Santiago, Vasco da Gama (ca. 1469–1524), to command four caravels for the journey to India. Da Gama, an experienced mariner, made good use of the accumulated Portuguese knowledge of seafaring in the Atlantic and guidance by Arab sailors in the Indian Ocean. After a journey of 6 months, the ships arrived in Calicut, the main spice trade center on the Indian west coast.

The first Portuguese mariner sent ashore by da Gama in Calicut encountered two North African Muslims, who addressed him in Castilian Spanish and Genoese Italian: "The Devil take you! What brought you here?" The mariner replied: "We came to seek Christians and spices." When da Gama went inland to see the ruler of Calicut, he was optimistic that he had indeed found what he had come for. Ignorant of Hinduism, he mistook the Indian religion for the Christianity of Prester John. Similarly ignorant of the conventions of the India trade, he offered woolen textiles and metal goods in exchange for pepper, cinnamon, and cloves. The Muslim and Hindu merchants were uninterested in these goods designed for the African market and demanded gold or silver, which the Portuguese had only in small amounts. Rumors spread about the Muslims plotting with the Hindus against the apparently penniless Christian intruders. Prudently, da Gama lifted anchor and returned home with small quantities of spices.

> "We [da Gama and his crew] were so amazed at this that we heard him [the mariner] speak and we could not believe it—that there could be anyone so far away from Portugal who could understand our speech."
>
> —Álvaro Velho

After these modest beginnings, however, within a short time Portugal had mastered the India trade. The Portuguese crown organized regular journeys around Africa, and when Portuguese mariners on one such journey—taking a far western route in the Atlantic—landed in northeast Brazil they claimed it for their expanding commercial network. During the early sixteenth century, the Portuguese India fleets brought considerable amounts of spices from India back to Portugal, threatening the profits of the Egyptian and Venetian merchants who had hitherto dominated the trade. Prester John, of course, was never found, and the project of retaking Jerusalem receded into the background.

Rise of the Ottomans and Struggle with the Habsburgs for Dominance, 1300–1609

While Muslim rule disappeared in the late fifteenth century from the Iberian Peninsula, the opposite was happening in the Balkans. Here, the Ottoman Turks spearheaded the expansion of Islamic rule over Christians. By the late sixteenth century, when the East–West conflict between the Habsburgs and Ottomans reached its peak, entire generations of Croats, Germans, and Italians lived in mortal fear of the "terrible Turk" who might conquer all of Christian Europe.

Late Byzantium and Ottoman Origins   The rise of the Ottomans was closely related to the decline of Byzantium. The emperors of Byzantium had been able to reclaim their "empire" in 1261 from its Latin rulers and Venetian troops by allying themselves with the Genoese. This empire, which during the early fourteenth century included Greece and a few domains in western Anatolia, was no more than a midsize kingdom with modest agricultural resources. But it was still a valuable trading hub, thanks to Constantinople's strategic position as a market linking the Mediterranean with Slavic kingdoms in the Balkans and the Ukrainian–Russian principality of Kiev. Thanks to its commercial wealth, Byzantium experienced a cultural revival, which at its height featured the lively scholarly debate over Plato and Aristotle that exerted a profound influence on the western Renaissance in Italy (see Chapter 10).

Inevitably, however, both Balkan Slavs and Anatolian Turks appropriated Byzantine provinces in the late thirteenth century, further reducing the empire. One of the lost provinces was Bithynia, across the Bosporus in Anatolia. Here, in 1299, the Turkish warlord Osman (1299–1326) gathered his clan and a motley assembly of Islamic holy warriors (Turkish *gazis*, including a local saint and his followers), as well as adventurers (including renegade Byzantines) and declared himself an independent ruler. Osman and a number of other Turkish lords in the region were nominally subject to the Seljuks, the Turkish dynasty which had conquered Anatolia from the Byzantines two centuries earlier but by the early 1300s had disintegrated.

During the first half of the fourteenth century, Osman and his successors emerged as the most powerful emirs by conquering further Anatolian provinces from Byzantium. The Moroccan Abu Abdallah Ibn Battuta (1304–1369), famous for his journeys through the Islamic world, Africa, and China, passed through western Anatolia and Constantinople during the 1330s, visiting several Turkish principalities. He was duly impressed by the rising power of the Ottomans, noting approvingly that they manned nearly 100 forts and castles and maintained pressure on the eastern Christian infidels. In 1354, the Ottomans gained their first European foothold on a peninsula about 100 miles southwest of Constantinople. Thereafter, it seemed only a matter of time before the Ottomans would conquer Constantinople.

Through a skillful mixture of military defense, tribute payments, and dynastic marriages of princesses with Osman's descendants, however, the Byzantine emperors salvaged their rule for another century. They were also helped by Timur the Great

"We journeyed next to Bursa [the capital of the Ottomans, conquered in 1326 from Byzantium], a great city with fine bazaars, surrounded by orchards and springs. Outside it are two thermal establishments, one for men and the other for women to which patients come."

—Ibn Battuta

Shipbuilding

With the appearance of empires during the Iron Age, four regional but interconnected traditions—Mediterranean, North Sea, Indian Ocean, and Chinese Sea—emerged.

In the Mediterranean, around 500 BCE, shipwrights began to use nailed planks for their war galleys as well as cargo transports, as evidenced by shipwrecks of the period. In the Roman Empire (ca. 200 BCE–500 CE), nailed planking allowed the development of the roundship (image *a*), a large transport of 120 feet in length with a capacity of 400 tons of cargo transporting grain from Egypt to Italy. The roundship and its variations had double planking, multiple masts, and multiple square sails. After 100 BCE, the triangular (lateen) sail allowed for zigzagging (tacking) against the wind, greatly expanding shipping during a summer sailing season.

The Celtic North Sea tradition adapted to the Mediterranean patterns of the Romans. When the Roman Empire receded during the 300s CE, shipwrights in Celtic regions continued with their own innovations, shifting to frame-first construction for small boats in the 300s. At the same time, Norsemen, or Vikings, innovated by introducing overlapping (clinkered) plank joining for their eminently seagoing boats. The North Sea innovations, arriving as they did at the end of the western Roman Empire, remained local for nearly half a millennium.

The evolution of China into an empire resulted in major Chinese contributions to ship construction. In the Han period (206 BCE–220 CE) there is evidence from clay models of riverboats for the use of nailed planks. One model, dating to the first century CE, shows a central steering rudder at the end of the boat. At the same time, similar stern rudders appeared in the Roman Empire. Who adopted what from whom, if at all, is still an unanswered question.

Patterns of Shipbuilding. Left to right: (*a*) Hellenistic-Roman roundship, (*b*) Chinese junk, (*c*) Indian Ocean dhow.

(r. 1370–1405), a Turkish-descended ruler from central Asia who sought to rebuild the Mongol Empire. He surprised the Ottomans, who were distracted by their ongoing conquests in the Balkans, and defeated them decisively in 1402. Timur and his successors were unsuccessful with their dream of neo-Mongol world rule, but the Ottomans needed nearly two decades (1402–1421) to recover from their collapse and reconstitute their empire in the Balkans and Anatolia. Under Mehmet II, "the Conqueror" (r. 1451–1481), they finally assembled all their resources to lay siege to the Byzantine capital.

Shipbuilding innovations continued after 600 CE. In Tang China, junks with multiple watertight compartments (bulkheads) and multiple layers of planks appeared. The average junk was 140 feet long, had a cargo capacity of 600 tons, and could carry on its three or four decks several hundred mariners and passengers (see image *b*). Junks had multiple masts and trapezoidal (lug) and square sails made of matted fibers and strengthened (battened) with poles sewed to the surface. The less innovative Middle Eastern, eastern African, and Indian dhow was built with sewed or nailed planks and sailed with lateen and square sails, traveling as far as southern China (see image *c*).

In western Europe, the patterns of Mediterranean and North Sea ship-building merged during the thirteenth century. At that time, northern shipwrights developed the cog as the main transport for Baltic grain to ports around the North Sea. The cog was a ship of some 60 feet in length and 30 tons in cargo capacity, with square sails and flush planking below and clinkered planking above the water line. Northern European crusaders traveled during 1150–1300 on cogs via the Atlantic to the Mediterranean. Builders adapted the cog's clinker technique to the roundship tradition that Muslims as well as eastern and western Christians had modified in the previous centuries. Genoese clinkered roundships pioneered the Mediterranean–North Sea trade in the early fourteenth century (see image *d*).

Lisbon shipwrights in Portugal, learning from Genoese masters, borrowed from local shipbuilding traditions and Genoese roundship construction patterns for the development of the caravel around 1430. The caravel was a small and slender 60-foot-long ship with a 50-ton freight capacity, a stern rudder, square and lateen sails, and a magnetic compass (of Chinese origin). The caravel and, after 1500, the similarly built but much larger galleon were the main vessels the Portuguese, Spanish, Dutch, and English used during their oceanic voyages from the mid-fifteenth to mid-eighteenth centuries (see image *e*).

(d)

(e)

Patterns of Shipbuilding (Continued). From top: (*d*) Baltic cog, (*e*) Iberian caravel. These ships illustrate the varieties of shipbuilding traditions that developed over thousands of years.

Questions

- How does the history of shipbuilding demonstrate the ways in which innovations spread from one place to another?

- Do the adaptations in shipbuilding that flowed between cultures that were nominally in conflict with each other provide a different perspective on the way these cultures interacted?

From Istanbul to the Adriatic Sea   Similar to Isabella and Ferdinand's siege of Granada, Mehmet's siege and conquest of Constantinople (April 5–May 29, 1453) is one of the stirring events of world history. The Byzantines were severely undermanned and short of gunpowder, unable to defend the full length of the imposing land walls that protected the city. Although they had some help from Genoese, papal, and Aragonese forces, it was not nearly enough to make a difference. Using their superiority in troop strength of 11 to 1 for a tight siege, the Ottomans bombarded Constantinople's walls with heavy cannons. The weakest

Siege of Constantinople, 1453.
Note the soldiers on the left pulling boats on rollers and wheels over the Galata hillside. With this maneuver, Sultan Mehmet II was able to circumvent the chain stretched across the entrance to the Golden Horn (in place of the anachronistic bridge in the image). This allowed him to speed up his conquest of Constantinople by forcing the defenders to spread their forces thinly over the entire length of the walls.

part of the Byzantine defenses was the central section of the western walls, where it was relatively easy to tunnel into the soil underneath. Here, Mehmet stationed his heaviest guns to bombard the masonry and had his sappers undermine the foundations of the walls.

Another weak section was on the northeastern side, along the harbor in the Golden Horn, where the walls were low. Here, the Byzantines had blocked off the entrance to the Golden Horn with a huge chain. In a brilliant tactical move, Mehmet circumvented the chain. He had troops drag ships on rollers over a hillside into the harbor. The soldiers massed on these ships were ready to disembark and assault the walls with the help of ladders. On the first sign of cracks in the northeastern walls, the Ottoman besiegers stormed the city. The last Byzantine emperor, Constantine XI, perished in the general massacre and pillage which followed the Ottoman occupation of the city.

Mehmet quickly repopulated Constantinople ("Istanbul" in Turkish, from Greek "to the city," *istin polin*) and appointed a new patriarch at the head of the eastern Christians, to whom he promised full protection as his subjects. In quick succession, he ordered the construction of the Topkapı Palace (1459), the transfer of the administration from Edirne (which had been the capital since 1365) to Istanbul, and the resumption of expansion in the Balkans, where he succeeded in forcing the majority of rulers into submitting to vassal status. One of the Balkan lords resisting the sultan was Vlad III Dracul of Wallachia, who according to tradition in 1461–1462 impaled a contingent of Ottoman troops sent against him on sharpened tree trunks. Mehmet replaced Vlad with his more compliant brother, but the memory of the impalements lived on to inspire vampire folktales and, eventually, in 1897, the famous Gothic horror novel *Dracula*.

Mehmet's ongoing conquests eventually brought him to the Adriatic Sea, where one of his generals occupied Otranto on the heel of the Italian peninsula. The Ottomans were poised to launch a full-scale invasion of Italy from Otranto, when the sultan died unexpectedly. His successor evacuated Otranto, preferring to consolidate the Ottoman Empire in the Middle East, North Africa, and the Balkans before reconsidering an invasion of central and western Europe.

Imperial Apogee   Between 1500 and 1600 the Ottoman sultans succeeded magnificently in the consolidation of their empire. In 1514, with superior cavalry and infantry forces, cannons, and muskets, the Ottomans defeated the Persian Safavids in Iran, who had risen in 1501 to form a rival Shiite empire in opposition to the Sunni Ottomans. In the southern Middle East, intermittent tensions between the Ottomans and the Mamluk Turks in Egypt, Syria, and eastern Arabia gave way to open war in 1517. The Ottomans, again due to superior firepower, defeated the Mamluks and took control of western Arabia, including the holy pilgrimage city of Mecca. A year later, in 1518, Sultan Süleyman I, "the Magnificent" (r. 1520–1566), appointed a naval commander to drive the Spanish from a series of fortifications and cities in North Africa, which the latter had conquered in the name of the *Reconquista* in the 1490s and early 1500s.

In the Balkans, the Ottomans completed their conquests of Serbia and Hungary with the annexation of Belgrade and Buda (now part of Budapest) as well as a brief siege of Vienna in 1529, begun too late in the year and eventually stopped by the approaching winter. By the second half of the sixteenth century, when the submission of most of Hungary had been secured, the Ottoman Empire was a vast multiethnic and multireligious state of some 15 million inhabitants extending from Algeria in the Maghreb to Yemen in Arabia and from Upper Egypt to the Balkans and the northern shores of the Black Sea (see Map 16.2).

Morocco and Persia   In the period of 1450–1600, the two large empires of the Ottomans and Indian Mughals dominated Islamic civilization. Two smaller and more short-lived realms existed in Morocco and Persia, ruled by the Saadid (1509–1659) and Safavid (1501–1722) dynasties, respectively. The Saadid sultans defended themselves successfully against the Ottoman expansion and liberated themselves from the Portuguese occupation of Morocco's Atlantic ports which had followed the conquest of Ceuta in 1415. In 1591, after their liberation, the Saadids sent a firearm-equipped army to West Africa in order to revive the gold trade, which had dwindled to a trickle after the Portuguese arrival in Ghana. The army succeeded in destroying the West African empire of Songhay but failed to revive the gold trade. Moroccan army officers assumed power in Timbuktu, and their descendants, the Ruma, became provincial lords independent of Morocco. The Saadids, unable to improve their finances, split into provincial realms. The still-reigning Alaouite dynasty of Moroccan kings replaced them in 1659.

Vlad Dracul next to Impaled Ottoman Soldiers. The woodcut depicts the alleged impalement of 1,000 Ottoman soldiers sent against Vlad Dracul, prior to Sultan Mehmet II leading a victorious campaign into Wallachia and removing Dracul from power. Dracul's cannibalism, suggested in the image, is not confirmed by historical sources.

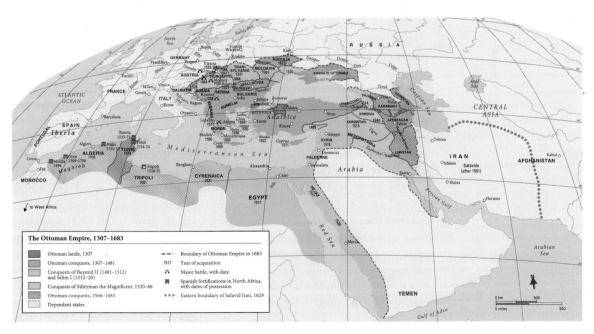

MAP **16.2** The Ottoman Empire, 1307–1683.

The Safavids grew in the mid-1400s from a Kurdish mystical brotherhood in northwestern Iran into a Shiite warrior organization (similar to the Sunni one participating in the early Ottoman expansion) that carried out raids against Christians in the Caucasus. In 1501, the leadership of the brotherhood put forward the 14-year-old Ismail as the Hidden Twelfth Imam. According to Shiite doctrine, the Hidden Imam, or Messiah, was expected to arrive and establish a Muslim apocalyptic realm of justice at the end of time, before God's Last Judgment. This realm would replace the "unjust" Sunni Ottoman Empire. The Ottomans countered the Safavid challenge in 1514 with the Battle of Chaldiran, where they crushed the underprepared Safavids with their superior cannon and musket firepower. After his humiliating defeat, Ismail dropped his claim to messianic status, and his successors assumed the more modest title of king (Persian *shah*) as the head of state, quite similar in many respects to that of the Ottomans.

Learning from their defeat, the Safavids recruited a standing firearm-equipped army from among young Christians on lands conquered in the Caucasus. They held fast to Shiism, thereby continuing their opposition to the Sunni Ottomans, and supported the formation of a clerical hierarchy, which made this form of Islam dominant in Iran. As sponsors of construction projects, the Safavids greatly improved urbanism in the country. After moving the capital from Tabriz to the centrally located Isfahan in 1590, they built an imposing palace, administration, and mosque complex in the city. In a suburb they settled a large colony of Armenians, who held the monopoly in the production of Caspian Sea silk, a high-quality export product which the Dutch—successors of the Portuguese in the Indian Ocean trade—distributed in Europe.

As patrons of the arts, the shahs revived the ancient traditions of Persian culture to such heights that even the archrival Ottomans felt compelled to adopt Persian manners, literature, and architectural styles. Persian royal culture similarly radiated to the Mughals in India. Not everyone accepted Shiism, however. An attempt to force the Shiite doctrines on the Afghanis backfired badly when enraged Sunni tribes formed a coalition, defeated the Safavids, and ended their regime in 1722.

Rise of the Habsburgs   Parallel to the rise and development of the Ottomans and Safavids, Castile–Aragon on the Iberian Peninsula evolved into the center of a vast empire of its own. A daughter of Isabella and Ferdinand married a member of the Habsburg dynastic family, which ruled Flanders, Burgundy, Naples, Sicily, and Austria, as well as Germany (the "Holy Roman Empire of the German Nation," as this collection of principalities was called). Their son, Charles V (r. 1516–1558), not only inherited Castile–Aragon, now merged and called "Spain," and the Habsburg territories but also became the ruler of the Aztec and Inca Empires in the Americas, which Spanish adventurers had conquered in his name between 1521 and 1536 (see Chapter 18). In both Austria and the western Mediterranean the Habsburgs were direct neighbors of the Ottomans (see Map 16.3).

After a victorious battle against France in 1519, Charles V also won the title of emperor from the pope, which made him the overlord of all German principalities and supreme among the monarchs of western Christianity. Although this title did not mean much in terms of power and financial gain in either the German

MAP **16.3** **Europe and the Mediterranean, ca. 1560.**

principalities or western Christianity as a whole, it made him the titular political head of western Christianity and thereby the direct counterpart of Sultan Süleyman in the struggle for dominance in the Christian–Muslim world of Europe, the Middle East, and northern Africa. Both the Habsburgs and the Ottomans renewed the traditional Islamic–Christian imperialism which had characterized the period 600–950 and which had been replaced by the Muslim and Christian common-wealths of 950–1450.

Habsburg Distractions   Charles V faced a daunting task in his effort to pre-vent the Ottomans from advancing against the Christians in the Balkans and Mediterranean. Multiple problems in his European territories diverted his atten-tion and forced him to spend far less time than he wanted on what Christians in most parts of Europe perceived as a pervasive Ottoman–Muslim threat. During the first three decades of the sixteenth century, revolts in Iberia, the Protestant Reformation in the German states, and renewed war with France for control of Burgundy and Italy commanded Charles's attention.

The emperor's distractions increased further in 1534 when, in an attempt to drive the Habsburgs out of Italy, France forged an alliance with the Ottomans. This alliance horrified western Europe. It demonstrated, however, that the Ottomans, on account of their military advances against the Christians in eastern Europe and the western Mediterranean, had become a crucial player in European politics. As fierce as the struggle between Muslims and Christians for dominance was, when the French king found himself squeezed on both sides of his kingdom by his archrival, Charles V, the Ottomans became his natural allies.

Habsburg and Ottoman Losses All these diversions seriously strained Habsburg resources against the Ottomans, who pressed relentlessly ahead on the two fronts of the Balkans and North Africa. Although Charles V deputized his younger brother Ferdinand I to the duchy of Austria in 1521 to shore up the Balkan defenses, he was able to send him significant numbers of troops only once. After a series of dramatic defeats, Austria had to pay the Ottomans tribute and, eventually, even sign a humiliating truce (1562). On the western Mediterranean front, the Habsburgs did not do well either. Even though Charles V campaigned several times in person, most garrisons on the coast of Algeria, Tunisia, and Tripoli were too exposed to withstand the Ottoman onslaught by sea and by land. In 1556, at the end of Charles V's reign, only two of eight Habsburg garrisons had survived.

A third frontier of the Muslim–Christian struggle for dominance was the Indian Ocean. After Vasco da Gama had returned from India in 1498, the Portuguese kings invested major resources into breaking into the Muslim-dominated Indian Ocean trade. In response, the Ottomans made great efforts to protect existing Muslim commercial interests in the Indian Ocean. They blocked Portuguese military support for Ethiopia and strengthened their ally and main pepper supplier, the sultan of Aceh on the Indonesian island of Sumatra, by providing him with troops and weapons. War on land and on sea, directly and by proxy, raged in the Indian Ocean through most of the sixteenth century.

In the long run, the Portuguese were successful in destroying the Ottoman fleets sent against them, but smaller convoys of Ottoman galleys continued to harass Portuguese shipping interests. As new research on the Ottoman "age of exploration" in the Indian Ocean has demonstrated, by 1570 the Muslims traded again as much via the Red Sea route to the Mediterranean as the Portuguese did by circumnavigating Africa. In addition, the Ottomans benefited from the trade of a new commodity—coffee, produced in Ethiopia and Yemen. Portugal (under Spanish rule 1580–1640) reduced its unsustainably large military presence in the Indian Ocean, followed by the Ottomans, which allowed the Netherlands in the early seventeenth century to overtake both Portugal and the Ottoman Empire in the Indian Ocean spice trade (see Map 16.4).

Habsburg–Ottoman Balance In the 1550s, Charles V despaired of being able to ever master the many challenges posed by the Ottomans as well as by France and

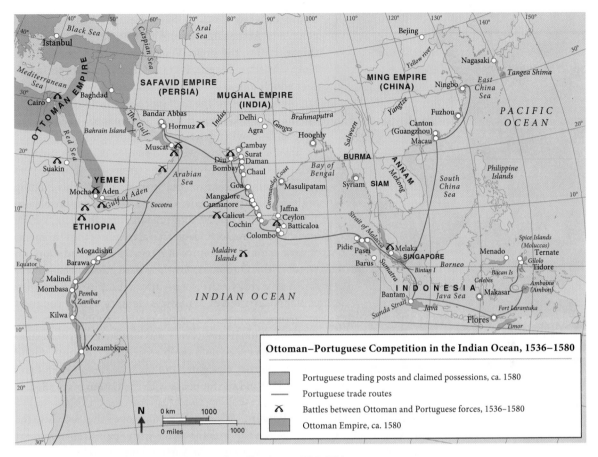

MAP **16.4** **Ottoman–Portuguese Competition in the Indian Ocean, 1536–1580.**

the Protestants. He decided that the only way to ensure the continuation of Habsburg power would be a division of his western and eastern territories. Accordingly, he bestowed Spain, Naples, the Netherlands, and the Americas on his son Philip II (r. 1556–1598). The Habsburg possessions of Austria, Bohemia, and the remnant of Hungary not lost to the Ottomans, as well as the Holy Roman Empire (Germany), went to his brother Ferdinand I (r. 1558–1564). Charles hoped that his son and brother would cooperate and help each other militarily against the Ottomans.

When Philip took over the Spanish throne, he realized, to his concern, that most of the Habsburg military was stationed outside Spain, leaving that country vulnerable to attack. As the Ottomans had recently conquered most Spanish strongholds in North Africa, a Muslim invasion of Spain was a distinct possibility. Fearful of morisco support for an Ottoman invasion of Spain, Philip's administration and the Inquisition renewed their decrees of conversion which had lain dormant for half a century.

This sparked a massive revolt among the moriscos of Granada in 1568–1570, supported by Ottoman soldiers and Moroccan arms. Philip was able to suppress the revolt only after recourse to troops and firearms from Italy. To break up the dangerously large concentrations of Granadan moriscos in the south of Spain,

Paolo Veronese, *Battle of Lepanto*, altar painting with four saints beseeching the Virgin Mary to grant victory to the Christians (ca. 1572). In the sixteenth century, the entire Mediterranean, from Gibraltar to Cyprus, was a naval battleground between Christians and Muslims. The Battle of Lepanto was the first major sea battle in world history to be decided by firepower: Even though Christian forces had slightly fewer ships, they had more, and heavier, artillery pieces. At the end of the battle "the sea was entirely covered, not just with masts, spars, oars, and broken wood, but with an innumerable quantity of blood that turned the water as red as blood."

Philip ordered them to be dispersed throughout the peninsula. At the same time, to alleviate the Ottoman naval threat, Philip, the pope, Venice, and Genoa formed the Holy Christian League. Its task was the construction of a fleet which was to destroy Ottoman sea power in the eastern Mediterranean. The fleet succeeded in 1571 in bottling up the entire Ottoman navy at Lepanto, in Ottoman Greece, destroying it in the ensuing firefight.

The Ottomans, however, had enough resources not only to rebuild their navy but also to capture the strategic port city of Tunis in 1574 from the Spaniards. With this evening of the scores, the two sides decided to end their unsustainable naval war in the Mediterranean. After this date, Venice was the only (but formidable) naval enemy of the Ottomans, at various times in control of Aegean islands and southern Greece. The Ottomans, for their part, turned their attention eastward, to the rival Safavid Empire, where they exploited a period of dynastic instability for the conquest of territories in the Caucasus (1578–1590). The staunch Catholic Philip II, for his part, was faced with the Protestant war of independence in the Netherlands. This war was so expensive that, in a desperate effort to straighten out his state finances, Philip II had to declare bankruptcy (1575) and sue for peace with the Ottomans (1580).

The Limits of Ottoman Power After their victory over the Safavids, the Ottomans looked again to the west. While the peace with Spain was too recent to be broken, a long peace with Ferdinand I in Austria (since 1562) was ready to collapse. A series of raids and counter-raids at the Austrian and Transylvanian borders had inflamed tempers, and in 1593 the Ottomans went on the attack. Austria, however, was no longer the weak state it had been a generation earlier. Had it not been for a lack of support from the Transylvanian and Hungarian Protestants, who preferred the sultan to the Catholic emperor as overlord, the Austrians might have actually prevailed over the Ottomans.

However, thanks to the Protestants' support, the Ottomans drew even on the battlefield with the Austrians. In 1606, the Ottomans and Austrian Habsburgs made peace again. With minor modifications in favor of the Austrians, the two sides returned to their earlier borders. The Austrians made one more tribute payment and then let their obligation lapse. Officially, the Ottomans conceded nothing, but in practical terms Austria was no longer a vassal state.

Expulsion of the Moriscos In the western Mediterranean, the peace between the Ottomans and Spanish Habsburgs held. But Philip and his successors remained aware of the possibility of renewed Ottoman aid to the Iberian Muslims, called *moriscos* ("little Moors"). Even though they had been scattered across the peninsula after 1570, the moriscos continued to resist conversion. Among Castilians, an intense debate began about the apparent impossibility of assimilating them to Catholicism in order to create a religiously unified state. The church advocated the expulsion of the moriscos, arguing that the allegedly high Muslim birthrate in a population of 7.5 million (mostly rural) Spaniards was a serious threat.

Fierce resistance against the proposed expulsion, however, rose among the Christian landowners in the southeastern province of Valencia. These landowners benefited greatly from the farming skills of the estimated 250,000 morisco tenant farmers who worked their irrigated rice and sugarcane estates. Weighing the potential Ottoman threat against the possibility of economic damage, the government decided in 1580 in favor of expulsion. Clearly, they valued Christian unity against the Ottomans more than the prosperity of a few hundred landowners in Valencia.

It took until 1609, however, before a compensation deal with the landowners in Valencia was worked out. In the following 5 years, some 300,000 moriscos were forcibly expelled from Spain, under often appalling circumstances: They had to leave all their possessions behind, including money and jewelry, taking only whatever clothes and household utensils they could carry. As in the case of the Jews a century earlier, Spain's loss was the Ottoman Empire's gain, this time mostly in the form of skilled irrigation farmers.

Expulsion of the Moriscos (secret Muslims) from Spain, 1609–1614. The Moriscos had to leave all their valuables behind, carrying only their barest belongings and watched closely by soldiers, as seen in this etching.

The Centralizing State: Origins and Interactions

The major technological change that occurred in the Middle East and Europe during 1250–1350 was the growing use of firearms. It took until the mid-1400s, however, before cannons and muskets were technically effective and reliable enough to make a difference in warfare. At this time, a pattern emerged whereby rulers created centralized states to finance their strategic shift to firearm-bearing infantries. They resumed the policy of conquest and imperialism, which had lain dormant during the preceding period, when the religious civilizations of Islam and Christianity had evolved into commonwealths of many competing realms. Both the Ottomans and the Habsburgs raised immense amounts of cash in silver and gold to spend on cannons, muskets, and ships for achieving world rule.

State Transformation, Money, and Firearms

In the early stages of their realms, the kings of Iberia (1150–1400) and the Ottoman sultans (1300–1400), with little cash on hand, compensated military commanders for their service in battle with parcels of conquered land, or land grants. That land, farmed by villagers, generated rental income in kind for the officers. Once the Iberian and Ottoman rulers had conquered cities and gained control over long-distance trade, however, patterns changed. Rulers began collecting taxes in cash, with which they paid regiments of personal guards to supplement the army of land-grant officers and their retainers. They created the centralizing state, forerunner of the absolutist state of the early seventeenth century.

Money economy:
Form of economic
organization in which
mutual obligations
are settled through
monetary exchanges;
in contrast, a system of
land grants obliges the
landholders to provide
military service, without
payment, to the grantee
(sultan or king).

The Land-Grant System   When the Ottoman *beys*, or military lords, embarked on their conquests in the early 1300s, they created personal domains on the choice lands they had conquered. Here, they took rents in kind from the resident villagers to finance their small dynastic households. Their comrades in arms, such as members of their clan or adherents (many of whom were holy warriors and/or adventurers), received other conquered lands, from which they also collected rents. As the Ottomans conquered Byzantine cities, first in Anatolia and then, in the second half of the 1300s, in the Balkans, they gained access to the **money economy**. They collected taxes in coins from the markets and tollbooths at city gates where foods and crafts goods were exchanged, as well as from the Christians and Jews subject to the head tax. The taxes helped in adding luxuries to the households of the Ottoman beys and enabling them to build palaces.

As a consequence of the full conquest of the southern Balkans by the Ottoman Empire in the fifteenth and sixteenth centuries, both the land-grant system and the money economy expanded exponentially. An entire military ruling class of grant holders emerged, forming the backbone of the early Ottoman army and administration. The grant holders were cavalrymen who lived with their households of retainers in the villages and towns of the interior of Anatolia and the Balkans.

Janissaries: Centrally
paid infantry soldiers
recruited among the
Christian population
of the Ottoman Empire.

**Boy Levy (*devşirme*) in a
Christian Village.** This
miniature graphically depicts the
trauma of conscription, including
the wailing of the village women
and the assembly of boys waiting
to be taken away by implacable
representatives of the sultan.

Most of the time, they were away on campaign with the sultans, leaving managers in charge of the collection of rents from the villagers on their lands. At the conclusion of the period of rapid growth of the Ottoman Empire in the early years of the sixteenth century, the landed ruling class of cavalrymen numbered some 80,000, constituting a vast reserve of warriors for the mobilization of troops each summer.

The Janissaries   An early indicator of the significance of the money economy in the Ottoman Empire was the military institution of the **Janissaries**—troops which received salaries from the central treasury. This institution probably appeared during the second half of the fourteenth century and is first documented in 1395. It was based on a practice (called ***devşirme*** [dev-SHIR-me]) of conscripting young boys, which palace officers carried out irregularly every few years among the empire's Christian population. For this purpose, the palace officers traveled to Christian villages, towns, and cities in the Balkans, Greece, and Anatolia. At each occasion, they selected boys between the ages of 6 and 16 and marched them off to Istanbul, where they were converted to Islam and trained as future soldiers and administrators. The boys and young men then entered the central system of palace slaves under the direct orders of the sultan and his viziers or ministers.

The *devşirme* contradicted Islamic law, which forbade the enslavement of "peoples of the Book" (Jews, Christians, and Zoroastrians). Its existence, therefore, documents the extent to which the sultans reasserted the Roman–Sasanid–Arab imperial traditions of the ruler making doctrine and law. Ruling by divine grace, the Ottomans were makers of their own law, called *kanun* (from Greek *kanon*). Muslim religious scholars, who had assumed the role of guardians of law and doctrine during the preceding commonwealth period of Islamic civilization (950–1300), had no choice but to accept sultanic imperialism and seek to adapt it to the Sharia as best they could.

Toward the first half of the fifteenth century, the sultans equipped their Janissaries with cannons and matchlock muskets. According to reports in Arabic chronicles, firearms first appeared around 1250 in the Middle East, probably coming from China. When the Janissaries received them, firearms had therefore undergone some 150 years of experimentation and development in the Middle East and North Africa. Even though the cannons and muskets were still far from being decisive in battle, they had become sophisticated enough to make a difference. By the mid-1400s, gigantic siege cannons and slow but reliable matchlock muskets were the standard equipment of Ottoman and other armies. The sultans relied on large numbers of indigenous, rather than European, gunsmiths, as new research in Ottoman archives has revealed.

Revenues and Money   The maintenance of a salaried standing army of infantry soldiers and a central administration to provide the fiscal foundation would have been impossible without precious metals. Therefore, the Ottoman imperial expansion was driven by the need to acquire mineral deposits. During the fifteenth century the Ottomans captured the rich silver, lead, and iron mines of Serbia and Bosnia. Together with Anatolian copper, iron, and silver mines conquered earlier, the Balkan mines made the Ottomans the owners of the largest precious metal production centers prior to the Habsburg acquisition of the Mexican and Andean mines in the mid-1500s.

The sultans left the Balkan mining and smelting operations in the hands of preconquest Christian entrepreneurs from the autonomous Adriatic coastal city-state of Ragusa or Dubrovnik. These entrepreneurs were integrated into the Ottoman imperial money economy as tax farmers obliged to buy their right of operation from the government in return for reimbursing themselves from the mining and smelting profits. **Tax farming** was the preferred method of producing cash revenues for the central administration. The holders of tax farms delivered the profits from the production of metals, salt, saltpeter, and other minerals to the state, minus the commission they were entitled to subtract for themselves. They also collected the head tax—payable in money—from the Jews and Christians and the profits from the sale of the agricultural dues from state domains. Thus, tax farmers were crucial members of the ruling class, responsible for the cash flow in the state.

The right to mint silver into the basic coin of the empire was similarly part of the tax-farm regime, as were the market, city gate, and port duties. The tax-farm regime, of course, was crucially dependent on a strong sultan or chief minister, the grand vizier. Without close supervision, this regime could easily deteriorate into a state of decentralization, something which indeed eventually happened in the Ottoman Empire on a large scale, although not before the eighteenth century.

Devşirme: The levy on boys in the Ottoman Empire; that is, the obligation of the Christian population to contribute adolescent males to the military and administrative classes.

Tax farming: Governmental auction of the right to collect taxes in a district. The tax farmer advanced these taxes to the treasury and retained a commission.

Ottoman Siege of a Christian Fortress. By the middle of the fifteenth century, cannons had revolutionized warfare. Niccolò Machiavelli, ever attuned to new developments, noted in 1519 that "no wall exists, however thick, that artillery cannot destroy in a few days." Machiavelli could have been commenting on the Ottomans, who were masters of siege warfare. Sultan Mehmet II, the conqueror of Constantinople in 1453, founded the Imperial Cannon Foundry shortly thereafter; it would go on to make some of the biggest cannons of the period.

Süleyman's Central State   The centralizing state of the Ottomans reached its apogee under Sultan Süleyman I, "the Magnificent." At the beginning of the sultan's reign, the amount of money available for expenditures was twice that of half a century earlier. By the end of his reign, this amount had again doubled. With this money, the sultan financed a massive expansion of the military and bureaucracy. Palace, military, and bureaucracy formed a centralized state, the purpose of which was to project power and cultural splendor toward its predominantly rural subjects in the interior as well as Christian enemies outside the empire.

The bureaucrats were recruited from two population groups. Most top ministers and officers in the fifteenth and sixteenth centuries came from the *devşirme* among the Christians. The conscripted boys learned Turkish, received an Islamic education, and underwent intensive firearm and (for some) horsemanship training, in preparation for salaried service in the Janissary army or administration.

The empire's other recruits came from colleges in Istanbul and provincial cities to which the Muslim population of the empire had access. Colleges were institutions through which ambitious villagers far from major urban centers could gain upward mobility. Graduates with law degrees found employment in the bureaucracy or as judges in the villages, towns, and cities. Muslims of Christian parentage made up the top layer of the elite, while Muslims of Islamic descent occupied the middle ranks.

Under Süleyman, the Janissaries comprised about 18,000 soldiers, divided into 11,000 musket-equipped troopers, a cavalry of 5,000, and 2,000 gunners who formed the artillery regiments. Most were stationed in barracks in and near the Topkapı Palace in Istanbul, ready to go on campaign at the sultan's command. Other Janissaries provided service in provincial cities and border fortresses. For his campaigns, the sultan added levies from among the cavalry troops in the towns and villages of the empire.

Typical campaigns involved 70,000 soldiers and required sophisticated logistics. All wages, gunpowder, and weapons and the majority of the foodstuffs were carried on wagons and barges, since soldiers were not permitted to provision themselves from the belongings of the villagers, whether friend or foe. Although the state collected heavy taxes, it had a strong interest in not destroying the productivity of the villagers.

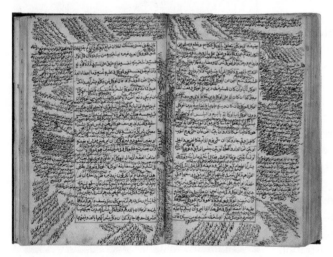

Ottoman Law Book. Covering the entire range of human activity—from spiritual matters, family relations, and inheritances to business transactions and crimes—the *Multaqa al-abhur* (*The Confluence of the Currents*) was completed in 1517 and remained for hundreds of years the authoritative source for many of the laws in the Ottoman Empire. It was written in Arabic by the legal scholar Ibrahim al-Halabi; later commentators added annotations in the margins and within the body of the text itself.

Charles V's Centralizing State   The centralizing state began in Iberia with the political and fiscal reforms of Isabella and Ferdinand and reached its mature phase under Charles V. From the late fifteenth century onward, Castile and Aragon shared many fiscal characteristics with those of the Ottomans. The Spanish monarchs derived cash advances from tax farmers, who organized the production and sale of minerals and salt. From other tax farmers, they received advances on the taxes collected in money from the movement of goods in and out of ports, cities, and markets, as well as on taxes collected in kind from independent farmers and converted through sale on urban markets. In addition, Muslims paid head taxes in cash. Most of the money taxes were also enforced in Flanders, Burgundy, Naples, Sicily, and Austria, after Iberia's incorporation into the Habsburg domain in 1516. Together, these taxes were more substantial than those of Spain, especially in highly urbanized Flanders, where the percentage of the urban population was about twice that of Spain.

From 1521 to 1536, the Spanish crown enlarged its money income by the one-fifth share to which it was entitled from looted Aztec and Inca gold and silver treasures. Charles V used these treasures to finance his expedition against Tunis. Thereafter, he collected a one-quarter share from the silver mines in the Americas that were brought into production beginning in 1545. Full production in the mines was not reached until the second half of the sixteenth century, but already under Charles V Habsburg imperial revenues doubled, reaching about the same level as those of the Ottomans. Thus, at the height of their struggle for dominance in the Muslim–Christian world, the Habsburgs and the Ottomans expended roughly the same amounts of resources to hurl against each other in the form of troops, cannons, muskets, and war galleys.

In one significant respect, however, the two empires differed. The cavalry ruling class of the Ottoman Empire was nonhereditary. Although land-grant holdings went in practice from father to son and then grandson, their holders had no recourse to the law if the sultans decided to replace them. By contrast, ever since the first half of the thirteenth century, when the Iberian kings were still lacking appreciable monetary resources, their landholders possessed a legal right to inheritance. The landholders met more or less regularly in parliaments (Spanish *cortes*), where they could enforce their property rights against the kings through majority decisions. When Isabella and Ferdinand embarked on state centralization, they had to wrestle with a powerful, landed aristocracy that had taken over royal jurisdiction and tax prerogatives (especially market taxes) on their often vast lands, including cities as well as towns and villages. The two monarchs took back much of the jurisdiction but were unable to do much about the taxes, thus failing in one crucial respect in their centralization effort. Although Habsburg Spain relied on precious metals as heavily as the Ottoman Empire did, it was in the end less centralized than that of the Ottomans.

The Habsburgs sought to overcome their lack of power over the aristocracy and the weakness of their Spanish tax base by squeezing as much as they could out of the Italian and Flemish cities and the American colonies. But in the long run their finances remained precarious, plentiful in some years but sparse in others. Relatively few Spanish aristocrats bothered to fulfill their traditional obligation to unpaid military service. Others who did serve forced the kings to pay them like mercenaries. As a result, in the administration and especially in the military, the kings hired as many Italians, Flemings, and Germans as possible. At times, they even had to deploy them to Spain in order to maintain peace there. Most of these foreigners were foot soldiers, equipped with muskets.

The Ottoman and Habsburg patterns of centralized state formation bore similarities to patterns in the Roman and Arab Empires half a millennium earlier. At that time, however, the scale was more modest, given that the precious metals from West Africa and the Americas were not yet part of the trade network.

In addition, earlier empires did not yet possess firearms, requiring an expensive infrastructure of charcoal and metal production, gunsmithing, saltpeter mining, and gunpowder manufacture. Thanks to firearms, the centralizing states of the period after 1450 were much more potent enterprises. They were established polities, evolving into absolutist and eventually national states.

Imperial Courts, Urban Festivities, and the Arts

Ottoman and Habsburg rulers set aside a portion of revenues to project the splendor and glory of their states to subjects at home as well as enemies abroad. They commissioned the building of palaces, mosques, and churches and sponsored public festivities. Since the administrators, nobility, tax farmers, and merchants had considerable funds, they also patronized writers, artists, and architects. Although Christian and Muslim artists and artisans belonged to different religious and cultural traditions and expressed themselves through different media, their artistic achievements were inspired by the same impulse: to glorify their states through religious expression.

The Ottoman Empire: Palaces, Festivities, and the Arts

The Ottomans built palaces and celebrated public feasts to demonstrate their imperial power and wealth. In Ottoman Islamic civilization, however, there were no traditions of official public art. The exception was architecture, where a veritable explosion of mosque construction occurred during the sixteenth century. Refined pictorial artistry, in the form of portraits, book illustrations, and miniatures, was found only inside the privacy of the Ottoman palace and wealthy administrative households. As in Habsburg Spain, theater and music enjoyed much support on the popular level, in defiance of official religious restrictions against these forms of entertainment.

The Topkapı Palace   When the Ottoman sultans conquered the Byzantine capital Constantinople in 1453, they acquired one of the great cities of the world. Although richly endowed with Roman monuments and churches, it was dilapidated and depopulated when the Ottomans took over. The sultans initiated large construction projects, such as covered markets, and populated the city with craftspeople and traders drawn from both the Asian and European sides of their empire. By 1600 Istanbul was again an imposing metropolis with close to half a million inhabitants, easily the largest city in Europe at that time.

One of the construction projects was a new palace for the sultans, the Topkapı Sarayı, or "Palace of the Gun Gate," begun in 1459. The Topkapı was a veritable minicity, with three courtyards, formal gardens, and forested hunting grounds. It also included the main administrative school for the training of imperial bureaucrats, barracks for the standing troops of the Janissaries, an armory, a hospital, and—most important—the living quarters, or harem, for the ruling family. Subjects were permitted access only through the first courtyard—reserved for imperial festivities—to submit their petitions to the sultan's council of ministers.

The institution of the harem rose to prominence toward the end of the reign of Süleyman. At that time, sultans no longer pursued marriage alliances with neighboring Islamic rulers. Instead, they chose slave concubines for the procreation of children, preferably boys. Concubines were usually from the Caucasus or other frontier regions, often Christian, and, since they were slaves, deprived of family attachments. A concubine who bore a son to the reigning sultan acquired privileges, such as influence on decisions made by the central administration.

The head eunuch of the harem guard evolved into a powerful intermediary for all manner of small and large diplomatic and military decisions between the sultan's mother, who was confined to the harem, and the ministers or generals she sought to influence. In addition, the sultan's mother arranged marriages of her daughters to members of the council of ministers and other high-ranking officials. In the strong patriarchal order of the Ottoman Empire, it might come as a surprise to see women exercise such power, but this power evidently had its roots in the tutelage exercised by mothers over sons who were potential future sultans.

Imperial Hall, Topkapı Palace. The Ottomans never forgot their nomadic roots. Topkapı Palace, completed in 1479 and expanded and redecorated several times, resembles in many ways a vast encampment, with a series of enclosed courtyards. At the center of the palace complex were the harem and the private apartments of the sultan, which included the Imperial Hall, where the sultan would receive members of his family and closest advisors.

Public Festivities   As in Habsburg Spain, feasts and celebrations were events that displayed the state's largesse and benevolence. Typical festivities were the Feast of Breaking the Fast, which came at the end of the fasting month of Ramadan, and the Feast of Sacrifice, which took place a month and a half later at the end of the Meccan pilgrimage. Festive processions and fairs welcomed the return of the Meccan pilgrimage caravan. Other feasts were connected with the birthday of the Prophet Muhammad and his journey to heaven and hell. Muslims believed that the Prophet's birth was accompanied by miracles and that the angel Gabriel accompanied him on his journey, showing him the joys of heaven and the horrors of hell. Processions with banners, music, and communal meals commemorated the birthdays of local Muslim saints in many cities and towns. As in Christian Spain, these feasts attracted large crowds.

Wrestlers, ram handlers, and horsemen performed in the Hippodrome, the stadium for public festivities. Elimination matches in wrestling determined the eventual champion. Ram handlers spurred their animals to gore one another with their horns. Horsemen stood upright on horses, galloping toward a mound, which they had to hit with a javelin. At the harbor of the Golden Horn, tightrope artists stood high above the water, balancing themselves on cables stretched between the masts of ships, as they performed juggling feats. Fireworks—featuring a variety of effects, noises, and colors—completed the circumcision festival in the evening. Court painters recorded the procession and performance scenes in picture albums. The sultans incorporated these albums into their libraries, together with history books recording in word and image their military victories against the Habsburgs.

Popular Theater   The evenings of the fasting month of Ramadan were filled with festive meals and a special form of entertainment, the Karagöz ("Black Eye")

Ottoman Festivities, 1720.
The sultan watches from a kiosk
on the shore of the Golden Horn
as artists perform high-wire acts,
musicians and dancers perform
from rowboats offshore, and high
officials and foreign dignitaries
view the festivities from a galleon.

shadow theater. This form of theater came from Egypt, although it probably had Javanese–Chinese roots. The actors in the Karagöz theater used figures cut from thin, transparent leather, painted in primary colors, and fashioned with movable jaws and limbs. With brightly burning lamps behind them, actors manipulated the figures against a cloth screen. The audience was seated on the other side of the screen, following the plays with rapt attention (or not).

Among boys, a performance of the Karagöz theater accompanied the ritual of circumcision, a rite of passage from the ancient Near East adopted in Islamic civilization. The custom called for boys between the ages of 6 and 12 to be circumcised. Circumcision signified the passage from the nurturing care of the mother to the educational discipline of the father. Groups of newly circumcised boys were placed in beds from which they watched the Karagöz plays.

Mosque Architecture   During the sixteenth century, the extraordinarily prolific architect Sinan (ca. 1492–1588) filled Istanbul and the earlier Ottoman capital Edirne with a number of imperial mosques, defined by their characteristic slender minarets. According to his autobiography, Sinan designed more than 300 religious and secular buildings, from mosques, colleges, and hospitals to aqueducts and bridges. Sultan Süleyman, wealthy officials, and private donors provided the funds. Sinan was able to hire as many as 25,000 laborers, enabling him to build most of his mosques in six years or less.

Selimiye and Hagia Sophia.
The architect Sinan elegantly
melded the eight, comparatively
thin, columns inside the mosque
(a) with the surrounding walls and
allowed for a maximum of light
to enter the building. In addition,
light enters through the dome (b).
Compare this mosque with the
much more heavily built, late-
Roman-founded Hagia Sophia (c).

Sinan described the Shehzade and Süleymaniye mosques in Istanbul and the Selimiye mosque in Edirne as his apprentice, journeyman, and master achievements. All three followed the central dome-over-a-square concept of the Hagia Sophia, which in turn is built in the tradition of Persian and Roman dome architecture. His primary, and most original, contribution to the history of architecture was the replacement of the highly visible and massive four exterior buttresses, which marked the square ground plan of the Hagia Sophia, with up to eight slender pillars as hidden internal supports of the dome. His intention with each of these mosques was not massive monumentality but elegant spaciousness, giving the skylines of Istanbul and Edirne their unmistakable identity.

The Spanish Habsburg Empire: Popular Festivities and the Arts

The centrality of Catholicism gave the culture of the Habsburg Empire a strongly religious coloration. Both state-sponsored spectacles and popular festivities displayed devotion to the Catholic faith. More secular tendencies, however, began to appear as well, if only because new forms of literature and theater emerged outside the religious sphere as a result of the Renaissance. Originating in Italy and the Netherlands, Renaissance aesthetics emphasized pre-Christian Greek and Roman heritages, which had not been available to medieval Christian artists.

Capital and Palace   The Habsburgs focused relatively late on creating the typical symbols of state power and splendor—that is, a capital city and a palace. Most Spaniards lived in the northern third and along the southern and eastern rims of the Iberian Peninsula, leaving the inhospitable central high plateau, the Meseta, thinly inhabited. Catholicism was the majority religion by the sixteenth century and a powerful unifying force, but there were strong linguistic differences among the provinces of the Iberian Peninsula. Charles V resided for a while in a palace in Granada next door to the formerly Muslim Alhambra palace. Built in an Italian Renaissance-derived style and appearing overwhelming and bombastic in comparison to the outwardly unprepossessing Alhambra, Granada was too Moorish and, geographically, too far away in the south for more than a few Spanish subjects to be properly awed.

Only a few places in the river valleys traversing the Meseta were suited for the location of a central palace and administration. Philip II eventually found such a place near the city of Madrid (built on Roman-Visigothic foundations), which in the early sixteenth century had some 12,000 inhabitants. There, he had his royal architect in chief and sculptor Juan Bautista de Toledo (ca. 1515–1567), a student of Michelangelo, build the imposing Renaissance-style palace and monastery complex of El Escorial (1563–1584).

As a result, Madrid became the seat of the administration and later of the court. A large central square and broad avenue were cut across the narrow alleys of the old city, which had once been a Muslim provincial capital. People of all classes gathered in the square and avenue, to participate in public festivities and learn the latest news "about the intentions of the Grand Turk, revolutions in the Netherlands, the state of things in Italy, and the latest discoveries made in the Indies," as the writer Antonio de Liñán y Verdugo remarked in a work published in 1620.

Like its Italian paradigm, the architecture of the Spanish Renaissance empha-sized the Roman imperial style—itself derived from the Greeks—with long friezes, round arches, freestanding columns, and rotunda-based domes. With this style, Spanish architects departed from the preceding Gothic, stressing horizon-tal extension rather than height and plain rather than relief or ornament-filled surfaces.

Christian State Festivities   Given the close association between the state and the church, the Spanish crown expressed its glory through the observance of feast days of the Christian calendar. Christmas, Easter, Pentecost, Trinity Sunday, Corpus Christi, and the birthdays of numerous saints were the occasion for pro-cessions and/or **passion plays**, during which urban residents affirmed the purity of their Catholic faith. Throngs lined the streets or marched in procession, pray-ing, singing, weeping, and exclaiming. During Holy Week, the week preceding Easter, Catholics—wearing white robes, tall white or black pointed hats, and veils over their faces—marched through the streets, carrying heavy crosses or shoul-dering wooden platforms with statues of Jesus and Mary. A variety of religious lay groups or confraternities competed to build the most elaborately decorated plat-forms. Members of flagellant confraternities whipped themselves. The physical rigors of the Holy Week processions were collective reenactments of Jesus' suffer-ing on the Cross.

> **Passion play:** Dramatic representation of the trial, suffering, and death of Jesus Christ; passion plays are still an integral part of Holy Week in many Catholic countries today.

By contrast, the Corpus Christi (Latin, meaning "body of Christ") proces-sions that took place on the Sunday after Trinity Sunday (several weeks after Easter) were joyous celebrations. Central to these processions was a platform with a canopy covering the consecrated host (bread believed to have been transfigured into the body of Jesus). Marchers dressed as giants, serpents, dragons, devils, angels, patriarchs, and saints participated in jostling and pushing contests. Others wore masks, played music, performed dances, and enacted scenes from the Bible. Being part of the crowd in the Corpus Christi processions meant partaking in a joyful anticipation of salvation.

The Auto-da-Fé   The investigation or proceeding of faith (Portuguese *auto-da-fé*, "act of faith") was a show trial in which the state, through the Spanish Inqui-sition, judged a person's commitment to Catholicism. Inquisitional trials were intended to display the all-important unity and purity of the Catholic Reforma-tion. The Inquisition employed thousands of state-appointed church officials to investigate anonymous denunciations of individuals failing to conform to the prescribed doctrines and liturgy of the Catholic faith.

Suspected offenders, such as Jewish or Muslim converts to Catholicism or per-ceived deviants from Catholicism, had to appear before one of the 15 tribunals distributed throughout the country. In secret trials, officials determined the degree of the offense and the appropriate punishment. These trials often employed torture, such as stretching the accused on the rack, suspending them with weights, crushing hands and feet in an apparatus called "the boot," and burning them with firebrands. In contrast to the wide perception of the Inquisition as marked by pervasive cruelties, however, scholarship has emphasized that in the great major-ity of cases the punishments were minor, or the investigations did not lead to convictions.

Popular Festivities *Jousts* (mock combats between contestants mounted on horseback) were secular, primarily aristocratic events, also frequently connected with dynastic occurrences. The contestants, colorfully costumed as Muslims, Turks, and Christians, rode their horses into the city square accompanied by trumpets and drums and led their horses through a precise and complex series of movements. At the height of the spectacle, contestants divided into groups of three or four at each end of the square. At a signal, they galloped at full speed past each other, hurling their javelins at one another while protecting themselves with their shields. The joust evolved eventually into exhibitions of dressage ("training"), cultivated by the Austrian Habsburgs, who in 1572 founded the Spanish Court Riding School in Vienna.

Bullfights, also fought on horseback, often followed the jousts. Fighting wild animals, including bulls, in spectacles was originally a Roman custom that had evolved from older bovine sacrifices in temples around the Mediterranean. During the Middle Ages, bullfights were aristocratic pastimes that drew spectators from local estates. Bullfighters, armed with detachable metal points on 3-foot-long spears, tackled several bulls in a town square, together with footmen who sought to distract the bulls by waving red capes at them. The bullfighter who stuck the largest number of points into the shoulders of the bull was the winner.

Theater and Literature The dramatic enactments of biblical scenes in the passion plays and Corpus Christi processions were the origin of a new phenomenon in Italy and Spain, the secular theater. During earlier centuries, traveling troupes had often performed on wagons after processions. Stationary theaters with stages, main floors, balconies, and boxes appeared in the main cities of Spain during the sixteenth century. A performance typically began with a musical prelude and a prologue describing the piece, followed by the three acts of a drama or comedy. Brief sketches, humorous or earnest, filled the breaks. Plays dealt with betrayed or unrequited love, honor, justice, or peasant–nobility conflicts. Many

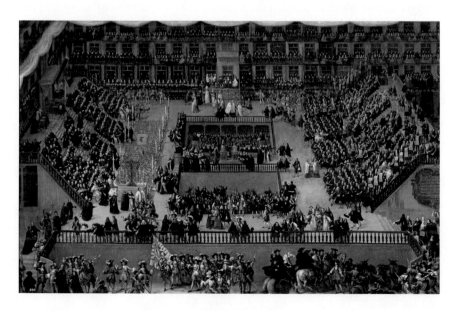

Auto-da-Fé, Madrid. This detail from a painting showing a huge assembly in the Plaza Mayor, Madrid, in 1683, captures the drama and spectacle of the auto-da-fé. In the center, below a raised platform, the accused stand in the docket waiting for their convictions to be pronounced; ecclesiastical and civil authorities follow the proceedings from huge grandstands set up for the event. On the left, an outdoor altar is visible—the celebration of Mass was a common feature of the auto-da-fé, which would often last for several hours.

El Greco, *View of Toledo*, ca. 1610–1614. The painting, now in the Metropolitan Museum of Art in New York City, illustrates El Greco's predilection for color contrasts and dramatic motion. Baroque and Mannerist painters rarely depicted landscapes, and this particular landscape is represented in eerie green, gray, and blue colors, giving the impression of a city enveloped in a mysterious natural or perhaps spiritual force.

were hugely successful, enjoying the attendance or even sponsorship of courtiers, magistrates, and merchants.

An important writer of the period was Miguel de Cervantes (1547–1616), who wrote his masterpiece, *Don Quixote*, in the new literary form of the novel. Don Quixote describes the adventures of a poverty-stricken knight and his attendant, the peasant Sancho Panza, as they wander around Spain searching for the life of bygone *Reconquista* chivalry. Their journey includes many hilarious escapades during which they run into the reality of the early modern centralizing state dominated by monetary concerns. Cervantes confronts the vanished virtues of knighthood with the novel values of the life with money.

Painters The outstanding painter of Spain during Philip II's reign was El Greco (Domenikos Theotokopoulos, ca. 1546–1614), a native of the island of Crete. After early training in Crete as a painter of eastern Christian icons, El Greco went to Venice for further studies. In 1577, the Catholic hierarchy hired him to paint the altarpieces of a church in Toledo, the city in central Spain that was one of the residences of the kings prior to the construction of El Escorial in Madrid. El Greco's works reflect the spirit of Spanish Catholicism, with its emphasis on strict obedience to traditional faith and fervent personal piety. His characteristic style features elongated, pale figures surrounded by vibrant colors and represents a variation of the so-called mannerist style (with its perspective exaggerations), which succeeded the Renaissance style in Venice during the later sixteenth century.

Putting It All Together

The Ottoman–Habsburg struggle can be seen as another chapter in the long history of competition that began when the Achaemenid Persian Empire expanded into the Mediterranean and was resisted by the Greeks in the middle of the first millennium BCE. Although India and China were frequently subjected to incursions from central Asia, neither of the two had to compete for long with any of its neighbors. Sooner or later the central Asians either retreated or were absorbed by their victims. The Ottomans' brief experience with Timur was on the same order. But the Middle East and Europe were always connected, and this chapter, once more, draws attention to this connectedness.

There were obvious religious and cultural differences between the Islamic and western Christian civilizations as they encountered each other during the Ottoman–Habsburg period. But their commonalities are equally, if not more, interesting. Most importantly, both Ottomans and Habsburgs were representatives of the return to imperialism, and in the pursuit of their imperial goals, both adopted the policy of the centralizing state with its firearm infantries and pervasive urban money economy. Both found it crucial to their existence to project their glory to the population at large and to sponsor artistic expression. In the long run, however, the imperial ambitions of the Ottomans and Habsburgs exceeded their ability to raise cash. Although firearms and a monetized urban economy made them different from previous empires, they were as unstable as all their imperial predecessors. Eventually, around 1600, they reached the limits of their conquests.

▶ For additional resources, including maps, primary sources, visuals, and quizzes, please go to www.oup.com/us/vonsivers. Please see the Further Resources section at the back of the book for additional readings and suggested websites.

Against the Grain

Tilting at Windmills

Cervantes's *The Ingenious Gentleman Don Quixote of La Mancha* was an instant hit in the Spanish-speaking literary world of the early 1600s and contributed to the rise of the novel as a characteristic European form of literary expression. As stated in his preface, Cervantes composed his novel in opposition to the dominant literary conventions of his time, to "ridicule the absurdity of those books of chivalry, which have, as it were, fascinated the eyes and judgement of the world, and in particular of the vulgar."

Every episode in this novel, from the literary frame to its most famous story, Don Quixote's joust against windmills he believes to be fantastic giants, is cast in the forms of gentle, hilarious, or biting parodies of one or another absurdity in society. The frame is provided by the fictional figure of Cide Hamete Benengeli, a purportedly perfidious Muslim and historian who might or might not have been lying when he chronicled the lives of the knight Don Quixote and his squire Sancho Panza in the 74 episodes of the novel. Don Quixote's joust, or "tilting," against windmills has become a powerful metaphor for rebelling against the often overpowering conventions of society.

Don Quixote is today acclaimed as the second most printed text after the Bible. Over the past four centuries, each generation has interpreted the text anew. Revolutionary France saw Don Quixote as a doomed visionary; German Romantics, as a hero destined to fail; Communists, as an anti-capitalist rebel before his time; and secular progressives, as an unconventional hero at the dawn of modern free society. For Karl Marx, Don Quixote was the hidalgo who yearned for a return to the feudal aristocracy of the past which in his time was becoming a pleasure aristocracy, enjoying its useless life at the royal court and imitated later by the bourgeoisie. Sigmund Freud enjoyed reading and rereading *Don Quixote* throughout his life, looking at the knight-errant as "tragic in his helplessness while the plot is unraveled." In our own time, Don Quixote became the quintessential postmodern figure; in the words of Michel Foucault, his "truth is not in the relation of the words to the world but in that slender and constant relation woven between themselves as verbal signs. The hollow fiction of epic exploits has become the representative power of language. Words have swallowed up their own nature as signs." As a tragic or comic figure, Don Quixote continues to be the irresistible symbol of opposition.

- What explains the lasting literary success of Don Quixote?

- Why has the phrase "tilting at windmills" undergone a change of meaning from the original "fighting imaginary foes" to "taking on a situation against all seeming evidence" in our own time?

Thinking Through Patterns

▶ **What patterns characterized the Christian and Muslim imperial competition in the period 1300–1600? Which elements distinguished them from each other, and which elements were similar? How did the pattern change over time?**

In 1300, the Ottomans renewed the Arab-Islamic tradition of jihad against the eastern Christian empire of Byzantium, conquering the Balkans and eventually defeating the empire with the conquest of Constantinople in 1453. They also carried the war into the western Mediterranean and Indian Ocean. In western Christian Iberia, the rekindling of the reconquest after the lull of the thirteenth and fourteenth centuries was more successful. Invigorated by a merging of the concepts of the Crusade and the *Reconquista*, the Iberians expanded overseas to circumvent the Muslims and trade for Indian spices directly. The so-called Age of Exploration, during which western Christians traveled to and settled in overseas lands, is deeply rooted in the Western traditions of war against Islamic civilization.

In the mid-1400s, the Middle East and Europe returned to the pattern of imperial state formation after a lull of several centuries, during which states had competed against each other within their respective commonwealths. The element which fueled this return was gunpowder weaponry. The use of cannons and handheld firearms became widespread during this time but required major financial outlays on the part of the states. The Ottomans and Habsburgs were the states with the most resources, and the Ottomans even assembled the first standing armies. To pay the musket-equipped soldiers, huge amounts of silver were necessary. The two empires became states based on a money economy: Bureaucracies maintained centralized departments that regulated the collection of taxes and the payroll of soldiers.

▶ **How did the centralizing state in the Middle East and Europe function in the period 1450–1600? How did economics, military power, and imperial objectives interact to create the centralizing state?**

▶ **Which patterns did cultural expressions follow in the Habsburg and Ottoman Empires? Why did the ruling classes of these empires sponsor these expressions?**

The rulers of these empires were concerned to portray themselves, their military, and their bureaucracies as highly successful and just. The state had to be as visible and benevolent as possible. Rulers, therefore, were builders of palaces, churches, or mosques. They celebrated religious and secular festivities with great pomp and encouraged ministers and the nobility to do likewise. In the imperial capitals, they patronized architects, artists, and writers, resulting in a veritable explosion of intellectual and artistic creativity. In this regard, the Ottomans and the Habsburgs followed similar patterns of cultural expression.

Chapter 17 1450–1750

The Renaissance, New Sciences, and Religious Wars in Europe

Though less celebrated than many of her male contemporaries, one of the most remarkable scientific minds of the seventeenth century was Maria Cunitz (ca. 1607–1664). Under the tutorship of her father, a physician, she became accomplished in six languages (Hebrew, Greek, Latin, Italian, French, and Polish), the humanities, and the sciences. For a number of years, while the Thirty Years' War (1618–1648) raged in Germany and her home province of Silesia, Cunitz and her Protestant family sought refuge in a Cistercian monastery in neighboring Catholic Poland. There, under difficult living conditions, she wrote *Urania propitia* (*Companion to Urania*), in praise of the Greek muse and patron of astronomy. When the family returned to Silesia after the war, Cunitz lost her scientific papers and instruments in a fire, but she continued to devote her life to science through her careful astronomical observations.

Cunitz's book is a popularization of the astronomical tables of Johannes Kepler (1571–1630), the major scientific innovator remembered today for his discovery of the elliptical trajectories of the planets. Cunitz's book makes corrections in Kepler's tables and offers simplified calculations of star positions. Writing in both Latin and German, she published it privately in 1650. It was generally well received, although there were a few detractors who

URBAN POPULATION OF EUROPE IN 1700

London Amsterdam
Paris
Naples

- Over 30%
- 25-30%
- 10-15%
- 5-10%
- 1-5%
- 0-1%
- city with population over 200,000

ABOVE: **Telescopic drawing of the moon by Galileo Galilei (1564–1642), showing the moon as a solid body—an observation that led him to argue that the earth was not unique.**

found it hard to believe that a woman could succeed in the sciences. Whatever injustice was done to her during her lifetime, today the scientific community has made amends. A crater on Venus has been named after her, and a statue of her stands in the town where she grew up.

Cunitz lived in a time when western Christianity had entered the age of early global interaction, from 1450 until 1750. During most of this time, Europe remained institutionally similar to the other parts of the world, especially the Middle East, India, China, and Japan. Rulers throughout Eurasia governed by divine grace. All large states followed patterns of political centralization. Their urban populations were nowhere more than 40 percent, and their economies depended on the productivity of agriculture. As research on China, the Middle East, and India during 1450–1750 has shown, there was no "great divergence" in the patterns of political organization, social formation, and economic production between western Christianity and the other religious civilizations until around 1750.

Culturally, however, northwestern Europe began to move in a different direction from Islamic, Hindu, Neo-Confucian, and Buddhist civilizations after 1500. New developments in the sciences and philosophy in England, France, the Netherlands, and parts of Germany initiated new cultural patterns for which there was no equivalent in the other parts of Eurasia, including southern Europe. As significant as these patterns were, for almost the entire span of time between 1500 and 1750 the new mathematized sciences remained limited to a few hundred and later to a few thousand educated persons, largely outside the ruling classes. Their ideas and outlooks diverged substantially from those represented by the Catholic and Protestant ruling classes and resulted frequently in tensions or, in a few cases, even repression of scientists by the authorities. The new scientific and intellectual culture broadened into a mass movement only after 1750. The subsequent Industrial Revolution of modernity was rooted in this movement.

The European Renaissance, Baroque, and New Sciences formed a cultural sequence that broke with much that had been inherited from medieval times. It began with the appropriation of the Greek and Roman cultural heritage, allegedly absent from the Middle Ages, by a small educated elite. In their enthusiasm for all things Greek and Roman, however, the members of this elite overestimated the extent of their break from the Middle Ages. In today's view from a greater distance, we think of this break as far less radical, with much in culture remaining unchanged. Many centuries were needed before the new cultural pattern initiated by Renaissance, Baroque, and the New Sciences became a general phenomenon.

Seeing Patterns

▶ What were the reasons for the cultural change that began in Europe with the Renaissance around 1400? In which ways were the subsequent patterns of cultural change different from those in the other religious civilizations of Eurasia?

▶ When and how did the mathematization of the sciences begin, and how did it gain popularity in northwestern Europe? Why is the popularization of the sciences important for understanding the period 1500–1750?

▶ What were the patterns of centralized state formation and transformation in the period 1400–1750? How did the Protestant Reformation and religious wars modify these patterns?

Chapter Outline

- Cultural Transformations: Renaissance, Baroque, and New Sciences

- Centralizing States and Religious Upheavals

- Putting It All Together

Similarly, the political and social changes of the period 1400–1750 have to be balanced against the inherited continuities. The rise of firearm-equipped armies of foot soldiers was a new phenomenon, but the use of these infantries by rulers to further increase their centralizing powers was an inheritance from the Middle Ages. The idea of a religious return to the roots of Christianity, pursued by the leaders of the Protestant Reformation, can also be traced back to the Middle Ages. When rulers used the Reformation for their centralizing ambitions, however, the ensuing religious wars became a new phenomenon. Overall, the seeds of an eventual departure of western Christianity from the general patterns of agrarian–urban society were planted around 1500. But for a long time thereafter these seeds remained largely underground, and the "great divergence" from the agrarian–urban patterns of Islamic, Hindu, and Chinese civilizations began only after 1750.

Cultural Transformations: Renaissance, Baroque, and New Sciences

Renaissance: "Rebirth" of culture based on new publications and translations of Greek, Hellenistic, and Roman authors whose writings were previously unknown in western Christianity.

The **Renaissance** was a period of cultural transformation which in the fifteenth century followed the scholastic Middle Ages in western Christianity. In many ways, the Renaissance was an outgrowth of scholasticism, but its thinkers and artists saw themselves as having broken away from scholastic precepts. They considered their period a time of "rebirth" (which is the literal meaning of "renaissance" in French). During this period they were powerfully influenced by the writings of Greek and Hellenistic-Roman authors who had been unknown during the scholastic age. In the sixteenth century, the Renaissance gave way to the Baroque in the arts and the **New Sciences**. Thus, the Renaissance was just the first of a sequence of periods of cultural transformation following each other in rapid succession.

New Sciences: Mathematized sciences, such as physics, introduced in the 1500s.

The Renaissance and Baroque Arts

Beginning around 1400 in Italy and spreading later through northwestern Europe, an outpouring of learning, scholarship, and art came from theologians, philosophers, writers, painters, architects, and musical composers. These thinkers and artists benefited from Greek and Hellenistic-Roman texts which scholars had discovered recently in mostly eastern Christian archives in Byzantium. In addition, in the early fifteenth century Byzantine scholars from Constantinople arrived in Italy with further newly rediscovered texts, which had a profound impact. The emerging cultures of the Renaissance and Baroque were creative adaptations of those Greek and Hellenistic-Roman writings to the cultural heritage of western Christianity. Out of this vibrant mixture arose the overarching concept of **humanism**.

Humanism: Intellectual movement focusing on human culture, in such fields as philosophy, philology, and literature, and based on the corpus of Greek and Roman texts.

New Manuscripts and Printing   Eastern Christian Byzantium experienced a cultural revival between its recovery in 1261 from the Latin interlude and its collapse in 1453 when the Muslim Ottomans conquered Constantinople. During this revival, for example, scholars engaged in a vigorous debate about the compatibility of Plato and Aristotle with each other. The debate made Italian scholars fully aware of how much of Greek literature was still absent from western Christianity. For example, at the time they possessed just two of Plato's 44 dialogues. Italians invited about a dozen eastern Christian scholars, who brought manuscripts to Florence, Rome, and Venice to translate and teach. Their students became fluent in Greek and translated Hesiod and Homer, some Greek tragedies and comedies, Plato and the Neo-Platonists, the remaining works of Aristotle, Hellenistic scientific texts, and the Greek church fathers. Western Christianity had finally absorbed the ancient heritage.

The work of translation was helped by the development of a more rounded, simplified Latin script, which replaced the angled, dense Gothic script used since the 1150s. In addition, the costly vellum (scraped leather) writing material on which many manuscripts had been laboriously written was replaced by cheaper paper, which had been introduced from Islamic Spain in the early twelfth century and had become common in the rest of Europe by 1400. Experimentation in the 1430s with movable metal typeface resulted in the innovation of the printing press. A half century later, with more than 1,000 printers all over Europe and more than 8 million books in the hands of readers, a veritable printing revolution had taken place in Europe.

Philology and Political Theory   The flood of new manuscripts and the renewed examination of existing manuscripts in libraries encouraged the study of Greek, Latin, and Hebrew philology. Scholars trained in these languages edited critical texts based on multiple manuscripts. The best known among these philologists was the Dutchman Desiderius Erasmus (1466–1536), who published an edition of the Greek and Latin New Testaments in 1516. Critical textual research, which became central to subsequent scholarship, can trace its foundations to the Renaissance.

Another type of critical stance emerged as a central element in political thought. In *The Prince*, Niccolò Machiavelli (1469–1527) reflected on the ruthless political competition among the princes of Europe for dominance over his hopelessly disunited native Italy. What Italy needed in his own generation, Machiavelli argued, was a unifier who possessed what Aristotle discussed in Book 5 of his *Politics*, namely a person of intuitive strength, valor, or indomitable spirit (Italian, *virtù*) to take the proper steps—subtle or brutal—when political success was to be achieved. Many Renaissance scholars preferred Plato, but Machiavelli remained faithful to Aristotle, the superior political realist—an Aristotle held in high esteem centuries later by the American founding fathers.

Bookseller. By 1600, the increase in literacy levels combined with widespread printing of books, pamphlets, and tracts had made people like this itinerant bookseller in Italy a commonplace sight throughout much of Europe.

1506–1558 Reign of King Charles V of Spain	**1517** Martin Luther posts his 95 theses; beginning of Protestant Reformation	**1561** Beginning of Catholic Reformation	**1565–1620** Dutch Protestant war of liberation from Spain	**1589–1610** Reign of King Henry IV of France
1514 First formulation of the heliocentric solar system by Nicolaus Copernicus		**1524–1525** German Peasants' War	**1562–1598** French war of religion	**1571–1630** Johannes Kepler, discoverer of the elliptical paths of the planets
1556–1598 Reign of King Philip II of Spain, the Netherlands, and the Americas	**1618–1648** Thirty Years' War in Germany	**1643–1715** King Louis XIV of France	**1688** "Glorious Revolution" in England	**1740–1786** Frederick II, builder of the centralizing state of Prussia
1604 Galileo Galilei's first formulation of the mathematical law of falling bodies		**1642–1661** English Civil War and Puritan Republic	**1687** Isaac Newton unifies physics and astronomy	**1690** Denis Papin's first steam engine

"But the duke [of Milan, Francesco Sforza, 1401–1466] possessed such indomitable spirit [*virtù*] and so much ability, he was so well aware that men must either be won over or else destroyed, and had such a sound basis for his power, which he had established in such a short period, that he would have overcome all of the difficulties if he had not had those two armies on top of him, or if he had been in good health."

—Machiavelli

The Renaissance Arts   In Italy, the reception of the new texts of the fifteenth century was paralleled by a new artistic way of looking at the Roman past and the natural world. The first artists to adopt this perspective were the sculptor Donatello (ca. 1386–1466) and the architect Filippo Brunelleschi (1377–1446), who received their inspiration from Roman imperial statues and ruins. The artistic triumvirate of the high Italian Renaissance was composed of Leonardo da Vinci (1452–1519), Michelangelo (1475–1564), and Raphael (1483–1520). Inspired by the Italian creative outburst, the Renaissance flourished also in Germany, the Netherlands, and France, making it a Europe-wide phenomenon.

The earliest musical composers of the Renaissance in the first half of the fifteenth century were Platonists, who considered music a part of a well-rounded education. The difficulty, however, was that the music of the Greeks or Romans was completely unknown. A partial solution for this difficulty was found through emphasizing the relationship between the word—that is, rhetoric— and music. In the sixteenth century this emphasis coincided with the Protestant and Catholic demand for liturgical music, such as hymns, masses, and *madrigals* (verses sung by unaccompanied voices). A pioneer of this music was the Italian composer Giovanni Pierluigi da Palestrina (ca. 1525–1594), who represented Renaissance music at its most exquisite.

The theater was a relatively late expression of the Renaissance. The popular mystery, passion, and morality plays from the centuries prior to 1400 continued in Catholic countries. In Italy, in the course of the fifteenth century, the *commedia dell'arte* (a secular popular theater) emerged, often using masked actors in plays of forbidden love, jealousy, and adultery. In England during the sixteenth century the popular traveling theater troupes became stationary and professional, attracting playwrights who composed more elaborate plays. Sponsored by the aristocracy and the Elizabethan court, playwrights wrote hundreds of scripts—some 600 are still extant—beginning in the 1580s. The best known among these playwrights was William Shakespeare (1564–1616), who also acted in his tragedies and comedies.

The Baroque Arts   The Renaissance gave way around 1600 to the Baroque, which dominated the arts until about 1750. Two factors influenced its emergence. First, the Protestant Reformation, Catholic Reformation, and religious wars changed the nature of patronage, on which architects, painters, and musicians depended. Many Protestant churches, opposed to imagery as incompatible with their view of early Christianity, did not sponsor artists for the adornment of their buildings with religious art. Wealthy urban merchants, often Protestant, stepped into the breach but avoided paintings with religious themes, preferring instead secular portraits, still lifes, village scenes, and landscapes.

Second, the predilection for Renaissance measurement, balance, and restraint gave way in both Catholic and Protestant regions to greater spontaneity and dramatic effect. Even more pronounced was the parallel shift in church and palace architecture to a "baroque" voluptuousness of forms and decorations, exemplified by Bavarian and Austrian Catholic churches, the Versailles Palace, and

Renaissance Art. Brunelleschi's cupola for the cathedral of Florence, completed in 1436, was one of the greatest achievements of the early Renaissance (*a*). Raphael's *School of Athens* (1509–1510) depicts some 50 philosophers and scientists, with Plato (in red tunic) and Aristotle (blue) in the center of the painting (*b*). Peter Brueghel's *The Harvesters* (1565) shows peasants taking a lunch break (*c*).

St. Paul's Cathedral in London, all completed between 1670 and 1750. Baroque music, benefitting from ample church and palace patronage and exemplified by the Italian Antonio Vivaldi (1678–1741) and the German Johann Sebastian Bach (1685–1750), experienced a veritable explosion of unrestrained exploration.

The New Sciences

Eastern Christian scholars invited from Byzantium to Florence in Italy during the first half of the fifteenth century brought with them Hellenistic scientific treatises, which aroused great interest among Italian Renaissance scholars. Battle lines were drawn between those scholars who continued to adhere to the Aristotelian-scholastic scientific method, even though this method had undergone significant changes during the 1300s, and scholars (such as Copernicus) who were more interested in newly translated mathematical, astronomical, and geographical texts. Eventually, in the 1600s, two scientific pioneers—Galileo and Newton—abandoned much of the *qualitative* scientific method of Aristotelian scholasticism in favor of the *mathematized* science of physics. In the eighteenth century, Newton's unified astronomical-physical-based science of a mechanical, deterministic universe became the foundation for the development of modern scientific–industrial society.

Copernicus's Incipient New Science   According to Aristotle, nature was composed of the four elements of (in ascending order of lightness) earth, water, air, and fire. In astronomical terms, he thought that these elements formed distinct layers, together shaping the world. In geographical terms, however, it was obvious to Aristotle that not all earth was submerged by water. He knew that Europe, Asia, and Africa formed a contiguous land mass of continents above water. Aristotle did not resolve the contradiction in his writings, but subsequent medieval scholars sought to find a resolution. They developed the theory of the "floating apple," whereby they assumed that most of earth was submerged, and a minimal protruding amount—the three continents—was surrounded everywhere by water.

During the Renaissance, the *Geography*, written by the Hellenistic cosmographer Ptolemy (see Chapter 5), became available from Constantinople (a Latin translation was printed in 1477). This important work proposed the geographical concept of a globe composed of a single sphere of intermingled earth and water. When Nicolaus Copernicus (1473–1543) appeared on the scene, scholars were still grappling with these competing theories of the floating apple and the intermingled earth-water spheres.

Copernicus was born in Torun, a German-founded city which had come under Polish rule a few years before his birth. He began his studies at the University of Kraków, the only eastern European school to offer courses in astronomy. During the years 1495–1504, he continued his studies—of canon law, medicine, geography, cosmography, and astrology—at Italian universities. In 1500 he briefly taught mathematics in Rome and perhaps read Greek astronomical texts translated from Arabic in the library of the Vatican. Eventually, Copernicus graduated with a degree in canon law and took up an administrative position at the cathedral of Torun, which allowed him time to pursue astronomical research.

Sometime between 1507 and 1514 Copernicus realized that the discovery of the Americas in 1492 provided a decisive empirical proof for the theory of the world as a single earth-water sphere. During this time, it is likely that he saw the new world map by the German cartographer Martin Waldseemüller (ca. 1470–1520), which made him aware of the existence of the Americas as hitherto unknown inhabited lands on the other side of the world. Much more land protruded from the water and was not limited to the interconnected land mass of Eurasia-Africa, than had been previously assumed in the floating-apple theory.

> "To these regions [Eurasia-Africa], moreover, should be added the islands discovered in our time under the rulers of Spain and Portugal, and especially America, named after the ship's captain who found them. On account of their still undisclosed size they are thought to be a second group of inhabited countries."
>
> —Copernicus

As a result, this theory became questionable. Copernicus firmly espoused the Ptolemaic theory of the single intermingled water-earth sphere with mountainous protrusions. A globe with well-distributed water and land masses is a perfect body that moves in perfect circular paths, so he argued further, and formulated his hypothesis, according to which the earth is a body that performs the same motions as the other bodies in the planetary system. The discovery of the Americas, therefore, can be considered as the empirical trigger that convinced Copernicus of the correctness of his trigonometric calculations, which removed the earth from the center of the planetary system and made it revolve around the sun.

Galileo's Mathematical Physics   During the near century between the births of Copernicus and Galileo Galilei (1564–1642), mathematics—with its two branches of Greek geometry and Arabic algebra—improved considerably. Euclid's *Elements*, badly translated from Arabic in the late twelfth century, with a garbled definition of proportions, was retranslated correctly from the original Greek in 1543. Shortly thereafter, the new translation in 1544 of a text on floating and descending

Waldseemüller's 1507 World Map. The German mapmaker Martin Waldseemüller (ca. 1470–1520) was the first western Christian to draw a world map which included the newly discovered Americas. He gave them the name "America" after the Italian explorer Amerigo Vespucci (1454–1512), who was the first to state that the Americas were a separate land mass, unconnected to Asia. The single copy of Waldseemüller's map still extant is among the holdings of the US Library of Congress.

bodies by the Hellenistic scholar Archimedes (287–212 BCE) attracted intense scholarly attention. The text, unknown to the Arabs, had been translated from the Greek in the thirteenth century but subsequently remained unappreciated, on account of its incompatibility with the then-prevailing Aristotelian scholasticism.

What was required for a scholar critical of scholastic traditions was to combine geometry, algebra, and Archimedean physics. In 1604, that scholar appeared in the person of Galileo, when he formulated his famous mathematical "law of falling bodies." It is true that this law had been foreshadowed by the reflections of scholastic scholars at the University of Oxford's Merton College and the University of Paris in the 1300s. But these earlier scholars reflected on the logical and/or geometric properties of motion only "according to imagination." Galileo was the scholar who systematically combined imagination with empirical research and experimentation and thereby became the founder of what we now call the (mathematized) New Sciences.

Running Afoul of the Church   Galileo was not only a physicist but also a first-rate astronomer, one of the first to use a telescope, which had been recently invented in Flanders. On the basis of his astronomical work, in 1610 he received a richly endowed appointment as chief mathematician and philosopher at the court of the Medici, the ruling family of Florence. But his increasing fame also attracted the enmity of the Catholic Church.

As a proponent of Copernican heliocentrism, Galileo seemed to contradict the passage in the Hebrew Bible where God recognized the motion of the sun around the earth. (In Joshua 10:12–13, he stopped the sun's revolution for a day, in order to allow the Israelites to win a critical battle against the Amorites.) In contrast to the more tolerant pope at the time of Copernicus, the Roman Inquisition favored a strictly literal interpretation of this passage, which implied that God had halted the sun's motion. In 1632 Galileo found himself condemned to house arrest and forced to make a public repudiation of heliocentrism.

The condemnation of Galileo had a chilling effect on scientists in the southern European countries where the Catholic Reformation was dominant (see p. 503). Prudent patrons reduced their stipends to scientists, and scientific research subsequently declined. During the seventeenth century, interest in the New Sciences shifted increasingly to France, Germany, the Netherlands, and England. In these countries, no single church authority, of either the Catholic or the Protestant variety, was sufficiently dominant to enforce the literal understanding of scripture. As a result, these countries produced numerous mathematicians, astronomers, physicists, and inventors, Catholic as well as Protestant. The New Scientists in northern Europe had a certain liberty that their southern colleagues lacked. It was this relative intellectual freedom, not any great sympathy on the part of religious authorities for the New Sciences, which allowed the latter to flourish, especially in the Netherlands and England.

Iberian Natural Sciences   The shift of New Sciences research to northwestern Europe notwithstanding, southern European countries such as Spain were well situated to make substantial scientific contributions, even if not in the New Sciences. Hundreds of botanists, geographers, ethnographers, physicians, and metallurgists fanned out across the new colonies to take advantage of what their northern colleagues in the New Sciences could not do: They researched the new plants, diseases, peoples, and mineral resources of the New World, Africa, and Asia with the traditional descriptive and qualitative methods of the natural sciences and accumulated a voluminous amount of knowledge. For long periods, the Habsburg monarch kept the manuscripts with this knowledge under wraps, fearful that his colonial competitors would benefit from them—hence it was only through recent research efforts that the Iberian contributions to the sciences in the 1500s and 1600s have become more widely known.

Isaac Newton's Mechanics   In the middle of the English struggles between the Protestants and the Catholic/Catholicizing Stuart monarchs, Isaac Newton (1643–1727) brought the New Sciences of Copernicus and Galileo to their culmination. As a professor at the University of Cambridge, he worked in the fields of mathematics, optics, astronomy, physics, alchemy, and theology. His primary early contribution was calculus, a new field in mathematics, which he developed at the same time as the German philosopher Gottfried Wilhelm Leibniz (1646–1716). Later in his career, Newton unified the fields of physics and astronomy, establishing the so-called Newtonian synthesis. His *Mathematical Principles of Natural Philosophy*, published in 1687, was the towering achievement of the New Sciences. It established a deterministic universe following mathematical rules and formed the basis of science until the early twentieth century, when Albert Einstein's relativity theory superseded Newtonianism.

The New Sciences and Their Social Impact

Scientists in the seventeenth century were in close communication with each other. They met in scientific societies or residential salons. Popularizers introduced an increasingly large public to the New Sciences. Scientists carried out experiments with constantly improved scientific instruments, such as telescopes, microscopes, thermometers, and barometers. Experience with barometers led technically versatile scientists and engineers to experiment with vacuum chambers and cylinders operating with condensing steam. Experimentation culminated with the invention of the steam engine in England in 1712.

New Science Societies   When the Catholic Reformation drove the New Sciences to northwestern Europe, the Italian-style academies gave way to chartered scientific societies, such as the Royal Society of London (1660) and the Paris Academy of Sciences (1666). Other countries, like Prussia, Russia, and Sweden, soon followed suit. These societies employed staffs of administrators, co-opted scientists as fellows, held regular discussion meetings, challenged their fellows to answer scientific questions, awarded prizes, and organized field trips and expeditions. They also published transactions, correspondences, and monographs. Many societies attracted thousands of members—famous pioneers, obscure amateurs, technically proficient tinkerers, theoretical mathematicians, daring experimenters, and flighty dreamers—representing an important cross section of seventeenth-century urban society in northwest Europe (see Map 17.1).

Other popularizers were textbook authors and itinerant lecturers who addressed audiences of middle-class amateurs, instrument makers, and specialized craftspeople, especially in England and the Netherlands. Many lecturers toured coffeehouses, urban residences, country estates, and provincial schools. Coffeehouses allowed the literate urban public to meet, read the daily newspapers (first appearing in the early seventeenth century), and exchange ideas. Coffee, introduced from Ethiopia and Yemen via the Ottoman Empire in the sixteenth century, was the preferred nonalcoholic social drink before the arrival of tea in the later eighteenth century. Male urban literacy is estimated to have exceeded 50 percent in England and the Netherlands during this period, although it remained considerably lower in France, Germany, and Italy.

Some lecturers were veritable entrepreneurs of the speaking circuit, teaching a kind of "Newtonianism lite" for ladies and gentlemen with little time or patience for serious study. Other lecturers set up subscriptions for month-long courses. Wealthy businessmen endowed public lectures and supported increasingly elaborate experiments and expensive laboratory equipment. In the first half of the eighteenth century, the New Science triumphed in northwestern Europe among a large, scientifically and technically interested public of experimenters, engineers, instrument makers, artisans, business people, and lay folk.

Women, Social Salons, and the New Science   Women formed a significant part of this public. In the fields of mathematics and astronomy, Sophie Brahe (1556–1643), sister of the Danish astronomer Tycho Brahe (1546–1601), and Maria Cunitz (see chapter-opening vignette) were the first to make contributions to the new astronomy of Copernicus and Kepler. According to estimates, in the second half of the seventeenth century some 14 percent of German astronomers were women. A dozen particularly prominent female astronomers practiced their science privately in Germany, Poland, the Netherlands, France, and England.

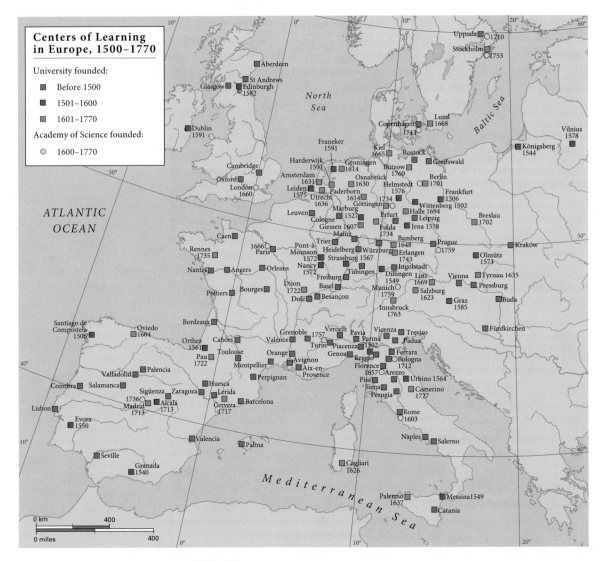

MAP **17.1 Centers of Learning in Europe, 1500–1770.**

Another institution which helped in the popularization of the New Sciences was the salon. As the well-furnished, elegant living room of an urban residence, the salon was both a domestic chamber and a semipublic meeting place for the urban social elite to engage in conversations, presentations, and experiments. The culture of the salon emerged first in Paris sometime after the closure of the court-centered Palace Academy in the 1580s. Since the Catholic French universities remained committed to Aristotelian scholasticism, the emerging stratum of educated urban aristocrats and middle-class professionals turned to the salons as places to inform themselves about new scientific developments. Furthermore, French universities as well as scientific academies refused to admit women, in contrast to Italian and German institutions. The French salon, therefore, became a bastion of well-placed and respected female scholars.

One outstanding example of French salon science was Gabrielle-Emilie du Châtelet (1706–1749). In her youth, Châtelet fulfilled her marital duties to her husband, the Marquis of Châtelet. She had three children before turning to the sciences. In one of the Paris salons she met François Marie Arouet, known as Voltaire (1694–1778), the eighteenth-century Enlightenment writer, skeptic, satirist, and amateur Newtonian. Châtelet and Voltaire became intimate companions under the benevolent eyes of the Marquis at the family estate in Lorraine in northeastern France. Although Voltaire published prolifically, Châtelet eventually outstripped him both in research and scientific understanding. Her lasting achievement was the translation of Newton's *Mathematical Principles* into French, published in 1759.

Discovery of the Vacuum   Among the important scientific instruments of the day were telescopes, microscopes, and thermometers. It was the barometer, however, that was the crucial instrument for the exploration of the properties of the vacuum and condensing steam, eventually leading to the invention of the steam engine. The scientist laying the groundwork for the construction of the barometer was Evangelista Torricelli (1608–1647), a mathematician and assistant of Galileo. In collaboration with Florentine engineers, he experimented with mercury-filled glass tubes, demonstrating the existence of atmospheric pressure by the air and of vacuums in the tubes.

New Scientist. Maria Cunitz is honored today with a sculpture in Świdnica, Poland, where she grew up.

A few years later, the French mathematician and philosopher Blaise Pascal (1623–1662) had his brother-in-law haul a mercury barometer up a mountain to demonstrate lower air pressures at higher altitudes. Soon thereafter, scientists discovered the connection between changing atmospheric pressures and the weather, laying the foundations for weather forecasting. The discovery of the vacuum, the existence of which Aristotle had held to be impossible, made a deep impression on the scientific community in the seventeenth century and was an important step toward the practical application of the New Sciences to mechanical engineering in the eighteenth century.

The Steam Engine   The French Huguenot scientist and engineer Denis Papin (ca. 1647–1712) took the first crucial step from the vacuum chamber to the steam engine. In 1690, when he was a court engineer and professor in Germany, Papin constructed a cylinder with a piston. Weights, via a cord and two pulleys, held the piston at the top of the cylinder. When heated, water in the bottom of the cylinder turned into steam. When subsequently cooled through the injection of water, the steam condensed, forcing the piston down and lifting the weights up. Papin spent his last years (1707–1712) in London, where the Royal Society of London held discussions of his papers, thereby alerting engineers, craftspeople, and entrepreneurs in England to the steam engine as a labor-saving machine. In 1712, the mechanic Thomas Newcomen built the first steam engine to pump water from coal mine shafts.

Vacuum Power. In 1672, the mayor of Magdeburg, the New Scientist Otto von Guericke, demonstrated the experiment that made him a pioneer in the understanding of the physical properties of the vacuum. In the presence of German emperor Ferdinand III, two teams of horses were unable to pull the two sealed hemispheres apart. Guericke had created a vacuum by pumping out the air from the two sealed copper spheres.

Altogether, it took a little over a century, from 1604 (Galileo) to 1712 (Newcomen), for Europeans to apply the New Sciences to engineering—that is, the construction of the steam engine. Had it not been for the New Sciences, this engine—based on contracting steam—would not have been invented. (Hero of Alexandria, who invented steam-driven machines in the first century CE, made use of the expanding force of steam.) Prior to 1600, mechanical inventions—such as the wheel, the compass, the stern rudder, and the firearm—were constructed by anonymous tinkerers with a good commonsense understanding of nature. In 1700, engineers had to have at least a basic understanding of mathematics and such abstract physical phenomena as inertia, gravity, vacuums, and condensing steam if they wanted to build a steam engine or other complex machinery.

The New Sciences: Philosophical Interpretations

The New Sciences engendered a pattern of radically new intellectual, religious, and political thinking, which evolved in the course of the seventeenth and early eighteenth centuries. This thought was largely incompatible with the inherited medieval scholasticism. It eventually evolved into a powerful instrument of critique of Christian doctrine and the constitutional order of the absolutist states. Initially, the new philosophical interpretations were confined to a few thinkers, but through the new concept of the social contract in the course of the 1700s they became a potent political force.

Descartes's New Philosophy   After the replacement of qualitative with mathematical physics, brought about by Galileo with his law of descending bodies, the question arose whether Aristotelian philosophy and Catholic theology were still adequate for the understanding of reality. New Scientists perceived the need to start philosophizing and theologizing from scratch. The first major New Scientist who, in his own judgment, started a radical reconsideration of philosophy from the ground up was the Frenchman René Descartes (1596–1650). He earned a degree in law, traveling widely after graduation. In the service of the Dutch and Bavarian courts, he bore witness to the beginning of the Thirty Years' War and its atrocities committed in the name of religious doctrines. During the war, he spent two decades in the Netherlands, studying and teaching the New Sciences.

His principal innovation in mathematics was the discovery that geometry could be converted through algebra into analytic geometry.

Descartes was shocked by the condemnation of Galileo and decided to abandon all traditional propositions and doctrines of the church as well as Aristotelianism. Realizing that his common sense (that is, the five senses of seeing, hearing, touching, smelling, and tasting) was unreliable, he determined that the only reliable body of knowledge was thought, especially mathematical thought. As a person capable of thought, he concluded—bypassing his unreliable senses—that he existed: "I think, therefore I am" (*cogito ergo sum*). A further conclusion from this argument was that he was composed of two radically different substances, a material substance consisting of his body (that is, his senses) and another, immaterial substance consisting of his thinking mind. According to Descartes, body and mind, although joined through consciousness, belonged to two profoundly different realms of reality.

Variations on Descartes's New Philosophy   Descartes's radical distinction between body and mind stimulated a lively debate, not only among a growing circle of philosophers of the New Sciences. Was this distinction only conceptual while reality was experienced as a unified whole? If the dualism was real as well as conceptual, which substance was more fundamental, sensual bodily experience or mental activity, as the creator of the concepts of experience? The answers of three philosophers—Baruch Spinoza, Thomas Hobbes, and John Locke—stood out in the 1600s. They set the course for two major directions of philosophy during the so-called Enlightenment of the 1700s (see Chapter 23), one Continental European and the other Anglo-American.

For Baruch Spinoza (1632–1677), Descartes's distinction between body and mind was to be understood only in a conceptual sense. In our daily experience we do not encounter either bodies or minds but persons endowed with both together. He therefore abandoned Descartes's distinction and developed a complicated philosophical system that sought to integrate Galilean nature with the ideas of God, the Good in ethics, and the Just in politics into a unified whole. The Jewish community of Amsterdam, into which he had been born, excommunicated him for heresy, since he seemed to make God immanent to the world. But he enjoyed a high esteem among fellow philosophers on the continent who appreciated his effort to moderate Descartes's radical mind/body distinction.

Both Thomas Hobbes (1588–1679) and John Locke (1632–1704) not only accepted Descartes's radical distinction; they furthermore made the body the fundamental reality and the mind a dependent function. Consequently, they focused on the bodily passions, not reason, as the principal human character trait. For Hobbes, the violent passions of aggression and fear were constitutive of human nature. He speculated that individuals in the primordial state of nature were engaged in a "war of all against all." To survive, they forged a social contract in which they transferred all power to a sovereign. Hobbes's famous book *Leviathan* (1651) can be read as a political theory of absolute rule, but his ideas of a social contract and transfer of power nevertheless imply a sprinkling of constitutionalism.

Locke, who lived through the less violent phases of the English religious wars, focused on the more benign bodily passion of acquisitiveness. Primordial individuals, so he argued, engaged as equals in a social contract for the purpose of erecting

Patterns Up Close

Mapping the World

The world—its shape, its size, its orientation—has been rendered so thoroughly knowable by modern technology that we fail to appreciate how long it took to map the planet scientifically.

In 1400, no accurate map of the world existed anywhere on the planet. Prior to the first Portuguese sailing expeditions down the west coast of Africa in the 1420s and 1430s, mariners all over the world relied upon local knowledge of winds, waves, and stars to navigate. The Portuguese were the first to use science to sail, adapting highly sophisticated scholarship in trigonometry, astronomy, and solar timekeeping developed in previous centuries by Jewish and Muslim scientists in Iberia.

Crucial to this novel approach was latitude. Mathematically challenging, fixing exact latitude required precise calculations of the daily changes in the path of the sun relative to the earth and determination of the exact height of the sun. The invention of the nautical astrolabe in 1497 by the Jewish scientist Abraham Zacuto aided this process tremendously. Determining longitude was also important, and Jewish scientists in Portugal adapted a method based on the pioneering work of the Islamic astronomer al-Biruni (973–1048).

Although primarily resting upon achievements in astronomical observation and measurement in the Jewish and Islamic scientific traditions, the new maps of the fifteenth century also drew upon an innovation from another part of the world: the

a government that protected their properties and, more generally, established a civil society governed by law. With Hobbes and Locke a line of new thought came to its conclusion, leading from Galileo's mathematized physics and Descartes's two substances to the ideas of absolutism as well as democratic constitutionalism.

Centralizing States and Religious Upheavals

The pattern of the centralizing state transforming the institutional structures of society was characteristic not only of the Ottoman and Habsburg Empires during 1450–1750, as we have seen in Chapter 16, but also of other countries of Europe, the Middle East, and India. The financial requirements for sustaining such a state required everywhere a reorganization of the relationship between rulers, ruling classes, and regional as well as local forces. The Protestant Reformation and religious wars slowed the pattern of central state formation, but once the religious fervor died down, two types of states emerged: the French, Russian, and Prussian landed centralizing state and the Dutch and English naval centralizing state.

The Rise of Centralized Kingdoms

The shift from feudal mounted and armored knights to firearm-equipped professional infantries led to the emergence of states whose rulers sought to strengthen the power of their administrations. Rulers sought to centralize state power, collect

compass. Originating in China, the compass was first widely used as a navigational instrument by Muslim sailors during the twelfth century. In the thirteenth century, mapmakers in the Mediterranean began to include compasses on portolans, or nautical charts, enabling sailors to follow their direction on a map.

With an accurate science for fixing latitude and improved knowledge for longitude (determining precise longitude would not be achieved until 1774 with the invention of the marine chronometer), the science of cartography was transformed in the fifteenth and sixteenth centuries. Any place on earth could be mapped mathematically in relation to any other place, and the direction in which one place lay in relation to another could be plotted using compass lines. By 1500 mapmakers could locate any newly discovered place in the world on a map, no matter how remote.

Portolan by Pedro Reinel. Drawn in 1504 by the great Portuguese cartographer Pedro Reinel (ca. 1462–ca. 1542), this nautical chart (portolan) shows compass lines and is the earliest known map to include lines of latitude.

Questions

- How were adaptations from various cultural traditions essential to the transformation of cartography in the fifteenth and sixteenth centuries?

- How are developments in cartography in this time period an example of the shift from descriptive science to mathematical science?

higher taxes to subsidize their infantries, and curb the decentralizing forces of the nobility, cities, and other local institutions. Not all autonomous units (such as city-states, city-leagues, and religious orders dating to the previous period, 600–1450) were able to survive the race to centralization. A winnowing process occurred during 1450–1550, which left a few territorially coherent kingdoms in control of European politics.

The Demographic Curve   Following the demographic disaster of the Black Death in 1348 and its many subsequent cycles, the population of the European states expanded again after 1470. It reached its pre-1348 levels around 1550, with some 85 million inhabitants (not counting the Spanish Habsburg and Ottoman Empires). The population continued to grow until about 1600 (90 million), when it entered a half century of stagnation during the coldest and wettest period in recorded history, the Little Ice Age (1550–1750).

During 1650–1750, the population rose slowly at a moderate rate from 105 to 140 million. In 1750, France (28 million) and Russia (21 million) were the most populous countries, followed by Germany (18 million), Italy (15 million), Poland (13 million), England (7 million), and the Netherlands and Sweden (2 million each). While the population figures of the individual countries for the most part bore little resemblance to their political importance during 1450–1750, as we shall see, the overall figures for Europe demonstrate that western Christianity had risen by 1750 to the status of demographic equivalence to the two leading religious civilizations of India (155 million) and China (225 million).

A Heritage of Decentralization   Bracketed between the two empires of the Ottomans and Habsburgs at either geographical end, western Christian Europe during the second half of the fifteenth century was a quilt of numerous independent or autonomous units, including the nascent centralizing kingdoms of France and England, the Hanseatic League of trading cities, the territory ruled by the Catholic crusading order of Teutonic Knights, and the small kingdoms of Denmark, Sweden, Norway, Poland–Lithuania, Bohemia, and Hungary. It furthermore comprised the principalities and cities of Germany, the duchy of Burgundy, the Alpine republic of Switzerland, and the city-states of Italy. At the northeastern periphery was the Grand Duchy of Moscow, representing eastern Christianity after the fall of Byzantium to the Ottomans in 1453. In this quilt, the majority of units competed vigorously with each other, seeking either to exploit the new possibilities which armies of mercenaries with firearms gave them or to survive as best as possible with just a handful of mercenaries.

Table 17.1 Victims of State Centralization in Europe, 1450–1600.

- Duchy of Burgundy, absorbed by France, 1477
- City-states Milan, Naples, taken by France 1499–1501
- Rest of Italy, except Venice, taken by Spain, 1550s
- Kingdoms of Bohemia and rump Hungary taken by Austrian Habsburgs, 1526; majority of Hungary to the Ottoman Empire
- Calais, last toehold of England on continent, to France, 1558
- Hanseatic League of ports in northern Europe, centered on the Free Cities of Lübeck and Hamburg, de facto dissolved 1669
- Duchy of Prussia lost by Teutonic Order to the kingdom of Poland, 1525; Prussia as fief of the kingdom of Poland, under its own dynasty of the Hohenzollern
- Prussia united with Brandenburg, 1618; Hohenzollerns as Polish vassals in Prussia and Habsburg vassals in Brandenburg
- Sweden independent from Denmark, 1523

Military and Administrative Capacities   In the course of the sixteenth century, some kingdoms turned their mercenary troops into standing armies and stationed them in star-shaped forts. These forts were a fifteenth-century Italian innovation that made walls more resistant to artillery fire and trapped attackers in cross fires. Sweden introduced the line infantry in the mid-seventeenth century. In this formation, three-deep lines of musketeers advanced on a broad front toward the enemy, with the front line firing, stepping back to reload, and making room for the next line to step forward and repeat the actions. Since the line formation required extensive peacetime drills and maneuvers, the regimental system came into use. Soldiers formed permanent regiments and wore standardized, multicolored uniforms.

The French-invented flintlock gradually replaced the matchlock musket during 1620–1630, the advantage being that the flint produced a spark more quickly than the wick fuse. Similarly, during 1660–1700 the French introduced and gradually improved the bayonet—a sharp knife fixed to the end of the muzzle. With the appearance of the bayonet, pikemen, equipped with thrusting spears-cum-battle-axes for the protection of musketeers in hand-to-hand combat, were

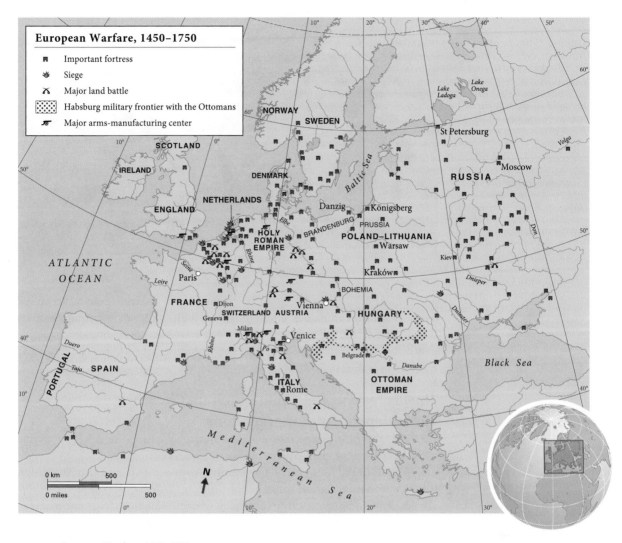

MAP 17.2 **European Warfare, 1450–1750.**

phased out. By 1750, armies in the larger European countries were both more uniform in their armaments and larger, increasing from a few thousand to tens of thousands of soldiers (see Map 17.2).

The military forces devoured copious amounts of tax money. Accordingly, taxes expanded substantially during the period 1450–1550. But rulers could not raise land, head, and commerce taxes without the formal (in assemblies) or informal (based on customs and traditions) assent of the ruling classes and cities. Similarly, villagers voted with their feet when taxes became too oppressive. The taxation limits were reached in most European countries in the mid-sixteenth century, and for the next two centuries rulers could raise additional finances only to the detriment of their previously acquired central powers, such as by borrowing from merchants and selling offices. The Netherlands was an exception. Only there did the urban population rise from 10 to 40 percent, willing to pay higher taxes on expanded urban manufactures and commercial suburban farming. The Dutch

Musketeers. These pictures from an English illustrated drill manual demonstrate the steps by which a seventeenth-century musketeer "makes ready" his weapon, typically in less than 30 seconds. In battle, a sergeant would stand alongside each company of musketeers, organizing its movements and volley fire. Once a rank of musketeers had discharged its weapons, it would move out of the way for another rank to fire. If combat was joined at close quarters, the musketeers would use their rifle butts as clubs.

government also derived substantial revenues from charters granted to armed overseas trading companies. Given the severe limits on revenue-raising measures in most of Europe, the eighteenth century saw a general deterioration of state finances, which eventually became major contributing factors to the American and French Revolutions.

The Protestant Reformation, State Churches, and Independent Congregations

Parallel to the growing centralism of the kings, the popes restored the central role of the Vatican in the church hierarchy, after the devastating Great Schism of competing papal lines (1305–1415). Outwardly, the popes displayed this restoration through expensive Vatican construction projects that aroused considerable criticism outside Rome, especially in Germany, where the leading clergy under a weak emperor was more strongly identified with Rome than elsewhere. Growing literacy and lay religiosity helped in the growth of a profound theological dissatisfaction, which exploded in the **Protestant Reformation**. The Reformation began as an antipapal movement of reform in the early sixteenth century that demanded a return to the simplicity of early Christianity. The movement quickly engulfed the kingdoms and divided their ruling classes and populations alike. Vicious religious wars were the consequence. Although these wars eventually subsided, the divisions were never healed completely and mark the culture of many areas in Europe even today.

Protestant Reformation: Broad movement to reform the Roman Catholic Church, the beginnings of which are usually associated with Martin Luther.

Background to the Reformation   Several religious and political changes in the fifteenth century led to the Protestant Reformation. One important religious shift was the growth of popular theology, a consequence of the introduction of the printing press (1454/1455) and the distribution of printed materials. A flood of devotional tracts, often read aloud to congregations of illiterate believers, catered to the spiritual interests of ordinary people. Many Christians attended Mass daily, confessed, and did penance for their sins. Wealthy Christians endowed saint cults, charitable institutions, or confraternities devoted to the organization of processions and passion plays. Poor people formed lay groups or studied scripture on their own and devoted themselves to the simple life of the early Christians. More Europeans than in previous centuries had a basic, though mostly literal, understanding of Christianity.

An important political change in the fifteenth century was an increasing inability for the popes, powerful in Rome, to appoint archbishops and bishops outside Italy. The kings of France, Spain, England, and Sweden were busy transforming their kingdoms into centralized states, in which they reduced the influence of the popes. Only in Germany, where the powers of the emperor and the rulers in the various principalities canceled each other out, was the influence of the popes still strong. What remained to the popes was the right to collect a variety of dues in the kingdoms of Europe. They used these dues to finance their expensive and, in the eyes of many, luxuriously worldly administration and court in Rome, from which they engaged in European politics. One of the dues was the sale of **indulgences**, which, in popular understanding, were tickets to heaven. Many contemporary observers found the discrepancy between declining papal power and the remaining financial privileges disturbing and demanded reforms.

Indulgence: Partial remission of sins after payment of a fine or presentation of a donation. Remission would mean the forgiveness of sins by the Church, but the sinner still remained responsible for his or her sins before God.

Luther's Reformation   One such observer was Martin Luther (1483–1546), an Augustinian monk, ordained priest, and New Testament professor in northeastern Germany. Luther was imbued with deep personal piety and confessed his sins daily, doing extensive penance. After a particularly egregious sale of indulgences in his area, in 1517 he wrote his archbishop a letter with 95 theses in which he condemned the indulgences and other matters as contrary to scripture. Friends translated the theses from Latin into German and made them public. What was to become the Protestant Reformation had begun.

News of Luther's public protest traveled quickly across Europe. Sales of indulgences fell off sharply. In a series of writings, Luther spelled out the details of the church reform he envisaged. One reform proposal was the elevation of original New Testament scripture over tradition—that is, over canon law and papal decisions. Salvation was to be by faith alone; good works were irrelevant. Another reform was the declaration of the priesthood of all Christians, doing away with the privileged position of the clergy as mediators between God and believers who could forgive sins. A third reform was a call to German princes to begin church reform in their own lands through their power over clerical appointments, even if the Habsburg emperor was opposed. Finally, by translating the Bible into German, Luther made the full sacred text available to all who, by reading or listening, wanted to rely solely on scripture as the source of their faith. Luther's Bible was a monument of the emerging literary German language. A forceful and clear writer in his translation and own publications, Luther fully explicated the basics of Protestantism.

Reaction to Luther's Demands   Both emperor and pope failed in their efforts to arrest Luther and suppress his call for church reform. The duke of Saxony was successful in protecting the reformer from seizure. Emperor Charles V, a devout Catholic, considered Castile's successful church reform of half a century earlier to be fully sufficient. In his mind, Luther's demands for church reform were to be resisted. Two other pressing concerns, however, diverted the emperor's attention.

Anti-Catholic Propaganda.
This anonymous woodcut of 1520 by a German satirist depicts the devil (complete with wings and clawed feet) sitting on a letter of indulgence and holding a money collection box. The devil's mouth is filled with sinners who presumably bought letters of indulgence in good faith, thinking they had been absolved of their sins.

First, the Ottoman-led Islamic threat, in eastern Europe and the western Mediterranean, had to be met with decisive action. Second, his rivalry with the French king precluded the formation of a common Catholic front against Luther. Enthusiastic villagers and townspeople in Germany exploited Charles's divided attention and abandoned both Catholicism and secular obedience. A savage civil war, called the Peasants' War, engulfed Germany from 1524 to 1525, killing perhaps as many as 100,000 people.

Luther and other prominent reformers were horrified by the carnage. They drew up church ordinances that regulated preaching, church services, administrative councils, education, charity, and consistories for handling disciplinary matters. In Saxony, the duke endorsed this order in 1528. He thereby created the model of Lutheran Protestantism as a state religion, in which the rulers were protectors and supervisors of the churches in their territories. A decade later, Saxony was fully Lutheran.

A minority of about half a dozen German princes and the kings of Denmark and Sweden followed suit. In England, Protestants gained strength in the wake of the break with Rome by Henry VIII (r. 1509–1547) and his assumption of church leadership in his kingdom (1534). Although remaining Catholic, he surrounded himself with religious reformers and proclaimed an Anglican state church whose creed and rites combined elements of Catholicism and Protestantism. In Switzerland, several cantons adopted the religious reforms of Huldrych Zwingli (1484–1531). In Scotland, the reforms of John Knox (1514–1572) became the foundation for the state church. Thus, most of northern Europe followed a pattern of alliances between Protestant reformers and the state (see Map 17.3).

Calvinism in Geneva and France   In France, as in England, the king controlled all church appointments. King Francis I, however, did not take the final step toward the creation of an independent state church. Since he competed with Charles V of the Habsburg Empire for dominance over the papacy in Italy, he had to appear especially loyal and devout. When a few Protestants in France went public with their demands for church reform, Francis I gave them the stark choice of exile or burning at the stake.

One reformer who chose exile was the French lawyer John Calvin (Jean Cauvin, 1509–1564). During his exile, he passed at one point (in 1536) through Geneva, where a French friend of his beseeched him to help him in preaching the faith. Calvin relented and began a stormy and at one point interrupted career as the city's religious reformer. Geneva's city council—not yet part of Switzerland and under the nominal rule of the duke of Savoy (himself under the nominal rule of the Habsburgs)—was unsure about which path of reform to embrace. It took Calvin well into the 1550s before his form of Protestantism prevailed in the city.

As expressed in Calvin's central work, *Institutes of the Christian Religion* (1536), and numerous other writings, a crucial doctrine of Calvin's was *predestination*. According to this doctrine, God has "predestined" each human prior to birth for

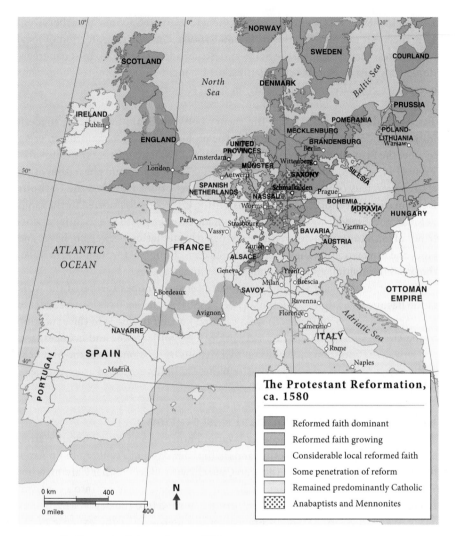

MAP **17.3** **The Protestant Reformation, ca. 1580.**

heaven or hell. Believers could only hope, through faith alone, that sometime during a life of moral living they would receive a glimpse of their fate. In contrast to Luther, however, Calvin made the enforcement of morality through a formal code, administered by local authorities, part of his version of Protestantism.

Interestingly, this code did not prohibit the taking of interest on loans. While Luther as well as the Catholic Church, in accordance with scripture, condemned all interest as usury, Calvin considered a few percentage points to be entirely justifiable. The strong condemnation of interest on loans in the Hebrew Bible was rooted in the precariousness of Palestinian rain-fed agriculture: Several years of drought could drive farmers into total dependence on landlords if the latter demanded interest on loans. By placing moneylending into the increasingly urban context of the 1500s, Calvin displayed a greater sense of economic reality than Luther. Acquiring wealth with the help of money and thereby perhaps gaining a glimpse of one's fate became one of the hallmarks of Calvinism. Wealth began to become respectable in Christian society.

Calvin died in his Genevan exile, but Geneva-trained Calvinist preachers went to France and the Netherlands in the mid-1500s. Under the protection of local magistrates, they organized the first clandestine independent Calvinist congregations. Calvinist religious self-organization by independent congregations thus became a viable alternative to Lutheran state religion.

The Catholic Reformation   The rivalry between Spain and France made it initially difficult for the popes to tackle the problem of Catholic reforms in order to meet the Protestant challenge. When they finally called together the Council of Trent (1545–1563), they abolished payment for indulgences and phased out other church practices considered to be corrupt. These actions launched the **Catholic Reformation**, an effort to gain back dissenting Catholics. Supported by the kings of Spain and France, however, the popes made no changes to the traditional doctrines of faith together with good works, priestly mediation between believer and God, and monasticism. They even tightened church control through the revival of the papal Inquisition and a new Index of Prohibited Books.

Catholic Reformation: Reaffirmation of Catholic papal supremacy and the doctrine of faith together with works as preparatory to salvation; such practices as absenteeism (bishops in Rome instead of their bishoprics) and pluralism (bishops and abbots holding multiple appointments) were abolished.

To counterbalance these punitive institutions, the popes furthered the work of the Basque priest Ignatius Loyola (1491–1556). At the head of the new order of the Society of Jesus, or Jesuits, Loyola devoted himself tirelessly to the education of the clergy, establishment of a network of Catholic schools and colleges, and conversion of Protestants as well as non-Christians by missionaries to the Americas and eastern Asia. Thanks to Jesuit discipline, Catholics regained a semblance of self-assurance against the Protestants.

Religious Wars and Political Restoration

The growth of Calvinism led to a civil war in France and a war of liberation from Spanish Catholic rule in the Netherlands in the later sixteenth century. In England, the slow pace of reform in the Anglican Church, with which neither Calvinists nor Catholics could identify, erupted in the early seventeenth century into a civil war. In Germany, the Catholic–Protestant struggle turned into the devastating Thirty Years' War (1618–1648), which France and Sweden won at the expense of the Habsburgs. On the religious level, western Christians grudgingly accepted denominational toleration; on the political level, the centralizing states evolved into polities based on absolutism, tempered by provincial and local administrative practices.

Civil War in France   During the mid-1500s, Calvinism in France grew to about 1,200 congregations, mostly in the western cities of the kingdom, where literate merchants and craftspeople catering to trade overseas were receptive to Protestant publications. Calvinism was essentially an urban denomination, and peasants did not join in large numbers. Some 2 million, or 10 percent of the total population of 18.5 million, were Huguenots, as the Protestants were called in France. They continued to be persecuted, but given their numbers, it was impossible for the government to imprison and execute them all. In 1571, they even met in a kingdom-wide synod, where they ratified their congregational church order. They posed a formidable challenge to French Catholicism.

In many cities, relations between Huguenots and Catholics were uneasy. From time to time, groups of agitators crashed each other's church services. The arrival of a child king to the French throne in 1560 was an open invitation to escalate hostilities. In vain, the queen mother, Catherine de' Medici (1519–1589), who acted as the king's regent, sought to rein in the passions. The first three rounds of war ended with the victorious Huguenots achieving full freedom of religious practice and self-government in four western cities. In this new situation, she arranged in 1572 for the marriage of her daughter to King Henry III of Navarre (later King Henry IV of France, 1589–1610), a Protestant of the Bourbon family in southwestern France. Henry had risen to the leadership of the Huguenots a few years earlier, but he detested the fanaticism that surrounded him.

The prospect of a Huguenot king drove the Catholic aristocracy into a renewed frenzy of religious persecution. On St. Bartholomew's Day (August 24, 1572), just 6 days after the wedding of the future Henry IV, they perpetrated a wholesale slaughter of thousands of Huguenots. This massacre, in response to the assassination of a French admiral, occurred with the apparent connivance of the queen. For over a decade and a half, civil war raged, in which Spain aided the Catholics and Henry enrolled German and Swiss Protestant mercenaries.

A turning point came only in 1589 when Henry of Navarre became King Henry IV. Surviving nearly three dozen plots against his life, the new king needed 9 years and two conversions to Catholicism—"Paris is well worth a Mass," he is supposed to have quipped—before he was able to calm the religious fanaticism among the majority of French people. With the Edict of Nantes in 1598, he decreed freedom of religion for Protestants. A number of staunch Catholic adherents were deeply offended by the edict as well as the alleged antipapal policies of Henry IV. The king fell victim to an assassin in 1610. Catholic resentment continued until 1685, when King Louis XIV revoked the edict and triggered a large-scale emigration of Huguenots to the Netherlands, Germany, and England. At last, France was Catholic again.

Dutch War of Independence   In the Netherlands, the Spanish overlords were even more determined to keep the country Catholic than the French monarchs prior to Henry IV. When Charles V resigned in 1556 (effective 1558), his son Philip II (r. 1556–1598) became king of Spain and the Netherlands, consisting of the French-speaking regions of Wallonia in the south and the Dutch-speaking regions of Flanders and Holland in the north. Like his father, Philip was a staunch supporter of the Catholic Reformation. He asked the Jesuits and the Inquisition to aggressively persecute the Calvinists. For better effect, Philip subdivided the bishoprics into smaller units and recruited clergymen in place of members of the nobility.

In response, in 1565 the nobility and Calvinist congregations rose in revolt. They dismantled the bishoprics and cleansed the churches of images and sculptures, thereby triggering what was to become a Protestant war of Dutch liberation from Catholic Spanish overlordship (1565–1620). Philip retaliated by sending in an army that succeeded in suppressing the liberation movement. He reimposed Catholicism, and executed thousands of rebels, many of them members of the Dutch aristocracy.

Remnants of the rebellion struggled on and, in 1579, renewed the war of liberation in three of the 17 northern provinces making up the Netherlands. Later joined by four more provinces, the people in these breakaway regions called themselves members of the "United Provinces of the Dutch Republic." Spain refused to recognize the republic and kept fighting until acute Spanish financial difficulties prompted the truce of 1609–1621. Although drawn into fighting again during the Thirty Years' War, the Netherlands gained its full independence in 1648.

At the head of the Dutch republic was a governor (*stadhouder*) from the House of Orange-Nassau, one of the leading aristocratic families of the Netherlands. The representative body, with which the *stadhouder* governed, was the States General, and the privileged religious body was the Calvinist Dutch Reformed Church. About 20 percent of the population of 1 million was Calvinist, double the percentage in France and England. But there were also sizeable groups of Catholics and other Protestants. Among the latter, the Anabaptists and Mennonites (characterized by the doctrines of adult baptism and pacifism, respectively) were prominent. The Netherlands was also a haven for Jews, who had originally arrived there after their expulsion from Spain and Portugal in 1492–1498 (see above, on Baruch Spinoza, p. 507). Gradually, the Dutch accepted each other's doctrinal differences, and the Netherlands became a model of religious tolerance.

Civil War in England   As in the Netherlands, the prevalent form of Protestantism in England was Calvinism. During the sixteenth century, the Calvinists numbered about 10 percent in a kingdom in which the Anglican Church encompassed the vast majority of subjects in a total population of 7 million. English Catholics, who refused to recognize the king as the head of the Anglican Church, numbered 3 percent. The percentage of Calvinists was the same as in France before 1685, but the partially reformed Anglican Church was able to hold them in check. The Calvinists were, furthermore, a fractious group, encompassing moderate and radical tendencies that neutralized each other. Among the radicals were the Puritans, who demanded the abolition of the Anglican clerical hierarchy and a new church order of independent congregations. In the early seventeenth century, when Anglican Church reform slowed under the Catholic successors of Elizabeth I (r. 1558–1603), the Puritan cause began to acquire traction. Realizing that these Stuart successors and their bishops were immovable, some Puritans emigrated to North America rather than continue to chafe under the Anglican yoke. Other Puritans began to agitate openly.

Along with their efforts to restrain would-be reformers, the Stuart kings were busy building their version of the centralized state. They collected taxes without the approval of Parliament. Many members resented being bypassed since Parliament was the constitutional cosovereign of the kingdom. A slight majority in the House of Commons was Puritan, and the stalled church reform added to their resentment. Eventually, when all tax resources were exhausted, the king, Charles I (r. 1625–1649), had to call Parliament back together. Mutual resentment was so deep, however, that the two sides were unable to make any decisions on either financial or religious matters. The standoff erupted into civil war, leading to the king's execution and ending the monarchy.

Despite the brutal fate of Charles I, the English civil war of 1642–1651 was generally less vicious than that in France. Nevertheless, because of widespread pillage and destruction of crops and houses, the indirect effects of the war for the population of thousands of villages were severe. The New Model Army, a professional body of 22,000 troops raised by the Puritan-dominated Parliament against the king, caused further upheavals by cleansing villages of their "frivolous" seasonal festivals, deeply rooted in local pagan traditions and featuring pranks, games, dances, drunkenness, and free-wheeling behavior. A republican theocracy emerged, with preachers enforcing Calvinist morality among the population.

Republic, Restoration, and Revolution   The ruler of this theocracy, Oliver Cromwell (r. 1649–1658), was a Puritan member of the lower nobility (the gentry) and a commander in the New Model Army. After dissolving Parliament, Cromwell handpicked a new parliament but ruled for the most part without its consent. Since both Scotland and Ireland had opposed the Puritans in the civil war, Cromwell waged a savage war of submission against the Scottish Presbyterians (Calvinists organized in a state church) and Irish Catholics. The Dutch and Spanish, also opponents of the Puritans in the Civil War, were defeated in naval wars that substantially increased English shipping power in the Atlantic. But fear among the gentry in Parliament of a permanent centralized state led to a refusal of further financial subsidies for the army. After Cromwell's death in 1658, it took just 3 years to restore the Stuart monarchy and the Anglican state church to their previous places.

The recalled Stuart kings, however, resumed the policies of centralization and Catholicism. As before, the kings called Parliament together only sparingly and raised funds without its authorization. But their standing army of 30,000, partially stationed near London, was intended more to intimidate the parliamentarians than to actually wage war. In 1687, the king even espoused a major plan of reform, as new research has shown. In the "Glorious Revolution" of 1688, the defiant Parliament, dominated since the Restoration by mostly Anglican gentry, seized the initiative for reform and deposed the Catholic king, James II (r. 1685–1688). It feared that the recent birth of a royal son threatened the succession of the king's daughter by his first marriage, Mary, a Protestant married to William of Nassau-Orange, the *stadhouder* of the Netherlands. It offered the throne to William and Mary as joint monarchs, and the Stuarts went into exile in France.

The Thirty Years' War in Germany   As religious tensions were mounting in England during the early seventeenth century, similar tensions erupted into a full-blown war in Germany, bringing about the second such conflagration in a century, the Thirty Years' War. As we saw earlier, even though the rulers of the German principalities had made either Catholicism or Protestantism their state religion, minorities were tolerated or even admitted to offices. The Jesuit-educated Ferdinand II (r. 1619–1637), ruler of the Holy Roman Empire, however, refused to appoint Protestants in majority-Protestant Bohemia, of which the Habsburgs were kings since 1526. In response, Protestant leaders in 1618 renounced Ferdinand's authority and made the Calvinist prince of the Palatinate in the Rhineland their new king. With these events in Protestant Bohemia, open hostilities between the religious denominations began in Germany.

In a first round of war (1619–1630), Ferdinand and the Catholic princes suppressed the Bohemian rebellion and slowly advanced toward northern Germany, capturing territories for reconversion to Catholicism. When the Danish king intervened in favor of Lutheranism (1625–1629), he was crushed, and the Protestant cause seemed to be doomed. In 1630, however, the Lutheran king

Centralizing States at War. German imperial troops besiege Swedish troops in the northern German city of Stralsund in 1628. The etching shows typical features of the centralizing state, from top to bottom: galleon-style warships (successors of the caravel); a star-shaped fort (an Italian innovation) designed to withstand artillery barrages; the medieval walls of the city; musket-equipped infantry troops; field cannons; and the colorful Baroque uniforms worn by the musketeers of the period.

Gustavus II Adolphus (r. 1611–1632) of Sweden intervened. The king's main goal was the creation of a Swedish-Lutheran centralized state around the Baltic Sea, a project begun before the Thirty Years' War. By aiding the German Lutherans, he hoped to consolidate or even increase his predominance in the region. Louis XIII (r. 1610–1643) of France granted Sweden financial subsidies, since he was concerned that Ferdinand's victories would further strengthen the Habsburg Spanish–Flemish–Austrian–German–Italian grip around France. With the politically motivated alliance between Sweden and France, the German Catholic–Protestant war turned into a war for state dominance in Europe.

At first, the Swedes were successful, advancing victoriously as far as Bavaria in the south. But when Gustavus fell unexpectedly in battle, Ferdinand II—fearful that the Swedish ally France would enter the war—decided to compromise with the Protestant princes of Germany. In the peace of 1635, the two sides agreed to a return to the prewar territorial division between Catholic and Protestant princes in northern Germany. But the French entered the war anyway. During the next 13 years, French armies sought to cut the Habsburg supply lines from Italy to the Netherlands by occupying Habsburg Alsace. Swedish armies, exploiting the French successes against the Habsburgs, fought their way back into Germany. In the end, the Austrian–German Habsburgs, pressured on two sides, agreed in October 1648 to the Peace of Westphalia.

The agreement provided for religious freedom in Germany and ceded territories in Alsace to France and the southern side of the Baltic Sea to Sweden. It granted territorial integrity to all European powers. The Spanish Habsburgs continued their war against France until 1659, when they also bowed to superior French strength, giving up parts of Flanders and northeastern Spain. In the Caribbean, Spain also lost territories to France, the Netherlands, and England, accelerating the decline of Spain's overseas power. France emerged as the strongest country in Europe, and the Spanish-dominated Caribbean became an area of open power rivalry (see Map 17.4).

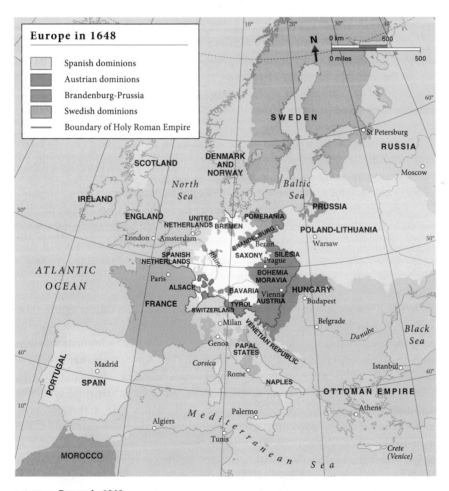

MAP **17.4** **Europe in 1648.**

Absolutism in France?   During its period of greatest political dominance, France came under the rule of its longest-reigning monarch, King Louis XIV (1643–1715). He was of small stature—for which he compensated with high-heeled shoes—but his hardy constitution and strong self-discipline helped him to dominate even the most grueling meetings with his advisors. He enjoyed pomp and circumstance and built Versailles—his gigantic palace and gardens near Paris, populated with 10,000 courtiers, attendants, and servants—into a site of almost continuous feasting, entertainment, and intrigue. It was here that Louis, the "Sun King," beamed benevolently with his "absolute" divine mandate upon his aristocracy and commoners alike.

Versailles played an important role in Louis's efforts to undercut the power of the nobility. Anyone with any aspirations of attracting the king's attention had to come to the palace to attend him. By keeping both friends and potential enemies close by and forcing them to spend lavishly to keep up with the fashions inspired by the king and vie for his attention, he was able, like the Tokugawa shoguns in Edo, Japan, to bypass them administratively and rule through central bureaucratic institutions.

Absolutism: Theory of the state in which the unlimited power of the king, ruling under God's divine mandate, was emphasized. In practice, it was neutralized by the nobility and provincial and local communities.

In practice, the French **absolutism** of Louis XIV and his eighteenth-century successors, as well as absolutism in other European countries, was a complex mixture of centralized and decentralized forces. On the one hand, after the end of the religious wars in 1648, mercenary armies under autonomous dukes and counts disappeared from the European scene, replaced by permanent armies or navies under the central command of royal or princely dynasties. The kings also no longer called their respective assemblies of nobles and notables together to have new taxes approved (in France from 1614 to 1789), and thus, many of the nobility's tax privileges disappeared.

On the other hand, the kings of the seventeenth century were acutely aware that true absolutism was possible only if centrally salaried employees collected taxes. It was physically impossible, however, to transport tax revenues, in the form of silver money and grain, from the provinces to the capital, pay the central bureaucrats, and then cart the remaining money back to the provinces to pay salaried tax collectors there. A centrally paid bureaucracy would have required a central bank with provincial branches, using paper money. The failed experiment with such a bank in Paris from 1714 to 1720 demonstrates one such effort to find a solution to the central salarization problem. The bank's short life demonstrates that absolute central control was beyond the powers of the kings.

Instead, the kings had to rely on subcontracting out most offices and the collection of most taxes to the highest bidders, who then helped themselves to the collection of their incomes. Under Louis XIV, a total of 46,000 administrative jobs were available for purchase in Paris and the provinces. Anyone who had money or borrowed it from financiers was encouraged to buy an office—from the old aristocracy of the "sword" receiving rents from the farmers on their rural estates to ordinary merchants' sons with law degrees borrowing money from their fathers.

Once in office, the government often forced these officers to grant additional loans to the crown. To retain their loyalty, the government rewarded them with first picks for retaining their offices within the family. They were also privileged to buy landed estates or acquire titles of nobility to the secondary (and less prestigious) tier of the "nobility of the robe" (as opposed to the first-tier "nobility of the sword," which by the seventeenth century was demilitarized). With this system of offering offices and titles for sale, the king sought to bind the financial interests of the two nobilities to those of his own.

About the only way for Louis XIV to keep a semblance of a watchful eye on the officeholders was to send salaried, itinerant *intendants* around the provinces to ensure that collecting taxes, rendering justice, and policing functioned properly within the allowable limits of the "venality of office," as the subcontracting system was called. Louis XIV had roughly one intendant for each province. About half of the provinces had *parlements*—appointed assemblies for the ratification of decrees from Paris—whose officeholders, drawn from the local noble, clerical, and commoner classes, frequently resisted the intendants. The Paris *parlement* even refused to accept royal writs carried by the intendants.

In later years, when Louis XIV was less successful in his many wars against the rival Habsburgs and Protestant Dutch than previously, the crown overspent and had to borrow heavily with little regard for the future. Louis's successors in the second half of the eighteenth century were saddled with crippling debts. French-inspired European "absolutism" was thus in practice a careful (or not so careful) balancing act between the forces of centralization and decentralization in the states of Europe.

The Rise of Russia   Although France's absolutism was more theory than practice, its glorious ideological embodiment in the Versailles of Louis XIV spawned adaptations across Europe. These adaptations were most visible in eastern Europe, which was populated more thinly and had far fewer towns and cities. Since rulers in those areas did not have a large reservoir of urban commoners to aid them as administrators in building the centralized state, they had to make do with the landowning aristocracy. As a result, rulers and aristocracy connived to finance

A World Turned Upside Down. In this popular satirical woodcut of 1766, based on a similar woodcut from the early 1700s, the mice are capturing and burying the cat: In other words, Peter the Great has turned the world upside down with his reforms.

state centralization through an increased exploitation of the farmers in the villages: In the 1600s, their legal status deteriorated, their tax liabilities increased continuously, and they became serfs.

In Russia, Tsar Peter I, "the Great" (r. 1682–1725), of the eastern Christian Romanov dynasty, was a towering figure who singlehandedly sought to establish the French-type centralized state during his lifetime. At nearly 7 feet tall, Peter was an imposing, energetic ruler, controllable only by his second wife (and former mistress) Catherine, a warmhearted woman and beloved tsarina. Peter invited western European soldiers, mariners, administrators, craftspeople, scholars, and artists into his service and succeeded within just a few years in building a disciplined army and imposing navy. He built ports on the Baltic Sea and established the new capital of St. Petersburg, distinguished by many very beautiful palaces and official buildings.

A typical example among the thousands invited to Russia by the tsar was Peter von Sivers, a Danish mariner (and ancestor of one of the coauthors of the book) who rose to the position of admiral in the Baltic fleet that broke Swedish dominance in northern Europe. Since the tsar was not able to pay these advisors salaries (any more than Louis XIV could pay salaries to advisors to the French court), he gave many western guests estates with serfs in the Baltic provinces and Finland, conquered from Sweden, and made them aristocrats in his retinue.

The Russian military was completely reorganized by the tsar. After an early rebellion, Peter savagely decimated the inherited firearm regiments and made them part of a new army recruited from the traditional Russian landed nobility. Both classes of soldiers received education at military schools and academies and were required to provide lifelong service. In order to make his soldiers look more urban, Peter decreed that they shave their traditional beards and wear European uniforms or clothes. Every twentieth peasant household had to deliver one foot soldier to conscription. A census was taken to facilitate the shift from the inherited household tax on the villagers to a new capitation tax collected by military officers. In the process, the remaining free farmers outside the estate system of the aristocracy found themselves classified and taxed as serfs, unfree to leave their villages. The result of Peter's reforms was a powerful, expansionary centralizing state that played an increasingly important role among European kingdoms during the eighteenth century (see Map 17.5).

The Rise of Prussia   Similar to Russia, the principality of Prussia-Brandenburg was underurbanized. It had furthermore suffered destruction and depopulation during the Thirty Years' War. When the Lutheran Hohenzollern monarchs embarked on the construction of a centralized state in the later seventeenth century, they first broke the tax privileges of the landowning aristocracy in the estates general and raised taxes themselves. As in Russia, farmers who worked on estates held by landlords were serfs. Since there were few urban middle-class merchants and professionals, the kings enrolled members of the landlord aristocracy in the army and civilian administration.

Elevated by the Habsburg Holy Roman emperor from the status of dukes to that of kings in 1701, the Hohenzollern rulers systematically enlarged the army, employing it during peacetime for drainage and canal projects as well as palace construction in Berlin, the capital. Under Frederick II, "the Great" (1740–1786),

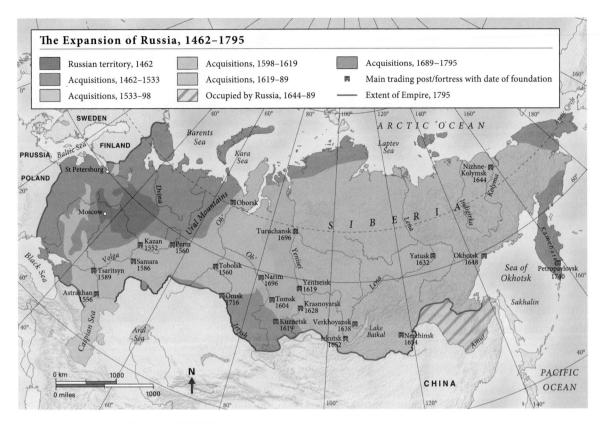

MAP **17.5 The Expansion of Russia, 1462–1795.**

Prussia pursued an aggressive foreign policy, capturing Silesia from the Habsburgs in a military campaign. Frederick also expended major efforts to attracting immigrants, intensifying agriculture, and establishing manufacturing enterprises. Prussia emerged as a serious competitor of the Habsburgs in the Holy Roman Empire of Germany.

English Constitutionalism   In contrast to Prussia, France, Spain, Austria, and other European states, England had since 1450 a political system ruled by a king or a queen, with a parliament composed of the aristocracy as well as representatives of towns and cities. Only in England did the interests of the nobility and the urban merchants gradually converge. Rulers on the European continent financed their early centralizing states through raising indirect taxes on sales, commerce, imports, and exports, affecting cities more than noble estates. In England, the cities allied with the aristocracy in resisting indirect tax increases and forcing the throne to use the less ample revenues of its royal estates to pay soldiers. Efforts of the Stuart kings to create a centralized land-based state based on firearm infantries failed. Instead, the ruling class preferred to build a centralized naval state. After the Glorious Revolution of 1688, England became the dominant power on the world's oceans.

After its victory over the Stuart kings, Parliament consolidated its financial powers through the creation of the Bank of England in 1694, two decades before a

Prussian Military Discipline. The Prussian line infantry made full use in the mid-1700s of flintlock muskets, bayonets, and drilling.

similar but ill-fated attempt in France. When first Mary and then William died without children, England continued in 1714 with a king from a distantly related dynasty from the principality of Hanover in Germany. Around the same time, England and Scotland united, creating the United Kingdom. Parliament collected higher taxes than France and, through its bank, was able to keep its debt service low during the early 1700s. The navy grew twice as large as that of France and was staffed by a well-salaried, disciplined military, while the few land troops, deemed superfluous, were mostly low-paid Hessian–German mercenaries. A rudimentary two-party system of two aristocracy–merchant alliances came into being. The two parties were known as the Whigs and the Tories, the former more parliamentarian and the latter more royalist, with the Whigs in power for most of the first half of the eighteenth century.

Putting It All Together

Prior to 1500, all religious civilizations possessed sophisticated mathematics and practiced variations of qualitative sciences, such as astrology, geography, alchemy, and medicine. The one exception was trigonometry-based astronomy in Islamic, Hindu, and Christian religious civilizations, pioneered by the Hellenistic scholar Ptolemy (Chapter 5). Physics became the second mathematical science in the early 1500s, but only in western Christianity. This transformation of the sciences, however, had no practical (that is, engineering) consequences prior to the invention of the steam engine in the 1700s and the subsequent industrialization of England in the 1800s. Furthermore, the mathematization of physics did little to influence the continued prevalence of qualitative description as the methodology of the other sciences. Astrology, chemistry, and medicine continued with what we regard today as outmoded qualitative theories well into the nineteenth century.

Most importantly, the rise of the New Sciences should not be confused with the vast political, social, economic, and cultural changes, called "modernity" after 1800, which propelled the West on its trajectory of world dominance. Although the West began to acquire its specific scientific and philosophical identity with the introduction of the mathematical sciences in the 100-year span between Copernicus and Galileo, the impact of these sciences on the world became felt only after 1800 when it was applied to industry. Once this application gathered momentum, in the nineteenth century, Asia and Africa had no choice but to adapt to modern science and industrialization.

For additional resources, including maps, primary sources, visuals, and quizzes, please go to www.oup.com/us/vonsivers. Please see the Further Resources section at the back of the book for additional readings and suggested websites.

Against the Grain

The Digger Movement

In April 1649, toward the end of the English Civil War and just three months after the execution of King Charles I, a group of 70 mostly landless farmers and day laborers occupied "common" (public) land near Walton, Surrey (about 25 miles south of London), to establish a colony. As the farmers and laborers dug up the soil and sowed the ground with parsnips, carrots, and beans, they came to be called the "Diggers."

Driven off by enraged small landowners who benefited greatly from the use of common land for grazing sheep and cutting timber, a much-reduced group of colonists moved on to common land in nearby Cobham in August 1649. After some delay, this time it was the gentry with their manor rights to the common land who destroyed the Diggers' cottages and fields in the winter of 1650. The Diggers, although ultimately unsuccessful, made a much-publicized statement that public land was "the treasure of all people" and should not be reserved for the benefit of anyone, be they gentry or even small property owners—a bold demand which ran counter to the rapidly increasing privatization of land and commercialization of agriculture.

The leader of the group was Gerrard Winstanley (1609–1670), an embittered former cloth merchant in London who had to abandon his trade in 1643 after he became insolvent. He struggled to regain his solvency in the countryside of Surrey, at one point working as a grazier of cattle. Parts of Surrey had suffered substantial hardship during the Civil War, having been forced to provision and quarter troops. In a flurry of pamphlets between 1648 and 1650 Winstanley explained the motives and goals of the Diggers most eloquently, displaying a remarkable familiarity with local affairs. In addition, he had a superb ability to make these affairs relevant, in the religious idiom of Protestantism, for England as a whole. He was the first to clearly identify the problem of the rising numbers of rural landless laborers victimized by the increasing commercialization of agriculture in England—a labor force that continued to increase until the industrializing cities of the later 1700s eventually absorbed them.

- **Was Winstanley hopelessly utopian in his efforts to establish farmer communities on common land in England?**

- **How have other figures in world history sympathized with the lot of poor and landless farmers and attempted reform (or revolution) on their behalf?**

Thinking Through Patterns

▶ **What were the reasons for the cultural changes that began in Europe around 1450? In which ways were the patterns of cultural changes during 1450–1750 different from those in the other religious civilizations of Eurasia?**

Located far from the traditional agrarian–urban centers of Eurasia, western Christianity repeatedly adapted its culture (particularly theological, philosophical, scientific, and artistic forms of expression) in response to outside stimuli coming from Islamic and eastern Christian civilizations. Without these stimuli, the Renaissance, Baroque, New Science, and Enlightenment would not have developed. In contrast, the Middle East, Byzantium, India, and China, originating firmly within the traditional agrarian–urban centers, received far fewer outside stimuli prior to the scientific–industrial age. Scholars and thinkers in these religious civilizations did not feel the same pressure to change their cultural heritage as their colleagues in western Christianity did.

The discovery of the two new continents of the Americas prompted Nicolaus Copernicus to reject Aristotle's astronomical theory of spheres and to posit a sun-centered planetary system. Copernicus's new approach to science continued with Galileo Galilei's discovery of the mathematical law of falling bodies in physics and was completed when Isaac Newton unified physics and astronomy. The New Sciences became popular in educated urban circles in northwestern Europe, where Catholic and Protestant church authorities were largely divided. In southern Europe, where the Catholic Reformation was powerful and rejected Galileo, the adoption of the New Sciences occurred more slowly. As scientists in northwestern Europe discovered, the New Sciences possessed practical applicability: After studying the properties of condensing steam and the vacuum, scientists and mechanics began experimenting with steam engines, which served as the principal catalysts for the launching of the scientific–industrial age.

▶ **When and how did the New Sciences begin, and how did they gain popularity in northwestern European society? Why is the popularization of the New Sciences important for understanding the period 1450–1750?**

▶ **What were the patterns of centralized state formation and transformation in the period 1450–1750? How did the Protestant Reformation and religious wars modify these patterns?**

European kingdoms, such as France, Sweden, and Prussia, expanded their powers of taxation to the detriment of the nobility. With the accumulated funds, they hired and salaried mercenary infantries equipped with firearms, using them to conquer land from their neighbors. The religious wars of the 1500s and 1600s strengthened centralization efforts and hastened the demise of the nobility as an obstacle to the centralized state. In England, Parliament blocked the Stuart kings from building a landed central state and instead pursued the construction of a naval state, which succeeded a similar one built by the Netherlands in 1688.

Chapter 18 1500–1800

New Patterns in New Worlds

COLONIALISM AND INDIGENOUS RESPONSES IN THE AMERICAS

Alonso Ortíz was a deadbeat. He fled from his creditors in Zafra, Estremadura, in southwestern Spain, in the early 1770s to find a new life in the Americas. In Mexico City, with the help of borrowed money, he set up shop as a tanner. His business flourished, and, with a partner, Ortíz expanded into two rented buildings. Eight Native American employees, whom he had trained, did the actual labor of stomping the hides in the vats filled with tanning acids. A black slave, belonging to his partner, was the supervisor. Happy that he no longer had to take his shoes off to work, Ortíz concentrated on giving instructions and hustling up business.

Ortíz's situation in Mexico City was not entirely legal, however. He had left his wife, Eleanor González, and children alone in Zafra, though the law required that families should be united. The authorities rarely enforced this law, but that was no guarantee for Ortíz. Furthermore, he had not yet sent his family any remittances, leaving Eleanor to rely on the largesse of her two brothers back home for survival. And then there was still the debt. Ortíz had reasons to be afraid of the law.

To avoid prosecution, Ortíz wrote a letter to Eleanor. In this letter, he proudly described the comfortable position he had achieved. He announced that his kind business partner was sending her a sum of money sufficient to begin preparations for her departure from Spain. To his creditors, Ortíz

ATLANTIC
OCEAN

PACIFIC
OCEAN

THE AMERICAS
IN 1750

Spanish
Portuguese
British
French
Dutch

ABOVE: The meeting of Moctezuma and Cortés, from The History of the Conquest of Mexico by the Spaniards, by Spanish historian Antonio de Solís (1610–1686).

promised to send 100 tanned hides within a year. "Your arrival would bring me great joy," he wrote to Eleanor, reneging on an original promise to have already returned home to Spain. Evidently aware of her reluctance to join him in Mexico, Ortíz closed his letter with a request to grant him 4 more years abroad and to do so with a notarized document from her hand. Unfortunately, we do not know her answer.

The Ortíz family drama gives a human face to European colonialism and emigration from Europe to the Americas. Like Alonso Ortíz, some 300,000 other Spaniards emigrated between 1500 and 1800. They came alone or with family, temporarily or for good, and either failed or succeeded in their new lives. A few hundred letters by emigrants exist, giving us glimpses of their lives in Mexico, Peru, and other parts of the Americas conquered by the Spanish and Portuguese in the sixteenth century. As these relatively privileged immigrants settled, they hoped to build successful enterprises using the labor of Native Americans as well as black slaves imported from Africa. The example of Ortíz shows that even in the socially not very prestigious craft of tanning a man could achieve a measure of comfort by having people of even lower status working for him.

Seeing Patterns

▶ What is the significance of western Europeans acquiring the Americas as a warm-weather extension of their northern continent?

▶ What was the main pattern of social development in colonial America during the period 1500–1800?

▶ Why and how did European settlers in South and North America strive for self-government, and how successful were they in achieving their goals?

Beginning in the sixteenth century, the Americas became an extension of Europe. European settlers extracted mineral and agricultural resources from these new lands. In Europe these resources had become increasingly expensive and impractical to produce (if they could be produced at all). A pattern emerged in which gold and silver, as well as agricultural products that could not be grown in Europe's cooler climate, were intensively exploited. In their role as supplementary subtropical and tropical extensions of Europe, the Americas became a crucial factor in Europe's changing position in the world. First, Europe acquired large quantities of precious metals, which its two largest competitors, India and China, lacked. Second, with its new access to warm-weather agricultural products, Europe rose to a position of agrarian autonomy similar to that of India and China. In terms of resources, compared with the principal religious civilizations of India and China, Europe grew between 1550 and 1800 from a position of inferiority to one of near parity.

The Colonial Americas: Europe's Warm-Weather Extension

The European extension into the subtropical and tropical Americas followed Columbus's pursuit of a sea route to India and its spices that would circumvent the Mediterranean and its dominance by Muslim traders. The Spaniards justified the conquest of these new continents and their Native American inhabitants with Christ's command to convert the heathen in the Spanish Habsburg World Empire, the glorious final empire before Christ's return. They financed their imperial expansion as well as their wars against Ottoman and European rivals with American gold and silver, leaving little for domestic investment in productive enterprises. A pattern evolved in which Iberian settlers transformed the Americas into mineral-extracting and agrarian colonies based on either cheap or forced labor.

The Conquest of Mexico and Peru

The Spanish conquerors of the Aztec and Inca Empires, although few in number, succeeded by exploiting internal weaknesses in the empires. They swiftly eliminated the top of the power structures, paralyzing the decision-making apparatuses long enough for their conquests to succeed. Soon after the conquests, the Old World disease of smallpox—to which New World inhabitants had never been exposed and therefore had never developed immunity—ravaged the Native American population and dramatically reduced the indigenous labor force. To make up for this reduction, colonial authorities imported black slaves from Africa for employment in mines and in agriculture. Black Africans, who had long been in contact with Eurasia, were, like Europeans, less susceptible to smallpox. A three-tiered society of European immigrants, Native Americans, and black slaves emerged in the Spanish and Portuguese Americas.

From Trading Posts to Conquest   Columbus had discovered the Caribbean islands under a royal commission, which entitled him to build fortified posts and to trade with the indigenous Taínos. Friendly trade relations with the Taínos, however, quickly deteriorated into outright exploitation, with the Spaniards usurping the traditional entitlements of the Taíno chiefs to the labor of their fellow men, who panned gold in rivers or mined it in shallow shafts. With the help of **land-labor grants** (Spanish *encomiendas*), the Spanish took over from the Taíno chiefs and, through forced labor, amassed sizeable quantities of gold. What had begun as trade-post settlement turned into full-blown conquest of land.

The Spaniards conquered the Caribbean islands not only through force. Much more severe in its consequences was the indirect conquest through disease. The Old World disease of smallpox quickly wiped out an estimated 250,000 to 1 million Taínos on the larger northern islands as well as the less numerous Caribs on the smaller southern islands. Isolated for more than 10,000 years from the rest of humankind, Native Americans possessed no immunity against smallpox and were similarly ravaged by other introduced diseases.

Protests, mostly among members of the clergy, arose against both the brutal labor exploitation by the conquerors and the helplessness of the Taínos against disease. Unfortunately, the protesters remained a small minority, even within the clergy. One notable protestor was Bartolomé de las Casas (1474–1566), from a family of merchants in Seville. Las Casas had practiced law before emigrating to Hispaniola, where he received an *encomienda*. After becoming a priest in 1510 and later a Dominican monk, however, he became a bitter opponent of the land-labor grant system, which finally came to an end after 1542 with the introduction of the *repartimiento* system (see p. 540).

First Mainland Conquests   Another early settler on Hispaniola was Hernán Cortés (1485–1547). His father was a lower-level nobleman in Estremadura,

Land-labor grant (encomienda): Land grant by the government to an entrepreneur entitling him to use forced indigenous or imported slave labor on that land for the exploitation of agricultural and mineral resources.

Chapter Outline

• The Colonial Americas: Europe's Warm-Weather Extension

• The Making of American Societies: Origins and Transformations

• Putting It All Together

a rough, formerly Islamic frontier region in southwestern Iberia. Chosen by his parents for a career in law, Cortés learned Latin but left the university before graduation. After his arrival in the New World in 1504, he advanced quickly from governmental scribe in Hispaniola to mayor of Santiago in Cuba. Thanks to several labor grants, he became rich. When the Cuban governor asked him in the fall of 1518 to equip and lead a small preparatory expedition for trade and exploration to the Yucatán Peninsula in southeastern Mexico, Cortés enthusiastically agreed. Within a month he assembled 300 men, considerably exceeding his contract. The governor tried to stop him, but Cortés departed quickly for the American mainland.

Cultural Intermediary.
The Tabascans gave Malinche, or Doña Marina, to Hernán Cortés as a form of tribute after they were defeated by the Spanish. Malinche served Cortés as a translator and mistress, playing a central role in Cortés's eventual victory over the Aztecs. She was in many respects the principal face of the Spanish and is always depicted center stage in Native American visual accounts of the conquest.

As the Cuban governor had feared, Cortés did not bother with trading posts in Yucatán. The Spanish had previously learned of the existence of the Aztec Empire, with its immense silver and gold treasures. In a first encounter, Cortés's motley force—numbering by now about 530 Spanish men—defeated a much larger indigenous force at Tabasco. The Spaniards' steel weapons and armor proved superior in hand-to-hand combat to the obsidian-spiked lances and wooden swords, as well as quilted cotton vests of the defenders.

Among the gifts of submission presented by the defeated Native Americans in Tabasco was Malinche, a Nahuatl [NA-hua]-speaking woman. Her widowed Aztec mother had sold her into slavery to the Tabascans after her remarriage. Malinche quickly learned Spanish and became the consort of Cortés, teaching him about the subtleties of Aztec culture. In her role as translator, Malinche was nearly as decisive as Cortés in shaping events. Indeed, Aztecs often used the name of Malinche when addressing Cortés, forgetting that her voice was not that of Cortés. With Tabasco conquered, Cortés quickly moved on; he was afraid that the Cuban governor, who was in pursuit, would otherwise force him to return to Cuba.

Conquest of the Aztec Empire   On the southeast coast of Mexico, Cortés founded the city of Veracruz as a base from which to move inland. In the city, he had his followers elect a town council, which made Cortés their head and chief justice, allowing Cortés to claim legitimacy for his march inland. To prevent opponents in his camp from notifying the Cuban governor of his usurpation of authority, Cortés had all ships stripped of their gear and the hulls sunk. Marching inland, the Spaniards ran into resistance from indigenous people, suffering their first losses of horses and men. Although bloodied, they continued their march

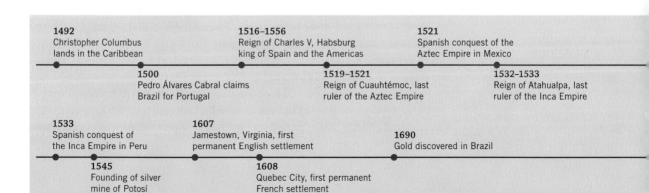

1492 Christopher Columbus lands in the Caribbean	1516–1556 Reign of Charles V, Habsburg king of Spain and the Americas	1521 Spanish conquest of the Aztec Empire in Mexico
1500 Pedro Álvares Cabral claims Brazil for Portugal	1519–1521 Reign of Cuauhtémoc, last ruler of the Aztec Empire	1532–1533 Reign of Atahualpa, last ruler of the Inca Empire
1533 Spanish conquest of the Inca Empire in Peru	1607 Jamestown, Virginia, first permanent English settlement	1690 Gold discovered in Brazil
1545 Founding of silver mine of Potosí	1608 Quebec City, first permanent French settlement	

with thousands of Native American allies, most notably the Tlaxcalans, traditional enemies of the Aztecs. The support from these indigenous peoples made a crucial difference when Cortés and his army reached the court of the Aztecs.

"Xicotenga [shee-co-TEN-ga, ruler of Tlaxcala] made many complaints about Montezuma [Moctezuma] and his allies, for they were all enemies of the Tlaxcalans and made war on them."

—Bernal Díaz del Castillo

When Cortés arrived at the city of Tenochtitlán on November 2, 1519, the emperor Moctezuma II (r. 1502–1519) was in a quandary over how to react to these invaders whose depredations neither his tributaries nor his enemies had been able to stop. To gain time, Moctezuma greeted the Spaniard in person on one of the causeways leading to the city and invited him to his palace. Cortés and his company, now numbering some 600 Spaniards, took up quarters in the palace precincts. After a week of gradually deteriorating discussions, Cortés suddenly put the incredulous emperor under house arrest and made him swear allegiance to Charles V.

Before being able to contemplate his next move, however, Cortés was diverted by the need to march back east, where troops from Cuba had arrived to arrest him. After defeating those troops, he pressed the remnants into his own service and returned to Tenochtitlán. During his absence, the Spaniards who had remained in Moctezuma's palace had massacred a number of unarmed Aztec nobles participating in a religious ceremony. An infuriated crowd of Tenochtitlán's inhabitants invaded the palace. In the melee, Moctezuma and some 200 Spaniards died. The rest of the Spanish fled for their lives, retreating east to their Tlaxcalan allies, who, fortunately, remained loyal. Here, after his return, Cortés devised a new plan for capturing Tenochtitlán.

After 10 months of preparations, the Spaniards returned to the Aztec capital. In command now of about 2,000 Spanish soldiers and assisted by some 50,000 Native American troops, Cortés laid siege to the city, bombarding it from ships he had built in the lake and razing buildings during forays onto land. After nearly 3 months, much of the city was in ruins, fresh water and food became scarce, and smallpox began to decimate the population of some 3–4 million inhabitants in the Mexican Basin and 25 million throughout the Aztec Empire. On August 21, 1521, the Spaniards and their allies stormed the city and looted its gold treasury. They captured the fiercely resisting last emperor, Cuauhtémoc [cu-aw-TAY-moc], a few days later and executed him in 1525, thus ending the Aztec Empire (see Map 18.1).

Conquest of the Inca Empire   At about the same time, a relative of Cortés, Francisco Pizarro (ca. 1475–1541), conceived a plan to conquer the Andean empire of the Incas (which, in 1492, comprised some 9–12 million inhabitants). Pizarro, like Cortés born in Estremadura, was an illegitimate and uneducated son of an infantry captain from the lower nobility. Arriving in Hispaniola as part of an expedition in 1513 that went on to discover Panama and the Pacific, he became mayor of Panama City, acquired some wealth, and began to hear rumors about an empire of gold and silver to the south. After a failed initial expedition, he and 13 followers captured some precious metal from an oceangoing Inca sailing raft. After receiving a permit to establish a trading post from Charles V, Pizarro departed with a host of 183 men in late December 1530.

In a grimly fortuitous bit of luck for Pizarro, smallpox had preceded him in his expedition. In the later 1520s, the disease had ravaged the Inca Empire, killing the emperor and his heir apparent and leading to a protracted war of succession

MAP **18.1 The European Exploration of the Americas, 1519–1542.**

between two surviving sons. Atahualpa, in the north, sent his army south to the capital, Cuzco, where it defeated his half-brother, Huáscar. When Pizarro entered the Inca Empire, Atahualpa was encamped with an army of 40,000 men near the northern town of Cajamarca, on his way south to Cuzco to install himself as emperor.

ATAHUALLPA. INCA XIIII.

Conquest by Surprise.
The Spanish conqueror Francisco Pizarro captured Emperor Atahualpa (top) in an ambush. Atahualpa promised a roomful of gold in return for his release, but the Spaniards collected the gold and murdered Atahualpa (bottom) before generals of the Inca army could organize an armed resistance.

Arriving at Cajamarca, Pizarro succeeded in arranging an unarmed audience with Atahualpa in the town square. On November 16, 1532, Atahualpa came to this audience, surrounded by several thousand unarmed retainers, while Pizarro hid his soldiers in and behind the buildings around the square. At a signal, these soldiers rushed into the square. Some soldiers captured Atahualpa to hold him hostage. In the ensuing bloodbath, not one Spanish soldier was killed. The whole massacre was over in less than an hour.

With his ambush, Pizarro succeeded in paralyzing the Inca Empire at the very top. Without their emperor, Atahualpa, none of the generals in Cuzco dared to seize the initiative. Instead of ordering his generals to liberate him, Atahualpa sought to satisfy the greed of his captors with a room full of gold and silver as ransom. In the following 2 months, Inca administrators delivered immense quantities of precious metals to Pizarro in Cajamarca. During the same time, however, the Spanish were in fear of being attacked from the north. Spanish officers subjected Atahualpa to a mock trial and executed the hapless king on July 26, 1533, hoping to keep the Incas disorganized.

And indeed, the northern forces broke off their march and thereby allowed the Spaniards to take the capital. The Spaniards did so against minimal resistance, massacring the inhabitants and stripping Cuzco of its immense gold and silver treasures. Pizarro did not stay long in the now worthless, isolated city in the Andes. In 1535 he founded a new capital, Lima, which was more conveniently located on the coast and about halfway between Cajamarca and Cuzco. At this time, Incas in the south finally overcame their paralysis. Learning from past mistakes, they avoided mass battles, focused on deadly guerilla strikes, and rebuilt a kingdom that held out until 1572. It was only then that the Spanish gained full control of the Inca Empire.

The Portuguese Conquest of Brazil   The Portuguese were not far behind the Spaniards in their pursuit of conquest. Navigators from both Spain and Portugal had first sighted the Brazilian coast in 1499–1500, and the Portuguese quickly claimed it for themselves. Brazil's indigenous population at that time is estimated to have amounted to nearly 5 million. The great majority lived in temporary or permanent villages based on agriculture, fishing, and hunting. Only a small minority in remote areas of the Amazon were pure foragers.

The Portuguese were interested initially in trade with the villagers, mostly for a type of hardwood called brazilwood which was used as a red dye. When French traders appeared, ignoring the Portuguese commercial treaties with the tribes, the Portuguese crown shifted from simple trade agreements to trading-post settlements. This involved giving land grants to commoners and lower noblemen with the obligation to build fortified coastal villages for settlers and to engage in agriculture and friendly trade. By the mid-sixteenth century, a handful of these villages became successful, their inhabitants intermarrying with the surrounding indigenous chieftain families and establishing sugarcane plantations.

Explanations for the Spanish Success   The slow progression of the Portuguese in Brazil is readily understood. But the stupendous victories of handfuls of Spaniards over huge empires with millions of inhabitants and large cities defy easy explanation. Five factors invite consideration.

First, and most important, the conquistadors went straight to the top of the imperial pyramid. The emperors and their courts expected diplomatic deference from inferiors, among whom they included the minuscule band of Spaniards. Confronted, instead, with a calculated combination of arrogance and brutality, the emperors and courts were thrown off balance by the Spaniards, who ruthlessly exploited their opportunity. As the emperors were removed from the top level, the administration immediately below them fell into paralysis, unable to seize the initiative and respond in a timely fashion.

Second, both the Aztec and Inca Empires were relatively recent creations in which there were individuals and groups who contested the hierarchical power structure. The conquistadors either found allies among the subject populations or encountered a divided leadership. In either case, they were able to exploit divisions in the empires.

Brazil in 1519. This early map is fairly accurate for the northern coast but increasingly less accurate as one moves south. First explorations of the south by both Portuguese and Spanish mariners date to 1513–1516. Ferdinand Magellan passed through several places along the southern coast on his journey around the world in 1520–1521. The scenes on the map depict Native Americans cutting and collecting brazilwood, the source of a red dye much in demand by the Portuguese during the early period of colonization.

Third, European-introduced diseases, traveling with or ahead of the conquerors, took a devastating toll. In both empires, smallpox hit at critical moments during or right before the Spanish invasions, causing major disruptions.

Fourth, thanks to horses and superior European steel weapons and armor, primarily pikes, swords, and breast plates, small numbers of Spaniards were able to hold large numbers of attacking Aztecs and Incas at bay in hand-to-hand combat. Contrary to widespread belief, cannons and matchlock muskets were less important, since they were useless in close encounters. Firearms were still too slow and inaccurate to be decisive.

A fifth factor, indigenous religion, was probably of least significance. According to some now-outdated interpretations, Moctezuma was immobilized by his belief in a prophecy that he would have to relinquish his power to the savior Quetzalcoatl returning from his mythical city of Tlapallan on the east coast (see Chapter 15). Modern scholarship provides convincing reasons, however, to declare this prophecy a postconquest legend, circulated by Cortés both to flatter Charles V and to aggrandize himself as the predicted savior figure bringing Christianity.

The Establishment of Colonial Institutions

The Spanish crown established administrative hierarchies in the Americas, similar to those of the Aztecs and Incas, with governors at the top of the hierarchy and descending through lower ranks of functionaries. A small degree of

Spanish Steel. The *Lienzo de Tlaxcala*, from the middle part of the sixteenth century, is our best visual source for the conquest of Mexico. In this scene, Malinche, protected by a shield, directs the battle on the causeway leading to Tenochtitlán. The two Spanish soldiers behind her, one fully armored, brandish steel swords, which were more effective than the obsidian blades carried by the Aztec defenders (one of whom is dressed in leopard skins), shown on the left.

Creoles: American-born descendants of European, primarily Iberian, immigrants.

settler autonomy was permitted through town and city councils, but the crown was determined to make the Americas a territorial extension of the European pattern of centralized state formation. Several hundred thousand settlers (including Alonso Ortíz) found a new life in the Americas, mostly as urban craftspeople, administrators, and professionals. By the early seventeenth century, a powerful elite of Spanish who had been born in America, called **Creoles** (Spanish *criollos*, Portuguese *crioulos*, natives) was in place, first to assist and later to replace most of the administrators sent from Spain in the governance of the Americas (see Map 18.2).

From Conquest to Colonialism   The unimaginable riches of Cortés and Pizarro inspired numerous further expeditions. Adventurers struck out with small bands of followers into Central and North America, Chile, and the Amazon. Their expeditions, however, yielded only modest amounts of gold and earned more from selling captured Native Americans into slavery. In the north, expeditions penetrated as far as Arizona, New Mexico, Texas, Oklahoma, Kansas, and Florida but encountered only villagers and the relatively poor Pueblo towns. No new golden kingdoms (the mythical El Dorado, or "golden city") beyond the Aztec and Inca Empires were discovered in the Americas.

In the mid-sixteenth century, easy looting was replaced by a search for the mines from where the precious metals came. In northern Mexico, Native Americans led a group of soldiers and missionaries in 1547 to a number of rich silver mines. In addition, explorers discovered silver in Bolivia (1545) and northern Mexico (1556), gold in Chile (1552), and mercury in Peru (1563). The conquistadors shifted from looting to the exploitation of Native American labor in mines and in agriculture.

In a small number of areas, indigenous peoples resisted incorporation into the Spanish colonies. Notably, in southern Chile the Mapuche repulsed all attempts by the Spanish to subdue them. They had already prevented the Incas from expanding their empire to the southern tip of the continent. Initially, in 1550–1553 the Spanish succeeded in establishing a number of forts and opening a gold mine. But in campaign after campaign they failed to gain more than a border strip with an adjacent no-man's-land. In 1612 they agreed to a temporary peace which left the majority of the Mapuche independent.

Another Native American people who successfully resisted the Spanish conquest were the Asháninka in the Peruvian rain forest. Located along the Eno River, one of the headwater tributaries of the Amazon, they were the first standing in the way of the Spanish attempts to extend their dominance from Peru eastward. The Asháninka exploited hillside salt veins in their region and were traders of goods between the Andes and the rain forest. Although Jesuits and later Franciscans established missions among the Asháninka in the 1600s, they failed to make many converts. It was only in 1737 that the Spanish finally built a fort in the region—a first step toward projecting colonial power into the rain forest.

Bureaucratic Efficiency   During the first two generations after the conquest, Spain maintained an efficient colonial administration, which delivered between

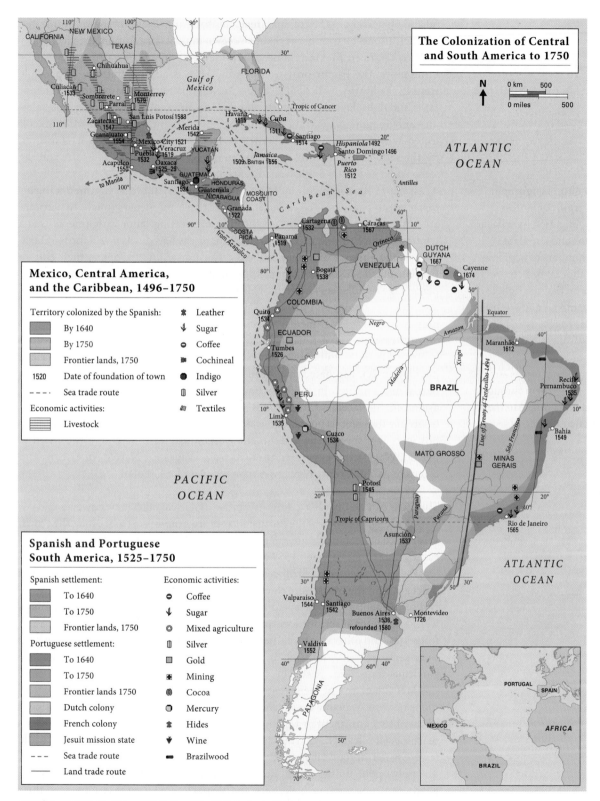

The Colonization of Central and South America to 1750

N

0 km — 500
0 miles — 500

Mexico, Central America, and the Caribbean, 1496–1750

Territory colonized by the Spanish:
- By 1640
- By 1750
- Frontier lands, 1750

1520   Date of foundation of town
- - - - Sea trade route

Economic activities:
- Livestock

- ✹ Leather
- ⬇ Sugar
- ⊖ Coffee
- 🐛 Cochineal
- ● Indigo
- ▯ Silver
- ▨ Textiles

Spanish and Portuguese South America, 1525–1750

Spanish settlement:
- To 1640
- To 1750
- Frontier lands, 1750

Portuguese settlement:
- To 1640
- To 1750
- Frontier lands 1750
- Dutch colony
- French colony
- Jesuit mission state

- - - Sea trade route
—— Land trade route

Economic activities:
- ⊖ Coffee
- ⬇ Sugar
- ◉ Mixed agriculture
- ▯ Silver
- ◼ Gold
- ✦ Mining
- ◍ Cocoa
- ◑ Mercury
- ✹ Hides
- ♣ Wine
- ▬ Brazilwood

MAP 18.2 **The Colonization of Central and South America to 1750.**

50 and 60 percent of the colonies' revenues to Spain. These revenues contributed as much as one-quarter of the Spanish crown budget. In addition, the viceroyalty of New Spain in Mexico remitted another 25 percent of its revenues to the Philippines, the Pacific province for which it was administratively responsible from 1571 onward. As in Spain, settlers in New Spain had to pay up to 40 different taxes and dues, levied on imports and exports, internal trade, mining, and sales. The only income tax was the tithe to the church, which the administration collected and, at times, used for its own budgetary purposes. Altogether, however, for the settlers the tax level was lower in the New World than in Spain, and the same was true for the English and French colonies in North America.

Labor assignment (*repartimiento*): Obligation by villagers to send stipulated numbers of people as laborers to a contractor, who had the right to exploit a mine or other labor-intensive enterprise; the contractors paid the laborers minimal wages and bound them through debt peonage to their businesses.

In the 1540s the government introduced rotating **labor assignments** (*repartimientos*) to phase out the *encomiendas* that powerful owners sought to perpetuate within their families. This institution of rotating labor assignments was a continuation of the *mit'a* system, which the Incas had devised as a form of taxation, in the absence of money and easy transportation of crops in their empire (see Chapter 15). Rotating labor assignments meant that for fixed times a certain percentage of villagers had to provide labor to the state for road building, drainage, transportation, and mining. Private entrepreneurs could also contract for indigenous labor assignments, especially in mining regions.

In Mexico the *repartimiento* fell out of use in the first half of the seventeenth century due to the toll of recurring smallpox epidemics on the Native American population. It is estimated that the indigenous population in the Americas, from a height of 54 million in 1550, declined to 10 million by 1700 before recovering again. The replacement for the lost workers was wage labor. In highland Peru, where the indigenous population was less densely settled and the effects of smallpox were less severe, the assignment system lasted to the end of the colonial period. Wage labor expanded there as well. Wages for Native Americans and blacks remained everywhere lower than for those for Creoles.

The Rise of the Creoles   Administrative and fiscal efficiency, however, did not last very long. The wars of the Spanish Habsburg Empire cost more than the crown was able to collect in revenues. King Philip II (r. 1556–1598) had to declare bankruptcy four times between 1557 and 1596. In order to make up the financial deficit, the crown began to sell offices in the Americas to the highest bidders. The first offices put on the block were elective positions in the municipal councils. By the end of the century, Creoles had purchased life appointments in city councils as well as positions as scribes, local judges, police chiefs, directors of processions and festivities, and other sinecures. In these positions, they collected fees and rents for their services. Local oligarchies emerged, effectively ending whatever elective, participatory politics existed in Spanish colonial America.

Over the course of the seventeenth century a majority of administrative positions became available for purchase. The effects of the change from recruitment by merit to recruitment by wealth on the functioning of the bureaucracy were far-reaching. Creoles advanced on a broad front in the administrative positions, while fewer Spaniards found it attractive to buy their American positions from overseas. The only opportunities which European Spaniards still found enticing were the nearly 300 positions of governors and inspectors, since these jobs gave their owners the right to subject the Native Americans to forced purchases of goods, yielding huge profits. For the most part, wealthy Spanish merchants delegated junior partners to these highly lucrative activities. By 1700, the consequences of the Spanish crown selling most of its American administrative offices were a decline in the competence of office holders, the emergence of a Creole elite able to bend the Spanish administration increasingly to its will, and a decentralization of the decision-making processes.

Northwest European Interference As Spain's administrative grip on the Americas weakened during the seventeenth century, the need to defend the continents militarily against European interlopers arose. At the beginning, there were European privateers, holding royal charters, who harassed Spanish silver shipments and ports in the Caribbean. In the early seventeenth century, the French, English, and Dutch governments sent ships to occupy the smaller Caribbean islands not claimed by Spain. Privateer and contraband traders stationed on these islands engaged in further raiding and pillaging, severely damaging Spain's monopoly of shipping between Europe and the Caribbean.

Conquests of Spanish islands followed in the second half of the century. England captured Jamaica in 1655, and France colonized western Hispaniola (Saint-Domingue) in 1665, making it one of their most profitable sugar-producing colonies. Along the Pacific coast, depredations continued into the middle of the eighteenth century. Here, the galleons of the annual Acapulco–Manila fleet carrying silver from Mexico to China and returning with Chinese silks, porcelain, and lacquerware were the targets of English privateers. Over the course of the seventeenth century, Spain allocated one-half to two-thirds of its American revenues to the increasingly difficult defense of its annual treasure fleets and Caribbean possessions.

Bourbon Reforms After the death of the last, childless Habsburg king of Spain in 1700, the new French-descended dynasty of the Bourbons made major efforts to regain control over their American possessions. They had to begin from a discouragingly weak position as nearly 90 percent of all goods traded from Europe to the Americas were of non-Spanish origin. Fortunately, population increases among the settlers as well as the Native Americans (after having overcome their horrific losses to disease) offered opportunities to Spanish manufacturers and merchants. After several false starts, in the middle of the eighteenth century the Bourbon reform program began to show results.

The reforms aimed at improved naval connections and administrative control between the mother country and the colonies. The monopolistic annual armed silver fleet was greatly reduced. Instead, the government authorized more frequent single sailings at different times of the year. Newly formed Spanish companies, receiving exclusive rights at specific ports, succeeded in reducing contraband trade. Elections took place again for municipal councils. Spanish-born salaried officials replaced scores of Creole tax and office farmers. The original two viceroyalties were subdivided into four, to improve administrative control. The sale of tobacco and brandy became state monopolies. Silver mining and cotton textile manufacturing were expanded. By the second half of the eighteenth century, Spain had regained a measure of control over its colonies.

As a result, government revenues rose substantially. Tax receipts increased more than twofold, even taking into account the inflation of the late eighteenth century. In the end, however, the reforms remained incomplete. Since the Spanish economy was not also reformed, in terms of expanding crafts production and urbanization, the changes did not diminish the English and French dominance of the import market by much. Spain failed to produce textiles, metalwares, and household goods at competitive prices for the colonies; thus the level of English and French exports to the Americas remained high.

Early Portuguese Colonialism   In contrast to the Spanish Americas, the Portuguese overseas province of Brazil remained initially confined to a broad coastal strip, which developed only slowly during the sixteenth century. The first governor-general, whose rank was equivalent to a Spanish viceroy, arrived in 1549. He and his successors were members of the high aristocracy, but their positions were salaried and subject to term limits. As the colony grew, the crown created a council in the capital of Lisbon for all Brazilian appointments and established a high court for all judicial affairs in Bahia in northern Brazil. Commoners with law degrees filled the nonmilitary colonial positions. In the early seventeenth century, however, offices became as open to purchase as in the Spanish colonies, although not on the city council level, where a complex indirect electoral process survived.

Jesuits converted the Native Americans, whom they transported to Jesuit-administered villages. Colonial cities and Jesuits repeatedly clashed over the slave raids of the "pioneers" (*bandeirantes*) in village territories. The bandeirantes came mostly from São Paulo in the south and roamed the interior in search of human prey. Native American slaves were in demand on the wheat farms and cattle ranches of São Paulo as well as the sugar plantations of the northeast. Although the Portuguese crown and church had, like the Spanish, forbidden the enslavement of Native Americans, the bandeirantes exploited a loophole. The law was interpreted as allowing the enslavement of Native Americans who resisted conversion to Christianity. For a long time, Lisbon and the Jesuits were powerless against this flagrantly self-interested interpretation.

Expansion into the Interior   In the middle of the seventeenth century, the Jesuits and Native Americans finally succeeded in pushing many bandeirantes west and north, where they switched from slave raiding to prospecting for gold. In the far north, however, the raids continued until 1680, when the Portuguese administration finally prevailed and ended Native American slavery, almost a century and a half after Spain. Ironically, it was mostly thanks to the "pioneer" raids for slaves that Brazil expanded westward, to assume the borders it has today.

As a result of gold discoveries in Minas Gerais in 1690 by bandeirantes, the European immigrant population increased rapidly, from 1 to 2 million during the 1700s. Minas Gerais, located north of Rio de Janeiro, was the first inland region of the colony to attract settlers. By contrast, as a result of smallpox epidemics beginning in the 1650s in the Brazilian interior, the Native American population declined massively, not to expand again until the end of the eighteenth century. To replace the lost labor, Brazilians imported slaves from Africa, at first to work in the sugar plantations and, after 1690, in the mines, where their numbers increased to two-thirds of the labor force. In contrast to Spanish mines, Brazilian mines were surface operations requiring only minimal equipment outlays. Most blacks worked with pickaxes and shovels. The peak of the gold boom came in the 1750s, when the importance of gold was second only to that of sugar among Brazilian exports to Europe.

Early in the gold boom, the crown created the new Ministry of the Navy and Overseas Territories, which greatly expanded the administrative structure in Brazil. It established 14 regions and a second high court in Rio de Janeiro, which replaced Bahia as the capital in 1736. The ministry in Lisbon ended the sale of offices, increased the efficiency of tax collection, and encouraged Brazilian textile manufacturing to render the province more independent from English imports. By the mid-1700s, Brazil was a flourishing overseas colony of Portugal, producing brazilwood, sugar, gold, tobacco, cacao, and vanilla for export.

North American Settlements Efforts at settlement in the less hospitable North America in the sixteenth century were unsuccessful. Only in the early part of the seventeenth century did French, English, and Dutch merchant investors succeed in establishing small communities of settlers on the northeastern coast, who grew their own food on land purchased from the local Native American villagers. These settlements were Jamestown (founded in 1607 in today's Virginia), Quebec (1608, Canada), Plymouth and Boston (1620 and 1630, respectively, in today's Massachusetts), and New Amsterdam (1625, today's New York). Subsistence agriculture and fur, however, were meager ingredients if the settlements were to prosper. The northerly settlements struggled through the seventeenth century, sustained either by Catholic missionary efforts or by the Protestant enthusiasm of the Puritans who had escaped persecution in England. Southern places like Jamestown survived because they adopted tobacco, a warm-weather plant, as a cash crop for export to Europe. In contrast to Mexico and Peru, the North American settlements were not followed—at least not at first—by territorial conquests (see Map 18.3).

Native Americans European arrivals in North America soon began supplementing agriculture with trade. They exchanged metal and glass wares, beads, and seashells for furs, especially beaver pelts, with the Native American groups of the interior. The more these groups came into contact with the European traders, however, the more dramatic the demographic impact of the trade on them was: Smallpox, already a menace during the 1500s in North America, became devastating as contacts intensified. In New England, for example, of the ca. 144,000 estimated Native Americans in 1600, fewer than 15,000 remained in 1620.

The introduction of guns contributed an additional lethal factor to trading arrangements, as English, French, and Dutch traders provided their favorite Native

Mine Workers. The discovery of gold and diamonds in Minas Gerais led to a boom, but did little to contribute to the long-term health of the Brazilian economy. With the Native American population decimated by disease, African slaves performed the backbreaking work.

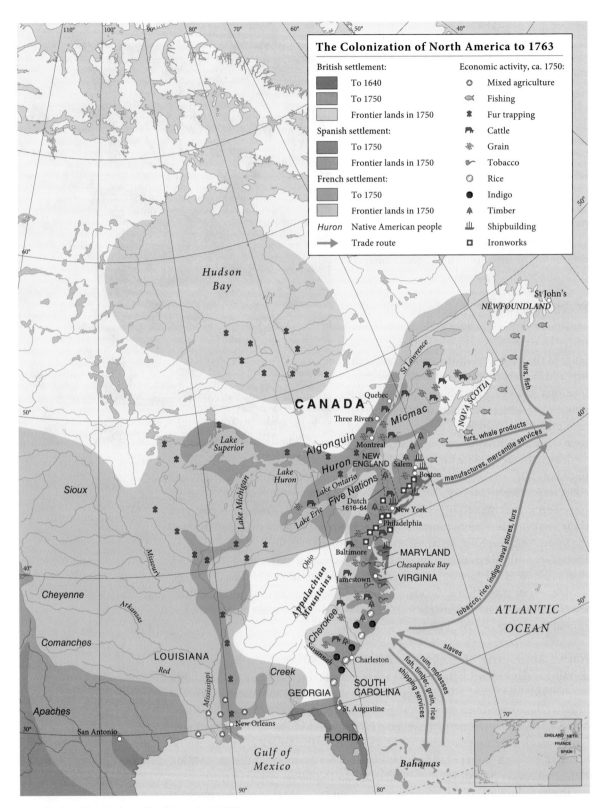

The Colonization of North America to 1763

British settlement:
- To 1640
- To 1750
- Frontier lands in 1750

Spanish settlement:
- To 1750
- Frontier lands in 1750

French settlement:
- To 1750
- Frontier lands in 1750

Huron   Native American people

→   Trade route

Economic activity, ca. 1750:
- Mixed agriculture
- Fishing
- Fur trapping
- Cattle
- Grain
- Tobacco
- Rice
- Indigo
- Timber
- Shipbuilding
- Ironworks

MAP 18.3 **The Colonization of North America to 1763.**

American trading partners with flintlocks, in order to increase the yield of furs. As a result, in the course of the 1600s the Iroquois in the northeast were able to organize themselves into a heavily armed and independent-minded federation, capable of inflicting heavy losses on rival groups as well as on European traders and settlers.

Further south, in Virginia, the Jamestown settlers encountered the Powhatan confederacy. These Native Americans, living in some 200 well-fortified, palisaded villages, dominated the region between the Chesapeake Bay and the Appalachian Mountains. Initially, the Powhatan supplied Jamestown with foodstuffs and sought to integrate the settlement into their confederation. When this attempt at integration failed, however, benevolence turned to hostility, and the confederacy raided Jamestown twice in an attempt to rid their region of foreign settlers. But the latter were able to turn the tables and defeat the Powhatan in 1646, thereafter occupying their lands and reducing them to small scattered remnants. Pocahontas, the daughter of the Powhatan chief at the time of the foundation of Jamestown, was captured during one of the raids, converted to Christianity, and lived in England for a number of years as the wife of a returning settler. The decline of the Powhatan in the later 1600s allowed English settlers to move westward, in contrast to New England in the north, where the Iroquois, although allied with the English against the French, blocked any western expansion.

The Iroquois were fiercely determined to maintain their dominance of the fur trade and wrought havoc among the Native American groups living between New England and the Great Lakes. In the course of the second half of the 1600s they drove many smaller groups westward into the Great Lakes region and Mississippi plains, where these groups settled as refugees. French officials and Jesuit missionaries sought to create some sort of alliance with the refugee peoples, to counterbalance the powerful Iroquois to the east. Many Native Americans converted to Christianity, creating a Creole Christianity similar to that of the Africans of Kongo and the Mexicans after the Spanish conquest of the Aztecs.

Major population movements also occurred further west on the Great Plains, where the Apaches arrived from the Great Basin in the Rockies. They had captured horses which had escaped during the Pueblo uprising of 1680–1695 against Spain. The Comanches, who arrived at the same time also from the west and on horses, had, in addition, acquired firearms and around 1725 began their expansion at the expense of the Apaches. The Sioux from the northern forests and the Cheyenne from the Great Basin added to the mix of federations on the Great Plains in the early 1700s. At this time, the great transformation of the Native Americans in the center of North America into horse breeders and horsemen warriors began. Smallpox epidemics did not reach the Plains until the mid-1700s while in the east the ravages of this epidemic had weakened the Iroquois so much that they concluded a peace with the French in 1701.

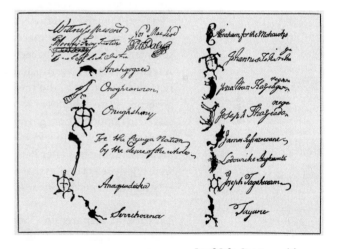

Land Sale. Signatures of the leaders of the Iroquois federation on a treaty with Thomas and Richard Penn in 1736. By the terms of this treaty the Iroquois sold land to the founders of the English colony of Pennsylvania. The leaders of the six nations that made up the Iroquois federation (Mohawk, Oneida, Onondaga, Cayuga, Seneca, and Tuscarora) signed with their pictograms. The names were added later.

French Canada   The involvement of the French in the Great Lakes region with refugees fleeing from the Iroquois was part of a program of expansion into the center of North America, begun in 1663. The governor of Quebec had dispatched explorers, fur traders, and missionaries not only into the Great Lakes region but also the Mississippi valley. The French government then sent farmers, crafts-people, and young single women from France with government-issued agricul-tural implements and livestock to establish settlements. The most successful settlement was in the subtropical district at the mouth of the Mississippi, called "La Louisiane," where some 300 settlers with 4,000 African slaves founded sugar plantations. Immigration was restricted to French subjects and excluded Protestants. Given these restrictions, Louisiana received only some 30,000 settlers by 1750, in contrast to English North America, with nearly 1.2 million settlers by the same time.

Colonial Assemblies   As immigration to New England picked up, the mer-chant companies in Europe, which had financed the journeys of the settlers, were initially responsible for the administration of about a dozen settlement colonies. The first settlers to demand participation in the colonial administration were Virginian tobacco growers with interests in the European trade. In 1619 they deputized delegates from their villages to meet as the House of Burgesses. They thereby created an early popular assembly in North America, assisting their governor in running the colony. The other English colonies soon followed suit, creating their own assemblies. In contrast to Spain and Portugal, England—racked by its internal Anglican–Puritan conflict—was initially uninvolved in the governance of the overseas territories.

When England eventually stepped in and took the governance of the colonies away from the charter merchants and companies in the second half of the seventeenth century, it faced entrenched settler assemblies, especially in New England. Only in New Amsterdam, conquered from the Dutch in 1664–1674 and renamed "New York," did the governor initially rule without an assembly. Many governors were deputies of wealthy aristocrats who never traveled to America but stayed in London. These governors were powerless to prevent the assemblies from appropriating rights to levy taxes and making appointments. The assemblies thus modeled themselves after Parliament in London. As in England, these assemblies were highly select bodies that excluded poorer settlers, who did not meet the prop-erty requirements to vote or stand for elections.

Territorial Expansion   Steady immigration, also from the European main-land, encouraged land speculators in the British colonies to cast their sights beyond the Appalachian Mountains. (According to historical convention, the English are called "British" after the English–Scottish union in 1707.) In 1749, the Ohio Com-pany of Virginia received a royal permit to develop land, together with a protective fort, south of the Ohio River. The French, however, also claimed the Ohio valley, considering it a part of their Canada–Mississippi–Louisiana territory. A few years later, tensions over the valley erupted into open hostility. Initially, the local en-counters went badly for the Virginian militia and British army. In 1755, however, the British and French broadened their clash into a worldwide war for dominance in the colonies and Europe, the Seven Years' War of 1756–1763.

The Seven Years' War   Both France and Great Britain borrowed heavily to pour resources into the war. England had the superior navy and France the superior army. Since the British navy succeeded in choking off French supplies to its increasingly isolated land troops, Britain won the war overseas. In Europe, Britain's failure to supply the troops of its ally Prussia against the Austrian–French alliance caused the war on that front to end in a draw. Overseas, the British gained most of the French holdings in India, several islands in the Caribbean, all of Canada, and all the land east of the Mississippi. The war costs and land swaps, however, proved to be unmanageable for both the vanquished and the victor. The unpaid debts became the root cause of the American, French, and Haitian constitutional revolutions that began 13 years later. Those revolutions, along with the emerging industrialization of Great Britain, signaled the beginning of the modern scientific–industrial age in world history.

The Making of American Societies: Origins and Transformations

The patterns which made the Americas an extension of Europe emerged gradually and displayed characteristics specific to each region. On the one hand, there was the slow transfer of the plants and animals native to each continent, called the **Columbian Exchange** (see "Patterns Up Close"). On the other hand, Spain and Portugal adopted different strategies of mineral and agricultural exploitation. In spite of these different strategies, however, the settler societies of the two countries in the end displayed similar characteristics.

Columbian Exchange: Exchange of plants, animals, and diseases between the Americas and the rest of the world.

Exploitation of Mineral and Tropical Resources

The pattern of European expansion into subtropical and tropical lands began with the Spanish colonization of the Caribbean islands. When the Spanish crown ran out of gold in the Caribbean, it exported silver from Mexico and Peru in great quantities to finance a centralizing state that could compete with the Ottomans and European kings. By contrast, Portugal's colony of Brazil did not at first mine for precious metals, and consequently the Portuguese crown pioneered the growing of sugar on plantations. Mining would be developed later. The North American colonies of England and France had, in comparison, little native industry at first. By moving farther south, however, they adopted the plantation system for indigo and rice and thus joined their Spanish and Portuguese predecessors in exploiting the subtropical–tropical agricultural potential of the Americas.

Silver Mines   When the interest of the Spaniards turned from looting to the exploitation of mineral resources, two main mining centers emerged: Potosí in southeastern Peru (today Bolivia) and Zacatecas and Guanajuato in northern Mexico. For the first 200 years after its founding in 1545, Potosí produced over half of the silver of Spanish America. In the eighteenth century, Zacatecas and Guanajuato jumped ahead of Potosí, churning out almost three times as much of the precious metal. During the same century, gold mining in Colombia and Chile rose to importance as well, making the mining of precious metals the most important economic activity in the Americas.

The Columbian Exchange

Few of us can imagine an Italian kitchen without tomatoes or an Irish meal without potatoes or Chinese or Indian cuisine without the piquant presence of chilies, but until fairly recently each of these foods was unknown to the Old World. Likewise, the expression "As American as apple pie" obscures the fact that for millennia apples, as well as many other frequently consumed fruits, such as peaches, pears, plums, cherries, bananas, oranges, and lemons, were absent from the New World. It was not until the sixteenth century, when plants, animals, and microbes began to flow from one end of the planet to another, that new patterns of ecology and biology changed the course of millions of years of divergent evolution.

When historians catalog the long list of life forms that moved across the oceans in the Columbian Exchange, pride of place is usually reserved for the bigger, better-known migrants like cattle, sheep, pigs, and horses. However, the impact of European weeds and grasses on American grasslands, which made it possible for the North American prairie and the South American pampas to support livestock, should not be overlooked. By binding the soil together with their long, tough roots, these "empires of the dandelion" provided the conditions for the grazing of sheep, cattle, and horses, as well as the planting of crops like wheat.

The other, silent invader that accompanied the conquistadors was, of course, disease. Thousands of years of mutual isolation between the Americas and Afro-Eurasia rendered the immune systems of Native Americans vulnerable to the scourges that European colonists unwittingly brought with them. Smallpox, influenza, diphtheria, whooping cough, typhoid, chicken pox, measles, and meningitis wiped out millions of Native Americans—by some estimates, the native populations of Mesoamerica and the Andes plummeted by 90 percent in the period 1500–1700. In comparison, the contagions the New World was able to reciprocate upon the Old World—syphilis and tuberculosis—did not unleash nearly the same devastation, and the New World origin of these diseases is still debated.

It is therefore obvious that the big winner in the Columbian Exchange was western Europe, though the effects of the New World bounty took centuries to be fully discerned. While Asia and Africa also benefited from the Columbian Exchange in the forms of new foods that enriched diets, the Europeans got a continent endowed with a warm climate in which they could create new and improved versions of their homelands.

Innovations, such as the "patio" method, which facilitated the extraction process through the use of mercury, and the unrestrained exploitation of indigenous labor made American silver highly competitive in the world market. Conditions among the Native Americans and blacks employed as labor were truly abominable. Few laborers lasted through more than two forced recruitment (*repartimiento*) cycles before they were incapacitated or dead.

Given gaps in bookkeeping and high levels of smuggling, scholars have found it extremely difficult to estimate the total production of the American mines from 1550 to 1750. The best current estimate is that Spanish America produced

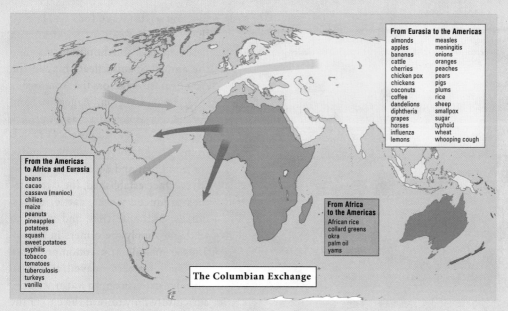

From Eurasia to the Americas

almonds	measles
apples	meningitis
bananas	onions
cattle	oranges
cherries	peaches
chicken pox	pears
chickens	pigs
coconuts	plums
coffee	rice
dandelions	sheep
diphtheria	smallpox
grapes	sugar
horses	typhoid
influenza	wheat
lemons	whooping cough

From the Americas to Africa and Eurasia

beans
cacao
cassava (manioc)
chilies
maize
peanuts
pineapples
potatoes
squash
sweet potatoes
syphilis
tobacco
tomatoes
tuberculosis
turkeys
vanilla

From Africa to the Americas

African rice
collard greens
okra
palm oil
yams

The Columbian Exchange

MAP 18.4 **The Columbian Exchange.**

The Native Americans were nearly wiped out by disease, their lands appropriated, and the survivors either enslaved or marginalized. The precipitous drop in the population of Native Americans, combined with the tropical and semitropical climate of much of the Americas, created the necessary conditions for the Atlantic slave trade. The population losses from this trade were monumental, although the Columbian Exchange, which brought manioc and corn to Africa, balanced these losses to a degree.

Questions

- Can the Columbian Exchange be considered one of the origins of the modern world? How? Why? How does the Columbian Exchange demonstrate the origins, interactions, and adaptations model that is used throughout this book?

- Weigh the positive and negative outcomes of the Columbian Exchange. Is it possible to determine whether the overall effects of the Columbian Exchange on human society and the natural environment were for the better or for the worse?

150,000 tons of silver (including gold converted into silver weight). This quantity corresponded to roughly 85 percent of world production. The figures underline the extraordinary role of American silver for the money economies of Europe, the Middle East, and Asia, especially China.

Since the exploitation of the mines was of such central importance, for the first century and a half of New World colonization the Spanish crown organized its other provinces around the needs of the mining centers. Hispaniola and Cuba in the Caribbean were islands which had produced foodstuffs, sugar, and tobacco from the time of Columbus but only in small quantities. Their main

The Silver Mountain of Potosí. Note the patios in the left foreground and the water-driven crushing mill in the center, which ground the silver-bearing ore into a fine sand that then was moistened, caked, amalgamated with mercury, and dried on the patio. The mine workers' insect-like shapes reinforce the dehumanizing effects of their labor.

function was to feed and protect Havana, the collection point for Mexican and Peruvian silver and the port from where the annual Spanish fleet shipped the American silver across the Atlantic.

A second region, Argentina and Paraguay, was colonized as a bulwark to prevent the Portuguese and Dutch from cutting across the southern end of the continent and accessing Peruvian silver. Once established, the two colonies produced wheat, cattle, mules, horses, cotton, textiles, and tallow to feed and supply the miners in Potosí. The subtropical crop of cotton, produced by small farmers, played a role in Europe's extension into warm-weather agriculture only toward the end of the colonial period.

A third colonial region, Venezuela, began as a grain and cattle supply base for Cartagena, the port for the shipment of Colombian gold, and Panama and Portobelo, ports for the transshipment of Peruvian silver from the Pacific to Havana. Its cocoa and tobacco exports flourished only after the Dutch established themselves in 1624 in the southern Caribbean and provided the shipping. Thus, three major regions of the Spanish overseas empire in the Americas were mostly peripheral as agricultural producers during the sixteenth century. Only after the middle of the century did they begin to specialize in tropical agricultural goods, and they were exporters only in the eighteenth century. By that time, the Dutch and English provided more and more shipping in the place of the Spanish.

Wheat Farming and Cattle Ranching   To support the mining centers and administrative cities, the Spanish colonial government encouraged the development of agricultural estates (*haciendas*). These estates first emerged when conquistadors used their *encomienda* rights to round up Native American labor to produce subsistence crops. Native American tenant farmers were forced to grow wheat and raise cattle, pigs, sheep, and goats for the conquerors, who were now agricultural entrepreneurs. In the latter part of the sixteenth century, the land grants gave way to rotating forced labor as well as wage labor. Owners established their residences and built dwellings for tenant farmers on their estates. A landowner class emerged.

Like the conquistadors before, a majority of landowners produced wheat and animals for sale to urban and mining centers. Cities purchased wheat and maintained granaries in order to provide for urban dwellers in times of harvest failure. Entrepreneurs received commissions to provide slaughterhouses with regular supplies of animals. As the Native American population declined in the seventeenth century and the church helped in consolidating the remaining population in large villages, additional land became available for the establishment of estates. From 1631 onward, authorities granted Spanish settler families the right to maintain their estates undivided from generation to generation. Through donations, the church also acquired considerable agricultural lands. Secular and clerical land-owning interests supported a powerful upper social stratum of Creoles from the eighteenth century onward.

Plantations and Gold Mining in Brazil   Brazil's economic activities began with brazilwood, followed by sugar plantations, before gold mining rose to prominence in the eighteenth century. A crisis hit sugar production in 1680–1700, mostly as a result of the Dutch beginning production of sugar in the Antilles. It was at that time that the gold of Minas Gerais, in the interior of Brazil, was discovered.

Gold-mining operations in Brazil during the eighteenth century were considerably less capital-intensive than the silver mines in Spanish America. Most miners were relatively small operators with sieves, pickaxes, and a few black slaves as unskilled laborers. Many entrepreneurs were indebted for their slaves to absentee capitalists, with whom they shared the profits. Since prospecting took place on the land of Native Americans, bloody encounters were frequent. Most entrepreneurs were ruthless frontiersmen who exploited their slaves and took no chances with the indigenous people. Brazil produced a total of 1,000 tons of gold in the eighteenth century, a welcome bonanza for Portugal at a time of low agricultural prices. Overall, minerals were just as valuable for the Portuguese as they were for the Spanish.

Plantations in Spanish and English America   The expansion of plantation farming in the Spanish colonies was a result of the Bourbon reforms. Although sugar, tobacco, and rice had been introduced early into the Caribbean and southern Mexico, it was only in the expanded plantation system of the eighteenth century that these crops (plus indigo, cacao, and cactuses as host plants for cochineal) were produced on a large scale for export to Europe. The owners of plantations did not need expensive machinery and invested instead in African slave labor, with the result that the slave trade hit full stride, beginning around 1750.

English North American settlements in Virginia and Carolina exported tobacco and rice beginning in the 1660s. Georgia was the thirteenth British colony, founded in 1733 as a bulwark against Spanish Florida and a haven for poor Europeans. In 1750 it joined southern Carolina as a major plantation colony and rice and indigo producer. In the eighteenth century, even New England finally had its own export crop, in the form of timber for shipbuilding and charcoal production in Great Britain, at the amazing rate of 250 million board-feet per year by the start of the nineteenth century. These timber exports illustrate an important new factor appearing in the Americas in the eighteenth century. Apart from the cheap production of precious metals and warm-weather crops, the American extension of Europe became increasingly important as a replacement for dwindling fuel resources across much of northern Europe. Altogether, it was thanks to the Americas that cold and rainy Europe rose successfully into the ranks of the wealthy, climatically balanced, and populated Indian and Chinese empires.

Social Strata, Castes, and Ethnic Groups
The population of settlers in the New World consisted primarily of Europeans who came from a continent that had barely emerged from its population losses to

the Black Death. Although population numbers were rising again in the sixteenth century, Europe did not have masses of emigrants to the Americas to spare. Given the small settler population of the Americas, the temptation to develop a system of forced labor in agriculture and mining was irresistible. Since the Native Americans and African slaves pressed into labor were ethnically so completely different from the Europeans, however, a social system evolved in which the latter two not only were economically underprivileged but also made up the ethnically nonintegrated lowest rungs of the social ladder. A pattern of legal and customary discrimination evolved which, even though partially vitiated by the rise of ethnically mixed groups, prevented the integration of American ethnicities into settler society.

The Social Elite   The heirs of the Spanish conquistadors and estate owners—farmers, ranchers, and planters—maintained city residences and employed managers on their agricultural properties. In Brazil, cities emerged more slowly, and for a long time estate owners maintained their manor houses as small urban islands. Estate owners mixed with the Madrid- and Lisbon-appointed administrators and, during the seventeenth century, intermarried with them, creating the top tier of settler society known as Creoles, some 4 percent of the population. In a wider sense, the tier included also merchants, professionals, clerks, militia officers, and the clergy. They formed a relatively closed society in which descent, intermarriage, landed property, and a government position counted more than money and education.

> "And now the Indians of that town [Tejupan, southern Mexico] appeared before me and reported that the time of the contract [with the Spaniards] was finished and that they wished to raise silk on their own for the profit and usefulness that [the industry] would bring them."
>
> —Petition by Native Americans, 1543

In the seventeenth and eighteenth centuries, the estate owners farmed predominantly with Native American forced labor. They produced grain and/or cattle, legumes, sheep, and pigs for local urban markets or mining towns. In contrast to the black slave plantation estates of the Caribbean and coastal regions of Spanish and Portuguese America, these farming estates did not export their goods to Europe. From the beginning of colonialism, furthermore, Madrid and Lisbon discouraged estate owners, as well as farmers in general, from producing olive oil, wine, or silk, to protect their home production.

As local producers with little competition, farming and ranching estate owners did not feel market pressures. Since they lived for the most part in the cities, they exploited their estates with minimal investments and usually drew profits of less than 5 percent of annual revenues. They were often heavily indebted, and as a result there was often more glitter than substance among the landowning Creoles.

Lower Creoles   The second tier of Creole society consisted of people like Alonzo Ortíz, the tanner introduced at the beginning of this chapter. Even though of second rank, they were privileged European settlers who, as craftspeople and traders, theoretically worked with their hands. In practice, many of them were owner-operators who employed Native Americans and/or black slaves as apprentices and journeymen. Many invested in small plots of land in the vicinity of their cities, striving to rise into the ranks of the landowning Creoles.

Wealthy weavers ran textile manufactures mostly concentrated in the cities of Mexico, Peru, Paraguay, and Argentina. In some of these manufactures, up to

Textile Production. Immigrants from Spain (like Alonso Ortíz, discussed at the beginning of the chapter), maintained workshops (*obrajes*) as tanners, weavers, carpenters, or wheelwrights. As craftspeople producing simple but affordable goods for the poor, they remained competitive throughout the colonial period, in spite of increasingly large textile, utensil, and furniture imports from Europe. At the same time, indigenous textile production by native women continued as in the preconquest period, albeit under the constraints of labor services imposed by officials or clergy, as shown in these examples.

300 Native American and black workers produced cheap, coarse woolens and a variety of cottons on dozens of looms. Men were the weavers and women the spinners—in contrast to the pre-Columbian period, when textile manufacture was entirely a woman's job. On a smaller scale, manufactures also existed for pottery and leather goods. On the whole, the urban manufacturing activities of the popular people, serving the poor in local markets, remained vibrant until well into the nineteenth century, in spite of massive European imports.

Mestizos and Mulattoes   The mixed European–Native American and European–African population had the collective name of "caste" (*casta*), or ethnic group. The term originated in the desire of the Iberian and Creole settlers to draw distinctions among degrees of mixture in order to counterbalance as much as possible the masses of Native Americans and Africans, especially from the eighteenth century onward. The two most important castes were the *mestizos* (Spanish), or *mestiços* (Portuguese), who had Iberian fathers and Native American mothers, and *mulatos*, who had Iberian fathers and black mothers. By 1800 the castas as a whole formed the third largest population category in Latin America (20 percent), after Native Americans (40 percent) and Creoles (30 percent). In Brazil, black freedmen and mulattoes were numerically even with Creoles (28 percent each), after black slaves (38 percent) and before Native Americans (6 percent in the settled provinces outside Amazonia). In both Spanish and Portuguese America, there was also a small percentage of people descended from Native American and black unions. Thus, most of the intermediate population groups were sizeable, playing important neutralizing roles in colonial society, as they had one foot in both the Creole and subordinate social strata (see Figure 18.1).

As such neutralizing elements, mestizos and mulattoes filled lower levels of the bureaucracy and the lay hierarchy in the church. They held skilled and supervisory positions in mines and on estates. In addition, in the armed forces mulattoes dominated the ranks of enlisted men; in the defense militias, they even held officer ranks. In Brazil, many mulattoes and black freedmen were farmers. Much of the craft production was in their hands. A wide array of laws existed to keep mestizos and mulattoes in their peculiarly intermediate social and political positions.

Women The roles played by women depended strongly on their social position. Well-appointed elite Creole households followed the Mediterranean tradition of secluding women from men. Within the confines of the household, elite women were persons of means and influence. They were the owners of substantial dowries and legally stipulated grooms' gifts. Often, they actively managed the investment of their assets. Outside their confines, however, even elite women lost all protection. Crimes of passion, committed by honor-obsessed fathers or husbands, went unpunished. Husbands and fathers who did not resort to violence nevertheless did not need witnesses to obtain court judgments to banish daughters or wives to convents for alleged lapses in chastity. Thus, even elite women were bound by definite limits set by a patriarchal society.

On the lower rungs of society, be it popular Creole, mestizo, mulatto, or Native American, gender separation was much less prevalent. After all, everyone in the family had to work in order to make ends meet. Men, women, and children shared labor in the fields and workshops. Girls or wives took in clothes to wash or went out to work as domestics in wealthy households. Older women dominated retail in market stalls. As in elite society, wives tended to outlive husbands. In addition, working families with few assets suffered abandonment by males. Women headed one-third of all households in Mexico City, according to an 1811 census. Among black slaves in the region of São Paulo, 70 percent of women were without formal ties to the men who fathered their children. Thus, the most pronounced division in colonial society was that of a patriarchy among the Creoles and a slave society dominated by women, with frequently absent men—an unbridgeable division that persists today.

Race, Class, and Gender in Colonial Mexico. An outraged mulatta defends herself against an aggressive Creole, with a fearful child clinging to the woman's skirt.

Figure 18.1 Ethnic Composition of Latin America, ca. 1800.

American Indian 40%, Mestizo 30%, Creole 15%, Mulatto 10%, African 5%

Native Americans In the immediate aftermath of the conquest, Native Americans could be found at all levels of the social scale. Some were completely marginalized in remote corners of the American continents. Others acculturated into the ranks of the working poor in the silver mines or textile manufactures.

Illustration from an Indian Land Record. The Spaniards almost completely wiped out the Aztec archives after the conquest of Mexico; surviving examples of Indian manuscripts are thus extremely rare. Although the example shown here, made from the bark of a fig tree, claims to date from the early 1500s, it is part of the so-called Techialoyan land records created in the seventeenth century to substantiate native land claims. These "títulos primordiales," as they were called, were essentially municipal histories that documented in text and pictures local accounts of important events and territorial boundaries.

A few even formed an educated Aztec or Inca propertied upper class, exercising administrative functions in Spanish civil service. Social distinctions, however, disappeared rapidly during the first 150 years of Spanish colonialism. Smallpox reduced the Native American population by nearly 80 percent. Diseases were more virulent in humid, tropical parts of the continent than in deserts, and the epidemics took a far greater toll on dense, settled populations than they did on dispersed forager bands in dry regions. In the Caribbean and on the Brazilian coast, Native Americans disappeared almost completely; in central and southern Mexico, their population shrank by two-thirds. It was only in the twentieth century that population figures reached the preconquest level again in most parts of Latin America.

Apart from European diseases, the native forager and agrarian Native Americans in the Amazon, Orinoco, and Maracaibo rain forests were the least affected by European colonials during the period 1500–1800. Not only were their lands economically the least promising, but they also defended those lands successfully with blowguns, poison darts, and bow and arrow. In many cold and hot arid or semiarid regions, such as Patagonia, southern Chile, the Argentine grasslands (*pampas*), the Paraguayan salt marshes and deserts, and northern Mexican mountains and steppes, the situation was similar. In these lands, the seminomadic Native Americans quickly adopted the European horse and became highly mobile warrior peoples in defense of their mostly independent territories.

The villagers of Mexico, Yucatán, Guatemala, Colombia, Ecuador, and Peru had fewer choices. When smallpox reduced their numbers in the second half of the sixteenth century, state and church authorities razed many villages and concentrated the survivors in *pueblos de indios*. Initially, the Native Americans put up strong resistance against these resettlements, by repeatedly returning to their destroyed old settlements. From the middle of the seventeenth century, however, the pueblos were fully functional, self-administering units, with councils (*cabildos*), churches, schools, communal lands, and family parcels.

The councils were important institutions of legal training and social mobility for ordinary Native Americans. Initially, the traditional "noble" chiefly families descending from the preconquest Aztec and Inca ruling classes were in control as administrators. The many village functions, however, for which the *cabildos* were responsible allowed commoners to move up into auxiliary roles. In some of these roles, they had opportunities to learn the system and acquire modest wealth. Settlers constantly complained about insubordinate Native Americans pursuing lawsuits in the courts. Native American villages were closed to settlers, and the only outsiders admitted were Catholic priests. Contact with the Spanish world remained minimal, and acculturation went little beyond official conversion to Catholicism. Village notaries and scribes were instrumental in preserving Nahuatl in Mexico and Quechua in Peru, making them into functional, written languages. Thus, even in the heartlands of Spanish America, Native American adaptation to the rulers remained limited.

Unfortunately, however, tremendous demographic losses made the Native Americans in the pueblos vulnerable to the loss of their land. Estate owners expanded their holdings, legally and illegally, in spite of the heroic litigation efforts of the villages opposed to this expansion. When the population rebounded, many estates had grown to immense sizes. Villages began to run out of land for their inhabitants. Increasing numbers of Native Americans had to rent land from estate owners or find work on estates as farmhands. They became estranged from their villages, fell into debt peonage, and entered the ranks of the working poor in the countryside or city, bearing the full brunt of colonial inequities.

New England Society   For a long time in the early modern period, the small family farm, where everyone had to work to eke out a precarious living, remained the norm for the majority of New England's population. Family members specializing in construction, carpentry, spinning, weaving, or iron works continued to be restricted to small perimeters around their villages and towns. An acute lack of money and cheap means of transportation hampered the development of market networks in the interior well into the 1770s. The situation was better in the agriculturally more favored colonies in the Mid-Atlantic, especially in Pennsylvania. Here, farmers were able to produce marketable quantities of wheat and legumes for urban markets. The number of plantations in the south rose steadily, demanding increasing numbers of slaves (from 28,000 in 1700 to 575,000 in 1776), although world market fluctuations left planters vulnerable. Except for boom periods in the plantation sector, the rural areas remained largely poor.

Real changes occurred during the early eighteenth century in the urban regions. Large port cities emerged which shipped in textiles and ironwares from Europe in return for timber at relatively cheap rates. The most important were Philadelphia (28,000 inhabitants), New York (25,000), Boston (16,000), and Newport, Rhode Island (11,000). A wealthy merchant class formed, spawning urban strata of professionals (such as lawyers, teachers, and newspaper journalists). Primary school education was provided by municipal public schools as well as some churches, and evening schools for craftspeople existed in some measure. By the middle of the eighteenth century a majority of men could read and write, although female literacy was minimal. Finally, in contrast to Latin America, social ranks in New England were less elaborate.

The Adaptation of the Americas to European Culture

European settlers brought two distinct cultures to the Americas. In the Mid-Atlantic, Caribbean, and Central and South America, they brought with them the Catholic Reformation, a culture and perspective that resisted the New Science of Galileo and the Enlightenment thought of Locke until the late eighteenth century. In the northeast, colonists implanted dissident Protestantism as well as the Anglicanism of Great Britain. The rising number of adherents of the New Science and Enlightenment in northwestern Europe had also a parallel in North America. Settlers and their locally born offspring were proud of their respective cultures, which, even though provincial, were dominant in what they prejudicially viewed as a less civilized, if not barbaric, Native American environment.

Catholic Missionary Work   From the beginning, Spanish and Portuguese monarchs relied heavily on the Catholic Church for their rule in the new American provinces. The pope granted them patronage over the organization and all appointments on the new continents. A strong motive driving many in the church as well as society at large was the belief in the imminent Second Coming of Jesus. This belief was one inspiration for the original Atlantic expansion (see Chapter 16). When the Aztec and Inca Empires fell, members of the Franciscan order, the main proponents of the belief in the imminence of the Second Coming, interpreted it as a sign of the urgent duty to convert the Native Americans to Christianity. If Jesus' kingdom was soon to come, according to this interpretation, all humans in the Americas should be Christians.

Thousands of Franciscan, Dominican, and other preaching monks, later followed by the Jesuits, fanned out among the Native Americans. They baptized them, introduced the sacraments (Eucharist, baptism, confession, confirmation, marriage, last rites, and priesthood), and taught them basic theological concepts of Christianity. The missionaries learned native languages, translated the catechism and New Testament into those languages, and taught the children of the ruling native families how to read and write. Thanks to their genuine efforts to understand the Native Americans on their own terms, a good deal of preconquest Native American culture was recorded without too much distortion.

The role and function of saints as mediators between humans and God formed one element of Catholic Christianity to which Native Americans acculturated early. Good works as God-pleasing human efforts to gain salvation in the afterlife formed another. The veneration of images of the Virgin Mary and pilgrimages to the chapels and churches where they were kept constituted a third element. The best-known example of the last element is Our Lady of Guadalupe, near Mexico City, who in 1531 appeared in a vision to a Native American in the place where the native goddess Tonantzin used to be venerated. On the other hand, the Spanish Inquisition also operated in the Spanish and Portuguese colonies, seeking to limit the degree to which Catholicism and traditional religion mingled. The church treaded a fine line between enforcement of doctrine and leniency toward what it determined were lax or heretical believers.

Education and the Arts   The Catholic Reformation expressed itself also in the organization of education. The Franciscans and Dominicans had offered general

Spanish Cruelty to Incas.
Felipe Guamán Poma de Ayala,
a Peruvian claiming noble
Inca descent, was a colonial
administrator, well educated
and an ardent Christian. He is
remembered today as a biting
critic of the colonial administration and the clergy, whom
he accused of mistreating and
exploiting the Andean population,
as in this colored wood print.

education to the children of settlers early on and, in colleges, trained graduates for missionary work. The first New World universities, such as Santo Domingo (1538), Mexico City, and Lima (both 1553), taught theology, church law, and Native American languages. Under the impact of the Jesuits, universities broadened the curriculum, offering degrees also in secular law, Aristotelian philosophy, the natural sciences, and medicine. Although the universities did not admit the New Sciences and Enlightenment of northwestern Europe into their curriculum, there was nevertheless considerable scientific research on tropical diseases, plants, and animals as a counterbalance. The vast extent of this research, long kept secret by the Spanish and Portuguese monarchs from their European competitors, is becoming gradually known only now.

Furthermore, missionary monks collected and recorded Native American manuscripts and oral traditions, such as the Aztec *Anales de Tula* and the Maya *Popol Vuh*. Others wrote histories and ethnographies of the Taíno, Aztec, Maya, Inca, and Tupí peoples. Bartolomé de las Casas, Toribio Motolonía de Benavente, Bernardino de Sahagún, Diego de Landa, Bernabé Cobo, and Manoel da Nóbrega are merely a handful of noteworthy authors who wrote about the Native Americans. Many labored for years, worked with legions of informers, and produced monumental tomes.

A number of Native American and mestizo chroniclers, historians, and commentators on the early modern state and society are similarly noteworthy. Muñoz Camargo was a Tlaxcaltecan; Fernando de Alva Ixtlixóchitl and Fernando Alvarado Tezózomoc were Mexican mestizos; and Juan de Santa Cruz Pachacuti Yamqui and Felipe Inca Garcilaso de la Vega were Peruvian mestizos, all writing on their native regions. Felipe Guamán Poma de Ayala (ca. 1535–1616), a native Peruvian, is of particular interest. He accompanied his 800-page manuscript, entitled (in English translation) *The First New Chronicle and Good Government*, with some 400 drawings of daily-life activities in the Peruvian villages. These drawings provide us with invaluable cultural details, which would be difficult to render in writing. Unfortunately, King Philip II of Spain, a relentless proponent of the Catholic Reformation, took a dim view of authors writing on Native American society and history. In 1577 he forbade the publication of all manuscripts dealing with what he called idolatry and superstition. Many manuscripts lay hidden in archives and did not see the light of day until modern times.

Protestantism in New England   From the start, religious diversity was a defining cultural trait of English settlements in North America. The spectrum of Christian denominations ranged from a host of English and continental European versions of Protestantism to Anglicanism and a minority of Catholics. As if this spectrum had not been sufficiently broad, dissenters frequently split from the existing denominations, moved into new territory, and founded new settlements. Religiosity was a major characteristic of the early settlers.

An early example of religious splintering was the rise of an antinomian ("anti-law") group within Puritan-dominated Massachusetts. The Puritans dominant in this colony generally recognized the authority of the Anglican Church but strove to move it toward Protestantism from within. The preachers and settlers represented in the General Court, as their assembly was called, were committed to the Calvinist balance between "inner" personal grace obtained from God and "outer" works according to the law. The antinomian group, however, digging deep into early traditions in Christianity, advocated an exclusive commitment to inner grace through spiritual perfection.

Their leader was Anne Hutchinson, an early and tireless proponent of women's rights and an inspiring preacher. She was accused of arguing that she could recognize those believers in Calvinist Protestantism who were predestined for salvation and that these believers would be saved even if they had sinned. After a power struggle with the deeply misogynistic magistrates opposed to influential women, the General Court prevailed and forced the antinomians to move to Rhode Island in 1638.

The New Sciences in the New World. This painting by Samuel Collings, *The Magnetic Dispensary* (1790), shows how men and women, of lay background, participated in scientific experiments in the English colonies of North America, similar to educated middle-class people in western Europe at the same time.

The example is noteworthy because it led to the founding of Harvard College in 1636 by the General Court. Harvard was the first institution of higher learning in North America, devoted to teaching the "correct" balanced Calvinist Protestantism. Later, the college functioned as the main center for training the colony's ministers in Puritan theology and morality, although it was not affiliated with any specific denomination.

New Sciences Research　As discussed in Chapter 17, the New Sciences had found their most hospitable home in northwestern Europe by default. The rivalry between Protestantism and Catholicism had left enough of an authority-free space for the New Sciences to flourish. Under similar circumstances—intense rivalry among denominations—English North America also proved hospitable to the New Sciences. An early practitioner was Benjamin Franklin (1706–1790), who began his career as a printer, journalist, and newspaper editor. Franklin founded the University of Pennsylvania (1740), the first secular university in North America, and the American Philosophical Society (1743), the first scientific society. This hospitality for the New Sciences in North America was quite in contrast to Latin America, where a uniform Catholic Reformation prevented its rise.

Witch Hunts　In the last decade of the seventeenth century, a high level of religious intensity and rivalry was at the root of a witchcraft frenzy which seized New England. The belief in witchcraft was the survival on the popular level of the ancient concept of a shared mind or spirit that allows people to influence each other, either positively or negatively. Witches, male and female, were persons exerting a negative influence, or black magic, on their victims. In medieval Europe, the church had kept witchcraft out of sight, but in the wake of Protestantism and the many challenges to church authority it had become more visible. In the North American colonies, with no overarching religious authority, the visibility of witchcraft was particularly high.

Witch Trial. In the course of the 1600s, in the relatively autonomous English colonies of North America, more persons were accused, tried, and convicted of witchcraft than anywhere else. Of the 140 persons coming to trial between 1620 and 1725, 86 percent were women. Three witch panics are recorded: Bermuda, 1651; Hartford, Connecticut, 1652–1665; and Salem, Massachusetts, 1692–1693. This anonymous American woodcut of the early 1600s shows one method to try someone for witchcraft: swim or float if guilty, or sink if innocent.

The one case where this sensitivity erupted into hysteria was that of Salem, Massachusetts. Here, the excitement erupted in 1692 with Tituba, a Native American slave from Barbados who worked in the household of a pastor. Tituba practiced voodoo, the West African–originated, part-African and part-Christian religious practice of influencing others. When a young daughter and niece in the pastor's household suffered from convulsions, mass rioting broke out, in which 20 women accused of being witches were executed, although Tituba, ironically, survived. A new governor finally calmed the passions and restored order.

Revivalism   Religious fervor expressed itself also in periodic Protestant renewal movements, among which the "Great Awakening" of the 1730s and 1740s was the most important. The main impulse for this revivalist movement came from the brothers John and Charles Wesley, two Methodist preachers in England who toured Georgia in 1735. Preachers from other denominations joined, all exhorting Protestants to literally "start anew" in their relationship with God. Fire-and-brimstone sermons rained down on the pews, reminding the faithful of the absolute sovereignty of God, the depravity of humans, predestination to hell and heaven, the inner experience of election, and salvation by God's grace alone. Thus, revivalism, recurring with great regularity to the present, became a potent force in Protestant America, at opposing purposes with secular founding-father constitutionalism.

Putting It All Together

During the period 1500–1800 the contours of a new pattern in which the Americas formed a resource-rich and warm-weather extension of Europe took shape. During this time, China and India continued to be the most populous and wealthiest agrarian–urban regions of the world. Scholars have estimated China's share of the world economy during this period as comprising 40 percent. India probably did not lag far behind. In 1500, Europe was barely an upstart, forced to defend itself against the push of the Ottoman Empire into eastern Europe and the western Mediterranean. But its successful conquest of Iberia from the Muslims led to the discovery of the Americas. Possession of the Americas made Europe similar to China and India in that it now encompassed, in addition to its northerly cold climates, subtropical and tropical regions which produced rich cash crops as well as precious metals. Over the course of 300 years, with the help of its American extension, Europe narrowed the gap between itself and China and India, although it was only after the beginning of industrialization, around 1800, that it eventually was able to close this gap.

Narrowing the gap, of course, was not a conscious policy in Europe. Quite the contrary, because of fierce competition both with the Ottoman Empire and internally, much of the wealth Europe gained in the Americas, especially silver, was wasted on warfare. The centralizing state, created in part to support war, ran into insurmountable budgetary barriers, which forced Spain into several state bankruptcies. Even mercantilism, a logical extension of the centralizing state, had limited effects. Its centerpiece, state support for the export of manufactures to the American colonies, functioned unevenly. The Spanish and Portuguese governments, with weak urban infrastructures and low manufacturing capabilities, especially in textiles, were unable to enforce this state-supported trade until the eighteenth century and even then only in very limited ways. France and especially England practiced mercantilism more successfully but were able to do so in the Americas only from the late seventeenth century onward, when their plantation systems began to take shape. Although the American extension of Europe had the potential of making Europe self-sufficient, this potential was realized only partially during the colonial period.

A fierce debate has raged over the question of the degree of wealth the Americas added to Europe. On the one hand, considerable quantitative research has established that the British slave trade for sugar plantations added at best 1 percent to the British gross domestic product (GDP). The profits from the production of sugar on the English island of Jamaica may have added another 4 percent to the British GDP. Without doubt, private slave-trading and sugar-producing enterprises were at times immensely profitable to individuals and groups, not to mention the mining of silver through forced labor. In the larger picture, however, these profits were considerably smaller if one takes into account the immense waste of revenues on military ventures—hence, the doubts raised by scholars today about large gains made by Europe through its American colonial acquisitions.

On the other hand, the European extension to the Americas was clearly a momentous event in world history. It might have produced dubious overall profits for Europe, but it definitely encouraged the parting of ways between Europe and Asia and Africa, once a new scientific–industrial society began to emerge around 1800.

▶ For additional resources, including maps, primary sources, visuals, and quizzes, please go to www.oup.com/us/vonsivers. Please see the Further Resources section at the back of the book for additional readings and suggested websites.

Against the Grain

Juana Inés de la Cruz

I n the wake of the Protestant and Catholic Reformations of the 1500s, it was no longer unusual for European women to pursue higher education. In the considerably more conservative Latin American colonies of Spain, Juana Inés de la Cruz (1651–1695) was less fortunate, even though her fame as the intellectually most brilliant figure of the seventeenth century in the colonies endured.

De la Cruz was the illegitimate child of a Spanish immigrant father and a Creole mother. She grew up on the hacienda of her maternal grandfather, in whose library she secretly studied Latin, Greek, and Nahuatl, and also composed her first poems. Unable as a woman to be admitted to the university in Mexico City, de la Cruz nevertheless was fortunate to receive further education from the wife of the vice regent of New Spain. In order to continue her studies and eschewing married life in the ruling class, in 1668 she entered a convent. Here, she continued to study and write hundreds of poems, comedies, religious dramas, and theological texts. Her seminars with courtiers and scholarly visitors were a major attraction in Mexico City.

In 1688, however, she lost her protection at court with the departure of her vice-regal supporters for Spain. Her superior, the archbishop of Mexico, was an open misogynist, and even though her confessor and the bishop of Puebla were admirers, their admiration had limits. A crisis came in 1690 when the bishop of Puebla published de la Cruz's critique of a famous sermon of 1650 by the Portuguese Jesuit António Vieira on Jesus' act of washing his disciples' feet, together with his own critique of de la Cruz. The complex theological arguments addressed the question of whether the foot washing was an inversion of the master/slave (Vieira) or master/servant (de la Cruz) relationship—a theological question unresolved in the Gospels, as well as among the Christian churches in the subsequent centuries. De la Cruz viewed Vieira's interpretation as more hierarchical/male and her own interpretation as more humble/female.

A year later, in 1691, de la Cruz wrote a highly spirited, lengthy riposte to the bishop's apparently well-meaning advice to her in his critique to be more conscious of her status as a woman. Her message was clear: Even though women had to be silent in church, as St. Paul had taught, neither study nor writing were prohibited for women. Before the church could censor her, in 1693 Juana Inés de la Cruz stopped writing. She died two years later.

- **Why were the Latin American colonies more socially conservative than Europe?**

- **Was de la Cruz right to stop her correspondence with the Mexican clergy in 1693?**

Thinking Through Patterns

▶ **What is the significance of western Europeans acquiring the Americas as a warm-weather extension of their northern continent?**

In their role as supplementary subtropical and tropical extensions of Europe, the Americas exerted considerable impact on Europe's changing position in the world. First, Europe acquired large quantities of precious metals, which its two largest competitors, India and China, lacked. Second, with its new access to warm-weather agricultural products, Europe rose to a position of agrarian autonomy similar to that of India and China. In terms of resources, compared with the principal religious civilizations of India and China, Europe grew between 1550 and 1800 from a position of inferiority to one of near parity.

Because the numbers of Europeans who emigrated to the Americas was low for most of the colonial period—just 300,000 Spaniards left for the New World between 1500 and 1800—they never exceeded the numbers of Native Americans or African slaves. The result was a highly privileged settler society that held superior positions on the top rung of the social hierarchy. In principle, given an initially large indigenous population, labor was cheap and should have become more expensive as diseases reduced the Native Americans. In fact, labor always remained cheap, in part because of the politically supported institution of forced labor and in part because of racial prejudice.

▶ **What was the main pattern of social development in colonial America during the period 1500–1800?**

▶ **Why and how did European settlers in South and North America strive for self-government, and how successful were they in achieving their goals?**

Two contrasting patterns characterized the way in which European colonies were governed. The Spanish and Portuguese crowns, primarily interested in extracting minerals and warm-weather products from the colonies, had a strong interest in exercising as much centralized control over their possessions in the Americas as they could. In contrast, the British crown granted self-government to the North American colonies from the start, in part because the colonies were initially far less important economically and in part because of a long tradition of self-rule at home. Nevertheless, even though Latin American settlers achieved only partial self-rule in their towns and cities, they destroyed central rule indirectly through the purchase of offices. After financial reforms, Spain and Portugal reestablished a degree of central rule through the appointment of officers from the home countries.

Chapter 19 1450–1800

African Kingdoms, the Atlantic Slave Trade, and the Origins of Black America

I t was a claim the Catholic Capuchin monks of the kingdom of Kongo had just vigorously denounced as a heretical abomination. Dona Beatriz Kimpa Vita (1684–1706), it was said, had been reborn as St. Anthony of Padua. For many subjects of the kingdom, however, this claim was perfectly reasonable as part of an African Christian spirituality in which a gifted person could enter other people's minds and assume their identity. But the monks prevailed. One of the claimants to the throne of Kongo had Dona Beatriz condemned after a trial and burned at the stake.

Dona Beatriz had been intellectually precocious. In her childhood, her family had her initiated in a *kimpasi* enclosure as a *nganga marinda* (a Kikongo word derived from "knowledge" or "skill"). Such enclosures at the edges of towns and cities had become common and contained altars with crosses and censers (for burning incense). They also, however, included statues believed to be capable of recognizing evildoers, animal claws to grab them, horns to mark the line between the worlds of nature and the spirit, and animal tails as symbols of power. In her initiation ceremony, the head woman of the enclosure put the young Dona Beatriz into a trance that enabled her to

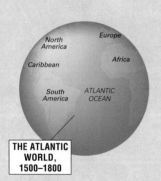

THE ATLANTIC WORLD, 1500–1800

ABOVE: In this watercolor by Capuchin monk Antonio Cavazzi (1621–1678), a European monk and Kongo natives participate in a religious procession.

recognize and repel all the troubling forces that might disturb a person or the community. The people in Kongo were very much aware, however, that not all *ngangas* were benevolent. Some *ngangas* were thought to misuse their spiritual powers and engage in witchcraft. For the missionary Capuchin monks, preaching the Catholic Reformation, all *ngangas* were seen as witches. Whether the young Dona Beatriz was intimidated by their denunciations or not, she followed the church's rulings, renounced her initiation, married, and pursued the domestic life of any other young woman in Kongo society.

But Dona Beatriz's spiritual path did not end here. In 1704, she again underwent a series of deep religious transformations in which she "died," only to be reborn as St. Anthony of Padua (1195–1231), a Portuguese Franciscan monk and one of the patron saints of Portugal. Devotees of the saint believe he blesses marriages and helps people find lost items. With her new saintly and male identity, more powerful than her earlier one as a *nganga*, Dona Beatriz preached a novel and inspiring vision: She was God's providential figure, arrived to restore the Catholic faith and reunify the kingdom of Kongo, both of which she saw as having been torn asunder during nearly half a century of dynastic disunity and civil war (1665–1709).

After her spiritual rebirth, Dona Beatriz immediately went to Pedro IV, king of Kongo (r. 1695–1718), and his Capuchin ally, the chief missionary Bernardo da Gallo, and accused them of being laggards in their efforts to restore the faith and unity of the kingdom. Pedro, perhaps impressed with her claims and the potential power at her command, temporized in his response. Bernardo, however, subjected Dona Beatriz to an angry interrogation about her faith and alleged saintly possession. In a startling and, for Bernardo, alarming parallel to Martin Luther's arguments nearly two centuries before, Beatriz countered with a remarkable attack on the Catholic cornerstone of sacraments. Intention or faith alone, she argued, not the sacraments of the church, would bring salvation. Unlike Luther, however, Dona Beatriz did not derive her convictions from the letters of St. Paul in the New Testament but from her *nganga* initiation: Here, good intentions distinguished the inspired preacher from the witch.

Unable to arrive at a plan of action, the king and Bernardo let Beatriz go. In a journey reminiscent of that of Joan of Arc, she led a growing crowd of followers to the ruined capital of Kongo, M'banza (called São Salvador by the Portuguese). There, she trained "little Anthonies" as missionaries to convert the Kongolese to her new Antonian-African Christianity. Under the protection of a rival of the king, Beatriz was at the pinnacle of her spiritual power when everything unraveled. Though married, she gave birth to a child conceived with one of her followers. She did so secretly at her ancestral home

Seeing Patterns

▶ What was the pattern of kingdom and empire formation in Africa during the period 1500–1800?

▶ How did patterns of plantation slavery evolve in the Atlantic and the Americas?

▶ What are the historic roots from which modern racism evolved?

Chapter Outline

- African States and the Slave Trade

- American Plantation Slavery and Atlantic Mercantilism

- Culture and Identity in the African Diaspora

- Putting It All Together

in King Pedro's territory, evidently in a deep crisis over her spiritual mission. Allies of the king discovered the lovers by accident and arrested them. They brought them before Pedro, who, in the meantime, had decided to reject Beatriz's challenge and silence her. After a state trial—the church stayed out of the proceedings—Beatriz, her companion, and the baby were executed by the favored means of punishing heretics—burning at the stake.

The story of Dona Beatriz illustrates a major pattern discussed in this chapter: the process by which many Africans adapted their religious heritage to the challenge of European Christianity. Europeans arrived on the western coast of Africa in the fifteenth century as both missionaries and merchants—at times also as slave traders and slave raiders. Africans responded with gold, goods, and their own adaptive forms of Christianity, as well as efforts—as in Kongo, Angola, and Benin—to limit the slave trade in accordance with their own political interests. Elsewhere, however, Africans also exploited and adapted indigenous systems of household, agricultural, administrative, and military slavery to reap voluminous profits from the developing Atlantic human traffic. The unprecedented massive transfer of African slaves to the plantations and mines of the Americas brought to those continents a vast and complex array of peoples from foragers and herders to villagers and city dwellers, representing a wide variety of religious experiences—including those of both Islam and Christianity. In many cases, their cultures would not only survive in the Americas under extraordinarily difficult circumstances but become foundational in the new societies being created there.

African States and the Slave Trade

In the north of sub-Saharan Africa the pattern of Islamic and Christian dynastic state formation that had been ongoing for centuries continued to dominate herder and village societies in the period 1500–1800. An invasion by Muslim forces from Morocco during the sixteenth century, however, ended the trend toward empire building and strengthened the forces of decentralization. By contrast, in the savanna and Great Lakes regions of central Africa, improved agricultural wealth and intensified regional trade helped perpetuate the kingdom formation already under way. An important set of institutions in the chiefdoms and states of Africa was slavery, though its form and character were far different from the chattel slavery that would characterize the Americas. When the Europeans inserted themselves into these systems, they profoundly altered them to benefit their own interests in the production of warm-weather cash crops on American plantations. The implications of the new trade provided both enormous opportunities and horrific challenges for African traders and local leaders. As the Mediterranean slave trade had for Venetian, Genoese, and North African traffickers, the growing Atlantic slave trade appealed to some West African rulers as a path to enhanced wealth and power, and they enriched themselves through warfare, raids, and trading. More often, however, rulers tried by various means to resist what ultimately became the greatest forced migration in human history.

The End of Empires in the North and the Rise of States in the Center

The Eurasian empires with universal ambitions of the premodern world united peoples of many different religions, languages, and ethnic affiliations. Mali (1240–1460) was the first African empire that was similar to the empires of Eurasia in this respect. Mali's successor state, the focus of this section, was the even larger Songhay Empire (1460–1591). Though vast, it lasted only a short time.

Origins of the Songhay   Songhay was initially a tributary state of Mali. It was centered on the city of Gao downstream on the Niger River from the agricultural center of Jenné-jeno and the commercial and scholarly center of Timbuktu. Gao's origins dated to 850, when it emerged as the end point of the eastern trans-Saharan route from Tunisia and Algeria, parallel to the more heavily traveled western route from Morocco. Gao was located at the northern end of the Songhay Empire, near the Niger Bend, and was inhabited by the Songhay, an ethnic grouping composed of herders, villagers, and fishermen.

The Songhay were ethnically distinct from the Soninke of the kingdom of ancient Ghana and the Malinke of the Mali Empire further west. Their homeland was located to the east and southeast of the Niger Bend. At the end of the eleventh century, the leading clans of the Songhay, profiting from the trans-Saharan trade, converted to Islam. Two centuries later the warriors among them assumed positions of leadership as vassals of the *mansa*, or emperor, of Mali.

The Songhay Empire   The Songhay began their imperial expansion in the mid-1400s, toward the end of the dry period in West Africa (1100–1500), during which control of the steppe region was sometimes difficult to maintain. Mali, which had its center in the much wetter savanna, lost its northern outpost, Timbuktu, to the Songhay in 1469. In the following decades, Mali slowly retreated southwestward. Eventually, it became a minor vassal of the Songhay. At its height, the Songhay Empire stretched from Hausaland in the savanna southeast of Gao all the way westward to the Atlantic coast (see Map 19.1).

As in the previous centuries in ancient Ghana and Mali, the decisive difference that elevated the Songhay emperors (*askiyas*) above their vassals was their taxation of the gold trade. The gold fields of the Upper Niger, Senegal, and Black Volta Rivers in the southern rain forest were outside the empire, but merchant clans, often accompanied by troop detachments, transported the gold to Timbuktu and Gao. Here, North African merchants exchanged their Mediterranean manufactures and salt for gold, slaves, and kola nuts. Agents of the *askiyas* in these cities

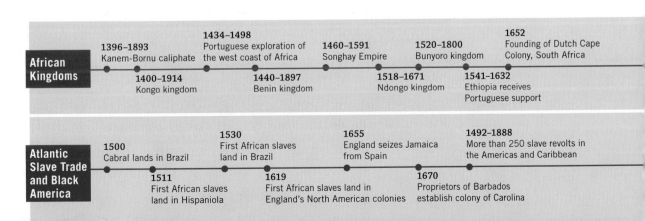

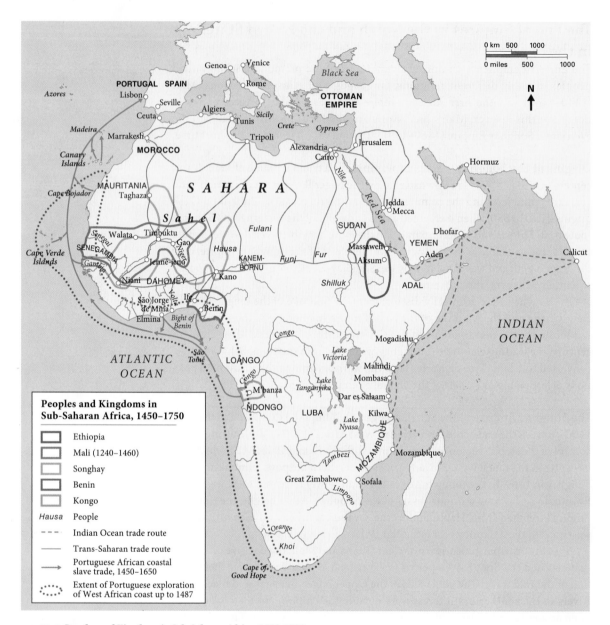

MAP **19.1** **Peoples and Kingdoms in Sub-Saharan Africa, 1450–1750.**

collected market taxes in the form of gold. Agricultural taxes and tributes supported kingdoms; long-distance trade was needed in addition for an empire to come into being.

Songhay's Sudden End   After the initial conquests, the Songhay Empire had little time to consolidate its territory on a more peaceful footing. After just over a century of dominance, the Songhay Empire came to a sudden end in 1591 when a Moroccan force invaded from the north. The invasion was prompted by Moroccan sultans who had successfully driven the Portuguese from their Atlantic coast but were concerned about the flourishing Portuguese trade for gold on the West African coast. They therefore decided to find and occupy the West African gold fields in the rain forest, thus depriving the Portuguese of their supply.

However, after defeating Songhay, they were unable to march any farther, lacking necessary logistical support from Morocco through the Sahara. Although the officers initially turned the Niger delta and bend into a Moroccan province, within a generation they assimilated into the West African royal clans. As a result, imperial politics in West Africa disintegrated, together with much of the trans-Saharan gold trade, which was siphoned off by the Portuguese on what became known as the Gold Coast (modern Ghana).

The Eastern Sahel and Savanna   The steppes between Songhay in the west and Ethiopia in the northeastern highlands near the Red Sea also were home to Islamic regimes governing moderate to large territories. Kanem-Bornu (1396–1893) was a long-lived Islamic realm, calling itself a caliphate, but with a majority of subjects following local African religious traditions. Located in both the steppe and savanna, it was based on a slave and ivory trade with the Mediterranean and on agriculture and fishing for its internal organization on the south side of Lake Chad. Kanem-Bornu's imperial frontier was in the southwest, where it waged long intermittent wars with the savanna kingdoms of Hausaland.

The Hausa kingdoms, numbering about half a dozen, had formed during the height of the Mali-dominated trans-Saharan trade as southeastern extensions of this trade into rain-forest Africa. Although they were under frequent attack by Songhay and Kanem-Bornu during the period 1500–1800, the Hausa kingdoms enjoyed periods of independence during which many of the ruling clans converted to Islam. Like their northern neighbors, they maintained cavalry forces, which—apart from military purposes—served to protect the caravans of the traders. In addition to taxing these traders, the Hausa kings collected dues from the villagers. Craftspeople produced pottery, iron implements and utensils, cotton cloth, basketry, leather goods, and iron weapons. Miners and smiths smelted and forged copper, iron, and steel. Although more agricultural in orientation, the Hausa kingdoms closely resembled their northern neighbors in the steppe.

Farther east, in the steppe between Lake Chad and the Nile, the Fur and the Funj, cattle-breeding clan-lineage federations, converted fully to Islam, from the royal clans down to the commoners. In contrast, in West Africa only the dynasties and merchants became Muslim. Their leaders adopted the title "sultan" and became increasingly Arabized in the period 1500–1800, while Christianity along the upper Nile disappeared completely.

South Central Africa   On the southern side of the rain forest, the eastern part of the southern savanna and the Great Lakes area in central Africa remained outside the reach of the slave trade. As a result, their populations continued to grow. Large numbers of farmer and cattle herder groups, organized in chiefdoms, inhabited these regions. In the eastern savanna, the kingdom of Luba emerged before 1500, while others followed at various intervals thereafter.

A steady increase in regional trade for copper, iron, salt, dried fish, beads, cloth, and palm oil enabled chieftain clans to consolidate their rule and enlarge their holdings into kingdoms. Living in enclosures and surrounded by "courts," or dense ruling-class settlements, kings maintained agricultural domains worked by slaves. Villages nearby delivered tribute in the form of foodstuffs. From the mid-seventeenth century onward, the American-origin staples corn and cassava (manioc) broadened the food supply. Tributaries at some distance delivered prestige goods, especially copper and ironware, as well as beads. At times, the kings mobilized thousands of workers to build moats and earthworks around their courts, which became centers of incipient urbanization processes.

The Great Lakes region, to the north, south, and west of Lake Victoria, was a highly fertile eastward extension of the southern savanna supporting two annual crops of sorghum and sesame, as well as banana groves and herds of cattle. Traders distributed salt, iron, and dried fish. Agriculture, cattle breeding, and trade supported intense political competition in the region. Small agricultural–mercantile kingdoms shared the region, but sometime in the sixteenth century cattle breeders—the Luo, relatives of the Shilluk—arrived from southern Sudan and shook up the existing political and social structures. Pronounced disparities in cattle ownership emerged on the rich pasture lands. Cattle lords, bolstered by their new wealth and status, rose as competitors of the kings.

North of Lake Victoria, the Bunyoro kingdom, based on agriculture and regional trade, held the cattle lords at bay, while on the south side of the lake the cattle lords created new small kingdoms. After a while cattle breeders and farmers settled into more or less unequal relations of mutual dependence. Under the colonial system in the nineteenth century, these unequal relations froze into a caste system in which the minority Tutsi cattle breeders were continually at odds with the majority Hutu farmers. (The tensions in this social situation were part of a combination of factors that ultimately led to the mass killings and genocide committed by the Hutus against the Tutsis in the modern state of Rwanda in 1993–1994.) Farther south the pre-1500 tradition of gold-mining kingdoms, such as Great Zimbabwe, continued. But here the interaction of Africa with Portugal set the kingdoms on a different historical trajectory.

Portugal's Explorations along the African Coast and Contacts with Ethiopia

The Portuguese expansion into North Africa and the exploration of the African coast were outgrowths of both the *Reconquista* and crusading impulses. Mixed in with these religious motives was the practical necessity of financing the journeys of exploration through profits from trade. The combination of the two guided Portugal within a single century around the African continent to India. Along the coast, the Portuguese established forts as points of protection for their merchants. In Ethiopia they supported the Christian kingdom there with military aid, providing protection against the Ottomans in Yemen, just across the Red Sea.

Chartered Explorations in West Africa   Henry the Navigator (1394–1460), brother of the ruling king, a principal figure of the Portuguese *Reconquista* and chief embodiment of the crusading zeal, occupied the Moroccan port of Ceuta in 1415. He claimed that Ceuta had been Christian prior to the Berber-Arab conquest and subsequent Islamization of Iberia. He also wished to renew crusading for the reconquest of Jerusalem, lost to the Muslims in 1291. But the merchant wing of the Lisbon court was wary of the military expenditures. During the fifteenth century, campaigns for the military occupation of other cities of Morocco, mostly along the Atlantic coast, alternated with voyages financed by Portuguese groups of merchants and aristocrats for commerce along the West African coast.

In 1434, mariners discovered that ships could overcome adverse currents and winds and return from the West African coast by sailing out into the Atlantic, setting course for the newly discovered islands of the Canaries, Madeira, and Azores, before turning east toward Lisbon. It was the impossibility of returning along the coast from the southern part of West Africa that had doomed all previous efforts. Sailors either had to return by land, via the Sahara to the Mediterranean, or they disappeared without a trace. Thus, sailing south in the Atlantic and developing a route by which to return was a decisive step toward circumnavigating the continent.

Between 1434 and 1472, through a combination of royally chartered, merchant-financed voyages, as well as public state-organized expeditions, Portuguese mariners explored the coast as far east as the Bight of Benin. Trade items included European woolens and linens, which were exchanged for gold, cottons, and Guinea pepper. Small numbers of African slaves were included early on as trade items, mostly through purchases from chieftains and kings. Several uninhabited tropical islands off the coast were discovered during this time, and the Portuguese used slaves for the establishment of sugar plantations on them. They shipped other slaves to Europe for domestic employment, adding to the long-standing Mediterranean and trans-Saharan practice of household slavery.

Portugal and Ethiopia   By the second half of the fifteenth century, private merchant interests focused on developing trade in West Africa provided few incentives for further explorations. It required the military wing of the Portuguese court to revive crusading. From 1483 through 1486 the king organized state expeditions for further expansion from the Bight of Benin south to the Congo River. Here, mariners sailed upstream in hopes of linking up with Prester John (see Chapter 16), a mythical Christian king believed to live in Ethiopia or India who could help Portugal in the reconquest of Jerusalem. Instead of Prester John, the Portuguese mariners encountered the ruler of the powerful kingdom of Kongo, who converted to Christianity and established close relations with Portugal.

A few years later, after Christopher Columbus had sailed to the Americas for Castile–Aragon in 1492, the Portuguese crown continued the search for a way to Ethiopia or India, a route presumed to lie around the southern tip of Africa. Eventually, Vasco da Gama circumnavigated the southern tip, established trade outposts in Swahili city-states of East Africa, and reached India in 1498. From this point Portuguese development of the Indian spice trade grew in importance.

The Portuguese discovered in the early sixteenth century that the Ethiopian kingdom was extremely weak in the face of the aggressive Muslim sultanate of Adal, on the Red Sea to the east. Until the end of the fifteenth century, Ethiopia had been a powerful Coptic Christian kingdom in the highlands of northeastern Africa. Its people practiced a productive plow-based agriculture for wheat and teff (a local grain), and its kings controlled a rich trade of gold, ivory, animal skins, and slaves from the southern Sudan through the Rift Valley to the Red Sea. Possession of a Red Sea port for this trade, however, was a bone of contention between Ethiopia and Adal during the first half of the sixteenth century.

Prester John. The legend of Prester John, a Christian ruler whose lost kingdom in northeast Africa, surrounded by Muslims and pagans, captivated the European imagination from the twelfth through the seventeenth centuries. Purportedly a descendant of one of the Three Magi, Prester John (or Presbyter John) presided over a realm full of riches and fabulous creatures.

A Christian incursion into Muslim territory in 1529 triggered a response by Adal in the form of a furiously destructive Muslim holy war. Ethiopia would have been destroyed in this war had it not been for the timely arrival in 1541 of a Portuguese fleet with artillery and musketeers. For its part, Adal received Ottoman Muslim artillery and musketeer support from Yemen, but 2 years later, after several fierce battles, the Christians prevailed.

Ethiopia paid a high price for its victory, however. Adal Muslim power was destroyed, but in its place, the Ottomans took over the entire west coast of the Red Sea, mostly in order to keep out Portugal. Non-Christian cattle breeders from the southwest occupied the Rift Valley, which separated the northern and southern Ethiopian highlands and had been depopulated during the Christian–Muslim wars. Cut off by the newcomers, Christians in the southern highlands were left to their own devices, surviving in small states. Small numbers of Portuguese stayed in Ethiopia, with Jesuit missionaries threatening to dominate the Ethiopian church, which had long followed its own traditions, as well as the kings. In 1632 the Ethiopian king expelled the Jesuits and consolidated the kingdom as a shrunken power within much smaller borders.

Initially, Ethiopian culture continued to be active under a strong court, expressed mostly through theological writings and iconic paintings. But from about 1700 Ethiopia decentralized into provincial lordships with little interest in their cultural heritage. Only in the mid-nineteenth century, in response to the Western challenge, did the kings take back their power from the provincial lords.

Coastal Africa and the Atlantic Slave Trade

After Portuguese mariners had circumnavigated Africa, they initially focused on developing their spice trade with India. Gradually, however, they also built their Atlantic slave trade, which took off in the early seventeenth century, to be followed by mariner-merchants from other European countries. To understand the pattern underlying the slave trade from 1500–1800 it is crucial to be aware of the importance of slavery within the African historical context. Different kinds of

(a) **Elmina as it appeared in a European etching from 1562.**

(b) **Outer defensive walls.**

Elmina. This town in present-day Ghana was, along with the village of São Jorge da Mina, the first Portuguese fortified trading post on the African coast, from 1482 until it passed to the Dutch in 1637. Merchants used it for storing the goods they traded and for protection in case of conflicts with Africans. It was staffed by a governor and 20–60 soldiers along with a priest, surgeon, apothecary, and a variety of craftspeople. Throughout the first half of the sixteenth century Elmina was also the center of Portuguese slaving activities.

slavery existed in a number of regions in Africa. In many places, a form of slavery existed in the place of land ownership. The more slaves a household, clan leader, chief, or king owned, to work at home or in the fields, the wealthier he was. This form of **household slavery** was the most common variety.

Trade Forts   Early on, in the 1440s, Portuguese mariners raided the West African coast in the region defined by the Senegal and Gambia Rivers—Senegambia—for slaves. But they suffered losses since the performance and reliability of their muskets was not yet superior to the precisely aimed poisoned arrows of the Africans. Furthermore, dwelling in a rain forest with its many rivers opening to the coast, West Africans possessed a well-developed tradition of boat building and coastal navigation. Boats hollowed out from tree trunks could hold as many as 50 warriors. These warriors paddled swiftly through the estuaries and mangrove swamps along the coast and picked off the mariners from their caravels if they approached the coast in a hostile manner. The Portuguese thus learned to set foot on the beach in a less threatening way and began what developed into a lucrative coastal fort trade in a variety of items, including slaves.

Through treaties with local African leaders, Portugal acquired the right to build posts or forts from which to trade. Africans involved in trade in these regions produced a variety of items that were soon in demand in Europe. They wove colorful cotton cloth and wore it by the yard. A particular kind of bark or leaf cloth from central West Africa was at times highly sought in Portugal and the Caribbean. For a long time, Senegambian mats were preferred as bedcovers in Europe. In many places, Africans smelted iron and forged steel that was of higher quality than that of iron-poor Portugal.

Trade, as in most other parts in the world during the period 1500–1800, was for expensive luxury goods, not ordinary articles of daily life. Merchants had to be able to achieve high profits while carrying comparatively little to weigh them down. African rulers purchased luxuries in order to engage in conspicuous consumption, fashion display, and lavish gift giving—all ways to enhance their status and cement power relations. They sold slaves to the Europeans in a similar fashion, as luxuries in return for luxuries. Thus, scarcity raised demand on both sides in their respective quest for luxury items.

Household slavery: African chiefs and kings maintained large households of retainers, such as administrators, soldiers, domestics, craftspeople, and farmers; many among these were slaves, acquired through raids and wars but also as a form of punishment for infractions of royal, chiefly, or clan law.

Portuguese Traders. This brass plaque, from about the middle of the sixteenth century, decorated the palace of the Benin *obo* and shows two Portuguese traders. The fact they are holding hands suggests that they could be father and son.

African Slavery Sub-Saharan Africa—with few long rivers and immense equatorial rain forests—was a vast region with enormous hurdles to a shift in patterns from local self-sufficiency to exchange agriculture and urbanization. Inland exchanges of food for manufactured goods over distances greater than 20 miles were for the most part prohibitively expensive. Human portage or donkey transport, the only available forms of moving goods, were limited to highly valuable merchandise, such as salt, copper, and iron. Everything else was manufactured within self-sufficient households, such as pottery, textiles, mats, basketry, utensils, implements, leather goods, and weapons, alongside a full range of agricultural goods.

Such self-sufficiency required large households. In villages with limited outside trade, the polygamous household with the largest number of males and females employed at home and in the fields was the wealthiest. To increase his wealth further, a household master often raided neighboring villages and acquired captives, to be enslaved and put to work inside and outside the household. Not surprisingly, therefore, slave raiding and household slavery were general features in sub-Saharan African societies, though some peoples like the San of southern Africa lacked the institution altogether. The more stratified slaveholding societies were—with chiefly or royal institutions such as central administrations, armies, and juridical and fiscal offices—the more slaves rose into positions of responsibility and, frequently, autonomy. This was especially the case in the large empires like Mali and Songhay, where a variety of institutions of servitude existed outside of the category of household slaves. Thus, as in a number of societies outside of Africa, the varieties of slavery in sub-Saharan Africa tended to be highly complex and flexible in structure and function.

Limited Slave Trade from Benin When Portugal began the slave trade to supply labor for its sugar plantations on West African offshore islands, African chiefs and kings had to evaluate the comparative value of slaves for their households or for sale. The kingdom of Benin in the rain-forest region west of the Niger delta was an early example of this calculation. The ruler Ewuare (r. 1440–1473) was the first to rise to dominance over chiefs (*azuma*) and assume the title of king (*obo*). Through conquests in all directions, Ewuare acquired large numbers of slaves who were employed in his army and for the construction of extensive earthworks protecting the capital, Benin City.

Early trade contacts between Portuguese mariners and Benin intensified when the successor of Ewuare granted permission to build a fort on the coast in 1487. But the king kept the exchange of palm oil, ivory, woolens, beads, pepper, and slaves for guns, powder, metalware, salt, and cottons under close control. A generation later, when the kings prohibited the sale of male slaves, the Portuguese promptly abandoned their fort. Later, a compromise was reached whereby a limited number of slaves were traded, perhaps some 30 percent of the total trade volume between Portugal and Benin, in return for firearms. The kingdom admitted missionaries and members of the dynasty acculturated to the Portuguese, making Benin increasingly economically diversified and culturally complex.

Slave exports remained restricted during the following two centuries, when Benin was a strong, centralized state. Under subsequent weak kings, decentralization set in. Provincial chiefs began to compete with each other, requiring increased numbers of firearms. To buy more weapons, toward the end of the seventeenth century a weak Benin palace lifted the restrictions on the slave trade. Even more weapons were purchased and slaves were sold during a civil war in the first half of the eighteenth century. But the kingdom reunified, and the palace never lost complete control over Benin's trade with the Portuguese and, from the mid-seventeenth century onward, Dutch and British merchants. Compared to the slave trade farther west on the West African coast, the large centralized kingdom of Benin with its high internal demand for slave labor remained a modest exporter of slaves and thus retained a considerable degree of autonomy and agency.

The Kingdom of Kongo   Farther south, on the central West African coast, the Portuguese established trade relations with several coastal kingdoms, among which Kongo and Ndongo were the most important. These kingdoms were located south of the Congo River, with rain forest to the north and savanna to the south. Kongo, the oldest and most centralized kingdom in the region, emerged about 1400, or a century before the arrival of the Portuguese. Its capital, M'banza (São Salvador), was 20 miles inland in the fertile highlands. With 60,000 inhabitants in the sixteenth century, its size was comparable to such European cities as London, Amsterdam, Moscow, and Rome at the time. M'banza also contained a large palace population and a royal domain, where slaves farmed sorghum, millet, and corn.

Within a radius of some 20 miles, the kings governed a region of about 300,000 independent villagers directly. To defend their rule, they relied on a standing army of 5,000 troops, including 500 musketeers, in the sixteenth century. They appointed members of the royal family as governors, who were entitled to rents but were also obliged to deliver taxes in kind to the palace. In addition, the kings collected a head tax in the form of cowrie shells, an indication that farmers engaged in a limited form of trading their agricultural surplus on markets in the capital to obtain the shells for the tax. This region of direct rule was marked by a unified law and administration. Royal appointees traveled around to represent the royal writ. Farther away, vassal kings, called dukes (Portuguese *duque*), governed and sent tribute or gifts to the capital. They sometimes rebelled and broke away; thus, the territory of Kongo, similar to that of Songhay, shifted constantly in size.

The kings of Kongo converted to Christianity early and sent members of the ruling family to Portugal for their education. Portuguese missionaries converted the court and a number of provincial chiefs. Among the ruling class, many read and wrote Portuguese and Latin fluently, impressing European aristocrats with their comportment whenever they went on missions. Muslim ethnic stereotypes against "reddish" Christians and Christian stereotypes and patronizing attitudes against dark Muslims, called *moros*, and, by extension, black people from sub-Saharan Africa had existed for a long time in Iberia and expressed themselves in Portugal's dealings with Kongo.

Kongolese royalty wore Portuguese dress, listened to church music and hymns, and drank wine imported from the Canaries. Lay assistants converted many urban and villager commoners to Catholicism, and schoolmasters instructed children at churches and chapels. The result was an African Creole culture, in which the veneration of territorial and ancestral spirits was combined with Catholicism. As the story of Dona Beatriz Kimpa Vita demonstrates, this Creole culture should not be viewed as a simple copy of European culture. Instead, as with the Creole cultures of the Americas, it was a creative adaptation of traditions: in this case, of Portuguese Catholicism to the indigenous African spiritual and cultural heritage, in the same way that East and West Africa adapted to Coptic Christianity or Islam and represented genuine variations of African culture.

Kongo began to sell slaves to Portuguese traders as early as 1502 for labor on the sugar plantations of the island of São Tomé. By the mid-1500s, the kings permitted the export of a few thousand slaves a year. But Portugal wanted more slaves, and in 1571 the crusader king Sebastião I (r. 1557–1578), who renewed Henry the Navigator's devotion to territorial conquest, chartered a member of the aristocracy with creating a colony in the adjacent kingdom of Ndongo for the mining of salt and silver by slaves. At first, this holder of the charter assisted the king of Ndongo in defeating rebels; but when his colonial aims became clear, the king turned against him, and a full-scale Portuguese war of conquest and for slaves erupted.

In this war, which lasted with short interruptions from 1579 to 1657, the Portuguese allied themselves with Ibangala bands. The Ibangala were a large group of loosely organized, fierce warriors from the eastern outreaches of Kongo and Ndongo into central Africa who raided in both kingdoms for slaves. Their propaganda as well as their swift campaigns threw the population into fear and turmoil. Tales of cannibalism and the forcible recruitment of child soldiers spread by word of mouth. The Ibangala reputation for fierceness was enhanced by their consumption of large quantities of palm wine and imported Portuguese wine from the Canaries, the latter received from traders in payment for slaves. Together, a few hundred Portuguese musketeers and tens of thousands of Ibangalas raided the kingdoms of Ndongo and Kongo for slaves, often capturing as many as 15,000 a year.

Kongolese Cross of St. Anthony. Considered an emblem of spiritual authority and power, the Christian cross was integrated into Kongo ancestral cults and burial rituals and was believed to contain magical protective properties. In Antonianism, the religious reform movement launched by Dona Beatriz, or Kimpa Vita, in 1704, St. Anthony of Padua, a thirteenth-century Portuguese-born saint, became known as Toni Malau, or "Anthony of Good Fortune," and was the patron of the movement. His image was widely incorporated into religious objects and personal items, such as this cross.

The war reduced the resourceful Queen Nzinga (r. 1624–1663) of Ndongo to a guerilla fighter. In the end, thanks to an alliance with some Ibangalas, she recreated a kingdom, greatly reduced in size, that also engaged in the slave trade. The widening conflict also spilled over into Kongo, where Portuguese and allied Ibangala troops exploited a long civil war (1665–1709) and enslaved even Catholic and Antonian Christians. The war expanded further when new entrants onto the scene, the Dutch West India Company, mistakenly assumed that the small numbers of Portuguese troops would be no match in a quick conquest for the coastal forts. Thanks to Brazilian help, however, Portugal was able to drive out the Dutch. The latter decided to return to a more peaceful trade for slaves from other fortified strongholds on the African west coast.

The Dutch in South Africa   In 1652, the Dutch built a fort on the South African coast to supply fresh water and food to ships traveling around the Cape of Good Hope. Employees of the company, working on time contracts, grew wheat on

Queen Nzinga. In this contemporary engraving, Queen Nzinga is shown conducting negotiations with the Portuguese in 1622. She sits on a slave's back to avoid having to stand in the presence of a person beneath her rank.

small lots and bought cattle from the Khoi, local cattle breeders. A few wealthy landowners imported the first black slaves in 1658, from Dahomey, on the West African coast, to convert the original Dutch smallholdings into larger wheat and grape plantations. Gradually, a culturally Dutch settler society emerged, which included Protestants fleeing religious persecution in France and Germany.

The majority of these settlers were urban craftspeople and traders, while most of the actual farmers employed slaves from Mozambique, the island of Madagascar, and even as far away as Indonesia, the epicenter of Dutch colonial ambitions in the East Indies. Around 1750, there were about 10,000 *Boers* (Dutch for "farmer") in the Cape Colony, easily outnumbered by slaves. Through relentless land expansion into the interior, ranchers destroyed the Khoi, forcing their absorption into other local groups. The Boers governed themselves, following the model of Dutch representative institutions. Their descendants, who called themselves "Afrikaners," would one day fight the Zulu for land and the British for independence and create the system of apartheid in South Africa. Today, they share political power and a troubled political legacy with their black African countrymen.

American Plantation Slavery and Atlantic Mercantilism

The patterns of African slavery were quite different from the patterns of American plantation slavery. While European slave traders exploited existing African slave systems, the American plantation slave system had its roots in the eastern Christian religious civilization of Byzantium. There, the Roman institution of agricultural estate slavery survived, in both law and practice. Imperial estates on the Mediterranean islands of Cyprus and Crete employed Muslim prisoners as well as captives from the Russian steppes as slaves for the cultivation of such labor-intensive crops as wine and olive oil. After 1191, when crusaders conquered Cyprus from Byzantium, crusader landlords and Venetian and Genoese merchants expanded into sugar production, which had been introduced in the eastern Mediterranean by Arabs in the period 800–1000. Two and a half centuries later, Venetians, Spaniards, and Portuguese established slave-based sugarcane plantations on the islands of Madeira, the Canaries, and São Tomé off the West African coast.

The Special Case of Plantation Slavery in the Americas

Plantation slavery: Economic system in which slave labor was used to grow cash crops such as sugarcane, tobacco, and cotton on large estates.

In examining the rise and perpetuation for more than three centuries of the patterns of American **plantation slavery**, a number of questions arise: How many Africans were forcibly taken from Africa to the Americas? Who were they, and who were the people who exploited their labor? What institutions were created to capture, transport, supply, and work slaves? What did the labor of the African slaves help to build? And, perhaps most of all, why did this system develop the way it did—and last so long?

Numbers   The enslavement of Africans for labor in the Western Hemisphere constituted the largest human migration—voluntary or involuntary—in world history before the later nineteenth century. Though it is estimated that millions of Africans had earlier been taken into servitude in the Muslim world from the eighth to the fourteenth century, their numbers are dwarfed by those shipped across the Atlantic from the fifteenth through the early nineteenth century.

While the figures have been hotly debated by scholars and activists over recent decades, the latest estimates put the numbers of Africans shipped out of Africa at around 12.5 million—more than twice the number taken in the so-called Oriental slave trade to the Middle East and Indian Ocean basin during the period 700–1400. Nearly half of these slaves, 5.8 million, went to Brazil. While historical demographers and other scholars try to determine how many slaves died in the process of being transferred to the African coast after their initial capture and how many more perished at sea, their conclusions are at present only tentative. However, most estimates place the numbers of slaves lost during these transfers at another 1.4 million, or 12 percent, with a total of 11 million reaching the American shores. These figures, it should be noted, exclude the numbers killed in the African slave raids and wars themselves, which will probably never be precisely known (see Map 19.2).

Chattel: Literally, an item of moveable personal property; chattel slavery is the reduction of the status of the slave to an item of personal property of the owner, to dispose of as he or she sees fit.

Chattel Slavery   By the mid-eighteenth century African slaves everywhere in the New World had been reduced to the status of **chattel**. The perfect expression of this condition may be found in the famous Dred Scott decision, handed down by the US Supreme Court a century later, in 1857. In the court's opinion, the chief justice, Roger B. Taney, forcefully stated that black African slaves "had no rights which a white man was bound to respect."

Within this statement we see another qualitatively different element from earlier kinds of slavery: what came to be known as the "color line." While color was sometimes not the determining factor in the early years of American slavery, it had very much come to be that by the eighteenth century. The equation of blackness with slavery prompted assumptions over time of African inferiority and

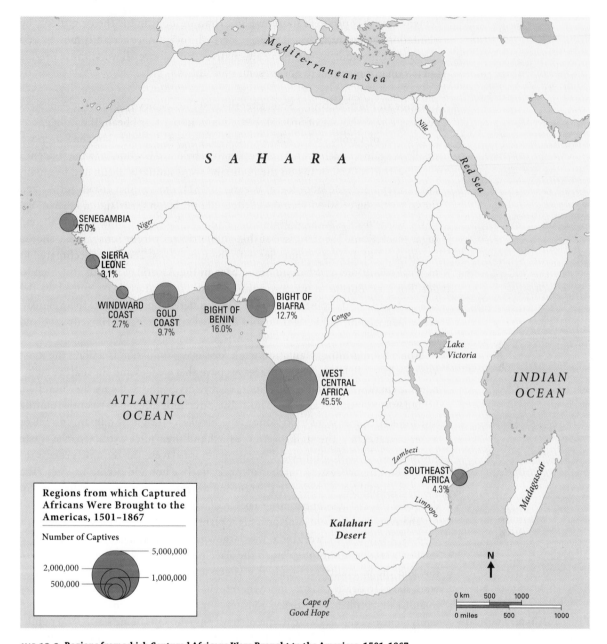

MAP **19.2** **Regions from which Captured Africans Were Brought to the Americas, 1501–1867.**

created the basis for the modern expression of the phenomenon of racism, a problem that has plagued all societies touched by the institutions of African slavery to this day.

Historians have long debated the role of present-day sensibilities and issues in the study of the past. The practice of looking at the past through the lens of the present is called **presentism**. Of course, everyone brings his or her own views and biases along when studying history. Historians, however, consciously try to distance themselves from these while attempting to empathetically enter the past.

Presentism: A bias toward present-day attitudes, especially in the interpretation of history.

Nowhere is this problem more evident than in looking for the origins of the plantation system and African slavery. Here, the origins are certainly modest and distant in time and present many alternatives. But, above all, what those origins led to remains repellent to our present sensibilities.

Caribbean Plantations Soon after the first European voyages to the Americas and the establishment of Spanish settlements in the Caribbean, the indigenous population of Taínos and Caribs all but disappeared, decimated by the European smallpox against which the native peoples were helpless. Beginning in the sixteenth century, Native Americans on the mainland were similarly decimated by small-pox. To replenish the labor force, as early as 1511, the Spanish crown authorized the importation of 50 African slaves for gold mining on the island of Hispaniola. In the following decades thousands more followed for work on newly established sugar plantations. The Africans, at this point primarily from Senegambia, shared a similar set of disease immunities with the Europeans. They were acclimated to tropical conditions and had no home base in the American islands to which to flee. For their European overlords, this made them ideal workers. Indeed, by the late sixteenth century African slaves outnumbered Europeans in the Spanish-controlled islands and in Mexico and Peru, where they were primarily involved in mining.

Apart from mining, plantation work for sugar production is among the most arduous forms of labor. Sugarcane leaves have sharp edges and the mature stalks must be cut down with *machetes*—long, heavy knives. The stalks are then bundled, loaded into a cart, and carried to a mill. The early mills utilized horizontal rotating millstones (later versions used stone or metal rollers) turned by human, animal, or water power. Once the stalks were crushed and their juice extracted, the waste was used as food for animals, or occasionally for slaves. The refining process involved boiling successive batches of juice, itself a hot and taxing process. The charred animal bones added to the refining were often supplemented by those of deceased slaves, thus contributing a particularly sinister element to the process.

The average slave field hand on a sugar plantation was estimated to live just 5 or 6 years. Early on, the workforce was largely male, which meant that there were relatively few children to replenish the slave population. With the price of slaves low and the mortality rate high, it was economically more desirable to literally work slaves to death and buy more than to make the extra investments necessary to cultivate families. Not surprisingly, revolts, work slowdowns, and sabotage of equipment and cargoes were frequent, with punishments being severe and public. Slaves were flogged and branded for minor infractions and maimed, castrated, hanged, burned, and sometimes dismembered for more severe crimes.

Mercantilism: Political theory according to which the wealth derived from the mining of silver and gold and the production of agricultural commodities should be restricted to each country's market, with as little as possible expended on imports from another country.

Mercantilism in Action in the Caribbean With the decline of Spanish power and the rise of the North Atlantic maritime states during the seventeenth century, a profound shift of the political balance in the Caribbean took place. Portugal, Spain, the Netherlands, Great Britain, and France all followed a similar path to enrichment that came to be known as **mercantilism**—that is, when the wealth of the state depends on having the maximum amount of gold and silver in its treasury. Thus, states should keep their economies blocked off from competitors and import as little and export as much as possible. Colonies were seen as vital

Grinding Sugarcane. The steps in the making of refined sugar were elaborate and backbreaking. In the center, a wagon brings the harvested cane in from the fields, while slaves in the foreground sort the stalks under the watchful eyes of an overseer. The wind-powered mill uses rollers to crush the cane and extract its juice for boiling.

to this economic system, because they supplied raw materials to the European homeland and provided safe markets for goods manufactured in the home country.

It followed that one way to enhance your riches was to capture those of your rivals. Thus, from the late sixteenth through the early eighteenth centuries, the navies of the Dutch, English, French, Spanish, and Portuguese all attacked each other's shipping interests and maritime colonies. The Spanish, with their lucrative treasure fleets from Acapulco and through the Caribbean along the Spanish Main, were the favorite targets of all. Moreover, all of these governments issued "letters of marque" allowing warships owned by individuals or companies called **privateers** to prey on the shipping of rival powers for a share in the prize money they obtained. Not surprisingly, a number of individuals also went into this business for themselves as pirates.

The growing trade in plantation commodities from the Caribbean compelled Spain's European competitors to oust the Spanish from their valuable sugar islands. Thus, the rising naval power of England seized Jamaica from Spain in 1655. France, by the mid-seventeenth century the premier continental European power, followed a decade later in seizing the western part of Hispaniola, which came to be called Saint-Domingue.

This process was accompanied by two developments that enhanced the mercantilist economics of both powers. First, English and French as well as Dutch merchants became involved in the African slave trade, usurping the Portuguese near-monopoly on the traffic. The second was that the growing demand for molasses (a syrup that is a by-product of sugar refining) and the even greater popularity of its fermented and distilled end product, rum, pushed both sugar planting and slavery to heights that would not reach their peak until after 1750. As we will see in more detail, sugar, slaves, molasses, and rum form the vital legs of the famous triangular trade that sustained the Atlantic economic system.

Privateers: Individuals or ships granted permission to attack enemy shipping and to keep a percentage of the prize money the captured ships brought at auction; in practice, privateers were often indistinguishable from pirates.

Indentured laborers:
Poor workers enrolled in European states with an obligation to work in the Americas for 5–7 years in return for their prepaid passage across the Atlantic.

"The Negroes are so wilful and loth to leave their own country, that they have often leap'd out of the canoes . . . into the sea, and kept under water until they were drowned. . . . They have a more dreadful apprehension of Barbadoes than we can have of hell."

—Thomas Phillips, "The Voyage of the Ship *Hannibal* of London," 1693

The human toll, however, was appalling. Barbados, for example, was settled initially in 1627 by English planters, who grew tobacco, cotton, indigo, and ginger, employing English and Irish **indentured laborers**. In 1640, however, planters switched to the more profitable sugarcane. English and Irish indentured laborers now proved so unwilling to leave their home countries for Barbados that law courts in the home ports resorted to convicting them on trumped-up charges and sentencing them to "transportation." Many others were tricked or seized by press-gangs and sent there. So great was the mortality of their African counterparts that they had to be shipped to the sugar islands at a rate of two to one in order to keep the population from declining.

The Sugar Empire: Brazil   The Portuguese first planted sugarcane as a crop in Brazil in the 1530s, well before Caribbean planters began to grow it and a generation after the original trade in brazilwood (a red dye) was established. Portuguese colonists turned to the production of sugar because, unlike their counterparts in the Caribbean, Mexico, and Peru, they did not find any gold or silver. Like the Spanish, the Portuguese crown repeatedly issued edicts to the colonists to refrain from enslaving indigenous people for work on the sugar plantations; these edicts, however, were widely ignored. In addition, in the 1530s, the Portuguese trading network on the central African coast began to supply the colony with African slaves. By the end of the century, a dramatic rise in demand for sugar in Europe increased the importation of African slaves, of which the Portuguese carefully cultivated their carrying monopoly. The insatiable demand of the sugar industry for slaves received a further boost in 1680 when enslavement of Indians was finally abolished, and in 1690 the discovery of gold in Minas Gerais, in the interior, led to a gold boom and increased demand for labor even more. Brazil ultimately became the final destination of nearly half of all the slaves transported to the Americas. Indeed, Brazil went on to be the largest slave state in the world, with about two-fifths of its entire population consisting of people of African descent, and was the last country in the Americas to give up the institution, in 1888 (see Map 19.3).

Slavery in British North America

Modern historians have identified a plantation zone which, in 1750, extended unbroken from the Chesapeake Bay in England's North American colonies to Brazil, embracing the entire Caribbean. This zone represented a pattern unprecedented in world history. No system of cash cropping had ever extended over so much territory or brought so much profit to its owners and investors. It created the largest demand for human labor yet seen, which after 1700 was satisfied almost exclusively through the African slave trade. As we noted in the beginning of this section, this in turn created a nearly immutable color line that defined a permanent underclass and identified blackness with slavery and inferiority. Though it was eventually destined to die out in the northernmost British and French possessions as well as the northern United States, legal slavery at one time extended far beyond the plantation zone into what is now Canada.

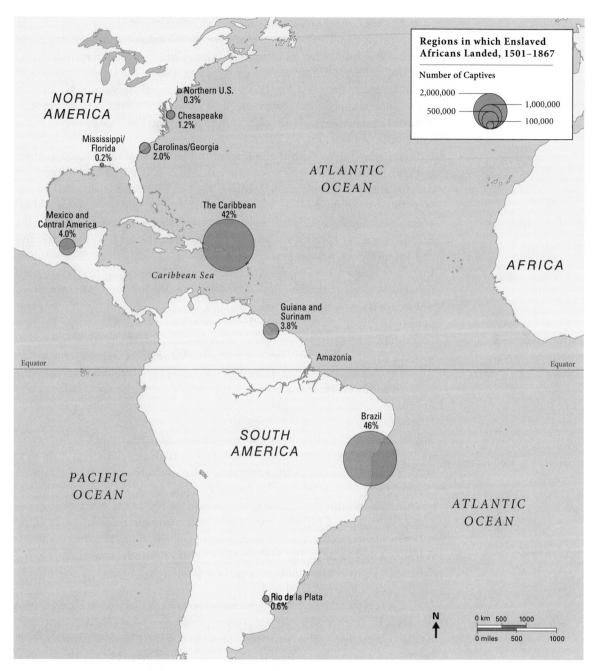

MAP **19.3 Regions in which Enslaved Africans Landed, 1501–1867.**

The "Sot Weed" Enterprise   As we saw in preceding chapters, the first permanent English settlements in the Americas were the for-profit enterprise at Jamestown in 1607 and the religious "errand in the wilderness" of the initial settlements in Massachusetts from 1620 on. Both would soon count Africans among them, though their descendants in Jamestown would be by far the more economically important. In August of 1619 a Dutch privateer surprised a Portuguese slaver en route to Vera Cruz, Mexico, and relieved her of 60 of her African slaves. By the end of the month, the ship put in at the struggling enterprise of Jamestown and disembarked "twenty and odd Negroes," some of whom were Christians from the kingdom of Kongo. These were the first slaves sold in the English colonies of North America. They would be far from the last. Though only about 3–5 percent of the slaves shipped from Africa ended up in North America, through procreation on the continent their numbers grew to more than 4 million by the eve of the American Civil War.

Their labor, along with that of increasing numbers of indentured workers from Europe, was needed for a new enterprise that, it was hoped, would save the colonial enterprise from failure: tobacco. The Powhatan and other local peoples grew tobacco for themselves, but it was considered by the increasing numbers of European smokers to be inferior to the varieties grown in the Caribbean. The English, however, had acquired some of the Caribbean plants and begun intensive cultivation in the Chesapeake Bay region of this "sot weed," as it came to be called. Indentured labor was widely used, but those workers were bound to stay only until they had worked off the cost of their passage, usually 5–7 years. After that, they worked for wages or acquired their own land. Under these conditions, slaves came to be the preferred labor source in the colony of Virginia.

Manumission: The process by which slaves are legally given freedom.

Though a surprising number of Africans earned **manumission** from their owners, gaining their freedom, acquiring land, and on occasion even starting their own plantations with their own slaves during the seventeenth century, the colonial authorities eventually passed laws firmly fixing the slave underclass as one based on color.

Sugar, Rice, and Indigo in the Lower South The colony of Carolina came under the purview of the Lords Proprietors in Barbados, who began sending settlers in 1670 as a way to transport religious dissenters and to form a bulwark against the Spanish in Florida. As part of a vast pine forest running from southern Virginia to northern Florida, its position as a provider of naval stores—pitch, tar, rosin, and turpentine—as well as tall, straight tree trunks for ships' masts, was vital in the age of wooden vessels. Even today, the state of North Carolina's nickname is "the Tarheel State." Although indentured laborers and slaves were involved in these enterprises, plantation crops were destined to see the largest demand for their labor.

In the seventeenth and early eighteenth centuries, settlers in the Carolinas ran what was by far the most successful attempt ever to enslave Native Americans. As many as 50,000 Native American slaves labored there by the early eighteenth century. Native resistance to slaving resulted in war between the settlers and a Native American alliance in 1715–1717 that almost lost the colony for the Lords Proprietors. The settlers, angry with what they considered the mismanagement of the Lords Proprietors, appealed to the crown, and South Carolina was split off in 1719 and set up as a royal colony shortly thereafter. Deprived of Native Americans for slaves, the colonies began to import large numbers of West African slaves as the Dutch dominance of the trade gave way to the British. This initial wave of slave immigration ultimately grew to a point that made South Carolina the only North American colony, and later state, in which African Americans outnumbered those of European descent.

In addition, South Carolina produced many of the same plantation commodities as Brazil and the Caribbean (such as sugarcane, molasses, and rice), along with one vitally important new addition: indigo, which was destined to become the colony's most important cash crop until the cotton boom of the nineteenth century.

The dark blue dye produced from the tropical plant *Indigofera tinctoria* had been grown extensively throughout Asia, the ancient Mediterranean, and North and West Africa. A similar American species, *Indigofera suffruticosa*, had long been in use in Mexico and Central America. Maritime countries with Indian and East Asian connections imported vast quantities of it into Europe, while the Spanish began to cultivate the American variety. Sales in northern Europe were initially hampered because there indigo competed with the local production of dyes made from the woad plant. Restrictions on imports were gradually lifted, and South Carolina entered an indigo boom starting in the 1740s. The burgeoning need for labor in planting, stripping the leaves, fermenting, cleaning, draining, scraping, and molding the residue into balls or blocks—all accompanied by a considerable stench—drove the slave trade even further.

Advertisement for a Slave Auction. In this notice from 1766, potential slave buyers in Charleston, South Carolina, are informed of the time and place for the sale of a "choice cargo" of recently arrived Africans. As Charleston was undergoing a smallpox epidemic at the time, potential customers are reassured that the captives are healthy and likely to be immune to the disease.

The last new English possession in southern North America prior to 1750 was Georgia. The southern regions of what was to become the colony of Georgia had been claimed by the Spanish as early as 1526 as part of their exploration of Florida and the Gulf Coast. Attempts by the French to found a colony near Port Royal, South Carolina, and Fort Caroline (near present-day Jacksonville) in the 1560s were ultimately undone. With the expansion of the English presence in the seventeenth century and the French concentrating on their vast claims in Canada and the Mississippi valley, the territory between Carolina and the Spanish fort at St. Augustine became increasingly disputed.

Into this situation stepped James Oglethorpe (1696–1785), the only founder of an English colony in North America who lived to see it become part of the United States. Oglethorpe's vision was to set up a colony for England's poor, debtors (who would otherwise be imprisoned), and dispossessed. He obtained a royal charter for his idea and in 1733 landed with his first band of settlers at the site of the modern city of Savannah. After buying land from the local Native Americans, he began to develop the colony as a free area in which slavery was banned. The Spanish attempted to claim Georgia in 1742 but were repulsed. Pressed by settlers bringing their slaves in from South Carolina, Georgia's ban on slave labor was soon rescinded. By the end of Oglethorpe's life, which he spent in retirement in England, Georgia had developed its own slave-based plantation economy, producing rice, sugar, indigo, and, on the Sea Islands along the coast, a fine, long-fiber variety of cotton, which proved to be a harbinger of the commodity that would ensure slavery's survival in the United States until 1865.

The Fatal Triangle: The Economic Patterns of the Atlantic Slave Trade

As mentioned, the European countries that successively dominated the transportation of slaves from the West African coast moved steadily northward in a pattern that paralleled their naval and merchant marine power. That is, during the fifteenth and sixteenth centuries, Portugal had an effective monopoly on the trade from outposts in Senegambia, Elmina, and Ndongo. The success of Dutch and English privateers encouraged more concerted economic warfare and, with it, the seizure by the Dutch of Elmina in 1637. Now it was the Dutch who became the principal slave carriers, part of a pattern of aggressive colonizing that made the Netherlands the world's richest country in per capita terms through much of the seventeenth century. The rise of England's naval power at the expense of the Dutch and the fading of the Spanish and Portuguese naval presence allowed the English—and, to a lesser extent, the French—to dominate the slave trade. By the mid-eighteenth century, as the trade approached its height, it had become the base upon which the world's most lucrative economic triangle was constructed (see Map 19.4).

MAP **19.4** **The North Atlantic System, ca. 1750.**

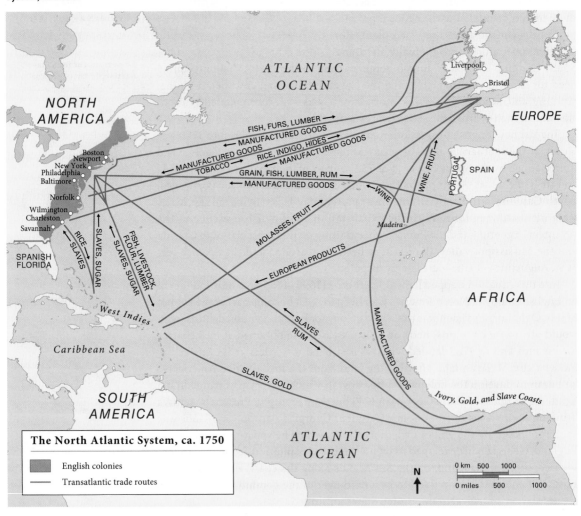

Rum, Guns, and Slaves   As we have seen, England's colonies in the Americas, especially those in the Caribbean, were by the eighteenth century producing valuable crops, including sugar, tobacco, cotton, and indigo, for export to the Old World. Tobacco was raised mainly in England's North American colonies, along with some cotton for export to England, though at this point England still imported most of its cotton from India. So profitable were these exports that, in keeping with the policy of mercantilism, the crown passed a series of acts in 1651 and 1660 that produced even greater profits for merchants in the motherland. The Navigation Acts required that all goods imported to England from American colonies had to be transported only on English ships, thereby guaranteeing a virtual monopoly on transatlantic trade.

British merchants acquired enormous profits through their colonial trading practices, particularly with the Atlantic colonies. We are afforded a good example of how this worked through an analysis of the **Atlantic system**, or the "triangular trade." In general terms, British ships would leave home ports in either their North American colonies or Britain with goods of various kinds, then travel to ports along the western coast of Africa, where these goods would be exchanged for African slaves; these ships would then sail across the Atlantic, where slaves would be exchanged for goods produced in western Atlantic colonies; and finally, these goods would be carried back to the home port.

One common pattern consisted of the following stages: An English ship loaded with New England rum would sail from Europe to the western coast of Africa, where the rum would be exchanged for a cargo of slaves; laden with slaves, the ship would then sail westward across the Atlantic to sugar colonies in the Caribbean, where the slaves would be exchanged for a cargo of molasses; the ship would sail to New England, where the molasses would be processed into rum. A variant pattern consisted of British ships leaving their home ports—increasingly Liverpool and Bristol, the ports that benefited most dramatically from the slave trade—loaded with manufactured goods, such as guns, knives, textiles, and assorted household wares. They would sail to the western coast of Africa, where these goods would be exchanged for a cargo of slaves, then sail westward across the Atlantic to the British colony of Virginia, where their human cargo would be exchanged for tobacco; they would then sail eastward across the Atlantic to their home ports in Britain, where the tobacco would be unloaded and then sold to British and European merchants.

The Middle Passage   Following capture in Africa, prisoners were usually marched to slave markets and embarkation ports roped, chained, or ganged together by forked tree limbs. Slave lots were then wholesaled to middlemen or auctioned directly to foreign factors. From this point they would be imprisoned in fortified slave pens called "barracoons" until the next ship bound for their sale destination arrived. But it was on the voyage from Africa to the Americas, the infamous "Middle Passage," that the full horror of the slave's condition was most fully demonstrated.

Because the profits involved in transportation were so high for captains, officers, and even crewmen, they constantly experimented with ways to pack the maximum number of human beings into the holds of their ships. Because a certain percentage of mortality was expected during a voyage that lasted from a few weeks to

Atlantic system: Economic system in which European ships would exchange goods for slaves in West Africa and slaves would then be brought to America and exchanged for goods that would be carried back to the home port.

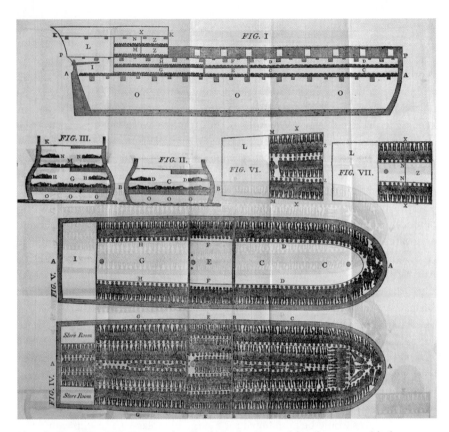

Plan of a Slave Ship, 1789. This image, based on the *Brooks*, a Liverpool slave ship, was one of the first to document the horrors of the slave trade. It shows the captives laid like sardines below deck. In such conditions slaves perished at the rate of 10–30 percent during the Middle Passage. The engraving was widely distributed by British abolitionists, who eventually succeeded in banning the trade in 1807.

nearly 2 months, some ship captains favored "tight packing"—deliberate overcrowding on the assumption that a few more captives might survive than on a ship with fewer captives but a higher rate of survival. On the other hand, some captains favored the "loose pack" method, with the assumption that a higher number would survive if given marginally more room. In either case, conditions were abominable.

Due to well-founded fears of slave mutiny, the holds of slave ships were locked and barred and the hatchways and vents covered with iron gratings. The slaves were chained to tiny bunks arranged in tiers configured to maximize the space of the hold. Food was minimal, usually corn mush, and sanitation nonexistent. Small groups of captives would be brought up on deck on a rotating basis to be haphazardly washed of their vomit and feces with buckets of frigid ocean water thrown at them by the crew. They would then be "danced" for minimal exercise and sent back down, and the next group would be brought up. The dead, sick, and resistant would simply be thrown overboard. The ship and crew were also well armed to fight off mutineers and attacks by competitors or pirates. On landing at their destination, the slaves were again barracooned, cleaned up, and given better meals pending their auction to individual buyers. In the process somewhere between 10 and 30 percent of them died en route.

Culture and Identity in the African Diaspora

The original meaning of the term "diaspora" referred to the dispersal of the Jews around the Roman Empire after their revolt of the first century CE was put down. Scholars now use the term more generally for the wide dispersal by forced or voluntary migration of any large group. In the case of the **African diaspora**, in which Africans moved to nearly all parts of the Americas primarily through the slave trade, the story is far too varied and complex for us to do more than note some general patterns related to culture and identity.

A New Society: Creolization of the Early Atlantic World

As discussed earlier in this chapter, one of the effects of the Portuguese implantation on African coasts through trade forts and colonies was the adaptation of coastal African societies to western Christianity and Portuguese culture. These societies were highly diverse. Some were clan- or lineage-based and welcomed trade with outsiders; others were militarily oriented and saw the new arrivals as unwelcome competitors; still others were kingdoms, some of which cooperated intermittently or permanently with the Portuguese and later with the Dutch, English, and French. Depending on the type or intensity of interaction, African Creole cultures emerged—that is, cultures in which some adaptation to Catholicism occurred and in which Africans appropriated certain outside cultural elements into their own heritage.

In earlier scholarship this creolization was often described as resulting in certain elements of an alien, colonizing culture uneasily grafted onto "genuine" Africanness. As in the case of Dona Beatriz and the rise of a Kongolese Catholicism, however, Creole culture has to be seen as an "authentic" phenomenon in its own right. This is similarly true for black Creole cultures in the Americas. Africans arrived with either their own local spiritual traditions or as Christians and Muslims, since foreign and indigenous slave raiders penetrating inland Africa made no religious distinctions among their victims. Either way, African slaves adapted to their plantation life through creolization or, as African Christian or Muslim Creoles, through further creolization, a process that expressed itself in distinct languages or dialects as well as synthetic (or hybrid) religious customs. Adaptation was thus not simple imitation but a creative transformation of cultural elements to fit the new conditions of a life of forced labor abroad.

Recent scholarship suggests that a key formative element in the development of culture and identity of Africans in the Americas lay in the influence of the central African Creoles from Kongo and Ndongo (today's Congo and Angola) up to the middle of the seventeenth century. The Christianity of some believers and its later variants helped to nurture this religion among Africans in the new lands, especially when it was reinforced by the religious practices of the slave owners. The mix of language and terms for a multitude of objects similarly gave the early arrivals a certain degree of agency and skill in navigating the institutions of slavery as they were being established.

An example of a Creole language that has survived for centuries is Gullah, used by the isolated slave communities along the coastal islands of South Carolina and

African diaspora: Dispersal of African peoples throughout the world, particularly the Americas, as part of the transatlantic slave trade.

Patterns Up Close | Voodoo and Other New World Slave Religions

One prominent pattern of world history that we have seen a number of times already is the way indigenous elements work to shape the identity of imported religions as they are taken up by their new believers. Buddhism in China and Japan, for example, adopted elements from Daoism and Chinese folk beliefs as well as spirits and demons from Shinto. Christianity added Roman and Germanic elements to its calendar of holidays, architecture, and cult of saints. Islam in Iran and India and Christianity in Africa underwent similar processes. In Kongo, for example, the African Christian cult of St. Anthony merged Portuguese

Altar and Shrine from the Interior of the Historic Voodoo Museum in New Orleans.

Catholic and Kongolese spiritual traditions into a new church. This trend of interaction continues today, where we find the African Christian churches among the fastest growing in the world and increasingly sending clergy and missionaries to Europe and the United States.

In the Americas three main strains of this kind of interaction and adaptation of imported and indigenous traditions developed over time and are still widely practiced today: Santeria is found primarily in Cuba and among the Spanish-speaking Africans of the Caribbean but is now also in the larger cities of North America with communities of Caribbean immigrants; vodoun, usually written as "voodoo," developed in Haiti

Georgia and still spoken by their descendants today. In Haiti, Creole (*Kreyòl*) is not only the daily spoken language but one also used in the media and in literary works. (French is recognized as the other national language, especially in law and official pronouncements.) Creole cultures thus typically involve not only the phenomenon of adaptation but also multiple identities—in language, religion, and culture.

Music and Food   It can justifiably be said that the roots of most popular music in the Americas may be found in Africa. Regardless of where they came from in Africa, slaves brought with them a wide variety of musical instruments, songs, and chants, all of which contributed to shaping the musical tastes of their owners and society at large. The widespread use of rhythmic drumming and dance in African celebrations, funerals, and even coded communications has come down to us today as the basis for music as diverse as Brazilian samba, Cuban and Dominican rumba and meringue, New Orleans jazz, and American blues, rock and roll, soul, and hip-hop. It is difficult to imagine American country and western music, or bluegrass, without the modern

and old Saint-Domingue and is widely practiced among African-descended French speakers around the Caribbean and in areas of Louisiana; and the adherents of Candomblé are mostly confined to Brazil.

All three are syncretic religions composed of elements that appear disconnected to outsiders but which practitioners see as part of an integrated whole. They intermingle Roman Catholic saints with West African natural and ancestral spirits and gods, see spiritual power as resident in natural things, and incorporate images of objects to represent a person or thing whose power the believer wants to tap or disperse (as in the use of so-called voodoo dolls). They also hold that proper ritual and sacrifices by priests and priestesses can tune into the spirits of the natural world. In some cases, they see these practices as curing sicknesses and raising the dead—the source of the famous "zombie" legends. Such innovations allowed the slaves to create a religious and cultural space in which they carved out autonomy from their masters—indeed, in which they *were* the masters. They also provided a kind of alternate set of beliefs which could be invoked alongside more mainstream Christian practices. In a real sense, they provided a precious degree of freedom for people who had almost no other form of it.

Mami Wata. Both a protector and a seducer, Mami Wata is an important spirit figure throughout much of Africa and the African Atlantic. She is usually portrayed as a mermaid, a snake charmer, or a combination of both. She embodies the essential, sacred nature of water, across which so many African Americans traveled in their diaspora.

Questions

- How do black Christianity and voodoo religion show the new patterns of origins, interaction, and adoption that emerged after 1500?

- Can you think of more recent examples of syncretic religions? If so, which ones? Why are they syncretic?

descendant of a West African stringed instrument we know today as the banjo. The chants of field hands, rhyming contests, and gospel music contributed mightily to many of these genres.

Like music, cuisine passed easily across institutional barriers. Here, the dishes that most Americans consider "southern" have in many cases deep African roots. The first rice brought to the Carolinas was a variety native to the Niger inland delta in West Africa. Africans brought with them the knowledge of setting up and running an entire rice-based food system, which was established in the Carolina lowlands and Gulf Coast. The yam, the staple of West African diets, also made its way to the Americas. The heart of Louisiana Creole cooking, including rich and spicy gumbos, "dirty rice," jambalaya, and other dishes, comes from the use of the African vegetable okra and a heady mixture of African, American, and Asian spices along with rice.

Plantation Life and Resistance   Although nineteenth-century apologists for slavery frequently portrayed life under it as tranquil, the system was in fact one of constant real and implied violence.

Slave Culture. This ca. 1790 painting from Beaufort, South Carolina, shows the vibrancy of African American culture in the face of great hardship. Note the banjo, whose origins lie in West Africa and which would have a great impact on the development of American music.

"I hold that in the present state of civilization, where two races of different origin, and distinguished by color . . . are brought together, the relation now existing in the slaveholding states between the two, is, instead of an evil, a good— a positive good."

—Senator John C. Calhoun

Most slaves reconciled themselves to their condition and navigated it as best they could, but the reminders of their status were constantly around them. Obviously, those who endured the Middle Passage had violence thrust upon them immediately upon capture. Even those born into slavery, however, lived in squalid shacks or cabins; ate inadequate rations, perhaps supplemented with vegetables they were allowed to grow themselves; and spent most of their waking hours at labor.

Those working as house servants had a somewhat easier life than field hands. In some cases, they were the primary guardians, midwives, wet nurses, and even confidants of their masters' families. Often, there was considerable expressed affection between the household slaves and the master's family. But more often, this was tempered by the knowledge that they or their family members could be sold at any time, that infractions would be severely punished, and that they would be treated as unruly, temperamental children at best.

As we saw earlier, field hands led a far harder and shorter life. The price of slavery for the master was eternal vigilance; his nightmare was slave revolt. Over the years a variety of methods were developed to keep slaves in line and at their work. Overseers ran the work schedules and supervised punishments; drivers kept slaves at their work with a long bullwhip in hand to beat the slow or hesitant. Slaves leaving plantations on errands had to carry passes, and elaborate precautions were taken to discourage escape or even unauthorized visits to neighboring plantations. In the Carolinas, for example, owners spread tar on fence rails so that slaves attempting to climb or vault them would be marked for easy detection. Runaways were pursued with relentless determination by trackers with bloodhounds and flogged, branded, maimed, or castrated when returned.

Punishing Slave Revolts. John Gabriel Stedman (1744–1797) was a British–Dutch soldier and writer whose years in Surinam, on the northern coast of South America, were recorded in *The Narrative of a Five Year Expedition against the Revolted Negroes of Surinam* (1796). With its graphic depictions of slavery it became an important tract in the abolitionist cause. In this illustration, *A Negro Hung Alive by the Ribs to a Gallows*, engraved by the famous artist and Romantic poet William Blake (1757–1827), Stedman shows a rebel who was hung by his ribs for two days as punishment for his crimes. Masters routinely cut off the noses of their slaves, burnt them alive, and whipped them to death with impunity.

Given these conditions, slave behaviors designed to try to manage their work on their own terms or to get back at their owners were frequent. Slaves staged work slowdowns, feigned illnesses, sabotaged tools and equipment, or pretended not to understand how to perform certain tasks. Kitchen slaves would sometimes spit or urinate into soups or gravies. Despite the risks involved, runaways were quite common. Later, in the United States in the 1850s, enforcement of the Fugitive Slave Act would be a prime factor driving the country toward civil war.

Despite all their precautions, slave owners throughout the Americas constantly faced the prospect of slave insurrection. By some estimates, there were more than 250 slave uprisings involving 10 or more slaves during the four centuries of Atlantic slavery. In some cases, these rebellions were successful enough for the slaves to create their own isolated settlements where they could, for a time, live in freedom. These escapees were called *Maroons*. Three of the more successful

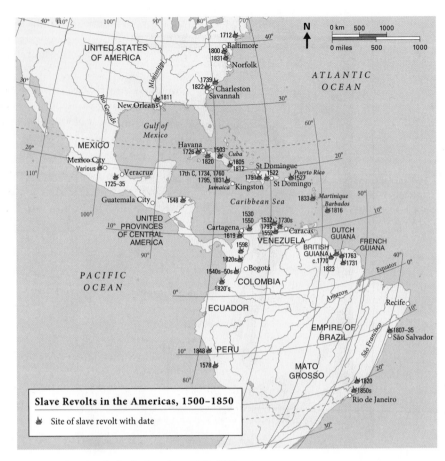

MAP **19.5** **Slave Revolts in the Americas, 1500–1850.**

Maroon settlements existed in Jamaica, Colombia, and Surinam. In Brazil, slaves developed their own system of weaponless martial arts called *capoeira*, in which fighters walk on their hands and use their legs to strike. Map 19.5 lists some of the larger slave insurrections from 1500 to 1850.

Putting It All Together

Portugal, the Netherlands, England, France, and Spain built up a fully evolved pattern of trading for plantation slaves on the Atlantic coast of Africa in the course of the sixteenth and seventeenth centuries. The trade took off toward the end of the sixteenth century, with 28,000 slaves annually, and by 1700 it had reached 80,000 annually, where it stayed until the early nineteenth century, when the slave trade was abolished. As for the patterns of state formation in Africa, on the whole, the more powerful a kingdom was, the fewer slaves it sold, given its own labor requirements. Conversely, the more conducive the circumstances were to the collapse of chiefly or royal rule and the emergence of raider societies such as the Imbangala, Ashante, or Dahomey, the more damaging the impact was on a given population.

Thus, no global judgment is possible. Undoubtedly, in some regions of western and central Africa the effects were grave, while in others, often directly adjacent, the impact was less decisive. Nonetheless, the period marked a profound transformation, with many areas depopulated by the slave trade, some enhanced through the trade and the introduction of new food crops like maize and cassava, and others undergoing creolization to some degree.

The interaction and adaptation patterns of Europeans and Africans in Africa and Europeans, Africans, and Native Americans in the Caribbean and Americas over the course of three centuries (1500–1800) created not just a new, two-hemisphere world system of trade but a new kind of society as well. The Atlantic slave trade was the foundation on which the mass production of cash crops and commodities, the first world pattern of its kind, was brought into being. This economic sphere was by far the richest of its kind in the world, but with it came the creation of an enduring social underclass and the foundation of modern racism.

Yet even as early as the 1750s, one finds the origins of the abolition movement—the international movement to end first the slave trade and ultimately slavery itself. Among the leaders of Europe's Enlightenment, thinkers were already calling for the end of the trade and institution. Within a few decades, works like the memoirs of the former slave and abolitionist Olaudah Equiano (ca. 1745–1797) would push the movement forward, as would the work of England's William Wilberforce (1759–1833), who actually lived to see the outlawing of the trade and of English slavery itself. Elsewhere, it would take a revolution, as in Haiti, or a civil war, as in the United States, for abolition to occur. In the Atlantic world, slavery finally ended in Brazil in 1888. But it persists informally in India, Africa, and the Middle East even today.

▶ For additional resources, including maps, primary sources, visuals, and quizzes, please go to www.oup.com/us/vonsivers. Please see the Further Resources section at the back of the book for additional readings and suggested websites.

Against the Grain

Oglethorpe's Free Colony

Set against the backdrop of both expanding colonial slavery and the hardening of the so-called color line, James Oglethorpe's dream of a colony of Georgia in which both slavery and rum were to be banned, and where the colonists were to consist of the "worthy poor" freed from the threat of debtor's prison, would appear to defy the patterns of the times. Oglethorpe, as a young member of the House of Commons, was appalled at the conditions of London prisons, and perhaps even more by the practice of imprisoning debtors and forcing them to pay for their own upkeep while incarcerated. Appointed to a parliamentary committee investigating the situation, he developed a scheme that he hoped would solve several problems plaguing English society: growing indebtedness on the part of the working poor and the jobless; rampant alcoholism fueled by cheap rum and gin; and migration to cities by the landless.

His solution was to found a colony as a haven for those most afflicted by these ills. He bought land at fair prices from the Creek people, ensured that skilled craftsmen and laborers were among the initial settlers, and laid out what became the city of Savannah in a design that called for houses with ample lots, a 45-acre farm outside the city for self-sufficiency, and numerous common areas and squares to create close-knit neighborhoods. To ensure that the labor of the immigrants would be valued, slavery was strictly forbidden, as was the slave-produced product of rum. While scholars differ on whether he was a true abolitionist, he did declare slavery to be "immoral" and felt that it violated English law.

As we saw in this chapter, however, his visionary aims ultimately ran aground on the shoals of the colony's position on the border with Spanish Florida. With Oglethorpe's retirement to England in 1750, his fellow trustees returned control of the colony to the British crown, and the ban on slavery was rescinded. The invention of the cotton gin in the 1790s began a process by which that commodity would become the most valuable export in the world and the bulwark of the US economy. And as cotton became king, the slave state of Georgia would be at the epicenter of its expansion.

- **Why were institutions of slavery so prevalent in so many places in the world?**

- **Even though many people found slavery to be immoral on humanitarian and even economic grounds, the institution persisted for centuries in the Atlantic world. Why do you think it proved so difficult to dismantle?**

Thinking Through Patterns

▶ **On what was the pattern of kingdom and empire formation in Africa based during the period 1500–1800?**

What is remarkable about Africa during these 300 years is that it continued its pattern of kingdom and empire formation and actually did so on an accelerated pace, on the basis of increased intra-African trade. The half-dozen examples analyzed in this chapter could be applied to another dozen states. In the interior of Africa the pattern continued in spite of the demographic effects (in whatever form they had in specific regions) of the Atlantic slave trade.

The pattern of plantation production evolved over several centuries before it was transplanted to the islands of the Atlantic and the Caribbean as well as the Americas. It was above all a system for growing labor-intensive cash crops—indigo, sugar, tobacco—that relied increasingly on African slave labor. By 1800, the demand for plantation commodities by Europeans and the guns, textiles, rum, and other manufactured goods that Africans took in trade for slaves swelled the system to huge proportions. In turn, the mercantilist economics of western Europe regulated the trade within an efficient, tightly controlled, triangular system.

The gradual domination of African slavery in the Americas and Caribbean over other kinds of servitude created a pattern of racism, in which blackness was permanently associated with slavery. As the economics of slavery became entrenched, the participants in the system answered the criticism of slavery on moral grounds by claiming that black Africans were inherently inferior and thus deserved to be enslaved. The argument was essentially circular: They were enslaved because they were inferior, and they were inferior because they were slaves.

▶ **How did the patterns of slave trade and plantation slavery evolve in the Atlantic and the Americas?**

▶ **What are the historic roots from which modern racism evolved?**

In North America, long after slavery was abolished, these attitudes were preserved in law and custom in many places and reinforced during the colonization of Africa in the nineteenth century and in the practice of segregation in the United States. In Latin America—although racism is no less pervasive—racial views are more subtle. People describing themselves as *mulato*, *sambo*, or *pardo* have had a better chance to be recognized as members of their own distinct ethnic groups than in the United States, where until recently the census classified people simply as either black or Caucasian. The 2010 census form, however, expanded its choices to 14 racial categories and allowed people to check multiple boxes. Clearly, the complexities of race and ethnicity in the Americas are continuing to evolve.

Chapter 20 1400–1750

The Mughal Empire

MUSLIM RULERS AND HINDU SUBJECTS

June 17, 1631, could hardly have been a less auspicious day for the family of the Mughal emperor Shah Jahan. Though he ruled over the most powerful empire in India's history and commanded unprecedented wealth, the emperor's beloved wife, Mumtaz Mahal, had just died in giving birth to their fourteenth child. The royal family was naturally plunged into mourning, a grief conveyed by the following lines read at the announcement of her death:

> The world is a paradise full of delights,
>
> Yet also a rose bush filled with thorns;
>
> He who picks the rose of happiness
>
> Has his heart pierced by a thorn.

Shah Jahan himself, however, plumbed far greater depths of depression. His beard turned gray, and it was said that he wept for nearly 2 years afterward. Indeed, his eyes grew so weak from his tears that he needed to wear glasses to read his daily correspondence. Inconsolable for months on end, he finally resolved to build a magnificent tomb complex for Mumtaz Mahal over her burial site along the Jumna (or Yamuna) River near the giant fortress at Agra. At a time when monumental building projects were the order of the day for Mughal rulers, this tomb, with its balance of deceptively simple lines,

Central
Asia

Southeast
Asia

**MUGHAL
INDIA,
ca. 1700**

INDIAN
OCEAN

ABOVE: The Taj Mahal (1631–1653), a magnificent architectural synthesis
of Hindu and Muslim influences and Persian classicism.

harmony of proportion, and technical skill, would become the most recognized symbol of India throughout the world: the Taj Mahal.

Beyond its architectural elegance, however, the Taj Mahal also conveys a great deal of information about the circumstances of Mughal rule in India, particularly about the syncretism of Muslim rulers and Hindu subjects we first saw in Chapter 12. Like their predecessors, the Mughals discovered the difficulties of being an ethnic and religious minority ruling a huge and diverse population. By Shah Jahan's time, moreover, religious revival was sweeping Islamic India and earlier Mughal rulers were subject to criticism about their laxity in ruling according to Islamic law and the accommodations they had made with India's other religious communities. Shah Jahan therefore devoted himself anew to a study of the Quran and resolved to rule insofar as it was possible according to Islamic precepts. Over the coming decades, such policy changes would raise tensions between Hindus and Muslims.

Seeing Patterns

▶ What were the strengths and weaknesses of Mughal rule?

▶ What was the Mughal policy toward religious accommodation? How did it change over time?

▶ What factors account for the Mughal decline during the eighteenth century?

The gleaming white stone dome and minarets of Shah Jahan's architectural masterpiece are the centerpiece of a much larger complex that is, in fact, a vision of the entrance to paradise recreated on earth. The complex is, as one scholar put it, a vast **allegory** of Allah's judgment in paradise on the day of the resurrection. In the end, Mughal ambition to create an empire as the earthly expression of this vision lent itself to that empire's ultimate decline. The constant drive to bring the remaining independent Indian states under Mughal control continually strained imperial resources. Dynastic succession almost always resulted in internal wars fought by rival claimants to the Mughal mantle. By the eighteenth century, prolonged rebellion and the growing power of the East India companies of the European powers would conspire to send the dynasty into a downward spiral from which it never recovered. But its most visible symbol, the Taj Mahal—literally the "Crown Palace"—remains the emblem of India's peak as a syncretic religious civilization in the modern period.

Allegory: A literary, poetic, dramatic, pictorial, or architectural device in which the parts have symbolic value in depicting the meaning of the whole.

History and Political Life of the Mughals

Though we have noted previously that relations between Muslims and India's other religions were *syncretic*—that despite attempts to integrate them more thoroughly into India's larger religious mosaic, they coexisted, sometimes on difficult or hostile terms, but remained largely separate from the other traditions. Yet the political and social systems created by the Mughals were in many respects a successful *synthesis*. That is, the Mughals brought with them a tradition that blended the practices of what social scientists call an "extraction state"—one that supplies itself by conquest and plunder—with several centuries of ruling more settled areas. This legacy would guide them as they struggled with a set of problems similar to those faced by rulers in other areas in creating an empire centered on one religion. Aided in their conquests by the new military technologies of cannon and small firearms, the Mughals created a flexible bureaucracy with a

Chapter Outline

- History and Political Life of the Mughals

- Administration, Society, and Economics

- Science, Religion, and the Arts

- Putting It All Together

strict hierarchy of ranks and sophisticated separation of powers but with ultimate power concentrated in the hands of the emperors. Like those of the Chinese and Ottomans, the system was easily expanded into newly conquered areas, gave considerable free rein to the ambitious, and weathered all the major political storms it encountered until its decline during the eighteenth century.

From Samarkand to Hindustan

As we have seen in earlier chapters, the rise to prominence of speakers of Turkic languages of the Altaic group had taken place over the course of many centuries. From at least the time of the Huns, these groups regularly coalesced into potent raiding and fighting forces, often putting together short-lived states such as those of the Toba in fifth- and sixth-century China, the Uighurs in the eighth and ninth centuries, and, most importantly, the Mongols in the twelfth and thirteenth centuries. But the Mongol Empire, the largest in world history, soon fell apart, and in its wake the central Asian heartland of the Turkic peoples—roughly speaking, from the Sea of Azov to the western reaches of present-day Mongolia—evolved into a patchwork of smaller states, many of whose rulers claimed descent from Genghis Khan. With the ousting of the Mongol Yuan dynasty from China in 1368, the eastern regions of this vast territory were thrown into further disarray, which set the stage for another movement toward consolidation.

The Empire of Timur   Aided by the ease of travel within the Mongol Empire, Islam had by the fourteenth century become the dominant religion among the central Asian Turkic peoples. By this time some of the Turkic groups, like the Seljuks and the Ottomans, had long since moved into the eastern Mediterranean region and Anatolia. In the interior of central Asia, however, the memory of the accomplishments of the Mongol Empire among the inhabitants of Chaghatay—the area given to Genghis Khan's son of that name—was still fresh. Their desire for a new Mongol Empire, now coupled with Islam, created opportunities for military action to unite the settled and nomadic tribes of Chaghatay. The result by the end of the fourteenth century was the stunning rise of Temur Gurgan (r. 1370–1405), more widely known by a variation of the Persian rendering of his name, Timur-i Lang, as Timur the Lame, or Tamerlane.

> "I am not a man of blood; and God is my witness that in all my wars I have never been the aggressor, and that my enemies have always been the authors of their own calamity."
>
> —Timur-i Lang

What little is known about Timur's early years has been clouded by the mystique he cultivated as a ruler, which continued to grow long after his death. Though he came close to matching the conquests of Genghis Khan, his forebearers were not direct descendants of the conqueror. He therefore devised genealogies connecting him to the dominant Mongol lines to give him legitimacy as a ruler, and he even found a direct descendant of Genghis Khan to use as a figurehead for his regime. He also portrayed himself as a man whose destiny was guided by God from humble beginnings to world domination.

From 1382, when he secured the region of his homeland around the capital, the Silk Road trading center of Samarkand, until his death in 1405, Timur ranged widely through western central Asia, Afghanistan, northern India, Iran, Anatolia, and the eastern Mediterranean lands (see Map 20.1). Like his model, Genghis Khan, he proved surprisingly liberal in his treatment of certain cities that surrendered peacefully. Many more times, however, he reduced besieged cities to rubble, slaughtered the inhabitants, and erected pyramids of skulls as a warning to others to submit. "Your sins must be great indeed for God to send me to punish you," he would tell his unfortunate opponents.

At the time of his death in 1405, Timur was contemplating the invasion of Ming China. This, however, never came to pass, and Timur's empire, like that of Genghis Khan, did not long outlast him. As it fell apart, the various Chaghatay peoples largely resumed their local feuds, once again leaving the way open for a strong military force to impose order.

Babur and the Timurid Line in India By the beginning of the sixteenth century, the region from Samarkand south into the Punjab in northern India had largely become the province of feuding Turkic tribes and clans of Afghan fighters, many of whom had migrated south to serve with the Lodi sultans of India. Into this

MAP **20.1 Area Subjugated by Timur-i Lang, 1360–1405.**

volatile environment was born Zahir ud-Din Muhammad Babur (1483–1530, r. 1526–1530), more commonly known as simply Babur (though the Turkic *babur* means "lion," Zahir's nickname was from the Persian *babr* for "leopard" or "tiger") in 1483. Babur's claims to legitimate rule were considerable: His father was a direct descendant of Timur, while his mother claimed the lineage of Genghis Khan.

At 14, Babur conquered Samarkand, though he was soon forced out by a competing tribe. Like Timur and Genghis Khan, his accomplishments as a youthful prodigy led him to believe that God had provided him with a special destiny to fulfill. This belief sustained him during the next several years when, out of favor with certain powerful relatives, he roamed the border regions seeking an opportunity to return to power.

In 1504, accompanied on a campaign by his strong-willed mother, Babur moved into Afghanistan, captured Kabul, and went on to raid points farther south over the following decade. By 1519, he stepped up his raids into northern India with a view to subjugating and ruling it. After 7 more years of campaigning, this goal was achieved. In 1526, Babur's army of approximately 12,000 met the forces of Sultan Ibrahim Lodi, whose army boasted perhaps 100,000 men and 1,000 elephants, at Panipat, near Delhi. Though the sultan enjoyed such vast numerical superiority, Babur's forces employed the new technologies of matchlock muskets and field cannon to devastating effect. In the end, the Lodi sultan was killed, along with many of the Afghan tribal chiefs whose forces made up the bulk of his army, and Babur's way was now clear to consolidate his new Indian territories.

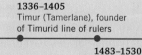

| 1336–1405 Timur (Tamerlane), founder of Timurid line of rulers | 1542–1605 Akbar, most innovative of Mughal rulers | 1618–1707 Aurangzeb, last powerful Mughal ruler | 1739 Invasion by Persians; looting of Delhi; taking of Peacock Throne |
| 1483–1530 Babur, founder of Timurid line in India—the Mughals | 1627–1657 Shah Jahan, builder of the Taj Mahal | 1707–1858 Ebbing of Mughal power in India; rise of British influence | |

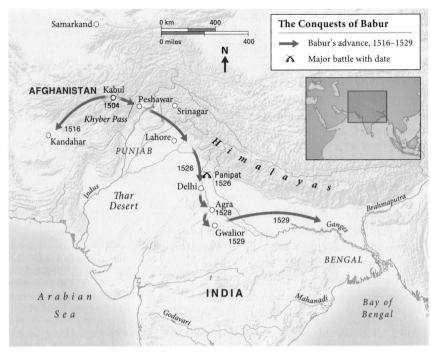

MAP 20.2 **The Conquests of Babur.**

Institutionalization: The creation of a regular system for previously improvised or ad hoc activities or things, such as law codes to replace local customs.

Portrait of Babur. This imagined portrait of Babur was done about 60 years after his death. He is shown receiving representatives of the Uzbeks of central Asia and the Rajputs of India in an audience dated December 18, 1528.

Victory at Panipat was swiftly followed by conquest of the Lodi capital of Agra and further success over the Hindu Rajputs in 1528. On the eve of his death in December 1530, Babur controlled an enormous swath of territory extending from Samarkand in the north to Gwalior in India in the south (see Map 20.2). For Babur and his successors, their ruling family would always be the "House of Timur," prompting historians to sometimes refer to the line as the Timurids. Because of their claims to the legacy of Genghis Khan, however, they would be better known to the world as the Mughals (from "Mongols").

Loss and Recovery of Empire As had been the case so many times in the past with other newly conquered empires, the House of Timur's new rulers were now faced with the problem of consolidating, organizing, and administering Babur's vast domain. Like Timur before him, Babur had given comparatively little thought to the arts of peace. Now it fell upon his son Humayun (r. 1530–1556) to create a state. Unfortunately, Humayun's interests were aimed more toward Islamic Sufi mysticism, poetry, astrology, and at times wine and opium than they were toward responsible leadership. Though chroniclers have generally been critical of him for losing much of Babur's legacy, he tapped a considerable reservoir of courage and determination to ultimately win it back.

A chronic problem for the long-term health of the dynasty was the **institutionalization** of traditional nomadic succession practices among the Mughal rulers. Though only one son was designated as the ruler's successor, the others were given substantial territories to govern within the empire, a situation that frequently led to conflict. In addition to such ongoing family difficulties, Humayun faced various hostile military forces still active in unconquered areas of northern India and Afghanistan. An Afghan leader named Sher Khan Sur managed to unite many of these forces and invaded the extreme eastern region of Bengal. Twice routed, Humayun fled to Persia in 1540, where, utterly humiliated, he was forced to convert to Shia Islam in a desperate bid to court the favor of the Safavid ruler, Shah Tahmasp. As distasteful as this was for him as a Sunni Muslim, he now at least had Persian backing and proceeded to move into Afghanistan and, ultimately, to Delhi. By 1555, after 15 years of exile and fighting, the dynasty was restored. For Humayun, however, the peace brought only a brief respite. In a final irony for this bookish man, he fell from the roof terrace of his palace library and died in January 1556.

Regency: The setting up of a guardian for an underage or incapacitated monarch to rule in his or her stead.

Consolidation and Expansion   Because of the difficulties involved in Humayun's own accession to the throne, his death was kept secret for several weeks, while the court worked out plans for a **regency** for the emperor's son, 14-year-old Jalal ud-Din Akbar (r. 1556–1605). His military education began quickly as Humayun's old enemy, Sher Khan Sur, sent an army to attack Delhi in 1557. In a close fight, Mughal forces finally carried the day. Over the next year and a half, they secured the eastern, southern, and western flanks of their lands, bringing them conclusively into the Mughal fold and again anchoring Islam in the former areas of its influence—"Hindustan."

Upon finally seizing power in a palace coup, Akbar plunged into renewed campaigning in quest of more territory. Along the way, he seemed at once determined to master all India by any military means necessary yet also intolerant of cruelties practiced by his subordinates in his name. Akbar abhorred religious violence of any kind and spent much of his rule attempting to reconcile the different religious traditions of his empire. In the end his attempts, though remarkably farsighted, would prove futile and earn him the enmity of many of his fellow Muslims, who felt he had become an unbeliever.

As a warrior Akbar was far more successful. Through the 1560s, aided by capable military advisors, Mughal armies continued to push the boundaries of the empire west, south, and east. In 1562 they subdued Malwa and in 1564 Gondwana; in 1568, the great Rajput fortress of Chitor fell. This string of victories continued into the next decade, with the long-sought conquest of Gujarat taking place in 1573. Turning eastward, Akbar set his sights on Bengal, which, along with the neighboring regions of Bihar and Orissa, fell to the Mughals by the mid-1570s. They remained, however, volatile and hostile to Mughal occupation. Both Muslim and Hindu princes in the region continued their campaigns of resistance into the following decades (see Map 20.3).

In the meantime, resistance and rebellion periodically plagued other areas of the empire. In central Asia, as early as 1564, a rebellion of Uzbek Mughal allies required a skilled combination of violence and diplomacy to defuse. At the same time, revolts in Malwa and Gujarat required reconquest of those territories. In order to keep the old Islamic heartland of northern India—Hindustan—under

Humayun Being Received by the Persian Shah Tahmasp. This gouache rendering of a pivotal moment in Mughal dynastic history is from a painting on a wall at Chel Soloun in Isfahan. Although all seems cordial between the two men and Humayun was treated well by the Shah, a number of accounts claim that he was threatened with execution if he did not covert to Shia Islam.

Visions of Akbar. A depiction of Akbar from ca. 1630 (*above*) shows him in all of his religious glory: surrounded by a luminous halo, surmounted by angels glorifying him and holding his crown, and graced with the holiness to make the lion lie down with the heifer.

firm Mughal control, the Mughals built fortresses at strategic points throughout their inner domains as well as along the frontier. Among the most important of these were Allahabad, Lahore (in modern Pakistan), Ajmer (the Amber Fort in Jaipur), and the largest—the famous Red Fort in Delhi.

The New City   In addition to fielding large armies—one European observer estimated that the army he accompanied on one of Akbar's campaigns surpassed 100,000—and huge, expensive forts, the immense revenues of the Mughal lands allowed other monumental projects to be undertaken. In an effort to show solidarity with his non-Muslim subjects, Akbar had married a Hindu Rajput princess named Manmati. Manmati had twins, who tragically died, and a distraught Akbar sought advice from a famous Sufi holy man named Salim Chishti. Salim told Akbar that he would ultimately have a son. When that son—named Salim in honor of the holy man—was born, Akbar began to build a city on the site of Salim Chishti's village of Sikri. Fatehpur Sikri, as the new city was known when it was completed in 1571, was built from the same red sandstone as the great fort at Agra, 26 miles away. Akbar's instincts for design and dynastic propaganda were

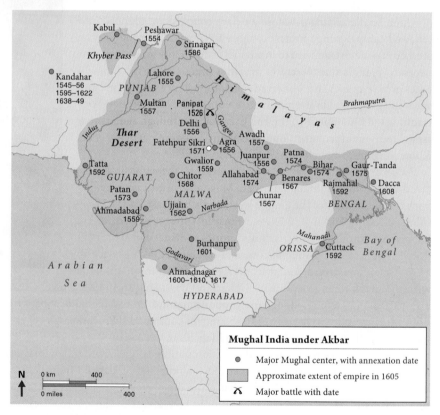

MAP **20.3** **Mughal India under Akbar.**

everywhere evident within the city. At its center was the mosque, which housed the tomb of Salim Chishti and became an object of veneration and pilgrimage for Indian Sufis. Despite its amenities, however, the city was untenable in the long run and ultimately abandoned because there was simply not enough available water to sustain the population.

The Summer and Autumn of Empire

In a way, the saga of Fatehpur Sikri runs parallel to Mughal fortunes over the next century. The military accomplishments of the dynasty are in many ways spectacular, but they were eventually worn down by internal rebellion and succession struggles; the immense fortunes of the rulers were ultimately squeezed by the needs of defense and of ostentation to demonstrate power; and new economic and, ultimately, military competitors arrived on the scene with the coming of the Europeans.

The Revolt of the Sons   In 1585, Akbar left Fatehpur Sikri with his army for Lahore, which he would make his temporary capital for most of the rest of his life. Once again, the Afghan princes were chafing under Mughal domination and intriguing with the Uzbeks and Safavid Persians to wrest local control for themselves. For Akbar, as for his predecessors, it was vital to maintain a hold over these areas because of their historical connection to the Chaghatay and the need to keep control of the essential Silk Road trade. Now the key city of Kandahar, in modern Afghanistan, was in Safavid hands, disrupting Mughal control of the trade. For the next 13 years, Akbar and his generals fought a long, stubborn war to subdue the Afghans and roll back the Safavids. Though his forces were defeated on several occasions, in the end the Mughals acquired Sind and Kashmir, subdued for a time the region of Swat, and, with the defection of a Safavid commander, occupied Kandahar. By 1598, the regions in question were secure enough for Akbar to move back to Agra.

In 1600, Akbar embarked on his last great campaign against the remaining free Muslim sultanates of central India. These were reduced within a year, but Akbar was now faced with a domestic crisis. His son Salim launched a coup and occupied the fort at Agra. Salim declared himself emperor, raised his own army,

Salim Chishti's Tomb at Fatehpur Sikri. The tomb of the Sufi mystic Salim Chishti shows the sense of restrained flamboyance that marks the mature Mughal architectural style. The Chishtis had long been revered by India's Sufis, and Salim's simple, elegant tomb, with its domed sarcophagus, multihued marble, and Quranic inscriptions, quickly became a favorite pilgrimage site. Surrounding it is one of the red sandstone courtyards of Akbar's Fatehpur Sikri.

and even had coins struck with his name on them. In the end, one of Akbar's wives and a group of court women were able to reconcile Akbar and Salim. Salim was confined within the palace amid intrigues that threatened to bypass him as heir in favor of his own son, Khusrau. In the end, however, he retained his position, and upon Akbar's death on October 25, 1605, Salim acceded to the throne as Jahangir (r. 1605–1627).

Renewed Expansion of the "War State"   As if to underscore the dynasty's continual problems with orderly succession, Jahangir's son Khusrau left the palace, quickly put a small army together, and marched on Lahore. When negotiations with his son went nowhere, Jahangir's forces swiftly defeated the insurgents. To impart to his son a special horror at what he had done, Khusrau was made to watch his comrades put to death by impalement—a punishment also used by the Ottomans and the famous Vlad "the Impaler" Dracula (Chapter 16). Sharpened posts were driven through their midsections and planted in the ground so that they would die slow, agonizing deaths suspended in the air. The doomed soldiers were made to salute Khusrau, who was forced to ride among them in a macabre military review. Undeterred, Khusrau rebelled again, and on failing this time, was blinded and imprisoned for his efforts.

As one scholar writes, "Under Jahangir the empire continued to be a war state attuned to aggressive conquest and territorial expansion." This now meant pushing south into the Deccan and periodically resecuring Afghanistan and its adjacent regions. A move into Bengal, however, foreshadowed a major clash with a very different kind of enemy: the Shan people of southeast Asia called the Ahoms. Southeast Asia was where the expanding cultural and political influence of China met that of Hindu and Buddhist India. In the case of the Ahoms, the territory in question was in the vicinity of Assam, along the Brahmaputra River to the north of Burma and Thailand. Though they had recently converted to Hinduism, the Ahoms had no caste system and drew upon a legacy of self-confident expansion that the Mughals had not encountered before in their opponents. With little fixed territory to defend because of their mobility, the Ahoms proved the most stubborn enemies the empire had yet encountered. Year after year, Jahangir's armies labored to secure the northeastern territories only to have the Ahoms bounce back and mount fresh offensives against them. Though both sides employed troops armed with matchlocks and cannon, neither side could obtain a clear tactical edge, and their wars dragged on for decades.

More culturally and psychologically threatening to the Mughals was their relationship with the empire to their west, Safavid Persia. Both sides constantly jockeyed for position against each other and periodically went to war. There was also intense religious rivalry, with the predominantly Sunni Mughals and Shiite Safavid Persians each denouncing the other as heretical unbelievers. For the Mughals, moreover, it was particularly galling that they owed the survival of their dynasty in part to the Persian shah Tahmasp, who had given aid to Humayun—forcing him to convert to Shiism in return.

In addition, among the sizeable number of Persians and Shiites within the Mughal elites there was a pronounced feeling that Persian culture, language, and literature were superior to those of the Turks and Muslim India as a whole. In some respects, both Persians and "Persianized" Indians saw Muslim India as a kind of cultural colonial outpost, in much the same way that Chinese sophisticates viewed the high cultures of Japan, Korea, and Vietnam. This made for a complex set of relations between the two empires, with both vying for power in religious and cultural terms as much as in the political and military realm.

New Directions in Religious Politics   After Jahangir died of a fever in October 1627, his oldest son, Khurram, outmaneuvered his younger brother for the throne and reigned as Shah Jahan (r. 1627–1657). His rule coincided with perhaps the high point of Mughal cultural power and prestige, as reflected in its iconic building, the Taj Mahal. However, his record is less spectacular in political and military terms. In this case, the Mughal obsession with controlling the northern trade routes coincided with the need to take back the long-contested great fort at Kandahar, once again in Persian hands. Thus, Shah Jahan spent much of his reign on the ultimately fruitless drive to finally subdue the northwest.

> "Nothing resulted from this expedition except the shedding of blood, the killing of thirty to forty thousand people, and the expenditure of thirty-five million rupees."
>
> —Sadiq

As we noted earlier, the reign of Akbar and, to a considerable extent, that of Jahangir had marked a time of extraordinary religious tolerance. The attraction of both men to the Sufi school of Salim Chishti, with its mystical leanings and parallels with similar Hindu movements, created a favorable emotional environment for religious pluralism. It also made Muslims, for whom strict adherence to Sunni doctrine was necessary to guard against undue Persian Shia influence, apprehensive. Others, noting the ability of Hindus to incorporate the gods and beliefs of other faiths into their own, feared that the ruling Muslim minority might ultimately be assimilated into the Hindu majority.

With Shah Jahan, however, we see a definite turn toward a more legalistic tradition. Under the influence of this trend among leading Sunni theologians, Shah Jahan began to block construction and repair of non-Muslim religious buildings, instituted more direct state support for Islamic festivals, and furnished lavish subsidies for Muslim pilgrims to Mecca. The old ideal of a unified Muslim world governed by Quranic law steadily gained ground at the Mughal court and would see its greatest champion in Shah Jahan's son Aurangzeb. In the meantime, the trend lent itself to the creation of a new capital, Shajahanabad Delhi, just south of Delhi, complete with the largest mosque, college (*madrasa*), and hospital complex in India—and, of course, the Taj Mahal at Agra.

The Pinnacle of Power   The ascendancy of Aurangzeb (r. 1658–1707) was marked yet again by the now all-too-familiar pattern of princely infighting. In this case it was brought on by the extended illness of Shah Jahan in 1657. A four-way struggle broke out among the sons of Shah Jahan and his beloved Mumtaz Mahal. Although Shah Jahan soon recovered, he returned to Agra broken and depressed, while his sons fought bitterly for control. By 1661 three had been defeated and killed, leaving Aurangzeb in control of the empire. Shah Jahan lived on in captivity until 1666.

Aurangzeb's long rule, despite its violent birth, seemed to begin auspiciously enough. Renewing the Mughal bid to expand into the northeastern areas controlled by the Ahoms, his armies fought them to a standstill in the early 1660s and made them Mughal clients. When Mughal control of the area around Kabul and the Khyber Pass was threatened by a revolt of local tribesmen, Aurangzeb fought

Patterns Up Close | Akbar's Attempt at Religious Synthesis

Like their predecessors, the Mughals as Muslim rulers in India were faced with an immense array of diverse, and sometimes antagonistic, religious and cultural traditions. Amid this "religious syncretism," as we have termed it, Akbar's innovation within the world-historical pattern of religious civilizations was to create a new religion that would encompass these traditions and bind his followers directly to him as emperor and religious leader: to create an Indian "religious synthesis."

Already graced with a larger-than-life reputation for charisma and openness, he was also resistant to the strictures of Sunni Islam or any other organized religion. As a boy, he was condemned by his tutors as uneducable because he remained unable to read or write. Some scholars have suggested that he was dyslexic. Perhaps because of this, he developed an extraordinary memory for literature and poetry. Some have also suggested that his illiteracy was in emulation of the stories of the early prophets, who found illumination directly from God. In any case, his tastes within Islam centered on Sufi mysticism, which had a long tradition of tolerance and eclecticism. This openness encouraged him to study the mystical traditions of the Hindus, Parsis (Zoroastrian immigrants from Persia), and Christians. After establishing himself at Fatehpur Sikri, he sponsored regular Thursday-night theological debates, mostly among Muslim scholars but gradually including Hindus, Parsis, and in 1578 Catholic missionaries. He honored many of the cultural traditions of India's various religions as well: He wore his hair long under his turban like the Sikhs and

Akbar Presiding Over a Religious Debate. Akbar's distaste for religious orthodoxy manifested itself most dramatically in his conducting regularly held debates among theologians from many of India's faiths. Here, a discussion is taking place with two Jesuit missionaries, Fathers Rudolph Aquaviva and Francis Henriquez (dressed in black) in 1578. Interestingly, the priests had unfettered access to Akbar, were free to preach, and even gave instruction to members of Akbar's family at his request.

several stubborn campaigns to retain control of the region and bought off other potentially troublesome groups with lavish gifts.

With these campaigns, the political power of the Mughals reached perhaps its greatest extent. But the period also marked a watershed in at least two respects. First, it saw the opening of decades-long wars with the Hindu Marathas, in which the empire's cohesion was steadily eroded. In addition, the various trading companies of the British, French, and Dutch expanded their own fortified outposts in Indian ports outside Mughal domains. As Mughal power was sapped by the revolts of the eighteenth century, the companies' armed forces became important players in regional politics.

The other watershed was Aurangzeb's bid for a more effective "Islamification" of Mughal India. Aurangzeb's vision for the empire was rule by Islamic Sharia law. As an Islamic state, connected to the larger commonwealth of Islamic states,

some Hindus, coined emblems of the sun to honor the Parsis, and kept paintings of the Virgin Mary as a nod to the Christians.

During one particularly lavish and bloody hunting party in 1578, he had a sudden, intense mystical experience. Like Ashoka so long before him—of whom Akbar was completely unaware—he was now appalled by the destruction and waste in which he had participated. Out of this experience and his religious consultations, he gradually developed a personal philosophy he called *sulh-i kull*—"at peace with all." While this did not end his military campaigns, which he saw as ordained by God, it did push him to develop a new religion he called *din-i ilahi* (divine faith). Akbar shrewdly directed the movement at key courtiers, nobles, and those aspiring to gain favor from the regime. He devised elaborate rituals in which adherents swore loyalty to him not only as emperor but as the enlightened religious master of the new sect. Borrowing heavily from Sufi mysticism, Persian court protocols, Zoroastrian sun and fire veneration, and even Muslim- and Christian-influenced spiritualism, he sought to at once limit the power of Sunni Islamic clerics and draw followers of other religions to what he taught was a "higher" realm, one that embraced all religions and provided the elect with secret insights into their ultimate truths.

In the end, however, despite its creative merging of the needs of state and religion to overcome what had been considered deep religious and cultural divisions, Akbar's attempt must be counted as a failure. While some Hindu and Muslim courtiers embraced *din-i ilahi* enthusiastically for its perceived religious truths, many did so for opportunistic reasons, and it was roundly condemned by most Sunni theologians. And while Akbar's personal magnetism was able to hold the sect together during his lifetime, his successors not only repudiated it but swung increasingly in the direction of stricter Sunni Islam.

Questions

- How does Akbar's attempt at religious syncretism demonstrate the pattern of origins–innovations–adaptations that informs the approach of this book?

- Why was Akbar's attempt to create a new divine faith doomed to failure?

he believed that Mughal rule should be primarily for the benefit of Muslims. This was an almost complete repudiation of his great-grandfather Akbar's vision of religious transcendence. While Aurangzeb stopped short of forcible conversion, he did offer multiple inducements to bring unbelievers into the faith. Elites who converted to Islam were given lavish gifts and preferential assignments, while those who did not convert found themselves isolated from the seat of power. Discriminatory taxes were also levied on unbelievers, including a new tax on Hindu pilgrims. Zealous Muslim judges in various cities prompted protests from Hindus regarding their rulings. Moving a step beyond the actions of Shah Jahan, Aurangzeb ordered the demolition of dozens of Hindu temples that had not been constructed or repaired according to state-approved provisions. The most unpopular measure, however, was the reimposition of the hated *jizya* tax on unbelievers, which had been abolished by Akbar.

The new religious policies also created problems in dealing with self-governing, non-Muslim groups within the empire. The legacy of distrust of the Mughals among the Sikhs, who blended Hindu and Muslim traditions, was enhanced by Aurangzeb's heavy-handed attempts to intervene in the selection of a new Sikh guru, or religious leader, and by the destruction of some Sikh temples. When the Sikhs did not choose the candidate Aurangzeb favored, the emperor arrested the other candidate for allegedly converting Muslims and had him executed. His son and successor, Gobind Singh, would later lead a full-blown Sikh revolt.

The Maratha Revolt   Notwithstanding these internal problems, Aurangzeb's military prowess netted him key areas that had long eluded Mughal efforts: Bijapur, Golconda, and much of the Maratha lands of the Deccan region of south central India. Yet even here, the preconditions were already in place for a rebellion that would sap the strength of the empire for generations.

The Hindu Marathas, like the inhabitants of many regions bordering Mughal India, had evolved working relationships with the old Muslim sultanates that, over time, were annexed by the Timurids. For the earlier Mughal rulers, it was often enough for these small states to remit tribute and, on occasion, supply troops in order to retain their autonomy. For Aurangzeb, however, commitment to a more robust and legalistic Islam also meant political expansion of the Mughal state. This was justified on the religious grounds that the sultanates to the south had drifted from correct observance of Quranic law, that it was permissible to confiscate the lands of unbelievers, and that unbelievers would more likely convert if guided by proper Muslim rulers. Hence, Aurangzeb spent much of the last two decades of his life campaigning to bring central India under his sway.

Despite the tenacity of Maratha resistance, Aurangzeb's carrot-and-stick strategy—supporting pro-Mughal factions among the Maratha leaders, lavishing money and gifts on Maratha converts and deserters, and fielding large armies to attack Maratha fortifications—was successful. In the early 1690s 11 Maratha strongholds fell to his forces. Yet prolonged fighting, with the emperor staying in the field year after year, also led to problems at court and in the interior of the empire.

The demands of constant campaigning reduced the flow of money and goods from south to north and east to west across central India. Moreover, by the early eighteenth century, the Maratha frontier, far from being steadily worn down, was actually expanding into Mughal areas. The Marathas had set up their own administrative system with its own forts and tax base and encouraged raids on Mughal caravans and pack trains. By the time of Aurangzeb's death in 1707, the Marathas were noticeably expanding their sway at Mughal expense. With the weakening of the Mughal interior, Persia took the opportunity to settle scores. The Persians sent an expeditionary force that sacked Delhi in 1739 and carried off Shah Jahan's fabled Peacock Throne—from this time forward associated with the monarchs of Persia and Iran, rather than with India and the Mughals.

The East India Companies   Within a dozen years of Vasco da Gama's first voyage to India in 1498, armed Portuguese merchant ships seized the port of Goa in 1510. Portugal's pioneering efforts in capturing the spice trade and setting up fortified bases from which to conduct business were swiftly imitated by other

European maritime countries. For the English, Dutch, and French, these enterprises were conducted by royally chartered companies, which were given a monopoly over their country's trade within a certain region. Because these companies were operating thousands of miles from home in areas that were often politically chaotic, they acted much like independent states. They maintained fortified warehouses, their armed merchant ships functioned as naval forces, and they assembled their own mercenary armies.

Throughout the seventeenth century English, French, and Dutch enterprises largely supplanted Portuguese influence in the region, while the location of their trading ports outside Mughal lands allowed them considerable freedom. European naval prowess had by this time also surpassed that of any of the Indian states, and European ships controlled the sea-lanes to Indian ports. Thus, the companies grew richer and more powerful and increasingly found themselves involved in local politics. For the English, the acquisition of Bombay (Mumbai) from Portugal in the 1660s gave the company a superb harbor. In 1690, after unwisely becoming involved in a struggle with Aurangzeb, British traders were pushed down the Hugli (also Hoogli or Hooghly) River in Bengal and began building a new trading station called Calcutta (not to be confused with the port of Calicut, on the west coast of India). By 1750, the power of the Dutch in India had been eclipsed by that of the British and French East India Companies. With the victory of the British East India Company commander, Robert Clive, at Plassey over the French forces in 1757 came British domination of Bengal and, by century's end, much of northern India.

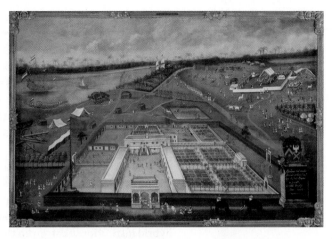

The Dutch Trading Post at Hugli, 1665. The mid-seventeenth century was the high point of Dutch influence and trade in Asia, and the Dutch East India Company was one of the most powerful entities in the region. This fortified outpost on the Hugli River was typical of European trading establishments in the region during the late sixteenth and most of the seventeenth century. By the end of the century, however, the Dutch would be supplanted on the Hugli by their archrivals, the English, who would establish their own base, which would swiftly grow into the great trading center of Calcutta.

Administration, Society, and Economics

One of the large patterns characteristic of the period under consideration in this section is a pronounced trend toward centralization. In a way, this phenomenon is not surprising, since the creation of states and empires requires power at the center to hold the state together, ensure consistent governance, provide for revenues, and maintain defense. What is noteworthy, however, is that in widely separate regions throughout Eurasia a variety of states concurrently reached a point where their governments, with armies now aided by firearms, made concerted efforts to focus more power than ever at the center. As part of this trend toward the development of centralizing states, some form of enforcement of approved religion or belief system legitimating the rulers was also present. As we saw in the Ottoman and Habsburg Empires in Chapter 16 and in seventeenth-century France and other European countries in Chapter 17, the trend was toward what came to be called "absolutism," with vast powers concentrated in the person of the monarch. In China and Japan, as we will see in Chapter 21, it meant additional powers concentrated in the hands of the emperor (China) and shogun (Japan). For Mughal

India, the system that attempted to coordinate and balance so many disparate and often hostile elements of society is sometimes called "autocratic centralism." While never as effective as the Chinese bureaucratic system or as tightly regulated as absolutist France, its policies and demands stretched into the lives of its inhabitants in often unexpected ways.

Mansabdars and Bureaucracy

As we saw earlier, Babur and his successors found themselves forced to govern a largely settled, farming and city-dwelling society, whose traditions, habits, and (for the majority) religious affiliations were different from their own. While not unfamiliar with settled societies, the nomadic Timurids initially felt more comfortable in adapting their own institutions to their new situation and then grafting them onto the existing political and social structures. The result was a series of hybrid institutions that, given the tensions within Indian society, worked remarkably well when the empire was guided by relatively tolerant rulers but became increasingly problematic under more dogmatic ones.

Political Structure　　The main early challenge faced by the Timurids was how to create a uniform administrative structure that did not rely on the unusual gifts of a particular ruler. It was the problem of moving from what social scientists call "charismatic leadership" (in which loyalty is invested in a leader because of his personal qualities) to "rational-legal" leadership (in which the institution itself commands primary respect and loyalty). Thus, Akbar created four principal ministries: one for army and military matters; one for taxation and revenue; one for legal and religious affairs; and one for the royal household.

Under the broad central powers of these ministries, things functioned much the same on the provincial and local levels. The provincial governors held political and military power and were responsible directly to the emperor. In order to prevent their having too much power, however, the fiscal responsibility for both the civil and military affairs of the provinces was in the hands of officers who reported to the finance minister. Thus, arbitrary or rebellious behavior could, in theory at least, be checked by the separation of financial control.

Administrative Personnel　　One key problem faced by the Mughals was similar to that confronting the French king Louis XIV and the Tokugawa shoguns in Japan during the following century—that is, how to impose a centralized administrative system on a state whose nobles were used to wielding power themselves. In all three cases, the solutions were remarkably similar. For the Mughals, India's vast diversity of peoples and patchwork of small states offered a large pool of potential noble recruits, and the competition among the ambitious for imperial favor was intense. The Timurid rulers were careful to avoid overt favoritism toward particular ethnic, or even religious, groups; and though most of their recruited nobility were Sunni Muslims, Hindus and even Shiite Muslims were also represented.

The primary criteria—as one would expect in a centralizing state—were military and administrative skills. An elaborate, graded system of official ranks was created in which the recipients, called *mansabdars*, were awarded grants of land and the revenues those working the land generated. In turn the mansabdars were responsible for remitting the correct taxes and, above a certain rank, for furnishing men and materiel for the army. Standards for horses, weapons, and physical qualities for soldiers, to which recruiters were expected to adhere, were established by the central government. The positions in the provincial governments and state ministries were filled by candidates from this new mansabdar elite chosen by the court. Thus, although the nobles retained considerable power in their own regions, they owed their positions to the court and had no hope of political advancement if they did not get court preferment.

The Mughals and Early Modern Economics

Mughal India had a vigorous trade and manufacturing economy, though, as with all agrarian-based societies, land issues and agriculture occupied the greatest part of the population. Unlike the societies of China, Japan, Korea, and Vietnam, which were influenced to a greater or lesser degree by Neo-Confucian ideas that regarded commerce as vaguely disreputable, Hindu, Muslim, Buddhist, and Jain traditions reserved an honored place for commerce and those who conducted it. Thus, Mughal economic interests routinely revolved around keeping the flow of goods moving around the empire, maintaining a vigorous import and export trade, and, as we have seen, safeguarding access to the Silk Road routes.

Agriculture and Rural Life   The basic administrative unit of rural India at the time of the Mughals was the *pargana*, a unit comprising an area usually containing a town and from a dozen to about 100 villages. It was in the pargana that the lowest levels of officialdom had met the network of clan and caste leaders of the villages under both the Hindu rajas and the Muslim sultans before the Timurids, and this pattern continued over the coming centuries. But because the earliest years of the Mughals were marked by conquest and plunder, and later by an administrative apparatus that contented itself with taxation and defense at the local level, life in the villages tended to go on much as it had before the conquest. Thus, the chief duties of the *zamindars*, as the local chiefs and headmen were called, were to channel the expansive and competitive energies among local clans, castes, and ethnic and religious groups into activities the Mughals considered productive. In border areas especially, this frequently involved clearing forests for farmland, harvesting tropical woods and products for market, and often driving off bands of foragers from the forests and hills.

Agricultural expansion went hand in hand with systematic integration of the rural and urban economies. One enormous obstacle facing the Mughals, which had faced previous regimes, was efficiency and equity in rural taxation. Grain and other agricultural commodities provided the bulk of Indian tax revenues, but vast differences in regional soil conditions, climate, and productivity made uniform tax rates extremely difficult to enforce. During Akbar's reign, therefore, massive surveys of local conditions were conducted to monitor harvests and grain prices over 10-year periods. These were then compiled into data tables used by local officials to calculate expected harvests and tax obligations. Imperial and local officials would sign agreements as to grain amounts to meet tax obligations over a set period. These obligations, like the Chinese "single-whip" system (see Chapter 21), would then be paid in silver or copper coin in four installments.

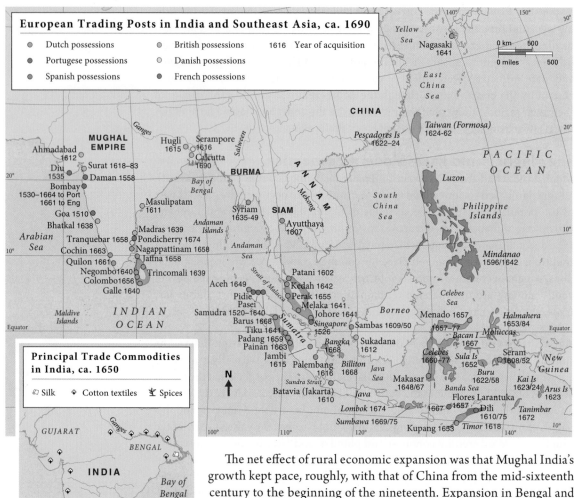

European Trading Posts in India and Southeast Asia, ca. 1690

- Dutch possessions
- Portugese possessions
- Spanish possessions
- British possessions
- Danish possessions
- French possessions

1616 Year of acquisition

Principal Trade Commodities in India, ca. 1650

Silk   Cotton textiles   Spices

MAP 20.4 **European Trading Ports in India and Southeast Asia, ca. 1690.**

The net effect of rural economic expansion was that Mughal India's growth kept pace, roughly, with that of China from the mid-sixteenth century to the beginning of the nineteenth. Expansion in Bengal and northeast India of wet rice cultivation and the introduction of American crops such as maize and potatoes in dryer areas allowed for a population increase from about 150 million in 1600 to 200 million in 1800. Moreover, acreage under cultivation increased by perhaps as much as one-third over this same period. Preferential tax rates on tobacco, indigo, sugarcane, cotton, pepper, ginger, and opium ensured that supplies of these coveted trade items would be secure. India began a burgeoning silk industry during this time as well. Thus, revenues more than doubled between Akbar's and Aurangzeb's reigns, to about 333.5 million rupees a year, while the increase in population meant that the per capita tax burden actually went down.

International Trade   India had been the center of Indian Ocean trade for nearly two millennia before the rise of the Mughals, but the advent of the world trading systems being created by the Atlantic maritime states added a vastly expanded dimension to this commerce. The intense and growing competition among the English, Dutch, and French East India Companies meant that Indian commodities were now being shipped globally, while imports of American silver and food and cash crops were growing annually. By the mid-seventeenth century, the Dutch and British dominated maritime trade in Indian spices. Between 1621 and 1670, for example, Indian exports of pepper to Europe doubled to 13.5 million pounds. An often added bonus was Indian saltpeter, a vital component of gunpowder, used as ships' ballast (see Map 20.4).

Perhaps of even more long-term importance, however, was the growth of India's textile trade. Here, French access to Bengali silk contributed immensely to French leadership in European silk products, while Indian indigo supplied European needs for this dye until slave production of it in the Americas lowered its cost still further. Most momentous of all, though, was the rapid rise of Indian cotton exports. Lighter and more comfortable than wool or linen, Indian cotton *calicoes* (named for Indian port of Calicut) proved immensely popular for underwear and summer clothing. Indeed, the familiar term "pajamas" comes from the Hindi word *pajama*, the lightweight summer garments worn in India and popularized as sleepwear in Europe.

Society, Family, and Gender

Though the majority of the material in this chapter describes the activities of the Muslim Timurids in Indian history and society, it must be kept in mind that the vast majority of people in all areas of India were Hindus rather than Muslims. Thus, although the laws and customs of the areas controlled by the Mughals had a considerable effect on all members of Indian society, most of the everyday lives of Indians at the pargana, village, clan, and family levels went on much as it had before the arrival of the Mughals—or, for that matter, before the arrival of Islam.

Caste, Clan, and Village   As we saw in earlier chapters, the ties of family, clan, and caste were the most important for the majority of Indians (most of whom were Hindu), particularly in rural society, which comprised perhaps 90 percent of the subcontinent's population. Even after the reimposition of the tax on unbelievers by Aurangzeb and the restrictions on the building and rehabilitating of Hindu temples, Hindu life at the local level went on much as it had before. Indeed, many new converts to Islam retained their caste and clan affiliations, especially in areas in which caste affiliation was determined by language, village designation, or profession.

For rural Indian society, however, even in areas under Muslim control for centuries, religious and cultural tensions as well as local friction with central authority were present. Thus, during the reign of Akbar, whose tolerant rule eased tensions somewhat, clan archives are relatively quiet; in contrast, during Aurangzeb's long rule and periods of internal conflict, these same archives bristle with militia drives and petitions for redress of assorted grievances. In areas only marginally under Mughal control, clan councils offered resources for potential rebels.

Family and Gender   For the Indian elites outside the areas of Mughal control, family life of the higher castes went on largely as it had from the time of the Guptas. The "twice-born" Hindus of the brahman varna went through lengthy training and apprenticeship in the household of a trusted guru in preparation for their roles as religious and societal leaders through their various stages of life. Women, who

Jahangir's Influential Wife, the Former Persian Princess Nur Jahan, in Her Silk Gauze Inner-Court Dress.

in the pursuit of dharma it was said are "worthy of worship," nevertheless spent most of their lives in seclusion. Whether among the highest castes or the lowest, their primary duties still included the running of the household and childrearing. Among the elites, where education in literature, poetry, and basic mathematics was also available to certain women, maintaining the household accounts, supervising servants, as well as education in the arts of living and loving as depicted in the *Kama Sutra* were also considered part of a wife's proper knowledge. In all cases, however, as in China, the "inner" world of the household and the "outer" world of business, politics, warfare, and so on were clearly defined by gender. In rural areas, the lives and work of peasant families, though generally guided by traditional gender roles, were more flexible in that large collective tasks such as planting and harvesting required the participation of both men and women.

The conquests of the Mughals brought with them a somewhat different temperament among their elites. The nomadic Turkic peoples of the Asian steppes, with their reliance on mobility and herding and organization around small groups of fiercely independent families and clans, had not developed the elaborate class, caste, and gender hierarchies of their settled neighbors. Women could, and often did, exercise a far greater degree of power and influence than even among the Hindu, Sikh, or Muslim elites in India.

Even after the conversion of these nomadic peoples to Islam, this tradition of female independence continued among the Timurids. As we saw earlier, for example, Babur's mother played a vital role in his rise to power, and emperors' wives, like Mumtaz Mahal, exercised a considerable degree of control in the imperial household. Moreover, since marriages played a vital role in cementing diplomatic and internal relations, women exercised a good deal of influence in terms of the extension of imperial power. Nur Jahan (d. 1645), the striking Persian princess married to Jahangir, played a leading role in court politics and in mediation during the succession wars at the end of Jahangir's reign. Indeed, Jahangir turned the running of the empire over to her on several occasions, stating that he felt quite secure with it in her capable hands.

As the Mughals assimilated local Muslim elites, the court quickly set up the harem as an institution of seclusion and protection for court women. Yet within the harem, women enjoyed considerable freedom, constructed their own hierarchies among the imperial wives and their attendants, and celebrated their own holidays and ceremonies largely insulated from the influence of men. It was in many respects a kind of alternative women's society, in which a distinct system of values was instilled in daughters and, crucially, women newly married into the household. For these women, navigating the harem's social relationships was of supreme importance, since the inner harmony of the court—and sometimes human lives—depended on it.

Science, Religion, and the Arts

While the advancement of science and technology in Mughal India did not match the pace set during the scientific revolution in western Europe, there were nonetheless several noteworthy developments in weaponry, mathematics, and astronomy. In terms of religion, as we have seen, the great theological differences between Hindus and Muslims persisted—and with the reign of Aurangzeb increased. Again, however, the tendency of Hinduism to assimilate other traditions and the relative compatibility of Islamic Sufi practices with other mystical traditions did sometimes decrease tensions. This, of course, was most dramatically seen with Akbar's efforts at bridging the religious gaps of his empire. Finally, one could say that where attempts at reconciling religions failed, language, literature, art, and architecture often succeeded and left a brilliant legacy of cultural synthesis.

Science and Technology

As they had done for centuries already, Muslim scholars in India drew upon the rich scientific history of the subcontinent and merged it with their efforts at preserving, commenting on, and transmitting the ancient Greco-Roman and Persian achievements. Among the most important developments in this regard, as we have seen in other chapters, was the spreading of the Indian decimal number system and the use of zero as a placeholder in mathematical computations. This had already had a profound effect on the development of European science, which forever after referred to that system as "Arabic numerals." Among the developments that directly fostered the rise of Muslim empires, none was more important than the rapid development of gunpowder weapons.

New Directions in Firearms in the Gunpowder Empires   The spread of firearms from China and the shift in emphasis among weapons developers from rockets to tubular weapons firing projectiles is an extraordinarily complex subject and one littered with claims and counterclaims for the ultimate sources of particular innovations. We can say, however, that by the beginning of the sixteenth century, the armies of the major European kingdoms, Ming China, Ottoman Turkey, and Persia had all become accustomed to employing cannons and explosive charges for besieging fortresses, were developing more convenient and effective small arms for their infantries, and were beginning to employ lighter, more portable cannons as field guns for pitched battles. The use of these weapons became so pervasive and the changes that accompanied them so important that scholars often refer to the states of the Mughals, Persians, and Ottomans as the **gunpowder empires**.

Given the desire on the part of all armies to expand their firepower, it is not surprising that a gifted engineer, astronomer, and philosopher named Fathullah Shirazi (ca. 1580) came up with a design for a multibarreled gun—similar to one designed by Leonardo da Vinci—for Akbar's armies. In this case, 12–16 light cannons were mounted side by side on a gun carriage and fired by the operator in quick succession.

Gunpowder empires: Muslim-ruled empires of the Ottomans, Safavids, and Mughals that used cannons and small arms in their military campaigns, 1450–1750.

Mathematics and Astronomy   India's long history of mathematical innovation merged with Muslim work on astronomical observation to make impressive

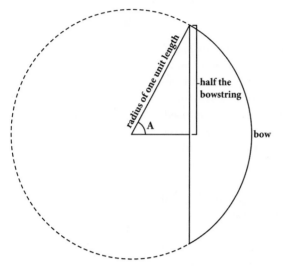

Origins of the Trigonometric Sine of an Angle as Described by Indian Mathematicians. Indian mathematicians did pioneering work in all of the areas of mathematics, particularly arithmetic and geometry. Hindu geometers knew of the trigonometric sine of an angle from at least the eighth century CE, if not earlier. In the early ninth century, the great Arabic mathematician al-Khwarizmi described the sine of an angle in his treatise on "Hindu" numbers, which was subsequently translated into Latin in the twelfth century. Through a series of mistranslations from one language to another, the original Sanskrit word for sine, *jya-ardha* ("half the bowstring"), ended up being rendered as "sinus" in Latin and other European languages—the modern sine.

advances in celestial calculation. A century before Akbar, Indian mathematicians had pushed their calculations of the value of pi to nine decimal places and expanded their facility with trigonometry to the point where some of the fundamental concepts of infinite series and calculus had been worked out.

Like other agrarian peoples reliant on an accurate calendar for the yearly agricultural and ceremonial cycle, Mughal rulers had a vital interest in knowing when unusual celestial phenomena such as comets, eclipses, and meteor showers were due and in having explanations for them ready at hand. Using extremely fine calculations and careful observation, the astronomers of the Kerala school, active from the fourteenth to the sixteenth centuries, had calculated elliptical orbits for the visible planets a century in advance of Johannes Kepler and suggested systems of planetary orbits similar to those of both Tycho Brahe and Copernicus (Chapter 17).

Religion: In Search of Balance

As scholars have often noted, Indian Islam went through relatively open, inclusive, and Sufi-oriented cycles—most notably in this chapter during the reigns of Babur, Humayun, and Akbar—and phases in which a more rigorous attention to orthodox Sunni practices and the desire to connect with Muslim communities beyond India prevailed, such as during the reigns of Jahangir, Shah Jahan, and especially Aurangzeb. These periods, as we have already seen, had a profound effect on the relations of minority Muslim rulers with non-Muslim subjects. But they also played an important role in mandating which forms of Islam would be most influential in Mughal India and the relations of the Mughals with the Muslims of other regions.

The Position of Non-Muslims in Mughal India   As we have seen in earlier chapters, despite profound theological differences between the monotheism of Islam and the profuse polytheism of popular Hindu religious traditions, there was a degree of attraction between the adherents of the two religions. As was the case with mystical and devotional sects of both, they saw a commonality in their ways of encountering the profound mysteries of faith. Thus, Akbar's grounding in Islamic Sufi mysticism made him interested in and receptive to Hindu mystical traditions. For their part, in addition to the mystical elements of Islam—in any case accessible only to a relative few—far more Hindus of the lower castes were attracted to the equality before God of all Islamic believers. Thus, like Buddhism before it, Islam promised emancipation from the restrictions of the caste system and a shared brotherhood of believers without regard for ethnicity, race, job, or social position.

More generally, however, the religious divisions remained difficult to reconcile. From the time of the first occupation of territories by Muslim armies in the seventh century, nonbelievers had been granted the legal status of protected peoples (Chapter 10). That is, they were allowed to worship as they pleased and govern according to their own religious laws. There were also inducements and penalties aimed at conversion to Islam. Unbelievers were subject to the *jizya* and pilgrimage taxes, and they suffered job discrimination in official circles, all of which disappeared once they converted. For their part, Hindus considered Muslims to be ritually unclean (*mleccha*), and upper-caste members underwent elaborate purification rites after coming into contact with them.

Yet the presence of a vastly larger Hindu population also meant that considerable accommodation had to be made by the rulers in order to run the empire effectively and even more to maintain order at the local level. Akbar, as we noted earlier, banned the discriminatory taxes on unbelievers. In addition, the financial skills of Hindus and Jains were increasingly sought by the court, and their status rose further when Akbar made a Hindu his finance minister and employed Hindu court astrologers. Perhaps of even more symbolic and political importance was the habit of Mughal rulers of occasionally marrying Hindu women.

The position of Christians was similar. They, along with Jews, were considered "people of the Book" and therefore protected but still subject to the same taxes and impediments before the reign of Akbar. While the position of Christian missionaries in Mughal lands was often precarious, the reverence with which Muslims regarded the biblical prophets and Jesus also helped to smooth diplomatic relations at court. Akbar invited Jesuits to his debates, and paintings of Christian religious figures, especially the Virgin Mary, can be found in Mughal depictions of court life.

Yet this period of relative religious openness peaked with Akbar, and the pendulum soon began to swing back with increasing speed. Mughal receptiveness of Islamic mysticism and other religions, as most dramatically displayed by Akbar's new *din-i ilahi* religion, offended more orthodox Sunni Muslims. Their influence was felt at court during the reign of Jahangir and especially during that of Shah Jahan, who merged love and piety in the form of the Taj Mahal. It reached its zenith during Aurangzeb's reign. As Mughal lands stretched to their greatest extent, the austere Aurangzeb reimposed the taxes on unbelievers and purged many Hindus from his court.

Islamic Developments   While the vast majority of India's Muslims remained adherents of the Sunni branch of Islam and Hanafi school of interpretation of Islamic law, there were also several noteworthy developments in other areas. First, as we have noted several times already, there was an influential Shiite presence in India. For centuries, Shiites had migrated into Hindu areas of southern India, where, despite being a notable minority, they generally escaped the discrimination at the hands of Sunnis characteristic of the north. In addition, Mughal relations with Safavid Persia, where Shia Islam was the official state religion, meant a certain influence on the Mughal court was unavoidable. Hence, Akbar studied mystical elements of Shiism, while Jahangir married the Safavid princess Nur Jahan, probably the most powerful woman of the Mughal period.

One branch of Shiism that attained considerable influence despite its small numbers was that of the Ismailis. Like a number of Muslim mystical brotherhoods, the Ismailis, originally refugees from the fall of the Fatimid caliphate, blended Shiite mysticism with practices borrowed from the devotional (*bhakti*) cults of Hinduism. During Aurangzeb's reign they were suppressed as part of his general drive to bring Indian Islam more in accordance with Islamic law. They survived and later prospered, however, and in the twentieth century, their leader, the Aga Khan, was one of the world's wealthiest men.

Literature and Art

The Mughal period was one of India's most prolific in terms of its profusion of literary genres. Moreover, literature, art, and architecture were the areas in which India's rich multicultural environment produced its most arrestingly synthetic works. In translation projects, classical Persian works, poetry in nearly all of India's languages, and even treatises on law and theology, Indian writers borrowed freely and frequently from each other. In painting, realistic portraits of personages and dramatic contemporary and historical scenes were recorded; and of course the great buildings of the era remain for many the "authentic" symbols of India.

New Literary Directions   As they had been for centuries in Islamic India, Arabic and Persian remained the principal literary languages. The use of both, however, was considerably enlivened by the introduction of the latest wave of Turkic terms by the Chaghatay–Turkic Mughals. Chaghatay itself remained in use among the elites until the nineteenth century, while many of its loan words, along with a considerable Persian and Arabic vocabulary, were grafted onto the base of Sanskrit to form the modern languages of Hindi and Urdu. Regional languages, such as Kashmiri and Bengali, also rose to prominence for both literary and general use.

Ironically, one of the catalysts for the explosion of literary work from the mid-sixteenth to the mid-seventeenth centuries came from the Mughals' most humiliating period. The exile of Humayun to Persia in the 1540s coincided with the Persian Shah Tahmasp embarking on a program of self-denial and abstinence in response to criticism about the worldliness of his court. Writers, painters, and poets who suddenly found themselves out of favor at the Persian court attached themselves to Humayun. They followed him to India, where their talents enlivened the arts already developing there. Their classical Arab and Persian verse forms were ultimately adopted into Urdu, as seen in the classical verse forms of *qasida* and *mathnavi*. By the following century, these forms had matured with the verses of Qudsi and Abu Talib Kalim (d. 1602), whose verses were considered models of adept compression of emotion.

> "Life's tragedy lasts but two days.
>   I'll tell you what these two are for;
>   One day, to attach the heart to this and that;
>   One day, to detach it again."
> —Abu Talib Kalim

Though Sunni scholarship languished somewhat under Akbar, Sufi works proliferated, many borrowing concepts and terminology from non-Islamic sources. The most famous of these was Muhammad Ghauth Gwaliori's *The Five Jewels*, which tapped sources from Hindu and Muslim astrology and Jewish Kabbala traditions, as well as Sufi mysticism. By Aurangzeb's reign, the pendulum had swung back to the more Mecca-centered, prophetic, and exclusive strain in Indian Islam. Thus, the works tended to be more often treatises on Islamic law, interpretation of *hadith*—the traditions of the Prophet—and Sunni works on science and philosophy.

Art and Painting   One of the more interesting aspects of Islam as practiced by the Mughals—as well as the Safavid Persians and Ottomans—is that the injunctions against depicting human beings in art were often widely ignored in the inner chambers and private rooms of the court. Of course, during Aurangzeb's long reign, there was a marked drop in artistic output because of his much stricter interpretation of proper Islamic behavior.

Not surprisingly, Akbar had a direct hand in the creation of what is considered to be the first painting in the "Mughal style"—a combination of the extreme delicacy of Persian miniature work with the vibrant colors and taste for bold themes of Hindu painters. Akbar inherited two of the master painters who accompanied Humayun from Persia, and the contact they acquired with Hindu works under Akbar's patronage resulted in hundreds of Mughal **gouache** works, including the colossal illustrated *Hamzanama* of 1570. The Persian tradition of miniature painting flourished under the Mughals. Illustrations of Muslim and Hindu religious themes and epics were perennial favorites, as were numerous depictions of imperial *durbars*—receptions requiring noble attendance at court. These usually included authentic portraits of key individuals and provide scholars with important clues as to the identities of courtiers and dignitaries. Mughal artists often passed their skills on within their families over generations and represented an important subset of members at the imperial court and among the entourages of regional elites.

By the end of the sixteenth century, a new influence was beginning to affect Mughal art: Europeans. The realistic approach of European artists and their use of perspective began to be felt at the courts of Akbar and Jahangir. One prominent female artist, Nadira Banu, specialized in producing Flemish-style works. Some took European paintings and added Mughal touches—flatter backgrounds, gold leaf, and mosques in the distance. The period of Akbar's religious experiments also prompted an unparalleled interest among Mughal painters in Christian religious figures. Depictions of Christ from the gospels and from Muslim tales were popular fare, as were angels; even more so was the figure of the Virgin, a picture of whom even appears in a portrait of Jahangir. It was perhaps the most dramatic meeting of cultural influences since the era of the Gandharan Buddhas that were fashioned in the style of the Greek god Apollo.

The *Hamzanama* (Book of Hamza). Akbar so enjoyed the *Hamzanama*, a heroic romance about the legendary adventures of the Prophet Mohammad's uncle Amir Hamza, that he commissioned an illustrated version in 1562. This painting from Akbar's version shows the prophet Elijah rescuing Hamza's nephew Prince Nur ad-Dahr.

Gouache: Watercolors with a gum base.

Architecture   Nowhere was the Mughal style more in evidence than in the construction of tombs and mausoleums. The most prominent of these, the Taj Mahal, was introduced in the opening to this chapter and needs little additional discussion. The ethereal lightness of so colossal a construction and the perfection of its layout make it the most distinctive construction of its kind. Europeans sometimes assumed that its architects were influenced by French or Italian artistic trends, though this remains a subject of debate. The chief architect, Ustad Ahmad Lahori (d. 1649), also designed the famous Red Fort of Shah Jahan's city, Shahjahanabad.

During the high point of Mughal wealth and power, several Mughal emperors built entire cities. By far the most famous of these, as we have previously seen, was Akbar's Fatehpur Sikri. Indeed, as an idealized tribute to the inclusive Sufi master Salim Chishti, with architectural influences from Hindu and Muslim sources, materials from all over India, and a quote from Jesus, as handed down in Islamic lore, over its gateway—"The world is but a bridge; cross over it but build no house upon it"—it does indeed reflect Akbar's vision of what his realm should be. Not to be outdone, of course, Shah Jahan created his own city complex at Delhi, Shahjahanabad.

As one would expect, just as they were integral to the tomb complexes of the Mughals, mosques would be among the empire's most important constructions. Many were built as shrines at holy sites or to mark significant events in the lives of holy men or martyrs. Once again, a distinctive style emerged in which the basic form of the dome symbolically covering the world and the slender arrow of the minaret pointing heavenward interacted with central Asian, Persian, and even Hindu architectural influences. The largest Mughal mosques, like the Friday Delhi Mosque (Jama Masjid) in Shahjahanabad and Aurangzeb's huge Badshahi Mosque in Lahore, contain immense courtyards, surrounded by cloisters leading to small rooms for intimate gatherings, domed areas for men and women, and distinctive minarets with fluted columns and bell-shaped roofs. One mosque in Burhanpur built by Shah Jahan even has Sanskrit translations of Quranic verses in it. As scholars have noted, the location of many of the largest mosques, like those of some European cathedrals, is adjacent to government buildings and forts in order to demonstrate the seamless connections of these religious civilizations.

Putting It All Together

The rise of the Turkic central Asian peoples to prominence and power, from the borders of successive Chinese dynasties to Anatolia and the domains of the Ottomans, and with the Timurids or Mughals in India, is one of the most dramatic sagas of world history. In India, this latest group of outside conquerors faced what might be called the "great question" of the subcontinent: how to create a viable state out of so many long-standing religious traditions, many of which are in direct opposition to each other. Even before the coming of Islam, rulers such as Ashoka felt the need to use transcendent concepts, such as dharma, to try to bridge cultural and religious gaps. The Guptas, for their part, tried to use state-supported Hinduism. With the arrival of Islam, a new religion that stood in opposition to the older Hindu pattern of assimilation of gods and favored instead the conquest and conversion of opponents, a divide was created, which persists to this day. It should be remembered that, as recent scholarship has shown, even within these dramatically opposed religious traditions, much more accommodation than previously supposed took place. The later development of Sikhism, as another attempt at a syncretic bridge across India's religious divide, both added to attempts at greater tolerance and at times contributed to religious tensions.

Against this backdrop the accomplishments of the Mughals must be weighed as significant in terms of statecraft and artistic and cultural achievement, and perhaps less so in religious areas. At its height, Mughal India was the most populous, wealthy, politically powerful, and economically vibrant empire in the world next to China. It thus allowed the Mughal rulers unprecedented wealth and financed the proliferation of monumental architecture that became forever identified with India: the Red Fort, Fatehpur Sikri, and, above all, the Taj Mahal.

Yet, for all its wealth and power, the Mughal dynasty was plagued by problems that ultimately proved insoluble. The old nomadic succession practices of the Timurids repeatedly led to palace revolts by potential heirs. These wars in turn encouraged conflict with internal and external enemies who sensed weakness at the core of the regime. Protracted conflicts in Afghanistan, with Safavid Persia, and in Bengal also bled this centralized state of resources. Finally, the Maratha wars slowly wore down even the semblance of unity among the rulers following Aurangzeb.

But perhaps an equally important factor in the ultimate dissolution of the empire was that of Hindu–Muslim syncretism. Here, we have two of the world's great religions interacting with each other in prolonged and profound ways, with the added complication of Muslim rulers and Muslims in general being a minority among the subcontinent's people. Despite the flexibility of the early rulers in trying to deemphasize the more oppressive elements of Islamic rule in Hindu India— most dramatically, Akbar through his effort to create an entirely new religion— the attempt at a stricter orthodoxy under Aurangzeb hardened Hindu–Muslim and Sikh divisions for centuries to come.

Throughout the period, one other factor loomed larger day by day as the dynasty went into decline. The well-financed and well-armed trading companies of the Europeans, increasingly adept at reading Indian politics, gradually moved into positions of regional power. By 1750, they were on the cusp of changing the political situation completely. Indeed, the seeds that had been planted by 1750 would soon be reaped as the first great clash of mature religious civilizations with the new industrially based societies. By 1920, all of these religious civilizations would be gone.

▶ For additional resources, including maps, primary sources, visuals, and quizzes, please go to www.oup.com/us/vonsivers. Please see the Further Resources section at the back of the book for additional readings and suggested websites.

Against the Grain

Sikhism in Transition

As we saw in Chapter 13, the example of Zen Buddhism affords an example of a pacifistic religious tradition that was taken up by warrior classes. In some respects, Sikhism underwent a similar transformation, though not as thoroughgoing as that of Zen, and one that took place for very different reasons. As we remember from Chapter 12, the Sikhs had started from an avowedly peaceful premise: that the tension, and even all-out warfare, between Hindus and Muslims must somehow be transcended. Influenced by poets and mystics like Kabir and Guru Nanak, and drawing upon the emotional connections experienced by Muslim Sufis and Hindu Bhakti devotees who proclaimed that "there is no Hindu; there is no Musselman [Muslim]," the Sikhs had emerged during the sixteenth century as an entirely new religious movement.

Yet, far from providing a model for the two contending religions to emulate, Sikhs were viewed with suspicion by both. Although they attracted enough of a following to remain vital to the present day, their attempts at transcendence were viewed in much the same light as Akbar's attempts at a new religious synthesis were. Though they were awarded the city of Amritsar, the Golden Temple of which became their religious center, Mughal repression of the Sikhs under Aurangzeb in the seventeenth century provoked a prolonged rebellion, which turned them into a fierce fighting faith in self-defense. The Sikhs established control of most of the Punjab region during the eighteenth-century decline of the Mughals. During the days of British control, the reputation of the Sikhs as fierce fighters prompted the British to employ them as colonial troops and policemen throughout their empire. Even after independence, smoldering disputes between the government and Sikhs urging local autonomy for Punjab led to the assassination of Indian prime minister Indira Gandhi in retaliation for a government operation to forcibly remove a Sikh splinter group from the Golden Temple in 1984.

- **Why would both Hindus and Muslims express hostility toward a religion that claims to want to transcend the differences between them? Did the Sikhs appear to have any alternatives to becoming a fighting faith in order to ensure their survival?**

- **Why does it seem that, on the whole, what we have termed "religious civilizations" have difficulty tolerating different religious traditions within their domains? Does loyalty to a state require loyalty to its approved religion(s) as well? Why?**

Thinking Through Patterns

▶ **What were the strengths and weaknesses of Mughal rule?**

The weaknesses are probably more obvious than the strengths at first glance. Two things are immediately apparent: first, the position of the Mughals as an ethnic and religious minority ruling a vastly larger majority population and, second, the conflict-prone succession practices of the older central Asian Turkic leaders. The minority position of the Mughals aggravated long-existing tensions between Hindu subjects and Muslim rulers in India, of which the Mughals were to be the last line. In an age of religious civilizations, where some kind of unity of religion was the ideal, this put considerable strains on the Mughals as rulers—as it did the Ottomans in predominantly Christian lands and Catholics and Protestants in Europe. Central Asian Turkic succession practices almost always guaranteed conflict when it was time for a new ruler to accede the throne. Nearly every Mughal successor during this period ended up having to fight factions and family to gain the empire.

In some respects the strengths of Mughal rule developed in reaction to these problems. Babur and Akbar, in particular, were extraordinarily tolerant rulers in terms of religion. When later rulers like Aurangzeb returned to strict Sunni Islamic policies, it prompted resistance, especially among Hindus. Also, while Mughal rulers were never able to completely free themselves from succession struggles, they succeeded in setting up a well-run fiscal–military state with the mansabdar system, largely undercutting old local and regional loyalties and tying the new loyalty to the state. Like France, the Ottomans, and the Confucian states of eastern Asia, the development of bureaucratic forms was an important earmark of the early modern era.

As we noted, Mughal rulers faced the problem confronted by nearly all "religious civilizations": Religious orthodoxy was seen, in theory, as a vital element of loyalty to the state. But for the Mughals, as for previous Muslim rulers in India, the desire for strict adherence to Muslim law was always tempered by the problem of Islam being a minority religion in India. Here, as we saw, the early Mughal rulers—Babur, Humayun, Akbar—were far less tied to strict Sunni Islam than their successors. Thus, their way of ruling was to uphold Sunni Islam as the approved state religion but to scrupulously refrain from forcing Muslim practices on other religious groups. Akbar went so far as to create a new religion and held Thursday-night discussions with leaders of other religions to find ways to satisfy the desires of all. With Shah Jahan, however, the reaction building among reform-minded Sunni Muslims to this liberalization turned into enforcing more strict practices, which peaked during the long reign of Aurangzeb. By the end of Aurangzeb's reign the Sikhs were near revolt and the long Hindu Maratha revolt was in full swing. But even during this period, local religious customs remained largely intact and, indeed, often thrived.

▶ **What was the Mughal policy toward religious accommodation? How did it change over time?**

▶ **What factors account for the Mughal decline during the eighteenth century?**

At the beginning and for much of the eighteenth century, Mughal India was the second richest and most prosperous empire in the world, after China. But by 1750 it was already in pronounced decline. A large part of this was due to rebellions by the Sikhs, Rajputs, and especially the Marathas that raged off and on through the century. By the 1750s as well, the European trading companies with their small but well-trained armies were becoming locally powerful. Here, the great milestone would take place during the Seven Years' War (1756–1763), when the British East India Company eliminated its French competitors and in essence took over the rule of Bengal from its headquarters in Calcutta. Within 100 years it would take over all of India.

Chapter 21 1500–1800

Regulating the "Inner" and "Outer" Domains

CHINA AND JAPAN

The time seemed right for a letter home. In only 2 weeks the Japanese invasion force had captured the Korean capital of Seoul, and the skill and firepower of the Japanese warriors seemed to let them brush their opponents aside at will. The Japanese commander, Toyotomi Hideyoshi, was a battle-hardened commoner who had risen through the ranks of his patron, Oda Nobunaga, as Oda fought to unite Japan before his assassination in 1582. Now, a decade later, Hideyoshi, as he was still known (as a commoner he had no surname and had only been given the family name Toyotomi by the imperial court in 1586) had embarked on an audacious campaign to extend his power to the Asian mainland. Six years before, he had written his mother that he contemplated nothing less than the conquest of China. Now seemed like a good time to inform her that his goal might actually be within his grasp.

As if in an eerie foreshadowing of another Korean conflict to come centuries later, however, the Japanese soon faced a massive Chinese and Korean counterattack and became mired in a bloody stalemate, their guns and tactics barely enough to compensate for the determination and numbers of their

ABOVE: This scene, one of 15 from the handscroll painting A Visit to the Yoshiwara by Hishikawa Mononobu (ca. 1625–1694), depicts the "floating world" of Tokugawa Japan.

enemies. After 4 more years of negotiation punctuated by bitter fighting, Hideyoshi finally withdrew to Japan. One final invasion attempt of Korea in 1597 collapsed when his death the following year set off a bloody struggle for succession, which ultimately placed in power the Tokugawa family, who would go on to rule Japan for more than 250 years.

Hideyoshi's dream of conquering China was, in a sense, a quest to claim the wellsprings of Japanese civilization as well. The episode brought together the politics, cultures, and fortunes of three of the four fiercely independent realms that together wove the primary strands of an east Asian pattern of history. The fourth, Vietnam, while not involved in this particular struggle, had been subject to similar pressures of Chinese cultural and political diffusion for eighteen centuries. The rise of Japanese power represents a vitally important pattern of world history, which we have seen in other areas, such as the Mediterranean and the expanding kingdoms of Europe: A state on the periphery absorbs innovation from a cultural center, in this case China, and then becomes a vital center itself. And like the other states in the region, Japan had absorbed the structures of "religious civilizations," as we have termed them—in this case, the philosophical system of Neo-Confucianism.

Of equal importance, Hideyoshi's invasion was made possible in part by the arrival of a new factor: the appearance of the first Europeans in the region. While their arrival in the sixteenth century provided only the smallest inkling of the reversals of fortune to come, by the middle of the nineteenth century their presence would create a crisis of power and acculturation for all of east Asia. For Japan, the industrializing West would then become a new center from which to draw innovation. For the present, however, European intrusions provided powerful incentives for both China and Japan to turn inward to safeguard their own security and stability.

Late Ming and Qing China to 1750

Proclaimed as a new dynasty in 1368, the Ming in its early years appears to have followed the familiar pattern of the "dynastic cycle" of previous dynasties. Having driven out the Mongol remnant, the Hongwu emperor and his immediate successors consolidated their rule, elevated the Confucian bureaucracy to its former place, and set up an administrative structure more focused on the person of the emperor than in previous dynasties. In 1382, the Grand Secretariat was created as the top governmental board below the emperor. Under the Grand Secretariat were the six boards, the governors and governors-general of the provinces, and lower-level officials of various degrees down to the district magistrate.

In this section we will also take up the question of China's retreat from its greatest period of maritime expansion in the early 1400s—and sudden withdrawal to concentrate on domestic matters. Why such an abrupt change in policy? What factors led to the ultimate decline of the Ming dynasty and the rise to power of the Manchus, a bordering nomadic people who drove out the Ming and created China's last imperial dynasty, the Qing [ching]? By what means did the Manchus

Seeing Patterns

▶ Why did late Ming and early Qing China look inward after such a successful period of overseas exploration?

▶ How do the goals of social stability drive the policies of agrarian states? How does the history of China and Japan in this period show these policies in action?

▶ In what ways did contact with the maritime states of Europe alter the patterns of trade and politics in eastern Asia?

▶ How did Neo-Confucianism in China differ from that of Tokugawa Japan?

Chapter Outline

- Late Ming and Qing China to 1750

- The Long War and Longer Peace: Japan, 1450–1750

- Putting It All Together

create a state in which, despite being a tiny ruling minority, they held their grip on power into the twentieth century? Finally, what faint hints of the dynasty's problems appeared during its time of greatest power in the mid-eighteenth century?

From Expansion to Exclusion

During the late fourteenth and early fifteenth centuries, while China was rebuilding from the war to drive out the Mongols, the more pressing problems of land distribution and tenancy had abated somewhat. As in Europe, the depopulation of some areas from fighting and banditry and the lingering effects of the Black Death (which had reduced China's population from perhaps 100 million to about 60 million) had raised the value of labor, depressed the price of land, and increased the proportional amount of money in circulation. While the problems of land tenure would recur, another period of relief from their full effects soon came, albeit indirectly, from the creation of overseas empires by the Portuguese and the Spanish in the sixteenth century. The resulting Columbian Exchange saw the circulation of a number of new food crops on a global scale that had a substantial impact on the world's agricultural productivity (see Chapter 18).

New Food Crops   In addition to new, higher-yielding rice strains from southeast Asia, the Chinese began to cultivate sugarcane, indigo, potatoes, sweet potatoes, maize (corn), peanuts, and tobacco that came from Africa and the Americas by way of the Spanish in the Philippines and the Portuguese at Macau. Corn and potatoes, versatile crops suitable for cultivation in a variety of marginal environments, accounted for a considerable increase in the arable land within China. Peanuts, sugarcane, indigo, and tobacco quickly established themselves as important cash crops.

Aided by the productivity of these new crops, China's population grew from its low of perhaps 60 million at the beginning of the Ming period to an estimated 150 million by 1600. There was also a marked growth in urbanism as market towns and regional transshipment points multiplied. The efficiency of Chinese agriculture, the continued incorporation of marginal and border lands into production, and the refinement of the empire's immense internal trade all contributed to another doubling of the population to perhaps 300 million by 1800. This accelerating growth began China's movement toward what some historical demographers have called a *high-level equilibrium trap*—a condition in which the land has reached its maximum potential for feeding an increasing population; that population then (barring radical improvements in crops or technology) becomes slowly squeezed into impoverishment (see Map 21.1).

China and the World Commercial Revolution   China's rapid recovery, particularly as the sixteenth century brought new crops from the Americas, placed the late Ming and Qing Empires in the center of an increasingly extensive and complex worldwide commercial revolution (see "Patterns Up Close: The 'China' Trade"). The competition for markets among the emerging maritime Atlantic states of Europe pushed them to develop ever-widening trade networks in the Indian and Pacific Oceans, along the African coast, and in the Americas. In all of these regions (except the Americas) they faced stiff competition from local traders long involved in regional networks, particularly in the Indian Ocean, among the many ports of what is now Indonesia.

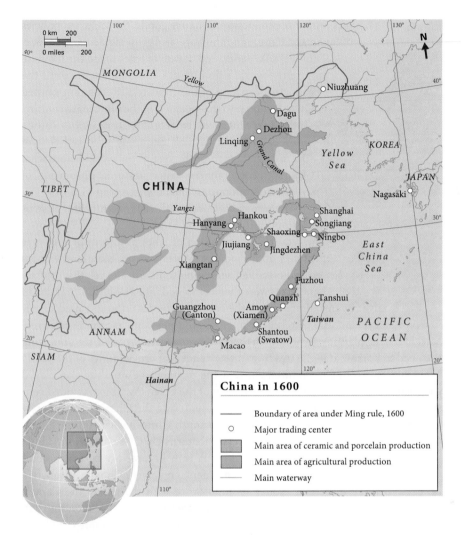

MAP **21.1** **China in 1600.**

Among the European states, commercial, political, and religious competition resulted in policies of mercantilism (see Chapters 17, 18, and 19) in which countries strove to control sources of raw materials and markets. Similarly, China and Japan (by the early seventeenth century) sought to tightly control imports, regulate the export trade, and keep potentially subversive foreign influences in check.

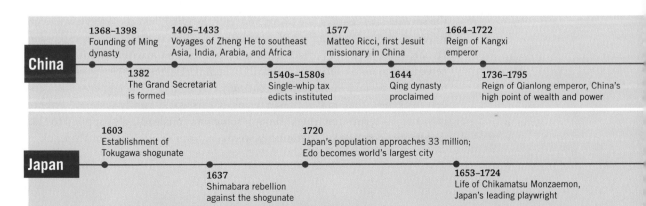

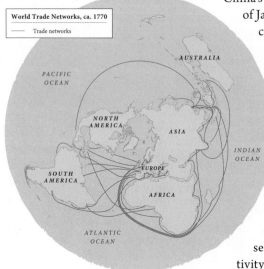

World Trade Networks, ca. 1770
—— Trade networks

AUSTRALIA

PACIFIC
OCEAN

NORTH
AMERICA

ASIA

INDIAN
OCEAN

EUROPE

SOUTH
AMERICA

AFRICA

ATLANTIC
OCEAN

MAP **21.2 World Trade Networks, ca. 1770.**

China's immense production of luxury goods, the seclusion policies of Japan and Korea, and the huge and growing demand for porcelain, tea, silk, paper, and cotton textiles made the Chinese empire the world's dominant economic engine until the productive capacity of the Industrial Revolution vaulted Great Britain into that position in the nineteenth century. Indeed, recent work by world historians has shown how extensively China's economy powered that of Eurasia and much of the rest of the world before what Kenneth Pomeranz has called "the great divergence" of Western economic ascendancy (see Map 21.2).

In the midst of this growth, the government took steps to simplify the system of land taxation. *Corvée* labor—the required contribution of labor as a form of tax—was effectively abolished. As in previous regimes, land was assessed and classified according to its use and relative productivity. Land taxes were then combined into a single bill, payable in silver by installments over the course of the year: the so-called single-whip tax system. The installment plan allowed peasants to remain relatively solvent during planting season when their resources were depleted, thus reducing the need to borrow at high rates from moneylenders at crucial times of the yearly cycle. Significantly, the requirement that the payment be in silver also played a crucial role in the increasing monetization of the economy. This was aided considerably by the increasing amounts of silver entering the Chinese economy by means of the Manila trade. Merchants from south China exchanged spices and Chinese luxury goods such as porcelain (see Patterns Up Close below) in Manila for Spanish silver from the Americas. Manila thus became a vital axis around which the trade economies of three continents revolved. Though ultimately eclipsed in trade share and economic importance with the rise of the Canton system in the eighteenth century, Spanish (and later Mexican) silver continued to be the preferred medium of exchange for Chinese merchants for more than three centuries.

Regulating the Outer Barbarians   By the late fifteenth century, Ming China had made considerable progress toward establishing the peace and stability long sought by Chinese regimes. In addition to the practical requirements of defending the historic avenues of invasion in China's remote interior, the view of the empire cultivated by China's elites placed it at the center of a world order defined by Neo-Confucian philosophy and supported by a host of Chinese cultural assumptions. As we will see in the following sections, like the Tokugawa shogunate in Japan in the seventeenth century, the Ming, and later the Qing, had come to view foreign influence as less "civilized" and far too often injurious to established social order. Hence, successive rulers placed severe restrictions on maritime trade and conceived of diplomatic relations primarily in commercial terms. "All the world is one family," imperial proclamations routinely claimed, and the emperor was conceived as the father, in Confucian terms, of this world-family system. "Tribute missions," a term sometimes (though somewhat misleadingly) applied to this diplomatic–commercial relationship, were sent from Korea, Vietnam, the Ryukyu

Islands, and occasionally Japan to pay periodic ceremonial visits to the emperor, who then bestowed presents on the envoys and granted them permission to trade in China. This arrangement worked reasonably well within the long-standing hierarchy of the Confucian cultural sphere. By the late eighteenth century, however, it came into direct conflict with the more egalitarian system of international trade and diplomacy that had evolved in the West.

The Ming in Decline   Despite the increased attention directed at the Mongol resurgence of the 1440s, periodic rebellions in the north and northwest punctuated the late fifteenth and sixteenth centuries. The huge commitment of Chinese troops in Korea against the forces of the Japanese leader Hideyoshi during his attempted invasion of Korea and China from 1592 to 1598 weakened the dynasty further during a crucial period that saw the rise of another regional power: the Manchus. By the turn of the seventeenth century, under the leadership of Nurhachi (r. 1616–1626) and Abahai (r. 1636–1643), the Manchus, an Altaic-speaking nomadic people inhabiting the northeastern section of the Ming domain, had become the prime military force of the area, and dissident Chinese sought them as allies. In 1642, the Chinese general Wu Sangui invited the Manchu leader Dorgon to cross the Great Wall where it approaches the sea at Shanhaiguan. For the Chinese, this event would come to carry the same sense of finality as Caesar's crossing of the Rubicon: The Manchus soon captured Beijing and declared the founding of a new regime, the Qing, or "pure," dynasty. Like the defeated remnant of the Nationalist regime in 1949, some Ming loyalists fled to the island of Taiwan, where they expelled the Dutch (who had established a trading base there) and held on until succumbing to Qing forces in 1683.

Manchu Bannermen, Canton, ca. 1872. Until the twentieth century, the Qing maintained garrisons of Manchu soldiers organized under the old "banner system" in all of China's major cities. The bannermen lived in their own quarter, often in reduced circumstances, as a check on the local Chinese population. Significantly, in terms of China's difficulties with Western imperialism in the later nineteenth century, the group pictured here was part of the guard of the British consul.

The Spring and Summer of Power: The Qing to 1750

Like the Toba and Mongols before them, the Manchus now found themselves in the position of having to "dismount and rule." A good deal of preparation for this had already taken place within the borderland state they had created for themselves—for a time, successfully isolated by the Ming—on the Liaodong Peninsula of south Manchuria. Long exposure to Chinese culture and Confucian administrative practices provided models that soon proved adaptable by Manchu leaders within the larger environment of China proper.

The Banner System   The **banner system**, under which the Manchus were organized for military and tax purposes, was also expanded under the Qing to provide for segregated Manchu elites and garrisons in major cities and towns. Under the banner system, the Manchu state had been divided into eight major military and ethnic (Manchu, Han Chinese, and Mongolian) divisions, each represented by a distinctive banner. Within each division, companies were formed of 300 fighters recruited from families represented by that banner. Originally devised for a

Banner system: The organizational system of the Manchus for military and taxation purposes; there were eight banners under which all military houses were arranged, and each was further divided into blocks of families required to furnish units of 300 soldiers to the Manchu government.

Patterns Up Close | The "China" Trade

Ming and Qing China may be said to be at the heart of two innovations of enormous importance to the patterns of world history. The first is one that we have tracked through all of the chapters in this book pertaining to China: the technical and aesthetic development of ceramics, culminating in the creation of true porcelain during the Song period (960–1279). The early Ming period saw the elaboration of the use of kaolin white clays with what are called "flux" materials—minerals, metals, and compounds—that can fuse with the clay under extremely high temperatures to form durable glazes and striking artistic features. Thus, the Song and Yuan periods were characterized by pure white and celadon green wares, some with a purposely created "crackle" glaze on them, while by the Ming period, highly distinctive blue and white ware—the result of employing pigments with cobalt oxide imported from the areas around modern Iran and Iraq—set the world standard for elegance.

The artistic excellence of Chinese porcelain, like earlier styles of Chinese ceramics, spawned imitations throughout the Chinese periphery. By 1500, porcelain works in Korea, Japan, and Vietnam supplied a burgeoning market both at home and throughout east and southeast Asia. While these regional manufacturers for the most part followed the designs of the Chinese imperial works at Jingdezhen, some, especially the Japanese ceramicist Chojiro, preferred highly rustic, rough-hewn earthenware designs with glazes that formed spontaneous designs as the pieces were fired—the famous raku ware. Thus, there was already a highly developed regional market for what was, at the time, arguably the world's most highly developed technology.

Porcelain Vase, Ming Period. Porcelain ware of the Song and Ming periods is among the most coveted Chinese art objects even today. Here we have a Ming vase showing characteristically vibrant colors and a degree of technical perfection indicative of the best Chinese pottery works, such as Jingdezhen. The motif of the grass carp on the vase is symbolic of endurance and perseverance, and thus associated with the god of literature and scholarship.

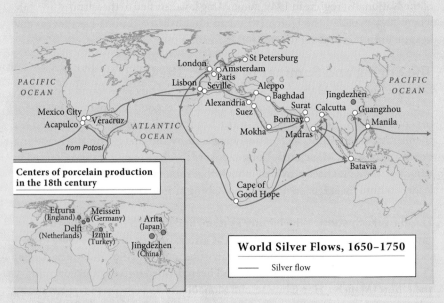

Centers of porcelain production in the 18th century

Etruria (England) Meissen (Germany) Arita (Japan)
Delft (Netherlands) Izmir (Turkey) Jingdezhen (China)

World Silver Flows, 1650–1750

——— Silver flow

MAP 21.3 **Silver Flows and Centers of Porcelain Production.**

The period from 1500 to the mid-nineteenth century brings us to the second great innovation in which China was the driving force: the world market for porcelain. China's wares had found customers for centuries in nearly every corner of Eurasia and North and East Africa. Shipwrecks have been found in the Straits of Malacca laden with Ming porcelain; traders in the Swahili cities along the East African coast were avid collectors, while Africans farther inland decorated their graves with Chinese bowls. All stops on the Silk Road had their precious supplies of porcelain, while the Ottoman Turks did their best to copy the blue and white Ming wares in their own factories at Izmir.

Before the sixteenth century, a trickle of Ming porcelain also made its way to Europe. With the establishment of the first European trade empires, however, the demand for porcelain skyrocketed. Portuguese, Spanish, and later Dutch, French, English, and (after 1784) American merchants all sought porcelain in ever-increasing amounts. From 1500 to 1800 it was arguably the single most important commodity in the unfolding world commercial revolution. While estimates vary, economic historians have suggested that between one-third to one-half of all the silver produced in the Americas during this time went to pay for porcelain. Incoming ships often used the bulk cargoes of porcelain as ballast, and foreign merchants sent custom orders to their Chinese counterparts for Chinese-style wares designed for use at Western tables. Such was the prominence of this "export porcelain" in the furnishings of period homes that scarcely any family of means was without it (see Map 21.3).

With the prominence of mercantilist theory and protectionism toward home markets during the seventeenth and eighteenth centuries, it is not surprising that foreign manufacturers sought to break the Chinese monopoly. During Tokugawa times, the Japanese, for example, forced a group of Korean potters to labor at the famous Arita works to turn out Sino–Korean designs; the Dutch marketed delftware as an attempt to copy Chinese "blue willow" porcelain. It was not until German experimenters in Saxony happened upon a workable formula for hard-paste porcelain—after years of trial and error, even melting down Chinese wares for analysis—that their facility at Meissen began to produce true porcelain in 1710. Josiah Wedgwood set up his own porcelain factory in 1759 in England. But Chinese manufacturers would still drive the market until the end of the nineteenth century. And fine porcelain would forever carry the generic name of "china" regardless of its origins.

Porcelain Candlestick for the Export Market, Qing Period. By the early 1700s, luxury exports from China such as porcelain, lacquerware, and, of course, tea had become important staples of European maritime trade. Export porcelain—either items made to order by Chinese porcelain works for overseas buyers or generic ones made to suit European and colonial tastes—had become such a big business that cheaper pieces were sometimes actually used as ship's ballast on the homeward voyages. Shown here is a candlestick for use in a European home with Chinese motifs of vessels at the top. The cobalt blue color is characteristic of the Ming and Qing designs.

Questions

• How does the development of porcelain serve as an example of Chinese leadership in technical innovation during the premodern and early modern periods?

• How did the emergence of a global trading network after 1500 affect both the demand for porcelain and its impact on consumer tastes?

mobile warrior people, the system eventually became the chief administrative tool of the Manchu leadership. It was now introduced into China in such a way as to establish the Manchus as a hereditary warrior class occupying its own sections of major Chinese cities. The Han, or ethnic Chinese, forces were organized into their own "Armies of the Green Standard," so named for the color of the flags they carried.

Minority Rule   Always conscious of their position as a ruling minority in China, with their numbers comprising only about 2 percent of the population, the Manchus, like the Mongols before them, sought to walk a fine line between administrative and cultural adaptation and the kind of complete assimilation that had characterized previous invaders. Thus, under what is sometimes termed the Sino–Manchu **dyarchy**, Chinese and Manchus were scrupulously recruited in equal numbers for high administrative posts; Manchu quotas in the examination system were instituted; edicts and memorials were issued in both Chinese and Manchu; Qing emperors sought to control the empire's high culture; and, of course, Manchu "bannermen" of the various garrisons were kept in their own special quarters in the towns and cities. In addition, the Manchu conqueror Dorgon instituted the infamous "queue edict" in 1645: All males, regardless of ethnicity, were required on pain of death to adopt the Manchu hairstyle of a shaved forehead and long pigtail in the back—the queue—as the outward sign of loyalty to the new order. This hairstyle can be seen in early photographs taken of Chinese men until the Qing dynasty fell in 1912. As a darkly whimsical saying put it, "Keep the hair, lose the head; keep the head, lose the hair."

> **Dyarchy:** A system of administration consisting of two equal or parallel parts.

The results, however, were bloody and long-lasting. The queue edict provoked revolts in several cities, and the casualties caused by its suppression may have numbered in the hundreds of thousands. For the remainder of the Qing era, rebels and protestors routinely cut their queues as the first order of business; during China's Taiping Rebellion (1851–1864), perhaps the bloodiest civil war in human history, insurgents were known as "the long-haired rebels" for their immediate abandonment of the Qing hairstyle.

Creating the New Order   Though the Qing kept the centralized imperial system of the Ming largely intact, while importing the banner system as a kind of Manchu parallel administrative apparatus, they also made one significant addition to the uppermost level of the bureaucracy. While retaining the Ming Grand Secretariat, the emperor Kangxi's successor, Yongzheng, set up an ad hoc inner advisory body called the Grand Council in 1733. Over the succeeding decades the Grand Council became the supreme inner advisory group to the emperor, while the Grand Secretariat was relegated to handling less crucial "outer" matters of policy making and implementation.

For much of the seventeenth century, however, the pacification of the empire remained the primary task. Under the able leadership of Nurhachi's great-grandson the Kangxi Emperor (r. 1661–1722), the difficult subjugation of the south was concluded, the Revolt of the Three Feudatories (1673–1681) ultimately crushed, and the naval stronghold of the Ming pretender called Koxinga by the Dutch captured on Taiwan in 1683.

As had been the case in past dynasties, the Qing sought to safeguard the borders of the empire by bringing peoples on the periphery into the imperial system through a judicious application of the carrot and the stick, or, as it was known to generations of Chinese strategists, the "loose rein" and "using barbarians to check barbarians." In practical terms, this meant a final reckoning with the Mongols in the 1720s by means of improved cannon and small arms, along with bribes and presents to friendly chieftains, and the intervention of the Qing in religious disputes regarding Tibetan Buddhism, which had also been adopted by a number of the Mongol groups. Toward this end, the Qing established a protectorate over Tibet in 1727, with the Dalai Lama ruling as the approved temporal and religious leader. To cement the relationship further, the emperor built a replica of a Tibetan stupa just outside the Manchu quarter in Beijing and a model of the Dalai Lama's Potala Palace at the emperor's summer retreat in Jehol [yeh-HOLE].

The Qianlong Emperor   With the traditional threats from the borders now quashed, the reign of the Qianlong [chien-LUNG] emperor, from 1736 to 1795, marked both the high point and the beginning of the decline of the Qing dynasty—and of imperial China itself. The period witnessed China's expansion to its greatest size during the imperial era. This was accompanied by a doubling of its population to perhaps 300 million by 1800. By almost any measure, its internal economy dwarfed that of any other country and equaled or surpassed that of Europe as a whole until the Industrial Revolution was well under way.

The Qing army, though perhaps already eclipsed in terms of efficiency and weaponry by the leading nations of Europe, was still many times larger than that of any potential competitor. Moreover, Qianlong wielded this power successfully a number of times during his reign, with expeditions against pirates and rebels on Taiwan and in punitive campaigns against Vietnam, Nepal, and Burma between 1766 and 1792 (see Map 21.4). During his long life, he also tried, with limited success, to take up the writing brush of a scholar and connoisseur, creating the collection of art that is today the core of the National Palace Museum's holdings on Taiwan. Under his direction, the state sponsored monumental literary enterprises on a scale still awesome to contemplate today. Based on the small but steady stream of information on the Qing empire circulating around Europe, it seemed to some that the Chinese had solved a number of the problems of good government and might provide practical models of statecraft for Europeans to emulate.

Early European Contacts   Ironically, it was precisely at the time that China abandoned its oceanic expeditions that tiny Portugal on the Atlantic coast surmounted its first big hurdle in pursuit of what would become a worldwide maritime trade empire (see Chapters 16, 18, 19). By the 1440s, Portuguese navigators had rounded the bulge of West Africa and opened commercial relations with the coastal kingdoms there. Scarcely a decade after Vasco da Gama arrived in Calicut in 1498, the first Portuguese ships appeared in Chinese waters. By 1557, these *Folangqi*—the Chinese transliteration of "Franks," a generic term for Europeans transmitted

Tibetan Stupa and Temple, Beijing. This marble *chorten*, the Tibetan version of the Buddhist stupa, or reliquary, was built by the Qianlong emperor for the visit of the Panchen Lama in 1779, in part to cement the new Sino–Tibetan relationship growing from the establishment of a Qing protectorate over Tibet.

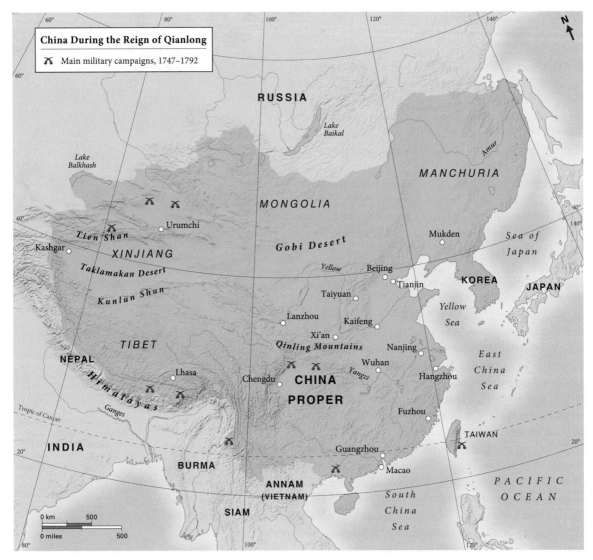

MAP **21.4** **China during the Reign of Qianlong.**

by the Arabs to Malacca, where it was transformed into *Ferenghi* [fa-REN-gee]—had wrested the first European colony from the Chinese at Macau. It was destined to be the longest-lived European colony as well, remaining under Portuguese control until 1999. From this point on, through merchants and missionaries, the contacts would frequently be profitable—and, sometimes, disastrous. Ultimately, they provided some of the most far-reaching interactions of world history.

Missionaries   The arrival of the first European merchants in east Asia was followed shortly by that of the first Catholic missionaries. Although the crusading impulse was still very much alive in Christian dealings with Muslim merchants in the Indies, Christian missionaries (at first from the Franciscan and Dominican orders and later from the Jesuits) were quick to realize the vast potential for religious conversions in China and Japan. The various missionary orders set up headquarters in Malacca, and in 1549 the Franciscan Francis Xavier landed in Japan. The endemic conflict among the *daimyo* (regional warlords) of Japan helped create a demand for Western goods, especially firearms, and the association of these with Christianity allowed considerable progress to be made in gaining conversions. China, however, required a vastly different strategy.

Wary of potentially disruptive foreign influences, the Ming at first refused entry to missionaries. Once admitted, the Franciscans and Dominicans, with their limited training in Chinese language and culture, made little headway. Additionally, their efforts were largely aimed at seeking conversions among the poor, which won them scant respect or influence among China's elite. The Jesuits, however, tried a different tack. Led by Matteo Ricci (1552–1610) and his successors Adam Schall von Bell (1591–1666) and Ferdinand Verbiest (1623–1688), they immersed themselves in the classical language and high culture of the empire and gained recognition through their expertise in mathematics, astronomy, military science, and other European learning sought by the imperial court. Jesuit advisors served the last Ming emperors as court astronomers and military engineers and successfully made the transition to the new dynasty. The high point of their influence was reached during the reign of the Qing Kangxi Emperor. With Schall as the official court astronomer and mathematician and an entire European-style observatory set up in Beijing, Kangxi actively considered conversion to Catholicism.

Matteo Ricci and Li Paul. The cross-cultural possibilities of sixteenth- and seventeenth-century Sino–Western contact were perhaps best exemplified by the activities of the Jesuit Matteo Ricci (1552–1610). Ricci predicated his mission in China on a respectful study of the language and classical canon of the empire coupled with a thorough knowledge of the new mathematics and astronomy of the West. Here, he is pictured with one of his most prominent converts, a literatus and veteran of the war against the Japanese in Korea, Li Yingshi. Upon his conversion in 1602, Li took the Christian name of Paul.

The papacy, however, had long considered Jesuit liturgical and doctrinal adaptations to local sensibilities problematic. In the case of China, competition among the three orders for converts and disturbing reports from the Franciscans and Dominicans regarding the Jesuits' alleged tolerance of their converts' continued veneration of Confucius and maintenance of ancestral shrines set off the "rites controversy." This was worsened in the eyes of the papacy by the Jesuits' acquiescence to the use of tea and rice for the Eucharist instead of bread and wine. After several decades of intermittent discussion, Kangxi's successor, Yongzheng, banned the order's activities in China in 1724. Christianity and missionary activity were thus driven underground, though the Qing would retain a Jesuit court astronomer into the nineteenth century.

The Canton Trade   While China's commerce with the maritime Atlantic states grew rapidly in the eighteenth century, the Europeans had not yet been fully incorporated into the Qing diplomatic system. A century before, the expansion of

Canton Factories, ca. 1800. Under the "Canton system" begun in 1699, all maritime trade with the Europeans was tightly controlled and conducted through the single port of Canton, or Guangzhou. Foreign merchants were not allowed to reside within the walled city, so they constructed their own facilities along the Pearl River waterfront. Though it kept profits high for the concerned parties, the restrictiveness of the system caused nineteenth-century merchants and diplomats to push the Chinese to open more ports to trade, which proved to be a major sticking point in Sino–Western relations.

Factory: Here, the place where various "factors" (merchants, agents, etc.) gathered to conduct business.

Russia into Siberia and the region around the Amur River had prompted the Qing to negotiate the Treaty of Nerchinsk in 1689. Under its terms, negotiated with Kangxi's Jesuit advisors acting as interpreters and go-betweens, the Russians agreed to abandon their last forts along the Amur and were given rights to continue their lucrative caravan trade in the interior. Formal borders were established in Manchuria, and the first attempts at settling claims to the central Asian regions of Ili and Kuldja were made. Significantly, Russian envoys were also permitted to reside in Beijing but in a residence like those used by the temporary envoys of tribute missions.

The situation among the European traders attempting to enter Chinese seaports, however, was quite different. The British East India Company, having established its base at Calcutta in 1690, soon sought to expand its operations to China. At the same time, the Qing, fresh from capturing the last Ming bastion on Taiwan and worried about Ming loyalists in other areas, sought to control contact with foreign and overseas Chinese traders as much as possible, while keeping their lucrative export trade at a sustainable level. Their solution, implemented in 1699, was to permit overseas trade only at the southern port of Guangzhou [GWAHNG-joe], more widely known as Canton. The local merchants' guild, or *cohong* (in pinyin, *gonghang*), was granted a monopoly on the trade and was supervised by a special official from the imperial Board of Revenue. Much like the Tokugawa in seventeenth-century Japan, the Qing permitted only a small number of foreigners, mostly traders from the English, French, and Dutch East India Companies, to reside at the port. They were confined to a small compound of foreign "**factories**," were not permitted inside the city walls, and could not bring their wives or families along. Even small violations of the regulations could result in a suspension of trading privileges, and all infractions and disputes were judged according to Chinese law. Finally, since foreign affairs under these circumstances were considered a dimension of trade, all diplomatic issues were settled by local officials in Canton.

The eighteenth century proved to be a boom time for all involved in the Canton trade, and the British in particular increasingly viewed it as a valuable part of their growing commercial power. While the spread of tea drinking through Europe and its colonies meant that tea rapidly grew to challenge porcelain for trade supremacy, silk also grew in importance, as well as lacquerware, wicker and rattan furniture, and dozens of other local specialties increasingly targeted at the export market. After 1784, the United States joined the trade; but despite the growing American presence, it was the British East India Company that dominated the Canton factories. Both the cohong and foreign chartered companies carefully guarded their respective monopolies, and the system worked reasonably well in keeping competition low and profits high on all sides.

Village and Family Life

Just as the effort toward greater control and centralization was visible in the government and economy of China during the Ming and Qing, it also reverberated within the structures of Chinese village life. While much of local custom and social relations among the peasants still revolved around family, clan, and lineage—with the scholar-gentry setting the pace—new institutions perfected under the Ming and Qing had a lasting impact into the twentieth century.

Organizing the Countryside   During the sixteenth century, the administrative restructuring related to the consolidation of the tax system into the single-whip arrangement led to the creation of the *lijia* system. All families were placed into officially designated *li*, or "villages," for tax purposes; 10 households made up a *jia*, and 100 households composed a *li*, whose headmen, appointed by the magistrate, were responsible for keeping tax records and labor dues.

While the lijia system was geared primarily toward more efficient tax collection and record keeping, the *baojia* (Chapter 12) system functioned as a more far-reaching means of government surveillance and control. The baojia system required families to register all members and be organized into units of 10 families, with one family in each unit assuming responsibility for the other nine. Each of these responsible families was arranged in groups of 10, and a member of each was selected to be responsible for that group of 100 households, and so on up to the *bao*, or 1,000-household level. Baojia representatives at each level were to be chosen by the families in the group. These representatives were to report to the magistrate on the doings of their respective groups and held accountable for the group's behavior.

Glimpses of Rural Life   As with other agrarian–urban empires, much of what little we know about Chinese peasant life comes to us through literary sources. Most of these were compiled by the scholar-gentry, though starting in the seventeenth century a small but influential number of chronicles were also produced by Westerners traveling in China. Based on these accounts, some generalizations can be made about rural and family life in Ming and Qing times.

First, while the introduction of new crops during the period had brought more marginal land under cultivation, allowed for a huge increase in the population, and helped lend momentum to the trend toward more commercialization of

Chinese Commercial Enterprises. The growing volume and profits of the export trade encouraged further development and specialization of long-standing Chinese domestic industries during the eighteenth and nineteenth centuries. Moneychangers known as *shroffs* (a), were involved in testing the quality of silver taken from foreign concerns in exchange for Chinese goods. A worker and overseer demonstrate the operation of a silk reeling machine (b). Women worked to sort tea; in this photograph (c), packing chests for tea are stacked behind the sorters. The hairstyle of the men in these photos—shaved forehead with long braid called a queue—was mandatory for all Chinese males as a sign of submission to the Qing.

agriculture, the work, technology, and overall rhythms of peasant life had changed little over the centuries.

Second, as with gathering political tensions, some early signs of economic stress were already present toward the end of Qianlong's reign. Chief among these was the problem of absentee landlordism. This would grow increasingly acute as the vitality of the commercial networks and market towns of central and southern China increased and the gentry were drawn away from the countryside by urban opportunities and amenities. In addition, successful tea, cotton, silk, and luxury goods traders frequently retained their compounds in the cities while buying land and degrees and becoming scholar-gentry, further increasing the incidence of absenteeism in the countryside. During the next century, with the dislocations of the Opium Wars, the Taiping Rebellion, and the foreign treaty ports, the problem of absentee landlordism greatly accelerated.

Third, as we have seen before, pressures on patterns of village life tended to be magnified in the lives of women and girls. Elite women were routinely educated to be as marriageable as possible. Study of proper Confucian decorum, writing model essays, chanting poetry, and developing a firm grasp of the *Xiaojing* (*Classic of Filial Piety*) were central to their lessons. As noted earlier, women were expected to be modest and obedient and were usually separated from and subordinate to men. Marriage and property laws were set up to reinforce these qualities. In addition to the emphasis placed on mourning by both sexes, widows were expected to remain single and be subordinate to their oldest sons. As also noted previously, the custom of foot binding had long since become institutionalized, though in some areas—among southern China's Hakka minority, for example—it never caught on. The sale of infant girls and, in extreme cases, female infanticide rose markedly in rural areas during times of war, famine, or other social stresses. It should be remembered, however, that, as in previous Chinese dynasties, the dominance of women over the "inner realm" of the family remained largely complete, though this realm was never considered equal in importance to the outer sphere of men's activities.

Science, Culture, and Intellectual Life

As we saw in Chapter 12, the Ming dynasty in many ways marked the high point as well as the beginning of the decline of China's preeminent place as a world technological innovator. One area in which this became painfully evident by the eighteenth and nineteenth centuries was in military matters.

Superpower   The Ming at their height have been described by some Chinese scholars as a military superpower. Perhaps most important in this regard was that the ascendancy of the Ming in 1368 marked the beginning of what one historian has called a "military revolution" in the use of firearms. The first use of metal gun barrels in the late thirteenth century spurred the rapid development of both

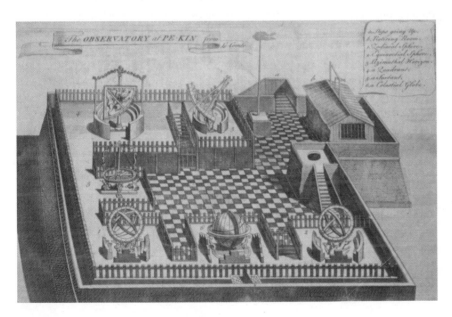

Observatory in Beijing. One of the ways the Jesuits were able to gain favor at the imperial courts of two successive dynasties was through the New Sciences of the West. Jesuit mathematicians, technical advisors, mapmakers, and astronomers found an eager reception among their Chinese counterparts, the fruits of which included armillary spheres (pictured on the left and right foreground) and the celestial globe (center). The instruments were cast by Chinese artisans to the specifications of the Jesuit court mathematician Ferdinand Verbiest in the 1680s.

cannon and small arms—so much so that by the mid-fifteenth century the Ming arsenal at Junqiju [JWUN-chee-joo] was producing thousands of cannon, handguns, and "fire lances" every year. By one estimate, in 1450 over half of the Ming frontier military units had cannon and one-third of all troops carried firearms. As early as the 1390s large shipborne cannon were already being installed in naval vessels. Indeed, court historians of the late Ming credited nearly all the military successes of the dynasty to the superiority of their firearms.

By the Qing period, however, following the pacification of the realm, the need for constant improvement of arms was seen as increasingly costly and unnecessary. While marginal improvements were made in the **matchlock** firing mechanisms of Chinese small arms, such improvements as were made in larger guns were largely directed by European missionary advisors to the throne.

Matchlock: An early type of gun in which the gunpowder charge is ignited by a burning taper (the "match") attached to the trigger mechanism.

Science and Literature   In geography, mathematics, and astronomy a fruitful exchange was inaugurated between European Jesuit missionaries and a small but influential group of Chinese officials in the seventeenth and eighteenth centuries. The most lasting legacy of this meeting was the European-style observatory in Beijing and a number of new maps of the world based on sixteenth- and seventeenth-century explorations. Unfortunately, by the nineteenth century these were all but forgotten, and the inadequacy of the geographical knowledge of Chinese officials in policy-making positions was soon all too apparent.

As in seventeenth-century France, the centralizing tendency of the government of China led to the exercise of considerable control in the cultural realm through patronage, monopoly, and licensing. As Manchus, the Kangxi, Yongzheng, and Qianlong emperors strove to validate their reigns by being patrons of the arts and aspiring to high levels of connoisseurship and cultivation of the best of the literati. As in other centralizing realms, they not only set the tone in matters of aesthetics but also used mammoth cultural projects to direct the energies of scholars and officials into approved areas. At the same time, they sought to quash unorthodox views through lack of support and, more directly, through literary inquisitions. Kangxi, for example, sponsored the compilation of a huge dictionary of approved definitions of Chinese characters—still considered a primary reference work today. Under his direction, the commentaries and interpretations of Neo-Confucianism championed by the Song philosopher Zhu Xi became the approved versions. Kangxi's 13 sacred edicts, embodying maxims distilled in part from Zhu Xi's thought, became the official Qing creed from 1670 on. Anxious to legitimize themselves as culturally "Chinese," Kangxi and Qianlong sponsored huge encyclopedia projects. Qianlong's effort, at 36,000 volumes, was perhaps the most ambitious undertaking of its kind ever attempted.

Neo-Confucian Philosophy   While the urge to orthodoxy pervaded both dynasties, considerable intellectual ferment was also brewing beneath the surface of the official world. As we saw in Chapter 12, in the sixteenth century the first major new directions in Neo-Confucianism were being explored by Wang Yangming (1472–1529). While Wang's school remained a popular one, his emphasis on intuition, on a kind of enlightenment open to all, and, more and more, on a unity of opposites embracing different religious and philosophical traditions placed his more radical followers increasingly on the fringes of intellectual life. In addition, the Qing victory ushered in an era of soul-searching among Chinese literati and a wholesale questioning of the systems that had failed in the face of foreign conquest.

Two of the most important later figures in Qing philosophy were Huang Zongxi [hwang zung-SHEE] (1610–1695) and Gu Yanwu [goo yen-WOO] (1613–1682). Both men's lives spanned the Qing conquest, and like many of their fellow officials, both men concluded that the collapse of the old order was in part due to a retreat from practical politics and too much indulgence in the excesses of the radicals of the Wang Yangming school. With a group of like-minded scholars, they based themselves at the Donglin Academy, founded in 1604. There, they devoted themselves to reconstituting an activist Confucianism based on rigorous self-cultivation and on remonstrating with officials and even the court. One outgrowth of this development, which shares interesting parallels with the critical textual scholarship of the European Renaissance, was the so-called Han learning movement. Convinced that centuries of Buddhism, religious Daoism, and Confucian commentaries of questionable value had diverted Confucianism from the intent of the sages, Han learning sought to recover the original meaning of classic Confucian works through exacting textual scholarship and systematic philology, or historical linguistics. The movement, though always on the fringe of approved official activities, peaked in the eighteenth century and successfully uncovered a number of fraudulent texts, while setting the tone for critical textual analysis during the remainder of the imperial era.

The Arts and Popular Culture   Although China's artists and writers clung to an amateur ideal of the "three excellences" of poetry, painting, and calligraphy, increasing official patronage ensured that approved schools and genres of art would be maintained at a consistent, if not inspired, level of quality. Here, the Qianlong emperor was perhaps the most influential force. Motivated in part by a lifelong quest to master the fine arts, he collected thousands of paintings—to which he added, in the tradition of Chinese connoisseurs, his own colophons—rare manuscripts, jade, porcelain, lacquerware, and other objets d'art. Because the force of imperial patronage was directed at conserving past models rather than creating new ones, the period is not noteworthy for stylistic innovation. One interesting exception to this, however, was the work of the Jesuit painter Giuseppe Castiglione (1688–1766). Castiglione's access to Qianlong resulted in a number of portraits of the emperor and court in a style that merged traditional Chinese subjects and media with Western perspective and technique. Evidence of this synthesis can also be seen in the Italianate and Versailles-inspired architecture at the emperor's Summer Palace just outside of Beijing.

Local Custom and Religion   Chinese cities and villages were populated by storytellers, corner poets, spirit mediums, diviners, and a variety of other sorts of entertainers. While village social life revolved principally around clan and family functions, popular culture was also dominated by Daoism, Buddhism, and older

> "The great man regards Heaven and earth and the myriad things as one body. He regards the world as one family and the country as one person. Even the mind of the small man is no different. Only he himself makes it small.'"
>
> —Wang Yangming, *Inquiry on the Great Learning*

Qianlong Emperor (1736–1795). One of the more interesting cross-cultural interactions during the early Qing period was that inspired by the Jesuit missionary Giuseppe Castiglione (1688–1766). Trained as an architect and painter, Castiglione (Chinese name Lang Shining) arrived in Beijing in 1715 and served as court painter to emperors Kangxi, Yongzheng, and Qianlong. He influenced Chinese painters in the use of Western perspective and also absorbed Chinese techniques of portraiture and landscape painting. Here, the young Qianlong emperor is shown in his imperial regalia—including his robes of imperial yellow with dragon motifs—but with an authentically detailed face gazing confidently at the viewer.

traditions of local worship, all with their own temples, shrines, and festivals. The oldest beliefs of the countryside involving ancestral spirits, "hungry ghosts" (roaming spirits of those not properly cared for in death), fairies, and demons were enhanced over the centuries by a rich infusion of tales of Daoist adepts and "immortals," *yijing* diviners, Buddhist bodhisattvas, and underworld demons. Popular stories incorporating all of these, like *A Journey to the West*, continued to be popular fare for the literate as well as for storytellers and street performers.

One of the richest glimpses into local society comes from Pu Songling's (1640–1715) *Strange Tales from the "Make-Do" Studio*, sometimes rendered in English as *Strange Tales from a Chinese Studio*. Though considered a master stylist among his circle of friends, Pu never progressed beyond the provincial-level examinations and spent most of his life in genteel poverty. He traveled extensively, collecting folktales, accounts of local curiosities, and especially stories of the supernatural. His stories are available to us today thanks to the foresight of his grandson, who published them in 1740. In Pu's world, "fox-fairies" appear as beautiful women, men are transformed into tigers, the young are duped into degenerate behavior—with predictable consequences—and crooked mediums and storytellers take advantage of the unwary.

The Long War and Longer Peace: Japan, 1450–1750

As we recall from Chapter 13, the struggles by court factions in Japan's capital of Heian-Kyo (Kyoto) had ultimately resulted in the creation of the office of the *shogun*, the chief military officer of the realm, in 1185. Actual executive power gradually receded from the emperor's hands, however, into the shogun's, and by the fourteenth century the emperor had become in reality the puppet of his first officer. As we also saw, a fundamental shift occurred with the attempt by Emperor Go-Daigo to reassert his prerogatives in 1333. When his one-time supporter Ashikaga Takauji expelled him and set up his headquarters in the capital, power and prestige were pressed together once again, with profound political and cultural consequences for Japan. Courtly elegance insinuated itself into the brutal world of the warrior, while power, intrigue, and ultimately a prolonged and debilitating civil war would ravage the capital until it ended with Japan's unification.

The price of unification, however, was high. As we saw in the opening vignette of this chapter, the first of Japan's unifiers, Oda Nobunaga, was assassinated for his efforts; the invasions of Korea undertaken by his successor Hideyoshi resulted in the loss of hundreds of thousands of lives. The final custodians of Japanese unification, the Tokugawa family, created a system over several generations that they hoped would preserve Japan forever in a state of unity and seclusion. Yet over the two and a half centuries of the Tokugawa peace, forces were building that would allow Japan to vault into the modern world with unprecedented speed in the late nineteenth century.

The Struggle for Unification

As we have seen, the fundamental instability of the Ashikaga regime lent itself to the continual contesting for the shogun's office among the more powerful daimyo, or regional warlords. In 1467, these factional battles finally erupted into a devastating civil war that would last off and on for more than a century. The opening phase of this struggle, the Onin War, lasted 10 years and devastated the city of Kyoto, while leaving the imperial court barely functional and the shogunate in tatters. With no real center of power, a bitter struggle of all against all among the daimyos continued into the 1570s.

Oda Nobunaga and Toyotomi Hideyoshi   For the Japanese, the period was called *Gekokujo*, or "those below toppling those above." By the mid-sixteenth century, a handful of daimyo began the painful process of consolidating their power and securing allies. One important factor in deciding the outcome of these wars was the result of intrusion from the outside. By the 1540s, the first Portuguese and Spanish merchants and missionaries had arrived in southern Japan. One daimyo who was quick to use the newcomers and their improved small arms to his advantage was Oda Nobunaga, the son of a small landholder who had risen through the ranks to command. Oda employed newly converted Christian musketeers to secure the area around Kyoto and had largely succeeded in unifying the country when he was assassinated in 1582. His second in command, Hideyoshi, whom we met in the opening of this chapter, was another commoner who had risen through the ranks. Now he assumed Oda's mantle and systematically brought the remaining daimyo under his sway over the next nine years.

Hideyoshi viewed a foreign adventure at this point as an excellent way to cement the loyalties of the newly subdued daimyo. In addition, the army he had put together—battle-hardened, well trained, with perhaps the largest number of guns of any force in the world at the time—might prove dangerous to disband. Hence, as early as 1586 he announced his grandiose plans to conquer China itself. Thus, in 1592 he set out with a massive expeditionary force, which at its peak numbered over 200,000 men. Though his supply lines were harassed unmercifully by the Korean naval forces in their well-armored "turtle ships," the Japanese made good progress up the peninsula until massive Chinese counterattacks slowly eroded their gains and decimated large stretches of Korea.

Hideyoshi's adventure ended when he turned homeward to Japan with the remnants of his army in 1596. His stature as a commander and force of personality kept his coalition of daimyo together until his death during his troubled second Korean campaign in 1598.

The coalition then broke in two, and a civil war began between Tokugawa Ieyasu, the charismatic leader of the eastern coalition of daimyos, and their western counterparts. In the fall of 1600, the back of the western coalition was broken by the Tokugawa victory at the Battle of Sekigahara, near Kyoto. Ieyasu, who claimed

Toyotomi Hideyoshi (1536–1598). Portraits of Japanese daimyo and shoguns tend to position them in similar ways, looking to the front left, with stiff, heavily starched official robes that reflect their austerity and dignity. In this 1601 portrait, done several years after his death, Hideyoshi is shown in a typical pose, with the signs of his adopted family and imperial crests around the canopy to denote his role of imperial guardian.

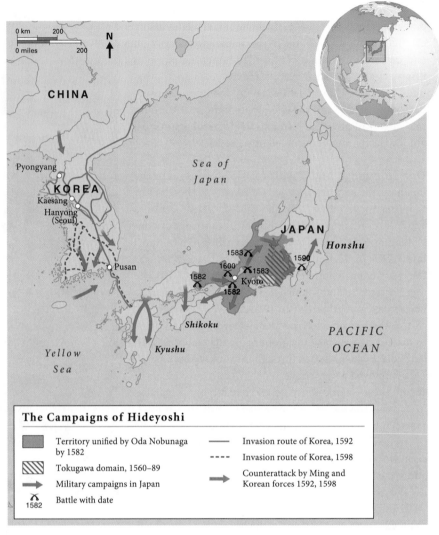

MAP **21.5** **The Campaigns of Hideyoshi.**

> "Don't let my soldiers become spirits in a foreign land."
>
> —Toyotomi Hideyoshi to his commanders shortly before his death

to be a descendant of the Minamoto clan, the original shoguns, laid claim to the office and was officially invested with it in 1603. His accession marked the beginning of Japan's most peaceful, most secluded, and perhaps most thoroughly regulated and policed interval in its long history. Breaking precedent, the Tokugawas would create a hereditary shogunate, organized along Chinese Neo-Confucian models of morality and government, that would last until 1867 (see Map 21.5).

The Tokugawa *Bakufu* to 1750

The realm that Tokugawa Ieyasu (1542–1616) had won at the Battle of Sekigahara was one that had been scarred by seemingly endless warfare and social disruption. The daimyo and samurai, their armies as large as hundreds of thousands of soldiers in some cases, employed some of the most advanced military technology in the world, but their depredations had broken old loyalties and alliances. The intrusion of European missionaries and merchants, along with their converts and agents, contributed to the social ferment. The brief interlude of unity behind Hideyoshi's continental adventures had thoroughly unraveled and, indeed, had been a contributing cause of the civil war that had brought Ieyasu to power.

Ieyasu's assumption of the shogunate in 1603 thus began a process of unparalleled centralization and stabilization in Japan that would last until 1867. Initially, however, seclusion did not figure among its principles. In fact, under the direction of European advisors, Ieyasu and his son Hidetada (1579–1632) laid plans to build a powerful naval and merchant fleet during their first decade of rule. Seclusion did not emerge as the shogunate's policy until the 1630s. The most pressing order of business was to erect a system within which to place all the daimyo that would at once reward the loyal and keep a watchful eye on the defeated.

"Tent Government"   The system devised under the Tokugawa *bakufu* ("tent government," referring to the shogun's official status as the emperor's mobile deputy) was called *sankin kotai*, the "rule of alternate attendance." An inner ring of daimyo holdings was annexed by the Tokugawa family and administered by their retainers. All daimyo were then given either *fudai*, or "inner" domains, if they had been allies of the Tokugawa, or *tozama*, "outer" domains, if they had ultimately surrendered to Ieyasu's eastern coalition. The shogunate placed its new headquarters in the Tokugawa castle in Edo, the future city of Tokyo. In order to ensure their loyalty, all outer daimyo were required to reside in the capital in alternate years and return to their domains during the off years. Members of their families were required to stay as permanent hostages in Edo. Daimyo were also required to bring their most important retainers and their households with them during their stays. Almost from the beginning, therefore, the main roads to Edo, most famously the Tokaido, were the scene of constant daimyo processions. Like the great pilgrimage routes of Islam, Buddhism, and Christianity, these roads spurred enormous commerce and the creation of an array of services to meet the needs of the constant traffic. And like the French nobility a few decades later at Versailles, the daimyo found both their power and their purses increasingly depleted.

Freezing Society   In turning the office of shogun over to his son Hidetada in 1605, Ieyasu made it legally hereditary for the first time. With the possibility of revolt always just under the surface, Ieyasu stayed on as regent and pursued further measures to enhance the stability of the regime. Under his grandson Iemitsu (1604–1651), most of the characteristic Tokugawa policies in this regard became institutionalized. The shogunate declared that, like in the jati system in India, the members of the officially recognized classes in Japan—daimyo, samurai, peasants, artisans, merchants—and their descendants would be required to stay in those classes forever. The Tokugawa adopted Neo-Confucianism as the governing ideology, thus joining the commonwealth of Confucian "religious civilizations" in the region, and its long-established precepts of filial piety, models of ethical behavior, and unswerving loyalty to the government were incorporated into the new law codes.

Significant differences, however, separated the practice of this system in Japan from similar, concurrent systems in China, Korea, and Vietnam. In China and Vietnam, a civil service had long been in place, complete with a graded system of examinations from which the best candidates would be drawn for duty. The situation in Japan was closer to that of Korea, in which the *Yangban* were already a hereditary aristocracy in the countryside and so monopolized the official classes. Japan, though, differed even further because the samurai and daimyo were now not just a hereditary class of officials but a military aristocracy as well. Not only was the low position traditionally given to the military in Chinese Confucianism totally reversed, but the daimyo and samurai had absolute, unquestioned power of life and death over all commoners. Like their counterparts in China, they were expected to have mastered the classics and the refined arts of painting, poetry, and calligraphy. But official reports and popular literature are full of accounts of samurai cutting down hapless peasants who failed to bow quickly enough to daimyo processions or who committed other infractions, no matter how trivial.

Giving Up the Gun   In order to ensure that the samurai class would be free from any serious challenge, the government required them to practice the time-honored skills of swordsmanship, archery, and other forms of individual martial arts. But the rapid development of firearms and their pervasive presence in the realm remained a threat to any class whose skills were built entirely around hand-to-hand combat. Thus, in a way perhaps unique among the world's nations, the Tokugawa literally "gave up the gun." Tokugawa police conducted searches for forbidden weapons among commoners and destroyed almost the entire stock of the nation's firearms. A few museum pieces were kept as curiosities, as were the bronze cannon in some of the Tokugawa seaside forts. Thus, weapons that had been among the most advanced in the world when they were cast in the 1600s were the ones that confronted the first foreign ships nearly 250 years later in 1853.

As the shogunate strove to impose peace on the daimyo and bring stability to the populace, it became increasingly anxious to weed out disruptive influences. In addition to the unsettling potential of the country's guns, therefore, they began to restrict the movements of foreigners, particularly missionaries. From the earliest days of European arrivals in Japan, subjects of competing countries and religions had brought their quarrels with them, often involving Japanese as allies or objects of intrigue. The influence of the missionaries on the growing numbers of Japanese Christians—perhaps 200,000 by the 1630s—was especially worrisome to those intent on firmly establishing Neo-Confucian beliefs and rituals among the commoners. Moreover, the bitter duel between Catholic and Protestant missionaries and merchants carried its own set of problems for social stability, especially in the ports, where the majority of such activities tended to take place.

Christian Martyrs. Beginning in 1617 and culminating in the suppression of a rebellion by impoverished Christian peasants in 1637–1638, missionaries and their converts to the foreign faith were brutally persecuted by the Tokugawa. Wholesale massacres and even crucifixions along the main roads were not uncommon, or, as in this engraving, hanging criminals—in this case Jesuits—upside down and setting them on fire.

Tokugawa Seclusion   Ultimately, therefore, missionaries were ordered to leave the country, followed by their merchants. The English and Spanish withdrew in the 1620s, while the Portuguese stayed until 1639. Ultimately, only the Dutch, Koreans, and Chinese were allowed to remain, in small, limited numbers and subject to the pleasure of the shogunate. Further, in 1635 it was ruled that Japanese subjects would be forbidden to leave the islands and that no oceangoing ships were to be built. Any Japanese who left would be considered traitors and executed upon return. Like the Canton system later in Qing China, foreign merchants would be permitted only in designated areas in port cities and could not bring their families with them. The only Europeans permitted to stay, the Dutch, were chosen because they appeared to be the least affected by the religious bickering that characterized their European counterparts. They were, however, restricted to a tiny island called Dejima (also known as Deshima) built on a landfill in Nagasaki harbor. In return for the privilege, they were required to make yearly reports in person to the shogun's ministers on world events. Over time, the collections of these reports found a small but willing readership among educated and cultured Japanese. This "Dutch learning" and the accounts of Chinese and Korean observers formed the basis of the Japanese view of the outside world for over two centuries. Like European learning in Korea and Vietnam, it also provided useful examples for reformers to use in critiquing Neo-Confucian society.

Trampling the Crucifix Much less tolerance was shown to Japan's Christian community. Dissatisfaction with the new Tokugawa strictures provoked a rebellion at Shimabara just outside Nagasaki in 1637 by Christian converts and disaffected samurai. As the revolt was suppressed, many of those facing the prospect of capture and execution by the Tokugawa flung themselves into the volcanic hot springs nearby. Those who were captured were subjected to what their captors understood to be appropriate European-style punishment: Instead of being burned at the stake, they were clustered together and roasted to death inside a wide ring of fire. Subsequently, remaining missionaries were sometimes crucified upside down, while suspected converts were given an opportunity to "trample the crucifix" to show they had discarded the new faith. Those who refused to convert back to

Dutch Ships in Nagasaki Harbor. This detail from a 1764 map shows Dutch and Japanese ships in Nagasaki harbor. The Japanese ships are dwarfed by the much larger Dutch sailing vessels. The small fan-shaped area connected to the town of Nagasaki was the only place where the Dutch were allowed to disembark and trade. They were forbidden to cross the causeway into the city itself.

approved faiths were imprisoned or executed. In the end, perhaps 37,000 people were killed. For all their attempts at suppressing the religion, however, tens of thousands continued to practice in secret until Christianity was declared legal again during the reign of Emperor Meiji (r. 1867–1912). Though foreign ships would occasionally attempt to call at Japanese ports, by the eighteenth century Europeans generally steered clear of the islands. As we will see in Chapter 24, however, by the middle decade of the nineteenth century the opening of more ports in China for trade, the growth of the whaling industry, and the quest for gold in California would all conspire to change this situation forever.

Growth and Stagnation: Economy and Society

While a number of the processes begun under earlier shogunates continued during the seventeenth and eighteenth centuries, their pace quickened immensely. Perhaps most dramatically, by 1750, Japan had become the most urbanized society on earth. Edo itself reached a million people, making it arguably the world's largest city. Osaka and Kyoto were both approaching 400,000, and perhaps as much as 10 percent of Japan's population lived in cities with populations above 10,000 (see Map 21.6). In a way, such explosive growth is even more remarkable given that the Tokugawa placed strict curbs on travel within their realms. Commoners, for example, were not to leave their home districts without permission from the local authorities. On the other hand, as we have seen, the law of alternate attendance ensured an immense and growing traffic in and out of the major cities along the major routes into Edo. The vast array of services required to support that traffic aided urban and suburban growth and had the effect of spreading the wealth down to the urban merchants, artisans, entertainers, bathhouse proprietors, and even refuse collectors.

Population, Food, and Commerce   Perhaps a more direct cause of this urbanization may be found in the growth of the population as a whole. By various estimates, Japan may have had as many as 33 million people in 1720. The efficiency of small-scale, intensive rice and vegetable farming, aided by easy-to-operate, simple machines such as the Chinese-style "climbing stair" or "dragon wheel" pump made Japanese agriculture the most efficient in the preindustrial world. Such efficiencies would create one of the most densely populated rural landscapes in the world even into the twentieth century.

As we have noted, various Tokugawa policies aimed at stabilizing the country politically and socially had the unanticipated effect of spurring the economy. A number of factors contributed to this in addition to the forced movement of the daimyo and their retinues in alternate years. The Tokugawa tax structure set quotas of rice for each village, rather than for individuals, and left the individual daimyos responsible for remitting these to the capital. Thus, an immense traffic in bulk rice further spurred the carrying trade along the roads and in the coastal waters. In addition to guaranteeing provisions for the cities, the need to convert rice to cash for the treasury contributed greatly to building a banking and credit infrastructure. Indeed, the practice of merchant bankers advancing credit to wholesalers against anticipated rice crops created what some scholars have called an early kind of futures market. The progress of the famous Mitsui *zaibatsu*, or cartel, of the nineteenth and twentieth centuries followed such a route, its members starting

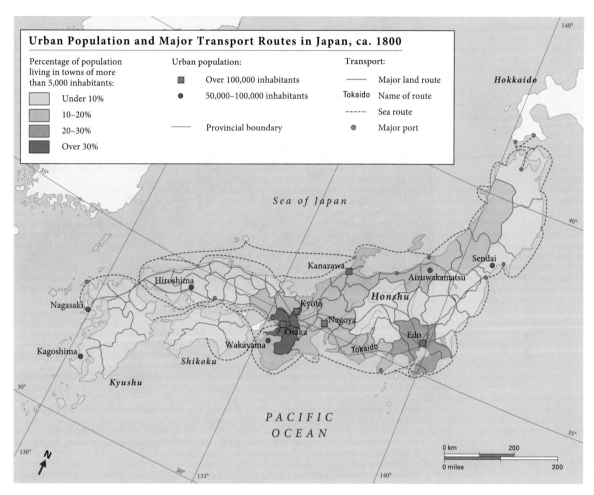

MAP **21.6** **Urban Population and Major Transport Routes in Japan, ca. 1800.**

in 1670 as dry goods merchants and gradually moving into the position of bankers for the shogunate.

The tastes of the three largest cities—Edo, with its high concentration of the wealthy and well-connected; Kyoto, with its large retinue of the imperial household; and Osaka, the chief port—created a huge demand for ever more sophisticated consumer goods and services. Such enterprises as sake brewing, wholesaling dried and prepared foods, running bathhouses, and managing large studios of artisans all became booming businesses. Even the import and export trades, slowed to a relative trickle by government regulations, proved quite lucrative for the few engaged in them. Books, porcelains, lacquerware, and objets d'art were exchanged for Japanese hard currency. Indeed, the vibrancy of Japanese urban life and a burgeoning middle class created what scholars have sometimes called the "democratization of taste." That is, what was once the strict province of the court, daimyo, and samurai was now widely available to anyone who had the money and interest to afford it. Moreover, the new moneyed classes were also creating new directions in the arts and entertainment.

Woodblock Print of the Fish Market at the East Side of Nihonbashi (The Bridge of Japan). The Tokugawa period, with its long interlude of peace and prosperity, was Japan's first great age of urban life. The constant traffic of daimyo progressions along the main roads and the large coasting trade along the Inland Sea ensured a growing middle class of artisans, tradespeople, and merchants. The capital, Edo, had ballooned to over a million people on the eve of the American intrusion; and the bustle of the capital is illustrated in this panel depicting a famous fish market.

Rural Transformations   Life in rural areas underwent certain changes as well. As they had with the military houses, the Tokugawa promulgated Neo-Confucian rules for the comportment of families and their individual members. Like parish churches in Europe, each local Buddhist temple was to keep registers of the villagers in its district. Weddings, funerals, travel, rents, taxes, and so forth were subject to official permission through either the village headman or the samurai holding a position equivalent to a magistrate. Within these strictures, however, and subject to the hereditary occupation laws, families, clans, and villages were relatively autonomous.

This was especially true of rural families, in which men, women, and children commonly worked together on their plots. While the "inner domain," so central to Neo-Confucian thought as the strict province of women, retained a good deal of that character, there were also many areas that mitigated it. Men, for example, routinely helped in the everyday tasks of childrearing. As late as the 1860s, foreign observers reported watching rural groups of men minding infants while their wives were engaged in some collective task. Women in cities and larger villages routinely ran businesses, especially those involved in entertainment. Indeed, the women of the famous geisha houses, owned and run by women, were renowned for their skills, education, wit, and refinement. Even on a more humble level, women ran bathhouses, taverns, restaurants, and retail establishments of all sorts. Interestingly, by the eighteenth century, merchants increasingly utilized the spinning and weaving talents of rural and semirural women in parceling out the various steps in textile manufacturing to them—a Japanese version of the English "putting out system."

The Samurai in Peacetime   As time went by, the position of the samurai in rural society changed as well. Though he was expected to hone his military skills, his role as an official and Neo-Confucian role model gradually became paramount. Samurai existed on stipends, either directly from the Tokugawa or from their local daimyo. These, however, were no guarantee of prosperity, and by the later eighteenth century the samurai living in genteel poverty had become something of a popular stereotype. In many areas, they functioned as schoolmasters and founded village academies in the local temples for the teaching of practical literacy and correct moral behavior. By the mid-nineteenth century Japan may have had the world's highest level of functional literacy. As in Korea, this proved important in popularizing new crops or agricultural techniques.

By the middle of the eighteenth century there were signs of tension among the aims of the government in ensuring peace and stability, the dynamism of the internal economy, and the boom in population. Like China a century later, some scholars contend that Japan had approached the limit of the ability of the land to support its people. In fact, Japan's population remained remarkably steady from the middle of the eighteenth century to the latter nineteenth. Repeated signs of creeping rural impoverishment and social unrest manifested themselves, however, and were often noted by commentators. Inflation in commodity prices ran ahead of efforts to increase domain revenues, squeezing those on fixed incomes and stipends. Efforts to keep rural families small enough to subsist on their plots led to an increasing frequency of infanticide. Compounding such problems were large-scale famines in 1782 and 1830. By the early nineteenth century, there was an increasing perception that the government was gradually losing its ability to care for the populace.

Hothousing "Japaneseness": Culture, Science, and Intellectual Life

As with so many elements of Japanese cultural history, existing genres of art—major styles of painting, poetry, and calligraphy—continued to flourish among the daimyo and samurai, while exerting an increasing pull on the tastes of the new middle classes. Indeed, Zen-influenced **monochrome** painting, the ideals of the tea ceremony championed by Sen Rikyu, the austere Noh theater, and the abstract principles of interior design and landscape gardening were carefully preserved and popularized until they became universally recognized as "Japanese."

Monochrome: Single-color; in east Asian painting, a very austere style popular in the fourteenth and fifteenth centuries, particularly among Zen-influenced artists.

New Theater Traditions   Traditional cultural elements coexisted with new forms, with some adapting aspects of these earlier arts and others conceived as mass entertainment. Among the former was the development of *bunraku*, the elaborate puppet theater still popular in Japan today. Bunraku puppets, perhaps one-third life size, generally took three puppeteers to manipulate. Their highly facile movements and facial expressions staged against a black backdrop to conceal their handlers readily allowed the audience to suspend disbelief and proved a highly effective way to popularize the older Noh plays. But renowned playwrights soon wrote special works for these theaters as well. The most revered was Chikamatsu Monzaemon [chick-ah-MAT-soo mon-ZAE-mon] (1653–1724), who skillfully transferred the tragically noble sentiments of the best Noh works into contemporary themes. The fatal tension between love and social obligation, for example, made his *Love Suicide at Sonezaki* wildly popular with Edo audiences. His most famous work, *The Forty-Seven Ronin*, written in 1706, is based on a 1703 incident in which the daimyo of 47 samurai was killed by a political opponent, leaving them as *ronin*—masterless. Out of loyalty to their dead daimyo the ronin kill his assassin in full knowledge that their lives will then be forfeit to the authorities, a price they stoically go on to pay.

Originally written for bunraku, *The Forty-Seven Ronin* was adapted a few decades later as a work for *kabuki*, the other great mass entertainment art of

"Summer grass;
Great warriors;
Remains of dreams"

　夏草や
　兵どもが
　夢の跡
　　　—Basho

Tokugawa Japan. Because kabuki was originally a satirical and explicitly bawdy form of theater, the government banned women from appearing in it, hoping to sever its association with prostitution. Female impersonators as actors continued its risqué reputation, however, while more serious works also drew immense crowds to the pleasure districts, to which the theaters were by law segregated. Kabuki remained by far the most popular Japanese mass entertainment, and interestingly, given the medium's off-color reputation, *The Forty-Seven Ronin* remained the most frequently performed play throughout the Tokugawa period.

The era also marked the golden age of the powerfully brief poetic form of *haiku*, the most famous practitioner of which was the renowned Matsuo Basho (1644–1694). As a poet he used a dozen pen names; he took "Basho" from the banana plant he especially liked in his yard. In poems like "Old Battlefield" the 17-syllable couplets compressed unbearable emotion and release in a way that has made them a treasured form in Japan and, more recently, in much of the world.

The visual arts found new forms of expression through the widespread use of fine woodblock printing, which allowed popular works to be widely duplicated. The new genre was called *ukiyo-e*, "pictures of the floating world," a reference to the pleasure quarters on the edge of the cities that furnished many of its subjects. Though largely scorned by the upper classes, it remained the most popular form of advertising, portraiture, and news distribution until the end of the nineteenth century, when it began to be supplanted by photography. During Tokugawa times, one of the most famous practitioners of the art was Kitagawa Utamaro (1753–1806), whose studies of women became forever associated with Japanese perceptions of female beauty. In the works of Katsushika Hokusai (1760–1849) and Ando Hiroshige (1797–1858) scenes like Hokusai's *Thirty-Six Views of Mt. Fuji*, or, like Utamaro's work, gentle snowfalls on temples, formed many of the first popular images that nineteenth-century Westerners had of Japan.

Two Courtesans. During the late seventeenth century, the new genre of *ukiyo-e*, "pictures of the floating world," developed and remained popular through the nineteenth century. Finely wrought woodblock prints in both monochrome and color, they take their name from the pleasure districts whose people and scenes were favorite subjects. This work is from a series by the noted artist Kitagawa Utamaro (ca. 1753–1806) on famous courtesans of the "Southern District," part of the Shinagawa section of Edo.

Putting It All Together

During the late Ming and early Qing periods, imperial China achieved social and political stability and developed the world's largest economy. Yet, by the second part of the eighteenth century, internal problems were already germinating that would come to the surface in succeeding decades. In the following century, these initial cracks in the empire's structure would continue to grow and have a profound impact on China's fortunes.

The arrival of large numbers of foreign traders who brought with them the new technologies of the first scientific–industrial societies, combined with China's profound self-confidence in its own culture and institutions, added more pressure to an already volatile internal situation and ultimately created an unprecedented challenge for China. Over the coming decades, Chinese expectations of being able to civilize and assimilate all comers would dissolve, along with the hope that a renewed faithfulness to Confucian fundamentals would produce the leaders necessary to navigate such perilous times. But at the halfway mark of the eighteenth century, the Chinese still expected that they would successfully regulate the "inner" and "outer" domains of their empire and keep pernicious foreign influences at arm's length.

Ravaged by a century of warfare and foreign intrusion, Japan also sought to regulate its inner and outer domains and minimize outside influences. As with China, however, the stability perfected by the Tokugawa shogunate in the seventeenth and eighteenth centuries would be increasingly threatened in the nineteenth by the growing commercial power of the Europeans and Americans. Before the nineteenth century was finished, China would be rent by the bloodiest civil war in human history, while Japan would experience its own civil war and, in its aftermath, install a unified government under an emperor for the first time since the twelfth century. In the final years of the nineteenth century, Japan would once again invade Korea to attack China—this time with very different results. In the process, the historical relationship of more than two millennia between the two countries would be altered forever.

▶ For additional resources, including maps, primary sources, visuals, and quizzes, please go to www.oup.com/us/vonsivers. Please see the Further Resources section at the back of the book for additional readings and suggested websites.

Against the Grain

Seclusion's Exceptions

Despite Japan's *sakoku* (closed country) policies of seclusion during the Tokugawa era, scholars have long understood that the country was more porous than popularly supposed. This was of course most true for Chinese and Korean merchants doing business in Japan. Formal relations of a sort with Korea on a more or less equal footing were maintained by the Tokugawa through the lord of the Tsushima *han*, or feudal domain, who also maintained a trading post in the Korean port of Pusan. Korean vessels, like those of the Chinese, were permitted to put in at Nagasaki, and Korean goods were in high enough demand that the shogunate's attempts to curtail silver exports were generally waived for Korean trade. Moreover, more than a dozen Korean trade missions traveled to the shogun's court during the Tokugawa period.

No official exchanges with Chinese representatives took place either in Edo or Beijing, since neither side wanted to be seen as the junior partner in the Neo-Confucian hierarchy of diplomacy by the so-called tribute mission system. In addition to the predominance of Chinese ships at Nagasaki, however, both Chinese and Japanese merchants took advantage of a loophole in the sovereignty of the Ryukyu Islands to trade there. China and Japan both insisted that the islands were their protectorate, though the Japanese domain of Satsuma had captured Okinawa in 1609. The leaders in Okinawa, however, sent trade and tribute missions to both China and the Japan in order to safeguard their freedom of action, thus keeping the conduit for trade semiofficially open for both sides.

The Dutch remained the European exceptions. In part, this was a condition they had helped engineer themselves: They had continually warned the Tokugawa about the sinister religious intentions of their Iberian competitors, suggesting that the Dutch alone should handle Japan's European trade. Indeed, though the volume of China's trade in Japan was many times larger, it was the Dutch who retained yearly access to the shogunate. Though their power and influence in European markets ebbed considerably during the eighteenth and early nineteenth centuries, their influence among the small but intellectually vital circle of Japanese scholars and leaders engaged in *rangaku*—"Dutch learning"—remained strong right up to the time of the coming of Perry's "Black Ships" in 1853. Thus, as one scholar of Japan has put it, "The Nagasaki door was always ajar and sometimes wide open."

- While the attempts by China, Korea, and Japan to keep out foreign influences may strike us as impractical, many nations today still seek to limit foreign influences, particularly in the realm of culture. What are the advantages and disadvantages of such policies? Are they inevitably self-defeating?

- Were the policies of turning inward among these agrarian–urban societies part of larger historical patterns at work during this time? Why or why not?

Thinking Through Patterns

▶ **Why did late Ming and early Qing China look inward after such a successful period of overseas exploration?**

In some respects the problem is similar to that faced by planners for defense spending in nations today: Why maintain huge, expensive systems when there are no enemies against which to use them? While the commercial prospects for China's fleets grew in prominence, maritime trade was simply not essential to the Chinese economy at that point. Moreover, urgent defense preparations were needed in the overland north against the resurgent Mongols. It is important to remember that the discontinuing of the fleets seems like a mistake in hindsight because of what happened to China hundreds of years later due to a lack of adequate naval defenses. At the time, however, these measures seemed both rational and appropriate to the Chinese and outside observers.

One almost universal pattern of world history among agrarian states is that their governments adopt policies aimed at promoting social stability. The reason for this is that, in short, nearly everything depends on having reliable harvests. Given the agricultural techniques and technology of preindustrial societies, the majority of the population must be engaged in food production to ensure sufficient surpluses to feed the nonproducing classes. If such a society places a premium on change and social mobility, it risks chronic manpower shortages and insufficient harvests. Thus, social classes—whether in feudal Europe, India, China, or Japan—are carefully delineated, and the state directs its policies toward eliminating social upheaval.

▶ **How do the goals of social stability drive the policies of agrarian states? How does the history of China and Japan in this period show these policies in action?**

▶ **In what ways did contact with the maritime states of Europe alter the patterns of trade and politics in eastern Asia?**

In both China and Japan, these connections resulted in severe restrictions on maritime trade: the Canton system in China and the seclusion policies of the Tokugawa in Japan. Earlier, the Chinese emperor had welcomed Jesuit missionaries for their expertise in mathematics and science and even considered conversion to Catholicism. But the backlash against "subversive" influence induced the Qing to drive Christianity underground. In Japan such contact had earlier injected European influences into Japan's civil wars, and the reaction against this was Tokugawa seclusion.

The fundamental difference was that Japan was a military society, which adopted the forms and structures of Neo-Confucianism to make the daimyo and samurai into officials. They therefore were expected to maintain this civil role as bureaucrats but also to stand ready to fight if need be. The low esteem in which the military was held in China was just the inverse of that of the martial elites of Japan. Another key difference was that officials in China were selected on the basis of competitive examinations, thus creating some social mobility. In Japan, the social classes were frozen and no exams were offered for potential officials.

▶ **How did Neo-Confucianism in China differ from that of Tokugawa Japan?**

PART FIVE

The Origins
of Modernity

1750–1900

What we have termed "modernity" in this section may be said to have begun roughly around 1800 in western Europe and may be characterized as the product of what historian Eric Hobsbawm (1917–2012) called the "twin revolutions" of the late eighteenth century. One of these was the new political landscape brought into being by the trio of constitutional revolutions in North America, France, and Haiti, which dealt a telling blow to the concept of traditional monarchial rule by divine right and introduced popular sovereignty as the new justification for political power. The other was the Industrial Revolution, which began in England with the introduction of steam-driven machine–produced textiles and other goods. Scientific–industrial modernity, with its developing constellation of values marked by experimentation; political, social, and technological progress; social mobility; and secularism, was thus set on a path to displacing the older agrarian–urban order of religious civilizations that had been characterized by hierarchy, natural order, and divinely ordained law and morality. This transition is, in fact, still ongoing. Although the old agrarian–urban political order has been almost universally superseded, its values still contend with those of modernity in many parts of the world today.

The Origins of Modernity

The political and industrial revolutions that define modernity have intellectual roots reaching back to the 1500s. As scholars increasingly recognize, the discovery of the Americas, as well as the Copernican revolution in astronomy, provided powerful incentives for the introduction of new patterns of science and political philosophy. For more than two centuries, however, these ideas remained the province of only a small intellectual elite.

Political and Industrial Revolutions

By the 1700s, however, adherents of the new science and philosophy among urban, educated administrators and professionals in northwestern Europe had grown in numbers and began to become influential in society. In Britain, the *theory* of the social contract entered into the *practice* of constitutionalism following the Glorious

1765
James Watt perfects the steam engine

1776–1804
American, French, and Haitian revolutions

1798–1801
Napoleon's occupation of Egypt

1815
Congress of Vienna

1832
Greece wins independence from the Ottomans

1839–1876
Tanzimat reforms in the Ottoman Empire

1848
Karl Marx and Friedrich Engels publish *The Communist Manifesto*

1853–1854
Commodore Perry opens trade and diplomatic relations with Japan

Revolution of 1688. Both were vastly expanded by thinkers during the eighteenth-century Enlightenment and helped to inspire the American, French, and Haitian Revolutions. These were narrow revolutions in the sense of ending monarchial–aristocratic rule—courageous revolts during still deeply religious times. Nonetheless, this era set the emancipation of humanity from the confining traditions of the past as a goal to be achieved. And in the case of Haiti, the idea that "all men are created equal," emblazoned earlier in the American Declaration of Independence and echoed in the French Declaration of the Rights of Man, formed the basis of a successful slave rebellion against revolutionary France itself.

The Industrial Revolution, beginning around 1800 in Great Britain, was a socially transformative and self-sustaining sequence of technical inventions and their commercial applications. Britain industrialized during the first half of the 1800s through steam-driven iron foundries, textile factories, overland transportation, and ocean travel. In a second wave, Germany and the United States industrialized, with the introduction of chemicals, electricity, and motorcars into the factory system. The two waves of industrialization created an unequal class system, with a citizenry composed of both landed aristocrats—fading in power as the old agrarian–urban order decayed—and a new, dynamic urban middle class amassing political and economic power. But the equally new phenomenon of the industrial working class, bidding for political, social, and economic equality, added a volatile social factor to the mix as its members sought to make good on the promises of the constitutional revolutions.

Resistance and Adaptation to the Western Challenge

The twin political–industrial revolutions in Europe were a major factor in the mid-nineteenth-century expansion of the existing seaborne European empires in Asia and Africa. Postrevolutionary France renewed its competition with Britain, and both later used "gunboat diplomacy" to establish favorable commercial conditions and trade outposts. From here, these two European nations, and others, proceeded to compete in imperial conquests for what they now considered to be strategically important territories across the globe.

The traditional agrarian and religious empires and states of Asia and Africa responded to the increasingly superior military power of the European maritime empires and the United States during the 1800s with both resistance and adaptation. Resisting with traditional armies and weapons, however, became more difficult as the 1800s unfolded and the industrial development of the West spawned new and sophisticated weaponry. "Adaptation," as it occurred under the duress of imperialism, was a creative process in which the states under challenge selected generic elements from the constitutional and industrial revolutions that had made the West powerful and attempted to harmonize them with their inherited traditions.

Thinking Like a World Historian

▶ What were the origins of the "twin revolutions" of the late eighteenth century? How did they combine to create what we call "modernity"?

▶ Why were the values of scientific–industrial society opposed to the older agrarian–urban order? Why does this conflict still persist in many parts of the world today?

▶ What patterns of resistance and adaptation characterized the responses of traditional agrarian and religious empires to European military power and expansion?

1857
Sepoy Mutiny, India

1868–1912
Reign of Emperor Meiji, Japan

1878–1885
Independence of Serbia, Montenegro, Romania, and Bulgaria

1888
End of slavery, Brazil

1894–1895
Sino-Japanese War

1904–1905
Russo-Japanese War

1861
Emancipation of serfs in Russian Empire

1869
Opening of Suez Canal

1884
Hiram Maxim invents the first fully automatic machine gun

1900
Boxer Rebellion

1905
Albert Einstein publishes theory of relativity

1908
"Young Turks" rise to power in Ottoman Empire

Chapter 22 1750–1871

Patterns of Nation-States and Culture in the Atlantic World

When the French Revolution broke out in 1789, a young Caribbean mulatto named Vincent Ogé (ca. 1755–1791) was in France on business. His extended family of free light-skinned blacks owned a coffee plantation and a commercial business with black slaves on Saint-Domingue [SAN-dow-MANG] (modern Haiti). Caught up in the excitement of 1789, Ogé embraced the French revolutionary principles of liberty, equality, and fraternity with great enthusiasm and quickly became an adherent of French constitutional nationalism: The former absolute monarchy in France was swiftly reorganized to incorporate a written constitution and an elected National Assembly. As part of the general atmosphere of emancipation so prevalent during the early part of the revolution, he joined the antislavery Society of the Friends of Blacks in Paris and demanded that French constitutionalism be extended to Saint-Domingue.

In a short time the society's efforts appeared to bear fruit. In March 1790, the National Assembly granted self-administration to the colonies, and Ogé returned to Saint-Domingue full of hope that he would be able to participate as a free citizen in the island's governance. But the governor stubbornly refused to admit mulattoes as citizens of the new order. Ogé and a group of friends therefore joined a band of 250–300 freedmen and took up arms to

THE NORTH ATLANTIC, 1750-1880

Canada
United States
Haiti
ATLANTIC OCEAN
Western Europe

ABOVE: Thousands of Polish soldiers joined Napoleon's forces sent to Haiti in 1802, depicted here in Battle on Santo Domingo by Polish painter January Sucholdoski (1797-1875).

carve out a stronghold for themselves in the north of the island by arresting plantation owners and occupying their properties. One plantation owner later testified that the rebels looted and killed during their uprising but that Ogé himself was a man of honor who treated his prisoners fairly and even left him in the possession of his personal arms.

After only a few weeks of fighting, however, government troops pushed the rebels into the Spanish eastern part of the island. Ogé and his followers surrendered after being guaranteed their safety. But the Spanish governor betrayed his prisoners, turning them over to the French. After a trial for insurrection in February 1791, Ogé and 19 followers were condemned to death. Ogé suffered particularly barbaric tortures before expiring: Executioners strapped him spread-eagle on a wagon wheel and systematically broke his bones with an iron bar until he was dead.

Seeing Patterns

▶ How did the pattern of constitutional nationalism, emerging from the American and French Revolutions, affect the course of events in the Western world during the first half of the nineteenth century?

▶ In what ways did ethnolinguistic nationalism differ from constitutional nationalism, and what was its influence on the formation of nation-states in the second half of the nineteenth century?

▶ What were the reactions among thinkers and artists to the developing pattern of nation-state formation? How did they define the intellectual–artistic movements of romanticism and realism?

The Ogé insurrection was a prelude of the Haitian Revolution, which began in August 1791 as a rebellion against discrimination and culminated with the achievement of independence under a black government in 1804. It was the third of the great constitutional-nationalist revolutions—after the American and French Revolutions—that inaugurated, with the Industrial Revolution, the modern period of world history. The new pattern of constitutional nation formation encouraged other peoples who possessed a cultural but not political unity to strive for their own ethnolinguistic nation-states. Italians and Germans united in their own states and Irish, Scots, and Welsh strove for autonomy within the United Kingdom.

The political ferment which led to the three constitutional revolutions was part of a larger cultural ferment called the Enlightenment. The rising urban middle classes of professionals, officials, and entrepreneurs embraced the New Sciences and their philosophical interpretations, which not only provided the intellectual ammunition for the revolutions but also stimulated entirely new forms of cultural creativity in the movements of romanticism and realism.

Origins of the Nation-State, 1750–1815

The Glorious Revolution of 1688 in England (Great Britain after 1707) bestowed rights and duties on English subjects who had never enjoyed them before. In this revolution, for the first time in Europe, the traditional divine rights of a monarch were curbed. A century later, the innovative ideas of *subjects* becoming *citizens* with constitutionally guaranteed rights and duties and of Parliament representing the citizens spread from Great Britain to North America, France, and Haiti. Beyond the Glorious Revolution, however, the American, French, and Haitian Revolutions were more radical in the sense that they rejected the British compromise of royal and parliamentary power and led to republican, middle-class or liberated slave nation-states without traditional divine-right monarchies.

Chapter Outline

- Origins of the Nation-State, 1750–1815

- Enlightenment Culture: Radicalism and Moderation

- The Growth of the Nation-State, 1815–1871

- Romanticism and Realism: Philosophical and Artistic Expression to 1850

- Putting It All Together

The American, French, and Haitian Revolutions

The American and French Revolutions were outgrowths of the Seven Years' War, in which Great Britain and France fought for the dominance of their respective seaborne empires in the world. The governments of both kingdoms went deeply into debt to wage the war. They owed this debt to their wealthy subjects, many of whom were landowners and administrators forming the ruling class. To pay back the debt, the kings had to go to all of their subjects and raise their taxes. The incongruence of monarchs holding the mass of their subjects responsible for their debts to a few wealthy subjects was apparent to a large number of people, who therefore formulated political principles of reform and, ultimately, revolution. Once the revolutions were under way, the American and French revolutionary principles of freedom and equality had repercussions in the wider Atlantic world, first in Haiti and ultimately the Latin American colonies of Spain and Portugal (Chapter 27).

Conditions for Revolution in North America   When Britain won the Seven Years' War, it acquired France's trade forts in India as well as French possessions in Canada and the Ohio–Mississippi River valley. France turned what remained of Louisiana over to its ally Spain (which had lost Florida to Britain) and retreated entirely from the continent of North America. But the British victory and territorial gains came at the price of a huge debt: The payment of the interest alone devoured most of the country's regular annual budget. Taxes had to be raised domestically as well as overseas, and in order to do so the government had to strengthen its administrative hand in an empire that had grown haphazardly and, in North America, without much oversight.

By 1763, the 13 North American colonies had experienced both rapid demographic and powerful economic growth. Opening lands beyond the Appalachian Mountains into the Ohio valley would relieve a growing population pressure on the strip of land along the Atlantic coast that the colonies occupied. Environmental degradation, through overplanting and deforestation, had increased the landless population and contributed to the presence of growing numbers of poor people in the burgeoning cities of Philadelphia, Boston, and New York.

The occupation of new land across the Appalachians, on the other hand, increased the administrative challenges for the British. They had to employ large numbers of standing troops to protect not only the settlers from the hostility of the Native Americans but also the Native Americans from aggression by settlers. Grain, timber, and tobacco exports had made the colonies rich prior to 1763, but the war boom inevitably gave way to a postwar bust. While new land created new opportunities, the economic slump created hardships (see Map 22.1).

In view of the complicated political and economic situation in the North American colonies, the British government failed to devise a clear plan for strengthening its administrative as well as taxing powers. It was particularly inept with the imposition of new taxes intended to help in the reduction of the national debt. In 1765, it introduced the Stamp Act, forcing everyone to pay a tax on the use of paper, whether for legal documents, newspapers, or even playing cards. The tax was to be used for the upkeep of the standing troops, many of which were withdrawn from the Ohio valley and ordered to be quartered in the colonies for the enforcement of the increased taxes.

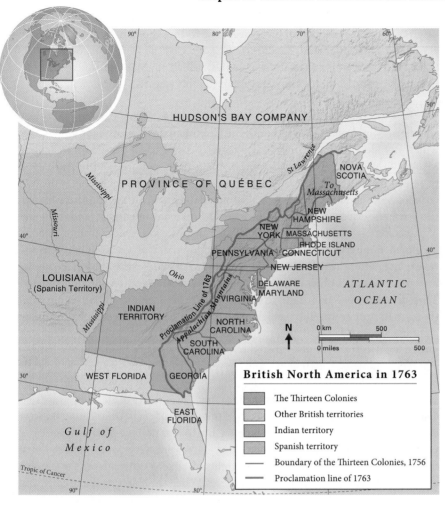

MAP 22.1 **British North America in 1763.**

Countdown to War   A firestorm of protest against the Stamp Act broke out among the urban lower-middle ranks of shopkeepers, small merchants, mechanics, and printers, who organized themselves in groups such as the Daughters of Liberty and Sons of Liberty. The Daughters declared a highly successful boycott of British goods and promoted the production of homespun textiles. In Boston, one of the flashpoints of unrest, the British administration offended colonists of the upper urban class when it dissolved the Massachusetts Assembly for opposing the tax. The British Parliament withdrew the Stamp Act in 1766 when exports fell, but replaced it with indirect taxes on a variety of commodities. Although these taxes were less visible, there were still levied without the colonies' consent.

The one indirect tax which aroused particular anger among the American colonists was the tea tax. This tax was actually a subsidy to keep the near-bankrupt East India Company afloat and had nothing to do either with America or Britain's debt. In 1773 the colonists protested the tax with the symbolic dumping of a

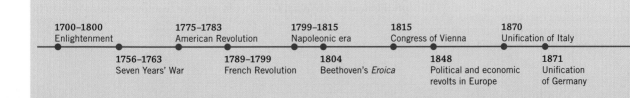

cargo of tea into Boston Harbor. In response to this "Boston Tea Party," Britain closed the harbor, demanded restitution, and passed the so-called Coercive Acts (called the "Intolerable Acts" in the colonies), which put Massachusetts into effective bankruptcy. Both sides now moved inexorably toward a showdown.

The War of Independence   To countermand the British Coercive Acts, the colonial assemblies came together in the Continental Association of 1774–1776, which decided on an economic boycott of Britain. In an effort to isolate Massachusetts from the Association, British troops ventured out in April 1775 to seize an assumed cache of arms and ammunition in Concord. A militia of farmers—the famous "minutemen"—stopped the British, inflicting heavy casualties on them. After this clash of forces, war broke out in earnest, and delegates of the colonies appointed George Washington, a former officer from a wealthy Virginian family of tobacco planters, as commander of the colonists' troops. A year later, after the mobilization of popular forces and in the hope of garnering foreign support, delegates of the colonies issued the Declaration of Independence. This declaration was a highly literate document steeped in Enlightenment thought. Its author was Thomas Jefferson, like Washington the son of a Virginian planter, with an advanced university education that included the New Sciences. The great majority of the delegates who signed were also educated men of means— planters, landowners, merchants, and lawyers. The urban middle class was clearly in command.

Central to the declaration was the idea that the equality of all "men" was "self-evident." The declaration tacitly excluded the one-fifth of all Americans who were black slaves and the half who were women, not to mention the Native Americans. On the other hand, the signers also excluded Locke's property ownership from what they considered to be the most valuable rights of citizens and rendered these rights as "life, liberty, and the pursuit of happiness." When the colonists eventually won the War of Independence in 1783, the founders created a revolutionary federal republic with a Congress that was more representative of its citizens than the Parliament in Great Britain but still excluded a substantial proportion of inhabitants.

The Early United States   The new republic's initial years were fraught with organizational difficulties. The governing document, the Articles of Confederation, granted so much power to the individual states that they operated de facto like separate countries. In 1787, a constitutional convention came together in Philadelphia to create a far more effective federal constitution. Careful to add checks and balances in the form of a bicameral legislature and separation of powers into legislative, executive, and judicial branches, the new constitution seemed to embody many of the ideals of the Enlightenment—including a set of 10 initial amendments: the Bill of Rights. Though still imperfect—particularly in sidestepping the contentious issue of slavery—it provided a model for nearly all the world's constitutions that followed. A later commentator praised it as "a machine that would go of itself"; another, more critical one called its checks and balances "a harmonious system of mutual frustration." In 1789, under the new system, George Washington was elected the first president of the United States.

Though the new republic fell far short of what we would consider today to be "representative"—until 1820 voting rights were restricted to white males with property—its abolition of the divine right of monarchial rule and its replacement by the sovereignty of the people was for most people a previously unimaginable reversal of the natural order of things. In this respect, the American and French Revolutions signaled the inauguration of a new pattern of state formation and the advent of modernity.

Conditions for the French Revolution   King Louis XVI (r. 1774–1792) and the French government had watched the American War of Independence with great sympathy, hoping for an opportunity to avenge the kingdom's defeat in the Seven Years' War. France supplied the Americans with money, arms, and officers, and in 1778–1779, in alliance with Spain, waged war on Great Britain. The French–Spanish entry into the war forced Britain into an impossible defense of its entire colonial empire. Although mounting a creditable military effort, Britain conceded defeat in 1783 in the hope of escaping with minimal territorial losses, apart from the North American colonies. Indeed, in the peace negotiations France and Spain made few territorial gains. The French government furthermore had to begin exorbitant payments—much higher than what Britain faced after the Seven Years' War—on the interest for the loans to carry out the war. Crippling debt, which the French government was ultimately unable to pay, played a large role in establishing the preconditions underlying the outbreak of the French Revolution.

As in America, the French population had increased sharply during the 1700s. Food production could barely keep up, and inflation increased. As new scholarship has shown, the rural economy responded to the rising demand, though with difficulty, and in the region of Paris, production for the market was highly profitable. Furthermore, colonial trade with the Caribbean colonies boomed. Had it not been for the debt, the government would have been well-financed: It collected direct taxes as well as monies from compulsory loans and the sale of titles and offices to a large upper stratum of ordinary people of means—merchants, lawyers, and administrators. These people were deeply invested in the regime, buying themselves into the ranks of the aristocracy and benefiting from administrative offices handling the kingdom's tax revenue. Although claiming to be the absolute authority, the king in reality shared power and wealth with a large ruling class of old and new aristocrats as well as aspiring ordinary urban people of wealth.

In 1781, suspicions arose about the solvency of the regime when the finance minister quit. He had kept the extent of the subsidies for the American revolutionaries a government secret. But the government continued to borrow, even though bad weather leading to two poor harvests in 1786–1787 diminished tax revenues. The hardship caused by these two years became crucial for the eventual revolution in 1789: Without reserves in grain and animals, the peasants suffered severe famine and grew increasingly angry when government imports intended to help ended up in the hands of profiteers and hoarders.

By 1788, the government was unable to make payments on short-term loans and had to hand out promissory notes, with bankruptcy looming in the background. As in Britain in the 1760s, a reform of the tax system became unavoidable. At first, the king sought to initiate this reform with the help of a council of appointed notables. When this failed, he held general elections for a popular assembly to meet in Versailles (called the Estates-General, last convened in 1614). Voters, defined as males over 25 who were French and paid taxes, met in constituent meetings in their districts across France, according to their "estate" as clergy, aristocrats, or commoners. Peasants met in large numbers in the "third estate," or commoner meetings; but the deputies they elected to meet in Paris were overwhelmingly administrators, lawyers, doctors, academics, businessmen, and debt holders. At the request of the king, the deputies composed petitions in which they listed their grievances about taxes, waste, luxury at court, and ministerial "despotism" to form the basis for the reform legislation.

The most famous among the petitions was the pamphlet of the priest Emmanuel-Joseph Sieyès [see-YES], entitled *What Is the Third Estate?* Sieyès was elected as a commoner from Paris and became one of the leading intellectual figures in the revolution. In his pamphlet he put forward the revolutionary idea that the French nation of 25 million *was* the third estate, while the other two estates, totaling 200,000 members, were no more than a tiny fraction. The third estate, embodying Rousseau's idea of the "general will" of the nation, should alone form a "national assembly" and translate this general will into a constitution, fiscal reform, and the abolition of aristocratic privileges.

Amid widespread unrest and rioting among peasants in many places in France and workers in Paris, the third estate now outmaneuvered the other estates and the king. In June 1789 it seceded from the Estates-General and declared itself the National Assembly. Pressured by the pro-aristocracy faction at court, the king issued a veiled threat: If the Assembly would not accept his reform proposals, he said, "I alone should consider myself their [the people's] representative." The king then reinforced his troops in and around Paris and Versailles and dismissed his popular finance minister, who had brought some famine relief in spring. Parisians, afraid of an imminent military occupation of the city, swarmed through the streets on July 14, 1789. They provisioned themselves with arms and gunpowder from arsenals, gunsmith shops, and the Bastille, the royal fortress and prison inside Paris, which they stormed.

Three Phases of the Revolution The French Revolution, unfolding from 1789 to 1799, went through the three phases of constitutional monarchy (1789–1792), radical republicanism (1792–1795), and military consolidation (1795–1799). The first phase began with the "great fear" of near anarchy, which reigned during July and August 1789. People in the provinces, mostly peasants, chased many of their aristocratic and commoner landlords from their estates. Paris, too, remained in an uproar, since food supplies, in spite of a good harvest, remained spotty. Agitation climaxed in October when thousands of working women, many with arms, marched from Paris to Versailles, forcing the king to move to Paris and concern himself directly with their plight. No longer threatened by the king, the National Assembly issued the Declaration of the Rights of Man and of the Citizen (1789), subjected the Catholic Church to French civil law (1790), established a constitutional monarchy (1791), and issued laws ending the unequal taxes of the Old Regime (1792)—four major reforms carried out in the spirit of constitutional nationalism.

The second phase of the revolution (1792–1795), the period of radical republicanism, began when the revolutionaries found themselves unable to establish a stable constitutional regime. After the king tried unsuccessfully to flee Paris with his unpopular Austrian-born, Habsburg wife, Marie-Antoinette, to a monarchist

stronghold in eastern France in the summer of 1791, Austria and Prussia threatened to intervene if the king and queen were harmed. Patriotic feelings were aroused, and the idea of preventive war gained adherents. In April 1792 the government declared war on its eastern neighbors, to which many aristocratic families had fled.

Events quickly escalated, with republicans deposing the king and holding elections for a new assembly, the National Convention, to draw up a constitution. In the following year, the republicans executed the royal couple and created a conscript army, to regain control of the borders. Fears of plots from outside France as well as among the revolutionaries led to the formation of the Committee of Public Safety. This committee, the executive organ of the National Convention, ruthlessly eliminated some 30,000 real and suspected "reactionaries" during its "Reign of Terror," making mockery of the Revolution's Declaration of the Rights of Man and universal male suffrage.

The Revolution entered its third phase (1795–1799) after the army had succeeded in securing the borders at the end of 1793. A growing revulsion at the Reign of Terror led to the emasculation of the Committee of Public Safety and its eventual replacement by the Directory in November 1795. A new constitution and bicameral legislature were created, but political and financial stability remained elusive. The Directory depended increasingly on the army to survive. What was originally an untrained conscript army of able-bodied male civilians had become highly professionalized during two years of constant warfare and was the only stable institution in France.

Within the army, a brash young brigadier general named Napoleon Bonaparte (1769–1821), of minor aristocratic Corsican descent, was the most promising commander. From 1796 to 1798 Napoleon scored major victories against the Austrians in northern Italy and invaded Egypt, which he occupied in preparation for an invasion of British India. But, thwarted by a pursuing British fleet, he returned to France and overthrew the ineffective Directory in November 1799, thus ending the Revolution.

The French Revolution. After the storming of the Bastille (top left), the French Revolution gained momentum when Parisian women marched to Versailles, demanding that the king reside in Paris and end the famine there (top right). The inevitability of a republic became clear when the king and queen were captured after they attempted to flee (bottom left).

Patterns
Up Close

The Guillotine

It is estimated that during the period of the Terror (June 1793–July 1794) the guillotine was responsible for around 1,000 executions in Paris alone and for perhaps as many as 30,000 throughout France. This iconic symbol of grisly public executions is attended by many myths. Among these is the idea that the guillotine was invented by—and took its name from—one Dr. Guillotin solely for the purpose of speeding up executions of perceived enemies of the republic during the infamous Reign of Terror. Neither of these notions is true, however. Indeed, the actual train of events is far more compelling—and ironic.

Far from appearing for the first time during the French Revolution, the first known model of a "decapitation machine" is probably the Halifax Gibbet, in use in England from around 1300 until 1650. Another model, the Scottish Maiden, was derived from the Halifax Gibbet and used in 150 executions from 1565 until 1708. It was subsequently turned over to a museum in Edinburgh in 1797 and may have earlier served as a model for the French machine.

When and how did the instrument first appear in France? Ironically, it came as an indirect result of efforts to end the death penalty. During the early days of the revolution the National Assembly pondered the abolition of the death penalty in France altogether. On October 10, 1789, the Assembly was addressed by Dr. Joseph Ignace Guillotin (1738–1814), founder of the French Academy of Medicine and a staunch opponent of capital punishment, who urged the assembly to at the very least find "a machine that beheads painlessly," if they could not ultimately agree to stop executions altogether. Toward this end Guillotin presented sketches of the kind

The Execution of Marie-Antoinette. During the radical republican period of the French Revolution, the Committee of Public Safety had Queen Marie-Antoinette condemned to death for treason after a show trial. She was executed on October 16, 1793, 9 months after the execution of her husband, Louis XVI.

Revival of Empire   Once in power, Napoleon embarked on sweeping domestic reforms that, taken together, curtailed much of the revolutionary fervor and restored order and stability in France. His crowning achievement was the reform of the French legal system, promulgated in the Civil Code of 1804, which in theory established the equality of all male citizens before the law but in reality imposed restrictions on many revolutionary freedoms. In 1804 Napoleon sealed his power by crowning himself emperor of the French. Secure in his authority at home, he now struck out on a lengthy campaign of conquest in Europe. Victory followed upon victory from 1805 to 1810, resulting in the French domination of most of Continental Europe.

The goal was the construction of an Enlightenment-influenced but newly aristocratic European empire, land-based and in the tradition of the Habsburgs, Ottomans, and Russians (see Map 22.3). With this empire, he planned to form a

of machine he had in mind, but his initial design was rejected, followed by a second rejection on December 1 of the same year. In 1791 the Assembly finally agreed to retain the death penalty, noting that "every person condemned to the death penalty shall have his head severed." But instead of adopting Dr. Guillotin's design, the Assembly accepted a model designed by Dr. Antoine Louis, secretary of the Academy of Surgery; Dr. Louis then turned to a German engineer, Tobias Schmidt, who constructed the first version of the "painless" decapitation machine. It was not until April 25, 1792, that the guillotine, nicknamed "Louisette" after Dr. Louis, claimed its first victim. It is not clear when the name was changed to "guillotine" (the final "e" was added later), but historians speculate that Dr. Guillotin's early advocacy of quick and painless executions was a major factor. As for Dr. Guillotin himself, the crowning irony was that, after fighting a losing battle with the government to change the name of the machine because of embarrassment to his family, he changed his own name and retreated to the obscurity he had come to crave.

Execution by Guillotine in France, 1929. An Enlightenment innovation, the guillotine was intended to execute humans swiftly and humanely. But the mass executions of the French Revolution turned the guillotine into a symbol of barbarism. It was not until 1977 that France executed its last criminal by guillotine. Today, most countries subscribe to the belief that even criminals have inalienable human rights, the most basic being the right to live.

Questions

• Can the guillotine be viewed as a practical adaptation of Enlightenment ideas? If so, how?

• Why do societies like France in the late eighteenth century debate the means they use to execute prisoners? What are the criteria by which one form of execution is considered more humane than others?

Continental counterweight to the maritime British Empire that was unchallengeable in the Atlantic and Indian Oceans. The failure of Napoleon's Russian campaign in 1812, however, marked the beginning of the end of Napoleon's grand scheme. An alliance of Great Britain, Austria, Prussia, and Russia ended Napoleon's empire in 1815 and inaugurated the restoration of the pre–French Revolution regimes in Europe.

Conditions for the Haitian Revolution   French Saint-Domingue was one of the richest European colonies, based on plantations that produced vast amounts of sugar, indigo, coffee, and cotton for export to the Old World. At the time of the French Revolution, the colony produced nearly half of the world's sugar and coffee. Originally, it had been a Spanish possession. But as Spain's power slipped during the seventeenth and eighteenth centuries, France took advantage of the

Punishment of a slave on the estate of Charles Balthazar Julien Févret de Saint-Mémin. This watercolor vividly depicts the vast differences between the slave strapped to a frame and the completely unconcerned estate owner on horseback. During the uprising of 1791 slaves occupied the great majority of estates, ended slavery, and drove their owners into exile. Saint-Mémin, whose mother was Creole, waited for a decade in the United States for the return of his estate before giving up and returning to France.

situation and established its colony on the western part of the island. In the following century, settlers enjoyed French mercantilist protectionism for splendid profits from their slave plantations.

In the second half of the 1700s, some 30,000 white settlers, 28,000 mulattos (holding about one-third of the slaves), and about 500,000 black plantation and household slaves formed an extremely unequal colonial society. Similarly extreme inequalities existed only in Brazil and Jamaica. When France, like Britain and Spain after the Seven Years' War, tightened colonial controls, the French administrators in Haiti were afraid that the white and mulatto plantation owners would form a united resistance. In order to split the two, they introduced increasingly racist measures to deprive the mulattos of their privileges. It was this increasing split which created the conditions for Vincent Ogé's uprising discussed in the vignette of this chapter and eventually for the slave rebellion once the French Revolution itself was under way.

Revolt of the Slaves   After the failure of Ogé's uprising, resentment continued to simmer among the mulattos in the south as well as the black slaves in the north of Haiti. Resentment turned into fury when the white settler Provincial Assembly refused any concessions even though the French revolutionary National Constituent Assembly in May 1791 granted citizen rights to mulattos whose parents were free. Aware of the by now open hostility between the mulattos and whites, slaves seized the opportunity for their own rebellion in August 1791. The leaders of the slaves were overseers, coachmen, or managers on plantations who called the slaves under their authority to arms. Almost simultaneously, but with little coordination, the mulattos of the south rose in rebellion as well. Within weeks, the slave and mulatto rebellion had 100,000 followers and encompassed the entire northern and southern provinces of the colony. The settlers were well armed but suffered heavy losses under the onslaught of overwhelming numbers.

With the rebellion taking an increasingly severe toll on the economy, the Assembly in Paris sent commissioners and troops in November 1791 and April 1792 to reestablish order. Neither commission made much headway, largely because of the unrelenting hostility of the whites, especially lower-class whites in urban centers. In their desperation to gain support, even from the blacks, the second commission made the momentous decision in August 1793 to abolish slavery. This decision, however, failed to rally the black military leaders who had allied themselves with the Spanish, rulers of the eastern half of Santo Domingo. Revolutionary France was embroiled in war against Spain and Britain since early 1793, and the latter had invaded Haiti in the summer of 1793. Spain and Britain looked like inevitable victors, and the commissioners' emancipation declaration appeared to have been too little too late.

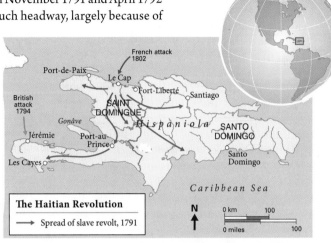

MAP 22.2 **The Haitian Revolution.**

Both invasions stalled, however, largely because of the impact of tropical diseases catching up with the British occupation forces (1793–1797). A by now sympathetic Assembly in Paris confirmed the emancipation declaration in February 1794, and the French position on the island began to improve. In May 1794, a shrewd black rebel leader from the north, François-Dominique Toussaint Louverture (ca. 1743–1803), decided that the tide was turning. He left the Spanish with his 4,000 troops and joined the French, whose numbers had dwindled to a few thousand (see Map 22.2). Toussaint, grandson of a vassal king (*onto*) in Benin, West Africa, had obtained his freedom in the 1770s. For a short period he had leased a coffee farm with a number of slaves, but after financial difficulties he went back to the plantations of his former owner as a coachman. Upon his return to the French in 1794, he accommodated himself with the mulatto faction of the rebellion in the south. In the following years, the northern blacks and southern mulattos transformed the rebellion into a full-fledged revolution.

Nation-State Building   During the violent events of 1791–1794, many plantation owners had fled the colony. The former slaves carved out plots for themselves on deserted plantations and grew subsistence crops for their families. Toussaint remained committed to the plantation system, however, in order to supply revenues for his state-building ambitions. He dispatched his officers to the countryside to force former slaves to resume production, with moderate success. In 1801, Toussaint was sufficiently powerful to assume the governorship of Saint-Domingue from the French officials in a soft coup and proclaim a constitution that incorporated the basic principles of French constitutional nationalism. By this time, the civil administration was reasonably functional again, and efforts were under way to build local courts and schools to broaden the revolution.

But Toussaint still had to reckon with Atlantic politics. Napoleon Bonaparte, in control of France since 1799, was determined to rebuild the French overseas empire. In Egypt (perhaps with plans to continue to India) he was thwarted by the British, but in the Americas he was successful in purchasing Louisiana from Spain

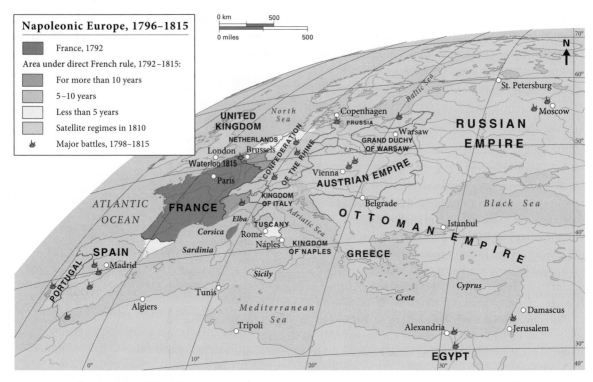

MAP 22.3 **Napoleonic Europe, 1796–1815.**

in 1800 (ceded after the Seven Years' War of 1758–1763). With the defeat of Austria in 1802, Napoleon was able to get its ally Britain to recognize the French Republic and make peace. Immediately, Napoleon dispatched troops to Saint-Domingue to add the colony to Louisiana and revive the French Atlantic empire. Toussaint was well prepared for the invasion, but when the French landed in February 1802 several of his officers surrendered without a fight. As the French advanced into the island against declining resistance, one general, Jean-Jacques Dessalines, betrayed Toussaint to the French in June 1802. After his arrest, Toussaint was sent to France, where he died in April 1803. The revolution seemed to be finished.

Jean-Jacques Dessalines (r. 1802–1806) was a former slave from northern Haiti who, as a roofer, was of higher rank than the plantation slaves. Toussaint had made him the point man for the repair of the plantation system but without giving him the preferential role that he thought he deserved. Seemingly obedient to the French, Dessalines waited for the dreaded yellow fever to take its toll among the invaders. When more than two-thirds of the French forces were dead by the summer of 1802, Napoleon realized that his Atlantic dream was unrealizable. He sold Louisiana to the United States in April 1803 and withdrew the remnants of his troops from Saint-Domingue in November 1803. On January 1, 1804, Dessalines assumed power and declared the colony's independence.

Subsequently, he made himself emperor, to counter Napoleon, and renamed the country Haiti, its supposed original Taíno name. When he changed the constitution in favor of autocratic rule, he provoked a conspiracy against him, which culminated in his assassination in 1806. In the aftermath, the state split into an autocratically ruled black north with a state-run plantation economy and a more democratic mulatto south with privatized economy of small farms (1806–1821).

Of the three revolutions resulting in the new form of the republican nation-state based on a constitution, that of Haiti is clearly the one that realized the Enlightenment principles of liberty, equality, and fraternity most fully. By demonstrating the power of the new ideology of constitutional nationalism, it inaugurated a new pattern of state formation in world history not only among the new white and colored urban middle classes but also among the uprooted black African underclass of slaves.

Enlightenment Culture: Radicalism and Moderation

The American, French, and Haitian Revolutions were embedded in the culture of the **Enlightenment** (ca. 1700–1800). The origins of this culture lay in the new mathematized sciences, which inspired a number of thinkers, such as Descartes, Spinoza, Hobbes, and Locke, to create new philosophical interpretations (see Chapter 17). The radical interpretation was materialism, according to which all of reality consisted of matter and Descartes's separate substance of mind or reason could either be dispensed with or be explained as a byproduct of matter. Moderates held on to Descartes's mind or reason as a separate substance, struggling to explain its presence in reality. The radical Enlightenment tradition evolved primarily in France, most prominently among the so-called Encyclopedists, who were materialists and agnostics or even atheists. The moderate tradition found adherents in Germany, where the Enlightenment mingled with ethnolinguist awareness.

Enlightenment: European intellectual movement (1700–1800) growing out of the New Sciences and based largely on Descartes's concept of reality consisting of the two separate substances of matter and mind.

The Enlightenment and Its Many Expressions

Energetic writers popularized the new, science-derived philosophy in eighteenth-century France, Holland, England and Germany. Thousands subscribed to Enlightenment-themed books, pamphlets, and newspapers and attended academies, salons, and lectures. The audiences were still a minority, however, even among the growing middle class of urban administrators, professionals, merchants, and landowners, not to mention the 80 percent of the population engaged in the crafts and in farming. But their voices as radical or moderate "progressives" opposing tradition-bound ministers, aristocrats, and clergy became measurably louder.

It was the late eighteenth-century generation of this vociferous minority that was central to the revolutions in America and France and—a minority within the minority—in the French slave colony Haiti. They translated their New Sciences–derived conception of reality into such "self-evident" ideals as life, liberty, equality, social contract, property, representation, nation, popular sovereignty, and constitution. In the wider, more broadly conceived culture of the Enlightenment, they fashioned new forms of expression in the arts and thereby made the Enlightenment a broad movement.

Denis Diderot and the *Encyclopédie* The idea to bring together all the new knowledge accumulated since the Renaissance and the advent of the New Sciences in an alphabetically organized encyclopedia appeared first in England in 1728. A French publisher decided in 1751 to have it translated. But under the editorship of Denis Diderot (1713–1784) and (until 1759) Jean le Rond d'Alembert (1717–1783) it became a massively expanded work in its own right. Both poured all their energy into writing entries and soliciting contributions from the "republic of letters," as the French Enlightenment thinkers were called.

Many entries dealt with delicate subjects, such as science, industry, commerce, freedom of thought, slavery, and religious tolerance, sometimes edited by the cautious publisher without Diderot's knowledge. Publication itself was not easy, since the Catholic Church and the French crown banned the project as subversive for several years and forced it to continue in secret. But the roughly 4,000 subscribers received their twenty-eighth and last volume in 1772, ready and able to assimilate everything modern, urbane gentlemen and gentlewomen should know.

Philosophy and Morality   Jean-Jacques Rousseau (1712–1778), in contrast to his atheist Enlightenment colleagues of the *Encyclopédie*, was a firm believer in the religious morality of the masses. The son of a cultivated and music-loving Geneva watchmaker, Rousseau was philosophically moderate, even if emotionally fragile and at times given to paranoia. To the consternation of the radicals in France, he espoused in his *Social Contract* (1762) the notion that humans had suffered a steady decline from their "natural" state ever since civilization began and imposed its own arbitrary authority on them. The radicals held that even though humans had lost their natural state of freedom and equality and had come under arbitrary authority, they were experiencing a steady progress of civilization toward ever-improving degrees of freedom and equality. Rousseau did share with his former friends a low opinion of the absolutist French regime, of which he ran afoul just as much as they did. But he had little faith in such concepts as popular sovereignty, elections, and electoral reforms that they propagated. Instead, he believed that people, rallying in a nation, should express their unity directly through a "general will," a sort of direct democracy—more applicable to his native city of Geneva than a large nation like France.

Philosophy and the Categorical Imperative   Immanuel Kant (1724–1804), a much more disciplined philosopher than Rousseau, was a firm believer in the progress of civilization and history, as expressed in his *Perpetual Peace* (1795). In fact, he quite immodestly thought of himself as having performed a second "Copernican turn" in modernity with his two main books, *Critique of Pure Reason* and *Critique of Practical Reason* (1781–1787). Like all Enlightenment thinkers, Kant took his departure from Descartes. But he rejected the materialist turn of Locke and the radical French Enlightenment. Even though he admitted that sensory or bodily experience was primary, he insisted that this experience could be understood only through the categories of the mind or reason which were not found in experience. Reason transcended experience.

In contrast to Rousseau with his traditional Christian ethics, Kant sought to build morality on transcendent reason. He came to the conclusion, therefore, that this morality had to be erected on the basis of the *categorical imperative*: to act in such a way that the principle of your action can be a principle for anyone's action.

This highly abstract principle later entered modern thought as the basis for human rights, with their claim to universality, as in the Charter of the United Nations (1945).

Economic Liberalism   The Enlightenment also saw the birth of the academic discipline of economics. French and British thinkers who were appalled by the inefficient administration of finances, taxes, and trade by the regimes in their countries found the official pursuit of mercantilism wanting. As discussed in previous chapters, mercantilism was the effort to import as little as possible, except from the warm-weather colonies, and develop domestic crafts so as to export manufactured goods in exchange for the commodities of the colonies. Opposed to mercantilist state control in France, the so-called physiocrats argued that individual freedom and equality should be the principles of the economy. The state should reduce taxes and other means of control to a minimum so that entrepreneurism in the general population could flourish. It should adopt a policy of *laissez-faire* [les-say-FAIR]—that is, "hands-off."

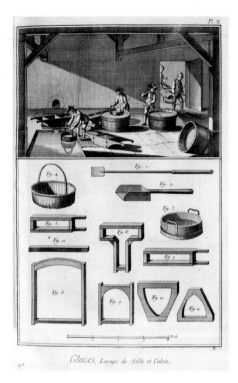

The *Encyclopédie*. Denis Diderot's massive work promoted practical, applied science, such as this illustration showing glassmaking.

The Scottish economist Adam Smith (1723–1790), who spent some time in Paris and was familiar with many of the physiocrats, developed a British version of laissez-faire economics. In his *Inquiry into the Nature and Causes of the Wealth of Nations* (1776) Smith argued that if the market were largely left to its own devices, without many state regulations and restrictions, it would regulate itself through the forces of supply and demand, appropriate prices, and so forth. It would then move in the direction of increasing efficiency as if guided by "an unseen hand." Smith became the founding father of modern economics, whose ideas are still regularly invoked today.

Literature and Music   As in the other fields of modern cultural expression, the Enlightenment also inspired writers and composers. Noteworthy among them were Johann Wolfgang von Goethe (1749–1832) and Wolfgang Amadeus Mozart (1756–1791), sons of a lawyer and a court musician, respectively. Among Goethe's numerous poems, novels, plays, and even scientific works (on color) was his drama *Faust* about an ambitious scientific experimenter who sells his soul to the devil to acquire mastery of nature. Faust became a metaphor for modernity—for the technicians and engineers whose dominance of natural forces runs roughshod over environmental concerns. Mozart was a child prodigy who composed an astounding number of symphonies, operas, and chamber music pieces. One of his best-known operas is *The Magic Flute*, a work displaying the influence of the Freemasons, a fraternal association popular in Enlightenment Europe devoted to "liberty, fraternity, and equality"—principles which the French Revolution borrowed as its motto.

The imperial turn of the French Revolution under Napoleon may be said to have effectively ended the Enlightenment. A few years later, with the fall of Napoleon and the restoration of monarchies, the European kings actively worked to rescind its effects, and in the face of overwhelming power, the Enlightenment constitutionalists went either silent or underground.

Grimm's Fairy Tales. Perhaps the most famous collection of folktales in the Western tradition, *Children's and Household Stories* (1812) was assembled by Wilhelm and Jakob Grimm as a way to preserve their country's cultural commonality and to rekindle in their countrymen an appreciation for their Germanic roots. The stories they collected, such as "Rapunzel," shown in this illustration, were brought together through fieldwork and by peasant women who would visit the brothers Grimm and recite stories that awoke "thoughts of the heart."

The Other Enlightenment: The Ideology of Ethnolinguistic Nationalism

The constitutional nationalists who led the revolutions of 1776–1804 in America, France, and Haiti proclaimed universal human rights in centuries-old monarchical states that had evolved into overseas empires. Ethnic descent or linguistic affiliations did not play a part in their revolutionary actions. After 1815, however, these affiliations began to play increasingly important roles.

Constitutional versus Ethnic Nationalism In North America, prior to the revolution the great majority of the constitutional nationalists were "British," which meant that they were Englishmen, with minorities from among the Irish, Welsh, and Scots. These minorities did not express their ethnolinguistic autonomy until the later 1800s. France was a similarly old monarchy at the heart of an Atlantic empire. A grammatically complex "high" French spoken in the Paris region set the national linguistic standard, while some of the provincial dialects spoken by nearly half of the population were mutually incomprehensible. The other half spoke no French at all and were ethnically either Celtic or German. These two minorities did not emphasize any ethnolinguistic autonomy in the 1700s, and—in contrast to Britain—not even in the 1800s.

Overseas Haiti presents the remarkable case of a rebellion in favor of the French metropolitan constitutional nationalism which transformed itself gradually into a revolutionary ethnolinguistic nationalism. After the Haitians achieved their independence, they elevated their West/Central African ethnic heritage and spoken language, Kreyòl, into their national identity, deemphasizing their French constitutional heritage.

German Cultural Nationalism In contrast to Great Britain and France, Germany was politically fragmented during the 1700s. Even though it had always possessed a central ruling institution, its imperial, rather than royal, constitution made for a much higher degree of political decentralization than in the English and French kingdoms. In addition, many Germans in eastern Europe were widely dispersed among people with different cultural and even religious heritages, such as Czechs, Slovaks, Hungarians, Poles, and Russians. Educated Germans, such as urban professionals, administrators, and educators, clearly shared a common culture wherever they lived, but in the absence of a strong central state, this culture was largely nonpolitical.

A central figure in articulating the commonly shared culture into an ethnolinguistic ideology was Johann Gottfried Herder (1744–1803). Herder's father was an elementary school teacher and Lutheran church warden in eastern Germany. At college, Herder studied with Kant but also with others under whose influence he became familiar with Pietism, a Lutheran version of the medieval Catholic mystical tradition. Employed first as a preacher and then as an administrator at assorted courts in central Germany, he published widely as a literary critic and was on close terms with Goethe and other German Enlightenment figures. In his writings, such as *On the Origin of Language* (1772), Herder sought to meld the diffuse cultural heritage into a more or less coherent ideology of Germanness combined with the Enlightenment. This ideology, so he hoped, would be preached not only to the educated but to the people in general through school curricula, history, and the arts.

The Herder-inspired ethnolinguistic version of the Enlightenment received a major boost during the French Revolution. Many Germans began to realize that any adoption of French constitutional nationalism made sense only in a politically united Germany. Before any unification plan could mature, however, Napoleon ended the French Revolution, declared himself emperor, and proceeded to defeat Prussia and Austria. With this, he aroused patriotic passions for liberation from French rule and hopes for a unified Germany under a constitutional government. Times seemed to be ripe for the realization of political unification on the basis of a combined constitutional and ethnolinguistic nationalism.

> "Thus was the German nation [*Volk*] placed—sufficiently united within itself by a common language and a common way of thinking and sharply enough severed from other peoples."
>
> —Johann Gottlieb Fichte, 1808

The Growth of the Nation-State, 1815–1871

Napoleon's defeat in Russia in 1812 and the Congress in Vienna of 1815 were the principal occasions for rulers to turn back the clock in Europe. Monarchies and aristocracies reappeared throughout the continent, and the restored kings allowed only for the barest minimum of popular representation in parliaments. By contrast, in Anglo-America, the supremacy of constitutionalism was unchallenged during the 1800s. Here, a pattern of increasing citizen participation in the constitutional process manifested itself, although not without challenges, which culminated in the American Civil War.

Restoration Monarchies, 1815–1848

For a full generation, monarchists in Europe sought to return to the politics of absolutism. This return required repression and elaborate political manipulation to keep the now-identifiable middle class of public employees, professionals, schoolteachers, and factory entrepreneurs away from meaningful political participation. A "Concert of Europe" emerged in which rulers avoided intervention in the domestic politics of fellow monarchs, except in cases of internal unrest.

The Congress of Vienna European leaders met in 1815 at Vienna after the fall of Napoleon in an effort to restore order to a war-torn continent. The driving principle at the session was monarchical conservatism, articulated mainly by Prince Klemens von Metternich (1773–1859), Austria's prime minister. An opponent of constitutional nationalism, Metternich was determined to resist the aspirations of the still-struggling middle classes outside France, which he regarded with contempt.

To accomplish his objective of reinstituting kings and emperors ruling by divine grace, Metternich had the Congress hammer

> "We see this intermediary [middle] class abandon itself with a blind fury and animosity . . . applying itself to the task of persuading kings that their rights are confined to sitting upon a throne, while those of the people are to govern, and to attack all that centuries have bequeathed as holy and worthy of man's respect."
>
> —Klemens von Metternich, 1820

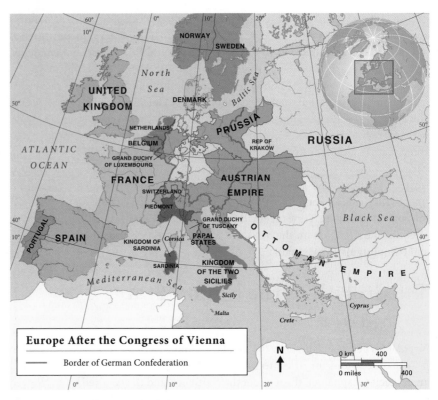

MAP 22.4 **Europe after the Congress of Vienna.**

out two principles: legitimacy and balance of power. The principle of legitimacy was conceived as a way to both recognize exclusive monarchial rule in Europe and to reestablish the borders of France as they were in 1789. The principle of the balance of power involved a basic policy of preventing any one state from rising to dominance over any other. Members agreed to convene at regular intervals in the future in what they called the "Concert," so as to ensure peace and tranquility in Europe. What is remarkable about this is that, with only minor exceptions, this policy of the balance of power remained intact down to 1914 (see Map 22.4).

As successful as the implementation of these two principles was, the solution devised for the German territories—now no longer with an overall ruler since the Holy Roman Empire was dissolved in 1806—was less satisfactory. The Congress of Vienna created an unwieldy and weak confederation of 39 German states, including the empire of Austria and the kingdoms of Prussia, Denmark, and the Netherlands. Prussia and Austria promptly embarked on a collision course over dominance in the confederation, with Prussia keeping the initiative and creating a customs union in 1834. Prussia's main purpose in this was to find outlets for its rising industrial and commercial interests in the northern German Ruhr region. Constitutionalist and republican Germans disliked the confederation as well, since they had no meaningful voice in it. Thus, by resolving the overall issue of coexistence among the German states, but not of their fragmentation, the Congress was only partially successful.

Further Revolutions in France   In keeping with the principle of legitimacy, the Congress restored the French Bourbon monarchy with the coronation of King Louis XVIII (r. 1814–1824), a brother of Louis XVI. Louis, even though determined to restore full absolutist powers, was indecisive as to which republican institutions to abolish first. Playing for time, he tolerated the "White Terror," during which the returning aristocracy and other royalists pursued revenge for their sufferings during the revolution. When Louis died in 1824 the conservatives succeeded in putting Charles X (1824–1830), a second brother of Louis XVI, on the throne. Charles took the extreme course of restoring the property of the aristocracy lost during the revolution and reestablishing the crown's ties to the Catholic Church.

Republican reaction to Charles's restoration policy was swift. In two elections, the republicans won a majority and overthrew the king. But they stopped short of abolishing the monarchy and elevated Louis-Philippe (1830–1848), son of a pro-republican duke who had been guillotined and had fought in the republican guards during 1789–1792, to the throne. Under this "bourgeois king," as he was sometimes caricatured, however, rising income gaps in the middle class as well as difficult living conditions among the nascent industrial working class led to new tensions. In the ensuing revolution of 1848, in which thousands of workers perished, the adherents of restoration and republicanism attempted another compromise: Louis-Philippe went into exile, and the parliament elected Louis-Napoleon Bonaparte (r. 1848–1852; self-declared emperor 1852–1870), a nephew of the former emperor, as president.

Rebellion. Following the successful revolution of 1848 that ended the monarchy of Louis-Philippe in France, similar uprisings broke out across Europe. This image shows the Berlin Alexander Square barricades of March 1848.

Uprisings across Europe   After the revolution in Paris, uprisings occurred in the spring of 1848 in cities such as Berlin, Vienna, Prague, Budapest, Palermo, and Milan, as well as in three Irish counties. In Prussia the king seemingly bowed to pressure from revolutionaries and promised constitutional reforms. In Austria, hit by uprisings in multiple cities and by multiple nationalities, both the emperor and Metternich, the driving forces of 1815, resigned. The successors, with Russian help, slowly regained military control over the Italians, Czechs, and Hungarians, as well as his own Austrians.

In the German Confederation, also hit by uprisings, moderate and republican delegates convened a constitutional assembly in Frankfurt in May 1848. This assembly elaborated the basic law for a new, unified state for German speakers and elected a provisional government. The new hard-line Austrian emperor, however, refused to let go of his non-German subjects. Therefore, the constitution joined only the German Federation and Prussia (also with non-German minorities) into a unitary state, with the provision for a future addition of German-speaking Austria. Against strong resistance by republicans, the delegates offered the Prussian king a new hereditary imperial crown in the name of the German people. But the king, unwilling to accept the principle of popular sovereignty, refused the crown "of clay." This refusal turned the tide against the Frankfurt Assembly. Moderate delegates departed, and radical ones instigated revolts. Prussian troops stepped in and relieved a group of grateful regional monarchs of their insurrectionists. By July 1849, the provisional Frankfurt government had come to an end and Germany's constitutional experiment was over.

Ethnolinguistic Nationalism in Italy   Italy was as fragmented politically as Germany, but unlike Germany it was also largely under foreign domination. Austria controlled the north directly and the center indirectly through relatives from the house of Habsburg. The monarchy of Piedmont in the northwest, the Papal States in the center, and the kingdom of Naples and Sicily (the "Two Sicilies") were independent but administratively and financially weak. After the Metternich restoration, the Italian dynasties had made concessions to constitutionalists, but Austria repressed uprisings in 1820–1821 and 1831–1832 without granting liberties. The republican Carbonari inspired both uprisings; they were members of the crafts guild of charcoal burners who had formed Enlightenment fraternities similar to the Freemasons during the eighteenth century. After their decisive defeat in 1831, the remnants formed the Young Italy movement.

Realistic second-generation politicians of the Restoration recognized that the middle-class ethnolinguistic nationalism coming to the fore in 1848 was a potent force that could be harnessed. By remobilizing this force in the 1860s, they would be able to end state fragmentation and make Italy and Germany serious players in the European Concert. These politicians were more sympathetic to French-style constitutionalism than the Restoration politicians but still opposed to republicanism. Their pursuit of realpolitik—exploitation of political opportunities—resulted in 1870–1871 in the transformations of the Italian kingdom of Piedmont and the German Empire of Prussia into the nation-states of Italy and Germany.

The Italian politician who did the most to realize Italy's unification was the prime minister of Piedmont-Sardinia, Count Camillo di Cavour (1810–1861).

Cavour was the scion of an old aristocratic family in northwestern Italy with training as a military officer. While in the army, he read widely among French and British political philosophers and became a constitutional nationalist. A supporter of Adam Smith's liberal trade economics, he imported South American guano fertilizer and grew cash crops, like sugar beets, on his estate. As prime minister he was the driving force behind the development of railroads, first in Piedmont and later in Italy. With the backing of his similarly liberal-minded king, Victor Emanuel II (r. 1849–1878), he began the Italian unification process under decidedly trying circumstances. Through adroit maneuvering, he was able to arrange for a favorable plebiscite in north-central Tuscany and Emilia in 1859, gaining these two regions from Austria for Piedmont. A year later Cavour occupied the Papal States and accepted the offer of Giuseppe Garibaldi (1807–1882) to add adjoining Naples and Sicily to a now nearly unified Italy.

Garibaldi, a mariner from Nice in the northwest (present-day France), was a Carbonaro and Young Italy republican nationalist with a colorful career as a freedom fighter not only in Italy but also in Brazil and Uruguay. Dressed in his trademark red gaucho shirt with poncho and sombrero, the inspiring Garibaldi attracted large numbers of volunteers wherever he went to fight. Cavour died shortly afterward and did not live to see Piedmont transform itself into Italy in 1870, when it gained Venice from Austria and Rome from France in the wake of the Prussian–Austrian war of 1866. But he clearly was the power politician who laid the decisive groundwork.

Bismarck and Germany   In contrast to Italy, neither King Wilhelm I (r. 1861–1888) nor his chancellor (prime minister) Otto von Bismarck (in office 1862–1890) in Prussia had deep sympathies for constitutionalism. By combining their antipathies and forming a coalition of convenience, they succeeded in keeping the constitutionalists in the Prussian parliament in check. But they realized they could dip into the ethnolinguistic nationalism that had poured forth in 1848, using it for power politics: realpolitik.

Bismarck was a Prussian aristocrat with a legal education rather than a military career. He was multilingual, widely read, and experienced in the diplomacy of the European Concert. He realized that Prussia, a weak player in the Concert, had a chance for greater influence only if the kingdom could absorb the German Federation. For Prussia to do so, Bismarck argued, it had to progress from talk about unification, as in Frankfurt, to military action, using "blood and iron." From the time of his appointment to 1871, he systematically maneuvered Prussia into an internationally favorable position for the coup that would eventually bring unification: war with France.

First, he exploited a succession crisis in Denmark for a combined Prussian–Austrian campaign to annex Denmark's southern province of Schleswig-Holstein in 1865. Then, when Austria objected to the terms of annexation, he declared war on Austria (1866). After Prussia won, Bismarck dissolved the German Confederation and annexed several German principalities. In France, Louis-Napoleon Bonaparte

Giuseppe Garibaldi. Garibaldi was an Italian nationalist who, in collaboration with Count Cavour, prime minister of the kingdom of Piedmont, contributed decisively to the unification of Italy. Garibaldi and his "Red Shirts" were able to seize Sicily and Naples from its Bourbon-descended monarch in 1860. He then unified his conquests with the constitutional kingdom of Piedmont to form the nucleus of Italy, which was fully unified a decade later.

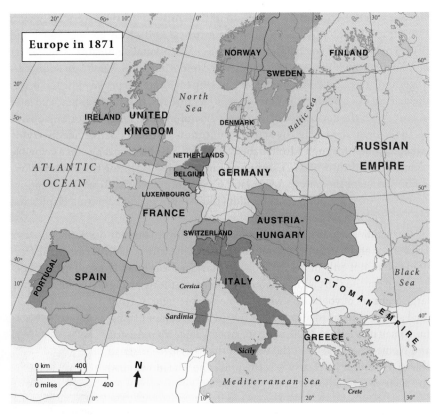

MAP 22.5 **Europe in 1871.**

was greatly concerned about the rising power of Prussia. He had carried out a coup d'état in 1852, ending the Second Republic and declaring himself emperor—an act that prompted the readily quotable Karl Marx to claim that "history always repeats itself, the first time as tragedy, the second time as farce." A distraction on his eastern flank was not at all what Emperor Napoleon III desired.

But he carelessly undermined his own position. First, he prevented a relative of King Wilhelm from succeeding to the throne of Spain after it fell vacant. But when he demanded additional assurances that Prussia would not put forward candidates for any other thrones in the future, the canny Bismarck outmaneuvered him. He advised King Wilhelm to refuse the demand and edited the refusal in such a way as to make it insulting to the French. France then declared war on Prussia but was defeated (1870). Now Bismarck had the upper hand that he had been diligently working to gain. He used it to annex Alsace-Lorraine from the French, carried out the final unification of Germany, and elevated the new state to the status of empire in 1871 (see Map 22.5).

Nation-State Building in Anglo-America, 1783–1900

After the independence of the United States in 1783, both the United States and Great Britain were free to pursue their versions of constitutional nation-state development. The old and new monarchies and ethnolinguistic movements which complicated nation-state formation in central Europe did not affect the United States, giving rise instead to a long tradition among American historians of claiming American "exceptionalism." While it is indeed true that the growth of the United States in the 1800s followed its own trajectory, there is also no question that the underlying pattern of modern nation-state formation was not unlike that of the other two constitutional nations, France and Great Britain: Neither was much affected by ethnolinguistic nationalism (although Britain was more than France, as we shall see below).

The United States   During the first half of the nineteenth century the newly independent North American states not only prospered but also began a rapid westward expansion. As this process unfolded, toward 1850 it became increasingly apparent that sectional differences were developing in the process. Whereas the North developed an industrial and market-driven agricultural economy, the South remained primarily agrarian, relying heavily upon the production of cotton for its economic vitality. Even more, the South relied upon vast numbers of slaves to work the fields of the cotton plantations. Cotton was the main fiber for the industrial production of textiles, and it not only defined the wealth of the plantation owners but led them to see chattel slavery as the only viable means to keep the "cotton kingdom" prosperous. In defense of its stance, the South increasingly relied upon the notion of states' rights in opposition to federal control. With the acquisition of new territory extending to the Pacific coast after the war with Mexico from 1846 to 1848 and the push of settlement beyond the Mississippi, the vital question of which of the new territories would become "free states" and "slave states" resulted in increasing tensions between North and South.

The result was an attempt by a number of southern states to secede and form a new union, the Confederate States of America. When the new administration of President Abraham Lincoln attempted to suppress this movement, the disastrous American Civil War (1861–1865) ensued. Resulting in an enormous loss of life—more than 600,000 combatants on both sides were killed—the Civil War finally ended with a northern victory in 1865. There were several major results of the conflict, not least of which was an enhanced unification of the country during the occupation of the southern states. Here, federal troops enforced the policies of the Reconstruction (1865–1877). First, Lincoln's concept of the primacy of national government over individual assertions of states' rights was now guaranteed. Second, slavery was abolished and slaves were granted full citizenship. Third, the rebuilding of the country and opening of the west resulted in a period of remarkable growth, facilitated especially by the expansion of a national network of railroads. By 1900, about 200,000 miles of uniform-gauge track crisscrossed the country, and the United States was on its way to becoming the world's predominant industrial power (see Map 22.6).

The price of reintegrating the old South into the new order was the end of Reconstruction and the reversion over the course of two generations to an imposition of de facto peonage on its black citizens. Indeed, between 1877 and 1914 state legislatures in the South systematically stripped African Americans of voting rights by means of poll taxes and literacy tests and imposed formal and informal segregation in social and public accommodations. These were enforced by law and all too often by lynchings and other forms of violence. In order to accommodate the sensibilities of white southerners regarding race, most northern policy and opinion makers gradually backed away from the views espoused by the champions

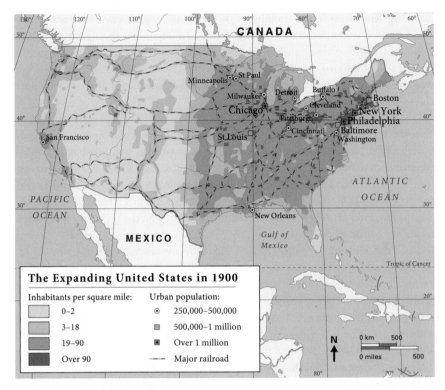

MAP 22.6 **The Expanding United States in 1900.**

of racial equality during Reconstruction and gave tacit acquiescence to southern efforts to maintain white hegemony. The drive for full civil rights would thus occupy a sizeable share of American domestic policy debates throughout the twentieth century.

Native Americans   While blacks made uneven advances during the 1800s, Native Americans suffered unmitigated disasters. When the Louisiana Purchase in 1803 (see above, p. 671) nearly doubled the size of the United States, politicians quickly conceived of the idea of moving Native Americans from their eastern homelands to the new territories. For their part, Native Americans realized that only a large-scale unification would help them to stay put, especially in the South (Georgia, Alabama, and Florida) and the Midwest (Ohio, Indiana) where white settler encroachment was strong after independence.

In the Midwest, Tecumseh (1768–1812) and his brother Tenskwatawa (1775–1836) renewed the prophecies of unification that had been in circulation since the mid-1700s. Tecumseh traveled widely between the Midwest and South, seeking to forge a Native American resistance federation. Tenskwatawa, claiming his authority from visions of the Master of Life, the spirit of spirits in the world, preached that Native Americans needed to reject white culture and return to traditional life. In Tippecanoe, a newly founded town in Indiana, thousands of followers from a variety of nations came together, but suffered a severe defeat at the hands of US troops in 1812. The defeat ended the dream of Native American unity.

In the South, discriminatory legislation and brutal assaults by the states made it more and more difficult for Native American nations to survive on their lands. With the declared intention of helping these nations against the states, in 1830 the federal government issued the Indian Removal Act. In fact, however, this act only deepened the sufferings of the Native Americans: A quarter never made it on the "Trail of Tears" to their designated new homeland Oklahoma, dying on the way from disease and deprivation. The survivors settled and reconstructed their agriculture, schools, and councils as best as they could, having to accommodate the regular arrival of newly displaced Native Americans from the east in the subsequent decades.

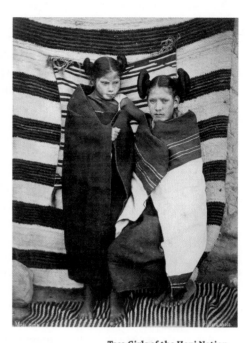

Destruction of the Buffalo Herds   By mid-century, white ranchers and miners began to encroach on the lands farther west of the Mississippi, and beyond Missouri, already a state in 1821. Again, the federal government passed a law supposedly protecting the Native Americans of the Plains from increasingly bloody clashes with advancing whites by creating "reservations" (1851). The obligation, especially for such free-roaming groups as the Sioux and Apache, to stay on reservations rather than to hunt freely was a first aggravation. Further affronts came through the Homestead Act (1862), the construction of the transcontinental railroad (1863–1869), and the rapid appearance of towns and cities along the railroad corridors. The worst injury was the destruction of the gigantic herds of buffalo (bison), the hunting of which formed the principal livelihood of the Native Americans on the Plains.

Within a mere two decades (1865–1884), some 10–15 million animals were slaughtered until fewer than 1,000 remained. Research in the early 2000s has demonstrated that new chemical methods developed in 1871 in Britain and Germany made the tanning of the thick buffalo skin feasible for high-quality shoe leather and industrial belting, greatly stimulating the hunt for hides. In the American Indian Wars (1862–1890), the Native Americans defended their homelands tenaciously but ultimately in vain. Once more, visionaries sought to unify the various groups through the Ghost Dance, enacting a prophecy of the return of the buffalo herds and the disappearance of the whites. Their last stand was at Wounded Knee Creek, South Dakota, in December 1890. Defeated and demoralized by 1900, under a quarter million Native Americans (down from 600,000 in 1800) found themselves on 310 reservations on 2.3 percent of American soil.

Two Girls of the Hopi Nation with Their Characteristic Hairstyles and Blankets. The Hopi live in the American Southwest, today's Arizona. They are best known as sophisticated farmers in adobe pueblos, some of which were built into the rock walls of canyons. In 1680, the Hopi rebelled for a dozen years against Spanish missionaries and colonists in their midst, achieving a degree of autonomy as a result. The United States organized the nation in 1882 into the Hopi Reservation.

Reform Measures   As in other Western nation-states, rapid industrialization produced social and labor unrest in the United States, resulting in the reforming initiatives of the Progressive era, which extended from 1890 to 1914. Although the later nineteenth century is referred to as the Gilded Age, epitomized by the staggering wealth of industrial tycoons like Andrew Carnegie (1835–1919) and John D. Rockefeller (1839–1937), all was not well beneath the surface. Big business had grown to such an extent that in the early 1900s a few hundred firms controlled two-fifths of all American manufacturing. The "trust buster" president, Theodore

Roosevelt (r. 1901–1909), and Congress ended the monopolies of many firms, Rockefeller's Standard Oil among them, which had to divide itself into 30 smaller companies. A new Department of Commerce and Labor (1903) and the Pure Food and Drug and Meat Inspection Acts (1906) helped the hard-pressed workers and consumers. With the Federal Reserve Act (1913) and the Federal Trade Commission Act (1914) Congress created an overall framework for the supervision of the financial and business sectors. As many people at the time realized, a free market prospered only with at least a minimum of regulations.

Great Britain   The pattern of constitutional nation-state construction that Britain followed in the eighteenth and nineteenth centuries was gradual and uninterrupted by wars. Challenges did not come from a civil war but from the rise of ethnolinguistic nationalisms outside the English core. The first signs of Irish nationalism, based not only in ethnic and linguistic but also religious traditions, appeared after the Great Famine of 1845–1849. Rural production and land issues were the main points of contention, leading to demands for home rule or even independence. A Protestant landlord class still controlled most of the land, which was farmed by Catholic tenant farmers. During the worldwide Long Depression of 1873–1896 Irish farmers received low prices for their crops but no reductions in rent. A "land war" (mass protests against tenant evictions) ensued which the British Army sought to quell. This eventually led in 1898 to local self-rule for the Irish and in 1903–1909 to land reform.

Scotland, traditionally divided between the Highlands and Lowlands, developed an ethnolinguistic sense of its identity only slowly. The development began on the level of folklore, with the revival of Scottish dress and music (clan tartans, kilts, and bagpipes). More serious issues came to the fore in 1853 when the Scots, upset by what their perception that the British government paid more attention to Ireland, founded an association for the vindication of Scottish rights. But they had to wait until 1885, when the British Liberal Party wrested power from the conservative Tories, thanks to the support of Irish members of Parliament. With the creation of the position of a secretary for Scotland, the nationalists found their first recognition.

Welsh nationalism arose in the context of industrialization and the development of a Welsh working class, which organized uprisings in the 1830s. Religious issues, mostly related to opposition to the Church of England among nonconformists (e.g., Methodists, Quakers, and Presbyterians), and education issues surrounding the so-called Treachery of the Blue Books added to the unrest. A governmental report of 1847, bound in blue covers, found that education in Wales was substandard: Sunday schools were the only schools offering education in Welsh, while regular schools used English as the language of instruction for children who spoke only Welsh. Both issues were the focus of most Welsh nationalist agitation in the second half of the 1800s, and it was not until 1925, with the foundation of the Party of Wales, that Welsh nationalism became a force of its own.

While ethnolinguistic nationalisms arose around the English core, Parliament, the guardian of British constitutional nationalism, undertook major legal reforms of its constitutional order in the course of the 1800s. As industrialization progressed, both Liberals and Tories took cognizance of the growing middle and working classes. The Great Reform Bill of 1832 shifted seats from southern districts to the more populated and industrialized center and north. The repeal of the Corn Laws in 1846 liberated imports and made grain cheaper, and the Second Reform Act of 1867 extended the franchise to larger numbers of working-class voters. The end result was not only that Britain escaped the revolutions of 1848 but also that the British electorate was largely united during the Victorian period (1837–1901) in its support for British imperialism around the globe.

Romanticism and Realism: Philosophical and Artistic Expression to 1850

Parallel to the evolution of the patterns of constitutional and ethnolinguistic nationalism, the two movements of romanticism and realism patterned the evolution of culture on both sides of the Atlantic. Romanticism was an outgrowth of strains in the Enlightenment in which the independence of the mind from matter was emphasized. Taking their cue from Rousseau and Kant, romantics emphasized unrestrained individual creativity and spontaneity for the expression of their feelings. As industrialization progressed, however, a growing sense of realism concerning material conditions set in, expressing itself in the arts by greater social awareness.

Romanticism

Inspired by the Enlightenment and the revolutions, a number of philosophers, writers, composers, and painters of the period of **romanticism** in the early 1800s drew the conclusion that humans possessed a fullness of freedom to remake themselves. To them, the mind was entirely independent, creating new aesthetic categories out of its own powers. Not all thinkers and artists went this far, but for romantics creativity became absolute. Indeed, the stereotype of the bohemian creative "genius" crossing new imaginative thresholds became firmly implanted in the public imagination during this time.

Romanticism: Intellectual and artistic movement that emphasized emotion and imagination over reason and sought the sublime in nature.

Philosophers and Artists   The one philosopher who, building on Kant, postulated the complete freedom of mind or spirit was Georg Wilhelm Friedrich Hegel (1770–1831). The most systematic of the so-called idealist philosophers in Germany, Hegel asserted that all thought proceeded dialectically from the "transcendental ego" to its opposite, matter, and from there to the spiritualized synthesis of nature. This **dialectic** permeates his entire system of philosophy.

Even more than philosophy, music became the medium for expressing the creative genius. The German Ludwig van Beethoven (1770–1827) and the Frenchman Hector Berlioz (1803–1869) pioneered the new genre of program music, with the *Pastoral Symphony* (Symphony no. 6) and the *Symphonie phantastique*, respectively, emphasizing passion and emotional intensity and the freedom of the musical spirit over traditional form. From among the emerging middle class, eager to develop their romantic sensibilities and play music at home, a veritable explosion of composers erupted during the first half of the 1800s. Often composing at a furious rate, these musicians were also virtuosi on the violin or piano, playing their own new musical forms and traveling on concert circuits all across Europe.

Dialectic: The investigation of truth by discussion; in Hegel's thought, the belief that a higher truth is comprehended by a continuous unification of opposites.

The medium of painting also lent itself to the expression of romantic feelings of passion and the mind's overflowing imaginative aesthetics. Not surprisingly, the proliferation of romantic painters numbered in the hundreds. The common feature of these painters was that they departed from the established academic practices and styles. They either let nature dictate the direction and extent of their absorption into it or expressed their personal impressions forcefully with new, dramatic topics.

As in the other art forms, romanticism in literature appears in heroines or heroes and their passions and sentiments. In the still late-Enlightenment-informed prose of the British author Jane Austen (1775–1817), witty and educated urbane society shapes the character and sensibilities of young women and prepares them for their reward, namely the love of the proper gentleman and marriage to him. A generation later, also in Britain, the three Brontë sisters, Charlotte (1816–1855), Emily (1818–1848), and Anne (1820–1849), published novels with equally complex plots but much greater emphasis on romantic passion on the one hand and character flaws or social ills on the other. The novels also contain mysterious, seemingly inexplicable happenings—artistic devices which the American Edgar Allan Poe (1809–1849) used more explicitly in his thematic Gothic stories and tales, such as "The Fall of the House of Usher" (1839).

Realism

Realism: The belief that material reality exists independently of the people who observe it.

Toward the middle of the 1800s, many artists and writers shifted their focus from the romanticism of the self and its aesthetic or moral sentiments to the **realism** of the middle classes whose constitutionalist dreams had been smothered by the repression of the revolutions of 1848. In philosophy, thinkers identified stages leading progressively to the rise of middle classes and industrialism. And in literature, the complex and tangled relationships that characterized the plots of the romantics continued, but now set in the more prosaic urban world of factories and working classes.

Philosophy of History   Toward the middle of the 1800s, the French thinker Auguste Comte (1798–1857) composed a six-volume work entitled *The Positive Philosophy* (1830–1842). In it he arranged world history into the three successive stages of the theological, metaphysical, and scientific. In his view, the scientific advances of the sciences had all but eclipsed the metaphysical stage and had ushered in the last, scientific era. For Comte this was a sign of Europe's progress and a "positive" stage. His philosophy, labeled "positivism," exerted a major influence in Europe as well as in Latin America. Comte further argued that the only sure way of arriving at truth was based on scientific facts and knowledge of the world acquired through the senses. In Comte's view, the laws governing human behavior could be ascertained with the same degree of precision as the laws of nature: a utopian ideology still with us today.

Prose Literature   Realistic writers of fiction moved away from personal sentiments to realistic scenes as they were encountered in middle-class society. New aesthetic experimentations ensued so that the ordinary could be a heightened reflection of the new "reality" of life in the industrial age. William Makepeace Thackeray (1811–1863) in England, for example, was a supreme satirist, as

(a)

(b)

Romantic Art. Romantic painters expressed an absorbing, encompassing nature in their art. Note the barely recognizable steam-powered train in this painting (*a*) by J. M. W. Turner, *Rain, Steam, and Speed: The Great Western Railway* (1844). Romantic painters also depicted dramatic or exotic scenes relating to revolutions or foreign lands, such as the languid harem in *The Women of Algiers in Their Apartment* (1834) by Eugène Delacroix (*b*).

displayed in *Vanity Fair,* a book on bourgeois human foibles and peccadilloes. His compatriot Charles Dickens (1812–1870) had a similar focus but centered on working- and lower-middle-class characters in his many novels. The English-woman George Eliot, born Mary Ann Evans (1819–1880), was politically oriented,

Realism. The documentary power of photography spurred the new impulses of realism that emerged around 1850. The photograph here shows the execution of hostages in the Commune of Paris in the spring of 1871 shortly before its final defeat by troops of the provisional French national government. One of the executed hostages was Georges Darboy, archbishop of Paris, a critic of the pope and strong patriot who cared for the wounded of the war against Prussia in 1870.

ASSASSINAT des OTAGES à la PRISON de LA ROQUETTE le 24 MAI 1871
Mr Darboy   Bonjean   Duguerry   Ducoudray   Clerc   Allard

placing small-town social relations within the context of concrete political events in Great Britain, as in *Middlemarch* (1874). Gustave Flaubert (1821–1880) in France experimented with a variety of styles, among which those featuring extremely precise and unadorned descriptions of objects and situations are perhaps the most important (*Madame Bovary*, 1857). Henry James (1843–1916), an American living in Britain, in his self-declared masterpiece, *The Ambassadors* (1903), explored the psychological complexities of individuals whose entwined lives crossed both sides of the Atlantic. In the end, realism, with its individuals firmly anchored in the new class society of the 1800s, moved far from the freedom and exuberance celebrated by the romantics.

Putting It All Together

Though the pattern of nation-state building in Europe and North America was relatively slow and, in places, painful, it has become the dominant mode of political organization in the world today. As we will see in subsequent chapters, the aftermath of World War I and the decolonization movement following World War II gave a tremendous boost to the process of nation-state formation around the world. Here, the legacy of European colonialism both planted these ideas among the colonized and, by supplying the Enlightenment ideas of revolution and the radical remaking of society, gave them the ideological means of achieving their own liberation from foreign rule. In both cases, the aspirations of peoples to "nationhood" followed older European models as the colonies were either granted independence or fought to gain it from declining empires. But, in many respects, their efforts mirrored the difficulties of the first constitutional and ethnolinguistic nation-states.

Take the example of the United States. Though it achieved world economic leadership by 1914, it had faced an early constitutional crisis, endured a prolonged sectional struggle in which slavery marred the constitutional order for almost three-quarters of a century, fought a bloody civil war for national unification that very nearly destroyed it, and remained united in part by acquiescing in practices of overt segregation and discrimination against the 10 percent of its population that was of African descent. Or take the case of France. Its people adopted constitutional nationalism in 1789, but the monarchy it seemingly replaced bounced back three times. Thus, even in the later nineteenth century, Abraham Lincoln's resolution that "government of the people, by the people, for the people shall not perish from the earth" was still far from guaranteed.

Yet another example is the case of Germany, where ethnolinguistic nationalism diluted the straightforward enthusiasm for the constitution and the symbols accompanying it. Historians continue to argue over whether Germany, and by extension other central and eastern European nations, took a special route (*Sonderweg*) to constitutional normality or whether the path was the same except that the pace slowed at critical times. In retrospect, it is impossible to say which of the speed bumps on the way toward the nation-state—slavery/racism, residual monarchism, or the twentieth-century experiments of communism and supremacist nationalism—were responsible for the longest delay. In Part 6 we will consider all of these developments in more detail.

For additional resources, including maps, primary sources, visuals, and quizzes, please go to www.oup.com/us/vonsivers. Please see the Further Resources section at the back of the book for additional readings and suggested websites.

Against the Grain

Defying the Third Republic

Republican and socialist Parisians despised the new conservative Third Republic of France, which was dominated by two monarchist factions. They considered it defeatist against the Prussians who had been victorious in the war of 1870. After two failed protests, the final trigger for an outright revolution was the government's attempt, on March 18, 1871, to collect some 400 guns under the command of the Parisian National Guard. The attempt turned into a fiasco. The number of horses to pull the hundreds of cannons away was insufficient, and the troops fraternized with the crowds who swarmed around the cannons, offering flowers and food to the soldiers. In the melee, however, several government soldiers and two generals were killed (the latter probably by army deserters in Paris, not guardsmen). Seizing the opportunity, the central committee of the National Guard declared its independence and held elections on the basis of male suffrage for a communal council on March 26 (Commune of Paris: March 18 to May 28, 1871).

The council of mostly workers and craftsmen plus a strong contingent of professionals issued a flurry of new laws. All deputies were under binding mandates and could be recalled anytime. As a commune of a desired universal republic, Paris considered all foreigners as equals. France itself was to become a federation of communes. Abandoned factories and workshops were to be directed by workers' councils. Church properties were confiscated, and the separation of church and state was declared. Under the auspices of the women-run Union of Women for the Defense of Paris and the Care of the Injured, measures for equal pay and pensions for retired survivors, regardless of marital status, were envisaged. The official symbol of the Commune was the red flag of the radical French Revolution of 1792, not the republican tricolor. In short, as Haiti had done in 1794, the Commune pushed equality much further than the American and French revolutions had ever done, frightening the middle classes to their core.

The Commune had no chance of survival against the superior troops of the Third Republic. It was bloodily repressed, although with far fewer victims, according to new documentation analyzed in 2012. The total of communards killed is now estimated to be at most 7,400. The symbolical significance of the Commune, however, was immense: Socialists and communists made it the mythical dawn of world revolution, working class dictatorship, and the eventual withering away of the (national) state in the utopia of a classless society.

- Did the members of the Commune of Paris opponents run counter to the pattern of nation-state formation in the nineteenth century, and if so, how did they want to replace it?

- Did the ideas of small communities and opposition to centralized national governments retain their attraction in the twentieth and twenty-first centuries? If yes, which examples come to mind and for which reasons?

Thinking Through Patterns

▶ How did the pattern of constitutional nationalism, emerging from the American and French Revolutions, affect the course of events in the Western world during the first half of the nineteenth century?

Constitutional nationalism emerged as a result of the success of American and French revolutionaries in overthrowing absolute rule. The constitutional revolutionaries replaced the loyalty of subjects to a monarch with that of free and equal citizens to the national constitution. This form of nationalism called for unity among the citizens regardless of ethnic, linguistic, or religious identity. In the United States, this nationalism had to overcome a conservative adherence to slavery in the South before it gained general recognition after the end of the Civil War. In France, republican nationalists battled conservative monarchists for nearly a century before they were able to finally defeat them in the Third Republic.

Constitutional nationalists emphasized the principles of freedom, equality, constitution, rule of law, elections, and representative assembly regardless of ethnicity, language, or religion. However, nationalists in areas of Europe lacking centralized monarchies sought to first unify what they identified as dispersed members of their nation through ideologies that emphasized common origin, centuries of collective history, and shared literary, artistic, and religious traditions. In these ethnolinguistic (and sometimes religious) ideologies constitutional principles were secondary. Only once unification in a nation-state was achieved would the form of government—monarchist, constitutional-monarchist, republican—then be chosen.

▶ In what ways did ethnolinguistic nationalism differ from constitutional nationalism, and what was its influence on the formation of nation-states in the second half of the nineteenth century?

▶ What were the reactions among thinkers and artists to the developing pattern of nation-state formation? How did they define the intellectual-artistic movements of romanticism and realism?

Philosophers and artists in the romantic period put a strong emphasis on individual creativity. They either viewed this creativity as an upwelling of impulses and sentiments pouring forth with little intellectual control or, conversely, considered their creativity to be the result of an absolute or transcendent mind working through them as individuals. By the 1850s, with the rise of the middle class, individual creativity gave way to a greater awareness, called "realism," of the social environment with its class structure and industrial characteristics.

Chapter 23 1790–1917

Creoles and Caudillos

LATIN AMERICA IN THE NINETEENTH CENTURY

Among the leaders of the Latin American wars of independence (1810–1826) from Spain, a woman named Juana Azurduy de Padilla (1781–1862) stands out for her bravery. Azurduy was a mestiza military commander in what are today the countries of Bolivia and Argentina. Her father was a Creole landowner near the city of Chuquisaca [choo-kee-SA-ca], and her mother was a Quechua-speaking Amerindian. Sent by her parents to a convent for her education and perhaps the life of a nun, Azurduy preferred the stories of heroic women warrior saints to a more sedate life of contemplation. After she completed her schooling, she married Manuel Ascencio Padilla, the son of a Creole landowner in Upper Peru, a military man in his youth and a law student after that. Together, the two enthusiastically joined the cause of independence in 1810, creating a mini republic (*republiquita*) in the mountains.

Here, Azurduy learned swordsmanship, firearms handling, and logistics for fighting guerilla wars. Well versed in Quechua and Aymara, Azurduy and Ascencio recruited some 6,000 locals, armed with the traditional Inca arms of clubs and slings. Azurduy, adored by these locals as Mother Earth (*pachamamba*), and Ascencio with their men joined in 1813 an expeditionary force of independence fighters from Buenos Aires. This force suffered a crushing defeat, however, at the hands of royal troops sent by the vice-regent

LATIN AMERICA AND THE CARIBBEAN

ABOVE: Amerindian laundry women in Rio de Janeiro, 1835.

of Peru. In an effort to recover, Azurduy borrowed a training manual and drilled what she called her "Loyal Battalion" for ambushes and quick retreats. But under the relentless pressure of the viceregal troops, the battalion suffered a constant loss of men, including her husband in 1816. Azurduy had no choice but to retreat to what is today northwestern Argentina, where she was incorporated as a lieutenant colonel in the regular independence army, in recognition of her bravery.

In 1825 Upper Peru finally gained its independence, under the name of Bolivia (in honor of the Venezuelan independence leader Simón Bolívar). Azurduy returned from Argentina to retire in her birthplace, renamed Sucre, after the first president of Bolivia. Four of her children had died of malaria, and only her daughter Lisa remained of her family. When Azurduy died in 1862 she was largely forgotten, but in the early 1900s Bolivians remembered her again and named a town near her birthplace after her.

Seeing Patterns

▶ Which factors in the complex ethnic and social structures of Latin America were responsible for the emergence of authoritarian politicians, or caudillos?

▶ After achieving independence, why did Latin American countries opt for a continuation of mineral and agricultural commodity exports?

▶ How do the social and economic structures of this period continue to affect the course of Latin America today?

The story of Juana Azurduy highlights important elements in the wars of independence in Latin America. Much more than in the United States, these wars as well as the subsequent creation of republican constitutions were the work not only of European American settlers but also of Amerindians, mestizos, black freedmen, and black slaves. In the United States, only a smattering of Native and African Americans participated in the wars, while independence in Mexico, Colombia, Bolivia, Peru, and Chile would be unthinkable without the prominent participation of Native and/or African Americans. Finally, the fact that a woman was able to buck patriarchal conventions in the early 1800s and rise in the ranks of the military demonstrates the power of the revolutionary ideas of liberty and of the republican and constitutional nation-state—a power that still inspires today.

Independence, Constitutionalism, and Landed Elites

In Latin America, the eighteenth-century Enlightenment was far less an intellectual incubator of independence and constitutionalism than in North America. In a few places, notably New Granada (today Colombia, Venezuela, Ecuador, and Panama), there was actually some limited awareness of the New Sciences and social contract theories. But the American and French revolutions had a limited intellectual impact, and the Haitian slave revolution raised apprehension among Creoles. Although the struggle for independence was clearly another chapter in the history of the revolutionary wars of independence since 1776, its prehistory was much shorter.

This is not to say that there were not tensions between the Spanish or Portuguese reforming administrators of the second half of the 1700s and the Creoles who had to accept the reforms, or that there were not indigenous rebellions against the

Chapter Outline

- Independence, Constitutionalism, and Landed Elites

- Latin American Society and Economy in the Nineteenth Century

- Putting It All Together

reforming colonial regimes, notably among the Guajira in Colombia (1769) and the Quechua and Aymara in Peru (1780–1781). But the catalyst for people of all ranks and even races to come together for the cause of independence from Spain and eventually nation-state republicanism in Latin America was Napoleon's occupation of Spain and Portugal (1807–1814). The occupation confronted Creoles, mestizos, Amerindians, mulattoes, and African American slaves with the choice of continued loyalty to the deposed absolutist Bourbon dynasty or full republican independence, notably after the collapse of Napoleon's regime in Iberia. (In Brazil, the monarch declared independence in the place of the nation in 1822.) Thus the constitutional crisis of the colonial regime itself made a decision about the constitutional future of Latin America unavoidable.

Independence and Southern and Western South American Politics

Independence movements in the far south of South America began in June 1810. Under the guise of loyalty to the deposed Fernando VII of Spain, Creoles in Buenos Aires seized the initiative to establish a junta rejecting the viceregal Spanish authorities. By contrast, Creoles in the Andes avoided declarations of loyalty to Napoleon but supported the existing colonial administration, even after 1814 when fresh Spanish troops arrived. The figure who eventually broke the logjam between the two sides of pro- and anti-Spanish Creole parties in 1816–1822 was José de San Martín, one of the heroes of Latin American independence.

Independence in Argentina   The viceroyalty of La Plata, comprising the modern countries of Argentina, Uruguay, Paraguay, and Bolivia, was the youngest of Spain's colonial units. In the course of the Bourbon reforms, Spain had separated it in 1776 from the viceroyalty of Peru, where declining silver exports diminished the importance of the port of Lima. La Plata, with the rising port of Buenos Aires, had grown through contraband trade with Great Britain, and the Bourbon reformers wanted to redirect its trade more firmly back to Spain. Buenos Aires was so important to the British, however, that they occupied Buenos Aires in 1806–1807, until Spanish colonial forces drove them out again.

Creoles in La Plata had far fewer Amerindians, African slaves, mestizos, and mulattoes to deal with—or fear—than in any of the other viceroyalties. But in 1810, when the first independence movements formed, there was a clear distinction between the pro-independence Creoles of Buenos Aires, or *porteños*, and the Creoles of the *pampas* (grasslands of the temperate interior of Argentina and Uruguay) and the subtropical plains and hills of Paraguay, who favored continued colonialism. The latter were either royalists or strove for independence separate from La Plata.

Uruguay, furthermore, was initially claimed by Brazil and eventually achieved its own independence only in 1828. Upper Peru, or modern Bolivia, with its high-elevation plains, lowland Amazon basin rain forest, large Native American population, and Potosí silver mines, was heavily defended by colonial and Spanish troops. Given these various urban–rural and geographical circumstances, the porteño independence fighters achieved only a standstill during the initial period of 1810–1816, as mentioned in the vignette at the beginning of the chapter.

The breakthrough for independence eventually came via an experienced military figure, the highly popular José de San Martín (ca. 1778–1850). San Martín was a Creole from northeastern Argentina. His father, an immigrant from Spain, was a military officer and administrator of a Jesuit-founded Native American mission district. The son, educated from an early age in a Spanish military academy, began service in the porteño independence movement in 1812, where he distinguished himself in the Argentine struggle for independence.

During his service, San Martín realized that ultimate success in the struggle for independence in the south would require the liberation of the Andes provinces. Accordingly, he trained the Army of the Andes, which included large numbers of mulatto and black volunteers. With this army, he crossed the mountains to Chile in 1818, liberating the country from royalist forces. With the help of a newly established navy composed of ships acquired from the United States and Britain, he conquered Lima in Peru. However, San Martín was defied by the local Creoles when he sought to introduce social reforms, such as an end to the Native American tribute system, the *mit'a*, and the emancipation of the children of African slaves. When he was also unable to dislodge Spanish troops from Peru, he left for Argentina to complete the fight for independence against the royalist Creoles and Spanish troops. The capture of Peru was left to Simón Bolívar, the second liberation hero of South America (see below, p. 700).

Independent Peru   Peru's independence came following the defeat of Spanish forces in 1824–1826. As with the other new states in South America, it took decades for Peru, Chile, and Bolivia to work out territorial disputes. The most serious of these by far was the War of the Pacific from 1879 to 1884, resulting in a victorious Chile annexing Peruvian and Bolivian lands. Most devastating for Peru was the destruction that Chilean troops wrought in southern Peru. The economy, which had made modest progress by using nitrate exports in the form of guano to fund railroad building and mining, was only painfully rebuilt after the destructions of war. Political stability for several decades returned under the presidency of Nicolás de Piérola, who introduced a number of belated reforms during his terms (1879–1881 and 1895–1899). As the presidency from this time until the 1920s was held by men from the upper landowning Creole class, it is sometimes called the period of the "Aristocratic Republic."

Caudillos and Oligarchic Rule   During the later 1820s the independence junta in Buenos Aires solidified into an oligarchy of the city's landowning Creole elite, but the vast, largely undeveloped areas of the pampas with their small floating population of Amerindians and Creole *gauchos*, or cowboys, remained largely outside the new state. A war with Brazil drained the country of much of its manpower and resources. The political circles in Buenos Aires began to solidify around those favoring a central government to conduct a strong foreign policy and exercise control over the provinces, which—by contrast—advocated a looser federal

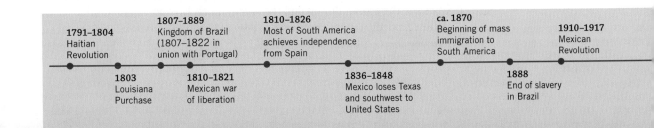

1791–1804
Haitian
Revolution

1807–1889
Kingdom of Brazil
(1807–1822 in
union with Portugal)

1810–1826
Most of South America
achieves independence
from Spain

ca. 1870
Beginning of mass
immigration to
South America

1910–1917
Mexican
Revolution

1803
Louisiana
Purchase

1810–1821
Mexican war
of liberation

1836–1848
Mexico loses Texas
and southwest to
United States

1888
End of slavery
in Brazil

Fiercely Independent Gauchos, around 1900. Gauchos, shown here sharpening their long knives (*facónes*), were recognizable by their ponchos or wool blankets which doubled as winter coats and saddle cloths. As in North America, they were expert riders, calf ropers, and—with their dogs shown in front—cattle herders.

Caudillo: Political-military leader with authoritarian tendencies.

system. By the 1830s these unsettled conditions gave rise to the first of many Argentine **caudillos**, Juan Manuel de Rosas (in office 1829–1852).

De Rosas was descended from a wealthy Creole ranching family and tended to identify with the gauchos. But he saw himself as a champion of national unity rather than one who sought to limit the role of the government in regional affairs. After becoming governor of Buenos Aires in 1829, he systematically extended his personal influence (*personalismo*) over his fellow governors until he was named caudillo in 1835, imposing a severe and fundamentally conservative brand of autocratic rule on the country.

Ultimately, his centralism and appetite for expansion contributed to his downfall. Fiercely opposed to British annexation of the Malvinas Islands—or Falklands, as the British called them—though frustrated by not being able to reverse it, he unwisely intervened in a civil war in Uruguay in 1843. His popularity flagged as the war dragged on for 9 years. Finally, the unsuccessful war, coupled with his unwillingness to lend his support to a constitution favorable to the provinces, led to his ouster in 1852.

The Settling of the Pampas The victor was a provincial governor named Justo José de Urquisa, who became the new caudillo. Urquisa swiftly extricated Argentina from Uruguay, defeated an army of de Rosas loyalists, and successfully sponsored a constitutional convention in 1853, lessening political centralism. In 1854 he was elected president, and it seemed for the moment that Argentina was on the road to a more open, representative government. But the presidency remained the property of a small Creole oligarchy from the provincial landowning elite. Not surprisingly, renewed conflict broke out over the issue of a centralized regime versus a projected new federal arrangement. In 1861, the forces of Buenos Aires defeated Urquisa's provincial forces and the country was reunited, with Buenos Aires as the national capital.

In the following years, many of the same forces that were shaping the North American West were also actively transforming the pampas. Encouraged by the government, European immigrants streamed into the country. The land was opened to settlement, driving the gauchos from their independent existence into becoming hired hands. The railroad was spurring settlement, and the remaining Amerindians were driven south to Patagonia or exterminated. In contrast to the homesteading policies in the United States, however, the pampas were divided up into huge estates (*estancias*) of tens of thousands of acres, aided by the introduction of barbed wire to fence in the ranges. The old system of rounding up essentially wild livestock and driving it to market now gave way to the ranching of cattle, sheep, and goats. As in other areas of South America, the new landed Creole elite dominated politics and the economy long into the twentieth century.

While landed interests continued to prevail, the urban center of Buenos Aires, expanding through waves of Spanish and Italian immigrants, grew restless under the rotating presidency that characterized the period of 1880–1900. Spurred by the development of radical politics in Europe, especially versions of Marxism and socialism, two major urban opposition parties took shape in the 1890s: the Radical Party and the Socialists. As the influence of these parties grew, electoral reforms were forced on an unwilling landed oligarchy. In 1912, universal male suffrage was passed, and voting by secret ballot was established. By 1916, the closed oligarchy was at last cracked open by the arrival of a new president, Hipólito Yrigoyen (1916–1922, 1928–1930). He relied for support mostly on an urban constituency, which dominated politics in the early twentieth century.

Independence and Development in Northern South America

Compared to the viceroyalty of La Plata (Argentina), the viceroyalty of New Granada in northern South America, with today's countries of Venezuela, Colombia, Ecuador, and Panama, had far fewer Creoles. For its struggle for independence to succeed, leaders had to seek support from the *pardos*, as the majority population of free black and mulatto craftspeople in the cities was called. Independence eventually came through the building of strong armies from these diverse elements, mostly by Simón Bolívar, the liberator of northern South America. After independence, however, the Creoles quickly moved to dissolve their coalitions with the lower classes and embraced the caudillo politics that were also practiced in other parts of South America.

Creoles and Pardos   In contrast to Mexico, with its relatively large Creole and mestizo populations in the cities and countryside, New Granada's Creole population was small in relation to mestizos and pardos. The latter constituted over half of the urban and two-thirds of the rural people. In 1810, the New Granadans created *juntas*, or committees, among which the junta of Cartagena was the most important, and drove the colonial Spaniards from their administrative positions. Initially, the Creole-led juntas agreed on the equality of all ethnicities and worked on constitutions that provided for elections by all free men. But they were also suspicious of each other, denouncing their allegedly aristocratic, nondemocratic aspirations.

In 1811, cooperation broke down and the pardos assumed power in a coup. The Creoles struck back a year later when they declared the First Republic of Cartagena. Their power was limited by the pardo-dominated militias, however, and in a compromise they agreed on the continuation of full voting rights. In the long run, during the 1800s, this revolutionary achievement did not last, and the Creoles established oligarchic rule.

Bolívar the Liberator   The junta of Cartagena, together with other juntas, formed the federation of the United Provinces of New Granada in 1811, with a weak executive unable to prevent squabbling among the juntas or even defend their independence. The Spanish king, Fernando VII, after returning to the throne in 1813, was determined to reestablish colonial control by dispatching armies to Latin America. The largest forces, comprising some 10,000 troops, landed in the United Provinces in 1814, taking Cartagena after a siege, and resurrected the viceroyalty of New Granada.

Simón Bolívar Liberating Slaves in Colombia. As a Creole growing up on his father's cacao plantation, worked by slaves, Bolívar was intimately familiar with slavery. But his exile in post-revolutionary Haiti 1814–1816 demonstrated to him that slavery was incompatible not only with the principles of the American and French Revolutions but also with the revolutions in Spanish America, of which he was one of the main leaders.

The eventual liberator of northern South America from renewed Spanish rule in 1819 was Simón Bolívar (1783–1830). Bolívar was born in Venezuela, into a wealthy Creole family; it owned cacao plantations worked by African slaves and was engaged in colonial trade. Although lacking a formal education, thanks to his tutor Bolívar was familiar with Enlightenment literature. In 1799, he visited Spain, where he met his future wife, and he later returned to Europe after her death. In 1804, he was deeply impressed when he watched the lavish spectacle of Napoleon crowning himself emperor in Paris. These European visits instilled in Bolívar a lasting admiration for European ideals of liberty and popular sovereignty, and he longed to create a constitutional republic in his homeland.

In 1810, as in Cartagena, Venezuelan cities formed Creole-led juntas with pardo participation. A young Bolívar participated in the congress of juntas that declared outright independence for Venezuela in 1812, against the resistance of royalists who remained faithful to Fernando VII. A civil war ensued, which made Bolívar's tenure in Venezuela insecure and, after the arrival of the Spanish expeditionary force of 1814, impossible. He went into exile first to British Jamaica and then to revolutionary Haiti. In 1816 Bolívar returned from exile to Venezuela with a military force, partly supplied by Haiti. After some initial difficulties, he succeeded in defeating the Spanish troops. In 1822, he assumed the presidency of "Gran Colombia," an independent republic comprising the later states of Colombia, Venezuela, Ecuador, and Panama.

The Bolívar–San Martín Encounter After their defeat in Gran Colombia, Spanish troops continued to occupy Peru in the Andes, where an independence movement supported by Argentina—including Juana Azurduy, discussed in the opening vignette of this chapter—was active but had made little progress against Spanish and royalist Creole troops. In the face of this situation, the Argentinean liberator José de San Martín (discussed above) and Bolívar met in 1822 to deliberate on how to drive the Spanish from Peru and to shape the future of an independent Latin America.

As for fighting Spain, they agreed that Bolívar was in a better geographical position than San Martín to send military forces to Peru. But even with these forces the task of attacking the Spanish was daunting for Bolívar. The troops were unaccustomed to high-altitude fighting and were hindered as much by mountain sickness as by enemy resistance. After two years of fighting, one of Bolívar's lieutenants finally got the better of the fiercely resisting Spanish. Two years later, in 1826, Spanish colonialism in Latin America finally ended when the last troops surrendered on an island off the Chilean coast.

The content of the discussion for the future of Latin America between San Martín and Bolívar never became public and has remained a bone of contention among historians. San Martín, bitterly disappointed by endless disputes among liberal constitutionalists and royalists, federalists and centralists, as well as Creole elitists and mestizo, pardo, and mulatto populists, favored monarchical rule to bring stability to Latin America. Bolívar preferred republicanism and Creole oligarchical rule. Both sought limited mestizo and pardo collaboration, especially in their armies. Apart from their awareness of the need for ethnic and racial integration, there was not much common ground between the two independence leaders.

San Martín's sudden withdrawal from the Andes after the meeting and his subsequent resignation from politics, however, can be taken as an indication of his realization that the chances for a South American monarchy were small indeed. Bolívar, also acutely aware of the multiple cleavages in Latin American politics, more realistically envisioned the future of Latin America as that of relatively small independent republics, held together by strong, lifelong presidencies and hereditary senates. He actually implemented this vision in the 1825 constitution of independent Upper Peru, renamed Bolivia after him.

> "Without envy, San Martín accepted that Bolívar, with whom he shared the glory of liberating half a world, would wear the laurels of victory, and he even recognized the modest inferiority of his own accomplishments, although he was morally and militarily the better man."
>
> —Bartolomé Mitre, 1882

Ironically, in his own country of Gran Colombia Bolívar was denied the role of strong president. Although he made himself a caudillo, he was unable to coax recalcitrant politicians into an agreement on a constitution for Gran Colombia similar to that of Bolivia. Eventually, in 1830 Bolívar resigned, dying shortly afterward of tuberculosis. In 1831 Gran Colombia divided into its component parts of Colombia, Venezuela, Ecuador, and (later) Panama.

Caudillo Rule   Independent Venezuela, as perhaps the poorest and most underpopulated of northern South America's newly independent countries, became the politically most turbulent Latin American republic. In Carácas, the capital, caudillos from the landowning Creole families displaced each other at a rapid rate. By one estimate, there were 41 presidencies and 30 insurrections in the period of 1830–1899. Although many of the presidents sought foreign financial support for development, little was accomplished and much of the money went into the private coffers of the leaders. The main issue that kept rival factions at odds was federalism versus tighter central control, with at least one all-out war being fought over the issue during the 1860s.

Venezuela's neighboring countries followed a similar pattern of caudillo politics. Though enjoying longer periods of stability, Colombia—the name adopted in 1861 to replace that of New Granada—also saw a continuing struggle between federalists and centralizers, with each side seeking the support of the Catholic Church. From 1899 until 1902, the two sides fought the War of a Thousand Days, leaving the country sufficiently weak for Panamanian rebels to establish an independent state of Panama in 1903, supported by the United States.

After independence, the administration of Theodore Roosevelt (1901–1909) swiftly concluded a treaty with the new country. In this treaty, the United States was to take control of a 10-mile-wide strip bisecting the narrow isthmus for the completion of the construction of the Panama Canal. A French consortium had begun gigantic earth-moving work in 1879 but was constantly behind schedule, as a result of landslides, flooding, tropical diseases, and engineering disputes, and went bankrupt in 1888. The government-sponsored construction took only seven years (1904–1911), but at the cost of appalling conditions for the Caribbean

Land and Liberty. This enormous mural by Diego Rivera (1886–1957), in the National Palace in Mexico City, shows Father Hidalgo above the Mexican eagle, flanked by other independence fighters. Above them are Emiliano Zapata and Pancho Villa, the heroes of the Revolution of 1910, holding a banner, "Tierra y Libertad." The other parts of the mural show historical scenes from the Spanish conquest to the twentieth century.

(African American) and European (Spanish) workers, who received half of the wages of their American counterparts on the railroad carrying the spoils.

Independence and Political Development in the North: Mexico

In contrast to the central Spanish colony of New Granada with its substantial black and mulatto populations and relatively few Amerindians, New Spain (Mexico) had few inhabitants of African descent and large numbers of indigenous Americans. Therefore, from the beginning of the independence struggle mestizos and Amerindians had prominent and ongoing roles in the political development of the nineteenth century. As in the other two regions, however, conservative landowning Creoles were for most of the time dominant in the political process. Only toward the end of the 1800s did urban white, mestizo, and Amerindian residents acquire a voice. Landless rural laborers entered the political stage in the early twentieth century, during the Mexican Revolution.

The Mexican Uprising   In New Spain (modern Mexico), Miguel Hidalgo y Costilla (1753–1811), the son of a Creole hacienda estate administrator and his Creole wife, launched a movement for independence from Spain in 1810. A churchman since his youth, Hidalgo was broadly educated, well versed in Enlightenment literature, conversant in Nahuatl, and on the margins of strict Catholicism. As a young adult, he became a parish priest and devoted himself to creating employment opportunities for Amerindians in a province southeast of Mexico City.

In 1808, Hidalgo participated in a conspiracy of Creoles, some of them members of the military, to overthrow a group of Spanish colonial military officers who had staged a successful coup d'état against the civilian colonial administration of New Spain in 1808. Just before being discovered, the conspiracy launched a popular rebellion in 1810, declaring itself in favor of Fernando VII, the Spanish king deposed by Napoleon, whom the members considered to be the legitimate ruler.

Under the leadership of Hidalgo, tens of thousands of poor Creoles, mestizos, and Amerindians, who had suffered in a recent drought, marched on Guanajuato (in south-central Mexico), indiscriminately looting and killing both Spaniards and Creoles. Initially, they were successful in defeating the Spanish troops marching against them. When Hidalgo, shocked by the violence, called off an attack on Mexico City, however, the rebellion began to sputter and was eventually defeated in 1811. Loyal Spanish forces ultimately captured and executed Hidalgo.

War of Independence   After the defeat, associates of Hidalgo carried on in several southwestern provinces of Mexico but failed to make a comeback in the heartland around Mexico City, where royalists intent on preserving the union between Spain and Mexico remained supreme. In 1813, the pro-independence nationalist rebels adopted a program for independence that envisioned a constitutional government, abolished slavery, and declared all native-born inhabitants of New Spain "Americans," without regard to ethnic differences. A year later they promulgated a constitution providing for a strong legislature and a weak executive. Both program and constitution, however, still awaited the conclusion of the civil war between nationalists and royalists for their implementation.

The war ended in 1821 with Mexico's independence, based on a compromise between the nationalist Vicente Guerrero (1782–1831) and the royalist Agustín de Iturbide (1783–1824). Both leaders came from wealthy landowning families, although the Guerreros also owned transportation enterprises and gunsmithies. Guerrero's father was a mestizo, his mother an African slave; Iturbide was a Creole of Basque gentry descent who insisted—against some doubts—that his mother was also Creole. According to the compromise, Mexico was to become an independent constitutional "empire," give full citizenship rights to all inhabitants regardless of race and ethnicity, and adhere to Catholicism.

Revolutionary Women. Women, such as these *soldaderas* taking rifle practice, played many significant roles in the Mexican Revolution, 1910–1920.

Iturbide became Mexico's first ruler, with the title "emperor," but abdicated in 1823 when his prolandowner policies and continued tolerance of slavery provoked a military uprising. By that time, Mexico was no longer an empire; already in 1821, El Salvador, Nicaragua, Costa Rica, and Honduras had declared their independence. With a new constitution in 1824, Mexico became a republic. For eight months in 1829, the liberation hero Guerrero was the republic's second president. During his short tenure he officially abolished slavery, before losing both his office and his life in another military uprising. As in other parts of Latin America during the period of early independence, politics remained unstable, pitting federalists and centralists against each other. Centralists eventually triumphed and, for a long period under Santa Anna, maintained authoritarian rule until 1857.

Northern Mexico and the Comanches   Initially, Mexico had a number of advantages as an independent nation. It had abundant natural resources, and its nominal northern territories—Texas, New Mexico, and California—contained much valuable pasture and agricultural land. These territories were inhabited by numerous Native American peoples, among whom the Comanches were the most powerful. Originally from the Great Basin, they had migrated to the Colorado plains around the Arkansas River in the 1600s. Here, they acquired horses after the Pueblo Revolt (1680) against Spain. As migrants, they adopted more readily to the opportunities offered through horse breeding and contraband firearms than other, more settled Native American peoples.

In the course of the mid-1700s, they built a 400-mile-wide empire from the Arkansas River to just north of San Antonio. They raided regularly into New Mexico and maintained a flourishing trade of horses, cattle, bison hides, and enslaved war

TA·HER·YE·QUA·HIP or HORSE-BACKS CAMP. *B.*

NO·CO·NIE. COMANCHES.

Highly Mobile Comanches.
The Comanches, having acquired horses and muskets, became the most efficient bison hunters prior to white Americans moving in with modern breechloaders. Living in tents, as shown here in a late nineteenth century photograph, the highly mobile Comanches maintained a militarily powerful trading and raiding empire on the southwestern plains (1700–1875).

captives, including blacks, on their borders. In the last decades of Spanish rule, colonial reformers, intent on creating a northern buffer zone to protect their silver mines, dispatched troops to check the Comanche expansion. But during the war of Mexican independence, Comanche raids resumed and wiped out the recent gains.

Northern Immigration   To diminish the endemic insecurity in the northern borderlands resulting from the Comanches, beginning in the early 1820s Mexico supported immigration from the United States. It sold land to settlers on generous terms and allowed them to be largely self-governing as long as taxes were duly paid. At the same time, the United States entered a protracted period of growth. Settlement of the rich agricultural areas of

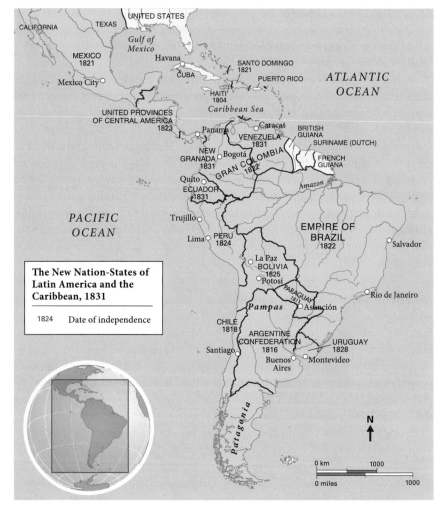

MAP 23.1 **The New Nation-States of Latin America and the Caribbean, 1831.**

the formerly French Ohio and Mississippi valleys moved with astonishing speed. The new demand for American cotton in British and American factories drove a frenetic expansion into Alabama, Mississippi, Louisiana, and Arkansas. Cotton exhausted the soil quickly, and the availability of cheap land made it more efficient to abandon the depleted lands and keep pushing the realm of "King Cotton" ever westward.

Many US citizens emigrated to Mexico to take advantage of its generous land policy and autonomy. The Mexican province of Texas was particularly attractive, especially to southerners, because of its nearness to the settled southern states and its suitability for cotton cultivation. While Mexico had outlawed slavery, most slave owners who migrated to Texas ignored these restrictions. The increasingly blatant violation of the antislavery laws and the swelling numbers of immigrants seeking opportunity in Texas came to alarm the Mexican national government by the 1830s.

The US–Mexico War   In 1836, the Mexican president Antonio López Santa Anna led some 4,000 troops against the militias maintained by the Texans. At first, these troops were successful, decimating Texan militiamen and US volunteers defending the Alamo, a fort near San Antonio. But then Texan forces defeated Santa Anna, and the state declared its independence (1836). Mexico refused to recognize Texas, and nine years later Texas opted for the security of union with the United States. It had also settled with the Comanches for an end to the raiding which had wrought havoc in western Texas.

When the United States declared war on Mexico over a Texas border dispute in the following year (1846), the other northern territories of Mexico had suffered such debilitating devastations from Comanche raids that the government found it impossible to build strong defenses against the US invasion. Within two years, Santa Anna's troops were defeated and Mexico was forced to give up over half of its territory (everything north of the Rio Grande and Gila Rivers), in return for 18 million dollars as part of a previous purchase offer and the Mexican state debt, as well as a promise of protection from future Comanche raids (see Map 23.2).

The French Interlude in Mexico   After the crushing losses of land to the United States, Santa Anna eventually fell from power, and in 1855 liberals gained the upper hand. They introduced a new constitution in 1857 which reaffirmed federalism, guaranteed individual liberties, and separated church and state. The conservatives in Mexico detested this new constitution and waged the "Reform War" (1857–1861) to abolish it. They lost, and the liberals elected Benito Juárez (1861–1864) president, the first Amerindian to accede to the office.

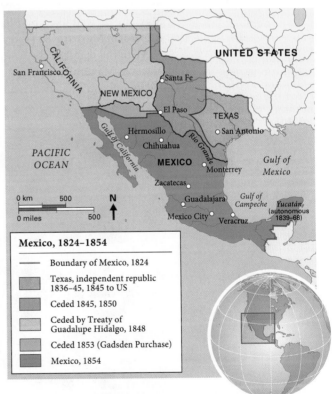

MAP 23.2 **Mexico's Loss of Territory to the United States, 1824–1854.**

As soon as he was in office, however, he discovered that the war had drained Mexico's financial reserves, obliging him to suspend payment on the state debt. International reaction was swift, with British, Spanish, and France forces seizing the customs house in the port city of Veracruz, making a mockery of the US Monroe Doctrine of 1823, which had been inspired by the Latin American independence wars. According to the doctrine, no foreign intervention would be tolerated again in the Americas. For four decades the doctrine had been remarkably successful at deterring the European powers, largely because it suited British trade policy as well. Mexico had easily beaten back two invasion attempts by small expeditionary forces, one from Spain in 1829 and another from France in 1838. Not wishing to violate the pan-American opposition to European intervention with a prolonged occupation, Britain and Spain withdrew their forces quickly.

The French, however, stayed, exploiting the inability of the United States to intervene as a result of the outbreak of the Civil War. Louis-Napoleon III Bonaparte, nephew of Napoleon and self-declared emperor (r. 1852–1870), was determined to return France to imperial glory overseas. He seized on the issue of suspended debt payments and, with an eye on the Mexican silver mines, set in motion an ambitious plan of imposing a pliable ruler in the country. In 1862, he provided military backing to the Austrian prince Maximilian, well liked by Mexican conservatives, who installed himself as the emperor of Mexico (1864–1867).

With the defeat of the Confederate states in the US Civil War in April 1865, however, Maximilian's position became precarious. The Union army was ballooning to over a million men, many of whom had just been sent to Texas to suppress

> "With good reason the public now feels that constitutions are born and die, that governments succeed each other, that codes are enlarged and made intricate, that pronouncements and plans come and go, and that after so many mutations and upheavals, so much inquietude and so many sacrifices, nothing positive has been done for the people."
>
> —Ponciano Arriaga, "Father of the 1857 Constitution"

The Execution of Emperor Maximilian of Mexico, June 19, 1867. Édouard Manet has been characterized as the "inventor of modernity," not only for his technique but for the way he portrayed events, even significant political events, in a calm and composed manner. The soldiers who dispatch the hapless emperor come across as cool and professional—what they are doing is all in a day's work.

the last Confederate holdouts. In 1866, after some discreet aid from the US government, an uprising broke out in Mexico. With Maximilian cut off from any hope of quick support from France, liberal forces defeated and captured him, executing him by firing squad in 1867.

Díaz's Long Peace   A period of relative peace arrived at last with the withdrawal of most US government troops from Texas at the end of Reconstruction—ending the potential threat of invasion or border incursions—and the rise of Mexico's next caudillo, Porfirio Díaz (in office 1876–1880 and 1884–1911). Díaz's lengthy hold on power allowed a degree of conservative stability to settle over Mexico's turbulent politics. Moreover, the period also coincided with the defeat of the last Amerindians north of the border and the settlement and development of the American West.

In addition, Díaz, like his contemporary President José Balmaceda (1886–1891) of Chile, was the first to favor infrastructural and industrial development. The two realized that mineral and agricultural exports made their countries too dependent on the world market with its periodic depressions, such as the Long Depression of 1873–1896. The basic infrastructure of Mexico's rail, telegraph, and telephone systems were laid during this time; textile factories and some basic heavy industries were set up; oil was produced in quantity; and modest agricultural improvements were made. Overall, the economy expanded by 6 percent annually during the Porfiriato, as the period of Díaz's government was called.

Much of Díaz's conservative stability was built on the faction of Creole landowners with whom Díaz had come to power. This faction had grown through the addition of groups of technocrat administrators (*científicos*), financiers, land speculators, and industrialists. As in all ruling classes, personal connections and mutual promotions provided the glue for cohesiveness; but what characterized the Porfiriato regime in addition was the undisguised desire for self-enrichment while disregarding the law and even resorting to physical violence. Critics of the regime were arrested, beaten, and sent to exile on the Yucatán peninsula as the Porfiriato became increasingly repressive.

The number of critics rose steadily, however, in tandem with the growth of cities and the urban middle classes of professionals (journalists, lawyers, doctors, teachers, small businessmen, accountants, etc.). They found themselves excluded from economic or even political participation. Meeting in liberal clubs, they demanded a return to the constitution of 1857. Critics also arose among the working classes (miners, railroad and streetcar workers, textile and steel workers, and some craftsmen) who found themselves prohibited from forming trade unions and carrying out strikes, although there were nevertheless frequent strikes in the textile factories. In the early 1900s, an aging Díaz and his septuagenarian *científicos* faced an increasingly restless urban population.

The countryside, where the large majority of Mexicans still lived and worked, was just as restless. Ever since colonial times, there was a profound division between Creole estate (*hacienda*) owners, as well as mestizo and Amerindian rurals (that is, people farming or working on the estates and peasants in their own villages). For most of the 1800s, the economy of the countryside had been typified by self-sufficiency: Nearly everything was produced and consumed there, as transportation costs were prohibitive.

But with the construction of the railroad system under Díaz, the transportation costs of sending a ton of cotton from the provinces to Mexico City sank from $63 to $3. Now the hacienda landlords could produce crops for the market and, accordingly, gobbled up acres of farmland by the millions from villagers who could not show legal titles to the land. Even if villagers did legally own the land, corrupt lawyers outmaneuvered them. The wealthiest landlord was Luis Terrazas, with 50 haciendas totaling nearly 7 million acres, mostly in the northern state of Chihuahua. Asked whether he was *from* Chihuahua, Terrazas was reported to have said, "*I am* Chihuahua!"

The Early Mexican Revolution   Middle-class discontent was the first to manifest itself in the elections of 1910, which Díaz had to hold according to the constitution. As before, this election had once more been manipulated in favor of Díaz. But the president, currying the favor of a fawning US journalist, had declared in 1908 that he would like to have an opposition party in Mexico. For a short time, liberals in the country were greatly encouraged, and they found a surprisingly popular candidate.

This candidate was Francisco Madero (1873–1913), the dissident son of a wealthy Creole landowner family who was deeply committed to the social justice proclaimed in the 1857 constitution. Madero refused to recognize the election

Emiliano Zapata and Fellow Revolutionaries in Mexico City, June 4, 1911. Shortly after the fall of Díaz, his opponents Madero, Villa, and Zapata (seated, second from left) entered Mexico City in triumph, to celebrate the end of the regime of Díaz. But already by June 8, Zapata and Madero disagreed on the issue of land reform. The moderate Madero wanted to halt it; Zapata wanted to continue it in his state of Morelos. This disagreement, among other internal rifts in the revolutionary camp, was responsible for the revolution dragging on to 1920.

and called on the middle classes, working classes, and peasants to rise up against the tyrant Díaz. The call was couched in cautious terms, making the case for a return to the constitutional revolution of the early 1800s. But by mentioning also the right of workers to organize in trade unions and of peasants to receive their own plots of land, he inevitably opened the floodgates for a full social and economic revolution.

Among the first to respond was Pancho Villa (1878–1923), a muleteer-cum-cattle rustler asked by a motley of miners, ranch hands, cowboys, and military colonists to lead them in their rebellion in the northern state of Chihuahua. Another rebel leader was Emiliano Zapata (1879–1919), head of a village in the state of Morelos in south-central Mexico, who had begun with his *campesinos* (tenant farmers, laborers, and village peasants) to occupy sugar plantations and distribute plantation land to them. Victories of Villa in the north and Zapata as close as 20 miles from Mexico City against federal troops persuaded Díaz to step down in May 1911 and leave for exile in France.

Madero was sworn in as the new president. But soon into his tenure it became clear that his vision for a constitutional revolution was incompatible with the social and economic revolutions pursued by Zapata and Villa. Madero sent federal troops against Zapata to force an end to his land distributions. Compromising and pacific, Madero was increasingly driven into the arms of Porfiriato officers who, supported by the US government, were nervous about the events in Mexico. The officers had no use for Madero, however, and deposed and executed him in February 1913.

The Later Revolution   During the subsequent 15 months, power in Mexico was disputed between Porfiriato reactionaries in Mexico City and the Constitutionalists (those faithful to the liberal constitution of 1857) in the wealthy states of the north, along the US border. Many of the Constitutionalists were from the urban middle classes whose ambitions had been thwarted during Díaz's regime. They were opposed to land distribution, but they needed more troops to overthrow the reactionaries. Constitutionalists, Pancho Villa, and Emiliano Zapata, therefore, forged an alliance that made Venustiano Carranza (1859–1920), from a wealthy but liberal Creole family, their leader. Together, they ended the reactionary regime in Mexico City in July 1914.

Once in power, the Constitutionalists dissolved the reactionary federal army but then broke apart over the issue of land reform. The antireform minority left Mexico City and retreated to Veracruz on the east coast to reorganize itself. Villa and Zapata, at the head of the pro-reform majority, entered Mexico City. But they were too committed to the continuing land reforms in their respective northern and south-central states to form a functional central government. By default, the working classes and their union representatives began to assume their own role in the revolution. They decided to support Álvaro Obregón (1880–1928), a rising commander among the Constitutionalists from the northern state of Sonora, where he had been a commercial farmer and businessman opposed to Díaz. After the departure of Villa and Zapata for their home states, Obregón entered Mexico City in February 1915.

Although the Constitutionalists had overcome the reactionary Creole landowner interests, they were deeply divided between a policy of a constitutional revolution under a strong central government with a modest land and labor reform program and a policy of agrarian revolutions in autonomous states. The supporters of the constitutional revolution gained the initiative when Obregón succeeded in driving Villa in the north from power. Carranza followed by having Zapata eliminated by treachery.

Carranza, in office as president of Mexico from 1915 to 1920, systematically removed a host of minor agrarian revolutionaries from their states and villages and ended all land distributions. But Obregón, more sympathetic to labor and land reform (albeit guided from the top and carried out in moderation), successfully challenged Carranza for the presidency in the next elections. With the support of the Constitutional army he forced Carranza to surrender and ended the Mexican Revolution late in 1920.

All constitutional revolutions of 1776–1826 in Europe and the Americas were works in progress, because they proclaimed universal liberty, equality, and brotherhood without initially granting it to all inhabitants of the nation. In Mexico, as in the other Latin American nation-states, only the estate-owning Creole oligarchy embodied the nation in the years after 1826. The Mexican Revolution expanded the constitutional process to the urban middle class, workers, farmers, and villagers. It did so because it also brought about real social and economic gains for men and women other than the landowners. All this happened at the tremendous human cost of one million victims, but as complex as the events of 1910–1920 were, they made the Mexican nation much more cohesive than it had been a century earlier.

Brazil: From Kingdom to Republic

During the late colonial period, Brazil underwent the same centralizing administrative, fiscal, and trade reforms as the Spanish possessions. These reforms were resented as much by the Brazilian planters and urban Creoles (Portuguese *crioulos*) as by their Spanish counterparts, but their fear of rebellion among the huge population of black slaves held them back from openly demanding independence. As it happened, independence arrived without bloody internecine wars, through the relocation of the monarchy from Portugal to Brazil in the wake of Napoleon's invasion of Iberia in 1807. Brazil had since become an empire, and when the second emperor, Dom Pedro II (r. 1831–1889), under pressure from Britain, finally abolished slavery in 1888, the politically abandoned plantation oligarchy avenged itself by deposing him and switching to a republican regime under the military in 1889. Given the enormous size of the country, as well as the split of the Creole oligarchy into groups with mining, sugar, and coffee interests, the regime became solidly federal, making it difficult for caudillos to succeed and eventually allowing for the rise of civilian presidents.

Relocation of the Dynasty   Portugal's royal family fled the country in advance of Napoleon's armies in 1807. Escorted by British ships, they took refuge in Brazil and elevated the colony to the status of a coequal kingdom in union with Portugal but governed from Brazil after Napoleon's defeat in 1815. The arrival of some 15,000 Portuguese together with the dynasty, however, created resentment among the Brazilian Creoles, sharpening the traditional tension between Creoles and Portuguese-born reformers. A crisis point was reached in 1820 when rebels in Portugal adopted a liberal constitution, which demanded the return of Brazil to colonial status as well as the transfer of the dynasty back to Portugal. The reigning king went back but left his son, Pedro I (r. 1822–1831), behind in Brazil. On the advice of both his father and courtiers, Pedro uttered in 1822 his famous "*Fico*" ("I remain"), and proclaimed, "Independence or death!" thereby making Brazil an independent kingdom.

Pedro I's Authoritarianism   On acceding to the throne, Pedro declared Brazil an empire because of its size and diversity. His rule at the head of the Creole landowner ruling class, however, shared many of the same characteristics as that of the early caudillos in the Spanish-speaking South American countries. In addition, like the restoration monarchs of Europe in the early 1800s, he firmly adhered to his belief in divine right, which was incompatible with more than token constitutionalism. Consequently, he rejected an attempt by the landed oligarchy to introduce limited monarchical rule. Instead, he issued his own constitution in 1823, which concentrated most powers in his hands, as well as a council of state, with a weak lifetime senate and a legislative chamber based on severely limited voting rights. Since he also reserved for himself the nomination and dismissal of ministers, the dissolution of the chamber, and, above all, the appointment of provincial governors, his rule was far too authoritarian even for the conservative planter elite.

In reaction, in 1824 six northeastern provinces attempted to secede. They proclaimed the republican Federation of the Equator and, somewhat illogically, demanded more central government support for the traditional northern sugar and cotton plantations, neglected by a rising emphasis on south-central coffee plantations. Increased British patrols in the Atlantic to suppress the slave trade had increased the price for slaves. The sugar planters could ill afford the increased prices, but the expanding coffee market enabled its planters to pay (see "Patterns Up Close").

Given the close ties between Britain and Brazil, Pedro found it difficult to resist mounting British demands for the abolition of slavery. As a result, early signs of alienation between the crown and the Creole planter elite crept in. It also did not help that Pedro supported the open immigration to Brazil of skilled foreigners from Europe, as well as foreign loans and investments for development. As the sources document, Pedro's policy was directed at increasing the number of whites in order to decrease the proportion of blacks and Amerindians.

By contrast, the plantation elites were primarily interested in acquiring servile labor and control of the courts to ensure severe punishments for infractions by slaves. They voiced their opposition to internal improvements, like railroads, for fear of disrupting the stability of the plantation system. Ultimately, a succession crisis in Portugal in 1830 led to a conservative revolt against Pedro. In 1831, he lost his nerve and abdicated, sailing back to Portugal. He left the throne to his 5-year-old son, Pedro II (r. 1831–1889), who required a regent. The landowning elite exploited the opportunity of the temporarily weak monarchy by renewing its demands for federalism.

The Federalist Interlude   After lengthy debates, in 1834 the government granted the provinces their own legislative assemblies with strong tax and budget powers, effectively strengthening the provincial landholding elites with their various regional interests. It also abolished the council of state but created a national guard to suppress slave revolts and urban mobs. This mixed bag of reforms was too much for some provinces. The most dangerous revolt against the reforms was that of 1835 in Rio Grande do Sul, a southern province dominated by cattle owners who did not own many slaves and commanded military forces composed of gauchos. These owners established an independent republic that attracted many domestic and foreign radicals opposed to slavery, including Giuseppe Garibaldi, the Italian nationalist who played a crucial role in the unification of Italy. In reaction to the coexistence of a now weak and decentralized monarchy and an antislavery republic offering refuge to runaways on Brazilian soil, the centralists reasserted themselves. In 1840 they proclaimed the 14-year-old Pedro II king and curbed the powers of the provincial assemblies. In 1845 they negotiated a return of Rio Grande do Sul to Brazil.

The End of Slavery   The 1830s and 1840s coincided with a transition in Brazil from sugar to coffee as a major export commodity on the world market. The old sugar plantation elite lost clout, and a newer coffee planter oligarchy ascended to prominence. Both needed slaves, and as long as the crown did not seriously seek to fulfill its promises of 1831 to the British to curb the importation of slaves, there was no more than unease about the mutual dependence of the king and the oligarchy on the continued existence of slave labor. But when the British in 1849 authorized warships to enter Brazilian waters to intercept slave ships, the importation of slaves virtually ceased, causing a serious labor shortage. Sugar, cotton, and coffee plantation owners began to think of ridding themselves of a monarchy that was unable to maintain the flow of slaves from overseas.

Slave Rebellions in Cuba and Brazil

Blacks had gained little from the American and French Revolutions, and the pattern of brutal exploitation continued in many parts of the Americas. Not surprisingly, therefore, blacks sought to emulate the example of Haiti's successful slave revolt during the first half of the 1800s. However, none of the subsequent Haiti-inspired revolts were any more successful against the well-prepared authorities than previous revolts had been in the 1700s, as a look at rebellions in Cuba and Brazil during the first half of the nineteenth century shows.

In Cuba, the decline of sugar production in Haiti during the revolution encouraged a rapid expansion of plantations and the importation of African slaves. As previously in Haiti, a relatively diversified eighteenth-century society of whites, free mulattoes, and blacks, as well as urban and rural black slaves, was transformed into a heavily African-born plantation slave society, forming a large majority in many rural districts. The black freedman José Antonio Aponte (ca. 1756–1812),

Slave Revolt Aboard Ship. Rebellions aboard ship, such as the famous 1839 mutiny aboard the *Amistad* shown here, were common occurrences. The Amistad was engaged in intra-American slave trafficking, and the slaves overpowered the crew shortly after embarkation in Cuba. After protracted legal negotiations, the slaves were eventually freed and returned to Africa.

In the 1860s and 1870s, antimonarchy agitation gathered speed. Brazilians, especially professionals and intellectuals in the cities, became sensitive to their country being isolated in the world on the issue of slavery. After the United States emancipated slaves in 1863, the Spanish colonies of Puerto Rico and Cuba followed suit by ending slavery for all elderly slaves and newborn children. Brazil was now left as the only unreformed slaveholding country in the Western Hemisphere.

In the following decade and a half, the antislavery chorus increased in volume. While the government introduced a few cosmetic changes, it fell to the provinces to take more serious steps. Planters, who began to see the demise of the system on the horizon, encouraged their provinces to increase the flow of foreign immigrants, to be employed as wage labor on the coffee plantations. The political situation neared the point of anarchy in 1885, with mass flights of slaves from

a militiaman and head of the Yoruba confraternity (*cabilde*) in Havana, led an abortive revolt in 1812 that drew support from both sectors. In the subsequent revolts of 1825, 1835, and 1843, the urban element was less evident. Authorities and planters, heavily invested in new industrial equipment for sugar production and railroads, and exhausted by the unending sequence of uprisings, unleashed a campaign of sweeping arrests of free blacks and mulattoes that cut the urban–rural link once and for all.

Brazil, like Cuba, also benefited from the collapse of sugar production on Haiti in the 1790s and the first half of the 1800s. It expanded its plantation sector, particularly in the province of Bahia, and imported large numbers of slaves from Africa. But here distrust divided those born in Africa from Brazilian-born slaves, freedmen, and mulattoes. Many freedmen and mulattoes served in the militias that the authorities used to suppress the revolts. Furthermore, in contrast to the narrow island of Cuba, plantation slaves could run away more easily to independent settlements (called *quilombos*) in the wide-open Brazilian interior, from where revolts were more easily organized than in cities or on plantations. In fact, no fewer than a dozen quilombo revolts extending into plantations occurred in Bahia during 1807–1828, revolts which the militias found difficult to crush, having to march into often remote areas.

Two urban revolts of the period were remarkable for their exceptional mix of insurgents, unparalleled in Cuba or elsewhere in Latin America. The first was the Tailor's Rebellion of 1798 in Salvador, Bahia's capital. Freedmen, mulattoes, and white craftspeople cooperated in the name of freedom and equality against the Creole oligarchy. The second was the Muslim uprising of 1835, also in Bahia, organized by African-born freedmen as well as slaves with Islamic clerical educations that they had received in West Africa before their enslavement.

Questions

- Do the slave rebellions in Cuba and Brazil in the early nineteenth century confirm or complicate the pattern of slave revolutions that was manifested first in Haiti?

- What role did geography play in the success or failure of a revolution?

plantations and armed clashes to keep them there. Only in 1888 did the central government finally end slavery.

The Coffee Boom Predictably, given the grip of the planter elite on the labor force, little changed in social relations after the abolition of slavery. The coffee growers, enjoying high international coffee prices and the benefits of infrastructure improvements through railroads and telegraph lines since the 1850s, could afford low-wage hired labor. The now-free blacks received no land, education, or urban jobs, scraping by with low wages on the coffee and sugar plantations. Economically, however, after freeing itself from the burdens of slavery, Brazil expanded its economy in the 5 years following 1888 as much as in the 70 years of slavery since independence.

The monarchy, having dragged its feet for half a century on the slavery issue, was thoroughly discredited among the landowners and their military offshoot, the officer corps. By the 1880s, officers were also drawn from professional and intellectual urban circles. Increasingly, they subscribed to the ideology of *positivism* coming from France, which celebrated the idea of secular scientific and technological progress (see Chapter 22). Positivists, almost by definition, were liberal and republican in political orientation. In 1889, a revolt in the military supported by the Creole plantation oligarchy resulted in the abolition of the monarchy and proclamation of a republic, with practically no resistance from any quarter.

Two political tendencies emerged in the constituent assembly 2 years after the proclamation of the republic. The coffee interests of the south-central states favored federalism, with the right of the provinces to collect export taxes and maintain militias. The urban professional and intellectual interests, especially lawyers, supported a strong presidency with control over tariffs and import taxes as well as powers to use the federal military against provinces in cases of national emergency. The two tendencies resulted in a compromise with a tilt toward federalism, which produced provincial caudillos on the one hand but also regularly elected presidents on the other.

Following this tilt, in the 1890s the government was strongly supportive of agricultural commodity exports. Coffee, rubber, and sugar exports yielded high profits and taxes until 1896, when overproduction of coffee resulted in diminishing returns. The state of São Paulo then regulated the sale of coffee on the world market through a state purchase scheme, which brought some stabilization to coffee production. At the same time and continuing into the early twentieth century (and without much state or central government support), immigrants and foreign investors laid the foundation for **import-substitution industrialization**, beginning with textile and food-processing factories. The comparative advantage afforded by commodity exports had run its course by the late 1800s and early 1900s and now had to be supplemented with industrialization.

Import-substitution industrialization: The practice by which countries protect their economies by setting high tariffs and construct factories for the production of consumer goods (textiles, furniture, shoes, followed later by appliances, automobiles, electronics) and/or capital goods (steel, chemicals, machinery).

Latin American Society and Economy in the Nineteenth Century

Independence meant both disruptions and continuities in the economy just as much as in politics (discussed in the first half of this chapter). In Spanish America, four colonial regions broke apart into what were eventually 21 independent republics, organized around the pattern of constitutional nationalism. Trade with Europe was thus radically altered. What continued were deep divisions between the small landowning elites and the urban masses of officials, professionals, craftspeople, and laborers. Although many members of the elites and urban middle and lower classes had collaborated in the drive for independence, afterward the Creole landowning elite made participation of the urban classes in the constitutional process increasingly difficult. Correspondingly, when trade with Europe resumed, this elite was primarily interested in the export of mineral and agricultural commodities, from which it reaped the most benefits (see Map 23.3).

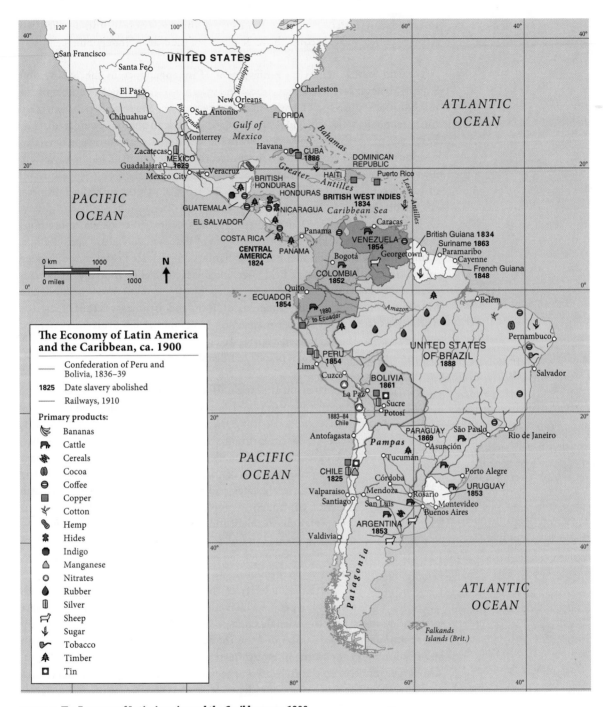

The Economy of Latin America and the Caribbean, ca. 1900

——— Confederation of Peru and Bolivia, 1836–39

1825 Date slavery abolished

——— Railways, 1910

Primary products:

- Bananas
- Cattle
- Cereals
- Cocoa
- Coffee
- Copper
- Cotton
- Hemp
- Hides
- Indigo
- Manganese
- Nitrates
- Rubber
- Silver
- Sheep
- Sugar
- Tobacco
- Timber
- Tin

MAP 23.3 **The Economy of Latin America and the Caribbean, ca. 1900.**

Rebuilding Societies and Economies

Reconstruction in the independent Spanish-speaking republics and the Brazilian monarchy took several decades. Mercantilist trade was gone, replaced by free trade on the world market. Production in the mines and on the estates had to be restarted with fresh capital. All this took time, and it was only by mid-century that Latin America had overcome the after-effects of the wars of independence.

After Independence   The achievement of independence in the 1820s, after lengthy struggles with Spain and local and internal conflicts, had a number of far-reaching consequences. The most important result was the end of Spain's mercantilist monopoly, weak as it had been. The Latin American republics were free to buy or sell and to borrow money anywhere in the world. Among trading partners, this freedom benefited Great Britain most directly. Its merchants had already established themselves in several Latin American cities during the Continental boycott of Napoleon, which had shut out Great Britain from trade with the European continent.

Initially, however, for Latin Americans the freedom to trade was more hope than reality. Dislocations from the struggle of independence were considerable. Capital had fled the continent and left behind uncultivated estates and flooded mines. The Catholic Church held huge, uncollectable debts. In many areas taxes could not be collected. Troops helped themselves to payment through plunder. In Mexico, where the struggle between republicans and royalists was the fiercest, the disruptions were worst and reconstruction took longest. Chile also experienced violent struggles but stabilized itself relatively quickly. On average, though, it took until around 1850 for Latin America to fully recover.

"There were drawing rooms where only those [Creoles] with certain surnames could enter and which were closed to those who had only the power of money; there were families before which one knelt with respect, awe, and adulation. The daughter of one of these said in Europe, 'In my country I am like a princess.'"

—Jorge Basadre, 1946

Constitutional Nationalism and Society   The Creoles were in many countries the leaders in the wars of independence. The most powerful among them were large landowners—that is, owners of grain-farming self-sufficiency estates, cattle ranches, and sugar, indigo, cacao, coffee, or cotton plantations. Independence did not produce much change in agrarian relations: Landowners of self-sufficient estates and plantations in many parts of Latin America continued to employ tenant farmers and slaves. Their interpretation of constitutionalism tended toward *caudillismo*— that is, the same kind of authoritarian and paternalistic form of action that they practiced on their estates. They were the conservatives of independence.

The large majority of the Creoles, however, were not landowners but people who made their money in the cities. They were urban administrators, professionals, craftspeople, and laborers. Their leaders, ardent constitutional nationalists, tended toward political and economic liberalism. In many countries they were joined by mestizos, mulattoes, and black freedmen, also largely craftspeople and laborers. The main issue dividing the conservatives and liberals in the early years of independence was the extent of voting rights: Conservatives sought to limit the vote to a minority of males through literacy and property requirements, while liberals wanted to extend it to all males. No influential group at this point considered extending voting rights to women.

Political Divisions   Once independence was won, distrust between the two groups with very different property interests set in, and the political consensus fell apart. Accordingly, landed constitutional conservatives restricted voting rights, to the detriment of the urban constitutional liberals. The exceptions were Argentina and, for a time during the mid-nineteenth century, Peru: The former had few mestizos and mulattoes but a relatively large urban Creole population that gained the upper hand, and the latter had large numbers of urban mestizos and Amerindians who could not be ignored. Nevertheless, even if liberal constitutionalism was submerged for periods of time under caudillo authoritarianism in the mid-1800s, the expansion of constitutionalism from the landowning oligarchy to larger segments of the population remained a permanent fixture in the minds of many, especially intellectuals and political activists in cities. It was this early presence of constitutionalism in the wider population which distinguished Latin America from the Ottoman Empire, Russia, China, and Japan and made its constitutional process similar to the United States and France.

Split over State–Church Relations   Among the many issues over which conservatives and liberals split, the relationship between state and church was the deepest. Initially, given the more or less close collaboration between conservatives and liberals during the struggle for independence, Catholicism remained the national religion for all. Accordingly, education and extensive property remained under church control, as guaranteed by the constitutions.

But the new republics ended the powers of the Inquisition and claimed the right of *patronato*—that is, of naming bishops. At the behest of Spain, however, the pope left bishoprics empty rather than agreeing to this new form of lay investiture. In fact, Rome would not even recognize the independence of the Latin American nations until the mid-1830s. The conflict was aggravated by the church's focus on its institutional rather than pastoral role. The Catholic clergy provided little guidance later on during the 1800s when rapid urbanization and industrial modernity were crying out for spiritual reorientation. At the same time, papal pronouncements made plain the church's hostility toward the developing capitalist industrial order.

This hostility of the church was thus one of the factors that in the mid-1800s contributed to a swing back to liberalism, beginning with Colombia in 1849. Many countries adopted a formal separation between church and state and introduced secular educational systems. But the state–church issue remained bitter, especially in Mexico, Guatemala, Ecuador, and Venezuela, where it was often at the center of political shifts between liberals and conservatives. In Colombia, for example, it even led to a complete reversal of liberal trends in the mid-1880s, with the reintroduction of Catholicism as the state religion.

Economic Recovery   Given the shifts of leadership between conservatism and liberalism during the period of recovery after independence (ca. 1820–1850), the reconstruction of a coherent fiscal system to support the governments was difficult to accomplish. For example, governments often resorted to taxation of trade, even if this interfered with declared policies of free trade. The yields on tariffs and export taxes, however, were inevitably low and made the financing of strong central governments difficult. Consequently, maneuvering for the most productive mix of the two taxes trumped official pronouncements in favor of free trade and often eroded confidence among trade partners.

This maneuvering had little effect on the domestic economy—self-sufficiency agriculture and urban crafts production—which represented the great bulk of economic activities in Latin America. Grain production on large estates and small farms, especially in Brazil, where gold production declined in late colonial times, had escaped the turbulence of the independence-war and recovery periods relatively unscathed. Land remained plentiful, and the main bottleneck continued to be labor. The distribution of marketable surpluses declined, however, given the new internal borders in Latin America with their accompanying tariffs and export taxes. Self-sufficiency agriculture, and local economies relying on it, thus remained largely unchanged throughout the 1800s.

The crafts workshops, especially for textiles, suffered from the arrival of cheap British factory-produced cottons, which represented the majority of imports by the mid-1800s. Their impact, however, remained relatively limited, mostly to the coasts, since in the absence of railroads transportation costs to the interior were prohibitively expensive. Only Mexico encouraged the financing of machine-driven textile factories, but the failure of its state bank in 1842—from issuing too many loans— ended this policy for a number of decades. On the one hand, there was a definite awareness in most countries of the benefits of factories, using domestic resources, and linking the self-sufficiency agricultural sector to modern industrial development. On the other hand, its necessity in the face of traditional opposition was not demonstrated until later in the nineteenth century.

Export-Led Growth

The pursuit of a policy of commodity exports—export-led growth—from about 1850 led to rises in the standard of living for many Latin Americans. The industrializing countries in Europe and North America were voracious consumers of the minerals that Latin America had in abundance, as well as of its tropical agricultural products. More could have been sold, had there not been a chronic labor shortage.

Raw Materials and Cash Crops   Mining and agricultural cash crop production recovered gradually, so that by the 1850s nearly all Latin American governments had adopted export-led economic growth as their basic policy. This was about all the conservatives and liberals were able to agree on, since land distribution to poor farmers and a system of income taxes were beyond any consensus. Mexican and Peruvian silver production, the mainstay of the colonial mercantilist economy, became strong again, although the British adoption of the gold standard in 1821 imposed limits on silver exports. Peru found a partial replacement for silver with guano, which was mined and exported for use as an organic fertilizer and as a source of nitrates for explosives. Chile hit the jackpot with guano, nitrate, and copper exports, of crucial importance during the chemical- and electricity-driven second Industrial Revolution in Germany and the United States.

In other Latin American countries, tropical and subtropical cash crops defined export-led economic growth during the mid-1800s. In Brazil, Colombia, and Costa Rica, labor-intensive coffee growing redefined the agricultural sector. In Argentina, the production of jerked (dried) beef, similarly labor-intensive, refashioned the ranching economy. The main importers of this beef were regions in the Americas where plantation slavery continued into the second half of the 1800s, especially the United States, Brazil, and Cuba. The latter, which remained a Spanish colony until 1895, profited from the relocation of sugarcane plantations from the mainland and

Caribbean islands after the British outlawing of the slave trade (1807) and slavery itself (1834) as well as the Latin American wars of independence (1810–1826).

In the long run, however, like silver, cane sugar had a limited future, given the rise of beet sugar production in Europe. Minerals and cash crops were excellent for export-led economic growth, especially if they required secondary activities such as the processing of meat or the use of mining machinery. But competition on the world market increased during the 1800s, and thus there was ultimately a ceiling, which was reached in the 1890s.

Broadening of Exports   With their eyes increasingly focused on exports, Latin American governments responded quickly to the increased market opportunities resulting from the Industrial Revolution in Great Britain, the European continent, and the United States. Peru broadened its mineral exports with copper, Bolivia with tin, and Chile with nitrates. Brazil and Peru added rubber, Argentina and Uruguay wool, and Mexico *henequen* (a fiber for ropes and sacks) to its traditional exports. Luxuries from tropical Latin America, like coffee, cacao (for chocolate bars, invented in 1847), vanilla, and bananas, joined sugar after 1850 in becoming affordable mass consumer items in the industrialized countries. Argentina, with investments in refrigeration made by Britain, added frozen meat to this list in 1883. This commodity diversification met not only the broadened demand of the second Industrial Revolution, with its need for chemicals and electricity, but also the demand for consumer goods among the newly affluent middle classes.

Since the choice among minerals and crops was limited, however, most nations remained wedded to one commodity only (50 percent of exports or more). Only two, Argentina and Peru, were able to diversify (exports of less than 25 percent for the leading commodity). They were more successful at distributing their exports over the four main industrial markets of Great Britain, Germany, France, and the United States. On the eve of World War I the United States had grown to be the most important trading partner in 11 of the 21 Latin American countries. Given its own endowments and under the conditions of world trade in the second half of the nineteenth century, the continent's trade was relatively well diversified.

The prices of all Latin American commodities fluctuated substantially during the second half of the nineteenth century, in contrast to the imported manufactured goods (primarily textiles, metal utensils, and implements), which became cheaper over time. In fact, Brazil's government was so concerned about fluctuating coffee prices in the 1890s that it introduced the Taubaté coffee valorization scheme in 1906. As the largest producer, it regulated the amount of coffee offered on the world market, carefully adjusting production to keep market prices relatively stable in much the same way that oil-producing countries would later do with petroleum.

Since coffee trees need 5 years to mature, Brazil was largely successful with its scheme until World War I, when global conditions changed. An American oligopoly (the United and Standard Fruit Companies) in control of banana production in Central America from the 1890s controlled prices similarly. A careful investigation of commodity prices by economic historians has resulted in the conclusion that, in spite of all fluctuations, commodity prices rose overall during 1850–1914.

Rising Living Standards   From all evidence, in the period from the middle of the 1800s to the eve of World War I, Latin American governments can be judged as having been successful with their choice of export-led growth as their consensus policy. Living standards rose, as measured in gross domestic product (GDP). At various times during 1850–1900, between five and eight Latin American countries kept pace with the living standards in the industrialized countries. Argentina and Chile were the most consistent leaders throughout the period. Thus, although many politicians were aware that at some point their countries would have to industrialize in addition to relying on commodity export growth, they can perhaps be forgiven for keeping their faith in exports as the engine for improved living standards right up to World War I.

Labor and Immigrants   As in the industrialized countries, the profitability of exports was achieved through low wages. Together with the rest of the world, Latin America experienced high population increases during the 1800s. The population grew sevenfold, to 74 million, although it remained small in comparison to the populations of Europe, which doubled to 408 million, and Africa and Asia, which each grew by one-third to 113 and 947 million, respectively. The increases were not large enough to alter the favorable land–person ratio, so it is not surprising that the high demand for labor continued during the 1800s. This demand, of course, was the reason the institution of forced labor—revolving labor duties (*mit'a*) among Amerindians in the Andes and slavery—had come into existence in the first place.

Not surprisingly, *mit'a* and slavery continued during the 1800s, liberal constitutionalism notwithstanding, in a number of countries. Even where forced labor was abolished early, moreover, low wages continued. One would have expected wages to rise rapidly, given the continuing conditions of labor shortage and land availability. Mine operators and landowners, however, were reluctant to raise wages

Dining Hall for Recently Arrived Immigrants, Buenos Aires. Immigrants, all male, and more than likely all Spanish and Italian, rub shoulders sometime around 1900 in a dining hall in Buenos Aires set up for newly arrived immigrants. By 1914, 20 percent each of the population of Argentina had been born in Spain and Italy.

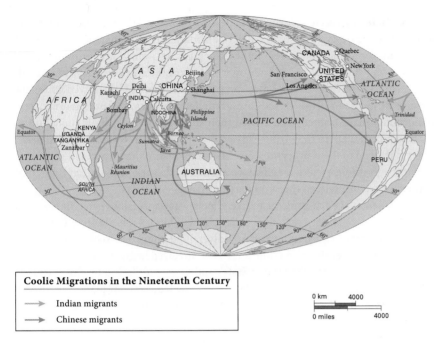

Coolie Migrations in the Nineteenth Century

→ Indian migrants

→ Chinese migrants

0 km — 4000
0 miles — 4000

MAP 23.4 **Non-Western Migrations in the Nineteenth Century.**

because they feared for the competitiveness of their commodities on the world market. They could get away with low wages because of ethnic discrimination: Racism trumped market conditions. Nevertheless, on occasion labor shortages were so severe and European immigration so insufficient that governments resorted to measures of selective mass immigration, in order to enlarge the labor pool.

Typical examples of selective immigration were *coolies* (from Urdu *kuli*, hireling)—that is, indentured laborers recruited from India and China on 5- or 10-year contracts working off the costs of their transportation. During 1847–1874, nearly half a million East Indians traveled to various European colonies in the Caribbean. Similarly, 235,000 Chinese came to Peru, Cuba, and Costa Rica, working in guano pits and silver mines, on sugar and cotton plantations, and later on railroads. If the experience of five Caribbean islands can be taken as a guide, only about 10 percent of the coolies returned home. Coolie migration to Latin America, therefore, can be described as a major part of the pattern of massive migration streams across the world that typified the nineteenth century (see Map 23.4).

Immigration to Latin America from Europe was less controlled, more regular, and on a much bigger scale. In Argentina, Uruguay, Brazil, and Chile, Italians and Spaniards settled in large numbers from around 1870 on. In Argentina, nearly one-third of the population consisted of immigrants, a share much higher than at any time in the United States. The Italian population of Argentina numbered close to 1 million by the turn of the century. Most immigrants settled in cities, and Buenos Aires became the first city on the continent with more than a million people. Only here did a semiregular labor market develop, with rising urban and rural wages prior to World War I. Elsewhere in Latin America, governments, beholden to large landowners, feared the rise of cities with immigrant laborers who did not share their interests. They, therefore, opposed mass immigration.

Self-Sufficiency Agriculture   Except for Argentina, Chile, and Uruguay, the levels of commodity exports did not rise sufficiently to reduce the size of the rural labor force engaged in self-sufficiency farming—a major condition for improved living standards. On the eve of World War I, between two-thirds and half of the laborers in most Latin American countries were still employed as tenant farmers or farmhands on large estates. Smaller numbers of these laborers were indigenous village farmers who owned their small farmsteads. Their contribution to the national GDP in Brazil and Mexico, for example, was less than one-quarter. Toward the end of the century, observers began to realize that export-led growth—even though it looked like an effective economic driver—did not have much of a transformative effect on the rural masses in most countries.

The absence of such transformative effects was especially visible in the high levels of illiteracy among rural inhabitants. Adult illiteracy rates of up to 80 percent were not uncommon, even in relatively diversified countries, such as Brazil and Mexico. Only Argentina and Chile after 1860 invested heavily in primary education, on levels similar to the United States and Britain, followed by Costa Rica in the 1890s. Literate self-sufficiency farmers, knowledgeable in plant and animal selection as well as fertilizers, were practically nonexistent prior to the Mexican Revolution.

Governments paid greater attention to the improvement of rural infrastructures from about 1870 onward, with the development of railroads. Almost everywhere, they looked to direct foreign investment, given the low-yielding and highly regressive trade taxes on which the relatively slim central domestic revenues depended. The foreign investors or consortiums built these railroads primarily for the transportation of commodities to ports. Many self-sufficiency farmers and even landlords, therefore, received little encouragement to produce more food staples for urban markets inland. Argentina and Chile, followed by Costa Rica and Uruguay, built the most railroads. Correspondingly, with fertilizers and better implements available via railroads, corn yields quintupled in Argentina. Conversely, these yields changed little in Mexico outside the railroad corridors concentrated in the north and center. Overall, the Latin American railroad network represented only about one-fifth to one-third of that in other Western developing settler countries, such as Australia, Canada, and New Zealand.

Mexican Textile Factory.
Cocolapam in the state of Veracruz was the site of the first Mexican cotton textile factory, founded in 1836 by Lucas Alamán, a Mexican government minister and investment banker. Its machinery, imported from Great Britain, was water-driven. The textiles it produced remained inferior to imports, but they were cheap and satisfied the needs of most Mexicans.

Factories   Until about 1870, the handicrafts sector met the demands of the rural and low-earning urban populations. It produced cheap, low-quality textiles, shoes, soap, candles, tools, implements, cutlery, and horse tack. As is well known, this sector failed in most parts of the world during the 1800s or 1900s to mechanize itself and establish a modern factory system. Latin America was no exception. Most crafts shops were based on family labor, with a high degree of self-exploitation, unconnected to the landowning elite and deemed too small by lending banks. There was no path from workshops to factories.

However, even entrepreneurial investors interested in building factories for the manufacture of yarn or textiles were hampered in their efforts. They had little chance of success prior to the appearance of public utilities in the 1880s, providing water during the dry season and electricity as an energy source, in the absence of high-quality coal in most parts of Latin America. Even then, the risk of engaging in manufacturing, requiring long-term strategies with no or low profits, was so great that the typical founders of factories were not Creoles but European immigrants.

In Argentina and Chile these immigrants labored hard during their first years after arrival and saved the start-up capital necessary to launch small but modern textile, food-processing, and beverage factories. Argentina, Chile, Mexico, and Peru made the greatest advances toward factory industrialization, producing import-substituting consumer goods to the tune of 50–80 percent. Prior to World War I, the only country that took the step from consumer goods to capital goods (goods for building and equipping factories) was Mexico. This occurred with the foundation of the Fundidora Iron and Steel Mill in 1910 in Monterrey, which, however, was unprofitable for a long time. Full capital goods industrialization had to await the postwar period.

Culture, Family, and the Status of Women

Economic growth and urbanization added considerably to the growth of constitutional-nationalist modernity in Latin America. But the absence of industrialization until the end of the nineteenth century slowed the transformation of society and its cultural institutions. The law and custom represented by the Catholic Church remained pervasive. In the second half of the nineteenth century, however, with the diversification of the urban population, the idea of separating church and state gained adherents, with some major legal consequences for social institutions.

Role of the Church   In most countries, repeated attempts by governments after independence to reduce the role of the Catholic Church in society remained unsuccessful. The church resisted the efforts of the constitutional nationalists to carry out land expropriations and to separate state and church in social legislation. In a number of civil codes women's rights in inheritance and property control improved, but overall husbands retained their patriarchal rights over their families. Typically, they were entitled to the control over the family budget, contractual engagements, choice of husbands for their daughters (up to age 25 in some countries), or residence of unmarried daughters (at home, up to age 30). Only from the middle of the nineteenth century did the influence of the Catholic Church diminish sufficiently to allow legislation for secular marriages and divorce in a number of countries. Catholicism remained doctrinally unchanged.

Family Relations   As it also developed in the Euro-American Victorian world, on the cultural level there was a popular ideal in nineteenth-century Latin America of nuclear-family domesticity. But, as research has also shown, in both places this was often honored more in the breach than the observance. That is to say, in Mexico and South America, despite the long-standing proverb *El hombre en la calle, la mujer en la casa* ("Men in the street, women in the home"), it was often the case that the two spheres were intermingled. In urban areas, women frequently ran shops, managed markets, were proprietors of *cantinas*, and performed a host of skilled and unskilled jobs, particularly in the textile and food trades. In rural areas, farm work on small holdings and peonages was often shared by men and women, though a number of individual tasks—plowing, for example—were most frequently done by men.

As in Europe and North America, too, there was a remarkably high level of widowhood and spinsterhood. In areas where the predominant form of employment was dangerous—mining, for example—the incidence of widowhood was very high. Widows often could not or chose not to remarry, especially if they had relatives to fall back on or were left an income. The stereotype of the stern patriarchal husband was also pervasive enough so that many middle-class women, often to the consternation of their families, chose not to marry at all.

Both of these conditions were common enough so that by one estimate one-third of all the households in Mexico City in the early nineteenth century were headed by women. Widows were entitled to their dowries and half of the community property, while boys and girls received equal portions of the inheritance. Thus, despite society's pressures to marry and raise children, many women did not marry or, after becoming widowed, remained single. In this sense, they achieved a considerable degree of autonomy in a male-dominated society. Thus social realities and legal rights diverged in early independent Latin America, even before legal reform.

The Visual and Literary Arts   To try to encapsulate the culture and arts of more than a continent—and one so vast and diverse as Latin America—is far beyond the scope of this textbook. Suffice it to say that the trend in nineteenth-century culture under the aegis of Spanish and Portuguese influences after independence was toward "indigenization": Much like the way the United States attempted during this time to break away from European art and literary influences, a similar movement pervaded the Latin American world. Along with attempts to form national and regional styles of their own, many countries also engaged in art as a nation-building exercise—artistic and literary celebrations of new national heroes or famous historic events through portraiture and landscape painting. Finally, there were also periodic engagements with the popular or folk arts of Amerindian peoples, mulattoes, mestizos, and Africans in celebration of regional uniqueness.

Literature to some extent paralleled the trajectory of the other arts. In the later eighteenth and early nineteenth centuries, an indigenous style developed, called *criollo*, for its inception and popularity in the Creole class. Literature often turned to themes befitting countries trying to establish themselves as nations with distinct historic pasts and great future potential. In some cases, critique of the present was the order of the day. Artists had a keen eye for a society caught between the specific kind of preindustrial tradition and modernity that characterized the Spanish- and Portuguese-speaking countries of the Americas during the nineteenth century.

Putting It All Together

The term "banana republic" appeared for the first time in 1904. The American humorist O. Henry (1862–1910) coined it to represent politically unstable and economically poor Latin American countries, governed by small elites and relying on tropical exports, such as bananas. O. Henry had spent several years at the end of the nineteenth century in Honduras, hiding from US authorities. Thus, he knew whereof he spoke.

Today, political stability is much greater; but many parts of Latin America are still poor and underindustrialized. Consequently, the expression "banana republic" still resonates. Were Latin American elites, therefore, wrong to engage in a pattern of export-led growth through mineral and agricultural commodities? And did they collude with elites in the industrial countries to maneuver the continent into permanent dependence on the latter? Indeed, an entire generation of scholars in the second half of the twentieth century answered the question in the affirmative and wrote the history of the 1800s in gloomy and condemnatory tones. They called their analysis "dependency theory."

Contemporary historians are less certain about many of these conclusions. They compare Latin America not with the United States or western Europe but with the settler colonies of South Africa, Australia, and New Zealand or the old empires of the Middle East and Asia. In these comparisons, Latin America did very well and was not any more dependent on the industrializing countries than the latter were on Latin America.

Dependence increased only at the very end of the 1800s when industrial countries like the United States and Britain began to make significant capital investments. It was then that foreign companies, such as those that owned railroads in Nicaragua and Honduras, succeeded in exploiting and controlling production and export. The question we may need to ask then is not why Latin America failed to industrialize in the 1800s but, rather, whether Latin America, selecting from the available choices, made the right decision when it opted for export-led growth up to about 1890. Did such a choice represent a "third way" toward economic growth, separate from industrial capitalism and tenacious attempts to keep economies closed off from the vagaries of world trade? Perhaps it did.

▶ For additional resources, including maps, primary sources, visuals, and quizzes, please go to www.oup.com/us/vonsivers. Please see the Further Resources section at the back of the book for additional readings and suggested websites.

Against the Grain

Early Industrialization in Chile?

In the early 1880s, Chilean businessmen began to discuss the idea of moving away from exclusive reliance on the export of coal and copper, as world market prices for those commodities fluctuated widely, and encouraging the turn to industrialization. They founded the Society for the Stimulation of Manufacturing in 1883, with the purpose of building factories for the transformation of raw materials into finished goods. Their ideas turned into a concrete governmental program under the presidency of José Manuel Balmaceda Fernández (1886–1891), who in 1888 created a ministry for industry and public works. Balmaceda, a black sheep of Chile's conservative Creole class, had strong liberal-constitutionalist convictions and was acutely aware of Chile's changing economic and social conditions in the last quarter of the century.

Chile had experienced a substantial population increase, from 2 to 2.5 million during 1875–1885. The urban population had grown even faster, rising from half to two-thirds the size of the rural population during the same time. Farmers and farmhands were particularly drawn to the mining cities in the newly acquired north (as the result of Chile winning the War of the Pacific during 1879–1884 against Peru and Bolivia), with its nitrate deposits. Other cities had grown near the existing coal and copper mines further south. Santiago, Valparaíso, and Concepción had evolved into major urban centers. Although farming still supported the majority of Chileans, urban employments had risen greatly in numbers and importance.

Balmaceda's new ministry for industry and public works engaged in a massive investment program in education, railroads, ports, armaments, and naval ships, financed with the revenue from mining exports, including the northern nitrates. Keeping at least a portion of these nitrates in the country and making them the foundation for a chemical industry became a newly envisaged option. The second Industrial Revolution had begun during the 1860s in Germany and the United States on the basis of nitrates, crucial for the production of sulfuric acid, which, in turn, was used for the production of glass, soap, bleach, paper, dyes, pottery, and nitroglycerin—all transformative industries absorbing large numbers of the urban population of unskilled and skilled laborers.

Unfortunately, Balmaceda's energetic program of import-substitution industrialization fell apart as soon as 1891, without any outside imperialist British or other foreign intervention. Perhaps Balmaceda's investment program was too much, introduced too fast. Favoritism in appointments and corruption among office holders aroused opposition not only among the conservative Creole landowners but also among dissident liberals who disliked Balmaceda's imperious style. The opposition unleashed a civil war, in which Balmaceda was deposed. With Balmaceda's suicide the incipient indigenous industrialization program ended, apparently still too weak against the dominant policy of export-led economic growth based on mineral extraction.

- **Why and how does rapid urbanization create the demand for industrialization?**
- **Was Balmaceda too progressive for the Chilean Creole class? Should he have attempted a different course?**

Thinking Through Patterns

▶ **Which factors in the complex ethnic and social structures of Latin America were responsible for the emergence of authoritarian politicians, or caudillos?**

Similar to the United States and France, which also underwent revolutions in the late 1700s and early 1800s, Latin America's independence movements (1810–1824) did not extend the constitutional revolution beyond a small number of property owners who inhabited the highest levels of the social strata. The dominant class of large landlords and plantation owners was conservative and did not favor land reform for the benefit of small farmers. Urban professionals and craftspeople, divided in many places by ethnicity, did not share common interests that allowed them to provide an effective opposition to the landed class. Landowning and plantation interests thus protected themselves through authoritarian caudillo politics and sought to keep the opposition weak.

In colonial times, Latin America was the warm-weather extension of Europe, sending its mineral and agricultural commodities to Europe. When it acquired its independence and Europe industrialized during the 1800s, these commodities became even more important, and the continent opted for a pattern of export-led development. This meant the systematic increase of mineral and agricultural commodity exports, with rising living standards not only for those who profited directly from the exports but also for many in the urban centers. Even with rising living standards it became clear by the turn of the century that a supplementary policy of industrialization had to be pursued.

▶ **Why did Latin American countries, after achieving independence, opt for a continuation of mineral and agricultural commodity exports?**

▶ **How do the social and economic structures of this period continue to affect the course of Latin America today?**

Many countries in Latin America are barely richer than they were in the 1800s. Even though industry, mineral and commodity exports, and services expanded in urban centers in the early part of the twentieth century, poor farmers with low incomes continued to be a drag on development. This phenomenon still characterizes many parts of Latin America today.

Chapter 24 1750–1910

The Challenge of Modernity

EAST ASIA

In Asia, our two countries, China and Japan, are the closest neighbors, and more-over have the same [written] language. How could we be enemies? Now for the time being we are fighting each other, but eventually we should work for perma-nent friendship . . . so that our Asiatic yellow race will not be encroached upon by the white race of Europe.

So commented the Chinese statesman Li Hongzhang to his Japanese counterpart, Ito Hirobumi, as they discussed terms to end the Sino–Japanese War in the Japanese town of Shimonoseki in the spring of 1895. For Li it was the culmination of more than three decades of frustration as China's most powerful advocate of *self-strengthening*—using new foreign technologies and concepts to preserve China's Confucian society in the face of European and American intrusion. During Li's lifetime such intrusions had come with alarming frequency. Now, at 71, he was forced to go to Japan to sue for peace as Japanese troops occupied Korea and southern Manchuria. To add injury to insult, he had just narrowly survived being shot in the face by a Japanese fanatic while en route to the peace talks.

For Ito, one of the architects of Japan's astonishing rise to power, the vic-tory over China was tinged with sadness and puzzlement as he responded: "Ten years ago when I was at Tientsin [Tianjin], I talked about reform with [you]. . . . Why is it that up to now not a single thing has been changed or

EAST ASIA
1750–1900

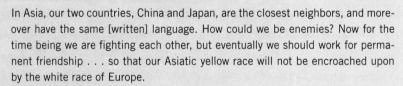

ABOVE: A Japanese print (1895) depicting negotiations held in the Japanese town of Shimonoseki to end the Sino–Japanese War.

reformed? This I deeply regret." This feeling was shared by Li, whose reply betrays a weary bitterness at China's deteriorating position: "At that time when I heard you . . . I was overcome with admiration . . . [at] your having vigorously changed your customs in Japan so as to reach the present stage. Affairs in my country have been so confined by tradition that I could not accomplish what I desired. . . . I am ashamed of having excessive wishes and lacking the power to fulfill them."

The significance of this rueful exchange was not lost on the other countries with interests in east Asia, who viewed the war's outcome with a mixture of fascination and alarm. Japan's surprisingly complete victory over China was cited as proof that it was now ready to join the ranks of the great powers. It also upset a shaky balance of power that was dependent on China's feeble Qing dynasty not collapsing altogether. Now Japan had dramatically raised the stakes. In addition to imposing a crippling indemnity on the Qing, reducing Korea to a client state, and annexing the island of Taiwan, the new Treaty of Shimonoseki called for the occupation by Japan of Manchuria's Liaodong Peninsula, which guarded the approaches to Beijing.

For Russia, France, and Germany, who saw their own interests threatened by this move, it was time to act. In what became known as the Triple Intervention, they threatened Japan with joint action if it did not abandon its claims to Liaodong. Unable to take on all three powers, the Japanese bitterly acquiesced. They grew more bitter the following year when the Qing secretly leased the territory to Russia in a desperate attempt to counter Japanese expansion. For the Japanese, this began a decade-long state of tension with Russia that would culminate in the Russo–Japanese War of 1904–1905. For the other powers in east Asia, it began a "race for concessions" in China that stopped just short of dismembering the empire.

For the Chinese, however, it marked the most dramatic and humiliating role reversal of the past 1,500 years. China had always viewed Japan in Confucian terms as a younger brother. Like Korea and Vietnam, Japan was considered to be on the cultural periphery of the Chinese world, acculturating to Chinese institutions and following Chinese examples in those things considered "civilized." Now, after barely a generation of exposure to Euro-American influence, Japan had eclipsed China as a military power and threatened to extend its sway throughout the region.

T he new order in east Asia brought about by the Sino–Japanese War underscores the larger effects of one of the most momentous patterns of world history: the phenomenon of imperialism growing from the innovations that created scientific–industrial society—one of the foundations of modernity

Seeing Patterns

▶ What was the impact of Western imperialism on the "regulated societies" of China and Japan?

▶ Why did European empire building in Asia have such dramatically different effects on China and Japan?

▶ How have historians seen the nature of these outside forces and their influences in east Asia?

Chapter Outline

- China and Japan in the Age of Imperialism

- Economics and Society in Late Qing China

- Zaibatsu and Political Parties: Economics and Society in Meiji Japan

- Putting It All Together

that we have examined in this part of the text. As we began to see in the previous two chapters, in less than a century, European countries and their offshoots—and now Japan—expanded their power so rapidly and completely that on the eve of World War I in 1914 more than 85 percent of the world's people were under their control or influence. How were a very few countries like Japan able to resist and adapt to the broad forces of modernity, while China struggled to cope with its effects through most of the nineteenth and twentieth centuries?

China and Japan in the Age of Imperialism

As we saw in Chapter 21, the reign of the Qing emperor Qianlong (r. 1736–1795) marked perhaps the high point of China's power in the early modern world and the period in which the first hints appeared of trouble to come. Some of the problems facing the Qing began to emerge within a year after Qianlong stepped down from the throne in 1795. A Buddhist sect called the White Lotus sparked a rebellion, which took years to suppress while at the same time highlighting the limitations of the Manchu bannermen as a military force. Less obvious, but perhaps more debilitating for the agrarian imperial order as a whole, were the new directions in economics. China was steadily drawn into the emerging European global commercial system, but the increasing forces of free trade were eroding its established systems of exchange control. Specifically, China's efforts to retain close control over its export trade in luxury goods coupled with efforts to eradicate the lucrative but illegal opium trade created a crisis with Great Britain in the summer of 1839. This crisis led to the First Opium War, China's first military encounter with the industrializing West.

China and Maritime Trade, 1750–1839

By the 1790s, with the China trade at record levels and the French Revolution making European trade increasingly problematic, the British government sought to establish diplomatic relations with the Qing. In the summer of 1793, they dispatched Lord George Macartney, an experienced diplomat and colonial governor, to Beijing with a sizeable entourage and boatloads of presents. His mission was twofold: to persuade the Qianlong emperor to allow the stationing of diplomatic personnel in the Chinese capital and create a system for the separate handling of ordinary commercial matters and diplomacy along the lines of European practices. Qianlong, however, politely but firmly rebuffed Macartney's attempts to establish a British embassy, observing that China really had "no need of your country's ingenious manufactures." A second British mission in 1816 met with similar results.

The Imbalance of Trade?   One important reason that Europeans and Americans were anxious to bring the Chinese into their diplomatic system was the widespread perception that China was benefiting from a huge trade imbalance. Though recent scholarship has shown that China's economy actually supported much of the interconnected Eurasian commercial system, contemporary merchants and political economists were convinced that China's control of trade functioned in the same way as European mercantilism. Thus, they believed that the money paid to Chinese merchants essentially stayed in the "closed" economy of the Qing Empire, draining the West of its stocks of silver. However, as Qianlong's reply to Macartney noted, European merchants offered little that the Chinese needed or wanted.

Thus, by the end of the eighteenth century, European and American traders had become increasingly anxious to find something that Chinese merchants would buy in sufficient quantities to stem the flow of Western silver into China. By the beginning of the nineteenth century, a growing number of merchants were clandestinely turning to a lucrative new commodity, with tragic consequences. When tobacco was introduced into China from the Americas, the innovation of smoking quickly spread. In southwestern China, tribesmen living in remote mountain villages began combining small quantities of powdered opium with tobacco. The Dutch, who briefly maintained bases on Taiwan, also introduced the practice there, from which it spread gradually to the maritime provinces of south China. Disturbed by the growing use of opium beyond normal medicinal practice in the area, the Qing banned the smoking of the substance as early as 1729. For the rest of the century opium use remained a strictly local problem in China's south.

Smugglers, Pirates, and "Foreign Mud"   By the end of the eighteenth century, the British East India Company's territory in Bengal had come to include the area around Patna, historically a center of medicinal opium production. While company traders were strictly prohibited from carrying opium to China as contraband, an increasing number of noncompany merchants willing to take the risk discovered that they could circumvent Chinese regulations and sell small quantities of the drug for a tidy profit. Initially, their customers were the wealthy of Canton society; and the exotic "foreign mud," as opium was nicknamed, soon became a favorite local diversion. With success came increased demand, and by the early decades of the nineteenth century, an elaborate illicit system of delivery had been set up along the south China coast. Heavily armed ships unloaded their cargo of opium on small, sparsely inhabited offshore islands, from which Chinese middlemen picked up the drug and made their rounds on the mainland (see Map 24.1). The ever-rising profits from this illegal enterprise encouraged piracy and lawlessness along the coast, and the opium trade soon became a major irritant in relations between China and the West.

The relationship that the British East India Company and the government-licensed Chinese merchant guild, or *cohong,* had so carefully developed over the previous century was now being rapidly undermined by the new commerce.

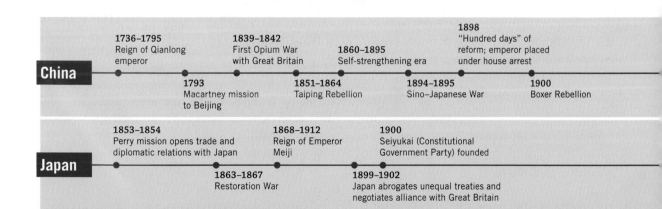

	China			
1736–1795 Reign of Qianlong emperor	**1839–1842** First Opium War with Great Britain	**1860–1895** Self-strengthening era	**1898** "Hundred days" of reform; emperor placed under house arrest	
	1793 Macartney mission to Beijing	**1851–1864** Taiping Rebellion	**1894–1895** Sino–Japanese War	**1900** Boxer Rebellion

	Japan		
1853–1854 Perry mission opens trade and diplomatic relations with Japan	**1868–1912** Reign of Emperor Meiji	**1900** Seiyukai (Constitutional Government Party) founded	
	1863–1867 Restoration War	**1899–1902** Japan abrogates unequal treaties and negotiates alliance with Great Britain	

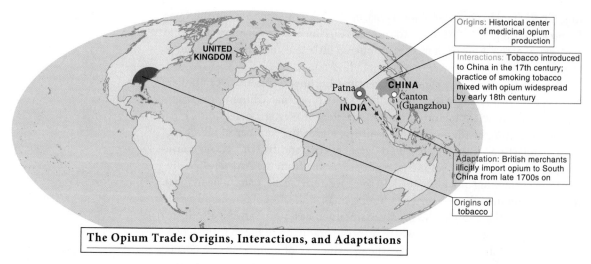

MAP 24.1 **The Opium Trade: Origins, Interactions, Adaptations.**

Moreover, growing free-trade agitation in England put an end to the East India Company's monopoly on the China trade in 1833. With the monopoly lifted, the number of entrepreneurs seeking quick riches in the opium trade exploded. With wealth came power, and in the foreign trading "factories" in Canton, newcomers engaged in the opium trade vied for prestige with older firms involved in legitimate goods.

The push for legitimacy among the opium merchants coincided with an aggressive attempt by Westerners to force China to open additional trading ports for legal items. Chinese authorities, however, viewed this Western assertiveness as driven primarily by opium and Christian evangelism. The East India Company itself was now fatally compromised as well, since an estimated one-quarter of its revenues in India were directly tied to opium production.

Far worse, however, were the effects on the ordinary inhabitants of south China. The huge rise in availability and consequent plunge in prices increased opium usage to catastrophic levels. Its power to suppress pain and hunger made it attractive to the poor engaged in physical labor, though the dreamlike state it induced often made it dangerous to work under its influence. Its addictive properties led people to seek it even at the expense of food, thus creating a health crisis for tens of thousands, made infinitely worse by the drug's notoriously difficult withdrawal symptoms.

"Let us ask, where is your conscience? I have heard that the smoking of opium is very strictly forbidden by your country. . . . Since it is not permitted to do harm to your own country, then even less should you let it be passed on to the harm of other countries—how much less to China!"

—Lin Zexu, "A Letter to the English Ruler"

Commissioner Lin Zexu   Matters came to a head in the spring of 1839. The Daoguang emperor sent Lin Zexu (1785–1850), a widely respected official with a reputation for courage and honesty, to Canton as an imperial commissioner. Lin, charged with cutting off the opium trade at its source, was given wide-ranging powers to deal with both Chinese and foreign traffickers. In addition to setting up facilities for the recovery of addicts, he demanded that all foreign merchants surrender their opium stocks and sign a pledge that they would not, under penalty of death,

Chinese Opium Smoker. This photograph, taken in the early 1870s, shows the pervasiveness of the opium habit among ordinary Chinese. These men are smoking in the back room of a restaurant, a common practice, even here in British-controlled Hong Kong.

Commissioner Lin Destroys the Opium. This drawing depicts Lin Zexu "burning" 20,000 chests of opium surrendered by the foreign merchants. In fact, however, he did not actually the burn the drug, but mixed it with water, salt, and lime and flushed it through sluiceways out to sea. The mixture created clouds of fumes, which misled some onlookers into believing it had been burned. The legend was perpetuated by depictions like this one in a 1909 Canton newspaper as part of a series called "Portraits of the Achievements of Our Dynasty's Illustrious Officials."

deal in the drug anymore. He even wrote a letter to the young Queen Victoria in which he lectured her on the morality of the opium trade.

When the foreign community balked at surrendering the goods, Lin blockaded the port and withdrew all Chinese personnel from Western firms. His determined stance finally ended the stalemate, and the dealers eventually surrendered 20,000 chests of opium, with most also signing the pledge. Lin then publicly treated the opium with lime and water and flushed the resulting slurry into the sea. Following Lin's actions, however, the dealers appealed to the British government for compensation.

The British government decided to use the incident to settle the long-standing diplomatic impasse with the Qing over foreign representation and open ports. In a show of force, the British sent a fleet of warships to Canton to demand reparations for the destroyed opium, pressure the Qing to establish diplomatic relations, and open more ports. In sad contrast to the days four centuries earlier when Zheng He commanded his great fleets, the Chinese now had no real naval forces to contest the British. What vessels they had were modestly armed with seventeenth-century cannon and used for customs collection. The British fleet, on the other hand, was the most powerful in the world and in a high state of readiness. When negotiations broke down, a small Chinese squadron sailed out to confront the British men-o'-war. The British ships sank a number of the junks and easily scattered the Chinese squadron. Such inauspicious circumstances marked the beginning of the First Opium War (1839–1842) and, with it, a long, painful century of foreign intrusion, domination, and ultimately revolution for China.

The Opium Wars and the Treaty Port Era

The hostilities that began in the fall of 1839 between China and Great Britain exposed the growing gap between the military capabilities of industrializing countries and those, like China, whose armed forces had fallen into disuse. The military had never been an honored profession in China, and the consequences of maintaining scattered Manchu banner garrisons, discouraging militia recruiting, and underfunding the Chinese regular forces (Armies of the Green Standard) were immediately evident.

Over the next 2 years, with a brief truce called in 1841, the British methodically attacked and occupied ports along the Chinese coast from Canton to Shanghai at the mouth of the Yangzi River, for the most part without serious opposition. As the British planned to move north to put pressure on Beijing, Chinese officials opened negotiations in August 1842. The resulting Treaty of Nanjing (Nanking) marked the first of the century's "unequal treaties" that would be imposed throughout east Asia by European powers.

The Treaty of Nanjing   Curiously, the treaty ending the First Opium War did not mention opium. In the final agreement, the British claimed the island of Hong Kong, with its excellent deep-water harbor; levied an indemnity on the Chinese to pay the costs of the war; and forced the Chinese to open the ports of Shanghai, Ningbo, Fuzhou, and Xiamen (Amoy), in addition to Canton. The Chinese were also confronted with British insistence on **nontariff autonomy**: By treaty they could now charge no more than a 5 percent tariff on British goods. The British also imposed the policy of **extraterritoriality** in the newly open ports: British subjects who violated Chinese laws would be tried and punished by British consuls.

Over the next several years, the Chinese signed similar treaties with France and the United States. An important addition in these later treaties was the *most-favored nation* clause: Any new concessions granted to one country automatically reverted to those who by treaty were "most-favored nations." Thus, the time-honored Chinese diplomatic strategy of "using barbarians to check barbarians" was dealt a near-fatal blow (see Map 24.2).

Nontariff autonomy: The loss by a country of its right to set its own tariffs.

Extraterritoriality: The immunity of a country's nationals from the laws of their host country.

Steam Power Comes to China. The new technologies of the Industrial Revolution were on painful display in China in 1840 as the British gunboat HMS *Nemesis* took on provincial warships down the river from Canton. The *Nemesis* featured an armored hull put together in detachable sections, shallow draft and steam-powered paddle wheel propulsion for river fighting, and a large pivot gun to take on shore batteries. Its power and versatility convinced Lin Zexu and a growing number of Chinese officials over the coming decades that China needed, at the very least, the same kinds of "strong ships and effective cannon" if they were to defend their coasts and rivers. By the 1860s the first attempts at such craft were finally under way.

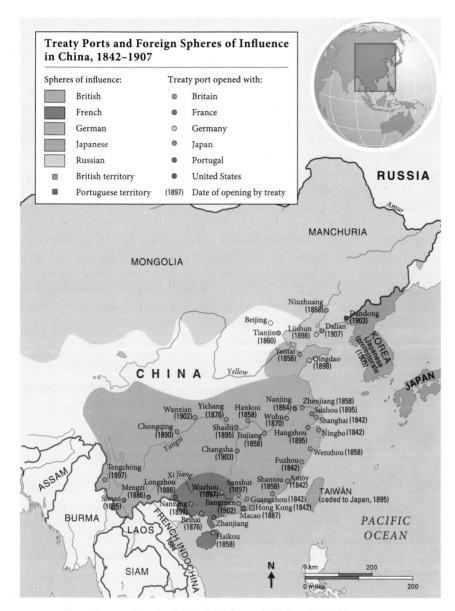

MAP **24.2** **Treaty Ports and Foreign Spheres of Influence in China, 1842–1907.**

The Taiping Movement, 1851–1864   In addition to the spread of the opium trade to the newly opened ports, long-established trade routes for more licit items swiftly shifted from Guangzhou to more convenient outlets. The growth of Shanghai was especially important in this regard because it served the Yangzi River, the greatest highway through China's heartland. Coastal trade also increased, while Hong Kong grew as the primary point of opium transfer to small smuggling vessels. The swiftness of all of these changes and their accompanying economic dislocation, along with smoldering discontent at the inability of the Qing government to resist foreign demands, made south China particularly volatile. In 1851 the region exploded in rebellion. Before it was over, this largest civil war in world history and its related conflicts would claim as many as 30 million lives.

The catalyst for revolt symbolized the diverse cultural influences penetrating the area. Though Christian proselytizing had been banned by the Qing since the early eighteenth century, missionary activity was protected in the foreign enclaves and now increased dramatically with the enactment of the new treaties. A candidate for the local Confucian examinations, Hong Xiuquan [hung SHIOO-chwahn] (1813–1864), read some Christian missionary tracts passed on by a colleague. Not long after, he failed the examination for the third time and suffered a nervous breakdown. When he eventually recovered, Hong came to believe that the Christian God had taken him up to heaven and informed him that he was in fact Christ's younger brother. Hong told his startled listeners that it had been revealed to him that he must now work to bring about the Heavenly Kingdom of Great Peace (*taiping tianguo*) on earth. The movement became known as the Taiping Rebellion and lasted from 1851 until 1864.

Hounded from their community, Hong and his group moved into a mountain stronghold and began to gather followers from the disillusioned and unemployed, anti-Manchu elements, religious dissidents, and fellow members of south China's Hakka minority. By 1851 they had created a society based on Protestant Christian theology, Chinese traditions, and a vision of equality in which all goods were held in common; women worked, fought, and prayed alongside men; and foot binding, opium smoking, and gambling were forbidden. As a sign that they were no longer loyal to the Qing, the men cut their queues and let the hair grow in on their foreheads, prompting the Qing to refer to them as "the long-haired rebels." Repudiating Confucian tradition, the rebels targeted the scholar-gentry in their land seizures and executions.

By late 1851, the movement had gathered enough strength to stand against local government forces and began an advance to the north. By 1853 they had captured the city of Nanjing and made it their capital. That winter the Taipings were narrowly thwarted from driving the Qing from Beijing and were pushed back to central China by the revived imperial forces. For the next decade, however, Hong's movement would remain in control of the Chinese heartland, and the long, bloody contest to subdue them would leave thousands of towns and villages devastated for decades to come.

For the foreigners in China, the prospect of a Christian movement taking power seemed like a dream about to come true. However, missionaries and diplomats gradually became less sure of the movement's aims. On the one hand, Hong and his advisors talked about instituting Western-style administrative reforms and building a modern industrial base—things Western well-wishers had continually urged on Chinese officials. On the other hand, a powerful Taiping China might repudiate the unequal treaties and throw the new trade arrangements into disarray. Thus, the foreign powers in the end grudgingly elected to continue recognizing the Qing as China's legitimate rulers (see Map 24.3).

The Second Opium War, 1856–1860   At the height of the rebellion in 1856, a new dispute arose between the Qing and the British and French. After 4 years of intermittent fighting, this conflict produced the next round of "unequal treaties" that greatly expanded foreign interests and control in the empire. Britain,

France, and the United States all felt by the mid-1850s that the vastly expanded trade in China—and now Japan—called for the opening of still more ports, an end to Qing prohibitions on missionary activity, and diplomatic relations along Western lines.

The catalyst came in late 1856. A Chinese customs patrol in Canton hauled down the British flag on the *Arrow*, a Chinese vessel whose registry had been falsified to take advantage of British trading privileges. The British used this purported insult to their flag as an opportunity to force treaty revision. The French, who considered themselves the protectors of Catholic missionaries and their converts, saw an excellent opening to pressure China on the missionary issue and so joined the British.

The war itself was fought intermittently in a highly localized fashion. The British seized the

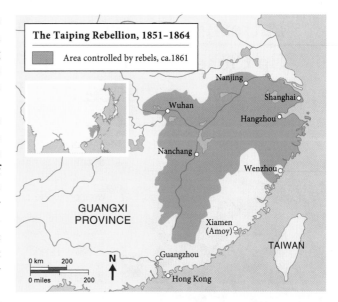

MAP **24.3 The Taiping Rebellion, 1851–1864.**

walled city of Canton, captured the governor-general of the region's two provinces, and sent him into exile in India. But by 1857 the Great Rebellion in India consumed British attention, while in China negotiations dragged on intermittently and the Qing remained preoccupied with the Taipings. In 1858 the Qing court refused a draft treaty. Returning in 1860 with a large expeditionary force, British and French troops advanced to Beijing, drove the emperor from the city, and burned and looted his summer palace. The final treaty stipulated that a dozen ports be opened to foreign trade, that opium be recognized as a legal commodity, that extraterritoriality be expanded, and that foreign embassies be set up in the capital. A newly created Chinese board, the Zongli Yamen, was to handle Qing foreign relations, and the Chinese were invited to send their own ambassadors abroad.

Self-Strengtheners. Two of the key figures in China's self-strengthening movement were Zeng Guofan (left) and Li Hongzhang (right). The two men began working together during the last years of the Taiping Rebellion, both having formed and led militia armies in their home provinces of Hunan (Zeng) and Anhui (Li). Both men also pioneered the use of modern weapons by their troops. After Zeng's death in 1872, Li emerged as the most active proponent of self-strengthening and China's most powerful official.

Patterns Up Close | Interaction and Adaptation: "Self-Strengthening" and "Western Science and Eastern Ethics"

Most of the important technical innovations taking place in China and Japan during the late eighteenth and early nineteenth centuries came from outside east Asia. This,  of course, is not surprising, since the scientific and industrial revolutions were largely focused on developing labor-saving machinery and weaponry and improving the speed and efficiency of transportation—matters of lesser priority in these labor-rich societies. Confronted by the expansive, newly industrialized countries of Europe and America, their possible responses were largely confined to what might be called the "three Rs"—reaction, reform, and revolution. Perhaps most interesting in this regard is the middle path of reform taken by both countries in attempting to create a synthesis of tried-and-true Confucian social structures and what were considered to be the best of the new technologies and institutions.

As we have seen in past chapters, Chinese philosophical concepts tended toward the desire for correlation and the reconciliation of opposites. In this tradition, *ti* and *yong*, or "essence" and "function/application," became the two key terms in the popular self-strengthening formulation *Zhongxue wei ti; Xixue wei yong* ("Chinese studies for the essence; Western studies for the practical application"). Thus, Chinese thinkers were able to accommodate the need for new foreign technologies within historically and philosophically acceptable terminology.

Interaction and Adaptation in China and Japan. Weapons on display at the Nanjing Arsenal in 1868 include an early Gatling-type rotary machine gun and a pyramid of round explosive shells (a), while an 1890 lithograph of a Japanese seamstress (b) shows the delicate balance between "essence" and "function" that Japan has tried to maintain since the middle of the nineteenth century. The woman is attired in Western dress, and she works a Western-style sewing machine. Has the "function" degraded the essence of what she is doing? It is a question that many in Japan still ask today.

Self-Strengthening Chinese officials, desperate to roll back the foreign threat and suppress the Taipings, favored a diverse array of strategies. Few advocated simply fighting the foreigners with whatever means were at hand. Most, like the emperor's brother Prince Gong, felt that over time these new peoples would be assimilated to Chinese norms, like invaders and border peoples of the past. In the meantime, however, they should be "soothed and pacified," but not unconditionally. As the prince later remarked to the British ambassador, "Take away your opium and your missionaries and you will be welcome."

Similarly, the Japanese, also schooled in Neo-Confucianism, were able to justify an even more thoroughgoing transformation of society by means of the balanced formula they called "Western science and Eastern ethics."

However, the two sides of the concept were not evenly balanced. As with many Neo-Confucian formulae, the "essence" and "ethics" elements were considered to be primary and the method of implementation—"function"—secondary. Thus, their proponents could argue that their chief aim was the preservation of the fundamentals of Confucian society while remaining flexible about the appropriate means of attaining their goals. Opponents, however, argued that the formula could—and eventually would—be reversed: that "function" would eventually degrade the "essence." Here, they pointed to the alleged Westernization of students sent abroad and the wearing of Western clothes in Japan as examples of the dangers of this approach.

Yet in both countries, one can argue that this has remained a favored approach, even through war and revolution. Though societal and generational tensions over "tradition" and "modernity" have been present for nearly a century and a half in Japan, the Japanese have made foreign technologies and institutions their own, while retaining some of their most cherished Shinto and Buddhist practices alongside social customs still tinged with Neo-Confucianism. Similarly, in China, since the beginning of the Four Modernizations in 1978, coupling technological and institutional modernization with an effort to rediscover and preserve what is considered to be the best of traditional Chinese civilization has been the dominant approach. Thus, the present regime pursues a policy of "socialism with Chinese characteristics" and supports the founding of Confucius Institutes alongside computer factories—all in the service of creating what the Communist Party calls "the harmonious society."

Questions

- How were the Chinese and Japanese adaptations to Western innovations similar? How were they different? What do these similarities and differences say about the cultures of these two countries?

- Do you believe that, over the course of time, the "function" of foreign innovations has degraded the "essence" in China and Japan?

In order to do this, however, China needed to be able to halt further encroachments by the Western powers. Toward this end, a growing number of prominent officials advocated a policy that came to be called "self-strengthening." During the 1860s, the two most prominent were Li Hongzhang (1823–1901) and his senior colleague Zeng Guofan (1811–1872). Both men had distinguished themselves as Confucian scholars and as leaders of militia armies during the Taiping years. In 1864, their combined forces finally captured the Taiping capital at Nanjing and forced the suicide of Hong Xiuquan, bringing the movement to an end.

Like a number of leaders during these desperate times, Li and Zeng were also distinguished by the flexibility of their thinking and, increasingly, by their growing familiarity with the new weapons and techniques brought to China by foreign forces. By the end of the rebellion, they had begun to move toward a strategy of what a later slogan called "Chinese studies for the essence; Western studies for practical application." In the 1860s and early 1870s they sponsored a foreign language and technical school, modern arsenals and factories at Nanjing and Jiangnan (Kiangnan), a modern navy yard at Fuzhou, initiatives to send Chinese students to the United States and Europe, a modern shipping concern, and the first moves toward sending representatives abroad.

Toward Revolution: Reform and Reaction to 1900

While China's efforts at self-strengthening seemed promising to contemporaries during the 1870s, signs of their underlying weakness were already emerging. As we have seen, the architect of many of these efforts, Li Hongzhang, was all too aware of the political constraints he faced. With the ascension of the infant Guangxu as emperor in 1874 came the regency of Empress Dowager Cixi. Desperate to preserve Manchu power, Cixi constantly manipulated factions at court and among the high officials to avoid concentration of power in any particular area. Such maneuverings, sometimes favoring Li's colleagues and as often opposing them, severely hampered the long-term health of many self-strengthening measures. In addition, the new programs were costly, usually requiring foreign experts, and China's finances were continually strained by the artificially low treaty tariffs and the obligation to pay old indemnities.

China and Imperialism in Southeast Asia and Korea   By the 1880s foreign tensions exposed more problems. France had been steadily encroaching upon southeast Asia since the late 1850s. By the early 1890s rising tensions surrounding the Korean court and intrigues by Japanese and Chinese agents involving various factions threatened war. Japan sent a force which they claimed to be "diplomatic"; troops of a Chinese counterforce were killed when a Japanese warship sunk their transport. By the fall of 1894, both sides were sending troops and naval forces to Korea, and a full-scale war over the fate of Korea and northeast Asia was under way.

The Sino–Japanese War   As we noted at the beginning of this chapter, the war between China and Japan over control of Korea graphically exposed the problems of China's self-strengthening efforts. China's arms procurement, for example, was not carried out under a centralized program, as Japan's was. The result was that different Chinese military units were armed with a wide variety of noninterchangeable weapons and ammunition, making it difficult for them to support each other. China's rebuilt fleet, though impressive in size and armament, faced similar problems.

While many of the land battles were hotly contested, superior organization and morale enabled the Japanese to drive steadily through Korea. A second force landed in southern Manchuria to secure the territory around the approaches to Beijing, while Japanese naval forces reduced the fortress across from it at Weihaiwei. By spring 1895, after some preliminary negotiations, Li made his humiliating trip

Scenes from the Sino–Japanese War. News accounts of the Sino–Japanese War aroused great interest and an unprecedented wave of nationalism in Japan. They also marked the last extensive use of *ukiyo-e* woodblock printing in the news media, as the technology of reproducing photos in newspapers was introduced to Japan shortly after the conflict. Because few of the artists actually traveled with the troops, the great majority of these works came from reporters' dispatches and the artists' imaginations. In these representative samples from the assault on Pyongyang showing the use of the new technology of the electric searchlight to illuminate an enemy fort (a), the pride in Japan's modernization and the disdain for China's "backwardness" are all too evident. Note the almost demon-like faces and garish uniforms of the Chinese as they are invariably depicted as being killed or cowering before the Japanese; note, too, the modern, Western uniforms and beards and mustaches of the Japanese (b).

to Shimonoseki and was forced to agree to Japan's terms. The severity of the provisions, especially the annexation of Taiwan, the control of Korea, and, temporarily at least, the seizure of Liaodong, signaled to the Western powers in east Asia that China was weak enough to have to acquiesce to massive economic and territorial demands.

Thus, a "race for concessions" began in which France demanded economic and territorial rights in south China adjacent to Indochina, Great Britain did the same in the Yangzi River valley, Russia and Japan made demands in the north for rights in Manchuria, and a newcomer, Germany, demanded naval bases and rights at Qingdao [ching-DOW] (Tsingtao) on the Shandong Peninsula. China's total dismemberment was avoided in 1899 when John Hay, the US secretary of state, circulated a note with British backing suggesting that all powers refrain from securing exclusive concessions and instead maintain an "open door" for all to trade in China.

The Hundred Days of Reform Amid this growing foreign crisis, the aftermath of the war produced a domestic crisis as well. The terms of the Shimonoseki

EN CHINE
Le gâteau des Rois et... des Empereurs

Dismembering China. The weakness of the Qing during the final years of the nineteenth century prompted the so-called race for concessions among the imperial powers in east Asia. In this French cartoon, China is depicted as a cake around which caricatures of the monarchs and national symbols of the various powers sit with their knives poised arguing over who should get the best pieces. A desperate Chinese official—perhaps Li Hongzhang himself—with his long fingernails and flapping queue, holds up his hands imploring them to stop. The French caption says, "In China: The cake of kings and emperors."

treaty had prompted patriotic demonstrations in Beijing and raised levels of discussion about reform to new levels of urgency. A group of younger officials headed by Kang Youwei (1858–1927) petitioned Emperor Guangxu, now ruling in his own right, to implement a list of widespread reforms, many modeled on those recently enacted in Japan. Guangxu issued a flurry of edicts from June through September 1898, attempting to completely revamp China's government and many of its leading institutions. Resistance to this "hundred days' reform" program, however, was extensive, and much of it was centered on the emperor's aunt, the empress dowager. With support from her inner circle at court, she had the young emperor placed under house arrest and rounded up and executed those of Kang's supporters who could be found. Kang and his junior colleague, the writer and political theorist Liang Qichao [leeahng chee-CHOW] (1873–1929), managed to escape to the treaty ports. For the next decade they traveled to overseas Chinese communities attempting to gather support for their Constitutional Monarchy Party.

The Boxer Rebellion and War The turmoil set off by the "race for concessions" among the imperial powers was particularly intense in north China, where the ambitions of Russia, Japan, and Germany clashed. The increased activity of German missionaries on the Shandong Peninsula sparked renewed antiforeign sentiment, increasingly perpetrated by a Chinese group calling itself the Society of the Harmonious Fists. This group was anti-Qing as well as antiforeign, and the members' ritual exercises and name prompted the foreign community to refer to them as the "Boxers." By late 1899 the Boxers were regularly provoking the foreign and Christian communities, hoping that foreign governments would pressure the Qing to suppress the movement, thereby fomenting a larger rebellion against the Qing.

In the spring of 1900 matters came to a crisis when Boxers assassinated the German ambassador. The Germans demanded that the Qing crush the movement, pay a huge indemnity, and erect a statue to their ambassador as a public apology. In the midst of this crisis, the empress dowager, who had been negotiating in secret with the Boxers, declared war on all the foreign powers in China and openly threw the court's support behind the movement. The result was civil war across northern China, as Boxer units hunted down missionaries and Chinese Christians, many Chinese army units aided the Boxers in attacking foreigners, and the foreign diplomatic quarter in Beijing was besieged.

The foreign governments quickly put together a multinational relief force led by the Germans and British and largely manned by the Japanese but including

The Empress Dowager Cixi.
Following the rout of the Qing and Boxer forces in the fall of 1900, the empress dowager made herself more accessible to Western diplomats and photographers. There are numerous pictures of her in various royal poses; here, she sits with her court ladies-in-waiting. The legend above her throne reads from right to left: "The reigning Saintly Mother, Empress Dowager of the Great Qing, [may she rule] 10,000 years! 10,000 years! 10,000, 10,000 years!"—the last exhortation (*wan sui, wan sui, wan wan sui*) the Chinese rendering of the more familiar Japanese "Banzai."

units of nearly all the countries with interests in China. By August they had fought their way to the capital and chased the imperial court nearly to Xi'an. Amid considerable carnage in the mopping up of Boxer sympathizers, Li Hongzhang, in his last official duty before his death, was commissioned to negotiate an end to the conflict for the court. With Qing power utterly routed, the foreign governments were able to impose the most severe "unequal treaty" yet: They extracted the right to post troops in major Chinese cities, demanded the total suppression of any antiforeign movements, and received such a huge indemnity that China had to borrow money from foreign banks in order to service the interest on the loan. One positive outcome of the Boxer Protocols of 1901 was that the United States agreed to return its share of the indemnity money to China on the condition that it would be used to send Chinese students to study in American institutions. This resulted in considerable goodwill toward the United States; indeed, in subsequent decades a significant portion of Chinese leaders were educated in the United States.

In Search of Security through Empire: Japan in the Meiji Era

As we have just seen, the close of the nineteenth century saw Japan looming larger and larger as China's chief threat. Yet they both faced similar pressures and, as Li Hongzhang observed, shared a common culture and in many ways a common cause. How, then, was Japan, with only a fraction of China's population and resources, able not only to survive in the face of foreign pressure but join the imperial powers itself?

The Decline of Tokugawa Seclusion   Though the eighteenth century saw occasional attempts by foreign ships to put in at Japanese ports, Europeans generally

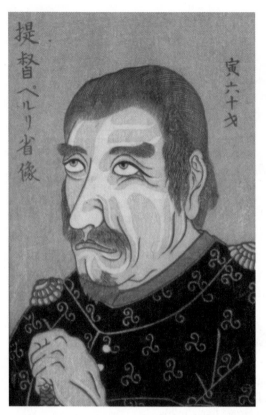

提督ペルリ肖像

寅六十戈

"Blue-eyed Barbarians." The Japanese commonly referred to Westerners as "blue-eyed barbarians." In this sketch, part of a long series that artists made after Commodore Perry's four heavily armed steamships sailed into Tokyo Bay in July 1853, Perry's son Oliver, who served as his father's personal secretary, is portrayed as jowly and slightly demonic looking.

Coolies: Poor migrant laborers from China and India who performed menial work in other parts of the world in the nineteenth century.

honored Japan's seclusion policies. Moreover, since all maritime trade with China took ships along a southerly route to Canton, the opportunity to go to Japan seldom presented itself. By the first decades of the nineteenth century, however, the situation was changing. The vastly expanded legitimate trade with China and the development of the opium trade increased the volume of shipping closer to Japanese waters. Moreover, the rapid growth of the whaling industry in the northern Pacific increasingly brought European and American ships into waters adjacent to Japan. From their perspective, the need for establishing relations for the disposition of shipwreck survivors and perhaps trade was therefore becoming ever more urgent.

By the 1840s the pressure to establish relations with the Tokugawa shogunate became even more intense for the Western powers with interests in China. The treaty ports created in the wake of the First Opium War included Shanghai, which was rapidly becoming east Asia's chief commercial enclave. Because of its geographical position, major shipping routes to Shanghai now ran directly adjacent to southern Japan. Moreover, the Mexican-American War (1846–1848) (see Chapter 23) brought the Pacific coast of North America under the control of the United States. At the same time, the discovery of gold in California made San Francisco the premier port for all American transpacific trade. In addition, increasing numbers of Chinese sought passage to the gold fields and the promise of employment in the American West, while the infamous **"coolie** trade" continually increased human traffic to Cuba and Peru. Plans to open steamship service along the great circle route from San Francisco to Shanghai, and the need for coaling stations to supply it, now threatened to place Japan squarely in the path of maritime traffic.

The Coming of the "Black Ships"   The Tokugawa were well aware of the humiliation of the Qing at the hands of the British in 1842 and watched nervously as foreign commerce mounted in the Chinese treaty ports. As pressure increased on Japan to open its ports, divided counsels plagued the shogunate. The influential Mito School, long exposed to "Dutch learning" (see Chapter 21), feared the growing military and technological power of the Europeans and Americans and advocated a military response to any attempt at opening the country. Others looking at the situation in China felt that negotiation was the only possible way for Japan to avoid invasion.

The Americans, taking the lead in seeking diplomatic and commercial relations, put together a fleet of their newest and most powerful warships, which arrived in Japan in July 1853. Their commander, Matthew C. Perry, assembled multiracial and multiethnic crews in order to impress his Japanese hosts with the reach and power of the United States. Anxious to awe them as well with the new technologies available, he brought along as presents a telegraph set and a model railroad, both of which proved immediately popular with the Japanese. When negotiations flagged, the shogun's men gleefully amused themselves aboard the miniature train, smacking the engine and its operator with their fans to make it go faster.

On Perry's return trip in 1854 with even more of the "black ships," as the Japanese dubbed them, the Treaty of Kanagawa was signed, Japan's first with an outside power. Like China, Japan had now entered the treaty port era.

"Honor the Emperor and Expel the Barbarian!"   The widely differing attitudes toward foreign contact expressed within the shogunate were reflected among the daimyo and samurai as well. The treaty with the Americans, and the rapid conclusion of treaties with other foreigners, tended to reinforce antiforeignism among many of the warrior elite, while emphasizing the weakness of the Tokugawa to resist further demands. Moreover, the new cultural contacts taking place in treaty ports like Yokohama and Nagasaki hardened positions and raised tensions further. Many samurai felt that dramatic gestures were called for to rouse the country to action. Hence, as with the Boxers later in China, they attacked foreigners and even assassinated Tokugawa officials in an effort to precipitate antiforeign conflict. By 1863, a movement aimed at driving out the Tokugawa and restoring imperial rule had coalesced around the samurai of two southern domains, Satsuma and Choshu. Taking the slogan *Sonno joi* ("Honor the emperor, expel the barbarian") members of this "Satcho" (*Satsuma* and *Choshu*) clique challenged the shogunate and fought the smoldering Restoration War, which by the end of 1867 forced the Tokugawa to capitulate. In short order, the new regime moved to the Tokugawa capital of Edo and renamed it Tokyo (Eastern Capital).

The new emperor, 15-year-old Mutsuhito, took the reign name of Meiji (Enlightened Rule) and quickly moved to make good on its promise. As proof that the new regime would adopt progressive measures, in April 1868 the throne issued a "charter oath" in which the new emperor renounced the restrictive measures of the past. A constitution was also promulgated, which spelled out in more detail how the new government was to be set up.

Creating a Nation-State   While the Tokugawa had created an efficient warrior bureaucracy based on Neo-Confucianism, Japan was still dominated by regional loyalties and fealty to the daimyo of one's *han*, or feudal domain. The foreign threat and restoration of the emperor provided the opportunity as well as the necessity to forge a more thoroughgoing national unification. Thus, the new government quickly set about dismantling the feudal han and replacing them with a centralized provincial structure; the daimyo were replaced by governors, and the samurai were disbanded, given stipends, and encouraged to form business enterprises or to teach. In their place, a new conscript army modeled after that of Germany was created, and a navy modeled on Great Britain's was established. In addition, the new order was to be held together by a national system of compulsory education in which loyalty to the emperor and state was carefully nurtured at every level.

Emperor Meiji. A number of portraits and photographs of Emperor Meiji were done during his lifetime, particularly in his twenties and thirties. Here, in a portrait probably done in the late 1870s or early 1880s, he is shown as a vigorous and decisive man at the height of his powers. Note the European-style military uniform and Van Dyke beard of the kind frequently sported by Western monarchs and leaders.

The 1870s also marked the flourishing of government-managed social experimentation. Like the Chinese "self-strengtheners," Japanese senior advisors to the emperor, or *genro* [GEN-row, with a hard g], sought to use new foreign technologies and institutions to strengthen the state against further foreign intrusion. Japan's planners, however, proved more systematic and determined in their efforts and, unlike their Chinese counterparts, had the full backing of the imperial court. Thus, Japan's proclaimed goals of using "Western science and Eastern ethics" in the service of "civilization and enlightenment" were seen as the primary tools in reaching eventual equality with the Western imperial powers and rolling back Japan's unequal treaties.

Creating an Empire   As we saw earlier in this chapter, rising tensions between Japan and China over the disposition of Korea ultimately led to the Sino–Japanese War of 1894–1895. The issue was temporarily held in abeyance by the Treaty of Tianjin of 1885, but continuing difficulties arising from the instability of the

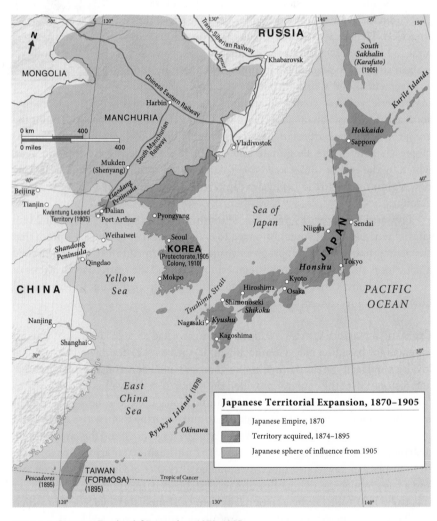

MAP **24.4 Japanese Territorial Expansion, 1870–1905.**

Korean government, feuding pro-Chinese and pro-Japanese factions within it, and the *Tonghak*, or "Eastern learning," movement, kept the region a volatile one. Combining elements of Confucianism, Buddhism, and a pronounced strain of antiforeignism, Tonghak-led peasant rebellions had erupted in 1810 and 1860. Though the rebellion had been suppressed in the 1860s, the forced opening of Korea to trade in the following decade and the constant intrigues of the Qing and the Japanese surrounding the Yi court in succeeding decades brought about the movement's revival in the 1890s.

As we have seen, Japan's successful showing in the war surprised and alarmed the Western powers in the region. The Triple Intervention, in which Russia, Germany, and France forced Japan to return the Liaodong Peninsula to China, only to have the Chinese lease it to Russia the following year, put that empire on a collision course with Japanese aspirations on the Asian mainland. Japan's control of Korea made it intensely interested in acquiring concessions in Manchuria. For Russia, it was vital to build rail links from the Trans-Siberian Railway to their new outposts of Port Arthur and Dairen (Dalian) in Liaodong and to extend the line across Manchuria to Vladivostok on the Pacific. As the twentieth century began, the Russians pressured the Chinese into allowing them the rights to build the Chinese Eastern Railway across Manchuria and the South Manchurian Railway to Port Arthur, with a vital junction at Mukden, known today as Shenyang. Japan and Russia would shortly fight a war that would secure Japan's dominant position in northeast Asia and begin a long train of events that would end in revolution for Russia (see Map 24.4).

Economics and Society in Late Qing China

The century and a half from 1750 to 1900 marked the structural, cultural, and economic decline of the great agrarian empires. Nowhere was this more evident than in Qing China. By 1900, China's treasury was bankrupt; its finances increasingly were controlled by foreign concerns; its export trade was outstripped by European and Japanese competitors; its domestic markets turned to factory-produced foreign commodities; and its land, ravaged by war, eroded by declining productivity, and squeezed by the world's largest population, grew less and less capable of sustaining its society.

The Seeds of Modernity and the New Economic Order

As we have seen a number of times in this chapter, the economic policies of late imperial China were increasingly at odds with those of the industrializing and commercially expanding West. For Chinese thinkers, this was considered sound in both ideological and economic terms. Confucianism held that agriculture was China's primary concern; that the values of humanity, loyalty, and filial piety were tied to agrarian society; and that the values of the merchant—particularly the drive for profit—were in direct opposition to these agrarian values. As the nineteenth century advanced, the opium trade provided ample evidence to Confucian officials of the correctness of this stance.

While opium was the great entering wedge, the building pressures on China and other regulated societies to lower their barriers to legitimate trade and the steps taken by those countries exerting the pressure to safeguard their own markets had equally severe long-term effects. Briefly, China was squeezed both ways in terms of trade. That is, the unequal treaties imposed artificially low tariff rates on the empire, making it increasingly difficult to protect its markets; at the same time, trading nations in the West increased tariffs on their own imports and, in some cases, developed their own substitutes for Chinese products.

Self-Strengthening and Economics   The programs to improve China's economics and trade were set up as "government-sponsored/merchant-operated" enterprises. Amid the halting attempts at government-sponsored innovation, however, other economic forces at work would also have a profound effect on China's later economic development. The first was that in the treaty ports themselves the economic climate created by the Western powers for their own benefit exposed much of China's urban population to aspects of modern industrial and commercial society. A substantial class of Chinese people who made a living mediating between Westerners and Chinese interests had developed by the end of the nineteenth century.

The other long-term process at work was the growing influx and popularity of European, Japanese, and American consumer goods diffused from the treaty ports to the interior. While foreign curiosities had been popular with Chinese elites since the eighteenth century, Qing efforts to safeguard domestic markets through the Canton system and internal transit taxes had been steadily beaten down. By the end of the nineteenth century, foreign machine-made cotton cloth dominated the Chinese interior; John D. Rockefeller's Standard Oil Company was giving away kerosene lamps to market their fuel; the British–American Tobacco Company had established its products in the empire; and even the Japanese invention of the rickshaw had become a popular mode of transport in China's cities. With the Qing finally committed to railroad and telegraph construction and modern deep mining and with China's commercial ports resembling more and more those of their foreign counterparts, the seeds of economic modernity had been at least fitfully planted.

Rural Economics and Society   While about 80–85 percent of China's population remained rural, the old structures of the empire's peasant-based society were slowly beginning to crumble. As we saw during the Taiping era, tensions among peasants, village headmen, scholar-gentry, and local officials were never far from the surface. Landlordism, especially the growing incidence of absentee landlordism, exacerbated these tensions. Living on the edge of poverty in many areas, with old trade routes and handicrafts disrupted by the treaty ports, many peasants saw in the Taipings, the Nian, and other local rebellions a desperate way to change their situations. But in the end, the radical ideologies and ruthlessness of the rebels disillusioned the peasantry, while in many places their poverty increased due to the immense destruction caused by rebel clashes and the flight of many wealthy scholar-gentry to the treaty ports. As a result, by the beginning of the twentieth century, absentee landlordism had become an increasingly acute problem. As some scholars have noted, the land problems of China—and their parallels in India and the Ottoman Empire—were an important impediment to an effective response to the scientific–industrial challenge of Europe and America.

Social Trends   While changes were certainly noticeable in the family, in relationships between men and women, and in the level of confidence the Chinese

Chinese Family, ca. 1873. While the later nineteenth century marked changes on a number of fronts, the centrality of the family and its Confucian hierarchy remained largely intact. In the portrait here of the Yang family of Beijing, the father and eldest son occupy the places of honor under the central window of the ground floor, while the wives, concubines, infants, and servants are arrayed on the upper veranda. In most cases, the seclusion of such wealthy women was nearly complete. The photographer reported, however, that these women frequently moistened their fingertips and rubbed them on the paper windowpanes to make them transparent so they could secretly watch events outside.

displayed in the Confucian system—particularly among urban Chinese—the durability of long-standing traditions is probably far more striking. As we have seen in every chapter on China, the family remained the central Chinese institution. Within it, the father continued to be the most powerful figure, and the Confucian ideal of hierarchical relationships between husband and wife, father and son, and elder brother and younger brother remained in force. Daughters, though most often treated with affection, were also considered a net drain on family resources because they would marry outside the family. Thus, the education they received was generally aimed at fostering the skills the family of their husbands-to-be would consider valuable—cooking, sewing, running a household, and perhaps singing and poetry. It was also desirable for girls to acquire enough literacy to read such classics as *Admonitions for Women*, the *Classic of Filial Piety*, and other guides to proper behavior. But the proverbial wisdom remained that "a woman with talent is without virtue." Hence, the daughters of the wealthy were kept secluded in the home, and most—with the exception of the Manchus and certain minorities like south China's Hakkas—continued the practice of foot binding.

Culture, Arts, and Science

Though the late Qing period is often seen by scholars as one more concerned with cataloging and preserving older literary works than innovation, there was nevertheless considerable invigoration due to foreign influences toward the end of the dynasty. Indeed, one could say that the era begins with one of China's great literary masterpieces and ends with China's first modern writers pointing toward a vernacular-language literary renaissance starting around 1915. Reversing the trend of thousands of years, the most significant Chinese developments in science and technology were those arriving from the West as products of the Industrial Revolution and the new kind of society emerging there.

The Dream of the Red Chamber   Though the novel during Ming and Qing times was not considered high literature by Chinese scholars, the form, as with Europeans in the eighteenth and nineteenth centuries, proved immensely popular. During the mid-eighteenth century, what many consider to be China's greatest novel, *Hong Lou Meng* (*The Dream of the Red Chamber*), was written by the shadowy Cao Xueqin [sow shway-CHIN] (ca. 1715–ca. 1764). The novel, which chronicles the decline and fall of a powerful family, is seen by some scholars as a loose autobiography of Cao's own family and a thinly veiled account of events in the early days of the Qing. In fact, the novel has been so closely studied and analyzed that in China there is an entire field called "red studies" or "redology" (*hong xue*) devoted to examination of the work.

Poetry, Travel Accounts, and Newspapers   China's increasing need to understand new threats as well as opportunities prompted publication of a great number of atlases, gazetteers of foreign lands, and eyewitness travel accounts. Many of the early attempts at compiling information about foreign countries were copies of Western works. The most significant of these were the *Illustrated Gazetteer of the Maritime Countries* of 1844 by Wei Yuan (1794–1856) and the *Record of the World* of 1848 by Xu Jiyu (1795–1873). These accounts, especially Xu's, formed the backbone of what Chinese officials knew about the outside world until the first eyewitness accounts of travelers and diplomats began to arrive in the late 1860s.

Though hundreds of thousands of Chinese had emigrated to various parts of the world by the mid-1860s, it was only in 1866 that the first authorized officials began to visit foreign countries and not until 1876 that diplomats began to take up their posts in foreign capitals and ports. All of these men, however, were required to keep official journals of their experiences for use by the government and/or for publication, and by the later part of the century China began to acquire a far more complete sense of what the outside world was like. The journals of the diplomats Zhang Deyi (1847–1919) and Guo Songtao (1818–1891) were particularly significant in this regard.

The popular newspaper also emerged in the treaty ports and eventually in most Chinese cities during this time. For centuries newsletters tracking official doings at the capital had been circulated among the elites. However, the 1860s saw the first popular Chinese-language papers, the most prominent of which was *Shenbao*. By the turn of the century, Liang Qichao (1873–1929) had emerged as China's most influential journalist and scholar, having started and edited five newspapers, each heavily influenced by his views on reform. Such publications and the growing numbers of journals and popular magazines, many started by missionaries anxious to use science and Western material culture as a vehicle for their work, were vitally important in the transfer of ideas between Chinese and foreigners.

Science and Technology   The most pressing need for China during the early nineteenth century was military technology. During the period between the two Opium Wars, Chinese officials attempted with some success to purchase guns and cannon from European and American manufacturers to bolster their coastal defenses. It was quickly apparent to the self-strengtheners, however, that China must understand the basic principles behind these revolutionary weapons and begin to manufacture them on its own. Moreover, this would be impossible to do unless the infrastructure was in place and such supporting industries as mining, railroads, and telegraphy were also established.

Despite the general animosity directed against them by Chinese officials, missionaries ironically were key players in transfers of science and technology. Unlike the Jesuit missionaries of the seventeenth century, Protestant missionaries in the nineteenth century directed their efforts at ordinary Chinese, but often did so by attracting them with the new advantages of science. Central to their efforts was the role of medical missionaries in setting up clinics and using their presence in the community to foster conversion. The missionary community was also active in popularizing developments in Western science and technology through journals like the *Globe Magazine*. By the latter part of the century, increasing numbers of Chinese scholars were becoming involved in the study of foreign subjects, going abroad for education, and in the translation of Western works into Chinese. The Chinese mathematician Li Shanlan (1810–1882), for example, collaborated with Shanghai missionaries in translating works on algebra, calculus, and analytical geometry. Later, Liang Qichao and Yan Fu (1854–1921) studied and translated a wide range of foreign scientific and social science works.

Thus, while China had not yet completed its move to the new scientific–industrial society, the momentum had already begun to build among the empire's intellectual leaders. Even so, nearly all agreed that the future would not lie in slavish imitation of the West. In the meantime, however, the example of Japan confronted them only a short distance away.

Zaibatsu and Political Parties: Economics and Society in Meiji Japan

Scholars of Japan's economic history have often pointed out that the commercial environment developing through the Tokugawa period was well suited to the nurturing of capitalism and industrialism in the nineteenth century. As we saw in Chapter 21, for example, the imposition of the law of alternate attendance created a great deal of traffic to and from Edo as daimyo processions made their biannual trips to the capital. This guaranteed traffic supported numerous hostels, restaurants, stables, supply stores, theaters, and all the other commercial establishments necessary to maintain the travelers in safety and comfort. The infrastructure of the major roads also required constant tending and improvement, as did the port facilities for coastal shipping and fishing industries. Towns and cities along the routes also grew, as did the regionally specialized crafts and industries they supported. By 1850, for example, Edo had well over 1 million inhabitants, while Osaka and Kyoto both had about 375,000. Finally, commercial credit establishments, craft guilds, and large-scale industries in ceramics, sake brewing, fine arts, fishing, and coastal shipping—all intensified by being compressed into a relatively small area—had already regularized many of the institutions characteristic of the development of a modern economy.

Commerce and Cartels

Perhaps because of the urgency of their situation following Perry's visits, the Japanese were quicker to go abroad to study the industrially advanced countries of Europe and the United States. In 1860, for example, they sent an embassy to America in which the participants—including the future journalist Fukuzawa Yukichi (1835–1901)—were expected to keep diaries of everything they saw. Even during the last days of the Tokugawa regime, Japanese entrepreneurs were already experimenting with Western steamships and production techniques.

Cooperation and Capitalism   When the Meiji government began its economic reforms, its overall strategy included elements that still mark Japanese policy today. The first was to make sure that ownership, insofar as possible, would remain in Japanese hands. The second was that, taking its cue from the success of the leading commercial nations of the West, Japan would develop its exports to the utmost while attempting to keep imports to a minimum. Japanese entrepreneurship also received an enormous boost from the cashing out of the samurai. While many of the former warriors found anything to do with commerce distasteful, some took to heart the government's injunction that starting economic enterprises was a patriotic duty. By the end of the century, Japan's industrial statistics were impressive by any standards: Coal production had increased to six times its 1860 base level, and iron, copper, and other mining industries expanded at a similar rate—but still could not keep pace with Japan's industrial needs. By the turn of the century Japan needed to import much of its raw material, a situation that has continued to this day.

Not surprisingly, families with long-standing connections to capital swiftly moved to unite their enterprises to gain market share. The Mitsui Company, for example, used its extensive brewing profits to fund a host of other enterprises, soon becoming one of Japan's largest industrial concerns. Similarly, the Mitsubishi Company expanded from coastal shipping to manufacturing—later creating military vehicles and aircraft during World War II as well as popular cars today. The encouragement of the government and the cooperation of social networks among elites in finance and industry led to the creation of a number of **cartels** called *zaibatsu*. By the end of the nineteenth century, the zaibatsu would control nearly all major Japanese industries.

The Transportation and Communications Revolutions   The rapid development of railroads and telegraphs was one of the most stunning transformations of the Meiji era. The Japanese pursued these devices with an enthusiasm scarcely paralleled anywhere else in the world at the time. By the mid-1870s Japan had in place a trunk railroad line along the main coastal road and several branches to major cities in the interior. Though Westerners found Japanese trains quaint—along with the custom of leaving one's clogs on the platform before boarding the cars—they were efficient and marked a trend for railroad building wherever the Japanese went. Similarly, telegraph—and, by the end of the century,

Cartel: A group of domestic or international businesses that form a group to control or monopolize an industry.

Visions of the New Railroads.
The marvels of the new systems of railroads and telegraphs springing up in Japan provided practitioners of *ukiyo-e* woodblock art a host of new subjects to depict in the 1870s and 1880s. Here is one of a number of views of new stations, in this case, Ueno on the Ueno–Nakasendo–Tokyo Railway, with small commuter trains arriving and departing.

telephone—lines were swiftly strung between the major cities and towns, followed by undersea cables to the Asian mainland and North America. By 1895, Japan was estimated to have over 2,000 miles of private and government railroads in operation and over 4,000 miles of telegraph wires in place (see Map 24.5).

The Meiji Constitution and Political Life   While the charter oath and constitution of 1868 were instituted with considerable success, a debate had already begun among the genro concerning the liberalization of representative government in Japan. In 1881 the emperor approved a plan whereby Ito Hirobumi (1841–1909)

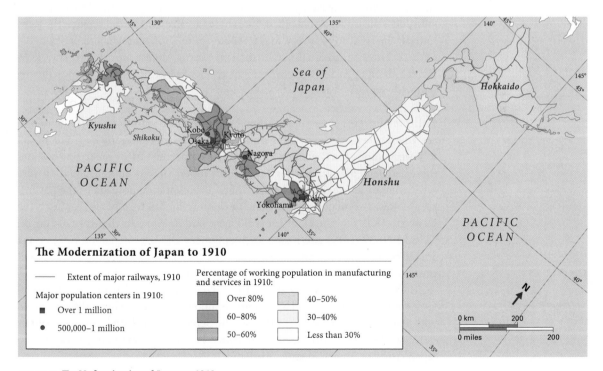

The Modernization of Japan to 1910

—— Extent of major railways, 1910

Major population centers in 1910:
■ Over 1 million
● 500,000–1 million

Percentage of working population in manufacturing and services in 1910:

Over 80%   40–50%
60–80%   30–40%
50–60%   Less than 30%

MAP 24.5 **The Modernization of Japan to 1910.**

and several senior colleagues would launch a study of the constitutional governments of the United States, Great Britain, France, Germany, and other countries, to see what aspects of them might be suitable for Japan's needs. The Meiji Constitution, as it came to be called, was promulgated in 1889 and remained in force until it was supplanted by the constitution composed during the Allied occupation of Japan after World War II.

While borrowing elements from the US and British models, Ito's constitution drew most heavily from that of Germany. Much of it was also aimed at preserving the traditions of Japan's Confucian society that Ito and the genro most valued. Chief among these was the concept of *kokutai*, the "national polity." In this view, Japan was unique among nations because of its unbroken line of emperors and the singular familial and spiritual relationship between the emperor and his people. Thus, the Meiji Constitution is presented, in Ito's words, as "the gift of a benevolent and charitable emperor to the people of his country." The sovereignty of the country was placed in the person of the emperor as the embodiment of kokutai; the emperor's Privy Council, the army and navy, and the ministers of state were answerable directly to him. There was also a bicameral parliamentary body called the Diet, with an upper House of Peers and a lower House of Representatives. Like the House of Lords in Great Britain, Japan's House of Peers consisted of members of the nobility; the representatives were elected by the people. The primary purpose of the Diet in this arrangement was to vote on financing, deliberate on the everyday items of governance, and provide advice and consent to the Privy Council, Ministry of State, and Imperial Court.

As for the people themselves, 15 articles spelled out "the rights and duties of subjects." Duties included liability for taxes and service in the military, while the rights enumerated are similar to those found in European and American constitutions: the right to hold office, guarantees against search and seizure, the right to trial, the right to property, and freedoms of religion, speech, and petition. All of these, however, are qualified by such phrases as "unless provided by law," leaving the door open for the government to invoke extraordinary powers during national emergencies.

Political Parties   As constitutional government began to be implemented in the 1890s, the factional debates among senior advisors naturally began to attract followers among the Diet members and their supporters. In the preceding decades there had been political parties, but their membership was limited, and they were seen by many as illegitimate because of their potential opposition to the government. Now, two major parties came to the fore by the turn of the century. The Kenseito [KEN-say-toe], or Liberal Party, had its roots in the work of Itagaki Taisuke (1837–1919) and his political opponent Okuma Shigenobu [OH-ku-ma SHIH-geh-no-bu]. The two merged their followers but later split into factions at the turn of the century. It later was reestablished as the Minseito.

The more powerful party during this time was the Seiyukai, or Constitutional Government Party, founded by Ito and his followers in 1900. Generally associated with the government and the zaibatsu, the Seiyukai dominated Japanese politics in the era before World War I; after World War II, its adherents coalesced into Japan's present Liberal Democratic Party.

Social Experiments   In addition to creating an industrial base and a constitutional government, Japan's rulers attempted to curb practices in Japan that were believed to offend foreign sensibilities as part of its program of "civilization and enlightenment." Bathhouses, for example, were now required to have separate entrances for men and women, and pleasure quarters were restricted in areas near foreign enclaves; meat eating was even encouraged in largely Buddhist Japan, resulting in the new dish *sukiyaki*. In the boldest experiment of all, the government mandated the use of Western dress for men and women, accompanied by a propaganda campaign depicting the advantages of this "modern" and "civilized" clothing. Criticism from a variety of quarters, however, including many Westerners, ultimately forced the government to relent and make the new dress optional.

In the same vein, traditional restrictions on women were altered. Though the home remained the primary domain for women, as it does even today, women were far more often seen in public. Concubines were now accorded the same rights as wives. Courtesans and prostitutes were no longer legally considered servants. Among elites, the fad of following all things Western established to some degree Victorian European standards of family decorum. More far-reaching, however, was the role of the new education system. Even before the Meiji Restoration, Japan had one of the highest levels of preindustrial literacy in the world—40 percent for males and 15 percent for females. With the introduction of compulsory public education, literacy would become nearly universal, and the upsurge in specialized women's education created entire new avenues of employment for women.

This same trend toward emancipation was evident among the rural population. The formal class barriers between peasants and samurai were eliminated, though informal deference to elites continued. In addition, some barriers between ordinary Japanese and outcast groups, such as the Eta, were also reduced. During the latter part of the nineteenth century, aided by better transportation, improved crops, maximum utilization of marginal lands, and the opening up of Hokkaido for development, Japan became the most intensely farmed nation in the world. Japan's already well-developed fishing industry contributed mightily by introducing commercial fish-based fertilizers that boosted yields enormously. The result was that although Japan's population increased to 40 million by 1890, it was a net exporter of food until the turn of the century.

"Enlightenment and Progress":
Science, Culture, and the Arts

As we saw in Chapter 21, while the Tokugawa sought seclusion, they were by no means cut off entirely from developments in other nations. Of particular importance in this regard was the requirement imposed on the Dutch merchants at Deshima to make their annual reports to the Shogun on the state of the world. By the time of Commodore Perry's visit the accumulated amount of "Dutch learning" was impressive. Much of it consisted of notes on scientific and technical developments.

Engaging "Western Science"   Nevertheless, at the time of their initial contact with the Western powers, the Tokugawa were stunned at the degree to which the accelerating technologies of the Industrial Revolution had armed their adversaries. During Perry's visits Japanese sketch artists frantically sought to capture the details of the ships' gun ports and cannon and the outward signs of their steam power. The Japanese were also immediately engaged with the notion of the railroad; just as quickly they sought to create oceangoing steamships. By 1860, they had built and manned steamers and insisted that their embassy to the United States travel aboard a ship the Japanese had built themselves.

The demand for industrial and military technology encouraged large numbers of Japanese to seek technical education. During the initial stages of the Meiji era, thousands of Japanese students studied in Europe and the United States, and the Japanese government and private concerns hired hundreds of foreign advisors to aid in science and technical training. By the 1880s a university system anchored by Tokyo Imperial University was offering courses in medicine, physics, chemistry, engineering, and geology, among other advanced disciplines. On the whole, however, the bulk of the nation's efforts went into the practical application of science to technology and agriculture in order to support the government's modernization efforts.

Culture and the Arts   As was the case a decade later in China, Japanese intellectuals eagerly absorbed copies of Western Enlightenment, philosophical, and social science works in translation. As was also true in China, journalism played a dominant role in disseminating information to the public. Here, Fukuzawa Yukichi, like Liang Qichao in China, held a central place both in fostering the growth of newspapers and in articulating the role of journalists in a modern society.

> "In editing the paper [*Jiji-shimpo*] I encouraged the reporters to write bravely and freely. I have no objection to any severe criticism or extreme statements, but I warned them that they must limit their statements to what they would be willing to say to the victim face to face."
>
> —Fukuzawa Yukichi

As with nearly all the arts in late nineteenth-century Japan, the novel was also heavily influenced by Western examples. In some respects, the culmination of this trend was *Kokoro*, by Natsume Soseki (1867–1916), published in 1914. Soseki utilizes the wrenching changes in Meiji Japan set against traditional and generational values to create the tension and ultimate tragic end of the central character in his work.

More traditional arts such as Noh and kabuki theater and *ukiyo-e* printing survived, but often in a somewhat altered state. Updated kabuki variations now featured contemporary themes and often had female actors playing female parts. In addition, European plays such as Ibsen's *A Doll's House* enjoyed considerable vogue. As for *ukiyo-e*, it remained the cheapest and most popular outlet for depictions of contemporary events until the development of newspaper photography. Especially telling in this regard are *ukiyo-e* artists' interpretations of the Sino–Japanese War.

Putting It All Together

Scholars of China and Japan have long debated the reasons for the apparent success of Japan and failure of China. One school of thought sees the fundamental reasons growing from the respective cultural outlooks of the two countries.

China, it is argued, assumed that outsiders would simply be won over to Confucian norms and modes of behavior, because this is what China's historical experience had been for the last 2,000 years. When it became apparent that defensive measures were necessary, it was still assumed that China's superior culture would win out. Japan, on the other hand, because of its long history of cultural borrowing and its much smaller size, assumed a more urgent defensive posture. In addition, the Japanese had the advantage of watching events unfold in China before the danger reached their own shores. This allowed them to act in a more united and pragmatic fashion when resisting the Western threat.

Some historians, however, disagree with this analysis. They argue instead that the cultural differences between China and Japan were secondary in the face of the foreign threat. According to this school of thought, the primary cause of the radically different outcomes for China and Japan was that China was victimized by foreign imperialism much earlier and much more thoroughly than Japan. Once Japanese modernization efforts were under way, the Japanese won for themselves a breathing spell with which to keep imperialism at bay and ultimately fought their way into the great power club themselves.

▶ **For additional resources, including maps, primary sources, visuals, and quizzes, please go to www.oup.com/us/vonsivers. Please see the Further Resources section at the back of the book for additional readings and suggested websites.**

Against the Grain
Reacting to Modernity

One of the enduring patterns of world history has been the complexity of acculturation to innovation from outside—particularly if it is perceived to be forced. As scientific and industrial society developed and expanded its control and influence into the old agrarian–urban empires in the nineteenth century, the clashes, as we have seen, were particularly fierce, and all the more so, since societies like those of China or Japan felt themselves to be culturally superior to the invaders.

Not surprisingly, given the categories of choices we have outlined in this chapter's Patterns Up Close feature—reform, reaction, or revolution—many people in a variety of places in different parts of the world chose what we might term a "culturally fundamentalist" approach. That is, faced with a growing threat that seems increasingly insurmountable by the more conventional approaches of reform or resistance, they chose to take radical action by harkening back to a time when the virtues that first made their societies great prevailed. By bringing such virtues back into play, they believed they could restore the country's greatness. In almost every case this involved considerable invented nostalgia and often a charismatic messiah figure. To cite just a few examples of this phenomenon, the Taipings and Boxers in China, the Tonghaks in Korea, the followers of the Mahdi in the Sudan, the Ghost Dancers of the Native Americans in the United States, and the Samurai Rebellion in Japan all held out a kind of mystical view that proper prayers, ritual, and confidence in the rightness of their cause would win the day. In some cases, they believed that their ritual purity and correctness, along with certain sacred gestures or garments, made them invulnerable to the enemy's weapons. In the end, however, all of these movements were ultimately crushed by the modern or modernizing forces arrayed against them. Yet the bootless courage of their stands is often celebrated today—ironically by the representatives of the very societies that they sought to turn back.

- **What factors make people turn to solutions during times of extreme stress that they wouldn't consider otherwise? Can you think of other instances in history where this phenomenon has taken place?**

- **Are there current movements you can think of that seem to fit this phenomenon? What stresses in their societies do you think are provoking such movements?**

Thinking Through Patterns

▶ **What was the impact of Western imperialism on the "regulated societies" of China and Japan?**

The impact of the intrusion of Great Britain, France, the United States, and later Germany and Russia forced both China and Japan into defensive postures. Both countries had sought to keep out what they considered subversive foreign influences after an earlier period of exposure to Western traders and missionaries. China had created a tightly controlled system of overseas trade based in Guangzhou (Canton); Japan allowed only the Dutch to trade with them. But the expansion of trade in both legitimate goods and opium and the need of the British for regularization of diplomatic practices pushed Britain and China into a cycle of war and "unequal treaties" under which China was at an increasing disadvantage. Japan, suddenly thrust into international commerce and diplomacy by the young United States, now sought to protect its borders without pushing the Western powers into seizing any of its territory.

China's long history of absorbing and acculturating outside invaders to Confucian norms encouraged its leaders to assume that the Westerners would be no different. Though many officials realized the qualitative difference between the industrializing Euro-American countries and invaders from the Chinese past, they were divided about what to do. Thus, attempts at reform were often undercut by political infighting at court and in the bureaucracy. The Taiping Rebellion also played a central role in further depleting China's strength and resources. As time went on, increasing Western control of China's ports and tariffs, absentee landlordism, and declining agricultural productivity also played a role.

▶ **Why did European empire building in Asia have such dramatically different effects on China and Japan?**

For Japan, after a decade of indecision about how to handle the foreign intrusion, a civil war ended in the dismantling of the shogunate and the unification of the country under Emperor Meiji. With remarkable unity born of a deep sense of urgency, Japan embarked upon a thoroughgoing reform program aimed at remaking the country along avowedly Western lines. The focus and consistency displayed by Meiji and his advisors avoided many of the problems China experienced, and Japan's late Tokugawa economics to some degree had predisposed the country toward a smoother transition into scientific–industrial society.

▶ **How have historians seen the nature of these outside forces and their influences in east Asia?**

Historians have long debated the relative weight that should be assigned to cultural and material reasons for the differing paths of China and Japan. China's long history as the region's cultural leader, some have argued, made it difficult for the empire to remake itself to face the Western challenge; Japan, on the other hand, has a long history of cultural borrowing and thus found it easier to borrow from the Euro-American world. Some historians have argued that China's earlier experience with imperialism hobbled the modernizing tendencies within the empire and kept it from responding; they argue that Japan had the advantage of being "opened" later and so could respond more effectively. Others have argued that Japan's tradition of military prowess played a role, and still others contend that China's more complete incorporation into the modern "world system" hampered its ability to respond more independently.

Chapter 25 1683–1908

Adaptation and Resistance

THE OTTOMAN AND RUSSIAN EMPIRES

Serfdom: Legal and cultural institution in which peasants are bound to the land.

RUSSIAN AND OTTOMAN EMPIRES, 1683–1908

October 13, 1824, saw a most unusual event in Russia. On this date, Aleksander Nikitenko, born into serfdom, received his freedom at the age of 20 from his lord, a fabulously wealthy landowning count. Even more remarkable is the subsequent course of Nikitenko's life and career. After earning a university degree, he went on to become a professor of literature at St. Petersburg University, a member of the distinguished Academy of Sciences, and a censor in the Ministry of Education.

Beginning in 1818 at the age of 14, the precocious Nikitenko kept a diary, which provides insights into the role of serfdom in the Russian Empire. He writes that "when the inevitable happened," the errant serfs were turned over to a lackey in charge of meting out punishment in the form of flogging with birch rods: "Woe to the unfortunates who fell into [his] hands! He was a master and enthusiast of flogging, especially of girls, and they were terrified by the mere sight of him." Nikitenko's curse, Russian serfdom, was scarcely different from plantation slavery in the Americas or from untouchability in the Indian caste system. Slavery was also the common lot of many in the neighboring Ottoman Empire, where, though limited to households, it was no less demeaning. The end of serfdom in Russia would not come until 1861 and that of slavery in the Ottoman Empire not until 1890.

ABOVE: Auction of Serfs (1910), a painting by Klavdiy Vasilievich Lebedev (1852–1916), shows a wealthy Russian family auctioning off its valuables—and its serfs.

Serfdom and slavery were dramatic examples of the kinds of practices that the new Enlightenment constitutionalism, in theory at least, stood firmly against. As such, they were among the first of many challenges the world outside western Europe and North America faced from the West in the nineteenth century. Russia was an empire that had inherited Byzantine Christian civilization but had not adopted the New Sciences and their offspring, the twin revolutions of the Enlightenment and Industrial Revolution. For its part, the Ottoman Empire was heir to both Islamic and Byzantine traditions but also had not participated in the transition to the New Sciences, Enlightenment, and industrialization. Even though Enlightenment thought had produced and elaborated the political theories of the social contract and popular sovereignty, which were realized in the American, French, and Haitian Revolutions, shortly before the onset of the Industrial Revolution in Great Britain, it would be the campaigns of Napoleon in the early nineteenth century that sowed these ideas throughout Europe.

They also would cast these seeds on the initially unpromising soil of the Russian and Ottoman Empires. Napoleon's invasions of Ottoman Egypt in 1798 and Russia in 1812 drove home to their rulers that his new armies of mass conscripts, equipped with flintlock muskets and light, mobile artillery and drilled to fight in flexible formations, were superior to their own military forces. It became essential for the Ottomans and Russians, if they were to keep their independence, to update their armies and training and to respond somehow to the constitutional nationalism arising from the French Revolution and carried by Napoleon's armies, which now attracted rising numbers of adherents among their subjects.

At the same time, the two empires became mortal enemies: An expanding eastern (Orthodox) Christian Russia declared its goal to be conquest of the former eastern Christian capital Constantinople (Istanbul) and to drive a shrinking Ottoman Empire from Europe back into "Asia" (Asia Minor, or Anatolia). Since both empires were members of the Concert of Europe, their conflict involved the other European powers as well. These powers found themselves increasingly drawn into confrontation, culminating in the Crimean War of 1853–1856, that was only partially European and increasingly involved Russia and the Ottomans in Asia. For the monarchs, politicians, and diplomats focused after 1815 on the balance of power in western and central Europe, such a power struggle between the Russians and Ottomans held little interest: For them, this contest was "Oriental" and therefore alien.

It is important that we keep this partially non-Western identity of the Russian and Ottoman Empires in mind for this chapter: As forcefully as Russia asserted itself in the European Concert in the early years after 1815 and again at the end of the nineteenth century, it was in reality—despite its Christian character—not any more or less "European" than the increasingly harried Muslim Ottoman Empire. Indeed, as we will see, both empires had far more in common with each other, and to some degree with the empire of the Qing in China, than they did with the evolving nation-states of western Europe. Furthermore, their reactions to the challenges posed by the new nation-states paralleled each other to a degree not often appreciated by students and scholars studying them outside of a world context. Therefore, we consider them together here as their own case studies in the overall patterns of constitutionalism, nation-state formation, and the challenge of modernity.

Seeing Patterns

▶ Which new models did the Ottomans adopt during the nineteenth century to adapt themselves to the Western challenge?

▶ How did the agrarian Ottoman and Russian Empires, both with large landholding ruling classes, respond to the western European industrial challenge during the 1800s?

▶ Why did large, well-established empires like the Russian and the Ottoman Empires struggle with the forces of modernity, while a small, secluded island nation like Japan seemed to adapt so quickly and successfully?

Chapter Outline

• Decentralization and Reforms in the Ottoman Empire

• Westernization, Reforms, and Industrialization in Russia

• Putting It All Together

Decentralization and Reforms in the Ottoman Empire

Prior to the Russian–Ottoman rivalry in the 1800s, the traditional enemies of the Ottomans were the Austrian Habsburgs. This enmity had reached its climax in the second half of the 1600s. The Habsburgs ultimately won but in the course of the 1700s were increasingly sidelined by the rise of Russia as a new, Orthodox Christian empire, whose rulers, the tsars, saw themselves as representatives of the "third Rome"—that is, Moscow as the successor of Rome and Constantinople. After consolidating itself on the fertile northeast European plains, Russia expanded eastward and southward, clashing with the Muslim Ottomans, conquerors of Constantinople. Because the Russians adapted themselves earlier than the Ottomans to new western European military tactics, the Ottomans found it increasingly difficult to defend themselves in the later 1700s. They sought to improve their defenses through military and constitutional–nationalist reforms in the mid-1800s but were only partly successful. Russia became the patron of nationalist movements among the Slavic populations in the European provinces of the Ottoman Empire. Although they strengthened themselves through reforms, the Ottomans were no match for the combined Russian–southern Slavic aggression. At the end of the Second Balkan War of 1913, they had lost nearly the entire European part of their empire to ethnic–nationalist liberation movements and were barely able to hang on to Istanbul (see Map 25.1).

Ottoman Imperialism in the 1600s and 1700s

In the period from 1500 to 1700 the Ottoman Empire was the dominant political power in the Middle East and North Africa, flanked by the two lesser realms of Persia in the east and Morocco in the west. At that time, the main enemy of the Ottomans was not yet Russia but the Habsburg Empire in Spain, Germany, and Austria. The two were fighting each other on dual fronts, the Balkans in the east and North Africa in the western Mediterranean, each gaining and losing in the process and eventually establishing a more or less stable disengagement. It was during this disengagement period that Russia began its expansion southward at the increasing expense of the Ottomans.

Demographic Considerations   As with the other agrarian–urban regions of Asia and Europe, the Middle East had experienced a sustained recovery of population levels after the Black Death of the mid-1400s. This recovery came to an end around 1600, with 25 million inhabitants, though with slow increases reaching 27 million by 1700 and about 30 million by 1800. The population figures were thus smaller than those of the Habsburg countries, with 37 million in 1700 and 42 million in 1800. If one takes into consideration, however, that the Spanish Habsburg line died out in Spain in 1700 and the Austrian Habsburgs governed only indirectly in Germany, the resulting figure for the smaller territory in 1800 is a comparable 25 million. Russia, for its part, had population figures roughly comparable to those of the Ottoman Empire. As the Ottomans approached the era of the challenge of modernity, they formed part of a relatively sparsely populated eastern Europe and Middle East.

From Conquests to Retreats   At the end of the 1500s, after a long period of military showdowns, the Ottomans and Habsburgs were beset by problems of military overextension. Therefore, in 1606 they concluded a peace to gain time for recovery, during which the Ottomans recognized the Habsburgs for the first time as a de facto Christian power on the border of the Ottoman province of Hungary. The peace lasted until the end of the 1600s, when both were sufficiently recovered to renew their competition. The Ottoman recovery was based on the recruitment of the Janissary infantry from exclusively rural Christian boys and young, mostly urban Muslims. By shifting from the increasingly less important cavalry to their firearm-equipped infantry and artillery, the Ottoman army regained its edge.

In 1683 the Ottomans renewed their competition with the Habsburgs and marched with a giant force to their northwestern border. For a second time in their history, they laid siege to Vienna (the first siege was in 1529), the capital of the Austrian Habsburgs. But even though sappers and siege cannons succeeded in breaching the walls in several places, a Polish relief army allied with the Habsburgs arrived just in time to drive the besiegers, who had neglected to fortify their camp, into a retreat. The Habsburgs followed up on this retreat by seizing Hungary, Transylvania, and northern Serbia, thus making a third siege of Vienna impossible. In the peace of 1699, the Ottomans and Habsburgs finally agreed to recognize each other fully in the territories they possessed.

Renewed Reforms   During the war years of the later 1600s, the Janissary force had swollen to some 70,000 soldiers. In the end, however, only about 10,000 were on active duty. Since they were all on the payroll, and given renewed fiscal shortfalls, the money was often debased or in arrears, forcing them to earn a living as craftspeople. In short, the Janissary force was in the process of becoming a collection of crafts guilds on a kind of government welfare.

New reforms were clearly necessary. In the early 1700s the sultan's government cut the Janissary rolls by half and enlisted Anatolian farmers to supplement the active Janissaries. In order to increase revenues with which to pay the Janissaries, the reformers introduced the new institution of the lifetime tax farm, or **life lease**, for agricultural rents from village farmers. As in France, which developed a similar tax-farm regime at the time, the idea was to diminish the temptation—endemic among the annual tax farmers—to squeeze farmers dry so that they would flee from the countryside to the cities. Wealthy and high-ranking courtiers, officers, administrators, and Islamic clerics in Istanbul bought these life leases. Thus, here in the early 1700s was the beginning of a development parallel to similar developments in France and England, with efforts to organize a kind of capital market.

Life lease: Lifelong tax farm, awarded to a wealthy member of the ruling class, in return for advances to the central imperial treasury on the taxes to be collected from village farmers.

1683	1768–1774	1832
Second Ottoman siege of Vienna	First Ottoman–Russian war	Greece secures independence from Ottomans

	1762–1796	1798–1801	1839–1876
	Catherine II of Russia	Napoleon's occupation of Egypt	Tanzimat reforms in Ottoman Empire

1853–1856	1878–1885	1908
Crimean War of Great Britain, France, and Ottoman Empire against Russia	Independence of Serbia, Montenegro, Romania, and Bulgaria	"Young Turks" rise to power in Ottoman Empire

	1861	1904–1905
	Emancipation of serfs in Russian Empire	Russo–Japanese War, followed by abortive Russian revolution

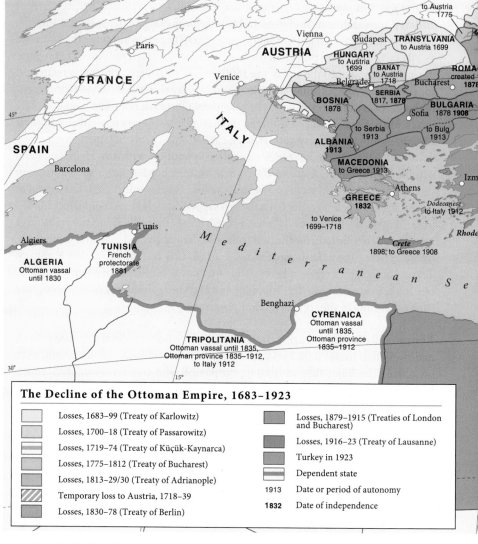

The Decline of the Ottoman Empire, 1683–1923

Losses, 1683–99 (Treaty of Karlowitz)	Losses, 1879–1915 (Treaties of London and Bucharest)
Losses, 1700–18 (Treaty of Passarowitz)	Losses, 1916–23 (Treaty of Lausanne)
Losses, 1719–74 (Treaty of Küçük-Kaynarca)	Turkey in 1923
Losses, 1775–1812 (Treaty of Bucharest)	Dependent state
Losses, 1813–29/30 (Treaty of Adrianople)	1913 Date or period of autonomy
Temporary loss to Austria, 1718–39	1832 Date of independence
Losses, 1830–78 (Treaty of Berlin)	

MAP 25.1 **The Decline of the Ottoman Empire, 1683–1923.**

As a result of the reforms, in 1720, for the first time in a century and a half, the central budget was balanced again.

Decentralization An accelerating transformation of cavalry-held lands into tax farms started a pattern of political decentralization in the Ottoman Empire. Agents responsible for the collection of taxes for their superiors succeeded in withholding increasing amounts from the treasury in Istanbul. By the mid-1700s, these agents were in positions of considerable provincial power as "notables" in the Balkans or "valley lords" in western Anatolia. Starved for funds, the sultan and central administration were no longer able to support a large standing army of infantry and cavalry in the capital.

In 1768–1774 the notables and valley lords played a crucial role not only in financing a major war against Russia but also in recruiting troops—untrained and underarmed peasants—since the numbers of government forces in fighting order had shrunk to minimal levels. The war was the first in which the Russian tsars exploited Ottoman decentralization for a systematic expansion southward. When the sultan lost the war, he was at the mercy of these notables and lords in the provinces.

The Western Challenge and Ottoman Responses

Soon after this Ottoman–Russian war, the Ottoman Empire began to face the challenge of Western modernity. As with China and Japan, the increasing military, political, and economic strength of the West allowed it to force the traditional Asian empires to adapt to its challenges. This adaptation was extremely difficult and entailed severe territorial losses for the Ottoman Empire. But after initial humiliations, the ruling class was able to develop a pattern of responses to the Western challenge, by reducing the power of the provincial magnates, modernizing the army, introducing constitutional reforms, and eventually transforming its manufacturing sector.

External and Internal Blows   During the period 1774–1808, the Ottoman central government suffered a series of humiliations which were comparable in their destabilizing effects to those in the later Opium Wars and the Taiping and Boxer Rebellions in China. Russia gained the north coast of the Black Sea and Georgia in the Caucasus. Napoleon invaded Egypt and destroyed the local regime of Ottoman military vassals in 1798. But a British fleet sent after him succeeded in destroying his navy, and a subsequent land campaign forced him to return to France in 1801. As he was victimizing the Ottoman Empire, Napoleon apparently wanted to demonstrate the ineffectiveness of Great Britain's European continental blockade and teach it a lesson about the vulnerability of its control of India. Napoleon's sudden imperialist venture produced a deep shock in the Middle East: For the first time a Western ruler had penetrated deep into the Ottoman Empire, cutting it effectively in half.

Internally, the lessening of central control in the second half of the 1700s left the provinces virtually independent. Most notables and lords were satisfied with local autonomy, but a few became warlords, engaging in campaigns to become regional leaders. In other cases, especially in Egypt, Syria, and Iraq, *Mamluks*— that is, military slaves from the northern Caucasus whom Ottoman governors had previously employed as auxiliaries in the military—seized power. In eastern Arabia, a local Sunni cleric, Muhammad ibn Abd al-Wahhab [wah-HAHB], exploited Ottoman decentralization to ally himself with the head of a powerful family in command of a number of oases, Ibn Saud [sa-OOD], to establish an autonomous polity in the desert, which today is the most powerful oil state in the world—Saudi Arabia. None of these ambitious leaders, however, renounced allegiance to the sultan, who at least remained a figurehead.

To reclaim power, the sultan and his viziers once more sought for ways to reform the empire. In 1792, they proclaimed a "new order," defined by a reorganization of the army with the creation of a new, separate artillery and flintlock musket corps of some 22,000 soldiers alongside the Janissaries. The ad hoc financing of the new order, however, came to haunt the reformers. During a severe fiscal crisis in 1807, auxiliary Janissaries, refusing to wear new uniforms, assassinated a new-order officer. Inept handling of this incident resulted in a full-scale revolt of Janissaries as well as religious scholars and students, costing the sultan his life and ushering in the dissolution of the new troops. In a counter-revolt, thanks to the timely arrival from northern Bulgaria of a Ukrainian-born notable with his private army, a new sultan came to power in 1808. As a price for his accession, the sultan had to agree to power sharing with the provincial lords.

Renewed Difficulties   After a dozen years of careful maneuvering, during which the sultan reconstituted the core of another new army and neutralized many notables and valley lords, he was able to crush the Janissaries in a bloody massacre (1826).

But the new corps was in no shape yet to provide the backbone for a sustained recentralization of the empire. New internal enemies arose, in the form of Greek ethnic nationalists, whom the Ottomans would have defeated had it not been for the military intervention of the European powers. As a result, Greece became independent in a war of liberation (1821–1832). It was the first country, prior to Italy and Germany, in which ethnic nationalism was an element in its foundation.

Russia, providing support for its fellow Orthodox Christian Greeks, acquired new territories from the Ottomans around the Black Sea. Several Balkan provinces achieved administrative autonomy. Algiers in North Africa was lost in 1830, falling to an invading French force. Worst of all, in 1831, the new Ottoman vassal in Egypt, the Albanian-born officer Muhammad Ali (r. 1805–1848), seeking greater influence within the empire, rose in rebellion. After occupying Syria (1831–1840), he would have conquered Istanbul had he not been stopped by Russian, British, and French intervention. Without the diplomacy of Great Britain, which carefully sought to balance the European powers after the end of the Napoleonic empire, the Ottoman Empire would not have survived the 1830s.

Muhammad Ali. Muhammad Ali transformed Egypt during the first half of the nineteenth century more thoroughly than the Ottoman overlord sultan could in his far-flung empire. He astutely realized that long-staple cotton, bred first in Egypt, could make Egypt a wealthy state in the beginning industrial transformation of the world.

Life, Honor, and Property   The cumulative effect of these setbacks was a realization among Ottoman administrators that only a serious effort at recentralization would save the empire. In 1839, with a change of sultans, the government issued the Rose Garden Edict, the first of three reform edicts, plus more specific additional ones in between, which are collectively known as **Tanzimat** ("Reorganizations"). In the Rose Garden Edict, the government bound itself to three basic principles: the guarantee of life, honor, and property of all subjects regardless of religion; the replacement of tax farms and life leases with an equitable tax system; and the introduction of a military conscription system, all in accordance with the Sharia, the compendium of Islamic morality and law. The edict carefully avoided a definition of the position of the Christians and Jews in the empire before the law, offering them the rights of life, honor, and property while maintaining their inequality vis-à-vis the Muslims proclaimed in Islamic law.

Tanzimat: Ottoman reforms inspired by constitutional nationalism in Europe, including the adoption of basic rights, a legal reform, and a land code.

The edict addressed the two fundamental problems of the empire (that is, taxes and the military), carefully emphasizing the Islamic justification. It also enumerated basic human rights, inspired by the American Declaration of Independence and the French Rights of Man. Here, we can see a first adaptation of the Ottoman Empire to the Western challenge: The Ottoman Empire adapted, at least in an initial and partial way, to constitutional nationalism, the outgrowth of Enlightenment thought.

Further Reforms   As these reforms were being implemented, a new European political initiative challenged the Ottoman Empire. The aggressively imperialistic Napoleon III (president 1848–1852, emperor 1852–1870), self-declared emperor of France, challenged the Russian tsar's claim to be the protector of the Christian holy places in Palestine, a claim which the Ottoman sultan had acceded to after his defeat in 1774. As we saw in Chapter 24, the French joined the British during the Second Opium War for much the same reason: protection of Catholics and French missionaries in China. While the French and Russian diplomats each sought to influence a vacillating sultan, the political situation turned increasingly tense. Through careful maneuvering, Ottoman diplomats were able to strengthen themselves in a coalition with Great Britain and France. In the Crimean War of 1853–1856 this coalition was victorious against an isolated Russia. It forced Russia in the subsequent peace to recognize the Ottoman Empire's right to full integrity, provided the latter would continue the reforms announced in 1839.

Accordingly, the sultan promulgated the "Fortunate Edict" of 1856, in which he clarified the question of equality left open in the earlier edict: Regardless of religion, all subjects had the right to education, employment, and administration of justice. A number of subsequent measures spelled out this right and the earlier edicts in greater detail. To begin with, the reformers reorganized the judiciary by establishing law courts for the application of newly introduced commercial, maritime, and criminal legal codes, based on European models. A further reform measure was the introduction of a system of secular schools, initially for males, from age 10 through high school. But a lack of funds delayed the building of this system, which at the end of the 1800s still lagged far behind the traditional religious primary schools and colleges as well as the more rapidly expanding Christian, Jewish, and foreign missionary schools.

A measure that worked out quite differently from what was intended was the Land Code of 1858. The code reaffirmed the sultan as the owner of all land unless subjects or religious foundations possessed title to specific parcels of private property. But it also confirmed all users of the sultan's land—that is, farmers who produced harvests on family plots as well as landowners collecting rents from the farmers of entire villages. Theoretically, the code subjected all users, family farmers as well as landowners, to taxation. But in practice the central administration had no money to appoint tax collectors (or even establish a land registry prior to 1908). It could not do without tax farmers, who still collected what they could get and transmitted to the government as little as they were able to get away with.

> "The land of an inhabited village cannot be given to one person independently in order to make a [family plot]."
>
> —The Ottoman Land Code

Highly uneven forms of landownership thus developed. Overall, tax yields remained as low as ever, improving only toward the end of the nineteenth century, long after the introduction of the Tanzimat. The much-needed land reform remained incomplete.

Constitution and War   Seen in the context of the centralization reforms in previous centuries, the Tanzimat decrees of 1839 and 1856 were little more than enactments of traditional policies. In the context of nineteenth-century constitutional nationalism, however, they appeared like autocratic dictates from above, lacking popular approval. In the 1860s, younger Tanzimat bureaucrats and journalists working for the first Ottoman newspapers, meeting in loose circles in Istanbul and Paris under the name of "Young Ottomans," became advocates for the introduction of a constitution as the crowning element of the Tanzimat, to end the autocracy of the sultan.

The idea of a constitution became reality in the midst of a deep crisis in which the empire found itself embroiled from 1873 to 1878. The crisis began when the Ottoman government defaulted on its foreign loans. In order to service the renegotiated loans, it had to increase taxes. This increase triggered ethnic–nationalist uprisings in Herzegovina, Bosnia, and Bulgaria in the Balkans in 1875 and 1876. The heavy-handed repression of these uprisings resulted in a political crisis, with a palace coup d'état by the Young Ottomans, during which a new sultan, Abdülhamit II (r. 1876–1909), ascended the throne and a constitution was adopted. Finally, in this sequence of events, the Russians exploited the perceived political weakness of the new constitutional Ottoman regime for a new Russo–Ottoman war in support of the Balkan nationalist uprisings.

Ottoman Parliament. The constitutional reforms (Tanzimat) of the Ottoman Empire culminated in elections for a parliament and two sessions, uniting deputies from a multiplicity of ethnic backgrounds (1876–1878). It met during the Russian–Ottoman War of 1877–1878, which the Ottomans lost. The newly installed Sultan Abdülhamit used the war as an excuse for ending constitutional rule and governing by decree.

Amid a rapid advance of Russian troops against a crumbling Ottoman army, the Ottomans held elections for the constitutionally decreed parliament between December 1876 and January 1877. Provincial and county councils elected 130 deputies to meet for two sessions in Istanbul. With the invading Russian forces practically at the gates of Istanbul in February 1878, the deputies engaged in a spirited criticism of the government. Irritated, the sultan dismissed the parliament and ruled by decree.

A few months later, at the Congress of Berlin, the sultan had to accept the loss of two-thirds of the empire's European provinces. Montenegro, Serbia, Romania, and (after a delay of 7 years) Bulgaria gained their independence. Bosnia-Herzegovina and Cyprus, although still Ottoman, received an Austrian administration and a British administration, respectively. Sultan Abdülhamit never reconvened the parliament, and the empire reverted back to autocratic rule.

Autocracy   Sultan Abdülhamit surrounded himself with capable second-generation Tanzimat bureaucrats who did not have the constitutionalist leanings of the Young Ottomans. He had very little financial leeway, since the Public Debt Administration, imposed by the European powers in 1881, collected about one-third of the empire's income to pay for its accumulated foreign debt. Furthermore, the European price depression in the second half of the nineteenth century (1873–1896) was not favorable to foreign investments in the empire. Nevertheless, a few short-distance railroads connecting the fertile Anatolian valleys and their agricultural produce with Mediterranean ports were built thanks to French capital. A postal service and telegraph system connected all provinces, and steamship lines connected the ports. Once the depression was over, foreign investors enabled the government to build long-distance railroads across Anatolia. By the early 1900s, a basic communication infrastructure was in place in the Ottoman Empire.

Given his fiscal limits, the sultan was all the more active as a propagandist, burnishing his credentials as the pan-Islamic caliph of Muslims in Eurasia, from

Austrian Bosnia and Russian Asia to British India. He astutely sensed that the Balkan events of 1875/1876 and subsequent Congress of Berlin had been a watershed in European politics. The Concert of Europe, with its Britain-supported concept of a balance of power, was no more. It was being replaced by the beginning of an imperial rivalry between Germany and Great Britain. France, Austria-Hungary, and Russia played their own subsidiary imperial roles. Since France and Great Britain, furthermore, carried out their imperialism against the Ottoman Empire, with the conquests of Tunisia in 1881 and Egypt in 1882, respectively, Abdülhamit was particularly affected. His pan-Islamism was therefore a carefully executed effort to instill the fear of jihad in European politicians and their publics.

Although most of the Ottoman Balkan provinces had become independent nations by 1878, three ethnic–nationalist movements were still left inside the empire. Abdülhamit met them with an iron fist. The first movement consisted of Serb, Bulgarian, Vlah, and Greek nationalists agitating in Macedonia during 1893–1895. Without outside support, none of these feuding groups could impose itself on the province, and Ottoman troops were therefore able to repress them.

The next were the Armenians, who formed sizeable minorities in the six eastern provinces of Anatolia. Most Armenian farmers and craftspeople in these provinces were politically quiet but urban-based and secularized Armenian ethnic nationalists organized terrorist incidents. In reaction, the sultan armed Kurdish tribal units, which massacred thousands of Anatolian Armenian villagers from 1894 to 1896. Finally, the Ottomans met a revolt in Crete in 1897, in favor of union with Greece, with an invasion and defeat of Greece itself, which had to pay an indemnity. Europe, busy with its imperialist competition in Africa and Asia, had no time to help the remaining ethnic–nationalist movements of the Macedonians and Armenians in the Ottoman Empire.

In the later years of his rule, Abdülhamit increasingly failed to stem dissatisfaction with the lack of political freedom among the graduates of the elite administrative and military academies. As so often prior to revolts or revolutions, improved economic conditions—as they materialized after the end of the worldwide recession of 1893—stoked political ambitions to create a condition social scientists sometimes call a "revolution of rising expectations." In a pattern similar to that unfolding in Qing China at the same time, oppositional circles among Ottoman intellectuals abroad merged with secret junior officer groups in Macedonia and Thrace in 1907. Barely one step ahead of the sultan's secret service, the officers launched a coup d'état in 1908, which urban Ottomans generally received with great relief. The officers forced the sultan to reinstate the constitution of 1878 and, after elections, accept a new parliament.

Decline of the Ottomans   Emboldened by their success, leaders of the coup formed the Committee of Union and Progress (CUP), commonly referred to as the "Young Turks," and in 1909 they forcibly deposed Abdülhamit. The CUP then embarked on a policy of self-strengthening and modernization in order to create a new, Turkish national identity for the Ottoman Empire.

A series of unanticipated reactions to what was perceived as a reassertion of Ottoman power in the Balkans produced a sequence of cascading events that threatened to undermine the CUP and to bring down the empire. Austria-Hungary and Bulgaria formally annexed Bosnia-Herzegovina and northern Rumelia, respectively, in 1908. Albania revolted in 1910 and Italy invaded Tripolitania in 1911. In the following year Serbia, Montenegro, Bulgaria, and Greece collaborated in the First Balkan War, forcing Ottoman forces to retreat from the strategically important city of Erdine and to move back toward Istanbul. Fortunately for the CUP, the four victorious Balkan states were unable to agree on the division of the spoils. The Ottomans exploited the disagreements and retook Edirne, succeeding in a new peace settlement to push the imperial border westward into Thrace. Nevertheless, the overall losses were horrendous; the Ottoman Empire had now been driven out of Europe, ending more than half a millennium of rule in the Balkans.

Economic Development   While the empire was disintegrating politically, the economic situation improved. The main factor was the end of the depression of 1873–1896 and a renewed interest among European investors in creating industrial enterprises in the agrarian but export-oriented independent and colonial countries of the Middle East, Asia, and South America. When Abdülhamit II was at the peak of his power in the 1890s and early 1900s, investors perceived the Ottoman Empire as sufficiently stable for the creation of industrial enterprises.

The Ottoman Empire in the 1800s can be described as a state in which the traditional crafts-based textile industry initially suffered under the invasion of cheap industrially produced English cottons in the period 1820–1850. But a recovery took place in the second half of the 1800s, both in the crafts sector and in a newly mechanized small factory sector of textile manufacturing, producing cottons, woolens, silks, and rugs. This recovery was driven largely by domestic demand and investments, because the European price depression of 1873–1896 was not conducive to much inflow of foreign capital. Operating with low wages and even more low-paid female labor, domestic small-scale manufacturing was able to hold foreign factory-produced goods at bay.

Throughout the 1800s, the empire was also an exporter of agricultural commodities. But the recovery of domestic textile production demonstrates that the Ottomans did not succumb completely to the British free market system. When foreign investments resumed in the 1890s and early 1900s, there was a base on which industrialization could build, similar to conditions in the Netherlands, France, and Latin America when they industrialized.

Iran's Effort to Cope with the Western Challenge

Iran (also called Persia, in recognition of its long heritage) had risen in the 1500s as the Shiite alternative to the Sunni Ottomans. The two dynasties of kings (*shahs*) who ruled Iran, the Safavids (1501–1722) and Qajars (1795–1925), nurtured a hierarchy of Shiite clerics who formed an autonomous religious institution in their state. While the Ottoman sultans always kept their leading Sunni religious leaders under firm control, the Iranian rulers had to respect a delicate balance of power with their Shiite leaders. Therefore, when Iran in the 1800s faced the Western challenges, reformers had to establish an alliance with the Shiite clerics to bring about constitutional reforms.

Safavid and Qajar Kings   The Safavid Empire was a less powerful state than that of the Ottomans. It comprised Shiite Iran, the Caucasus, Sunni Afghanistan,

Patterns Up Close | Sunni and Shiite Islam

Like all revealed religions, Islam followed the pattern of splitting into multiple denominations. Revelation is centered on God, whose covenant with humans includes, among several theological teachings, the idea of providence. God's providence is contained in his promise of salvation in the future, on the Day of Judgment, both for the believers and for the world as a whole. How quickly and under whom this providential future prior to the Judgment unfolds, however, was a major source of conflict. Some of the fiercest theological debates raged around the providential future of Islam and have led to the foundation of the two major branches of Islam, Sunnism and Shiism.

During the formative period of Islam in the 800s and 900s, Muslims were deeply divided over the question of providential leadership. Was the leader of the Muslim community until the Day of Judgment a caliph (or representative) of the Prophet Muhammad and descended from the Quraysh, the dominant lineage of Mecca? Sunnis answered this question in the affirmative and regarded the caliphate as an institution guaranteeing the future of Islam until the Judgment in the distant future.

Husayn, Comforting His Dying Son Ali Akbar. In the early stage of the battle of Karbala, the Umayyad soldiers killed Ali Akbar, before Husayn himself was martyred. Processions and performances in remembrance of Karbala during the month of Muharram passed frequently by Shiite shrines which were embellished by local painters with frescoes showing imagined scenes of Karbala. This image, painted in 1905, is from the Imamzadeh Shah Zayd shrine in Isfahan, Iran.

Shiites denied this answer and saw the future of Islam in a community led by the Imam (or leader), who was a descendant of Fatima and Ali, the daughter and cousin of Muhammad, respectively. Until 874, the eldest son in each generation was entitled to lead the Muslims, at which time the last Imam was believed to have entered "occultation"—that is, a state of concealment from where he would return as the Mahdi ("rightly guided leader") at the end of time, just before God's Judgment. In contrast to Sunni Islam, the Shiite Imam was believed to be endowed with divine inspiration, a special kind of inner knowledge received from God and shared with Muhammad but no other human. This inspiration made the Imams sinless and infallible, enabling them to pronounce authoritative interpretations of the Quran and Islamic Tradition. No Sunni caliph ever claimed inspiration, sinlessness, or infallibility.

Just before 900, a conflict broke out among the Shiites over the imminence of the Imam's return. A minority, the Ismailis, believed that the seventh Imam (in the line of descent from Fatima and Ali) would emerge from hiding already in the early 900s. Their returned Imam and Mahdi founded the Ismaili, or Fatimid, Empire in Tunisia, Egypt, and Syria. The majority, the Twelver Shiites, adhered to the belief that it would be the twelfth Imam who would return from occultation in the distant future. They were the founders of the Buyid dynasty of emirs in Iran and Iraq (934–1055) and, much later, of the Safavid dynasty in Iran (1501–1722). Both dynasties sponsored large establishments of jurists and religious scholars who created a body of traditions and legal interpretations which made Twelver Shiism comparable to legalism in Sunni Islam.

The particular legal school that came to dominate in Twelver Shiism was Usulism. It emerged in the second half of the 1700s and is still dominant in contemporary Iran. Its central characteristic is its emphasis on the special status of a small number of senior legal scholars (ayatollahs ["signs of God"], today about half a dozen in number) who are distinguished by their knowledge of the Quran and Islamic tradition, power of reason, and inspiration. This combination of special qualifications enables them to collectively interpret theology and law in an authoritative manner, binding for everyone, even in the absence of the Hidden Imam. Among Sunnis, anyone can acquire learning and practice interpretation, although traditionally theological schools also awarded, and still award, diplomas.

In a further interpretation, Ayatollah Ruhollah Khomeini (1902–1989), leader of the Islamic Revolution of Iran in 1979, expanded the religious guardianship of the jurist—that is, of all Shiite clerics with himself at the head—to include that of political rulership. Accordingly, Iran is a partially elective Islamic theocracy, governed by certified pious Shiites and the Shiite hierarchy of clerics, from mosque preachers and middle-ranking jurists ("proofs of Islam" or *hojjatalislams*) to ayatollahs. Sunnis do not have such a hierarchy and today not even a corporate clerical establishment.

In the history of Islamic civilization, Shiites were always a minority, today about 10–20 percent among the totality of Muslims. At times, therefore, they suffered persecution from the Sunnis. In order to survive, Shiites developed the theological concept of dissimulation (*taqiyya*), which allows Shiites to pretend that they are Sunnis. Even in places where they could live under their own authorities, however, they developed customs which celebrate their minority status, making Shiism a religion of sufferance. In annual processions in the month of Muharram Shiites reenact the martyrdom of two of Imam Ali's sons, Husayn and Abbas, who perished in 680 at Karbala, Iraq, with 71 followers in a desperate uprising against the Sunni caliph. Participants in these processions often flagellate themselves in their fervor for suffering. Today, the two mausoleums for Husayn and Abbas are important pilgrimage sites for Shiites, together with those of the other nine Imams. Nearby Najaf, the burial place of Imam Ali, is also the site of one of the leading Shiite seminaries for the training of Shiite clerics.

Although overall they constitute a minority, today Shiites are a majority in Iran and pluralities in Iraq and Lebanon, making them important political actors in the Middle East. Their importance has led to restlessness among Shiite minorities in Bahrain and eastern Saudi Arabia as well as major clashes between Sunnis and Shiites in Pakistan and Yemen (where the Shiites base themselves on the Fifth Imam). Thus, in present times relations between Sunnis and Shiites are shifting from the relative mutual tolerance of the 1800s and 1900s to increasing tension.

Questions

- Which other revealed religions split into denominations, and over which issues?

- Which questions do rulers face when they declare themselves the returned Imam and Mahdi, as in the case of the founders of the Fatimid Empire in the early tenth century CE and the Safavid Empire in 1501?

Isfahan, Naqsh-i Jahan Square. At its southeastern end is the majestic Shah (today Imam) Mosque (1611–1629), a major example of the Iranian and Central Asian open courtyard mosque style.

and parts of Sunni central Asia. The Safavid kings, whose lands were limited in most provinces to oasis agriculture, were not wealthy enough to recruit a large firearm infantry to match the Janissaries. As a result, for most of the time the Ottomans were able to keep the Safavid rivalry at a manageable level, especially from the mid-1600s onward.

At this time, the Safavids ruled Iran from their newly founded capital of Isfahan in the center of the country, which they embellished with palaces and mosques. Safavid Iran was a major exporter of silk yarn and clothes, second in quality only to Chinese wares, and thus supplemented its limited agrarian revenues with an international trade in silk.

The Safavids were vulnerable not only to the military challenges of their Ottoman neighbors to the west but also to those of tribal federations in the Sunni provinces to the east. In Afghanistan, one of the two major Pashtu tribal federations revolted repeatedly against the efforts of the Safavids to convert them to Shiite Islam. Eventually, in 1722, this federation succeeded in conquering Iran and ending Safavid rule, at a time of advanced decentralization in the empire. The Afghanis, however, were unable to establish a stable new regime. Instead, provincial Iranian rulers reunified and even expanded the empire for short periods during the 1700s. Stabilization finally occurred in 1796, with the accession of the new Qajar dynasty.

The Qajars had been among the founding Shiite Turkic tribal federation of the Safavids, but in contrast to their brethren, they had no Shiite aspirations of their own. Instead, they paid respect to the clerical hierarchy that had become powerful in the aftermath of the Afghani conquest in the 1700s. The clerics supported themselves through their own independent revenues from landholdings in the vicinity of their mosques and colleges, and the Qajars were not powerful enough to interfere.

During the 1800s, two developments dominated Iran's historical evolution. First, like the Ottoman Empire, primarily agrarian Iran was subject to oscillating periods of decentralization and recentralization, following the decline or rise of tax revenues from the countryside. Second, the increasingly hierarchical and theologically rigid Shiite clerics were challenged by the popular, theologically less tradition-bound Babi movement. This movement, begun in 1844, rallied around a figure who claimed to be the promised returned Twelfth Imam or Mahdi with a new law superseding the body of legal interpretations of the Shiite clergy. A combination of Qajar troops and clerically organized mobs succeeded in suppressing this widespread movement, which subsequently evolved into the Baha'i faith.

The Qajars not only faced an unstable internal situation but also suffered from Russian imperialism. The declared Russian goal of liberating Constantinople implied the conquest of the central Asian Turkic sultanates as well as the north face of the Caucasus Mountains astride the land bridge between the Black and Caspian Seas. Accordingly, Russian armies sought to drive the Qajars from their Caucasus provinces. In response, the Qajar kings embarked on centralizing military and administrative reforms, which were similar to those of the Ottomans though less pervasive. In the absence of sizeable groups of reformers of their own and bowing to Russian pressures, they hired Russian officers to train a small corps of new troops, the Cossack Brigade. (The tsar, although bent on expanding into the Caucasus, did not want Iran to collapse and cease being a counterweight to the Ottomans.) Swedish advisors trained the police force, in an effort to improve civil peace. British subjects acquired economic concessions, such as monopolies on minerals and telegraph connections or the manufacture of tobacco. The increasing foreign influence in Iran aroused the ire of the conservative clerical hierarchy, and the kings had to withdraw the concessions. The Qajar ruling class was acutely aware of the Western challenge, but its reformist power vis-à-vis the clerical establishment was limited.

Perceptive Iranian constitutional nationalists from among the educated younger ruling class were less numerous than their Young Ottoman colleagues. They therefore founded a tactical alliance toward the end of the 1800s with conservative clerics and merchants. In 1906, after widespread revolts against tax increases to cover a lavish European trip by the shah, this alliance mounted a successful constitutional revolution, imposing parliamentary limits on the Qajar regime. The constitutional–nationalist alliance with the clerics was, however, inherently unstable, and parliamentary rule failed to become a reality. As World War I drew near, Iran reverted to autocratic rule by the shahs. Nevertheless, the memory of the abortive Constitutional Revolution of 1906 lived on, becoming decisive in the later twentieth century with the formation of the Islamic Republic in 1979 and the enactment of a hybrid Islamic–democratic constitution.

Westernization, Reforms, and Industrialization in Russia

The Russian Empire that expanded during the 1800s southward at the expense of the Qajar and Ottoman Empires had arisen in 1547 as a tsardom in Moscow, succeeding the Byzantine eastern Christian "caesars" (from which the Russian term "tsar," or "czar," is derived). It was a relatively late empire, succeeding that of the Mongols; and it spanned eastern Europe as well as Asia. Given this geographical location at the eastern edge of Europe and outside western Christian civilization, Russia developed along an uneven pattern of relations with western Europe. Unlike the Qing, but like the Meiji and the Ottomans, Russia aspired to adapt western values and practices. Western culture became a force only around 1700 when the tsar Peter the Great (r. 1682–1725) became its advocate. The idea of constitutionalism arrived in the wake of the French Revolution and Napoleon's failed invasion of Russia (1812). But it remained weak and was diluted by pan-Slavic ethnic nationalism, an ideology whereby Russians sought unification with the Slavic peoples of the Balkans. Multiple small political groups competed with each other, with no single united reformist force emerging. These groups rose amid the social dislocations that followed the Russian industrialization effort at the end of the nineteenth century, but none was able to take over leadership in the abortive revolution following the disastrous defeat at the hands of a modernizing Japan in 1905. Although this uprising produced a weak Russian parliament, the Duma, the autocratic tsarist regime tottered on until collapsing under the unbearable strain of World War I.

Russia and Westernization

The states of western Europe were, of course, aware of a large empire on their eastern flank but did not consider it fully European. Indeed, at a time when feudal practices were dying in western Europe, Russia under the Romanov dynasty *institutionalized* serfdom. Half a century earlier, Tsar Peter the Great went on a mission of investigation to western Europe and began a reform and urbanization process from the top, against an often-fierce resistance in both the ruling class and the population at large, to bring Russia more in line with the western European norms. His legacy was the new capital of St. Petersburg, extensive military reorganization, and concerted attempts to rein in the power of Russia's high nobility, the *boyars*. But another legacy was political and cultural resistance to any such measures coming from outside Russia, not unlike the cultural resistance that would plague Chinese reformers in the nineteenth century.

The German-born "enlightened despot" Tsarina Catherine II, "the Great" (r. 1762–1796), continued the reform process from the top; however, it was slow to trickle down. When the constitutional–nationalist revolutions broke out in the United States, France, and Haiti, the Russian Empire was an autocratic, fiscal–military state that had expanded in all directions.

Catherine II's Reforms   Catherine the Great, the dominant figure of tsarist Russia during the eighteenth century, was intellectually engaged with Enlightenment concepts that spread among the European courts. Rulers were to remain firmly committed to absolute rule but should also pursue administrative, judicial, and educational reforms in order to increase the welfare of their subjects. Her Enlightenment outlook made Catherine far ahead of the Russian aristocracy, not to mention the small urban educated upper strata, both of which were still much beholden to eastern Christian traditions.

As much an activist as Peter the Great but more subtle, the energetic Catherine pushed through a number of major reforms. Urban manufactures, especially of linen and woolen cloth, had greatly expanded in the early 1700s, and Catherine strengthened urban development with a provincial reform in 1775 and a town reform in 1785 that allowed local nonaristocratic participation. But in 1785 she also strengthened the aristocracy with a charter that exempted its members from the poll tax and increased their property rights, including the purchase of serfs. This was largely a measure to head off a repetition of the terrible peasant rebellions of 1762–1775, which had culminated with Pugachev's Cossack revolt, which had the effect of limiting Catherine's implementation of enlightened policies. Yet, in a reform of the educational system (1782), the government set up a free, mostly clergy-staffed educational system, from urban primary schools to high schools. Catherine's legal reform project, however, apart from a police ordinance issued in 1782, remained incomplete, and the codification and humanization of Russia's laws had to wait for another 80 years.

In foreign affairs, Catherine was determined to continue and even exceed Peter the Great's expansionism. She first undertook the dismemberment of the Kingdom of Poland, accomplished together with Prussia and the Austrian Habsburgs in three stages, from 1772 to 1795. Then, in two wars with the Ottoman Empire (1768–1792), Catherine waged a successful campaign to expand Russian power over the Tatars, a Turkic-speaking population of mixed ethnic descent that had succeeded the Mongols of the Golden Horde (ca. 1240–1502) in Crimea and adjacent northern Black Sea lands. Catherine's modernized infantry forces were successful in humbling the considerably larger but disorganized Ottoman army and navy. In the first war, Russia gained access to the Black Sea, ending the Tatar–Ottoman alliance and gaining free access for Russian ships to the Mediterranean. In the second war, Russia absorbed the Tatars within its imperial borders, which now advanced to the northern coast of the Black Sea.

Russia in the Early Nineteenth Century

The ideas of the French Revolution made their first fleeting mark on Russia in the form of the Decembrist Revolt in 1825, several decades before they did in the Ottoman Empire. But since in the pattern of traditional empire formation the personality of the ruler still counted more than the continuity of the administration, the reign of the deeply monarchical Nicholas I for a generation in mid-1800s Russia meant that whatever the Decembrists had set in motion could only spread under the surface. Above ground, Nicholas pursued an aggressive foreign policy of expansion, in the tradition of Catherine the Great (see Map 25.2).

Russia and the French Revolution   In her old age, Catherine was aghast at the monarchical constitutionalism of the French Revolution, not to mention its republicanism and radicalism. In an abrupt about-face, her government had Voltaire's books burned and other Enlightenment books banned. The situation eased under Catherine's grandson, Alexander I (r. 1801–1825), who was educated in Enlightenment ideas. He initially showed inclinations toward constitutionalism, coaxed by his discreetly constitutionalist minister Mikhail Speranskii (1772–1839), but Napoleon's imperial designs interrupted any idea of implementation.

Russia emerged as a key power in efforts to undo Napoleon's takeover of Europe. In 1805 Russia joined Britain and Austria in the Third Coalition against France. After a long and initially humiliating war, Russia defeated Napoleon during his disastrous invasion of 1812. At the Congress of Vienna in 1815, Alexander assumed a prominent role in the negotiations for the territorial settlements and reestablishment of peace, advocating a "holy alliance" of monarchs to be its guarantors. As a result, Napoleon's Duchy of Warsaw became the Kingdom of Poland, with the Russian tsar as its king. In contrast to his monarchical colleagues in Europe, however, Alexander remained open to Enlightenment reforms, initiating the liberation of serfs in Russia's Baltic provinces, pursuing constitutional reform in Finland and Poland, and mapping out a new status for eastern Christianity. But Russia also experienced unrest, so Alexander gradually lost interest in the continuation of his reforms.

Orthodoxy, Autocracy, and Nationality   No sooner did Nicholas I (1825–1855) ascend the throne in 1825 than a bloody revolt broke out, led by a small number of Russian officers who had been exposed to the ideas of constitutional nationalism. Known as the Decembrist Revolt, the uprising was quickly suppressed and its leaders were hanged. Nevertheless, the revolt had a decided effect on the intelligentsia, who vowed to avenge tsarist repression. The revolt had few connections

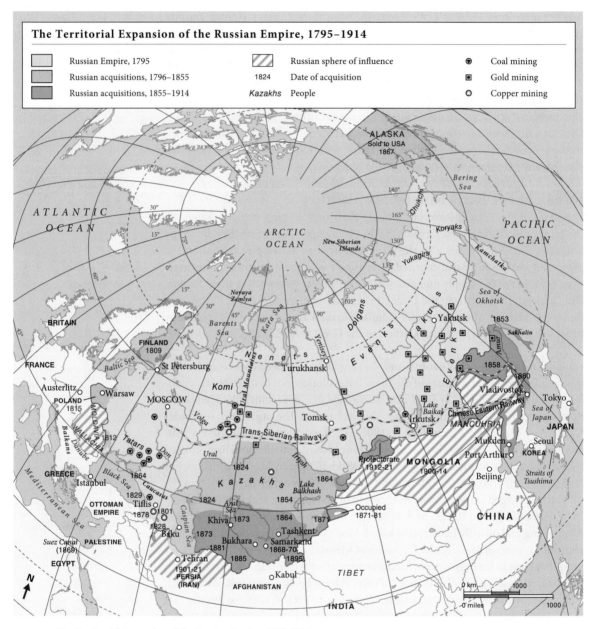

The Territorial Expansion of the Russian Empire, 1795–1914

	Russian Empire, 1795		Russian sphere of influence	●	Coal mining
	Russian acquisitions, 1796–1855	1824	Date of acquisition	▣	Gold mining
	Russian acquisitions, 1855–1914	*Kazakhs*	People	○	Copper mining

MAP 25.2 **The Territorial Expansion of the Russian Empire, 1795–1914.**

with civilians and was furthermore intellectually divided between federalists and unionists. The former serf Nikitenko, introduced at the beginning of this chapter, was fortunate to escape with his life from his contacts with Decembrists. Despite this relative lack of impact, the revolt represented the first antitsarist, constitutional-revolutionary movement and thus became a harbinger of things to come.

Determined to preclude any future constitutional revolts, in 1833 Nicholas implemented the doctrine known as "official nationality," aimed particularly at the suppression of constitutional movements sweeping the European continent in the early 1830s. According to this new formulation of tsarist policy, three fundamental concepts would in the future guide the government: *orthodoxy*, reaffirming the adherence to eastern Christianity and rejection of secularist notions originating in the Enlightenment; *autocracy*, meaning the absolute authority of the tsar; and *nationality*, or the equivalent of something like the "spirit" of Russian identity. In order to enforce these directives, Nicholas created a secret police agency known as the Third Section, which vigorously suppressed dissidence against the government in any form.

Nicholas also carried through on his conservative policies by joining other conservative European rulers in suppressing constitutional revolts. When a revolt in Poland in 1830 threatened to topple the viceroy (meaning ultimately the tsar himself as overlord), Nicholas intervened by suppressing it and abolishing the country's autonomy. Then, during the widespread agitation of revolutionary constitutional movements across Europe in 1848, Nicholas supported the Austrian emperor in suppressing the Hungarian nationalists. The failure of the attempted constitutional revolutions of 1848 was largely attributable to Nicholas's determined intervention.

In larger terms, Nicholas was determined to continue Russia's drive toward Constantinople (Istanbul). In the Russo–Ottoman War of 1828–1829 Russia succeeded in helping the Greeks achieve independence. With Russian help Serbia attained autonomy, while Moldavia and Wallachia—technically still within the Ottoman Empire—became protectorates of Russia. However, when Napoleon III of France in 1853 demanded recognition as protector of the Christians in Palestine under Ottoman rule, Russia did not fare as well. After Nicholas responded by insisting that the Ottomans honor their agreement with the Russian tsars as the actual protectors, the ensuing diplomatic wrangling ended in the outbreak of the Crimean War (1853–1856) between Britain, France, and the Ottoman Empire on one side and Russia, on the other.

Poor planning, missed opportunities, language barriers, and a lack of coordination between soldiers and officers plagued both sides in the Crimean War. One of the first products of the mid-nineteenth-century industrial weapons revolution, the French Minié ball, whose hollow expanding base allowed for ease of ramming in muzzle-loading rifles, quadrupled the effective range of infantry weapons and vastly increased their accuracy. As they would a few years later during the American Civil War, armies fighting with increasingly obsolescent tactics would suffer fearful losses from these new weapons. French steam-powered and iron-hulled floating batteries inaugurated the age of ironclad navies. Telegraph lines permitted correspondents to send frontline reports to their London newspapers. And the nascent technology of photography was there to document the conflict. To lessen the sufferings of the wounded, doctors and nurses on both sides staffed field hospitals—including the English nurse Florence Nightingale (1820–1910), the founder of modern medical care on battlefields and the first prominent advocate of nursing as a profession for women. The new scientific–industrial age had manifested itself for the first time in war.

The Ottomans, still in the initial stages of their military reform, did not acquit themselves well, suffering from a weak officer corps and the absence of noncommissioned officers. They would have

> "They came closer and closer. Suddenly, right across the line, our bugles sounded, followed by the booming of our cannon and the firing of our guns; the earth shook, there was a thunderous echo, and it was so dark from the gunsmoke that nothing could be seen. When it cleared we could see that the ground in front of us was covered with the bodies of the fallen French."
>
> —Prokofii Podpalov, a Russian officer describing the Battle of Malakoff, September 1855

Hospital Ward, Scutari, Ottoman Empire, 1856. This airy, uncluttered, warm hospital room shows injured and recovering soldiers. Florence Nightingale is depicted in the middle ground, in conversation with an officer.

been defeated, had it not been for allied participation. The Russians did not perform well either, except for their navy with its superior shells. The Russian army suffered from overextending its battle lines on too many fronts, from the Danube and Crimea to the Caucasus. Thus, as far as the two imperial foes, the Russian and Ottoman Empires, were concerned, the war was a setback for both in their effort to meet the challenges of the West. Like their counterparts in China during the Second Opium War, also fought in the mid-1850s, however, they did receive a renewed taste of the state of the art in military technology and usage. This would mark many of the reform efforts of all three empires in the coming decades.

The Golden Age   During the period 1810–1853, in spite of periods of censorship and repression, Russia enjoyed an outburst of intellectual and cultural activity. Taken as a whole, this period was considered the golden age of Russian culture. Inspired by European romantics, a Russian intelligentsia—many of whom were Western-educated intellectuals predominantly from the ranks of the landowner nobility—met in the salons of Moscow and St. Petersburg, where they considered and debated issues related to religion and philosophy, as well as Russian history. A significant development was the appearance of literary journals, which introduced new literary forms as well as new ideas. Many of these ideas were potentially seditious, since they concerned ways to end the autocracy of the tsars and to reform serfdom. More important, the first stirrings of reform movements emanated from these circles—as illustrated below in Against the Grain.

The Great Reforms

The Russian defeat in the Crimean War convinced the newly enthroned Alexander II (r. 1855–1881) of the need for reforms. Russia, so he believed, lost the war because of a technologically inferior army, a lack of infrastructure, and the unwillingness of the serf-owning aristocracy to shift from subsistence to market agriculture. He implemented major reforms, which, however, took time to produce the intended effects. Many Russians did not want to wait, and the empire entered a time of social destabilization, balanced abroad to a degree by successes against the Ottoman Empire.

Russian Serfdom   Serfdom in Russia varied according to factors including topography, economic status, and dispositions of landlords. Settlements were similar to medieval manorial villages, with dwellings clustered in the center, surrounded by arable fields. These were organized into *mirs*, or communes, which oversaw economic and legal affairs. Many Russian peasants lived near the subsistence level; dependent upon agriculture, economies fluctuated owing to frequent poor harvests and famines. Peasant dwellings were modest, consisting of small log houses covered by thatched roofs. Interiors featured a small stove for cooking and heating, along with wooden shelves that served as beds. Livestock were occasionally admitted as well. Most serfs had a small plot of land on which to grow vegetables, and they owned livestock of various sorts, including pigs, goats, sheep, and chickens. Diets consisted mainly of grains (mostly rye), meat, and dairy products, as well as foraged nuts, berries, fruits, and occasionally fish. Households consisted of husbands, wives, and children, and occasionally extended to nuclear families consisting of relatives and in-laws. Organized along patriarchal lines, families were dominated by husbands. Misogyny was common—a Russian folk saying translates as "A hen is not a bird and a woman is not a person"— as was wife beating. Nevertheless, Russian women were considered important helpmates in agricultural labors as well as in cooking and other household chores; and although accorded second-class status in Russian society, they were not without some legal rights.

The Emancipation of Serfs   Nicholas tackled serfdom first. In 1861, Alexander (the "tsar liberator") issued the Emancipation Edict, in which peasants were ostensibly freed from their bondage to their villages and their dues and labor services to the Russian landowning aristocracy. On the face of it, the edict ended the centuries-old system of serfdom, affecting some 50 million serfs. But the edict fell far short of liberating the peasantry for three key reasons. First, the decree of emancipation did not go into effect immediately but took 2 years to be fully enacted. Second, peasants were not given land titles directly; rather, the land was turned over to the control of local mirs, which then in turn allocated parcels to individual serfs. Finally, serfs had to redeem their new holdings by making annual payments to the state to pay back long-term government loans, the proceeds from which were then used to compensate the landowning nobility. Even worse, these payments were often higher than the former dues that serfs had owed the aristocracy. In effect, then, tens of millions of farmers remained mired in poverty-stricken agricultural self-sufficiency.

Following Western models, Alexander enacted further reforms. For example, in 1864 the administration of government at the local level was reorganized by the establishment of regional councils known as *zemstvos*. Each zemstvo was in reality controlled by the local aristocracy, although peasants had a say in their election. Whatever their drawbacks, it must be said that zemstvos made advances in education, health, and the maintenance of roads within their regions. Legal reforms were enacted shortly afterward; these provided all Russians access to courts, trial by jury, and especially the concept of equality before the law. Then, in 1874, a series of reforms aimed at modernizing the military and bringing it closer to Western standards was enacted. Among these was the reduction of active duty service in the military from 25 to 6 years, followed by several years of service in the reserves, along with an overall improvement in the quality of life in the ranks. Planned infrastructure reforms, however, remained limited by lack of funds. As in the Ottoman Empire, the reforms brought important changes to Russia, but in many cases, their effects would not be known until years later.

Starving Russian Peasants. Severe weather in 1890–1891 resulted in poor harvests, which in turn led to a period of famine during the 1890s. Russian peasants were especially hard hit by grain shortages and by the government's policy of exporting surpluses in order to boost the Russian economy. Here, peasants beg food from a horse-mounted soldier in St. Petersburg.

Pan-Slavism: Ideology that espoused the brotherhood of all Slavic peoples and gave Russia the mission to aid Slavs in the Balkans suffering from alleged Ottoman misrule.

Pan-Slavism and Balkan Affairs   In the 1870s, conservative intellectuals broadened Tsar Nicholas's concept of the Russian nationality into the ideology of **pan-Slavism**.

Two issues contributed to mounting Russian pan-Slavic engagement in the Balkans. First, across the nineteenth century the Ottomans had been forced to relinquish control of large areas of their empire in the Balkans. Second, the increasingly popular appeal of ethnolinguistic nationalism in Europe—embodied in Italian unification in 1870, followed by German unification in 1871—strengthened the assertiveness of the Balkan nationalities. In 1875 Bosnia-Herzegovina revolted against the Ottomans, and the rebellion then spread to Bulgaria, Serbia, and Montenegro. What would happen if these provinces did in fact break away from the Ottoman Empire? Which of the European powers might then take them over and thus increase its presence in this vital region? Thus, the Balkans became an area of increasing attention for the leading powers, while at the same time resembling a powder keg ready to ignite.

The Russo–Ottoman War   Encouraged by Russian popular support for pan-Slavism and sensing an opportunity to exploit rising anti-Ottoman sentiments among ethnic national movements in the Balkans, the tsar reopened the war front against the Ottomans in July 1877. The pretext was the Ottoman repression of uprisings in Bosnia-Herzegovina and Bulgaria, which had led to a declaration of war by neighboring Montenegro and Serbia in June 1876 and a call for Russian military aid. The Russians invaded across the Danube and by December had advanced as far as Rumelia. Serbia, claiming complete independence, and Bulgaria, under Russian tutelage, were now poised to gain control of Istanbul. The other European powers stood by, anxiously waiting to see whether Russia would advance on the Ottoman capital.

In 1878, alarmed over what appeared to be an imminent Russian occupation of Istanbul, Austria and Britain persuaded Germany to convene the Congress of Berlin. In order to preserve peace among the great powers and to diffuse rising tensions over this "eastern question," the congress decided to amputate from the Ottoman Empire most of its European provinces. For its part, Russia agreed to give up its designs on Istanbul in return for maintaining control over lands it had secured in the Caucasus Mountains. Serbia, Romania, and Montenegro became independent states. Austria acquired the right to "occupy and administer" the provinces of Bosnia and Herzegovina. There things stood for the rest of the nineteenth century, as the European powers began their imperial scramble, and Russia, forced to deal with renewed internal unrest, turned its attention away from the Balkans.

Russian Industrialization

Following the assassination of Alexander II in 1881 by a leftist terrorist organization impatient for further reforms, the next Romanov tsars reaffirmed autocratic authority and exercised tight political control, harkening back to the policies of Nicholas I. They surrounded themselves with conservative advisors and buttressed their hold on absolute rule by connecting loyalty to the state with adherence to eastern Christianity. These tsarist policies provoked renewed calls for constitutional reforms and generated new movements opposed to the autocracy of the regime. At the same time, when the depression of 1873–1896 began to ease in the 1890s, the country enjoyed a surge in industrialization, aggravating the political and social contradictions in Russia.

The Reassertion of Tsarist Authority   In the face of increasing demands by constitutionalists and social reformers, Alexander III (r. 1881–1894) unleashed a broad program of "counter-reforms" in order to shore up autocratic control over the country. These actions turned Russia into a police state, in which political trials before military courts were commonplace. Revolutionaries, terrorists, and opponents among the intelligentsia were especially targeted for intimidation, exile, or even death. Outside Russia, Alexander insisted on a program of *Russification*, or forced assimilation to Russian culture, especially language, for Poles, Ukrainians, and the Muslim populations of central Asia. For the time being, the regime maintained its grip on power.

Nicholas II (r. 1894–1917), regarded by many contemporaries as a narrow-minded, unimaginative, and ultimately tragic figure, followed in his father's footsteps. Nicholas's paramount concern was loyalty not only to the state but also to the church. Any deviations were considered treasonous. He felt a special contempt for revolutionary groups and individuals, who therefore retaliated with increasingly strident demands for the overthrow of the tsarist government. In addition to continuing the repressive policies of his father, Nicholas held an enduring distrust of Russian Jews as unpatriotic, which climaxed in the pogroms of 1903–1906. These pogroms, repetitions of earlier ones in 1881–1884 following the assassination of Alexander II, triggered mass emigrations to the United States and smaller ones to Britain, South America, South Africa, and Palestine as Russian Jews sought to escape persecution.

Industrialization   Industrial development was as slow in Russia as it was in the Ottoman Empire, and for many of the same reasons. For one thing, the empire suffered from a poor transportation infrastructure. Although canal construction had started under Peter the Great, road construction did not follow until the early 1800s. Railroad construction was even slower, owing to the great distances in the empire that made large capital investments from abroad necessary. The first line, from St. Petersburg to Moscow, opened in 1851, but only a few thousand miles of track were laid until 1890 when the European depression of the previous three decades lifted. A major reason for the defeat in the Crimean War was the absence of railroad connections from Moscow to the Black Sea, forcing the army to rely on water transport and horse-drawn carts. Moreover, Russian railroads never adopted the standard gauge of their Western counterparts, necessitating costly and time-consuming changes of carriages and rolling stock at border crossings.

Among other factors driving the push toward accelerated industrialization was the dawning recognition of the regime that Russia was falling behind the industrialized nations of Europe in the race for economic—and thus political—global

Aristocratic Splendor. This oil painting of the wedding of Nicholas II and Alexandra in 1894, by the Danish painter Laurits Regner Tuxen (1853–1927), shows the rich glory of the Eastern Christian Church and the empire in ascendancy, with the couple's iconic art, ermine furs, veiled ladies in waiting, and decorated officers.

political influence. But the driving force in Russia's push for industrialization in the 1890s was the minister of finance, Sergei Witte (1849–1915, in office 1892–1903). His "Witte system" included an acceleration of heavy industrial output, the establishment of import tariffs, increased taxes on the peasantry, and conversion to the gold standard in order to stabilize the currency. Although historians debate the overall success of Witte's reforms, there is no question that Russia made tremendous progress in heavy industrialization during the late nineteenth century.

Witte's crowning achievement was the Trans-Siberian Railroad, built during 1891–1905 and connecting Moscow with Vladivostok on the Pacific coast. During Catherine's time, it took 3 years for communications to be sent to and from Vladivostok; now, the distance was covered in 8 days. Witte's objective was not only to make Russia more competitive but also to extend Russia's reach into Siberia with its rich agricultural and mineral resources, while at the same time extending Russia's influence in east Asia. Russia's policy of opening east Asia was the equivalent of Western imperialism in Asia and Africa and was designed to ensure that Russia enjoyed a share of the global race for empire.

Industrialism and Society   In the 1890s, British, French, and Belgian capital poured into the empire and helped in building railroads, mining ventures, iron smelters, and textile factories. It is estimated that during this decade Russia's industrial output increased at an annual rate of nearly 8 percent. Owing, however, to Russia's late start in industrializing, as well as to a lack of abundant reserves of financial capital, many of the factories were technologically inferior to those of the west.

In other ways social adjustments and changes similar to those experienced in industrialized cities in the west occurred in major Russian industrial centers. The populations of Moscow and St. Petersburg in the second half of the nineteenth century soared from around 250,000 to 1 million. And, like their western counterparts, industrialized urban centers consisted of overcrowded and unhealthy slums adjacent to factories.

Again, as in the west, industrialism spawned changes in social structures. Factories and mines employed a new class of workers. Their working conditions were oppressive, including 11 hours and more a day of manual labor in less-than-ideal circumstances. Mounting calls for reforms throughout the later nineteenth century led to the formation of several protest and socialist groups, all of whom contributed to the increasing pressures and chaos that would explode in the 1905 Revolution.

There was, however, one striking difference between the Russian and western industrial experiences. While it is true that the economic upturn in Russia produced a rising urban middle class, the numbers of wealthy factory owners, entrepreneurs, and merchants pales in comparison with the west. Many factors account for this disparity, but perhaps the most important was that many Russian manufacturing plants were controlled by western investors, and those that were not were under the supervision of the Russian government.

The Russo–Japanese War   The dramatic surge in industrialization, in conjunction with imperial ambitions in east Asia, brought Russia into conflict with Japan. As we saw in Chapter 24, with the Meiji Restoration in 1867–1868, Japan had embarked on a systematic program of modernization and industrialization. Like western Europe and Russia, it developed imperial ambitions in the 1890s, seeking to replace China as the dominant power in east Asia. To this end Japan provoked war with China and in the Sino–Japanese War (1894–1895) occupied Taiwan and the Liaodong Peninsula of Manchuria. Although Japan was successful in defeating China and replacing it as the protector of Korea, the European powers forced Japan to give up the Liaodong Peninsula in the Triple Intervention (1895), which was in turn leased to Russia the following year. Determined to continue Russian expansion in east Asia, Witte completed the construction of a railway spur from the Trans-Siberian Railroad through Manchuria to the warm-water fortress city of Port Arthur on the southern tip of Liaodong.

The construction of this spur was the final straw for Japan, whose imperial goals seemed suddenly threatened by Russian expansion. Already smarting from what they considered Russia's double-dealing in helping to engineer the Triple Intervention and leasing the naval base at Port Arthur from the Qing, in early 1904 Japanese naval forces suddenly attacked the Russian fleet moored at Port Arthur, destroying several of its ships and laying siege to the fortress. The Russian Baltic fleet, sent for relief, not only arrived too late to prevent the fall of Port Arthur but was destroyed in May 1905 by Japan when it tried to reach Vladivostok. In the peace settlement, Japan gained control of the Liaodong Peninsula and southern Manchuria, as well as increased influence over Korea, which it finally annexed in 1910.

The Abortive Russian Revolution of 1905

In addition to Russia's mauling by the Japanese in the war of 1904–1905, a variety of factors coalesced in the early 1900s that sparked the first revolution against tsarist rule. One of these was a rising discontent among the peasantry, who continued to chafe under injustices such as the redemption payments for landownership. Another was the demand by factory workers for reform of working conditions: The workday ran to 11.5 hours and wages were pitifully low. Although the government had allowed for the formation of labor unions, their grievances fell on deaf ears. In response, workers in major manufacturing centers across the country, especially in St. Petersburg, mounted massive protests and occasional strikes.

Revolutionary Parties   The discontent among workers and peasants spurred calls for reforms, resulting in the creation of new political parties. One of these was the Social Democratic Labor Party, formed in 1898 by Vladimir Ilyich Lenin (1870–1924), a staunch adherent of Marxism (discussed in Chapter 26). This group sought support from workers, whom they urged to stage a socialist revolution by rising up and overthrowing the bourgeois capitalist tsarist government.

During its meeting in London in 1903 the Social Democratic Labor Party developed two competing factions. The more moderate group, the Mensheviks ("minority," though they were actually numerically in the majority), was willing to follow classical Marxism, which allowed for an evolutionary process from fully evolved capitalism to social revolution and then on to the eventual overthrow of capitalism and tsarist rule. The more radical faction, known as Bolsheviks ("majority"), led by Lenin, was unwilling to wait for the evolutionary process to unfold and instead called for revolution in the near term. In 1902 Lenin had sketched out his agenda in *What Is to Be Done?* which laid out the principal Bolshevik aims. Foremost among these was a demand for the overthrow of the tsar, which could be accomplished only by relying on a highly disciplined core of dedicated revolutionaries leading the masses, whom Lenin distrusted as unwieldy and potentially unreliable. Even after the split in the Social Democratic Labor Party, however, the Bolsheviks were still a long way away from the kind of elite "vanguard of the revolution" party Lenin envisaged.

The Revolution of 1905   Events moved toward a violent climax in the Revolution of 1905. Amid mounting calls for political and economic reforms during the early 1900s, two concurrent events in 1904 shook the government to its foundations. First, reports of the humiliating defeats during the ongoing Russo–Japanese War began to filter to the home front. These made apparent the government's mismanagement of the war. Second, in January 1905, 100,000 workers went on strike in St. Petersburg, resulting in massive disruptions and loss of life commemorated later by Lenin.

> "Today is the twelfth anniversary of 'Bloody Sunday,' . . . which is rightly regarded as the beginning of the Russian revolution."
>
> —Vladimir Lenin

Then, from September to October, workers in all the major industrial centers staged a general strike, which brought the country to a standstill. Finally forced to make concessions, Nicholas issued the "October Manifesto," in which he promised to establish a constitutional government. Among other things, the manifesto guaranteed individual civil liberties, universal suffrage, and the creation of a representative assembly, the Duma. During 1905–1907, however, Nicholas repudiated the concessions granted in the manifesto, especially an independent Duma, which remained a rubber-stamp parliament until Nicholas abdicated in 1917. Its momentum sapped, the revolution withered.

The main reason for the failure of the revolution was the absence of a broadly based constitutionalism. Its replacement was small revolutionary parties which lacked popular backing. This failure of constitutionalism made the formation of broader reformist coalitions, perhaps even with military participation, as in the Ottoman Empire, impossible. The tsarist regime, though humbled by Japan, still had enough military resources to wear down the combination of small groups of Marxist revolutionaries and street demonstrators. Without sympathizers in the army, a determined tsarist regime was impossible to bring down. But like Qing China during these years, whatever belated reforms were initiated by the government would increasingly be seen as irrelevant.

Vladimir Yegorovich Makovsky (1846–1920), *Death in the Snow* **(1905).** This dramatic oil painting of the crowd protesting against the tsarist regime during the abortive revolution of 1905 is one of the greatest Russian realist paintings. Makovsky was one of the founders of the Moscow Art School and continued to paint after the Russian Revolution of 1917.

It was now felt that nothing short of changing the system would be effective. For both empires, the revolutionaries would now dominate the scene.

Putting It All Together

Both the Ottoman and Russian Empires faced the initial Western military and constitutional challenges directly on their doorsteps, not from across the ocean, as China and Japan did. Of course, once military technology had undergone its own industrial transformation in Europe during the first half of the 1800s, China was no longer too far away for British steam-powered gunboats and rifled breech-loading weapons. The Ottoman Empire, as a mature empire struggling to regain its traditional centralism, fought largely defensive wars. Russia, still a young empire, expanded aggressively against the defensive Ottomans and its weaker Asian neighbors (except Japan), all the while suffering occasional military and diplomatic setbacks. India failed to master the Western military challenge altogether. China, the Ottoman Empire, and Qajar Iran survived at the price of diminished territories. The Western challenge was pervasive across the world.

Western constitutional nationalism was another powerful and corrosive pattern. The transformation of kingdoms or colonies into nations in which subjects would become citizens, regardless of language or dialect, social rank, or religion, was difficult enough in Europe. France, with its uneasy shifts between monarchy and republic during the 1800s, demonstrated this difficulty. In the Ottoman Empire, a wide gap existed between constitutional theory and practice, especially as far as religion was concerned. Russia, plagued by the reluctance of its aristocracy to give up serfdom even after emancipation, left its constitutionalists out in the cold. Japan created a constitutional state but, like Germany, left the great majority of real power in the hands of its emperor and his advisors. China's bid for a constitutional monarchy died once in 1898 and was never fully reborn before its revolution in 1911. Sultans, emperors, and kings knew well that none of their constitutions would fully satisfy the demands for liberty, equality, and fraternity.

To complicate matters for both the Ottoman and Russian Empires, in the second half of the 1800s, many members of the rising educated urban middle class deserted constitutional nationalism and turned to ethnic nationalism (in the Ottoman Empire) or pan-Slavism and Marxism (in the Russian Empire). By contrast, both the Ottoman and Russian Empires met the Western *industrial* challenge—cheap, factory-produced cotton textiles—without completely surrendering their markets. Once they were able to attract foreign capital for the construction of expensive railroads and factories at the end of the 1800s, they even started on their own paths to industrialization—the seemingly stable Russia faster than the apparently sick Ottoman Empire. In spite of wrenching transformations, the two were still empires in control of themselves when World War I broke out. Neither would survive the war. Instead, they would be transformed by the forces that had beset them throughout the nineteenth century: Turkey would become a modern, secular nation-state, though always running somewhat behind its European contemporaries in economic development. Inspired by the Revolution of 1905, and influenced by its tremendous losses in World War I, Russia would be transformed into the world's first Marxist state, pursue breakneck industrial and economic development at a tragic cost, and emerge after World War II as one of two "superpowers" with the United States.

For additional resources, including maps, primary sources, visuals, and quizzes, please go to www.oup.com/us/vonsivers. Please see the Further Resources section at the back of the book for additional readings and suggested websites.

Against the Grain

Precursor to Lenin

As noted earlier in this chapter (pp. 780) Russia's humiliating defeat in the Crimean War inspired Alexander II to enact a series of reforms in order to advance Russia into the age of modernity. At the forefront was the Emancipation Edict, issued in 1861, which was touted as making vast improvements in the lives of Russia's peasantry. When it became apparent in the 1860s that reform measures fell far short of the mark, enhancing rather than limiting autocracy, radical and even terrorist political factions demanded more far-reaching reforms. In the vanguard was a group of Russian intelligentsia who spread their notions and ideas by widely circulating them in pamphlets and literary journals.

Of these activists, one of the most notable was Nikolai Chernyshevsky (1828–1889), who defied conventional approaches to Russia's problems. In Chernyshevsky's view, Alexander's reforms were either ineffective or wrong-headed from the start. As editor of the radical journal *Contemporary*, and inspired by western intellectuals like Hegel, Chernyshevsky wrote numerous critiques of moderate reforms, especially those advocated by liberals and intelligentsia. The only way to resolve the current status quo, according to Chernyshevsky, was through outright revolution, and the Russian peasantry was designated as the dynamo that would drive meaningful reforms. To this end Chernyshevsky advocated the formation of social collectives, or communes, based on the utopian models of Charles Fourier and others.

Chernyshevsky's writing finally resulted in his imprisonment in 1862. During this time he wrote the inflammatory novel *What Is to Be Done?*, frequently referred to as a "handbook of radicalism." In it, Chernyshevsky called for innovative actions and policies informed by socialist ideals, including women's liberation, and broad programs of social justice. Running as a subtle thread through the novel was an oblique call for outright revolution. As such, the book served as an inspiration for radical activists and terrorists during the 1870s and 1880s, and earned for Chernyshevsky the distinction of being labeled the first revolutionary socialist as well as both the inspiration for and forerunner of the 1905 revolution. Lenin was so impressed by Chernyshevsky's novel that he not only referred to it as one of the most influential books he had ever read—including those of Marx—but he also entitled his own manual of revolution *What Is to Be Done?*

- In what ways does Chernyshevsky epitomize radical socialist ideas?

- How does Chernyshevsky compare to earlier contrarians like Thomas Paine and Joseph Sieyès?

Thinking Through Patterns

▶ **Which new models did the Ottomans adopt during the nineteenth century to adapt themselves to the Western challenge?**

The traditional model for reform in the Ottoman Empire was based on the Islamic concept of the divinely sanctioned, absolute authority of the sultan: Officials could be appointed or dismissed at will. The later history of the Ottoman Empire is significant in world history because it shows the *adaptation pattern* to the Western challenge, in this case the borrowing of constitutional nationalism and modern military technology from Europe.

As agrarian polities with large landowning classes collecting rents from tenant farmers or serfs, the Ottoman and Russian Empires found it difficult to respond to the European industrial challenge. Large foreign investments were necessary for the building of steelworks, factories, and railroads. Given the long economic recession of the last quarter of the 1800s, these investments—coming from France and Germany—went to an expanding Russia, more than the shrinking Ottoman Empire, as the safer bet.

▶ **How did the agrarian Ottoman and Russian Empires, both with large landholding ruling classes, respond to the western European industrial challenge during the 1800s?**

▶ **Why did large, well-established empires like the Russian and the Ottoman Empires struggle with the forces of modernity, while a small, secluded island nation like Japan seemed to adapt so quickly and successfully?**

This is in many respects a tantalizing question for world historians. Aside from philosophical debates about what actually constitutes "success," one avenue of inquiry is cultural: How receptive were the Russians and Ottomans—or the Qing, for that matter—to the ideas of the Enlightenment? The short answer must be "Not very." Even the most willing leaders in these empires risked alienating a host of entrenched interests by attempting the most modest reforms. They therefore walked a very fine political line in what they attempted, and they often found that the reforms disrupted traditional routines but left little or nothing to replace them with effectively. In addition, such large multiethnic empires as those of Russia and the Ottomans found it difficult to rally subjects around a distinct "nationality," since they encompassed so many divergent ones. In contrast, the Meiji reformers had the advantage of a unity derived from outside pressures. With the old shogunate gone, the emperor could formulate completely new institutions and count on the loyalty of subjects who had seen him as a semidivine figure. Moreover, the new regime immediately began creating an ideology of Japaneseness—a form of ethnic nationalism—and institutionalized it in education and national policy. There was, to be sure, opposition; but it was scattered, class-based, and not effective against the modern army and industrial power the new regime created. Japan's legacy of cultural borrowing may also have been an advantage, as well as a nascent capitalist system developing in the late Tokugawa era. Finally, the goal of using its progress toward "enlightenment and civilization" according to Western standards could be measured along the way, as were the power and prestige of its new programs.

Chapter **26** 1750–1914

Industrialization and Its Discontents

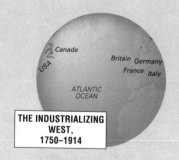

THE INDUSTRIALIZING WEST, 1750–1914

I n the late summer of 1845, Mary Paul, age 15, made a life-altering decision. Having already realized just how limited her prospects were in the hardscrabble farm country of rural Vermont, she decided to head for Massachusetts and stake her future on a job in the newly expanding textile industry.

Exactly how that future would unfold can be seen in letters she wrote to her widowed father, Bela. Her correspondence reveals that the primary reason behind her dramatic decision was simply to earn steady wages, rather than rely on the uncertainties and drudgery of farm work. On September 13, 1845, Mary wrote for her father's consent to leave her nearby domestic job and seek employment in the booming mill town of Lowell, Massachusetts. On November 20, Mary wrote that she had already "found a place in a spinning room and the next morning [she] went to work." She continued, "I like very well have [sic] 50cts first payment increasing every payment as I get along in work. [I] have a first rate overseer and a very good boarding place." Shortly before Christmas, Mary reported that her wages had increased: "Last Tuesday we were paid. In all I had six dollars and sixty cents paid $4.68 for board. With the rest I got me a pair of rubbers and a pair of 50.cts shoes. Next payment I am to have a dollar a week beside my board." She then offered her father glimpses into her daily routine in the mill, one with which millions of

ABOVE: American photojournalist Lewis Hine (1874–1940) documented child labor, including these girls in a North Carolina textile mill in 1910.

workers around the world would soon grow quite familiar: "At 5 o'clock in the morning the bell rings for the folks to get up and get breakfast. At half past six it rings for the girls to get up and at seven they are called into the mill. At half past 12 we have dinner are called back again at one and stay till half past seven." Mary closes by pointing out, "I think that the factory is the best place for me and if any girl wants employment I advise them to come to Lowell."

Mary Paul's experiences, shared by thousands of other young, unmarried women in rural farming regions, signaled a momentous change in the patterns of American and world history. Like Great Britain and areas throughout northern Europe, the northeastern United States was now in the initial stages of what we have termed "scientific–industrial society." The agrarian–urban model, which had lasted for millennia on every inhabited continent except Australia, was now slowly giving way to a society based on machine-made goods, large-scale factories, regimented work hours, and wage labor. Moreover, the economies of the industrializing states would increasingly be dominated by capitalism. An ideology of progress (a legacy of the Enlightenment), backed by the acceleration of technology and science, constituted what we term the "challenge of modernity." That challenge was already being spread globally through innovations in transportation, communications, and weaponry produced by this Industrial Revolution.

Origins and Growth of Industrialism, 1750–1914

Like the agricultural revolution of the Neolithic age, which resulted in humankind's transition from foragers to food producers and made urbanization possible, the Industrial Revolution forever altered the lives of tens of millions around the globe. Whether or not this movement was in fact a "revolution," however, is a matter of some debate. It is perhaps more accurate to say that the process of industrialization evolved gradually, originating in Britain in the eighteenth century, then spreading to the European continent and North America in the nineteenth century and subsequently around the globe, interacting with and adapting to local circumstances and cultures along the way. But there is no question that the transition from manual labor and natural sources of power to the implementation of mechanical forms of power and machine-driven production resulted in a vast increase in the production of goods, new modes of transportation, and new economic policies and business procedures.

Early Industrialism, 1750–1870

The industrialization of western Europe began in Britain. As with all transformative events in history, however, a number of important questions arise: Why did the industrial movement begin in Britain? Why not, say, in China in the Song or Ming period? Why in the eighteenth century? Why in such areas as textiles, iron, mining, and transport? How did these changes become not only self-sustaining but also able to transform so many other manufacturing processes? And was this

Seeing Patterns

▶ Where and when did the Industrial Revolution originate?

▶ What were some effects of industrialization on Western society? How did social patterns change?

▶ In what ways did industrialization contribute to innovations in technology? How did these technological advances contribute to Western imperialism in the late nineteenth century?

▶ What new directions in science, philosophy, religion, and the arts did industrialism generate? What kind of responses did it provoke?

Chapter Outline

- Origins and Growth of Industrialism, 1750–1914

- The Social and Economic Impact of Industrialism, 1750–1914

- Intellectual and Cultural Responses to Industrialism

- Putting It All Together

process "inevitable," as some have claimed, or was it contingent on a myriad of complex interactions that we are still struggling to comprehend?

Preconditions   Although there are no simple answers to these questions, it is possible to cite several distinct conditions and advantages enjoyed by both Europe in general and Britain in particular. For one thing, unlike China, Europeans had earlier seen the rise to prominence of a prosperous and largely independent middle class consisting of merchants and manufacturers. In addition, Europe was unique among global civilizations in that it had experienced an earlier scientific revolution, essential for providing the technological foundation for the creation and application of machine technology to production.

Three key factors made Britain especially suitable for launching the industrial movement. First, Britain benefited from what some historians refer to as the "coal and colonies" theory. Large reserves of coal and iron ore, combined with the establishment of overseas colonies and subsequent global trading networks, provided a foundation for commercial expansion, which in turn created capital to fund new enterprises. Second, a thriving merchant class, empowered by the Glorious Revolution of 1688, grew in significance in the House of Commons of the British Parliament and supported legislation that promoted economic development. Finally, Britain developed a flourishing banking system: the Bank of England (founded in 1694) provided needed funds to entrepreneurs willing to make risky investments in new ventures.

Thanks to agricultural improvements, in part coming from the introduction of new crops from the Americas, Britain experienced a surge in population. Whereas in 1600 Britain's population was around 5 million, by 1700 it had nearly doubled to around 9 million. At the same time, a demographic shift in which displaced tenant farmers migrated to towns and cities caused a rapid increase in urban growth and created greater demand for food and consumer goods, such as textiles.

Indeed, the impact of these changes was especially notable in the textile industry. Although woolen cloth had long been the staple of the British textile industry, the introduction of new fabrics from Asia, such as silk and cotton, began to gain in popularity among consumers. Cotton's advantages of light weight and ease of cleaning resulted in a growing demand for the domestic production of affordable cotton clothing, or "calicoes." At first, the demand for finished cloth goods was satisfied by weavers working in the older, domestic cottage industries, a system known as "protoindustrialism." Due in large part to concerns for the woolen industry, however, Parliament enacted the protectionist Calico Acts of 1700 and 1720, which prohibited the importation of cotton goods from India. But this legislation had the unintended consequence of increasing domestic demand for English-made cotton textiles, which quickly outstripped available supplies. Given soaring demand, it was apparent that some sort of means was needed to speed up production.

British Resources   The impasse was resolved by a combination of factors peculiar to Britain at this time, which taken together made the use of machines more practical and cost-efficient than it might have been somewhere else. Since wages for workers in rural industries were high, the use of labor-saving machinery was increasingly seen as a means to help firms be profitable. By contrast, where wages were relatively low (such as in the Dutch Republic and France), there was no urgent need to develop more cost-effective means of production. At the same time, Britain's vast reserves of coal resulted in cheap energy.

Moreover, Britain was singularly fortunate in its social and cultural capital. The composition of British society in the seventeenth and eighteenth centuries was unusually attuned to what historians sometimes call the "Industrial Enlightenment." As discussed in Chapter 17, eighteenth-century Britain was at the center of the European scientific revolution, which was realized in a more widespread fashion in Britain than elsewhere. The majority of British inventors had interests in and ties to societies aligned with scientific aspects of the Enlightenment, which served as centers of discourse and exchange between leading scientists, inventors, experimenters, and mechanics.

New Technologies and Sources of Power   These factors produced an explosion of technological innovation in Britain. From 1700 to 1800 over 1,000 inventions were developed, most of which were related to the textile industry. Among the most prominent were the flying shuttle (1733), the spinning jenny (1764), the water frame (1769), and the spinning mule (1779). Each of these devices greatly increased the speed and quality of spinning or weaving; the mule combined both operations into one machine. The power loom (1787) then set the technological stage for full-scale machine production of textiles, gradually replacing manually operated looms. This in turn resulted in the decline of handicraftsmen, particularly hand weavers, whose livelihoods were threatened by the new power-driven looms. In desperation, handicrafters of all sorts mounted an organized and combined campaign to sabotage the increasing use of machines in textile factories (see "Against the Grain" on p. 820).

Even these improvements were not enough, however, to supply both domestic and colonial markets with sufficient quantities of textiles. What was needed in order to speed up production was some sort of reliable mechanical power to drive the looms. The solution was provided by the development of the steam engine, easily the most important—and iconic—innovation of the industrial era.

The Factory System   The growing dependence on large machinery, the necessity of transporting fuel and raw materials to centers of production, and the efficiency afforded by housing a multitude of machines under one roof necessitated the construction of large manufacturing buildings. These facilities were initially located near sources of running water in order to provide the power to run mechanical looms. The implementation of steam power to drive machinery allowed entrepreneurs to move mills and production centers away from water sources in rural areas to urban settings, where there were large pools of cheap labor. Another attraction of urban areas

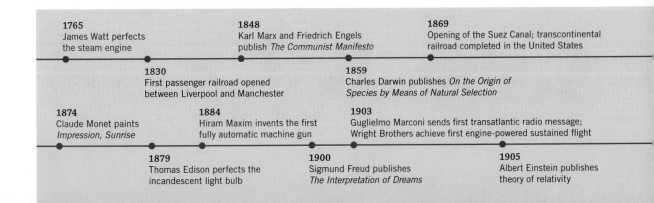

1765
James Watt perfects the steam engine

1848
Karl Marx and Friedrich Engels publish *The Communist Manifesto*

1869
Opening of the Suez Canal; transcontinental railroad completed in the United States

1830
First passenger railroad opened between Liverpool and Manchester

1859
Charles Darwin publishes *On the Origin of Species by Means of Natural Selection*

1874
Claude Monet paints *Impression, Sunrise*

1884
Hiram Maxim invents the first fully automatic machine gun

1903
Guglielmo Marconi sends first transatlantic radio message; Wright Brothers achieve first engine-powered sustained flight

1879
Thomas Edison perfects the incandescent light bulb

1900
Sigmund Freud publishes *The Interpretation of Dreams*

1905
Albert Einstein publishes theory of relativity

was their greater accessibility to roads, canals, and, later, railroads. Once established, these factories in their turn drew increasing numbers of workers, which contributed to urban population surges, particularly in the north and Midlands of England. By the 1830s over 1 million people drew wages from textile factories, and close to 25 percent of Britain's industrial production came from factories (see Map 26.1).

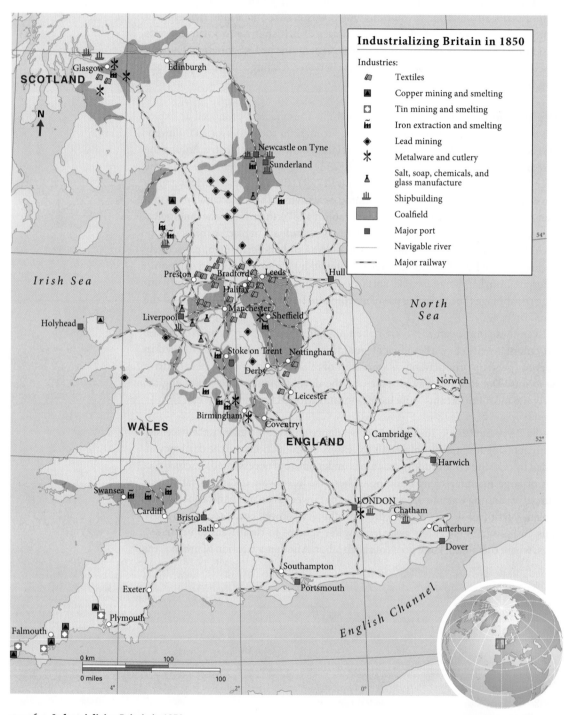

MAP **26.1** **Industrializing Britain in 1850.**

Global Commerce   The application of machines to the production of textile manufactures resulted in Britain's increasingly important role in the development of intercontinental trade and commerce. Prior to the Industrial Revolution, India and China dominated global trade in textiles. But thanks to its vast holdings in American and Asia, combined with mercantilist policies, Britain had ready-made markets for the distribution and sale of its increased output of goods. Britain also benefited from slave labor in its former colonies, which kept the price of commodities like American cotton low. One result was growing demand among colonial markets for textile products, which in turn stimulated the necessity to step up production. Yet another consequence of the surge in the volume of textile production was that manufacturers were able to lower the prices of their goods, making them more competitive in global markets.

Transportation   While steam-powered factories provided much of the muscle of the Industrial Revolution, it was the steam railroad that captivated the imagination of the public. Its origins, like those of the earlier stationary pumping engines, began at the mines. For more than a century, miners had used track-mounted cars to pull loads of coal and iron out of mines. By the 1820s experiments were already under way to attach engines to moving carriages. Whereas in 1840 Great Britain counted only 1,800 miles of rail, by 1870 the figure had jumped nearly ninefold to 15,600 miles. Railroads vastly improved the shipping of coal and other bulk commodities and greatly enhanced the sale and distribution of manufactures of all kinds. The railroad itself developed into a self-sustaining industry, employing thousands in all sorts of related jobs and spurring further investment by wealthy entrepreneurs.

Although their impact was realized somewhat later, the application of steam to ships had far-reaching ramifications, especially in the second half of the nineteenth century. Credit for the first practical steam-powered riverboat goes to the American engineer and inventor Robert Fulton (1765–1815). Fulton's *Clermont*, constructed in 1807, plied the Hudson River from New York to Albany. English engineers were quick to copy Fulton's lead; by 1815 there were 10 steamboats hauling coal across the Clyde River in Scotland. During the 1820s and 1830s steamboats were in regular use on Europe's principal rivers. Steamboats also played a vital role in opening up the Great Lakes and the Ohio and Mississippi Rivers to commerce in the United States. By the 1830s and 1840s the British East India Company used iron-hulled steamers to facilitate maritime trade with its markets in India. Military uses soon followed.

The Spread of Early Industrialism

By the 1830s, in Belgium, northern France, and the northern German states—all of which had coal reserves—conditions had grown more suitable for industrialization than earlier when wages were low. More settled political conditions after the Napoleonic Wars led to population increases, contributing to higher consumer demand. At the same time, larger urban areas provided greater pools of available workers for factories. Moreover, within these regions improved networks of roads, canals, and now railways facilitated the movement of both raw materials to industrial centers and manufactured goods to markets. In addition, governmental involvement greatly enhanced the investment climate; protective tariffs for manufactures and the gradual removal of internal toll restrictions, particularly in the northern German states, opened up the trading industry.

The United States   Industrialism was imported to the United States toward the end of the eighteenth century by Samuel Slater (1768–1835), a British engineer. Slater established the first water-powered textile factory in America, in Rhode Island in 1793. By 1825 factories in the northeastern section of the country were producing vast quantities of textile goods on mechanically powered looms.

After a brief interruption during the American Civil War—during which the majority of factories on both sides were engaged in producing munitions and war materiel—industrialization in America resumed at a greatly accelerated pace. As production data indicate, by 1870 America was producing far more spindles of cotton than Great Britain, and its production of iron ingots was swiftly catching up to that of British and European producers. By 1914 the United States had become the world's single largest industrial economy.

In addition to manufacturing, trade and commerce across the vast American continent were facilitated by a national network of railroads, which swiftly took over the carrying trade from the canal networks created in the early nineteenth century. Data for US rail construction show this astonishing growth: from 2,800 miles of rail in 1840 to about 35,000 miles by the conclusion of the Civil War—more than the rest of the world combined. By 1869 the first transcontinental railroad was joined with a final golden spike at Promontory Point, Utah, resulting in an astonishing total of 53,000 rail miles by 1870.

Later Industrialism, 1871–1914

In many ways the next stage of industrialism, often referred to as "the second Industrial Revolution," grew out of the first phase. Perhaps the best measure of the difference in the two periods, however, is that while the first stage relied upon steam power, the second introduced several high-technology innovations that, taken together, altered the course not only of the Industrial Revolution but also of world history. Among the most significant were steel, electricity, and chemicals (see Map 26.2).

New Materials: Steel   An important element in the second Industrial Revolution was the increasing use of steel instead of iron. Refined techniques for making steel had existed for many hundreds of years in different parts of the world but were largely the province of highly skilled craftspeople such as swordsmiths. New technical advances, however, now made it possible to produce large quantities of high-grade yet *inexpensive* steel. Subsequent improvements in production in the 1860s and 1870s included the blast furnace and the open-hearth smelting method.

Following the conclusion of the Franco–Prussian war, Germany's annexation of the ore-rich regions of Alsace-Lorraine led to a dramatic increase in industrial production. Starting with almost no measurable steel production in the 1870s, Germany managed to catch up to British annual steel production in 1893 and then went on to surge far ahead: By 1914 its annual tonnage of steel was more than twice that of Britain. One advantage enjoyed by Germany was that it was able to model its new industrial facilities on those of its most modern competitors, saving substantial time and investment capital and resulting in newer and more efficient equipment and business methods. Yet another advantage was Germany's development of sophisticated scientific research capabilities at universities.

Industrialization also spread further afield during the second half of the nineteenth century. Aware of the growing power and influence of western European industrial powers, both Russia and Japan implemented economic reforms to compete on a more equal footing with the West. One factor in Russia's decision to convert from an agrarian to an industrial economy was their defeat by French and British forces in the Crimean War (1853–1856). Following the emancipation of serfs in 1861, Russia embarked on an ambitious plan to industrialize, as discussed in greater detail in Chapter 25. Stunned by the bold intrusion of the West into its waters by Commodore Matthew Perry in 1853, which led to the Meiji Constitution in 1868, Japan also adapted its economy to industrialism in order to keep pace with the West (see Chapter 24).

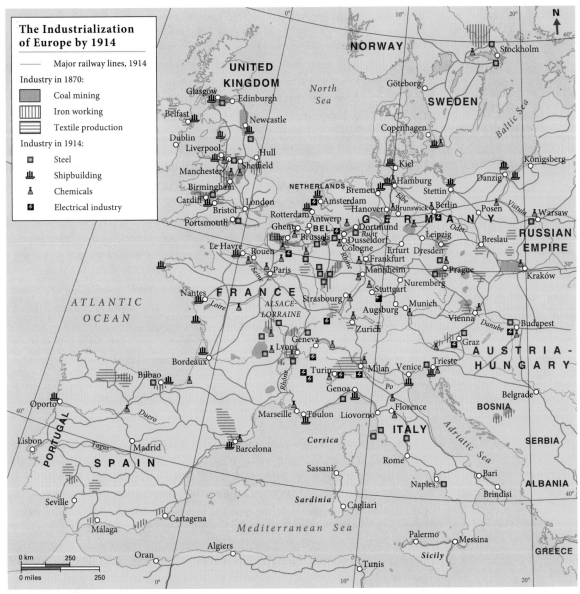

MAP 26.2 **The Industrialization of Europe by 1914.**

Patterns Up Close | "The Age of Steam"

More than any other innovation of the industrial age, the advent of practical steam power revolutionized manufacturing, transportation, communications, economics, and even politics and military matters. Indeed, at the height of steam's dominance, many people saw its ability to move freight and people and to run myriad kinds of machines as close to divine. Frederic A. Bartholdi, builder of the Statue of Liberty, rhapsodized at the American Centennial Exhibition in 1876 that the mammoth Corliss steam engine dominating the Machinery Hall there had "the beauty and almost the grace of human form" in its operation.

The origins of the steam age lie in an environmental crisis. A growing shortage of wood for fuel and charcoal making in Britain in the early 1700s forced manufacturers to turn to another fuel source: coal. As we have seen, Britain was blessed with vast amounts of coal, but getting to it was difficult because of a high water table: Mineshafts often flooded after only a few feet and had to be abandoned. Early methods of water extraction featured pumps operated by either human or animal power, but these were inefficient, expensive, and limited in power.

The first steam-driven piston engine based on experimentation with vacuum chambers and condensing steam came from the French Huguenot Denis Papin (1647–ca. 1712), who spent his later career in England. Thomas Savery (ca. 1650–1715), also taking up the idea of condensing steam and vacuum power, built a system of pipes employing the suction produced by this process dubbed the "Miner's Friend" that was able to extract water from shallow shafts but was useless for the deeper mines that were more common in rural Britain.

This drawback was partially addressed by Thomas Newcomen (1663–1729), who in 1712 vastly improved the efficiency of Papin's piston-and-cylinder design. Though over 100 Newcomen engines were in place throughout Britain and Europe at the time of Newcomen's death in 1729, a number of flaws still rendered them very slow and energy-inefficient. It remained for James Watt (1736–1819), a Scottish engineer, to make the final changes needed to create the prototype for fast engines sufficiently

Corliss Steam Engine. A tribute to the new power of the steam engine was this huge power plant in the Machinery Hall of the American Centennial Exposition in 1876. The Corliss engine pictured here produced over 1,400 horsepower and drove nearly all the machines in the exhibition hall—with the distinct exception of those in the British display. Along with the arm of the Statue of Liberty, also on exhibition there, it became the most recognized symbol of America's first world's fair.

The advantages of steel over iron were that it was lighter, harder, and more durable. Thus, it provided better rails for railroads and, increasingly, girders for the construction of high-rise buildings. Indeed, structural steel and steel-reinforced concrete made possible the construction of high-rise "skyscrapers," which by the turn of the century were soaring past the tallest masonry buildings. The switch from iron to steel construction of ships also marked a significant advance in steamship technology during the third quarter of the nineteenth century. Steel ships greatly improved the travel time between far-flung continents. By 1900, 95 percent of all commercial ocean liners were being constructed of steel. Steel also made possible stronger, faster, and roomier ships, while steel warships also proved far more durable in battle and set the tone for naval construction to this day.

efficient and versatile to drive factory machinery. Watt had been engaged in repairing Newcomen engines and quickly realized their limitations. His newly refined model, completed in 1765 and patented in 1769, was five times as efficient as Newcomen's engine and used 75 percent less coal.

After making several refinements Watt introduced a further improved model in 1783 that incorporated more advances. First, by injecting steam into both the top and bottom of the piston cylinder, its motion was converted to double action, making it more powerful and efficient. Second, through a system of "planetary gearing"—in which the piston shaft was connected by a circular gear to the hub of a flywheel—the back-and-forth rhythm of the piston was converted to smooth, rotary motion, suitable for driving machines in factories and mills. Watt's steam engines proved so popular that by 1790 they had replaced all of the Newcomen engines and by 1800 nearly 500 Watt engines were in operation in mines and factories.

Within a few decades, adaptations of this design were being used not just for stationary engines to run machinery but also to move vehicles along tracks and turn paddle wheels and screw propellers on boats—the first railroad engines and steamships. Both of these innovations soon provided the muscle and sinew of enhanced commerce and empire building among the newly industrializing nations. Indeed, by 1914, there was scarcely a place on the globe not accessible by either railroad or steamship. Although societies seeking to protect themselves from outside influence saw the railroad and steamer as forces of chaos, the web of railroad lines grew denser on every inhabited continent, and the continents themselves were connected by the tissue of shipping lines. Steam may indeed be said to be the power behind the creation of modern global society.

Questions

- How is the innovation of steam power the culmination of a pattern that began with the rise of the New Sciences in western Europe in the sixteenth and seventeenth centuries?

- Does Frederic A. Bartholdi's statement in 1876 that the Corliss steam engine "had the beauty and almost the grace of the human form" reflect a romantic outlook? If so, how?

Chemicals   Advances were also made in the use of chemicals. Here, the most significant developments were initiated by academic scientists, whose work resulted in later advances in the chemical industry. In 1856 the first synthetic dye, mauveine, was created, which initiated the synthetic dyestuffs industry. The result of these advances was not only a wider array of textiles but also new chemical compounds important in the refinement of wood pulp products, ranging from cheaper paper in the 1870s to artificial silk, known as rayon. Later discoveries, such as the synthesizing of ammonia and its conversion to nitrate for use in fertilizers and explosives, were to have far-reaching effects during World War I. The invention of dynamite by the Swedish chemist and engineer Alfred Bernhard

Nobel (1833–1896) provided the means to blast through rock formations, resulting in great tunnels and massive excavation projects like the Panama Canal (1914). In yet another chemical advance, Charles Goodyear (1800–1860) invented a process in 1839 that produced vulcanized rubber, and celluloid—the first synthetic plastic—was developed in 1869. Other innovations in chemistry, ranging from pharmaceuticals and drugs like aspirin to soap products, contributed to improved health. By the early part of the twentieth century, these developments had led to a "hygiene revolution" among the industrialized countries.

New Energies: Electricity and the Internal Combustion Engine   Although electricity had been in use during the first period of industrialization, its development and application were greatly advanced after 1850, especially in the generation of electrical power. The first step came with Michael Faraday (1791–1867) patenting the electromagnetic generator in 1861. But large-scale electrical generation would require a number of other innovations before it became a reality. Perhaps the most important devices in this regard were developed by engineer Nikola Tesla (1856–1943). Among Tesla's inventions were the alternating current (AC), the Tesla Coil (1891) for the more efficient transmission of electricity, and a host of generators, motors, and transformers. In 1888 the introduction of Tesla's "electric induction engine" led to the widespread adoption of electricity-generating power plants throughout industrialized Europe.

Another key source of energy to power the industrial revolution was the internal combustion engine. When oil, or liquid petroleum, was commercially developed in the 1860s and 1870s, it was at first refined into kerosene and used for illumination. One of the by-products of this process, gasoline, however, soon revealed its potential as a new fuel source. The first experimental internal combustion engines utilizing the new fuel appeared in the 1860s. Their light weight relative to their power was superior to steam engines of comparable size, and the first practical attempts to use them in powering vehicles came along in the next decade.

Who invented the automobile? Although two Germans, Gottlieb Daimler (1834–1900) and Karl Benz (1844–1929), are usually credited with the invention, the first true automobile was invented by an unheralded Austrian mechanic and inventor named Siegfried Marcus (1831–1898). As early as 1864 Marcus harnessed his own experimental internal combustion engine to a cart, which moved under its own power for over 200 yards. Over the next several years Marcus tinkered with several gadgets and devices in order to perfect his self-propelled contraption. Among these were the carburetor, the magneto ignition, various gears, the clutch, a steering mechanism, and a braking system. All of these inventions were included in the first real combustion-engine automobile, which Marcus drove through the streets of Vienna in 1874.

Internal combustion engines were also applied to early attempts at sustained flight. In 1900 Ferdinand von Zeppelin (1838–1917) constructed a rigid airship—a *dirigible*—consisting of a fabric-covered aluminum frame that was kept aloft by the incorporation of bags filled with hydrogen gas and powered by two 16-horsepower engines. Zeppelin's airships thus became the ancestors of the blimps that even today still ply the airways. Perhaps more momentous was the marriage of the gasoline engine to the glider, thus creating the first airplanes. Though there were several claimants to this honor, the Wright brothers are usually credited with the first sustained engine-powered flight in Kitty Hawk, North Carolina, on December 17, 1903. By 1909, the first flight across the English Channel had been completed; in 1911 the first transcontinental airplane flight across the United States took place, though by taking 82 hours of flight time over a span of 2 months it could scarcely compete with railroad travel. Still, the potential of both the automobile and the airplane were to be starkly revealed within a few years during the Great War.

The Communication Revolution Although electric telegraph messages were transmitted as early as the 1840s with the advent of the devices and code devised by Samuel F. B. Morse (1791–1872), it was only in the 1860s and 1870s that major continental landmasses were linked by submarine transoceanic cables. The first successful link from Britain to India was installed in 1865. The first transatlantic cable, from Britain to America, was laid as early as 1858, though it was only in 1866 that the cable was deemed operationally successful. By the latter part of the nineteenth century, telegraphic communication was a worldwide phenomenon, which has been likened to the Internet in its impact on human contact. This was vastly augmented with the telephone, invented by Alexander Graham Bell (1847–1922) in 1876, which made voice communication possible by wire.

But perhaps most revolutionary of all was the advent of wireless communication. The theoretical groundwork for this had been laid by James Clerk Maxwell (1831–1879), a Scottish physicist researching the theoretical properties of electromagnetism, and Heinrich Rudolf Hertz (1857–1894). In 1885 Hertz—whose name was later given to the unit of measurement for radio wave cycles—discovered that electromagnetic radiation actually produces unseen waves that emanate through the universe. In the later 1890s, Guglielmo Marconi (1874–1937) developed a device using these radio waves generated by electric sparks controlled by a telegraph key to send and receive messages over several miles. By 1903 Marconi had enhanced the power and range of the device enough to send the first transatlantic radio message, from Cape Cod in the United States to Cornwall in England. The "wireless telegraph" was quickly adopted by ships for reliable communication at sea. Subsequent improvements, such as the development of the vacuum tube amplifier and oscillator, resulted in greater power and reliability and, within a few years, the ability to transmit sound wirelessly.

The Weapons Revolution The advances in chemistry and explosives, metallurgy, and machine tooling during the second half of the nineteenth century also contributed to a vastly enhanced lethality among weapons. Earlier advances from the 1830s to the early 1860s (including the percussion cap, the conical bullet, the revolver, and the rifled musket) provided the base for of the development of ever more sophisticated firearms. Breech-loading weapons, in their infancy during the early 1860s, rapidly came of age with the advent of the brass cartridge. By 1865, a number of manufacturers were marketing repeating rifles, some of whose designs, like the famous Winchester lever-action models, are still popular today. Rifles designed by the German firms of Krupp and Mauser pioneered the bolt-action, magazine, and clip-fed rifles that remained the staple of infantry weapons through two world wars.

Artillery went through a similar transformation. Breech-loading artillery, made possible by precision machining of breech locks and the introduction of metallic cartridges for artillery shells, made loading and firing large guns far more efficient.

By the early 1880s the invention of the recoil cylinder—a spring or hydraulic device like an automobile shock absorber—to cushion the force of the gun's recoil eliminated the necessity of reaiming the piece after every shot. Field artillery could now be anchored, aimed, and fired continuously with enhanced accuracy: It had become "rapid-fire artillery." Its effectiveness was enhanced further by the new explosives like guncotton, dynamite, and later TNT, for use in its shells. Another innovation in this regard was the development of smokeless powder, or *cordite*, which, in addition to eliminating much of the battlefield smoke generated by black powder, was three times more powerful as a propellant. Thus, the range and accuracy of small arms and artillery were pushed even further.

By far, the most significant—and lethal—advance in weaponry during the later nineteenth century, however, was the invention of the machine gun, the deadliest weapon ever developed. Though many quick-firing weapons had been developed with varying degrees of success during these years—the most famous being the Gatling Gun (1861)—the first fully automatic machine gun was conceived by Hiram Maxim (1840–1916), an American inventor and dabbler in electricity.

"In 1882 I was in Vienna . . . [an acquaintance] said: . . . 'If you want to make a pile of money, invent something that will enable these Europeans to cut each others' throats with greater facility.'"

—Hiram Maxim

By the outbreak of World War I, every major army in the world was equipping itself with Maxim's guns, now manufactured in licensed factories in Europe and the United States. Perhaps more than any other single weapon, the machine gun made the western front in Europe from 1914 to 1918 the most devastating killing field in human history. In his memoirs, Maxim notes somewhat ruefully that he was applauded more highly for inventing his "killing machine" than for inventing a steam inhaler for those suffering from bronchitis.

Hiram Maxim. In this 1900 photo, the proud inventor of the machine gun looks on with self-satisfied pride as Albert Edward, Prince of Wales (the future King Edward VII), experiences for himself the awesome firepower of Maxim's "little daisy of a gun." In 1885 Maxim put on a similar demonstration for Lord Wolseley, commander in chief of the British Army. The British War Office adopted the gun 3 years later. The lethal power of the machine gun was first put to use in Africa at the Battle of Omdurman in 1898, where 20,000 Sudanese cavalrymen were slaughtered in fruitless charges against a line of 20 Maxim guns.

The Social and Economic Impact of Industrialism, 1750–1914

All of these changes in modes of production, particularly the emergence of the factory system, resulted in wholesale transformations in the daily lives of millions around the globe. Along with new networks of transportation and communication, new materials, and new sources of energy, the industrialized nations underwent significant changes in how they viewed politics, social institutions, and economic relationships during this time.

Demographic Changes

Changes in the demographics of industrialized nations followed the development of new industries. Perhaps most significantly, the populations of these countries grew at unprecedented rates and became increasingly urbanized. Indeed, Great Britain became by the latter half of the nineteenth century the first country to have more urban dwellers than rural inhabitants. This trend would continue among the industrialized nations through the twentieth century.

Population Surge and Urbanization   As data from 1700 to around 1914 reveal, the industrialized nations experienced a significant population explosion (see Map 26.3). Advances in industrial production, expansion of factories, and improved agriculture during the first Industrial Revolution combined to produce increasing opportunities for jobs as well as more plentiful and nutritious food in order to sustain a larger population. In the second Industrial Revolution scientific advances in medicine, including drugs and vaccinations, along with notions of sanitation, contributed to a declining mortality rate. For example, the population of Britain grew from around 9 million in 1700 to around 20 million in 1850. Then from 1871 to 1914 Britain's population soared from 31 million to nearly 50 million. Other industrialized states experienced similar population increases; in Germany, for example, the population grew from around 41 million in 1871 to 58 million in 1914.

More revealing than overall population figures is the shift of populations from rural to urban areas. For example, in Great Britain in 1800 around 60 percent of the population lived in rural areas. By 1850, however, about 50 percent of the population lived in cities. In numerical terms, the population of London amounted to around 1 million in 1800, but by 1850 that figure had more than doubled to around 2.5 million. Moreover, in 1801 only 21 cities in Europe (including London) could boast of populations over 100,000. By 1850, this had doubled to 42. Significant in this respect was the appearance of new industrial and commercial centers such as Manchester, Liverpool, Birmingham, and Glasgow, as well as vast increases in the size of older capital cities such as Paris, Berlin, and St. Petersburg.

European Migrations   Another social change during the industrial era concerns overseas emigrations of Europeans. In part, this movement was sparked by the dramatic rise in population in industrialized areas of Europe. Another contributing factor, however, was the desire to escape the grinding poverty of underdeveloped regions of Europe—particularly Ireland and southeast Europe—in order to seek better opportunities in developing industrial parts of America. In

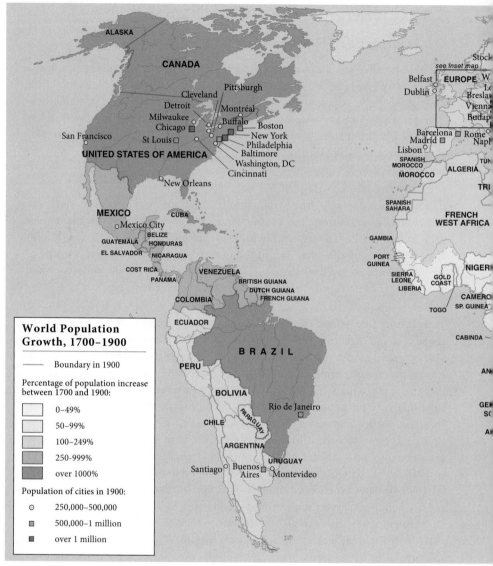

MAP **26.3** **World Population Growth, 1700–1900.**

addition, advances in transportation made it easier for Europeans to emigrate. In all, some 60 million Europeans left for other parts of the world (North and South America, Australia, and Asiatic Russia) between 1800 and 1914. Of these, the majority emigrated to the United States and Canada (see Map 26.4).

Industrial Society

Industrialization led to significant changes in the hierarchy of social ranks. Although the elites continued to enjoy their privileged status, the "new money" of the rising middle classes began to eclipse "old money" in terms of social status and influence. The increasing importance of capitalism and commerce, and with it the accumulation of significant wealth, greatly enhanced the status and influence of the upper echelons

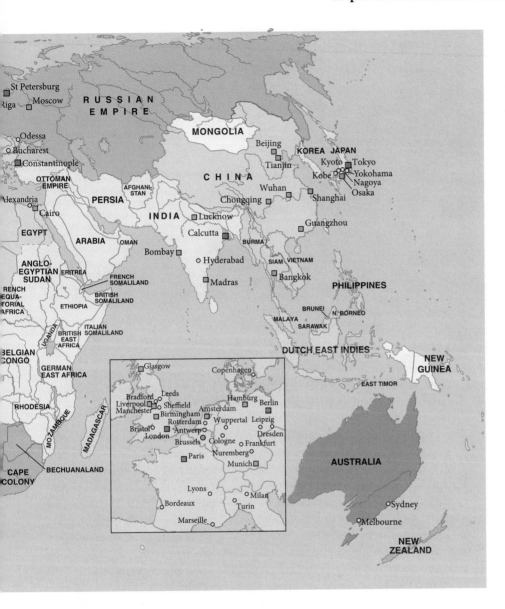

of the middle class, or bourgeoisie. No longer were status and power determined solely by aristocratic birth or privilege. The principal alteration in the social hierarchy, however, was the appearance of a new rank: the working class. For the first time, the advent of industrialism created the concept of "class consciousness," or growing awareness of, and emphasis on, social standing determined by occupation and income.

The Upper Classes   At the top of the European social scene, members of the landed aristocracy were joined by the new urban elites. Together, they constituted only 5 percent of the total population. These urban elites were the extremely rich factory owners, bankers, and merchants who had made personal fortunes from industrial pursuits. Although a tiny minority, they managed to control almost

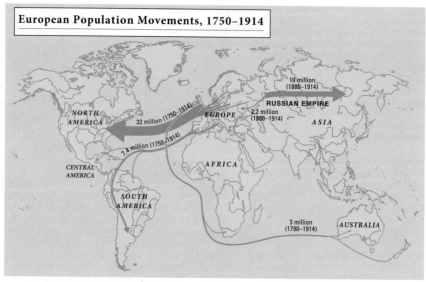

MAP **26.4 European Population Movements, 1750–1914.**

40 percent of Europe's wealth. Below these were the bourgeoisie, who had either married into the highest social rank or whose wealth was not quite at the level of the aristocrats and urban elites.

The Middle Classes   A notch down from the upper classes were the middle classes, who constituted around 15 percent of Europe's total population. This rank was peopled mostly by professionals (lawyers, physicians), high-ranking government officials, and prosperous businessmen and merchants, who rose to prominence in the new age thanks largely to their acquisition of cash. Distinguished from the landed aristocracy above them and from the working classes below, the middle classes were themselves divided by a sense of class consciousness. They enjoyed better lifestyles in terms of education, fine homes, and as measured by conspicuous consumption of luxury goods. The lower middle class was itself divided into two social strata. The upper tier was made up for the most part by artisans and skilled workers in factories, mines, and other places, while beneath them were unskilled workers, tradespeople, and handcrafters.

It was the middle class, particularly concerned with "respectability," which set the cultural and moral tone for the second half of the nineteenth century. Impropriety and sexual scandal were not to be tolerated; indeed, in 1867 the English parliament passed the Obscene Publications Bill in an attempt to crack down on pornographic literature. They set themselves apart from the elites above, and especially from those below, by emphasizing what they considered their respectability, frugality, and industry. Determined to succeed at all costs, the industrial middle classes eagerly consumed numerous "self-help" books, of which the most famous was Samuel Smiles's *Self-Help* (1859). The book went through several editions in subsequent years, and emerged as the most popular of the self-help books in Victorian England.

The Working Class   Urban factory workers were distinguished from farmers and workers in rural areas by their daily routine regulated by the factory time clock and by selling their labor in return for cash wages. Among the working classes, divisions existed between skilled and unskilled workers, largely determined by familiarity with the intricacies of industrial machinery and its maintenance.

Woman and Children Coal Putters, Mid and East Lothian, Scotland ca. 1848. Women and children (some as young as 5 or 6 years old) worked long hours in terrible conditions in underground mines. Here, a woman and two children, known as "putters," struggle to push a wagon of coal to the surface. Other children, called "trappers," maintained airflow in the tunnels by operating ventilation doors.

Typical working conditions in British textile mills in the early 1800s were deplorable. Without traditional protective guilds or associations, workers were at the mercy of factory owners. The factory clock and the pace of factory machinery determined the day's work, which was repetitive, dirty, and dangerous. Even young children—some as young as 7 years old—worked in factories, some alongside their parents as family units and others who had been orphaned or turned over to local parishes by parents who could no longer provide for their care. Working long hours—12- to 14-hour days were common in the early 1800s—children were constantly urged to speed up production and severely disciplined for "idling." Indeed, they were commonly beaten for falling asleep and to keep them from falling into the machinery, which, because of the lack of protection from its moving parts, could easily maim or kill them. In fact, until the 1840s in Britain, the majority of "hands," or factory workers, were women and children, who, by virtue of their inexperience and expendability, could be paid less than their male counterparts.

Conditions were often even worse in the mines. Children frequently began work in mines as early as age 6 or 7, most often as "trappers," responsible for opening and shutting ventilation doors in mineshafts. Because of their small size, children were put to work "hurrying," or lugging newly dug coal along long, low underground passageways for conveyance to the surface. Girls were especially victimized in underground mines, where they not only had to drag heavy coal-filled carts by chains fixed to leather belts around their waists but also were frequently sexually abused by their supervisors.

Factory Towns   Because industrial cities expanded close to factories and mills, conditions there were as grim as within the factories themselves. Clouds of coal smoke blackened buildings, acidified the rain and soil, and caused respiratory ailments among the citizens, prompting the poet William Blake's famous allusion to "dark Satanic Mills." In addition to the acrid smell of coal, a variety of other stenches assaulted the nostrils of the inhabitants. Piles of coal ash and clinker, pungent waste materials from coking or from gas works, and vile outpourings from tanneries and dye works combined with household waste, sewage, and horse manure. With the population exploding and only rudimentary waste disposal and access to clean water, diseases like cholera, typhus, and tuberculosis were rampant.

Adding to the miseries of the inhabitants of factory towns were their wretched living conditions. The working classes lived in

"In one of these courts there stands . . . a privy without a door, so dirty that the inhabitants can pass . . . only by passing through foul pools of stagnant urine and excrement."

—Friedrich Engels

Working-Class Tenements in English Industrial Cities. In this engraving, entitled *Over London by Rail*, the celebrated engraver Gustave Doré (1832–1883) depicts the overcrowded and squalid living conditions in working-class tenements during the early years of the Industrial Revolution. Notice the long rows of houses separated by walls and arranged in back-to-back fashion. Notice also the stretched lines for drying clothes, as well as the large number of occupants in each outdoor area.

crowded tenements consisting of row after row of shoddily built houses packed together in narrow, dark streets. One social activist, Friedrich Engels (1820–1895), the son of a wealthy mill owner and later collaborator with Karl Marx, was determined to call attention to such abysmal conditions.

Critics of Industrialism

It was not long before Engels and other socially conscious observers began to draw attention to the obvious abuses of the industrial movement and to stimulate reform of working conditions. Efforts to improve these sordid conditions were launched in Great Britain in the 1820s and 1830s and carried over into the 1870s.

Socialists   The plight of the working classes inspired many social activists to take up the fight for reform, among them French and English "utopian socialists"— a term originally used derisively to describe the presumed impracticality of their schemes. One of the earliest of these activists was Henri de Saint-Simon (1760–1825), whose view of humanity defied industrial society's competition for individual wealth. In Saint-Simon's view, private property should be more equally distributed, according to the notion "From each according to his abilities, to each according to his works." Louis Blanc (1811–1882) criticized the capitalist system in his *The Organization of Work* (1839), urging workers to agitate for voting rights and espousing radical ideas like the right to work. He reconfigured Saint-Simon's memorable phrase to read "From each according to his abilities, to each according to his needs." Charles Fourier (1772–1837) advocated the founding of self-sustaining model communities in which jobs were apportioned according to ability and interest, with a sliding scale of wages tailored to highly compensate those doing the most dangerous or unattractive jobs. Fourier's concept of such "phalanxes" was the one adopted by the North American Phalanx, in which Mary Paul spent time (see the opening of this chapter).

Robert Owen (1771–1858), a factory owner in the north of England, led a movement to establish the Grand National Consolidated Trades Union. Its objective was a national strike of all trade unions, but owing to a lack of participation among workers, the movement was disbanded. Owen had previously established a model community in Scotland called New Lanark, where more humane living and working conditions for workers resulted in greater profits. After campaigning for the formation of workers' unions, Owen left for America, where he set up a model socialist community in Indiana called New Harmony, which eventually dissolved amid internal quarrels when he returned to England.

Chartism was another organized labor movement in Britain. Taking its name from the People's Charter (1838), Chartism was formed by the London Working Men's Association, and its primary goal, among others, was universal male suffrage. Millions of workers signed petitions, which were presented to Parliament in 1839 and 1842; these were rejected. Nevertheless, the chartist movement galvanized for the first time workers' sentiments and aspirations, and it served as a model for future attempts at labor reform.

Karl Marx   By far the most famous of the social reformers was Karl Marx (1818–1883). The son of a prosperous German attorney, Marx proved a brilliant student, eventually earning a PhD in philosophy from the University of Berlin. Marx's activities, however, resulted in his being exiled from Germany and then from France. During a visit to the industrial center of Manchester, where he met and befriended Friedrich Engels, Marx observed both the miserable lives of factory workers and the patent inequities of industrialism. From this, Marx developed his theory, which he termed "scientific socialism," that all of history involved class struggles. Borrowing the dialectical schema of the German philosopher Georg Wilhelm Friedrich Hegel (1770–1831), Marx replaced its idealism with his own materialist concept based on economic class struggle: *dialectical materialism*. Moreover, Marx saw revolution as the means by which the industrial working classes will ultimately topple the capitalist order: Just as the Third Estate and bourgeoisie had overthrown the aristocracy during the French Revolution, the current struggle between the working classes and the capitalist entrepreneurs would ultimately result in the demise of capitalism.

Karl Marx. In this photo, taken in London in 1875, Marx displays many of the character traits for which he is best known. Following the publication of his *Das Kapital* in 1871, Marx had established his reputation as a scholar of economic theory. Notice his self-satisfied and confident demeanor as he stares at the camera in an almost defiant manner. Notice as well his attire, ironically suggestive of a successful member of the bourgeoisie. After Marx's death, his longtime friend Friedrich Engels distributed 1,200 copies of this photo to communists around the world.

Convinced of the need to overthrow the capitalist system, Marx and Engels joined the nascent Communist Party in London. In preparation for a meeting in 1848, the two collaborators dashed off a pamphlet entitled *The Communist Manifesto* (1848), propaganda designed to rally support among the working classes, or *proletariat,* and to encourage them to rise up and overthrow the capitalist factory owners, or *bourgeoisie.* Compiled from a variety of French socialist, German philosophical, and personal interpretations of past history, the *Manifesto* reflects Marx's vision that "the history of all hitherto existing society is the history of class struggle" and that the time had come for the working classes to follow earlier examples and to overthrow the capitalists: "The proletarians have nothing to lose but their chains. They have a world to win. WORKING MEN OF ALL COUNTRIES, UNITE!"

Inquiries and Reforms   As critics of industrialism cried out against the abuses of the industrial movement, many—including some factory owners inspired by humanitarian concerns—called for governments to reform working conditions. In 1832 Parliament launched an inquiry into abuses within factories, resulting in the Sadler Report, which pointed out abuses related to child labor. In 1833 the Factory Act was passed, which set a minimum age of 9 for child employees and limited the workday to 8 hours for children between the ages of 9 and 13 and to 12 hours for those aged 13–18. Further reforms in 1847 and 1848 limited women and children to a maximum of 58 hours a week (the Ten Hours Act). Working conditions in mines were equally harsh, especially for women and children. Accordingly, similar inquiries were conducted concerning working conditions within mines, resulting in the Mines Act of 1842. It forbade the underground employment of all girls and women and set a minimum age of 10 for child laborers.

Improved Standards of Living

Although still a matter of debate among historians, contemporary data suggest that in overall terms living and working conditions began to improve in Britain from around the 1830s to the end of the century. Thanks to the series of reforms already mentioned, conditions in factories and mines were substantially better than at the beginning of the century. Textile factories were now located in urban areas, and housing conditions for workers were more amenable. Most important, wage levels increased across the nineteenth century for industrial workers. For example, from 1850 to 1875 wages of British workers increased by around one-third and by nearly one-half by 1900.

New Jobs for Women   As a result of the second Industrial Revolution, many women fared far better in terms of employment. In overall terms, women represented around one-third of the workers in later nineteenth-century industrial jobs. The data from textile mills offer supporting evidence. While fewer than 2,000 women were employed in the mills in 1837, that figure nearly doubled by 1865, and by around 1900 the number of female textile workers had increased to nearly 6,000. But factory work in textile mills was not the only avenue open to women as the industrial era unfolded in the later years of the nineteenth century.

When new technologies and social trends created new employment possibilities, women constituted a readily available pool of workers. Inventions like the typewriter (perfected in the 1870s), the telephone (invented by Alexander Graham Bell in 1876), and calculating machines (in use in the 1890s), for instance, required workers to handle related jobs, the majority of which went mostly to single women and widows. As a result, women became particularly prominent in secretarial

Women Working as Telephone Operators. The first telephone exchange appeared in 1879. Women were selected as operators because their voices were considered pleasing to the ear and because they were considered more polite than men.

office jobs. In addition, the explosion of business firms created countless jobs for secretaries, while department stores opened up jobs for women as clerks.

Women's Suffrage Movement   Although many women were afforded new opportunities in business and in professions like nursing and education after 1871, in many other areas women remained second-class citizens. Women in both the United States and Europe did not begin to gain the right to own property or to sue for divorce until the third quarter of the nineteenth century, as exemplified by the passage of the English Married Woman's Property Act in 1882.

More urgent for many female reformers was the right to vote. Throughout Europe during the late nineteenth and early twentieth centuries, women formed political groups to press for the vote. The most active of these groups was in Britain, where in 1867 the National Society for Women's Suffrage was founded. The most famous—and most radical—of British political feminists was Emmeline Pankhurst (1858–1928), who together with her daughters formed the Women's Social and Political Union in 1903. They and their supporters, known as *suffragettes*, resorted to public acts of protest and civil disobedience in order to call attention to their cause. Although these tactics were of no avail prior to 1914, the right to vote was extended to some British women after the war.

Political feminists were also active on the Continent. The French League of Women's Rights was founded in the 1870s, and the Union of German Women's Organizations was formed in 1894; in neither country was the right to vote granted women until after World War I. Women in the United States pursued a parallel course with similar results: After decades of lobbying before the war, women's suffrage was finally granted by constitutional amendment in 1920.

Improved Urban Living

Living conditions within the major urban areas in industrialized nations improved significantly during the late nineteenth and early twentieth centuries. Largely the result of the application of new technologies emerging from the industrial movement, there is no question that the lives of urban dwellers were improved in the second half of the nineteenth century.

Sanitation and Electricity   One measure of improved living conditions was in the provision of better sanitation. Beginning in the 1860s and 1870s large cities in Britain and Europe established public water services and began to construct underground sewage systems to carry waste from houses, outfitted with running water, to rivers and other locations beyond urban areas. By the latter part of the nineteenth century, the widespread use of gas lighting gradually began to give way to electrical varieties. Thomas Edison (1847–1931) perfected the incandescent light bulb in 1879, making the lighting of homes and business interiors more affordable and practical and gradually replacing gas lighting.

Paris represents a good example of the implementation of these reforms. In the 1850s and 1860s Napoleon III (r. 1852–1870) appointed the urban planner Georges Haussmann (1809–1891) to begin a massive reconstruction of the city. Haussmann tore down close-packed tenements in order to construct modernized buildings and wide boulevards. This was driven by a desire to beautify the city as well as the need to provide better access for government troops in the event of public demonstrations; barricaded streets, a feature of the revolutions of 1830 and 1848, thus became a thing of the past. And, like most cities of the industrialized West by the turn of the twentieth century, Paris featured lighted and paved streets, public water systems, parks, hospitals, and police. A dramatic symbol of both the newly redesigned city of Paris and the triumph of industry and science during the second Industrial Revolution was the Eiffel Tower, designed by Alexandre Gustave Eiffel (1832–1923). Erected for the Paris Exposition of 1889, the tower took years to construct, and at nearly 1,000 feet in height was the tallest structure in the world until the construction of the Empire State building in New York in 1931.

Leisure and Sport   Another advance in urban life in the "age of materialism" was an increase in leisure and sporting activities. The later nineteenth century saw the emergence of sporting organizations and clubs, along with the establishment of rules for play. Games played by professional teams, another innovation in sport, provided recreation for working-class men. In Britain, for example, rules for playing soccer were established in 1863 by the Football Association, and in 1888 the English Football League was established. In 1871 the Rugby Football Union was formed. In the 1870s and 1880s British cricket teams took the game abroad to compete with teams in their far-flung colonies. In 1901 the championship game of the British FA Cup competition drew over 100,000 spectators.

Nor was this trend confined to Britain. In 1896 the first modern Olympic Games took place in Athens, Greece. In 1903 the first Tour de France was run through the French countryside. In 1904 the game of soccer was given international rules by a meeting of the International Federation of Association Football in Paris. By the early 1900s the game of baseball in America had been formalized into two leagues, the National League and the American League.

Big Business

As the scale of urban planning and renewal increased toward the end of the nineteenth century, business flourished. As manufacturing, transportation, and financing matured, entrepreneurs and businessmen became concerned about competition and falling profit rates. Since governments generally pursued hands-off liberalism (*laissez-faire*; see Chapter 22) in the economy, except for protective tariffs, entrepreneurs sought to establish cartels and monopolies, creating big business enterprises in the process.

Large Firms   As Britain industrialized, it gradually shifted from a closed mercantilist economy to the liberal free-trade policy Adam Smith advocated (see Chapter 22). Britain's competitors, especially Germany and the United States, by contrast, erected high tariff walls around their borders in order to help their fledgling industries. After the second wave of steel, chemical, and electrical industrialization in the second half of the nineteenth century, the scale of industrial investments rose exponentially. On domestic markets, governments did not interfere with business organization and practice, except for labor protection in Europe. As a result, in several branches of the economy, big businesses emerged during the second half of the nineteenth century that protected their profit rates through *cartels* (market-sharing agreements) or strove for outright monopolies.

Large firms typically developed in Germany and the United States, the leaders of the second wave of industrialization. By the 1890s, corporations like the Krupp steelworks in Germany and Standard Oil Company in the United States controlled large shares of their markets. Standard Oil at its height, for example, produced over 90 percent of the country's petroleum. The United States Steel Corporation, founded in 1901 by Andrew Carnegie (1835–1919), dominated the production of American steel. Carnegie himself amassed a huge personal fortune of almost $250 million, making him the richest man in the world at the time.

New Management Styles   In addition, new technologies in all industrial sectors offered more efficient means of production; the result was a series of significant changes in production processes during the second phase of European industrialism. One example is the implementation of the so-called American System, incorporating the use of interchangeable parts, which greatly enhanced mass production. A related development was the appearance of "continuous-flow production," wherein workers performed specialized tasks at stationary positions along an assembly line. In addition, new "scientific management" tactics were employed in mass-production assembly plants. Since no more than basic skills were required on many assembly lines, labor costs could be kept low.

The best known of the new management systems was Taylorism, named after Frederick W. Taylor (1856–1915), an American engineer. Its objective was to measure each factory worker's production based on how many units were completed in an hour's time. The result was that workers were not only more carefully managed by their superiors but also paid in accordance with their productivity. The combined result was a rapid escalation in the speed of production, which in turn contributed to a marked increase in the production of goods for daily consumption and, therefore, in the development of a consumer market at the turn of the twentieth century.

The Assembly Line. The American System of interchangeable parts for muskets of the early nineteenth century had evolved into the assembly line by the early twentieth. Here, Ford Model T automobiles are moved along a conveyor to different stations, where workers assemble them in simple, repetitive steps, resulting in production efficiency and low prices for the cars.

Intellectual and Cultural Responses to Industrialism

The impressive achievements of industrialism contributed to social and cultural shifts in western society toward the close of the nineteenth century. The advent of modernity was initially celebrated as an age of progress in science, industry, and the development of a mass culture. Nevertheless, the new age of prosperity and materialism gradually provoked a growing sense of unease concerning what these advances had wrought. The rising chorus of doubt, initiated by new discoveries in the scientific community, generated similar reactions among intellectuals and artists. In the process alternative and startlingly innovative modes of cultural expression, particularly in the expressive arts, upset traditional and conventional forms. Taken together the intellectual and cultural scene in Europe was convulsive and chaotic, resulting in a mood of anxiety and uncertainty on the eve of the Great War.

Scientific and Intellectual Developments

The latter half of the nineteenth century saw advances in both theoretical and empirical sciences that laid the basis for many of the staples of the twentieth century. Among the most far-reaching were atomic physics and relativity theory, Darwinism and evolution, and the foundations of modern psychology. Scientists also made great strides in medicine, although here the most important breakthroughs had to await the twentieth century.

New Theories of Matter   Quests for understanding the nature of matter, under way since Galileo (see Chapter 17), became systematic with the establishment of technical universities and science faculties in existing universities in the second half of the 1800s. Researchers made important discoveries in the 1890s that would have far-reaching consequences in the development of atomic physics and the theories of relativity. In 1892 the Dutch physicist Hendrik Lorentz (1853–1928) demonstrated that the atom, far from being a solid billiard ball, actually contained smaller particles, which he named "corpuscles"; these were later renamed electrons. A few years later, Wilhelm Roentgen (1845–1923) discovered a mysterious form of emission he called X-rays. The ability to generate these rays would shortly lead to the development of the X-ray machine. The following year, 1896, saw the first experiments in assessing radioactivity in uranium and radium by Antoine Becquerel (1852–1908) and Marie Curie (1867–1934).

As a result of these experimental findings, theoretical physics advanced new theories on the nature of light and energy. In 1900 Max Planck (1858–1947) proposed that instead of the accepted notion that energy is emitted in steady streams or waves, it is issued in bursts, or what he termed "quanta." This idea, later developed into quantum theory, suggested that matter and energy might be interchangeable. Ernest Rutherford (1871–1937), interested in this interchangeability, demonstrated in 1911 that radioactive atoms release a form of energy in the process of their disintegration. Thus, nearly three centuries of speculation about atoms as the building blocks of nature led to experimentally verified theories of subatomic particles.

Albert Einstein   These discoveries in the physical sciences set the stage for the appearance of perhaps the most sensational of the turn-of-the-century scientific theories: the theory of relativity of Albert Einstein (1879–1955). In 1905 and then again in 1915 Einstein published papers in which he destroyed the Newtonian notion of a certain, absolute, and mechanistic universe that obeys unvarying and objectively verifiable laws. Instead, Einstein argued that there are no absolutes of time, space, and motion; rather, these are relative to each other and depend on the position of the observer.

Moreover, Einstein demonstrated that Newton was incorrect in thinking that matter and energy were separate entities; they were, in fact, equivalent, and he developed the corresponding mathematical formula. In his equation $E = mc^2$, Einstein theorized that the atom contains an amount of energy equal to its mass multiplied by the square of the speed of light. In other words, relatively small amounts of matter could be converted into massive amounts of energy. This discovery, developed further in the twentieth century, provided the foundation for a better understanding of the forces among subatomic particles and the construction of nuclear weapons.

Charles Darwin   The basis of modern theories of evolution was first proposed by Charles Darwin (1809–1882). Darwin's *On the Origin of Species by Means of Natural Selection* (1859) argued that species gradually evolved from lower to higher forms. As a young man Darwin sailed on an exploratory mission on the HMS *Beagle* from 1831 to 1836 to the waters off the South American Pacific coast. Observing the tremendous variability of species on the string of the isolated Galapagos Islands, he found himself at a loss to explain why so many different species cohabited within such close geographical areas.

It occurred to Darwin—and independently to another English naturalist, Alfred Russell Wallace (1823–1913)—that an explanation for the appearance of new species in nature might lie in the struggle for food: Only those species equipped with the tools to survive in their environments would win out; those without these characteristics would become extinct.

The most controversial part of the Darwinian theory of evolution as spelled out in the *Origin* rests in the notion that characteristics are passed on by means of "natural selection." In other words, there is no intelligence or plan in the universe—only random chance and haphazard process, resulting in a pessimistic view of "nature, red in tooth and claw."

Although the *Origin* said nothing about the theory of evolution as applied to humankind—this appeared later in *The Descent of Man* (1871)—there were those who quickly applied it to society and nations. The English philosopher Herbert Spencer (1820–1903) was instrumental in proposing a theory that came to be called "social Darwinism," which sought to apply ideas of natural selection to races, ethnicities, and peoples. Spencer's ideas were frequently used to support imperial ventures aimed at the conquest and sometimes the "uplift" of non-European or American peoples as well as to justify increasingly virulent nationalism in the years leading to World War I.

Sigmund Freud   Victorians were especially concerned with apparently unconscious impulses for actions not subject to human will. The best known of the early

Charles Darwin as Ape.
Darwin's theories about the evolution of humankind aroused enormous scorn. In this scathing 1861 cartoon, Darwin, with the body of a monkey, holds a mirror to a simian-looking creature. The original caption quoted a line from Shakespeare's *Love's Labour's Lost:* "This is the ape of form."

psychologists was Sigmund Freud (1856–1939), an Austrian physician. Freud specialized in treating patients suffering from what was then called "hysteria," which he treated using a technique he labeled "psychoanalysis." In 1900 Freud published his highly influential *The Interpretation of Dreams*, in which he drew connections between dreams and the unconscious in humans. The sum total of Freudian psychological theories is that humans, so far from being rational creatures, are in fact irrational creatures, driven by subconscious, and not conscious, urges. Today, Freud's ideas no longer enjoy the unquestioned dominance they once did in the field, which has largely become a branch of medicine and, in particular, the study of brain chemicals. But his influence still survives on the practical level in the form of therapeutic counseling and behavior modification.

The Meaning of the New Scientific Discoveries
Physics, biology, and psychology were not the only sciences contributing to the emergence of scientific–industrial society at the end of the nineteenth century. Medicine began to acquire a scientific character, for example, with the discoveries of vaccines by Louis Pasteur (1822–1895). But it had to await the twentieth century before it reached maturity. With the arrival of the theories of relativity, Darwinian selection, and the psychological unconscious, however, the transition toward the scientific–industrial age was sufficiently under way to throw people into deep philosophical and religious confusion.

In a sense, the path of reductionism begun in the seventeenth century and discussed in Chapter 17 was being reached. In previous centuries, the Hobbesian embodied mind, fear of death, "war of all against all," and religious skepticism, secularism, and atheism of the Enlightenment were merely speculations that remained ultimately unproved. Now, the specter of a meaningless universe inhabited by beings devoid of free will and driven by biological forces over which they have no control seemed to many to be inescapable. Thus, the new era seemed to usher in a profoundly disturbing devil's bargain: The sciences had created so many useful things to ease the burdens of human life but had taken away the sense of purpose that made that life worth living. It was left to philosophers, religious leaders, intellectuals, and artists to wrestle with the implications of this central problem of scientific–industrial society.

Toward Modernity in Philosophy and Religion
Despite the impressive achievements of Western industrialized society during the late nineteenth century, there were many who felt uneasy about the results. Scores

of detractors—mostly in the intellectual community of western Europe—decried the boastful claims of a "superior" scientific civilization. These voices ridiculed Western bourgeois values and advocated alternative approaches to personal fulfillment.

Friedrich Nietzsche   The most celebrated of these detractors was the German philosopher Friedrich Nietzsche (1844–1900), a brilliant but mentally unstable professor at the University of Basel. Nietzsche, who railed against the conventions of Western civilization and criticized the perceived decadence of modern culture, represents a tendency toward pessimism and doubt about the progress of Western culture near the end of the nineteenth century.

Nietzsche began his assault on Western culture in 1872 with the publication of *The Birth of Tragedy*, which was followed in later years by works like *Beyond Good and Evil* (1886) and *On the Genealogy of Morals* (1887). One object of derision for Nietzsche was the entire notion of scientific, rational thought as the best path toward intellectual truth. For Nietzsche, and for others of like mind, rational thought will not improve either the individual or the welfare of humankind; only recourse to "will" instead of intellect—what Nietzsche called the "will to power"—will suffice. The individual who follows this path will become a "superman" and will lead others toward truth. Another target of Nietzsche's wrath was Christianity, which in his eyes led its believers into a "slave morality"; he infamously declared that "God is dead."

> "I call Christianity the one great curse . . . the one immortal blemish of mankind."
>
> —Friedrich Nietzsche

Toward Modernity in Literature and the Arts

As we have seen throughout this chapter, the creation of scientific–industrial society—modernity—was a slow and very traumatic process. The social realities of interacting and adapting to the new order were already on painful display in the postromantic period of realism in the arts and literature that marked the second half of the nineteenth century (see Chapter 22). The succeeding decades were to yield what in many ways was an even grimmer and more disjointed view of the new scientific–industrial society.

Literature   Literary expression was generally negative toward the popularization of "soulless" science and the materialism of the second half of the industrial revolution. Thomas Hardy (1840–1928), for example, in his *Far from the Madding Crowd* (1874) emphasized the despair resulting from the futility of fighting against the grinding forces of modernity. The plays of George Bernard Shaw (1856–1950) reflect the influence of Darwin, Nietzsche, and others and mock the shallowness and pretension of urban, bourgeois *fin de siècle* ("end of the century") society. In the mid-1880s two new movements in literature, decadence and symbolism, appeared. The decadents rejected prevailing bourgeois conventions and pretensions. For their part, symbolists preferred to revert to a form of the earlier romantic era and in the process to emphasize the ideal, the aesthetic, and the beautiful side of life.

Modernism in Art   Like their counterparts in literature, visual artists in the period 1871–1914 were confronted by the sweeping changes in life brought on by industrialism and science. The world of artistic expression in this period, often collectively labeled "modernism," in fact consisted of a great variety of successive movements, all of them skeptical of accepted middle-class conventions and truths. These movements became increasingly abstract and avant-garde as the Great War approached.

The first group of painters was known as the impressionists, and their style dominated from the 1870s until around 1890. The movement takes its name from a painting by Claude Monet (1840–1926) entitled *Impression, Sunrise* (1874). By around 1890 the impressionist school had been superseded by a more freewheeling style known as postimpressionism, which ran into the new century.

The period of art history from 1905 to 1914 saw numerous offshoots of the postimpressionists, each one more revolutionary and experimental than the last. These various artistic "schools" truly represent the beginnings of twentieth-century avant-garde art. Perhaps the best known of these, cubism, is represented in the works of Pablo Picasso (1881–1973). Picasso stretched fascination with geometric forms to their limits to deliberately fly in the face of accepted artistic conventions. In such works as *Les Demoiselles d'Avignon* (1907), for example, often considered the first of the cubist paintings, Picasso reveals his interest in African masks as an alternative to conventional European motifs.

Modernism in Music   During the 1870s, musical expression followed two separate tracks until 1914. One of these tracks is known as modernism, which was more attuned to cultural developments evolving in other fields during the waning years of the nineteenth century and early years of the twentieth.

An emerging trend in the period 1905–1914 was a movement in music often labeled "primitivism," in which composers abandoned the constraints of formal structure and convention to express their personal musical perceptions. Other musicians were even more outrageous and unconventional—and more typical of avant-garde rejections of Western musical conventions. In 1911 the Austrian composer and theoretician Arnold Schoenberg (1874–1951) published *Theory of Harmony*, in which he announced the inauguration of a new, modern style of musical composition featuring themes reflecting Freudian theories of the unconscious along with the noises and dissonances of engines, machines, and urban life.

Modernism in Art. Pablo Picasso's *Les Demoiselles d'Avignon* was unveiled in Paris in 1907. Its distorted and broken forms of expression set in a fractured and flattened space mark a conscious break with the Western artistic tradition. The painting's borrowing from "primitivist" African and ancient Iberian sources, and its forceful and unsettling depiction of *demoiselles*, a euphemism for prostitutes, unsettle the viewer.

Putting It All Together

The series of dramatic and sweeping changes associated with the Industrial Revolution had profound implications for both the industrializing countries and the nonindustrialized world. Thanks in large part to new technologies and facilitated by advances in transportation and communication, the period from 1871 to 1914 saw world trade networks and empires dominated by the newly industrialized nations.

The Industrial Revolution began in Britain in the early eighteenth century and eventually spread to Europe and North America during the nineteenth century.

Britain began the revolution when it employed steam engines in the rapid production of textiles. The subsequent development of the factory system along with more efficient transportation systems facilitated by railroads greatly expanded British manufacturing. Not everyone benefited, however, from the emergence of the factory system; capitalist entrepreneurs were reluctant to share with workers their slice of the economic pie, which in turn led to social unrest and calls for reform.

During the second Industrial Revolution in the later nineteenth century, advanced technologies led to the development of steel, electricity, and chemicals, which in turn greatly expanded the industrial economies of highly industrialized countries beyond Britain, including those of America and Germany. The daily lives of most citizens in industrialized nations were also improved by the application of industrial technologies to advances in transportation, communication, and even safety and sanitation.

These same advances also contributed to a new and greatly expanded surge of European imperialism. The explosive growth of industry and commerce, aided and abetted by new technologies and inventions, resulted in a quest among highly industrialized nations for raw materials, cheap labor, and new markets in order to sustain and expand their developing industries. Moreover, Western industrial nations soon discovered that new needs required the importation of not only raw materials but also foodstuffs. It is important to point out that nineteenth-century imperialism was made possible in the first place by technological innovations associated with advances in science and industrialism. Steam-powered gunboats, rapid-firing breechloaders, and the machine gun provided the overwhelming firepower to subdue nonindustrial societies and to open up interior regions of continents to Western colonialism. By the 1880s sailing ships were eclipsed by faster ones powered by much more efficient steam engines, and submarine cables provided for more efficient overseas communications and for the setting of more exact timetables. After 1871, the world's economy was increasingly divided into those who produced the world's manufactured products and those who both supplied the requisite raw materials and made up the growing pool of consumers.

Amid this process the basis for many of the patterns of twentieth-century modernity was being laid, as well as the foundations of its opposition. With the coming of World War I, and in its aftermath, many of the cleavages created by modernity and its scientific–technological underpinnings were laid bare. Yet, as a new form of society, its interaction and adaptation with older forms continued unabated. Today, the two places that contain the largest number of "Mary Pauls"—young women migrating from their farms to find work in urban factories—are the successors to the agrarian–urban religious civilizations that held out against the new order most tenaciously: India and China, both of whose economies now increasingly set the pace for twenty-first-century industrial development. It is the story of the impact of modernity on these societies and others around the globe to which we now turn.

▶ For additional resources, including maps, primary sources, visuals, and quizzes, please go to www.oup.com/us/vonsivers. Please see the Further Resources section at the back of the book for additional readings and suggested websites.

Against the Grain
The Luddites

Although the mechanization of textile production during the early phase of the Industrial Revolution was welcomed by some as providing new opportunities for better lives, and by others as an indication of technological progress, still others were hardline opponents of the new industrial movement. Deeply skeptical of the new era in the production of cloth goods, one group of workers in early-nineteenth-century Britain, known as "Luddites," fiercely opposed the application of machines in the textile industry.

While the term "Luddite" now refers to those who oppose new technologies of any kind, the original Luddites feared the widespread use of new machinery that lowered their wages and threatened their livelihoods. Composed primarily of skilled artisans in the knitting and hosiery trades, Luddites mounted a series of violent protests against the use of vastly improved mechanical knitting frames and steam-powered looms. Referring to themselves as soldiers in the army of General Ludd, a mythical figure, Luddites began their assaults on the night of November 4, 1811. Breaking into the home of a weaver in Nottinghamshire containing several power looms, they smashed the machines to bits and then quickly dispersed under cover of darkness. During 1812 and 1813 Luddites expanded their assaults into neighboring Yorkshire and Lancashire. Across a span of only 14 months Luddite "armies" smashed and destroyed around 1,000 machines.

The British government was quick to respond. At the height of the disturbances around 14,000 troops were dispatched to suppress the Luddite movement, and in February of 1812 Parliament passed the Frame Breaking Act, which made attacks on textile machinery punishable by death. This was followed by the trial and hanging of eight Luddites later in the year. After a quick show trial in January of 1813 that was designed to serve as a stark lesson, 14 followers of the movement were executed. This event effectively ended the movement, although occasional outbreaks of Luddism lingered on for another few years.

Even though the Luddite movement was relatively short-lived, it nevertheless called attention to disparities and inequalities inherent in early industrialism, particularly related to factory workers. This in turn prompted a series of parliamentary reforms in the 1830s and 1840s, which when taken together improved working conditions for workers in factories, mines, and other occupations.

- **Why did the British government react with such urgency to suppress the Luddite movement?**

- **How does the Luddite revolt compare with other protest movements against modernity in the later nineteenth century?**

Thinking Through Patterns

▶ **Where and when did the Industrial Revolution originate?**

Because of several advantageous factors, the Industrial Revolution began in Britain in the early eighteenth century. Among these were an earlier political revolution that empowered the merchant classes over the landed aristocracy, along with a prior agricultural revolution, and abundance of raw materials like coal.

Industrialization resulted in several social changes and adjustments. The capitalist middle classes were enriched and empowered by the growth of industrialism, as were the working classes, which did not exist as a group prior to industrialism. The benefits of industrialism were not evenly distributed across social strata; factory and mine workers were frequently exploited by the entrepreneurial and prosperous middle classes.

▶ **What were some effects of industrialization on Western society? How did social patterns change?**

▶ **In what ways did industrialization contribute to innovations in technology? How did these technological advances contribute to Western imperialism in the late nineteenth century?**

With the invention and perfection of the steam engine, capitalist entrepreneurs were able to substitute mechanical power for natural power and thus to develop the factory system. The factory system spread to the Continent and America as middle-class capitalism eclipsed mercantilism. Further advances contributed to a second Industrial Revolution beginning around 1850 based in steel, chemistry, and electricity.

Progress in industrial technology during the second Industrial Revolution led to innovations ranging from practical inventions like the light bulb to advances in communication and transportation. Inventions developed from industrial advances included the machine gun, new medicines, and startling developments in communications, to name a few. These tools facilitated the expansion of Western imperialism in Africa and Asia during the closing years of the nineteenth century

The new society that industrialism was creating not surprisingly spawned entirely new directions in science, philosophy, religion, and the creative fields such as literature and art. It generated new kinds of popular expression, from dime novels to photography. The advent of *mass society* also led to the beginnings of a mass culture, in which widespread literacy and public education allowed a far greater percentage of the populace access to what had largely been the province of elites. Yet there was also a profound disquiet among scientists, intellectuals, and artists. With so many of the old standards falling by the wayside, tremendous uncertainty lay present just under the surface of material progress. This disquiet would come to the surface with a vengeance in the immediate years after World War I.

▶ **What new directions in science, philosophy, religion, and the arts did industrialism generate? What kind of responses did it provoke?**

Chapter 27 1750–1914

The New Imperialism
in the Nineteenth Century

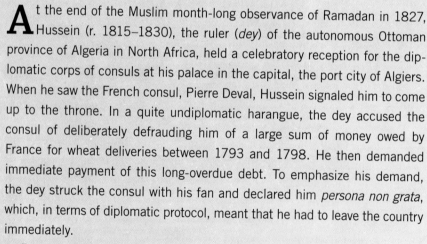

THE NEW
IMPERIALISM

A t the end of the Muslim month-long observance of Ramadan in 1827, Hussein (r. 1815–1830), the ruler (*dey*) of the autonomous Ottoman province of Algeria in North Africa, held a celebratory reception for the diplomatic corps of consuls at his palace in the capital, the port city of Algiers. When he saw the French consul, Pierre Deval, Hussein signaled him to come up to the throne. In a quite undiplomatic harangue, the dey accused the consul of deliberately defrauding him of a large sum of money owed by France for wheat deliveries between 1793 and 1798. He then demanded immediate payment of this long-overdue debt. To emphasize his demand, the dey struck the consul with his fan and declared him *persona non grata*, which, in terms of diplomatic protocol, meant that he had to leave the country immediately.

France's restored Bourbon king, Charles X (r. 1824–1830), found this insult by the Algerian dey to an appointee of the French court intolerably injurious to his own divinely ordained dignity. He dispatched a naval detachment to Algiers in 1828, demanding an apology, declaring the debt liquidated, and asking for reparations for a number of piracy depredations that had occurred in the preceding years. When the dey rejected the demands, the French mounted a blockade of the port. In 1830, they followed up on

ABOVE: Illustrations from a French schoolbook (c. 1910) show the cultivation of rice in French colonies.

this blockade with an expeditionary force that conquered Algiers, deposed the dey, and sent him into exile. Less than two decades later Algeria became a colony of France.

The incident illustrates the changing fortunes of those countries that were the beneficiaries of the new forces of modernity—in this case, France—and those like the Ottoman Empire and its territories in Algeria that largely were not. In this chapter, our focus will be on those parts of the world outside east Asia (see Chapter 24) that were unable to preserve, even in a tenuous fashion, their political independence while adapting to the colonial challenge through military, constitutional, and economic reforms. Here, we will study the victims of conquest and occupation in south and southeast Asia, the Middle East, Africa, and the Pacific Ocean that most clearly make visible the underlying patterns of imperialism and colonialism.

=========

Two patterns characterize the evolution of imperialism–colonialism in the period 1750–1900. The first was a shift from coastal trade forts under chartered companies—the old imperialism on the cheap—to government takeover, territorial conquest, and **colonialism**. Great Britain pioneered this "new imperialism" in India but also prevented the other European countries from following in its footsteps for a century.

The second pattern was the rise of direct territorial imperialism–colonialism by European countries in the course of the disintegration of the Ottoman Empire, under assault by Russia since the end of the eighteenth century, and, in the course of the nineteenth century, in Asia and Africa. The Europeans first protected the Ottomans from Russia, only later to help themselves to Ottoman provinces, beginning with the capture of Algeria by France. Thus the dey's fan slap in Algeria may be viewed as the unlikely catalyst that launched the competitive European imperialism–colonialism in Asia and Africa that characterized the remainder of the nineteenth century.

The British Colonies of India, Australia, and New Zealand

The transition in India from European trade-fort activities to governmental colonialism coincided with the decline of the Mughal dynasty (see Chapter 20). The British East India Company exploited the Mughal decline to become a government in all but name. Its notorious corruption and ultimate inability to conduct military affairs, however, forced the British government to assume direct control. As a result, Britain became a colonial power in the Eastern Hemisphere, making India its center for the delivery of the cotton on which early British industrialization depended. Later on, sparsely inhabited Australia and New Zealand began as small British settler colonies, the former as a penal colony and the latter against fierce indigenous resistance.

Seeing Patterns

▶ What new patterns emerged in the transition from trade-fort imperialism to the new imperialism?

▶ How did European colonizers develop their colonies economically, given that they were industrializing themselves at the same time?

▶ What were the experiences of the indigenous people under the new imperialism? How did they adapt to colonialism? How did they resist?

Colonialism: A system in which people from one country settle in another, ruling it and maintaining connections to the mother country; term now used most often to describe the contemporary exploitation of weaker countries by imperial powers.

Chapter Outline

- The British Colonies of India, Australia, and New Zealand

- European Imperialism in the Middle East and Africa

- Western Imperialism and Colonialism in Southeast Asia

- Putting It All Together

The British East India Company

An important factor in the rise of British power in India was the Seven Years' War. As we have seen, the Seven Years' War could be considered a kind of "first world war" in that fighting took place in Europe, in the Americas, on the high seas, and in India. It was the war in India, along with the deepening political difficulties of the Mughals, that enabled the rise of the British to supremacy not only on the subcontinent but later in Burma and Malaya as well.

The Seven Years' War   By the early eighteenth century Britain emerged as a strong contender for a larger share of global commerce among European trading companies. As we saw in Chapter 20, the British had joined forces at Surat on the west coast of India with the Dutch in the lucrative spice trade. But they had also established their own posts in provincial cities that would over time be transformed into India's greatest metropolises: Madras (Chennai), Bombay (Mumbai), and one created from scratch: Calcutta (Kolkata). By 1750 their chief commercial competitors were the French, who were aggressively building up both trade and political power from a base in Pondicherry in the southern part of peninsular India.

For the British East India Company, its evolution into a kind of shadow government in the area around Calcutta in Bengal on the northeast coast would now bear dividends. The decline of Mughal central power meant that regional leaders were being enlisted as French or British allies. If they were more powerful, they sought to use the sepoy (from Persian *sipahi* [see-pa-HEE], "soldier") armies of the European companies as support in their own struggles. Out of this confused political and volatile military situation, the ambitious East India Company leader, Robert Clive (1725–1774), won a victory over the Indian French allies at Plassey in 1757 and soon eliminated the French from power on the subcontinent. By the terms of the treaty ending the war in 1763, the East India Company ended up as the sole European power of consequence in India, and Clive set about consolidating his position from Calcutta.

Going Native: the Nabobs   Clive's aggressive style of economic aggrandizement set the tone for what Indian scholars have often called the "rape of Bengal" in the latter eighteenth century. The East India Company began to expand its holdings across northern India, extorting funds from pliant local princes. The company men had no interest in changing India or reforming Indian institutions. Indeed, many, inspired by Enlightenment ideals of cosmopolitanism, became great admirers of Indian culture. Some went so far as to "go native": After making their fortunes, they took Indian wives, dressed as Indian princes, and on occasion wielded power as local magnates, or **nabobs** (from Urdu *nawwab* [naw-WAHB], "deputy," "viceroy").

Nabob: A person who acquired a large fortune in India during the period of British rule.

The vast distances separating the company's London directors from operations in India, southeast Asia, and China made its local activities more or less autonomous. Its power, organization, and, most important, its army increasingly became the determining factors in local disputes across northern India; its attractiveness to ambitious young men on the margins of British society who wished to quickly "make their pile" left it vulnerable to corruption. This was particularly true because of the company's policy of paying low wages while turning a blind eye to employees trading locally for their private benefit.

By 1800, through the company's efforts to pacify turbulent territories adjacent to its holdings, British possessions extended across most of northern India (see Map 27.1). This extension prompted a shift in the variety of trading goods toward the beginning of the nineteenth century. Spices had been replaced by cotton goods—and, increasingly, by raw cotton—as the most lucrative commodity, due to Britain's mechanized textile revolution. Indian cotton would later be supplemented and eventually supplanted by cotton from the American South, Egypt, and Sudan.

The Perils of Reform While the nineteenth century is commonly perceived as the beginning of Western supremacy, it is well to remember—as we have noted in previous chapters—that even at this late date India and China were still the primary economic engines of Eurasia. As late as 1800, for example, Indian goods and services accounted for perhaps 20 percent of the world's output, while Britain's came to only 3 percent. As the Industrial Revolution kicked into high gear by the mid-1800s, however, these numbers began to reverse (see Figure 27.1). As Britain's share of India's economy grew, moreover, the British increasingly sought to create markets for their own goods there and to shunt Indian exports exclusively into the British domestic market. As we saw in Chapter 24, the early acquisition of Patna by the British enabled the creation of the Chinese opium trade, which by 1830 accounted for nearly one-quarter of company revenues in India. In addition, officials of the East India Company arbitrated disputes among Indian rulers, taking over their lands as payment for loans, and strong-arming many into becoming wards of the British. Because of this continuous attrition, by the end of the Napoleonic Wars, the Mughal emperor's lands had been reduced to the region immediately surrounding Delhi and Agra.

Perceptions of Empire. The British East India Company's real ascent to power in India began with Robert Clive's victory at Plassey in 1757, the symbolism of which is depicted here. Note the deference with which the assorted Indian princes treat the conqueror (top). Below, the second-from-last Mughal emperor, Akbar Shah II (r. 1806–1837), receives the British resident, ca. 1815. Despite the fact that the British East India Company had extended its sway over much of northern India by this time, the Indian artist depicts the British government official in a pose of supplication to Akbar Shah—in almost a mirror image of the imagined Indian princes in the painting of Clive.

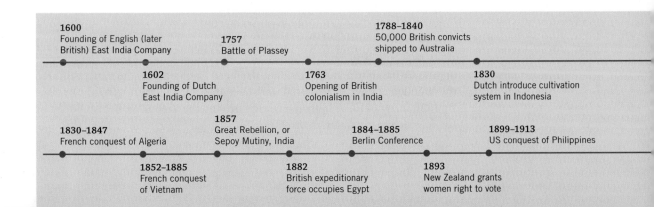

| 1600 Founding of English (later British) East India Company | 1757 Battle of Plassey | 1788–1840 50,000 British convicts shipped to Australia | |
| 1602 Founding of Dutch East India Company | 1763 Opening of British colonialism in India | 1830 Dutch introduce cultivation system in Indonesia | |

| 1830–1847 French conquest of Algeria | 1857 Great Rebellion, or Sepoy Mutiny, India | 1884–1885 Berlin Conference | 1899–1913 US conquest of Philippines |
| | 1852–1885 French conquest of Vietnam | 1882 British expeditionary force occupies Egypt | 1893 New Zealand grants women right to vote |

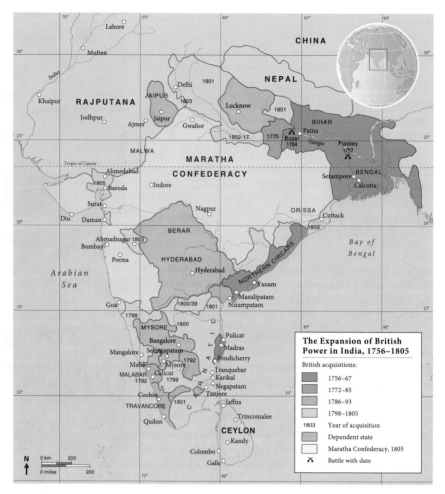

MAP **27.1** **The Expansion of British Power in India, 1756–1805.**

India's history, however, had long been marked by outsiders conquering large parts of the subcontinent, and while many chafed at company rule, its policy of noninterference with Indian customs and institutions softened the blow of the conquest somewhat. The period following the Napoleonic Wars, however, saw changes in this regard that had far-reaching consequences, by bringing the British government into a more direct role.

Clashes between factory owners and labor and the drive for political reform in Britain during this period found echoes in policy toward India. From the opening decades of the century, increasing numbers of Protestant missionaries, especially those of the new evangelical denominations, saw India as promising missionary ground. As was the case in China, many missionaries brought with them practical skills, particularly in medicine, education, and engineering. Many of those active in mission-based reform in India had also been involved with the movements for the abolition of slavery, industrial workers' rights, and electoral reform in Britain. By 1830 many of these individuals were driving the agenda on British policy in India, which increasingly asserted that India should be reformed along the lines

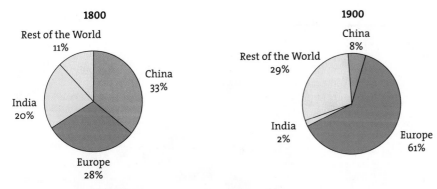

Figure 27.1 Share of World Manufacturing Output, 1800 and 1900.

they envisioned for Britain: better working conditions for the poor, free trade, the abolition of "barbaric" customs, and a vigorous Christian missionary effort.

In addition, the company reformed the tax system into a money-based land fee for greater efficiency of collection. At the same time, new industrial enterprises and transport and communication advances—steamboats, railroads, and telegraph lines—were constructed, benefiting the economy at large but also disrupting the livelihoods of many. Coupled with these changes was a perception on the part of opponents, and even some supporters, that these efforts in both India and England were characterized by smug righteousness and arrogance of the English toward Indian society. Perhaps the most famous expression of this was found in the parliamentary reformer and historian Thomas B. Macaulay's 1835 "Minute on Education," where he asserted that "a single shelf of European books is worth more than all the literatures of Asia and Arabia."

The Great Mutiny   The grim result of several decades of such wholesale change exploded in northern India in 1857. General disillusionment with the pace of change and the fear that British missionaries were attempting, with government connivance, to Christianize India came to a head among the company's sepoy troops. With the introduction of the new Enfield rifle, which required its operator to bite the end off a greased paper cartridge full of gunpowder, a rumor started that the grease had been concocted of cow and pig fat. Since this would violate the dietary restrictions of both Hindus and Muslims, the troops saw this as a plot to leave the followers of both religions ritually unclean and thus open to conversion to Christianity. Though the rumors proved untrue, a revolt raced through many of the sepoy barracks and in short order became a wholesale rebellion aimed at throwing the British out of India and restoring the aged Mughal emperor, Bahadur Shah Zafar (r. 1837–1857), to full power. The accumulated rage against the perceived insults to Indian religions and culture pushed the troops and their allies to frightful atrocities.

The Great Mutiny (also known by the British as the Sepoy Mutiny and by the Indians as the Great Rebellion, or First War of Independence) swiftly turned into a civil war as pro- and anti-British Indian forces clashed. The British shipped troops just sent to China for the Second Opium War back to India in a desperate attempt to crush the insurgency. Through a number of hard-fought engagements they were ultimately able to reassert control, but not without committing

Execution of Indian Rebels.
After British troops and loyalist Indian sepoys had restored order in northern India, retribution was unleashed on the rebels. Here, the most spectacular mode of execution is being carried out. Mutineers are tied across the mouths of cannons and blown to pieces while the troops stand in formation and are forced to watch.

atrocities of their own in retribution for the rebels' excesses. The occupation of many towns was accompanied by mass hangings and indiscriminate shootings of suspected rebels and collaborators.

Direct British Rule

After assuming direct rule (Hindi *raj*, hence the term "Raj" for the colonial government), the British were crucially concerned to keep their apparatus of civilian administrators as small as possible while maintaining an army large enough to avoid a repeat of 1857. These administrators made use of Indian administrators who, however, did not have any real decision-making powers. The Raj functioned because of a "divide and rule" policy that exploited the many divisions existing in Indian society, which prevented the Indians from making common cause and challenging British rule.

Creation of the Civil Service   Even as the pacification was winding down, the British government conducted an investigation which led to sweeping reforms in 1858. The East India Company was dismantled, and the British government itself took up the task of governing India. In a proclamation to England and India, Queen Victoria announced that British policy would no longer attempt to "impose Our convictions on any of Our subjects." An Indian civil service was created and made open to British and Indians alike to administer the subcontinent's affairs. The incorporation of India as the linchpin of the British Empire was completed when Queen Victoria assumed, among her many titles, that of Empress of India in 1877. India had now become, it was said, the "jewel in the crown" of the empire (see Map 27.2).

Less than a decade later, the fruits of the new civil service and the Indian schools feeding it were already evident, though perhaps not in the way its creators envisioned or desired. In 1885, Indians first convened the National Congress, the

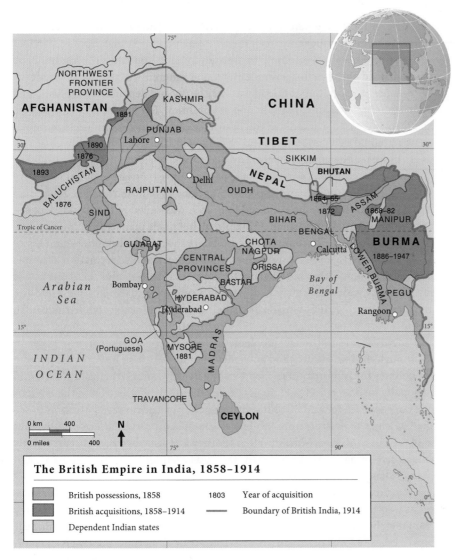

MAP 27.2 **The British Empire in India, 1858–1914.**

ancestor of India's present Congress Party. The congress's mission was to win greater autonomy for India within the structure of the British Empire and, by the opening decades of the twentieth century, to push for Indian independence. Already by the early 1890s, a young British-trained lawyer named Mohandas K. Gandhi (1869–1948) was actively campaigning for the rights of Indians in British-controlled South Africa. There, he developed the strategies that would make him among the most recognized world figures of the twentieth century as he pursued his quest to oust the British from India through nonviolence and noncooperation.

Divide and Rule   The Indian civil service, among the most difficult bureaucracies in the world into which to gain admission, seldom had more than 1,000 "Anglo-Indian" (ethnically British subjects who were either born in India or longtime residents there) and Indian officials to govern a quarter of a billion people. The civil service was intended as a showpiece of British incorruptibility and professionalism, in stark contrast to the perception of endemic graft and petty bribery customary among the Indian princes. Some of the ablest men in the British Empire, particularly those whose class or ethnic background might have proven a hindrance at home, passed the grueling examinations and entered the service as "readers." With so few officials, the workload was very heavy and demanded a sophisticated understanding of local conditions and sensibilities. The numbers of civil service members increased markedly in the twentieth century as Britain began to implement a gradual devolution to a kind of federated Indian autonomy. Even at this point, however, the numbers were only slightly above 3,000.

How did such a small government apparatus and expatriate population control such a large country? In many respects it was done by bluff and artifice. The Indian Army of Great Britain, the "thin red line" as it was called in the days before the uniforms were khaki, was small, well trained, but made up mostly of Indians. The British officers and noncommissioned officers included substantial numbers of Scots and Irish, themselves minorities often subject to discrimination at home. But the incipient threat of the army to suppress rebellion and the fruits of the revolution in weapons of the late nineteenth century—machine guns, rapid-fire artillery, repeating rifles—made any small revolt unthinkable, while the British divide-and-rule tactics made large-scale organization across caste, religious, ethnic, and linguistic lines extremely problematic.

Though the bureaucracy and political structure of British India served to unite the country for administrative purposes, the British secured their rule locally and regionally by divide-and-rule tactics. A key divide they utilized was the obvious one between Hindus and Muslims. British policy had encouraged Muslims to see the British as their protectors, while also often leaning in their favor in disputes with the Hindus. Thus, Muslims often felt they had a stake in the Raj, particularly when the alternative that presented itself was a Hindu-controlled India should independence from Britain ever come.

Other divides exploited differences among the Hindus. Rajputs and Gurkhas, for example, as military castes, were widely employed in the army in areas away from their home regions; this was also true of the Sikhs. In order to undermine the power bases of local Brahmans, lower castes were sometimes subtly given favorable treatment. Depending on the circumstances, different regions might be given preferential treatment as well.

The British also successfully exploited the sense of grandeur of the Indian elites, staging elaborate durbars (see Chapter 20) at the Raj's showpiece capital of New Delhi, built under the aegis of the British resident Lord Curzon (1859–1925). Curzon used these occasions to bolster the prestige, if not the actual power, of the Indian maharajas, and to reinforce traditional notions of deference and hierarchy.

The British administration created new systems of honorary ranks and revived older ones. By identifying British rule with India's historic past, it was hoped that the perception of strength and legitimacy would be enhanced. This effort to co-opt local rulers into upholding the British government as the historically destined status quo is sometimes called by historians a **subaltern** relationship. Yet a small but growing elite of Western-educated, often accomplished Indian leaders began to use the arguments of empire against their occupiers. By the 1920s many of these people—lawyers, journalists, and other professionals—would make up

Subaltern: A person or thing considered subordinate to another.

the burgeoning national movement associated with Gandhi's strategy of nonviolent noncooperation and the Indian National Congress's outlines for government when Britain was finally forced to "quit India."

British Settler Colonies: Australia

India was merely one area in Asia and the Pacific where the British advanced from exploration and trade forts to imperial expansion and colonial settlement. In the continent of Australia and on the islands of New Zealand they colonized indigenous forager and agrarian populations. In contrast to India, the British also encouraged large-scale immigration of European settlers to these regions. The evolution of Australia from a colony to a white immigrant–dominated dominion is the topic of the discussion below.

White Settlement in Australia   Dutch navigators, blown off course on their way to Indonesia, initially discovered the western coast of Australia in 1606, but when profitable trade opportunities with the forager Aborigines (the name given to the indigenous Australians) failed to materialize, they did not pursue any further contacts. The British navigator James Cook (1728–1779), during one of his many exploratory journeys in the Pacific, landed in 1770 on the Australian east coast and claimed it for Great Britain. After the United States wrested its independence from Britain in 1783, the British government looked to Australia as a place where it could ship convicts. Between 1788 and 1840, some 50,000 British convicts were shipped to the penal colony.

Immigration by free British subjects, begun a decade before the end of convict shipments, led to a pastoral and agricultural boom. Settlers pioneered agriculture in south Australia, where rainfall, fluctuating according to dry and wet *El Niño/La Niña* cycles, was relatively reliable and provided the population with most of its cereal needs. Sugar and rice cultivation, introduced to the tropical northeast in the 1860s, was performed with indentured labor recruited from Pacific islands. Even during penal colony times, sheep ranching in the east and the exportation of wool developed into a thriving business; eventually, half of the wool needed by the British textile industry was supplied by Australia. Even more important for the evolution of the Australian colony was the mining of gold and silver, beginning in the east in 1851 and continuing thereafter in nearly all parts of the continent. Although a colony, Australia was very similar to independent Latin America (see Chapter 23) in that it was a labor-poor but commodity-rich region, seeking its wealth through export-led growth.

Mining generated several gold-rush immigration waves, not only from Britain but also from China, as well as internal migrations from mining towns to cities when the gold rushes ended. Cities like Sydney and Melbourne expanded continuously during the 1800s and encompassed more than two-thirds of the total white population of about 5 million by 1914. The indigenous population of Aborigines, who had inhabited the continent for over 50,000 years, shrank during the same time from several hundred thousand to 67,000, mostly as a result of diseases but also after confrontations with ranchers intruding on their hunting and gathering lands. As in North America, whites were relentless in taking possession of an allegedly empty—or expected soon to be empty—continent.

Patterns Up Close | Military Transformations and the New Imperialism

French Defeat of the Mamluks at the Battle of the Pyramids, 1798. This painting shows the clear advantage of the military innovation of the line drill. The orderly French forces on the right, commanded by officers on horseback, mow down the cavalry charges of the Mamluks.

Between 1450 and 1750 firearm-equipped infantries rose to prominence throughout Eurasia. Recently, scholars have hotly debated the significance of the differences among the infantries and military organization more generally during this age of empire.

Historians believed for a long time that western Europeans had superior firearms, cannons, and cannon-equipped ships that enabled them to embark on overseas expansion, establish trade-fort mercantile empires, and eventually achieve imperial conquest and colonization of the Middle East, Africa, and southeast Asia. However, most scholars are now of the opinion that, beginning in the late seventeenth century, it was the flintlock muskets, bayonets, and line drill that distinguished western European infantries from other armies in Asia and Africa and gave Europeans an advantage. (The *line drill* was the Swedish-introduced innovation of training infantry soldiers stretched out in long lines three to six deep to fire, step back, allow the next line to fire, reload their muzzle-loaded flintlock muskets, and so on with the third to sixth lines.) These advantages were manifested in the Ottoman–Russian War of 1768–1774 and in Napoleon's invasion of Egypt in 1798.

In the early 1730s, the Ottomans realized that they could not match other powers with their matchlock muskets and that their infantry, the Janissaries, lacked sufficient discipline. Although their gunsmiths switched to flintlocks, the largely part-time and poorly paid Janissaries resisted all efforts at drills. Lack of finances caused these military reforms to grind to a halt. The Russian military, by contrast, learned much from the Seven Years' War (1756–1763), in which it was allied with Austria and France against Prussia and Great Britain. Its sizeable line infantries were of great importance during the war of 1768–1774 against the uncoordinated and untrained Ottoman foot soldiers. Similarly, Napoleon successfully employed his small, highly mobile, and

The Difficult Turn of the Century   The boom years ended for Australia around 1890. During the last quarter of the nineteenth century, the economies of the three leading industrial countries of the world—Great Britain, the United States, and Germany—slowed, with first a financial depression in 1873–1879 and another more economy-wide one in 1890–1896. Australia had been able to ride out the first depression, mainly thanks to continuing gold finds. But in the 1890s, construction as well as banking collapsed and factories closed. Coincidentally, a dry El Niño cycle devastated free selection farming. Labor unrest followed; although widespread strikes failed, the newly founded Labor Party (1891) immediately became a major political force. The country adopted labor reforms, an old-age pension, fiscal reforms, and a white-only immigration policy. The discovery of huge gold deposits in western Australia in 1892–1894 helped to redress the

flexible units (composed of mixed infantry, cavalry, and artillery) in his victory against the lopsidedly cavalry-dominated Egyptian Mamluks in 1798.

The Mughals in India and the Qing in China did not have to worry about flintlock, bayonet, and line infantry attacks in the eighteenth century, either from their neighbors or from the faraway Europeans. Like the Ottomans, who continued to maintain large cavalry forces against their no-madic neighbors in the Middle East and central Asia, the Mughals and Qing privileged their cavalries. However, once British East India Company officers elevated indigenous infantry soldiers to the privileged ranks of the sepoy regiments, their efficiency ultimately created such problems for the company that the British Crown had to take over the governance of India in 1858.

When European innovators introduced workable breech-loading rifles and artil-lery in the late 1850s, the technological balance shifted decisively toward Europe. The addition of rapid-firing mechanisms in the second half of the 1800s to these improved weapons further cemented Europe's technological superiority.

Thus, in this shift from an initially slight to an eventually pronounced superior-ity of European arms during this period, the new imperialism and the Industrial Revolution were parallel developments engendered by the same modernity that also saw the rise of constitutional nationalism and the formation of a new type of polity, the nation-state. Certainly, industrially produced weapons in the later nineteenth century greatly enhanced Europe's ability to dominate much of the Middle East, Africa, and Asia.

Ethiopian Forces Defeating an Italian Army at Adowa, 1896. A hundred years after Napoleon's victory, the tables were turned when an Ethiopian army equipped with repeating rifles, machine guns, and cannon routed an Italian invasion force. In response to the defeat, the *Times* of London complained that "the prestige of European arms as a whole is considerably impaired."

Questions

- Examine the painting showing French forces defeating the Mamluk cavalry. Are the military advantages of the line drill evident? If so, what are they?

- Does the painting of Ethiopian forces defeating an Italian army in 1896 show that in-digenous peoples could adapt Western innovations to their own purposes? If so, how?

economic problems. In 1900, Australia finally adopted a federal constitution, which made the country the second fully autonomous British "dominion," after Canada (1867) but before New Zealand (1907), Newfoundland (1907), South Africa (1910), and Ireland (1922).

European Imperialism in the Middle East and Africa

The British role in the Middle East during the eighteenth and early nineteenth centuries was much more modest, as was that of Europeans in general. Their function was limited to that of merchants, diplomats, or military advisors in an

Ottoman Empire with a long tradition of conquering European lands. The situation changed at the end of the eighteenth century when Russia adopted a plan of southern expansion designed to drive the Ottomans back into Asia, take Istanbul, and convert it back into an eastern Christian capital. The other European powers sought to slow the Russian advances, with Great Britain assuming the lead role in protecting the Ottomans. In the long run, this policy of containment failed. Under Russian pressure, Ottoman territory shrank, the Europeans joined Russia in dismembering the Ottoman Empire, and a general imperialist competition for carving up other parts of the world—notably south and east Asia as well as Africa—ensued.

The Rising Appeal of Imperialism in the West

Empires (multiethnic, multilinguistic, and multireligious polities) were, as we have repeatedly seen, of old lineage in world history. Their current embodiments were the Ottoman, Habsburg, and Russian Empires. The Russian Empire, a late-comer, saw its mission as replacing the Ottoman Empire as the dominant eastern European power and, by expanding eastward across the steppe, becoming the leading Asian power. Its ambition became the catalyst for France, Great Britain, Belgium, Germany, and even late-industrializing Italy to embark on competitive imperialism in other parts of the world (see Map 27.3).

The Ottoman, Russian, and British Empires   After the failure in 1815 of Napoleon's imperial schemes in both Egypt and Europe, Great Britain was the

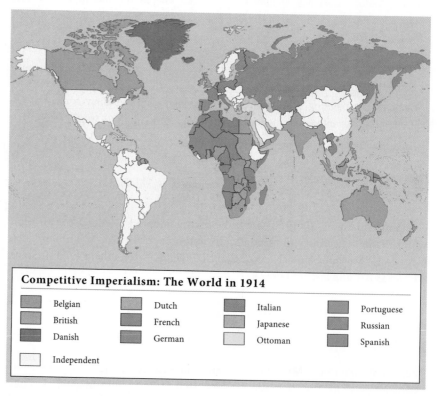

Competitive Imperialism: The World in 1914

Belgian	Dutch	Italian	Portuguese
British	French	Japanese	Russian
Danish	German	Ottoman	Spanish
Independent			

MAP **27.3 Competitive Imperialism: The World in 1914.**

undisputed leading empire in the world. No country had a navy that could rival it, British trade posts and colonies were widely distributed over the world, and British colonialism in India provided Indian cotton to fuel British industrialization. On the European continent, Britain worked to restore the monarchies of France, Austria, Prussia, and Russia so that they would balance each other as "great powers" in a **Concert of Europe**. Britain would not tolerate any renewed European imperialism of the kind that Napoleon had pursued. Meeting more or less regularly in congresses, the great powers were remarkably successful at maintaining peace in Europe. For an entire century not a single war engulfed the continent as a whole.

The Concert of Europe, however, was less successful at curbing the imperial ambitions of its members reaching for lands outside of western Europe. Russia did not hide its goal of throwing the Ottoman Empire (admitted to the Concert for better protection of its integrity in 1856) back into "Asia"—that is, Asia Minor, or Anatolia. Great Britain, although it made itself the protector of the integrity of the Ottoman Empire, could at best only slow the ambitions of Russia. The movement to secure the independence of Greece (1821–1832) is a good example of this pattern. Russia, as the Greeks' coreligionist and protector, was centrally involved in initiating a pattern of ethnolinguistic nationalism that replaced constitutional nationalism as the organizing ideology for many Europeans in the nineteenth century.

Concert of Europe: International political system that dominated Europe from 1815 to 1914, which advocated a balance of power among states.

The French Conquest of Algeria   Britain, unable to prevent the renewal of French imperialism, directed it outside Europe against Ottoman Algiers. The French naval expedition—the circumstances of which were described at the beginning of this chapter—conveniently took place in 1830 while British attention was still focused on the negotiations for Greece's independence. In its North African expedition, France followed an earlier short-lived blueprint of Napoleon's, which envisaged the creation of a Mediterranean empire encompassing Algeria and/or Egypt, prior to his lightning imperialism in Europe, possibly to signal to Britain the ease of reaching India via the Mediterranean.

Algeria was the crucial first step of a European power—in this instance France—seizing provinces of the Ottoman Empire in competition with the Russians, while officially protecting its integrity. This first step was still full of hesitations and counter-maneuvers. At first, the French stayed on a small coastal strip around Algiers and other places, encouraging the rise of indigenous leaders to take over from the Ottoman corsairs and Janissaries and share the country with the French. The British discreetly supported Algerian leaders with weapons to be used against the French.

In the end, however, coexistence proved impossible, and the French military—against strong Algerian resistance—undertook an all-out conquest. The civilian colonial administration after 1870 encouraged large-scale immigration of French and Spanish farmers, who settled on small plots, as well as French corporate investments in vineyards and citrus plantations on the coast. The indigenous population of Arabs and Berbers, decimated by cholera epidemics in the 1860s, found itself largely reduced to less fertile lands in the interior.

Britain's Containment Policy   Great Britain sought to limit Russian ambitions not only in Europe; it also opposed Russia in its own backyard of central Asia,

The Great Game: Competition between Great Britain and Russia for conquest or control of Asian countries north of India and south of Russia, principally Afghanistan.

inaugurating what was called the **Great Game** against Russia in Asia with the first Anglo–Afghan war in 1838. Although Great Britain failed to occupy Afghanistan and make it an advance protectorate against the approaching Russians, it eventually succeeded in turning Afghanistan into a buffer state keeping Russia away from India. A little later, in 1853–1856, Britain and France teamed up in the Crimean War to stop Russia from renewing its drive for Istanbul. This defeat, demonstrating the superiority of new industrially produced rifles and breech-loading artillery, chastened Russia for the next two decades.

In the second half of the nineteenth century, however, the ethnic–nationalist unification of Germany in 1870–1871, engineered by Prussia through a successful war against France (the Franco–Prussian War), destroyed the balance of the European Concert. Germany, much larger than Prussia and strengthened further through the annexation of the French industrializing region of Alsace-Lorraine, was now the dominant power in western Europe. Russia promptly exploited the new imbalance in Europe during anti-Ottoman uprisings in the Balkans in 1876. Leaving the humiliation of the Crimean War behind, Russian troops broke through Ottoman lines of defense and marched within a few miles of Istanbul. However, Great Britain, although no longer the arbiter of the European Concert, still had enough clout to force Russia into retreating.

Scottish Troops at the Sphinx, 1882. The British occupied Egypt as a means to secure the Suez Canal and guarantee the repayment of Egyptian debts. Subsequent negotiations with the Ottoman sultan for the status of Egypt failed, and the province became an unofficial protectorate of Britain. Although granted internal independence in 1922, Egypt remained in a semicolonial relationship with Britain until 1956.

British Imperialism in Egypt and Sudan To prevent a repeat of the Russian invasion, Britain and the Ottomans agreed in 1878 to turn the island of Cyprus over to the British as a protectorate. This protectorate would have British advisors and troops, ready to defend Istanbul against a renewed Russian invasion. Thus, in the name of curbing Russian imperialism, Great Britain became an imperial power itself in the Mediterranean.

Events after the occupation of Cyprus, however, followed a dramatically different course. Instead of watching Russia, the commanders of the British navy squadron in Cyprus had to turn their attention to Egypt. This province was the wealthiest part of the Ottoman Empire. It was governed by a dynasty of autonomous rulers, beginning with Muhammad Ali (r. 1805–1848), an Albanian officer in the Ottoman army who assumed political control after Napoleon's troops had evacuated Egypt. Although his efforts to use his new army to conquer Istanbul and take over the Ottoman Empire were thwarted by a Great Britain anxious to protect the sultans, Muhammad Ali had a huge impact on Egypt. In a major reform effort, similar to the Tanzimat constitutional reforms in Istanbul, Cairo and Alexandria became centers of adaptation to European arts and letters as well as a reformed Islam.

Muhammad Ali's successors were less able rulers who incurred considerable debts, in part for the French-led construction of the Suez Canal in 1869. Britain took over a large part of the canal shares from the debt-ridden Egyptian ruler in 1857. A year later, Britain and France imposed a joint debt commission that garnished a portion of Egyptian tax revenue. Opposition in Egypt to this foreign interference grew in the following years, both inside and outside the Egyptian government, and culminated in 1881 with a revolt in the Egyptian army that endangered the debt repayments.

British-initiated negotiations between the Ottoman sultan and the leader of the army revolt, Colonel Ahmad Urabi (1841–1911), over the issue of the debt collapsed after riots in Alexandria and a careless British bombardment of the port in response to Egyptian fortification efforts. Interventionists in London, fearing for their bonds and the supply of Egyptian cotton for the British textile industry, gained the upper hand. Overcoming the fiercely resisting Egyptian army, a British expeditionary force occupied Egypt in 1882.

> "I have always, and do now recommend it [the purchase of the Suez Canal shares] . . . which I believe is calculated to strengthen the Empire."
>
> —Benjamin Disraeli

The Ottoman sultan acquiesced to the occupation because the appointment of a British-appointed high commissioner, charged with the reorganization of the Egyptian finances, was supposed to be only temporary. Costly campaigns by British-led Egyptian troops in Sudan during 1883–1885, however, derailed any early departure plans. Egypt had occupied Sudan in the 1820s and, as in Egypt, had made cotton a major export crop for the British textile industry. Sudanese resentment over the occupation and anxiety over the accompanying social changes led to a religiously inspired uprising in Khartoum in 1883.

The leader of the uprising was Muhammad Ahmad Ibn Abdallah (1844–1885), head of an Islamic Sufi brotherhood and self-styled Mahdi ("rightly guided" or "Messiah"), sent to establish a realm of justice. After the Mahdi succeeded in driving the British–Egyptian forces from Sudan and establishing an independent state, he was left alone for the next decade.

Until the British slaughtered Abdallah's forces at the Battle of Omdurman in 1898, Egypt's finances, aggravated by problems in Sudan, were sufficiently in disarray to keep the British focused on Egypt. On the one hand, the British wanted to put Egyptian finances on a sound footing again, but on the other hand, they wanted out to avoid responsibility for the country's governance. They had no plans yet for a full-fledged Mediterranean imperialism. As a compromise, they conceived of a conditional departure, with the right of return at times of internal unrest or external danger. The Ottoman sultan, however, refused to sign this compromise. He was grateful to Britain for recognizing Ottoman sovereignty but sought to avoid the responsibility of governance. In the end, Britain stayed for almost three-quarters of a century, running Egypt as an undeclared colony for the first 40 years. Without a clear plan, Britain had nonetheless transplanted the pattern of imperialism–colonialism it had first experimented with in India.

France's Tunisian Protectorate   Similar to Algeria and Egypt, Tunisia was an autonomous Ottoman province, ruled by its own dynasty of *beys*. The dynasty had been founded by a Janissary officer in 1705 when the military ruling class began to shift from corsair raids against Christian shipping to the fiscal exploitation of the villages and nomadic tribes of the interior. Fertile northern Tunisia provided limited but fairly reliable tax revenues from olive oil, barley, wheat, fruits, and nuts. Annual tax expeditions to the south among the seminomadic sheep and camel tribes usually yielded few taxes and served mostly to demonstrate the dynasty's sovereignty.

The beys responded to the Western challenge early, being the first in the Muslim Middle East and North Africa to modernize their military and adopt a constitution (1857). With their more limited revenues, they hit the debt ceiling already in 1869, much earlier than the Ottomans and Egyptians, and had to accept a British–French–Italian debt commission for the reorganization of the country's revenues. When the French took over in 1881, they began with the same thankless task of balancing the budget as the British had in Egypt. Only later did they benefit from the French and Italian settlers they invited to the protectorate to intensify agriculture.

The Scramble for Africa

Competitive European imperialism exploded beyond the Mediterranean in early 1884 as Germany claimed its first protectorates in Africa. Conveniently, after having secured lands for his country, the German chancellor Otto von Bismarck (in various offices 1862–1890) called a conference in Berlin, which met from late 1884 to early 1885. The main agenda of the Berlin conference was a discussion on how the 14 invited European countries and the United States should "define the conditions under which future territorial annexations in Africa might be recognized." Bismarck's proposed main condition was "effective occupation," with the creation of spheres of influence around the occupied places. The first protectorates, confirmed at the conference, were Cameroon in west central Africa for Germany and Congo as a private possession of King Leopold II of Belgium. The **Scramble for Africa** was on (see Map 27.4).

Scramble for Africa:
Competition among European powers from 1884 to 1912 to acquire African colonies.

Explorers, Missionaries, and the Civilizing Mission Sub-Saharan Africa was still little known and often misunderstood by most Europeans in the 1800s. The Enlightenment had instilled curiosity about the geography, flora, fauna, and ethnology of Africa among the European reading public. As a result, intrepid explorers descended on the "Dark Continent," and in order to gain access to the interior explorers utilized trade routes and caravans, long in use by Africans. But enduring the hardships of traveling in the savanna, rain forest, and desert required strong commitment. David Livingstone (1813–1873), a tireless missionary and passionate opponent of slavery, was the best known among the pioneers who explored much of south central Africa. Livingstone's ultimate goals were not only to terminate trafficking in slaves but also to "civilize" Africans by broadcasting the blessings of Christianity and commerce.

The generation of explorers after Livingstone was better equipped, led larger expeditions, and composed more precise accounts. Here, the outstanding figure was Henry Morton Stanley (1841–1904), a Welsh journalist who worked in the United States and became famous for his encounter with Livingstone ("Dr. Livingstone, I presume?") at Lake Tanganyika in east central Africa. Still, in spite of extensive explorations, European politicians at the end of the century had only the vaguest idea of the geography of the "dark continent."

Civilizing mission:
Belief that European colonizers had a duty to extend the benefits of European civilization to "backward" peoples.

The exploits of Christian missionaries created a sense of both responsibility for and superiority to the Africans in the European public. They were at the forefront of the **civilizing mission**, the belief prevalent in the West in the nineteenth

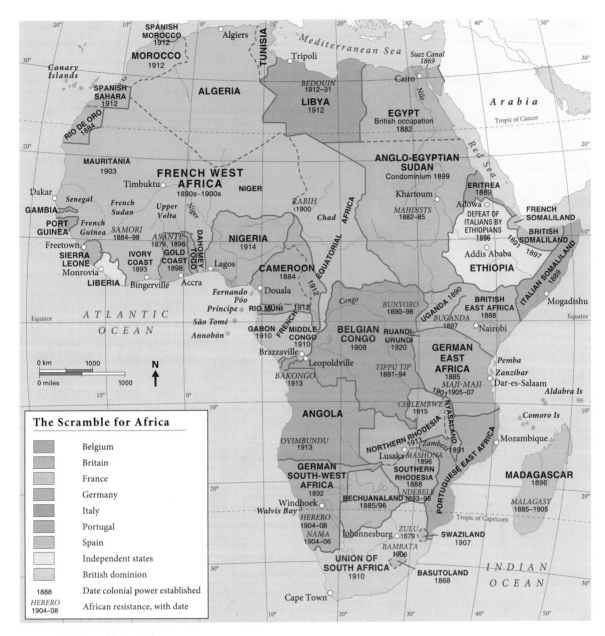

MAP 27.4 **The Scramble for Africa.**

century that colonists had a duty to extend the benefits of civilization (that is, European civilization) to the "backward" people they ruled.

In the early 1800s, malaria and yellow fever confined missionaries to the coasts of Africa. There, supported by missionary societies in Europe, they trained indigenous missionaries to translate tracts and scriptures for the conversion of Africans in the interior. When quinine (made from the bark of a Brazilian tree) became

"We must say openly that indeed the higher races have a right over the lower races . . . I repeat, that the superior races have a right because they have a duty. They have the duty to civilize the inferior races."

—Jules Ferry, French statesman

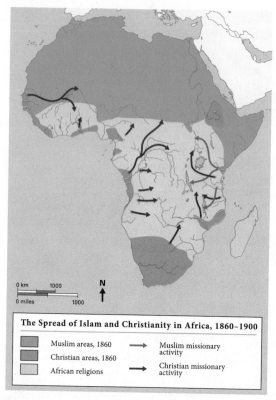

MAP 27.5 **The Spread of Islam and Christianity in Africa, 1860–1900.**

available in the middle of the 1800s, allowing for treatment of malaria, missionaries were able to follow their indigenous colleagues into the interior (see Map 27.5). At that time, tensions often arose between the two groups. African converts preached the gospel in the spirit of Christian equality, as did the former slave and later Anglican bishop Samuel Adjai Crowther (ca. 1809–1891), but many Western missionaries considered African Christianity to be contaminated by animist "superstitions" and did not accept Africans as equal.

Conquest and Resistance in West Africa Colonialism on the coast of West Africa after 1885 was an outgrowth of the traditional trade-fort system. By the 1800s, the British had ousted the Dutch and the French from most of the trading forts and had become the dominant European presence in the region. Ghana is a particularly instructive example of the pattern of conquest and resistance. Ghana, previously known as the Gold Coast, was the land of the Ashante kingdom. The Ashante had emerged back in the time of the empire of Songhay, when they mined the gold of the Akan fields that caravans carried across the Sahara. When gold declined in importance, the kingdom turned to the Atlantic slave trade and benefited handsomely from it. After the 1807 British prohibition of slavery, Ashante merchants switched to commodities (especially palm oil, used for lubricating machinery and for making soap) that were in great demand in industrializing Europe.

But the Ashante and British traders were in constant conflict over the terms of trade in the forts. Disciplined and well-armed Ashante troops defeated the British repeatedly. In 1874 British troops seized control of the Ashante capital at Kumasi. Only in 1896, when the British sent regular troops with breechloader rifles and machine guns to put down the Ashante with their now-antiquated muskets, was Ghana finally turned into a protectorate. Later on, after well over a half-century of colonialism, the memory of Ashante nineteenth-century prowess was an important factor in the Ghanaian struggle for independence.

France lost its West African trade forts to Britain after the Seven Years' War (1756–1763) but later received one of them back, a fortified island at the mouth of the Senegal River. It was from this base that career-hungry French officers after 1850 carried out expeditions into the interior of the river rain forest, for alliances and trade purposes. In 1857 they came into conflict with al-Hajj Umar (ca. 1791–1864), an Islamic reformer in the interior savanna who was in the process of building a state in what is today Guinea, Senegal, and Mali. The French barely survived a siege in a border fort and for decades could advance no further. Once the scramble was on, however, the West African Islamic state was doomed. In 1891, despite stiff resistance from the Islamists, the French began to carve out the huge colony in the steppe and savanna of West Africa that formed the core of their colonial empire.

Al-Hajj Umar was one of several West African Muslim religious scholars who became holy warriors (jihadis) seeking to rejuvenate Islam through a return to the study of the original Islamic sources. In the footsteps of what they perceived as the Prophet Muhammad's original state in Mecca, rising among the defeated unbelievers, the West African reformers forcibly converted black animists to Islam. In contrast to the Islamic kings and emperors of the previous centuries who made little or no efforts to convert their subjects, the jihadists of the 1800s succeeded in making Islam the dominant religion of West Africa.

Conquest and Resistance in East Africa   The arrival of colonialism in East Africa differed from the pattern in West Africa. Here, as early as the sixteenth century, the Portuguese had established trade forts in the south to acquire gold and ivory for their spice purchases in India. When Swahili patricians in the city-states farther north resisted this intrusion into their traditional Indian Ocean trade, the Portuguese responded with piracy and the construction of coastal forts in their midst. But the arrival of the Dutch with more powerful and numerous ships in the 1630s to take over the spice trade forced the Portuguese to curtail their East African engagement. An Omani Arab expeditionary force exploited the reduced Portuguese presence in 1698 by conquering the Swahili city-state of Mombasa after a 2-year siege. Oman had long-standing trade relations with East Africa and seized the opportunity to expand its limited domestic agricultural base on the Arabian Peninsula. Once in control, the Omanis developed a flourishing plantation system for sugar, rice, grain, and cotton on the coastal islands, along with slaves imported from the African interior. In the 1820s, the Omanis—by now under their separate sultan residing on the island of Zanzibar—began to specialize in cloves, becoming the main exporters of this precious spice on the world market. Thanks to the Omanis, the Swahili coast was prosperous again.

Zanzibar was the staging ground for adventurers, explorers, and missionaries in the nineteenth century to enter the African interior. It was here that they vied for places to occupy and spheres of influence to declare. Accordingly, in 1886 Germany received the lion's share on the coast and in the interior, Belgium's claims in the Congo were recognized, and Zanzibar somewhat later became a British protectorate. In its colony of Tanganyika (in current Tanzania), Germany used forced labor for the growing of cotton, provoking the fierce but in the end brutally suppressed Maji Maji Rebellion of 1905–1907.

Atrocities and Genocides   Similar atrocities stalked the European civilizing mission. As Germany was quelling rebellion in Tanganyika, it led a ferocious campaign on the other side of the continent against the Herero and Nama people of southwest Africa (modern Namibia). In their determination to establish colonial rule in the region, the German general staff ordered the extermination of the Herero in terms that can only be described as genocide: "I believe that the nation as such must be destroyed," commented General Lothar von Trotha (1848–1920 [TROH-tuh]). From 1904 to 1908 the war on the Herero resulted in 80,000 deaths.

A Slave Who Became Bishop. The remarkable life of Samuel Adjai Crowther shows that Africans also participated in the "civilizing mission." Born in Yorubaland in present-day West Africa, Crowther was enslaved as a young man but was rescued by the British navy and freed in 1821. He then converted to Christianity, and after training in London he was ordained an Anglican priest in 1841. He was appointed the first African Anglican bishop in 1864 and went on to produce Yoruba translations of the Bible and the Book of Common Prayer.

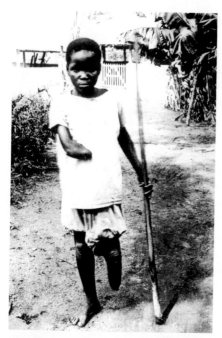

Colonial Brutality in the Congo. A young African boy whose hand and foot were severed by sentries after his village failed to meet its rubber quota. The Belgian Congo under King Leopold II employed mass forced labor of the indigenous population to extract rubber from the jungle. As the demand for rubber grew King Leopold's private army of 16,000 mercenaries was given leave to use any method to coerce the population into meeting quotas, including random killing, mutilation, village burning, starvation and hostage taking.

North of Namibia, King Leopold II (r. 1865–1909) of Belgium turned his personal colony of the Congo into a vast forced-labor camp for the production of rubber. The wild rubber tree, native to Africa, gained great importance in Europe for a variety of industrial applications. Leopold was particularly sadistic in his exploitation of the native workforce, using beatings and mutilations if collection quotas were not filled. Recent research indicates that an astonishing 10,000,000 Congolese were either killed or starved to death.

The scramble finally ended in 1912 with the French declaration of a protectorate over Morocco. By this time, the political competition in Europe had narrowed to the struggle between Germany and Great Britain for political predominance in western Europe. Italy's imperialist dreams were stymied by its crushing defeat at the battle of Adowa in 1896, in which one-third of its army was killed by Ethiopian forces (see "Patterns Up Close"). Ethiopia emerged from the scramble as the only noncolonized state in Africa. French and British rivalry in Africa, which had cropped up during the scramble and had even led to a confrontation at Fashoda over the control of Sudan in 1898, ended between 1905 and 1911, when Britain allied with France to counterbalance Germany. As a result of this alliance, Britain recognized France's interests in Morocco, adjacent to the two French territories of Algeria and Tunisia, over protests by Germany.

European Colonization   European colonial powers had many common interests as they plunged into the Scramble for Africa. They all participated in the exploitation of African raw materials and minerals, as well as the quest for overseas markets and territories in order to demonstrate their power and influence as rivalries among them heated up in the later nineteenth century.

But there were differences in the methods used to realize their ambitions. Portugal was the first European state to establish bases of power in Africa. In order to develop profitable plantations, the Portuguese adopted a policy of direct rule, administered by a centralized bureaucracy. In addition, by the policy of assimilation, qualified colonists could eventually attain citizenship status. Since the Portuguese had established port colonies in Angola and Mozambique in the 1600s, they attempted to expand their holdings during the early phase of the Scramble for Africa. As a result of the Berlin conference in 1884–1885, Portugal claimed a wide swath of sub-Saharan central Africa extending from Angola in the west to Mozambique in the east, in order to create a continent-wide swath across central Africa. Owing, however, to its relatively small size, its economy was not strong enough to sustain expansion, and as a result Portuguese interests were edged out by the larger colonial powers of Germany and Britain.

King Leopold of Belgium began the rush for African territories, concentrating on developing Belgian interests in Central Africa. After establishing the International Association for the Exploration and Civilization of Central Africa in 1876, the Belgian ruler commissioned Henry Morton Stanley to assist in the creation of the Congo Free State. Stanley trudged around the region, ostensibly making treaty arrangements with local rulers, but in reality "claiming" these lands for the Belgian crown. In order to convert these acquisitions into profitable commercial enterprises, Leopold set up vast plantations, adopting a policy of brutality in order to maintain control over their holdings.

Germany began to pursue its colonial ambitions in Africa in the 1880s and 1890s. Although Bismarck was initially reluctant, the growing need to make Germany competitive with other industrial powers, especially Britain, finally inspired Bismarck to join in the race for African possessions. Germany developed colonies in East Africa and West Africa, as well as in the Cameroons. The Germans quickly converted these lands into plantation economies, which in turn produced much-needed raw materials for burgeoning German industrialism. Like many other European colonizers, Germany relied upon brutality to render its plantations profitable.

Because it achieved unification as the Kingdom of Italy only in 1870, by the time Italian efforts were under way to establish colonies in Africa much of the continent had already been claimed. As a result, Italians had to settle for what was left, primarily regions in the Horn of Africa, increasingly important because of its proximity to the Suez Canal. In 1869 Italy acquired rights to the port of Assab on the coast of the Red Sea, and subsequently declared it a colony in 1882. From there Italians expanded their holdings into Somaliland in 1888, followed by Ethiopia in 1889; each of these was declared an Italian protectorate. But when the Ethiopian ruler discovered that he had been deceived, he mounted a fierce resistance movement that led to the defeat of Italian forces at the battle of Adowa in 1896.

Resistance   Resistance to European colonialism took different forms depending on a variety of factors. Among these were ongoing and systemic warfare among African societies, resulting in disunity and the resultant inability to mount an effective Africa-wide effort to oust the Europeans. A good example is afforded by Ghana, where opponents of the Ashante sided with the British in their effort to annex Ashante lands. Another form of resistance was the adoption of noncooperation tactics by colonized Africans. Termed "weapons of the weak" by a noted scholar of Africa, these included work slowdowns, desertion, arson, and even sabotage.

Resistance was also dependent on the size and power of assorted indigenous chiefdoms and kingdoms. For smaller communities, the preferred tactic was guerilla warfare; for larger and better-organized societies full-fledged armed confrontation was the method of choice. Many African rulers possessed European weapons, including rapid-fire rifles, through contacts with European traders. Moreover, some rulers also manufactured their own ammunition and gunpowder. Ethiopia, for example, amassed a huge fighting force of some 100,000 troops, which won a significant victory over Italian soldiers at the Battle of Adowa in 1896.

Although African societies mounted a variety of resistance movements, it was ultimately the superior technologies of Europeans that prevailed. The by-products of industrialization, these advances included gunboats, telegraph communications, and others. But by far the most lethal weapons in European arsenals were breech-loading rifles and especially machine guns. These advanced weapons proved far superior to the weapons available to Africans, weapons like bows and arrows, spears, and muskets. The disparity enabled relatively small contingents of European soldiers, numbering sometimes only in the hundreds, to fend off thousands of charging African warriors in pitched battles.

Western Imperialism and Colonialism in Southeast Asia

Parallel to developments in Africa, the new imperialism made its appearance also in southeast Asia, specifically Indonesia, the Philippines, Vietnam, Cambodia, and Laos. While the new imperialism in southeast Asia was an outgrowth of the earlier trade-fort presence of Portugal, Spain, and the Netherlands, it also included the return of France to imperial glory.

The Dutch in Indonesia

The Dutch were heirs of the Portuguese, who had set up forts that traded for spices in Indonesia during the sixteenth century and for the next 100 years were the middlemen for the distribution of spices from Portugal to northern Europe. But after liberating themselves from Habsburg–Spanish rule, the Netherlands displaced Portugal from its dominant position as a spice importer to Europe. From 1650 to 1750, the Netherlands was the leading naval power in the world. After 1750, they shifted from the trade of spices in their trade forts in Indonesia to the planting of cash crops, such as sugar, cacao, coffee, and tobacco—the mild- and warm-weather commodities that Europeans consumed in ever-larger quantities. The aim of the full colonization of Indonesia during the nineteenth century was to profit from European industrial demand for agricultural and mineral commodities.

Portuguese and Dutch Trade Forts   Portuguese sailors arrived in the strategic Strait of Malacca, which separates Sumatra from the Malay Peninsula and divides the Indian Ocean from the Chinese Sea, in 1511. They defeated the local sultanate and established a fort in the Malaysian capital, Malacca. Their main interest, however, given the power of Aceh on Sumatra, was to push onward to the spice-producing Maluku Islands (known in English as the Moluccas) in eastern Indonesia (between Sulawesi and New Guinea), where they established a trade fort in 1522, amid several Islamic island lords. From there, the Portuguese pushed on to China and finally Japan, where they arrived in the mid-1500s. Overall, their role in the Indonesian spice trade remained small, and indigenous Islamic merchants maintained their dominance.

After declaring their independence from Spain in 1581, the northern provinces of the Netherlands formed the Republic of the United Netherlands and pushed for their own overseas network of trade forts. In 1602, the Dutch government chartered the Dutch United East India Company (VOC), which spearheaded the expansion of Dutch possessions in India and southeast Asia. After a slow start, the company erected outposts on many Indonesian islands and in the mid-1600s founded Batavia (today Jakarta) on the island of Java as its main southeast Asian center. The VOC was by far the largest and wealthiest commercial company in the world during the seventeenth century, with a fleet consisting of nearly 5,000 merchant ships supported by large naval and land forces.

When the Dutch *stadhouder* (governor) of the Netherlands, William of Orange (1650–1702), became king of England after the English Glorious Revolution (see Chapter 17), the Dutch and English overseas trade interests were pooled. Great

Britain (as the country was known after England's union with Scotland in 1707) deepened its Indian interests through the British East India Company, and the Dutch pursued their engagements in Indonesia. Like the British company in India, the VOC was increasingly drawn during the early 1700s into local dynastic wars. Supported by some 1,000 Dutch soldiers and 3,000 indigenous auxiliaries, the VOC established peace in 1755 in the fragmenting Islamic sultanate of Banten (1527–1808). Thereafter, it became the de facto government on the island of Java over a set of pacified Islamic protectorates.

Several decades earlier than its British counterpart in India, the VOC fell on hard times. Governing and maintaining troops was expensive. VOC employees often paid their expenses out of their own pockets, since contact with the Netherlands in pretelegraph times was slow and sporadic. In the late eighteenth century, trade shifted from spices to bulk commodities, such as sugar, cacao, coffee, tobacco, indigo, and cotton. The inability of the VOC to shift from spices to commodities, which required investments in plantations and accompanying transportation infrastructures, was the decisive factor that led in 1799 to the liquidation of the VOC. Similar to the British experience in India, the government of the Netherlands then became the ruler of Indonesian possessions that had grown from trade forts into small colonies, surrounded by dependent indigenous principalities as well as independent sultanates.

Dutch Colonialism   The Dutch government took the decisive step toward investments in 1830 when Belgium separated from the large Dutch kingdom created after the Napoleonic Wars to form an independent Catholic monarchy. Faced with severe budgetary constraints and cut off from industrializing Belgium, the Dutch government adopted the **cultivation system** in Indonesia. According to this system, indigenous Indonesian subsistence farmers were forced into compulsory planting and labor schemes which required them to either grow government crops on 20 percent of their land or work for 60 days on Dutch plantations. Overnight, the Dutch and collaborating Indonesian ruling classes turned into landowners. They reaped huge profits while Indonesian subsistence farmers, having to replace many of their rice paddies with commercial crops, suffered in many places from famines. In the course of the nineteenth century, Indonesia became a major or even the largest exporter of sugar, tea, coffee, palm oil, coconut products, tropical hardwoods, rubber, quinine, and pepper to the industrial nations.

To keep pace with demand, the Dutch pursued a program of systematic conquest and colonization. They conquered the Indonesian archipelago, finally subduing the most stubborn opponents, the Muslim guerillas of Aceh, in 1903 (see Map 27.6). Even then, the conquest was incomplete, and inland rain forests remained outside Dutch government control. Conquered lands were turned over to private investors who established plantations. To deflect criticism at home and abroad, the Dutch also introduced reform measures. In 1870 they liberated farmers from the compulsory planting of government crops, and in 1901 they issued an "ethical policy," announcing measures such as land distribution, irrigation, and education. Severe underfunding, however, kept these measures largely on paper, and it was clear that the profits from colonialism were more important than investment for indigenous people.

Cultivation system: Dutch colonial scheme of compulsory labor and planting of crops imposed on indigenous Indonesian self-sufficiency farmers.

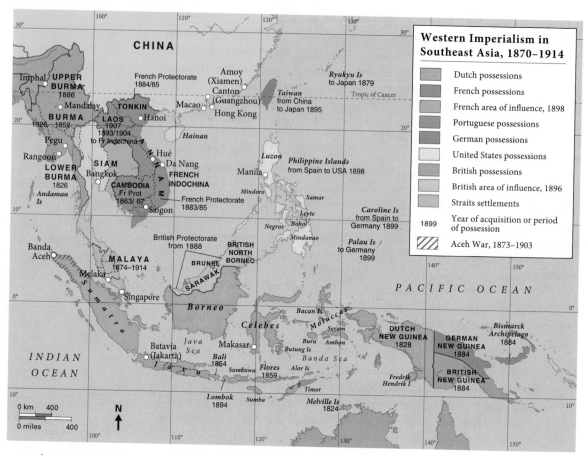

MAP 27.6 **Western Imperialism in Southeast Asia, 1870–1914.**

Spain in the Philippines

The Philippines are adjacent to the Indonesian islands in the northeast. The Spanish had built their first trade fort of Manila there shortly after conquering Mexico from the Aztecs, using it as a port from which to trade Mexican silver with China for luxury manufactures. Manila expanded only slowly, suffering from constant raids by indigenous highlanders from the interior, Islamic rulers from the southern islands, and Dutch interlopers. Imperial conquest had to await the later eighteenth century, and colonization followed in the middle of the nineteenth century with the introduction of sugarcane.

Galleons and Trade with China   Spain expanded early on from the Americas farther west in order to prevent Portugal from claiming all the lucrative spice islands of Indonesia. A Portuguese explorer in Spanish service, Ferdinand Magellan (ca. 1480–1521), successfully crossed the sea channels at the southern tip of South America in 1520 and, on a journey that took his fleet eventually around the entire globe, discovered what later became known as the Philippines, in honor of King Phillip II of Spain. It took another half century, however, before Spain could spare ships and men for the construction of a first trade fort and small colony. This fort,

Manila, became the base for subsequent biannual silver fleets from Mexico. Spanish merchants based in Mexico, from which Manila was administered, benefited greatly from the trade of silver for Chinese silk, porcelain, and lacquerware. Thus, Manila began as a small subcolony of the large Spanish colony of Mexico, or New Spain.

As the Spanish gradually expanded their hold on the coastal lowlands outside Manila on Luzon and Visaya (where the local king had converted to Christianity), they established estates, thus advancing from trade-fort imperialism to the beginnings of territorial expansion.

Incipient Colonialism   The indigenous farmers on the Philippine estates were obliged to deliver rents, in the form of rice and animals, to ensure the food supply for some 30,000 inhabitants of Manila, mostly merchants of Spanish, Chinese, and Japanese origin. Warrior chieftains outside Spanish lands who converted to Catholicism were confirmed as owners on their lands and transformed themselves into a Hispanicized landowner class. By the early eighteenth century, the Spanish controlled a critical mass on the two islands of Luzon and Visaya such that they were able to establish a regular administration for fiscal and juridical matters. The beginnings of colonialism in the Philippines had emerged.

The balance sheet for the colonial administration was always in the red, however, since the fiscal revenue did not yield surpluses and villagers produced only small quantities of exportable ginger, cinnamon, and gold. Much money had to be invested in defending the Spanish-controlled territory from attacks by independent Filipinos in the mountainous upland interiors of Luzon and Visaya who resisted conquest and conversion. Even more vexing were raids supported by Islamic sultanates which had formed in the south based in trading hardwoods for luxuries with China.

Full Colonialism   Major reforms, shifting the economy from silver to commodity exports, began in the early 1800s, motivated by the Spanish loss of Mexico to independence. These reforms resulted in the liberalization of trade and the beginnings of commercial agriculture for export. Ports were opened to ships from all countries, discrimination against Chinese settlements ended, and Spanish administrators and churchmen lost their trade privileges. Foreign entrepreneurs cleared rain forests and exported hardwoods. On the new land they grew cash crops, such as sugar, tobacco, hemp (for ropes and sacks), indigo, coffee, and cotton. Large-scale rice farms replaced a great number of small-scale village self-sufficiency plots, and thus, commercialization even usurped subsistence agriculture.

Strong resistance by landowners against a reform of the land regime and tax system until the very end of the nineteenth century, however, ensured that Spain did not benefit much from the liberalization of trade. Additionally, Philippine society stratified rapidly into a wealthy minority and a large mass of landless rural workers and urban day laborers. Manila had over 100,000 inhabitants in the early nineteenth century. This stratification, however, was very different from that in the Americas. There was no real Creole class—that is, a Spanish–Philippine upper stratum of landowners and urban people. Although the French Revolution and subsequent Napoleonic upheavals in Spain had their impact on the islands, agitation for independence and constitutionalism was largely limited to urban intellectuals.

American Soldiers in the Philippines. The victory of the United States over Spain in 1898 and its decision to annex the Philippines created for the first time an American overseas empire. Resistance was immediate, and a brutal war against Philippine fighters lasted from 1902 until 1913, with isolated outbreaks continuing until Philippine independence in 1946. Here, American troops dig in and fortify an outpost in Luzon.

The Philippines remained a colony, producing no revenue and still demanding costly administrative (especially fiscal) reforms and infrastructural investments, both of which Spain was unable to afford.

The first stirrings of Filipino nationalism, primarily among Hispanicized Filipinos of mixed Spanish and indigenous or Chinese descent, made themselves felt in the second half of the nineteenth century. The principal spokesman was José Rizal (1861–1896), whose subversive novels were a response to the Spanish justification of continued colonialism.

Colonial authorities promptly arrested Rizal for his activities, banishing him to Hong Kong, but he returned to Manila in 1892, inspiring both overt and underground resistance groups. One of these groups, Katipunan, operated in secret, advocating Filipino independence through armed struggle. In 1896 the government discovered the existence of the organization in Manila and executed hundreds of revolutionaries, including Rizal, before firing squads. But it was unable to destroy Katipunan in the provinces, and the two sides agreed in 1897 to a truce which included the end of armed revolt in return for exile of the leadership to Hong Kong.

Philippine–American War   Although it appeared that the colonial government was successful in suppressing the Filipino revolt for independence, events took a dramatic turn when the Spanish–American War broke out in 1898. The mysterious explosion of an American warship in Cuba—newly autonomous under Spanish suzerainty—had led to mutual declarations of war. The two sides fought their first battle in Manila Bay, where the United States routed a Spanish squadron. An American ship fetched the exiled Filipino rebel Emilio Aguinaldo (1869–1964) from Hong Kong, and he quickly defeated the Spanish and declared independence. Over four centuries of Spanish colonialism in the Pacific had come to an end.

After 4 months of fighting, Spain was defeated not only in Cuba, Puerto Rico, and Guam but also in the Philippines. The United States and Spain made peace at the end of 1898, ignoring the independent Philippine government in their agreement. Accordingly, US forces took possession of Manila in 1899 and within a year defeated the troops of the protesting Filipino government under the elected president, Emilio Aguinaldo. The Filipinos shifted to guerilla war, but US troops were able to capture Aguinaldo in 1901. The United States declared the war over in 1902 but had to fight remnants of the guerillas as well as southern rebels until 1913. Thus, the United States had joined the European race for imperial and colonial control of the non-Western world.

The French in Vietnam

North of Indonesia and west of the Philippines is Vietnam. Indochina, the peninsula on which Vietnam is located, also includes Cambodia, Laos, and Thailand. Portuguese monks in the sixteenth century were the first western Europeans to go to Indochina, seeking converts among the Buddhist, neo-Confucian, and animist indigenous inhabitants. French imperial and colonial involvement began in 1858, at a time when Europe was industrializing and competition in the Concert of Europe was beginning to spill over from the Balkans and Middle East into Africa. At first focusing on the south of Indochina, France gradually expanded northward, establishing protectorates over the Nguyen royal dynasty, which was the last of a succession of kingdoms that had begun in the third century CE.

French Interests in Vietnam   French royal efforts in the seventeenth and early eighteenth centuries to sponsor Catholic missions and trading companies were largely unsuccessful and ended altogether after their defeat in the Seven Years' War (1756–1763). When France renewed these efforts after the French Revolution and Napoleon, it was rebuffed by the Vietnamese kings, who shared Chinese concerns about the Western challenge. Both China and Vietnam adopted a policy of isolationism as their first answer to Western patterns of challenge.

The French, however, were not deterred. Napoleon had considered the idea of a Mediterranean empire that included either Algeria or Egypt before embarking on his campaign of European imperialism. The French then actually conquered Algeria in 1830–1847, as detailed earlier in this chapter. The ruler who was subsequently most active in pushing for the renewal of Napoleon's imperialism outside Europe was his nephew, Napoleon III (r. 1848–1870). This self-styled emperor involved himself in a variety of short-lived ventures in Mexico, China, and Japan. His one enduring conquest was that of Cochinchina, or southern Vietnam, in the late 1850s. Taking as a pretext the renewed torture and execution of French missionaries and Vietnamese converts, the French dispatched a squadron that occupied the sparsely inhabited Mekong River delta in 1858–1862, annexing it as a protectorate.

Conquest and Colonialism   Serious colonization efforts by the French had to await the scramble for the division of Africa and what remained unclaimed in Asia in the mid-1880s. After Napoleon III's fall from power as a result of the lost war against Prussia and the establishment of the Third Republic, opinions among politicians about the wisdom of a French empire were divided. But a year after pro-imperialists came to power in 1883, the French challenged and ultimately defeated China in a war for the control of northern Vietnam. In contrast to the thinly settled south, the Red River estuary in the north with the capital of the kingdom, Hanoi, was densely populated. When the imperialist frenzy was at its peak during the Berlin conference of 1884–1885 for the partition of Africa, the French conquerors united southern and northern Vietnam into the French colony of Indochina. Two members of the deposed Vietnamese dynasty took to the mountains and waged a guerilla war against the occupation, called the Black Flag Revolt. But by the early twentieth century the French had captured both and were in full control.

The French government and French entrepreneurs invested substantial sums in the Mekong delta, establishing plantations for the production of coffee, tea, and rubber. Indigenous rice farmers had to deliver 40 percent of their crops to the co-lonial government. Hanoi was made the seat of the colonial administration in 1902 and was enlarged as an architecturally French city. The port of Haiphong, downriver from Hanoi, became the main entry point for ships to load agricultural commodities for export. The commodities for the world market, which French West Africa largely lacked, existed in Vietnam, Cambodia, and Laos (the latter two added in 1893–1904).

Early Nationalism   Given Vietnam's long tradition of Confucian scholar-administrators, it was only a question of time before the pre-1858 spirit of antiforeign Vietnamese patriotism reasserted itself. The driving force in this reassertion was Phan Boi Chau (1867–1940), trained by his father and other scholars and an eyewitness to the crushing by the French of a protest by scholars in 1885. Phan Boi Chau's activities and writings inspired antitax demonstrations and a provincial uprising in Vietnam in 1908–1909, which the French suppressed harshly. Under French pressure, the Japanese expelled Phan Boi Chau from Japan in 1909. By 1912, he had given up his royalism, and from then on a newly formed nationalist grouping favored the expulsion of the French and the formation of a Vietnamese democratic republic.

Putting It All Together

Ever since Vladimir Lenin, the founder of the Soviet Union, declared in 1916 that imperialism was "the highest stage of capitalism" (adopting a thesis first suggested by the English historian John A. Hobson in 1902), scholars have hotly debated the topic of whether or not the capitalist industrialization process in Europe, North America, and Japan needed colonies to sustain its growth. Most recent historians, beginning with David K. Fieldhouse in 1984, have concluded that imperialism and colonialism were not needed and that all the mineral and agrarian commodities crucial for industrialization during the first and second Industrial Revolutions could have been bought from independent countries on the world market. It so happened, of course, that Great Britain had transformed its activity in India from trade-fort imperialism to territorial imperialism just prior to its industrialization and used Indian cotton as raw material for its textile factories. But this raises the reverse question: Would industrialization have happened had Great Britain not conquered India? This counterfactual question has no easy answer.

Perhaps a better approach to the question is to think of trade-fort and territorial imperialism as world-historical patterns of long standing. By contrast, industrialization was a much later phenomenon that arose out of the application of the New Sciences to practical mechanical uses, of which steam engines and textile factories were the first examples, appearing around 1800. Thus, old patterns of imperialism persisted during the rise of the new pattern of industrialization. These old patterns were tremendously amplified by the new power that industrialization gave the European countries. Therefore, the new imperialism of the nineteenth century, and the colonialism that followed in its wake, can be seen as phenomena in which old patterns continued but were superimposed on and enlarged by new patterns of industrial power.

▶ For additional resources, including maps, primary sources, visuals, and quizzes, please go to www.oup.com/us/vonsivers. Please see the Further Resources section at the back of the book for additional readings and suggested websites.

Against the Grain

An Anti-Imperial Perspective

During the heyday of Western imperialism in the later nineteenth century, many popular European writers justified the conquest of foreign lands and the exploitation of native peoples by expressing attitudes reflected in social Darwinism. Seen from this perspective, Europeans were doing God's work by pursuing a "civilizing mission," thus exposing "lesser breeds" to the benefits of Christianity and commerce. For proponents of imperialism, it was fitting and just to pursue a policy of civilizing the "inferior races." Perhaps the best known of these condescending works was Rudyard Kipling's "The White Man's Burden," published in 1899 in response to America's takeover of the Philippines after their victory in the Spanish–American war of 1898. According to this poem it was the duty, or "burden," of Western imperialists to "serve your captives' need / Your new-caught, sullen peoples / Half-devil and half-child."

Not all Europeans, however, were of like mind; there were many who refused to follow suit, and who expressed views contrary to the majority opinion. Among the most outspoken critics of European imperialism was a contemporary of Kipling, the British journalist E. D. Morel (1873–1924). Initially employed as a clerk in an English trading firm with commercial interests in the Belgian Congo, Morel had access to records and documents that revealed the mistreatment and exploitation of African slave labor on Belgian rubber plantations. Determined to expose these atrocities, Morel published a series of scathing denunciations in 1900.

Forced to leave his job, Morel continued his activist campaign against Belgian atrocities by launching a newspaper, the *West African Mail*, in 1903, followed by his foundation of the Congo Reform Association in 1904. Two particularly trenchant books exposing Leopold II's brutal policies soon followed: *King Leopold's Role in Africa* (1904) and *Red Rubber* (1906). By far the most famous of Morel's indictments, however, was *The Black Man's Burden* (1920), a condemnation of the evils of European capitalism and industrialism: "Its destructive effects are . . . permanent. . . . It kills not the body merely, but the soul. It breaks the spirit." For his pacifist activities Morel was sentenced to prison in 1917, but subsequently went on to win a seat in Parliament in 1922 as a Labour candidate, defeating Winston Churchill in the process. Although he played only a minor role in Parliament, Morel is often considered the father of international activism on behalf of human rights.

- In what ways is Morel a good example of nonconformity with European imperialism in Africa?

- How would you compare Morel's actions with current protest movements around the world?

Thinking Through Patterns

▶ **What new patterns emerged in the transition from trade-fort imperialism to the new imperialism?**

During the early modern period, European monarchs commissioned merchant marine companies, such as the British East India Company and the Dutch United East India Company, in order to avoid military expeditions of their own but still receive a share of the profits of trade. The mariner-merchants built coastal forts for storage and protection, granted to them by the local rulers with whom they traded. In the seventeenth and eighteenth centuries, much larger trading companies were formed, in which investors pooled their resources, and large numbers of mariner-merchants now served in dozens of trade forts overseas. In India and Indonesia, these companies became "too big to fail" and needed their governments in England and the Netherlands to rescue them. Thus, through the back door, governments found themselves forced to conquer and to colonize—they had become imperialist colonizers.

Great Britain was the pioneer in the development of exportable agricultural and mineral commodities in its colonies for the support of its expanding industries. By the middle of the nineteenth century, other industrializing countries either embarked on imperial conquests or shifted to full colonialism in order to obtain necessary commodities. As a rule, labor for the production of these commodities was scarce. Workers had to be recruited forcibly and were routinely paid low wages.

▶ **How did European colonizers develop their colonies economically, given that they were industrializing themselves at the same time?**

▶ **What were the experiences of the indigenous people under the new imperialism? How did they adapt to colonialism? How did they resist?**

Many imperial conquests involved protracted campaigns that claimed many indigenous victims. If one of the goals of the ensuing colonization was commodity production, the indigenous population was recruited, often forcibly and with low wages. Resistance to European colonialism manifested itself in ethnic nationalism, as demonstrated by the examples of José Rizal, Phan Boi Chau, and Emilio Aguinaldo discussed in this chapter. In Australia and New Zealand and other colonies where European settlement was encouraged, colonial governments or settlers ousted the indigenous population from the most fertile lands, often in the face of fierce resistance.

PART SIX

From Three Modernities to One

1914–PRESENT

World War I and the Interwar Period

The first great crisis in the evolution of modern scientific–industrial society was World War I (1914–1918). Although imperial competition in the Balkans triggered the war, there were even stronger forces at work in the background, together with other reasons still hotly contested by historians today.

For our purposes, the most dramatic effect of the war was that the single nineteenth-century pattern of modernity—constitutional and ethnic–linguistic nationalism and scientific–industrial society—splintered into the three subpatterns: capitalism–democracy, socialism–communism, and supremacist nationalism. The countries representing these subpatterns of modernity formed camps that were bitterly hostile to each other:

- Capitalist democracy (most notably in the United States, Britain, France, and parts of Latin America): support for the concepts of freedom (especially the free market), capitalism, and international institutions for maintaining peace

- Communism–socialism (the Soviet Union): professed support for equality over freedom and a command economy controlled from the top

- Supremacist nationalism (Italy, Germany, and Japan): contempt for both democracy and communism, the celebration of racial supremacy and authoritarian/dictatorial rule, a state-controlled economy, and territorial expansion through military conquest

In the period after World War I, the countries representing these three modernities moved in very different directions:

- The democratic victors, Great Britain and France, expanded their colonial empires by acquiring, under the rubric of "mandates," new territories taken from the liquidated Ottoman Empire in the Middle East and the Second German Empire in Africa. Since a variety of ethnolinguistic nationalisms in these territories were forming at the same time, future conflicts were inevitable.

1908 Oil discovered in the Middle East	**1914–1918** World War I	**1919** Versailles Treaty; League of Nations	**1937–1945** World War II in China, the Pacific, and (from 1939) Europe	**1947** Indian and Pakistani independence	**1950–1953** Korean War
1911–1912 Revolution in China; fall of Qing Dynasty	**1917** Bolshevik Revolution	**1929–1933** Stock market crash; Great Depression	**1942** Nazi Final Solution implemented	**1948** State of Israel founded; first Arab–Israeli War	**1957** USSR la of Sputr decolon begins i

- In Russia, a small but highly disciplined Communist Party managed to engineer a political takeover, withdraw the nation from the war, and build a communist state: the Union of Soviet Socialist Republics (Soviet Union, or USSR). The Soviet Union achieved full industrial strength in the 1930s.
- The loser of World War I, Germany, together with Italy and Japan (both of which had joined the Allies in hopes of territorial gains), turned toward supremacist nationalism.

World War II and the Rise of New Nations
In contrast to World War I, World War II was actively planned by the supremacist nationalists and was far less avoidable. Both World War I and the Great Depression effectively ended the global free trade that had characterized the nineteenth century. All countries, including the capitalist democracies, now subscribed to the idea that the future of industry lay in economic "spheres" dominated by one *autarkic*—that is, self-sufficient—industrial power. With the victory of the Allies, the United States and Soviet Union emerged after World War II as the leading examples of the two surviving patterns of modernity: capitalist democracy and socialism–communism. The proponents of each of these patterns competed with the other during the Cold War (1945–1991):

- The first, or "hot," phase, 1945–1962: The United States and Soviet Union surrounded themselves with allies in Europe and Asia and fought one another militarily through proxies—that is, smaller allied states. They also sought to align the new nations emerging in the wake of decolonization into their respective camps. The Cold War climaxed during the Cuban Missile Crisis of 1962.
- The second, "cooling" phase, 1962–1991: During this time, the two nuclear powers reduced tensions ("détente") and agreed on a mechanism to limit, and then to reduce, their nuclear arsenals. But they continued their proxy wars, in particular in Vietnam and Afghanistan.

Capitalist–Democratic Modernity
Perhaps the most significant event that put the United States on course for eventual victory over the Soviet Union in 1991 was the computer revolution—the third industrial revolution after those based on the steam engine (ca. 1800) and steel, electricity, and chemicals (ca. 1865). After fully adapting itself to this revolution, the United States became the unrivaled superpower, deriving its strength from its advanced computer technology, powerful financial services, and unmatched military strength.

Thinking Like a World Historian

▶ How are the three patterns that emerged after World War I different adaptations to modernity? Despite their marked differences, what common features do they share?

▶ Why, after World War II, was socialism–communism in many ways a more attractive pattern to decolonizing countries than capitalism–democracy?

▶ Why was the United States better able to adapt to technological innovation than the Soviet Union?

▶ How do consumerism and the widespread use of social networking show the emergence of a global culture in the twenty-first century? Can we predict what future patterns will look like?

| 1958 Great Leap Forward in China | 1963 Nuclear Test Ban Treaty | 1966–1969 Cultural Revolution in China | 1979 Shah of Iran overthrown; USSR invades Afghanistan | 1989–1991 Collapse of communism in eastern Europe and Soviet Union |

| 1962 Cuban Missile Crisis | 1965–1973 Vietnam War | 1978 "Four Modernizations" in China | 1985–1989 Perestroika and Glasnost in the USSR | 1989 Tiananmen Square demonstrations in China; Berlin Wall torn down |

| 1990 German unification | 1990–2000 Civil war and ethnic cleansing in former Yugoslavia | 1994 End of apartheid and election of Nelson Mandela as president in South Africa; genocide in Rwanda | 2001 Al-Qaeda attack on United States | 2008–2011 Global financial crisis and economic recession | 2011 Arab Spring uprisings; world population reaches 7 billion |

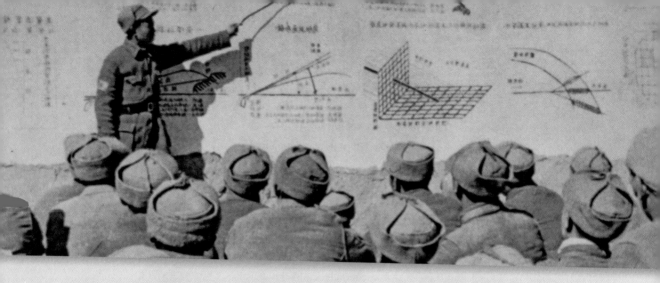

Chapter 28 1900–1945

World Wars and Competing Visions of Modernity

Professor Minobe seemed rattled. For 30 years he had been Japan's leading jurist and constitutional theorist. His decades of work in the law school of Japan's leading academic institution, Tokyo Imperial University, were celebrated not just in Japan but among scholars throughout the world. Indeed, such was his prestige that he had received a noble rank and occupied an honored place in Japan's House of Peers, the upper chamber of its Diet, or parliament. A self-confident, even combative, man, he was not ordinarily given to suffering fools or meekly taking a dressing down.

But today was different, and only later would Minobe Tatsukichi (1873–1948) realize what a dramatic turning point it was for him and for the direction of Japanese law and politics. On this bleak February day in 1934, his fellow peer Baron Takeo Kikuchi had taken the floor and publicly denounced Minobe's most famous legal theory. Decades earlier, Minobe had posited that the relationship of the emperor to the constitution was one in which the emperor was an organ of the state. More than a generation of Japanese lawyers and scholars had internalized and practiced law according to this "organ theory." But now, the baron had accused Minobe of belittling the emperor's role in Japan's unique *kokutai*, or "national polity/essence." This concept, as

A WORLD AT WAR, 1900–1945

ABOVE: **Members of the Chinese People's Liberation Army undergo artillery training.**

we shall see, played a key role in Japanese supremacist nationalism during the 1930s.

Though Minobe defended his position skillfully, reminding his colleagues that to say the emperor was an organ of the state simply means that he rules for the state and not for himself, the damage had been done. Following more attacks in the Diet, Minobe resigned from his position, narrowly escaped being tried for his views, and was nearly assassinated in 1936. Already, however, in their drive to "clarify" the meaning of the "national essence," the cabinet had eliminated all of Minobe's writings and banned his works from study or circulation. Minobe's experience personalizes a struggle to come to grips with new visions of modernity not only in Japan but in much of the world as well.

Seeing Patterns

▶ Which three patterns of modernity emerged after World War I? How and why did these patterns form?

▶ What were the strengths and flaws of each of the three visions of modernity?

▶ Why did supremacist nationalism disappear in the ashes of World War II?

By the 1930s, the liberal principles of modernity—constitutionalism, capitalism, science, and industry—were being tested in the crucible of the Great Depression and increasingly found wanting. In Japan, these values were already giving way to what we call "supremacist nationalism," offering close parallels to the ideologies of fascism in Italy and Nazism in Germany. In Russia, communism represented another new subpattern of modernity. Other nations—Spain, Portugal, and China, for example—struggled with variations of one or more of these competing ideologies.

In this chapter we will explore how the conflicts of spreading modernity spawned these new visions and how each fared through two world wars and the largest economic depression in history. We will also see how the supremacist nationalism that haunted Minobe, as embodied in the Axis powers, was utterly destroyed by the alliance of communism and capitalist democracy. Their interlude of victory, however, was destined to be short-lived. Within a few years the remaining two divisions of modernity renewed the struggle for dominance against each other under the shadow of potential nuclear annihilation.

The Great War and Its Aftermath

On July 27, 1914, the nations about to plunge into the abyss of total war the following day represented a host of different conditions on their way to modernity. As we saw in the preceding chapters, some, like Great Britain, Germany, and France, were, along with the United States, among the world leaders in the development of what we call "scientific–industrial society." Others, like Austria-Hungary, the Ottoman Empire, the newly independent Balkan nations, Russia, and even Japan, were at various stages of industrialization, more or less along the lines of the leading powers. In most cases, this latter group had come to this condition somewhat reluctantly, often after violent interactions with the new industrial powers. In terms of political modernity, all of these initial members of what would shortly be known as the Allies and Central powers—with the exception of France—were monarchies, though a number had become modified over the course of the nineteenth century with the addition of constitutions and legislative assemblies. The larger powers were also imperial powers that collectively had reduced much of Asia and effectively the entire

Chapter Outline

- The Great War and Its Aftermath

- New Variations on Modernity: The Soviet Union and Communism

- New Variations on Modernity: Supremacist Nationalism in Italy, Germany, and Japan

- Putting It All Together

Total War. By 1918, large swaths of northern France and Belgium resembled moonscapes from 4 years of destruction and carnage. One of the unluckiest places was the Belgian city of Ypres, which suffered three battles and was all but completely obliterated by war's end.

continent of Africa to the status of colonies. Over the next 4 years, this picture would change so completely that the old order could only be dimly glimpsed through the fog of memory of the diminished numbers who could recall it.

A Savage War and a Flawed Peace

Time-honored imperial competition, tempered by the need for a balance of power among the major states, dominated Europe during the century following the Napoleonic Wars. This intersected with the two trends of nineteenth-century modernity we have identified in the last several chapters: the political patterns of constitutional nationalism and ethnolinguistic nationalism and the pattern of industrialization. The rise of the new imperialism in the nineteenth century, itself part of the growth of nationalism and industrialism accompanying modernity, carried a logic of its own that seemed destined to disrupt the ongoing efforts of statesmen to adjust the balance of power to ever-shifting political conditions.

Empires and Nations in the Balkans   After decades of consensus and revision, modern scholars have begun to emphasize German aspirations for expansion into eastern Europe as one of the prime catalysts for its support of Austria against Serbia in 1914. For its part, France had sought at various times *revanche*—revenge—for Germany's annexing of its "amputated provinces" of Alsace and Lorraine in 1870, though this was tempered by the painful awareness of Germany's superior might. In the first decade of the twentieth century, however, the key to the preservation of peace in Europe was seen as maintaining the balance among the three unequal empires that met in the Balkans.

The shrinking Ottoman Empire, beset by continuing demands from ethnic-nationalist minorities for independence, struggled to survive. The expanding Russian Empire, despite having suffered a defeat at the hands of Japan and an abortive revolution in 1904–1905, was rapidly recovering its aggressiveness, if not its military strength. For its part, the opportunistic Habsburg Empire of Austria-Hungary opposed Russian expansionism but also sought to benefit from Ottoman weakness. Germany had largely replaced Great Britain as the protector of the Ottomans and assisted the latter in strengthening their army. Though it had taken

Mediterranean territories from the Ottomans, Britain still had a stake in keeping the rest of the Ottoman Empire in existence, as did the other powers, all of whom feared the results of a territorial scramble if the Ottoman Empire collapsed altogether. Hence, as there had been in China during the scramble for concessions of the late 1890s, there was a rough community of interest aimed at strengthening the Ottoman Empire, whose leaders were themselves seeking to improve their military posture.

One unresolved ethnic-nationalist issue of concern to the three empires was Bosnia-Herzegovina. After the Balkan war of 1878, Austria-Hungary had become the territory's administrator—but not sovereign—as a compromise with the Ottomans, who were unable to keep Serbs, Croats, and Muslims apart. When Russia renewed its support for Serb ethnic nationalism in the Balkans after 1905, Austria-Hungary felt compelled to assume sovereignty of Bosnia-Herzegovina in a protective move in 1908. This in return offered Russia support for its demand for open shipping through the Bosporus. Britain and Germany, however, forced Russia to withdraw this demand. Russia, committed to a policy of pan-Slavism—support for the aspirations of Slavs everywhere—avenged itself by stirring up Serb nationalists. On June 28, 1914, members of a Bosnian Serb nationalist group assassinated the Austrian heir to the throne, Franz Ferdinand, and his wife while they toured the Bosnian city of Sarajevo. This assassination began the tragic slide of the two rival alliances that maintained the balance of power into the cataclysm of World War I. Yet even this occurred only after a month of intense diplomacy and increasing desperation among most of the politicians involved. In the end, each country's perceived military necessities were invoked to trump any diplomatic solution to the crisis.

The Early Course of the War   In contrast with past conflicts, this war was no longer limited and localized but comprehensive from the start: **total war**. In addition, the contingency plans of the combatants' general staffs in many cases relied on precise timing and speedy mobilization of their forces. Here, the most dramatic example was that of Germany. In order to avoid a two-front war, Germany, with its allies Austria-Hungary and the Ottoman Empire (the Central powers), had to defeat France before Russia's massive army was fully mobilized. The German Schlieffen Plan therefore called for a massive assault on northern France through Belgium that would take Paris in 6 weeks, while trapping and isolating the Allied armies seeking to invade Alsace and Lorraine, taken by Germany after the Franco–Prussian War of 1870.

Though the German plan came close to succeeding, it ultimately failed after the desperate French–British victory in the first Battle of the Marne in early September 1914, a more rapid Russian mobilization than expected, and a poor showing by the Austrians against Russia. After several months of seesaw fighting along

Total war: A type of warfare in which all the resources of the nation—including all or most of the civilian population—are marshaled for the war effort. As total war became elaborated, all segments of society were increasingly seen as legitimate targets for the combatants.

1908
Oil discovered in
Middle East

1914–1918
World War I

1915–1916
Massacre of Armenians
in Ottoman Empire

1919
Versailles Treaty; founding
of League of Nations

1929
Stock market crash; Great
Depression begins

1911–1912
Revolution in China;
fall of Qing Dynasty

1917
Balfour Declaration promises
Jews a homeland in Palestine

1917
Bolshevik
Revolution

1922
Mussolini's March on Rome

1931
Japanese annexation
of Manchuria

1932–1945
New Deal in
United States

1936–1939
Spanish Civil
War

1937
Rape of Nanjing

1942
Hitler implements the
Final Solution: genocide
of European Jews

1929–1932
Collectivization of
agriculture in Soviet Union

1933
Hitler becomes
chancellor in Germany

1937–1945
World War II in China
and the Pacific

1939–1945
World War II in Europe, the
Mediterranean, and North Africa

the lines of the initial German advance into France, the Germans and the French and British dug in. By 1915 the two sides were forced to conduct grinding trench warfare in northeastern France and an inconclusive war in the east.

The Germans, with superior firepower and mobility, were able to keep the Russians at bay and inflicted heavy losses on their troops—many of whom marched into battle without weapons, being expected to pick them up off their dead comrades. For its part, the Ottoman Empire suffered a crushing Russian invasion in the Caucasus, prompting it to carry out a wholesale massacre of its Armenian minority, which was alleged to have helped in the invasion. From official Turkish documents published in 2005 it can be concluded that the number of Armenians killed was close to 1 million. This planned massacre, the one large-scale atrocity of the war, still requires a full accounting today and is hotly debated by scholars, lawyers, and politicians.

> "Those three battalions [2,500 men] who went over were practically annihilated. Every man went to his death or got wounded without flinching. Yet in this war, nothing will be heard about it, the papers have glowing accounts of great British success."
>
> —British soldier Reginald Leetham, on the Battle of the Somme (July–November 1916)

As the war dragged on, both camps sought to recruit new countries to their sides. Italy, Greece, and Romania entered on the Allied side with the hope of gaining territory from Austria-Hungary and the Ottomans; Bulgaria joined the Central powers in the service of its own territorial ambitions. Japan declared war on Germany in 1914 as part of a previous alliance with Britain but used its occupation of German territories in the Pacific and China as a step toward expanding its own empire. The Allies also recruited volunteers from among their dominions and colonies in considerable numbers, some 800,000 from India alone. Thus, with soldiers from the mostly white dominions of Australia and New Zealand, as well as the African and Asian colonies of Britain and France fighting and dying in the trenches, the war became a true world war. With the token entrance of China in 1917 and the pivotal entrance of the United States that same year, the war now involved every major state in the world.

The Turning Point: 1917 By early 1917 the ever-intensifying slaughter took its first political toll. In March 1917, tsarist Russia collapsed in the face of horrendous casualties, crippled industry, extensive labor unrest, government ineptitude, and general internal weakness. The February Revolution (actually in March, so called because it took place during February in the old-style Julian calendar still in use in Russia at the time) forced Tsar Nicholas II to abdicate and created a provisional government. The new social-democratic government committed itself to carrying on the war, which now grew even more unpopular and impossible for Russia to manage. The communist Bolshevik Party of Vladimir Lenin (1870–1924), now liberated from persecution by the provisional government, steadily campaigned against continuing the war and in early November (October in the Julian calendar) launched a takeover of the government in the capital of Petrograd—as St. Petersburg had been renamed at the beginning of the war.

Seizing the reins of government, the Bolsheviks began tortuous negotiations with the Germans, which resulted in the disastrous Treaty of Brest-Litovsk in March 1918. Roughly one-third of the Russian Empire's population, territory, and resources were handed over to the Germans in return for Russia's peaceful withdrawal from the conflict. The Germans had now come close to achieving the secret war goal of the Supreme Army Command (*Oberste Heeresleitung*, OHL): the creation of *Lebensraum* (living space) for Germany in the industrialized European part of Russia.

Supporting the Empire. The colonies were drawn into the conflicts of their rulers. Over three-quarters of a million Indian troops such as the ones shown here fought with the British during World War I.

The United States had declared neutrality at the outset of the war, but despite President Woodrow Wilson's plea to Americans to stay "neutral in thought" as well as action, the course of the war had shifted US opinion decidedly toward the Allied side. The German violation of Belgian neutrality in the opening days of the war and extensive German use of the new technology of the submarine swung Americans toward a profound distaste for German actions. The German torpedoing and sinking of the British liner *Lusitania* on May 7, 1915, cost the lives of more than 100 Americans and brought the United States to the brink of war. Germany drew back for a while but then, in early 1917, resumed its unrestricted submarine warfare. Wilson had no choice but to ask Congress to declare war, which it did on April 6, 1917.

The entrance of the United States added the critical resources needed by the Allies to ultimately win the war. More important, Wilson's war aims, embodied in his war address to Congress and later in his Fourteen Points, sought to transform the conflict from one of failed diplomacy and territorial gain to a war to make "the world . . . safe for democracy." He called for freedom of the seas, the rights of neutral powers, self-determination for all peoples, and peace "without annexations or indemnities." These new causes not only represented American goals but now were presented as the Allies' war aims as well. For peoples in all the world's empires yearning for independence and self-determination, it appeared, briefly at least, that one side decisively championed their desires.

It was not until early 1918, however, that American troops began to land in France in appreciable numbers. This coincided with a spring offensive mounted by Germany. Bolstered by the addition of troops from the now-peaceful Russian front, the Germans threw everything they had at the Allies and once again came close to seizing Paris. But the new American troops in France gave the Allies the advantage they needed to stop the German effort, which soon collapsed. By June, more than 1 million Americans had arrived; by September, nearly 2 million; and by the end of fighting in November, 4 million more Americans were in various stages of progress to the western front. Faced with these new conditions and reeling from the Allies' September counteroffensive, which now threatened to advance into Germany, the Germans agreed to an armistice on November 11, 1918.

The Versailles Peace   As the staggering war toll sank in, the Allies settled down to make peace. About 20 million soldiers and civilians were dead, and 21 million were wounded. Military deaths were 5 million for the Allies and 4 million for the Central powers. Many more millions perished in the world's worst influenza pandemic, abetted by the massive transportation of goods and soldiers at war's end. The settlement, signed at Versailles on June 28, 1919—the fifth anniversary of the assassination of Franz Ferdinand—has been described unflatteringly as a "victor's peace."

The German, Austro-Hungarian, and Ottoman Empires were all dismantled, and new nation-states were created in their stead. Germany lost its overseas colonies, Alsace-Lorraine, and West Prussia. The Allies declared Germany responsible for the war and subjected it to substantial military restrictions and huge reparation payments. France did not prevail with plans to divide Germany again into its pre-1871 components but succeeded in acquiring temporary custody of the Saar province with its coal reserves and steel factories as a guarantee for the payment of war reparations. For a long time, historians considered the Allied-imposed reparations excessive, but more recent research has come to the conclusion that Germany, which was not destroyed by war, had the industrial-financial capacity to pay.

League of Nations: An international body of 58 states created as part of the Versailles Treaty and functioning between 1919 and 1946 that sought to ensure world peace.

A new supranational **League of Nations** was entrusted with the maintenance of peace. But since one of its clauses required collective military action in case of aggression, the US Senate refused ratification, rejecting this infringement on American sovereignty. Altogether, the Versailles peace was deeply flawed. Instead of binding Germany into a common western European framework, the Allies actually encouraged it to go it alone by flanking it in the east with small and weak countries that could be dominated in the future (see Map 28.1).

America First: The Beginnings of a Consumer Culture and the Great Depression

The United States emerged from the war as by far the strongest among the Allied democracies. It had turned from a debtor country into a creditor country; a majority of Americans now lived in nonrural environments; and the war economy shifted relatively easily into a sustained peacetime expansion. Far less hampered by old traditions than its European counterparts, it espoused modernity with a brusque enthusiasm, although its writers and intellectuals were often all too aware of modernity's contradictions.

Modernity Unfolding in the United States   Increased mechanization in industries such as construction materials, automobile assembly lines, and electrical appliance manufacturing spurred the economic expansion. A new dream arose among Americans: to move from countryside to city and to own a house (with indoor plumbing), car, refrigerator, radio, and telephone. Once in the city, during the Roaring Twenties, as the 1920s came to be called, Americans wanted to be

Europe, the Middle East, and North Africa, 1914

0 km — 400
0 miles — 400

N

NORWAY
SWEDEN
North Sea
DENMARK
BRITAIN
NETH.
BEL.
LUX.
GERMANY
RUSSIAN EMPIRE
ATLANTIC OCEAN
FRANCE
SWIT.
AUSTRIA-HUNGARY
ROMANIA
SERBIA
MONT.
ALB.
BULGARIA
Black Sea
ITALY
PORTUGAL
SPAIN
Mediterranean Sea
GREECE
OTTOMAN EMPIRE
PERSIA
SPANISH MOROCCO
ALGERIA (to France)
TUNISIA (to France)
DODECANESE (to Italy)
CYPRUS (to Britain)
MOROCCO (to France)
LIBYA (invaded by Italy, 1911)
EGYPT
ARABIA

Europe, the Middle East, and North Africa, 1923

0 km — 400
0 miles — 400

N

FINLAND
NORWAY
SWEDEN
North Sea
DENMARK
ESTONIA
LATVIA
LITHUANIA
GER.
BRITAIN
REPUBLIC OF IRELAND (after 1932)
NETH.
BEL.
LUX.
GERMANY
POLAND
SOVIET UNION
ATLANTIC OCEAN
SAAR
FRANCE
SWIT.
CZECHOSLOVAKIA
AUSTRIA
HUNGARY
ROMANIA
YUGOSLAVIA
BULGARIA
Black Sea
GEORGIA
ARMENIA
AZERBAIJAN
ITALY
ALB.
PORTUGAL
SPAIN
Mediterranean Sea
GREECE
TURKEY
IRAN
SPANISH MOROCCO
ALGERIA (to France)
TUNISIA (to France)
TRANS-JORDAN (Brit. mandate)
PALESTINE (Brit. mandate)
SYRIA (French mandate)
IRAQ (British mandate)
MOROCCO (to France)
LIBYA (to Italy)
EGYPT
SAUDI ARABIA (after 1932)

MAP 28.1 **Europe, the Middle East, and North Africa in 1914 and 1923.**

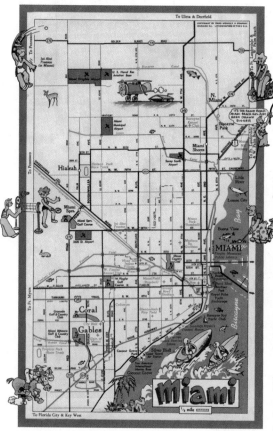

A Vision of American Modernity. This detail from a ca. 1930 Gulf Gasoline "Florida Info Map" vividly captures the vision of the American pattern of modernity—miles of roads and highways stretching in all directions, ample leisure opportunities, and a natural environment where the sun always shines.

entertained. A remarkable efflorescence of popular culture accompanied the rising urban prosperity. City and small-town dwellers alike were caught up in the mania of the movies, which, after 1927, came with sound. Americans frequented ballrooms to experiment with a wide range of dance steps and to listen to bands playing popular tunes. Jazz music in a large variety of styles found avid listeners. One could now listen to recorded sound on convenient 78-rpm records played on gramophones. The film industry of Hollywood and a recording industry came into being, churning out "hits," as their popular products came to be called, for the entertainment of the new consumers. And the rapid development of the radio now allowed news and entertainment to enter every household that could afford a set.

The New Woman   The Nineteenth Amendment of 1920 gave American women the right to vote, enormously expanding the promise of constitutional nationalism by half the population. In addition to winning political rights, American women heightened their social profile. Many colleges and universities went coed, although women often majored in education to become teachers, or in home economics to become good housewives for the husbands they met at school. Alternatively, they became secretaries skilled in shorthand and typing or nurses in hospitals. Indeed, the typewriter, developed in the late nineteenth century, directly contributed to the shift from secretaries being mostly men to overwhelmingly female. Its ease of operation and speed of copying and reproduction (through the use of carbon paper) was ideally suited to what were perceived to be women's skills and abilities. Similarly, women swiftly dominated the new occupation of telephone operator as the new century advanced.

For people of color, however, the situation was far different. Black women, if they were not agricultural laborers, rarely were able to become more than domestic servants or laundry workers in the growing urban economy. In larger segregated areas with more diversified economies, however, African American women often found similar kinds of opportunities as white women, though far more limited in scope and availability. Hence, although emancipation was expanding for white women, it clearly remained gendered, while the situation for black women continued to be additionally hampered by racism.

High Artistic Creativity   American intellectuals, writers, and artists viewed consumer and pop culture modernity with mixed feelings. On the one hand, they hailed what they viewed as the progress of liberal values. But on the other hand they were often uneasy about what they perceived as an increasing superficiality and materialism in modernity, furthered by ads, fashions, and fads. After World War I, the ambiguities of modernity engendered a veritable explosion of creativity in American culture.

The shattered illusions of the pre–world war era and search for a new beginning in modernity fueled much of this creativity. An entire cohort of artists and intellectuals viewed themselves as belonging to a "lost generation," referring to the sense that a generation that had lost its best years of life, or even life altogether, to a senseless world war. For African Americans, a new cultural touchstone was the Harlem Renaissance, featuring the leading innovators in jazz and literature (see "Patterns Up Close"). Few later authors plumbed modernity with the breadth of education as these "modernists" did, analyzing its contradictions, exposing its follies, articulating its inner emotional tensions in a "stream of consciousness," or offering counter-models of spirituality, naturalness, Greek classicism, or Chinese monism. Not only did the United States set the pace for mass culture; it also provided many of the literary tools to grapple with modernity and attempt to understand it, either by loathing it or by living with it critically.

Business and Labor   Just as much energy characterized American business. Presidents Harding, Coolidge, and Hoover along with the Congress exercised a minimum of political control, illustrated by Harding's campaign slogan "Less government in business and more business in government." While business boomed, trade and industrial unions stagnated. The American Federation of Labor (AFL), founded in 1886, was the largest trade union pushing for improved labor conditions. But, in contrast to European labor unions, it was always hampered by the fact that its members were unskilled workers of many ethnic, linguistic, and religious backgrounds and were therefore difficult to organize. Business easily quashed widespread strikes for the right to unionize in 1919. An anti-immigration hysteria followed, with laws that cut immigration by half. The hysteria, mixed with anticommunism, climaxed in 1927 with the trial of Ferdinando Nicola

Lynching. Outside the South, Indiana was the state that experienced the greatest surge in racial tensions in the period immediately after World War I. In 1925, the governor and half the state assembly were members of the Ku Klux Klan, as were about 30 percent of the state's white population. In this photo from August 1930, a crowd gathers to gawk at Tom Shipp and Abram Smith, two African American men who were lynched by a mob in Marion, Indiana, for allegedly committing robbery and rape.

Patterns Up Close | The Harlem Renaissance and the African Diaspora

Langston Hughes. The noted poet and writer Langston Hughes first emerged on the literary scene during the Harlem Renaissance and went on to influence the shaping of African and African American literary identity for decades afterwards.

As we have seen, the modern period up to the early twentieth century saw some of the largest migrations in human history. Such "diasporas"—a term originally used to describe the scattering of the Jews around Europe, the Middle East, and North Africa—not only threw those affected into new and sometimes hostile environments but over time also created rich and complex cultural conditions in which new generations struggled to forge their identities. In the case of African Americans in the 1920s, now several generations removed from slavery yet still hobbled by legal and social impediments, a new and vital cultural touchstone was the Harlem Renaissance.

Growing—though still severely limited—educational opportunities, a rapid increase in urbanization stemming from the "Great Migration" of rural southern African Americans seeking work in northern factory cities during World War I, and a new political assertiveness in the face of racism all contributed to a cultural explosion in a wide array of areas. As the largest African American enclave in America's largest city, New York, Harlem became the most vital black cultural center. Jazz and its offshoots came to dominate popular tastes; young people of all ethnicities sought to take up the latest dances from "uptown"; and writers such as Claude McKay (1889–1948), Langston Hughes (1902–1967), James Weldon Johnson (1871–1938), Zora Neale Hurston (1891–1960), and dozens of others achieved national and international recognition on an unprecedented scale.

Sacco and Bartolomeo Vanzetti, two Italian anarchist immigrants who were convicted for murder on contradictory evidence and executed.

The Backlash   The antiforeigner and anticommunist hysteria was part of a larger unease with modernity. Fundamentalist religion, intolerance toward Catholics and Jews, and fear and violence directed at African Americans rose visibly. The revival of the Ku Klux Klan was at the center of repeated waves of lynchings in the South and attempts to control the local politics of a number of states, most prominently Indiana. The Klan remained a powerful force in the South and Midwest until World War II.

The most startling offenses against the modern principles of liberty and equality, however, came from ideologues wrapping themselves in the mantle of modern science. Researchers at the leading private universities lent respectability to the

For many of these writers, a vision of Africa as their homeland hovered over their work. Though relatively few (such as Langston Hughes) actually visited Africa, its resonance as the center of their self-defined identity was powerful, and the legacy of this vision remains so even today. To be African in this sense was to be beyond the history of slavery and oppression and to be part of larger and richer collective history extending to the first human beings. Not surprisingly, this solidarity was expressed in the Pan-African movement of which the educator, activist, and cofounder of the NAACP W. E. B. DuBois (1868–1963) was a prominent popularizer. Indeed, during the 1920s the most popular mass movement among African Americans was the Universal Negro Improvement Association led by Marcus Garvey (1887–1940), which sought to help those of the African diaspora repatriate to the continent with a view to creating a strong and prosperous Africa for the Africans.

For its part, the Harlem Renaissance also had a profound effect on people of African descent in places far removed from the United States. Drawing from the revolutionary history of Haiti as well as the poetry of Hughes, African expatriates in Paris in the 1930s championed a cultural movement called Négritude, which called for a new pride in African history, culture, and "blackness" itself. Influenced by such writers as Aimé Césaire (1913–2008) and Léopold Senghor (1906–2001), the movement was powerfully influential in French-speaking Africa. Senghor himself became Senegal's first president and served for two decades. Through it all, however, these writers ultimately wrestled with a timeless, universal question, now burdened with all the urgency of modernity: "Who am I?"

Questions

- What were some of the factors that led to the Harlem Renaissance emerging in the 1920s, instead of some other time?

- Why were the questions these writers raised about identity so important to them? Why was this especially so in the new "modern" age?

pseudoscience of **eugenics**, conceptualizing an ideal of a "Nordic" race and searching for ways to produce more athletic, blond, and blue-eyed Americans. Foundations such as the Carnegie Endowment and businessmen such as Henry Ford financed research on how to prevent the reproduction of genetically "inferior" races. California and other states passed laws that allowed for the sterilization of nearly 10,000 patients—mostly women (black and white)—in state mental hospitals, and the Supreme Court in 1927 upheld these laws. Ironically, some of the practices that would inspire Hitler and the Nazis were already quietly put in place during the 1920s in the United States and actually regarded by some as progressive.

Eugenics: The discredited idea of the hereditary breeding of better human beings by genetic control.

The Great Depression   The Roaring Twenties came to a screeching halt in 1929, when saturation of the market for consumer goods behind high tariff walls during the later 1920s led to falling profit rates. Many of the wealthy had begun to shift their money from investments in manufacturing to speculation on the stock market. In addition, stocks began to be seen as a viable outlet for ordinary investors thanks to widespread margin borrowing with little money down. As long as the market boomed, investors made money, but if stocks went down, the margin calls went out, and investors could be wiped out.

By the late 1920s, a general slowdown in production shifted attention to unsustainable debt levels. Farmers were particularly deep in debt, having borrowed to mechanize while speculating wrongly on a continuation of high prices for commodities. In October 1929, the speculators panicked, selling their stock for pennies on the dollar. The panic rippled through both the finance and manufacturing sectors until it burst into a full-blown cascade. As banks began calling in loans at home and abroad, the panic swiftly became a worldwide crisis: the Great Depression of 1929–1933. Harrowing levels of unemployment and poverty put the American system of capitalist democratic modernity to a severe test.

Americans largely blamed their probusiness president, Herbert Hoover (in office 1929–1933), for failing to manage the crisis, and in 1932 they elected Franklin D. Roosevelt (in office 1933–1945). Hoover's approach had been one that previous administrations had turned to in times of economic crisis: cut government spending, raise tariffs to protect US industries, and let market forces correct themselves. But such measures only made things worse, while the Smoot-Hawley Tariff of 1930, with the highest tariff rates in American history, encouraged retaliatory tariffs in other countries and discouraged world commerce, thus contributing to a worldwide economic collapse.

Under Roosevelt's prodding, Congress immediately enacted what he called the "New Deal," in which the government engaged in deficit spending to enact a number of measures designed to help the unemployed and revive business and agriculture. One showpiece of the New Deal was the Tennessee Valley Authority, a government-owned corporation for the economic development of large parts of the southeastern United States particularly hard hit by the Depression. In addition, a social safety net was created for the first time, with unemployment benefits and the Social Security Act. Finally, a Securities and Exchange Commission (SEC) was created in 1934 to supervise and enforce regulations governing the stock market in order to prevent a number of the practices that had led to the collapse of 1929.

In 1937, however, a Congress frightened by the deficit slackened efforts to reduce unemployment, while the Supreme Court declared several of the New Deal programs unconstitutional. The result was a new slump, from which the economy finally recovered only with America's entry into World War II.

Great Britain and France: Slow Recovery and Troubled Empires

While the impact of World War I on the United States was relatively small, Britain and France suffered severely. A lack of finances hampered the recovery, as did the enormous debt both countries took on during the war. Conservative politicians relinquished the state capitalism of the war period and returned to politics favorable to private investors, without, however, allowing for the same uncontrolled speculations as in the United States. Although socialist politicians gained in importance, they did not succeed in improving working-class conditions or the safety net. Britain benefited from the discovery of oil in its mandates in the Middle East. Accordingly, the demands of the League of Nations mandate system, in which the colonies were to be prepared for future independence, were not pursued vigorously by either France or Britain.

Weak British Recovery   As the economy shifted from state control during the war back to market capitalism, industry was still in a leading role; but Britain was also heavily dependent on world trade, carried by its merchant fleet. Unfortunately for Britain, world trade declined dramatically after the war. In addition, the country owed a war debt of $4.3 billion to the United States for war materiel, which the United States insisted on receiving back (relenting only during the Depression). Since much of Britain's ability to repay these debts rested upon Germany's ability to pay its reparations, the entire European economic system remained fragile throughout the 1920s.

With the restructuring of Germany's debts under the Dawes Plan in 1924, some stability finally came to the international capital markets. Still, close to half of the annual British budgets in the interwar period went to paying off the war debt. In this situation, industrial investments were low and unemployment was high, dipping below 10 percent of the workforce only once during the 1920s. In addition, business lowered wages, causing labor to respond with a massive general strike in 1926. The strike collapsed after only 9 days, but business, without capital to make industry competitive again, did not benefit either. The British economy remained stagnant.

The dominant conservatives in the government could not bring themselves in the 1930s to accept deficit spending. At a minimum, however, they went off the gold standard and devalued the currency to make exports competitive again. World trade, of course, had declined; but by lowering tariffs within the empire, Britain created the equivalent of the **autarky** that Nazi Germany and militaristic Japan were dreaming of with their planned conquests. A semblance of prosperity returned to the country in the 1930s.

France: Moderate Recovery   Together with Russia, France suffered devastating human losses and destruction of property during the war. For every 10 men of working age, two were dead, one was disabled, and three were recuperating from their wounds. The population drop and consequent lack of replacement during the interwar period prompted some French observers to talk about the "hollow years." Alsace-Lorraine, the most important industrial region and the territory that France desperately wanted to recover from the Germans, was now a wasteland. The war had been fought with war materiel borrowed from the United States and Great Britain ($5 billion), to be paid for after the war. Some money for the reconstruction of industry and housing came from increased taxes, German

Down and Out in Wales. The prosperity of the 1930s was largely limited to southern England. Most of the rest of the British Isles, such as this unemployed miner in Wales, who here perhaps consoled by his two children, were largely left out.

Autarky: The condition of economic independence and self-sufficiency as state policy.

reparations, and taxes from German provinces occupied after the war. But reconstruction could be completed only in 1926–1929, when taxes were once more increased and Germany finally made full reparation payments.

Although French governments were dependent on coalitions among parties and therefore less stable, labor was more often than not represented in the governments. France did not suffer a traumatic general strike like England did, and even though it also returned to the gold standard (1928–1936), it wisely avoided the prewar parity, thereby making the low wages for its workers a bit more bearable. Since it had to reconstruct so much from the ground up, France modernized more successfully in many ways than Britain in the interwar period.

Thanks to its successful reconstruction, France weathered the Depression until 1931. Even then, conservative politicians found the idea of deficit spending as a way to get out of the Depression too counterintuitive. Instead, like the Hoover administration in America, they slashed government spending and refused to devalue the currency. Unrest in the population and rapidly changing governments were the consequences which in 1933–1934 made supremacist nationalism an attractive model, especially for business, which was afraid of labor strife. When fascist–communist street fighting broke out in Paris, the Communist Party initiated the formation of a Popular Front coalition with the Socialist Party and others (1936–1938). Although this coalition prevented a further slide into supremacist nationalism, it was too short-lived to allow the centrist middle-class core to broaden, with disastrous consequences for France's ability to resist Hitler in World War II.

Colonies and Mandates   The carefree consumer modernity in France and Britain during the 1920s contrasted sharply with the harsh reality of sustaining expensive colonial empires covering much of the world's land mass. After World War I, the British Empire grew by 2 million square miles to 14 million, or one-quarter of the earth's surface, adding 13 million more to its 458 million subjects, or one-quarter of the world population. The French Empire at the same time measured 5 million square miles, with a population of 113 million. Although the wisdom of maintaining empires was widely debated in the interwar period, in view of increased subsidies that had to be given to many of the colonies, conservatives held fast to the prestige that square mileage was presumed to bestow on its holders. Defense of these far-flung empires, interpreted as the "strategic interest" of the colonial powers, dominated the policies of Britain and France toward their dependencies and mandates during the interwar period (see Map 28.2).

The most important area strategically for both the British and the French after World War I was the Middle East. Under the postwar peace terms, the British and French had received the Arab provinces of the former Ottoman Empire (other than Egypt and Sudan, acquired in 1881) as *mandates*—that is, as territories to be prepared for independence. After a British geologist had in 1908 discovered oil in southwestern Iran, however, Britain and France put a high premium on their new Middle Eastern imperial possessions. Neither was in a hurry to guide its mandates to independent nationhood.

Twice-Promised Lands   As would be expected, Arab leaders were strongly opposed to the British and French mandates. Nationalism was on the rise, ironically

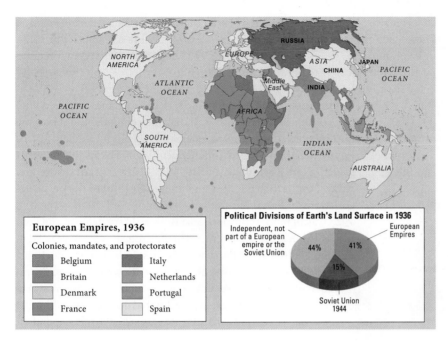

MAP 28.2 **European Empires, 1936.**

encouraged by the British during the war as they were searching for regional allies against the Ottomans. Their agent, T. E. Lawrence (1888–1935), the famous "Lawrence of Arabia," fluent in Arabic and Islamic customs, helped the members of a prominent family, the Hashemites from Mecca in western Arabia, to assume leadership of the Arabs for a promised national kingdom in Syria and Palestine in the so-called McMahon–Hussein correspondence of 1915–1916.

Since the British, seeking to rally support among Jews in Britain as well as Germany, Poland, and Russia, also promised the Jews a "national home" in Palestine in the Balfour Declaration of 1917, Arab nationalism was stymied even before it could unfold. The French ended a short-lived Arab-declared kingdom in 1920 in Damascus, and the British moved the Hashemites into their mandates of Iraq and Transjordan in 1921, in accordance with the Sykes–Picot agreement (1916) concerning the imperial division of the Middle East between the Allies. As Iraq was divided by majority Shiites and minority Sunnis, the British inaugurated a policy of divide and rule in their Middle Eastern mandates, while dangling the prospect of eventual independence in front of their populations.

In Palestine, the contradiction between the promises to Arabs and Jews during the war forced Britain to build an expensive direct administration under a high commissioner. In 1920, Palestine was inhabited by nearly 670,000 Arabs and 65,000 Jews. Many religious Jews had arrived as refugees from anti-Semitic riots, or pogroms, in Russia in the early 1880s and 1890s and the difficult postwar years in eastern Europe. When the Austrian Jewish journalist Theodor Herzl (1860–1904) made ethnic nationalism the ideology of secular Jews, early pioneers of **Zionism**, as secular Jewish nationalism was called, began to arrive as well. A Jewish National Fund collected money from Jews worldwide to buy land from willing Palestinian absentee landlords residing in Beirut and Jerusalem. As a

Zionism: The belief, based on the writings of Theodor Herzl, that European Jews—and by extension all Jews everywhere—were entitled to a national homeland corresponding to the territory of Biblical Israel. It grew into a form of ethnolinguistic-religious nationalism and ultimately led to the formation of the state of Israel in 1948.

consequence, Jewish settlers evicted the landlords' Palestinian tenant farmers. These evictions were the root cause of two Palestinian–Arab nationalist uprisings, in 1929 and 1936–1939, for which the British had no real answer except force and belated efforts in 1939 to limit Jewish immigration.

"We want it to be known—total independence is our goal! If only 'they' [the English] leave our nation! We could surpass Japan in civilization. Return to your country! Pick up your belongings! What audacity and rudeness. You are a true calamity! Do you have to stick to us like glue?"

—Popular Egyptian song, 1919

Secularizing Turkey. Atatürk was a committed educational reformer who sought to create a "public culture," and he was advised by the famous American philosopher of education John Dewey (1859–1952). Here, in 1928, dressed in a Western-style suit and necktie, he gives a lesson on the new Turkish alphabet, a variant of the Latin alphabet, whose use was mandated throughout the republic.

Egypt and Turkey After 1882, the Suez Canal acquired vital importance for the British in India, and relinquishing it became unthinkable. They rejected a demand in 1919 by a delegation of Egyptian nationalists for independence out of hand and exiled its leader, Saad Zaghlul (ca. 1859–1927). After deadly riots and strikes, the British relented and invited Zaghlul to the peace negotiations in Paris. But the independence the British granted in 1923 was of modest proportions: Both military defense and control of the Suez Canal were withheld from Egypt. A year later, Zaghlul and the Wafd Party won the first independent elections, with 90 percent of the vote. The ruling class, as in Iraq, was composed of landlords and urban professionals and, with few exceptions, was uninterested in industrial development. Thus, at the onset of World War II, Egypt was still entirely dependent on agricultural production and exports, though its strategic position was absolutely vital to the British Empire.

The severe punishment meted out to the Ottoman Empire by the Allies provoked the rise of local grassroots resistance groups in Anatolia. These groups merged under the leadership of General Mustafa Kemal "Atatürk" ("Father of the Turks," 1881–1938) into a national liberation movement, driving out the Greeks from western Anatolia, occupying one-half of Armenia (the other half was taken by the new Soviet Union), and ending the Ottoman sultanate/caliphate (1921–1924) altogether. Atatürk, the son of an Ottoman customs official in Salonika in what is now Greece, was among the relative few of the empire's militarily successful officers in World War I, most notably in his defense of Gallipoli against the British. Atatürk was the driving force behind the creation of a modern, secular Turkey that was able to stand up against the European powers.

Although he was authoritarian, Atatürk saw to it that the new Turkish parliament remained open to pluralism. Parliament adopted the French model of separation of state and religion, European family law, the Latin alphabet, the Western calendar, metric weights and measures, modern clothing, and women's suffrage. During the Depression, Atatürk's economic advisors launched *étatism*, the Turkish version of deficit spending. State capitalism, rather than private domestic or foreign capital, provided for the construction of steel and consumer goods factories, including textile plants. Both modernism and étatism showed only modest successes by 1939, and the rural masses in Anatolia remained mired in small-scale self-sufficiency farming and wedded to religious tradition. But the foundation was laid in Turkey not only for a Westernized ruling class but also for a much larger urbanized middle class.

Indian Demands for Independence The compromises negotiated during the Versailles Peace Conference, as we have seen, had a profound effect on the colonial world. Nowhere was this truer than in India. In April 1919, frustrated by a British crackdown on political protest, a large crowd gathered in a walled square in the Sikhs' sacred city of Amritsar. The British responded with a wholesale slaughter of the assembled men, women, and children by an elite unit of Gurkha troops. As the international furor over this "Amritsar Massacre" raged, the British, giving in to the inevitable, reformed the Indian Legislative Assembly by enlarging the portion of elected members to nearly three-quarters and the property-based franchise to 5 million, out of a population of 250 million. The Indian National Congress was infuriated by this minimal improvement and called for full self-rule (Hindi *swaraj*), urging nonviolent noncooperation, which, among other measures, called for a refusal to pay the land tax, for a boycott of British goods, and for people to spin and weave textiles at home.

Inevitably, civil disturbances accompanied the congress's push for self-rule. Mohandas Gandhi (1869–1948), a trained lawyer and the most prominent advocate of nonviolence, suspended the push in 1921. The leaders—lawyers, doctors, journalists, and teachers—exited the cities and, with the help of a large influx of party workers, scoured the countryside preaching nonviolent civil disobedience. It was during the 1920s and 1930s that the National Congress transformed itself from a small Westernized elite into a mass party.

In 1929, the new Labour government in Britain explored the possibility of giving India dominion status, but there was strong opposition from the other parties. When Labour could not deliver, Gandhi responded with the demand for complete independence and, on March 12, 1930, embarked on his famous 24-day Salt March to the sea in order for his followers to pan their own salt, which the government refused to free from taxation. Crowds in other places also marched to the sea. Disturbances accompanied the marches, and in a massive crackdown, with 100,000 arrests, the government succeeded in repressing the National Congress.

Nevertheless, after lengthy discussions the British government in 1935 passed the Government of India Act, which devolved all political functions except defense and foreign affairs to India. The members of the National Congress were unhappy, however, because of the decentralized structure of the reformed Indian government and particularly because the act recognized the Muslim League of Muhammad Ali Jinnah (1876–1948), not the Congress, as the representative of the Muslims. The British viceroy further inflamed matters in 1939 when he declared India in support of the British World War II effort, without even asking the Congress. As in Egypt and Iraq, there was a profound reluctance by the Western powers to relinquish colonialism. The legacy of this unwillingness would haunt the capitalist democracies well into the later twentieth century.

Swaraj: Literally, "self-rule" [*swa-RAJ*]. Gandhi interpreted this term as meaning "direct democracy," while the Congress Party identified it with complete independence from Great Britain.

Gandhi Leading the Salt March. Perhaps the most famous act of civil disobedience in Gandhi's career was the Salt March in 1930 to protest the British salt monopoly in India. It was a perfect embodiment of Gandhi's belief in nonviolent civil disobedience, which he called *satyagraha*, "soul-" or "truth-force." Though it failed to win major concessions from the British, it focused worldwide attention on the Indian independence movement.

Latin America: Independent Democracies and Authoritarian Regimes

Like Britain and France, Latin America remained faithful to its constitutional-nationalist heritage throughout the nineteenth century, though with a preference for authoritarian rule. In addition, a pattern of narrow elite rule had evolved in which large estate owners controlled the elections and politics of their countries and, through the military, kept rural black and indigenous Amerindian peoples, as well as the mixed urban populations, in check. Politicians in some countries realized the voting potential of the urban populations after World War I and pursued a new type of autocratic politics, called "populism," in conjunction with more or less extensive industrialization programs. Estate owner politics and populism, together with industrialization programs, characterized Latin America during the later interwar period.

Postwar Recovery   At the beginning of the 1900s, Mexico had enjoyed a long period of political stability and economic growth. It had a relatively diversified array of mineral and agricultural export commodities and began to exploit its mineral wealth to set up an iron and steel industry. But no change had taken place in agriculture, where the traditional oligarchy of rich ranching and plantation landowners continued to keep wages low. Thanks to US investments, railroad construction had progressed but more in order to support mining interests than agriculture, as there was no desire to improve the mobility of either the landless tenants or the indigenous Native American population engaged in subsistence farming.

The Years of Depression   In Mexico, a rapid urbanization process, begun in the late 1800s, continued during the interwar period. Immigration from overseas, mostly from southern and eastern Europe, as well as rural–urban migration fueled this process. In 1929 the newly created Institutional Revolutionary Party (Partido Revolucionario Institucional, PRI) brought the revolution of 1910–1917 to an end. A sufficiently strong government was in place again to complete land distribution to poor farmers, expand education, and begin social legislation. The PRI weathered the Depression with some difficulty, but thanks to increased state control of economic investments, it was able to maintain its footing until European and east Asian war preparations increased demand for commodities again.

Like Mexico, the countries with the largest internal markets, such as Argentina and Brazil, rode out the Depression more successfully than others. Nevertheless, overall the impact was substantial, with a reduction of commodity exports by over 50 percent. The Depression resulted in urban unrest, especially in countries with newly expanded mines or oil wells, such as Chile, Peru, and Venezuela, or expanded administrative bureaucracies, as in Brazil. At no time except the period of independence were there more coups, attempted coups, and uprisings than during 1930–1933.

An important shift away from landed oligarchies, however, began to appear among the ruling classes. Millions of people now lived in cities, although they did not have the clearly delineated social classes of workers or the nonindustrial lower classes that could be organized by communists, socialists, fascists, and militarists. Instead, a new generation of military officers, with urban backgrounds and no ties to the traditional oligarchy, appeared. They offered populist authoritarian programs that mixed elements from the prevailing European ideologies.

New Variations on Modernity: The Soviet Union and Communism

Communism was the second pattern of modernity that arose out of the ashes of World War I. Following their coup in November 1917, the Bolsheviks under Lenin ultimately triumphed in a debilitating civil war and established the Union of Soviet Socialist Republics. Lenin's successor, Joseph Stalin (1879–1953), built the Communist Party into an all-powerful apparatus that violently shifted resources from agriculture into industry and dealt ruthlessly with opposition to its policies. By World War II, Stalin's brutal policies had lifted the Soviet Union into the ranks of the industrialized powers.

The Communist Party and Regime in the Soviet Union

Karl Marx, the founder of communism, did not think that the underdeveloped Russian Empire, with its large majority of peasants, would be ready for a communist revolution for a long time to come. It was the achievement of Vladimir Lenin, however, as the leader of the Bolsheviks, a faction of the Russian Communist Party, to adapt Marxism to his circumstances. For him, the party was not the mass movement envisioned by Marx but rather the disciplined, armed vanguard that ruled with monopoly power and instilled the ideology of communism in a gradually expanding working class.

The Bolshevik Regime   Lenin was from a well-educated middle-class family; both of his parents were teachers, and his father had been given a patent of nobility; Lenin himself had a degree in law. The execution of his brother by the tsarist government for alleged complicity in the assassination of Tsar Alexander II (1881) imbued him with an implacable hatred for Russian autocracy. At the same time, he became steeped in the writings of Marx and radical thinkers across the political spectrum then circulating around Russia's intellectual underground. Contemplating the revolutionary potential of a communist party in Russia, he published a pamphlet in 1903 called *What Is to Be Done?* Here, he articulated for the first time the idea of professional revolutionaries forming an elite strike force. By eliminating the tsar and seizing control of the government, he argued, an ideologically trained communist party would be able, given Russia's highly centralized political structure, to implement its program of equality and industrialization from the top down.

The fall of the tsar's government in the spring of 1917 allowed Lenin and his fellow Bolsheviks to return from political exile. These included Leon Trotsky (1879–1940), the well-educated son of an affluent Ukrainian Jewish family, and Joseph Stalin, the hardnosed son of an impoverished Georgian cobbler who had escaped exile in Siberia seven times before the outbreak of World War I. Well aware of Lenin's subversive potential, the German government provided Lenin safe passage from Switzerland to Petrograd. By the summer of 1917, the Bolsheviks were mounting massive demonstrations with the slogans "Land, Peace, Bread" and "All Power to the Soviets" (councils of workers and soldiers that helped maintain order as the nation struggled to create a constitution). The collapse of a disastrous Russian summer offensive emboldened the Bolsheviks, who controlled the Petrograd Soviet, to make a bid for power. In early November 1917, the Bolsheviks staged a successful coup d'état in Petrograd.

Civil War and Reconstruction   The takeover of Russia by a tiny radical minority unleashed a storm of competing factions all across the political spectrum. For the Bolsheviks the first necessity therefore became building an army from scratch. Here, Trotsky proved a genius at inspiration and ruthless organization. From his armored train, flying the new "hammer and sickle" red flag, he continually rallied his forces against the far more numerous but utterly disunited "White" armies arrayed against his "Red" forces. From 1918 to 1921, the Ukraine, Georgia, Armenia, and Azerbaijan were each forced back into the new Bolshevik state.

The price for communist victory in the civil war was a complete collapse of the economy, amid a coincidental harvest failure. Lenin had initiated a policy of "war communism"—sending the Red Army into the countryside to requisition food, often with unrestrained brutality. Peasants fought back, and by 1922 a second civil war threatened. Only then did Lenin relent by inaugurating the temporary New Economic Policy (NEP), with a mixture of private and state investment in factories and small-scale food marketing by peasants. At the same time, however, the party—now several hundred thousand members strong—established an iron grip, with no deviation allowed. By 1928, a successful NEP had helped the Soviet Union to return to prewar levels of industrial production.

The Collectivization of Agriculture and Industrialization

Lenin suffered a stroke in 1922 and recovered only for short periods before he died in 1924. His successor was Joseph Stalin, who had garnered the key position of general secretary of the Communist Party in 1922. He had to fight a long struggle, from 1924 to 1930, to overcome potential or imagined rivals, a struggle which left in him a deep reservoir of permanent suspicion. His chief victim was Trotsky, whom he outmaneuvered, forced into exile, and ultimately had assassinated in Mexico in1940.

"Liquidation of the Kulaks as a Class"   When Stalin finally felt more secure, he decided that industrialization through the NEP was advancing too slowly. The most valuable source of funds to finance industrialization came from the sale of grain on the world market. But farmers had lost all trust in the communist regime after the forcible requisitions during the civil war and hoarded their grain. Grain production had fallen off and created a so-called Crisis of 1928. In November 1929, therefore, the party decreed the collectivization of agriculture as the necessary step for an accelerated industrialization. Over the next two years , in a carefully laid out plan, 3–5 percent of the "wealthiest" farmers on grain-producing lands, called *kulaks* (Russian for "fist," indicating the tightfistedness of wealthier farmers vis-à-vis poor indebted ones), were "liquidated"—selected for execution, removal to labor camps, or resettlement on inferior soils. Their properties were confiscated, and the remaining peasants were regrouped as employees either of state farms (*sovkhozy*) or of poorer collective farms (*kolkhozy*). Animals were declared collective property, with the result that many farmers slaughtered their cherished livestock rather than turn them over to the collectives. Between 6 and 14 million farmers were forcibly removed, with the majority killed outright or worked and starved to death.

Stalinism   The impact on agriculture was devastating. Grain, meat, and dairy production plummeted and failed to return to 1927 levels during the remainder of the interwar period. Food requisitions had to be resumed; bread had to be rationed on farms as well as in cities; and real wages on farms and in factories sank. On the other hand, the one-time transfer of confiscated wealth from the kulaks to industry was substantial. Income from accelerated oil exports and renewed grain exports from state farms in the 1930s was similarly poured into factory construction. By 1939, the rural population was down from 85 to 52 percent, and, for all practical purposes, industrialization had been accomplished, though at an unparalleled human cost.

The industrial and urban modernity that the Soviet Union reached was one of enforced solidarity without private enterprises and markets. The communist prestige objects were huge plant complexes producing the industrial basics of oil, coal, steel, cement, fertilizer, tractors, and farm combines. Little investment was left over for textiles, shoes, furniture, and household articles, not to mention cars, radios, and appliances. Consumers had to make do with shoddy goods, delivered irregularly to government outlets and requiring patient waiting in long lines.

The disaster of collectivization made Stalin even more concerned about any hidden pockets of potential resistance in the country. Regular party and army purges decimated the top echelons of the communist ruling apparatus. In 1937 alone, Stalin had 35,000 high-ranking officers shot, with disastrous effects for the conduct of World War II a few years later. Thus, in view of the enormity of Stalin's policies, scholars have since wondered about the viability of this attempt at accelerated modernity.

"Comrade, Come Join Us at the Collective Farm!" This is the call with which the woman on this wildly optimistic poster of 1930 is seen. In reality, Russian peasants experienced the collectivization program of 1929–1940 as a second serfdom, especially in the Ukraine, where private rather than collective village farming was widespread. They resisted it both passively and actively, through arson, theft, and especially the slaughtering of livestock.

New Variations on Modernity: Supremacist Nationalism in Italy, Germany, and Japan

The third vision of modernity was an ideology of supremacist nationalism. In contrast to communism, which was a relatively coherent ideology, the systems of fascism, Nazism, and Japanese militarism were far more diffuse and cobbled together from a wide variety of nineteenth-century intellectual sources. Fascism became a persuasive alternative to democracy and communism in Italy right after World War I. The much more brutal German Nazi and Japanese militarist ideologies became acceptable only once the Depression hit and appeared to reveal capitalist democracy to be incapable of weathering the crisis.

From Fascism in Italy to Nazism in the Third Reich

Benito Mussolini (1883–1945), the son of a blacksmith with anarchist leanings and a teacher, was well read in nineteenth-century philosophy and held positions as a journalist at various socialist newspapers. His support for the war as an instrument of radical change brought him into conflict with the majority of socialists, who bitterly opposed the war. As a result, he grew disillusioned with Marxism and founded the Italian Combat Squad (*Fasci italiani di combattimento*). War veterans, dressed in black shirts and organized in paramilitary units, roamed the streets and broke up communist labor rallies and strikes. The symbol of the movement was the *fasces* [FAS-sees]—derived from the old Roman emblem of authority in the form of a bundle of sticks and an ax, tied with a ribbon.

With their street brawls, the fascist "Blackshirts" contributed mightily to the impression of a breakdown of law and order, which the democratic government was apparently unable to control. Anticommunism thus was accompanied by denunciations of democracy as a chaotic form of government incapable of decisive action. Although Mussolini's party was still woefully behind the Socialist, Christian Democrat, and Conservative Parties in the parliament, he demanded and received the premiership by threatening a march on Rome by 10,000 Blackshirts. This turned into a victory parade, with the king acquiescing to the fascists' "third way" alternative to democracy and socialism.

Once given his chance, Mussolini transformed the Blackshirts into a militia for national security, paid for by the state. In 1923 he used the threat of their force again when he led his coalition government in the passing of a law that gave two-thirds of the seats in parliament to the party that garnered the most votes (at least 25 percent). A year later, Il Duce ("the Leader"), as he now styled himself, won his two-thirds and began to implement his fascist **corporate state**.

Corporate state: Sometimes called an "organic state"; based on a philosophy of government that sees all sectors of society contributing in a systematic, orderly, and hierarchical fashion to the health of the state, the way that the parts of the body do to a human being.

By 1926, elections were abolished, strict censorship of the press was in place, and the secret police kept a close eye on the population. Fascist party officials, provincial governorships, and mayors were appointed from above, and labor unions were closed down. In the Ministry of Corporations, industrialists and bureaucrats, representing labor, met and sharply curtailed wages and labor regulations. The Lateran Accords of 1926–1929 made Catholicism the Italian state religion in return for full support by the Vatican for the fascists.

Depression and Conquests   Italy weathered the Depression through deficit spending and state investments. In 1933, Mussolini formed the Industrial Reconstruction Institute, which took over the industrial and commercial holdings of the banks that had failed earlier. This institute was crucial in efforts to revive the Italian industrial sector, which was still much smaller than elsewhere in Europe. Only in the mid-1930s did the urban population, concentrated mostly in the north, come to outnumber its rural counterpart. In spite of a few swamp-reclamation and grain-procurement reforms, the fascists had no answer for the endemic underdevelopment of southern Italy, which remained overwhelmingly rural and poor.

Nevertheless, Italy's military industry was sufficiently advanced for Mussolini to proclaim a policy of autarky with the help of overseas territories. First, the conquest of formerly Ottoman Libya was completed with utmost brutality in 1931. Declaring Libya to be the "Fourth Shore," the fascists encouraged emigration into the largely infertile Sahara colony, which eventually numbered some 100,000 settlers. The other major colony was the proud Christian kingdom of Ethiopia, conquered by Italy in 1935–1936 and merged thereafter with the earlier territories of Italian Eritrea and Somalia into Italian East Africa. Eager to avenge Italy's defeat by the Ethiopians forty years before, Mussolini's forces invaded with airplanes, tanks, and poison gas and, after crushing Ethiopian resistance, pacified the new colony with the settlement of 200,000 Italians.

The Ethiopian conquest prompted protests by the League of Nations. Although these were ineffective, Mussolini felt sufficiently isolated that he sought closer relations with Adolf Hitler and the Nazis. He had formerly treated Hitler as a junior colleague but now found him to be a useful counterweight against international isolation. An increasingly close cooperation began between the two dictators, who formed the nucleus of the Axis powers, joined in 1941 by Japan.

The Founding of the Weimar Republic   In September 1918, the German Supreme Army Command (OHL) came to the conclusion that Germany had lost World War I. In the subsequent 2 months unrest broke out in the navy and among workers. German soldiers melted away from the western front, and communist worker councils formed in a number of major cities. Alarmed civilian politicians in Berlin did everything in their power to bring about a peaceful transition from empire to republic. When the emperor eventually abdicated, his last chancellor (head of the government) appointed Friedrich Ebert (1871–1925), a prominent member of the German Social Democratic Party, on November 9, 1918, as his successor. This appointment was not quite legal, but Ebert immediately contacted the OHL for armed support, and in the following months the two cooperated in crushing the well-organized and armed communist workers' councils.

The first test for the new republic (founded in nearby Weimar during the height of communist unrest in Berlin) came in the summer of 1919 when the Allies presented their peace settlement. The French, concerned about both their military security and future German economic power, would have liked to have Germany divided into individual states again, as it was before 1871. The British and Americans, however, were opposed to such a drastic settlement. Germany was let off with what historians now see in retrospect as relatively moderate reparations for civilian casualties, along with the loss of two western provinces, although it was also forced to accept responsibility for beginning the war. The compromise settlement was satisfactory to no one. France's security remained uncertain, German conservatives and nationalists screamed defiance, and the democrats of Weimar who accepted the settlement were embittered by its immediate consequence: inflation.

Asked to begin the payments immediately, Germany was unable to correct the general inflation when pent-up consumer demand exploded with the onset of peace. Instead, the inflation accelerated to a hyperinflation in which the German

Play Money. German children in 1923 playing with bundles of money in the streets. Hyperinflation had made money in the Weimar Republic worthless: At the height of the inflation, in November 1923, $0.24 US was worth 1 trillion "paper marks." To overcome the hyperinflation, the German Central Bank cut the "trillions" off the mark and created the "reichsmark." This currency was tied again to the gold standard and was in circulation until 1948.

mark became virtually worthless and Germany had to suspend payments. France and Belgium responded by occupying the industrial Ruhr province in 1923. German workers in the Ruhr retaliated with passive resistance, and a deadlock was the result.

Faced with this crisis, the new Weimar Republic made peace with the French by recognizing the new borders. Recognizing, too, the dire financial implications of an economically crippled Germany, the American-crafted Dawes Plan of 1924 had US banks advance credits to European banks to refinance the now considerably reduced German reparation payments. France and Belgium withdrew from the Ruhr, inflation was curtailed, and the currency stabilized. The newly solvent Weimar Republic then experienced a considerable economic and cultural efflorescence during the rest of the decade.

The Rise of the Nazis   This affluence disintegrated quickly in the months after the US stock market crash of 1929. American banks, desperate for cash, began to recall their loans made to Europe. Beginning in 1931 in Austria, European banks began to fail, and in the following 2 years world trade shrank by two-thirds, hitting an exporting nation like Germany particularly hard. Unemployment soared meanwhile to 30 percent of the workforce. The number of people voting for extremist opponents of democracy—communists and ultra-nationalists—rose from negligible to more than half of the electorate by July 1932. Among them, the National Socialist German Workers' Party (NSDAP, or Nazi Party), achieved 38 percent, becoming the largest party in parliament.

In early 1933, the Nazi leader, Adolf Hitler (1889–1945), a failed artist and son of an Austrian customs official, could look back on a checkered postwar political career. He had led a failed uprising in 1923, done time in prison, and in *Mein Kampf* (*My Struggle*), a book published in 1925, openly announced a frightening political program. Hitler advocated ridding Germany of its Jews, whom he blamed for World War I, and communists, whom he blamed for the Central powers losing the war, and sought to punish the Allies for the peace settlement they had imposed on Germany. In its most grandiose sections he supported the German conquest of a "living space" (*Lebensraum*) in Russia and eastern Europe for the superior "Aryan" (German) race, with the "inferior" Slavs reduced to forced labor. No one who followed politics in Germany during the 1920s could be in doubt about Hitler's unrestrained and violent supremacist nationalism. Throughout the decade, however, he remained marginalized and often ridiculed for his extreme views.

The Nazis in Power   When the Nazis won a plurality in parliament, however, not only in the spring of 1932 but again in the fall, Hitler demanded the chancellorship. Upon the advice of his counselors, President Paul von Hindenburg (in office 1925–1934), one of Germany's heroes as a leading general during World War I, nominated Hitler to the post on January 30, 1933, in an effort to neutralize Nazism and keep Hitler under control. Hitler, however, wasted no time in escaping all restraints. Following a major fire in the Reichstag (German parliament) building in February 1933, the causes of which have never been fully explained, but which Hitler blamed on the communists, the president allowed his new chancellor the right to declare martial law for a limited time. Two months later, the Nazi Party in parliament passed the Enabling Act with the votes of the mostly Catholic Centrist Party; its leaders calculated that they could control Hitler and also reach a much-desired agreement between the Vatican and Germany parallel to the one of Mussolini. According to the constitution, Hitler now had the power to rule by emergency decree for 4 years.

Taking their cue from Mussolini's policies, the Nazis abolished the federalist structure of the Weimar Republic, purged the civil service of Jews, closed down all parties except the NSDAP, enacted censorship laws, and sent communists to newly constructed concentration camps. Other inmates of these camps were Roma (Gypsies), homosexuals, and religious minorities. In order to gain the support of Germany's professional army, Hitler replaced his *Sturmabteilung* (SA) militias of thugs with the smartly outfitted *Schutzstaffel* (SS). A new secret police force (abbreviated *Gestapo*) established a pervasive surveillance system in what was now called the Third Empire (*Drittes Reich*), following that of the Holy Roman Empire and Germany after its unification in 1871.

At the same time, Hitler succeeded in gaining enthusiastic support among the population. Aided by a general recovery of the economy, within a year of coming to power he lowered unemployment to 10 percent. He had the support of able economists who advised him to reduce unemployment through deficit spending and build a mixed economy of state-subsidized private industrial cartels. Enthusiastic Germans built freeways, cleared slums, constructed housing, and, above all, made arms, for minimal wages. Hitler also denounced the "decadence" of modern art and pushed his planners to create monumental buildings in older neoclassical or Art Deco styles. In all of these endeavors he advocated a personal vision of a stridently "nationalist" German art. In his appeal to the patriotic and economic aspirations of so many Germans, Hitler thus succeeded in making himself a genuinely popular leader (*Führer*) among the great majority of Germans.

German rearmament was initially secret but, after 1935, became public knowledge, with the introduction of the draft and the repudiation of the peace settlement cap on troop numbers. During 1935–1939, the army grew from 100,000 to 950,000 men, warships from 30 to 95, and, most startling of all, the air force from 36 to over 8,000 planes. France, realizing the danger this rearmament signified for its security, signed a treaty of mutual military assistance with the Soviet Union, which Hitler took as a pretext for the remilitarization of the Rhineland (one of the German provinces temporarily occupied by France after World War I) in 1936.

This first step of German military assertion was followed with unofficial support for General Francisco Franco (1892–1975), who rose against the legitimate republican government in the Spanish Civil War (1936–1939), and the incorporation of Austria into Nazi Germany in 1938. Now alarmed at Germany's growing appetite for expansion and committed by treaty to defend the eastern European states created after the war, the heads of state of Britain and France met with Hitler and Mussolini in Munich in the summer of 1938 to hammer out a general agreement on German and Italian territorial claims. In the Munich Agreement, Hitler was allowed to occupy the Sudetenland, an area in Czechoslovakia largely inhabited by ethnic Germans, with the understanding that it represented his final territorial demand. The British prime minister, Neville Chamberlain (in office 1937–1940), seeking to mediate between the less-compromising France and Hitler, claimed that this appeasement of Germany promised "peace in our time." Hitler went to war, however, in little more than a year.

World War II in Poland and France   In 1939 Hitler decided that the German armed forces were ready to begin the quest for *Lebensraum* in eastern Europe. In a first step, Poland needed to be taken; and in order for this to happen, Stalin had to be led to believe that it was in the best interest of the Soviet Union and Germany to share in the division of eastern Europe. Stalin, of course, was under no illusions about Hitler's plans but needed time to rebuild his army after the purges of 1937 and found the idea of a Russian-dominated Polish buffer against Germany appealing. Accordingly, the two signed a nonaggression pact on August 23, 1939, and German troops invaded Poland on September 1, triggering declarations of war by Poland's allies Britain and France 2 days later. World War II had begun in Europe.

Having removed the two-front problem that had plagued Germany in World War I, Hitler had to eliminate Britain and France before turning to the next phase in the east. This he did by attacking France on May 10, 1940. The German army in Poland had pioneered a new kind of warfare: *Blitzkrieg,* or "lightning war." Using aircraft to cripple rear area defenses and harass enemy troops, while smashing enemy lines with tanks and motorized infantry, the Germans turned warfare from the stagnant defensive posture of World War I into a fast, highly mobile conflict. The French, bled dry of manpower in the previous war, had since relied largely on the highly elaborate but fixed defenses of their Maginot Line. Now, the German troops simply went around these fortifications on a broad front, from the Netherlands and Belgium to Luxembourg. After breaking through the thick unprotected Ardennes Forest in southern Belgium, to the great surprise of the French and British, the German troops turned northward, driving the Allies toward the Atlantic coast. Establishing a desperate defensive perimeter at Dunkirk, the encircled French and British troops used every available vessel to escape across the English Channel to Britain as the Germans regrouped for their final thrust.

France surrendered and agreed to an armistice. Hitler divided the country into a German-occupied part, consisting of Paris and the Atlantic coast, and a smaller unoccupied territory under German control, with its capital in Vichy. The German follow-up effort of an invasion of Britain failed when the air force, having suffered more losses than anticipated in the invasion of France, was unable to deliver the final blow. During the worst air raids the Conservative politician Winston Churchill (in office 1940–1945) replaced Neville Chamberlain as prime minister. Churchill's inspirational and unbending will during the aerial Battle of Britain proved to be a turning point in rallying the Allied cause.

The Eastern Front   A year after finishing with France, and with Britain only desperately hanging on, Hitler launched an invasion of the Soviet Union on June 22, 1941, to the surprise of an unprepared Stalin. Although the Soviet forces were initially severely beaten, they did not disintegrate, thanks in part to a force of new T-34 tanks that proved superior to German models and were four times more numerous than the Germans expected. The Soviets held out against the German attacks on Leningrad (the renamed St. Petersburg/ Petrograd), Moscow, and the Ukraine. Neither side made much progress in 1942, until the Soviets succeeded in trapping a large force of Germans in Stalingrad on the lower Volga, near the vital Caspian oil fields. The Soviet victory on February 2, 1943, became the turning point in the European war. Thereafter, it was an almost relentless and increasingly desperate retreat for the Germans, particularly after the western Allies invaded the continent in Italy and France.

The Final Solution As Hitler's *Mein Kampf* foretold, the war in the east became an ideological war of annihilation: Either the supremacist or the communist vision of modernity would prevail. The Soviets began early with their killings, when they massacred nearly 22,000 Polish prisoners of war in the forest of Katyn and sent hundreds of thousands of eastern Europeans to their eventual deaths in labor camps. The German SS and army, driven by their racism against Slavs, murdered soldiers and civilians alike, and German businesses worked their Slavic slave laborers to death. The so-called **Final Solution** (*Endlösung*), the genocide of the European Jews, was the horrendous culmination of this struggle. After Poland and the western Soviet Union were conquered, the number of Jews under German authority increased by several million. The Final Solution, set in motion in January 1942, entailed transporting Jews to extermination camps, the most infamous of which was at Auschwitz, in Poland, to be gassed in simulated shower stalls and their corpses burned in specially constructed ovens. In its technological sophistication in creating a kind of assembly line of death and the calm, bureaucratic efficiency with which its operators went about their business, the Holocaust (Hebrew *Shoah*) marks a milestone in twentieth-century inhumanity. It has since become the standard of genocide against which other planned mass murders are measured.

The Turn of the Tide in the West The first counteroffensives of the Allies in the west after their defeat in 1940 came in November 1942. After fighting a desperate rearguard action against the German general Erwin Rommel (1891–1944), "the Desert Fox," British forces in Egypt and American forces landing in occupied French North Africa launched a combined offensive, capturing Rommel's forces in a pincer movement and driving them to capitulate 6 months later. But it took another 2.5 years of long campaigning to grind down the forces of the Axis powers. Here, the industrial capacity of the United States proved to be the determining factor. For example, between 1942 and 1945 American factories produced 41,000 Sherman M4 tanks alone, which was more than the production of all German tank types taken together. German aircraft production peaked in 1944 at 44,000 planes; US manufacturers produced more than 100,000 the same year. The United States enjoyed similar advantages in manpower. By war's end, over 16 million American men and women, or 10 percent of the entire population, had served in

Genocide. The specters of the Holocaust that haunt us usually involve the infamous extermination camps—Auschwitz, Treblinka, Majdanek, Sobibor— but millions of Jews and other "undesirables"—Slavs, Gypsies (Roma), and homosexuals—were shot, such as this man calmly waiting for the bullet to penetrate his brain while SS executioners look on.

Final Solution: German supremacist-nationalist plan formulated in 1942 by Adolf Hitler and leading Nazis to annihilate Jews through factory-style mass extermination in concentration camps, resulting in the death of about 6 million Jews, or roughly two-thirds of European Jewry.

the armed forces. Finally, the natural barriers of the Atlantic and Pacific Oceans and American naval power ensured against invasion, while the lack of a long-range strategic bombing force prevented Axis air attacks on North America.

Furthermore, starting in 1943, the US Army Air Force and Britain's Royal Air Force began a furious campaign of around-the-clock bombing of military and civilian targets in Germany. Despite heavy Allied losses in planes and men, by war's end there was scarcely a German city or industrial center of any size that had not been reduced to rubble by air attack—quite a contrast to World War I, when Germany's interior was unscathed. With the landing of troops in Sicily in July 1943, the Italian Peninsula in early September, and Normandy in June 1944, along with the steady advance of Soviet forces in the east, the eventual unconditional German surrender on May 8, 1945 (VE, or "Victory in Europe" Day) was inevitable (see Map 28.3).

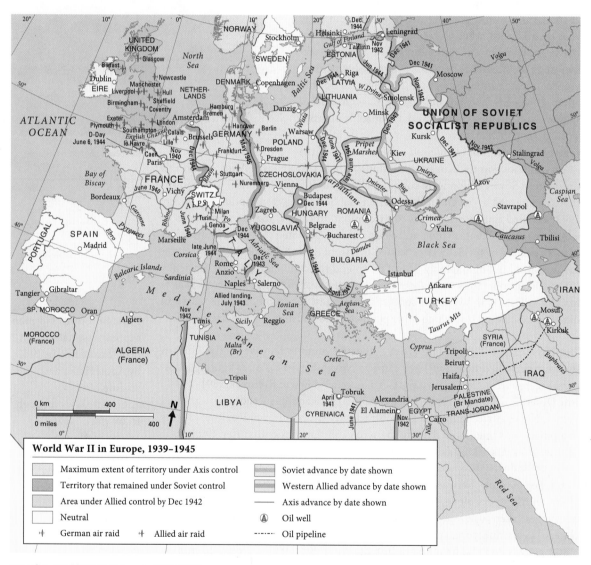

World War II in Europe, 1939–1945

	Maximum extent of territory under Axis control		Soviet advance by date shown
	Territory that remained under Soviet control		Western Allied advance by date shown
	Area under Allied control by Dec 1942	—	Axis advance by date shown
	Neutral	Ⓐ	Oil well
⊹	German air raid ⊹ Allied air raid	------	Oil pipeline

MAP **28.3 World War II in Europe, 1939–1945.**

Japan's "Greater East Asia Co-Prosperity Sphere" and China's Struggle for Unity

The Japanese ruling class that implemented the Meiji industrialization consisted for the most part of lower-ranking samurai "oligarchs." After World War I, this generation retired, and for the first time commoners entered politics. They formed two unstable conservative party coalitions, representing small-business and landowner interests, but were financed by big-business cartels, the zaibatsus (see Chapter 24). By the mid-1920s Japan's interwar liberalizing era had reached perhaps its high point, with universal male suffrage for those over the age of 25. Thereafter, however, and at an accelerated pace during the Depression of 1929–1933, the military increased its power and ended the liberalizing era.

Liberalism and Military Assertion   In the midst of the middle-class ferment of "Taisho Democracy," as Japan's politics during the reign of Emperor Taisho (r. 1912–1926) was known, the government not only broadened the suffrage but also enacted the first of what would be a long line of security laws. Worried about communist influence, the Peace Preservation Law of 1925 drew a line against frequent labor strikes and general leftist agitation. Anyone violating the "national essence" (*kokutai*) in thought or action could be arrested. A branch of the secret services, the *Tokko*, made widespread use of this law, with some 70,000 mostly arbitrary arrests during 1925–1945. The law was the turning point when Western-inspired liberalism began to swing toward militarism. Nowhere was this more dramatically on display than in the saga of Professor Minobe, described at the beginning of this chapter, who would go in a few short years from being Japan's leading legal theorist to being denounced as a traitor.

Military officers of modest rural origin, trained prior to World War I and without much general education, were unable or unwilling to comprehend the democracy, cultural transformation, and labor strikes of the 1920s. They became intoxicated with the staples of supremacist nationalism, such as the absolutism of the emperor, above law and parliament, and the right of junior officers to refuse to execute parliamentary laws. These two points were decisive for actions through which the military achieved dominance over parliament in the 1930s.

Militaristic Expansion   The early 1930s saw the end of a period of diplomacy by which Japan sought to consolidate its gains in international prestige from the Washington Naval Treaty and subsequent treaties stabilizing Japan's position in China. The growth of the power of the Chinese Nationalist Party (Guomindang, GMD) and its creation of a relatively stable regime in China after 1927 altered the fragile balance of power among the contending warlord regimes that Japan had exploited for over a decade in order to expand its influence. The junior officers who chafed at the liberalization of Japan and hearkened back to samurai values increasingly found a home and opportunity in the colonial armies of Manchuria.

The first step in this new direction was taken in 1928 when the Japanese Kwantung Army (Japan's force in Manchuria) blew up the train of the Chinese warlord Zhang Zuolin because of his leanings toward the GMD. This was followed by the Mukden Incident of 1931, in which the Japanese military engineered another railroad bombing, which was blamed on local warlords and used as the pretext for the annexation of Manchuria. Politicians in Tokyo, cowed by the aggressiveness of supremacist nationalist ideologues and by the select assassinations of political opponents of Japan's expansion, acquiesced. By way of making it a puppet state, they installed the last Manchu Qing Chinese emperor (Henry) Pu-Yi (r. 1908–1912; 1932–1945), deposed as a boy in the Chinese Republican Revolution of 1911–1912. Over the next several years, the Japanese army in Manchuria systematically moved into northern China. In July 1937, after a clash between Chinese and Japanese forces near the Marco Polo Bridge outside Beijing, Japan launched a full-scale invasion of China.

The Republican Revolution in China As we saw in Chapter 24, the Qing dynasty had failed to develop a sustained effort at reform in response to the Western challenge during the 1800s. Following belated attempts at institutional reform in the wake of the Boxer Rebellion in 1900, a variety of radical groups, aided by the growing numbers of overseas Chinese, began to work for the overthrow of the Qing. The most important figure among these groups was Sun Yat-sen (1866–1925), a medical doctor and son of peasants in south China, with his Revolutionary Alliance of 1905. Making common cause with a number of local revolutionary groups and Chinese secret societies, Sun's group formed an umbrella organization for a wide array of political ideas.

On October 10, 1911, an explosion in a Wuhan barracks signaled a takeover of the base. The movement quickly spread, and by the end of the year three groups of Qing opponents—provincial warlords, scholar-gentry, and nationalists—staged separate uprisings that reduced the Qing to a small territory in the north. The Qing commander, Yuan Shikai (1859–1916), struck a deal with the insurgents whereby he came over to them in return for the presidency of the new republic, formed upon the abdication of the Qing in February 1912. Sun was thus elbowed aside by the revolution he had done so much to begin. With Yuan's death in 1916, the remaining warlords feuded with each other for control of the country for the next decade.

Reemergence of Nationalism Sun Yat-sen, however, was not quite finished. With the republic in shambles and the provinces hijacked by the warlords, Sun remained a profoundly inspirational figure for Chinese nationalists, mostly through his numerous publications issued from exile in the Western treaty port of Canton (Guangzhou). Meanwhile, the decision announced on May 4, 1919, by the Allies at Versailles to allow Japan to keep the German territory in China it had seized at the beginning of the war set off mass demonstrations and a boycott of foreign businesses. This May Fourth Movement, as it came to be called, is often cited as the modern beginning of Chinese nationalism. Shortly thereafter, inspired by the Bolshevik Revolution in Russia, the Chinese Communist Party (CCP) was founded in 1921.

By 1923, encouraged by support from the Third Communist International (Comintern), Sun's Nationalist Party was being reorganized and supplied with Russian help, in return for which the party agreed to allow members of the CCP to join with it to form what became known as the First United Front (1924–1927). Sun died in 1925, and a year later Chiang K'ai-shek (1887–1975) ascended to the leadership of the army. Chiang came from a wealthy salt-merchant family and was a military officer trained in the Nationalist Party academy and in Moscow. The most pressing objective in 1926 was the unification of China. The two parties mobilized an army of some 85,000 men, and the so-called Northern Expedition of 1926–1927 became a remarkably successful effort that brought about the unification of southern China as far north as the Yangzi River.

In the middle of the campaign, however, the bonds between the GMD and CCP ruptured. The socialist wing of the GMD and the CCP had taken the important industrial centers of Wuhan and Shanghai in the Yangtze Delta from warlords, setting the stage for a showdown with the nationalist wing. Though he had been trained in Moscow, Chiang had grown intensely suspicious of Comintern and CCP motives and thus launched a preemptive purge of communists in nationalist-held areas. Though much of the leftist opposition was eliminated, a remnant under Mao Zedong (1893–1976) fled to the remote province of Jiangxi in the south to regroup and create their own socialist state. Mao, a librarian by training from a wealthy peasant family, was an inspiring rural organizer, and he set about developing his ideas of Marxist revolution with the heretical idea of having peasants in the vanguard.

By the early 1930s Mao's Chinese communists had developed this crucial variant of rural communism, which Marx and Lenin had found impossible to envisage. Mao replaced the capitalists with the landlords as the class enemy and promised a much-needed land reform to the downtrodden peasants. Moreover, the peasants would be the leading participants in the "People's War"—a three-stage guerilla conflict involving the entire populace and borrowing from sources as diverse as Sun Zi's *Art of War* and the colonists' tactics against the British in the American War for Independence.

Believing the communist threat to be effectively eliminated, Chiang resumed his Northern Expedition in 1928, subjugating Beijing but failing to eliminate the strongest northern warlords. Nevertheless, China was now at least nominally unified, with the capital in Nanjing, the National Party Congress functioning as a parliament, and Chiang as president. Chiang made substantial progress with railroad and road construction as well as cotton and silk textile exports. Thanks to the silver standard of its money, rather than the fatal gold standard of many other countries, the financial consequences of the Depression of 1929–1933 remained relatively mild. Chiang made little headway, however, with land reform. Furthermore, the volatile relations with the remaining warlords made the government vulnerable to border violence and corruption. Hovering above all after 1931 was the Japanese annexation of Manchuria and creeping encroachment on northern China.

Mao. The images of Mao that dominate our consciousness are usually the old Mao, when his health was failing, his youthful vigor long gone, and his political power diminished. But it is in the young Mao, such as in this photo from 1938, that we can best see his leadership skills in action.

"The Comrade's style of work incorporates the modesty and pragmatism of the Chinese people; the simplicity and diligence of the Chinese peasants; the love of study and profound thinking of an intellectual; the efficiency and steadfastness of a revolutionary soldier; and the persistence and indomitability of a Bolshevik."

—Zhou Enlai (1898–1976) describing Mao Zedong, 1943

The Long March and the Rape of Nanjing   In the early 1930s, Chiang knew that Japan was the enemy to watch, but he was painfully aware of the need to completely eliminate his internal opponents. Following the old proverbial warning of "Disorder within, disaster without" he resolved to eliminate the remaining threat from Mao's "Jiangxi Soviet." He mounted increasingly massive "bandit extermination" campaigns from 1931 to 1934, but each one was defeated by the superior mobility, local loyalty, and guerilla tactics of Mao's growing People's Liberation Army. With the help of German advisors, Chiang turned to encircling the CCP areas with a ring of trenches and blockhouses to limit the mobility of his opponents. By the fall of 1934 he had tightened the noose around the communists and almost succeeded in destroying their army.

But Mao and about 100,000 soldiers broke out in October 1934. Once free, the majority of the Red Army embarked on its epic Long March of 6,000 miles, describing a semicircle from the south through the far west and then northeast toward Beijing. Along the way harassment by nationalist troops, warlords, and local people as well as hunger, famine, heat, swamps, bridgeless rivers, and desertion decimated the bedraggled marchers. In the fall of 1935 some 10,000 communists eventually straggled into the small enclave of Yan'an (Yenan), out of Chiang's reach.

The communists had seized upon Japan's aggression as a valuable propaganda tool and declared war against Japan in 1932. Chiang's obsession with eliminating his internal enemies increasingly made him subject to criticism of appeasement toward Japan. In 1936, a group of dissident nationalist generals arrested Chiang outside the city of Xi'an and spirited him off to CCP headquarters at Yan'an. After weeks of fraught negotiations, Chiang was released as the leader of a China now brought together under a Second United Front, this time against Japan.

Seeing their prospects for gradual encroachment quickly fading, Japan seized on the so-called Marco Polo Bridge Incident and launched an all-out assault on China. The bridge was a key point along the front between Japanese and Chinese forces just outside Beijing, and on the night of July 7, 1937, a brief exchange of fire accidentally took place between the two sides. When a Japanese soldier seeking to relieve himself during the exchange did not return to post, the Japanese used this as a pretext to move against the Chinese. Though Chinese resistance was stiff in the opening months, the Japanese were able to use their superior mobility and airpower to flank the Chinese forces and take the capital of Nanjing (Nanking) by December 1937. Realizing the need to defeat China as quickly as possible in order to avoid a war of attrition, they subjected the capital to the first major atrocity of World War II: the "Rape of Nanjing." Though scholars are still debating the exact number of casualties, it is estimated that between 200,000 and 300,000 people were slaughtered in deliberately gruesome ways: hacked to death, burned or buried alive, and beheaded. Over and above this brutality, however, rape was systematically used as a means of terror and subjugation.

The direct message of all of this was that other Chinese cities could expect similar treatment if surrender was not swiftly forthcoming. Like the British and Germans under aerial bombardment a few years later, however, the destruction only stiffened the will to resist of the Chinese. Continually harassed as they retreated from Nanjing, the Chinese adopted the strategy of trading space for time to regroup, as did the Soviets a few years later. In an epic mass migration, Chinese soldiers and civilians stripped every usable article and moved it to the region around the remote city of Chongqing (Chungking), which became the wartime capital of China until 1945. Thereafter, both nationalists and communists used the vast interior as a base for hit-and-run tactics, effectively limiting Japan to the northeast and coastal urban centers but remaining incapable of mounting large offensives themselves.

World War II in the Pacific While Japan had used its control of Manchuria, Korea, and Taiwan in its quest for autarky and economic stability in the 1930s, it portrayed its imperial

The Rape of Nanjing. Of the many horrors of the twentieth century, few can match the Rape of Nanjing for its sadistic brutality, in which perhaps as many as 300,000 people lost their lives in a Japanese killing orgy.

bid in the Pacific as the construction of a "Greater East Asia Co-Prosperity Sphere." This expansion was considered essential because oil, metals, rubber, and other raw materials were still imported in large quantities from the United States and the Dutch and British possessions in southeast Asia. After Hitler invaded the Netherlands and France in 1940, the opportunity arrived for the Japanese could add to their power and remove the United States from the Pacific. Moreover, the stalemate in China was increasingly bleeding Japan of vital resources, while mounting tensions with the United States over China were already resulting in economic sanctions. Accordingly, in the summer of 1941, the Japanese government decided on extending the empire into the Dutch East Indies and southeast Asia, even if this meant war with the United States. Under the premiership of General Tojo Hideki (in office 1941–1944), Japan attacked Pearl Harbor in Hawaii, the Philippines, and Dutch and British territories on December 7–8, 1941. Within a few months, the Japanese completed the occupation of all the important southeast Asian and Pacific territories they had sought (see Map 28.4).

Japan's newfound autarky did not last long, however. Within 6 months, in the naval and air battle around Midway Atoll, American forces regained the initiative. The Japanese now exploited the populations of their new territories in extracting their raw materials with increasing urgency. As the American forces slowly deprived the Japanese of these resources through their highly effective "island-hopping" strategy, they came within bombing range of the Japanese home islands by late 1944. Starting in March 1945, they subjected Japan to the most devastating firebomb attacks ever mounted. Finally, President Harry S. Truman (in office 1945–1953) made the fateful decision to have two experimental atomic bombs dropped on Hiroshima and Nagasaki (August 6 and 9, 1945), effectively obliterating both cities. With the Soviets declaring war against Japan on August 8 and advancing into Manchuria, the Japanese were finally convinced that the war

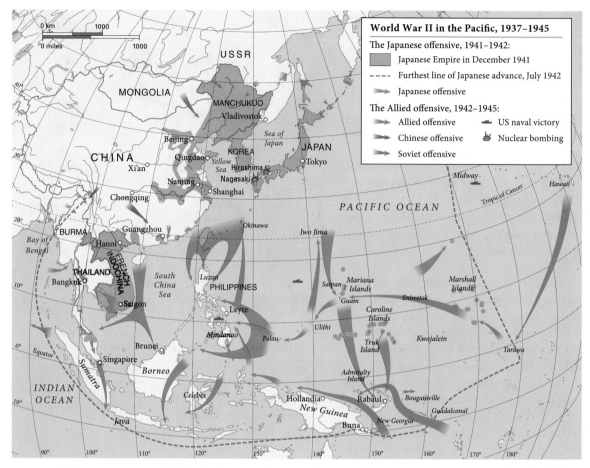

MAP 28.4 **World War II in the Pacific, 1937–1945.**

was lost. They surrendered on August 14, 1945, with the final ceremony taking place aboard the US battleship *Missouri* on September 2, 1945.

Putting It All Together

As discussed in previous chapters, the patterns of constitutional nationalism and industrialization in the late eighteenth and early nineteenth centuries were most visibly manifested in Great Britain, the United States, and France. Subsequently, two further patterns complicated the evolution of nations engaging in the pursuit of modernity: ethnolinguistic nationalism and the rise of the industrial working class. Abetted by the imperialistic tendencies inherited from before 1800, all of these patterns collided in World War I. After the war, they recombined into the three ideologies of modernity analyzed in this chapter: capitalist democracy, communism, and supremacist nationalism.

For the most part, only democracy and communism are considered to be genuine ideologies of modernity, in the sense of being based on relatively coherent programs. More recent historians, however, have come to the conclusion that supremacist nationalism was a genuine variety of modernity as well, though one defined more by what it opposed than by what it supported. The adherents of the three modernities bitterly denounced the ideologies of their rivals. All three considered themselves to be genuinely "progressive" or modern.

What is very difficult to understand in a country like the United States, still deeply loyal to its foundational national constitutionalism, is that someone could be an ardent ethnic nationalist, have little faith in constitutional liberties, find the conquest of a large and completely self-sufficient empire perfectly logical, and think of all this as the ideal of a future modernity. Indeed, historians have customarily thought of these views as revolts *against* modernity. Yet, as we have seen so often, innovations frequently create a "gelling" effect in which opposition to the new clarifies and solidifies, often in unexpected ways. The "modern" notion of ethnolinguistic nationalism thus created ways of opposing other modern innovations such as constitutionalism and industrialism—with their messy uncertainties and feelings of rootlessness—by insisting on a purer, more mystical bond for the modern nation-state that, ironically, harkened back to a simpler, reimagined past. But Mussolini, Hitler, and the Japanese generals all aspired to the same scientific–industrial future as Roosevelt, Churchill, Stalin, Chiang K'ai-shek, and Mao Zedong.

▶ For additional resources, including maps, primary sources, visuals, and quizzes, please go to www.oup.com/us/vonsivers. Please see the Further Resources section at the back of the book for additional readings and suggested websites.

Against the Grain

Righteous among the Nations

S ome 25,000 men and women bravely defied the German Nazi regime (1932–1945) during the Holocaust and saved Jews from arrest, deportation, and the gas chamber. Their acts of defiance are proof that ordinary citizens in Germany and the countries conquered by Germany during World War II carried out their human responsibility of saving other human beings. They did not cower before the seemingly all-powerful Gestapo, nor did they attempt to claim helplessness or ignorance regarding what was happening around them. They were aware, of course, that they risked their own lives by hiding Jews or smuggling them out of harm's way. Indeed, many were martyred at the hands of Nazi authorities. But they still acted as they did because they considered it their human calling.

Thousands of the saviors of Jews were Poles, Dutch, French, Ukrainians, and Belgians, all under German occupation during the war. By contrast, only 563 and 525 Italians and Germans, respectively, helped Jews to survive. The contrast in numbers illustrates the feelings of hatred among many in the conquered territories for the Germans on the one hand and the pervasiveness of the supremacist-nationalist fascist and Nazi ideologies in the populations of Italy and Germany on the other. Even if having the courage to help Jews was much easier in Nazi Germany than many Germans pretended after the war, their anti-Semitism prevented them from feeling any pangs of conscience.

Today, Israel recognizes 24,811 saviors of Jews as "Righteous among the Nations" and honors them in a special garden in the Yad Vashem Holocaust memorial museum in Jerusalem. One of them, Irena Sendler (1910–2008), may serve as an example for all. Sendler was a health worker, the daughter of a Polish physician who treated Jewish patients. When the Germans invaded she was an administrator for the Warsaw Social Welfare Department, responsible for providing food, clothing, medicine, and money for the poor and elderly. During the time of the Warsaw Ghetto (1940–1943), she was able to smuggle some 2,500 Jewish children out of the country, hiding them under loads of goods, in potato sacks or even in coffins. She provided them with false identities and had them taken to hiding places with Christian families. When the Nazis finally discovered her activities in 1943, they arrested and tortured her. But after members of the Polish resistance succeeded in bribing her would-be executioners, Sandler escaped and went into hiding until the end of the war. Yad Vashem honored Irena Sendler in 1965 as a righteous person and planted a tree in her name at the entrance of the Avenue of the Righteous among Nations.

- Faced with a situation similar to that of Irena Sendler, what would you do?

- Can you think of other 20th century mass atrocities in which people like Irena Sendler desperately tired to save innocent lives?

Thinking Through Patterns

▶ **Which three patterns of modernity emerged after World War I? How and why did these patterns form?**

Ethnic nationalism was difficult to accommodate in the nineteenth century, which began with the more inclusive constitutional nationalism of Great Britain, the United States, and France. New nations like Italy, Germany, and Japan were formed on the basis of an ethnic nationalism that in a sense created nations but not necessarily ones with the ideals of equality embodied in constitutional nation-states. World War I set back Germany, Italy, and Japan, but afterward they elevated their ethnic nationalism into supremacist nationalism and adopted imperialism, all under the banner of modernity. In Russia, communists seized the opportunity offered by the turmoil of World War I to turn a constitutionally as well as industrially underdeveloped empire into a communist, one-party industrial empire. The United States, Britain, and France, each based on variations of constitutionalism, industry, and smaller or larger empires, became advocates of a capitalist democratic modernity.

Capitalist democracy was a modernity that upheld free enterprise, the market, and consumerism. It succeeded in providing the modern items of daily life, but it suffered a major setback in the Depression and had to be reined in through tightened political controls. It also withheld freedom, equality, and the staples of daily life from minorities and the colonized. Communism succeeded in industrializing an underdeveloped empire and providing the bare necessities for modern life; it did so with untold human sacrifices. Supremacist nationalism was attractive to nationalists who were not workers and therefore afraid of communism. Supremacist nationalists held democracies in disdain because they considered constitutions meaningless pieces of paper.

▶ **What were the strengths and flaws of each of the three visions of modernity?**

▶ **Why did supremacist nationalism disappear in the ashes of World War II?**

Supremacist nationalism was a modernity that failed because the conquest of new, self-sufficient empires proved to be impossible. The advocates of democratic capitalist and communist modernity—most notably the United States, Great Britain, France, and the Soviet Union—were dangerously threatened by Germany, Italy, and Japan and came together to destroy these supremacist-nationalist countries.

Chapter 29 1945–1962

Reconstruction, Cold War, and Decolonization

THE COLD WAR
AND DECOLONIZATION

By any standard the event seemed symbolic of a new world order, one in which the emerging nonaligned nations would set the pace of innovation. Appropriately enough, it also marked the beginning of a new decade, one that would begin full of promise and peril and end in conflict and confusion for much of the world. The event was the 1960 election of the world's first female prime minister, Sirimavo Bandaranaike (1916–2000), of what was then called Ceylon (renamed Sri Lanka in 1972), a large island off the southeastern coast of India.

Coming from a prominent Buddhist family, she believed in a strong national foundation for her country as an independent nation beholden to neither West nor East. As a socialist, she continued the nationalization of the banking, insurance, and petroleum sectors begun by her husband, ordered the state to take over all Catholic schools, and joined the Non-Aligned Movement in 1961. The movement sought to bring India, Egypt, Yugoslavia, Indonesia, and a number of other states together as a bloc to retain their independence from the pressures of the Cold War between the two superpowers of the United States and the Soviet Union and their allies. Her strong commitment to a Sinhalese-only language policy, however, aroused considerable resistance in the country, especially

ABOVE: **Voters line up to cast their ballots in Ceylon (now Sri Lanka) on March 22, 1960. Sirimavo Bandaranaike was elected the world's first woman prime minister.**

from the Tamil minority in the north. The Theravada Buddhist Sinhalese compose about 74 percent and the Hindu Tamils 17 percent of the population. Only 2 years into Bandaranaike's tenure, the country was gripped by a Tamil civil disobedience campaign, and it rapidly became apparent that Ceylon was entering a time of political turbulence. Ultimately, anti-Tamil discrimination led to the abortive Tamil Tiger liberation war (1976–2009), pursued on both sides with the utmost brutality.

Seeing Patterns

▶ Why did the pattern of unfolding modernity, which offered three choices after World War I, shrink to just capitalist democracy and socialism–communism in 1945? How did each of these two patterns evolve between 1945 and 1962?

▶ What are the cultural premises of modernity?

▶ How did the newly independent countries of the Middle East, Asia, and Africa adapt to the divided world of the Cold War?

During her four terms as prime minister (1960–1965, 1970–1972, 1972–1977, and 1994–2000), Bandaranaike was a prominent leader on the world stage. Like her fellow female prime ministers Benazir Bhutto in Pakistan and Indira Gandhi in India and first-generation nonaligned leaders like Jawaharlal Nehru of India, Sukarno of Indonesia, and Gamal Abdel Nasser of Egypt, Bandaranaike tried to navigate the turbulent waters of ethnic and religious conflict, superpower pressure, and nation building in an increasingly competitive economic arena. The backdrop against which these nonaligned nations acted was woven from two main elements in the unfolding pattern of scientific–industrial modernity: the Cold War and decolonization. The capitalist–democratic and the socialist–communist spheres competed with each other for political, military, and economic dominance; at the same time, the West rid itself of what was now seen as its biggest curse—colonialism—which had severely detracted from its appeal during the interwar and early postwar periods.

Superpower Confrontation: Capitalist Democracy and Communism

World War II was the most destructive war in human history. After nearly 6 years of fighting in Europe and 9 years in Asia, the total loss of life (including combatants, civilians, and victims of the Holocaust) is estimated at over 50 million, three times as many as in World War I. With the exception of the continental United States, which was unreachable by enemy aircraft, all combatant countries in World War II suffered widespread destruction. Most ominous was the use of the first atomic weapons by the United States against Japan in the final days of the war. Yet, while the war raged, the foundations of a new world organization to replace the old League of Nations—the **United Nations (UN)**, whose charter was later signed by 51 nations in October 1945—were being laid. Remarkably, within a few years, the world's remaining patterns of modernity—capitalism–democracy and socialism–communism—would reemerge from the ruins stronger than ever, each according to its own vision.

United Nations: Successor of the League of Nations, founded in 1945 and today comprising about 200 countries, with a Secretary General, a General Assembly meeting annually, and a standing Security Council composed of permanent members (United States, China, Russia, the United Kingdom, and France) as well as five rotating temporary members.

The Cold War Era, 1945–1962
As the world rebuilt, the United States and the Soviet Union promoted their contrasting visions of modernity—capitalist–democratic and communist—with missionary fervor. For the next 45 years the two powers struggled to determine

Chapter Outline

- Superpower Confrontation: Capitalist Democracy and Communism

- Populism and Industrialization in Latin America

- The End of Colonialism and the Rise of New Nations

- Putting It All Together

Destruction and Despair in the Nuclear Age. World War II was the most destructive human conflict in history, far exceeding the damage of what had only a short time before been considered to be "the war to end all wars"—World War I. Nowhere was the damage more complete than in Japan, where an aerial campaign of firebombing Japanese cities by American B-29s had destroyed nearly every major Japanese center. The culmination of this campaign was the first—and, to date, last—use of nuclear weapons in warfare on the Japanese cities of Hiroshima and Nagasaki in August 1945. Here, a mother and child who survived the nuclear destruction of Hiroshima sit amid the utter devastation of their city in December 1945.

which approach would prevail. While each on occasion engaged in brinkmanship—pushing crises to the edge of nuclear war—as a rule both sought to avoid direct confrontation. Instead, they pursued their aims of expanding and consolidating their respective systems, in a conflict dubbed the "Cold War," through ideological struggle and proxy states (that is, states acting as substitutes against each other). Two phases can be discerned in the early Cold War. The first lasted from 1945 to 1956, when the Soviet Union continued to pursue Stalin's prewar policy of "socialism in one country," which was now extended to include Eastern Europe. The second comprised the years 1956–1962, when Stalin's successor, Nikita Khrushchev (1894–1971, in office 1953–1964), reformulated the policy to include spreading aid and influence to new nationalist regimes in Asia and Africa that had won their independence from Western colonialism, even if these regimes were not (yet) communist. This new policy, applied to Cuba, produced the near-disaster of the Cuban Missile Crisis in 1962, during which the United States and the Soviet Union almost came to blows (see Map 29.1).

Cold War: Ideological struggle between the United States and its allies and the Soviet Union and its allies that lasted from 1945 to 1989.

Cold War Origins   The origins of the **Cold War** have been bitterly debated since the 1940s, with apologists for each side tending to blame its inception on the actions of the other. While it may not be possible at this point to establish an exact time or event marking the beginning of the Cold War, we can point to certain mileposts in its development. It is important to note that tensions and distrust between the United States and the Soviet Union began to emerge earlier in the twentieth century. As early as the Bolshevik Revolution, concerns mounted in the West regarding communist expansion, prompting fear of communism in America during the 1920s. Awareness of Joseph Stalin's policies in the 1930s contributed to increasing doubts that delayed American recognition of the Soviet government until 1933.

Another milepost came in the spring of 1945, when the Soviet Red Army occupied German-held territories in Eastern Europe and communist guerilllas made rapid advances in the Balkans. In a secret deal between British prime minister Churchill and Soviet leader Stalin in May 1944, Greece became part of the British sphere, in return for Romania and Bulgaria being apportioned to the Soviet sphere of responsibility for occupation at war's end.

When it became increasingly clear that Stalin was determined to maintain the Russian presence in Eastern Europe, the United States formulated a policy designed to thwart Soviet expansion known as **containment**. First spelled out in 1946 by George F. Kennan, a diplomat in the State Department, the proposed policy served as the foundation for the administration's effort to confront communist expansion.

Containment: US foreign policy doctrine formulated in 1946 to limit as much as possible the spread of communism.

"It is clear that the United States cannot expect in the foreseeable future to enjoy political intimacy with the Soviet regime."

—George F. Kennan

Confrontations, 1947–1949 The apportionment of spheres of interest in the Balkans did not work out well. In Yugoslavia, the anti-Nazi resistance hero Josip Broz Tito (1892–1980) took over the government in November 1945 with the help of Soviet advisors. He then provided Greek communists with aid to overthrow the royal government that had returned to rule with British support in 1946. The United States stepped in with supplies for the Greek government in 1947, assuming that Stalin was orchestrating aid from Yugoslavia, Bulgaria, and Romania. Under the **Truman Doctrine**, the United States announced its support of all "free peoples who are resisting attempted subjugation by armed minorities or by outside pressures."

A 2-year proxy civil war between East and West in Greece ended in a split between Tito and Stalin. In 1948, Tito claimed his right to regional communism, against Stalin's insistence on unity in the Communist Bloc. Although Stalin had never supported the Greek communists directly, given his agreement with Churchill, a surprising majority of them opted for Stalin. Tito withdrew his support for the pro-Stalin Greek communists, and the bid for communism in Greece collapsed in 1949.

In keeping with his doctrine, Truman announced the **Marshall Plan** of aid to Europe, for the recovery of the continent from the ruins of the war. The plan was named after its architect, secretary of state George C. Marshall (1880–1959). Although invited to take part, Stalin flatly rejected American aid and forbade Hungary, Czechoslovakia, and Poland to ask for it. In addition to the political reasons behind Stalin's injunction, the Marshall Plan's requirement of free markets and convertible currencies contradicted the communist ideology of a central command economy. Stalin instead engineered fledgling communist governments in Eastern Europe and the Balkans, transforming them into the Communist Bloc and integrating their economies with that of the Soviet Union. This was formalized in 1949 as the Council for Mutual Economic Assistance (COMECON).

Truman Doctrine: Policy formulated in 1947, initially to outline steps directed at preventing Greece and Turkey from becoming communist, primarily through military and economic aid.

Marshall Plan: Financial program of $13 billion to support the reconstruction of the economies of 17 European countries during 1948–1952, with most of the aid going to France, Germany, Italy, and the Netherlands.

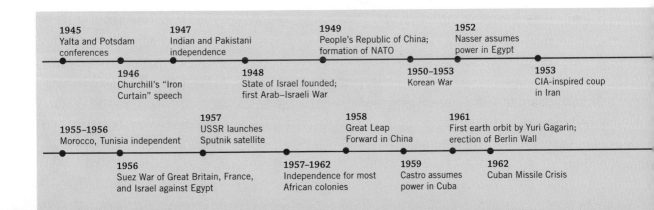

1945	1947	1949	1952
Yalta and Potsdam conferences	Indian and Pakistani independence	People's Republic of China; formation of NATO	Nasser assumes power in Egypt

1946	1948	1950–1953	1953
Churchill's "Iron Curtain" speech	State of Israel founded; first Arab–Israeli War	Korean War	CIA-inspired coup in Iran

1955–1956	1957	1958	1961
Morocco, Tunisia independent	USSR launches Sputnik satellite	Great Leap Forward in China	First earth orbit by Yuri Gagarin; erection of Berlin Wall

1956	1957–1962	1959	1962
Suez War of Great Britain, France, and Israel against Egypt	Independence for most African colonies	Castro assumes power in Cuba	Cuban Missile Crisis

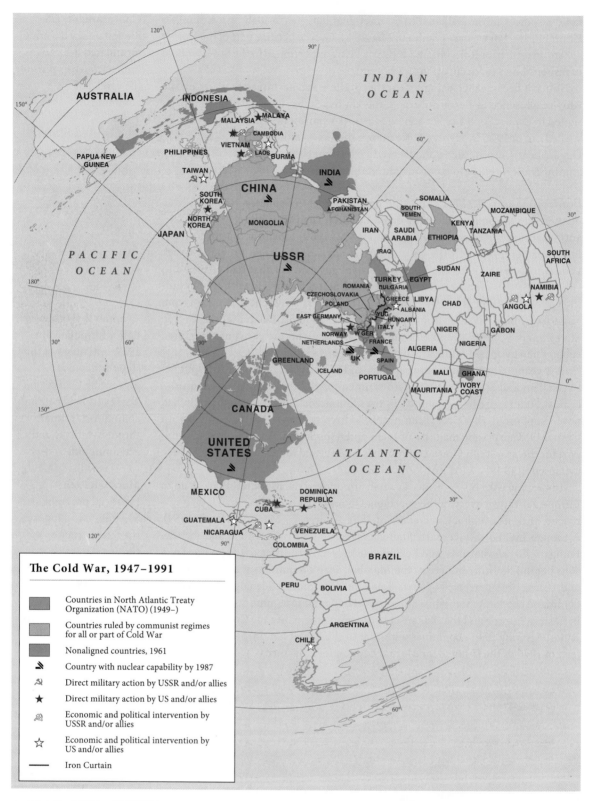

The Cold War, 1947–1991

■	Countries in North Atlantic Treaty Organization (NATO) (1949–)
■	Countries ruled by communist regimes for all or part of Cold War
■	Nonaligned countries, 1961
➘	Country with nuclear capability by 1987
⚒	Direct military action by USSR and/or allies
★	Direct military action by US and/or allies
⚒	Economic and political intervention by USSR and/or allies
☆	Economic and political intervention by US and/or allies
—	Iron Curtain

MAP **29.1** **The Cold War, 1947–1991.**

The Berlin Airlift. From June 1948 to May 1949, US, British, and British Commonwealth airplanes delivered more than 2 million tons of food and supplies to Berlin after Stalin had blocked all land access to the city. Here, Berlin children eagerly await the next delivery of supplies.

The success of the American Marshall Plan further irritated Stalin because it made the Western sectors of Germany and Berlin magnets for Eastern Europeans fleeing to the West. In 1948, therefore, the Soviets took the provocative step of setting up a highway and rail blockade of food and supplies to Berlin. The United States and Britain responded with the "Berlin Airlift," a demonstration of technological prowess as well as humanitarian compassion. For nearly a year, food, fuel, and other supplies required by this large city were flown in until Stalin finally gave up the blockade.

So far, the Cold War in Europe had been confined to diplomatic maneuvering between Washington and Moscow. During the Berlin crisis, however, the confrontation assumed military dimensions. Thanks in part to an elaborate espionage network embedded inside the nuclear programs of Britain and the United States, the Soviets had accelerated their efforts to build a nuclear bomb. In 1949, they detonated their first device 4 years earlier than anticipated. Now, with its advantage in nuclear weapons eliminated and concern increasing over the possibility of a communist takeover in Western Europe, the United States formed a defensive alliance known as the North Atlantic Treaty Organization (NATO) in 1949. In response, the Soviet Union later formed the Warsaw Pact in 1955 among the states of the Eastern Bloc.

The Central Intelligence Agency   In addition to military and diplomatic initiatives to contain the spread of communism, the United States used alternative means to overthrow left-leaning and socialist movements and governments around the globe. For these purposes the government relied primarily on the Central Intelligence Agency (CIA), an offshoot of the Office of Strategic Studies (OSS)

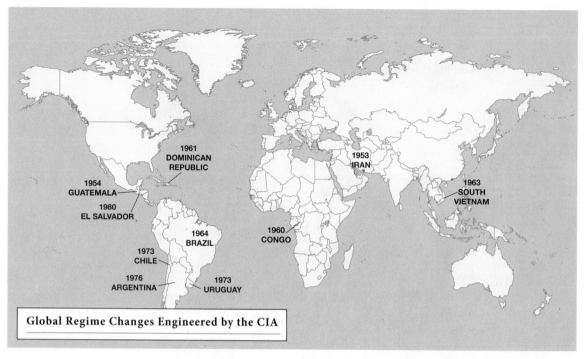

MAP 29.2 **Global Regime Changes Engineered by the CIA.**

developed during World War II. To carry out its mission the CIA employed a variety of covert operations including spy missions, electronic eavesdropping, photographs obtained by high-flying aircraft, and even outright assassination plots. As indicated in Map 29.2, CIA involvement in regime changes spanned the globe.

Hot War in Korea   Emboldened by the development of the nuclear bomb and the victory of the Chinese communists over the nationalists in October 1949, Stalin ratcheted up the Cold War. After a series of raids and counter-raids between communist North Korea and nationalist South Korea and Stalin's blessing for an invasion by the north, the Cold War turned hot. In June 1950, large numbers of North Korean communist troops invaded South Korea in an attempt at forcible unification. South Korean troops fought a desperate rearguard action at the southern end of the peninsula. Under US pressure and despite a Soviet boycott, the UN Security Council branded North Korea as the aggressor, entitling South Korea to UN intervention. At first, in July 1950, the North Korean invaders trapped US troops arriving from Japan and what remained of the South Korean defense forces in the southeast. But by October US troops, augmented by troops from a number of UN members, had mounted a surprise amphibious invasion and fought their way into North Korea, occupied the capital (Pyongyang), and advanced to the Chinese border.

In the meantime, the United States had sent a fleet to the remnant of the Chinese nationalists who had formed the Republic of China on the southern island of Taiwan, to protect it from a threatened invasion by a newly communist China. Thwarted in the south at Taiwan, Mao Zedong took the pronouncements of General Douglas MacArthur, the commander of the UN forces in Korea, about raiding Chinese supply bases on the North Korean border seriously. Stalin, on the other hand, opposed escalation and gave Mao only token support.

Secretly marching to the border in October 1950, communist Chinese troops launched a massive surprise offensive into the peninsula, pushing the UN forces back deep into South Korea. Over the next 3 years, the war seesawed back and forth over the old border of the 38th parallel, while negotiations dragged on. Unwilling to expand the war further or use nuclear weapons, the new Eisenhower administration and the North Koreans agreed to an armistice in 1953. The armistice has endured since that date, and no official peace treaty was ever signed. For more than half a century, the border between the two Koreas has remained a volatile flashpoint, with provocative incidents repeatedly threatening to reopen the conflict.

McCarthyism in the United States

The strains of a hot war in Korea had a troubling domestic impact in the United States as well. Amid the general atmosphere of anticommunism, Joseph McCarthy (1908–1957), a Republican senator from Wisconsin, sensationally announced in 1950 that he had a lengthy list of members of the Communist Party employed by the State Department. Though he never produced the list, his smear tactics, together with denunciations made by the House Committee on Un-American Activities, ruined the careers of hundreds of government employees, movie actors and writers, and private persons in many walks of life. McCarthy went as far as accusing Presidents Truman and Eisenhower of tolerating communist "fellow travelers" in their administrations. After 4 years of anticommunist hysteria, enough voices of reason arose in the Senate to censure McCarthy and relegate him to obscurity. The legacy of bitterness engendered by the "McCarthy era" remained for decades and generated abundant political accusations on both sides.

Revolt in East Germany

In April 1953, at the height of the McCarthy drama and the ongoing Korean armistice negotiations at Panmunjom, Stalin died of a stroke. The death of this powerful and paranoid dictator was profoundly unsettling for the governments of the Eastern Bloc, especially in the German Democratic Republic (East Germany). The East German government was nervously watching the rising wave of defections to the Federal Republic (West Germany)—nearly a million persons during 1949–1953. It had sealed off the border through a system of fences and watchtowers, but Berlin—also divided into East and West sectors—was still a gaping hole. The population was seething over rising production quotas, shortages resulting from the shipment of industrial goods to the Soviet Union (in the name of reparations), and the beginnings of a West German economic boom in which it could not share.

In June 1953, a strike among East Berlin workers quickly grew into a general uprising, encompassing some 500 cities and towns. East German police and Soviet troops, stunned at first, quickly moved to suppress the revolt. The Politburo (the Communist Party's Central Committee Political Bureau) in Moscow, still trying to determine Stalin's successor, refused any concessions, except for a few cosmetic changes in the reparations. The German Stalinist government obediently complied.

In the fall of 1953 Nikita Khrushchev was chosen to succeed Stalin. Khrushchev, a metalworker from a poor farming family on the Russian–Ukrainian border, had worked his way up through the party hierarchy during the war. It took him a year and a half to consolidate his power as party secretary and premier, during which he made substantial investments in agriculture, housing, and consumer goods. In February 1956 he gave a much-noted speech in which he denounced Stalin's "excesses" during collectivization and the purges of the 1930s. Thousands were released from prisons and labor camps (*gulags*). In the Communist Bloc Khrushchev pushed to replace Stalinist hard-liners with new faces willing to improve general living conditions for the population. To balance the new flexibility within the Soviet Bloc, Khrushchev was careful to maintain toughness toward the West. He alarmed leaders of the West when he announced that he was abandoning Stalin's doctrine of socialism in one country for a new policy that supported anticolonial nationalist independence movements around the globe even if the movements were not communist.

Revolt in Poland and Hungary   Khrushchev's reforms awakened hopes in Eastern Europe that new leaders would bring change there as well. In Poland, where collectivization and the command economy had progressed only slowly and the Catholic Church could not be intimidated, Khrushchev's speech resulted in workers' unrest similar to East Germany 3 years earlier. Nationalist reformists gained the upper hand over Stalinists in the Polish Politburo, and Khrushchev realized that he had to avoid another Tito-style secession at all costs. After a few tense days in mid-October, pitting Soviet troops and an angry population against each other, Poland received its limited autonomy.

Unrest in the Soviet Bloc. In the Hungarian uprising from October to November 1956, some 2,500 Hungarians and 700 Soviet troops were killed, while 200,000 fled to neighboring Austria and elsewhere in the West. Here, a young boy and older man watch while a Soviet tank rumbles through an intersection with barricades set up by Hungarian "freedom fighters."

In Hungary, the Politburo was similarly divided between reformers and Stalinists. People in Budapest and other cities, watching events in Poland with intense interest, took to the streets. The Politburo lost control, and the man appointed to lead the country to a national communist solution similar to that of Poland, Imre Nagy [noj] (1896–1958), felt emboldened by popular support to announce a multiparty system and the withdrawal of Hungary from the Warsaw Pact. This was too much for Khrushchev, who unleashed the Soviet troops stationed in Hungary to repress what had become a grassroots revolution.

Aware of British, French, and American preoccupation with the Suez Crisis, the Soviets crushed the uprising in November 1956. Nagy, finding sanctuary in the Yugoslav Embassy and promised safe conduct out of the country, was duped and arrested. The new pro-Moscow government executed him in 1958. During the brief uprising, perhaps a quarter of a million Hungarian citizens escaped to the West. For those who stayed, in the hopes of experiencing greater freedom, the events were a crushing blow.

ICBMs and Sputniks   The suppression of anticommunist unrest in the Eastern Bloc lessened the appeal of communism among many Marxists and revolutionary socialists in the West. But steady advancement in weapons technologies, including missiles and space flight, revealed a powerful military punch behind Soviet repression. In 1957 the Soviet Union announced the development of the world's first intercontinental ballistic missile (ICBM), with a range of around 3,500 miles, making it capable of reaching America's East Coast. In the same year, the Soviet Union launched the world's first orbiting satellite, named Sputnik, into space. Then, in 1961, Russian scientists sent the world's first cosmonaut, Yuri Gagarin (1934–1968), into space, followed 2 years later by Valentina Tereshkova (b. 1937), the world's first female cosmonaut.

These Soviet achievements frightened the Eisenhower administration and Congress as the implications of nuclear weapons descending from space with no practicable defense against them began to set in. Politicians played up the apparent technological leadership of the Soviet Union to goad Congress into accelerating the US missile and space program even at the risk of reheating the Cold War with the Soviet Union. Thus, in 1958 the United States successfully launched its first satellite, Explorer 1, and the following year its first ICBM, the Atlas. The space and missile races were now fully under way.

Communism in Cuba   In 1959, Fidel Castro (b. 1926), a nationalist guerilla fighter opposed to the influence of American companies over a government generally perceived as corrupt, seized power in Cuba. A lawyer, Castro was the son of a Spanish immigrant who had become a wealthy planter. About 6 months after the coup, Cuba was the new symbol of the Khrushchev government's widely hailed openness toward national liberation movements worthy of communist largesse. The Soviet Union lavished huge sums on the development of the island's economy. Khrushchev's instincts were proven right when Castro openly embraced communism in 1960.

To counter Khrushchev's overtures to national liberation movements, President Eisenhower and the head of the CIA, Allen Dulles (1893–1969), secretly supported and trained anticommunist dissidents in the Middle East, Africa, and

Aiming for the Stars. New scholarship sheds light on Sputnik's role in Russian cultural history. As this commemorative postcard reveals, the connection between the technological achievement of Sputnik and popular interest in space travel was strong. The legend reads in Russian: "4 October, the USSR launched Earth's first artificial satellite; 3 November, the USSR launched Earth's second artificial satellite."

Latin America. In the case of Latin America, a group of Cuban anticommunists trained in Guatemala with CIA support for an invasion and overthrow of Castro in Cuba. President John F. Kennedy (in office 1961–1963) inherited the initiative and, against his better judgment, decided to steer a middle course, sanctioning an invasion of Cuba by seemingly independent freedom fighters with no direct US military support. The so-called Bay of Pigs invasion in April 1961 (named for the small bay in southern Cuba where the anticommunist invasion began) was promptly intercepted and easily defeated by Castro's forces, to the great embarrassment of Kennedy.

The Berlin Wall   Fortunately for the United States, Khrushchev suffered a severe embarrassment of his own. East Germany, which retained its Stalinist leadership, pressured Khrushchev to close the last opening in Berlin through which its citizens could escape to West Germany. Between 1953 and 1961, the East German "brain drain" reached 3 million defectors, or nearly one-fifth of the population, most of them young and ambitious people whose talent and skills the regime coveted. The East German Stalinists, allied with a few remaining Stalinists in the Politburo, prevailed over Khrushchev's opposition and built the Berlin Wall in 1961, effectively turning the German Democratic Republic into a prison.

Post-War Eastern Europe   Behind the Iron Curtain eastern European countries freed from Nazism by advancing Red Armies, known collectively as the Eastern (or Soviet) Bloc, consisted of eight countries: Albania, Bulgaria, Czechoslovakia, East Germany, Hungary, Poland, Romania, and Yugoslavia. The social and cultural patterns of each of these nations were of different forms, but one theme that unites them all concerns their social and cultural experiences. Adherence to official Soviet policies was rigidly controlled by state centralization administered ultimately by the Communist Party in Moscow, enforced at the local level by Party committees.

Coercion was enforced through a network of secret police, the KGB, and concentration camps in the Russian gulag system. Although throughout the Stalinist era (1945–1953) and post-Stalinist period (1953–1968) industrialization was increased, often at the expense of agricultural production, shortages and even rationing of consumer goods were common. Employment opportunities were not on a par with those created by the Western economic postwar recovery, and although women were afforded jobs in the workforce, their principal responsibilities still lay within the home. State-sponsored educational programs stressed a program of Soviet propaganda and the sciences. The media were carefully monitored, cultural and religious expression was rigidly censored, and Western culture was condemned. Even so, some aspects of Western culture—especially jazz and rock music—found their way around the censors, along with diversions provided by television shows and athletic competitions.

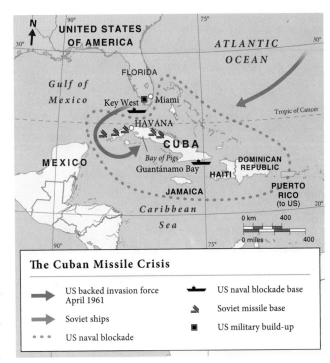

MAP **29.3** **The Cuban Missile Crisis.**

The playing field between East and West was now level, with setbacks on both sides, when the two reached the climax of the Cold War: the first direct confrontation between the Soviet Union and the United States, nearly two decades after the end of World War II. In October 1962, when US spy planes discovered the presence of missile launching pads in Cuba, President Kennedy demanded their immediate destruction and then followed up with a naval blockade of the island to prevent the arrival of Russian missiles. In defiance, Khrushchev dispatched Russian ships to Cuba; when it was discovered that they were bearing more missiles, President Kennedy demanded that Khrushchev recall the ships. The world held its breath for several days as the ships headed steadily for Cuba, raising the very real possibility of a nuclear exchange between the world's superpowers (see Map 29.3).

In the face of American determination, Khrushchev recalled the ships at the last minute. Kennedy, for his part, agreed to remove American missiles from Turkey. Realizing just how close the world had come to World War III, Kennedy and Khrushchev signed the Nuclear Test Ban Treaty in 1963, an agreement banning the aboveground testing of nuclear weapons. The treaty also sought to prevent the spread of these technologies to other countries. After this dramatic climax in the Cold War, relations gradually thawed.

Society and Culture in Postwar North America, Europe, and Japan

In the years after World War II, veterans sought to pursue civilian lives of normalcy and comfort. Intellectuals and artists again cast a critical eye on modern culture, as the previous generation had after World War I. Now, however, the political and ideological options were narrower. Supremacist nationalism in the form of fascism, Nazism, or militarism had been thoroughly bankrupted, and the

The GI Bill for African Americans. Staff Sergeant Herbert Ellison explains the GI Bill to members of his company. The bill, enacted in 1944, provided soldiers returning from the war with support for training and education as well as subsidized home loans. Some 7.8 million veterans benefited from the training and education it provided.

choices had shrunk to communism and capitalist democracy. Still, among the emerging nations, artists and intellectuals struggled to forge new paths, often attempting synthesis among indigenous culture and socialist and democratic ideas.

Mass Consumption Culture American soldiers returned to civilian life and started families, launching the so-called baby-boomer generation between 1945 and 1961. Families with four to six children were almost the norm. Medical advances and better diet and nutrition improved the health of parents and children. The growing population triggered increased consumer demand for such basics as food, clothes, and shelter, as well as consumer durables that increased the comfort of living, such as refrigerators, dishwashers, vacuum cleaners, radios, televisions, telephones, and cars. In the United States, the GI Bill supported not only a middle-class lifestyle but also university studies that led to better-paying jobs. In Europe, the Marshall Plan helped to provide Europeans with similar, if still somewhat lower, living standards. Americans increasingly took on credit to move into their middle-class lives, while Europeans tended to save first before purchasing consumer goods.

In the idealized family of the 1950s and early 1960s, husbands worked downtown from 9:00 to 5:00, while mothers and grandmothers were responsible for the household and children. Shopping was done in the new suburban mall, and everybody went to church or synagogue on weekends and occasionally treated themselves with a trip to the downtown department store and movie theater. This gendered and spatially segregated life was highly structured, corresponding to the yearning of the expanding middle classes for regularity and order after the years of economic depression and war. In Europe and Japan, with variations arising from cultural differences and a later suburbanization process, similar changes in consumer culture took place. An important minority of baby boomers eventually found this middle-class life so stultifying that they revolted in the 1960s, as we will see in Chapter 30.

Modernism: Any of various movements in philosophy and the arts characterized by a deliberate break with classical or traditional forms of thought or expression.

Existentialism: A form of thought built on the assumption that modern scientific–industrial society is without intrinsic meaning unless an answer to the question of what constitutes authentic existence is found.

Artistic Culture Consumerism, a central element in the capitalist–democratic order, was based on the belief in the autonomous individual as the basic component of society. The Enlightenment ideas of materialism and the social contract continued to dominate the Anglo-American cultural sphere and also became dominant in the European arts. They formed the background for the search for ever new forms of **modernism** in thought, writing, theater, painting, music, and film, such as neorealism, **existentialism**, abstract expressionism (see the images on p. 907), and serialism. After two world wars, however, the nineteenth century's optimism in an eternal progress was thoroughly discredited. Although intellectuals and artists remained strongly committed to modernism, they were now much more sensitive to its contradictions.

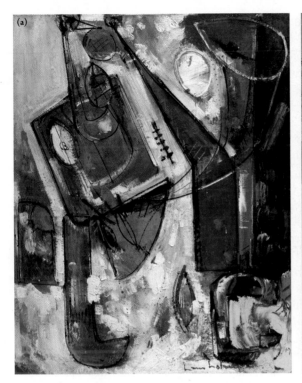 

Abstract Expressionism.
(a) Hans Hofmann (1880–1966), *Delight*, 1947. (b) Willem de Kooning (1904–1997), *Montauk Highway*, 1958. Abstract expressionism was a New York–centered artistic movement that combined the strong colors of World War I German expressionism with the abstract art pioneered by the Russian-born Wassily Kandinsky and the artists of the Bauhaus school. Before and during the Nazi period, many European artists had flocked to New York, including Hofmann and de Kooning. The movement caught the public eye when Jackson Pollock, following the surrealists, made the creation of a work of art—painting a large canvas on the floor through the dripping of paint—an art in itself.

Thinkers and artists reflecting on modernity versus tradition focused on such themes as individualism, loneliness, and alienation; conformism, freedom, and personal fulfillment; family bonds and parental relations; class, race, and gender sensibilities; and political persecution, torture, and mass murder. All provided for rich artistic post–World War II cultures in Western countries. As culture-specific as many artists were, by not merely dwelling on the inevitability of modernity but rather confronting it with their multiple inherited premodern traditions, they created works that could be understood across cultures.

Populism and Industrialization in Latin America

Western political and cultural modernity, as discussed above, was also a part of the Latin American experience. But the region also had a large population of Amerindians and blacks, who participated only marginally in this modernity and large majorities of whom were mired in rural subsistence. Since these populations increased rapidly after World War II, the region faced problems that did not exist in North America or Europe, where industry and its related service sector employed an overwhelmingly urban society. Latin America began to resemble Asia and Africa, which also had massive rural populations, small middle classes, and limited industrial sectors. Populist leaders relying on the urban poor thus sought to steer their countries toward greater industrialization, although with limited success.

Slow Social Change

Latin America had stayed out of World War II. The postwar aftermath therefore neither disrupted nor offered new opportunities to its pattern of social and economic development. The region had suffered from the disappearance of commodity export markets during the Depression of the 1930s, and politicians realized that import-substitution industrialization, replacing imported manufactures with domestically produced ones, had to be adopted as a postwar policy. Tackling industrialization, however, was not easy, since landowners opposed it and the great majority of rural and urban Latin Americans were too poor to become consumers.

Rural and Urban Society Prior to 1945, the rural population, though slowly decreasing, still composed about two-thirds of the total population. But during 1945–1962, the pace of urbanization picked up, with the proportions nearly reversing (see Map 29.4). While overall population growth during this period accelerated, poverty rates remained the same or even increased, making Latin America the world region with the greatest income disparities. The inequalities were exacerbated by the continuing presence of sizeable indigenous Amerindian farming populations in Guatemala, Ecuador, Peru, Bolivia, and parts of Mexico, as well as blacks in Brazil. Landowners continued to thwart efforts at land reform: Except for Mexico (in spurts after 1915) and Bolivia (1952) no country abolished landlordism prior to 1962. Cuba's land reform (1959) and the threat of local peasant revolutions made the issue urgent again, but agrarian reforms picked up only in the 1960s.

Much of the landless population migrated to the cities, making up nearly half of the arrivals. They settled in sprawling shantytowns with no urban services. Some migrants found employment in the expanding industrial sector, but more often than not they survived through occasional labor in the so-called informal sector, a new phenomenon of peddling, repairing, and recycling which composed the livelihood about one-third of the urban population. In contrast to the villages, rural–urban migrants benefited at least marginally from the health and education benefits that populist politicians introduced. The industrial labor force grew to about one-quarter of the total labor force, a growth that was far behind that of the east Asian "Tigers" or "Little Dragons" (terms meant to the connote rapid economic growth in this region) of Korea, Taiwan, and Hong Kong in the 1950s and reflected the hesitant attitude of the politicians toward industrialization in view of rebounding commodity exports in the 1950s.

At the end of World War II, industrialism was still confined mainly to food processing and textile manufacturing; only Mexico and Brazil had moved into basic goods, such as steel and chemicals. In the later 1940s and early 1950s, the larger Latin American countries moved to capital goods and consumer durables, such as machinery, tools, cars, and refrigerators. As a result, expanded production of manufactures reduced dependence on foreign imports. Unfortunately, however, very little private capital was available on the domestic market for risky industrialization ventures, requiring the state to allocate the necessary funds. Smaller countries, like Bolivia, Peru, and Paraguay, overextended themselves

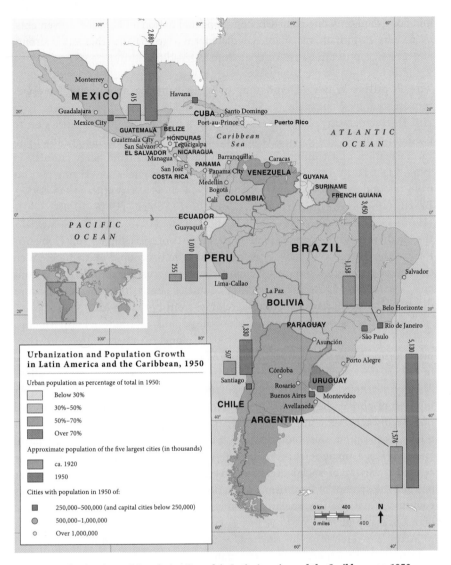

MAP 29.4 **Urbanization and Population Growth in Latin America and the Caribbean, ca. 1950.**

with industrial import substitution and, after a few years of trying, had to return in the early 1950s to a primacy of commodity exports.

Populist Guided Democracy

During the period 1945–1962, the influence of fascism and Nazism faded, and only democracy and communism remained as political and ideological choices. The attraction of democracy in its constitutional-nationalist North American and European forms, however, was limited, since the United States, in the grip of the Cold War, was primarily interested in the professed loyalty of autocratic rulers in its Latin American backyard. Communism was initially also of limited appeal, given Stalin's preference for large, obedient communist parties that toed his line,

Populism: Type of governance in which rulers seek support directly from the population, through organizing mass rallies, manipulating elections, and intimidating or bypassing parliament.

and flourished only once Khrushchev supported national liberation movements, as in Cuba. **Populism** was an intermediate form of governance that found strong, albeit brief, support in Latin America from 1945–1962.

The Populist Wave   Democracy in Latin America during this time was represented by Venezuela (1958), Colombia (1953–1964), and Costa Rica (1953). Democratic politicians, however, were unable to put Venezuela's oil to productive use or bring about land reform in Colombia, resulting eventually in the formation of a communist guerilla underground in the latter country in 1964. Eight Latin American countries had populist regimes for varying periods from the mid-1940s onward: Guatemala (1944–1954), Argentina (1946–1955), Brazil (1946–1954), Venezuela (1945–1948), Peru (1945–1948), Chile (1946–1952), Costa Rica (1948–1953), and Ecuador (1948–1961). In Guatemala, the Cold War and the banana plantation interests of the United Fruit Company formed the background for a CIA-fomented military coup d'état which ended the rule of the elected populist Jacobo Árbenz and was the prelude to a vicious civil war (1960–1996). The remaining countries similarly saw waves of coups d'état and authoritarian or dictatorial regimes from 1945 to 1962.

Peronism is the best-known example of the populist interlude in Latin America that characterized the period of 1945–1962. Colonel Juan Perón (1895–1974), of modest rural background, was a member of a group of officers who staged a coup in 1943 against the traditional landowners and their conservative military allies. They sympathized with the urban population of workers as well as the poor. As minister of labor in the junta, Perón entered into an alliance with labor unions and improved wages, set a minimum wage, and increased pensions. After an earthquake, as the junta solicited donations from celebrities, Perón met Eva Duarte (1919–1952), a movie actress. An attractive, popular person in her own right, she headed a variety of social organizations and charities; and the two together became the symbol of Peronism. In elections in 1946, at the head of a fractious coalition of nationalists, socialists, and communists, Perón gained a legitimate mandate as president.

After the elections he started a 5-year plan of nationalization and industrialization—the characteristic state socialism pursued also in Asia and Africa. Banks, phone companies, railroads, and streetcars, mostly in the hands of British and French capital, were nationalized, as was the entire export of agricultural commodities. A year later, construction of plants for the production of primary and intermediate industrial goods got under way. During Perón's tenure, the economy expanded by 40 percent.

To get the national factories going, however, they had to be equipped with imported machinery. Initially, Perón paid for these imports with reserves accumulated from commodity exports during World War II. But soon the costs of the imported machinery exceeded the internal reserves and revenues of Argentina, leading to inflation and strikes. What eventually derailed Perón, however, was the Cold War. President Truman refused to include Argentina in the list of recipients for Marshall Plan aid. He disliked the presence in his own hemisphere of a populist regime that strove to leap into full industrialization through state socialism. Plagued by chronic deficits and unable to pay its foreign debts, Perón was overthrown by a conservative-led coup in 1955. Thus, Argentina, instead of leaping into industrialization, stumbled—not unlike China in the later 1950s.

The End of Colonialism and the Rise of New Nations

Like Latin America, Asia and Africa also experienced rapid population growth and urbanization in the period 1945–1962. But in contrast to the politically independent American continent, colonialism was still dominant in Asia and Africa at the end of World War II. The governments of Great Britain and France had no inclination to relinquish their empires at this point, but both were too exhausted by the war to hold them completely. Thus, in a first wave after the end of war, a few independence movements succeeded, notably in the Middle East and Asia. A major shift in the perception of the benefits of colonialism during the mid-1950s, however, had to take place before Britain and France were willing to loosen their colonial grip in Africa.

"China Has Stood Up"

Japan maintained a short and brutal colonial regime from 1937 to 1945 in China. Given Japan's defeat in World War II by the Allies, the Chinese did not have to fight for their independence; but they were not spared conflict. In 1949 the communists finally prevailed over the nationalists after more than a decade of civil war. China was still fundamentally a peasant-based economy with scant industrial resources. Mao's theories of revolution had adopted Marxist principles to put peasants instead of industrial workers at the forefront of the movement toward socialism. For Mao, this reinterpretation of Marxism opened up fresh possibilities of development, with the expropriation of landlords, the construction of communal farms, and the eventual leap into decentralized village industrialization. During the Stalin years, China depended heavily on Soviet material aid and advisors. After Khrushchev introduced his consumer-oriented reforms in the mid-1950s and refused to share nuclear and space technology, estrangement set in, culminating in the Soviet Union's withdrawal of all advisors from China in 1960.

Victory of the Communists   China emerged from World War II on the winning side but was severely battered militarily, economically, and politically. The brutal war with Japan had taken 10–20 million lives, according to various estimates. Moreover, the shaky wartime alliance between the communists under Mao Zedong and the nationalists under Chiang K'ai-shek unraveled in the later civil war. The communists, deeply entrenched in the countryside, were at a strategic advantage in China's overwhelmingly rural society. Despite the nationalists' superiority, resulting from modern arms and American support, the communists were able to systematically choke the cities, causing hyperinflation in Shanghai and other urban centers in 1947.

By 1948 the size of the two armies had reached parity, but Mao's People's Liberation Army had unstoppable popular momentum, and the United States cut back on its aid to Chiang as he faced imminent defeat. By 1949, Chiang and most of his forces had fled to Taiwan, Mao's forces took Beijing, and the new People's Republic of China set about reshaping the country according to the Maoist vision of the communist pattern of collectivist modernity. For millions of Chinese,

Land Reform with a Vengeance, 1952. A Chinese farmer kneels at gunpoint before a communist court enforcing land redistribution policies. Like thousands of others, the landowner was convicted of being a "class enemy" and was executed.

Mao's pronouncement on October 1, 1949, from atop the Gate of Heavenly Peace in Beijing that "China has stood up" and would never be a victim of imperialism again was a source of enormous pride. What would follow in the next decade, however, would be met with more selective enthusiasm.

Land Reform   During the 1950s, a central aspect of Mao's thinking was the idea that Chinese peasants were the country's only reliable resource. With China lacking a workable industrial and transportation base, the early Maoist years were marked by repeated mass mobilization campaigns. Aside from the "Resist America/Aid Korea" campaign in support of Chinese intervention in Korea, the most important of these was the national effort at land reform. Party cadres moved into the remaining untouched rural areas and expropriated land, dividing it among the local peasants. Landlords who resisted were "struggled"—abused by tenants who were egged on by party cadres—and often lynched. By some estimates, land reform between 1950 and 1955 took as many as 2 million lives. As hoped for, peasant landownership caused agricultural productivity to increase.

Several years into the land reform program, party leaders decided it was time to take the next step toward socialized agriculture. Mao wanted to avoid the chaos that had accompanied Soviet collectivization of agriculture in 1930–1932. The party leadership felt that by going slowly they could greatly ease the transition. Thus, in 1953 peasants were encouraged to form "agricultural producers' cooperatives" in which villages would share scarce tools and machinery. Those who joined were given incentives in the form of tax breaks and higher prices. By 1956, agricultural production had recovered to pre–World War II levels and was registering impressive gains.

"Let a Hundred Flowers Bloom"   By 1957, Mao was ready to evaluate the commitment of the nation's intellectuals, many of whom had initially been enthusiastic about the reforms. Mao, however, was not sure whether these people truly supported his programs or were simply being circumspect. Adopting a slogan from China's philosophically rich late Zhou period, "Let a hundred flowers bloom, let a hundred schools of thought contend," the party invited intellectuals to submit public criticism of the party's record, assuring the intellectuals that offering their critique was patriotic.

By mid-1957 the trickle of criticisms had become a torrent, but when some critics suggested forming an opposition party, Mao acted swiftly. The "Hundred Flowers" campaign was terminated and the "Anti-Rightist" campaign was launched. Calls for an opposition party were denounced as the worst kind of right-wing thinking—as opposed to the "correct" left-wing thinking of the monopoly Communist Party. Those accused of rightism were rounded up and subjected to "reeducation." Even Deng Xiaoping (1904–1997), an old companion of Mao's and later the architect of China's present market economy, was forced to endure 5 years on a hog farm. In addition to being imprisoned and made to endure endless "self-criticism" sessions, many intellectuals were sentenced to long stretches of "reform through labor" in remote peasant villages.

The Great Leap Forward   At about the same time, Mao was growing impatient with the pace of Chinese agricultural collectivization. If production could be ramped up sufficiently, the surplus agricultural funds could then be used to fund 5-year plans for industrial development along the lines of those in the Soviet Union. Moreover, China had been borrowing heavily from the Soviet Union through the 1950s and had availed itself of Soviet technicians and engineers. All of the progress of the decade might be radically slowed or halted if agricultural revenues could not keep pace.

Mao therefore prodded the Communist Party into its most colossal mass mobilization project yet: the Great Leap Forward (1958–1961). The entire population of the country was to be pushed into a campaign to communalize agriculture into self-sustaining units that would function like factories in the fields. Men and women would work in shifts and live in barracks on enormous collective farms. Peasants were to surrender all their iron implements to be melted down and made into steel to build the new infrastructure of these communes. The most recognizable symbol of the campaign was the backyard steel furnace, which commune members were to build and run for their own needs. Technical problems were to be solved by the "wisdom of the masses" through politically correct "red" (revolutionary) thinking. The entire country would therefore modernize its rural areas and infrastructure in one grand campaign.

Predictably, the Great Leap was the most catastrophic policy failure in the history of the People's Republic. Knowledgeable critics had been cowed into silence by the Anti-Rightist campaign, and the initial wave of enthusiasm that greeted the mobilization ground to a halt as peasants began to actively resist the seizure of their land and implements. So many were forced into building the communal structures and making unneeded steel that by 1959 agricultural production in China had plummeted and the country experienced its worst famine in modern times. By 1962 an estimated 30 million people had died.

Conditions became so bleak that Mao stepped down from his party chairmanship in favor of "expert" Liu Shaoqi (1898–1969) and retreated into semiretirement. Liu, from a well-off peasant background in south-central China, and the rehabilitated Deng Xiaoping were now reinstated. Together they tackled the task of rebuilding the shattered economy and political structures. The next 5 years saw impressive gains in China's technical, health, and education sectors as the country returned to something like normalcy. But Mao was soon plotting his return.

Decolonization, Israel, and Arab Nationalism in the Middle East

Parallel to China ridding itself of Japanese colonialism after World War II, independence movements arose in the Middle East and North Africa against the British and French colonial regimes. Here, countries achieved their independence in two waves, the first following World War II and the second during

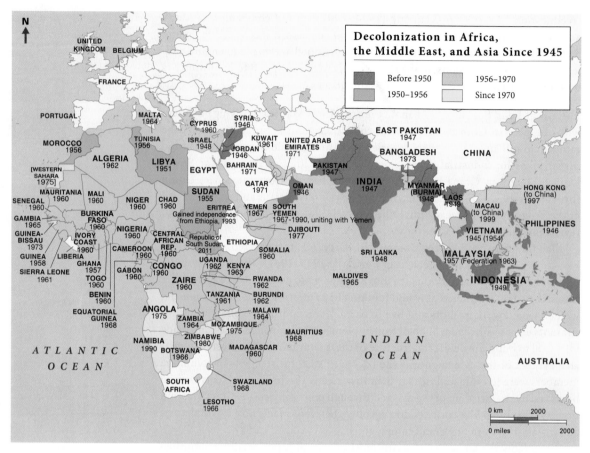

MAP 29.5 Decolonization in Africa, the Middle East, and Asia since 1945.

1956–1970 (see Map 29.5). The first wave was the result of local pressures, which colonial authorities found too costly to resist, as in the cases of Syria, Lebanon, Iraq, Jordan, and Israel. The second wave had to await the realization of the British and French governments that they were no longer powerful enough to maintain their empires in a world dominated by the United States and the Soviet Union.

Palestine and Israel   As World War II ended, Britain found itself in a tight spot in Palestine. After the suppression of the uprising of 1936–1939, the Arab Palestinians were relatively quiet but Zionist guerilla action protesting the restrictions on Jewish immigration and land acquisitions had begun in the middle of the war. Sooner or later some form of transition to self-rule had to be offered, but British politicians and the top military were determined to hold on to the empire's strategic interests (oil and the Suez Canal), especially once the Cold War heated up in 1946.

When it became impossible to find a formula for a transition acceptable to the Arabs, in February 1947 Britain turned the question of Palestinian independence over to the United Nations. After the collapse of the Soviet Union in 1991, documents surfaced showing—interestingly, given the Soviet Union's later animosity toward the Jewish state and support of the Arabs—that during the 1940s Stalin had used the United Nations to push for a weakening of the British imperial position in the Middle East by favoring the creation of the state of Israel. Accordingly, the United Nations adopted a partition plan worked out with American assistance in November, and Israel declared its independence on May 14, 1948 (see Map 29.6).

The Soviet Union backed up its tactical, Cold War–motivated support for Israel by releasing 200,000 Jewish emigrants from the Soviet Bloc and having Czechoslovakia deliver rifles, machine guns, and World War II–vintage planes to Israel. Israel was victorious against the Arab armies that invaded from surrounding countries, which, although determined to contest the new state, were unable to obtain weapons as the result of British and American embargoes. Only Jordan was partly successful, conquering the West Bank and the Old City of Jerusalem. Between November 1947 and the end of fighting in January 1949, the territory in and around the new state experienced, albeit on a smaller scale, the same kind of tragic and chaotic population shift that took place at about the same time in India and Pakistan. Some three-quarters of a million Palestinians were either forced from

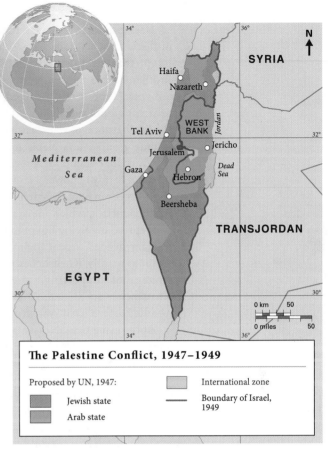

MAP **29.6 The Palestine Conflict, 1947–1949.**

their villages or fled, leaving only 150,000 in an Israeli territory now substantially larger than that of the original partition plan. In response, the Arab countries expelled about half a million Jews during the next decade from their countries. In the end, Stalin's early Cold War tactics were a grave miscalculation: Israel became a staunch Western ally. But the Western camp did not fare much better: The Arab "catastrophe" (Arabic *nakba*), as it was called, led to the replacement of liberal, landowning Arab nationalists by ardent military hard-liners of refugee background determined to end what remained of Western colonialism—which now, in their eyes, included the state of Israel.

The Officer Coup in Egypt   One Egyptian officer serving with distinction in the war against Israel was Colonel Gamal Abdel Nasser (1918–1970), the eldest son of a postal clerk from southern Egypt. Nasser had benefited from the opening of the officer corps to commoners. He was bitter toward the Egyptian royalty, supported by landowners who had done little to support the country with arms and supplies in the war. In the middle of a declining internal security situation—massive British retaliation against acts of sabotage in the Suez Canal Zone—the secret "Free Officers," with Nasser at the center, assumed power in a coup in July 1952. They closed down parliament and sent the king into exile on his private luxury yacht. The coup was bloodless, and there was little reaction in the streets.

Nasser quickly tightened the rule of his military regime. To break the power of the landowners, the Free Officers in 1952 initiated the first round of a land reform that eventually eliminated large estates. A rival for power was the Muslim Brotherhood, a militant organization founded in 1928 by the preacher Hasan al-Banna (1906–1949), who propagated a reformed Islam among poor and rural–urban migrants and advocated the establishment of an Islamic regime. Accusing the Brotherhood of an assassination attempt, Nasser outlawed it in 1954, driving it underground. In a plebiscite in 1956, Nasser made himself president, with a largely rubber-stamp parliament.

Once firmly in power, Nasser espoused the Arab nationalist cause. Palestinian Arab "freedom fighters" carried out raids against Israel from refugee camps in the Arab countries, which inevitably provoked Israeli reprisals. After the first raid and reprisal involving Egypt in February 1955, Nasser realized that the Egyptian military needed urgent improvements. When the United States would not sell weapons readily, Khrushchev jumped in 6 months later, based on his new Soviet strategy of supporting anticolonial nationalists. Where Stalin had failed, Khrushchev succeeded: After its failure in Israel, the Soviet Union was in the Middle Eastern Cold War struggle again.

At the same time, Nasser laid early plans for infrastructural improvements in advance of a later state-industrialization plan: He asked the World Bank for a loan to finance the Aswan High Dam. Initially, the United States and Britain, the main underwriters of the World Bank, were in support. But they withdrew this support in spring 1956 when Nasser pressured Egypt's neighbor Jordan into dismissing the British commander of its crack troops, the Arab Legion. Nasser responded with the nationalization of the Suez Canal (but with compensation of the share-holders) and closure of the Strait of Tiran (used by Israel for Indian Ocean shipping) in July 1956. Without the necessary loans, Nasser had to put the construction of the High Dam on hold.

Israel considered the closure of the Strait of Tiran an act of war and, with French participation, prepared for a campaign to reopen the straits. France, anxious to punish Nasser for weapons deliveries to Algerian fighters in the war of liberation that had begun in 1954, persuaded Britain to join in a plan that would be initiated with an attack on Egypt by Israel. If Nasser would close the Suez Canal, France and Britain would occupy it, ostensibly to separate the combatants but actually to reestablish Western control. The plan was hatched in secret because of US opposition to the use of force against Nasser. It unraveled badly when Israel ended its canal campaign victoriously on November 2 but the British and French troops were unable to complete the occupation of the Canal Zone before November 4, the day of the ceasefire called by the UN General Assembly and the United States. Although defeated militarily, Nasser scored a resounding diplomatic victory, effectively ending the last remnants of British and French imperialism in the Middle East.

After the Suez War, Nasser rode high on waves of pan-Arabism, nonalignment, and Arab socialism. The monarchical regimes in Arabia were on the defensive and maintained themselves only thanks to the United States, heir to the strategic oil interests of Britain after the demise of the latter's empire. Although unification with Syria as the United Arab Republic (1958–1961) did not work out, Egypt succeeded in establishing a cultural hegemony from North Africa to Yemen based on propaganda, movies, and music. The relationship with the Soviet Union deepened: Thanks to the Soviets, the Aswan Dam was completed, Soviet military and technical support grew, and Egyptian students received advanced educations in the Eastern Bloc. In 1961, the regime cofounded the **Non-Aligned Movement**, together with Indonesia's Sukarno, India's Nehru, Yugoslavia's Tito, and Ceylon's Bandaranaike. In the same year, Nasser announced his first 5-year plan, which included the nationalization of all large businesses and the construction of heavy steel, aluminum, cement, and chemical plants. Egypt embraced industrial modernity but under the aegis of state investments similar to what Stalin had pioneered in 1930. Nasser called this "Arab socialism."

Non-Aligned Movement: An international, anticolonialist movement of state leaders that promoted the interests of countries not aligned with the superpowers.

Decolonization and the Cold War in Asia

Nationalist forces similar to those in the Middle East arose also in south and east Asia as a consequence of World War II. The war had either thoroughly destroyed or considerably diminished the colonial holdings of Great Britain, France, the Netherlands, and Japan in Asia. With the destruction of Japan, the Greater East Asia Co-Prosperity Sphere around the Pacific Rim and its islands dissolved. In several colonies, existing independence movements established nationalist governments or fought against the attempted reimposition of European rule. In quick succession India and Pakistan (1947), Burma (1948), Malaysia (1957), Ceylon (1948), Indonesia (1949), and Vietnam (1954) achieved independence from the British and French. India and Vietnam merit a closer look as countries that played important roles during the Cold War competition between the two patterns of communism and capitalist democracy.

Independence and Partition on the Subcontinent   India, Pakistan, and Bangladesh form a prime example of the trials and tribulations encountered by the newly independent ethnic–religious nations in Asia. As the Indian crown colony emerged from the war, to which it had once again contributed huge numbers of volunteer soldiers, nationalists demanded nothing less than full independence. Gandhi, Nehru, and the majority of the Indian National Congress envisaged an Indian nation on the entire subcontinent in which a constitution, patterned after that of Britain, would trump any ethnic, linguistic, and/or religious identities, of which there were literally hundreds. For the Congress, to be an Indian meant adherence to the constitutional principles of equality before the law, due process, and freedom from oppression.

The Muslim minority, however, beginning in the 1930s, had drifted increasingly toward religious nationalism, demanding a separate state for themselves in regions where they formed a majority. The main advocate for this separatism was the Muslim League, led by Muhammad Ali Jinnah (1876–1948). Not surprisingly, there was also a small minority of Hindu religious nationalists who had already in the 1920s published pamphlets advocating independence under the banner of "Hindu-ness" (*hindutva*). To the dismay of the Indian National Congress, the British negotiators lent an ear to the demands of the Islamic religious nationalists and prevailed on Gandhi and Nehru to accept independence with partition— and the possibility of widespread disruption, given that even the northwest and northeast, with their Muslim majorities, were home to sizeable minorities of millions of Hindus.

When, on August 15, 1947, the two nations of India and Pakistan ("Land of the Pure") became independent, the jubilation of freedom was immediately mixed with the horrors of a population exchange on a massive scale. Desperate to save themselves, more than 2 million panicked people fled hundreds of miles on foot, by cart, or by railroad to settle in their respective countries. More than 100,000 Indians died in the accompanying communal violence. Gandhi himself fell victim 5 months later to an assassin from the hindutva supremacist-nationalist minority who was enraged by both the partition and Gandhi's principled adherence to constitutional nationalism, to which Hindu nationalism was to be subordinated.

While India settled into federal parliamentary democracy, Pakistan's constitution became disposable and the regime authoritarian. From the start, it was clear that religious nationalism was insufficient to define the identity of Pakistanis, distributed over two physically separated regions of the nation, Punjab in the west and East Bengal in the east. The capital, Islamabad, was in the west, and Urdu became the national language, relegating Bengali in the east to secondary status (to the dismay of its speakers, who eventually seceded in a bloody civil war and formed the nation of Bangladesh in 1971).

A decade into independence, a military officer, Field Marshal Ayub Khan (1907–1974) from the Pashtu minority in Waziristan on the western border, assumed power in a bloodless coup. Subsequently, he abrogated the 1948 British-style constitution and in 1962 imposed a new constitution, providing for a "guided democracy" of elected village councilors who voted for the president and the members of the national assembly. The constitution's definition of Islam as a national identity and its relationship to subsidiary ethnic and linguistic identities in the country, however, were so contentious that they remained unresolved.

Worst of all, given the role of Islam as the religious–nationalist foundation principle, Pakistan was in conflict with India over Kashmir, a province lying in the north between India and Pakistan. In 1947, its Hindu prince hesitated to join Pakistan, while its majority Muslim population demanded incorporation. In the ensuing first war between Indian and Pakistan, India succeeded in conquering most of the province, with Pakistan holding on to only a small sliver, but Kashmiri Muslims remained restive. As in so many other postcolonial territorial disputes, clashes between constitutional and ethnic–linguistic–religious nationalism became irresolvable.

Independent India   India's first prime minister, Jawaharlal Nehru (in office 1947–1964), had the formidable task of tying the subcontinent's disparate constituencies together into a united government. Within the British system, perhaps one-quarter of the territory had remained under the nominal rule of local princes, who now had to surrender their realms to the national government. The bewildering array of castes and the social inequalities built into the system also posed a powerful obstacle, especially since the British had frequently exploited these inequalities to divide and rule. The new government was itself in the uncomfortable situation of constitutionally mandating equality for women and outlawing caste discrimination, while being forced to acquiesce to the de facto absence of the former and continuation of the latter. In the end, the British parliamentary and court systems were adopted and the old civil service was retained, while the economy of the new government would officially be a modified, nonrevolutionary kind of socialism. Nehru's admiration for Soviet successes persuaded him to adopt the 5-year-plan system of development. Not surprisingly, India's first 5-year plan (1951–1955), like the early efforts in the Soviet Union and China, was geared toward raising agricultural productivity as a precondition for industrial development.

The most formidable problem was poverty. Though the cities were rapidly expanding beyond the ability of their local governments to keep pace with services, India, like China at the same time, was still fundamentally rural. The new nation's village population was second only to China's in size. The strains upon the land and reliance on the monsoon cycle meant a constant risk of famine. In the 1950s, India launched a family planning program, to encourage a slowing of the demographic expansion. As a democratic country, however, India had to rely on the voluntary cooperation of the villagers, a cooperation which was difficult to achieve as long as urbanization and industrialization were in their initial stages. For poor families, children were either important laborers in agriculture or, among the landless and the poor in city slums, crucial additional breadwinners as soon as they were old enough to work.

Political and Economic Nonalignment   Similar to the governments of the Soviet Union, China, and Egypt, Nehru and the Congress Party argued that the pressing rural poverty could be overcome only through rapid industrialization undertaken by the state. A hybrid regime of capitalist–democratic constitutionalism with private property (on a small scale) and guided "socialist" state investments came into being, which was officially aligned with neither the West nor the East. This nonalignment (Nehru coined this term in 1954) became the official policy of India and under its initiative also the founding principle of an entire organization, the Non-Aligned Movement, informally established in Bandung, Indonesia, in 1955, and formally inaugurated in 1961 (see "Patterns Up Close"). The Non-Aligned Movement, still in existence today, sought to maintain neutrality in the Cold War. It predictably incurred the wrath of Western Cold War warriors but was generally successful in maintaining its own course independent from the Western and Soviet Blocs.

Indian state socialism began with the state's second 5-year plan (1956–1961), which focused on state investments in heavy industry. Existing private enterprises were nationalized, and an immense hydroelectric complex and five steel plants were built, along with numerous cement works and an ambitious expansion of coal mines and railroads. In 1958, the Atomic Energy Commission was formed to pursue both peaceful and military applications of nuclear fission. With the iron, aluminum, cement, and chemicals from heavy industry, the planners hoped, private Indian investors, still minuscule in number but recipients of compensation for factories lost to nationalization, would buy the heavy industrial goods—iron, aluminum, and chemicals—to construct housing and build factories for the production of basic consumer goods. The giant domestic market of India was to become fully self-sufficient and independent of imports.

Though begun with much hope at a time of prosperity, the second plan failed to reach its goals. The government debt, owed both to domestic banks and to foreign lending institutions, grew astronomically. Tax collection was notoriously

Patterns Up Close | Bandung and the Origins of the Non-Aligned Movement

As we have noted in this chapter, one of the most momentous events of the post–World War II period was the dismantling of the vast colonial empires of the Western powers and Japan and the rapid emergence from them of dozens of new nation-states. While nationalist movements in these empires had long predated the war, the complete defeat of Japan accompanied by the exhaustion of Great Britain, France, and the Netherlands and the emergence of the Cold War proved powerful catalysts for independence—as had Allied propaganda during the war and the pronouncements and policies of the newly created United Nations after 1945.

As these new nations arrived on the scene in the 1940s and 1950s, however, they faced a host of unprecedented problems, ranging from poverty and developmental gaps to ethnic and religious conflicts. Looming over all of these emerging nations was the intensifying struggle between the United States and its allies in the capitalist camp and the Soviet Union and the Communist Bloc. As a result, many leaders of these new nations saw themselves as natural colleagues. They shared a common colonial experience, and many had also been fighters for national independence. Now, they also had to contend with both Cold War rivals attempting to enlist their support. By the early 1950s, the French scholar Alfred Sauvy had coined the term "third world" to describe these newly emergent nonaligned nations, whose situation he saw as parallel to the famous Third Estate of prerevolutionary France (Chapter 22).

Thus, led by the dynamic Indonesian president Sukarno and India's Prime Minister Nehru, Indonesia, India, Burma, Pakistan, and Ceylon (Sri Lanka) convened a conference in April 1955 attended by 25 countries, representing 1.5 billion people, at the Indonesian resort town of Bandung. Throughout the conference the words of Sukarno's opening speech seemed to sound a dramatic and prophetic note:

> The twentieth century has been a period of terrific dynamism. Perhaps the last fifty years have seen more development and more material progress than the previous five hundred years. . . . But has man's political skill marched hand-in-hand with his technical and scientific skill?

Indeed, although the Bandung Conference established the base on which Non-Aligned Movement was founded, politics proved a corrosive force in its interactions from the outset. Delegates on the whole agreed on the principle of Afro-Asian solidarity and cooperation, and were unanimous in their opposition to colonialism by any country. They were much less agreed, however, on exactly what constituted colonialism: Some equated the Soviet position in Eastern Europe with colonialism and worried about China's emergent predominance in east Asia. Others, more friendly toward Marxist developmental approaches and eager for aid from socialist countries, dismissed such ideas as Western propaganda. Zhou Enlai, the People's Republic of China's delegate, did much to calm the anxieties of those worried about his country's possible expansion and, indeed, attempted to place China firmly in the ranks of the nonaligned, despite China's close relationship with the Soviet Union at the time. The United States refused to attend, at least in part because of its policy of not recognizing the People's Republic, though American pronouncements offered aid and developmental expertise to the participants. (However, American congressman Adam Clayton Powell and the writer Richard Wright—both African American—did attend in unofficial capacities.) In the end, the conference unanimously adopted a 10-point declaration of "world peace and cooperation," very much in keeping with the tenets of the UN Charter.

Though regional rivalries and competing political aims, as well as the circumstances of the Cold War, never allowed the development of the kind of solidarity championed at Bandung, successive conferences in Cairo and Belgrade led to the official creation of the Non-Aligned Movement in 1961. Many of the leaders of Bandung, including Nehru, Sukarno, and Egypt's President Nasser, were there, as was the subject of this chapter's opening vignette, Sirimavo Bandaranaike. The movement marked the maturation of an important pattern that helped to regulate the behavior of the Cold War players to a considerable extent. The search for a third way beyond capitalism and Soviet communism spurred economic and developmental experimentation and encouraged both Cold War camps to woo nonaligned members into their respective ideological orbits. Politically, the growing number of new nations seeing security in a coalition opposed to superpower domination made the movement a genuine power of its own, particularly in international forums such as the UN General Assembly.

Bandung Conference.
(L-R) Dr. Ali Sastroamidjojo, Sir John Kotelawala, Pakistan's Premier Mohamed Ali, Jawaharlal Nehru, and U Nu at the Bandung Conference, April 1, 1955.

The pattern of resistance to superpower dominance continues today, decades after the end of the Cold War. The Non-Aligned Movement still casts itself as the champion of the developing "global south" in opposition to the economic power of the wealthy "north." Politically, however, its stance is now directed against membership in great power alliances such as NATO. With membership now including 120 countries and 17 observer nations, the Non-Aligned Movement's influence is arguably more widespread than ever, though the absence of the Cold War has made its focus more diffuse. One could say, however, that Sukarno's observation about politics remains as relevant and complex as ever: For the period 2012 to 2015, the presidency of the Non-Aligned Movement has moved to Iran, a country whose relationship with its neighbors and with the Western powers and the United States has been for decades one of extreme tension.

Questions

• How does the Non-Aligned Movement reflect the pattern of postwar developments regarding the trend toward anticolonialism?

• In what ways does Sukarno's opening speech anticipate postwar political and diplomatic relations among emerging independent states?

The Strains of Nonalignment. India's determined stance to navigate its own course between the superpowers was a difficult one, especially during the height of the Cold War. Here, however, a degree of diplomatic warmth appears to pervade the proceedings in Geneva, Switzerland, as the People's Republic of China's foreign minister, Chen Yi (left), toasts his Indian colleague, defense minister V. K. Krishna Menon (right), and the Soviet foreign minister, Andrei Gromyko (center background), smiles at them both. The date of this conference, however, formally convened to discuss issues between the Soviet and American sides over influence in the southeast Asian nation of Laos in July 1962, also coincided with rising border tensions between India and China. This photo was specifically released to show that both sides were still on friendly terms. Within a few months, however, they were shooting at each other.

difficult and unproductive, and chronic national and federal budget deficits drove up inflation. Bad monsoon seasons caused food shortages. In democratic India it was not possible to use the draconian dictatorial powers that Stalin had employed. India's difficulties were experienced time and again in other countries after independence.

Southeast Asia In contrast to India, where the postwar British imperialists gave in to the inevitable, the French under Charles de Gaulle (1890–1970) in 1944–1946 were determined to reconstitute their empire. De Gaulle and a majority of French politicians found it inconceivable that this new republic would be anything less than the imperially glorious Third Republic. To de Gaulle's chagrin, military efforts to hold on to Lebanon and Syria failed against discreet British support for independence and the unilateral establishment of national governments by the Lebanese and Syrians in 1943–1944. After these losses, the politicians of the Fourth Republic were determined not to lose more colonies.

Unfortunately for the French, however, when they returned to Indochina (composed of Vietnam, Laos, and Cambodia) in the fall of 1945, the prewar communist independence movement had already taken over. With covert American assistance, the communists had fought the Japanese occupiers in a guerilla war, and on

> "For more than eighty years, the French imperialists, abusing the standard of Liberty, Equality, and Fraternity, have violated our Fatherland and oppressed our fellow citizens."
>
> —Ho Chi Minh

September 2, 1945, the day of Japan's surrender to the United States, Ho Chi Minh, the leader, read a Vietnamese declaration of independence to half a million people in Hanoi.

Following protracted negotiations in early 1946 between Ho and the French, a stalemate ensued. Ho did not budge from his demand for independence, while the French insisted on returning to their "colony." The Vietminh promptly relaunched their guerilla war. Because of the rapid escalation of the Cold War, the French were successful at persuading the American administration that a Vietminh victory was tantamount to an expansion of communism in the world. By the early 1950s, the United States was providing much of the funding, and the French and allied Vietnamese troops did the actual fighting.

In May 1954, however, the Vietminh defeated the French decisively. During the Geneva negotiations carried out later that year, the French surrender resulted in a division of Vietnam into north and south along the 17th parallel, pending national elections, and the creation of the new nations of Laos and Cambodia.

The elections, however, never took place, and instead Ngo Dinh Diem [no deen jem] (in office 1955–1963), an authoritarian politician with a limited power base primarily composed of Catholics, emerged in the south. He legitimized his rule in 1955 through a fraudulent plebiscite. Although the new Kennedy administration (1961) was aware of Diem's unscrupulous rule, concerns about military successes being achieved by Laotian and South Vietnamese communists receiving North Vietnamese support led to the fateful American decision to carry the Western Cold War into Indochina. President Eisenhower had already sent several hundred military advisors to Diem, but President Kennedy, faced with the Bay of Pigs disaster in Cuba (April 1961) and the East German wall in Berlin (August 1961), increased the military presence to 16,000 by 1963. Since Diem was corrupt and unwilling to carry out much-needed land reforms, the United States engineered a coup in November 1963 that put a military government in place. This proxy regime was soon propped up by a growing American military presence that would reach a half-million men by 1967.

Decolonization and Cold War in Africa

Only 7 months after their defeat at Dien Bien Phu, the French had to face the declaration of a war for independence by the Algerian Front of National Liberation (November 1, 1954). Algeria, a French colony of 10 million Muslim Arabs and Berbers, had a European settler population of nearly 1 million. The French army was determined to prevent a repeat of the humiliation it had suffered in Indochina. But that is precisely what happened only 2 years later in the Suez war of 1956, and British and French politicians began to realize that the maintenance of colonies was becoming too costly. France hung on to Algeria and was even able to largely repress the liberation war by the later 1950s. But in the long run, Algerian independence (in 1962) could not be prevented, even though French military elements and settlers did everything (including two revolts in 1958 and 1961 against Paris) to keep the country French. France's colonial interests were too costly to be maintained, and the United States took over the West's strategic interests in the world. Since the colonies required immense expenditures to support newly burgeoning populations, and the reconstruction of Europe was still far from complete, both Britain and France were forced to rethink the idea of colonialism.

Amid much soul-searching, European governments began to liquidate their empires, beginning in 1957. Only Portugal and Spain continued to maintain their colonies of Angola, Mozambique, and Rio de Oro. South Africa introduced its apartheid regime (1948–1994), designed to segregate the white Afrikaner (Dutch-descended) ruling class from the black majority. As the British, French, and Belgians decolonized, however, they ensured that the governments of the newly independent African countries would remain their loyal subalterns. For them, African independence would be an exchange for support in the Cold War and continued economic dependence.

The Legacy of Colonialism   Between 1918 and 1957, even though the governments of Britain, France, Belgium, and Portugal had invested little state money in their colonies, vast changes had occurred in sub-Saharan Africa. The population had more than doubled from 142 to 300 million, mostly as a result of the reduction of tropical diseases through better medicine. Urbanization was accelerating; economies were coming to rely too heavily on commodity exports; and an emerging middle class was becoming restless. Heavy investments were required, not merely in mining and agriculture but also in social services to improve the lot of the growing African population. Faced with this financial burden, most of the colonial powers decided to grant independence rather than divert investments badly needed at home.

Ghana, the African Pioneer   Once Britain had decided to decolonize, the governmental strategy toward African independence was to support nationalist groups or parties that adopted British-inspired constitutions and the rule of law, guaranteed existing British economic interests, and abided by the rules of the British Commonwealth of Nations. The first to fit these criteria was Ghana in 1957. Its leader, Kwame Nkrumah (1909–1972), held a master's degree in education from the University of Pennsylvania and appeared to be a sound choice.

> "Capitalism is too complicated a system for a newly independent nation. Hence the need for a socialistic society."
>
> —Kwame Nkrumah

Ghana sought to be the pioneer of sub-Saharan independence and development. It had a healthy economy based on cocoa production as well as some mineral wealth. Its middle class was perhaps the most vital of any African colony's. Nkrumah had had a long career as an activist for African independence and a leading advocate of pan-African unity. Although he was jailed during the 1950s for his activism in the Convention People's Party and therefore viewed with some concern, the British nevertheless also realized that Nkrumah wielded genuine authority among a majority of politically inexperienced Ghanaians.

Only 2 years into his rule, however, Nkrumah discarded the independence constitution. Exploiting ethnic tensions among Ashante groups, where an emerging opposition to his rule was concentrated, he promulgated a new republican constitution, removing the country from the British Commonwealth. A year later, he turned to socialist state planning, similar to that of Egypt and India.

The construction of a massive hydroelectric dam on the Volta River, begun in 1961, was supposed to be the starting point of a heavy industrialization program, including aluminum, steel, glass, and consumer goods factories. But the country soon ran into financing problems, since prices for cocoa, the main export commodity, were declining on the world market and large foreign loans were required to continue the program. On the political front, Nkrumah in 1964 amended the constitution again, making Ghana a one-party state with Nkrumah himself as leader for life. An unmanageable foreign debt eventually stalled development, and an army coup, supported by the CIA in the name of Cold War anti-communism, ousted Nkrumah in 1966.

Resistance to Independence in Kenya   In some regions of Africa, particularly in Kenya, decolonization was not achieved as easily as in Ghana. Efforts to terminate British colonialism were advanced by Jomo Kenyatta (1894–1978), who founded the Kenya African National Union earlier in the 1940s. Interrupted by the war, Kenyatta's movement gathered momentum after the liberation of Ghana in 1957. But this was met with resistance by British settlers who had established profitable agricultural plantations earlier in the twentieth century, and who were therefore reluctant to relinquish control of their economic and political interests. In the face of British opposition, the African nationalists formed the Mau Mau movement, which resorted to terrorist attacks on British estates to achieve their ends. Finally, independence was granted Kenya in 1963, and in the following year Kenyatta was named as the first president of the newly created republic.

The Struggle for the Congo's Independence   Among the large group of sub-Saharan colonies achieving independence between 1957 and 1960, the Belgian Congo is an important case study because, like Vietnam, it became a battleground of the Cold War. The Belgian Congo had been under the authority of the Belgian government since the beginning of the twentieth century, when it took over from the king (see Chapter 27). During the interwar period, concession companies invested in mining, especially in the southern and central provinces of Katanga and Kisaï, where huge deposits of copper, cobalt, iron, uranium, and diamonds were discovered. Little money went into human development until after World War II, when Catholic mission schools, with state support, expanded the health and the primary school systems. The urban and mine workforce expanded considerably, but no commercial or professional middle classes existed.

Serious demands for independence arose in the Congo only after Ghana became independent in 1957. Several groups of nationalists, some advocating a federation and others a centralized state, competed with each other. The urban and mine worker–based National Congolese Movement (*Mouvement National Congolais*, MNC), founded in 1958 by the former postal clerk and salesman Patrice Lumumba (1925–1961), was the most popular group, favoring a centralized constitutional nationalism that transcended ethnicity, language, and religion. After riots in 1959 and the arrest of Lumumba, accused of stirring up the riots, Belgian authorities decided to act quickly so as not to lose control over events: They needed compliant nationalists who would continue existing economic arrangements. A Brussels conference with all nationalists—including Lumumba, freed from prison—decided to hold local and national elections in early 1960. To the dismay of Belgium, the centralists, led by Lumumba, won. On June 30, 1960, the Congo became independent, with Lumumba as prime minister and the federalist Joseph Kasa-Vubu (ca. 1910–1969) from Katanga as president.

Lumumba's first political act was the announcement of a general pay raise for state employees, which the Belgian army commander undermined by spreading a rumor that the Congolese foot soldiers would be left out. Outraged, the soldiers mutinied, and amid a general breakdown of public order, Katanga declared its independence. Lumumba fired the Belgian officers, but to restore order he turned to the United Nations. Order was indeed restored by the United Nations, but Belgium made sure that Katanga did not rejoin the Congo. To force Katanga, Lumumba turned for support to the Soviet Union, which airlifted advisors and equipment into the country. The Cold War had arrived in Africa.

Kasa-Vubu and Lumumba dismissed each other from the government on September 5, giving the new Congolese army chief, Mobutu Sese Seko (1930–1997), the opportunity to seize power on September 14. Mobutu was a soldier turned journalist and member of the MNC whom Lumumba had appointed as army chief, even though it was general knowledge that he was in the pay of the Belgians and the CIA. (Mobutu went on to become the dictator of the Congo, renamed Zaire, and was a close ally of the United States during the period he held power, 1965–1996.) He promptly had Lumumba arrested. Eventually, Belgian agents took Lumumba to Katanga, where they executed him on January 17, 1961.

At that time, as it is now known from documentary investigations in the 1990s, the Belgian government and the Eisenhower White House were convinced that Lumumba was another Castro in the making, a nationalist who would soon become a communist, influenced by Khrushchev's charm offensive among the African nationalists about to achieve independence. In the Cold War between the United States and the Soviet Union, the fierce but inexperienced Lumumba was given no chance by the Belgian and American governments acting with mutual consultation. At all costs, the Congo had to remain in the Western camp as a strategic, mineral-rich linchpin in central Africa.

Putting It All Together

Rapid, dizzying change characterized the pattern of modernity as it unfolded in the middle of the twentieth century. After only 150 years of constitutionalism and industry, 75 years of worldwide imperialism, and 15 years of a three-sided competition among the modernist ideologies of capitalist democracy, communism, and supremacist nationalism, the world changed drastically once more. An intense Cold War competition between the proponents of the ideologies of capitalist democracy and communism ensued. Imperialism and colonialism collapsed within a mere 17 years. And nearly 200 nations came to share the globe in the United Nations. Compared to the slow pace of change in the agrarian–urban period of world history for 5,300 years, the speed of development during just 145 years of scientific–industrial modernity was dizzying.

Perhaps the most noteworthy series of events characterizing the 17 years of the early and intense Cold War between capitalist democracy and communism in 1945–1962 was the sad fate of many countries as they emerged into independence or as they struggled to accommodate themselves as best they could in the Western camp, Eastern Bloc, or Non-Aligned Movement. As we have seen in this chapter, US and Soviet leaders were ruthless wherever they perceived communist or capitalist influence in their ranks. But even when new nations pursued a policy of nonalignment, there were subtler ways through which both West and East could apply financial pressures with devastating consequences: Egypt lost its finances for the Aswan Dam, and China lost its Soviet advisors during the Great Leap Forward.

Not that capitalist democracy and communism were on the same plane: The former, even if it did not readily offer meaning or equality to its adherents, provided greater political participation than the latter, which paid only lip service to its notions of equality, as became obvious in 1989. But the period of the early, active Cold War and decolonization from 1945 to 1962 was far less brutal than the preceding interwar period. Although several confrontations between East and West were hot, and nuclear war on one occasion posed a serious threat, humanity was spared the cataclysms of World War III.

▶ For additional resources, including maps, primary sources, visuals, and quizzes, please go to www.oup.com/us/vonsivers. Please see the Further Resources section at the back of the book for additional readings and suggested websites.

Against the Grain

Postwar Counterculture

Postwar Europe and North America during the 1950s embarked on programs of reconstruction, reflecting a yearning for normalcy following years of deprivation and hardship. Central to this agenda was a mood of conservatism and traditionalism. In America, however, fear of socialism and communism amid Cold War tensions generated a new element, provoked by fear of left-wing socialism and communism. Crackdowns on suspicious groups by the House Committee on Un-American Activities promoted a prevailing trend toward conformity with traditional Western social and cultural values.

Not everyone fell in line with this trend. The early 1950s witnessed the emergence of a countercultural movement known as the "Beat Generation," initiated by a group of writers and students affiliated with Columbia University. Finding prevailing conformity and uniformity stultifying and restrictive, Jack Kerouac, Allen Ginsberg, William Burroughs, and others sought new avenues of nonconformist expression, including experimentation with addictive drugs, alternative sexuality, and a fascination with Eastern religions—especially Buddhism—and music. Ginsberg's *Howl and Other Poems* (1956), an indictment of traditional societal and cultural norms, represents the earliest expression of the Beat ethic. *Howl* was followed by Kerouac's *On the Road* (1957); drawn from a series of road trips around America, the work expresses the emptiness of current culture.

Interestingly, Beats roamed the globe in quest of non-Western intellectual inspiration. Kerouac, Burroughs, and Ginsberg traveled widely; Ginsberg's visits to India introduced him to Eastern religions, particularly Buddhism and Krishnaism. In turn, Beat culture transcended American borders, and was assimilated into countercultural movements in Vienna, Prague, Istanbul, and Tokyo. Among the more telling instances of Beat influence abroad was John Lennon's meeting with a Beat poet in 1960, which resulted in changing the spelling of his famous rock group from "Beetles" to "Beatles."

The Beat Generation nurtured the emergence of later countercultures, including the hippies of the 1960s. Whereas the Beats simply explored alternative lifestyles, later exemplars were more motivated by, and interested in, political expressions. Their reach even extended to musical expressions of the 1960s; Bob Dylan, Jim Morrison, and the Beatles are among their many devotees.

- **What did the Beat Generation find so offensive and alienating about America during the postwar era of the 1950s?**

- **How does the Beat countercultural movement following World War II compare with expressions of the Lost Generation in the aftermath of World War I?**

Thinking Through Patterns

▶ **Why did the pattern of unfolding modernity, which offered three choices after World War I, shrink to just capitalist democracy and socialism–communism in 1945? How did each of these two patterns evolve between 1945 and 1962?**

The pattern of modernity evolved in the nineteenth century with four major ingredients: constitutional nationalism, ethnic–linguistic–religious nationalism, industrialism, and communism. However, traditional institutions such as monarchies and empires from times prior to 1800 continued to flourish. World War I wiped out most monarchies, but capitalist democracy continued, communism came into its own in the Soviet Union, imperialism and colonialism survived, and supremacist nationalism attracted all those who found democracy and communism wanting. World War II eliminated supremacist nationalism and, after a delay of 17 years, also imperialism and colonialism. The remaining choices of capitalist democracy and communism were divided between two power blocs, which during the early Cold War period of 1945–1962 shared the world almost evenly among themselves.

Modernity grew out of the philosophy of the New Sciences in the 1600s, with its assumptions of materialism and the social contract. After acquiring mass support, modernity with its twin ideologies of constitutional nationalism and industrialism evolved into scientific–industrial modernity, with profound cultural consequences. On the one hand, waves of increasingly modern artistic movements appeared, from early-nineteenth-century romanticism to mid-twentieth-century existentialism. On the other hand, these consecutive waves of newness were insufficient to address the basic materialist flaw of modernity, which in each generation gave rise to the question of the meaning of it all. Did a modern world of rampant consumerism and gaping social inequities have intrinsic meaning even if people continued to find thrilling possibilities in material and intellectual–artistic life? The question still haunts us today.

▶ **What are the cultural premises of modernity?**

▶ **How did the newly independent countries of the Middle East, Asia, and Africa adapt to the divided world of the Cold War?**

During 1945–1962 the number of nations on earth quadrupled to total (in 2011) approximately 200. The new nations, emerging from colonialism, were in theory, like the older nations of early modernity in the nineteenth century, countries with ethnic–linguistic–religious cores and functioning constitutional institutions. In fact, many were not. Since most, furthermore, were still overwhelmingly agrarian, industrialism was beyond reach. With great hope, the ruling elites in a number of large new nations embraced a mixed capitalist–democratic and socialist regime, with heavy state investments in basic industries. However, in contrast to Stalin, who introduced these types of investments under the label of state-guided socialism, none of the elites in the new nations had the will to collect the money for these investments from their rural population. Instead, they borrowed heavily from the capitalist–democratic countries. True independence remained elusive.

Chapter 30 1963–1991

The End of the Cold War, Western Social Transformation, and the Developing World

North America   Europe   Asia

Africa

South America

Australia

THE WORLD, 1963–1991

As the helicopter slowly approached the snow-capped mountain, the fighter on the ground recognized it immediately: *Shaitan Arba*— "Satan's Chariot," the Soviet MI-5 "Hind" attack helicopter. This new, heavily armed and armored helicopter gunship had proven largely impervious to the rifle and small arms fire with which the fighter and his *mujahideen* Afghan warriors vainly attempted to bring it down. Worse still, it carried a devastating array of rockets and machine cannon; the fighter had seen these gunships wipe out entire squads of his comrades. In this desperate fight in the Afghan high country, the Soviets, it appeared, had acquired a decisive technological edge as they sought to eliminate resistance to the client regime they had installed in the capital of Kabul in 1979.

But just before the soldier took cover, the helicopter exploded in a red and orange fireball, plummeting swiftly into the mountainside. A rapidly dissolving vapor trail marked a spot about 200 meters away from where it appeared a rocket had been fired. A small group of men shouted "God is great!" and cheered lustily at their victory.

ABOVE: Afghan Mujahideen soldiers, battling the Soviet invasion, celebrate the downing of a Russian helicopter in January 1980.

Similar scenes were repeated more than 300 times during the coming years. The weapon that had downed the helicopter was a new American "Stinger" shoulder-fired missile, which the United States was clandestinely supplying to the Afghan Muslim fighters attempting to expel the Soviet occupying forces. Perhaps more than any other weapon, the Stinger neutralized the Soviet technological advantage in airpower and enabled an international force of mujahideen to ultimately push the Soviets out of Afghanistan in this last contest of the Cold War, in much the same way that the United States had been forced from South Vietnam. In fact, as we will see in more detail in this chapter, the immense cost of the Soviet–Afghan War, added to the even higher price of trying to match the American effort to create a missile defense system against intercontinental ballistic missiles (ICBMs), contributed to the collapse of the Soviet economy by the end of the 1980s and led to the end of the Eastern Bloc and the Soviet Union itself. It thus appeared that the West and its version of modernity—capitalist democracy—had convincingly won both the physical and ideological contests of the Cold War.

In this chapter we will trace the progress of this struggle and the immense social changes associated with the period from 1963 to 1991 in the West and the progress of the struggle in the developing world. Although the end result was an apparent victory for democracy and capitalism—both of which were to be introduced into the successor states of the Soviet Union in the 1990s—the contest in the developing world was still active. From the triumph of Muslim resistance to the secular communist vision of modernity in Afghanistan would emerge a new global movement of resistance to the secular West and democratic capitalism: al-Qaeda and its affiliates.

The Climax of the Cold War

The Cold War continued into the 1980s when the power of the Soviet Union began to ebb. During the 1960s, despite the enactment of the Nuclear Test Ban Treaty, the United States and the Soviet Union remained bitter ideological enemies. The Soviet Union and the People's Republic of China both sent aid to Ho Chi Minh's forces fighting the Americans in Vietnam. The Soviets also supported the Arab efforts against US-backed Israel in 1967 and 1973. Moreover, both sides upgraded and expanded their nuclear arsenals. Despite this continuing hostility, the late 1960s and early 1970s also witnessed the era of *détente*: a downplaying of overt aggression toward one another and the pursuit of competition through diplomatic, social, and cultural means. The Soviet invasion of Afghanistan in 1979, however, ushered in a final phase of both openly hostile competition and covert warfare. In the end, the Soviet Union's resources were simply not sufficient to outlast those of the West in the struggle.

Seeing Patterns

▶ How did the political landscape of the Cold War change from 1963 to 1991?

▶ Why did such radically different lifestyles emerge in the United States and the West during the 1960s and 1970s? What is their legacy today?

▶ Why did some nations that had emerged from colonialism and war make great strides in their development while others seemed to stagnate?

Chapter Outline

- The Climax of the Cold War

- Transforming the West

- From "Underdeveloped" to "Developing" World, 1963–1991

- Putting It All Together

The Soviet Superpower in Slow Decline

In 1963, only a few months after the Cuban Missile Crisis, it still appeared that the Soviet Union was an adversary more or less equal to the United States. Indeed, in many respects, it seemed to have the momentum of history on its side. Yet, in less than 30 years the Soviet Union would fall apart, to be replaced by its core political unit of Russia and a host of newly independent former Soviet republics. What set this unexpected course of events in motion?

From the Brink of War to Détente   Nikita S. Khrushchev had cultivated a down-to-earth image that contributed to his popularity in the Soviet Union and, to some extent, on the international stage. But his initial success in rolling back some of the worst abuses of Stalinism had been overshadowed by three failures during the early 1960s. The first was allowing the Sino–Soviet split of 1960 to become a complete break. Moreover, Khrushchev's building of the Berlin Wall, though largely effective in its immediate objective of stopping the flood of refugees from East Berlin, had been a propaganda failure. His American counterpart, the youthful, charismatic president John F. Kennedy (in office 1961–1963), had rallied world opposition to the wall when he proclaimed, "Ich bin ein Berliner" ("I am a Berliner").

But Khrushchev's key blunder had been in appearing to back down during the Cuban Missile Crisis in October 1962. Seeking to test the resolve of the young American president by installing nuclear missiles on America's doorstep, the premier instead was forced to dismantle Soviet bases in Cuba. Though the United States also agreed to the face-saving gesture of dismantling its own medium-range missiles in Turkey, the Soviet Politburo shortly acted to oust Khrushchev, who duly resigned in October 1964.

The years of Leonid Brezhnev (in office 1960–1964; 1977–1982) were marked by actions demonstrating just how shaken the Soviet Union and United States were by how close they had come to all-out nuclear war in October 1962. One way that this danger had been partially defused was by the Nuclear Test Ban Treaty, signed in October 1963. Alert to the toxic effects of nuclear fallout and the possibility that tests may raise false alarms about attacks, the signatories agreed to abandon all aboveground nuclear testing. Nonnuclear nations were severely discouraged from developing their own weapons in subsequent "nonproliferation" treaties. Additional safeguards were built into the detection and early warning systems both sides used as part of missile defense. Finally, a hotline—a direct telephone link between the White House and the Kremlin—was created so that American and Soviet leaders could alert each other if an accident or false attack signal had been issued. Nonetheless, the mood of the 1960s remained one of nuclear tension on both sides, and American popular culture was rife with doomsday fantasies of the catastrophic effects of nuclear war.

By the late 1960s, the United States and the Soviet Union had entered into a period of relatively tranquil relations often referred to by historians as "**détente**," from the French term for "release of tension." However, for the Soviets, tensions were mounting with the People's Republic of China over disputed borders along the Amur River and the rising chaos of the Cultural Revolution. At several points, military engagements took place, and at least once, the Americans were approached by the Soviets about the possibility of a preemptive nuclear strike against China.

Détente. Following closer diplomatic contact between the United States and the Soviet Union in the wake of the Arab–Israeli War in the beginning of June 1967, President Lyndon Johnson and Soviet Premier Andrei Gromyko met at Glassboro State College (now Rowan University). The talks centered around the US position in Vietnam and the possibility of opening talks on lessening nuclear tensions. Here, President Johnson and Premier Gromyko are engaged in a frank discussion.

The era of détente abruptly ended in the fall of 1973, however, with the Egyptian and Syrian surprise attack on Israel, which coincided with both the Jewish holy day of Yom Kippur and the Muslim month of Ramadan and sparked the largest Arab–Israeli conflict to date. The Soviets actively supported the boycott by the largely Arab Organization of the Petroleum Exporting Countries (OPEC) of oil shipments to the United States during the mid-1970s and resumed support for North Vietnam's final drive to conquer South Vietnam after the American withdrawal in 1973.

"Prague Spring" in Czechoslovakia and "Solidarity" in Poland   The Brezhnev years were also marked by increasing dissent, both in the Soviet Union and, even more markedly, in its Eastern European client states (see Map 30.1). Since the uprising in Hungary in 1956, for example, government efforts to stifle dissent and reform had been increasingly difficult and threatened to stir up latent nationalistic feeling. One result was the evolution under János Kádár (in office 1956–1988), the Hungarian party secretary, of what came to be called "goulash communism": a relatively relaxed attitude toward criticism of the regime, the introduction of limited market reforms, some attention to consumer demands, and limited trade with the West.

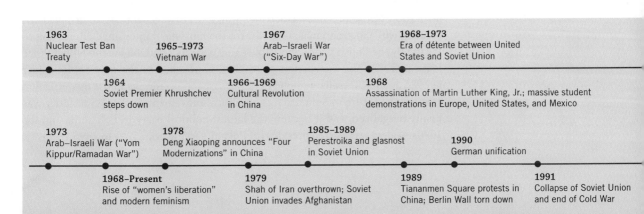

1963 Nuclear Test Ban Treaty	1965–1973 Vietnam War	1967 Arab–Israeli War ("Six-Day War")	1968–1973 Era of détente between United States and Soviet Union
	1964 Soviet Premier Khrushchev steps down	1966–1969 Cultural Revolution in China	1968 Assassination of Martin Luther King, Jr.; massive student demonstrations in Europe, United States, and Mexico

1973 Arab–Israeli War ("Yom Kippur/Ramadan War")	1978 Deng Xiaoping announces "Four Modernizations" in China	1985–1989 Perestroika and glasnost in Soviet Union	1990 German unification	
	1968–Present Rise of "women's liberation" and modern feminism	1979 Shah of Iran overthrown; Soviet Union invades Afghanistan	1989 Tiananmen Square protests in China; Berlin Wall torn down	1991 Collapse of Soviet Union and end of Cold War

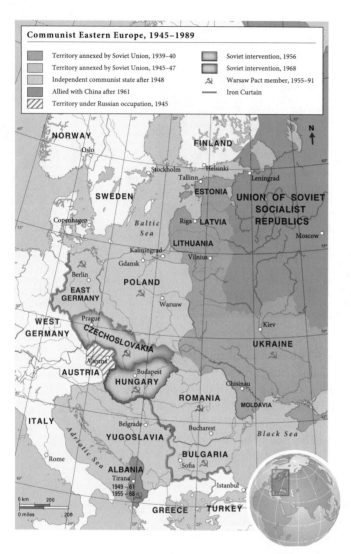

Communist Eastern Europe, 1945–1989

Territory annexed by Soviet Union, 1939–40	Soviet intervention, 1956
Territory annexed by Soviet Union, 1945–47	Soviet intervention, 1968
Independent communist state after 1948	Warsaw Pact member, 1955–91
Allied with China after 1961	Iron Curtain
Territory under Russian occupation, 1945	

MAP **30.1 Communist Eastern Europe, 1945–1989.**

In 1968, dissent took a more direct course in Czechoslovakia, in what came to be called the "Prague Spring." With the rise to power of Alexander Dubček (in office 1968–1969) in January 1968, a sweeping set of reforms, more extensive than those by Kádár in Hungary, was introduced. There were calls for a new decentralized administrative structure, relaxation of censorship, free speech, and opposition political parties. An atmosphere of excitement and expectation prevailed in the capital of Prague. Brezhnev's government, however, saw this as evidence of the Czechoslovak Communist Party's power slipping and entered into negotiations in order to bring the country back into line. By August, as the push for reform became more persistent, the Soviets sent Warsaw Pact forces into Czechoslovakia, where they ousted Dubček, installed Gustáv Husák (1913–1991), and dismantled the reforms of the previous 7 months. The Soviet move demonstrated what became known as the "Brezhnev Doctrine"—the right of the Soviets and Warsaw Pact to forcibly restrain any member country attempting to abandon socialism and the alliance with the Soviet Union.

With the shadow cast by the Brezhnev Doctrine, dissent once again went underground. In 1980, however, it reemerged in Poland with a strike by electrical workers at the Lenin Shipyard in Gdansk, which quickly spread to other port cities. A labor union was formed called "Solidarity," led by an electrician named Lech Walesa (b. 1943), which called for an end to censorship, the lifting of economic restrictions, and the right of workers to organize outside of the Communist Party. Despite arrests and government threats, by the end of 1980 one-fourth of Poland's population had joined the movement, including 80 percent of the country's workers.

The Polish government declared martial law in an attempt to stave off a Soviet invocation of the Brezhnev Doctrine. Still, a massive general strike crippled the country, while international sympathy for the movement intensified after a visit to Poland by the Polish pope John Paul II and Walesa's selection for the Nobel Peace Prize in 1983. The installation of Mikhail Gorbachev as the new Soviet leader in 1985 and his liberalizing policies of *glasnost* and *perestroika* in the Soviet Union ensured the future of Solidarity as a political movement. In 1989 Solidarity was finally relegalized, and it became the largest political party in Poland during the 1990s. Walesa was elected president of Poland, serving from 1991 to 1995.

The 1980s: Afghanistan and "Star Wars"   Despite the tensions following the collapse of détente and the Brezhnev Doctrine, some genuine progress on strategic arms limitation was achieved between the superpowers. The progress was motivated in part by the concept of "mutually assured destruction," which meant that nobody would "win" in an all-out atomic war. During the SALT II talks from 1977 to 1979, a historic agreement was reached in 1979 that would, for the first time, require the United States and the Soviet Union to limit certain types of nuclear weapons and begin a process of actually reducing them—a process that would later be known as START (Strategic Arms Reduction Talks/Treaty).

Much of the sense of progress achieved by this breakthrough was checked, however, by the Soviet invasion of Afghanistan in December 1979. The Egyptian–Israeli peace treaty of 1979 and the tilting of Saudi Arabia and Iraq toward the United States had altered the Middle Eastern landscape radically in favor of the West. Fearful of a weak, nominally communist Afghan government on its flank, adjacent to pro-American Pakistan and a China that appeared to have shifted toward the United States, the Soviets launched a swift coup in Afghanistan and installed a communist leader with a massive military force to back him up. The Soviets were immediately subjected to international condemnation, and the United States boycotted the 1980 Summer Olympics, which took place in Moscow.

At the same time, the new administration of President Ronald Reagan (in office 1981–1989) in the United States sought a more assertive policy toward the Soviet Union. The administration felt that the previous president, Jimmy Carter (in office 1977–1981), had been somewhat soft in response to both the Iranian taking of American hostages and the Soviet invasion of Afghanistan. At the same time, technological breakthroughs in computers and satellite communications made it theoretically possible for the United States to create an antiballistic missile system in outer space. Such a system was in violation of the antiballistic missile provisions of the 1969 SALT I accords, but the advantages of having a reliable missile defense in space—while at the same time retaining "first strike capability"—were overwhelming to American defense planners. Thus, over Soviet protests, the United States began to develop its Strategic Defense Initiative (SDI), nicknamed "Star Wars" after the popular movie of the same name.

From the mid-1980s, both superpowers thus began an enormously expensive strategic arms development race. For the Soviets, however, the drain of this new arms race, combined with the increasingly costly and unpopular war in Afghanistan, was simply unsustainable.

Glasnost and Perestroika   The death of Leonid Brezhnev in 1982 ushered in two short-lived successors before the relatively young Mikhail Gorbachev (b. 1931) took office as general secretary in the Politburo in 1985. Faced with growing dissent in Poland and other Eastern Bloc countries, an increasingly inefficient economy (the problems of which seemed to be highlighted by successful Chinese experiments with market economics), the endless war in Afghanistan,

Lech Walesa and Solidarity.
The strike at the Gdansk shipyard in Poland in 1980 brought to the fore an obscure electrician but able leader named Lech Walesa. Here, he is shown at a 1981 meeting of the organization he helped found, Solidarity, which ultimately helped topple Poland's communist government. Walesa himself went on to win the Nobel Peace Prize and was elected president of Poland in 1990.

and now the expensive arms race with the United States, Gorbachev called for large-scale structural reforms in the Soviet system.

Up until the 1980s, the Soviet economy had functioned as a giant economic command pyramid. Some 100 ministries in Moscow and 800 in the provinces oversaw some 50,000 enterprises, which produced some 24 million individual products. An army of ministerial bureaucrats oversaw every detail of the production and distribution process. The bureaucrats could never count on accurate figures, however, since both workers and managers had every incentive to overreport production figures and manufacture shoddy consumer goods as cheaply as possible. Periodic shortages were inevitable. As the saying on factory floors went, "They pretend to pay us and we pretend to work."

By the mid-1980s, however, Soviet planners had realized that their command system was delivering diminishing returns. Overall growth rates—in the 1950s and 1960s hovering around an impressive 10 percent—had declined to 3 percent. Several factors were responsible for the decline: fewer people were working in the factories; a lack of investment in new technologies and labor-saving machinery meant that factories were becoming less productive; and the percentage of people over 60 years of age had doubled between World War II and the mid-1980s, requiring the labor force to support more and more retirees.

Two years after becoming secretary of the Politburo in 1985, Gorbachev launched his two trademark economic and political programs, "restructuring" (**perestroika**) and "openness" (**glasnost**), which were intended to revitalize communism. Restructuring entailed the partial dismantling of the command economy. Freed to some degree from the planners' oversight, managers could sell up to one-third of what their factories produced on the market, instead of delivering everything to the state. Citizens were free to establish "cooperatives," the communist euphemism for private business enterprises. By the end of the 1980s, the law permitted co-ops in practically all branches of the economy. Gorbachev promoted the new mixed command and market economy as a "socialist" or "regulated" system, advertising it as the same order once pursued by Lenin (then called the New Economic Policy, or NEP).

In practice, perestroika did not work out as intended. Market production rose to a meager 5 percent of total production. Many managers were stuck with the manufacture of unprofitable goods, such as soap, toothpaste, matches, and children's clothes. Consumers complained about continued or even worse shortages in the stores. Other managers, eager to increase production, granted irresponsible wage increases to their workers as incentives. People of modest means established small businesses, charging outrageous prices and evading payment of taxes. Support structures for the co-ops, such as credit, banking, contract law, wholesale distribution centers, and wage bargaining mechanisms, were lacking. Gorbachev's measures, therefore, did little to end the stagnation of state factories and encouraged the rise of wild "carpetbagger" capitalism.

Parallel to economic restructuring, Gorbachev introduced political "openness," or glasnost. The catalyst for glasnost was the nuclear accident at Chernobyl in the Ukraine in April 1986. When it was impossible to conceal the magnitude of the disaster, reporting in the media became remarkably frank. This openness quickly extended to other hitherto suppressed topics. Gorbachev's glasnost was supposed to produce a "socialist pluralism," but the unintended result was a more

Perestroika: "Restructuring" of the Soviet bureaucracy and economic structure in an attempt to make it more efficient and responsive to market demand.

Glasnost: "Openness"; an attempt to loosen restrictions on media in the Soviet Union with an aim at more accurate reporting of events and the creation of "socialist pluralism."

spontaneous pluralism, reducing communism to just one of many competing ideologies in the rapidly evolving Soviet political scene.

Transformations in the Soviet Bloc   The countries of the Soviet Bloc, which were not oil producers, had borrowed heavily from the West in the 1970s and early 1980s for their costly oil imports and the renewal of their industrial base. Others borrowed to build oil and gas pipelines from Russia via their territories to Western Europe. But the oil price collapse of 1985–1986 forced all Soviet Bloc countries to reschedule their debts and cut their budgets, especially expenditures for their social safety nets and subsidies for basic consumer goods. Popular protests against these cuts in 1989 and 1990 in Poland, Hungary, and Czechoslovakia were accompanied by demands for power sharing.

As a result, dramatic and successful establishments of independent governments took place in Poland and Czechoslovakia. Yielding to increasing pressure, in 1989 the Communist Party in Poland permitted the first free elections in over 40 years, in which Solidarity won a landslide victory. Secure in its electoral majority, Solidarity formed a new coalition government, in which communists were a minority. When no reprisals from Moscow were forthcoming, Lech Walesa was elected Poland's president in 1990, a precedent which unleashed a wave of independence movements in the Soviet Bloc. In Czechoslovakia massive demonstrations in Prague and other cities toppled the ruling communist regime of President Husák in 1989 without bloodshed (the so-called Velvet Revolution). In its place, a coalition government consisting of the Party and members of the noncommunist Civic Forum was established. Its interim president was Vaclav [VATS-lav] Havel (1936–2011), a popular writer and dissident; in 1990 Havel was officially named president.

In the German Democratic Republic (GDR, East Germany), a particularly dramatic shift occurred. East Germans, after their summer vacations at the Black Sea in 1989, refused to return home, gathering instead at the Hungarian-Austrian border in hopes of being permitted to leave. Hungary, at that moment pursuing its own reforms, let the vacationers cross the border. Back in the GDR, massive demonstrations led to the fall first of the communist government and then of the Berlin Wall on the night of November 9, 1989. A year later, with Gorbachev's blessing, the two Germanys united, ending nearly a half century of division.

> "We were walled in, things were kept away from us, we were lied to. And then, all of a sudden, we realized things could also be done or organized differently, and that's when it all began, when we began to rethink everything . . ."
>
> —former East German factory worker, describing the events of 1989

Communist governments now fell in other Soviet Bloc countries as well (see Map 30.2). The governments of the Baltic states of Estonia, Latvia, and Lithuania, as well as that of Bulgaria, gave way more or less voluntarily to democracy. Albania followed suit in 1992. The only exception was Romania, where Nicolae Ceaușescu [chow-SHESS-coo] (in office 1974–1989) had built a strong personality cult and had put family members into key party and government offices. The botched eviction by the police of a Hungarian-minority Protestant pastor from his parish in western Romania in November 1989 resulted in scores of deaths. Following a mass demonstration in Bucharest protesting the deaths, portions of the army defected and arrested the fleeing Ceaușescu and his wife, Elena. Army elements assembled a tribunal, sentenced the two to death, and executed them summarily on

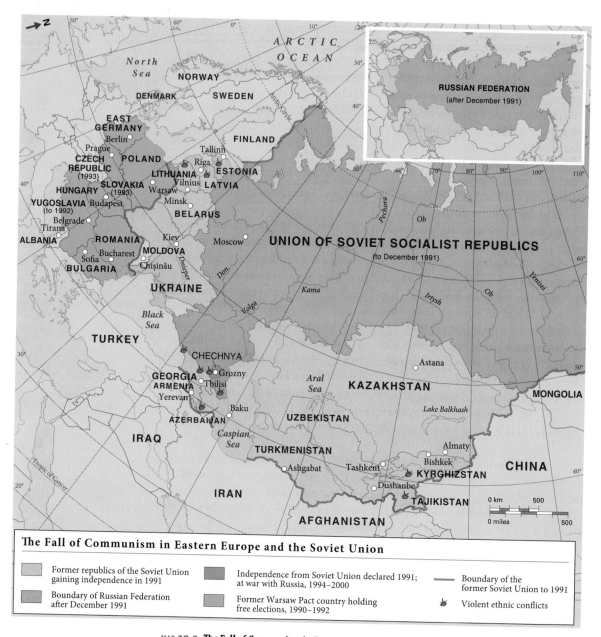

The Fall of Communism in Eastern Europe and the Soviet Union

Former republics of the Soviet Union gaining independence in 1991

Independence from Soviet Union declared 1991; at war with Russia, 1994–2000

Boundary of the former Soviet Union to 1991

Boundary of Russian Federation after December 1991

Former Warsaw Pact country holding free elections, 1990–1992

Violent ethnic conflicts

MAP 30.2 **The Fall of Communism in Eastern Europe and the Soviet Union.**

December 25, 1989. Subsequently, however, the army and the Communist Party reconciled, and the country returned to a dictatorship. It was not until 1996 that Romania adopted a democratic system.

The dissolution of communism in the Eastern Bloc eventually caught up with the 15 states making up the Soviet Union, most of which declared their sovereignty or independence in 1990. After arduous negotiations, Gorbachev agreed with President Boris Yeltsin and the other state presidents to a new federal union treaty for the Soviet Union in spring 1991, to be signed in August. This treaty triggered an abortive plot by eight communist hardliners who briefly succeeded in arresting Gorbachev as he was vacationing for a few days in his dacha on the Black Sea. The conspirators, however, showed their ineptitude by failing to arrest Yeltsin. In a tense showdown with troops sent to occupy the Russian parliament, Yeltsin and a large crowd of Muscovites forced the hardliners to relent. Officially, the Soviet Union ended on Christmas Day, 1991, replaced by the Commonwealth of Independent States with a democratic Russia under Yeltsin at its center.

Transforming the West

While North America and Western Europe enjoyed impressive growth and social change from the late 1940s through the early 1960s, scholars of popular culture have singled out the period from 1963 through the early 1970s as particularly dynamic. Social movements such as the African American civil rights movement in the United States moved to the center of the national agenda; the movements for equal rights for women and other historically marginalized groups also rose in prominence. Nearly all of these movements involved peaceful protests and civil disobedience, some borrowing directly from the strategies and philosophy of Gandhi and the powerful actions of Dr. Martin Luther King, Jr. Some, however, advocated violent confrontation.

Civil Rights Movements

The massive mobilization of Americans during World War II accelerated civil rights efforts. Vast numbers of African Americans serving in the armed forces, along with professed US and Allied repugnance regarding Nazi racial policies, made segregation in the military increasingly untenable. In 1947, therefore, President Truman signed an executive order desegregating the American armed forces. In 1954, the Supreme Court reversed its earlier stand on segregation in education in the momentous *Brown v. Board of Education* ruling. Overturning the 1896 *Plessy v. Ferguson* decision that "separate but equal" facilities were constitutional, the court now ruled that the separate facilities were by definition not equal. Schools were therefore ordered to desegregate "with all deliberate speed." This met with determined resistance in many communities; in 1957, President Dwight D. Eisenhower (in office 1953–1961) was compelled to deploy US Army troops to Little Rock, Arkansas, to enforce the ruling. Still, by the early 1960s there was a dramatic movement under way for civil rights and equal treatment for African Americans in the American south.

The Civil Rights Struggle. The career of the charismatic minister Dr. Martin Luther King, Jr., was launched during the 1955 Montgomery, Alabama, bus boycott. By the early 1960s he had emerged as America's preeminent civil rights leader. Here, he is shown at the peak of his influence, delivering his famous "I Have a Dream" speech on the Mall in Washington, DC, in August 1963.

The Postwar Drive for Civil Rights   The movement for desegregation was prompted by a domestic sense of urgency as well as international conditions. Postwar anticolonialism, particularly in Africa, where former European colonies secured their independence, had a powerful influence on the American civil rights movement. The Cold War also played a vital role, as Soviet propaganda had exploited the discrepancies between American claims of freedom and equality and its treatment of African Americans. Desegregation and guaranteeing civil rights would render that Soviet argument obsolete. Finally, when participants in civil rights marches and protests were brutally attacked by private citizens as well as law enforcement in some cities in the early 1960s, President John F. Kennedy reacted by sponsoring civil rights legislation to end discrimination.

> "I have a dream that one day this nation will rise up and live out the true meaning of its creed: 'We hold these truths to be self-evident; that all men are created equal.'"
>
> —Martin Luther King, Jr.

A high point of the civil rights movement occurred in August 1963 when the Reverend Martin Luther King, Jr. (1929–1968) delivered his electrifying "I Have a Dream" speech before a huge crowd at the Lincoln Memorial in Washington, DC.

After the assassination of Kennedy in November, his successor, Lyndon B. Johnson (in office 1963–1969), secured the passage of the Civil Rights Act of 1964, which provided significant protections for African Americans, including the prohibition of segregation in public places. This was followed by the 1965 Voting Rights Act, aimed at outlawing the poll taxes, literacy tests, and other means by which states attempted to limit their citizens' ability to vote. With legal remedies now in place for past discrimination, civil rights leaders increasingly turned their attention to economic and social justice. The Johnson administration program called "The Great Society" was aimed at eliminating poverty in America. Civil rights advocates lobbied for jobs, educational opportunities, and poverty-relief programs for their constituents.

Civil Rights for Native Americans   Native American activists in the 1960s and 1970s campaigned for social justice and to rectify previous abuses, including past treaty violations. Begun in Minneapolis in 1968, the American Indian Movement (AIM) initiated actions to end police mistreatment and harassment and advocate for better housing and other issues. In 1972, after a cross-country protest march, AIM activists occupied the Bureau of Indian Affairs offices in Washington, DC, to publicize a list of demands for change. In the following year armed AIM members laid siege to Wounded Knee, South Dakota, to commemorate the massacre of hundreds of Native Americans in 1890. After a 71-day standoff with federal troops, several AIM leaders were charged with numerous violations of federal laws; a negotiated settlement was finally reached when these charges were dismissed. The end result, however, was improved conditions for Native Americans.

Women's Rights and the Sexual Revolution   The success of the civil rights and antiwar movements encouraged the movement for women's rights. While the suffragist movement during World War I had led to voting rights for women in both Great Britain and the United States, the more sweeping social changes brought on by World War II and the Cold War advanced the movement for equality in gender relations further. A leading voice was that of Simone de Beauvoir (1908–1986), whose work *The Second Sex* (1949) challenged women to take more self-assertive actions in order to gain full equality with their male counterparts. De Beauvoir and other influential feminists also contributed to the so-called sexual revolution of the 1960s. European and American women now openly demanded an end to restrictions placed upon their reproductive and sexual freedoms. Laws prohibiting contraception and abortion were overturned in several Western countries during the 1960s and 1970s. The development and widespread use of oral contraceptives became commonplace, and the 1973 Supreme Court decision *Roe v. Wade* protected a woman's right to have an abortion. The loosening of postwar moral standards, along with relaxed censorship in the media as well as an increased emphasis on sex and eroticism in popular culture, also played a part in new attitudes toward female sexuality. By the late 1960s, the "women's liberation" movement worked toward equal pay for equal work and more social freedom for women to pursue careers outside the home.

Gay Rights Movement   Gay and lesbian Americans, whose push for equality and acceptance emerged during the countercultural era in the 1950s, also fought for their civil rights during this era. A single event in 1969, the so-called Stonewall Riot, is considered the flashpoint of the contemporary gay rights movement. On the night of June 28, 1969, New York City police raided the Stonewall Inn, a gay bar in Greenwich Village. (Police raids on gay bars were common at the time.) Accounts differ on what happened next, but for the first time gay patrons took the unusual step of fighting back, pelting police with coins and other objects and shouting "Gay power!" Large numbers of gay activists and protesters converged on the scene in subsequent days, demanding an end to discrimination against gays and lesbians. In the months that followed gay and lesbian activists launched the Gay Liberation Front (GLF), along with the publication of the first gay newspaper. The movement quickly spread around the globe, and gay pride parades are held annually around the end of June in New York and elsewhere in commemoration of Stonewall. These and other factors have produced greater social and legal equality, including same-sex marriages, for LGBT people, but subtle discrimination against them is still in evidence.

Stonewall Inn. Venerated by gays and lesbians, the Stonewall Inn in New York City was the site of the Stonewall riots. On June 28, 1970, the first annual gay pride (or simply "pride") parade was organized by gay-rights activists to commemorate the first demonstration of resistance to harassment and intimidation by New York City police. Here, unidentified revelers line up along the parade route at the Stonewall Inn on June 26, 2011.

Woodstock. The iconic event of the "hippie" or "counterculture" era of the late 1960s was the Woodstock music and art festival held in August 1969 in upstate New York. It was a massive event, attended by perhaps as many as 400,000 people. Of the dozens of performers playing over the 3 days of the event, one of the most electrifying was the guitarist Jimi Hendrix. Hendrix pioneered a wild, free-form, blues-inflected style that is still widely admired and imitated today.

The Global Youth Movement   A new global generation, known as "baby boomers" (those born during the postwar "baby boom" between 1945 and 1961), emerged during the postwar era. United by common bonds expressed in terms of dress, pop music, and shared ideologies, this new generation repudiated the rigidity of their parents by growing their hair long—in imitation of the Beatles and other rock bands—wearing jeans, T-shirts, and "workers'" clothing; dabbling in Asian philosophies; taking drugs; and engaging in sexual experimentation.

The early center for this movement of "hippies" was San Francisco, in which 1967 was proclaimed the "summer of love." Musical groups espousing hippie values—often crudely summed up as "sex, drugs, and rock and roll"—dominated much of the popular music scene during this time. Perhaps the peak of this movement came in August 1969, when the Woodstock Festival in New York State drew an estimated 300,000–500,000 attendees and sparked a decade of giant musical and cultural festivals attempting to capture the spirit of what became known as the "Woodstock generation." Though the hippie movement as a force for liberation from confining mainstream values had largely spent itself by the early 1970s, its influence in fashion, sexual attitudes, music, and drug use continues to some extent even today.

Student Demonstrations in the 1960s   Pent-up passions and discontent burst forth in a global movement of student demonstrations in the 1960s and 1970s. In protest against what they perceived as the excessive materialism, conformism, and sexual prudishness of the previous generation, student activists held marches, demonstrations, and protests in the United States, Japan, and several European and South American countries. Even third-world countries like Cuba and China, as well as Eastern Bloc countries, experienced similar protests. In each instance student activists shared similar ideologies and goals informed by the common thread of protest against existing polices on gender roles, abortion, gay rights, and other issues.

A prime example of global student activism is afforded by the antiwar movement. For many of the thousands of idealistic students who had taken part in civil rights demonstrations and programs to register African American voters in southern states in the early 1960s, it seemed to be a natural transition from activism in favor of civil rights to activism for other causes. By 1965, the American military effort in Vietnam began to attract protests against US involvement in southeast Asia. This was particularly true for young people of draft age, whether they had college deferments or not. The antiwar movement, initially limited to college campuses and other centers of left or liberal political leaning, increasingly became more mainstream over the next several years.

By 1968 additional factors adding to tensions on both sides were the assassinations of civil rights leaders Martin Luther King, Jr., and the antiwar presidential candidate Robert Kennedy in the spring of that year. In addition to anger and despair about creating change in the United States, student demonstrations now shook much of the Western world. The most serious of these took place in Paris, where rebelling students calling for major education reforms at the University of Paris took to the streets, a rebel movement that spread beyond the students to the labor sector and eventually brought down the French government. Massive demonstrations also took place in Mexico City in advance of the Olympic Games there that summer. In the wake of the quelling of these riots in Europe and the frustration felt by American radicals at their failure to stop the war, many now called for revolutionary violence directed against governments and programs funded by the military.

In Italy and West Germany, some rebel students joined violent revolutionary organizations such the Red Brigades and the Baader-Meinhof Gang. The most radical students expressed solidarity with third-world revolutionary efforts and such figures as Ernesto "Che" Guevara (1928–1967), Ho Chi Minh, and Mao Zedong. With the end of American involvement in Vietnam and the draft in the early 1970s, however, these groups either disbanded, went fully underground, or were dismantled by the authorities.

Economics and Politics in the 1970s and 1980s   Whereas the 1950s and 1960s represented unprecedented growth and prosperity, a sudden economic downturn in the early 1970s initiated a prolonged period of economic stagnation. Several factors were at work here. One cause was the ramping down of the Vietnam War effort, which had driven the US defense industry. Another cause stemmed from renewed hostilities between Arab and Israeli factions in 1973. In retaliation for American support of Israel, the newly formed OPEC, led by Arab states, dramatically increased the price of oil for export to America. The price per barrel of oil rose dramatically from $1.73 in 1973 to nearly $35 in 1981. The consequences of these economic downturns were at first inflation and then by the late 1970s **stagflation**. The emergence of developing economies in Asia and South America also began to lure American manufacturers to relocate to these countries in order to take advantage of lower labor costs, resulting in the decline of major industries in the United States.

Stagflation: Increased prices and record high interest rates but a stagnant economy overall.

The combined effect of these economic circumstances caused corresponding realignments in politics in the 1970s and 1980s. In some Western countries—the United States, Britain, and Germany—the trend shifted toward the adoption of more conservative policies. The most notable examples of what has been termed the "New Conservatism" were the policies of the American president Ronald Reagan and Britain's prime minister Margaret Thatcher (in office 1979–1990). Reagan's fiscal policies, by way of example (sometimes termed "Reaganomics"), featured lower taxes as a way to increase jobs, along with lower interest rates, and offset deficit spending. Although the subject of considerable debate, these policies have been credited with producing a period of sustained economic growth during his presidency. Both leaders orchestrated cutbacks in governmental spending for social services and welfare programs, and in both countries industrial strikes and the power of labor unions were restricted and the nationalization of major industries was replaced by privatization.

From Women's Liberation to Feminism

Historians often consider the 1960s and 1970s as particularly important. Indeed, the period is often considered to mark the beginning of "second-wave feminism," a renewal of the push that crested with "first-wave" feminism's achievement of suffrage and full political rights (see Map 30.3). A key reason for the importance of the period is that women seeking change had the examples of the African American civil rights movement and the growing antiwar movement on which to draw. Within both of these movements some attention was given to women's rights as part of a larger rubric of emancipation, but it remained largely a secondary issue.

By the mid-1960s growing numbers of American women were becoming dissatisfied with what they perceived as the latent *sexism*—the gender equivalent of racism—of other progressive organizations. In response, they founded the National Organization for Women (NOW) in 1966. At about this time the term "women's liberation" began to appear, first in the radical media and shortly thereafter in more mainstream media. At first, leaders of the movement agitated for such things as equity in the workplace. In the cultural realm, they led the call for women's studies and less gendered forms of address like "Ms." As the stakes of the movement turned toward more personal issues in women's lives, these became political and medical issues as well; for example, the availability of birth control and abortion was advocated by physicians in America and by population scientists in nondeveloped countries. Laws governing marriage became hot-button issues, reflected in the movement's motto, "The personal is political."

Although a "third wave" of feminism took hold in the 1990s and often projected a less restrictive attitude toward sexuality of all types than earlier feminism, feminist

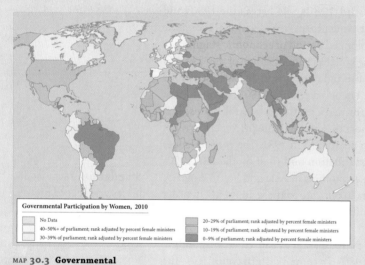

Governmental Participation by Women, 2010

| No Data |
| 40–50%+ of parliament; rank adjusted by percent female ministers |
| 30–39% of parliament; rank adjusted by percent female ministers |
| 20–29% of parliament; rank adjusted by percent female ministers |
| 10–19% of parliament; rank adjustzd by percent female ministers |
| 0–9% of parliament; rank adjusted by percent female ministers |

MAP 30.3 **Governmental Participation by Women.**

From "Underdeveloped" to "Developing" World, 1963–1991

As the Cold War reached its peak in the 1960s, the drive for independence in Africa also crested, with the last colonies finally achieving nationhood in the 1970s. At the same time the drive for economic development, national prestige, and

concerns became part of the ordinary political landscape of many countries. Indeed, "feminism" completely supplanted "women's liberation" as the term for a constellation of values and causes that includes equal pay in the workplace, free and full reproductive rights, greater sexual freedom for women, and a thoroughgoing lack of discrimination in society on the basis of gender. During this period, there was much theoretical groundwork laid for the problem of the "feminization of poverty" in the developing world: According to a United Nations report, women did 66 percent of the world's work, produced at least half of the food, but made only 10 percent of the income and owned a scant 1 percent of the property. Thus, female poverty was intricately linked with the patriarchy embedded in long-standing cultural practices.

Cross-cultural interactions and subsequent assimilations have greatly enhanced worldwide movements to advance women's rights. In 1977 the UN General Assembly declared the first annual International Women's Day. Similar initiatives were then undertaken in countries around the globe: the Progressive Organization for Women (POW) in India; the organization of feminist groups in Israel and Turkey; and the Japanese Equal Employment Opportunity Law, which outlawed gender discrimination in hiring. Feminist authors and activists found increasing audiences in countries around the world, Ding Ling in China, Huda Shaarawi and Nawal El-Saadawi in Egypt, Madhu Kishwar in India, and Fatima Mernissi in Morocco among them. As a measure of women's increasing importance in global politics, many countries have had female prime ministers and presidents; among them are Argentina, Bolivia, the United Kingdom, India, Israel, Liberia, Pakistan, Sri Lanka, and Turkey.

Women's Liberation in India. Members of the National Federation of Dalit Women demonstrate in support of rights for women of the dalit ("untouchables") caste in New Delhi, India, in 2008. While discrimination against dalit is proscribed by law in India, bias against dalit women is still widespread.

Questions

- How does the women's liberation movement demonstrate many of the characteristics of evolving modernity?

- Why does feminism promise to be the great emancipation movement of the twenty-first century?

national power continued to grow among newly independent nations everywhere. The 1960s through the 1980s marked the height of the contest among the nonaligned nations for preeminence between our two competing modernisms: market capitalism with democratic governments and variants of communism, based on the Soviet or Chinese model. Some newly independent governments attempted combinations of both forms of modernity as paths to development. Although many countries remained in dire poverty and were scarred by internal and external wars, the period also witnessed many more moving from the catchall category of "underdeveloped" to the more optimistic one of "developing."

While the unsurpassed prosperity of the West in this period impressed leaders in the developing world, many, if not most, continued to question whether capitalism was appropriate for their nations as an economic system. As we saw in Chapter 29, the socialist road also had a powerful theoretical appeal to many leaders in these emerging nations. The examples of the Soviet Union and China, and implicitly the Communist Bloc countries, appeared to show that formerly poor countries could quickly become rich and powerful—even to the point of being superpowers. Moreover, they were without the fatal stain of having been colonialists—at least in the sense that they had not created overseas empires—and thus could be perceived to be without a long-standing ulterior motive. Finally, one key development worth mentioning in this regard revolves around the ideological approaches of the rival camps. Marxist theorists had long argued that underdevelopment was *caused* by capitalism and imperialism.

> "Imperialism leaves behind germs of rot, which we must clinically detect and remove from our land, but from our minds as well."
>
> —Frantz Fanon

China: Cultural Revolution to Four Modernizations

Of all the major world powers, the People's Republic of China experienced perhaps the most wrenching policy changes during the period 1963–1991. Having just emerged from the first Maoist era of the 1950s, it entered into a relatively calm few years of Soviet-style socialist development, only to be catapulted into the frenzy of the Cultural Revolution in the late 1960s. The death of Mao in 1976, however, ushered in a complete reversal of economic course. In 1978, the Four Modernizations of Deng Xiaoping called for opening the country to foreign experts, aid, and investment and creating a market economy—that is, introducing capitalism. To this day, China's economic policy is officially called "socialism with Chinese characteristics."

China's "Thermidorean Reaction," 1960–1966   The turbulence of the first round of the Maoist years died down considerably under the leadership of Liu Shaoqi [shao-CHEE]. The decade began, however, with the "Sino–Soviet split," in which Soviet apprehensiveness about China's radical programs and Mao's distrust of Soviet policy changes under Khrushchev led to a complete withdrawal of Soviet aid and advisors in 1960. By the end of the decade, Chinese and Soviet forces would be exchanging fire at several disputed border crossings.

Nonetheless, the early 1960s saw a reassertion of the need for education and technical training in China under Liu, and China made several important technological advances with military implications: the detonation of China's first nuclear device in October 1964, the testing of a thermonuclear (hydrogen) device in 1966, and advances in missile technology that would yield the first Chinese satellites in the following decade. In addition, Liu's regime engaged in a more assertive policy of border rectification. Chinese forces had entered Tibet in 1959 to suppress an independence movement, resulting in the flight of the Dalai Lama to India. In securing Tibet, however, disputes arose regarding the actual border with India. In 1962, Chinese forces moved into the disputed regions and fought a brief undeclared war until withdrawing and submitting

Red Guards on the March. Mao Zedong's injunction to the youth of China to question the authority of party bureaucrats had swift effects on everything from the school system to factory production. The students banded together into Red Guard units and challenged their elders, often violently, on their adherence to Mao's thought as expressed in the famous "little red book," *Quotations from Chairman Mao Zedong.* In this photo from 1967, Red Guards parade with a portrait of Mao, while many carry the red book in their hands.

the issue to negotiation. This kind of display of force in order to make a point would be seen again in China's attack on Vietnam in 1979, though with far less effectiveness.

The Cultural Revolution   As China's Communist Party and government assumed a more Soviet-style approach to running the People's Republic, Mao Zedong grew uneasy about the direction of policy. For Mao, the party was reverting to a bureaucracy, uninterested in pushing the revolution forward toward a pure communism. Mao's position of politics taking command was in direct opposition to the increasingly technocratic stance he saw in Liu Shaoqi's policies. Thus, Mao spent several years writing widely circulated essays extolling the virtues of devoted communists and plotting his comeback. An important step was the publication of his famous "little red book," *Quotations from Chairman Mao Zedong*, in 1964. His ideological ally Lin Biao (in office 1954–1971), as vice premier and head of the People's Liberation Army, made it required reading for the troops and helped Mao establish an important power base.

In the spring of 1966, Mao launched a violent critique of the new direction of the party and called on the nation's youth to rededicate themselves to "continuous revolution." Young people were encouraged to criticize their elders and form their own pure "red" ideological path to socialism. Mao announced the launching of the Great Proletarian Cultural Revolution, the purpose of which was to stamp out the last vestiges of "bourgeois" and "feudal" Chinese society. Students formed squads of Red Guards with red armbands and attacked their teachers and elders. By August, millions of Red Guards converged on Beijing, where Mao addressed over 1 million of them in Tiananmen Square and symbolically donned their red armband as a show of solidarity.

From 1966 until 1969, when the Cultural Revolution was officially declared over, millions of people were persecuted or murdered by Red Guards and their allies. The "little red book" became the talisman of the movement, with people struggling to interpret it correctly to prove their ideological fitness. China's official ideology was now listed as "Marxism–Leninism–Mao Zedong Thought." Despite the atrocities committed by Mao, a cult of personality surrounding him and his book sprang up as people waved it at mass rallies and even attributed magical powers to it. By 1968 the country was in complete chaos as pro– and anti–Cultural Revolution factions battled each other in several regions. It was chiefly to end this endemic civil war that Mao declared the Cultural Revolution over in 1969. Its aftermath, however, continued until Mao's death in 1976.

"To Get Rich Is Glorious": China's Four Modernizations The final years of Mao's tenure as party chair saw at least one important change in policy. Despite the Sino–Soviet split, the People's Republic had maintained a strong anti-American posture in its domestic and foreign policy. This was matched by American Cold War antipathy toward "Red China" as a linchpin of the Communist Bloc. By the early 1970s, however, with the Vietnam War winding down and Soviet–Chinese tensions still high, President Richard Nixon made a bold visit to the People's Republic, which resulted in the Shanghai Communiqué of 1972. In this document, the United States and the People's Republic of China announced plans to initiate formal diplomatic and cultural relations (which went into effect in 1979), the United States pledged to no longer block the People's Republic's bid for a seat in the United Nations, and the United States agreed to downgrade its diplomatic presence in Taiwan.

The death of Mao Zedong in September 1976 opened the way for a new generation of Communist Party leadership in China. The result was a repudiation of the Cultural Revolution and those who promoted it and an entirely different direction in strategy for building a new China. After some jostling among the party factions, Deng Xiaoping ([hee-yao-PING]; in office 1978–1992) emerged in 1978 with the title of "vice premier" but in fact held the real power in the regime. The pragmatic Deng, whose motto was "It doesn't matter whether the cat is black or white, as long as it catches mice," implemented the fundamental policies that remain in force in China to the present: the Four Modernizations.

Aware of the difficulties of pursuing socialism in a country with little wealth to share, Deng's strategy relied on upgrading the quality of agriculture, industry, science, technology, and the military. China would pursue a new "open-door" policy with regard to foreign expertise from the West; it would allow its own students to study abroad and, most tellingly, allow the market forces of capitalism to create incentives for innovation in all sectors of the economy. China's new motto became "To get rich is glorious!"

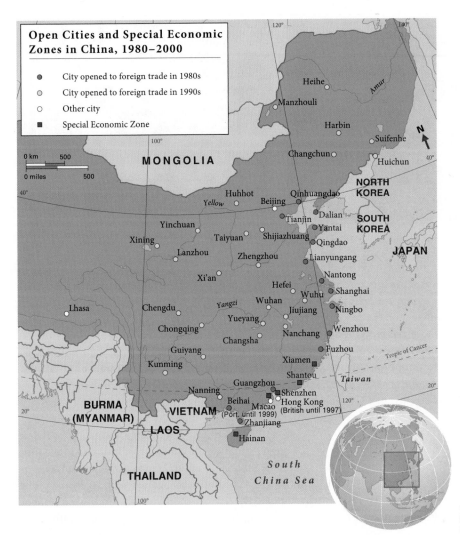

MAP 30.4 **Open Cities and Special Economic Zones in China, 1980–2000.**

The "responsibility system," as it was called, was introduced in a special economic zone set up in south China at Shenzhen to take advantage of capital and expertise from Hong Kong. The experiments in capitalism would then be expanded to the country at large once any flaws had been corrected. Peasants were among the first benefciaries as the communes were disbanded, individual plots assigned, and market incentives introduced. By the mid-1980s China, which had long been a byword in the West for hunger, was rapidly approaching self-sufficiency in food production and, by the 1990s, would register surpluses (see Map 30.4). Through the 1980s and 1990s China's gross domestic product (GDP) grew at an astonishing double-digit rate. In 2010 it surpassed Japan as the second largest economy in the world, after the United States.

Another more controversial innovation was the "one-child" policy. Mao felt that China's huge and growing population was an advantage because of its potential manpower and as a hedge against catastrophic losses from nuclear war. But population pressures were also a powerful brake on China's development. Thus, a policy was inaugurated in 1979 mandating that families (excluding those of most

Tiananmen Square Demonstrations. At their peak in May 1989, the demonstrations by students seeking greater government accountability and a more open political system were joined by workers and people from all walks of life (left). In this memorable image of the suppression of the demonstration, a lone man confronts a tank (right). The driver of the tank tried to get around the man and eventually stopped, together with the other tanks. At that point, demonstrators pulled the man back to safety. His subsequent fate is unknown. Both images were widely broadcast throughout the world.

minorities) were to have only one child. A second child would result in loss of subsidies for childrearing; a third pregnancy would result in mandatory abortion. Despite the many problems in enforcing such a policy, and its severe cultural impact on the male-centered traditional Chinese family structure, China's population has remained remarkably stable since the 1980s at around 1.3–1.5 billion. It has, however, abetted problems of selective female abortion, giving up girl babies for adoption, and even, in extreme cases, female infanticide. Moreover, all of these conditions have lent themselves to a large and growing gender imbalance: China currently has 117 male births for every 100 female births.

Tiananmen Square Massacre   The Chinese government managed a delicate balance between allowing foreign technology to come into China and preventing cultural items "injurious to public morals" to enter. Hence, IBM computers were welcome, but MTV was not. Repeated campaigns against such "spiritual pollution" were conducted throughout the 1980s, though with diminishing effect. Prodemocracy protests began taking place in Beijing following the death of the popular moderate leader Hu Yaobang in 1989. The gatherings grew in size and force as the seventieth anniversary of the May Fourth nationalist movement grew closer. At one point students constructed a large statue they called the Goddess of Democracy, which dominated the center of the square near the Monument to the People's Revolutionary Martyrs. By the beginning of June workers and citizens had joined the students in a generalized protest.

During the period of April 25 to May 19, the members of the Politburo engaged in intense discussions on how to deal with the protests. The hardliners eventually prevailed, but when they prepared the declaration of martial law, a number of high-ranking army officers weighed in with grave doubts. They argued that the People's Army could not possibly shoot on its own people. The most prominent figure refusing any order to shoot was Major General Xu Qinxian [hoo chin-HEEYAN], according to new documents publicized by the *New York Times* in June 2014 at the occasion of the twenty-fifth anniversary of the Tiananmen Massacre. But the Politburo prevailed and during June 2–4 soldiers crushed what to many among the leaders seemed to be an incipient rebellion. To this day, the number of killed is unknown, ranging between 300 (official number) to thousands. General Xu was court-martialed and imprisoned for four years, living in 2014 in a military sanatorium in northern China.

Vietnam: War and Unification

As we noted in Chapter 29, by the early 1960s Vietnam, having thrown off French colonialism in the 1950s, had failed to achieve final unification because of Cold War politics and remained divided into North and South Vietnam. The development of communist guerilla fighters, the Vietcong, in South Vietnam and similar guerilla threats in Laos had prompted the United States to send aid and military advisors to the shaky government of the Republic of Vietnam (South Vietnam) through the late 1950s. Rocked by clashes between Catholics and Buddhists, the government of South Vietnam was ousted in a coup with help from the American Central Intelligence Agency (CIA) in late 1963. Several weak governments took its place until a more stable one under Nguyen Van Thieu emerged and lasted from 1965 to 1975.

The American War In the summer of 1964 several alleged attacks on American ships in the Gulf of Tonkin (the truth of these allegations is still murky today) resulted in the United States radically ramping up its presence in Southeast Asia, effectively beginning what became known in Vietnam as the American War and in the United States as the Vietnam War. In retaliation for the attacks, American planes bombed

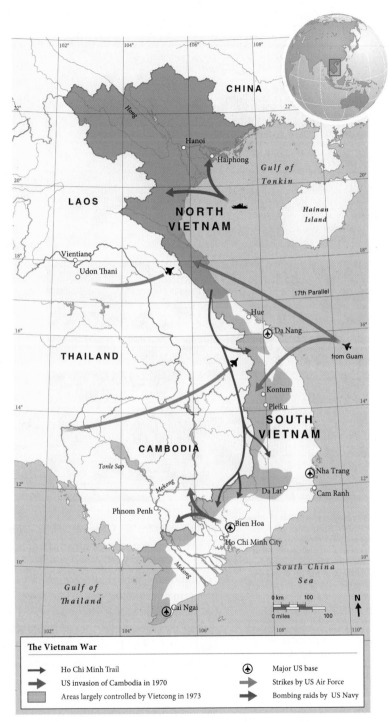

MAP **30.5** The Vietnam War.

sites in North Vietnam. By 1965 tens of thousands of American combat troops were being sent to support the South Vietnamese against the Vietcong. But, as in Korea, the Americans and their allies were plagued by unclear goals and the impatience of a public hoping for quick, decisive results. The task of "winning the hearts

The Arab–Israeli War of June 1967. The stunning victory of Israel over the combined armies of Syria and Egypt generated both admiration in the West and consternation in the Arab world and the Soviet Bloc. The Israelis' preemptive use of air power against Egyptian and Syrian air forces and tank and troop concentrations and their expert use of armor proved the deciding factors in the conflict. Here, Egyptian prisoners (in white underclothes in the truck to the right) are being transferred to holding camps (*top*). The war also led to a dramatic rise in the popularity of the Palestinian cause in the Arab and communist spheres. Here, Yasir Arafat marches with members of Fatah in 1970 (*bottom*).

and minds of the people," as the slogan went, however, was a long and tortuous one at best and always hampered by being a foreign presence in someone else's land. Thus, American forces were increased until they reached a high of over a half-million by 1967. Despite official optimism, there was little evidence that the war was being won (see Map 30.5).

In February 1968, on the Vietnamese lunar new year (*Tet*), the Vietcong, supported by North Vietnamese forces, launched an all-out assault on the South Vietnamese capital of Saigon and a number of other cities. American and Army of the Republic of Vietnam (South Vietnam) forces reeled for several days but launched a successful counterattack, finally destroying the Vietcong as an effective fighting force. In the United States, however, the Tet Offensive, as it came to be called, was seen as an American defeat. In the wake of massive protests against the war, President Johnson announced he would not seek re-election, and the way was clear for the United States to begin negotiations to end the war by political means. With the election of Richard Nixon in 1968, a combination of massive bombings of North Vietnam and Cambodian supply lines for North Vietnamese forces and peace talks in Paris over the next 5 years finally brought the war to an end.

Though South Vietnam survived the peace treaty in 1973, the American withdrawal spelled its demise within 2 years. The country was now finally united, but much of Vietnam, Cambodia, and Laos lay devastated from fighting and bombing. Over the next 2 years a Cambodian revolutionary group, the Khmer Rouge ("Red Khmers"), launched a radical program of urban depopulation, forced labor, and genocide against religious and political opponents. Perhaps one-third of the country's population was killed as a result. The ideas and practices of the Khmer Rouge leader, Pol Pot (1925–1998), were so radical and brutal that in 1977 Vietnam invaded the state and initiated his overthrow in favor of a more moderate and pliable candidate. In response, China briefly invaded northern Vietnam in 1979 but was soon repulsed by Vietnamese forces, the last and least successful of the many Chinese invasion attempts launched over two millennia.

The Middle East

One of the most troubled areas of the world during the twentieth century was also one that, as we have seen over the course of this book, has been the cradle of many influential religions: the Middle East. Since 1945, the area encompassing the

Arabian Peninsula, Iran, Iraq, and the eastern shores of the Mediterranean has seen a number of major wars and minor conflicts, innumerable guerilla raids and assaults, and attacks directed against the religious symbols of Judaism, Christianity, and Islam. As of this writing, despite peace talks that have been conducted over the course of decades, no comprehensive settlement has been reached.

Israeli and Arab Conflict In addition to competition arising from the demand for petroleum as a strategic commodity and Shiite–Sunni conflict within the context of Persian–Arab competition, by far the most contentious issue in the Middle East has been the presence of the Jewish state of Israel. During the 1950s and 1960s, Israel was largely seen in the West as a young country fighting democracy's battles against an array of authoritarian Arab states supported by the Soviet Union. A significant number of highly educated immigrants in the postwar decades helped the new state to build an efficient agriculture—often through the socialist device of the communal farm, or *kibbutz*—and an increasingly sophisticated manufacturing sector. West German reparations, compensating for Jewish losses during the Third Reich, helped financially. Mandatory military service and generous American support also contributed to the creation of superior armed forces equipped with the latest military technology.

MAP **30.6** The Arab–Israeli Wars, 1967 and 1973.

The "Six-Day War" For the Palestinian Arabs and their allies, however, the perspective was very different. For them it was "the disaster." Hundreds of thousands displaced since 1948 awaited their return in surrounding countries—often in camps—for decades, a situation that grew worse when new refugees arrived after every Arab–Israeli conflict. In the polarized Cold War climate, the Arab states viewed Israel as simply a new Western imperial outpost in what was rightfully Arab territory. Consequently, many subsequent attempts at Arab unity were premised on war with Israel. While Arab nationalism was largely secular, and often socialist-leaning with Soviet support, Muslim fundamentalist groups such as Egypt's Muslim Brotherhood gained adherents, despite government repression, as Western secular values came to be seen as causing Muslim difficulties.

In 1964, Yasir Arafat (1929–2004) and other like-minded Palestinian nationalists formed the Palestine Liberation Organization (PLO), whose militant wing, Fatah, began a guerilla war against Israel and its backers. Matters came to a head on May 22, 1967, when Egypt closed the Gulf of Aqaba to Israeli shipping, preventing the importation of oil. Following an Egyptian military buildup along the Sinai border and the expulsion of UN forces there, Iraq sent troops to Jordan at its invitation, and local Muslim leaders began to call for holy war against Israel. On June 5 the Israelis launched a massive preemptive air assault to neutralize the Egyptian and Syrian air forces. With an overwhelming advantage in number and quality of aircraft, Israel took out the Arab armor and ground troops with astonishing skill. The Six-Day War, as it came to be called, established Israel's reputation for military prowess and enlarged the state by conquering the eastern side of the Jordan River, the Golan Heights, and the Gaza Strip—territories belonging to Jordan, Syria, and Egypt, respectively. For many observers, Israel had now moved from a state simply fighting for its existence to one bent on expansion.

The Yom Kippur/Ramadan War   In early October 1973, Egypt, Syria, and a coalition of Arab states, stung by their defeat in 1967, launched a massive attack during the Jewish holy day of Yom Kippur, which in 1973 coincided with the Muslim holy month of Ramadan. This time, with Israel, the United States, and the Soviet Union caught unawares, Egyptian tanks crossed the Suez Canal on pontoon bridges and attacked Israel (see Map 30.6). Syria attacked the Golan Heights and contributed to the Egyptian crossing of the Canal. After taking severe losses and conceding ground for a week, Israeli forces managed to ultimately defeat the combined Arab armies once again. Having trapped Egyptian forces along the Suez Canal, Israeli units occupied the west bank of the Canal, pushing within 63 miles of Cairo. Other units drove 25 miles into Syria. A ceasefire was brokered by the United Nations, but the intensity of the fighting and the resupply efforts by the United States and Soviet Union moved both countries dangerously close to direct confrontation. For their part, the Arab oil producers and Iran immediately launched an oil embargo of the United States. Stringent measures and a degree of rationing and sharply higher gasoline prices drove home to Americans how dependent they had become on foreign oil, and encouraged new interests in solar and other alternative forms of energy.

For Egypt, the defeat resulted in a transformation of policy toward Israel. Under President Anwar el-Sadat (in office 1970–1981), Egypt took the initiative in undertaking peace talks by visiting Israel in 1977. The following year, the two sides reached an understanding about a basic framework for peace; and with the backing of the American president Jimmy Carter, Egypt and Israel signed the first treaty between an Arab country and the Jewish state at Camp David, Maryland, in 1979. Egypt and Jordan are the only Arab states to date to maintain diplomatic and cultural relations with Israel. While Egyptian–Israeli relations remained relatively cordial on the surface, no other Arab countries followed suit. Syria remained hostile, having lost the Golan Heights again, while the PLO stepped up its efforts throughout the 1980s. Profound resentment of Sadat for signing the treaty festered among many Egyptians. Despite some concessions to increasingly vocal fundamentalist Muslim groups—for example, agreeing to base Egyptian legislation on Islamic Sharia law—Sadat was killed by assassins in 1981.

Africa: From Independence to Development

During the period 1963–1991, the main struggles in Africa moved from ones mainly concerned with completing the pattern of decolonization and independence to ones involving development. As with other parts of the postcolonial world, vigorous internal debates were conducted about strategies for economic development, how best to deploy scarce resources, and the relative merits of a planned economy versus one governed by market forces. But in nearly all cases, the economies of the newly independent states, regardless of which economic system they favored, were problematic. In most cases they were tied to their former colonial regimes by means of the same raw materials—minerals, petroleum, agricultural or forest products— that had been exploitatively extracted during their colonial days. Moreover, they were more frequently than not competing in the markets for these products with other former colonies. Thus, they were at the mercy of world commodity prices but not insulated from the worst ups and downs by their former colonial regimes.

As in Chapter 29, far too many new nations emerged in Africa during this period for this chapter to cover them all. Therefore, we will focus on Nigeria, Zimbabwe, and South Africa as representative of the problems and prospects of the era.

Nigeria: Civil War and Troubled Legacies

While in the Congo the Cold War played out in dramatic fashion with the United States supporting the overthrow of Patrice Lumumba in favor of Mobutu Sese Seko in the early 1960s, Nigeria's independence had a more promising start. With a large and fairly prosperous population, sound agriculture, and abundant resources, it entered the postcolonial era as a republic with a British parliamentary system, Commonwealth membership, and a federal-style constitution. Like many African former colonies, however, it soon became apparent that Nigeria was also saddled with ethnic and religious conflicts that were a legacy from the old colonial divisions of the continent. Thus, its growing pains were marked by clashes between its established system of constitutional nationalism and the desires of its major constituent groups for their own nation-states more reflective of Nigeria's ethnic, linguistic, and religious makeup.

The new nation was marked by occasional conflicts and cooperation among three major antagonistic groups, the Hausa, Igbo, and Yoruba, divided by history, culture, religion, and language. The largest, the Hausa, were Muslims from the northern region who constituted nearly 30 percent of Nigeria's population. The Igbo, mostly living in the eastern region where valuable oil deposits had been recently discovered, were predominantly Christian or African-spiritual. The Yoruba, who controlled most of the national offices, were predominantly Muslim, although there were also Christian Yoruba.

Starting in 1966, the central government under strongman Yakubu Gowon (in office 1966–1975) had authorized raids to bring Igbo areas under greater control. In 1967, the eastern Igbo region declared itself independent as the state of Biafra under Colonel Chukwuemeka Odumegwu Ojukwu (b. 1933). What followed was perhaps the bloodiest civil war of the era. Both sides fought determinedly, and when a military stalemate was reached the Nigerian forces attempted to starve Biafra into submission. More than 1 million Biafrans died, mostly of starvation and malnutrition, before Biafra surrendered in early 1970. In the remainder of the period to 1991, Nigeria was ruled by a series of military strongmen, each in turn attempting to stabilize the volatile political situation of the central government. By 1991, the prosperous future that seemed so promising in 1960 seemed impossible to all but the most optimistic observers.

Zimbabwe: The Revolution Continued   Some of the former European colonies in Africa came to independence with substantial populations of white settlers, some of whose families had been there for several generations. Accustomed to a life of relative privilege, they had, in many cases, opposed independence, and when it came, they sought guarantees from the new governments against expropriation of land, discrimination, and reprisals. In 1964 the old colony of Northern Rhodesia gained independence as Zambia, breaking up a federation of the two colonies and Nyasaland, which subsequently became independent as Malawi. Threatened by the independence of nearby black African nations and confident of support from apartheid-based South Africa, the white leaders of the territory that now called itself simply "Rhodesia" declared unilateral independence in 1965 and set up a government in the colonial capital of Salisbury under Ian Smith (in office 1965–1970). Distressed at this move, Britain refused to recognize the new government and expelled Rhodesia from the Commonwealth. Few countries outside of South Africa recognized the regime, which now faced international sanctions and a guerilla movement from within.

Two rival groups, the Zimbabwe African National Union (ZANU) under Robert Mugabe (b. 1924) and the Zimbabwe African People's Union (ZAPU) led by Joshua Nkomo (1917–1999), struggled to bring Smith's regime down and create a majority-rule state. The long and bitter war lasted throughout the 1960s and 1970s, until Mugabe and ZANU finally triumphed and created a new state called "Zimbabwe" in 1980. Mugabe's regime pledged fairness to the remaining white settlers and, after changing the name of the capital to Harare, set about creating a socialist state. In this sense, despite constant condemnations of Africa's imperial legacy, Mugabe has been in constant need of the economic power of the country's white minority and thus initially trod fairly lightly on their rights. By the 1990s, however, vigilante seizures of white lands by "revolutionary veterans" became a regular occurrence. By the early 2000s, the chaotic agricultural sector combined with repression of opposition to ZANU one-party rule had plunged the country into a serious economic crisis.

Angola and Mozambique   Two colonies under Portuguese control, Angola and Mozambique, were among the last to gain independence from European rule. In spite of a series of uprisings in the early 1960s, the authoritarian government of Portugal refused to relinquish control of its possessions along the southwestern and southeastern coasts of Africa, respectively. Following a military coup in Portugal in 1974, however, during which the regime was overthrown, each was granted independence in the following year.

South Africa: From Apartheid to "Rainbow Nation"   South Africa, the richest of the continent's countries, also had the most complex and restrictive racial relations. From the seventeenth century, first Dutch, then English, settlers came to service the maritime traffic around the Cape of Good Hope. By the nineteenth century, the Dutch-descended Boers had moved inland from Cape Town to

Black Commuters in South Africa. The regime of apartheid (the strict separation of the races) that had been inaugurated by the white minority government in South Africa in 1948 obliged all black citizens, such as these workers congregating in a Johannesburg train station in the late 1950s, to carry "passbooks" that specified what areas they were permitted to enter. Resentment at the passbook requirement prompted mass demonstrations that resulted in the Sharpeville Massacre of March 21, 1960, which in turn sparked widespread protests against the apartheid system.

establish farms, ranches, and vineyards, pushing out the local people. The expansion of Zulu power at roughly the same time forced the British rulers and Dutch settlers into protracted Zulu wars that, climaxing in 1879, broke the last black empire in the region. By the end of the nineteenth century, the discovery of vast mineral wealth in gold and diamonds led to both the expansion of the colony's holdings and an influx of immigrants, including Chinese and Indians.

In the early twentieth century, the social divisions among whites, Africans, and "coloureds"—south and east Asians and peoples of mixed descent—were hardened into legal classifications. The Indian nationalist leader Mohandas Gandhi, for example, developed his successful nonviolent strategies by leading protests in South Africa for Indian rights. After 1910, immigration restrictions on Asians went into effect along with ever-more-restrictive laws governing relations between whites and Africans. This trend culminated in the institution of **apartheid** (Afrikaans, "apartness") in 1948. Black South Africans were relegated to a legal second-class status and were to live in designated "Bantustans"—that is, separate territories. They were required to carry passes when traveling; those commuting to work in white urban areas had to leave by sunset; and they were subject to curfew regulations.

Apartheid: System of social and legal segregation by race enforced by the government of South Africa from 1948 until 1994.

Through the 1950s South Africa faced international criticism for its policies, which the white government justified as necessary to maintain its rule, since whites made up less than one-sixth of the population. Moreover, as newly independent black majority countries came into being and completed the pattern of decolonization, the white government—resisting this pattern—felt itself increasingly besieged. It pointed out with some justification that a few of these emerging states were Marxist and thus claimed that it was fighting the free world's battle against the expansion of the Soviet Bloc in Africa. Nonetheless, it withdrew from the British Commonwealth in 1961, and a number of black political organizations—most prominently the African National Congress (ANC)—campaigned for the dismantling of apartheid. The brutality of the white armed forces and police and the constant harassment of dissenters, both white and black, added to the oppressive atmosphere.

By the 1980s it was clear that events in and outside the country would eventually force the dismantling of apartheid. International boycotts of South Africa had gained momentum, particularly after the public call for sanctions by the African Anglican bishop Desmond Tutu (b. 1931), who was awarded the Nobel Peace Prize in 1984. In the townships, the ANC, through a political and guerilla campaign, was making gradual gains. Massive strikes by black workers in 1987 and 1988 also led to increasing paralysis of the government. Finally, amidst the collapse of communism in the Soviet Bloc in 1990, the newly elected president, Frederik Willem de Klerk (b. 1936), began a set of sweeping reforms aimed ultimately at dismantling apartheid. In quick succession, the ANC was legalized and became South Africa's largest political party; its leader, Nelson Mandela (1918–2013), was released from prison; in 1991 all apartheid laws were repealed; and finally, in 1992 white voters amended the constitution to mandate racial equality among all citizens. By 1994, the first multiracial elections were held, and Mandela became president of the new South Africa, which Archbishop Tutu dubbed the "Rainbow Nation" in honor of its newly recognized diversity. Thus, the pattern of decolonization was completed.

Latin America: Proxy Wars

As in Africa, the 1960s in Latin American politics were marked in many ways by the forces contending for dominance against the backdrop of the Cold War. Here, however, because the countries in question had long since achieved their independence—if not yet long-term stability in government—the issues guiding the respective sides were largely ideological and economic, as well as centering around revolutionary politics.

By the 1970s, dissatisfaction with the authoritarian regimes of the region, particularly in Central America, resulted in several revolutionary efforts, the most notable being in Nicaragua and El Salvador. Since the mid-1930s, the United States had supported the family of the authoritarian Nicaraguan strongman Anastasio Somoza García (collectively in office from 1936–1979). Landlordism and rural poverty had been particularly acute problems in Nicaragua, and from the early 1960s a guerilla insurgency called the Sandinista National Liberation Front (FSLN) had sought to overthrow the Somozas and mount a socialist land-reform scheme. The Somoza regime fell in 1979, and a new government under the Sandinistas (invoking the name of Emilio Sandino, one of the original Somoza opponents) was led by Daniel Ortega (in office 1979–1990; 2007–).

The socialist direction of the new regime prompted the American administration of President Ronald Reagan to cut off aid to Nicaragua, begin a covert operation to destabilize Ortega through the funding and arming of opposition groups known collectively as the Contras, and end trade with the regime. With US support and fading aid from Cuba and the Soviet Bloc in the late 1980s, the two sides agreed to elections in 1990. These resulted in the presidency of the conservative opposition candidate, Violeta Barrios de Chamorro (in office 1990–1997).

In similar fashion, guerilla groups in El Salvador fought US-backed government forces, whose actions were sometimes directed against Catholic clergy believed to support the insurgents, in a bloody conflict throughout the 1980s, until elections were finally held in 1992. The death toll in this tiny country is estimated to be as high as 75,000. By the early 1990s, however, the two sides, as in Nicaragua, had resolved to work within the new political system.

The commitment of the United States to opposing any groups espousing Marxist or communist beliefs in Latin America also revealed itself in covert policy toward governments recognized as legitimate. As we saw in Chapter 29, for example, the CIA helped engineer a coup against Guatemalan leader Jacobo Árbenz (in office 1951–1954) in 1954 because he permitted the existence of a communist labor union. The most spectacular instance of American Cold War covert action, however, was directed at Chilean President Salvador Allende (in office 1970–1973) in 1973. Allende had led a coalition of socialists, communists, and liberal Christian Democrats to a plurality win in 1970. Many of his policies met opposition within Chile, while his ideology and nationalization of American interests in Chile's mines pushed the Nixon administration to back his opposition.

With American blessings and CIA help, Allende was overthrown, and the repressive regime of General Augusto Pinochet (in office 1973–1990) installed. Determined to suppress leftist groups and their sympathizers Pinochet launched Operation Colombo in 1975, resulting in the disappearance of over 100 activists and others perceived as threats to the government's plan to restore a capitalist economy. Throughout Pinochet's term of 16 years in power, his rule remained repressive, but Chile also became increasingly economically vibrant and slowly began to move toward a more open and democratic government. In 1998 Pinochet was arrested in London on charges of human rights violations and torture. After a lengthy court battle, he was ultimately released and returned to Chile, where he died in 2006.

"The Dirty War" and the "Disappeared"   As we have seen in this section, the damage inflicted by the Cold War and the actions of its combatants, real and proxy, upon Latin America was considerable. One of the most tragic and internationally condemned episodes of this struggle was the "Dirty War" (*Guerra Sucia*) carried out in Argentina from 1976 to 1983. The tangled politics of the post-Perón era resulted in a smoldering guerilla war against various regimes from the 1960s onward. By the early 1970s, many of these groups had coalesced into the Peronist Montoneros and the Marxist People's Revolutionary Army (ERP). While the Montoneros were essentially crushed in 1977, the ERP remained active, and under the cover of "Operation Condor" tens of thousands of Argentinians were kidnapped, imprisoned, and killed. Many of these men and women were not guerillas but writers, editors, labor organizers, teachers, and others suspected of having left-wing leanings or whom the government sought to eliminate for other reasons.

These victims became known as the "disappeared." Their fate is still poignantly brought to light by the Mothers of Plaza de Mayo, a group of women who have kept vigil for lost friends and relatives in that plaza in Buenos Aires since 1977 and grown into an internationally recognized human rights movement, spreading in the mid-1970s to other countries also suffering instances of "disappearances" under authoritarian rule such as Bolivia, Chile, Paraguay, and Uruguay. Already by 1979 the wholesale imprisonments prompted US president Carter to offer asylum to those languishing in Argentine jails.

In 1983, having deeply miscalculated in provoking and losing the Falklands War with Great Britain, the junta stepped down, elections were held, and a National Commission on the Disappearance of Persons (CONADEP) was established in December. While the figures vary greatly, from 15,000 to perhaps 30,000 "disappeared," the progress of the commission and its findings of torture, killing, and indefinite incarceration caused an international sensation. Today, most of the surviving military and political leaders held responsible are in prison or have already served lengthy terms.

Putting It All Together

During the years 1962 to 1991, from the Cuban Missile Crisis to the dissolution of the Soviet Union, the Cold War contest between the two remaining twentieth-century versions of modernity—capitalist democracy and the different varieties of communism–socialism—reached its climax. At the beginning of the period it seemed that communism was competing evenly, perhaps even winning, in its appeal to so many developing nations and their leaders. But in the end, the wealth and power of the West, particularly the United States, ultimately wore the Soviet Bloc down. Along the way, the most populous communist state, China, abruptly changed from extreme radical leftist programs during its Cultural Revolution to a capitalist style of market economics by 1991. Many other countries were now looking for some mixture of the two systems or a third way between the two for their own development. As the period drew to a close, it was, ironically, the two iconic communist regimes, the Soviet Union and the People's Republic of China, that were pioneering the way *out* of Marxist socialism. The Chinese sought to do this by retaining a powerful authoritarian government while embracing market economics. The former Soviet Union adopted democratic political values and guardedly introduced capitalism.

For the people of the world observing these changes it might indeed have seemed as if the triumphant words of Francis Fukuyama's 1989 essay "The End of History?" actually did sum up the age:

> A remarkable consensus concerning the legitimacy of liberal democracy as a system of government had emerged throughout the world over the past few years, as it conquered rival ideologies like hereditary monarchy, fascism, and most recently communism. More than that, however . . . liberal democracy may constitute the "end point of mankind's ideological evolution" . . . and as such . . . the end of history.

The next two decades, however, would see the emergence of new and unanticipated challenges to the domination of the capitalist-democratic order. For many, its secular character and its breaking down of traditional norms in the West was evidence that the evolving culture of this version of modernity would undermine the core values of their own societies. Hence, like the reformers in many of the old empires of the nineteenth century, they struggled to acquire the material advantages of modernity while isolating themselves from the cultural threat it presented. Still others in both the West and elsewhere had come to see the forces of modernity as threats to the delicate balance between human beings and the environment. They therefore sought to curtail the rapacity of capitalist-democratic countries and corporations in their contest for resources. In the final chapter of this book, both these trends—and the devil's bargain they present to so many—will occupy a considerable amount of our attention.

For additional resources, including maps, primary sources, visuals, and quizzes, please go to www.oup.com/us/vonsivers. Please see the Further Resources section at the back of the book for additional readings and suggested websites.

Against the Grain

The African National Congress

In the early 1900s, the Union of South Africa adopted laws which formed the backbone of what in 1948 was to become apartheid, an official program of racial segregation. According to these laws, blacks (who made up 5 million of the 6 million inhabitants of the country) were to be removed from the villages, towns, and cities of western South Africa to reservations and trust lands in the less fertile eastern part of the country, called "Bantustans."

In protest against segregation and demanding equal rights, in 1912 a few black professionals organized what was to become the African National Congress (ANC). Their demands were similar to those voiced by Indians and Egyptians around World War I and set the beginnings of the pattern of decolonization in the twentieth century. It required, however, another generation of younger professionals, including the law partners Oliver Thambo (1917–1993) and Nelson Mandela (1918–2013), before the ANC was able to become a mass movement among the impoverished and illiterate masses. They created a youth league within the ANC and formulated demands for land distribution, labor organization, and mass education.

After the Afrikaner nationalists came to power in 1948 and established outright apartheid, black South Africans were increasingly driven to join the ANC. During the 1950s, the government introduced race-marked passports, outlawed interracial marriages and sexual relations, demolished black shantytowns, resettled blacks, banned communism, and decreed segregated parks, beaches, buses, hospitals, schools, and universities. Determined to enforce apartheid, the government built up a massive bureaucracy, including an effective secret service.

Even though the events of the 1950s made the ANC a true representative of South African blacks, it held fast to its original program of multiracial and ideologically varied (including communism) integration, resisting any more narrowly defined black nationalist political orientation. Its mass protests and acts of sabotage through a newly created armed wing in 1961–1964 were met by the government with brutal acts of repression and mass arrest. In the so-called Rivonia trial, the arrested ANC leadership, including Mandela, was condemned to life or long-term imprisonment on Robben Island.

Courageous protests by student and labor organizations, churches, and white liberals continued, as did undiminished government brutality in response. The ANC was driven underground, from where it sought to make townships ungovernable. It also operated from abroad, where it helped in the creation by the 1980s of a broad coalition of Western states and organizations which sought to force South Africa to abolish apartheid through sanctions and boycotts. Ultimately, the ANC prevailed because of the collapse of the Soviet Bloc in 1989–1991; the apartheid regime could no longer claim that it was the final bulwark against world communism. In 1994, South Africa became a black-governed nation under the rule of the ANC.

- How does the ANC's support for racial integration, and its acceptance of differing political views, contrast with other nationalist and liberation movements from this period?

- Compare and contrast South African apartheid and segregation in the United States between 1918 and 1964. What are the similarities? What are the differences?

Thinking Through Patterns

▶ **How did the political landscape of the Cold War change from 1963 to 1991?**

Perhaps the biggest changes came in the 1980s. Though the United States had been defeated politically in Vietnam and was facing a recession at home, it still was the world's largest economy and could weather a protracted arms race. Though it was not fully perceived at the time, the Soviet Union was far more economically fragile—which ultimately made it ideologically fragile as well. The strains of Polish dissent, the Afghan War, and a renewed arms race with the United States simply wore the Soviet state down.

The unprecedented prosperity of the United States and the West more generally allowed younger people to attend universities in record numbers, experiment with new ideas of living, and simply indulge their desires for fun and new experiences. The idealism of the era also played a role, as did the threat of the military draft and the larger threat of nuclear war. For many, the materialism of the age repelled them and made them long for a simpler, more "authentic" existence. Thus, a popular motto from the time was "Turn on, tune in, drop out."

▶ **Why did such radically different lifestyles emerge in the United States and the West during the 1960s and 1970s? What is their legacy today?**

▶ **Why did some nations that had emerged from colonialism and war make great strides in their development while others seemed to stagnate?**

By and large, the nations that prospered were the ones that had already achieved self-sufficiency in agriculture, had at least a basic transportation and communications infrastructure, and were resourceful in adopting policies that maximized their labor force. Taiwan, South Korea, and Singapore are good examples of countries that made great strides in their development during this period. China, under Deng Xiaoping, followed a modified version of this strategy and was already growing at record levels by 1991. In the following decades, nearly all Asian countries (an exception being North Korea) would follow suit, with India moving into the top ranks of development and growth. Many Latin American countries—in particular, Brazil—also made great strides, and the drive to follow the example of using cheap labor to create a successful export manufacturing base also took hold in Africa.

In all cases, culture and ideology could and did play a powerful role in setting the psychological conditions for citizens to believe that progress was possible. Peace and stability also played an important role, for obvious reasons. The many internal conflicts that pockmarked Latin America and Africa held back development during this period.

Chapter 31 1991–2014
A Fragile Capitalist-Democratic World Order

I t was a scene that had been repeated hundreds of times across North Africa and the Middle East during the months of winter and spring of 2010–2011. First in Tunisia in December, then with daily regularity in Egypt, Libya, Bahrain, Yemen, and Syria, growing crowds gathered to remonstrate with authoritarian governments over a wide range of issues that had marked the process of modernity for two centuries: the constitutional rights of life, liberty, security, economic opportunity, emancipation of minorities and women, freedom of expression, and the rights of ethnic and religious groups to nationhood, autonomy, or even mere existence.

The governments challenged by these movements had long been propped up by brutal and repressive security services. Unable or unwilling to broaden political participation, aging authoritarian rulers had groomed their sons or favorites to succeed them. The rulers pretended to have liberalized the economies of their countries, but instead "crony capitalism" benefited their relatives and followers and discouraged entrepreneurial innovation. Chronic unemployment and underemployment left both the poor and the middle class in despair over their future. For many years, the unemployed youth of the Middle East had found solace in an Islamism whose preachers promised the

Population increase, 1950–2010
Country where population increased by:
☐ 0–100% ☐ 200–300%
☐ 100–200% ■ over 300%

ABOVE: **Activist and 2011 Nobel Peace Prize recipient Tawakkol Karman leads a rally for democracy in Sana, Yemen.**

solution for all ills. But these preachers had not turned out to be any more able than the increasingly despised rulers to improve the daily lives of the people. A general stagnation had set in throughout the region.

By mid-spring 2011 the relentlessly repeated, massive, and unarmed street protests had toppled the governments of Tunisia and Egypt. Crowds massed as well in Syria, Bahrain, Libya, and Yemen. Syria and Bahrain sought to suppress the democracy movements, while in Libya, Yemen, and Syria civil wars tore the populations apart. More remarkably, however, was that in Yemen, one of the many male-dominated bastions of conservative Islam, the movement was led by a charismatic female journalist and grassroots organizer. Armed with computers, smart phones burgeoning with apps such as Twitter, Facebook, and all the latest tools of social networking, Tawakkol Karman, 32, the leader of Women Journalists Without Chains and a mother of three, harangued mostly male crowds of thousands with calls for revolution. "We will make our revolution or we will die trying," she thundered, her words echoing those of so many insurgents of the recent past. "We are in need of heroes," said one Yemeni observer. "She manages to do what most men cannot do in a society that is highly prejudiced against women." But with her personal role models including Nelson Mandela of South Africa, Mohandas Gandhi of India, and Martin Luther King, Jr., and Hillary Clinton of the United States, Karman as much as any woman of her time embodied the choices and challenges marking the patterns of world history in the rapidly globalizing early twenty-first century. Not surprisingly, the Norwegian Nobel Committee made her the cowinner of the Peace Prize in 2013.

In the largest sense, achieving modernity through urbanization, science, industrialization, the accumulation of capital, and grassroots participation in political pluralism has become close to a universal goal in the world. Where it will lead is anyone's guess. But the story of how this pattern of modernity has grown to become nearly universal—and the old and new forces that oppose it—is the focus of this final chapter in our survey of world history.

Capitalist Democracy: The Dominant Pattern of Modernity

With the demise of communism, the struggle among the three ideologies of modernity that had characterized much of the twentieth century was now over. In the first flush of enthusiasm, some Western observers declared history to have ended, henceforth to be written merely as a series of footnotes to the triumph of capitalism and democracy. Other viewers argued that modernity had ended and we were

Seeing Patterns

▶ How did the United States demonstrate its dominant economic position toward the end of the twentieth century? How did it accelerate the pattern of globalization?

▶ What made capitalist democracy so attractive toward the end of the twentieth century that it became a generic model for many countries around the world to strive for?

▶ Which policies did China and India pursue so that they became the fastest industrializing countries in the early twenty-first century?

▶ How have information technology and social networking altered cultural, political, and economic interactions around the world?

▶ What is global warming, and why is it a source of grave concern for the future?

Chapter Outline

• Capitalist Democracy: The Dominant Pattern of Modernity

• The Environmental Limits of Modernity

• Putting It All Together

Postmodernism and postculturalism: Cultural movements influential across the world from ca. 1970 to 2010 which began with the adoption of eclectic styles in architecture. They evolved into a general "critical theory," according to which reality is constructed through discourse, the will to power determines society's institutions, and subaltern minorities in the new nations strive to overcome the hegemony of Western-centric culture.

at the beginning of a new age of **postmodernism** and **postcolonialism**. Less triumphant observers expressed the hope that capitalist modernity in the coming decades would become an increasingly generic pattern, adoptable in non-Western cultures. But they also realized that democracy would not spread rapidly as long as countries remained poor and stuck in inherited forms of authoritarianism or even autocracy.

More than a decade into the twenty-first century it has become clear that history not only did not end but is still in the middle of its scientific–industrial stage of modernity, which began around 1800. This stage of modernity, Western-centric during 1800–2000, has evolved into a generic modernity composed of capitalism, democracy, and consumerism spread across the globe.

A Decade of Global Expansion: The United States and the World in the 1990s

In the aftermath of the oil crisis of 1985–1986, and with even greater vigor after the collapse of communism in 1991, the United States advocated free trade, fiscal discipline, and transnational economic integration as the proper course for world development. It did so as the most economically and politically powerful country. Two characteristics made the United States the sole superpower it currently is. First, the United States dominated the so-called dollar regime—that is, dollars functioned as the currency for all oil sales and purchases. In fact, despite the growth in popularity of the European Union's euro and other major currencies like the English pound, Swiss franc, and Japanese yen, the dollar remained in a very real sense the world's currency. Second, with its giant consumer economy, the United States functioned as the world's favored destination for manufactured goods, particularly from east Asia. The leverage which the United States gained from these two economic functions was bolstered by overwhelming military force, which made the United States the principal enforcer of peace in the world. This enforcement function has earned the United States the opprobrium of many who criticize it for imperialism, materialism, and unrestrained spying.

A Hierarchy of Nations   During the 1990s, there were some 190 sovereign countries in the world, forming a three-tier hierarchy. At the top of the first tier, almost in a category of its own, was the United States. It was the richest, most evolved constitutional nation-state, based on a mature scientific–industrial society, sophisticated financial institutions, and by far the most powerful military. It boasted the densest infrastructure of universities, colleges, public libraries, museums, theaters, and other cultural institutions. Below the United States, the fully industrialized democracies in Europe, North America, and Australia occupied the rest of the first tier. In the course of the 1990s, four "newly industrialized countries" joined this tier, the Asian "Tigers" or "Dragons": Taiwan, South Korea, Hong Kong, and Singapore. Since the early 2000s, the so-called BRIC countries, Brazil, Russia, Indonesia, and China, as well as Turkey and Mexico, can be added. Such was the economic power of the fully industrialized and largely democratic countries (except for China) in the top tier that they alone still conducted nearly 60 percent of all world trade in goods and services.

In the second tier of the world hierarchy were 88 "middle-income countries," according to the United Nations' definition. These were developing countries in economic and democratic "transition." They were either industrializing states in the Middle East, south Asia, east Asia, and Latin America or reindustrializing states located in the former Communist Bloc. The reindustrializing states were replacing their obsolete communist-era manufacturing infrastructures with modern systems. In the broad bottom tier were 66 countries defined as "low-income" or "poor," located for the most part in sub-Saharan Africa and southeast Asia. Many of these countries were in early stages of economic development, with little or no democratization (see Map 31.1).

In 2000, about one-fifth of the world's population of 6 billion lived in fully industrialized countries, two-thirds in middle-income countries, and 15 percent in poor countries. The world population was still expanding, but the pace of the expansion was slowing, largely as a result of improved female education and contraceptives. The dominance of scientific–industrial society was such that only two centuries after its beginnings 90 percent of the world population was more or less integrated into the pattern of capitalist modernity characterized by market exchange and consumerism and no longer by traditional agrarian–urban subsistence agriculture.

MAP **31.1** **The Global Distribution of Wealth, 2012.**

The Dollar Regime The United States stood at the top of the world hierarchy thanks largely to the power of its financial system. The beginnings of this system date back to the years following 1971 when President Richard Nixon took the dollar off the gold standard. At that time, in a period of war expenditures in Vietnam and high inflation, the United States was running out of gold payable for dollars at the internationally agreed price of $35 an ounce. Two years later, Nixon persuaded the Middle East–dominated Organization of the Petroleum Exporting Countries (OPEC) to accept only dollars as payment for oil. In support of Egypt and Syria against Israel in the October War of 1973, OPEC had just quadrupled oil prices. Despite American support for Israel, however, OPEC was anxious to remain in the good graces of the United States as its largest buyer. As a result of

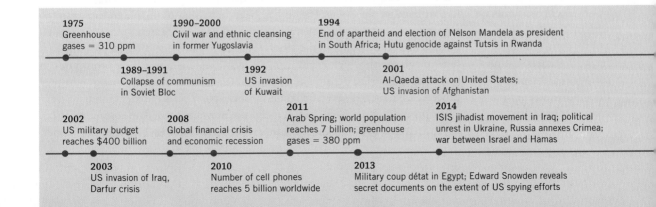

the Nixon–OPEC deal, the dollar took over from gold as the acknowledged international standard of exchange.

Dollar regime:
A system maintained by the United States whereby dollars are the sole currency in which the price of oil and most other commodities and goods in the world are denominated; the regime forces most countries to maintain two currencies, with consequent financial constraints.

Under the **dollar regime**, all oil-importing countries, except for the United States, had to manage two currencies. One, denominated in dollars, was for energy purchases; the other, in domestic currencies, was for the internal market of oil consumption. Countries had to carefully look after the strength of their domestic currency, as rising dollar prices could lead to severe crises in efforts to control inflationary domestic prices and pay back foreign, dollar-denominated loans. OPEC countries for their part invested their "petrodollars" in US Treasury bills ("T-bills"), as well as in American stocks and bonds. There were repeated grumblings among the non–oil producers of the world, both developed and developing, about being cheated by the dollar regime. But the US–OPEC deal did endure, backed up by a gigantic American financial system that emerged as a result of the dollar regime.

The United States as an Import Sinkhole In a development parallel to the creation of the dollar regime, the United States tied the industrializing countries of the world to itself by becoming the country to which everyone wanted to export. Building this tie was particularly important in east Asia. During the Cold War, the United States had encouraged import substitution industrialization along the lines of Japan in Korea, Taiwan, Hong Kong, Thailand, and southeast Asian countries. By becoming prosperous, so it was assumed, these countries would be less susceptible to the expansion of communism. Although uneven, the industrialization process advanced apace in most east Asian countries. In the 1990s, it reached levels where the United States began to pressure the Asian Tigers to reduce import substitution protectionism and replace it with free trade. In return for the United States buying their industrial goods, the countries of east Asia agreed to give free access to American financial institutions, such as banks and hedge funds.

"Although nobody loves the dollar standard, it is a remarkably robust institution that is too valuable to lose and too difficult to replace."

—Economist Ronald McKinnon, 2010

In the meantime, communism collapsed, and China, pushing its own import substitution industrialization, began to export cheap industrial goods as well to the United States. In the 1990s, aided by abundant cheap labor, these goods undercut those produced by the Asian Tigers, and the United States became an even deeper "sinkhole," this time for textiles, toys, and simple electrical and electronic devices made in the People's Republic of China. The United States in effect underwrote China's industrialization, binding the country's economic interests closely to its own financial interests within the dollar regime (see Map 31.2).

Information technology:
The array of computers, information, electronic services, entertainment, and storage available to business and consumers, with information increasingly stored in the "cloud"—that is, online storage centers rather than individual computer hard drives.

US Technological Renewal and Globalization Communism had collapsed in part because the Soviet Union had been unwilling or unable to leap into the new industrial age of consumer electronics. The United States, by contrast, transformed itself thoroughly in the 1990s. Electronics was one of those periodic new technologies with which capitalism, always threatened by falling profit rates in maturing industries, became more profitable again. By computerizing industrial processes, businesses saved on labor. Personal computers in offices made bureaucratic procedures more efficient. A fledgling Internet speeded up communication. An entirely new branch of industry, **information technology (IT)**, put cell phones,

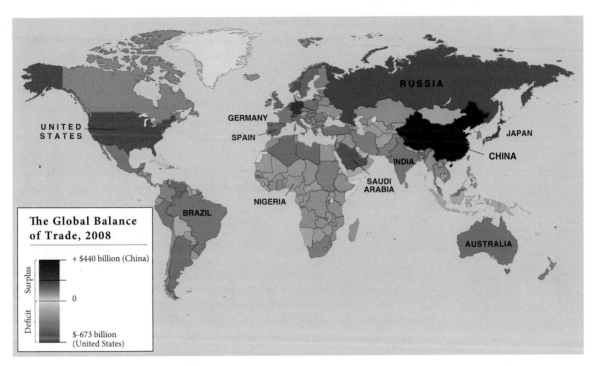

MAP **31.2** **The Global Balance of Trade, 2008.**

online delivery of music and entertainment, and a vast array of other services into the hands of consumers.

During this decade, the national budget was balanced; America became the leader in what was now called the "high-tech industry" of electronics, biotechnology, and pharmacology; unemployment shrank; inflation remained low; and the foreign debt was moderate. Worldwide, the volume of trade goods doubled and the volume of capital flows quadrupled. The US Federal Reserve kept up with demand and printed more than half as many dollars in the course of the 1990s as were already in circulation.

The only blemishes in the **globalization** process, from an American perspective, were continued protectionism and low consumption in many Asian countries. The closest economic advisors of President Bill Clinton (in office 1993–2001) were bankers and investors who had greatly expanded the size and influence of the financial services sector since the Nixon years. This sector handled the spectacularly enlarged volume of dollars floating around in the world. Alongside the traditional means of investment—stocks and bonds—new, more speculative instruments called "derivatives" gained in popularity. Derivatives were complex bets on higher or lower future prices of stocks, bonds, commodities, currencies, or anything else traded on the world market. The US globalization offensive in the 1990s was thus in large part an effort to open protected foreign markets to American financial institutions.

Globalization: The ongoing process of integrating the norms of market economies throughout the world and binding the economies of the world into a single uniform system.

Globalization and Its Critics   In many ways, the dollar- and import-sinkhole regimes were so complex that they attracted critics from the entire political spectrum dissatisfied with one or another specific aspect of the evolving system. Conservative critics were appalled that the United States no longer adhered to the gold standard and sacrificed its sovereignty to oil sheikhs trading oil for dollars. They furthermore bemoaned the disappearance of the traditional manufacturing sector and its replacement by financial institutions and Internet start-ups that produced nothing tangible. In their judgment, the United States could be held hostage to policy dictates by the foreign holders of T-bills.

Progressive critics accused the United States of using its arrangements with OPEC and the east Asian countries to exclude the poorer countries in the world that had little to offer. In their opinion, the United States pursued the maintenance of an imperialist capitalist system that limited wealth to a minority of industrialized and industrializing countries and refused to share it with the have-nots. Overall, however, both conservative and progressive criticisms remained marginal during the 1990s, given the general prosperity of the industrial countries.

US Military Dominance   In addition to pursuing global economic integration, the United States emphasized a number of basic political principles in the 1990s. A first principle was that America was and must continue to be the unchallenged military power in all regions of the world. It defined itself as the guarantor of last resort for the maintenance of world peace. Accordingly, by the year 2002, the US military budget had risen to $400 billion. This astronomical sum was considerably smaller than during the Cold War but still larger than the defense budgets of the next eight countries combined. On the basis of this military machine, President Bill Clinton operated from a position of de facto world dominance.

His successor, President George W. Bush (in office 2001–2009), articulated this dominance in an official doctrine, the National Security Strategy of 2002. American might was highly visible in all parts of the world, generating considerable resentment among those for whom the combined economic–military power of the United States amounted to a new kind of world dominance. Since 2009, however, President Barack Obama (in office 2009–) sought to reduce the American military posture by withdrawing troops from Iraq and Afghanistan and reducing the now-unsustainable military budget. In spite of these reductions, American predominance remained undiminished (see Map 31.3).

Intervention in Iraq   The National Security Strategy elevated two policies already in practice into doctrine: preventing countries from establishing dominance in a region and destroying terrorist organizations bent on destruction in the United States. The first policy was enacted after Saddam Hussein (1937–2006) and his Baath regime occupied Kuwait (1990–1991). President George H. W. Bush (in office 1989–1993) intervened when it became clear that Saddam Hussein, by invading Kuwait, sought dominance over Middle Eastern oil exports from Saudi Arabia and that the region was unable or unwilling to prevent him from achieving it. At the head of a coalition force and with UN backing, in 1992 Bush ordered US troops to evict the Iraqis from Kuwait in Operation Desert Storm. In a devastating combined air and ground war of 6 weeks, the coalition force drove the Iraqi occupiers from Kuwait.

In the following decade, the United States and United Nations subjected Iraq to a stringent military inspection regime to end Saddam Hussein's efforts to acquire nuclear and chemical weapons. The inspectors discovered large quantities of weapons and supervised their destruction. But in the face of massive Iraqi efforts at obstruction, the inspectors eventually left. Their departure was followed by a retaliatory US bombardment of Baghdad in 1998. After the US invasion of Afghanistan in 2001, a chastened Saddam Hussein readmitted the inspectors. Their inability to find anything significant touched off an intense debate among the members of the UN Security Council. The United States and Great Britain considered further inspections worthless, while France, Russia, and China argued that these inspections should be given more time. A stalemate ensued, and in an extraordinarily passionate worldwide discussion the multilateralists who advocated continued United Nations–led sanctions squared off against the unilateralists favoring a preemptive United States–led invasion of Iraq.

In the end, in March 2003, President George W. Bush espoused the unilateralist cause and ordered a preemptive invasion without Security Council backing, arguing that Iraq had once more become a regional threat. To the surprise of many, Saddam Hussein's regime put up little resistance and fell after just 3 weeks to the vastly superior US armed forces. Afterward, no weapons of mass destruction were discovered, in spite of an intense scouring of every corner of the country.

Intervention in Afghanistan   The second US principle announced in President George W. Bush's national security strategy was swift retaliation, prevention, and even preemption against nonstate challengers of American supremacy. This doctrine was a response to the rise of Islamic terrorism. In 1992, al-Qaeda ("the Base") under the leadership of Osama bin Laden (1957–2011) had emerged as the principal terrorist organization operating on an international scale.

Al-Qaeda's campaign of terrorism climaxed on September 11, 2001. Suicide commandos hijacked four commercial airliners in the northeastern United States and crashed them into the World Trade Center's Twin Towers in New York City, the Pentagon outside Washington, DC, and (after passengers on the plane disrupted the attempted hijacking) a field near Shanksville, Pennsylvania. Nearly 3,000 people died in the disasters. In response, US troops invaded Afghanistan on October 7, 2001, in an effort to eliminate bin Laden, who was protected by the regime in power. They destroyed the pro–al-Qaeda government of the Taliban, receiving support from anti-Taliban Afghans, and drove the al-Qaeda terrorists to western Pakistan. It took another decade for the United States to track down and assassinate bin Laden (May 2011) and several of his close collaborators and to come to grips with the resurgent Taliban terrorists in its ongoing war in Afghanistan.

Day of Infamy. Smoke billowing from the south tower of the World Trade Center in New York City on September 11, 2001. The north tower had already collapsed. Nearly 2,600 people died in the inferno, in which the heat of the exploding commercial airplanes in the interior of the high rises melted the steel girders supporting the buildings.

The United Nations and Regional Peace   Even though it was the United States and sometimes the North Atlantic Treaty Organization (NATO) that guaranteed peace in the 1990s and early 2000s and not the United Nations, the United Nations nevertheless fulfilled vital, if not always successful, peace

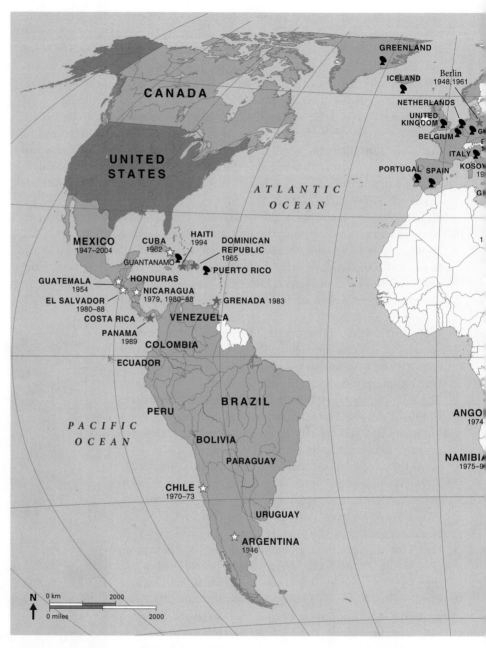

MAP **31.3** **US Security Commitments since 1945.**

missions in regional conflicts. An important example of a failure in this regard was the Rwandan civil war of 1994, in which mostly French peacekeeping troops serving under UN auspices stood by as the Hutu ethnic majority massacred the Tutsi ethnic minority by the hundreds of thousands.

On the other hand, despite the bloodshed on both sides, the crisis in the Sudan saw the United Nations fare somewhat better. Two vicious civil wars raged between Arab Muslim northern Sudan on the one hand and Christian and

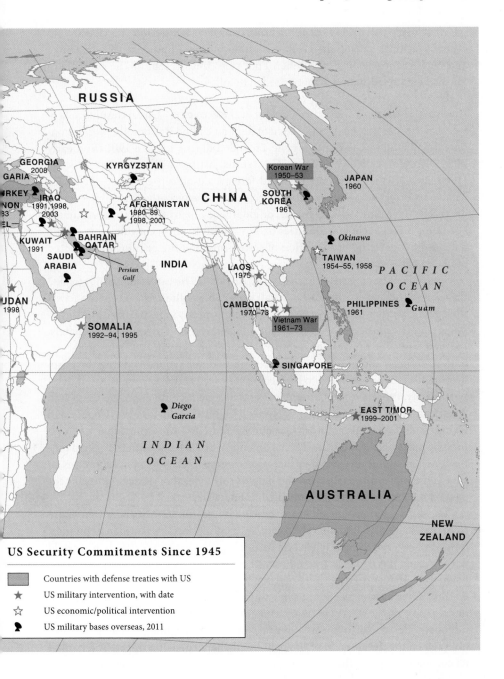

US Security Commitments Since 1945

▨ Countries with defense treaties with US

★ US military intervention, with date

☆ US economic/political intervention

♟ US military bases overseas, 2011

African-spiritual southern Sudan (1983–2005) and the non-Arab Muslim region of Darfur in western Sudan (2003–present), on the other. After lengthy efforts under UN mediation, the two sides in the first conflict agreed to the secession of South Sudan as an independent country in 2011. The Darfur conflict continued to smolder, with the United Nations pursuing criminal charges against the president of Sudan and an African Union force seeking to protect the refugees from Arab-inspired attacks. After barely two years of independence in South Sudan, the power struggle between two leading politicians degenerated into a civil war with ethnic overtones, pitting the president and former vice president and the Dinka and Nuer groups against each other. First steps toward settling the conflicts in Sudan were taken, but much more needed to follow.

American Finances Go Global: Crisis and Recovery   Under the umbrella of world peace maintained by the United States and United Nations, the world economy dominated by the dollar regime expanded during the late 1900s and early 2000s. In the so-called Washington Consensus, lasting a little more than a decade (1989–2002), Western economists and foreign aid officers preached the motto "Stabilize, Privatize, and Liberalize" to the governments of the emerging nations. To receive investments, foreign aid, or emergency loans to overcome recurrent economic crises, recipient countries had to submit to stringent rules concerning balanced budgets, the privatization of state firms, and the opening of protected branches of the economy.

Spurred by the consensus in the 1990s, private US investors had nearly tripled the value of their assets abroad, to a total of over $6.5 trillion. The now more accessible public and private financial systems in many newly industrialized and developing countries, however, were often not sufficiently robust to respond adequately. In a first crisis, the Mexican government—under pressure in 1994 from inflation, budget deficits, and political instability—could not avoid devaluing the peso. It promptly ran out of pesos to service its short-term, dollar-denominated debt. Fortunately, President Bill Clinton was at that time eager to complete the North American Free Trade Agreement (NAFTA) with Canada and Mexico. He had Congress and the International Monetary Fund (IMF) bail out Mexico with a massive infusion of loans. (The IMF is an international bank, with the US government as the largest shareholder, that provides emergency loans to countries in sudden financial distress.) With the help of this loan, the Mexican government paid off the foreign lenders and steadied its financial system.

The next crisis began in 1997 in Thailand. Here, the state finances were more solid than in Mexico. The liberalized private banking sector was still in its infancy, however, with huge unpaid loans on its books. When many private banks could not pay back their American creditors, the latter began withdrawing what they could from Thailand. American funds for derivatives moved in to speculate on the distress. Derivative managers specializing in currency bets sensed an imminent devaluation of the Thai currency, the *baht*. Since they bet with hundreds of billions of dollars, their speculation became a self-fulfilling prophecy. Accordingly, when the devaluation of the baht finally happened, it stripped Thailand of its currency reserves. Thailand—in good times one of the world's leading tourist destinations—scraped along the edge of bankruptcy, recovered in 1999, but was thrown again into turmoil in 2010–2011 and 2013–2014 in a near–civil war over allegations of corruption in the government.

From Thailand the crisis quickly expanded in 1998 to Malaysia, Indonesia, and finally even the newly industrialized Korea, Singapore, and Taiwan. These countries suffered from variations of the same problem of overcommitted banks with nonperforming portfolios. They thereby also made themselves vulnerable to American derivatives speculators invading their financial markets. The IMF had to move in with massive loans to the southeast and east Asian countries. In return, these countries had to tighten credit, close unprofitable banks and factories, tolerate higher unemployment, and promote increased exporting. Newly industrialized South Korea was relatively successful with its reforms and quickly cranked up its exports again.

Russia's Crisis and Recovery   Russia defaulted in 1998 on its internal bonds and from 1999 to 2001 on several of its external loans. These defaults were a culmination of the disastrous postcommunist economic free fall. In the decade after 1991, Russia's gross domestic product (GDP) dropped by nearly half, a decline far worse than that experienced by the United States during the Great Depression of the 1930s. Ordinary Russians had to reduce their already minimal consumption to half of what they had been used to under communism. Moreover, the government had yet to dismantle the system of unproductive former state enterprises financing themselves through local tax collection. Consequently, the state was periodically starved of funds needed for the repayment of its external loans. Fortunately, higher oil prices after 2001 eased the debt situation of Russia somewhat.

The oil and gas revenues from state firms available directly to the government, however, strengthened its autocratic tendencies. The former KGB officer Vladimir Putin, president of Russia 2000–2008 and again after 2012, was the principal engineer of this autocracy. Pervasive corruption and obedience to state directives undermined the legal system so severely that it was no longer possible to speak of the rule of law in Russia. Given the small size of the private sector in the early 2000s, the country was still years away from subjecting its state enterprises to market rules and creating a comprehensive market economy.

In addition, Putin has sharply curtailed civil rights, restricted press freedom, and made it difficult for NGOs and human rights organizations to operate in Russia. Putin has also encouraged a resurgent nationalism, a desire to restore the country to its former imperial greatness he exploits to promote his agenda of reasserting Russian hegemony. In August 2008, Putin provoked the former Soviet republic of Georgia, which was on track for admission into NATO, into a conflict that resulted in Russian control over both South Ossetia and Abkhazia. The biggest prize in Putin's imperial land grab so far is Crimea, part of Ukraine since 1954. When massive protests erupted in early 2014 against the pro-Russian Ukrainian president Viktor Yanukovych, who had scuttled a popular agreement to increase Ukraine's ties to the European Union, Yanukovych was overthrown. Putin used this opportunity to invade and seize Crimea in March 2014. A separatist, pro-Russian rebellion in eastern Ukraine has been strongly condemned by the international community.

Globalization and Poor Countries   The mixed record of development in the middle-income countries was mirrored in the bottom tier of poor countries. Since these countries still had weak manufacturing bases, their governments relied on the export of mineral or agricultural commodities to finance development. Apart from the oil-rich desert states of the Middle East, some 50 poor states depended on three or fewer commodities for over half of their export earnings. In about 20 of these states, these commodities even made up over 90 percent of export earnings. As a result of overproduction on the world market, commodity prices were depressed through most of the 1990s. The price depression imposed severe budget cutbacks on many poor countries, with consequent unemployment, middle-class shrinkage, reduction in education, and a rise in HIV infections.

In a world perspective, however, the developing world benefited from the globalization of the 1990s. Poverty declined up until the recession of 2008, although this decline was unevenly distributed among the regions of the world. The World Bank defines as "absolutely poor" a man or woman who has to live on less than $1.25 a day. According to statistics compiled during 1990–2000, the total number of the poor went down from 29 to 24 percent, even though the world population grew by nearly 1 billion. As encouraging as this figure was, the gains were concentrated almost exclusively in east and south Asia, particularly China, Vietnam, and India. The number of the absolute poor actually increased in sub-Saharan Africa, southeast Asia (except Vietnam), Russia and central Asia, and Latin America. Thus, while globalization benefited an absolute majority of humans, its uneven geographical distribution made the benefits look substantially smaller in many regions.

Two Communist Holdouts: China and Vietnam

Communism or socialism as an official ideology survived in North Korea, Cuba, China, Vietnam, North Korea, and Cuba. China and Vietnam opened their command economies to the market quite dramatically but maintained many large state firms and single-party control. In both cases, the parties remained communist in name but became in fact ordinary autocracies presiding over capitalist economies.

Two Views of China. Despite attempts to regulate its pace, China's economic acceleration continued at a torrid pace. In 2010, its GDP surpassed that of Japan to become second only to that of the United States. The new prosperity created startling contrasts and a growing diversity of lifestyles in the People's Republic. In the image above, young Chinese hipsters sport T-shirts harkening back with deliberate irony to revolutionary leaders Mao Zedong and Cuba's romantic figure of Che Guevara. In the lower panel, China's leadership—smartly decked out in Western suits and "power ties"—strive to steer the country toward continued growth as the means to preserve the ascendancy of the Chinese Communist Party.

The Chinese Economic Boom After the crushing experience of Tiananmen Square in 1989, the new Chinese middle class, benefiting from the economic reforms of the Open Door and Four Modernizations, had to accommodate itself as best it could to a repressive top layer and a corrosively corrupt bottom layer of a monopoly party that was communist in name but autocratic in practice. The basic characteristics of the middle class were remarkably similar to those of India and Turkey, discussed later in this chapter. Socially conservative migrants from the provinces to the cities found unskilled jobs in the early 1980s. They acquired skills and earned enough to send their children to school. From around 2005, the children, now with college degrees, took jobs as managers, technicians, professionals, and entrepreneurs in state companies, private firms, and Chinese branches of foreign firms. They began to flex their muscles as consumers.

To keep the middle class from demanding political participation outside the Communist Party, the government pursued accelerated annual GDP growth, which in some years went into double digits. Wages rose beyond those paid in

Vietnam, Bangladesh, India, and Pakistan. Instead of spending its earnings, however, the middle class saved at rates double those in Japan or Europe prior to the recession of 2008–2011. The only partially subsidized new health care and education systems consumed many of those savings, even though the payments were bearable under the continued conditions of the one-child law (relaxed somewhat in 2013). In addition, urban real estate and rental apartments became increasingly unaffordable in many Chinese cities during the early 2000s. Under the slogan of the "harmonious society"—in which all segments of the populace worked together with no toleration for "disruptive elements" or those advocating independence for Tibet or the ethnically Uighur region of Xinjiang—the government and party staked its continued legitimacy to ongoing economic progress.

Vietnam Taking Off   With stellar double-digit growth rates in the 1990s, Vietnam outpaced other poor Asian neighbors, such as Cambodia and Bangladesh, diversifying its manufacturing sector from textiles to footwear and electronics. Hong Kong, Taiwanese, and Korean companies, the principal foreign investors, showed a strong preference for Vietnam, on account of its advanced literacy rate and lower wages compared to China. A major new export sector from the later 1990s onward was aquaculture, the farming of shrimp, catfish, and tilapia. Vietnam moved in 2010 from the poor to the intermediate countries on the world list of nations.

A Decade of Global Shifts: Twenty-First-Century Currents and Cross-Currents

In the first and early second decade of the 2000s, there was a palpable swing toward pessimism in the West. Two recessions framed the decade, the Washington consensus fell apart over protests from borrower countries, and the problematic postwar settlement in Iraq demonstrated the limits of US power. The Middle East fared even worse, with terrorism, suicide bombings, the Syrian (2011–) and Iraqi (2014-) civil wars, no Arab–Israeli peace, and a potential Iranian nuclear bomb. By contrast, China and India, with strong economic growth rates, expanded their educated and entrepreneurial middle classes. Africa and Latin America, benefiting from the voracious demand for oil and minerals in China and India, experienced similarly strong growth. By the second decade of the 2000s, it was clear that, while there might be doubts about the course of modernity in the West, the commitment to it was growing everywhere else.

Unease in the West   Two recessions in the first decade of the 2000s in the United States sapped much of the enthusiasm about the future of modernity that had ridden so high after the fall of communism. The first—relatively mild—recession, of 2001–2003, was the so-called dot-com crisis, which had its origins in uncontrolled speculation about the expansion of the new medium of the Internet. The second—much more severe—recession of 2008–2011 began with the collapse of the housing market, as a result of the overly risky granting of real-estate mortgages to buyers with insufficient funds. Mortgage-backed uncollectable securities became "toxic," getting the banks holding them into deep financial trouble. The mortgage crisis snowballed into a general credit, credit card, and auto loan crisis, reducing consumer demand. Manufacturers, especially in the auto industry (General

Motors and Chrysler), became insolvent and mass unemployment deepened the recession. The unemployment rate reached 9.6 percent in 2010, compared to half the rate in 2000–2008. There were signs suggesting the recession of 2008–2011 could have reached the dimensions of the Great Depression of 1929–1932, had it been left unchecked.

The crisis of 2001–2003 hit the African American and Hispanic working class particularly hard; in the following recession of 2008–2011 many white workers lost their jobs. By contrast, a majority of employees in the financial sector, the upper management of large corporations, and in the information technology industry survived the recession relatively unscathed. The American public became increasingly aware of the gap that separated the top one percent of income earners and asset owners from the rest of the population.

In addition to the unease about economic inequalities, unhappiness about political and social issues grew, especially among white, middle-class, older, and evangelical voters. The Tea Party movement ("Taxed Enough Already") founded by these voters in 2009 introduced radically populist antiestablishment and anti-foreigner agendas into the political debate. This movement opted to work inside the Republican Party, seeking to reform it from within. It thereby began to push the party to the right, polarizing American politics as a result.

At first, the successful presidential campaign of Barack Obama (President 2009–), a law professor and the first African American president of the nation, gave a majority of Americans a much-needed boost of optimism to emerge from the depression. It appeared initially that the president's deficit spending helped in steadying the economy. But given the strong opposition of Congress, this spending turned out to be insufficient, and the grind of a continuing recession dragged the ebullient mood down again. Meanwhile, conservatives and Tea Party activists relentlessly criticized government spending, health-care reform, illegal immigration, and especially the slow economic recovery. In the 2010 elections, the Republicans regained the House and rejected tax increases to offset budget deficits out of hand.

A year later the Tea Party wing of the Republican Party held the nation hostage in the negotiations for an increase of the national debt ceiling. It nearly drove the country into default, and the creditworthiness of the United States was damaged. In 2013 Tea Party members repeated the action and, simultaneously, shut the government down for 16 days in a failed effort to defund the Affordable Health Care Act passed in 2010, which guaranteed health insurance for the large majority of Americans. Given the unwillingness of lawmakers to reform the tax code, the gap between the wealthy and poor continued to widen. This gap increasingly threatened the ability of middle-class Americans to consume and thereby sustain the capitalist system, given that 70 percent of the GDP was consumer-generated.

Europe saw a similar trend of rising income disparities, although this was mitigated by a stronger manufacturing sector (around 20 percent of GDP versus 11 percent in the United States in 2010) and a more generous social safety net. But the costs of this net weighed heavily on the budgets of many countries, seriously imperiling the future not only of Greece, Portugal, Spain, and Ireland (all of which fell into near-bankruptcy during the recession of 2008–2011), but also of the European Union itself. Questions arose whether the euro, which was launched with great fanfare in 1999, could be maintained as the common currency.

Since the unemployed (6.8–12 percent during 2008–2014) were entitled to long-term support in most European countries, the Tea Party-type angry populist debate was more muted during the early stages of the recession. But the rigorous policy of budget-cutting and public savings, largely imposed by Germany, slowed the recovery in 2011 to a crawl. Antiestablishment and antiforeign populism finally broke into the open in 2014 when between 19 and 27 percent of the electorate in Austria, Denmark, France, Italy, and the United Kingdom voted for anti-European candidates running for the European parliament. As in the United States, optimism about the future of modernity was at a low ebb in the second decade of the twenty-first century.

A Bloody Civil War in Yugoslavia   Eastern Europe and the Balkans went through an economic collapse and political restructuring during the 1990s similar to Russia, Ukraine, Belarus, and the other former Soviet republics. This collapse and restructuring was mostly peaceful except in Yugoslavia, where a civil war raged from 1990 to 1995. Until the 1980s, communism was the main ideology in Yugoslavia, through which the country's ethnic nationalisms of the Orthodox Christian Serbs (one-third of the population), Catholic Croats (20 percent), Muslim Bosnians (9 percent), Catholic Slovenes (8 percent), and mostly Muslim Kosovar Albanians (8 percent) were subsumed under the mantle of a federal constitution granting these ethnic groups a degree of autonomy. The main enforcer of communist unity, through carrot and stick, was President Josip Tito (1892–1980), a Croat whose authority—based on his legitimacy as an underground fighter against the Nazi occupation during World War II—was unimpeachable. After his death, however, the Serb president Slobodan Milošević ([mee-LOSH-e-vich], 1941–2006) exploited the demographic superiority of his ethnic community for the establishment of political dominance while holding on to communism as the pro forma ideology.

Yugoslavia, like many Eastern European communist states, had borrowed heavily from Western countries to keep its industries from collapsing during the oil price slump of 1985–1986. At the end of the 1980s it was practically bankrupt, with hundreds of thousands of unemployed workers carrying their dashed hopes for the good life of consumerism in the city back to their native villages. This disappointment exploded in 1990 with extraordinary fury into deadly religious–nationalist hatred, led by the smaller ethnic groups against Serbs on their territories. The Serb supremacist-nationalist backlash, with an effort to "cleanse" minorities from "greater Serbian" territory, was no less explosive. It took more than a decade for the European Union and the United States to stop the Orthodox Serbs from murdering Muslim Bosnians and Albanians and enforce a semblance of peace in the Balkans.

Since then, the five successor states of Yugoslavia have struggled to adapt to capitalism and democracy. Slovenia has done so relatively successfully, while others like Bosnia-Herzegovina, Serb-controlled Bosnia, and Kosovo have yet to master the basics, much less implement them. Serb supremacist nationalism survived the longest and only gradually began to subside when the democratically elected pro-European government decided to arrest the main perpetrators of ethnic cleansing, Radovan Karadžić ([KA-ra-jich], b. 1945) and Ratko Mladić ([my-LA-dich], b. 1943) in 2008 and 2011, respectively. The two had lived more or less openly in Serbia for years, protected by diehard followers. With these arrests and much relief, the Serbian government opened the way toward joining the European Union.

The Middle East: Paralysis, Liberation, and Islamism   As in the United States and Europe, the momentum that was generated after the collapse of communism had largely dissipated in the Middle East and North Africa by the early 2000s. In fact, with the exception of Turkey, a pall of economic and political paralysis hung over the region. The republics in the 1990s and early 2000s (e.g., Egypt, Syria, Algeria, Tunisia, and Yemen) inched intermittently toward privatization of state-run businesses but not at all toward democratization. Monarchies (Saudi Arabia, Jordan, Oman, and the Gulf sheikhdoms) actively encouraged private investment, especially in the oil sector, but were extremely cautious, if not altogether hostile, toward democratic reforms. Under the impact of the Arab Spring, in 2011 the kingdom of Morocco adopted constitutional reforms allowing for greater democracy. The "rejection front" of autocratic regimes in Iran and Syria, as well as the guerilla terrorist organizations Hezbollah in southern Lebanon and Hamas in the Gaza Strip, rejected Washington and globalization out of hand. Syria did, however, open its state-controlled economy ever so cautiously to privatization in the early 2000s.

Islamism: Religious-nationalist ideology in which the reformed Sunni or Shiite Islam of the twentieth century is used to define all institutions of the state and society.

Fear of **Islamism** was a major factor accounting for the immobility of "republican autocrats" as well as monarchs. Western secular observers often expressed surprise at the strength of the religious resurgence in the Middle East after watching its apparent demise with the rise of secular Arab nationalism and Arab socialism during the period 1952–1970. In this case, however, while Islam was less visible in the region in the twentieth century when the political elites consisted of secular liberals and nationalists, it had not receded at all from the villages and poor city quarters, where it remained as vital as ever.

The key to understanding the rise of Islamism lay in the acceleration of rural–urban migration in the Middle East in the late 1990s and early 2000s. Ever since the 1960s, when Middle Eastern and North African governments built the first large state-run manufacturing plants in their cities, the workers were largely peasants arriving from villages with highly localized cultures of saintly Sufi (mystical) Islam. They encountered militant preachers in the cities who—representing a reformed, standardized, urban Sunni Islam—were appalled by the "un-Islamic" saint cults among the workers. The children of these workers learned a similar standardized Islam in the schools, intended to buttress Arab nationalism, in which the Prophet Muhammad was the first nationalist. Standard Islam and militant urban Islamism gradually crowded out the rural saintly Islam and eventually produced small but potent offshoots of Islamist terrorism, such as al-Qaeda, the Taliban, and the Salafists.

In the 1990s and early 2000s Middle Eastern governments essentially barricaded themselves behind their secret services and armies against the onslaughts of these Islamists. Terrorists attacked tourists, as happened periodically in Egypt, seeking to bring down a government that relied heavily on Western tourism. Sometimes they picked weak states such as Yemen, which, relying on dwindling oil revenues, began to lose control of its nomadic groups in the east, agricultural minorities in the north, and urban secessionists in the south. In this condition, it became a haven for al-Qaeda terrorists. Even a stronger state, Algeria, suffered a devastating civil war that claimed 150,000 victims from 1992 to 2002. Under the threat of Islamist terrorism, Middle Eastern and North African governments found it impossible to pursue bold new initiatives of the kind that China or India advanced.

The Growth of Hezbollah   One area where Islamists achieved a breakthrough was Lebanon. Hezbollah ("Party of God"), an Islamist guerilla organization with attendant social services and recruiting from among the Shiite majority of Lebanese Muslims, waged an underground war against Israel. It succeeded in 2000 at driving Israel from southern Lebanon after an 18-year occupation that had begun with Israel expelling the Palestine Liberation Organization (PLO) from the country. Thereafter, it periodically fired rockets into Israel and repelled a retaliatory Israeli raid in 2006. During this time, Hezbollah was apparently also active abroad: It was accused of bombing the US embassy in Beirut in 1983, hijacking an American airliner in 1985, and carrying out two bombings against Jews in Argentina in 1992 and 1994 and the bombing of an Israeli tour bus in Bulgaria in 2012. By the second decade of the 2000s, Hezbollah had evolved into the most formidable enemy of Israel.

In 2013, Hezbollah even grew into the role of a regional, quasi-state actor. Not only did it come to dominate the Lebanese administration, it became a decisive force strengthening Bashar al-Assad in his civil war against his Arab Spring challengers (see below). Increasingly, Sunni terrorist groups were elbowing the challengers aside, seeking to turn the Syrian civil war into a sectarian conflict. Hezbollah and its patron, Iran, were determined to assert the role of Shiism in the contemporary Middle East. Given the internal conflicts in Egypt, Iran emerged as a main power in Middle Eastern politics.

Israel and Gaza   During the globalization of the 1990s, Israel developed an advanced economy specializing in high-tech software and microbiology. In 1994, it was officially at peace with two Arab neighbors, Egypt and Jordan. But it continued to face a hostile Arab Middle East in general and restless Palestinians in the occupied territories on the West Bank and in Gaza, in particular. To protect its citizens from guerilla attacks, the Israeli government built a border fence in 2002–2013, supplemented in places by a wall of concrete slabs, inside the entire length of the occupied West Bank. In many places, this fence veered into West Bank territory, separating Palestinian villagers from their farmland. In a parallel move it withdrew from the fenced-in Gaza Strip in 2005. Suicide attacks were fewer, but cross-border rocket attacks from Gaza increased, trapping Israel in a cat-and-mouse game of low-level cross-border warfare.

After 2006, Israel slid into an even worse trap. In the first-ever Palestinian elections the victory in Gaza went to the Islamic guerilla organization Hamas, founded in 1988, over the older, secular, ethnic-nationalist PLO. The PLO, deprived of its inspiring leader Yasir Arafat, was able to prevail only in the West Bank. The PLO refused to recognize the elections, and a civil war broke out, in which Hamas was victorious, forcing the PLO to retreat to the West Bank. Israel imposed a complete embargo on Hamas-ruled Gaza in an attempt to bring the organization down.

For those in Israel who wished to renew the Camp David peace process, left incomplete in 2000, the PLO–Hamas split was a disaster, since it threw the entire idea of a two-state solution into doubt. Hamas was happy to deepen this doubt in the following years by launching thousands of rockets against Israel. In retaliation, Israel invaded Gaza in December–January 2008–2009, causing unmitigated misery for the Palestinian population of Gaza, but was not able to defeat Hamas. Efforts at healing the split between PLO and Hamas produced no results. In the summer of 2014 vicious war between Israel and Hamas erupted once again.

Israel's Predicament and Iranian Ambitions   The failure of the Lebanon invasion in 2009 brought a conservative government into power in Israel. The government renewed the open pursuit of Israeli settlement construction in the West Bank while tightening the embargo on Gaza. But neither more Jewish settlements in the West Bank (making the two-state solution illusory) nor punishing Israel's neighbors Hezbollah and Hamas with invasions and/or embargoes brought the country closer to peace. In fact, a major US push toward a peace settlement in 2013–2014 ended not only without results but also with renewed mutual accusations. The formation of a PLO–Hamas unity government of technocrats in 2014 was greeted by Israel with further settlement plans. Israel's long dominance over its neighbors, gradually acquired in the last half of the twentieth century, appeared to have reached its limits in the early years of the twenty-first.

Hezbollah and Hamas were able to assert themselves against Israel thanks to Iran, which supplied them with rockets. Iran, a leader of the rejectionist front against Israel, had experienced a "pragmatic" period after the death of its spiritual guide, Ruhollah Khomeini, in 1989. This pragmatism had raised the hope that the Shiite Islamist regime was lessening its policy of fighting what it viewed as the "satanic" Western culture of secularism, liberalism, and pop culture. But the reformers were timid, and the still-powerful clerics systematically undermined attempts at democratic and cultural reforms.

Any remaining hopes for reform were dashed when Mahmoud Ahmadinejad [ah-ma-DEE-nay-jahd] (b. 1956), an engineer from a modest rural background, was elected president. He renewed the anti-Western crusade and adopted a policy of populism, with subsidies for food and gas as well as distributions of cash by the suitcase on his cross-country trips. Most important, under his leadership, the Revolutionary Guard became not only the most effective military organization but, by investing in a wide variety of businesses, also a huge patronage machine.

The precipitous decline of revenues from oil exports during the recession of 2008–2011, however, seriously reduced Ahmadinejad's populist appeal. Hence, he needed the Revolutionary Guard commanders to falsify the elections of 2009 to stay in power. Suspected Iranian ambitions for acquiring a nuclear bomb, coupled with North Korea's already existing nuclear arsenal, created recurrent nightmares in the world about nuclear proliferation, "dirty" nuclear material in the hands of terrorists, and the possibility of nuclear war by "rogue" nations. Put under a severe economic sanctions regime by the United Nations, Iran elected a less populist and more pragmatic president, Hasan Rouhani (b. 1948), in 2013 and began to search for ways to stabilize the dire economic situation. Rouhani negotiated an initial easing of some sanctions in return for increased inspections and a limitation on nuclear enrichment in November 2013.

The Ascent of Turkey   Turkey was the one Middle Eastern country to have largely escaped Islamist militancy and had become one of the most dynamic newly industrialized countries in the world. In contrast to other regimes in the Middle East, Turkish Muslims found access to the political process, thanks to a well-established and functioning multiparty system. After many false starts and interruptions by military coups d'état, a right-of-center party with a strong contingent of Islamists in 1983 not only captured the premiership of the country but simultaneously implemented bold new initiatives of economic privatization and industrial export orientation. Benefiting from these initiatives, an entire new middle class of socially conservative but economically liberal entrepreneurial businesspeople arose.

In an even more effective second wave of Islamist middle-class expansion after 2003 under Prime Minister Recep Erdoğan [RAY-jep er-dow-AHN] (b. 1954), Turkey's GDP grew to become the world's fifteenth largest. Elections in June 2011 enabled Erdoğan's party to garner slightly more than half of the vote and, on the basis of this vote, enacted constitutional reforms which rescinded the military's power in politics. His electoral strength, however, misled Erdoğan into believing that he could repress environmentally motivated popular protests in Istanbul in 2013 without damaging the democratic process. Even more damage occurred soon thereafter when he sought to quash a corruption scandal among a number of ministers and their sons by removing investigating police and state attorneys from their positions. The repression revealed a deep rift among factions in the ruling party. Thus, while Turkey largely completed its arrival in capitalist modernity, it has yet to complete the democratic counterpart.

The Arab Spring of 2011   Turkey was a model example for the compatibility of Islam and beginning democracy. But in spring 2011 Tunisia and Egypt each saw constitutional-nationalist revolutions, which demonstrated that democracy could sprout in Arab countries as well. On December 17, 2010, 26-year-old Mohamed Bouazizi set himself ablaze in a last spectacular act of despair brought about by the humiliations he had suffered at the hands of a Tunisian policewoman.

Democracy's Martyr.
A refashioned monument in the city of Sidi Bouzid, Tunisia, in honor of Mohamed Bouazizi, whose portrait is visible on top of the monument. Bouazizi was a street vendor, selling fruits and vegetables. After months of harassment by the police, he set himself afire in despair. His example galvanized young, educated, and social network–savvy Tunisians into their peaceful Arab Spring revolution.

Bouazizi's death touched off the mostly peaceful democratic revolutions dubbed the "Arab Spring," on which we centered this chapter's opening vignette. Beginning in Tunisia, they snowballed into Egypt, Libya, Bahrain, Yemen, and Syria in the course of early 2011. In Tunisia and Egypt they ousted longtime and aging autocrats, Tunisia's Zine El Abidine Ben Ali (r. 1987–2011) and Egypt's Hosni Mubarak (r. 1981–2011). After months of fighting, Libya's Muammar el-Qaddafi (r. 1969–2011) was finally toppled in September 2011 and killed a month later. Autocratic rulers in countries seeing similar protests held on with iron nerves and unrestrained brutality. Central to the nonviolent daily rallies in Tunisia and Egypt, continuing for days and weeks, were demands for freedom, equality, fair elections, the end of corruption (especially crony capitalism), new democratic constitutions, the rule of law, and, last but not least, jobs.

The demonstrators, for the most part young, Internet-savvy, educated, and fully conversant with international youth culture, documented the events through pictures, videos, and blogs and revealed police violence for the world to instantly see. Social connectedness and the direct transmission of facts on the ground gave these constitutional revolutions a new character. Now a world public watching these events could declare solidarity with the demonstrators and demand action from its own politicians. As these democratic revolutions were beginning to be implemented, however, they raised the question of how closely the young demonstrators were integrated into the rest of the population, such as Islamists, as well as the urban and rural traditional Muslims. Would they be able to relate to the population at large with their demonstrations?

> "When we took part in the protests it was just a protest for our basic human rights, but they [the regime] escalated it to a revolution . . . They empowered us through their violence; they made us hold onto the dream of freedom even more."
>
> —Egyptian filmmaker Salma El Tarzi, 2011

Unfortunately, the Arab Spring activists were too diverse in their interests to be able to translate their newfound power into electoral victories. In both Tunisia and Egypt, elections brought organizationally more unified Islamist parties to power, even if only by slim margins. These parties went to work immediately to Islamize Tunisia and Egypt, even though they had not participated much in the Arab Spring demonstrations. Renewed mass demonstrations in 2013, this time against the Islamization measures, became unmanageable, and in Egypt the military stepped in. In a coup d'état, the military ended both the tenure of President Muhammad Morsi (r. 2012–2013) and the Arab Spring. In Tunisia, the political process broke down as well in 2013, but in the absence of a large army the opponents sought to resolve the breakdown through negotiations. In Egypt, the military deepened its rule in 2014 through the adoption of a new constitution and the election of a new president, Abdel Fattah Sisi (b. 1954), even though only 38 and 46 percent of the citizens, respectively, voted. In Tunisia, by contrast, the Islamist government stepped aside in favor of a government of technocrats that is to complete work on a new constitution and hold new elections. Thus, Islamism entered a period of crisis, with further democratization slowing down.

In Syria, hopes for an Arab Spring were dashed almost immediately. The first pro-democracy protests began in mid-March, but the president, Bashar al-Assad (b. 1965), sought to suppress them with an iron fist, beginning in the end of April and continuing until early June when the protests turned into an armed rebellion. Assad was the heir of the secular Arab-socialist regime of the Baath Party in which members of the small Shiite sect of the Alawites from northwestern Syria held the key army and secret service positions. Baath bureaucrats pursued a policy of state capitalism as late as 1991 when first concessions to economic liberalization were finally granted.

Although a large majority of Sunni Arabs (64 percent of the population of 22 million), Sunni Kurds (10 percent), and Christian Arabs (9 percent) benefited from the Baath's policies of industrialization, urbanization, and education, income disparities grew during the period of economic liberalization in the 1990s and early 2000s. An uprising in 1982 by Islamists in Hama had been bloodily suppressed at the cost of some 20,000 lives and a brief "Damascus Spring" at the beginning of Assad's rule (2000–2001), during which prisoners were released and political pluralism was discussed, ended with rearrests and repression. Although Syria was led by a young president, it did not differ much from the old-men regimes of Tunisia and Egypt in early 2011.

During the summer of 2011, the Arab Spring uprising grew into a full-fledged civil war. The initially untrained rebels were increasingly joined in 2012 by hardened Sunni jihadists with battle experience from Afghanistan, Iraq, Yemen, and the Russian Caucasus. At the same time, Assad released Islamists from his own prisons to the rebels, so as to discourage the United States and Europe from arming the secular wing of the opposition, for fear of their weapons falling into the hands of the jihadists. The brutality with which Assad battled his opponents—he used chemical weapons (until stopped in 2013 by the United States) as well as indiscriminate barrel bombs, in addition to heavy artillery, airplanes, and helicopters—caused a mass exodus of refugees (over 9 million) to neighboring countries. Until the end of 2013 Assad was on the defensive, but thanks to unwavering support from Russia and Iran, as well as soldiers from Iran and the Lebanese Hezbollah, he regained the initiative. Even though he gave up large swaths of land in the north and northeast he made major gains in the populated corridor between Damascus and Aleppo.

In the northeast, Assad discreetly gave some of the most radical jihadists free rein, even though this meant allowing them to control Syria's oil wells in the region. The organization "Islamic State in Iraq and al-Sham [historical Syria]" or ISIS took advantage of Assad's ploy in 2013. Aiming not merely at terrorism but the reconstruction of the seventh-century caliphate allegedly based on the pristine Islam of the Quran and Sunna, ISIS developed its own forms of brutality which alienated it from the other anti-Assad jihadist groups in northern Syria. Led by the former Iraqi al-Qaeda operative Abu Bakr al-Baghdadi (b. 1971), a man from Samarra with a religious education, ISIS built a state in northeastern Syria based on draconic Islamic laws, steep taxes on non-Muslims, as well as money from hostages, bank heists, and oil.

In early 2014, well-paid and highly disciplined ISIS units crossed into Iraq and occupied parts of the cities of Falluja and Ramadi. In the middle of the year they followed up with a lightning campaign that netted them central Iraq, with the city of Mosul as the major prize. The troops of the largely impotent Iraqi government fled with hardly a shot fired. The result of this unexpected turn of events was not only the de facto division of Iraq into a triad of Kurdish, Sunni, and Shiite polities but also the utter evaporation of what were even the minimal achievements of the humanly and financially expensive US war in Iraq during 2003–2011.

Driving Toward Prosperity. The Bajaj scooter was the early status symbol of the emerging Indian middle class. On account of their size, the Indian and Chinese middle classes, numbering perhaps in the hundreds of millions, are powerful groups, representing a huge reservoir of ever-more-demanding consumers. This picture is from 2010, when the Indian middle class had come of age.

The New Middle Class in India   The rise of a conservative Islamic middle class in Turkey and other Middle Eastern countries had its parallel in India in the rise of a religiously conservative Hindu middle class of shopkeepers, traders, merchants, and small manufacturers. The new Indian middle class—defined by a cell phone, motorized transportation, and a color TV—includes anywhere between 60 and 300 million Indians, in a population of 1.2 billion in 2010. During the 1990s and early 2000s, the secular Congress Party enjoyed the trust of the new middle class. But an economic slowdown in 2013 and the perception of bureaucratic immobility, cronyism, and corruption returned the religiously oriented Bharatiya Janata Party to power in the 2014 elections.

The most dynamic members of the new middle class live and work in the southern heavy industry and high-tech hub of Bangalore. Because the city is 12.5 hours ahead of California, it is perfect for effecting linkages to maintain around-the-clock computing with Silicon Valley. By the second decade of the 2000s, these two leading world centers of information technology on opposite sides of the globe had become closely integrated.

The rapid expansion of urban centers such as Bangalore greatly contributed to the decline of the traditional caste divisions in Hinduism within the urban and even, to some degree, rural contexts. Widespread protests in 2006 against the complex affirmative action system introduced in the 1990s in favor of less-privileged social groups indicated the beginning of a dissolution of the caste divisions in the urban environment. Since descent could be hidden in the cities, even the untouchable caste (*dalit*) began to enter the new middle class.

The success of the middle class in India, impressive as it is, must be measured against conditions in the countryside, much of which is still largely outside the market economy. Almost three-quarters of the population lived in villages with poor or no water, electricity, and roads at the beginning of the twenty-first century. An overwhelming majority of villagers lived in extreme poverty (less than $1.25 per day), existing completely outside the market circuit and depending on handouts. This majority declined in the first decade of the 2000s, perhaps by one-quarter, helped by a sinking birth rate that stood at 2 percent in 2013. A major factor in the persistence of poverty was an incomplete land reform. Landlordism and tenancy continued to encompass nearly half of the rural population. Large landholdings had been abolished after independence, but medium and small landlordism persisted undiminished. As a major voting bloc in the Congress Party, the landlords were successful in resisting further land reform.

African Transformations   The half-decade between the oil price slump, debt crisis, and disappearance of communism (1985–1991) was as challenging for sub-Saharan Africa as it was for India. The continent's GDP in the early 1990s was down by almost half from what it was in 1975 when all main social and economic indicators were at their peak. The decline of living conditions was particularly devastating in the health services sector, cut back by half in almost all countries, in spite of a steady increase in HIV/AIDS. Many countries expended more hard currency on their debt services than on education. With a doubling of the population at the absolute poverty level ($1.25 per day), sub-Saharan Africa became by far the poorest region in the world.

During this time, the urban population of sub-Saharan Africa increased to almost one-third of the total population, making it more numerous than that of India but still smaller than that of China, where nearly half of the population was urban. The urbanization process was an important factor for the political consequences of the crisis: Students, civil servants, and journalists became restless and demanded political reforms. Up until the early 1990s, almost everywhere state structures were patronage hierarchies: The civilian or military rulers in power provided cushy government jobs for the ethnic groups from which they hailed. Although all 54 African countries were officially "nations" with seats in the United Nations, none (except South Africa) was either a functionally constitutional or ethnically uniform nation. Urban dwellers, however, were less tied to ethnicity and more committed to constitutionalism. They felt little sympathy for autocratic rulers and their kin running the states into financial ruin and pushed for democratic reforms in the late 1990s and early 2000s.

Unfortunately, the push for reforms had mixed results. On the one hand, while a majority of rulers in power prior to 1991 had exited office as a result of coups or assassinations, after 1991 they either resigned voluntarily or stepped down after losing elections. On the other hand, incumbents still won more often than not, and honest elections were rare. Some regime changes were truly thrilling, notably the end of apartheid and the election of Nelson Mandela (1918–2013, president 1994–1999) in the Republic of South Africa; three cycles (2004–2012) of clean multiparty elections in Ghana; the first election of a female African president, the Harvard-trained economist Ellen Johnson Sirleaf (b. 1938, elected 2006 and

Social Networking

As we have seen, the Tunisian revolution sparked a wave of revolts across North Africa and the Middle East in what has come to be called the Arab Spring. What makes these movements unique, however, is that they were organized and carried out by means of *social networking sites* (SNSs) like Twitter, Facebook, and YouTube, supported by cell phones and other modern communication technologies. But what are the origins of these devices, and how have they developed into such important tools of political and social revolution?

SNSs can ultimately be traced back to the origins of the Internet and the World Wide Web. The Internet is a product of the Cold War. In 1969 the US government initiated the Advanced Research Projects Agency (ARPA), which created a system linking computers at major universities into a network that allowed them to share vital information. From this small step the Internet expanded during the 1990s into a global computer network. The World Wide Web was conceived in 1989 and launched two years later as a part of the Internet. Simply put, the "web" uses the Internet to gain access to categories of data, documents, and other resources found within the larger network.

The Face of Revolution. Perhaps the most novel aspect of the ongoing "Arab Spring" has been the widespread use of social media in recruiting, organizing, and popularizing the efforts of activists in various countries. The inventiveness of the participants in avoiding government scrutiny and bypassing restrictions on SNSs has become legendary. Here a Syrian man logs into his Facebook account "legally" for perhaps the first time in February, 2011.

reelected 2011) in Liberia; and the relatively clean Nigerian presidential elections of 2007 and 2011.

Setbacks in 2012 and 2013, however, with coups d'état and armed revolts in Guinea Bissau, Mali, the Central African Republic, and South Sudan, were stark reminders that African democratization is still fragile. For a short period, Mali even split apart into a rump republic in the populated south and an Islamist state in the north (2012–2013). It was eventually reunited only after an armed intervention by France.

Islamism was also a factor in bloody conflicts engulfing the Central African Republic and northern Nigeria. In the Central African Republic, a rebellion by leaders from the Muslim minority in the north led to a ferocious backlash from the Christian majority in the south, requiring the intervention of a European Union peace contingent to establish a tenuous truce in 2014. In Northern Nigeria, the

SNSs sprang up in the 1990s when it was recognized that the Internet provided social groups the means to easily communicate with each other and to share information. By the 2000s, social networking sites represented a global explosion of instantaneously distributed information that revolutionized the nature of communication.

An early example of the power of SNSs to effect change was the so-called Twitter Revolution in Iran in 2009, during which antigovernment activists used the full range of SNSs while engaged in an ultimately futile effort to overthrow the Iranian regime. Following the success of the Tunisian revolution, however, an even more spectacular display of the power of SNSs erupted in Egypt on January 25, 2011, when thousands of protesters took to the streets to demand the ouster of the authoritarian president Hosni Mubarak. This "Facebook Revolution," was launched by the April 6 Youth Movement, a Facebook group composed of social and political activists.

For all their success in facilitating uprisings against authoritarian governments, however, SNSs are used with equal effectiveness by extremist terrorist groups. Al-Qaeda and the Taliban have learned to take advantage of Facebook and Twitter to broadcast their calls for global *jihad*. SNSs are also used to solicit financial support and share information concerning plans for forthcoming attacks. Moreover, SNSs—particularly Facebook—serve as effective recruitment tools. How ironic that Internet websites originally intended for exchanges among friends have been transformed into tools to spread revolution, violence, and terrorism.

Questions

- How do SNSs show how an innovation can be adapted for purposes wholly different from the original purposes for which they were intended?

- Do you believe SNSs have allowed young people around the world to make their wishes and aspirations more powerfully felt? If so, what does this say about the connection between technology and youth?

government proved to be completely incompetent against the rapidly expanding Islamist movement Boko Haram ("Western education is sin"). Founded in 2002, this jihadist organization intent on introducing Sharia law staged increasingly daring raids, beginning in 2009 and culminating in 2014 with the abduction of over 300 Christian schoolgirls. African as well as foreign observers note the rise in sectarian conflicts on the continent with growing concern.

The African economy picked up in the early 2000s, mostly because of rising commodity prices. The main oil exporters (Nigeria, Angola, Chad, Sudan, Gabon, Cameroon, Equatorial New Guinea, and the two Republics of the Congo) benefited from higher oil prices, as did the mining countries of South Africa, Zambia, both Congos, and Malawi with their diamonds, gold, copper, silver, zinc, lead, and other rare metals. In a United Nations–sponsored scheme in 1998, "blood diamonds" mined to finance civil wars, as in Angola, Sierra Leone, Liberia, Ivory

Freedom, Justice, and Dignity. The end of apartheid in 1994 and the election of Nelson Mandela (1918–2013), seen here visiting his former prison cell, was an inspiring event in Africa and the rest of the world. South Africa is the richest and most industrialized country of Africa, with large mineral and agricultural resources. Nearly 80 percent of the population is black, speaking its own languages, including isiZulu and isiXhosa. But Afrikaans (a Dutch-originated language) remained the dominant media language, with English being only the fifth most spoken language. In spite of South Africa's relative wealth, years of apartheid have resulted in vast income disparities.

Coast, and both Congos, were subjected to certification so as to prevent future wars. (Diamonds mined in Zimbabwe were exempted, since Zimbabwe's disintegration into a failed state was not considered to be the effect of a civil war.) Apart from minerals, agricultural products, such as coffee, cotton, and fresh flowers for the European market, also regained significance in the early 2000s. The global recessions of 2001 and 2008 did not have a major impact, largely because of the arrival of China on the scene as a major buyer and investor. Optimism about a sustained recovery and modernity within reach was clearly visible on the continent, even if tempered by continuing ethnic and sectarian conflicts.

Latin American Expansion   Elections after the scare of the financial meltdowns in the freewheeling 1990s produced more fiscally restrained, socially engaged governments in the large Latin American countries during the early 2000s. Democratic transitions in Mexico, Brazil, Argentina, and Chile (the latter three with socially oriented governments) demonstrated that the unhappy years of military dictatorships in the 1980s had been left behind. In Mexico the long rule of the Institutional Revolutionary Party (PRI) was interrupted from 2000 to 2012, with an orderly transition to less socially engaged Christian Democratic presidents. Only in 2012 did a markedly rejuvenated PRI return to power. It continued the pattern of economic liberalization begun at the beginning of the century.

Two extraconstitutional events in smaller Latin American countries, however, demonstrated that authoritarian temptations still survived. The first was an abortive uprising in 2002 of army units in Paraguay, allegedly instigated by a former commander outside the country who was wanted for an earlier coup attempt. The second, in Honduras in 2009, was the forcible removal of the president, who intended to hold a referendum on his plan for reelection, even though it had been forbidden by the Honduran constitutional court. More disruptive were continued efforts by revolutionary Marxists in Colombia to overthrow the government, even though their liberation movement, founded in 1964, declined in the early 2000s. In neighboring Venezuela, President Hugo Chávez (1954–2013), a former officer from a working-class background, was alone in mainland Latin America in his adherence to state socialism, encountering periodic middle-class resistance.

Industrialization, largely through foreign investments but increasingly also through internal financing, stimulated state-run firms to become competitive and even to privatize in several large Latin American countries. In some cases, as with Brazilian Embraer commercial airplanes or the electronics and information technology industry of Guadalajara in Mexico, Latin American countries have become world competitors. All four large economies—Brazil, Mexico, Argentina, and Chile—exported more manufactured goods than commodities by 2008. These countries clearly displayed the features of scientific–industrial modernity by the second decade of the 2000s.

The Environmental Limits of Modernity

What we have defined in the last two parts of this book as *modernity*—the political systems marked by constitutional and ethnic nationalism, as well as the economic systems propelled by science and industrialism—has now become not simply a regional or "Western" phenomenon but a global one. In the absence of the competing subpatterns of modernity—communism and supremacist nationalism—the systems of capitalism, consumerism, and democracy embodied by the United States, Canada, western Europe, and Australia have increasingly become the ones to emulate. All new nations in the world either are industrializing or seeking to do so if they have the financial means. The principal obstacle for these nations is the debilitating poverty of the great majority of their inhabitants, who are still mired in either subsistence farming or marginal work in the shantytowns of sprawling cities. The poorest are unskilled and uneducated and, because of high infant mortality rates and the need for farm labor and old-age support, still view large families as a necessity. Improved public health care is helping to raise life spans for the poorest people, but the combination of modern medicine and the desire for large families has caused a startling increase in the world population since the middle of the twentieth century.

Sustainability and Global Warming   In 1800, there was only one country (Great Britain) embarking on industrialization; by 1918, there were about a dozen countries (Europe and Japan), and by 1945 about three dozen countries (on three continents) had industrialized themselves. Today, about two-thirds of the 194 independent countries of the world are either industrialized or on the way toward full industrialization. We are only now, however, beginning to grasp the environmental consequences of this move to scientific–industrial modernity. Until about the last quarter of the twentieth century the carbon footprint of these countries had risen from 280 parts per million (ppm) of atmospheric carbon dioxide and

A Smoggy Future. China, the world's worst emitter of greenhouse gases, has large numbers of coal-fed power plants and factories which continue to belch out carbon dioxide as well as toxic substances into the air, with little scrubbing or other devices to clean the emissions before they reach the atmosphere. Here, a power plant on the outskirts of Linfen in Shanxi Province southwest of Beijing fouls the environment in 2009.

other chemical compounds—commonly called "greenhouse gases"—to 330 ppm. Between 1975 and 2010 the concentration of greenhouse gases in the atmosphere climbed to 380 ppm. In other words, a rise of 50 ppm in 175 years was followed by a rise of 70 ppm in only 35 years.

While there has been considerable debate over the last several decades on the nature and degree of global warming—whether it is a natural cyclical phenomenon or human-produced or even if it exists at all—there is a general scientific consensus that greenhouse gases are the main contributors to temperature increases on earth. Scientists generally assume that at current rates of greenhouse gas production the earth will reach a "tipping point" of 450 ppm, with irreversible consequences for the planet's climate, before the middle of this century.

What will happen when this tipping point is reached? If projections hold true, the polar ice caps and high mountain glaciers will melt. Ocean levels, rising from the melted ice, will submerge many islands and make inroads on the coasts of all continents. Widespread droughts and violent storms will regularly hit various parts of the earth, eroding by wind and flood what in many places had previously been fertile land. The world's tropical forests, already considerably reduced from timber harvesting and agricultural expansion, may well be wiped out, removing the most important agents for cleaning the atmosphere of greenhouse gases. Pollution and overfishing will leave little of the world's marine life. Biodiversity will be dramatically reduced, with many animal and plant species dying out. The consequence of these grim developments will likely be a severe reduction of the earth's arable land and fisheries needed for the production of food.

The ultimate outcome of this prospective climate transformation will be much worse for the new countries with less wealth to cushion them than for the older ones that industrialized early and have the resources to adjust. The crushing irony of such projections, therefore, is that the nations that viewed their adaptation to modernity as their salvation may well find themselves among the first to be doomed.

Scientific and Political Debate   There is a consensus among scientists that the warming trend in the world from greenhouse gases is real. Very few scientists still hold a skeptical view. The general public is gradually coming around to taking global warming seriously, though less so in the United States than in Europe. But vocal minorities still vociferously denounce climate warming as a hoax or conspiracy. So far, political responses have been tepid and largely divided.

By 2013, a total of nine UN conferences had been convened since the 1997 Kyoto Protocol that established benchmarks for the reduction of greenhouse gases in the European Union and 38 industrialized countries. But only the European Union was on track to meet its provision, mandating an annual reduction of 5.2 percent. The remaining countries were substantially off the mark. The 2013 Warsaw conference saw bitter conflicts over the inclusion of newly industrialized countries into the Kyoto Protocol and financial compensation demanded by

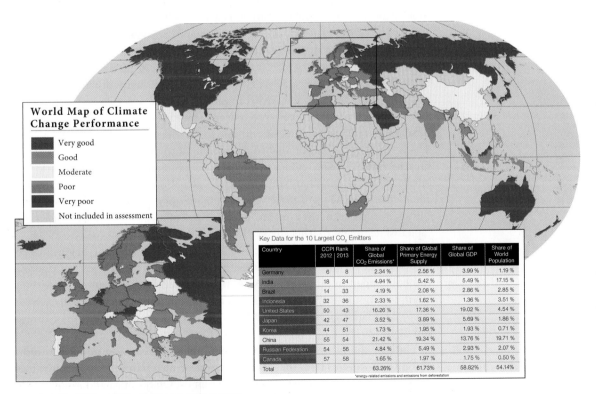

World Map of Climate Change Performance

- Very good
- Good
- Moderate
- Poor
- Very poor
- Not included in assessment

Country	CCPI Rank 2012	CCPI Rank 2013	Share of Global CO$_2$ Emissions*	Share of Global Primary Energy Supply	Share of Global GDP	Share of World Population
Germany	6	8	2.34 %	2.56 %	3.99 %	1.19 %
India	18	24	4.94 %	5.42 %	5.49 %	17.15 %
Brazil	14	33	4.19 %	2.08 %	2.86 %	2.85 %
Indonesia	32	36	2.33 %	1.62 %	1.36 %	3.51 %
United States	50	43	16.26 %	17.36 %	19.02 %	4.54 %
Japan	42	47	3.52 %	3.89 %	5.69 %	1.86 %
Korea	44	51	1.73 %	1.95 %	1.93 %	0.71 %
China	55	54	21.42 %	19.34 %	13.76 %	19.71 %
Russian Federation	54	56	4.84 %	5.49 %	2.93 %	2.07 %
Canada	57	58	1.65 %	1.97 %	1.75 %	0.50 %
Total			63.26%	61.73%	58.82%	54.14%

Key Data for the 10 Largest CO$_2$ Emitters

*energy-related emissions and emissions from deforestation

MAP **31.4 World Map of Climate Change Performance.**

developing countries for damages suffered from extreme weather. As agreed upon in Warsaw, governments are now supposed to formulate new targets for greenhouse gas emission curbs by 2015—curbs to begin in 2020.

At present, the consensus is that if the European 5.2 percent reduction rate were to continue after 2013 and everyone would sign on to this rate, the eventual decline in temperature by the middle of the twenty-first century would be 0.2 degree Fahrenheit below the current average temperature. Whether this would be sufficient to reverse the melting of polar ice and the onset of irregular weather patterns is debatable. But if present trends with minimal or no reductions continue, the projected temperature increase in 2050 will be more likely in the range of 3–4 degrees Fahrenheit—enough for the projections to indicate the catastrophic consequences we have mentioned, which are widely agreed to be irreversible.

> "Go back in your life to think about the hottest, most traumatic event you have experienced. What we're saying is that very soon [between 2047 and 2069], that event is going to become the norm."
>
> —Biogeographer Camilo Mora

Putting It All Together

The first decade of the twenty-first century witnessed the final transformation of the world from a millennia-old agrarian–urban pattern of life to a new scientific–industrial pattern. All of this was accomplished in the breathtakingly short span of 200 years. What had begun as a culturally specific, western European–pioneered transition, first from descriptive to mathematical science and then from agriculture to industry, had become ubiquitous. Everywhere in the world people have been adapting to a new role as individuals with well-defined "human rights," who aspire to be educated, find fulfilling jobs, become consumers, and achieve a materially secure life—in short, they are becoming *modern*.

The twentieth century also saw the original pattern of modernity split into three. World War I was a cataclysm that produced proponents of a first modernity, who sought to create competitive, capitalist, democratic societies; a second modernity, which sought to collapse power hierarchies and differences of wealth through equality in socialist–communist societies; and a third modernity, in which supremacist-nationalist societies sought to impose the will of allegedly superior races or ethnic groups through conquest (if not complete elimination) of inferior ones. Tremendous suffering and destruction accompanied the struggle among the proponents of these visions of modernity, and in a gradual process of elimination, it was the messiest and most unruly of the three forms of modernity—capitalist democracy—that survived.

Today, the faith in democracy that marked the exuberant beginnings of modernity at the end of the eighteenth century appears to be just as vigorous and unbounded in places far outside its birthplace. People—young, poor, educated, ambitious—continue to be its martyrs (Tiananmen Square, 1989; Tehran, 2009; Arab Spring, 2011; Kiev, 2014) as well as its proud flag bearers (Tunisia and Egypt, 2011).

Faith in the future of the environment at this point is a good deal more cautious, however. Here, the devil's bargain of materialism that accompanied the evolution of modernity continues to haunt us: On the one hand, it gave us the human right to a decent existence in material security; on the other hand, the means of achieving that security through exploitation of the earth's material resources has given us the nightmare prospect of an irreversibly changed nature that may allow for fewer and fewer of the comforts we currently enjoy. The pattern of modernity and the scientific–industrial society that supports it will no doubt continue, but its future shape will be just as unknowable to us as the patterns of society in the past were to those living through them.

▶ For additional resources, including maps, primary sources, visuals, and quizzes, please go to www.oup.com/us/vonsivers. Please see the Further Resources section at the back of the book for additional readings and suggested websites.

Against the Grain

North Korea: Lone Holdout against the World

In the second decade of the 2000s, North Korea was the laggard among the few countries that remained committed to socialism, such as China, Vietnam, and Cuba. While these latter countries enacted ambitious economic reforms since 1991, North Korea dragged its feet. Although it formally abandoned the ideologies of Marxism-Leninism and communism in its constitutions of 1972 and 2009, respectively, as unfulfillable, it retained its commitment to socialism, self-sufficiency, isolation, and militarism. The disappearance of all-important aid from the Soviet Bloc in 1991 plunged North Korea into hunger and starvation from which it barely reemerged after 2002.

The disappearance of Soviet Bloc aid, in combination with bad weather and several harvest failures during the 1990s, led to mass starvation on a scale similar to famines earlier in the century in the Soviet Union and China. It is estimated that hundreds of thousands died in this nation of 24.5 million inhabitants. Chinese, South Korean, and international food aid brought only minimal relief. Thereafter, massive malnourishment remained, accompanied by associated diseases. Reportedly, children were stunted in their growth by 1–3 inches in comparison to their South Korean counterparts. Adults had to subsist on 700 calories daily, as compared to 2,000–2,500 calories among Europeans. The constitutional principle of food self-sufficiency was a cruel joke.

In 2002 the regime enacted the first small steps of economic reform, recognizing the existence of the informal sector of private garden plots, mechanical workshops, and neighborhood markets. An economic free zone with South Korean factories was established near the border, and some foreign investment was allowed. Collective farmers were entitled to their own produce, in return for a steep 15 percent "rent" on their state-owned lands. After Kim Jong-un's succession to his father's position of supreme leader in 2013, reforms accelerated and North Korean businesses began to export cheap consumer products.

But sanctions imposed after the country's three nuclear tests in 2006 significantly slowed its small arms and missile exports to developing countries, which had provided revenue for keeping the regime in power and feed its outsized military program. With the country ranking lowest in the democracy index, around no. 70 in the poverty index (according to GDP), and no. 29 in military expenditures among the 194 nations in the world, North Korea is the most extreme example of a nation going against the grain of the twenty-first century.

- **Which factors explain the spectacular agricultural collapse in North Korea during the 1990s?**

- **Why is North Korea so steadfastly devoted to its military program? Why is this military program so worrisome for the world?**

Thinking Through Patterns

▶ **How did the United States demonstrate its dominant economic position toward the end of the twentieth century? How did it accelerate the pattern of globalization?**

The United States demonstrated its dominant economic position through the dollar regime and by becoming the sinkhole for industrial exports from developing countries. In compensation for the latter, it expanded the reach of its financial system worldwide. The result was the globalization of the world economy.

Capitalist democracy became the universal model of modernity in part because growing middle classes in cities demanded liberalized markets where they could develop personal initiative and accumulate capital for business ventures. Socially conservative new middle classes became the engines that powered more than half a dozen successful industrialization processes throughout Asia, Latin America, and Africa.

▶ **What made capitalist democracy so attractive toward the end of the twentieth century that it became a generic model for many countries around the world to strive for?**

▶ **Which policies did China and India pursue so that they became the fastest industrializing countries in the early twenty-first century?**

China and India accelerated their industrialization by systematically encouraging the expansion of their middle classes as the engines of investment and innovation. China, however, did not allow the development of a multiparty system, fearing the chaos of popular agitation. India, by contrast, possessed constitutional-nationalist traditions reaching back to the nineteenth century that included constraints against populism and allowed for peaceful democratic competition.

Perhaps more than any other innovation in the last 20 years, or even the last 200 years, the communications revolution has reshaped the way humans interact with each other. The exponential growth of networking boggles the mind. In 2006, 50 billion e-mails were sent. Just 4 years later, that number had risen to 300 billion. Because of this connectedness, politics, culture, and economic activity now mutate more rapidly—and with more volatility—than ever before.

▶ **How have information technology and social networking altered cultural, political, and economic interactions around the world?**

▶ **What is global warming, and why is it a source of grave concern for the future?**

Global warming is caused by carbon dioxide and other gases that accumulate in the upper atmosphere and trap the sun's heat in the lower atmosphere. Warming and cooling trends have occurred periodically since the end of the last ice age, and for a long time scientists labored to distinguish clearly between a temporary trend toward warmer temperatures and a permanent, greenhouse gas–caused trend toward a decisive tipping point that will permanently alter nature as we know it. Today, there is an overwhelming scientific consensus concerning the reality of global warming. But politicians and the general public are not yet entirely convinced that the efforts begun with the Kyoto Protocol of 2005 should be intensified.

Further Resources

Chapter 1

Burroughs, William J. *Climate Change in Prehistory: The End of the Reign of Chaos.* Cambridge, UK: Cambridge University Press, 2005. Very well-researched and up-to-date discussion of climate and human evolution.

Finlayson, Clive. *The Humans Who Went Extinct: Why Neanderthals Died Out and We Survived.* Oxford: Oxford University Press, 2010. A comprehensive history of human evolution in the context of geological and climatic changes, by the excavator of the last Neanderthal traces in Europe.

Flood, Josephine. *Archaeology of the Dreamtime: The Story of Prehistoric Australia and Its People.* New Haven, CT: Yale University Press, 1989. Overview of the Australian archaeological record; short on discussion of Aboriginal Dreamtime and myths.

Johanson, Donald, and Kate Wong. *Lucy: The Quest for Human Origins.* New York: Three Rivers, 2009.

Lawson, Andrew J. *Painted Caves: Palaeololithic Rock Art in Western Europe.* Oxford: Oxford University Press, 2012. Presents an extensive overview ("gazetteer") of the various sites and analyzes the rock art phenomenon in great detail.

McBrearty, Sally, and Allison S. Brooks. "The Revolution that Wasn't: A New Interpretation of the Origin of Modern Human Behavior." *Journal of Human Evolution* 39 (2000): 453–463. Crucial, pioneering article in which the authors grounded anatomically and intellectually modern *H. sapiens* in Africa.

Pauketat, Timothy, ed. *The Oxford North American Handbook of Archaeology.* New York: Oxford University Press, 2012. Very detailed coverage of Paleo-Indian migrations and settlements. Needs to be supplemented with the March 2014 article in *Science* by Dennis O'Rourke, John Hoffecker, and Scott Elias on humans being trapped for 10,000 years on the habitable south coast of Beringia.

Renfrew, Colin,. *Prehistory: The Making of the Human Mind.* New York: Modern Library, 2008. Renfrew, a senior British archaeologist, incorporates the history of human evolution into the process or world history.

Tattersall, Ian. *Masters of the Planet: The Search for Human Origins.* New York: Palgrave Macmillan, 2012. A scholarly well-founded overview for the general reader, by one of the leading senior paleoanthropologists.

WEBSITES

Bradshaw Foundation, http://www.bradshawfoundation.com/. The Bradshaw Foundation has a large website on human evolution and rock art, with many images, and a link to Stephen Oppenheimer's website Journey of Mankind: The Peopling of the World, an important overview of *Homo sapiens'* migrations.

Institute of Human Origins, Arizona State University, http://iho.asu.edu/. Arizona State University's Institute of Human Origins runs the popular but scholarly well-founded website Becoming Human (http://www.becominghuman.org/).

Chapter 2

Alcock, Susan E., John Bodel, and Richard J. A. Talbert, eds. *Highways, Byways, and Road Systems in the Pre-Modern World.* Chichester, UK: John Wiley & Sons, 2012. Fascinating global survey of methods of transport and communication.

Assmann, Jan. *The Search for God in Ancient Egypt.* Ithaca, NY: Cornell University Press, 2001. Reflective investigation of the dimensions of Egyptian polytheism by a leading Egyptologist.

Bottéro, Jean. *Mesopotamia: Writing, Reasoning, and the Gods.* Chicago: University of Chicago Press, 1992. Classic intellectual history of ancient Mesopotamia.

Drews, Robert. *The End of the Bronze Age: Changes in Warfare and the Catastrophe ca. 1200 B.C.* Princeton, NJ: Princeton University Press, 1993. Closely argued essay on the destruction of Mycenaean culture and its consequences for the eastern Mediterranean.

Finkelstein, Israel. *The Archaeology of the Israelite Settlement.* Jerusalem: Israel Exploration Society, 1988. Authoritative presentation of the archaeology of the earliest period of Israelite social formation.

Kuhrt, Amélie. *The Ancient Near East, c. 3000–330 BCE,* 2 vols. London: Routledge, 1994. Comprehensive handbook surveying all regions of the Middle East.

Mithen, Steven. *After the Ice: A Global Human History, 20,000–5000 B.C.* Cambridge, MA: Harvard University Press, 2003. Engagingly written story of humans settling, becoming farmers, and founding villages and towns, as seen through the eyes of a modern time traveler.

Podany, Amanda H. *The Ancient Near East: A Very Short Introduction.* New York: Oxford University Press, 2014. Readable survey of the origin and development of Near Eastern civilizations.

Van de Mieroop, Marc. *The Ancient Mesopotamian City.* Oxford: Clarendon, 1997. Full examination of Mesopotamian urban institutions, including city assemblies.

WEBSITES

British Museum. Ancient Egypt, http://www.ancientegypt.co.uk/menu.html. Pictorial introduction, with short texts.

Livius.org. "Mesopotamia," http://www.livius.org/babylonia.html. A large collection of translated texts and references to philological articles, with portals on Mesopotamia, Egypt, Anatolia, and Greece.

Oriental Institute, University of Chicago. Ancient Mesopotamia, http://mesopotamia.lib.uchicago.edu/. A user-friendly portal to the world-renowned Mesopotamia collection of the Oriental Institute.

Chapter 3

Bryant, Edwin. *The Quest for the Origins of Vedic Culture: The Indo-Aryan Migration Debate.* Oxford: Oxford University Press, 2001. A scholarly yet readable attempt to address the linguistic and archaeological evidence surrounding the thesis of Aryan migration versus the more recent theory of indigenous Vedic development.

Embree, Ainslee T., ed. *Sources of Indian Tradition,* vol. 1, 2nd ed. New York: Columbia University Press, 1988. Though the language is dated in places, this is still the most comprehensive sourcebook of Indian thought available. Recent additions on women and gender make it even more so. Sophisticated yet readable introductions, glosses, and commentary.

Eraly, Abraham. *Gem in the Lotus: The Seeding of Indian Civilization.* London: Weidenfeld & Nicholson, 2004. Readable, comprehensive survey of recent scholarship from prehistory to the reign of Ashoka during the Mauryan dynasty of the fourth and third centuries BCE. Emphasis on transitional period of sixth-century religious innovations, particularly Buddhism.

Fairservis, Walter A. *The Roots of Ancient India: The Archaeology of Early Indian Civilization.* New York: Macmillan, 1971. Classic, well-detailed, and well-documented treatment of Indian archaeology and history to 500 BCE. Particularly well done on the so-called Vedic dark ages to 800 BCE. More useful in general for experienced students.

Kenoyer, Jonathan Mark. *Ancient Cities of the Indus Valley Civilization*. New York: Oxford University Press, 1998. Comprehensive work by team leader of Harappan Research Project. Particularly good on Lothal.

Kinsley, David R. *Hinduism: A Cultural Perspective*. Englewood Cliffs, NJ: Prentice Hall, 1993. Short, highly accessible overview of the major traditions within the constellation of belief systems called by outsiders "Hinduism." Sound treatment of the formative Vedic and Upanishadic periods.

Possehl, Gregory L., ed. *Harappan Civilization: A Recent Perspective*, 2nd ed. New Delhi: Oxford University Press, 1993. Sound and extensive treatment of recent work and issues in Indus valley archaeology by one of the leading on-site researchers and a former student of Fairservis. Used to best advantage by experienced students.

Singh, Upinder. *A History of Ancient and Early Medieval India: From the Stone Age to the 12th Century*. New Delhi: Pearson, 2008. Sweeping text by a longtime instructor of Indian history at the University of Delhi. Suitable for undergraduates and current on the latest debates on ancient origins.

Trautmann, Thomas. *India: Brief History of a Civilization*. New York: Oxford University Press, 2011. A succinct and lucid account of 4,000 years of Indian history, with particular emphasis on early developments.

Wolpert, Stanley. *A New History of India*, 5th ed. New York: Oxford University Press, 2004. Another extremely useful, readable, one-volume history from Neolithic times to the present. Excellent first work for serious students.

WEBSITES

Columbia University Libraries. South and Southeast Asian Studies, www.columbia.edu/cu/lweb/indiv/southasia/cuvl/history.html. Run by Columbia University, this site contains links to "WWW .Virtual Library: Indian History"; "Regnal Chronologies"; "Internet Indian History Sourcebook"; and "Medical History of British India."

Harappa, http://www.harappa.com. Contains a wealth of images of artifacts and other archaeological treasures from the Indus Valley.

Chapter 4

Chang, Kwang-chih. *The Archaeology of Ancient China*, 4th ed. New Haven, CT: Yale University Press, 1986. Sophisticated treatment of archaeology of Shang China. Prime exponent of the view of overlapping periods and territories for the Sandai period. Erudite, yet accessible for experienced students.

Ebrey, Patricia Buckley, ed. *Chinese Civilization: A Sourcebook*, 2nd ed. New York: Free Press, 1993. Wonderful supplement to the preceding volume. Some different classical sources and considerable material on women and social history. Time frame of this work extends to the modern era.

Keightly, David N., ed. *The Origins of Chinese Civilization*. Berkeley: University of California Press, 1983. Symposium volume on a variety of Sandai topics by leading scholars. Some exposure to early Chinese history and archaeology is necessary in order to best appreciate these essays.

Keightly, David N., ed. *Sources of Shang History: The Oracle-Bone Inscriptions of Bronze Age China*. Berkeley: University of California Press, 1978. Benchmark in the authoritative interpretation and contextualization of ritual inscriptions. Some grounding in ancient Chinese history is helpful.

Linduff, Katheryn M., and Yan Sun, eds. *Gender and Chinese Archaeology*. Walnut Creek, CA: Altamira, 2004. Reexamines the role of gender in ancient China in the context of a critique of the general lack of gendered research in archaeology as a whole.

Lowe, Michael, and Edward L. Shaughnessy, eds. *The Cambridge History of Ancient China: From the Origins of Civilization to 221 B.C.*

Cambridge, UK: Cambridge University Press, 1999. The opening volume of the Cambridge History of China series, this is the most complete multiessay collection on all aspects of recent Chinese ancient historical and archaeological work. The place to start for the serious student contemplating in-depth research.

Schirokauer, Conrad. *A Brief History of Chinese Civilization*. New York: Harcourt Brace Jovanovich, 1991. Readable one-volume text on Chinese history up to the late twentieth century. More thorough treatment of Sandai period than is generally the case with other one-volume texts.

Thorp, Robert L. *China in the Early Bronze Age: Shang Civilization*. Philadelphia: University of Pennsylvania Press, 2006. Comprehensive yet accessible survey of recent archaeological work on the period 2070–1046 BCE, including traditional Xia and Shang periods under the heading of China's "bronze age."

Wang, Aihe. *Cosmology and Political Culture in Early China*. Cambridge, UK: Cambridge University Press, 2000. Part of the Cambridge Studies in Chinese History, Literature, and Institutions series. Wang argues that control of *cosmology*—how the world and universe operate—was a vital key to the wielding of power by the Shang and Zhou rulers. Recommended for serious students.

Watson, Burton, trans. *The Tso Chuan: Selections from China's Oldest Narrative History*. New York: Columbia University Press, 1989. Elegant translation by one of the most prolific of scholars working today. Excellent introduction to Zhou period and politics. Appropriate for beginning students, though more useful for those with some prior introduction to the period.

WEBSITES

http://lucian.uchicago.edu/blogs/earlychina/ssec/. This is the site of the journal *Early China*, published by the Society for the Study of Early China.

British Museum. Ancient China, http://www.ancientchina.co.uk. This site provides access to the British Museum's ancient Chinese collections and is highly useful for students seeking illustrations of assorted artifacts in a user-friendly environment.

Chapter 5

The Americas

Bellwood, Peter. *First Migrants: Ancient Migration in Global Perspective*. Chichester, UK: John Wiley & Sons, 2013. An intriguing study of prehistoric migration and its role in shaping the emergence of civilization.

Benson, Sonia, and Deborah J. Baker. *Early Civilizations in the Americas Reference Library*, 3 vols. Farmington Hills, MI: Gale UXL, 2009. Extensive three-volume encyclopedia available as a download or in hard copy. Contains an almanac of historical information and one of biographies and primary sources. Recommended for beginning and experienced students.

Bruhns, Karen Olsen, and Karen E. Stothert. *Women in Ancient America*. Norman: University of Oklahoma Press, 1999. A comprehensive account of women's roles in daily life, religion, politics, and war in foraging and farming as well as urban societies in the Americas.

Fiedel, Stuart J. *Prehistory of the Americas*, 2nd ed. Cambridge, UK: Cambridge University Press, 1992. Accessible, detailed survey of the archaeology of the Americas by a leading American scholar.

Thomas, David Hurst. *Exploring Native North America*. Oxford: Oxford University Press, 2000. Selected chapters are useful on the major early North American sites, particularly Adena and Hopewell.

Trigger, Bruce G., Wilcomb E. Washburn, Richard E. W. Adams, Murdo J. MacLeod, Frank Salomon, and Stuart B. Schwartz, eds. *Cambridge History of the Native Peoples of the Americas*, 3 vols. Cambridge, UK: Cambridge University Press, 1996–2000. As with all of the Cambridge histories, this is a highly useful set for beginner and accomplished scholar alike. Useful bibliographies with the article entries.

von Hagen, Adriana, and Craig Morris. *The Cities of the Ancient Andes.* New York: Thames & Hudson, 1999. While more geared to later periods, still a useful overview, with illustrations, by specialists on Andean cultures.

Oceania

Bellwood, Peter S. *Man's Conquest of the Pacific: The Prehistory of Southeast Asia and Oceania.* New York: Oxford University Press, 1979. Along with Bellwood's earlier volume, *The Polynesians* (1978), traces the migrations of succeeding groups through the archipelagoes of the Pacific. Balanced treatment of controversies over gradual versus episodic migrations of Lapita cultures. For advanced students.

Fagan, Brian M., ed. *The Oxford Companion to Archaeology.* New York: Oxford University Press, 1996. Perhaps the best place to start for students interested in archaeological and historical overviews of the peopling of the Pacific. Extensive coverage of Lapita culture and expansion into Micronesia and Polynesia.

Kirch, Patrick V. *The Lapita Peoples: Ancestors of the Oceanic World.* Cambridge, MA: Blackwell, 1997. Basic introduction by one of the pioneers of Polynesian research.

Vlchek, Andre. *Oceania: Neocolonialism, Nukes and Bones.* Auckland, New Zealand: Atuanui, 2013. Analysis and discussion of the harmful effects of colonialism and neocolonialism on the development of Oceania.

WEBSITES

Foundation for the Advancement of Mesoamerican Studies (FAMSI), http://www.famsi.org/. Home page for the foundation, which has recently begun collaboration with the Los Angeles County Museum of Art and runs a wide range of scholarly, funding, and educational outreach programs aimed at advancing studies of Mesoamerica.

http://www.britannica.com/EBchecked/topic/468832/Polynesian-culture. Good link leading to an 8,000-word essay on leading topics concerning Polynesia and Oceania. In order to access the complete essay the reader must apply for a free trial on the online *Encyclopedia Britannica.*

Chapter 6

Sub-Saharan Africa

Chami, Félix. *The Unity of African Ancient History: 3000 BC to 500 AD.* Dar es Salaam: E&D, 2006. General overview by one of the leading archaeologists of East Africa.

McIntosh, Roderick J. *Ancient Middle Niger: Urbanism and the Self-Organizing Landscape.* Cambridge, UK: Cambridge University Press, 2005. Important revisionist work on the origins of urbanism and kingship in West Africa.

Mitchell, Peter, and Paul Lane. *The Oxford Handbook of African Archaeology.* Oxford: Oxford University Press, 2013. A total of 70 essays by specialists on all aspects of human culture in Africa, with an emphasis on hunter-gatherers, agriculturalists, and early urbanists.

Vansina, Jan. *Paths in the Rainforests: Toward a History of Political Tradition in Equatorial Africa.* Madison: University of Wisconsin Press, 1990. Magisterial presentation of the Bantu dispersal and village life in the rain forest.

Mesoamerica and the Andes

Aveni, Anthony F. *Skywatchers*, rev. ed. Austin: University of Texas Press, 2001. Classic study on astronomy and calendars of pre-Columbian Americans, including a discussion of the Nazca lines.

Evans, Susan Tobey. *Ancient Mexico and Central America: Archaeology and Culture History.* London: Thames & Hudson, 2004. Densely

but clearly written and detailed, with many sidebars on special topics.

Grube, Nikolai, ed. *Maya: Divine Kings of the Rain Forest.* Cologne, Germany: Könemann, 2001. Lavishly illustrated book with short contributions by many hands.

Schele, Linda, and David Freidel. *A Forest of Kings: The Untold Story of the Ancient Maya.* New York: Quill-William Morrow, 1990. Classic study summarizing the results of the decipherment of Maya glyphs, by two pioneers.

Sharer, Robert J., *The Ancient Maya*, 6th ed. Stanford, CA: Stanford University Press, 2006. Standard academic work on the civilization of the Maya, by one of the leading Maya scholars until death in 2012.

WEBSITES

Museum of Native American History. http://www.monah.us/precolumbian: Basic but fairly comprehensive website on pre-Columbian peoples and civilizations.

Stanford University Libraries. Africa South of the Sahara, http://www-sul.stanford.edu/depts/ssrg/africa/history.html. A large, resource-filled website based at Stanford University.

Chapter 7

Boatwright, Mary, Daniel J. Gargola, and Richard J. A. Talbert. *The Romans: From Village to Empire.* New York: Oxford University Press, 2004. Clearly written, comprehensive introduction to Roman history.

Boyce, Mary. *A History of Zoroastrianism.* Vol. 1, *The Early Period*, rev. ed. Handbuch der Orientalistik. Leiden, the Netherlands: E. J. Brill, 1989. Standard work by the leading scholar on the subject.

Briant, Pierre. *From Cyrus to Alexander: A History of the Persian Empire.* Winona Lake, IN: Eisenbrauns, 2000. Monumental work; the most detailed and authoritative study of the topic to date.

Cameron, Averil. *The Mediterranean World in Late Antiquity, AD 395–600.* London: Routledge, 1993. New perspective on the strengths and weaknesses of the late empire.

Dignas, Beate, and Engelbert Winter. *Rome and Persia in Late Antiquity: Neighbours and Rivals.* Cambridge, UK: Cambridge University Press, 2007. Detailed historical investigation of the rivalry between Rome and Persia.

Freeman, Phillip. *Alexander the Great.* New York: Simon & Schuster, 2011. Illuminating study of Alexander the Great intended for a general audience.

Hubbard, Thomas K., ed. *A Companion to Greek and Roman Sexualities.* Chichester, UK: John Wiley & Sons, 2014. Far-ranging and informative collection of essays on all aspects of sexuality in ancient Greece and Rome.

Lehoux, Daryn. *What Did the Romans Know?: An Inquiry into Science and Worldmaking.* Chicago: University of Chicago Press, 2012. Sophisticated analysis of Roman science in both its derivative and unique aspects.

Shaked, Shaul. *Dualism in Transformation: Varieties of Religion in Sasanian Iran.* London: School of Oriental and African Studies, 1994. Short history of the different religions in Sasanid Persia.

Smith, Mark S. *The Early History of God: Yahweh and the Other Deities in Ancient Israel.* San Francisco: Harper & Row, 1990. Very readable introduction to the problem of early monotheism among Israelites.

WEBSITES

British Museum. Ancient Greece, http://www.ancientgreece.co.uk/menu.html. Open the door to the compelling world of Ancient Greece. The British Museum has compiled a collection of images and information on various aspects of Greek history such as the Acropolis, Athens, daily life, festivals and games, Sparta, war, and gods.

Harvard University. Digital Atlas of Roman and Medieval Civilizations, http://darmc.harvard.edu/icb/icb.do?keyword=k40248&pageid=icb.page188868. Harvard University allows students to tailor searches in order to access specific geopolitical and spatial cartographical representations of the Roman and medieval worlds.

Perseus Digital Library, http://www.perseus.tufts.edu/hopper/. Probably the largest website on Greece and Rome, with immense resources, hosted by Tufts University.

Chapter 8

Auboyer, Jeannine. *Daily Life in Ancient India*. London: Phoenix, 2002. Overview consisting of sections on social structures/religious principles; individual/collective existence; and royal and administrative existence. Multidisciplinary approach appropriate for most undergraduates.

Carter, John Ross, and Mahinda Palihawadana trans. *The Dhammapada*. New York: Oxford University Press, 1987. Erudite but accessible translation of one of the key texts in the Buddhist corpus. Students with some exposure to the introductory ideas of Buddhism will find it very useful in its step-by-step elucidation of a number of central concepts.

Chakravarti, Uma. *The Social Dimensions of Early Buddhism*. New Delhi: Oxford University Press, 1987. Thorough analysis, with extensive glossary, of the influence of the north Indian economic transition to peasant market farming on the social milieu of early Buddhism.

Doniger, Wendy. *The Hindus: An Alternative History*. New York: Penguin, 2009. Vivid but controversial new interpretation of the history of Hinduism by one of the leading scholars of Indian history. The book's portrayals of Hindu history, particularly in the area between myth and history, have prompted a lawsuit in India, which resulted in the withdrawal of the book there in early 2014.

Embree, Ainslee T. *Sources of Indian Tradition*, 2 vols, 2nd ed. New York: Columbia University Press, 1988. The latest edition contains a number of new selections useful for the study of social relations in addition to the older religious material. As with all of the works in this series, the level of writing is sophisticated, though accessible; the overviews are masterly; and the works are ably translated.

Keay, John. *India: A History*. New York: Grove, 2000. Lively, highly detailed narrative history, with a number of highly useful charts and genealogies of ruling houses. Sympathetic treatment of controversial matters.

Knott, Kim. *Hinduism: A Very Short Introduction*. New York: Oxford University Press, 1998. Sound, brief discussion of modern Hinduism and its formative influences. Asks provocative questions such as "What is a religion?" and "Is Hinduism something more than the Western conception of religion?"

Nikam, N. A., and Richard McKeon, eds. and trans. *The Edicts of Asoka*. Chicago: University of Chicago Press, 1959. Slim but useful volume for those interested in reading the entire collection of Ashoka's Pillar, Cave, and Rock Edicts. Short, accessible introduction.

Willis, Michael. *The Archaeology of Hindu Ritual*. Cambridge, UK: Cambridge University Press, 2009. Best utilized by experienced students, this book uses site archaeology, Sanskrit documents, and studies of ancient astronomy to plot the development of Hinduism under the Guptas and their use of it in statecraft as they created their vision of a universal empire.

Wolpert, Stanley. *A New History of India*, 6th ed. New York: Oxford University Press, 2000. The standard introductory work to the long sweep of Indian history. Evenly divided between the period up to and including the Mughals and the modern era. Good coverage of geography and environment, as well as social and gender

issues. Good select bibliography arranged by chapter; highly useful glossary of Indian terms.

WEBSITE

Digital Library of India, http://www.dli.ernet.in. This online resource, hosted by the Indian Institute of Science, Bangalore, contains primary and secondary sources not only for history but also for culture, economics, literature, and a host of other subjects.

Chapter 9

Ebrey, Patricia Buckley, ed. *Chinese Civilization: A Sourcebook*, 2nd ed. New York: Free Press, 1993. Varied primary sources with an accent on social history material: letters, diary excerpts, etc. Particularly strong on women's history sources.

Hinsch, Bret. *Women in Early Imperial China*. Lanham, MD: Rowman & Littlefield, 2002. Broad examination of the place of women, and transition of the place of women, during the crucial early Chinese dynasties.

Huang, Ray. *China: A Macro History*. Armonk, NY: M. E. Sharpe, 1997. Readable, entertaining, and highly useful one-volume history. Particularly good on the complex politics of the post-Han and Song–Yuan periods.

Keay, John. *China: A History*. New York: Basic Books, 2009. Adventurous and well-written general history of China from prehistory to the present. Especially good for students with some previous grounding in the essentials of Chinese history.

Lewis, Mark Edward. *The Early Chinese Empires: Qin and Han*. Cambridge, MA: Harvard University Press, 2007. Detailed exploration of the rise and adaptations of China's initial empires. Better for advanced students.

Loewe, Michael. *Everyday Life in Early Imperial China during the Han Period, 202 B.C.–A.D. 220*. New York: Harper & Row, 1968. Short, highly useful one-volume survey of Han social history by a preeminent scholar. Especially good on details of peasant and elite daily existence.

Qian, Sima. *Records of the Grand Historian*. Translated by Burton Watson. 3 vols. Revised edition. New York: Columbia University Press, 1993. Complete, powerful translation of China's supreme historical work by one of its best interpreters. Includes material from the Qin and Han Dynasties. Invaluable source for serious students.

Snow, Philip. *The Star Raft: China's Encounter with Africa*. Ithaca, NY: Cornell University Press, 1988. Important, accessible study of the little-known area of China's maritime trade with Africa from Han times to the epic fifteenth-century voyages of Zheng He and beyond.

WEBSITES

Asian Topics for Asian Educators. "Defining 'Daoism': A Complex History," http://afe.easia.columbia.edu/cosmos/ort/daoism.htm. Looks at Daoism as a term, its use, and its practice in terms of morality, society, nature, and the self.

http://bulldog2.redlands.edu/Dept/AsianStudiesDept/index.html. *East and Southeast Asia: An Annotated Directory of Internet Resources*. One of the most complete guides to websites dealing with all manner of Chinese and East Asian history and society.

Chapter 10

The Arabian Nights. Translated by Husain Haddawy. New York: Norton, 1990. Translation of the critical edition by Muhsin Mahdi, which reconstitutes the original thirteenth-century text.

Barry, Michael. *Figurative Art in Medieval Islam and the Riddle of Bihzâd of Herât (1465–1535)*. Paris: Flammarion, 2004.

Chaudhuri, K. N. *Trade and Civilization in the Indian Ocean*. Cambridge, UK: Cambridge University Press, 1985. Discusses the historical evolution of the trade and its various aspects (sea route, ships, commodities, and capital investments).

Fryde, Edmund. *The Early Palaeologan Renaissance (1261–c. 1360)*. Leiden, the Netherlands: E. J. Brill, 2000. Detailed presentation of the main philosophical and scientific figures of Byzantium after the recovery from the Latin interruption.

Khalili, Jim al-. *The House of Wisdom: How Arabic Science Saved Ancient Knowledge and Gave Us the Renaissance*. New York: Penguin, 2010. In spite of the somewhat overwrought title, an expertly written introduction to the golden age of Arabic science by a scientist.

Laiou, Angeliki E., and Cécile Morrisson. *The Byzantine Economy*. Cambridge, UK: Cambridge University Press, 2007. Comprehensive and well-researched study of ups and downs in the demography, productive capacity, and long-distance trade of Byzantium.

Lapidus, Ira. *Muslim Cities in the Later Middle Ages*. Cambridge, UK: Cambridge University Press, 1984. Seminal work and still the only study of Muslim urban society, although it should be supplemented by Shlomo D. Goitein's monumental study of Jews, *A Mediterranean Society* (1967–1993).

Rippin, Andrew. *Muslims: Their Religious Beliefs and Practices*, 2nd ed. London: Routledge, 2001. One of the best and most accessible introductions to the basic beliefs and practices of Islam, based on the reevaluation of Islamic origins also presented in this chapter.

Tyerman, Christopher. *God's War: A New History of the Crusades*. Cambridge, MA: Belknap, 2006. Persuasive revisionist history by a leading Crusade historian.

Whittow, Mark. *The Making of Byzantium, 600–1025*. Berkeley: University of California Press, 1996. Revisionist study of the Byzantine struggle for survival in the early years.

WEBSITES

BBC—Religion: Islam. http://www.bbc.co.uk/religion/religions/islam/. A very basic overview of Islamic Civilization. Most websites on Islam and Islamic civilization are apologetic (pro-Muslim or pro-Christian) and earlier scholarly websites are no longer available.

Asian Topics in World History. "The Mongols in World History," http://afe.easia.columbia.edu/mongols/. With a timeline spanning 1000–1500, "The Mongols in World History" delivers a concise and colorful history of the Mongols' impact on global history.

Chapter 11

Bartlett, Robert. *The Making of Europe: Conquest, Colonization, and Cultural Change, 950–1350*. Princeton, NJ: Princeton University Press, 1993. Analyzes the expansion of Europe from a cultural perspective.

Berend, Norma, Przemyslaw Urbanczlyk, and Przemyslaw Wiszewski. *Central Europe in the High Middle Ages: Bohemia, Hungary and Poland, ca. 900–ca. 1300*. New York: Cambridge University Press, 2013. Learned and insightful study that explores frequently overlooked aspects of medieval Europe.

Brown, Peter. *The Rise of Western Christendom: Triumph and Diversity, A.D. 200–1000*, 2nd ed. Oxford: Wiley-Blackwell, 2003. Traces the development of Christian Europe from the perspective of the church.

Grant, Edward. *The Foundation of Modern Science in the Middle Ages*. Cambridge, UK: Cambridge University Press, 1996. Seminal study of the contributions of medieval science to the scientific revolution of the seventeenth century.

Lawrence, C. H. *Medieval Monasticism: Forms of Religious Life in Western Europe in the Middle Ages*, 2nd ed. New York: Longman, 1984. Thorough survey of the development of the Western monastic tradition.

McKitterick, Rosamond. *Charlemagne: The Formation of a European Identity*. Cambridge, UK: Cambridge University Press, 2008. An examination of how Charlemagne's policies contributed to the idea of Europe.

Platt, Colin. *King Death: The Black Death and Its Aftermath in Late-Medieval England*. Toronto: University of Toronto Press, 1997. Riveting analysis of the effects of the Black Death on all aspects of society.

Reynolds, Susan. *Fiefs and Vassals: The Medieval Evidence Reinterpreted*. Oxford: Oxford University Press, 1994. Important revisionist study of medieval feudal institutions.

Riley-Smith, Jonathan, ed. *The Oxford Illustrated History of the Crusades*. New York: Oxford University Press, 1995. A very useful and readable history of the crusading movement.

Turner, Denys. *Thomas Aquinas: A Portrait*. New Haven, CT: Yale University Press, 2013. Up-to-date biography of one of the greatest figures in medieval philosophy.

WEBSITES

British Library. Treasures in Full: Magna Carta, http://www.bl.uk/treasures/magnacarta/virtual_curator/vc9.html. An excellent website that makes available a digitized version of Magna Carta. Audio files answer many FAQs about the manuscript and its significance.

Howe, Jeffery. A Digital Archive of Architecture, http://www.bc.edu/bc_org/avp/cas/fnart/arch/gothic_arch.html. Jeffery Howe's Digital Archive of Architecture has a quick index reference guide, which links to images of both early and high Gothic architecture.

Chapter 12

Bulag, Uradyn Erden. *The Mongols at China's Edge: History and the Politics of National Unity*. Lanham, MD: Rowman & Littlefield, 2002. New historical overview of the Mongols through historical and anthropological lenses that seeks to demythologize their experience and interactions with China and central Asian peoples.

De Bary, William T., ed. *Sources of Chinese Tradition*, vol. 1. New York: Columbia University Press, 1960. Excellent introduction to major Chinese philosophical schools. Extensive coverage of Buddhism and Neo-Confucianism with accessible, highly informative introductions to the documents themselves.

Ebrey, Patricia Buckley, ed. *Chinese Civilization: A Sourcebook*, 2nd ed. New York: Free Press, 1993. More varied than de Bary, with more social history material: letters, diary excerpts, etc. Particularly strong on women's history sources.

Ebrey, Patricia Buckley, ed. *The Inner Quarters*. Berkeley: University of California Press, 1993. Perhaps the best scholarly exploration of the roles of women in Song China.

Hansen, Valerie. *The Open Empire: A History of China to 1600*. New York: W. W. Norton, 2000. A fresh and accessible synthesis of pre-modern Chinese history.

Levathes, Louise. *When China Ruled the Seas: The Treasure Fleet of the Dragon Throne 1405–1433*. New York: Simon & Schuster, 1994. Delightful coverage of the voyages of Zheng He from 1405 to 1433. Particularly good on the aftermath of the voyages.

Mujeeb, M. *The Indian Muslims*. London: Allen & Unwin, 1967. Thorough historical overview from the eighth century to the twentieth. Especially useful on political and administrative systems of the early and middle periods of Muslim hegemony in north India.

Robinson, Francis. *Islam and Muslim History in South Asia*. New York: Oxford University Press, 2004. Compendium of essays and reviews by the author on a variety of subjects concerning the history and status of Islam in the subcontinent. Of particular interest is his response to Samuel Huntington's famous "clash of civilizations" thesis.

Singh, Patwant. *The Sikhs*. London: John Murray, 1999. Readable popular history of the Sikh experience to the present by an adherent. Especially useful on the years from Guru Nanak to the changes of the early eighteenth century and the transition to a more militant faith.

WEBSITES

Fordham University. Internet Indian History Sourcebook, http://www.fordham.edu/halsall/india/indiasbook.asp. One of series of online "sourcebooks" by Fordham containing links to important documents, secondary literature, and assorted other web resources.

Fordham University. Internet East Asian History Sourcebook, http://www.fordham.edu/halsall/eastasia/eastasiasbook.asp. As with its counterpart above, this is one in the series of useful online sources and links put together by Fordham, in this case about East Asia, with particular emphasis on the role of China as a center of cultural diffusion.

Chapter 13

General

Mann, Susan. *East Asia (China, Korea, Japan)*. Washington, DC: American Historical Association, 1999. The second volume in the Women's and Gender History in Global Perspective series. Short, informative volume with historiographic overviews and cross-cultural comparisons among the three countries named in the title. Critical annotated bibliographies on the use of standard texts in integrating women and gender into Asian studies.

Murphey, Rhoads. *East Asia: A New History*. New York: Longman, 1997. One of the few one-volume histories that include material on China, Japan, Korea, Vietnam, and southeast Asia. Written by a leading scholar of modern China and east Asia. Appropriate for beginning students but more useful for those with some background on the area.

Ramusack, Barbara N., and Sharon Sievers. *Women in Asia*. Bloomington: Indiana University Press, 1999. Part of the series Restoring Women to History. Far-ranging book divided into two parts, "Women in South and Southeast Asia" and "Women in East Asia." Coverage of individual countries, extensive chronologies, valuable bibliographies. Most useful for advanced undergraduates.

Korea

De Bary, William T., ed. *Sources of Korean Tradition*, vol. 1. Introduction to Asian Civilizations. New York: Columbia University Press, 1997. Part of the renowned Columbia series on the great traditions of east Asia. Perhaps the most complete body of accessible sources for undergraduates.

Korean Overseas Information Service. *A Handbook of Korea*. Seoul: KOIS, 1993. Wonderfully complete history, geography, guidebook, and sociology text. Excellent source, but students should keep in mind its provenance and treat some of its historical claims to uniqueness accordingly.

Japan

De Bary, William T., ed. *Sources of Japanese Tradition*, vol. 1. Introduction to Asian Civilizations. New York: Columbia University Press, 2002. Like the volume above on Korea and the others in this series on India and China, the sources are well selected, the glossaries are sound, and the overviews of the material are masterful. As with the other east Asia volumes, the complexities of the various Buddhist schools are especially well drawn. As with the others in the series, students with some previous experience will derive the most benefit from this volume.

Reischauer, Edwin O., and Albert Craig. *Japan: Tradition and Transformation*. Boston: Houghton Mifflin, 1989. The companion volume to J. K. Fairbank's *China*, by the leading American scholar of and former US ambassador to Japan. A one-volume history but with more emphasis on the modern than ancient periods.

Totman, Conrad. *A History of Japan*. Oxford: Blackwell, 2000. Part of Blackwell's History of the World series. A larger, more balanced, and comprehensive history than the Reischauer and Craig volume. More than half of the material is on the pre-1867 period, with extensive coverage of social history and demographics.

Vietnam

Steinberg, Joel David, ed. *In Search of Southeast Asia*, rev. ed. Honolulu: University of Hawaii Press, 1987. Extensive coverage of Vietnam within the context of an area study of southeast Asia. Though weighted toward the modern period, very good coverage of agricultural and religious life in the opening chapters.

Taylor, Keith W. *The Birth of Vietnam*. Berkeley: University of California Press, 1983. Comprehensive, magisterial volume on early Vietnamese history and historical identity amid the long Chinese occupation. Best for students with some background in southeast Asian and Chinese history.

WEBSITES

Department of Prints and Drawings, British Museum, http://www.britishmuseum.org/the_museum/departments/prints_and_drawings.aspx. A comprehensive source for all manner of interests related to Asian studies.

Public Broadcasting Service, Hidden Korea, http://www.pbs.org/hiddenkorea/history.htm, Sound introduction to the geography, people, history and culture of Korea, with links to additional source material.

Cambridge Journals Online, Journal of Southeast Asian Studies, http://journals.cambridge.org/action/displayJournal?jid=SEA. Online version of the scholarly publication of the same name, features articles on the history, sociology, cultural studies, and literature of the region. It aims for scholarly but accessible presentations. Recommended for advanced students.

Chapter 14

Birmingham, David, and Phyllis M. Martin, eds. *History of Central Africa*, vol. 1. London: Longman, 1983. The first chapter, by Birmingham, provides an excellent summary of the history of Luba prior to 1450.

Collins, Robert O., and James M. Burns. *A History of Subsaharan Africa*, 2nd ed. Cambridge, UK: Cambridge University Press, 2014. Updated authoritative history by two well-known Africanists.

Crummey, David. *Land and Society in the Christian Kingdom of Ethiopia: From the Thirteenth to the Twentieth Century*. Urbana: University of Illinois Press, 2000. The first book in which the rich land records of the church have been used for a reconstruction of agriculture and land tenure.

Horton, Mark, and John Middleton. *The Swahili: The Social Landscape of a Mercantile Society*. Oxford: Blackwell, 2000. A study that gives full attention to the larger context of East Africa in which the Swahilis flourished. Middleton is the author of another important study, *The World of the Swahili: An African Mercantile Civilization* (Yale University Press, 1992).

Huffman, Thomas N. *Mapungubwe: Ancient African Civilization on the Limpopo*. Johannesburg: Witwatersrand University Press, 2005. Short but illuminating summary of the archaeological record by a leading South African expert, although his interpretation of Zimbabwe in an earlier work (*Snakes and Crocodiles*, Witwatersrand University Press, 1996) is controversial.

Levtzion, Nehemia. *Ancient Ghana and Mali.* New York: Africana, 1980. Originally published London: Methuen, 1973. Standard history of ancient Ghana, Mali, and Songhay based on a thorough knowledge of the Arabic sources; a revision by David Conrad, Paulo Farias, Roderick J. McIntosh, and Susan McIntosh has been announced but has yet to appear.

Robinson, David. *Muslim Societies in African History.* Cambridge, UK: Cambridge University Press, 2004. Advertised as part of a series of new approaches, this book nevertheless presents a conventional view of Islam, albeit in its African context.

Trigger, Bruce. *History and Settlement in Lower Nubia.* Yale University Publications in Anthropology 69. New Haven, CT: Yale University Press, 1965. Chapter 9 is still the best overview of Nubian history, by a scholar with a broad understanding of early civilizations.

WEBSITES

Heilbrunn Timeline of Art History. "Ife (from ca. 350 B.C.)," http://www.metmuseum.org/toah/hd/ife/hd_ife.htm. An excellent introductory website hosted by the Metropolitan Museum of Art. It contains many links and presents clear overviews.

For a website by Patrick Darling, the principal archaeological investigator of the Nigerian earthworks, see http://cohesion.rice.edu/CentersAndInst/SAFA/emplibrary/49_ch09.pdf for a copy of a 1998 article.

Chapter 15

Bruhns, Karen Olsen, and Karen E. Stothert. *Women in Ancient America.* Norman: University of Oklahoma Press, 1999. Comprehensive account of women's role in daily life, religion, politics, and war in hunter–gatherer and agrarian–urban societies.

Brumfield, Elizabeth M., and Gary F. Feinman, eds. *The Aztec World.* New York: Abrams, 2008. Collection of expert short chapters on a variety of topics, richly illustrated.

Carrasco, Davíd. *The Aztecs: A Very Short Introduction.* Oxford: Oxford University Press, 2012. Clear, compressed account by a specialist, containing all essential information.

D'Altroy, Terence. *The Incas.* Malden, MA: Blackwell, 2002. Well-organized, comprehensive, and up-to-date overview.

Hassig, Ross. *War and Society in Ancient Mesoamerica.* Berkeley: University of California Press, 1992. Best study of the rising importance of militarism in Mesoamerican city-states, up to the Aztec Empire.

Julien, Catherine. *Reading Inca History.* Iowa City: University of Iowa Press, 2000. Ambitious "reading" of "genres" of memory in the available, mostly Spanish sources.

Malpass, Michael A. *Daily Life in the Inca Empire*, 2nd ed. Westport, CT: Greenwood, 2009. Clear, straightforward, and readable account of ordinary people's lives by a specialist.

Smith, Michael E., *The Aztecs*, 3rd ed. Hoboken, NJ: Wiley, 2013. Up-to-date, extensive account of all aspects of Inca history and civilization.

WEBSITE

Aztec History, http://www.aztec-history.com/. Introductory website, easily navigable, with links.

Chapter 16

Ágoston, Gábor. *Guns for the Sultan: Military Power and the Weapons Industry in the Ottoman Empire.* Cambridge, UK: Cambridge University Press, 2005. Thorough study, which is based on newly accessible Ottoman archival materials and emphasizes the technological prowess of Ottoman gunsmiths.

Casale, Giancarlo. *The Ottoman Age of Exploration.* New York: Oxford University Press, 2010. Detailed correction, based on Ottoman and Portuguese archives, of the traditional characterization of the Ottoman Empire as a land-oriented power.

Casey, James. *Early Modern Spain: A Social History.* London: Routledge, 1999. Detailed, well-documented analysis of rural–urban and royal–nobility tensions.

Elliott, John Huxtable. *Spain, Europe, and the Wider World: 1500–1800.* New Haven, CT: Yale University Press, 2009. A comprehensive overview, particularly strong on culture during the 1500s.

Glete, Jan. *War and the State in Early Modern Europe: Spain, the Dutch Republic, and Sweden as Fiscal–Military States, 1500–1660.* London: Routledge, 2002. A complex but persuasive construction of the forerunner to the absolute state. Unfortunately leaves out the Ottoman Empire.

Murphy, Rhoads. *Ottoman Warfare, 1500–1700.* New Brunswick, NJ: Rutgers University Press, 1999. Author presents a vivid picture of the Janissaries, their discipline, organization, campaigns, and voracious demands for salary increases.

Pamuk, Sevket. *A Monetary History of the Ottoman Empire.* Cambridge, UK: Cambridge University Press, 2000. Superb analysis of Ottoman archival resources on the role and function of American silver in the money economy of the Ottomans.

Ruiz, Teofilo R. *Spanish Society, 1400–1600.* London: Longman, 2001. Richly detailed social studies rewarding anyone interested in changing class structures, rural–urban movement, and extension of the money market into the countryside.

Subrahmanyam, Sanjay. *The Career and Legend of Vasco da Gama.* Cambridge, UK: Cambridge University Press, 1997. Focuses on the religious motivations in Vasco da Gama and the commercial impact of his journey to India.

WEBSITES

Frontline, "Apocalypse! The Evolution of Apocalyptic Belief and How It Shaped the Western World," PBS, 1995, http://www.pbs.org/wgbh/pages/frontline/shows/apocalypse/. The contribution by Bernard McGinn, University of Chicago, under the heading of "Apocalypticism Explained: Joachim of Fiore," is of particular relevance for the understanding of Christopher Columbus viewing himself as a precursor of Christ's Second Coming.

Islam: Empire of Faith: Timeline, http://www.pbs.org/empires/islam/timeline.html. Comprehensive and informative, this PBS website on the Ottoman Empire examines the various facets of this Islamic culture such as scientific innovations, faith and its leaders.

Chapter 17

Biro, Jacquelin. *On Earth as in Heaven: Cosmography and the Shape of the Earth from Copernicus to Descartes.* Saarbrücken, Germany: VDM Verlag Dr. Müller, 2009. Short study establishing the connection between geography and cosmology in Copernicus. Uses the pathbreaking articles by Thomas Goldberg.

Black, Jeremy. *Kings, Nobles, and Commoners: States and Societies in Early Modern Europe—A Revisionist History.* London: Tauris, 2004. Available also electronically on ebrary; persuasive thesis, largely accepted by scholars, of a continuity of institutional practices in Europe across the sixteenth and seventeenth centuries, casting doubt on absolutism as being more than a theory.

Cañizares-Esguerra, Jorge. *Nature, Empire, and Nation: Explorations of the History of Science in the Iberian World.* Stanford, CA: Stanford University Press, 2006. A collection of essays that provides new perspectives on the history of science in early modern Iberia.

Geanakoplos, Deno John. *Constantinople and the West: Essays on the Late Byzantine (Palaeologan) and Italian Renaissances and the Byzantine and Roman Churches.* Madison: University of Wisconsin Press, 1989. Fundamental discussion of the extensive transfer of texts and scholars during the 1400s.

Jacob, Margaret C. *Scientific Culture and the Making of the Industrial West.* Oxford: Oxford University Press, 1997. Widely cited short book emphasizing the connections between New Science, scientific societies, and the steam engine.

Margolis, Howard. *It Started with Copernicus: How Turning the World Inside Out Led to the Scientific Revolution.* New York: McGraw-Hill, 2002. Important scholarly study of the connection between the discovery of the Americas and Copernicus's formulation of a sun-centered planetary system.

Nexon, Daniel H. *The Struggle for Power in Early Modern Europe: Religious Conflict, Dynastic Empires and International Change.* Princeton, NJ: Princeton University Press, 2009. Charles Tilly–inspired re-evaluation of the changes occurring in sixteenth- and seventeenth-century Europe.

Park, Katharine, and Lorraine Daston, eds., *The Cambridge History of Science.* Vol. 3, *Early Modern Science.* Cambridge, UK: Cambridge University Press, 2006. Voluminous coverage of all aspects of science, under the currently paradigmatic thesis that there was no dramatic scientific revolution in Western Christian Civilization.

Rublack, Ulinka. *Reformation Europe.* Cambridge, UK: Cambridge University Press, 2006. Cultural history approach to the effects of Luther and Calvin on western Christians.

Schiebinger, Londa. *The Mind Has No Sex? Women in the Origins of Modern Science.* Cambridge, MA: Harvard University Press, 1989. A pioneering study presenting biographies and summaries of scientific contributions made by women. Discusses the importance of Marie Cunitz.

WEBSITES

Ames Research Center. "Johannes Kepler: His Life, His Laws and Times," http://kepler.nasa.gov/Mission/JohannesKepler/. This NASA website looks at the life and views of Johannes Kepler. It examines his discoveries, his contemporaries, and the events that shaped modern science.

Howard, Sharon. "Early Modern Resources," http://sharonhoward .org/earlymodern.html. Website with many links on the full range of institutional and cultural change.

Chapter 18

Alchon, Suzanne A. *A Pest in the Land: New World Epidemics in a Global Perspective.* Albuquerque: University of New Mexico Press, 2003. A broad overview, making medical history comprehensible.

Behringer, Wolfgang. *Witches and Witch-Hunts: A Global History.* Cambridge, UK: Polity, 2004. A well-grounded overview of the phenomenon of the fear of witches, summarizing the scholarship of the past decades.

Bulmer-Thomas, Victor, John S. Coatsworth, and Roberto Cortés Conde, eds. *The Cambridge Economic History of Latin America.* Vol. 1, *The Colonial Era and the Short Nineteenth Century.* Cambridge, UK: Cambridge University Press, 2006. Collection of specialized summary articles on aspects of Iberian colonialism.

Burkholder, Mark A., and Lyman L. Johnson. *Colonial Latin America,* 6th ed. Oxford: Oxford University Press, 2008. A well-established text, updated multiple times.

Eastman, Scott, *Preaching Spanish Nationalism across the Hispanic Atlantic, 1759–1823.* Baton Rouge: Louisiana State University Press, 2012. Close look at the national reform debates in the Iberian Atlantic world at the close of colonialism.

Ekberg, Carl J. *French Roots in the Illinois Country: The Mississippi Frontier in Colonial Times.* Urbana: University of Illinois Press, 1998. Detailed, deeply researched historical account.

Socolow, Susan M. *The Women of Latin America.* Cambridge, UK: Cambridge University Press, 2000. Surveys the patriarchal order and the function of women within it.

Stein, Stanley J., and Barbara H. Stein. *Silver, Trade, and War: Spain and America in the Making of Early Modern Europe.* Baltimore:

Johns Hopkins University Press, 2000. Covers the significance of American silver reaching as far as China.

Taylor, Alan. *American Colonies.* London: Penguin, 2001. History of the English colonies in New England, written from a broad Atlantic perspective.

Wood, Michael. *Conquistadors.* Berkeley: University of California Press, 2000. Accessible, richly illustrated history of the conquest period.

WEBSITE

Conquistadors, http://www.pbs.org/conquistadors/. Wonderful interactive website that allows you to track the journeys made by the Conquistadors such as Cortés, Pizarro, Orellana, and Cabeza de Vaca. Learn more about their conquests in the Americas and the legacy they left behind them.

Chapter 19

Carney, Judith A. *Black Rice: The African Origins of Rice Cultivation in the Americas.* Cambridge, MA: Harvard University Press, 2001. Study which goes a long way toward correcting the stereotype that black slaves were unskilled laborers, and carefully documents the transfer of rice-growing culture from West Africa to the Americas.

Dubois, Laurent, and Julius S. Scott. *Origins of the Black Atlantic: Rewriting Histories.* New York: Routledge, 2009. Book that focuses on African slaves in the Americas as they had to arrange themselves in their new lives.

Gray, Richard, and David Birmingham, eds. *Pre-Colonial African Trade.* London: Oxford University Press, 1970. Collective work in which contributors emphasize the growth and intensification of trade in the centuries of 1500–1800.

Hall, Gwendolyn Midlo. *Slavery and African Ethnicities in the Americas: Restoring the Links.* Chapel Hill: University of North Carolina Press, 2005. Study that focuses on slaves in the Americas according to their regions of origin in Africa.

Heywood, Linda M., and John K. Thornton. *Central Africans, Atlantic Creoles, and the Foundation of the Americas.* Cambridge, UK: Cambridge University Press, 2007. Pathbreaking investigation of the creation and role of Creole culture in Africa and the Americas.

Iliffe, John. *Africans: The History of a Continent.* Cambridge, UK: Cambridge University Press, 1995. Standard historical summary by an established African historian.

Kriger, Colleen E. *Cloth in West African History.* Lanham, MD: Altamira, 2006. Detailed investigation of the sophisticated indigenous West African cloth industry.

Oliver, Roland, and Anthony Atmore. *Medieval Africa, 1250–1800.* Cambridge, UK: Cambridge University Press, 2001. Revised and updated historical overview, divided into regions and providing detailed regional histories on the emerging kingdoms.

Thornton, John. *The Kongolese Saint Anthony: Dona Beatriz Kimpa Vita and the Antonian Movement, 1684–1706.* Cambridge, UK: Cambridge University Press, 1998. Detailed biography of Dona Beatriz, from which the vignette at the beginning of the chapter is borrowed; includes a general overview of the history of Kongo during the civil war.

WEBSITES

British Museum. "Benin: An African Kingdom," www.britishmuseum .org/PDF/british_museum_benin_art.pdf. In addition to offering a brief historical backdrop to the art of the Benin kingdom, the British Museum's PDF also depicts various artifacts taken by the British from the Royal Palace.

Voyages: The Atlantic Slave Trade Database, http://www.slavevoyages .org/tast/index.faces. A large electronic website based at Emory

University and sponsored by a number of American universities, presenting up-to-date demographic tables.

Chapter 20

Bernier, François. *Travels in the Mogul Empire, A.D. 1656–1668.* Translated by Archibald Constable. Delhi: S. Chand, 1968. One of many fascinating travel accounts by European diplomats, merchants, and missionaries.

Eaton, Richard M. *Essays on Islam and Indian History.* New York: Oxford University Press, 2002. A compendium of the new scholarly consensus on, among other things, the differences between the clerical view of Islamic observance and its actual impact in rural India. Contains both historiography and material on civilizational and cultural issues.

Gommans, J. J. L. *Mughal Warfare: Indian Frontiers and Highroads to Empire 1500–1700.* New York: Routledge, 2002. Sound examination of the Mughal Empire as a centralizing state increasingly reliant on a strong military for border defense and extending its sway. Examination of the structure of Mughal forces and the organization and weapons of the military.

Kearney, Milo. *The Indian Ocean in World History.* New York: Routledge, 2003. Long view of the history of Indian Ocean trade from ancient times. Particularly relevant in examining the vital period in which the Portuguese and later East Indian Companies come to dominate the trade.

Nizami, Khaliq A. *Akbar and Religion.* Delhi: IAD, 1989. Extensive treatment of Akbar's evolving move toward devising his Din-i Ilahi movement, by a leading scholar of Indian religious and intellectual history.

Richards, John F. *The Mughal Empire.* Cambridge, UK: Cambridge University Press, 1993. Comprehensive volume in the New Cambridge History of India series. Sophisticated treatment; best suited to advanced students. Extensive glossary and useful bibliographic essay.

Schimmel, Annemarie. *The Empire of the Great Mughals: History, Art, and Culture.* London: Reaktion, 2004. Revised edition of a volume published in German in 2000. Lavish illustrations, wonderfully drawn portraits of key individuals, and extensive treatment of social, family, and gender relations at the Mughal court.

Srivastava, M. P. *The Mughal Administration.* Delhi: Chugh, 1995. Solid overview and analysis of the development and workings of the Mughal bureaucracy. Best utilized by advanced students.

WEBSITES

Association for Asian Studies http://www. asian-studies.org/ As with other Asian topics, one of the most reliable websites are sponsored by the Association for Asian Studies, the largest professional organization for scholars of Asia.

BBC: Religions. "Mughal Empire (1500s, 1600s)" http://www.bbc .co.uk/religion/religions/islam/history/mughalempire_1.shtml. The Mughal Empire ruled most of India and Pakistan in the sixteenth and seventeenth centuries. Learn more about the religious divides and governance of Muslim Mughals in a country with a majority of Hindi populace.

Chapter 21

China

De Bary, William T., and Irene Bloom, comps. *Sources of Chinese Tradition*, 2 vols., 2nd ed. New York: Columbia University Press, 1999. Thoroughgoing update of the classic sourcebook for Chinese literature and philosophy, with a considerable amount of social, family, and women's works now included.

Fairbank, John K., and Edwin O. Reischauer. *China: Tradition and Transformation.* Boston: Houghton Mifflin, 1989. A complete textbook on Chinese history, with the majority of the material geared toward the modern era. Emphasis on the "change within tradition" model of Chinese history.

Mungello, D. E. *The Great Encounter of China and West.* Lanham, MD: Rowman & Littlefield, 1999. Sound historical overview of the period marking the first European maritime expeditions into East Asia and extending to the height of the Canton trade and the beginnings of the opium era.

Pomeranz, Kenneth. *The Great Divergence: China, Europe, and the Making of the Modern World Economy.* Princeton, NJ: Princeton University Press, 2001. Pathbreaking work mounting the strongest argument yet in favor of the balance of economic power remaining in east Asia until the Industrial Revolution was well under way.

Spence, Jonathan. *The Memory Palace of Matteo Ricci.* New York: Penguin, 1984. Highly original treatment of Ricci and the beginning of the Jesuit interlude in late Ming and early Qing China. Attempts to penetrate Ricci's world through the missionary's own memory techniques.

Japan

De Bary, William T., ed. *Sources of Japanese Tradition*, 2 vols. New York: Columbia University Press, 1964. The Tokugawa era spans volumes 1 and 2, with its inception and political and philosophical foundations thoroughly covered in volume 1 and the Shinto revival of national learning, the later Mito school, and various partisans of national unity in the face of foreign intrusion covered in the beginning of volume 2.

Duus, Peter. *Feudalism in Japan*, 3rd ed. New York: McGraw-Hill, 1993. Updated version of a short, handy volume spanning all of Japanese history to 1867, with special emphasis on the shogunates. Good introduction on the uses and limitations of the term "feudalism" with reference to Japan within a comparative framework.

Gordon, Andrew. *A Modern History of Japan from Tokugawa Times to the Present.* New York: Oxford University Press, 2009. One of the few treatments of Japanese history that spans both the Tokugawa and the modern eras, rather than making the usual break in either 1853 or 1867/1868. Both the continuity of the past and the novelty of the new era are therefore juxtaposed and highlighted. Most useful for students with a background at least equivalent to that supplied by this text.

WEBSITE

National Geographic. China's Great Armada, http://ngm.nationalgeographic.com/ngm/0507/feature2/map.html. Track the voyages made by Zheng He to southeast Asia, India, Arabia, and Africa.

Chapter 22

Herb, Guntram H. *Nations and Nationalism: A Global Historical Overview.* Santa Barbara, CA: ABC-Clio, 2008. Contains a large number of articles on the varieties of ethnic nationalism and culture and the proliferation of nationalism in Europe and Latin America.

Israel, Jonathan I. *A Revolution of the Mind: Radical Enlightenment and the Origins of Modern Democracy.* Princeton, NJ: Princeton University Press, 2010. Israel is a pioneer of the contemporary renewal of intellectual history, and his investigations of the Enlightenment tradition are pathbreaking.

Kaiser, Thomas E., and Dale K. Van Kley, eds. *From Deficit to Deluge: The Origins of the French Revolution.* Stanford, CA: Stanford University Press, 2011. Thoughtful reevaluation of the scholarly field that takes into account the latest interpretations.

Kitchen, Martin. *A History of Modern Germany: 1800 to the Present.* Hoboken, NJ: Wiley-Blackwell, 2011. A broadly conceived historical overview, ranging from politics and economics to culture.

Rakove, Jack. *Revolutionaries: A New History of the Invention of America.* Boston: Houghton Mifflin, 2010. A new narrative history focusing on the principal figures in the revolution.

Riall, Lucy. *Risorgimento: The History of Italy from Napoleon to Nation-State*. New York: Palgrave Macmillan, 2009. Historical summary, incorporating the research of the past half-century, presented in a clear overview.

West, Elliott. *The Last Indian War: the Nez Perce Story*. Oxford and New York: Oxford University Press, 2009. Vivid story of the end of the US wars for the subjugation of the Native Americans.

Wood, Gordon S. *The American Revolution: A History*. New York: Modern Library, 2002. A short, readable summary reflective of many decades of revisionism in the discussion of the American Revolution.

WEBSITES

Liberty, Equality, Fraternity: Exploring the French Revolution, http://chnm.gmu.edu/revolution/. This website boasts 250 images, 350 text documents, 13 songs, 13 maps, and a timeline all focused on the French Revolution.

Nationalism Project, http://www.nationalismproject.org/. A large website with links to bibliographies, essays, new books, and book reviews.

Chapter 23

Adelman, Jeremy. *Sovereignty and Revolution in the Iberian Atlantic*, Princeton, NJ: 2006. A leading study in a group of recent works on the transatlantic character of colonial and postcolonial Latin America.

Brown, Matthew. *The Struggle for Power in Post-Independence Colombia and Venezuela*. New York: Palgrave Macmillan, 2012. Detailed history of the forces pulling for democracy as well as authoritarianism on the north coast of South America.

Bulmer-Thomas, Victor. *The Economic History of Latin America since Independence*, 2nd ed. Cambridge, UK: Cambridge University Press, 2003. A highly analytical and sympathetic investigation of the Latin American export and self-sufficiency economies, calling into question the long-dominant dependency theories of Latin America.

Burkholder, Mark, and Lyman Johnson. *Colonial Latin America*, 6th ed. New York: Oxford University Press, 2008. Overview, with focus on social and cultural history.

Dawson, Alexander. *Latin America since Independence: A History with Primary Sources*. New York: Routledge, 2011. Selection of topics with documentary base; for the nineteenth century covers the topics of the nation-state, caudillo politics, race, and the policy of growth through commodity exports.

Drake, Paul W. *Between Tyranny and Anarchy: A History of Democracy in Latin America*. Stanford, CA: Stanford University Press, 2009. The author traces the concepts of constitutionalism, autocracy, and voting rights since independence in clear and persuasive strokes.

Girard, Philippe, *The Slaves Who Defeated Napoléon: Toussaint Louverture and the Haitian War of Independence, 1801–1804*. Tuscaloosa: University of Alabama Press, 2011. Thoroughly researched study of the leader of the revolution, with a number of revisionist conclusions.

Hämäläinen, Pekka. *The Comanche Empire*. New Haven, CT: Yale University Press, 2008. A revisionist account that puts the extraordinary importance of the Comanche empire for the history of Mexico and the United States in the 19th century into the proper perspective.

Moya, Jose C., ed. *The Oxford Handbook of Latin American History*. New York: Oxford University Press, 2011. Important collection of political, social, economic, and cultural essays by leading specialists on nineteenth-century Latin America.

Popkin, Jeremy D. *The Haitian Revolution and the Abolition of Slavery*. Cambridge, UK: Cambridge University Press, 2010.

Sater, William F. *Andean Tragedy: Fighting the War of the Pacific, 1879–1884*. Lincoln: University of Nebraska Press, 2007. Close examination of this destructive war on the South American west coast.

Skidmore, Thomas. *Brazil: Five Centuries of Change*, 2nd ed. New York: Oxford University Press, 2010. Short but magisterial text on the history of Brazil, with a detailed chapter on Brazil's path toward independence in the nineteenth century.

Wasserman, Mark, and Cheryl English Martin. *Latin America and Its People*, 2nd ed. New York: Pearson Longman, 2007. Thematic approach, drawing general conclusions by comparing and contrasting the individual countries of Latin America.

WEBSITE

Casahistoria. "19th Century Latin America," http://www.casahistoria .net/latin_american_history19.html. Website on nineteenth-century Latin America, for students.

Chapter 24

China

Cohen, Paul. *Discovering History in China*. New York: Columbia University Press, 1984. Important work on the historiography of American writers on China. Critiques their collective ethnocentrism in attempting to fit Chinese history into Western perspectives and approaches.

Fairbank, John K., and Su-yu Teng. *China's Response to the West*. Cambridge, MA: Harvard University Press, 1954. Though dated in approach, still a vitally important collection of sources in translation for the period from the late eighteenth century till 1923.

Kang, David C. *East Asia before the West: Five Centuries of Trade and Tribute*. New York: Columbia University Press, 2010. An excellent companion piece to D. E. Mungello's work covering the period from 1500–1800. Especially good on the Ming era.

Platt, Stephen R. *Autumn in the Heavenly Kingdom*. New York: Knopf, 2012. Reinterpretation of the Taiping era as a global political and economic phenomena involving the curtailing of US cotton exports during its civil war, their effects on the British textile industry, and the loss of Chinese markets during the Taiping Rebellion.

Spence, Jonathan D. *The Search for Modern China*. New York: Norton, 1990. Extensive, far-reaching interpretation of the period from China's nineteenth-century decline in the face of Western imperialism, through its revolutionary era, and finally to its recent bid for global preeminence.

Japan

Beasley, W. G. *The Meiji Restoration*. Stanford, CA: Stanford University Press, 1972.

Reischauer, Edwin O., and Albert M. Craig. *Japan: Tradition and Transformation*. Boston: Houghton Mifflin, 1989.

Totman, Conrad. *A History of Japan*. Oxford: Blackwell, 2000.

Totman, Conrad. *Japan before Perry*. Berkeley: University of California Press, 1981.

WEBSITES

Association for Asian Studies, http://www.asian-studies.org/. This website of the Association for Asian Studies has links to sources more suited to advanced term papers and seminar projects.

Education about Asia, http://www.asian-studies.org/eaa/. This site provides the best online sources for modern Chinese and Japanese history.

Sino-Japanese War 1894–5, http://sinojapanesewar.com/. Packed with maps, photographs and movies depicting the conflict between Japan and China at the end of the nineteenth century, students can learn more about causes and consequences of the Sino-Japanese War.

Chapter 25

Gaudin, Corinne. *Ruling Peasants: Village and State in Later Imperial Russia*. DeKalb: Northern Illinois University Press, 2007. A close and sympathetic analysis of rural Russia.

Inalcik, Halil, and Donald Quataert, eds. *An Economic and Social History of the Ottoman Empire*. Vol. 2, *1600–1914*. Cambridge, UK: Cambridge University Press, 1994. A pioneering work with contributions by leading Ottoman historians on rural structures, monetary developments, and industrialization efforts.

Kasaba, Resat, ed. *The Cambridge History of Turkey*. Vol. 5, *Turkey in the Modern World*. Cambridge, UK: Cambridge University Press, 2008. An ambitious effort to assemble the leading authorities on the Ottoman Empire and provide a comprehensive overview.

Lieven, Dominic. *Empire: The Russian Empire and Its Rivals*. New Haven, CT: Yale University Press, 2002. Broad, comparative history of the Russian Empire, in the context of the Habsburg, Ottoman, and British Empires.

Nikitenko, Aleksandr. *Up from Serfdom: My Childhood and Youth in Russia, 1804–1824*. Translated by Helen Saltz Jacobson. New Haven, CT: Yale University Press, 2001. Touching autobiography summarized at the beginning of the chapter.

Poe, Marshall T. *Russia's Moment in World History*. Princeton, NJ: Princeton University Press, 2003. A superb scholarly overview of Russian history, written from a broad perspective and taking into account a good number of Western stereotypes about Russia, especially in the nineteenth century.

Quataert, Donald. *Manufacturing in the Ottoman Empire and Turkey, 1500–1950*. Albany: State University of New York Press, 1994. The author is still the leading American historian on workers and the early industrialization of the Ottoman Empire.

Riasanovsky, Nicholas, and Mark Steinberg. *A History of Russia*, 8th ed., 2 vols. New York: Oxford University Press, 2011. A comprehensive, fully revised history, ranging from politics and economics to literature and the arts.

Uyar, Mesut, and Edward J. Erickson. *A Military History of the Ottomans: From Osman to Atatürk*. Santa Barbara, CA: Praeger Security International, 2009. A detailed, well-documented history of the Ottoman Empire from the perspective of its imperial designs and military forces, by two military officers in academic positions.

Zurcher, Erik J. *The Young Turk Legacy and Nation Building: From the Ottoman Empire to Ataturk's Turkey*. London: I. B. Tauris, 2010. Detailed yet readable account of how the Young Turk movement laid the foundation for the Kemal Ataturk's Republic of Turkey.

WEBSITE

Russian Legacy. "Russian Empire (1689–1825)," http://www.russian-legacy.com/en/go_to/history/russian_empire.htm. Russian Legacy, a website devoted to the Russian Empire, organized as a timeline with links.

Chapter 26

Allen, Robert C. *The British Industrial Revolution in Global Perspective*. Cambridge, UK: Cambridge University Press, 2009. An in-depth analysis, well supported by economic data, not only of why the Industrial Revolution occurred first in Britain but also of how new British technologies carried industrialism around the world.

Dublin, Thomas, ed. *Farm to Factory: Women's Letters, 1830–1860*. New York: Columbia University Press, 1981. A fascinating collection of correspondence written by women who describe their experiences in moving from rural areas of New England to urban centers in search of work in textile factories.

Griffin, Emma. *Liberty's Dawn: A People's History of the Industrial Revolution*. New Haven, CT: Yale University Press, 2013. Riveting study of the impact of the Industrial Revolution on the lives of working men and women in Britain, as told in autobiographies and memoirs.

Headrick, Daniel R. *The Tools of Empire: Technology and European Imperialism in the Nineteenth Century*. Oxford: Oxford University Press, 1981. A fascinating and clearly written analysis of the connections between the development of new technologies and their role in European imperialism.

Hobsbawm, Eric. *The Age of Revolution: 1789–1848*. London: Vintage, 1996. A sophisticated analysis of the Industrial Revolution (one element of the "dual revolution," the other being the French Revolution) that examines the effects of industrialism on social and cultural developments from a Marxist perspective.

Mokyr, Joel. "Accounting for the Industrial Revolution." In *The Cambridge Economic History of Modern Britain*, vol. 1, edited by Roderick Floud and Paul Johnson, pp. 1–27. Cambridge, UK: Cambridge University Press, 2004. An analysis of the industrial movement that emphasizes its intellectual sources, embraced in the term "Industrial Enlightenment."

More, Charles. *Understanding the Industrial Revolution*. London: Routledge, 2000. A comprehensive explanation of how theories of economic growth account for the development of the industrial movement in Britain.

Rosen, William. *The Most Powerful Idea in the World: A Story of Steam, Industry, and Innovation*. Chicago: University of Chicago Press, 2012. Absorbing history of the importance of steam technologies in the development of industrialism.

WEBSITES

Claude Monet: Life and Paintings, http://www.monetpainting.net/. A visually beautiful website which reproduces many of Monet's masterpieces; this site also includes an extensive biographical account of the famous painter's life and works. It also includes information about his wife Camille, his gardens at Giverny, and a chronology.

Darwin Online, http://darwin-online.org.uk/. This website has reproduced, in full, the works of Charles Darwin. In addition to providing digitized facsimiles of his works, private papers, and manuscripts, it has also added a concise biographical account and numerous images of Darwin throughout his life.

Einstein Archives Online, http://www.alberteinstein.info/. Fantastic and informative website that houses digitized manuscripts of Einstein's work. Also includes a gallery of images.

ThomasEdison.org, http://www.thomasedison.org/. Remarkable website that explores Thomas Edison's impact on modernity through his innovations and inventions. This site also reproduces all of Edison's scientific sketches, which are available to download as PDF files.

Chapter 27

Belich, James. *Replenishing the Earth: The Settler Revolution and the Rise of the Anglo-World, 1783–1939*. Oxford: Oxford University Press, 2009. Important study by an Australian historian, focusing on the British settler colonies.

Burbank, Jane, and Frederick Cooper. *Empires in World History: Power and Politics of Difference*. Princeton, NJ: Princeton University Press, 2010. Well-written and remarkably comprehensive comparative work.

Chamberlain, M. E. *The Scramble for Africa*. New York: Routledge, 2013. Insightful account of the European colonization of Africa during the period 1870 to 1914.

Ferguson, Niall. *Empire: The Rise and Demise of the British World Order and the Lessons for Global Power*. New York: Perseus, 2002. Controversial but widely acknowledged analysis of the question of whether imperialism deserves its negative reputation.

Hobsbawm, Eric. *The Age of Empire, 1875–1914*. New York: Vintage, 1989. Immensely well-informed investigation of the climactic period of the new imperialism at the end of the nineteenth century.

Hochschild, Adam. *King Leopold's Ghost: A Story of Greed, Terror, and Heroism in Colonial Africa*. New York: Houghton Mifflin, 1998. A gripping exposé of Leopold II's brutal tactics in seizing territory and exploiting African labor in the Congo.

Jefferies, Matthew. *Contesting the German Empire, 1871–1918*. Malden, MA: Blackwell, 2008. Up-to-date summary of the German historical debate on the colonial period.

Ricklefs, Merle Calvin. *A History of Modern Indonesia Since c. 1200*, 3rd ed. Stanford, CA: Stanford University Press, 2001. Standard history with relevant chapters on Dutch imperialism and colonialism.

Singer, Barnett, and John Langdon. *Cultured Force: Makers and Defenders of the French Colonial Empire*. Madison: University of Wisconsin Press, 2004. Study of the principal (military) figures who helped create the French nineteenth-century empire.

WEBSITES

The Colonization of Africa, http://exhibitions.nypl.org/africanaage/essay-colonization-of-africa.html. An academically based summary with further essays on African topics, as well as multimedia functions.

South Asian History—*Colonial* India, http://www.lib.berkeley.edu/SSEAL/SouthAsia/india_colonial.html. Very detailed website with primary documents and subtopics of nineteenth-century British India.

Chapter 28

Berend, Ivan T. *An Economic History of Twentieth-Century Europe: Economic Regimes from Laissez-Faire to Globalization*. Cambridge, UK: Cambridge University Press, 2006. Includes Europe-wide, comparative chapters on laissez-faire and state-directed economies, including deficit spending.

Bose, Sugata, and Ayesha Jalal. *Modern South Asia: History, Culture, Political Economy*. New York: Routledge, 2004. Well-informed analyses by two of the foremost South Asia specialists.

Clark, Christopher. *The Sleepwalkers: How Europe Went to War in 1914*. New York: HarperPerennial, 2014. One of a slew of new investigations into the origins of the war published to mark its centennial; emphasizes the Austrian-Serbian roots of the war.

Fritzsche, Peter. *Life and Death in the Third Reich*. Cambridge, MA: Harvard University Press, 2008. Book that seeks to understand the German nation's choice of arranging itself to Nazi rule.

Gelvin, James L. *The Modern Middle East: A History*, 3rd ed. Oxford: Oxford University Press, 2011. Contains chapters on Arab nationalism, British and French colonialism, and Turkey and Iran in the interwar period.

Gordon, Andrew. *A Modern History of Japan: From Tokugawa Times to the Present*, 2nd ed. Oxford: Oxford University Press, 2009. Detailed overview of Japan's interwar period in the middle chapters.

Grasso, June M., J. P. Corrin, and Michael Kort. *Modernization and Revolution in Modern China: From the Opium Wars to the Olympics*, 4th ed. Armonk, NY: M. E. Sharpe, 2009. General overview with a focus on modernization, in relation to the strong survival of tradition.

Lombardo, Paul A., ed. *A Century of Eugenics in America: From the Indiana Experiment to the Human Genome Era*. Bloomington: Indiana University Press, 2011. Study of a dark chapter in US history.

Martel, Gordon, ed. *A Companion to Europe 1900–1945*. Malden, MA: Wiley-Blackwell, 2010. Collective work covering a large variety of cultural, social, and political European topics in the interwar period.

Meade, Teresa A. *A History of Modern Latin America: 1800 to the Present*. Malden, MA: Wiley-Routledge, 2010. Topical discussion of the major issues in Latin American history, with chapters on the first half of the twentieth century.

Snyder, Timothy. *Bloodlands: Europe between Hitler and Stalin*. New York: Basic Books, 2010. Book that chronicles the horrific destruction left behind by these two dictators.

WEBSITES

BBC. World War One, http://www.bbc.co.uk/ww1, and World War Two, http://www.bbc.co.uk/history/worldwars/wwtwo/. The BBC's treatment of the causes, course, and consequences of both WWI and WWII from an Allied position.

Marxists Internet Archive. "The Bolsheviks," http://www.marxists.org/subject/bolsheviks/index.htm. A complete review of the Bolshevik party members, including biographies and links to archives which contain their works.

1937 Nanking Massacre, http://www.nanking-massacre.com/Home.html. A disturbing collection of pictures and articles tell the gruesome history of the Rape of Nanjing.

United States Holocaust Memorial Museum. Holocaust Encyclopedia, http://www.ushmm.org/wlc/en/article.php?ModuleId=10005151. The US Holocaust Memorial Museum looks back on one of the darkest times in Western history.

U.S. History, http://www.ushistory.org/us/. Maintained by Independence Hall Association in Philadelphia, this website contains many links to topics discussed in this chapter.

Chapter 29

Baret, Roby Carol. *The Greater Middle East and the Cold War: US Foreign Policy under Eisenhower and Kennedy*. London: Tauris, 2007. Thoroughly researched analysis of American policies in the Middle East, North Africa, and south Asia.

Birmingham, David. *Kwame Nkrumah: Father of African Nationalism*. Athens: University of Ohio Press, 1998. Short biography by a leading modern African historian.

Conniff, Michael L. *Populism in Latin America*. Tuscaloosa: University of Alabama Press, 1999. The author is a well-published scholar on modern Latin America.

Damrosch, David, David Lawrence Pike, Djelal Kadir, and Ursula K. Heise, eds. *The Longman Anthology of World Literature*. Vol. F, *The Twentieth Century*. New York: Longman/Pearson, 2008. A rich, diverse selection of texts. Alternatively, Norton published a similar, somewhat larger anthology of world literature in 2003.

De Witte, Ludo. *The Assassination of Lumumba*. Translated by Ann Wright and Renée Fenby. London: Verso, 2002. An admirably researched study of the machinations of the Belgian government in protecting its mining interests, with the connivance of CIA director Allen Dulles and President Dwight D. Eisenhower.

Goscha, Christopher E., and Christian F. Ostermann. *Connecting Histories: Decolonization and the Cold War in Southeast Asia, 1945–1962*. Stanford, CA: Stanford University Press, 2009.

Guha, Ramachandra. *India after Gandhi: A History of the World's Largest Democracy*. New York: Harper Collins, 2007. Highly readable, popular history with well-sketched biographical treatments of leading individuals, more obscure cultural figures, and ordinary people. Accessible to even beginning students.

Hasegawa, Tsuyoshi. *The Cold War in East Asia, 1945–1991*. Stanford, CA: Stanford University Press, 2011. A new summary, based on archival research by a leading Japanese historian teaching in the United States. New insights on the Soviet entry into World War II against Japan.

Herman, Arthur. *Joseph McCarthy: Reexamining the Life and Legacy of America's Most Hated Senator*. New York: Free Press, 2000. A fascinating study of the Wisconsin senator whose virulent campaign against communism launched decades of fear and reprisals in America during the Cold War era.

Meredith, Martin. *The Fate of Africa: A History of the Continent since Independence*. Philadelphia: Perseus, 2011. A revised and up-to-date study of a fundamental analysis of Africa during the modern era.

WEBSITES

Economist. "The Suez Crisis: An Affair to Remember," http://www.economist.com/node/7218678. The *Economist* magazine looks back on the Suez Crisis.

NASA. "Yuri Gagarin: First Man in Space," http://www.nasa.gov/mission_pages/shuttle/sts1/gagarin_anniversary.html. In addition to information and video footage regarding Yuri Gagarin's orbit of the earth, students will also find information on America's space history.

Newseum. The Berlin Wall, http://www.newseum.org/berlinwall/. The Newseum's interactive website looks at what life was like on both sides of the Berlin Wall.

Chapter 30

Ash, Timothy Garton. *The Magic Lantern: The Revolution of '89 Witnessed in Warsaw, Budapest, Berlin, and Prague*. New York: Random House, 1999. A gripping first-hand account of the wave of anticommunist revolutions that rocked Eastern Europe after 1989.

Duara, Prasenjit. *Decolonization: Perspectives from Now and Then*. London: Routledge, 2004. A leading scholar of China and postcolonial studies edits essays in this offering in the Rewriting Histories series on the fall of the colonial empires by scholars such as Michael Adas and John Voll and activists and leaders such as Frantz Fanon and Kwame Nkrumah.

Fanon, Frantz. *The Wretched of the Earth*. New York: Grove, 1961. One of the most provocative and influential treatments of theoretical and practical issues surrounding decolonization. Fanon champions violence as an essential part of the decolonization process and advocates a modified Marxist approach that takes into consideration the nuances of race and the legacies of colonialism.

Frieden, Jeffrey. *Global Capitalism: Its Fall and Rise in the Twentieth Century*. New York: W. W. Norton, 2006. Despite the title, a comprehensive history of global networks from the days of mercantilism to the twenty-first century. Predominant emphasis on twentieth century; highly readable, though the material is best suited for the nonbeginning student.

Gaddis, John Lewis. *The Cold War: A New History*. New York: Penguin, 2005. Though criticized by some scholars for his pro-American positions, America's foremost historian of the Cold War produces here a vivid, at times counterintuitive, view of the Cold War and its global impact. Readable even for beginning students.

Gitlin, Todd. *The Sixties: Years of Hope, Days of Rage*, rev. ed. New York: Bantam, 1993. Lively, provocative account of this pivotal decade by the former radical, now a sociologist. Especially effective at depicting the personalities of the pivotal period 1967–1969.

Harmer, Tanya. *Allende's Chile and the Inter-American Cold War*. Chapel Hill: University of North Carolina Press, 2014. A reinterpretation of American determination to overturn Allende's leftist government and its subsequent results.

Liang Heng and Judith Shapiro. *After the Nightmare: A Survivor of the Cultural Revolution Reports on China Today*. New York: Knopf, 1986. Highly readable, poignant, first-person accounts of people's experiences during the trauma of China's Cultural Revolution by a former husband-and-wife team. Especially interesting because China was at the beginning of its Four Modernizations when this was written, and the wounds of the Cultural Revolution were still fresh.

Raleigh, Donald J. *Soviet Baby Boomers: An Oral History of Russia's Cold War Generation*. New York: Oxford University Press, 2012. A revealing and entertaining account of new social and cultural trends among Russia's youth, as told in a series of interviews.

Smith, Bonnie. *Global Feminisms since 1945*. London: Routledge, 2000. Part of the Rewriting Histories series, this work brings together under the editorship of Smith a host of essays by writers such as Sara Evans, Mary Ann Tetreault, and Miriam Ching Yoon Louie on feminism in Asia, Africa, and Latin America, as well as Europe and the United States. Sections are thematically arranged under such headings as "Nation-Building," "Sources of Activism," "Women's Liberation," and "New Waves in the 1980s and 1990s." Comprehensive and readable, though some background in women's history is recommended.

WEBSITES

Cold War International History Project, http://www.wilsoncenter.org/program/cold-war-international-history-project. Run by the Woodrow Wilson International Center for Scholars. Rich archival materials including collections on the end of the Cold War, Soviet invasion of Afghanistan, Cuban Missile Crisis, and Chinese foreign policy documents.

College of DuPage Library, http:codlibrary.org. Entering "Research guide to 1960s websites" in the search box yields a wide-ranging set of relevant topics.

Chapter 31

Chau, Adam Yuet, ed. *Religion in Contemporary China*. New York: Routledge, 2011. Collection of fascinating chapters on the revival of Daoist, Confucian, and Buddhist traditions and their adaption to middle-class modernity, with their proponents operating often in a gray zone between official recognition and suppression.

Daniels, Robert V. *The Rise and Fall of Communism in the Soviet Union*. New Haven, CT: Yale University Press, 2010. A magisterial summary of the communist period by a specialist.

Dillon, Michael. *Contemporary China: An Introduction*. New York: Routledge, 2009. Concise yet quite specific overview of the economy, society, and politics of the country.

Eichengreen, Barry. *Exorbitant Privilege: The Rise and Fall of the Dollar and the Future of the Monetary System*. New York: Oxford University Press, 2011. The author is an academic specialist on US monetary policies, writing in an accessible style and presenting a fascinating picture of the role of something as prosaic as greenbacks.

Gelvin, James L. *The Arab Uprisings: What Everyone Needs to Know*. New York: Oxford University Press, 2012. Concise overview of the Arab Spring events with carefully selected background information.

Jacka, Tamara, Andrew Kipnis, and Sally Sargeson. *Contemporary China: Society and Social Change*. Cambridge, UK: Cambridge University Press, 2013. Ambitious sociological-historical study focusing on the many differences within Chinese society and the forces that drive change in contemporary China.

Meade, Teresa A. *A History of Modern Latin America: 1800 to the Present*. Malden, MA: Wiley-Blackwell, 2010. The book is an excellent, comprehensive analysis and has a strong final chapter on recent Latin America.

Saxonberg, Steven. *The Fall: A Comparative Study of the End of Communism in Czechoslovakia, East Germany, Hungary, and Poland*. Amsterdam: Harwood Academic, 2001. A well-informed overview of the different trajectories by an academic teaching in Prague.

Speth, James Gustav. *The Bridge at the Edge of the World: Capitalism, the Environment, and Crossing from Crisis to Sustainability*. New Haven, CT: Yale University Press, 2008. A strong plea to change our capitalist system.

Swanimathan, Jayshankar M. *Indian Economic Superpower: Fact or Fiction?* Singapore: World Scientific Publishing, 2009. A thoughtful evaluation of the pros and cons of economic growth in India, in concise overviews.

Wapner, Kevin. *Living through the End of Nature: The Future of American Environmentalism*. Cambridge, MA: MIT Press, 2010. A specialist's look at the vast transformation of nature which is taking place according to the best evidence science can marshal.

WEBSITES

BBC. Nelson Mandela's Life and Times, http://www.bbc.co.uk/news/world-africa-12305154. The BBC News looks back at the life and career of Nelson Mandela.

Environmental Protection Agency. Climate Change, http://www.epa.gov/climatechange/. The US Environmental Protection Agency's website on climate change reviews the threat to the world's climate and the implications of consistent abuse. The site also looks at various initiatives to help reverse some of the damage already done.

Sierra Club, http://sierraclub.org/. Balanced and informative environmental websites.

Credits

Chapter 1: © Christoph Hormann, 4; © Morton Beebe/Corbis. 7; (top left) RMN-Grand Palais/Art Resource, NY, 10; (top right) akg-images/CDA/Guillemot, 10; (bottom) National Museum of Tanzania, Dar es Salaam, 1985 David L. Brill, 10; © Kenneth Garrett Photography, 14; Photograph by Chris O'Connell, Bradshaw Foundation, Geneva, 18; (top) "Lion-man", statuette carved of mammouth-tusk, H 296 mm. Site: Hohlenstein-Stadel-cave, community. Asselfingen, Baden-Württemberg, Germany. Upper Paleolithic period (Aurignacien), approx. 32 000 BP. Inv. Ulmer Museum Prä Slg. Wetzel Ho-St. 39/88.1. Photo Thomas Stephan, © Ulmer Museum, 20; (bottom) Foto: Hilde Jensen, copyright University Tübingen, 20; (top) © Walter Geiersperger/Corbis, 21; (bottom) © Charles & Josette Lenars/CORBIS, 21; © UNESCO/Nathalie Valanchon, 26; AP Photo/Perfect Image, James Chatters, HO, 29.

Chapter 2: © The Trustees of the British Museum/Art Resource, NY, 32; adapted from Gianni Tortoli/ Photo Researchers, Inc, 39; Erich Lessing/Art Resource, NY, 41; RMN-Grand Palais/Art Resource, NY, 45; © Copyright Alfred Molon, 46; Werner Forman/Art Resource, NY, 46; © SOTK2011/Alamy, 52; © Ivy Close Images/Alamy, 60; (left) akg-images/John Hios, 61; (right, nude) Scala/Art Resource, NY, 61.

Chapter 3: DeA Picture Library/Art Resource, NY, 66; Photo courtesy of National Museum of Pakistan, Karachi, 73; © Harappa, 74; © Harappa, 75; bpk, Berlin . Museum fuer Asiatische Kunst, Staatliche Museen/Iris Papadopoulos/Art Resource, NY, 82; Firmin Didot, ~ 1810, Copyright: ImagesofAsia.com, 87; (top) © Doranne Jacobson, 88; (bottom) © Doranne Jacobson, 88.

Chapter 4: © Xiaoyang Liu/Corbis, 92; (top) Photo ChinaStock, 97; (middle) Photo ChinaStock, 97; (bottom) Photo ChinaStock, 97; © Asian Art & Archaeology, Inc./CORBIS, 98; V&A, London/Art Resource, NY, 102; photo by Gary Lee Todd, 103; © Lowell Georgia/Corbis, 113; © Asian Art & Archaeology, Inc./CORBIS, 114; joannawnuk/Shutterstock, 116.

Chapter 5: ERNESTO BENAVIDES/AFP/Getty Images/Newscom, 120; © David Muench/Corbis, 128; © Ricardo Azoury/CORBIS, 129; ©Sean Sprague/The Image Works, 133; © Charles & Josette Lenars/CORBIS, 134; © Charles & Josette Lenars/CORBIS, 136; Science © 2006, 139; ©Caroline Penn/Impact/HIP/The Image Works, 143; The Kon-Tiki Museum, no. 3241, 144.

Chapter 6: © Kazuyoshi Nomachi/Corbis, 150; Werner Forman/Art Resource, NY, 157; Werner Forman/Art Resource, NY, 162; Richard Maschmeyer, 165; bpk, Berlin/Ethnologisches Museum, Staatliche Museen /Art Resource, NY, 169; Photograph K2803© Justin Kerr, 170; DEA/G. DAGLI ORTI, 173; © Gianni Dagli Orti/Corbis, 174; © Karen Su/Corbis, 176.

Chapter 7: Vanni Archive/Art Resource, NY, 180; SEF/Art Resource, NY, 184; 205 Louis and Nancy Hatch Dupree Collection, Williams Afghan Media Project Archive, 188; Vanni Archive/Art Resource, NY, 191; © Vanni Archive/ Art Resource, NY, 192; © Wolfgang Kaehler/Corbis, 202; Dura-Europos Synagogue, National Museum of Damascus, Syria/Photo © Zev Radovan/Bridgeman Images, 205; akg-images/Gerard Degeorge, 208; The Metropolitan Museum of Art/Art Resource, NY, 210 (top) Dsmdgold/Wikimedia Commons , 211; (bottom) Erich Lessing/Art Resource, NY, 211.

Chapter 8: Courtesy of the Library of Congress, 216; Borromeo/Art Resource, NY, 222; (top) © Clive Friend, 223; (bottom) © Clive Friend, 223; © Jeremy Richards/iStock, 225; Roland and Sabrina Michaud/akg-images, 228; A.F.Kersting/akg-images, 230; © The Trustees of the British Museum, 236; The Metropolitan Museum of Art/Art Resource, NY, 239.

Chapter 9: The Trustees of the British Museum/Art Resource, NY, 244; © Glow Asia RF/Alamy, 248; akg-images/Laurent Lecat, 252; photo by Gary Lee Todd, 256; Courtesy of ChinaStock, 258; Courtesy of ChinaStock, 261; Photograph © 2015 Museum of Fine Arts, Boston. Francis Bartlett Donation of 1912, 266; (top) The Metropolitan Museum of Art/Art Resource, NY, 268; (bottom) Courtesy of the National Archive and Records Administration, 268.

Chapter 10: Courtesy of the Library of Congress, 274; The Trustees of the British Museum/Art Resource, NY, 277; ALIMDI.NET/Fabian von Poser, 282; © Bruno Morandi/SOPA/Corbis, 285; © Jon Hicks/Corbis, 285; Biblioteca Nacional, Madrid, Spain/Album/Art Resource, NY, 287; visualiseur.bnf.fr/Bibliothèque nationale de France, 289; British Library, London, UK/© British Library Board. All Rights Reserved/Bridgeman Images, 293; Scala/White Images/Art Resource, NY, 295; bpk, Berlin/Bibliotheque Nationale/Gerard le Gall /Art Resource, NY, 300; Gianni Dagli Orti/The Art Archive at Art Resource, NY, 305.

Chapter 11: Palazzo Pubblico, Siena, Italy/Erich Lessing/Art Resource, NY, 310; bpk, Berlin/Cathedral (Palatine Chapel), Aachen, Germany/Stefan Diller /Art Resource, NY, 314; bpk, Berlin/Hamburger Kunsthalle/Elke Walford/Art Resource, NY, 323; (left) Santa Sabina, Rome, Italy/Alinari/Bridgeman Images, 325; (right) akg-images/Henning Bock, 325; © Jorge Royan/Alamy, 330; Basilique Saint-Denis, France/Peter Willi/Bridgeman Images, 332; akg-images/VISIOARS, 334; Georgios Kollidas/Shutterstock, 337.

Chapter 12: akg-images, 344; © Michael S. Yamashita/Corbis, 347; akg-images/Gerard Degeorge, 349; National Museum of China/China Stock, 353; © British Library Board/Robana/Art Resource, NY, 356; The Art Archive at Art Resource, NY, 358; © All rights reserved by Seoul Korea, 359; illus. Jan Adkins, http://www.south chinasea.org, 361; Musee des Arts Asiatiques-Guimet, Paris, France/© RMN-Grand Palais/Art Resource, NY, 367.

Chapter 13: Photo © AISA, 372; © Carmen Redondo/CORBIS, 377; from A Handbook of Korea. Korean Overseas Information Service. Seoul, 1993. pg 50, 381; © Atlantide Phototravel/Corbis, 382; (left) The Metropolitan Museum of Art/Art Resource, NY, 383; (right) The Metropolitan Museum of Art/Art Resource, NY, 383; Plan of Heiankyo. Transcribed by Mori Koan in 1750. National Archives of Japan, 387; The Metropolitan Museum of Art/Art Resource, NY, 389; The Metropolitan Museum of Art/Art Resource, NY, 392; © Luca Tettoni/Robert Harding World Imagery/Corbis, 399.

Chapter 14: Bibliotheque Nationale, Paris, France/Bridgeman Images, 404; © Franck Guiziou/Hemis/Corbis, 410; Werner Forman/Art Resource, NY, 417; Mapungubwe Museum, Department of UP Arts, at the University of Pretoria, 418; © South African Railways & Amp Harbors/National Geographic Society/Corbis, 419; Werner

Forman/Art Resource, NY, 427; akg-images/André Held, 428; Image courtesy of The Minneapolis Institute of Arts, 429.

Chapter 15: © Margaret Sidlosky, 432; Gianni Dagli Orti/The Art Archive at Art Resource, NY, 438; © Christophe Boisvieux/Corbis, 439; bpk, Berlin/Ibero-Amerikanisches Institut, Stiftung Preussischer Kulturbesitz, Berlin, Germany/Dietmar Katz/Art Resource, NY, 443; © Gianni Dagli Orti/The Art Archive at Art Resource, NY, 445; (top) Robert Cortright, Bridge Ink, 448; (bottom) © RICKEY ROGERS/Reuters/Corbis, 448; © Ellisphotos/Alamy, 450; © Kelly-Mooney Photography/Corbis, 452; © Bettmann/CORBIS, 454.

Chapter 16: Erich Lessing/Art Resource, NY, 462; (left) DeA Picture Library/Art Resource, NY, 470; (middle) Eileen Tweedy/The Art Archive at Art Resource, NY, 470; (right) © John Warburton-Lee Photography/Alamy, 470; (top) AP Photo/Thomas Haentzschel, 471; (bottom) s70/ZUMA Press/Newscom, 471; © The Granger Collection, New York, 472; akg-images/ullstein bild/ullstein-Archiv Gerstenberg, 473; Cameraphoto Arte, Venice/Art Resource, NY, 478; © Image Asset Management Ltd./Alamy, 479; Topkapi Palace Museum, Istanbul, Turkey/Bridgeman Images, 480; Bridgeman-Giraudon/Art Resource, NY, 481; Courtesy of the Library of Congress, 482; Bob Krist/Corbis, 485; (top) Gianni Dagli Orti/The Art Archive at Art Resource, NY, 486; (middle left) Art Resource, NY, 486; (bottom right) Vanni Archive/Art Resource, NY, 486; (bottom left) © Simon Harris/Robert Harding World Imagery/Corbis, 486; Erich Lessing/Art Resource, NY, 489; The Metropolitan Museum of Art/Art Resource, NY, 490.

Chapter 17: Courtesy of the Library of Congress, 494; Courtesy of the Library of Congress, 497; (right) Alinari/Art Resource, NY, 499; (top left) RMN-Grand Palais/Art Resource, NY, 499; (bottom left) The Metropolitan Museum of Art/Art Resource, NY, 499; Courtesy of the Library of Congress, 501; © Witold Skrypczak/Lonely Planet Images, 505; akg-images, 506; Pedro Reinel/akg-images, 509; Private Collection/Peter Newark Military Pictures/Bridgeman Images, 512; Deutsches Historisches Museum, Berlin, Germany/© DHM/Bridgeman Images, 514; veröffentlicht in den Hogenbergschen Geschichtsblättern, 520; akg-images/RIA Nowosti, 523; akg-images, 526.

Chapter 18: Courtesy of the Library of Congress, 530; Private Collection/Archives Charmet/Bridgeman Images, 533; (top) bpk, Berlin/Ethnologisches Museum, Staatliche Museen, Berlin, Germany/Dietrich Graf /Art Resource, NY, 536; (bottom) Private Collection/Bridgeman Images, 536; Bibliotheque Nationale, Paris, France/Scala/White Images/Art Resource, NY, 537; Courtesy of the Library of Congress, 538; The Art Archive/Biblioteca National do Rio de Janiero Brazil/Gianni Dagli Orti, 543; © Lebrecht Music & Arts/Corbis, 545; Courtesy of The Hispanic Society of America, New York, 550; (left) Snark/Art Resource, NY, 553; (right) Snark/Art Resource, NY, 553; Museo de America, Madrid, Spain/Bridgeman Images, 554; Courtesy of the Library of Congress, 555; The Granger Collection, NYC — All rights reserved, 558; The Library Company of Philadelphia, 559; Private Collection/The Stapleton Collection/Bridgeman Images, 560.

Chapter 19: Courtesy of Michele Araldi, 564; Erich Lessing/Art Resource, NY, 572; (left) © CORBIS, 573; (right) Werner Forman/Art Resource, NY, 573; Werner Forman/Art Resource, NY, 574; © The Metropolitan Museum of Art/Art Resource, NY, 576; Art Resource/Art Resource, NY, 577; © British Library Board/Robana/Art Resource, NY, 581; Art Resource/Art Resource, NY, 585; Private Collection/© Michael Graham-Stewart/Bridgeman Images, 588; Abby Aldrich Rockefeller Fold Art Museum, The colonial Williamsburg

Foundation, Williamsburg, Va, 592; © Robert Holmes/CORBIS, 590; Collection of Herbert M. and Shelley Cole. Photo by Don Cole, 591; Private Collection/Archives Charmet/Bridgeman Images, 593.

Chapter 20: travelib prime/Alamy, 598; V&A Images/The Art Archive at Art Resource, NY, 602; © British Library Board/Robana/Art Resource, NY, 603; The Metropolitan Museum of Art/Art Resource, NY, 604; © Arthur Thévenart/CORBIS, 605; Courtesy of The Chester Beatty Library, 608; Rijksmuseum, Amsterdam, 611; © 2015 Museum Associates/LACMA. Licensed by Art Resource, NY, 616; British Museum, London, Great Britain/Erich Lessing/Art Resource, NY, 621.

Chapter 21: John C Weber Collection. Photo: John Bigelow Taylor, 626; © Hulton-Deutsch Collection/CORBIS, 631; The Metropolitan Museum of Art/Art Resource, NY, 632; The Metropolitan Museum of Art/Art Resource, NY, 633; © CHINASTOCK/QI WEN, 635; © Bettmann/CORBIS, 637; Private Collection/Roy Miles Fine Paintings/Bridgeman Images, 638; (top left) John Thomson, 640; (top right) John Thomson, 640; (bottom) John Thomson, 640; Courtesy of the Library of Congress, 641; RMN-Grand Palais/Art Resource, NY, 643; © The Granger Collection, New York, 645; Courtesy of the Library of Congress, 648; University of British Columbia Library, Rare Books and Special Collections, 649; akg-images, 652; V&A Images, London/Art Resource, NY, 654.

Chapter 22: Battle on Santo Domingo, a painting by January Suchodolski, 660; (top left) © Bettmann/CORBIS, 667; (bottom right) © Gianni Dagli Orti/CORBIS, 667; (top right) © Gianni Dagli Orti/CORBIS, 667; © Gianni Dagli Orti/CORBIS, 668; Courtesy of the Library of Congress, 669; Chateau de Blerancourt/Gianni Dagli Orti/The Art Archive at Art Resource, NY, 670; SSPL/Science Museum/Art Resource, NY, 675; bpk, Berlin/Hanna Forster/Art Resource, NY, 676; © Lebrecht Music & Arts/Corbis, 679; © The Print Collector/Corbis, 681; John K. Hillers/J. Paul Getty Museum, 685; (top) National Gallery, London/Art Resource, NY, 689; (bottom) Erich Lessing/Art Resource, NY, 689; © Hulton-Deutsch Collection/CORBIS, 690;

Chapter 23: Bibliotheque Nationale, Paris, France/Snark/Art Resource, NY, 694; Courtesy of the Library of Congress, 698; Gianni Dagli Orti/The Art Archive at Art Resource, NY, 700; Schalkwijk/Art Resource, NY, 702; ©CORBIS, 703; Courtesy of the Library of Congress, 704; Erich Lessing/Art Resource, NY, 706; Courtesy of the Library of Congress, 708; The Granger Collection, New York, 712; Courtesy of the Library of Congress, 720; ©akg-images/The Image Works, 722.

Chapter 24: © Philadelphia Museum of Art/CORBIS, 728; (left) Courtesy of the Library of Congress, 733; (right) The Art Archive at Art Resource, NY, 733; Eileen Tweedy/The Art Archive at Art Resource, NY, 734; (left) National Palace Museum, 737; (right) © The Print Collector/Heritage/The Image Works, 737; (top) akg-images/British Library, 738; (bottom) Private Collection/Peter Newark Pictures/Bridgeman Images, 738; (top) © Philadelphia Museum of Art/CORBIS, 741; (bottom) ©Mary Evans Picture Library/The Image Works, 741; © Mary Evans Picture Library/The Image Works, 742; Private Collection/Bridgeman Images, 743; Courtesy of the Library of Congress, 744; IAM/akg-images, 745; John Thomson, 749; Courtesy of the Library of Congress, 753.

Chapter 25: Arkhangelsk Museum, Russia/Bridgeman Images, 760; © Bettmann/CORBIS, 767; © Bettmann/CORBIS, 769; SEF/Art Resource, NY, 772; © Paule Seux/Hemis/Corbis, 774; © Heritage Images/Corbis, 780; © North Wind Picture Archives/Alamy, 781; © Reproduced by permission of The State Hermitage Museum, St. Petersburg, Russia/CORBIS, 783; Museum of the Revolution, Moscow, Russia/RIA Novosti/Bridgeman Images, 786.

Chapter 26: Courtesy of the Library of Congress, 790; SSPL via Getty Images, 798; Peter Newark Military Pictures, 802; © The Print Collector/Alamy, 807; Private Collection/The Stapleton Collection/Bridgeman Images, 808; © Bettmann/CORBIS, 809; Private Collection/Archives Charmet/Bridgeman Images, 810; Private Collection/Peter Newark Pictures/Bridgeman Images, 813; Natural History Museum, London, UK/Bridgeman Images, 816; Giraudon, 818.

Chapter 27: Kharbine Tapabor, 822; (top) © National Portrait Gallery, London, 825; (bottom) ©The British Library Board, Add. Or.3079, 825; © CORBIS, 828; RMN-Grand Palais/Art Resource, NY, 832; Private Collection/Archives Charmet/Bridgeman Images, 833; © Hulton-Deutsch Collection/CORBIS, 836; UniversalImagesGroup/Getty Images, 841; Anti-Slavery Internation/Panos Pictures, 842; Courtesy of the Library of Congress, 848.

Chapter 28: Courtesy of the Library of Congress, 856; © Hulton-Deutsch Collection/CORBIS, 858; Popperfoto/Getty Images, 861; Courtesy of the Library of Congress, 864; Huton Archive /Getty Images, 865; Courtesy of the Library of Congress, 866; The Granger Collection, NYC — All rights reserved, 869; Getty Images, 872; Central Press/Getty Images, 873; © Heritage Image Partnership Ltd/ Alamy, 877; © Hulton-Deutsch Collection/CORBIS, 880; Courtesy of the Library of Congress, 883; Hulton Archive/Getty Images, 887; © Bettmann/CORBIS, 889.

Chapter 29: Getty Images, 894; Time & Life Pictures/Getty Images, 896; AP Photo, 899; © Bettmann/CORBIS, 902; © Rykoff Collection/CORBIS, 904; © CORBIS, 906; (left) The Museum of Modern Art/SCALA/Art Resource, NY, 907; (right) © 2015 Museum Associates/LACMA. Licensed by Art Resource, NY, 907; Courtesy of the Library of Congress, 912; Lisa Larsen/The LIFE Picture Collection/Getty Images, 921; Courtesy of the Library of Congress, 922.

Chapter 30: © Alain DeJean/Sygma/CORBIS, 930; © CORBIS, 933; © Robert Maass/CORBIS, 935; © Bettmann/CORBIS, 939; lev raden/Shutterstock, 941; © Henry Diltz/CORBIS, 942; India Today Group/Getty Images, 945; © Bettmann/CORBIS, 947; (left) © Jacques Langevin/Sygma/Corbis, 950; (right) © Reuters/CORBIS, 950; (top) © Tim Page/CORBIS, 952; (bottom) © Bettmann/CORBIS, 952; Courtesy of the Library of Congress, 957.

Chapter 31: Getty Images Europe, 964; © Hubert Boesl/dpa/Corbis, 971; (top) AP Photo/str, 976; (bottom) AP Photo/Xinhua, Liu Weibing, 976; © Samuel Aranda /Corbis, 983; AP Photo/Manish Swarup, 986; Associated Press, 988; © Louise Gubb/CORBIS SABA, 990; AFP/Getty Images, 992.

Subject Index

Page numbers followed by *f* denote a figure or illustration. Page numbers followed by *m* denote a map.

Aachen, 314

Abahai, 631

Abbasid Dynasty, 198; Baghdad, city map, 280*m*; displacement of Umayyads, 320; empire building, 275; financial crisis, 282–3; slave revolt, 414; suppression of religion, 282; timeline placement, 277*f*; Umayyad comparison with, 278–9

Abd al-Malik, 277

Abelard, Peter, 329

Abolition of slavery: in Brazil, 711, 713–14; in China, 357; in Great Britain, 588, 595; international desires for, 595, 826; in the United States, 683

Aboriginals (Australia): described, 16; Dreamtime, 17–18, 31; rock art, 18–19; settlements, 16–17; social structures, cultural expressions, 17

Abortion, 941, 942, 944

Abortive Russian Revolution, 763*f*, 785–6

Absolutism, 508, 516, 522–3, 611, 677, 885

Abstract expressionism, 906, 907*f*

Abu Bakr, Swahili sheikh, 416–17

Academy of Florence, 306

Academy of Medicine (France), 668

Academy of Plato, 148*f*, 206

Academy of Sciences (Paris), 503

Achaemenid Persian Empire: administration, 183–5; Alexander's conquest of, 180, 188; cataphracts used by, 182–3; dates of, 148*f*, 183*f*; empire building by, 148, 181, 182; Greek city-states comparison, 185–7; hoplites (foot soldiers), 183; Jews/Judaism in, 203; military prowess of, 182–3; origins, 148*f*, 181–5; timeline placement, 183*f*. *See also* Sasanid Persian Empire

Acheulian tool technology, 9, 10*f*

Acropolis, 187, 188

Adena culture (North America), 123*f*, 139, 140*m*

Adrianople, Treaty of, 764*m*

Advanced Research Projects Agency (ARPA), 987

Aegean islands, 48, 478

Aegean Sea, 33, 51, 187

Aeneid (Virgil), 210, 211, 212

Aethiopica (Heliodorus of Emesa), 155

Affirmative action, 986

Afghanistan: agrarian activities, 35; Alexander's victories in, 186; Arab Spring participation, 985; Babur's invasion of, 601; Cyrus II's conquest of, 182; India's expansion into, 222, 348; literary achievements, 302; Mahmud of Ghazna's conquests in, 348–9; ouster

of Taliban regime, 967*f*; Pashtu tribal federation revolt, 774; Safavid Persia's conflicts in, 605, 623, 771–2; Soviet Union invasion of, 855*f*, 930–1, 935; Timur's travels in, 600; trade activities, 74; U.S. invasion of, 967*f*, 971

Africa: Americas, comparison with, 163; atrocities and genocides, 841–2; australopiths fossils, 7; Benin Kingdom, 427, 460*f*, 566, 567*f*, 571, 574–5, 671; Bunyoro Kingdom, 567*f*, 570; Central Africa chiefdoms, kingdoms, 420–1; Christian missionaries in, 406; Cold War in, 923–6, 944; Congo Reform Association, 852; Congo's independence struggle, 925–6; Da Gama's circumnavigation of, 460*f*, 465*f*; decolonization in, 854*f*, 914*m*, 924; Dhar Oualata village, 153; Dhar Tichitt village, 153; empire growth in, 3; European imperialism in, 838–43; fossil discoveries, 4–7, 10, 11; Hausa Kingdoms, 567, 569; *H. erectus* presence, 7; hominins origins, 7; Ibn Battuta's journeys, 469; Ice Age influences, 21, 22; independence of colonies, 897*f*; Indonesian contacts, 161–2; Islam, adaption to, 413–21; Islam/Christianity map, 840*m*; Kanem-Bornu caliphate, 567*f*, 569; Kenya's resistance to independence, 925; Luba Kingdom, 407*f*, 420–1, 421*m*, 431, 569; malaria/yellow fever in, 839–40; map (1415-1498), 465*m*; migration from, 5, 6, 10, 14, 15*m*; modern human origins in, 2, 5–14; music and food, 591–2; National Congolese Movement, 925; Nigerian civil war, 955–66; oil-exporting countries, 989; "out of Africa" theory, 10; Paleolithic rock paintings, 58; political transformations, 987–90; Portuguese circumnavigation of, 572; post-WW II growth, urbanization, 911; rain-forest kingdoms, 427; Rastafarianism in, 411–12; revolution in Zimbabwe, 956; rice cultivation, 158, 162, 414; Rift Valley, satellite view, 4*f*; sites in Mauritania, 152*m*; 600 BCE-600 CE, historical patterns, 162–3; South Central Africa, 569–70; Tichitt-Oualata villages, 152–3; trade networks, 321*m*, 408*m*; traditional rituals, 161; 2012, 2013, coups d'état, 988; Umayyad conquests in, 277; UN "blood diamonds" scheme, 989–90;

U.S. training of dissidents in, 903–4; weapons introduced to, 127. *See also* African slave trade; Aksum kingdom; Central Africa; East Africa; Ghana; Meroë kingdom; South Africa; Sub-Saharan Africa; West Africa

African Americans: civil rights movement and, 939–42, 944; consequences of economic crises, 978; G.I. bill for, 906*f*; Harlem Renaissance, 865–6; involuntary sterilization of women, 867; limited opportunities for women, 864; loss of voting rights, 683; lynching of, 683, 865*f*, 866; slavery of, 590*f*; 2001-2003 financial crisis impact, 978; women's employment opportunities, 864

African Christian spirituality, 564

African diaspora, 589, 591–3, 865–6

African National Congress (ANC), 957–8, 962

African slave trade: Brazil, 567*f*; East Africa, 415; England/North American colonies, 567*f*; Ghana, 415, 431; Hispaniola, 460, 567*f*; household slaves, 574; Mali, 415, 431; Mali Empire, 574; Muslim countries, 414; regions for capturing slaves, 579*m*; sales to Hispaniola, 460*f*; slave raids, 574; Songhay Empire, 567, 574; sub-Saharan Africa, 429; West Africa, 571. *See also* Atlantic slave trade; Plantation slavery, the Americas

African spirituality, 161

Afro-Eurasian Commercial World System, 298, 299*m*

Agincourt, Battle of, 336

Agrarian-urban society: in the Americas, 3; in Byzantium, 529; in China, 3, 37, 529, 560, 639; decline of, 791; defined, 33; in Egypt, 37, 46, 181; in Eurasia, 3, 452, 529; in Europe, 461; in the Fertile Crescent, 33–6; foraging transition to, 29, 33–5, 58, 128–9; gender role implications, 13, 43; in India, 3, 37, 72, 84, 90, 217, 529; in Japan, 403; in Mayan kingdom, 171; in the Middle East, 3, 29, 37, 40, 49, 496, 529, 762; in sub-Saharan Africa, 151. *See also* Agriculture; Urbanization

Agriculture: in Africa, 407–8; in the Americas, 3, 129–31, 134–5, 136; of the Assyrians, 452, 37; in Caral-Supé valley, Peru, 131; in China, 94–6, 95*f*, 96, 98, 99, 107–8, 109, 496; corn domestication, 3, 120, 122, 134–5, 176; in East Asia, 3, 100, 367, 374–5; European revolution in, 319–20;

Fertile Crescent origins, 3f, 29, 33, 34–5, 35f; foraging transition to, 33–5, 58, 128–9; in India, 613–14; in Latin America, 722; in Meroë kingdom, Africa, 152, 155; in Mesopotamia, 38, 41, 181; monsoon system influences, 68–9; Neolithic period, 36, 42; in the Neolithic period, 36, 42; origins of centers, 3; rice domestication, 70–80, 79–80, 95f, 98; role of women, 43; slash-and-burn method, 159; Soviet Union collectivization of, 859f, 866–77; spread to Western Europe, Central Asia, 48–9; in West Africa, 157–9. See also Agrarian-urban society

Aha (Egyptian king), 44

Ahimsa (nonviolence), 220, 227–8

Ahmadinejad, Mahmoud, 982

Ahuramazda (god of the Zoroastrians), 183, 201, 207

AIDS/HIV, 976, 987

Ainu, 28, 382, 389

Airplane development, 793f, 800–1

Akbar, Jalal ud-Din: abolishment of jizya tax on unbelievers, 609, 619; ascendancy of, 603; city-building skills, 604–5; grounding in Islamic Sufi mysticism, 618; map of empire under, 604m; marriage to Hindu princess, 604; military campaigns, 603, 604, 605–6; move to Lahore, 605; Mughal painting style contribution, 621; religious synthesis attempt, 371, 608–9, 623, 624; religious tolerance during reign, 607, 615, 617, 618, 625; timeline placement, 461f, 601f

Akkadian kingdom, 41–2, 42m

Aksum kingdom (Africa), 148; ascent of, 155–6; Coptic Christian Church in, 409–10; imperialism/crisis in, 156–7; loss of Yemen, 409; map, 154m; monasteries in, 410; Sasanid Persian invasion of, 157; slave trading, 409; splendor of, 156; timeline placement, 149f, 153f, 407f; trade networks, 157, 409

Alamo, Battle of, 705

Alaouite dynasty (Morocco), 473

Ala-ud-Din, 350

Alawites, Shiite Muslims, 964

Al-Biruni (Islamic astronomer), 508

Alexander I (Russian Tsar), 777

Alexander II (Russian Tsar), 780–1, 783, 788, 875

Alexander III (Russian Tsar), 783

Alexander the Great: Cleitus's conflicts with, 180–1; conquests in Persia, 180, 181, 188; dates of life, 183f; imperial pattern adoption, 148; map of empire, 189m; northern India campaigns, 188, 216, 217, 218–19, 219f, 242; successors of, 187–9, 189m, 203, 216–17; timeline placement, 183f; unification of Greece, 181

Alexander V (Pope), 337

Alexandria, 171, 206–7, 292, 293, 320, 407, 409–10, 836

Alexius I Comnenus, 289–90

Algeria: business privatization, 980; civil war in, 981; Fatimid rebellion in, 282; French conquest of, 822–3, 825f, 835, 842; independence of, 923; Islamic civilization in, 473; mosques in, 333

Algerian Front of National Liberation, 923

Ali, Muhammad (Ottoman vassal), 767, 836–7

Alighieri, Dante, 339

Allegory (defined), 599

Almohad Berber Dynasty, 277f

Alphabets, Phoenician, Greek, and Roman, 55f

Al-Qaeda terrorist group, 855f, 967f, 971, 981

Alsace-Lorraine, 682, 796, 836, 862, 869

Altaic-speaking peoples (Korea), 374

Altruism, 229, 247, 270

Amazon rainforest civilizations, 447, 458

The Ambassadors (James), 690

Amda Seyon, Ethiopian King, 412

Amenhotep III, Egyptian Pharoah, 64

Amenhotep IV, Egyptian Pharoah, 64

American Civil War, 584, 677, 683, 706–7, 779, 796

American Indian Movement (AIM), 940

American Indian Wars, 685

American Philosophical Society, 559

American Revolution, 658f, 661, 663–4, 663f

Americas (North, Central, South): African kingship comparison, 419; agrarian difficulties, 172; agrarian foundations, 3, 122; Amazonian culture, 140, 458; Andean, Mesoamerican villages, 123f; animal/plant domestication, 128, 129–30, 130f; archaeological studies, 120; Caribbean Islands, 123, 124, 140–1; Chavín de Huántar, mountain city, 123f, 132–6, 133f, 163, 173; Columbus's voyage to, 464, 465f, 571; communication systems development, 116; early evidence of humans, 2f, 5, 7f; environment of, 123–5, 126m; 1519-1532, European exploration, 535m; geographical regions, 123–4; human migrations, 5, 24, 25m, 26–8, 123f, 125, 127–8; hunters and foragers, 122–8; Neolithic settlements, 129–31; ocean currents, hurricanes, El Niño, 124–5; petroglyphs of Nazca, 174; plantation slavery, 578–82, 760; sculptures, figures, figurines, 428; settlements, development of, 127–8; shamanism practices, 391; shaman-led ceremonies, 128; slave revolts, 567f, 594f; smallpox epidemic, 147, 532, 534–5, 537, 540, 542, 555; Spain's discovery of, 460f; state formation patterns, 459; sub-Saharan Africa comparison, 151, 163; symbolic communication attempts, 116; timeline, early development, 123f; trade networks, 361; village settlement suitability, 179; wheel, development of, 130. See also Andes culture; Colonial North America; Mesoamerica; North America; South America

Americas and colonialism: adaptation to European culture, 557–60; agriculture, 531; Aztec empire, conquest of, 533–4; Catholic missionary work, 557; Central American settlements, 535m, 539m; Christian missionary establishments, 538; colonial assemblies, 546; economic activities, 539m; education and the arts, 557–8; European emigrations, 531–2; European explorations, 535m; first mainland conquests, 532–3; French Canada, 546; gold and silver mining, 531, 538; Inca empire, conquest of, 534–6; indigenous people's resistance, 538; interactions with Native Americans, 543, 545; labor assignments, 540; land-labor grants, 532; Mexico, conquest of, 532–3, 533f; New Sciences research, 559; North American colonization, 544m; North American settlements, 535m; Peru, conquest of, 532–3; Portuguese conquest of Brazil, 536; Portuguese settlements, 539m; post-conquests bureaucratic efficiency, 538, 540; South American settlements, 535m; territorial expansion, 546; timeline of events, 533f. See also Creoles; New England; Seven Years' War

Amerindians. See Native Americans

Amida Buddha, 392

Amun-Re worship, Egypt, 64

Anatolia, 33–4, 48–9, 52, 53, 55–6, 58; Alexander the Great in, 188; Crusades and, 290; grassroot resistance groups, 872; Greek city-states in, 209; iron making techniques, 77, 154; Janissaries in, 480, 763; Ottoman conquests, 464, 469–70, 480, 600, 761, 835; Persian expansion in, 182–4, 190, 276; railroads in, 769; religion and philosophy in, 201–2, 205; Roman expansion in, 192, 195; Seljuk Turks conquests, 288–9, 307; survival strategies, 284, 285

Anaximander, Greek visionary, 183f

Ancestor worship, 161

Andes culture: agrarian villages, 123f; animal/plant domestication, 129–30, 136; architectural discoveries, 131; Chavín de Huántar, city site, 123f, 132–6, 133f, 163, 173; early urban centers, 122, 130, 132m, 175m; geographical features, 123–4; Inca

Empire, 273f; metallurgy techniques, 135; pottery production, 130–1; textile production, 135; Wari state, 435f. *See also* Aztec Empire; Caral-Supé valley, Peru; Inca Empire; Tiwanaku state; Wari city-state

Anglican Church, 514, 516, 518, 519, 546

Anglo-American nation-state building: buffalo herds, destruction of, 685; Great Britain, 686–7; Native Americans, 684–5; reform measures, 685–6; United States, 683–4, 684m

Angola, independence of, 956

Animal domestication, 128, 129–30, 130f

Animals, selective breeding origins, 36

Animal sacrifice, 205

Anthony of Padua, Saint, 564–5

Antigonid Greece, 188, 189m

Anti-Rightist campaign (China), 912–13

Antonian-African Christianity, 565

Apaches, Native Americans, 545

Apartheid in South Africa, 577, 924, 956–8, 962; ending of, 855f, 958, 967f, 987, 990f

Apocalypse (defined), 466

Apocalyptic expectations (Iberia), 466

April 6 Youth Movement (Facebook group), 989

Aquinas, Saint Thomas, 326

Arab Empires: Abd al-Malik (caliph), 277; Battle of Tours, France, 278; conquests, 272f, 278m–279m, 352; state formation patterns, 483; trade networks, 413. *See also* Abbasid Dynasty; Umayyad Dynasty

Arab-Israeli conflicts, 854f, 897f, 933f, 952m, 953m

Arab-Israeli War (Six Day War), 933f, 953–4

Arab Spring (2011), 855f, 955, 967f, 980, 981–3, 988–9, 994

Arafat, Yasir, 954, 981

Aragon Dynasty (Spain), 465f

Árbenz, Jacobo, 910

Architecture: Chinese, 352, 643; Christian, 212; church, 285f, 332; Egyptian, 206; Harappan, 67; Indian, 239, 620, 621–2; Islamic, 212, 302–3, 333; Italian, 212, 487; Japanese, 384; Mayan, 172; Olmecs, 145; Ottoman Empire, 484, 486–7; Roman, 212; Sasanid palaces, 208; Spanish renaissance, 488

Ardi *(Ardipithecus ramidus)*, 6–7, 29

Argentina: caudillos in, 698; colonization of, 550, 696; democratic transition, 990; "Dirty War" in, 959; "disappearances" of citizens, 959; ethnic diversity in, 696; fight for/gaining of independence, 696–7; Hezbollah anti-Semitic bombings, 981; Native American culture, 555; Pampas settlements, 698–9; railroad building in, 722; reach of Inca empire, 446–7; San Martin's liberation of, 700; textile

manufacturing, 552–3; Yrigoyen's leadership, 699

Aristotle/Aristotelianism, 57, 214, 306, 328–30, 340, 343, 469, 496, 499–500, 507, 558

Articles of Confederation (U.S.), 664

Artistic achievements: abstract expressionism, 906, 907f; Andean cultures, 132; Aztec Empire, 456; Byzantium, 303, 306; cave paintings, 22, 40, 128, 129f, 152–3; Chavín de Huántar, 133; China, 103, 114, 268, 367–8; East Asia, 267; Egypt, 48, 61; Europe, rock art, 14f; European Enlightenment era, 675; Granada Kingdom, 303, 305; Greece, 209, 210; Harappa, 75; Ice Age art, 22f; Ife Kingdom, West Africa, 428–9; *Impression, Sunrise* (Monet), 793f; Inca Empire, 456; India, 82f, 240, 305, 620–1; industrialism period, 817; Iraq, 367, 632; Islamic civilization, 302–3; Japan, 387–8, 653–4, 756; Latin America, 724; La Venta, 137; Mayans, 166, 167; Mesopotamia, 59, 61; Ming Dynasty, China, 632–3; Moche culture, 173f; modernism period, 817–18; Mycenae, 61; Nubia, 152–3; Olmecs, 137; Ottoman Empire, 305, 485–6; post-World War II, 906–7; rock art, 14f, 18–19, 21, 21f, 58, 156; romantic era, 689f; Rome, 212; Safavid Empire, 474; Sasanid Persian Empire, 207–9; Spanish Habsburgs, 490; Teotihuacán, 172

Art of War (Sun Zi), 81, 887

Aryans (Indo-Europeans): caste system influences, 87; defined, 76; division with non-Aryans, 76, 86; inconclusive knowledge about, 77; Indo-Aryans, 78; Nazi term appropriation, 78; Sanskrit language roots, 78

Aryans (Nazi), 78, 880

Asceticism path (India), 87–8, 88f

Ashikaga Shogunate (Japan), 375f, 387, 388, 389, 644–5

Ashoka (Indian ruler): dharma path followed by, 220, 235; empire map, 221f; Harsha Vardhana comparison, 346; modernity of ideas of, 243; pillars of, 222f; police state-style leadership, 220–1; public works sponsorship, 221–2; support for Theravada Buddhism, 229; timeline placement, 219f; unification of commercial law, 221

Assad, Bashar al-, 981, 984–5

Assemblies, in Mesopotamia, 38

Assyrian Empire: contact with Egypt, 153; empire building, 52–3; gender relations, 296; Greece, contact with, 61; influence on Babylonian law codes, 45; map, 54m; Medes culture, 182; myths of, 209; origins, 35f, 52–3. *See also* Neo-Assyrian Empire

Astronomy, 62, 206, 207, 303, 313, 328, 426, 461f, 500, 502–3

Atahualpa (Inca Empire ruler), 533f, 535–6, 536f

Athens, Greek city-state, 56, 57, 185–7, 206, 214

Atlantic slave trade: Benin Kingdom, limited trade, 574–5; economic patterns of, 586–8; Kongo Kingdom, 575–6; middle passage, 587–8; North Atlantic system (defined), 586m, 587; rum and gun running, 587; timeline placement, 567f; trade forts, 573; underlying patterns, 572–3. *See also* African slave trade; plantation slavery, the Americas

Atomic bomb, 889

Augustus (Roman Emperor), 192, 192f, 193–4, 193m, 210

Aurangzeb (Mughal ruler): art suppressed during reign, 621; ascendancy of, 607–8; Britain's conflicts with, 611; destruction of Sikh temples, 610; Islamification efforts, 608–9; Maratha wars, 608, 610, 623, 625; religious suppression during reign, 619–20, 624; Sunni Islamic policies, 625; theological conflicts during reign, 617; timeline placement, 601f; unbelievers tax imposed by, 615

Australia: Aboriginal culture, 16–19, 31, 753, 757f; boomerang invention, 23; British colonialism in, 823, 825f, 831–3, 853; Ice Age influences, 22; migrations to, 14–19; shipping of British colonists to, 825f

Australopiths *(Australopithecus)*, 7–8, 7f, 10–11

Austria: alliances of, 547, 669, 678, 777, 832; Baroque arts in, 498–9; Habsburgs, 465f, 478, 489, 510, 520–1, 762–3, 776–7; Napoleon's defeat of, 672, 677; Prussian-Austrian War, 681–2; uprisings in, 680

Austria-Hungary, 770–1, 857–60

Austronesian cultural family, 141, 161

Autarky (defined), 869

Automobiles, 714, 800–2, 813f, 862

Avicenna (Ibn Sina), 301, 329

Avignon papacy, 336, 343

Aztec Empire (Mesopotamia), 273f; artistic achievements, 456; Charles V rulership, 474; conquest of, 533–4, 533f; corn domestication, 176; Cuauhtémoc's rulership, 533f, 534; founding myth, 442–3; governance, 444–5; human sacrifice, 454–5; map (1520 CE), 444m; military professionalism, 445, 449, 453; origins, 433, 442–3; power-enforced unilateralism, 447; reign of Cuauhtémoc, 533f, 534; rise of, 443–5; size comparison, 450; Spain's conquest of, 461f; Spanish conquest of, 461f, 474,

483, 532, 533–4, 533*f*; taxation method, 447; Tenochtitlán city-state, 443, 450–1, 451*m*, 454, 459, 534, 538*f*; timeline placement, 273*f*, 435*f*; trade activities, 451; weaponry, 445*f*, 449; writing development, 138

Azurduy de Padilla, Juana, 694–5

Baader-Meinhof Gang (West Germany), 943
Baath Party, 970, 984–5
Babur (Zahir ud-din Muhammad Babur): administrative challenges, 602, 612; conquests of, 349, 602*m*; Indian Timurid line founded by, 601–2; Mughal Empire, founding of, 349; religious tolerance during reign, 618, 625; timeline placement, 601*f*
Baby boomer generation, 906, 942
Babylonian Kingdom: Hammurabi, kingship of, 42, 43, 44–5; law codes, 42–5, 43; Minoan palace-state, 35*f. See also* Neo-Babylonians
Bactria-Margiana Archaeological Complex (BMAC), 72, 73
Balfour Declaration, 859*f*, 871
Balkan Slavs, 469
Balkan War (1878), 859
Balmaceda, José Manuel, 707, 726
Baluchistan (Neolithic Baluchistan), 70
Banana phytoliths, 159
Bandaranaike, Sirimavo, 894–5, 921, 945
Banner system, Qing Dynasty, 631, 634
Banpo Village (China), 96–7
Bantu people, 153*f*, 158, 159–61, 163, 179, 413–14, 418
Baronial courts, in England, 318
Baroque arts in, 498–9
Bartholdi, Frederic A., 798
Battle of Tours (France), 278, 312
Bay of Pigs invasion (1961), 904, 923
Bayonets, 359, 510, 525*f*, 832
Beat Generation, 928
Beatles, 928, 942
Beethoven, Ludwig van, 687
Belgium: imperialism of, 834, 838, 841–2; independence of, 845; industrialization in, 795, 845; Ruhr occupation and withdrawal, 880; World War I and, 858, 859
Bell, Alexander Graham, 801
Ben Ali, Zine El Abidine, 984
Benedict, Saint, 312–13
Benedictine monasteries, 312–13
Benin Kingdom (West Africa), 427, 460*f*, 566, 567*f*, 568*m*, 571, 574–5, 671
Benz, Karl, 800
Berber-Arab conquest, 466, 570
Berbers, 277–8, 306, 422–3, 426, 464, 835, 923
Beringia land bridge, 24, 26, 28
Berlin, Treaty of, 764*m*
Berlin Airlift, 899
Berlin Conference, 825*f*

Berlin Wall, 855*f*, 897*f*, 904, 932, 933*f*, 937
Beyond Good and Evil (Nietzsche), 817
Bhagavad Gita (Hindu spiritual text), 82, 83, 220, 232
Bharatiya Janata Party (India), 986
Bhutto, Benazir, 895
Bill of Rights (U.S.), 664
Bin Laden, Osama, 971
Bipedalism, 8
The Birth of Tragedy (Nietzsche), 817
Bismarck, Otto von (Chancellor of Germany), 681–2
Black Death (bubonic plague): in China, 360, 361, 628; demographic consequences, 509; in Egypt, 300; in Europe, 272*f*, 334, 335*m*, 762; in Middle East, 272*f*, 762; Mongols and, 299; physical characteristics, 332; in the Roman Empire, 196
The Black Man's Burden (Morel), 852
Blood diamonds, 989–90
Boccaccio, Giovanni, 339
Bohemia, 337, 339, 477, 510, 519
Boko Haram (Islamist movement), 989
Bolívar, Simón, 697*f*, 699–701
Bolshevik Party (Russia), 785–6, 860, 875
Bolshevik Revolution (Russia), 854*f*, 859*f*, 886, 896
Bonaparte, Louis-Napoleon (Napoleon III), 679, 681–2, 700, 706, 767–8, 779, 811, 849
Bonaparte, Napoleon, 658*f*, 663*f*; Continental boycott of, 716; defeat in Russia, 669, 677, 775, 777; domestic reforms, 668–9; Egypt invasions by, 658*f*, 761, 763*f*, 832, 836; ending of Enlightenment under, 675; ending of French Revolution, 677; French empire rebuilding efforts, 671, 672; Iberia, invasion of, 710; military victories, 667; Spain and Portugal, occupation of, 696
Boniface VIII (Pope), 326
The Book of Songs (ancient Chinese text), 115
Book of the Dead (Egypt), 35*f*
Boomerang invention, 23
Borana lunar calendar, 150
Bosnia, ethnic-nationalist uprisings, 769
Bosnia-Herzegovina, 769, 771, 782, 859, 979
Boston Tea Party, 664
Bouazizi, Mohamed, 983–4
Bourbon monarchy (France), 517, 541, 551, 679, 681*f*, 696, 822
Boxer Rebellion (China), 659*f*, 731*f*, 742–3, 766, 886
Brazil, 24, 128, 129*f*, 468; African slave trade in, 567*f*; Cabral's landing in, 533, 567*f*; coffee boom, 713–14, 718; democratic transition, 990; end of slavery, 659*f*; federalist interventions, 711; gold discovery, 533*f*; 1990s, global hierarchy, 966; Pedro II's leadership, 710; Pedro I's leadership, 710–11; Portuguese conquest of, 533*f*, 536, 537,

543; reconstruction of, 715–16; slave rebellions, 712–13; smallpox epidemic, 542; sugar plantation slavery, 582, 712–13
Brazilian Shield, 123*f*
Brest-Litovsk, Treaty of (Russia-Germany), 860
Brezhnev, Leonid, 932, 936
Brezhnev Doctrine, 932, 934, 935
British Coercive Acts, 664
British East India Company, 611, 625, 639, 731, 825*f*; Great (Sepoy) Mutiny, 827–8; nabobs (local magnates), 824–5; reform perils, 825–7; role in Seven Years' War, 625, 824
British North America, 582–5, 663*m*
Bronze Age: in China, 101, 115; collapse of, 35*f*, 51–2; historical background, 40; spread of crafts, technology, 77, 79
Brown v. Board of Education (1954), 939
Brunelleschi, Filippo, 498
Bubonic plague. *See* Black Death (bubonic plague)
Bucharest, Treaty of, 764*m*
Buddhism: *ahimsa* (nonviolence), 220, 227–8; Ashoka's conversion to, 220; in Ceylon (Sri Lanka), 220, 266, 375*f*, 395; challenges to caste system, 232, 233, 237–8; in China, 223, 226, 240, 247*f*, 258, 264, 266–7, 345; criticism of by Confucians, 355; description, 228–9; egalitarian influences of, 232; Empress Wu's embrace of, 351–2; Four Noble Truths, 229; in India, 66, 89, 218, 223, 235, 240, 245, 247*f*; influence on Confucianism, Daoism, 149; influences on caste system, 237–8; in Japan, 226, 345, 390, 391–2; in Korea, 230, 243, 258, 266, 272, 273, 345, 373, 376, 380; Mahayana school, 230–1, 239, 345, 352, 398–9; map of spread of, 231*m*; monastic Buddhism, 264; Nichiren Buddhism, 392, 402; origins, 219*f*, 228; in Southeast Asia, 221, 222, 226; spread of, from India, 345; texts, 229–30; Theravada school, 229, 230–1, 345; Tibetan Buddhism, 635; Zen Buddhism, 267, 377, 388, 392–3, 402, 624. *See also* Gautama
Buffalo herds, destruction of (U.S.), 685
Bulgaria, 659*f*; ethnic-nationalist uprisings, 769; First Balkan War collaboration, 771; independence from Ottomans, 763*f*, 782
Bunyoro Kingdom (Africa), 567*f*, 570
Burial sites and customs: of Africa, 414, 576*f*; of the Americas, 130, 137–8; of ancient Greece, 210*f*; of Aztecs (mummy burials), 453; of Buddha's relics, 230*f*; of China, 94, 101, 103, 111, 252*f*; of India, 598; of Japan, 383, 384, 391; of the Middle East, 773; of Moche culture, 174; of Natufians, 35;

of the Paracas, 174; of Peru, 432–3; of plague victims, 334f; Puruchuco burial place, 432

Burroughs, William, 928

Bus boycott, Montgomery, Alabama, 939f

Bush, George W., 971

Bushido ("Way of the Warrior"), 388, 402

Buyids Shiite Dynasty (Iran and Iraq), 415, 772

Byzantine Empire (Byzantium): Abbasid conquests in, 283; defeat of, 288–89; Berber conquests in, 277; Bulgars defeated by, 277f; Caliphs of, 277; *Codex* as legal foundation, 198; decline of, 469; difficult beginnings, 283–8; Eastern Christian civilization in, 277, 283–92; iconoclasm controversy, 284–5; landed aristocracy, 296–7; late empire, origins, 469–70; learning and the arts, 303, 306; map of empire, 286m; military changes in, 287–8; philosophy and sciences, 301–2; provincial/central organization, 296–7; recentralization of, 297; survival strategies, 284; tax farming system, 298; trade networks, 297–9, 299m; transformation into commonwealth, 285, 285f, 287; Umayyad conquest of, 276, 277; Varangian Guards, 287, 287f

Cabral, Pedro Álvares, 533f, 567f

Calendars: and African spirituality, 161; agrarian peoples' reliance on, 618; astronomical, 178; Borana, 177; Chinese lunar, 385; Christian, 488, 590; in Genesis, 201; Gregorian, 167; Indians, 240; Julian, 860; Mayan, 166–7, 439; in Mesoamerica, 150–1; Muslim, 282; Romans, 191; San Lorenzo religious cycle, 137

Calico Acts (Great Britain), 792

Calligraphy, in China, 117, 267, 268, 358, 386, 388, 393

Calvin, John, 514–16

Calvin Protestantism (Calvinism), 514–19, 559

Cambodia: Black Death origination, 331; Buddhism/"god-kings" in, 235; map location, 395m; Roman/Greek coins found in, 234

Camp David Accords, 954

Canada: Beringia land bridge, 24; early settlements, 543; European emigrations to, 804; French settlements, 546–7, 585, 662; geographical regions, 123; NAFTA participation, 974; railroad development, 722; Seven Years' War, 547, 625, 662, 663f, 665, 672

Canon of Medicine (Avicenna), 329, 330

Canterbury Tales (Chaucer), 340

Capetian kings (France), 317–18

Capitalism: in America, 821; condemnation of, 852; cooperation and, 752; defined, 322; in Europe, 322, 821; in industrializing states, 791; in industrial society, 804–5; in Japan, 751; Lenin on, 850; Marxism and, 785, 809

Capitalist democracy, 854, 855, 857, 878, 890, 893, 965–91; Chinese economic boom, 976–7; crony capitalism, 964, 984; global balance of trade, 969; global economic crisis, recovery, 855f, 967f, 974–5; global hierarchy, 966–7; globalization, 968–9; globalization, criticism of, 969–70; global wealth distribution, 967m; information technology, 968–9; 1990s, global expansion, 966–76; Russia's crisis and recovery, 975; UN, regional peace efforts, 971–4; U.S., Afghanistan intervention, 971; U.S., Iraq intervention, 970–1; U.S. as import sinkhole, 968; U.S. dollar regime, 967–8; U.S. military dominance, 970; U.S. technological renewal, 968–9

Capitulary for Saxony, 314

Capuchin Catholic monks, 564–5

Caral-Supé valley, Peru: archaeological findings, 120f, 121, 145, 151; chiefdoms of, 163, 438; historical background, 131, 145; khipu writing system, 131; origins, 3f, 120–1, 123f; societal development, 131

Caribbean Islands, 123, 124, 140–1; economy (ca. 1900), 715m; 1496-1750, colonization, 539m; indentured laborers, 582; mercantilism, 580–1; nation-state growth, 704m; plantation slavery, 580; populist-guided democracy, 909–10, 909f; privateers, 581; Santeria religion, 590; slave revolt, 567f; Spanish conquests of, 532

Carnegie, Andrew, 685

Carolinas, 584, 592

Carolingian Empire, 278, 280, 285, 311, 312, 317, 320, 343, 584, 592

Carranza, Venustiano, 709

Cartagena, Spain, 550, 699–700

Carter, Jimmy, 935, 954, 959

Caso, Alfonso, 150

Caste system (India), 69f, 84, 85, 86–7, 88–9, 91, 235–8, 351

Castiglione, Giuseppe, 643

Castile Dynasty (Spain): Aragon Dynasty union with, 465f, 474, 482, 571; conquests of, 464, 468; Fernando IV, 320; minting of gold coins, 424; reforms, 466; reforms in, 466

Castro, Fidel, 897f, 903–4, 926

Categorical imperative philosophy (Kant), 674–5

Cathar Heresy, 342

Catherine II (the Great), Tsarina of Russia, 763f, 776–7

Catholicism, 258, 267; in Africa, 576; in China, 637, 657; in Colombia, 717; conversions of Henry IV, 517; Creoles and, 589; in El Greco's art works, 490; in England, 519; in France, 516; in Germany, 519; Habsburg Empire, 487; Kongolese Catholicism, 589; Lateran Accords, Italy, 878; in Mexico, 702, 703; Native American conversions, 556; New Sciences and, 559; in Philippines, 847; Portuguese Catholicism, 576; Spanish Inquisition and, 488; in western Europe, 280

Catholic Reformation, 488, 497f, 498, 502, 503, 516, 517, 529, 557–9, 562, 565

Caudillo authoritarian regimes (Latin America), 697–701, 697f, 707, 710, 717, 727

Cell phones, global numbers of, 855f, 967f

Central Africa: agriculture, 566; chiefdoms and kingdoms, 420–1; Creoles from Kongo and Ndongo, 589; Imbangala warriors, 576; iron production, 155; kingship origins, 429; Kreyòl language, 676; Luba Kingdom, 407f, 420–1, 421m, 431, 569; rain forests, 22; South Central Africa, 569–70; trade networks, 566, 582

Central America: coffee boom, 713–14, 718; colonization to 1750, 539m; economy (ca. 1900), 715m; 1519-1532, European exploration, 535m; nation-state growth, 704m. *See also* individual countries

Central Asia: agriculture in, 48, 49; artistic achievements, 302; Buddhism in, 222, 230, 243, 266, 345; early human settlements, 19, 26; horse and chariots from, 49; horse domestication, 77; horse trade, 103; Hun invasions from, 183f, 197, 208, 223, 346; iron casting techniques, 114–15; map, 354m; migrations from, 190, 196, 219f, 288; monsoon system, 68; nomadic migrations, 3; Proto-Indo-Europeans in, 49, 77; slave recruitment, raids, 283, 288, 348–9; Tang invasions into, 352; tea's influence in, 355; Timur's invasions from, 350; trade network, 73–4, 110–11, 149, 190, 251, 260, 261; Umayyad expansion into, 277

Central Europe: Genghis Khan's conquests in, 349; Ice Age settlements, 22; Muslim conquests in, 463; nation-state formation in, 682; power struggles, 761

Central Intelligence Agency (CIA), 899–900, 903

Centralization of government: in China, 110, 364–5, 368, 389, 639; in Egypt, 296; in England, 519; in Eurasia, 495, 611; in Germany, 318, 678; in India, 80–1; in Japan, 647; in Oceania, 145; in Polynesia, 143; in Soviet Union, 904; in Spain, 483; victims of, in Europe, 510

Cervantes, Miguel de, 492

Césaire, Aimé, 867

Cesspits (toilets), 71

Ceylon (Sri Lanka): archaeological findings, 162; Bandaranaike's election, tenure, 894–5, 945; Bandung Conference, 920; Buddhism in, 220, 266, 375f, 395; Cholas invasion of, 347; independence gained by, 917

Chachnama (History of Sind), 344–5

Chaldiran, Battle of, 474

Chamberlain, Neville, 882

Charaka Samhita (Ayurvedic medical text), 240

Chariots, northern China, 95f

Charlemagne ("Charles the Great"): Capitulary for Saxony, 314; church role and interests, 311, 314; empire unification role, 313–14; legal practice reforms, 314; map of empire, 315m; papacy protected by, 319; timeline placement, 313f

Charles I, King of England, 335

Charles IV, King of France, 335

Charles V, King of Spain, Holy Roman Emperor: Aztec/Inca rulership, 474; central state creation, 482–3; efforts against the Ottomans, 475–6; Ferdinand I deputized by, 476; Francis I's competition against, 514; as Holy Roman Emperor, 474–5; occupation of Tunis, 463; Ottoman Empire alliance, 476; peacemaking efforts, 476–7; Phillip II's succession to, 517; residence in Granada palace, 487; victory over France, 474–5; view on Castile's church reform, 513; years of reign, 497f, 533f

Charles VII, King of France, 336

Charles X, French Bourbon King, 679

Charter of the United Nations, 675

Chaucer, Geoffrey, 340

Chávez, Hugo, 991

Chavín de Huántar (Andes mountain city), 123f, 132–6, 133f, 163, 173

Chemical manufacturing industry, 799–800

Chernyshevsky, Nikolai, 788

Cheyenne, Native Americans, 545

Chiang K'ai-shek, 886, 891, 911

Chichén Itzá Kingdom (Mesoamerica), 433, 437–8; agriculture, 437; flowering of, 433; origins, 438; timeline placement, 273f, 435f; trade networks, 438

Chiefdoms: Caral-Supé valley, Peru, 163, 438; Central Africa, 420–1; defined, 151; Jenné-jeno, West Africa, 153f, 157–8; Moche chiefdom, northern Peru, 149f, 153f, 173–4, 179; Paracas chiefdom, southern Peru, 153f, 174–5; Polynesian, kinship-based, 143; rainforest kingdoms, West Africa, 427; Saharan chiefdoms, 152; South Central Africa, 175–6, 569; Taíno chiefdom, Hispaniola, 141; Takrur, lower Senegal, 423; transformation to city-states, 459; Valley of Mexico, 434. *See also* Ghana

Childebert II, Frankish King, 313

Child labor, 790, 809–10

Chile: archaeological discoveries, 24; climate, 125, 555; democratic transition, 990; Depression years, 874; early industrialization in, 726; gold mining, 538, 547; Inca empire, 446, 447; increasing living standards, 720; infrastructural, industrial development, 707; liberation of, 697; migrations to, 25m, 720; populist wave in, 910; railroad building in, 722; Spanish explorations, 538; War of the Pacific victory, 726

China: agrarian-urban origins, 3, 99; agricultural developments, 95f, 96, 107–8; agricultural productivity, 260; antiforeign war, 731f; Anti-Rightist campaign, 912–13; artistic achievements, 268; *Art of War* (Sun Zi), 81; banning of foot binding, 365; Boxer Rebellion, 659f, 731f, 742–3, 766, 886; Buddhism in, 223, 240, 247f, 258, 264, 266–7, 345; calligraphy, 117, 267, 268, 358, 386, 388, 393; Canton trade, 637–9; Chiang K'ai-shek's leadership, 886, 891, 911; Christian missionaries in, 461f, 637; Communist victory in, 911–12; compass, invention of, 509; contact with East Africa, 362; cultural diffusion into Eurasia, 359; Cultural Revolution, 855f, 933f, 946, 947–8, 960; culture in, 112–14; Deng Xiaoping's leadership, 855f, 913, 946, 948; Ding Ling, feminist writer, 945; early political crises, 81; economy in, 107–12, 976–7; electronic product exports, 968; empire consolidation in, 148; Empress Wu, 351–2, 356, 356f, 370; entrepreneurial growth, 977; family adaptation in, 107–12; female infanticide in, 365; 589 CE, empire map, 256m; foot binding practice, 271, 365; foreign spheres of influence, 735m; fossil discoveries, 10; Four Modernizations, 855f, 948–50, 976; gender roles, 108, 111–12, 118, 262–4, 271; geography and climate, 94–6, 95m; Great Leap Forward in, 854f, 897f, 913; Hideyoshi's attempted invasion of, 631; horse trade, 103; Hundred Days of Reform, 731f; Hundred Flowers campaign, 912; Ibn Battuta's journeys, 469; Ice Age influence, 22; import substitution industrialization, 968; industry and commerce, 258–9, 260m; intellectual life, 267–8; iron and salt production, 259; Kangxi Emperor, 634, 637, 642; King Wu Ding, 92–3, 102, 104, 111, 113; land reforms, 259–60, 912; Legalism, morality system, 245, 246, 247f, 249, 250, 264, 269, 271; Lin

Zexu's destruction of opium, 732f, 733; Liu Shaoqi's leadership, 913, 946, 947; lunar calendar, 385; Macartney's Beijing mission, 731f; Manchu Emperors, 642; Mandate of Heaven, 104–6, 119, 246, 248, 265, 385; Maoist vision implementation, 911–12; Mao Zedong's leadership, 887, 888, 891, 900–1, 911, 943, 947–8; maritime trade, 730–3; May Fourth Movement, 886; Mencius (philosopher), 109–10, 244–5, 247–8, 265, 270; migrations to, 14; move from Marxist socialism, 960; mythological background, 99–100; negotiations with U.S., 948; Neo-Confucianism synthesis in, 273f, 356, 403, 642–3; Neolithic village findings, 119; 1990s, global hierarchy, 966; Nixon's visit to, 948; North and South Dynasties, 247f, 255; Northern Song Dynasty, 347f; "one-child" policy, 949–50; open cities, special economic zones, 949m; opium ("foreign mud") trade, 730–8, 732m, 744, 747, 759; Opium Wars, 730, 731f, 733, 734, 736–7, 744, 768; oracle bones, early writing, 93, 95f, 104, 105, 111, 112–13; People's Liberation Army, 811, 888, 911, 947; Persian Empire interaction, 190; printing developments, 268, 382–3; protection by U.S. military, 900–1; Qin Shi Huangdi, Emperor, 94, 252–3; Rape of Nanjing, 859f, 888–9; Red Guards, 947f, 948; reemergence of nationalism, 859f, 886–7; religion in, 112–14; "responsibility system," 949; reunification under the Sui, 247f, 376; rice cultivation, 3f, 79–80, 95f, 96, 98, 109, 257, 365, 637, 650; river systems, 94; Roman Empire comparison, 255–6; scholar-gentry, 363–4, 367, 379, 398, 639, 640, 736, 748, 886; scientific developments, 267–8, 734; self-strengthening era, 731f, 737f, 738–40; *Shujing* (historical text), 99, 100, 101, 105–6; Silk Road trade routes, 94, 111, 190, 196, 234, 235, 237m, 254, 261–2, 262m–263m, 298, 299, 319, 338, 345; sinicization in, 254; Sino-Japanese War, 659f, 728–30, 729–30, 731f, 746, 785, 886; Six Dynasties period, 247f, 255; society in, 107–12; Soviet tensions with, 932; Spanish trade with, 846–7; Spring and Autumn period, 95f, 112, 116, 247f; Taiping Rebellion, 634, 640, 731f, 735–6, 737m; taxation in, 109–10, 253, 255–6, 258–9, 353, 355, 360, 376, 378, 567–8, 748, 912; technology in, 114–15; terracotta warriors tomb, 252, 252f; Three Kingdoms period, 247f, 255, 374–6,

375f, 380; Tiananmen Square massacre, 855f, 950–1; trade imbalances, 730–1; Treaty of Nanjing with Great Britain, 734; Treaty of Tianjin, 746–7; treaty ports, 733–4, 735m; Vietnam attacked by, 947; warring states period, 247f; Western science, Eastern ethics, 738–9; world manufacturing data (1800, 1900), 827f; World War II campaigns, 854f, 886–7; writing developments, 95f, 99, 112–13, 116–17, 252, 266, 373, 400; Yongzheng Emperors, 637, 642; Zhou China states, 81. *See also* Confucianism; Daoism; Han Dynasty; Ming Dynasty; Neo-Confucianism; Qianlong Emperor; Qin Dynasty; Shang Dynasty; Song Empire; Sui Dynasty; Tang Dynasty; Xia Dynasty; Yellow River valley dynasties; Yuan Dynasty; Zhou Dynasty

"China's sorrow," 96

Chinese Communist Party (CCP), 119, 886–8, 947, 976f

Chinese Republican Revolution, 886

Christian Arabs, 985

Christian architecture, 212, 650

Christian Europe: Black Death, 331–5, 335m, 343; Carolingians, role in, 311, 312, 343; Cathar Heresy, 342; during Charlemagne's reign, 313–14; church crises, 336–7; early medieval church, 312–13; famine (14th century), 323; feudalism in, 315–17; formation of, 311–17; 14th century crises, 331–5; Jews in, 323; manorialism in, 316–17, 316f; Merovingians, role in, 311, 312, 343; monasteries, 264; the papacy, 313; post-Carolingian Europe, 314–15; Treaty of Verdun, 314; universities in, 241

Christianity: in Africa, 155, 156, 405–6, 575, 840m; Antonian-African Christianity, 565; in China, Ming Dynasty, 637; Christian Creoles, 545; Clovis's adoption of, 312; Coptic Christianity, 156, 406, 409–10; Eastern Christianity, 272, 275, 277f, 283–92; in Ethiopia, 405, 409–13; European piety popularization, 324–6; Greek Orthodox Christianity, 767; Jewish founding of, 149; Latin Christendom, 273, 296, 305, 306, 311–12; monotheism belief of, 203; Muslim competition with, 463–79; Native American conversion efforts, 531, 537, 557; Nestorian Christianity, 368; Nicene Creed, 195; Nietzsche's anger at, 817; origins of, 149, 205; Rastafarians, 411–12; Roman adoption of, 183f, 195–6, 198, 210, 218, 258; salvation/apocalypse themes, 201–2, 215; Sasanid Empire adoption of, 195–6; Trinitarian Byzantine Christianity, 277; unction ceremony,

312; western Christianity, 272, 278, 285, 289f, 290, 296, 301, 306, 311, 413

Christian missionaries, 406, 461f, 538, 637, 826, 838–9

Churchill, Winston, 882, 897, 897f

Ciompi rebellion, 334

Circumcision, 62, 161, 205

Cistercian monastic order (France), 323–4

The City of God (Augustine), 206

City-states (polis): Athens, 56, 57, 185–7, 206, 214; defined, 39; eastern Mediterranean region, 53; gender relation patterns, 44; Greek, 3f, 35f, 53, 57, 61; India, 3f; military/soldiers in, 57; origins/formation of, 56–7, 62; Phoenicia, 53; Sparta, 56, 57–8, 185; Syria, 53; Tenochtitlán, 443, 450–1, 451m, 454, 459, 534, 538f; Uruk, 35f; wars among, 42. *See also* Mexican Basin; Swahili city-states; Tenochtitlán; Wari city-state

Civil Rights Act of 1964 (U.S.), 940

Civil rights movements (U.S.), 939–40, 944

Civil service system: in China, 356, 399, 647; in India, 828–30, 918; in Vietnam, 647

Civil War (U.S.), 584, 677, 683, 706–7, 779, 796

Clay tablets, 40, 46, 48

Clement VII (Pope), 337

Climate change performance, 993m. *See also* Global warming

"Climbing 'Stork Pavilion'" poem (Wang Zhihuan), 93

Clinton, Bill, 969, 970, 974

Clinton, Hillary, 965

Clive, Robert, 824

Clovis (Frankish King), 312

Code of Manu (India), 84–5

Coffee: in Brazil, 710–11, 713–14, 718; Haitian plantations, 660, 669; in Indonesia, 844–5; in Latin America, 719; Ottoman introduction of, 476, 503

Coffee houses, 503

Cold War era (1945-1991), 855; in Africa, 923–6, 944; Berlin Wall, 855f, 897f, 904, 932, 933f, 937; Central Intelligence Agency, 899–900, 903; climax years, 933–8, 938m; Communism in Cuba, 903; "cooling" phase (1962-1991), 855; Cuban Missile Crisis, 854f, 855, 896, 897f, 905, 905m, 932, 960; defined, 896; East Germany's revolt, 901–2; economic modernisms competition, 945–6; ending of, 855f; "hot" phase (1945-1962), 855, 895–905; import substitution industrialization, 968; in Indochina, 922–3; Korean War, 854f, 897f, 900; map, 898m; McCarthyism in the U.S., 901; 1947-1949 confrontations, 897, 899; origins, 896–7; post-war Eastern Europe, 904–5; revolts by Poland and

Hungary, 902–3; role of Khrushchev, 896, 902–5, 910–11, 916; Soviet-Afghan War, 904–5; timeline of events, 897f

Colombia: Bolívar's liberation of slaves, 700f; Catholicism in, 717; gold mining, 547, 550; Guajira regime in, 696; independence and development, 699–700; Maroon settlements in, 593; populist wave in, 910; smallpox epidemic, 555

Colonialism: in Africa, 823, 838–43, 924; in Asia, 823; in Australia, 823, 825f, 831–3, 853; in Belgium, 421; defined, 823; in East Africa, 841; ending of, 911–19, 922–6; in Europe, 531, 690; in India, 825, 835, 837; in Indonesia, 845; in Philippines, 847–9; in Southeast Asia, 846m; in Vietnam, 825f, 849–50; as Western curse, 895. *See also* Americas and colonialism; Colonial North America

Colonial North America: African slave trade, 567f; British North America, 582–5, 663m; British slavery, 582–5, 583m; Continental Association, 664; Jamestown, Virginia, settlement, 461f, 533f, 543, 545, 583–4; "sot weed" enterprise, 583–4; sugar, rice, indigo, in the lower South, 584–5; Thirteen Colonies, 663m. *See also* New England

Columbian Exchange, 460f, 547, 548–9

Columbus, Christopher: Caribbean journey, 467–8, 532, 533f; route seeking voyages, 237, 464, 531; voyage to Americas, 464, 465f, 571; Zheng's ship comparison, 361

Comanches, Native Americans, 545, 703–4, 704f

The Commentaries of Mr. Zuo (Chinese text), 107

Committee of Union and Progress (CUP), 659f, 763f, 768–9, 770–1, 775

Communication revolution, 801

Communism: in China, 119, 886–8, 911–12; in Cuba, 903–4; in Eastern Europe, fall of, 855f, 937–9, 938m; in France, 870; in the Soviet Union, 875–6

The Communist Manifesto (Engels and Marx), 658f, 793f, 809

Communist Party (China), 119, 886–8, 947, 976f

Communist Party (Czechoslovakia), 934

Communist Party (France), 870

Communist Party (Poland), 937

Communist Party (Soviet Union), 875, 876, 904. *See also* Bolshevik Party

Compass, invention of, 321

Comte, Auguste, 688

CONADEP. *See* National Commission on the Disappearance of Persons

Concert of Europe, 835, 836

Confessions (Augustine), 206

Confucianism, 148f; Buddhism criticized by, 355; Buddhist influences on, 149; Christianity comparison, 340–1; doctrine (described), 246; Han-Confucian synthesis, 264–5, 352; influence on government, 245, 246, 247, 250, 269, 273368; legalism comparison, 249, 269; *shi* concept, 110; in Song Empire, China, 345; state sponsorship of, 112, 245; timeline placement, 247f; in Vietnam, 397, 850. *See also* Neo-Confucianism

Congo Reform Association, 852

Congress of Berlin, 769, 770, 782

Congress of Vienna, 658f, 663f, 677–8, 777

Constantinople: alliance with Jerusalem, 291–2; artistic decline in, 303; court of Versailles comparison, 297; decentralized government, 288; Eastern Greek church in, 311; Hagia Sophia in, 286; Khosrow II's arrival in, 212; Mehmet II's repopulation of, 472; Ottoman's conquest of, 272f, 277f, 292, 313f, 460f, 464, 469, 471–2, 484, 493, 496; post-1453 migrations from, 306; riots/destruction in, 198–9; Russia's goal for defeating, 761; Tang city (China) comparison, 352; trade networks, 320, 469; Venetian conquest of, 307, 327

Constitutional nationalism: in Austria, 677; in Britain, 686, 858, 893; of Creoles, 716; vs. ethnolinguistic nationalism, 693; in France, 660, 671, 677, 691; in Haiti, 673, 676, 776; in India, 918; in Latin America, 716; Napoleonic Wars and, 858; 19th-century evolution of, 929; of the Ottomans, 761, 767, 789; rise of, 833; in Spanish America, 714

Constitutions: of Africa, 925, 955; Austria's resistance to, 677; corrosive patterns of, 787; Creole adoption of, 716; of England, 525; of Ethiopia, 413; exposure of Russian officers to, 777; of France, 660, 671, 677, 691, 761; as French Revolution outcome, 761; Gandhi's adherence to, 918; of Great Britain, 686; of Greece, 186–7; of Haiti, 547, 673; of India, 232, 235, 242; of Japan, 385, 753, 797; of the Ottomans, 768–9; reforms of, 666; of Spanish America, 714; of United States, 684

Containment policy, of Great Britain, 835–6

Continental Association, 664

Convention Peoples' Party (Africa), 924

Cook, James, 831

Coolie trade (human trafficking), 721m, 744

Copernicus, Nicolaus, 207, 460f, 497f, 499–500, 502, 529, 618

Copper (*Chalcolithic*) Age, 39

Copper mining and smelting, 39

Coptic Christianity, 156, 406, 409–10

Coronation ceremony (defined), 312

Corpus Iuris Civilis (Justinian), 329

Cortés, Hernán, 532–4, 537, 538

Council for Mutual Economic Assistance (COMECON), 897

Council of Constance, 313f

Creoles: African Creole culture, 576, 589–90; Americas governance role, 538; Cartagena, Spain junta, 699; Christian Creoles, 545; defined, 538; divisions with mestizos, Amerindians, 707; early Atlantic world, 589, 591–2; gender roles, 554; in Haiti, 591; Latin America composition, 554m; music and food, 591–2; New Granada Creoles, 699; New Spain uprising, 702; rise of, 540–1; second tier social class of, 552–3; settlements, northern South America, 699; upper social stratum of, 551, 552; wages comparison, 540

Creolization, early Atlantic world, 589, 591–2

Crimean War, 761, 763f, 768, 779, 780, 783, 788, 797, 836

Critique of Practical Reason (Kant), 674

Critique of Pure Reason (Kant), 674

Cro-Magnon humans, 19

Cromwell, Oliver, 519

Crony capitalism, 964, 984

Crusades (to the Holy Land), 325–8; Byzantium initially aided by, 283; conquest of Constantinople, 272f, 277f; description, 326–8; Fatimids during, 282; First Crusade, 323, 327m; inspiration for, 326; Seljuk invasion and, 288–92; timeline placement, 313f

Cuauhtémoc (Aztec ruler), 533f, 534

Cuba: Bay of Pigs incident, 904, 923; Castro's leadership, 897f, 903–4, 926; Santeria religion, 590; slave rebellions, 712–13; student demonstrations, 942–3

Cuban Missile Crisis (1962), 854f, 855, 896, 897f, 905m, 932, 960

Cultivation scheme (defined), 845

Cultural Revolution (People's Republic of China), 855f, 933f, 946, 947–8, 960

Cuneiform writing development, 40, 41f, 44

Cunitz, Maria, 494–5, 503, 505f

Cunningham, Alexander, 66–7

Czechoslovakia, "Prague Spring" in, 933–4

Da Gama, Vasco, 460f, 465f, 468, 535, 571, 610

Daimler, Gottlieb, 800

Dalai Lama, 635

D'Alembert, Jean le Rond, 674

Däniken, Erich von, 178

Daoism, 149, 245, 249–50, 273, 352, 356

Darius I (the Great), King of Persia, 183

Darwin, Charles, 793f, 815

Daughters of Liberty, 663

Da Vinci, Leonardo, 498

Dawes Plan (Germany), 869

De Beauvoir, Simone, 940

Decameron (Boccaccio), 339

Decembrist Revolt (Russia), 777–8

Declaration of Independence (U.S.), 659, 664

Declaration of the Rights of Man and of the Citizen (France), 659, 666, 667, 767

De Gaulle, Charles, 922

De Klerk, Frederik Willem, 958

De la Cruz, Juana Inés, 562

Delhi Sultanate, India, 272f, 347f, 349–50, 350m

Democracy: in America, 271; in Athens, 186–7, 214; defined, 57, 214; in India, 242, 873; Taisho Democracy, Japan, 885; Wilson and, 861. *See also* Capitalist democracy

Democratic Republic of the Congo, 420

Les Demoiselles d'Avignon (Picasso), 818f

Deng Xiaoping, 855f, 913, 946, 948

De Pizan, Christine, 340

De Rosas, Juan Manuel, 698

Descartes, René, 506–8, 673, 674

The Descent of Man (Darwin), 815

Description of Africa (Leo Africanus), 463

Dessalines, Jean-Jacques, 672–3

Détente, between U.S. and Soviet Union, 855, 932–3, 933f

Dharma, 82, 83–5, 89

Dhar Oualata village (Africa), 153

Dhar Tichitt village (Africa), 153

Díaz, Porfirio, 707–9

Dickens, Charles, 689

Diderot, Denis, 674

Digger Movement (England), 528

Ding Ling (Chinese feminist author), 945

Divine Comedy, The (Dante), 339

DNA, 5, 19–20, 24

Dollar regime, in the U.S., 967–8

Dome of the Rock, 277

Dominic, Saint, 326

Dominican religious order, 325, 326, 342, 532, 557–8, 636–7

Don Quixote (Cervantes), 492

The Dream of the Red Chamber (Cao Xueqin), 750

Dreamtime (Australian Dreamtime), 17–18, 31

Duarte, Eva, 910

Dubček, Alexander, 934

DuBois, W. E. B., 867

Dulles, Allen, 903–4

Dutch Cape Colony (South Africa), 567f

Dutch East India Company, 611, 659f, 824, 825f, 827–8

Dutch Protestant War of Liberation (from Spain), 497f

Dutch West India Company, 576

Dyarchy administration system, Qing Dynasty, 633

Dylan, Bob, 928

Early Classic Period (Maya), 165–6

Early Dynastic Period (Egypt), 44–5

Earth orbit, by Gagarin, 897f

East Africa: agriculture in, 157, 161; Bantus in, 153*f*, 159; climatic conditions, 35, 162; conquest/resistance to colonialism, 841; Egyptian Nile origination, 37; fossil discoveries, 9–10; hominins in, 6; *Homo erectus* in, 6, 9–10; *Homo sapiens* in, 2*f*, 7*f*, 11–14; incipient urbanism in, 162; Kushite herders of, 150; Muslim merchants in, 414; pastoralism in, 161; Plague of Justinian, possible origination, 196, 196*m*; Sasanid control in, 157; slave trading, 414; Swahili city-states, 407*f*; trade activities, 162; village life in, 159–62. *See also* Swahili city-states

East Asia: agricultural developments, 3, 100, 109, 367, 374–5; artistic achievements, 267; Buddhism in, 243, 264, 392*f*, 395; challenges of modernity, 728–56; early human migrations, 19, 72, 115; 1150, map, 357*m*; fossil discoveries, analysis, 28; gender equity, 395; Japan's invasions in, 627; luxury item discoveries, 158; printing developments, 382–3; rice domestication, 79–80, 98, 101, 389–90; Shang dynasty's influence, 93, 101–2

Eastern Christianity, 272, 275, 277*f*, 283–92

Eastern Europe: Cold War and, 896–9; collapse of Communism, 855*f*, 938*m*; Communist map, 934*m*; Hitler and, 880–2; *Homo erectus* in, 9–10; horses in, 77; Jews in, 323; migrations from, 874; Mongol conquests in, 272*f*, 292; 1990s, economic collapse, 979; Ottoman dominance in, 476, 514, 560, 762, 834; route to constitutional normality, 691; Stalin and, 896. *See also* "Prague Spring" in Czechoslovakia

Eastern Mediterranean region: bronze, usefulness of, 40; city-states in, 53; climate variability, 37; farming and settlements, 33, 34*m*; geography, environment, 33–335; map, 50*m*; Mycenaeans, 35*f*, 54, 56

Eastern Zhou Dynasty (China), 95*f*, 106

East India companies: British East India Company, 611, 625, 639, 731, 825*f*; competition among, 614–15; dispute arbitration role, 825; Dutch East India Company, 611, 825*f*; founding of, 610–11; French East India Company, 611; growing power of, 599; near bankruptcy of, 663*f*

East India Railway, 66

Ecclesiastical History of the English People (Bede), 325

Economy: Atlantic slave trade patterns, 586–8; Caribbean Islands, 715*m*; China, 107–12, 357, 748, 976–7; Cold War era, 945–6; Eastern Europe, 1990s collapse, 979; Enlightenment Era, Europe, 675; Germany, crisis and recovery, 979; global economic crisis, recovery, 974–5; Great Britain, crisis, 978; India, 350–1, 919, 922; India, Mughal Empire, 613–15; Japan, 389; Latin America, 715*m*, 717–18; Mamluk Egypt, 294; money economy (defined), 480; Ottoman Empire, 480, 771; Portugal, crisis, 978; recession (ending 1893), 770, 789; recession of 2008-2011, 855*f*, 967*f*, 976, 977–8, 982; Roman Empire, 194–5; South America, 539*m*, 715*m*; Soviets, New Economic Policy, 936; Spain, 978; sub-Saharan Africa, 976, 987; Vietnam, 977; Yugoslavia (former), 979. *See also* Taxation

Edison, Thomas, 793*f*

Edward I (King of England), 318

Edwin Smith Papyrus, 62

Egypt: Arab Spring protests, 965, 983–4; architectural features, 70; British occupation of, 825*f*, 836–7; conquest of, 272*f*; Coptic Church, 156, 406, 409; creation myth, 60; Early Dynastic Period, 44–5; early towns, 38–9; empire building, 51–2; Euphrates/Nile floods, 37; feminist writers, 945; first written records, 152; gender roles, 43; hieroglyphic writing, 46*f*, 46; Hittite clashes with, 51; kingdoms in, 44–6; literature of, 60; *Mamluks* slave revolt, 766; Middle Kingdom, 48; military coup d'état, 967*f*, 984; Morsi removed from power, 967*f*, 984; Napoleon's occupation of, 658*f*, 761, 763*f*, 832; Nasser's leadership of, 895, 897*f*, 915–17, 921; New Kingdom Egypt, 43, 51, 59, 60*f*, 61; Nile River valley agriculture, 33, 152; Old Kingdom Egypt, 47*m*, 64; post-WW II officer coup, 915–17; Ptolemaic Egypt, 156, 162, 188, 189*m*, 190, 203, 206, 236; pyramids of, 46, 62, 121, 131; religion in, 64; science and math, 61–2; sculpture and paintings, 61, 61*f*; sharecroppers in, 38; Suez War against, 897*f*; temples in, 39; terrorist attacks, 980–1; as "the gift of the Nile," 70; trade networks, 321*m*; Upper/Lower, unification, 35*f*; urban centers in, 37–40, 38*f*. *See also* Mamluk Egypt

Einstein, Albert, 659*f*, 793*f*, 815

Eisenhower, Dwight D., 901, 923, 926

Electricity, 800–1, 811–12

Electromagnetism research, 801

Elements (Euclid), 330

Eliot, George (Mary Ann Evans), 689–90

El Niño weather phenomenon, 124–5, 831, 832

Emancipation Edict (Russia), 781, 788

Empress dowager (defined), 356

Empress Wu (Wu Zetian), 351–2, 356, 370

Encyclopédie (Diderot), 673–4

End of History?, The (Fukuyama), 960

Engels, Friedrich, 658*f*, 793*f*, 809

England: African slave trade, 567*f*; Anglican Church, 514, 516, 518, 519, 546; Battle of Hastings, 318; bubonic plague in, 196, 341; Christian conversions in, 310; civil war, 497*f*, 518–19; constitutionalism (political system), 525–6; Digger Movement, 528; expulsion of Jews, 323; 15th century reorganization, 337–8; Glorious Revolution, 497*f*, 519, 525, 658–9, 661; Henry II, 318; Henry VIII, 514; Ice Age influences, 22; Industrial Revolution, 658; Jews expelled from, 323; Magna Carta, 313*f*, 318; monasteries, 320; Norman and Angevin kings, 313*f*; North American settlements, 543, 544*m*; Obscene Publications Bill, 806; opening of passenger railroad, 793*f*; parliament of, 318; Plantagenet kings, 318; political recovery of, 317–18; post-Black Death population recovery, 509; Protestantism in, 514, 518, 528; Richard I, 327; rise of centralized government, 510*t*; scientific/philosophical developments, 495, 502; seaborne empire creation, 460; seizure of Jamaica from Spain, 567*f*; steam engine invention, 497*f*, 503, 505–6; theater in, 498; trade networks, 464; urban growth, 322; Vikings' arrival in, 314–15; wars against France, 331, 341; wool production, 320, 321

Enlightenment era, 663*f*, 673–7; Africa and, 838; American adaptations of, 557; American Revolution and, 664; capitalism as legacy of, 791; categorical imperative, 674–5; constitutionalism, 658–9, 676, 761; cosmopolitan ideals of, 824; Declaration of Independence and, 664; defined, 673; economic liberalism, 675–6; *Encyclopédie* (Diderot), 673–4; German cultural nationalism, 676–7; guillotine executions during, 669; Haiti and, 673; literature and music, 675; materialism, 906; Ottoman adaptations of, 767; philosophy, 674–5, 816; Russia and, 776, 777, 779; scientific aspects of, 793; social contract expansion during, 658–9, 906; stimulation for, 529, 661

Enuma Elish (Mesopotamian creation myth), 35*f*, 60

Environment: of Africa, 6, 122, 148–9; of the Americas, 123, 126*m*, 169, 442; of China, 98, 119, 628; of colonial North America, 662; of Eurasia, 122; genetic interactions with, 27–8; of Great Britain, 798; of India, 79; of Korea, 373–4; Kyoto Protocol agreement, 993, 994; limits of modernity, 991–4; of Middle East, Mediterranean region, 33–4; of Pacific Islands, 141; of rain-forest settlements, 158

Environmental adaptability, 7–8, 14
Epic of Gilgamesh, 60
Epistle to the God of Love (de Pizan), 340
Equal Employment Opportunity Law
    (Japan), 945
Erasmus, Desiderius, 497
Erdoğan, Recep, 983
Eroica (Beethoven), 663*f*
Estates-General, in France, 317–18
Ethiopia: agriculture, 155–6, 179;
    Christianity in, 405, 409–13, 571;
    coastal Muslims, 412–13; fossil
    discoveries, 4–5, 7, 11; highlands, 148,
    151–2, 155, 179, 409–10, 412*m*;
    invasions by, 200; Mussolini's invasion
    of, 879; Portugal's support of, 567*f*,
    572; Solomonid Dynasty, 407*f*, 409,
    411–13; sub-Saharan map, 568*m*;
    Zagwe Dynasty, 407*f*, 410–11. *See also*
    Aksum kingdom; Meroë kingdom;
    Middle Nile
Ethnic cleansing, in former Yugoslavia, 855*f*,
    967*f*, 979. *See also* Genocide
Ethnolinguistic nationalism: vs.
    constitutional nationalism, 676; in
    Germany, 676–7; in Italy, 680–1; *On
    the Origin of Language* (Herder), 676–7
Eubanks, Mary, 135
Eugenics (defined), 867
Eurasia: adaptation in, 11–21, 29; agrarian-
    urban society in, 3; Beringia land
    bridge, 23; China's cultural diffusion
    into, 359; early human migration to,
    5–6; *H. neanderthalensis* in, 26; *H.
    sapiens,* establishment in, 96; Ice Age
    influence, 22; India/China as economic
    drivers of, 825; interactions with sub-
    Saharan Africa, 149; migrations to,
    5–6, 7*f,* 10, 25; monotheism/monism
    religion, 149; trade routes, 348*m*;
    visionaries of reality in, 149; weaponry
    in, 16, 127, 832
Europe: agricultural revolution, 319–20;
    Baltic amber fossils, 23; Black Death,
    272*f,* 331–5, 335*m,* 343; boomerang
    invention, 23; bourgeoisie social class,
    322; canon law and medicine, 329;
    challenges of philosophy, 340;
    Christian piety popularization, 324–6;
    commerce and trade, 320–1, 321*m,* 338;
    Concert of Europe, 835, 836; Congress
    of Vienna, 658*f,* 663*f,* 677–8; the
    Crusades, 326–8; dominion map
    (1648), 521*m*; early capitalism, cash
    economy, 322; 1871 map, 682*m*; 15th
    century reorganization, 337–40;
    firearms, growing use of, 479; foraging
    culture in, 28; guilds, 322; Hanseatic
    League trading alliance, 338, 510; *H.
    sapiens* in, 7*f,* 9–10, 27, 31; Hundred
    Years' War, 335–6, 336*m*; Ice Age
    influence, 22; imperialism in Africa,
    838–43; industrial advances

(1750-1870), 784, 791–5, 794*m*;
    industrial advances (1871-1914),
    796–800; Jews expelled from, 323;
    literary achievements, 339–40;
    medieval math, 330; medieval science,
    330; middle class savings rate, 977;
    migrations to, 14, 19–20; Neanderthal
    in, 26; 1936 empire map, 871*m*; 1990s,
    global hierarchy, 966; nomadic steppe
    peoples in, 3; papal reforms, 324;
    political, economic, industrial revolts,
    659, 663*f*; political and industrial
    revolutions, 659; political recovery of,
    317–19; post-Black Death population
    recovery, 509; post-WW I recovery
    map, 863*f*; religious reform, expansion,
    323–8; return to imperial stage
    formation, 493; rising income dispar-
    ities, 978; rock art, 14*f,* 18–19, 20; social
    patterns, 322–3; student demon-
    strations, 855*f,* 942–3; territorial map
    (ca. 1560), 475*m*; universities and
    scholasticism, 328–9; urban growth,
    322; vernacular languages, 339; victims
    of state centralization, 510*f*; warfare
    map (1450-1750), 511*m*; weaponry
    developments, 510–11; women's right
    movement, 940–1; world manufac-
    turing data (1800, 1900), 827*f*; in World
    War II, 854*f*; World War II map, 884*m*.
    See also Americas and colonialism;
    Christian Europe; Crusades (to the Holy
    Land); individual countries
European Union (EU), 960, 978–80, 983, 988
"Exaltation of Inanna, The" poem
    (Enheduanna), 32
Exceptionalism, 682–3
Existentialism, 906, 929
Extraterritoriality (defined), 734

Facebook, 965, 987, 989
Facebook Revolution, 989
Factory Act, 809
Family: Aborigines, 17; in China, 101, 106,
    107–12, 355, 364–5, 749*f*; Confu-
    cianism and, 355; in India, 83–5,
    235–7, 615–16; in Japan, 639–41; in
    Latin America, 723–4; in Vietnam, 398
Faraday, Michael, 800
Far from the Madding Crowd (Hardy), 817
Fascism, 857, 877–8, 905, 909, 960
Fatimid Dynasty: commercial development,
    297–300; rebellion vs. Abbasids, 282;
    timeline placement, 277*f*
February Revolution (Russia), 860
Federal Reserve Act (U.S.), 686
Federal Trade Commission Act (U.S.), 686
Female infanticide, 365, 641, 950
Feminist movement: in China, 370;
    emergence of, 13, 855*f,* 933*f*; first-wave,
    second-wave, 944; in Great Britain, 811;
    third-wave, 944–5; writings of de
    Beauvoir, 940; writings of De Pizan, 340

Ferdinand I, King of Spain, 476
Fernando IV, King of Spain, 320
Fernando VII, King of Spain, 700
Fertile Crescent: agrarian origins in, 3, 29,
    33–48, 35*f,* 96; Natufian culture, 35–6
Feudalism: in Christian Europe, 315–18;
    consequences of, 340; defined, 106,
    315; demise of, 322; Gupta Empire,
    India, 347; in Japan, 387, 401; monastic
    reforms and, 323; in Nubia, 409; Zhou
    Dynasty (China), 106–7, 223, 387
Final Solution against Jews, 854*f,* 859*f,* 883
First Balkan War, 771
First Crusade, 323, 327*m*
First Emperors Tomb, terra-cotta warriors
    (China), 252, 252*f*
First-/second-wave feminism, 944
First Temple, destruction of, 411
Flaubert, Gustave, 690
Foot binding, 271, 365
Foragers (hunters and gatherers):
    agricultural innovations, 33; Amazon
    rainforest civilizations, 458; in the
    Americas, 122–8; Australian
    Aborigines, 14–19; climate influences,
    152–3; defined, 12; gender roles,
    12–13; in Ife Kingdom, Africa, 428;
    in the Middle East, 3, 33–6;
    Neanderthals, 19; Neolithic cultures,
    96, 129; Paleolithic foragers, 12, 13,
    59, 160; shift to agrarian-urban
    society, 29, 31, 89, 96, 115, 134, 151–2,
    459; social formation developments, 2,
    33, 174; in Southern and Central
    Africa, 417–18; Spirit Cave mummy,
    28; sub-Saharan Africa transition
    from, 151; by the Toltecs, 436
Ford, Henry, 867
Fossil discoveries: Anzick-1 fossil, 28; of
    Baltic amber, 23; in East Africa, 9–10;
    of *H. erectus,* 10; of *H. floresiensis,*
    10–11, 30; of *H. sapiens,* 11, 26–7, 29;
    of Kaddaba, 6; "Kennewick man," 7*f,* 28,
    29*f,* 125; Lucy (Hadar AL 288-1), 4–5,
    6*f,* 7–8; of Neanderthals, 19; of
    Orrorin, 6; of Paleoindians, 28; of
    Paleolithic humans, 19; of plants and
    insects, 24; in Portugal, 27; "Spirit
    Cave mummy" fossil, 7*f,* 28–9; of
    Toumaï, 2*f,* 6
Four Modernizations, 855*f,* 948–50
Four Noble Truths (of Buddhism), 229
France: absolutism in, 522–3; Academy of
    Medicine, 668; Academy of Sciences,
    503; Algeria conquered by, 825*f,* 835;
    Arab opposition to mandates, 870–1;
    Battle of Tours, 278, 312; bayonet-
    attachment invention, 510; Bourbon
    monarchy, 517, 541, 551, 679, 681*f,* 696,
    822; Calvinism in, 514–15; Capetian
    kings, 313*f,* 317–18; Cistercian
    monastic order, 323–4; civil war in,
    516–17; colonies and mandates, 870;

Committee of Public Safety, 667; Crimean War, 761, 763f, 768, 779, 780, 783, 788, 797, 836; Declaration of the Rights of Man and of the Citizen, 659, 666, 667, 767; demesne of, 317; Estates-General in, 317–18; expulsion of Jews, 323; 15-century reorganization, 337–8; Franco-Prussian War, 796, 859; Henry IV, rule of, 497f, 517; Huguenots in, 516, 517; Iberian Berbers/Arabs conquests, 278; Indochina involvement, 922–3; influence in China, 735m; Louis XIV, reign of, 497f, 517; Mamluk Egypt defeated by, 832f; monastery reform, 323–4; 1936 empire map, 871m; North American colonization, 544m; North American settlements, 543, 544m; political recovery of, 317–18; Popular Front Coalition, 870; post-Black Death population recovery, 509; post-WW I recovery, 869–70; reign of Henry IV, 497f; Reign of Terror, 667, 668; resistance to Nazi Germany, 882; rise of centralized government, 510; Second Opium War with China, 736–7, 768, 827; Seven Years' War, 547, 625, 662, 663f, 665, 672; Socialist Party, 870; Suez War vs. Egypt, 897f; Third Republic, 692, 693, 849, 922; trade networks, 321m; Treaty of Paris, 336; Triple Intervention against Japan, 729, 747, 785; Vietnam conquered by, 825f, 849–50; War of Religion, 497f; World War I, role in, 859–60; World War II in, 882. *See also* French Revolution

Franciscan religious order, 325–6, 342, 463, 538, 557–8, 636–7

Franco-Prussian War, 796, 859

Frankish Gaul, 311–17

Franklin, Benjamin, 559

Frederick I (German king), 319

Frederick II (King of Prussia), 497f

French Canada, 546

French East India Company, 611

French League of Women's Rights, 811

French Revolution, 658f, 661, 663f; aristocracy during, 809; conditions leading to, 512, 665–6; constitutional monarchy phase, 665; constitutional nationalism outcome, 761, 775; Estates-General, 318, 665, 666; "liberty, fraternity, equality" motto, 675; limited intellectual impact of, 695; military consolidation phase, 665; Napoleon's ending of, 677; Ogé, Vincent, and, 660, 670; Philippine Islands influenced by, 847; radical republicanism phase, 665; Reign of Terror, 667, 668; revival of empire, 668–9; Russia influenced by, 777; storming of the Bastille, 666, 667f; three phases of, 666–8; timeline

placement, 663f; trade problems outcome, 730

Freud, Sigmund, 793f, 815–16

Fukuyama, Francis, 960

Gagarin, Yuri, 897f

Galilei, Galileo, 207, 301, 461f, 497f, 500–2, 505–7

Gandhi, Indira, 624, 895

Gandhi, Mohandas K., 829, 831, 873, 917–18, 939, 957, 965

Ganges states (India), power centralization, 80–1

Gaozu (Han Dynasty ruler), 253

Garibaldi, Giuseppe, 681

Gatling gun, 802

Gautama (the Buddha or Enlightened One), 226, 228, 229, 239f

Gay rights movement (U.S.), 941

Gaza, Israel invasion of, 981–2

Gender roles and divisions: in China, 108, 111–12, 118, 262–4, 271, 365, 748–9; of Creoles, 554; in early Middle East society, 42–3; in forager/agrarian-urban society, 12–13; in Inca Empire, 454–5; in India, 84–5, 239, 615–16; Mamluk Sultanate, 296; Timur Empire, 616. *See also* Feminist movement; Women

Genghis Khan, 292, 349, 357, 600–2

Genocide: Final Solution against Jews, 854f, 859f, 883; in former Yugoslavia, 855f, 967f, 979; Germany vs. the Herero people, 841–2; Hutus vs. the Tutsis, 570, 855f, 967f; by Khmer Rouge, 952

Geoglyphs, Nazca chiefdom, 176

Germany: Baader-Meinhof Gang, 943; Berlin Airlift, 899; Berlin Wall, 855f, 897f, 904, 932, 933f, 937; Bismarck/Wilhelm I's coalition, 681–2; Christian conversions, 311; Congress of Berlin, 769, 770, 782; economic crisis, recovery, 979; ethnolinguistic nationalism in, 676–7; Franco-Prussian War, 796; Henry IV, 324, 343; influence in China, 735m; military assertion efforts, 881; papal reform, 324; Peasant's War, 497f; political recovery of, 318–19; post-Black Death population recovery, 509; post-WW I recovery, 869; Red Brigades, 943; Schlieffen Plan, 859; Social Democratic Party, 879; steel manufacturing, 797; Thirty Years' War, 494, 497f, 506, 516, 519–21, 524; trade networks, 321m; Treaty of Brest-Litovsk, 860; Triple Intervention against Japan, 729, 747, 785; unification of, 663f, 855f; Union of German Women's Organizations, 811; Weimar Republic founded by, 879–81; World War I participation, 859–62. *See also* Hitler, Adolf, Nazi Germany

Ghana: central administration, 426; Malian exploitation of, 426; map location,

425m; military power, 426; timeline placement, 407f

Ghaznavid Sultanate, India, 349–50

Ginsberg, Allen, 928

Glasnost policy (Soviet Union), 855f, 933f, 934, 935–7

Global financial crisis and recession (2008-1011), 855f, 967f, 974–5, 977–8

Globalization: criticism of, 969–70; defined, 969; Israel's technological developments, 981; and poor countries, 975–6; rejection, by Middle East autocratic regimes, 980; US technological renewal and, 968–9

Global shifts (21st century): African transformations, 987–90; Arab Spring, 855f, 955, 967f, 980, 981–3, 988–9, 994; ascent of Turkey, 983; growth of Hezbollah, 981; Iranian ambitions, 982; Israel and Gaza, 981–2; Latin American expansion, 990–1; Middle East/Islamism, 980–1; rise of India's middle class, 986–7; Western unease, 977–9; Yugoslavian civil war, 979–80

Global warming, 991–3, 997

Glorious Revolution (England), 497f, 519, 525, 658–9, 661

Glyphic alphabet, Maya, 153f

Göbekli Tepe sanctuary, 58

Goodyear, Charles, 800

Gorbachev, Mikhail, 934, 935–9

Grain, selective breeding origins, 36

Granada Kingdom: artistic achievements, 303, 305; as center or learning, 504f; Charles V residence in, 487; moriscos' revolt in, 477–8; Spain's conquests of, 460f, 464, 465f, 467, 468, 471; timeline placement, 272f, 277f

Grand Council, Qing Dynasty, 634

Gray, Tom, 4

Great Britain: American Revolution, 658f, 661, 663–4, 663f; Arab opposition to mandates, 870–1; Aurangzeb's conflicts with, 611; British Coercive Acts, 664; British North America, 582–5, 663m; Calico Acts, 792; colonialism in Australia, 823, 825f, 831–3, 853; colonialism in India, 824–31, 825f, 826m, 829m; colonies and mandates, 870; colonists shipped to Australia, 825f; containment policy, 835–6; Crimean War, 761, 763f, 768, 779, 780, 783, 788, 797, 836; direct rule in India, 828–31; early industrialism, 791–5, 794m; economic crisis, 978; Egypt occupied by, 825f; factory systems, 793–4; factory towns, abysmal conditions, 807–8; House of Commons, 318, 337, 518, 596, 792; House of Lords, 318, 754; imperialism in Egypt and Sudan, 836–7; India expansion map, 826m; India's demand for independence, 854f, 873; Industrial

Revolution, 658, 659, 825; influence in China, 735*m*; Japan's alliance with, 731*f*; Luddites movement, 820; nation-state building, 686–7; 1936 empire map, 871*m*; Opium Wars with China, 730, 731*f*, 733, 734, 736–7, 744, 827; post-WW I recovery, 869; Royal Air Force, 884; Seven Years' War, 547, 625, 662, 663*f*, 665, 672; social contract theory, 658–9; Suez War vs. Egypt, 897*f*; tax system reforms, 582–5, 665; technologies, power sources, 793; textile industry innovations, 793; Treaty of Nanjing with China, 734. *See also* England

Great Depression (U.S.), 854*f*, 855, 857, 859*f*, 867–8, 978

Great Lakes Native Americans, 545

Great Leap Forward (China), 854*f*, 897*f*, 913

Great Mutiny (India), 659*f*, 824, 825*f*, 827–8

Great Plains Native Americans, 545

Great Proletarian Cultural Revolution (China), 948

Great Pyramid of Egypt, 46, 131

Great Society, of Lyndon B. Johnson, 940

Great Zimbabwe Kingdom (South Africa), 273*f*, 407*f*, 413, 419, 420*m*, 570

Greece: Alexander's unification of, 181; alphabet, 55*f*; alphabet invention, 56; Antigonid Greece, 188, 189*m*; arts, development of, 61; Athens, city-state, 56, 57, 185–7, 206, 214; city-states, 35*f*; economic crisis, 978; 8th century BCE recovery, 56; First Balkan War collaboration, 771; gaining independence from Ottomans, 763*f*, 767; Hellenistic cultural influences, 188–9; interactions with Persia, 181–5; literature and art, 209–10; military formation development, 57; Minoans, 35*f*, 48, 56, 61, 138; Mycenaeans, 35*f*, 54, 56; oracles/Olympic games, 185; Orthodox Christianity, 767; Persian wars against, 187; political system, 57; repulsion of Persian invasions, 187; 6th century map, 185*m*; Sparta, city-state, 56, 57–8, 185; women in Athens, 214

Greek Orthodox Christianity, 767

Greenhouse gases, 967*f*

Gregory I (Pope), 310, 311, 313, 313*f*

Gregory VII (Pope), 324, 343

Gregory XI (Pope), 336

Gross domestic product (GDP): of Brazil, 722; of China, 949, 976–7; of India, 987; of Latin America, 720; of Mexico, 722; of North Korea, 996; of Russia, 975; of Turkey, 983

Grosseteste, Robert, 330

Guerrero, Vincent, 703

Guevara, Ernesto "Che," 943, 976

Guilds, growth of, in Europe, 322

Guillotine, 668–9

Gulf Stream current, 124–5

Gunpowder, 358–9

Gunpowder empires (defined), 359

Gupta Empire (India): artistic, literary achievements, 240; Buddhism/Hinduism, post-Gupta era, 346–8; court and culture, 223; decentralization, 235; decline of, 219*f*, 223, 346; feudalism in, 347; as "golden age" of India, 346; map of empire, 224*m*; origins, 222–3; religious foundations, 218, 223, 232, 236, 239, 368; reunification of India, 149*f*, 219*f*, 346; sciences development, 241; societal stability interests of, 235–6; Vijayanagar comparison, 347

Gu Yanwu (Qing philosopher), 643

Haas, Jonathan, 131

Habsburg Empire: Austrian Habsburgs, 465*f*, 478, 489, 510, 762–3, 776–7; centralized state formation, 483; Charles V, leadership, 475–6, 482–3; fundraising for resources, 479, 481, 483, 484; Iberia's incorporation of, 483; Islamic-Christian imperialism of, 475; losses in conflicts, 476; naval battle with Ottomans, 465*f*; peace treaty with Ottomans, 465*f*, 476–7, 478; power struggles with Ottomans, 469–78; rise of, 464, 474–5; state formation pattern, 483; territories of Ferdinand I, 477. *See also* Charles V; Spanish Habsburgs

Hadar AL 288-1 fossil ("Lucy"), 4–5, 6*f*, 7–8

Haiti: Bolívar's exile in, 700; constitutional nationalism in, 676, 776; Creole language of, 591; Dessalines' naming of, 672–3; migration to, 141; Ogé's imprisonment and torture, 660–1, 670; slave revolt, 670–1, 695, 712; sugar production collapse, 713; voodoo religion practices, 590–1

Haitian Revolution, 546, 658*f*, 661, 669, 671*m*, 697*f*, 761, 867

Halifax Gibbet (English guillotine), 668

Hammurabi (Babylonian king), 42, 43, 44–5. *See also* Law Code of Hammurabi

Han Dynasty (China): bureaucratic/political structure, 253, 353; decline of, 255; Han-Confucian synthesis, 264–5, 352; history during, 265–6; industry and commerce, 258–9, 260*m*; Korean occupation by, 374–5, 375*f*; map, 254*m*; shipbuilding, 470; sinicizing of nomadic peoples, 254; technological developments, 261*f*; trade networks, 254; Wang Mang, Red Eyebrow Revolt, 254–5; writing system development, 254; Wudi, Emperor, 190, 253–4, 259, 265, 375*f*, 396

Hanseatic League trading alliance, 338, 510

Harappa, 3*f*; archaeological investigations, 66–7; architectural uniformity in, 70–2; cesspits (toilets), 71; collapse of, 75–6; diet, 72; geographic description, 68; identity/government, 72–3; late and mature periods, 69*f*; Lothal seaport, 74–5, 74*f*, 75*f*; map, 71*m*; regional crafts of, 74–5; religion, 75; social organization, 68; as "the gift of the Indus," 70; trade networks, 73–4; urban planning system, 68; vanished origins of, 67–76; writing system, 67, 68

Hardy, Thomas, 817

Harlem Renaissance (U.S.), 865–6

Harsha Vardhana regime (India), 346–7, 347*f*

Hasmonean (Maccabean) kingdom, 183*f*, 203–4

Hastings, Battle of (England), 318

Hatshepsut (female "king" in New Kingdom Egypt), 43

Hausa Kingdoms (Africa), 567, 569

Hawley Tariff (1930), 868

Hebrew Bible, 55–6, 60

Hegel, Georg Wilhelm Friedrich, 809

Hegemony system (defined), 107

Heian period (Japan), 235, 267, 273*f*, 372, 375*f*, 379, 385–6, 386*m*, 390

Heliocentric model (of Copernicus), 460*f*, 497*f*

Heliodorus of Emesa, 155

Hellenistic period, Greece, 188–9

Hendrix, Jimi, 942*f*

Henry IV (German emperor), 324

Henry IV (King of France), 497*f*

Henry the Navigator, 466, 570–1, 576

Herder, Johann Gottfried, 676–7

Hertz, Heinrich Rudolf, 801

Herzegovina, ethnic-nationalist uprisings, 769

Heyerdahl, Thor, 146

Hezbollah, terrorist organization, 980, 981, 982, 985

Hidalgo y Costilla, Miguel, 702–3

Hideyoshi, Toyotomi: brief unification achieved by, 647; dream of conquering China, 627; military campaigns of, 626–7, 631, 644, 645–6, 646*m*

Hieroglyphic writing, Egypt, 46*f*, 46

Hindenberg, Paul von, 880

Hinduism: avatars and alvars, 232; caste system and, 235; contributions to cultural stability, 224; defined, 223; devotional branches, 224; Gupta leadership preference for, 218, 223, 232, 236, 239, 368; Maratha wars, 608, 610, 623, 625; maturation of, 231–3, 346; origins, 67, 85, 88, 91, 223 (*See also* Vedas); sacred texts of, 240; sexually-oriented temple carvings, 85; Shakti and tantra, 232–3; in southern India states, 347; spread of, 241; term derivation, 85

Hirobumi, Ito, 728–9, 753–4

Hiroshige, Ando, 654

Hispaniola: African slave trade, 460*f*, 567*f*, 580; colonization of, 141; Cortés, Hernán, 532–3, 532–4, 537, 538; French colonization, 541, 581; Pizarro, Francisco, 534; Saint-Domingue colony, 541, 581, 591, 660, 669, 672; trade network, 549

Hitler, Adolf, 76; eugenics and, 867; Final Solution against Jews, 854*f*, 859*f*, 883; invasion of Soviet Union, 882–3; *Mein Kampf*, 880, 883; Munich Agreement, 881–2; Mussolini's seeking of relations with, 879; rise to Chancellor, 859*f*; rise to power, 880–2; scientific-industrial future desired by, 891. *See also* Nazi Germany

Hittite Empire: collapse of, 54; empire building, 49–51; "great kings" self-labeling, 49–50; iron making mastery, 35*f*, 49; map, 50*m*; military preparedness, 49, 50; origins, 3*f*; political system, 57

Hobbes, Thomas, 507–8, 673

Hobsbawm, Eric, 658

Hobson, John A., 850

Ho Chi Minh, 922, 923, 931, 943

Hokusai, Katsushika, 654

Holy Christian League, 478

Hominins: Ardi (*Ardipithecus ramidus)*, 6–7, 29; australopiths, 7–8, 7*f*, 10–11; bipedalism of, 8; defined, 6; *Homo erectus*, 6, 7*f*, 8–10, 11, 19, 30, 31; Lucy (Hadar AL 288-1) discovery, 4–5, 7*f*, 8; Orrorins, 6, 7*f*; Toumaï, 2, 6, 7

Homo erectus, 6, 7*f*, 8–10, 11, 19, 30, 31

Homo floresiensis, 11

Homo habilis ("the handy human"), 8

Homo neanderthalensis, 26, 27

Homo sapiens (modern human): bow and arrow development, 26; brain size comparison, 9; characteristics, 13; creation of symbols, 13–14; Cro-Magnons, 19; Dreamtime, 17–18, 31; exodus from Africa, 14–15; figurines, rock paintings, 14, 20–2, 20*f*, 21*f*, 31; gender relations, 12–13; Ice Age survival challenges, 24; livelihood of, 11–12; mental life development, 13; migration to Australia, 16, 26; migration to Europe, 19, 26, 27; Neanderthal comparisons with, 19; origins, 2*f*, 7*f*, 11, 96; relation to *H. erectus*, 11; Siberian *H. sapiens*, 28; survival skills of, 23, 31; toolmaking skills, 11–12, 14

Hoover, Herbert, 868

Hopewell culture (North America), 139, 140*m*

Hothousing cultural traditions, Japan, 653–4

House Committee on Un-American Activities, 928

House of Burgesses (colonial America), 546

House of Commons (Britain), 318, 337, 518, 596, 792

House of Lords (Britain), 318, 754

Howl (Ginsberg), 928

Huang Zongxi (Qing philosopher), 643

Hughes, Langston, 866

Huguenots (Protestants), 516

Humanism, 339, 341496

Human origins, 4–31; African origins, 11–14; agricultural centers, 3; Americas, migrations to, 24, 25*m*, 26–7; Asia to Europe migration, 19–22; bipedalism/environmental adaptability, 8; empires, 3, 3*f*; hominins ancestry, 2, 4–11, 19, 29, 30–1; Ice Age crisis, 22–4, 23*m*; Kennewick Man, 28–9; Paleoindians, 28; South Asia to Australia migration, 14–19; up to 3 million years ago, 9*m*. *See also* Fossil discoveries

Human sacrifice: Aztec Empire, 454–5; propaganda and, 454–5; Teotihuacán kingdom, Mexican Basin, 172

Hundred Flowers campaign (China), 912

Hundred Years' War, 313*f*, 335–8, 336*f*, 343

Hungary, Cold War era revolt, 902–3

Hunting-and-gathering society. *See* Foragers (hunters and gatherers)

Hurston, Zora Neale, 866

Husák, Gustáv, 934

Hussein, Saddam, 970–1

Hutchinson, Anne, 559

Hutu genocide, 570, 855*f*, 967*f*

Ibangala, 576, 594

Iberia: apocalyptic expectations, 466; Christian expansion, 464, 466, 467–8; early human evidence, 7; Franciscan military orders of, 464, 466; Habsburg Empire incorporation, 483; land grants for military leaders, 479

Iberian Berbers, 278

Iberian Muslims (moriscos), 478–9

Ibn Abdallah, Muhammad Ahmad, 837

Ibn Abd al-Wahhab, Muhammad, 766

Ibn Ayyub, Salah al-Din Yusuf, 291

Ibn Battuta, Abu Abdallah, 356, 359, 416, 469

Ibn Khaldun, Abd al-Rahman, 301

Ibn Munqidh, Usama, 296

Ibn Musa al-Khwarizmi, Muhammad, 301

Ibn Qasim, Muhammad, 344–5

Ibn Rushd (Averroes), 301

Ibn Sina (Avicenna), 301, 329

Ibn Taymiyya, Taqi al-Din, 308

Ibn Tughluq, Muhammad ("Muhammad the Bloody"), 349–50

ICBMs. *See* Intercontinental ballistic missiles

Ice Age, 15; art, 22*f*; Beringia land bridge, 24, 26, 28; ending of, 2*f*, 35*f*; land bridge connections, 15–16; living conditions, 22–4, 29, 31; map of, 23*m*

Iconoclasm controversy, in Byzantium, 284–5

Ife Kingdom (West African rain forest), 273*f*, 407*f*, 427–9

"I Have a Dream" speech (King), 940

Illustrated Gazetteer of the Maritime Countries (Wei Yuan), 750

Imperialism: in Africa, 821; in the Aksum kingdom, 156–7; in Asia, 821; of the Aztecs, 445, 454; of China, 730–9; in Egypt, 51; of Europe, 819; of Great Britain, 687, 825*f*; of the Habsburgs, 475, 491; of the Incas, 454; of Japan, 740–1; in Korea, 740–1; in the Mediterranean, 148, 181; in the Middle East, 148, 181; of the Ottomans, 475, 479, 481, 491, 762–5; in Persian Empire, 187; of Russia, 774, 784. *See also* New imperialism

Impression, Sunrise painting (Monet), 793*f*, 818

Inca Empire (Andes), 273*f*; artistic achievements, 456; Atahualpa's leadership, 533*f*, 535–6, 536*f*; Charles V rulership, 474; communications structure, 449–50; conquest of, 534–6; Cuzco city, 176, 446–7, 449, 452–3, 535–6; founding myth, 446; government administration, 447–8; housing arrangements, 453; imperial expansion, 447; *khipu* coded communications, 121, 131, 448; map (1525 CE), 446*m*; military organization, 449; Ming/Qing government comparison, 447; *mit'a* taxation system, 447–8, 449, 453, 540, 697; mummy veneration, 455–6; origins, 433; road networks, 448*f*, 449; ruling class, gender relations, 454–5; sacred object arrangements, 176; size comparison, 450; Spain's conquest of, 461*f*; Spanish conquest of, 461*f*, 474, 483, 532, 534–6; Tawantinsuyu Empire, 446; timeline placement, 273*f*, 435*f*; Túpac Amaru burial site, 432–3; weaponry, 449

Indentured laborers, in the Caribbean, 582

India, 216–43; adaptation by Gangetic societies, 89; Alexander's campaigns, 188, 216, 217, 219, 219*f*, 242; ancient republics, 242; artistic, literary achievements, 240; Bharatiya Janata Party, 986; British "divide and rule" tactics, 829–31; British "new imperialism" in, 824–31, 825*f*, 826*m*, 829*m*; Buddhist archaeological sites, 66; caste system, 69*f*, 84, 85, 86–7, 88–9, 91, 235–8; Chola state, 347, 347*f*; Christian missionaries in, 826; civil service system, 828–30, 918; cultural clashes within, 345–51; Da Gama's journey to, 468, 476, 535, 610; Delhi Sultanate, 272*f*, 347*f*, 349–50, 350*m*; dharma, 82, 83–5, 89; economic/

political nonalignment, 919, 922; economics, of Islamic India, 350–1; empire consolidation in, 148; entrepreneurial growth, 977; family life/Hindu culture, 238; feminist writers, 945; Gandhi, Indira, leadership, 624, 895; Ganges River, urban life, 69f; Ganges states, power centralization, 80–1; gender roles, 84–5, 239; Ghaznavid Sultanate, 349–50; gods and priests, 85–6; "golden age," 346; Harsha Vardhana regime, 346–7, 347f; Hinduism, post-Guptas, 346–8; independence gained by, 854f, 873, 897f, 917–19; Indo-European migration to, 49, 69f; influence outside of India, 234–5; Islam in, 348–50; Maratha revolt, 610; Maratha wars, 608, 610, 623, 625; Mehrgarh culture, 69f, 70; monsoon system, 68–70, 69m; Mughal invasion of Delhi, 601f; Muslim trading in, 347; nabobs, 824–5; Nehru's leadership, 917, 918–19; new middle class, 986–7; Northern India, 66, 79–80, 83m; northern India map, 218m; Northern Sultanates, 349–50; Pallava state, 347f; patterns of state formation, 217–26; physical features, 69m; Progressive Organization for Women, 945; Rajputs, 349, 602, 625, 830; rape of Bengal, 824; regional struggles, 225–6; religion in, 76, 78–9, 85–9, 91; reunification under Gupta Empire, 149f, 219f, 346; rice cultivation, 79–80, 94, 218, 221, 614; rulership ideology, 81–2; Sanskrit language, 69f, 76, 77–8, 86, 208, 226, 229, 240, 266; Sanskrit language development, 69f; Sasanid transmission of texts of, 208; science, math achievements, 240–1; Sepoy Mutiny, 659f, 824, 825f, 827–8; shifting agrarian centers, 66–91; *smriti* law codes, 84; social class, 83–4; southern India dynasties, 348m; southern kingdoms, 223–6; spread of Buddhism from, 345; subalterns in, 830–1; taxation, acceleration of, 233–4; taxation in, 80, 347–8, 350, 609, 613–15, 619; temple complexes, 225; trade and expansion, 217, 219, 221, 225, 227, 234–5, 236–7, 237f, 348m; unification of, 219f; urban life, 69f, 70–5; Vijayanagar state, 272f, 347–8, 347f; wage comparison, 976–7. *See also* Aryans; Aurangzeb; Babur; Gandhi, Mohandas K.; Gupta Empire; Harappa; Hinduism; Indus Valley; Jainism; Mauryan Empire; Mohenjo-Daro; Mughal Empire; Northern India; Sikhs and Sikhism; Vedic society
Indian National Congress, 917
Indian Removal Act (U.S.), 685

Indian sacred texts: Bhagavad Gita, 82, 83, 220, 232; Puranas, 82, 238, 240; Upanishads, 69f, 88, 89, 218, 226, 227, 229, 240. *See also* Vedas
Indonesia: African contact, 161–2; agriculture, 143; animal domestication, 143; Buddhism in, 162f; commercial networks, 162; cultivation system in, 825f, 845; Dutch colonialism in, 845; employment of slaves, 577; fossil discoveries, 10–11, 30; Hinduism in, 241; Ice Age influences, 15, 22; Indianization in, 225, 234; Krakatau volcano eruption, 196; land bridge connections to, 15, 24; migrations to, 14, 24, 26, 131, 141, 151, 360, 382, 545; monsoon system, 68; 1990s, global hierarchy, 966; trade networks, 161–2, 234, 298, 347
Industrialism (1750–1870): in Belgium, 784; factory systems, 784, 793–4; in France, 784; global commerce, 795; in Great Britain, 784, 791–5, 794m; preconditions, 792; spread of, 795–6; technologies, power sources, 793; transportation, 795; in the U.S., 796
Industrialism (1871–1914): chemical manufacturing, 799–800; communication revolution, 801; electricity, development and applications, 800–1; in Europe (map), 797m; in Japan, 797; in Russia, 797; steel manufacturing, 796–7; weaponry advances, 801–2
Industrialism (1750–1914), social and economic impact, 803–13; demographic changes, 803–4; electricity/sanitation improvements, 811–12; European migrations, 803–4, 806m; factory towns, 807–8; inquiries and reforms, 809–10; intellectual/cultural responses to, 814–18; jobs for women, 810–11; large firms, growth of, 812–13; leisure time and sports, 812; literature and the arts, 817–18; management style advances, 813; middle class society, 806; philosophy and religion, 816–17; population surge, urbanization, 803; socialist criticism of, 808–9; upper class society, 805–6; woman's suffrage movement, 811; working class society, 806–7; world population growth, 804m–805m
Industrial Revolution, 352, 495, 630, 635, 718–19, 734f, 750, 761, 791
Indus Valley: Arab-Persian conquest of, 277f; archaeological discoveries, 66, 67, 72; collapse of civilization in, 76; Harappan system of cities in, 90; religion in, 85; rise of, as agrarian center, 37, 89, 115; urban life adaptations, 70–6. *See also* Harappa
Infanticide, 365, 641, 653, 950

Infant mortality rates, 991
Information technology, 968–9
The Ingenious Gentleman Don Quixote of La Mancha (Cervantes), 492
Innocent III (Pope), 325, 327, 342
Inquiry into the Nature and Causes of the Wealth of Nations (Smith), 675
Institutes of the Christian Religion (Calvin), 514–15
Institutional Revolutionary Party (Partido Revolucionario Institucional), 874
Intercontinental ballistic missiles (ICBMs), 903, 931
International Monetary Fund (IMF), 974–5
Internet, 801, 968, 970, 977, 984, 986. *See also* Social networking
The Interpretation of Dreams (Freud), 793f, 816
Inuit culture, 123f, 138–9
Ionia, 35f, 57
Iran: Ahmadinejad's leadership, 982; Buyids Shiite Dynasty, 415, 772; CIA inspired coup d'etat, 897f; conquests of, 272f, 292; discovery of oil, 859f; overthrow of Shah of Iran, 855f; potential nuclear bomb, 977; Qajar Dynasty, 771–2, 774–5, 787; Shiite Islam in, 281. *See also* Safavid Persian Empire; Sasanid Persian Empire
Iraq: Abbasid influences in, 279; agricultural limitations, 282; Arab conquests of, 272f, 276, 277f, 285, 288, 292, 406; Arab Spring participation, 985; Buyids Shiite Dynasty, 415, 772; coping with Western challenges, 771, 774–5; ISIS Jihadist movement, 967f; *Mamluks* slave revolt, 766; porcelain technology, 367, 632; Shiite Islam in, 281; U.S. invasion of, 967, 970–1. *See also* Abbasid Dynasty; Sasanid Persian Empire
Iron Age, 51–2; Hittite iron smelting, 35f; onset of, 51–2, 445; shipbuilding application, 470–1; South African site analysis, 161; western Mediterranean adaption to, 191
Iron casting technology (China), 114–15
Iroquois, Native Americans, 543, 546
ISIS (Islamic State in Iraq and al-Sham) jihadist organization, 967f, 985
Islamic civilization: Abbasids Dynasty, 198, 275; architectural achievements, 302–3; artistic achievements, 302–3; Christian architectures in, 212; commonwealth, development of, 275; educational sponsorships, 207; Ibn Battuta's journeys, 469; in India, 348–50; jihad (holy war), tenet of Islam, 281; legal/judicial system, 281; literary achievements, 302; map of commonwealth, 283m; map of conquests, 278m; in Nubia, Africa, 409; Ottoman dominance, 473; philosophy and sciences, 301–2;

religio-political crisis, 278–9; Saharan kingdoms, 162; scientific developments, 207; Sharia law, 281, 307, 308; spice trade, 237; state-religion separation, 281; Sunni Islam, 277*f*, 281, 282, 301, 309, 415; in Swahili city-states, 414–15. *See also* Byzantine Empire; Fatimid Dynasty; Islam religion; Mamluk Egypt; Seljuk Empire

Islamic Sufi brotherhood, 837

Islamism, 964–5, 980, 984, 988

Islam religion: origins, 276–9; Quran (holy scripture), 279–81, 305, 307, 308; Ramadan holy month, 281, 485–6, 822, 933, 954; salvation/apocalypse themes, 201–2; spread of, in Africa, 840*m*; Sunni-Sufi Islam, 300–1, 302, 307; theology and origins, 279–81; Umayyad Empire, 277. *See also* Muhammad (Prophet of Islam); Shiite Islam (Shiism); Sunni Islam (Sunnism)

Israel: Arab-Israeli conflicts, 854*f*, 897*f*, 933*f*; Balfour Declaration, 859*f*; failed Lebanon invasion, 982; founding of, 854*f*, 897*f*; invasion of Gaza and, 981–2; 1947-1949 Palestine Conflict, 914–15, 915*m*; post-WW II Soviet support for, 915; Six Day War, 933*f*, 953–4; Suez War vs. Egypt, 897*f*; Yom Kippur/Ramadan War, 933*f*, 954, 967. *See also* Jews and Judaism

Israelite Ark of the Covenant, 411

Israelites, 35*f*, 53, 55–6

Isthmus Declaration (Rome), 192

Italy: architecture, 212, 487; aristocracy/landholders, 192; Byzantium's influence on, 469; canon law development, 329; city-states, 185, 191, 339, 424, 464; ethnolinguistic nationalism in, 680–1; fascist ideology in, 857, 878; Germanic invasions of, 194, 198, 319, 463; Habsburg actions in, 483; Hanseatic League, 338; Leo Africanus visit, 463; literary achievements, 339; medieval medical advances, 329; Mussolini's march on Rome, 859*f*; 1936 empire map, 871*m*; Norman invasions, 320, 326, 328; plague outbreak, 331; post-Black Death population recovery, 509; Renaissance activities, 306, 487, 498; rise of centralized government, 510t; Roman papacy in, 313, 318; trade networks, 186, 292; unification of, 189, 191, 663*f*; urban growth, 322. *See also* Roman Empire

Ito Hirobumi, 728, 753–4

Iturbide, Agustín de, 703

Itzcóatl, 443

Ixtlixóchitl, Fernando de Alva, 558

Jainism, 67, 223; challenges created by, 232; description of doctrine, 227; Chandragupta Maurya embrace of,

223; influences on caste system, 237–8; origins, 67, 218, 219*f*, 226

Jamaica, 411–12, 541, 561, 567*f*, 581, 593

James, Henry, 690

Jamestown, Virginia, settlement, 461*f*, 533*f*, 543, 545, 583–4

Janissaries (military troops), 480–1, 482, 484, 763, 766–7, 774, 832

Japan: adaptations made by, 381–94; agricultural advances, 389–90; Ainu culture, 28, 382, 389; annexation of Manchuria, 859*f*, 886, 887; artistic achievements, 387–8, 756; Ashikaga Shogunate, 375*f*, 387, 388, 389, 644–5; Battle of Sekigahara, 646; Buddhism in, 345, 390, 391–2; Christian missionaries in, 637; climate, 381, 384*m*; cultural developments, 393–4; early settlement, 17; economy of, 389; Edo as largest city, 461*f*; empire creation, 746–7; Equal Employment Opportunity Law, 945; family structure, 390–1; feudalism in, 387, 401; geographic position, 381; Great Britain's alliance with, 731*f*; Heian period, 235, 267, 273*f*, 372, 375*f*, 379, 385–6, 386*m*, 390; imperial order in, 384–5; import substitution industrialization, 968; industrialism in, 797; influence in China, 735*m*; interwar militaristic expansion, 885–6; Jomon period, 374, 382–3; Kamakura Shogunate, 375*f*, 387; *kokutai*, 856–7; Korea occupation by, 728; land bridge, migration to, 14, 24; land limitations, 381; Liberal Democratic Party, 754; literary achievements, 273*f*, 372, 375*f*, 390, 393–4; Mandate of Heaven, 385; matriarchal/matrilineal clans, 382–3; Meiji Constitution, 797; Meiji Restoration era, 659*f*; microlith artifacts in, 382; middle class savings rate, 977; militaristic expansion, 885–6; modernization (to 1910), 753*m*; Mongol invasion attempts, 387, 388*m*; nation-state creation, 745–6; Neo-Confucianism in, 391; Nichiren Buddhism in, 392, 402; supremacist nationalism, 856–7; nuclear crisis, 855*f*, 967*f*; Onin War, 645; onset of Shogun title, 386; Perry's trade missions, 656, 658*f*, 731*f*, 744–5, 752, 755–6, 797; phallic symbols in, 382; population, food, commerce, 650–1; printing technology in, 382–3; Rape of Nanjing, 859*f*, 888–9; reaction to modernity, 758; Restoration War, 731*f*; rice cultivation, 383–4, 388, 389–90; Russo-Japanese War, 659*f*, 729, 763*f*, 782, 784–5; sake brewing, 389; sakoku seclusion policies, 656; samurai warriors, 387–9, 393, 401, 402, 648, 652–3; Seiyukai government founding,

731*f*; Shimonoseki Treaty with China, 728–9, 740–2; Shinto religion in, 380, 385, 390, 391, 590; Sino-Japanese War, 659*f*, 728–30, 729–30, 731*f*, 746, 785, 886; student demonstrations, 942–3; territorial expansion, 746*m*; theater traditions, 653–4; timeline of events, 375*f*; topography, 384*m*; transport routes (ca. 1800), 651*m*; Treaty of Shimonoseki, 729; Treaty of Tianjin, 746–7; Triple Intervention against, 729, 747, 785; unification struggles, 644–6; urban population (ca. 1800), 651*m*; World War II defeat, 911; World War I participation, 730, 860; Yamato period, 258, 373, 375*f*, 384–5, 389, 391; Yayoi period, 375*f*, 382–3, 388; Zen Buddhism in, 267, 377, 388, 392–3, 402, 624. *See also* Hideyoshi, Toyotomi; Meiji era; Tokugawa Shogunate

Jefferson, Thomas, 666

Jenné-jeno city-state, West Africa, 153*f*, 157–8

Jesuit missionaries, 461*f*

Jews and Judaism: adoption of Zoroastrianism, Greek philosophy, 149; beliefs of, 181; circumcision law, 205; England's expulsion of, 323; Final Solution of Hitler, 854*f*, 859*f*, 883; First Crusade, attacks against, 323; founding of Christianity, 149; founding of Second Temple, 203; genocide in Europe, 859*f*, 883; in Great Britain, 871; Kabbala traditions, 620; in Mamluk Egypt, 294; in medieval Europe, 323; migrations to Ottoman Empire, Portugal, 467; in Palestine, 203–4, 203*m*, 783, 871–2; in Persia, 195, 203; post-WW I anti-Semitism, 866; promise of a "national home," 871; Savior/apocalypse themes, 201–2; Second Temple kingdom, 206; settlements, map, 204*m*; Soviet release of Jews to Israel, 915; Spain's expulsion of, 460*f*, 467; synagogues, 204

Jihad (holy war), tenet of Islam, 281

Jinnah, Ali Muhammad, 917

Joan of Arc, 336

Johanson, Donald, 4, 7*f*

Johnson, James Weldon, 866

Johnson, Lyndon B., 933*f*, 940, 952

John XII (Pope), 318

Jomon period (Japan), 374, 382–3

Juárez, Benito, 705–6

Justinian, Plague of, 196, 196*m*, 299

Justinian I (the Great), Roman Emperor, 198–200, 262, 285*f*, 329

Justinian's *Codex*, 198, 281

Kabbala traditions, 620

Kádár, János, 933

Kahun Papyrus, 62

Kamakura Shogunate (Japan), 375*f*, 387

Kama Sutra, 85

Kanagawa, Treaty of, 745

Kanem-Bornu caliphate (Africa), 567*f*, 569

Kangxi Emperor (Ming Dynasty, China), 634, 637

Kant, Immanuel, 674–5, 687

Karadžić, Radovan, 979

Karlowitz, Treaty of, 764*m*

Karman, Tawakkol, 965

Karma-samsara concept, 88–9

Kebra Negast, 411

Kemal, Mustafa, 872

Kennan, George F., 897

Kennedy, John F., 904, 905, 923, 932, 940

Kennedy, Robert, 943

Kennewick man fossil, 7*f*, 28, 29*f*, 125

Kepler, Johannes, 497*f*

Kerouac, Jack, 928

Khipu writing system (Caral-Supé valley, Peru), 131

Khomeini, Ayatollah Ruhollah, 773, 982

Khosrow I, King of Persia, 199–200

Khosrow II, King of Persia, 212, 276

Khrushchev, Nikita, 896, 902–5, 910–11, 916, 932, 933*f*

Khubilai Khan, Yuan Emperor, 358, 359*f*

Khufu, Pharaoh of Egypt, 45

Kikuchi, Takeo, 856

King, Martin Luther, Jr., 940, 943

King Leopold's Role in Africa (Morel), 852

King List (2125 BCE), 41

King's Peace (Persia-Greece), 187

Kipling, Rudyard, 852

Kishwar, Madhu, 945

Knox, John, 514

Koguryo Kingdom (Korea), 376

Kongo Kingdom (Africa): Atlantic slave trade, 575–6; Capuchin Catholic monks, 564–5; Christianity in, 575; Pedro V (King), 565; relations with Portugal, 575–6; St. Anthony, Christian cult, 590; sub-Saharan map, 568*m*

Korea: agriculture, 374, 375; Altaic-speaking peoples, 374; Buddhism in, 230, 243, 258, 266, 272, 273, 345, 373, 376, 380; class structure, 379; climate, 374; egalitarianism in, 380; ethnic origins, 374; geography/environment, 373–4; Han China occupation, 374–5, 375*f*; *Han-gul* phonetic writing system, 375*f*, 380–1; Hideyoshi's attempted invasion of, 631; history/politics (to 1598), 374–8; iron smelting technology, 375; Japanese occupation of, 728; Koguryo Kingdom, 376; Koryo Kingdom, 273*f*, 375*f*, 377–8, 377*m*, 380; land bridge connections, 14, 24; land reforms, 378–9; language development, 117, 245; map, 500 CE, 376*m*; matrilocal marriage patterns, 380; Mongol expansion into, 377–8; name derivation, 273*f*; Neo-Confucian influences, 379; North Korea, 900–1,

963, 976, 982, 996; Paekche Kingdom, 376, 385, 391; Parhae Kingdom, 375*f*; printing advances in, 380; printing presses in, 268; printing technology in, 382–3; rice cultivation, 374, 378, 380; Silk Road trade route, 345; Silla Kingdom, 376, 377, 378–9, 380, 385; South Korea, 900–1, 963, 966, 975, 996; state formation tensions, 373; Sui Dynasty invasion, 257, 375*f*; Tang Dynasty invasion, 375*f*; Three Kingdoms era, 375*f*, 376, 377, 378–9, 380, 385; timeline of events, 375*f*; topography, precipitation, 375*m*; Treaty of Tianjin, 746–7; women and society, 379–80; Yi Dynasty, 375*f*, 378–80, 400; Zhou China contacts with, 374, 375

Korean War, 854*f*, 897*f*, 900

Koryo Kingdom (Korea), 273*f*, 375*f*, 377–8, 377*m*, 380

Kosok, Paul, 178

Kosygin, Aleksey, 933*f*

Ku Klux Klan, 865*f*, 866

Kuwait, U.S. invasion of, 967*f*

Kyoto Protocol (1997), 993, 994

Labor assignments (*repartimiento* system), 532, 540, 548

Labor unions, 707, 708, 808, 865, 878, 910, 943

Land Code (Ottomans), 768

Land-labor grants (Spanish *encomiendas*), 532, 533

Langland, William, 339–40

La Niña weather phenomenon, 125

Laozi, 247*f*

Lapita cultural complex (Western Pacific), 3*f*, 123*f*, 141–3, 145

Latin America: agricultural self-sufficiency, 722; American/French Revolution influences, 662; Azurduy's leadership, 694–5; "banana republic" labeling of, 724–5; Bolívar/San Martín's discussion, 700–1; Catholic Reformation influence, 559; caudillo authoritarian regimes, 697–701, 697*f*, 698, 701–2, 707, 710, 717, 727; coffee boom, 713–14, 718; constitutional nationalism in, 716; coolie migrations map, 721*m*; debt burden consequences, 975; democratic transitions, 990; "disappearances" of citizens, 959–60; economy/economic recovery, 715*m*, 717–18; 18th/19th century Enlightenment, 695–6; ethnic composition, 553–4, 554*f*, 597; expansion, 990–1; export-led growth, 718–23; factories, 722–3; family relations, 723–4; increasing poverty in, 976; independence achieved by, 716; labor and immigrants, 720–1; nation-state growth, 704*m*; nation-state republicanism, 696; political divisions,

post-independence, 716–17; populist wave, 909–10, 909*f*; "positivism" philosophy influences, 688; post-World War I recovery, 874; post-WW II, rural and urban society, 908–9; post-WW I recovery, 874; proxy wars, 958–60; raw materials, cash crops, 718–19; reconstruction era, 715–18; rise of living standards, 720; role of the church, 723; rural infrastructure development, 722; split over church-state relations, 717; transformations to democracy, 967; U.S. training of dissidents in, 903–4; visual and literary arts, 724. *See also* Central America; Creoles; Haiti; Mexico; South America

Latin Christendom, 273, 296, 305, 306, 311–12, 336

Law Code of Hammurabi, 42, 43, 44–5

The Law of the Kings (Fetha Nagast), 412–13

Lawrence, T. E., 871

League of Nations, 854*f*, 859*f*, 862, 869, 879

Le Dynasty (Vietnam), 375*f*, 397, 399–400

Legalism (Ancient China), 245, 246, 247*f*, 249, 250, 264, 269, 271

Legal systems: of the Achaemenid Empire, 183–4; of China, 269, 364; of France, 668; of India, 84, 221; of Italy, 329; Justinian's *Codex*, 198, 281; Law Code of Hammurabi, 42, 43, 44–5; of the Ottoman Empire, 480–1; of the Roman Empire, 198; of Russia, 975; of Sharia law, 281, 307, 308; Sumerian law code, 44

Legge, James, 244

Lejju, B. Julius, 159

Lenin, Vladimir Ilyich: Bolshevik Party leadership, 785–6, 860, 875–6; creation of provisional government, 860; founding of Soviet Union, 850; views on imperialism, capitalism, 850; *What Is to Be Done?*, 786, 788, 875

Lennon, John, 928

Leo Africanus ("Leo the African"), 462–3

Leo III (Pope), 314

Leo X (Pope), 462

Lepanto, Battle of, 465, 478, 478*f*

Leviathan (Hobbes), 507

Lewis-Williams, J. David, 21

Liberal Democratic Party (Japan), 754

Library of Alexandria, 206–7

The Life of Harsha (Bana), 346

Light bulb, incandescent (Edison), 793*f*

Lincoln, Abraham, 683, 691

Literary achievements: of Afghanistan, 302; of China, 111, 113, 117, 356, 367–8, 642, 750; of Egypt, 60; of Europe, 15th century, 339–40; of European Enlightenment era, 675; of European Renaissance, 487, 496–7; of Greece, 209–10; Harlem Renaissance, NY, 866; of India, 85, 240, 620; of the industrialism period, 817; of Islamic civilization, 302; of Italy, 339; of Japan,

273f, 372, 375f, 390, 393–4; of Latin America, 724; of Mesopotamia, 60, 209; of the Olmecs, 138; realism, in prose literature, 688–90; of Rome, 210, 212; of the Spanish Habsburgs, 489–90; of the U.S., post-WW II, 928. *See also* Writing developments

Liu Shaoqi, 913, 946, 947

Locke, John, 507–8, 557, 658–9, 664, 673, 674

Long Count Calendar (Mayas), 167

Longshan culture (China), 95f, 97–8

Lorentz, Hendrik, 814

Lothal seaport (Harappa), 74–5, 74f, 75f

Louis XIV, King of France, 497f, 664

Louis XVI, King of France, 679

Louis XVIII, King of France, 679

Luba Kingdom (Central Africa), 407f, 420–1, 421m, 431, 569

Lucy (Hadar AL 288-1), 4–5, 7f, 8

Luddites movement (Great Britain), 820

Lumumba, Patrice, 925–6

Luther, Martin, 339, 460f, 497f, 513–14. *See also* Protestant Reformation

Lynch, B. M., 150

Lynchings, of African Americans, 683, 865f, 866

MacArthur, Douglas, 901

Macartney, Lord George, 730–1

Macauley, Thomas B., 827

Macedonian Empire, 148, 181, 187–9, 215

Machiavelli, Niccolò, 497

Machine guns, 659f, 738, 793f, 802, 819, 821, 830, 840

Madame Bovary (Flaubert), 690

Madero, Francisco, 708

Magellan, Ferdinand, 537f, 846

The Magic Flute opera (Mozart), 675

Magna Carta ("the Great Charter"), 313f, 318

Mahayana Buddhism, 230–1, 239, 345, 352, 398–9

Mahmud of Ghazna, 347f, 348–9, 368

Mali Empire (West Africa): adaption to Islam in, 405; central administration, 426; decentralization of, 426; Eurasian empire comparison, 567; institutions of servitude, 574; Mansa Sundiata of, 407f, 430; military power, 426; origin, 422, 424–6; Sankoré Mosque, 427f; slave trade, 574; timeline placement, 273f, 407f; trade network, 424, 426, 569. *See also* Songhay Empire

Mamluk Egypt: Black Death in, 272f, 299–300; commercial development, 297–300; conquest of Nubia, 409; economy, 294; establishment in Egypt, 292; French defeat of, 832f; gender relations, 296; military units, 293f; Mongol campaigns against, 292; ruling class, 293–4; state and society in, 293–6; taxation in, 293–4, 296, 298–9;

timeline placement, 277f; urban working population, 294–5

Manchuria, 104; border uprisings, 355; Choson Kingdom in, 374; establishment of borders, 638; geography, 373–4; Japanese annexation of, 859f, 886, 887; Japanese invasion, occupation of, 729, 740, 785; Parhae Kingdom in, 375f; Sino-Japanese War and, 785; soybean introduced by, 109; Trans-Siberian Railroad passage through, 747, 785

Mandate of Heaven (China), 104–6, 119, 246, 248, 265, 385

Mandate of Heaven (Japan), 385

Mandela, Nelson, 855f, 958, 962, 965, 967f, 987, 990f

Manorialism, in medieval Europe, 316–17, 316f

Mansa Musa, King of Mali, 426

Manumission (defined), 584

Mao Zedong (Chairman Mao), 887, 888, 891, 900–1, 911, 943, 947–8

Mapping the world, 508–9

Mapungubwe Kingdom (Southern Africa), 407f, 418–19

Maratha wars (India), 608, 610, 623, 625

Marconi, Guglielmo, 793f, 801

Marcus, Siegfried, 800

Marie-Antoinette, Queen of France, 666–7, 666f

Maritime trade (China), 730–3

Marne, Battle of the (1914), 859

Marshall, George C., 897

Marshall Plan, 897, 899, 906, 910

Martel, Charles ("the Hammer"), 312

Marx, Karl, 492, 658f, 682, 788, 793f, 808, 809, 809f, 875, 887

Marxism, 699, 785, 787, 875, 878, 911

Mass consumption culture, post-World War II, 906

Mathematical physics (Galileo), 461f, 497f, 500–1, 508

Mathematics: beginnings of, 61–2; China and, 267; Descarte's contributions, 507; in Egypt, 62, 206; Euclid's contributions, 500–1; Grosseteste's contributions, 330; India and, 240–1, 616, 617–18; Jesuits' contributions, 637; Mayas and, 167; Newton's contributions, 502; women and, 503

Matriarchal/matrilineal clans, in Japan, 382–3

Mauritania sites, in Africa, 152m

Maurya, Chandragupta, 217, 219, 228

Mauryan Empire (India): Ashoka, reign of, 220–2, 221m, 235–6; burial mounds, 230f; decline of, 222, 234; onset of religious changes, 231–2; origins, 149f, 218–22; science/math ideas, 240; taxation of wealth, 233–4; unification of India, 219f

Maxim, Hiram, 659f, 793f, 802

Maximilian, Emperor of Mexico, 706–7

Maxwell, James Clerk, 801

Mayan Calendar Round, 167

Mayan kingdoms, southern Mesoamerica, 163–8; alliances of, 437; calendar development, 166–7; civilization map, 164m; classic period, dates, 149f; commoners, 167; crises of the kingdoms, 168–9; decline of, 437; early kingdoms, 165–6; glyphic alphabet, writing, 153f, 168; Mayaland, Yucatán Peninsula, 163–5; Olmec cultural influences, 164; realignment of power, 436–7; ruling classes, 166; spirituality/polytheism, 166; taxation in, 167; timeline placement, 435f. *See also* Chichén Itzá Kingdom

May Fourth Movement (China), 886

McCarthy, Joseph, and McCarthyism, 901

McIntosh, Roderick J., 158

McIntosh, Susan Keech, 158

McKay, Claude, 866

Meat Inspection Act (U.S.), 686

Mecca, 280–1, 414, 472, 485, 607, 620, 841, 871

Medici, Giovanni Leone di. *See* Leo Africanus ("Leo the African")

Medicine: Avicenna's contributions, 350; Byzantine contributions, 329; in China, 99, 731, 751, 826, 886; Copernicus's studies, 500; in early Egypt, 62; French Academy of Medicine, 668; Galen's contributions, 350; in Greece, 305; in India, 83–4, 208, 221–2, 236, 240; Industrial Revolution and, 803; Islamic contributions, 301, 329; Italy, medieval-era advances, 329; Nightingale and, 779; Pasteur's contributions, 816; in Rome, 329–30; use of gunpowder as, 358

Medina, 280

Mehmet II, Conqueror of Constantinople, 470, 471–2, 473f, 481f

Mehrgarh Neolithic culture (India), 69f, 70

Meiji Constitution (Japan), 797

Meiji (Japanese Emperor) era: allowance of Christianity, 650; commerce and cartels, 752–5; constitution and political life, 753–4; cooperation and capitalism, 752; photograph, 744m; political parties, 754; progressive measures of, 745; social experiments, 755; timeline placement, 659f, 731f; transportation, communications revolutions, 752–3

Mein Kampf (Hitler), 880, 883

Mencius (Chinese philosopher), 109–10, 244–5, 247–8, 265, 270

Menes (Egyptian king), 44

Mercantilism in the Caribbean, 580–1

Mernissi, Fatima, 945

Meroë kingdom, Middle Nile (Africa): agricultural production, 152, 155; cultural achievements, 155; decline of,

155–6, 406; description, 148, 152, 153; flourishing of, 151; geography, 155–6; map, 154m; Nubian kingdom and, 155; power structure, 153–4; Roman Empire skirmishes with, 155; timeline, 153f; trade network, 154

Merotic pyramids (Sudan), 150m

Merovingians, role in Christian Europe, 311, 312, 343

Mesoamerica (Mexico and Central America): agrarian villages, 123f; agricultural development, 129, 151, 163; animal/plant domestication, 129–30; ceremonial centers, chiefdoms, 434; Chichén Itzá Kingdom, 273f, 433, 435f, 437–8; climatic zones, 124; corn cultivation, 134–5; cultural prowess of, 150; divinity calendar discovery, 150; geographical regions, 123; kingdom formation, 148; map (1100 CE), 435; pottery production, 130–1; timeline of events, 153f; villages, settlements, 122, 136–8, 153f. See also Aztec Empire; Central America; Inca Empire; Mayan kingdom; Mayan kingdoms, southern Mesoamerica; Mexico; Olmec culture; Teotihuacán kingdom; Tiwanaku state; Toltec culture

Mesopotamia: architectural features, 70; assemblies in, 38; Aztec Empire, 273f; clay tablets, 40, 46, 48; creation myth, 60; cuneiform writing development, 40, 44; drought in, 76; early towns, 6, 38–9; Enuma Elish, creation myth, 35f; Euphrates/Nile floods, 37; kingship in, 41; literature of, 60; location description, 34–5; political system, 57; rule by Sargon of Akkad, 32; science and math, 61–2; sculpture and paintings, 61, 61f; sharecroppers in, 38; temples in, 35f, 39, 59; trade with Harappa, 73; Ubaid period, 59; urban centers in, 37–40, 38m

Mestizos, 553–4, 558, 695, 696, 699, 702, 716–17

Metternich, Klemens von (Chancellor of Austria), 677–8, 680

Mexican-American War, 744

Mexican Basin, 169–70, 173

Mexican Revolution, 697f, 702, 703f, 708, 709, 722

Mexican War of Liberation, 697f, 702–3, 704

Mexico: agriculture, 129; British, Spanish, French forces in, 706; ceremonial centers, chiefdoms, 433, 434; Comanches in northern Mexico, 703–4, 704f; conquest of, 533–4, 533f; corn cultivation, 134; decline of labor assignments, 540; democratic transition, 990; depression years, 874–5; Díaz's leadership, 707–9; early settlements, 122, 123f, 136; 1824–1854, map, 705m; 1496-1750, colonization

map, 539m; Institutional Revolutionary Party, 874; Iturbide's leadership of, 703; Juárez's leadership of, 705–6; map,nation-state growth, 704m; Maximilian's leadership, 706–7; NAFTA participation, 974; 1990s, global hierarchy, 966; Oaxaca stone carvings, 150; post-WW I recovery, 874; pottery making, 131; railroad construction, 708; "Reform War," 705; revolution, early, 708; revolution, late, 709; smallpox epidemic, 555; student demonstrations, 855f; textile manufacturing, 552–3; United States war with, 705; uprising in New Spain, 702; U.S. citizen's emigration to, 705; Valley of Mexico, 433–6, 444m. See also Aztec Empire; Inca Empire; New Spain (Spanish colonial Mexico); Olmec culture; Teotihuacán kingdom, Mexican Basin; Toltec culture

Michelangelo, 498

Microlith artifacts, in Japan, 382

Middens (defined), 128

Middle East: agricultural developments, 3, 29, 152; Arab-Israeli conflicts, 854f, 897f, 933f, 952m, 953m; Arab Spring, 855f, 955, 967f, 980, 981–3, 994; Black Death, 272f; bronze, usefulness of, 40; decolonization map, 914m; discovery of oil, 854f, 859f; farming and settlements, 34m; fear of Islamism, 980–1; firearms, growing use of, 479; foraging lifestyle, 33–6; fossil discoveries in, 19; geography, environment, 33–335; Indo-European migration to, 49; male dominance in, 13; migration from, 3; migration to, 10; monotheism/monism adoption, 200–6; 1990s, global hierarchy, 966; patriarchy and gender, 42–3; post-WW II independence movements, 913–17; post-WW I recovery map, 863f; return to imperial stage formation, 493; Roman expansion into, 148; shipbuilding, 471; 600 BCE–600 CE, cultural diversity, 181; Six Day War, 933f, 953–4; spread of agriculture from, 49; suicide bombings, 977, 981; taxation in, 509, 511; terrorism, suicide bombings, 977; transformations to democracy, 967; unemployment, consequences for youth, 964–5; U.S. training of dissidents, 903–4; Yom Kippur/Ramadan War, 933f, 954, 967. See also individual countries

Middle Kingdom, Egypt, 48

Middlemarch (Eliot), 689–90

Migrations (human migrations): from Africa, 5, 6, 10, 14, 15m; to the Americas, 24, 25m, 28, 125, 127–8; from Asia to Europe, 19–22, 26; to Eurasia, 3; to India, 49, 69f; to Indonesia, 14, 24, 26, 131, 141, 151,

360, 382, 545; multiple site identification, 27–8; South Asia to Australia, 14–19

Military: of the Achaemenid Empire, 181; of the Aztecs, 445; of China, 101, 104–9, 111, 114, 249, 250–1, 253–4, 352–4, 377, 631, 634, 641–2, 729, 730, 740; of Egypt, 51, 406; of Ethiopia, 570; of European maritime empires, 659; of Greece, 187; of the Habsburgs, 477; of the Hittite Empire, 49; of Incas, 449; of India, 599–600, 607, 612; of Japan, 386–9; of Luba Kingdom, 421; of Mayas, 165, 166; of Mesoamerica, 433–4, 444; of Mesopotamia, 41–3; of Nubia, 152; of the Ottomans, 482, 617, 761, 763, 766, 859; of the Persian Empire, 183, 187; of Portugal, 466, 476, 571; of Prussia, 526f; of Rome, 212, 276, 314; of Russia, 524, 761, 762, 832; of the Safavids, 617; of Sparta, 186; of the Toltecs, 436; of the United States, 855; of Wari, 440. See also Weaponry advances

Ming Dynasty (China): administrative policies, 634; Christian missionaries in, 637; commercial revolution during, 628; decline of, 363, 631; female infanticide in, 365; foot binding in, 365; founding of, 629f; gender roles, 111, 365; Grand Secretariat, 361, 634; Inca government comparison, 447; literary achievements, 750; magistrate system, 363; military superpower status, 641–2; Mongol rule replaced by, 338; naval power, 361–3; origins, 360; peace-seeking achievements, 630; peasant women's lives, 365; politics/government, 360–1, 363; population recovery, 361, 628; porcelain excellence, 632–3; Qing conquest of, 638; role in China's reconstitution, 361, 460; rural life in, 639–40; rural society, 363–4; scholar gentry, 363–4; science and literature, 642; technological achievements, 365, 366–7; timeline placement, 347f; Timur's contemplated invasion of, 601; view of foreign influences, 630; village and family life, 364–5, 639; weaponry of, 617; Zheng He, voyages of, 4`7, 347f, 361–3, 362m, 366; Zhu Yuanzhi's inauguration of, 378

Minoan kingdom (palace-state): artistic endeavors, 61; description, 48; Linear A script, 56, 138; Mycenaean war against, 56; origins, 35f

Minobe, Tatsukichi, 856

Minute on Education (Macauley), 827

Mit'a taxation system (Incas), 447–8, 449, 453, 540, 697

Mladić, Ratko, 979

Mobutu Sese Seko, 926

Moche chiefdom (northern Peru), 149f, 153f, 173–4, 179

Moctezuma II (Tenochtitlán Emperor), 534, 537

Modernism, 818, 872, 906, 945

Mohenjo-Daro (Indus civilization), 67, 70–1, 72, 72*m*, 75

Monasteries and monasticism: in Aksum Kingdom, 410; Benedictine, 312–13; Buddhist, in India, 240, 264; Capetian control of, 317; Capuchin Catholic monks, 564–5; in China, 266, 398; feudalism and, 323; iconoclasm controversy, 284; importance of icons, 304–5; Jain monasteries, 219, 228; in Japan, 398; in Korea, 398; reform of, 323–4; regular clergy in, 312; of Saint Andrew, Rome, 310; of Saint Catherine, Egypt, 305*f*; as Silk Road hostels, 235; St. Benedict model, 312–13; for women, 238

Monet, Claude, 793*f*, 818

Money economy (defined), 480

Mongol Empire: attempted invasions of Japan, 387, 388*m*; capture/sale of young boys, girls, 293; collapse of, 358460; explosives used by, 358; Genghis Khan, 292, 349, 357, 600–2; Iran/Iraq, conquests of, 292; Korean invasion by, 377–8; map of empire, 360*m*; Middle East conquests by, 277*f*, 292; Song Empire conquest by, 357–8; 13th/14th centuries expansion, 338; Timur's efforts at rebuilding, 470; Vietnam invasion by, 299; Vietnam's repulsion of invasions, 273*f*. *See also* Yuan Dynasty

Mongols of the Golden Horde, 777

Monotheism (and monism): adoption of, 195; in Christianity, 203; Eurasian formulations, 148; Middle East adaptations to, 200–6; 600 CE dominance of, 149; Sun religion comparison, 59

Monroe Doctrine (U.S.), 706

Monsoon system: in Africa, 35; in China, 35, 94, 124; in Egypt, Mesopotamia, 37; in India, 35, 68–70, 69*m*, 124

Montenegro, 659*f*, 763*f*, 769, 771, 782

Montgomery, Alabama bus boycott, 939*f*

Monumental architecture, 90, 121, 131, 144–5, 177, 212, 384, 450, 622

Morel, E. D., 852

Morocco: African invasions from, 566; Alaouite dynasty, 473; Berber empire in, 423; efforts at occupation of, 571; feminist writers, 945; fossil finds, 13; independence of, 897*f*; Leo Africanus' emigration to, 462; Phoenician expansion into, 54; Portuguese occupation of ports, 473; trade routes, 567

Morrison, Jim, 928

Morse, Samuel F. B., 801

Morsi, Muhammad, 967*f*, 984

Mothers of Plaza de Mayo (Argentina), 959

Mouvement National Congolais (MNC), 925

Mozambique, independence of, 956

Mozart, Wolfgang Amadeus, 675

Mubarak, Hosni, 984

Mughal Empire (India): administrative personnel, 612–13; agricultural and rural life, 613–14; Akbar, leadership of, 461*f*; architectural achievements, 621–2; artistic achievements, 305, 620–1; astronomy innovations, 618–19; caste, clan, and village ties, 615; consolidation and expansion, 603–4; decline of, 601*f*, 825; domination of India, 369; early modern economics, 613–15; family and gender, 615–16; as gunpowder empire, 359, 617; history and political life of, 599–611; international trade, 614–15, 614*m*; Islamic civilization, domination by, 473; Islamic culture in, 473, 619–20; literary achievements, 620; loss/recovery of, 602–3; mathematical innovations, 618–19; non-Muslims in, 618–19; origins, 349, 350, 460; persecution of Sikhs, 351; Persian cultural influences, 474, 606–7; political structure, 612; religious politics, new directions, 607; revolt of the sons, 605–6; war state, renewed expansion of, 606–7; weaponry/torture method, 606. *See also* Akbar, Jalal ud-Din; Aurangzeb; Babur (Zahir ud-din Muhammad Babur); Shah Jahan; Timur (Timur-i-lang)/Timurid Empire

Muhammad (Prophet of Islam), 277, 279–81, 304–5, 404, 415, 485, 620, 772, 841, 980

Mulattoes, 553–4, 660, 712–13, 716–17

Murasaki Shikibu, 273*f*, 372–3, 375*f*, 390, 393–4

Music: in Africa, 591; in the Americas, 128, 131, 133, 590*f*; Baroque, 498–9; in Byzantium, 303; in China, 353*f*, 355, 386, 417; of the European Enlightenment, 675; of the global youth movement, 942; in Habsburg Spain, 484; in the Inca Empire, 454; in Italy, 496; jazz, 864, 905; in the Kongo Kingdom, 576; modernism in, 818; in monasteries, 313; postwar counterculture, 928; of the Renaissance, 498; rock, 905; in Spain, 489

Muslim Brotherhood, 916

Muslim League (of Muhammad Ali), 873, 916

Muslims: Adal sultanate, Ethiopia, 571, 572; Afghan Muslim fighters, 931; in Africa, 566, 569, 570; African slave trade, 578, 589; Alexander's forced assimilation program, 783; Berber-Arab conquest, 570; Carolingian defeat of, 312; caste and, 351; Christian competition with, 463–79, 572, 575, 636; coastal

Muslims, 412; cultural synthesis of, 306; defined, 277; Delhi Sultanate, India, 347*f*; 1835 uprising, 713; ending of Fatimid dynasty by, 291; feudalism and, 316; Hindu-Muslim interactions, 345, 346, 349, 468, 623, 830, 918; Iberia/North Africa liberation from, 463; interest in Greek philosophical writings, 301; justifications for holy wars, 463; maritime trade, 321; mathematics development, 207; military modernization, 838; Nubian kingdom settlements, 408; Persian/Turkish Muslims, 302; raids on Anatolia, 284; Ramadan observance, 281, 485–6, 822, 933, 954; religious leadership divisions, 772; Spanish conquest of, 320; Sufism-Sunni Islam integration, 277*f*; in Swahili city-states, 415; trade networks, 322, 347; usury, prohibitions against, 351; West African Muslim scholars, 841. *See also* Abbasid Dynasty; Delhi Sultanate, India; Granada Kingdom; Islam religion; Mamluk Egypt; Ottoman Empire; Seljuk Empire; Timur (Timur-i-lang)/Timurid Empire

Mussolini, Benito, 859*f*, 878, 879, 891

Mycenaean palace-states, 35*f*, 54, 56, 61

Nabobs (in India), 824–5

NAFTA. *See* North American Free Trade Agreement

Nanjing, Treaty of, 734

Napoleonic era map, 672*m*

Napoleonic Wars, 795, 825–6, 845, 858

Naram-Sin of Akkad (King), 53

Narmer (Egyptian king), 44

Nasser, Gamal Abdel, 895, 897*f*, 915–17, 921

National Association for the Advancement of Colored People (NAACP), 867

National Commission on the Disappearance of Persons (CONADEP), 960

National Congolese Movement, 925

Nationalism: ethnolinguistic, 676–7, 680–1; reemergence in China, 859*f*, 886–7; in Vietnam, 850. *See also* Constitutional nationalism

National Organization for Women (NOW), 944

National Society for Women's Suffrage, 811

Nation-states, growth of (1815-1871), 677–87; Caribbean, 704*m*; Congress of Vienna, 677–8; Latin America, 704*m*; restoration monarchies, 677–82; revolutions in France, 679; uprisings across Europe, 680

Nation-states, origins (1750-1815), 661–73; Congress of Vienna, 658*f*, 663*f*; early United States, 664, 665; French Revolution, conditions for, 665–9; Haitian Revolution, conditions for, 669–73; North America, conditions for, 662–4

Native Americans: American Indian Wars, 685; Christianity and, 531, 537; civil rights for, 940; colonist interactions with, 543, 545; Comanches in northern Mexico, 703–4, 704f; conquest of, in Tabasco, 533; conversions to Christianity, 531, 545; defeat/mistreatment of, 684–5; DNA ancestry identification, 24; emergence of, 29; Indian Removal Act, 685; "Kennewick man" fossil, 7f, 28, 29f, 125; migrations, 125; Paleoindian ancestry, 28; Portugal's ending of slavery of, 542; smallpox decimation of, 532, 540, 545; "Spirit Cave mummy" fossil, 7f, 28–9; "Trail of Tears," 685; Wounded Knee massacre, 685, 940

Natufian culture, Fertile Crescent, 35–6

Naturalism, 58

Nature spirits worship, 161

Nazca chiefdom (Peru), 153f, 175–6, 177, 178, 179, 453

Nazca geoglyphs, 176, 178

Nazi Germany, 857; "Aryan" term appropriation, 78; autarky of, 869; brutality of, 878; Enabling Act, 881; final solution implementation, 854f, 859f; French resistance to, 882; German citizen defiance in, 892; Hitler's rise to power, 880–2; Munich Agreement, 881–2. See also Hitler, Adolf

Nazis, 76

Neanderthals, 19, 26, 27

Needham, Joseph, 365

Needham question, 365

Négritude cultural movement (France), 867

Nehru, Jawaharlal, 917, 918–19

Neo-Assyrian Empire, 3, 53, 148, 209

Neo-Babylonians, 55–6, 201, 411

Neo-Confucianism: in China, 273f, 356, 403, 642–3; description, 365–6; in Japan, 391; in Korea, 379–80; longevity/diversity of, 371; origins, 273, 345, 352, 369, 378; timeline placement, 375f; in Tokugawa Shogunate, Japan, 648

Neolithic Age (New Stone Age): defined, 36; grain/animals, selective breeding of, 36; Mehrgarh culture, India, 69f, 70; Yellow River settlements, 93–4, 95f, 96–9

Neo-Platonism, 497

Nestorian Christianity, 368

Netherlands: Calvinism in, 516; Catholic-Protestant conflict, 517; Descartes' studies, teaching, 506–7; New Sciences in, 495, 502; 1936 empire map, 871m; North American settlements, 543, 544m; post-Black Death population recovery, 509; post-plague population recovery, 509; Protestant war of independence in,

478; reign of Philip II, 497f; Renaissance aesthetics, 487, 498; science/philosophy developments, 495; South Africa, Dutch Cape Colony, 567f, 576–7; taxation in, 511–12; trade networks, 476; war of independence, 517–18; women scientists, 503

Newcomen, Thomas, 798–9

New Conservatism, 941

New Deal (U.S.), 859f, 868

New Economic Policy (NEP; Soviet Union), 936

New England: colonial assemblies, 546; English immigration to, 545, 546; export crops (18th century), 551; immigration to, 546; Native Americans in, 543, 546; New Sciences research, 559; Protestantism in, 558–9; religious revivalism, 560; society (18th century), 556; witch hunts, 559–60

New Granada Creoles, 699

New Imperialism (19th century): in Africa, 838–43; in France, 835; in India, 824–31, 825f, 826m, 829m; in Indonesia, 845; 1914, global competitive imperialism, 834m; in Southeast Asia, 846m

New Kingdom Egypt, 43, 51, 59, 60f, 61

New Sciences (Scientific Revolution): astronomic tables, 494; astronomy-physics unification, 497f; Catholic Reformation and, 503; Copernicus, Nicolaus, 207, 460f, 497f, 499–500, 502, 529, 618; cultural sequence created by, 495; Darwin/evolution theory, 793f, 815; defined, 496; Descartes' new philosophy, 506–7; Galileo's mathematical physics, 461f, 497f, 500–1, 508; Hobbes' philosophy, 507; Iberian natural sciences, 502; Locke's philosophy, 507–8; New England research, 559; new science societies, 503; new theories of matter, 814; Newton's mechanics, 497f, 502; philosophical interpretations, 506–8; radioactivity experimentation, 814; relativity theory (Einstein), 659f, 793f, 815; social impact of, 502–6; Spinoza's philosophy, 507; steam engine invention, 497f, 505–6; theoretical physics, 814; vacuum, discovery of, 505; women scientists, 503–5; X-ray technology, 814

New Spain (Spanish colonial Mexico), 540, 562, 702–3, 847

Newspapers, 503, 662, 673, 750, 756, 768, 878

Newton, Isaac, 461f, 497f, 502, 505, 529, 815

New Zealand, women's right to vote, 825f

Ngo Dinh Diem, 923

Nicene Creed, 195

Nichiren Buddhism, 392, 402

Nicholas I (Russian Tsar), 777–9

Nicholas II (Russian Tsar), 860

Nietzsche, Friedrich, 817

Nigeria, 159, 427

Nigerian civil war, 955–66

Nightingale, Florence, 779, 780f

Nikitenko, Aleksandr, 760, 778

Nile River valley, 33, 152

9/11 terrorist attack, 971

Nineteenth Amendment (U.S. Constitution), 864

Nixon, Richard, 948, 952, 959, 967–8

Nkrumah, Kwame, 924

Nobel, Alfred Bernhard, 799–800

Nobunaga, Oda, 626, 644, 645–6

Nomads, 38

Non-Aligned Movement, 817, 894, 919, 920–1, 926

Nontariff autonomy (defined), 734

Norsemen, 285, 287, 314, 316, 470

North Africa: agriculture, 65; Arabian camels in, 422; Berber conquests in, 277, 277f; French invasion, 767, 835; Muslim settlements, 408, 463, 468; 1914, 1923 map, 863m; Ottoman expansion into, 762, 822; Portuguese conquest, 464, 465f; post-WWI recovery map, 863f; Rome's expansion into, 192, 570; silk's influence in, 261; slave trade, 566; trade networks, 298, 422, 567; World War II in, 859f; World War II participation, 859f

North America: Adena villages, 123f, 139, 140m; Beringia land bridge, 24; British North America, 582–5, 663m; climatic zones, 123; Clovis points, 127; colonization map (to 1763), 544m; conditions for revolution in, 662–4; corn cultivation, 134–5; 1519-1532, European exploration, 535m; fossil discoveries, 7f; geographic regions, 123–4, 138; Hopewell villages, 139, 140m; Inuit migrations, 123f, 138–9; land bridge connections to, 24; map (1100 CE), 435; migration to, 14, 17, 24, 28; ocean currents, hurricanes, El Niño, 124–5; Powhatan Confederacy, 545; Siberian groups, migration to Alaska, 14. See also Colonial North America; New England

North American Free Trade Agreement (NAFTA), 974

North and South Dynasties (Ancient China), 247f, 255

North Atlantic Treaty Organization (NATO), 889, 971

Northern India, 66, 79–80, 83m

Northern Song Dynasty (China), 347f

Northern Sultanates (India), 349–50

North Korea, 900–1, 963, 976, 982, 996

Nubian kingdom: agricultural activities, 407–8; animal domestication, 36; Arab invasions, 406; archaeological

discoveries, 152; Christianity in, 405, 406, 409; conquest of, 51; feudalism in, 409; geography, 34; Islamic rule in, 409; Mamluk conquest of, 409; Meroë, kingdom and, 155; military prowess, 47, 152; mining, 48; origins/growth of, 151, 152; royal power and governance, 406–7; taxation in, 407–9; timeline placement, 407f; trade networks, 39, 407–8; waterwheel development, 406
Nuclear crisis in Japan, 855f, 967f
Nuclear Test Ban Treaty (1963), 855f, 905, 931, 933f

Oaxaca stone carvings (Mexico), 150
Obama, Barack, 970, 978
Obregón, Álvaro, 709
Obscene Publications Bill (England), 806
Oceania, 122, 123f, 141–2, 144–5, 146, 151
October Manifesto, 786
October War. See Yom Kippur/Ramadan War
Ogé, Vincent, 660, 661
Oglethorpe, James, 596
Old Kingdom Egypt, 47m, 64
Oldowan tools, 8, 9
Old Testament, 60
Olmec culture (Mesoamerica): archaeological discoveries, 136–7; architectural achievements, 145; La Venta settlement, 123f, 137–8; map, 137m; origins, 123f; religion/spirituality, 137, 166; Tres Zapotes settlement, 138; writing, 138
Omdurman, Battle of (Sudan), 837
Onin War (Japan), 645
On the Genealogy of Morals (Nietzsche), 817
On the Origin of Language (Herder), 676–7
On the Origin of Species by Means of Natural Selection (Darwin), 793f, 815
On the Road (Kerouac), 928
Opium Wars (China), 730, 731f, 733, 734, 736–7, 744, 768
Oracle bones (Ancient China), 93, 95f, 104, 105, 111, 112–13
Oral traditions (defined), 424
Organization of Petroleum Exporting Countries (OPEC), 933, 943, 967–8, 970
Origen of Alexandria, 206
Orrorin fossils, 6, 7f
Ortiz, Alonso, 530–1
Osman (Turkish war lord), 469
Otto I of Saxony (Germany), 318
Ottoman Empire: approaches to modernity, 762, 765–6; artistic achievements, 305, 485–6; Bosnia-Herzegovina revolt against, 782; British negotiations with, 837; capture of Constantinople, 272f, 313f, 460f, 465f, 469, 471–2; centralized state formation, 483; Charles V's alliance with, 476–7; Charles V's efforts against, 475–6;

consolidation of power, 467; constitution and war, 768–9; Crimean War, 761, 763f, 768, 779, 780, 783, 788, 797, 836; decentralization, 764–5; decline of, 764m, 770–1; economic development, 771; ethnic-nationalist uprisings, 769; exploitations of Safavids, 478; expulsion of moriscos, 478–9; external and internal blows, 766; First Balkan War collaboration, 771; Greece's independence from, 658f, 763f, 767; as "gunpowder empire," 359, 481; Habsburgs, peace treaty with, 465f; Habsburgs, power struggles with, 469–78; Islamic-Christian imperialism of, 475; Islamic civilization dominance, 473; Janissaries (military troops), 480–1, 482, 484, 763, 766–7, 774; Jewish migrations to, 467; Land Code, 768; land-grants for military leaders, 479, 480; life, honor, and property, 767; losses in conflicts, 476; Janissary 1807 revolt, 766; map (1307–1683), 473m; massacre of Armenians, 859f; massacre of Janissaries, 766; Mehmet II, leadership role, 470–1; money economy in, 480; mosque architecture, 486–7; Napoleon III's campaigns against, 767–8; naval battle with Habsburgs, 465f; origins, 293, 460, 464, 469–70; peace with Austrian Habsburgs, 465f; peace with Spanish Habsburgs, 478; Portuguese competition, Indian Ocean, 477m; power limitations, 478; public festivities, 485; rise of, 469–79; Rose Garden Edict, 767; rule by kanun law, 480–1; Russo-Ottoman war, 763f, 765, 769, 779, 782, 832; Safavid rivalries with, 478, 774; siege of Vienna, 763f; Siege of Vienna, 465f; slavery in, 760–1, 766; southern Balkan conquests by, 480; state formation pattern, 483; Tanzimat reforms, 658f, 767, 768; taxation in, 479, 480–2, 764, 767–9, 775; theater, 485–6; Timur's role in rebuilding, 470; Topkapı Palace, 484–5; treaties, 764m; weaponry development, 359, 617; Western challenges, 765–71; Young Ottomans, 659f, 763f, 768–9, 775
"Out of Africa" theory, 10
Owen, Robert, 808

Pacific Island migrations: colonization map, 142m; food issues, 147; Lapita cultural complex, 3f, 123f, 141–3, 145; Oceania, peopling of, 141, 145; Polynesia, creation of, 143–4
Paekche Kingdom (Korea), 376, 385, 391
Pakistan: Bhutto's leadership, 895; independence of, 854f, 897f; wage comparison, 976–7

Palace-state (defined), 48
Paleoamericans, 125
Paleolithic (Old Stone Age) era: ceramics, invention of, 20; forager period, 12, 13; gender roles, 13; Neanderthal fossils, 19; onset of, 8; population growth, 29; religious artifacts, 22
Palestine: Balfour Declaration, 859f, 871; conflict map, 915m; cultural influences in, 204; deportation of Neo-Babylonians, 201; Egyptian dynasty in, 51; emigrations to, 783; geographic features, 34; Jewish Second Temple kingdom in, 206; Judaism in, 203–4, 783, 871–2; loss of Crusader kingdom, 464; 1947-1949 conflict with Israel, 914–15, 915m; promise as Jewish homeland, 859f, 871
Palestinian Liberation Organization (PLO), 954, 981
Palestrina, Giovanni Pierluigi da, 498
Pampas settlements (South America), 698–9
Panama Canal, 701, 800
Pankhurst, Emmeline, 811
Pan-Slavism ideology (Russia), 782
Papacy: Avignon Papacy period, 336, 343; canon law utilized by, 329; challenges of, 331; Charlemagne's protection of, 319; establishment of, 313; Gregory I, elevation to, 310, 311, 313, 313f; iconoclasm controversy and, 284–5; Norman kings alliance with, 326; reform/investiture controversy, 324. See also individual Popes
Papin, Denis, 497f, 503, 505–6, 798
Papyrus, 46, 184
Paracas chiefdom (Peru), 153f, 174
Parhae Kingdom (Korea), 375f
Paris, Treaty of, 336
Paris Academy of Sciences, 503
Parthian Persian Empire, 183f, 190–1, 194, 204
Pascal, Blaise, 505
Passarowitz, Treaty of, 764m
Patriarchal society: in Athens, 214; Catholicism and, 723; in China, 108, 118, 119, 262–3, 390; in Creole culture, 554; female poverty and, 945; gender and, 42–4; in India, 78, 239; in Middle Eastern cultures, 296; in Nubia, 407, 409; origins, 13; in the Ottoman Empire, 485; in Rome, 210; in Russia, 781
Patterns Up Close: the "age of steam," 798–9; Akbar's attempt at religious synthesis, 371, 608–9; Babylonian law codes, 44–5; Bandung/origins of non-aligned movement, 920–1; Byzantine icons, Islamic miniatures, 304–5; the caste system, 86–7; the "China" trade, 632–3; Chinese writing system, 116–17; Columbian Exchange, 548–9; disappearance of Neanderthals, 26–7; global trade of Indian pepper, 236–7;

gothic cathedrals, 332–3; guillotine, 668–9; gunpowder, 358–9; Harlem Renaissance, African Diaspora, 865–6; human sacrifice and propaganda, 454–5; mapping the world, 508–9; Mayan ball game, 170–1; military transformations, new imperialism, 832–3; origin of corn, 134–5; Plague of Justinian, 196–7; printing, 382–3; sculptures of Ife, 428–9; self-strengthening, Western science, Eastern Ethics, 738–9; shipbuilding, 470–1; slave rebellions, Cuba and Brazil, 712–13; social networking, 988–9; the stirrup, 256–7; Sunni and Shiite Islam, 772–3; voodoo, other new world slave religions, 590–1; from women's liberation to feminism, 944–5

Paul, Mary, 790–1
Peace of Westphalia, 521
Pearl Harbor attack, by Japan, 889
Pearl River system (China), 94
Peasants' War (Germany), 497f
Pedro I, King of Brazil, 710–11
Pedro II, King of Brazil, 711
Pedro IV, King of Kongo, 565
Pedro V, King of Kongo, 565
Pelesets (Philistines), 35f, 55–6
Peloponnesian War, 187
People's Liberation Army (China), 811, 888, 911, 947
Pepin III ("the Short"), 312
Perestroika policy (Soviet Union), 855f, 933f, 934, 935–7
Perón, Eva, 910
Perón, Juan, 910
Perpetual Peace (Rousseau), 674
Perry, Matthew C., 656, 658f, 731f, 744–5, 752, 755–6, 797
Persian Empire: administration of, 183–5; Alexander's conquests in, 180, 181, 188; artistic influence in Tang China, 355–6; central Asian Huns invasion, 183f; communication networks, 184–5; conquests of, 182; culture and arts, 207–9; final Roman-Persian war, 276; Greece interactions with, 181–5, 187; Greece's repulsion of invasions, 187; imperial recovery in, 183f; Jewish population in, 195; mapping the world, 508–9; military power, 182–3; origins, 182; Parthian Persian Empire, 183f, 190–1, 194, 204; Roman Empire interactions with, 189–200; shahinshah ("king of kings") in, 184; weaponry of, 617; Zoroastrianism preference, 195. See also Achaemenid Persian Empire; Parthian Persian Empire
Peru: Caral-Supé city, 3f, 110–11, 113f; independence gained by, 695, 697; Moche chiefdom, 149f, 153f, 173–4, 179; Nazca chiefdom, 153f, 175–6, 177, 178, 179, 453; Paracas chiefdom, 153f, 174;

Puruchuco burial place, 432; Spanish conquests, 538; textile manufacturing, 552–3; Túpac Amaru burial site, 432–3. See also Wari city-state
Peter I (the Great) Tsar of Russia, 523
Phallic stones, 75
Phallic symbols (bo), in Japan, 382
Philip II (King of Spain), 465, 497f, 517
Philippine-American War, 848–9
Philippines: agriculture, 161, 628; colonialism in, 847–9; French Revolution influence on, 847; map, 395m; migrations to, 141; Spanish colonialism in, 846–8; trade networks, 143, 389; U.S. conquest of, 825f
Philistines (Pelesets), 35f, 55–6
Phillip II, King of France, 327
Phillip II, King of Macedonia, 188
Phillip II, King of Spain, 465f, 477, 478, 487, 490, 497f, 517, 540, 558
Phoenician kingdom: African port establishment, 191; letter alphabet invention, 54–5, 56; Syrian city-states, 182; timeline placement, 35f; trade activities, 53–4
Picasso, Pablo, 818
Pictographic symbols, Harappan civilization, 68
Piers Plowman (Langland), 339–40
Pietism, 676
Pillow Book (Sei Shonagon), 372
Pinochet, Augusto, 959
Piracy, 347, 731, 822, 841
Pizarro, Francisco, 534–6, 538
Plague of Justinian, 196–7, 196m, 299
Planck, Max, 814
Planetary elliptical paths, discovery of, 497f
Plantagenet kings (of England), 318
Plantation slavery, the Americas: Caribbean plantations, 580; chattel slavery, 578–80; defined, 578; indentured laborers, 582; mercantilism in the Caribbean, 580–2; numbers of slaves, 578; resistance of slaves, 592–3; sugar plantations, Brazil, 582
Plant domestication, 128, 129–30, 130f, 159
Plassey, Battle of, 824, 825f
Plato, 148f, 183f, 202–3, 206, 306, 496–7. See also Neo-Platonism
Platonic-Aristotelian thought, 301, 306
Plessy v. Ferguson (1896), 939
Plow and wheel, introduction of, 35f
Poetry Classic (ancient China text), 111
Poland: Catherine's dismemberment efforts, 776; 1830 revolt, 779; female astronomers in, 503; Jews in, 871; post-Black Death population recovery, 509; revolt during Cold War era, 902–3; rise of centralized government, 510f; 1650-1750, population growth, 509; Solidarity labor union, 934; state centralization in, 510; World War II in, 882; Yuan dynasty in, 358

Politics (Aristotle), 497
Polo, Marco, 356, 357, 359
Polynesia, 98, 123f, 142–4, 146, 159, 382
Polytheism: animism transition towards, 58–9; challenges to, 200–3; defined, 58, 166; kingship and, 59; in Mayan kingdoms, 58–9, 166; move to monotheism, 203
Popular Front Coalition (France), 870
Populist-guided democracy, in Latin America, 909–10, 909f
Portugal: agricultural exploitation, 547, 552; apocalyptic expeditions, 466; appearance of ghettos, 323; as Arab Empire component, 276; Brazil, conquest of, 533f, 536, 537, 543; Catholic Church, reliance on, 557; Creoles in, 538; da Gama's journey to India, 468; early colonialism, 542; economic crisis, 978; ending of Native American slavery, 542; Ethiopia supported by, 567f, 572; explorations of Africa, 572; fossil discovery, 27; Ice Age influences, 22; Jewish expulsions from, 518; Jewish migrations to, 467; maritime, shipbuilding activities, 460, 464, 471, 508, 537f; mineral exploitation, 547, 551; Napoleon's occupation of, 696; 1936 empire map, 871m; North Africa, conquest of, 465f; Ottoman competition, Indian Ocean, 477m; Reconquista policies, 464, 466, 570; Saadid sultan's liberation from, 473; shipbuilding, 471; slave trade, 532; spice trade activities, 237; trade networks, 237, 347, 361, 474, 476; West Africa, explorations, 567f, 571–2
The Positive Philosophy (Comte), 688
Postcolonialism, 966
Postmodernism, 906, 966
Potosí silver mine, 533f
Potsdam Conference (1945), 897f
Powhatan Confederacy, Native Americans, 545
"Prague Spring" in Czechoslovakia, 933–4
Presentism (defined), 579–80
The Prince (Machiavelli), 497
Printing developments: in China, 268, 382–3; in Japan, 382–3; in Korea, 268, 380, 382–3; in Renaissance Europe, 496; in Vietnam, 382–3
Privateers in the Caribbean, 581
Progressive Organization for Women (POW), 945
Protestantism: Calvin Protestantism, 514–19, 515, 516, 559; Catholic-Protestant clashes, 478, 495, 502, 516; Charles V interest in, 476–7; demand for liturgical music, 498; Lutheran Protestantism, 339, 460f, 497f, 513–14; in New England, 558–9; support of Ottomans, 478; War of Liberation from Spain, 339, 512–13

Protestant Reformation: alliances between reformers, 514; Baroque arts and, 498; central state formation and, 508; map, 515*m*; origins, 339, 496, 512–13; spread of religious tracts, 383

Proto-Indo-Europeans, 49

Prussia: Franco-Prussian War, 796, 859; Frederick II, reign of, 497*f*; rise of, 524–5; rise of centralized government, 510*t*; taxation in, 524; Teutonic Order of Knights, 510

Prussian-Austrian War, 681

Ptolemaic Egypt, 156, 162, 188, 189*m*, 190, 203, 206, 236

Pueblo Revolt, 703

Puranas (Indian folk tales, genealogies), 82

Puranas (Indian sacred text), 82, 238, 240

Pure Food and Drug Act (U.S.), 686

Puritans, 518, 519, 543, 558

Puruchuco burial place, 432

Putin, Vladimir, 975

Qaddafi, Muammar el-, 984

Qajar Dynasty (Iran), 771–2, 774–5, 787

Qianlong Emperor (China): Castiglione's artistic influence, 643; expansion during reign of, 635, 636*m*; patronage of the arts, 642; timeline placement, 461*f*, 731*f*

Qin Dynasty (China), 149*f*; conquest of Zhou, 250–1; empire map, 251*m*; hegemony system in, 107; intellectual exploration era, 245; Legalistic theories, 249, 250, 261; origins, 105; power struggles, 107, 244; regional commanderies, 253; timeline placement, 149*f*, 247*f*; unification of China, 245, 247*f*

Qing Dynasty (China): banner system expansion, 631, 631*f*, 634; "carrot and stick" imperialism, 634–5; commercial revolution during, 628, 640*f*; conquest of Ming Dynasty, 638; countryside organization, 639; culture, arts, and science, 749–51; decline of, 634, 635, 854*f*, 859*f*, 886; dyarchy administration system, 633; economics, 748; firearms development, 642; foreign "factories" in, 638; Grand Council, 634; hair styles of men, 634; Inca government comparison, 447; Kangxi Emperor leadership, 634, 637; local customs, religion, 643–4; Manchu soldiers maintained by, 631*f*, 634; minority rule status, 634; philosophy, 643; poetry, travel accounts, newspapers, 750; porcelain achievements, 633; "pure" dynasty reputation, 631; Revolt of the Three Feudatories, 634; rural life in, 639–40; science and technology, 751; self-strengthening, 748; social trends, 748–9; society and rural economics, 748; timeline placement, 629*f*; Treaty

of Nerchinsk with Russia, 638; underground Christianity in, 637; view of foreign influences, 630; village and family life, 639

Qin Shi Huangdi (Chinese Emperor), 94, 252–3

Quakers, 686

Quebec City, French settlement, 533*f*

Quetzalcóatl, Temple of the Feathered Serpent God, 173*f*

Quotations from Chairman Mao Zedong, 947

Quran (Islam holy scripture), 279–81, 305, 307, 308

Radical republicanism, 666

Railroads: in Anatolia, 769; in Argentina, 722; in Canada, 722; in Chile, 722; in England, 793*f*; in Manchuria, 747, 785; in Mexico, 708; in South America, 722; in the U.S., 793*f*, 796

Rain-forest settlements: Africa, 152, 157–9, 427; Mali, 426; Yucatán Peninsula, 163

Rajputanas, 223

Rajputs, 349, 602, 625, 830

Ramadan, 281, 485

Ramayana (Hindu spiritual text), 82, 84–5

Ranke, Leopold von, 271

Rapa Nui monoliths (Oceania), 144, 145

Rape of Bengal, 824

Rape of Nanjing, 859*f*, 888–9

Raphael, 498

Rastafarians, 411–12

Rational-legal leadership, 612

Re, sun god, Egypt, 64

Reagan, Ronald, 935, 943

Reaganomics, 943

Realism, in prose literature, 688–90

Recession of 1893, 770, 789

Recession of 2001-2003, 977

Recession of 2008-2011, 855*f*, 976, 977–8, 982

Reconquista: defined, 326; fall of Granada, as culmination, 467; Iberia's elimination of Muslim rule, 464*f*, 493; Portugal's policies of, 464, 466, 570

Record of the World (Xu Jiyu), 750

Records of the Historian (Sima Qian), 375

Red Brigades (West Germany), 943

Red Eyebrow Revolt (China), 254–5

Red Guards (China), 947*f*, 948

Red Rubber (Morel), 852

Reductionism philosophy, 816

Reform War, in Mexico, 705

Reich, David, 19

Reiche, Maria, 178

Reign of Terror (French Revolution), 667, 668

Relativity theory (Einstein), 659*f*, 793*f*, 815

Religion/spirituality: in Anatolia, 201–2, 205; in the Caribbean Islands, 590; in China, 112–14, 356, 643–4; in Cuba, 590; in Egypt, 59, 64; in Eurasia, 149; in Haiti, 590–1; in Harappa, 75; in

India, 76, 78–9, 85–9, 91; in Japan, 380, 385, 390, 391, 590; in Mesoamerica, 137, 166; in sub-Saharan Africa, 149; suppression of by Abbasid Dynasty, 282; in Sweden, 514. *See also* specific religions

Renaissance (European Renaissance): architectural style, 487–8; Baroque arts, 498–9; Byzantine's influence on, 469; Christian civilization transition to, 311, 331; cultural transformations, 495, 496; educational revolution during, 317, 328, 343; events leading to, 337, 341, 343; Gothic cathedral birth during, 328; humanism movement, 339, 496, 341496; literary achievements, 496–7; music, sculpture, theater arts, 487, 498; philology and political theory, 497; printing and new manuscripts, 496

Repartimiento system, 532, 540, 548

Republicanism: Bolívar's preference for, 701; defined, 57; French radical republicanism, 666, 679, 680, 777; in Latin America, 696; in Rome, 191–2

Republican Party (U.S.), 901, 978

Restoration War (Japan), 731*f*

Revolt of the Three Feudatories (Qing Dynasty), 634

Revolutionary Guard (Iran), 982

Rhind Mathematical Papyrus (Egypt), 62

Ricci, Matteo, 637

Rice: in Africa, 158, 162, 414; in Australia, 16; in the Caribbean, 551; in the Carolinas, 584–5; in China, 3*f*, 79–80, 95*f*, 96, 98, 109, 257, 365, 637, 650; in Colonial North America, 584–5; in East Asia, 79–80, 98, 101, 389–90; in Harappa, 72; in India, 79–80, 94, 218, 221, 614; in Japan, 383–4, 388, 389–90; in Korea, 374, 378, 380; in Neolithic cultures, 394; in Southeast Asia, 98, 390, 628; in Spain, 479; in Vietnam, 380, 397

Richard I, King of England, 327

Richard II, King of England, 337

Rig-Veda (Hindu text), 76, 78–9, 86, 91

Roads: in the Andes, 130; in Aztec Empire, 449; in Chavín de Huántar, 133; in China, 252, 257, 259, 353, 357, 447; in Inca Empire, 448*f*; in India, 221–2; in Japan, 647; in Persia, 184–5; in Rome, 194

Roaring 20s (U.S.), 862–3, 867–8

Robbins, L. H., 150

Rock art/paintings, 2; Australian rock art, 17–18; by *H. sapiens*, 14, 20–2, 20*f*, 21*f*; in Russia, 20; Spain, caves, 19

Rockefeller, John D., 685

Roentgen, Wilhelm, 814

Roe v. Wade (1973), 941

Roman Catholicism, 156, 246, 258, 512, 591

Roman Empire: Academy of Plato, 148*f*, 206; adoption of Christianity, 183*f*,

195–6, 198, 205–6, 210, 218, 258, 309, 310; alphabet, 55f; Augustan age, 193–4, 193m; dates, early empire, 149f, 183f; dates, late empire, 183f; empire building, 148, 191–2; end of, 149f; expansion into Middle East, 148; final Roman-Persian war, 276; imperial recovery in, 183f; Isthmus Declaration, 192; Italian peninsula unification, 183f; Justinian I, reconstruction of, 198–200; latifundia (large estates), 192; legionaries of, 191–2; Libary of Alexandria, 206–7; literature and art, 210, 212; Lyceum of Aristotle, 206; mathematics, scientific research, 206–7; Meroë kingdom skirmishes with, 155; monotheism, adoption of, 195; Persian Empire interactions with, 189–200; political/economic crises, 194–5; political system, 57; republican origins, 191; Sasanid war with, 148, 276, 277f; shipbuilding, 470; survival challenges, 309; western empire, end of, 183f

Romania, 659f, 763f
Roman-Sasanid-Arab imperial traditions, 480
Romanticism, 687–8
Rommel, Erwin, 883
Roosevelt, Franklin D., 868. See also New Deal
Roosevelt, Theodore, 685–6, 701
Rose Garden Edict (Ottomans), 767
Rouhani, Hasan, 982
Rousseau, Jean-Jacques, 666, 674, 687
Royal Air Force (Great Britain), 884
Russia: abortive 1905 revolution, 763f, 785–6; Abortive Russian Revolution, 763f, 785–6; Alexander II, reforms of, 780–1; Balkan engagements, 782; Bolshevik Party, 785–6, 860, 875; Bolshevik Revolution, 854f, 859f, 886, 896; Catherine II, reign of, 763f, 776–7; civil war and reconstruction, 876; Congress of Vienna participation, 777; Crimean War, 761, 763f, 768, 779, 780, 783, 788, 797, 836; Decembrist Revolt, 777–8; early 19th century, 777–80; economic crisis, recovery, 975; Emancipation Edict, 781, 788; expansion map, 526m; February Revolution, 860; French Revolution's influence, 777; Golden Age in, 780; H. sapiens migration from, 26; Ice Age influences, 22; increasing poverty in, 976; industrialism in, 797; industrialization in, 783–4, 789; influence in China, 735m; Khrushchev's leadership, 896, 902–5, 910–11, 916, 932, 933f; "matristic" society in, 13; Napoleon's defeat in, 669, 677, 775, 777; Nicholas I, reign of, 777–9; 1990s, global hierarchy, 966; pan-Slavism ideology, 782; Peter the Great, reign of,

776; post-Black Death population recovery, 509; Pugachev's Cossack revolt, 776; Putin's presidency, 975; rise of, 523–4; rock paintings in, 20; serfdom in, 760, 776, 780–1, 787; serfs, emancipation of, 659f, 763f, 781, 788; 1795-1914, territorial expansion map, 778m; Social Democratic Labor Party, 785, 786; taxation in, 523–4, 975; Third Coalition against France, 777; Treaty of Brest-Litovsk, 860; Treaty of Nerchinsk with China, 638; Triple Intervention against Japan, 729, 747, 785; weaponry developments, 779; westernization in, 776–7; World War I, role in, 859–60; World War I participation, 775–6, 787. See also Lenin, Vladimir Ilyich; Siberia
Russian Revolution, 786f
Russo-Japanese War, 659f, 729, 763f, 782, 784–5
Russo-Ottoman war, 763f, 765, 769, 779, 782, 832
Rutherford, Ernest, 814

El-Saadawi, Nawal, 945
El-Sadat, Anwar, 954
Safavid Persian Empire: artistic achievements, 474; domination of Morocco, Persia, 473; growth into Shiite warrior organization, 474; as "gunpowder empire," 359; Ottoman rivalries with, 478, 774
Sahagún, Bernardino de, 558
Saharan chiefdoms and kingdoms, 152
Saint-Domingue, 541, 581, 591, 660, 669, 672
Sakoku seclusion policies (Japan), 656
Salt March, India, 873
Samurai warriors (Japan), 387–9, 393, 401, 402, 648, 652–3
San Martín, José de, 700–1
Sanskrit language (India), 69f, 76, 77–8, 86, 208, 226, 229, 240, 266
Santa Anna, Antonio Lopez de, 703, 705
Sargon of Akkad, 32, 41–2. See also Akkadian kingdom
Sasanid Persian Empire: adoption of Christianity, 195–6; culture and arts, 207–9; empire map, 199m, 279m; Indian texts transmitted by, 208; invasions by, 157, 195; Khosrow I, 199–200; Khosrow II, 212, 276; origins of, 194; plague in, 200; repulsion of Hun invasion, 197; Roman competition with, 148, 276; timeline placement, 183f; Umayyad conquest of, 276; war of succession, 212–13; wars with Iran and Rome, 277f; Zoroastrianism in, 183f, 199, 309
Savery, Thomas, 798
Schall von Bell, Adam, 637
Schlieffen Plan (Germany), 859
Schoenberg, Arnold, 818

Scholar-gentry, of China, 363–4, 367, 379, 398, 639, 640, 736, 748, 886
Scientific advancements. See New Sciences (Scientific Revolution)
Scientific and political debate, 993–4
Scientific-industrial modernity, 658, 729–30
Scythic culture (central Asia), 110–11
Sea People, 51–2, 54
Sebastião I, King of Portugal, 576
Second Coming of Christ, 466, 468
Second Opium War, 736–7, 768, 827
The Second Sex (de Beauvoir), 940
Second-wave feminism, 944
Securities and Exchange Commission (SEC), 868
Sei Shonagon, 372
Seiyukai (Constitutional Government party; Japan), 731f, 754
Seleucid southwest Asia, 188, 189m
Seleucus Nikator, 81, 216–17, 219
Self-Strengthening Movement (China), 731f, 737f, 738–40
Seljuk Empire: artistic sponsorship, 303; conquests of the Byzantines, 288–92, 307, 309; Crusades and, 290, 326; disintegration/recovery of, 289–90; map of empire, 289m; religious revival sponsorship, 300; timeline placement, 277f; Turkish warlords subjection to, 469
Senghor, Léopold, 867
Sepoy Mutiny (India), 659f, 824, 825f, 827–8
September 11, 2001, terrorist attack, 971
Serbia, 659f, 763f, 771, 782
Serfdom: in China, 379; defined, 760; in Russia, 760, 776, 780–1, 787; Russia's abolition of, 763f, 781; in Ukraine, 877f
Seven Years' War: British East India Company role, 625, 824; causes, 547, 662, 665; Russia's lessons from, 832; timeline placement, 663f; victory of Great Britain, 662
Sexual revolution, 940–1
Shaarawi, Huda, 945
Shahinshah ("king of kings"), in Persia, 184
Shah Jahan (Mughal Emperor): arrest and captivity of, 607; building of Taj Mahal, 598–9, 601f, 619; legalistic ruling style, 607; Red Fort in Shahjahanabad, 621–2; reign of, 601f, 607; Sunni Muslim reaction to, 625
Shah of Iran, overthrow of, 855f
Shakespeare, William, 498
Shamanism: in the Americas, 391; Australian Dreamtime, 17, 18f; ceremonial caves, 21, 128; defined, 128; White Shaman, 128f
Shang Dynasty (China), 92–3; armies and expansions, 102; bronze articles and weapons, 113; chariot introduction, 79, 103, 103f; client states, relations with, 104; decline of, 106; dominance of, 101, 106; elite women in, 111; Erliang

city, 108; historical background, 101–2, 105; Longshan culture absorbed by, 97; Mandate of Heaven, 106; map, 102*m*; mythology, 100; origins, 3*f*, 87*f*, 93, 95*f*; politics and foreign relations, 104; religious influences, 113–14; social class and labor, 108; society in, 108; trade routes, 102*m*; traditional dates, 95*f*; weapons, example, 102*f*; Zhou Dynasty comparison, 104–5

Sharecroppers, 38

Sharia law, 281, 307, 308

Shaw, George Bernard, 817

Shiite Islam (Shiism), 277*f*, 281–3; doctrine, 474; in Egypt, 291; in India, 612, 619; in Iran, 288, 415, 472, 771; in Iraq, 871; origins, 281–2, 772–3; in Safavid Persia, 606, 771–2

Shimonoseki, Treaty of, 729

Shinto religion (Japan), 380, 385, 390, 391, 590

Shujing (Chinese historical text), 99, 100, 101, 105–6

Siberia: Beringia land bridge, 24; early human evidence, 7*f*; fossil discoveries, 19; Ice Age influences, 22, 24, 28; migrations from, 14, 22; migrations to, 14, 31

Sieyès, Emmanuel-Joseph, 666

Sikhs and Sikhism, 351; Aurangzeb destruction of temples, 610; Hindu/Muslim persecution of, 351; limitations of acceptance, 368; origins, 351, 371; transitional period, 624

Silk Road trade network: agricultural revolution and, 319; benefits to Turkish leaders, 288; China's passage through, 94, 111, 190, 196, 234, 235, 237*m*, 254, 261–2, 262*m*, 298, 299, 319, 338, 345; description, 261–2; gold-for-luxuries trade, 298; hostels and way stations on, 235; Mongol Empire and, 338; nomadic migrations using, 196, 357; opening up of, 190; raids on, 254; regions covered by, 94, 111, 149, 190, 234–5, 237*m*, 262*m*, 298; religion and, 345, 352, 353; stirrup invention, spread on, 256

Silla Kingdom (Korea), 376, 377, 378–9, 380, 385

Sinicization/sinicizing, 254, 396, 399–400

Sino-Japanese War, 659*f*, 728, 729–30, 731*f*, 746, 785, 886

Sioux, Native Americans, 545

Sirleaf, Ellen Johnson, 987–8

Six Day War (Arab-Israeli War), 933*f*, 953–4

Six Dynasties period (Ancient China), 247*f*, 255

Slash-and-burn farming, 159

Slave revolts: Abbasid Empire, 414; in the Americas, 567*f*, 594*f*; in Brazil, 712–13; in the Caribbean, 567*f*; in Cuba, 712–13; in Haiti, 712

Slavery: Aksum Kingdom, 409; Bolívar's liberation of Colombian slaves, 700; Brazil's slave rebellions, 712–13; British North America, 582–5, 583*m*; Central Asia, 283, 288, 348–9; China, 108, 114, 271; Cuba's slave rebellions, 712–13; Egypt, 292, 293, 294, 408; ending of, in Brazil, 659*f*; India, 76, 348; Indonesia, 162*f*, 577; Islamic culture, 288, 348–9; Korea, 379; Lincoln's abolishment of, 683; Middle East, 13, 42–3; Mongol Empire, 378; Ottoman Empire, 760–1, 766; Portugal, 532; Rome, 192, 214; smallpox epidemic, 532; Swahili city-states, 414; Syria, 277; Vietnam, 398; voodoo religion practices, 560, 590–1. *See also* Abolition of slavery; African slave trade; Atlantic slave trade; Plantation slavery, the Americas

Smail, Daniel Lord, 6

Smallpox epidemics: in the Americas, 147, 532, 534–5, 537, 540, 542, 555; in the Caribbean, 580; in Japan, 386; in South Carolina, 585

Smith, Adam, 675

Smoot-Hawley Tariff, 868

Smriti law codes (India), 84

Snowden, Edward, 967*f*

Social contract theory (Locke), 658–9

Social Darwinism, 815

Social Democratic Labor Party (Russia), 785, 786

Social Democratic Party (Germany), 879

Socialist criticism of industrialism, 808–9

Social networking, 965, 988–9

Social Security Act (U.S.), 868

Social stratification, 43, 101, 158, 165

Solidarity labor union, in Poland, 934

Solomonid Dynasty (Ethiopia), 407*f*, 409, 411–13

Song Empire (China): artistic achievement, 367–8; beliefs about Tang dynasty, 345; Confucianism in, 345; economy, 357; food binding practice, 271; gender roles, 111; literary achievement, 367–8; map location, 357*m*; modern period onset, 352; Mongol conquest of, 357–8; Northern Song Dynasty, 347*f*; porcelain crafts, 268, 367; printing presses in, 268; religion in, 356; Southern Song Dynasty, 347*f*; stirrups developed in, 256; tea and silk production, 355; technological achievements, 356, 365, 366–7; trade network, 357; Wang Anshi's reforms, 356–7; young girl issues, 263

Songhay Empire (West Africa), 567–9; gold mining, 567; slave trade, 567–8, 574; sub-Saharan map, 568*m*; sudden decline, 568–9; timeline placement, 567*f*

Sons of Liberty, 663

South Africa: apartheid, 577, 924, 956–8, 962; apartheid, ending of, 855*f*, 958, 967*f*, 987, 990*f*; bow and arrow development, 16; caudillo authoritarian regimes, 698, 701–2; de Klerk's leadership, 958; Dutch Cape Colony, 567*f*, 576–7; early human origins, 7, 9*m*; fossil discoveries, 7, 8; Great Zimbabwe Kingdom, 273*f*, 407*f*, 413, 419, 420*m*, 570; Mandela's leadership, 855*f*, 958, 962, 965, 967*f*, 987, 990*f*; Mapungubwe Kingdom, 407*f*, 418–19; Pardos settlements, 699; repeal of apartheid laws, 958; village life in, 159–62

South America: agricultural origins, 129; Bolívar as liberation hero, 697*f*, 699–700; climatic zones, 123; coffee boom, 713–14, 718; colonization settlements, 539*m*; Creole settlements, 699; early civilization, 16; economic activities, 539*m*; economy (ca. 1900), 715*m*; geographical regions, 123; nation-state growth, 704*m*; Pampas settlements, 698–9; Pardos settlements, 699; Radical Party, 699; railroad building in, 722; textile production, 131

South Asia: animal domestication, 98; industrialization in, 967; land bridge connections, 15–16; migrations to Australia, 14–15; rainfall variation, 68

South Central Africa, 569–70

Southeast Asia: Black Death origination in, 299, 331; bronze casting techniques, 113; Buddhism in, 221, 226, 243, 266, 375*f*, 399; Chinese imperialism in, 373, 608; European trading ports, 614*m*; fossil discoveries, 9–10; glass bead artifacts, 158; Hinduism in, 241; increasing poverty in, 976; Indianized territories, 225, 234–5, 368, 403; Indian pepper trade, 236; map of physical settings, 395*m*; Neolithic civilization, 79, 394; post-World War II, 922–3; Qin dynasty relations in, 251; rice experimentation, 98, 390; trade networks, 143, 234, 352, 355; Western imperialism in, 844–50. *See also* Cambodia; Indonesia; Vietnam

Southern India dynasties, 348*m*

South Korea, 900–1, 963, 966, 975, 996

Soviet Red Army, 896–7

Soviet Union: Afghanistan invaded by, 855*f*, 930–1, 935; bloc transformations, 937–9; Brezhnev's leadership, 932, 934, 935; collectivization of agriculture, 859*f*, 866–77; Communist Party, 875–6; decline of, 932–9; dissolution of Communism, 855*f*; Earth's political divisions, 871*m*; era of détente with U.S., 855, 932–3, 933*f*; glasnost policy, 855*f*, 933*f*, 934, 935–7; Gorbachev's leadership, 934, 935–9; Hitler's invasion of, 882–3; ICBMs, 903, 931; Khrushchev's leadership, 896, 902–5, 910–11, 916, 932, 933f; Kosygin's leadership, 933f; Lenin's founding of, 850; move from Marxist socialism, 960; New Economic Policy, 936; nuclear bomb building, 889; Nuclear Test Ban Treaty, 855f, 905, 931, 933f; perestroika policy, 855f, 933f, 934, 935–7; post-WW II support for Israel, 915; Sputnik satellite launch, 854f, 897f, 903; support of OPEC boycott, 933; taxation in, 936; tensions with People's Republic of China, 932; U.S. containment policy, 897. *See also* Lenin, Vladimir Ilyich; Stalin, Joseph

Spain: Americas discovered by, 460f; Aztec Empire, conquest of, 461f, 474, 483, 532, 533–4, 533f; cave paintings, 19; Columbus's Caribbean journey, 467–8; conquests, reasons for successes, 537; Donaña National Park, 26f; Dutch Protestant War of Liberation from, 497f; economic crisis, 978; El Escorial Palace construction, 465f; England's seizure of Jamaica from, 567f; expulsion of Jews, 460f, 467; expulsion of moriscos, 478–9; fossil discoveries, 19; Granada, conquest of, 460f, 465f; Ice Age influence, 22; Inca Empire, conquest of, 461f, 474, 483, 532, 533f, 534–6; Muslims expelled from, 465f; Napoleon's occupation of, 696; Neanderthal era, 27; 1936 empire map, 871m; North American colonization, 544m; Peru, conquests in, 538. *See also* Charles V

Spanish-American War, 852

Spanish Civil War (1936-1939), 859f

Spanish Habsburgs: *auto-da-fé* (act of faith) show trial, 488; capital and palace, 487–8; Native American conversion efforts, 531; Ottoman peace with, 478; painters, 490; popular festivities, 489; theater and literature, 489–90

Spanish Inquisition, 465f, 557

Sparta, Greek city-state, 56, 57–8, 185

Spencer, Herbert, 815

Spinoza, Baruch, 507, 518, 673

"Spirit Cave Mummy" fossil, 7f, 28–9

Spring and Autumn Chronicles (Chinese text), 107

Spring and Autumn period (China), 95f, 112, 116, 247f

Sputnik satellite launch (Soviet Union), 854f, 897f, 903

Sri Lanka. *See* Ceylon

Stagflation (defined), 943

Stalin, Joseph: actions in World War II, 882; building of Communist Party, 875, 876, 897; Churchill's secret agreement with, 897; collectivization of agriculture, 876–7; 1930s policies, 896;

scientific-industrial future desired by, 891; stance on Korean War, 901

Stamp Act (U.S.), 662

Statue of Liberty, 798

Steam, age of, 798–9

Steam engine: Papin's invention of, 497f, 503, 505–6, 798; Watt's perfection of, 658f, 793f, 798–9

Steel manufacturing industry, 796–7

Stirrup, development in China, 256–7

Stock market crash (U.S.), 854f, 859f, 868

Strategic Defense Initiative (SDI), 935

Student demonstrations, global (1960s), 942–3

Subaltern relationship (defined), 830–1

Submarine warfare (World War I), 861

Sub-Saharan Africa: agrarian-urban development, 151; Americas comparison, 151, 163; Bantu people, 153f, 158, 159–61, 163, 179, 413–14, 418; chiefdoms, 151; Christianity in, 405; cultural prowess of, 150; economic decline, 976, 987; Ghana's quest for independence, 924–5; interactions with Eurasia, 149; iron smelting, 148f, 153f; kingdoms and peoples, 568m; legacy of colonialism, 924; monotheism, monism religion, 405–6; Nile Valley domination, 405–6; Sahel (steppe), 157; transition from foraging, 151; villages, towns, kingdoms, 151–2, 157–61, 160m. *See also* Aksum kingdom; Meroë kingdom; West Africa

Sudan, 34, 37, 150m, 152, 570, 758, 825, 836–7

Suez Canal, 659f, 793f, 872

Suez War (1956), 897f

Suffrage movement for women, 811, 864, 940

Sufi Islam (Sufism): Akbar's grounding in, 618; defined, 602; Islamic Sufi brotherhood, 837; opposition to, 301; Sunni Islam integration with, 277f, 300–1

Sugar plantations, 542, 546, 551, 561, 571, 574, 576, 580, 708

Suicide bombings, 977, 981

Sui Dynasty (Ancient China): empire building, 257; internal power rebellion, 257–8; Korean invasion by, 375f; land redistribution, 259; reunification of China, 247f, 257, 351, 352, 376, 396; rise of, 385

Sumerian law code, 44

Summa Theologica (St. Thomas Aquinas), 272f, 313f

Summer of love (U.S., 1967), 942

Sumptuary laws, in China, 364

Sunni Arabs, 985

Sunni Islam (Sunnism), 277f, 301, 309, 415, 423; in Afghanistan, 771–2; in Africa, 323, 415; in central Asia, 774; in eastern Arabia, 766; historical

background, 301, 772–3; in Iraq, 871; in the Mughal Empire, 606–9, 608–9; in the Ottoman Empire, 472, 474, 771; Shiism comparison, 282; in the Umayyad Empire, 282

Sunni Kurds, 985

Sunni Muslims, 603, 612, 619, 625

Sunni-Sufi Islam, 300–1, 302, 307

Sun religion, Egypt, 59

Sun Zi, 887

Supreme Court rulings: *Brown v. Board of Education*, 939; *Plessy v. Ferguson*, 939; *Roe v. Wade*, 941

Sustainability, 991–3

Swahili city-states (East African coast), 162, 407f; adapting to Islam, 414–15; Chinese contacts with, 362; governance of, 415–17; map, 416m; origin, 405, 413, 414; slave trading, 414; timeline placement, 407f; trade network, 298, 413; urbanism in, 415; Zheng He, voyage to, 417

Sweden: intervention in Thirty Years' War, 516, 519–21; line infantry introduction, 510; New Sciences in, 503; post-Black Death population recovery, 509; religion in, 514; state centralization in, 510; taxation policy, 529

Sylvester II (Pope), 328

Syncretic social and political formations, 354

Syphilis, 147

Syria: Abbasids in, 279; agricultural settlements, 33; in Akkadian kingdom, 41–2; Arab conquest of, 272f, 276–7, 277f; Arab Spring protests, 965; Christianity in, 467; Civil War, 977; geographic boundaries, 41–2, 52, 53; Hittite control of, 51; independence of, 914; *Mamluks* slave revolt, 766; military slaves in, 766; Mongol conquests in, 308; Neo-Assyrian Empire and, 3, 209; Ottoman occupation of, 767; Phoenician city-states in, 182; Roman territories in, 195; Seleucids in, 190; "Sevener" Fatimids in, 288; spread of agriculture from, 48–9; trade networks, 320; writing system, 54

Taíno, indigenous culture, 532, 580

Taiping Rebellion, 634, 640, 731f, 735–6, 737m

Taiwan, 395m; aboriginal population of, 141; annexation of, 729, 741; early migrations from, 141; first migrations from, 123f; industrialization in, 966; Japan's occupation of, 785, 889; Ming loyalists in, 631; opium use in, 731; Qing conquests in, 635, 638, 729; Republic of China formed in, 900–1; U.S. diplomatic presence, 948

Taiwan, first migrations from, 123f

Taj Mahal, 60f, 598–9, 607, 619, 621, 622

Tale of Genji (Murasaki Shikibu), 273f, 375f, 390, 393–4

Taliban regime, 967f, 971, 980, 989

Tang Dynasty (China): Buddhism in, 258, 264, 266–7, 351–2; central Asia invasions by, 352; cosmopolitanism of, 355–6, 371; decline of, 268, 345, 352, 357; earthenware production, 258–9; exam/testing system, 353; founding of, 258, 266, 352; gender relations, 264; Korean invasion by, 375f; land distribution policies, 259; land losses, 357; map location, 354m; military losses, 354–5; occupation of Vietnam, 399; Persia's artistic influences in, 355–6; poetry accomplishments, 356; printing presses in, 268; prosperity/growth issues, 353, 355; religious influences in, 352–6; role in reconstitution of China, 351; Song Empire beliefs about, 345; technological achievements, 365, 366–7; timeline placement, 272f, 347f; trade network, 235, 352–3

Tanzimat reforms (Ottoman Empire), 658f, 767, 768

Tawantinsuyu Empire, 446

Taxation: in the Abbasid Empire, 282; in the Achaemenid Empire, 184; in Aksum, 156; in Aztec Empire, 447; in China, 109–10, 253, 255–6, 258–9, 353, 355, 360, 376, 378, 567–8, 748, 912; in colonial America, 662–6, 704, 711, 714; in Egypt, 45, 55, 837–8; in England, 318, 336–8; in France, 336, 522–3; in Germany, 870; in Iberia, 479; in Inca kingdom, 447; in India, 80, 347–8, 350, 609, 613–15, 619; in Japan, 754; in Korea, 377; in Latin America, 716–18; in Mamluk Egypt, 293–4, 296, 298–9; in Maya kingdoms, 167; in the Middle East, 509, 511; in the Netherlands, 511–12; in New Spain, 540–2; in Nubia, 407–9; in the Ottoman Empire, 479, 480–2, 764, 767–9, 775; in Persia, 184; in Prussia, 524; in Russia, 523–4, 975; in the Soviet Union, 936; in the United States, 940, 978

Tax farming system, Byzantium, 298

Tea Party movement (U.S.), 978–9

Technological renewal, in the U.S., 968–9

Tecumseh (Native American leader), 684

Temple Mound (Jerusalem), 277

Temple of Eridu, 39f

Temple of the Feathered Serpent God, 173f

Temple Pyramids of the Sun and Moon (Moche kingdom), 174

Temujin. *See* Genghis Khan

Tennessee Valley Authority (TVA), 868

Tenochtitlán (Aztec city-state), 443, 450–1, 451m, 454, 459, 534, 538f

Tenskwatawa (Native American leader), 684

Teotihuacán kingdom, Mexican Basin: alliances of, 437; building projects, 170–2; canal networks, 170; decline of, 172–3, 434, 435f; establishment, 153f, 170–2; geographic features, 169; human sacrifices, 172; legacy of, 433–8; map of, 172m; Temple of the Feathered Serpent God, 173f, 435, 454; timeline placement, 153f; trade network, 172–3; urban cultural development, 163

Tesla, Nikola, 800

Teutonic Order of Knights, 510

Textile industry innovations (Great Britain), 793

Thackery, William Makepeace, 688–9

Thambo, Oliver, 962

Thatcher, Margaret, 943

Theory of Harmony (Schoenberg), 818

Theravada Buddhism, 229, 230–1, 345, 375f

Third Coalition against France, 777

Third Communist International Party (China), 886

Third Republic of France, 692, 693, 849, 922

Third-wave feminism, 944–5

Thirteen Colonies (Colonial North America), 663m

Thirty Years' War (Germany), 494, 497f, 506, 516, 519–21, 524

Three Kingdoms era (Korea), 374–6, 375f, 385, 391

Three Kingdoms period (Ancient China), 247f, 255, 374–6, 375f, 380

Tiananmen Square massacre (People's Republic of China), 855f, 950–1

Tian ("heaven") concept (China), 114

Tianjin, Treaty of, 746–7

Tibet, 635

Tibetan Buddhism, 635

Tichitt-Oualata villages, Africa, 152–3

Tigris-Euphrates river valley, 33

Timur (Timur-i-lang)/Timur Empire: administration challenges, 612–13; agricultural and rural life, 613; annexation of Muslim sultanates, 610; gender equity, 616; India invaded by, 347f, 350; institutionalization challenges, 602–3; map of subjugated areras, 601m; Mongolian Empire, rebuilding efforts, 470; Ottoman encounters with, 490; palace revolts by heirs, 623; political challenges, 612; rebuilding of Ottoman Empire, 470; timeline placement, 601f; varied conquests of, 347f, 350, 600–1

Tiwanaku state (Mesoamerica): agriculture, 439; decline of, 445; expansion/colonization, 438–40; governmental authority, 440, 459; map, 441m; road networks, 449; ruling class, 459; timeline placement, 435f; Wari comparison with, 440; Wari-Tiwanaku frontier, 441–2

Tlaxcalans, indigenous culture, 534

Tokugawa Shogunate (Japan), 316, 359, 386, 391, 522, 612, 638; arrival of the "black ships," 744–5; *bakufu* ("tent government"), 647–50; Battle of Sekigahara victory, 645–6; decline of seclusion of, 743–4; establishment of, 629f; feudalism, 316; gunpowder use in battle, 359; intolerance of Christianity, 648–50; lifespan of leadership, 627, 646; limitations on foreigners, 638, 649; Louis XIV comparison, 522, 612; Ming/Qing comparison, 630; Mughal Empire comparison, 612; Neo-Confucianism in, 391, 648, 652; onset of Shogun title, 386; pottery production, 633; removal of guns, 648; rural transformations, 652; samurai warriors, 648, 652–3; unification efforts for Japan, 644; Western science engaged by, 755–6

Toltec culture (Mesoamerica): cultural expansion, 438; decline of, 436, 445; militarization, 436; origins, 434–5, 435f, 436; timeline placement, 435f; trade networks, 436; weaponry innovations, 436, 445

Tools and toolmaking: Acheulian tool technology, 9, 10f; in Africa, early humans, 2; in Asia, early humans, 3; *H. sapiens*, toolmaking skills, 11–12, 14; Oldowan tools, 8, 9

Tordesillas, Treaty of, 465f

Total war (definition), 859

Toumaï, 2, 6, 7

Tours, Battle of (France), 278

Toussaint Louverture, François-Dominique, 671–2

Trade activities: Afghanistan, 74; Aksum kingdom, 157; Americas, 361; Australian Aborigines, 17–18; Aztec Empire, 451; Byzantine Empire, 297–9, 299m; canoe innovation, 23; Canton China, 637–9; Central Africa, 566, 582; Central Asia, 73–4, 110–11; Chichén Itzá, Mesoamerica, 438; China, Han Dynasty, 254; China, opium trade, 730–8, 732m, 744, 747, 759; China, Song Empire, 357; China, Tang Dynasty, 235, 352–3; Constantinople, 320, 469; early African networks, 12; East Africa, 162; Egypt, 39, 73; England, 464; Eurasia, 348m; Europe, 12th/13th centuries, 321m; Hanseatic League trading alliance, 338, 510; Harappan civilization, 73–4; India, 217, 219, 221, 225, 227, 234–5, 236–7, 237f; Islamic spice trade, 237; Italy, 186, 292; Japan, 650–1, 651m; Mali Empire, West Africa, 424; Mapungubwe Kingdom, South Africa, 418; Mediterranean region, 320–1, 321m; Meroë kingdom,

154; Mesopotamia, 39, 73; Morocco, 567; Mughal Empire, 614–15, 614m; Muslims, 322; Mycenaeans, 54; Netherlands, 476; North Africa, 298; Nubian kingdom, 39, 407–8; Philippines, 143, 389; Phoenicians, 53–4; Portugal, 237, 347, 361, 474; reign of Philip II, 477; Teotihuacán kingdom, 172–3; Toltecs, Mesoamerica, 436; Valley of Mexico, 436; West Africa, 158. See also African slave trade; Atlantic slave trade; Plantation slavery, the Americas; Silk Road trade network

Trade unions, 707, 708, 808, 865, 878, 910, 943

"Trail of Tears" (U.S. Native Americans), 685

Transatlantic radio message (Marconi), 793f, 801

Transcontinental railroad (U.S.), 793f, 796

Transoceanic cable development, 801

Treaty ports (China), 733–4, 735m

Trigonometry, development of, 618f

Trinitarian Byzantine Christianity, 277

Triple Intervention against Japan, 729, 747, 785

Truman, Harry S, 889, 897, 901, 910, 939

Truman Doctrine, 897

Tunisia: Arab Spring protests, 965, 983–4; conquest of Byzantine Sicily by, 283; Fatamid rebellion in, 282; France as protectorate of, 837–78; independence of, 897f; Ottoman conquests of, 770; Rome's conquest of, 191

Túpac Amaru burial site, 432–3

Turkestan, Arab-Persian conquest of, 277f

Turkey: agricultural settlements, 33; American missiles removed from, 905, 932; ascent of, 983; feminist groups in, 945; increased modernity in, 787, 872, 968; middle class in, 976, 986; military weaponry, 617; Truman Doctrine and, 897. See also Anatolia

Tutankhamen of Egypt in Full Battle Regalia, 51f

Tutu, Desmond, 958

Twitter, 965, 987

Twitter Revolution, 989

Ubaid period, Mesopotamia, 59

Ukraine, 23, 104, 284, 285, 287, 876, 883, 936, 979

Umayyad Dynasty (Arab dynasty): Abbasid comparison with, 278–9; Abbasid displacement of, 320; empire building, 275, 276–7; overthrow of, 278–9; religious developments, 277; Shiite Islam origins, 281–2; timeline placement, 277f

Unction ceremony (defined), 312

Unequal treaties, 731f, 734, 736–7, 746, 748, 759

Union of German Women's Organizations, 811

Unions, labor and trade, 707, 708, 808, 865, 878, 910, 943

United Nations (UN): "blood diamonds" scheme, 989–90; Charter of the United Nations, 675, 895; definition of "middle-income countries," 966–7; environmental conferences, 993; feminism report, 945; Gorbachev's address to, 937; Iraq weapons inspections, 970–1; Israel independence plan, 915; Lumumba and, 926; middle-income countries survey, 966–7; Palestinian independence question, 914; regional peace efforts, 971–4; Stalin and, 914–15; Yom Kippur War ceasefire, 954

United States (U.S.): abortion rights, 941, 942, 944; Afghanistan invasion by, 967f; Al-Qaeda terrorist attack, 855f; American Indian Wars, 685; American Revolution, 658f, 663–4, 663f; anti-Soviet containment policy, 897; Articles of Confederation, 664; Bill of Rights, 664; Boston Tea Party, 664; buffalo herds, destruction of, 685; Bush presidency, 971; Carter's presidency, 935, 954, 959; Civil Rights Act (1964), 940; civil rights movements, 939–40, 944; Clinton's presidency, 969, 970, 974; Cuban Missile Crisis, 854f, 855, 896, 897f, 905m, 932, 960; Declaration of Independence, 659, 664; dollar regime, 967–8; early industrialism, 796; emigrations to Mexico, 705; era of détente with Soviet Union, 855, 932–3, 933f; financial crisis, recession, 855f, 967f, 974–5, 977–8; $400 billion military budget, 967f; gay rights movement, 941; Great Depression, 854f, 855, 857, 859f, 867–8, 978; Hawley Tariff, 868; as import sinkhole, 968; Indian Removal Act, 685; Johnson's presidency, 933f, 940, 952; Kennedy's presidency, 904, 905, 923, 932, 940; Kuwait invasion by, 967f; lynchings, of African Americans, 683, 865f, 866; Marshall Plan, 897, 899, 906, 910; McCarthyism in, 901; Meat Inspection Act, 686; Mexican-American War, 744; Mexico's war with, 705; military dominance (1990s), 970; Monroe Doctrine, 706; Montgomery, Alabama, bus boycott, 939f; NAFTA participation, 974; nation-state building, 683–4, 684m; negotiations with People's Republic of China, 948; New Deal, 859f, 868; 9/11 terrorist attack, 971; 1990s, global hierarchy, 966; Nixon's presidency, 948, 952, 959, 967–8; Nuclear Test Ban Treaty, 855f, 905, 931, 933f; Obama's presidency, 970, 978; Philippine-American War, 970, 978; Philippine-American War,

848–9; Philippines conquered by, 825f; post-1945 security commitments, 972m–973m; post-WW I, business and labor, 865–6; post-WW I, high artistic creativity, 864–5; post-WW II, artistic culture, 906–7; post-WW II, mass consumption culture, 906; post-WW II, society, culture, 905–7; Pure Food and Drug Act, 686; Reagan's presidency, 935, 943; Republican Party, 901, 978; Roaring 20s, 862–3, 867–8; scientific-industrial onset, 791; slavery, abolishment of, 683; Smoot-Hawley Tariff, 868; Spanish-American War, 852; Stamp Act, 662; stock market crash, 854f, 859f, 868; student demonstrations, 855f, 942–3; taxation in, 940, 978; Tea Party movement, 978–9; training of foreign dissidents, 903–4; transcontinental railroad, 793f, 796; Truman Doctrine, 897; Voting Rights Act (1965), 940; women's right movement, 940–1; women's suffrage movement, 864. See also Colonial North America

Upanishads (Hindu religious texts), 69f, 88, 89, 218, 226–7, 229, 240

Urania propitia (Companion to Urania) (Cunitz), 494

Urban II (Pope), 290, 326

Urbanization: in African inland delta, 158; in the Americas, 120, 128–38, 538, 542; in the Andes, 132m, 439; in Buenos Aires, 698–9; in Byzantium, 292; in China, 100, 108, 109, 264, 628, 748–9; in colonial America, 663, 664, 665; in Cuzco, 450; in East Africa, 162, 415; in East Asia, 353; in Great Britain, 803, 806, 810; in Harappa, 72, 76; in India, 67, 69f, 70, 83, 227, 233; in Iraq, 872; in Islamic civilization, 288; in Japan, 650–1, 651m; in Latin America, 908–9; in Mamluk Egypt, 294–5, 412; in Maya kingdoms, 172, 438; in Mexico, 874; in northwest Europe, 503; in the Ottoman Empire, 770; in Peru, 121; in Rome, 313, 322; in Russia, 776; in the Safavid Empire, 474; in South Central Africa, 570; in sub-Saharan Africa, 574; in Tenochtitlán, 450; in Turkey, 872; in the United States, 862, 864, 866; in Wari, 440; in West Africa, 151. See also Agrarian-urban society

Urquisa, José de, 698

Urukagina of Lagash (King), 44

Uruk city-state, 35f, 40

U.S Army Air Force, 884

U.S. Bureau of Indian Affairs, 940

U.S. Department of Commerce and Labor, 686

Utamaro, Kitagawa, 654

Utopian socialism, 788

Vajjian Confederacy (India), 80–1

Valley of Mexico: chiefdoms and kingdoms, 433, 434; late Toltec era, 436; map, 444m; militarism in, 434–6; Toltec state, 434–6; trade activities, 436. *See also* Aztec Empire; Teotihuacán kingdom

Vanity Fair (Thackeray), 688–9

Varna social structure (India). *See* Caste system

Vedas (Indian sacred texts): *Bhagavad Gita*, 82, 83, 220, 232; composition of, 69f; criticisms of rituals, sacrifices, 227; defined, 78; description, 220; four *varnas* of, 84, 85; *karma-samsara* concept in, 88–9; kingship connection to, 82; men's role in studying, 238; oral transmission of, 86; origins, 69f, 77–8; Ramayana, 82, 84–5; reformation, 226–31; *Rig-Veda* text, 76, 78–9, 86, 91; *Upanishads*, 69f, 88, 89, 218, 226, 227, 229, 240

Vedic society (India), 226–31; animal domestication, 79; caste system, 86–7; domestication of animals, 79; Indo-European origins, 77–9; *karma-samsara*, development of, 88–9; northern India, 79–80; religious directions, 86–8; rice cultivation, 79–80

Verbiest, Ferdinand, 637

Verdun, Treaty of, 314

Vernacular languages, in Europe, 339

Versailles Treaty, 854f, 859f, 862

Vietnam: artifact findings, 104234; Black Death origination, 331; Buddhism in, 235, 266, 272, 273, 345, 375f; China's attack on, 947; Confucianism in, 397, 850; cultural, political conflicts, 397; dynasty unification, 375f; French conquest of, 825f, 849–50; geographic features, 94; "god-kings" system in, 235; Han occupation of, 254, 396; Ho Chi Minh's leadership, 922, 923, 931, 943; independence from China, 396; Le Dynasty, 375f, 397, 399–400; map of physical setting, 395m; Mongol invasion of, 299; nationalism in, 850; Neo-Confucianism in, 272, 375f, 398; Ngo Dinh Diem's leadership, 923; 1990s economic growth, 977; politics, labor, trade, 397–8; printing technology in, 382–3; Qin China invasion of, 251; repulsion of Mongol invasions, 273f, 299, 375f; rice agriculture, 380; sinicization, 396; sinicization, resistance to, 399–400; state formation tensions, 373; Tang China occupation, 399; timeline of events, 375f; Tran Dynasty, 375f; Trung sisters revolt, 375f; wage comparison, 976–7; women in, 379–80, 395, 398

Vietnam War, 855f, 933f, 943, 948, 951–2, 951m

Vijayanagar ("City of Victory") state (India), 272f, 347–8, 347f

Vikings, 285, 314, 470

Villa, Pancho, 702f, 708–9, 708f

Vita Kimpa, Dona Beatriz, 564–6, 576

Voodoo religion, 560, 590–1

Voting rights/suffrage: of African Americans, 683; in Athens, 186, 214; in Brazil, 710; in colonial America, 664–5; in England, 546; in France, 667, 692; in Great Britain, 808; in Japan, 885; lack of, for Athenian women, 214; in Latin America, 718–19; in New Zealand, 825f; in South America, 699; universal male, 667, 692, 699, 808, 885; in the U.S., 864; for women, 811, 825f, 864, 872, 940

Wagadu, 405, 422–4, 426

Walesa, Lech, 934, 935f, 937

Wallace, Alfred Russell, 815

Wang Anshi, 356–7

Wang Mang, Emperor of China, 254–5, 266

Wang Yangming, 642

Wang Zhihuan, 93

Wari city-state (Mesoamerica): agriculture, 441, 447; decline of, 445; housing arrangements, 453; influence on the Nazca, 176; map, 441m; origins and expansion, 440; road networks, 449; timeline placement, 435f; Tiwanaku comparison with, 440

Wari-Tiwanaku frontier, 441–2

War of Liberation from Spain, 339, 512–13

Wars of Religion (France), 497f

Warsaw Conference (2013), 993

Warsaw Pact, 889, 903, 934, 937

Washington, George, 664

Waterwheel, animal-driven, development of, 406

Watt, James, 658f, 793f

Wealth, global distribution (2012), 967m

Weaponry advances: Aztec Empire, 445f, 449; bayonets, 359, 510, 525f, 832; 1830s-1918 period, 801–2; Europe, 510–11; Gatling gun invention, 802; gunpowder, 358–9; Inca Empire, 449; machine guns, 659f, 738, 793f, 802, 819, 821, 830, 840; Ming Dynasty, China, 617; Mughal Empire, India, 606; Ottoman Empire, 359, 617; Persian Empire, 617; Russia, 779; Toltec culture, 436, 445

Weimar Republic (Germany), 879–81

West Africa: agriculture, 157–8; banana phytoliths, 159; Benin Kingdom, 427, 460f, 566, 567f, 571, 574–5, 671; chartered exploration, 567f; chartered explorations in, 570–1; conquest/resistance to colonialism, 840–1; Ife Kingdom, 273f, 407f, 427–9; inland delta urbanism, 158; Jenné-jeno city-state, 153f, 157–8; Mali Empire, 273f,

407f; map of states, 425m; plant domestication, 159; Portuguese explorations, 567f, 571–2; rain-forest agriculture, 157–9; rain-forest settlements, 158–9; savannah, 157–9; slave trade, 571; trade networks, 158; village farming, 159

Western Christianity, 272, 278, 285, 289f, 290, 296, 301, 306, 311, 413

Western Schism (Latin Christendom), 336

Western Zhou Dynasty, 95f, 106

What Is the Third Estate? (Sieyès), 666

What Is to Be Done? (Lenin), 786, 788, 875

Wheel, development of, 130, 147, 406

The White Man's Burden (Kipling), 852

Wilhelm I, King of Germany, 681

William I, King of England, 318

Wilson, Woodrow, 861

Winstanley, Gerrard, 529

Witchcraft, 161, 559, 560f, 565

Women: in agricultural societies, 43; in ancient Egypt, 43; in China, 108, 111–12, 118, 262–4, 365; in Creole culture, 554; in democratic Athens, 214; Empress Wu's political authority, 356; in India, 83, 84–5; Industrial Revolution jobs for, 810–11; in Korea, 379–80; in medieval Europe, 322–3; New Zealand suffrage vote, 825f; Qing Dynasty, China, 748–9; role of, early humans, 12–13, 16, 29; suffrage movement, 811, 825f, 864, 872, 940; in Vietnam, 379–80, 395, 398. *See also* Feminist movement; Gender roles and divisions

Women Journalists Without Chains, 965

Women's rights movement, 940–1, 944–5

Women's Social and Political Union, 811

Woodstock generation, 942

The Works of Mencius (trans., Legge), 244

World population, 2011 data, 855f, 967f

World War I: Battle of the Marne, 859; Britain's post-war recovery, 869; collapse of Russia's terrorist regime, 775–6; early course of, 859–60; empires and Balkan nations, 858–9; explosives used during, 799; explosives/weaponry used during, 799, 802; French post-war recovery, 869–70; Germany's participation, 859–62; Japanese participation, 730, 860; Latin America's post-war recovery, 874; 1917 turning point, 860–2; Russia's participation, 775–6, 787; submarine warfare, 861; timeline placement, 854f, 859f; as total war, 859; U.S. participation, 861–2; Versailles Treaty, 854f, 859f, 862

World War II: Battle of Britain, 882; China's campaigns, 854f, 886–7; defeat of Japan, 911; eastern front action, 882–3; European map, 884m; in France, 882; Hitler's Final Solution against Jews,

854f, 859f, 883; Pacific campaigns, 889–90, 890f; Pearl Harbor attack, by Japan, 889; in Poland, 882; post-war counterculture, 928; post-war North American society, culture, 905–7; Stalin's actions in, 882; timeline placement, 854f, 859f; turn of the tide in the west, 883–4. *See also* Nazi Germany

World Wide Web (WWW), 987

Wounded Knee massacre (Native Americans), 685, 940

Wright, Wilbur and Orville, 793f, 800–1

Writing developments: Aztec Empire, 138; calligraphy, 117, 267, 268, 358, 386, 388, 393; Caral-Supé valley, *khipu*, 131; China, 93, 95f, 99, 104, 105, 111, 112–13, 116–17, 252, 254, 266, 373, 400; cuneiform, 40, 41f, 44; Egypt, hieroglyphics, 46f, 46; Harappan civilization, 67, 68; Korea, *han-gul* phonetics, 375f, 380–1; Mayan, glyphic alphabet, 153f, 168; Nazca geoglyphs, 176, 178; Olmecs, Mesoamerica, 138

Writs/jury system, in England, 318

Wudi (Han China Emperor), 190, 253–4, 259, 265, 375f, 396

Wu Ding, King of China, 92–3, 102, 104, 111, 113

Wu Zetian (Empress Wu), 351–2, 356, 356f, 370

Wycliffe, John, 337

Xesspe, Toribio Mejia, 178

Xia Dynasty (China), 106, 108, 114, 115; age of myth and, 99–101; chariot origins, 79; Erlitou palace complex, 95f, 100; origins, 96; society, 100–1; Zhou Dynasty comparison, 104–5

X-rays, discovery of, 814

Xuan Zang (Buddhist pilgrim), 346–7

Yalta Conference (1945), 897f

Yamato period (Japan), 258, 373, 375f, 384–5, 389, 391

Yangshao culture (China), 95f, 96, 97

Yangzi River system (China), 94

Yayoi period (Japan), 375f, 382–3, 388

Yellow River valley dynasties (China), 93; Banpo Village, 96–7; Dapenkeng culture, 98; geography and climate, 94–6, 95m, 98; Longshan culture, 95f, 97–8; Neolithic settlements, 93–4, 95f, 96–9; origins, 93–101; Yangshao culture, 95f, 96, 97

Yellow Turban Revolt, 255

Yemen, 14, 34, 35, 154, 157, 200; Aksum loss of, 409; Arab Spring in, 964–5, 984; business privatization in, 980; coffee trade, 476, 503; decolonization, 914m; Egypt hegemony in, 916–17; Portugal's protection of, 570; Sunni vs. Shiites in, 773; support of Ethiopia, 572

Yi Dynasty (Korea), 375f, 378–80, 400

Yom Kippur/Ramadan War, 933f, 954, 967

Yongzheng Emperors (China), 637, 642

Young Ottomans, 659f, 763f, 768–9, 775

Youth movement, global, 942

YouTube, 987

Yrigoyen, Hipólito, 699

Yuan Dynasty (China): appearance of novels, 367–8; creation of, 358–9, 359f, 396; as "darkest time" for China, 360; Mongol incorporation of, 256; timeline placement, 347f; Zhu Yuanzhi's conquest of, 378

Yugoslavia (former): civil war, 979–80; economic crisis, 979; ethnic cleansing in, 855f, 967f

Zacuto, Abraham, 508

Zagwe Dynasty (Ethiopia), 407f, 410–11

Zapata, Emiliano, 702f, 708–9, 708f

Zen Buddhism (Japan), 267, 377, 388, 392–3, 402, 624

Zeppelin, Ferdinand von, 800

Zheng He, voyages of, 347f, 361–3, 362m, 366, 417

Zhou Dynasty (China): agricultural innovation, adaptation, 98, 109; central Asian interactions, 110–11; decline of, 106–7; Eastern Zhou Dynasty, 95f, 106; Empress Wu's inauguration of, 356f; feudalism form of government, 106–7, 223; filial piety notions in, 108; historical records of, 104–5; iron casting technology, 114–15; Mandate of Heaven, 104–6, 119; map, 105m; merchants and *shi* class, 110; political crises in, 81; rural society, 109; *tian* ("heaven") concept, 114; *well-field* land division system, 109–10; Western Zhou Dynasty, 95f, 106

Zimbabwe, 298, 956. *See also* Great Zimbabwe Kingdom

Zimbabwe African National Union (ZANU), 956

Zimbabwe African People's Union (ZAPU), 956

Zionism, 409, 411, 871

Zoroastrianism: Ahuramazda (God), 183, 201, 207; fire temple communities, 203; Jewish adoption of elements, 149; as Persia's preferred religion, 195; Savior/apocalypse themes, 201–2; timeline placement, 183f

Zulus, 577, 957

Zwingli, Huldrych, 514